PRAISE FOR

SUPREME CITY

"A great skyscraper of a book. *Supreme City* is the improbable story not just of America's greatest metropolis during the Jazz Age, but the biography of an epoch."

—Rick Atkinson, author of *The Guns at Last Light:*
The War in Western Europe, 1944–1945

"Sparkling. . . . The history of dozens of astonishing newcomers who—largely in one tumultuous decade, the 1920s—made New York into what Duke Ellington called the capital of everything. . . . Miller skillfully weaves these different and colorful strands into a narrative both coherent and vivacious. . . . The full story richly deserves his original synthesis and, for me, makes New York even more fascinating."

—Robert MacNeil, *The Washington Post*

"Sweeping. . . . Enjoyable. . . . [In the 1920s] New York was the United States intensified, an electric vessel into which the hopes and desires of a nation were distilled. As Mr. Miller's vivid and exhaustive chronicle demonstrates, Jazz Age Manhattan was the progenitor of cultural movements—individualized fusions of art and commerce—that came to symbolize the American way of life."

—David Freeland, *The Wall Street Journal*

"Lower Manhattan dominated New York for three hundred years. In the 1920s, however, as Donald L. Miller makes clear in a page-turning book with an astonishing cast of characters, Midtown became the beating heart of the metropolis. *Supreme City* is about how these few square miles at the center of a small island gave birth to modern America. If you love Gotham, you will love this book."

—Kenneth T. Jackson, Barzun Professor of History, Columbia University
and Editor-in-Chief, *The Encyclopedia of New York City*

"[An] entertaining new history of Manhattan in its modern heyday. . . . Accessible, romantic, sweeping and celebratory."

—Beverly Gage, *The New York Times Book Review*

Simon & Schuster Paperbacks
An Imprint of Simon & Schuster, Inc.
1230 Avenue of the Americas
New York, NY 10020

First Simon & Schuster trade paperback edition May 2015

SIMON & SCHUSTER PAPERBACKS and colophon
are registered trademarks of Simon & Schuster, Inc.

For information about special discounts for bulk purchases, please contact
Simon & Schuster Special Sales at 1-866-506-1949
or business@simonandschuster.com.

The Simon & Schuster Speakers Bureau can bring authors to your
live event. For more information or to book an event contact
the Simon & Schuster Speakers Bureau at 1-866-248-3049
or visit our website at www.simonspeakers.com.

Designed by Paul Dippolito

Manufactured in the United States of America

1   3   5   7   9   10   8   6   4   2

The Library of Congress has cataloged the hardcover edition as follows:
Miller, Donald L., 1944–
Supreme City: How Jazz Age Manhattan Gave Birth to Modern America / Donald L. Miller
pages   cm
Includes bibliographical references and index.
1. Manhattan (New York, N.Y.)—Social life and customs—20th century.
2. New York (N.Y.)—Social life and customs—20th century. 3. Manhattan (New York, N.Y.)—
History—20th century. 4. New York (N.Y.)—History—20th century.
5. Manhattan (New York, N.Y.)—Social conditions—20th century. 6. New York (N.Y.)—
Social conditions—20th century. 7. Manhattan (New York, N.Y.)—Politics and government—
20th century. 8. New York (N.Y.)—Politics and government—1898–1951. I. Title.
F128.5.M54 2014
974.7'1043—dc23   2013020154

ISBN 978-1-4165-5019-8
ISBN 978-1-4165-5020-4 (pbk)
ISBN 978-1-4767-4564-0 (ebook)

SUPREME CITY

How Jazz Age Manhattan Gave Birth to Modern America

Donald L. Miller

Simon & Schuster Paperbacks

NEW YORK · LONDON · TORONTO · SYDNEY · NEW DELHI

Simon & Schuster Paperbacks
An Imprint of Simon & Schuster, Inc.
1230 Avenue of the Americas
New York, NY 10020

First Simon & Schuster trade paperback edition May 2015

SIMON & SCHUSTER PAPERBACKS and colophon
are registered trademarks of Simon & Schuster, Inc.

For information about special discounts for bulk purchases, please contact
Simon & Schuster Special Sales at 1-866-506-1949
or business@simonandschuster.com.

The Simon & Schuster Speakers Bureau can bring authors to your
live event. For more information or to book an event contact
the Simon & Schuster Speakers Bureau at 1-866-248-3049
or visit our website at www.simonspeakers.com.

Designed by Paul Dippolito

Manufactured in the United States of America

1   3   5   7   9   10   8   6   4   2

The Library of Congress has cataloged the hardcover edition as follows:
Miller, Donald L., 1944–
Supreme City: How Jazz Age Manhattan Gave Birth to Modern America / Donald L. Miller
pages   cm
Includes bibliographical references and index.
1. Manhattan (New York, N.Y.)—Social life and customs—20th century.
2. New York (N.Y.)—Social life and customs—20th century. 3. Manhattan (New York, N.Y.)—
History—20th century. 4. New York (N.Y.)—History—20th century.
5. Manhattan (New York, N.Y.)—Social conditions—20th century. 6. New York (N.Y.)—
Social conditions—20th century. 7. Manhattan (New York, N.Y.)—Politics and government—
20th century. 8. New York (N.Y.)—Politics and government—1898–1951. I. Title.
F128.5.M54 2014
974.7'1043—dc23   2013020154

ISBN 978-1-4165-5019-8
ISBN 978-1-4165-5020-4 (pbk)
ISBN 978-1-4767-4564-0 (ebook)

To Chuck Manoli, who got our minds moving

Every American is eaten up with a longing to rise.

—ALEXIS DE TOCQUEVILLE, *DEMOCRACY IN AMERICA*

There are roughly three New Yorks. There is, first, the New York of the man or woman who was born here. . . . Second, there is the New York of the commuter. . . . Third, there is the New York of the person who was born somewhere else and came to New York in quest of something. Of these three trembling cities the greatest is the last—the city of final destination, the city that is a goal. It is this third city that accounts for New York's high-strung disposition, its poetical deportment, its dedication to the arts, and its incomparable achievements.

—E. B. WHITE, *HERE IS NEW YORK*

CONTENTS

Preface   *xiii*

Cast of Characters   *xvii*

Prologue: The Jimmy Walker Era   *1*

PART ONE: POWER AND POLITICS

1. A Test for Tammany   *13*
2. Jimmy Walker's New York   *35*

PART TWO: CRIME AND PROHIBITION

3. Too Good to Be True   *65*
4. Owney Madden   *93*
5. "The Night Club Era"   *111*
6. "He Did It Alone"   *133*

PART THREE: THE MAKING OF MODERN MANHATTAN

7. Revenue Plucked from the Air   *151*
8. Street of Dreams   *169*
9. Vanishing Social Citadels   *181*
10. The Woman's City   *191*
11. Fred French   *216*
12. Masters of the Skyline   *231*
13. The Silver Spire   *249*
14. The Magic Carpet   *269*

PART FOUR: BRINGING IN THE FUTURE

15. Sarnoff   295
16. Paley   319
17. Jazz Age Baby   337
18. Sluggers   372
19. Tex   392
20. Pursuits   412
21. Visions   430
22. Highway Under the Hudson   454
23. Poet in Steel   472
24. A School of Minnows   487

PART FIVE: JAZZ AGE ICONS

25. Music Is My Mistress   503
26. Master of Allure   519
27. A Bag of Plums   543
    Epilogue: Blue Skies   575

    Acknowledgments   583
    Notes   587
    Bibliography   687
    Index   731
    Photo Credits   763

PREFACE

This book began as a vastly larger enterprise: a history of New York City—all five boroughs—in the years between World War I and World War II. Not long into the research, however, I was strongly drawn to a story within the larger story I had set out to tell—the transformation of Midtown Manhattan in the 1920s from a commercial backwater with one consequential skyscraper, the twenty-five-story Times Tower on Times Square at Forty-second Street and Broadway, into the entertainment and communications center of New York—and America—and a business district that rivaled Wall Street in power and consequence. This transformation began in earnest with the completion of Grand Central Terminal in 1913, the magnet project for the reconstruction of Midtown, and reached its apogee in 1927, the year David Sarnoff's new NBC radio network went national, the Roxy and Ziegfeld Theatres opened, and real estate prince Fred F. French completed his Art Deco skyscraper on Fifth Avenue, one of the first terrifically tall buildings north of Forty-second Street.

In 1927, the year of Charles Lindbergh's solo flight from New York to Paris, "the tempo of the city had changed sharply . . ." recalled F. Scott Fitzgerald. "The parties were bigger and the buildings were higher, the morals were looser and the liquor was cheaper. . . . The Jazz Age now raced along under its own power, served by great filling stations full of money."

I try to reimagine the city as it was then, to describe the lives of my characters—most of them from places other than New York—as they lived them, unsure of what lay ahead or of posterity's judgment. In 1927, it seemed unimaginable that the greatest urban building boom in modern history would soon collapse with shocking suddenness, and that stylish, high-living Jimmy Walker, the city's immensely popular mayor, would be brought low by charges of corruption and forced to resign.

1. Anne Vanderbilt's and Anne Morgan's Townhouses
2. Astor Mansion
3. Bergdorf Goodman Department Store
4. Boni & Liveright
5. CBS Studio
6. Chanin Building
7. Chrysler Building
8. Cornelius Vanderbilt II's Château
9. Cotton Club
10. Daily News Building
11. Elizabeth Arden's Salon
12. Empire State Building
13. Fred F. French Building
14. Garment District
15. George Washington Bridge
16. Grand Central Terminal
17. Helena Rubinstein's Salon
18. Hell's Kitchen
19. Holland Tunnel
20. Kentucky Club
21. Owney Madden's Phoenix Brewery
22. Madison Square Garden (1925–1968)
23. NBC Studios
24. New Amsterdam Theatre
25. New York Central Building
26. Pennsylvania Station
27. Random House
28. Simon and Schuster
29. Radiator Building
30. Roxy Theatre
31. Ritz Tower
32. Saks Fifth Avenue
33. Sutton Place
34. Texas Guinan's Club
35. *The New Yorker*
36. The "21" Club
37. Tudor City
38. Yankee Stadium
39. Ziegfeld Theatre

Central Park

FIFTH AVENUE
65TH STREET
SEVENTH AVENUE
BROADWAY
SIXTH AVENUE
FIFTH AVENUE
MADISON AVENUE
PARK AVENUE
LEXINGTON AVENUE
THIRD AVENUE
SECOND AVENUE
FIRST AVENUE
SUTTON PLACE
YORK AVENUE
59TH STREET
57TH STREET
48TH STREET
51ST STREET
42ND STREET

N
W E
S

Midtown Manhattan
Around 1927

0   1/4   1/2 mile
0   1/2   1 kilometer

East River

CAST OF CHARACTERS

(With Place of Origin)

Othmar Ammann	Designer & Engineer, GW Bridge	Schaffhausen, Switzerland
Elizabeth Arden	Cosmetics Entrepreneur	Ontario, Canada
Hattie Carnegie	Fashion Entrepreneur	Vienna, Austria
Irwin S. Chanin	Architect/Builder	Brooklyn, NYC
Walter P. Chrysler	Founder, Chrysler Motors	Wamego, KS
Frank Costello	Bootlegger/Mobster	Calabria, Italy
Jack Dempsey	Heavyweight Boxer	Manassa, CO
William "Big Bill" Dwyer	Bootlegger	Hell's Kitchen, NYC
Duke Ellington	Jazz Musician & Composer	Washington, DC
Fred F. French	Builder	Manhattan, NYC
Adam Gimbel	President, Saks Fifth Avenue	Philadelphia, PA*
Edwin Goodman	Department Store Mogul	Rochester, NY
"Texas" Guinan	Night Club Hostess	Waco, TX
Clifford M. Holland	Chief Engineer, Holland Tunnel	Somerset, MA
Raymond M. Hood	Architect	Pawtucket, RI
Abraham E. Lefcourt	Real Estate Developer	Birmingham, England
Horace Liveright	Publisher & Broadway Producer	Philadelphia, PA
Lois Long	Writer, *The New Yorker*	Stamford, CT
Owney Madden	Bootlegger/Mobster	Leeds, England
William S. Paley	Founder, CBS	Chicago, IL
Joseph Medill Patterson	Founder, New York *Daily News*	Chicago, IL
George "Tex" Rickard	Boxing Promoter	Sherman, TX**
Emery Roth	Builder	Gálszécs, Slovakia
Samuel "Roxy" Rothafel	Theatrical Impresario	Bromberg, Germany***

Helena Rubinstein	Cosmetics Entrepreneur	Kraków, Poland
Babe Ruth	New York Yankee	Baltimore, MD
David Sarnoff	Founder, NBC	Uzlyany, Belarus
Ruth Snyder	Executed Murderer	Queens, NYC
Gene Tunney	Heavyweight Boxer	Greenwich Village, NYC
Anne Harriman Vanderbilt	Philanthropist	Manhattan, NYC
James J. Walker	Mayor, NYC	Greenwich Village, NYC
William J. Wilgus	Engineer	Buffalo, NY
Florenz Ziegfeld, Jr.	Broadway Impresario	Chicago, IL

*Gimbel was born in Milwaukee and raised in Philadelphia.

**Rickard was born in Kansas City, Missouri, and moved to Sherman, Texas, with his parents when he was four.

***Roxy's birthplace remains a mystery, but he was probably born in Bromberg, Germany.

SUPREME CITY

THE JIMMY WALKER ERA

*Jimmy Walker somehow or other seemed to be New York
brought to life in one person.*

ED SULLIVAN

New York paid its final tribute to Jimmy Walker on November 21, 1946. The flags of civic buildings stood at half-staff, the business of the city was suspended, and a Solemn High Requiem Mass was celebrated at St. Patrick's Cathedral on Fifth Avenue, the street the former mayor "loved so well." In the year of the mayor's death, Fifth Avenue between Fiftieth and Fifty-first Streets, where the cathedral faces Rockefeller Center, was in the heart of Midtown Manhattan, the city's transportation, communications, cultural, entertainment, and fashion center. But when the cornerstone of St. Patrick's was laid in 1858 this slice of the city was a remote outpost of settlement, a long, wearying carriage ride from New York's port and population center on the southern rim of Manhattan Island. Mayor Walker had been born and raised down there, near the Hudson River piers, and had boldly promoted the explosive growth of Midtown, the city's main engine of entrepreneurial opportunity.

The Great Altar of St. Patrick's was resplendent with bouquets of autumn flowers—asters and goldenrod—that November morning when the mayor's mahogany coffin was carried down the central aisle at 10:25 A.M. Four thousand five hundred mourners, twice the cathedral's normal capacity, packed the pews and every open space in the massive nave and its side altars. Another ten thousand New Yorkers, most of them middle-aged and older, stood outside on the sidewalks and street corners to give a proper send-off to the most beloved, if hardly the greatest of the city's mayors, Beau James, who lived for the night, moving gaily from one glittering party to another in his long, chauffer-driven Duesenberg with chromium-plated wheels and doeskin upholstery.

Those attending the service "were people of importance in the three fields of [Walker's] pre-eminence, politics, the theatre and sports," reported *The New York Times*. There was current Mayor William O'Dwyer; former Mayor Fiorello La Guardia, one year out of office; and New York's senior senator, Robert F. Wagner, Sr., Walker's friend since their days together as young Albany legislators. New York Yankee center fielder Joe DiMaggio and former Yankee pitching ace Vernon "Lefty" Gomez, close friends of Jimmy's, arrived together. Founder and owner Tim Mara and his entire New York Giants football team created a stir when they marched into the church as a solid phalanx moments before the Mass began. Walker had followed both the Yankees and the Giants with fervor. He had his own box at the Polo Grounds, right on the field, behind the Giants' bench, and he rarely missed a big game at Yankee Stadium, especially when Babe Ruth, now old and broken-down, was still swinging for the seats. Two of the mayor's proudest accomplishments as an Albany lawmaker were the Walker Act of 1920, legalizing boxing in New York state, and a bill—passed at the same time—permitting professional baseball games on Sundays. "New York is the hub of the athletic wheel," wrote *New York Times* sportswriter Arthur Daley. "Unless it spins quickly and surely here, it doesn't spin anywhere. And Jimmy made it spin here."

Sitting in one of the front pews, his eyes filled with tears, was Bernard "Toots" Shor, the loud, backslapping owner and host of the legendary Midtown restaurant where Jimmy Walker had gathered with his cronies after Friday night fights at Madison Square Garden, then at Fiftieth Street and Eighth Avenue, lighting up the room with his Gaelic charm and cutting wisecracks, always delivered with a devilish smile. Sitting near Toots was Mike Jacobs, a former ticket scalper at the Garden who was now the biggest boxing promoter in the country. When Walker was riding high in his first term as mayor, from 1926 to 1930, Jacobs would meet him at the doors of the Garden and pilot him to his seat with a full police escort. Jimmy was more fun to watch than the fight itself, his friends claimed. "He'd duck, counter-punch and gesticulate in restless fashion," Arthur Daley described his antics. "Occasionally he'd finish up more wearied than the boxers." Walker loved boxing, he said, because it's "a sport in which you meet only one opponent at a time, and he is always in front of you."

Grover Whalen, Mayor Walker's official city greeter, had flown in from Los Angeles for the funeral. People smiled when they spotted him filing into a front pew. Still a smartly groomed fashion plate, he awakened memories of the lush years before the Crash of '29, a time of soaring prosperity and city pride. When Walker was mayor, in the second half of the 1920s, there was a blaze of publicity and a tremendous ticker tape parade, organized by Whalen, whenever a luminary like Charles Lindbergh, conqueror of the Atlantic, arrived in town. Beginning in 1927, these parades through the city's skyscraper canyons had become national celebrations after New York City was hooked up to the entire country by the coast-to-coast radio networks—NBC and CBS—formed by communications kings David Sarnoff and William Paley, friends of the mayor.

Largely unnoticed in the cathedral that gray morning were Al Smith, Jr., and William Randolph Hearst, Jr., sons of two of the titanic figures in Walker's life—one his political mentor, the other his longtime political nemesis, the crusading newspaper mogul who had tried to prevent him from becoming mayor. Three of the chief ushers were Charles S. Hand, Edward L. Stanton, and Thomas F. McAndrews, the mayor's secretaries. These hard-toiling loyalists had attended to the city's day-to-day business during Walker's scandalously frequent absences from City Hall—off on vacations in Havana or Palm Beach, or simply home in his bed nursing a hangover.

Standing in the back of the church was an old-time welterweight named Soldier Barfield, one of dozens of pugs Walker had known in their prime and helped out on their way down. Jimmy Walker was the regular feature speaker at the Boxing Writers Dinner and "never did he deliver anything but a stirring address. He was the only man," said Arthur Daley, "who could climb into the ring at the Garden and deliver a speech that would hold the impatient fight mob absolutely enthralled. . . . The proverbial pin could be heard dropping once his sonorous voice slid liquidly through the microphone."

Daley remembered Jimmy Walker as a memorable phrasemaker, quicker on his feet than anyone he knew. In June 1938, Walker met Joe Louis, the black heavyweight champion, after Louis knocked out Max Schmeling, the big German hailed by the Nazis as evidence of the doctrine of Aryan supremacy after he beat Louis in their first fight. Shaking his hand, Walker said memorably, "Joe, you have laid a rose on Abraham Lincoln's grave."

City reporters had celebrated Jimmy Walker as the very expression of Jazz Age New York; and that's how much of the country saw him. "[To] we hicks in the hinterland," said *New York Herald* sports reporter Red Smith, "he was the symbol of his city and his era. . . . To us he was New York"—its virtues and vices, its sin and sophistication. "He was the debonair prophet of gaiety and extravagance and glitter. He was the embodiment of all the qualities which hicks like us resented and admired about New York."

Walker's "virtues," wrote reporter Milton MacKaye, "were those of the time" and of the city he governed: moral tolerance, sympathy for the underdog, and an abhorrence of hypocrisy. "His vices were equally contemporary. He was glib, vain, prodigal, luxury-loving, and amazingly indifferent to the rules of common honesty. . . . He played all night and slept half the day, he drank too much and steamed out at health resorts, he praised his Church and ignored its commandments, he bought diamond bracelets at fifteen thousand dollars a crack and would not pay his bills. Yet the city loved him." As *The New York Times* noted, "few men in public office stood as high in public regard when he began his second term as Mayor of New York in 1930."

At 11:20 A.M., the body of James John Walker was carried out of the nave and down the marble steps from which he had regularly reviewed, with a boy's delight, the St. Patrick's Day Parade. People pressed in close to the coffin, a few reaching out to toss a flower, but were met by a solid wall of blue, part of a representation of three hundred of New York's finest. A cortege was formed and moved up Fifth and Madison Avenues, into the Bronx and out to Westchester County for burial in the Gate of Heaven Cemetery at Valhalla, where, two years later, Walker's ailing friend Babe Ruth would be put into the ground. Motorcycle patrolmen escorted the cortege all the way to the cemetery. With seven priests reciting the final prayers for the dead, the Jazz Age Mayor was lowered into a grave his family had only recently acquired.

Last to leave the burial site was Walker's younger sister, Anna Burke. "Nan" the family called her. A widow, she was the only surviving member of Walker's tight-knit Greenwich Village family; and she had been, at the end, the only woman in his life. Walker had never stopped loving his second wife, Betty Compton, after she divorced him in 1941 when he could no longer provide the excitement she craved. She was the apple-cheeked chorus girl turned actress he had openly cavorted with while he was married and mayor of the city, sneaking away with her to the penthouse apartments of discreet friends for weekend trysts. They had been married in Cannes, France, in 1933, just after Jimmy divorced Janet Allen Walker, his wife of twenty-one years. Betty Compton was the mother of Walker's two adopted children, Mary Ann, age ten, and James John Walker, Jr., eleven. When Betty Compton succumbed to cancer in 1944, Nan Walker Burke and her two older boys moved in with "Uncle Jimmy" and his two children, filling to capacity Walker's modest East Side apartment.

While he was mayor, Walker had received, under the table, over one million dollars in "beneficences," as he cagily called these handouts from well-heeled friends, but his total worth had been reduced to $40,000, the consequence of his earlier extravagance, but also of his continuing generosity to friends and charities. In his last years, he supported his own and Nan's family with a salary he received as president of Majestic Records, a largely ceremonial position he assumed after serving a four-year term as the impartial arbiter for the city's garment industry. Mayor La Guardia had provided him with that $20,000-a-year sinecure, a kindness to an old political enemy in his time of need. Walker disliked La Guardia personally, seeing him as a parading moralist, closing down newsstands that sold sexually suggestive magazines. Yet he supported most of La Guardia's reforms and proclaimed him "the greatest mayor New York ever had."

In his fading years, Walker had become, once again, "toastmaster to [the] town," the most popular after-dinner speaker in the city. When *New York Times* reporter S. J. Woolf met him for an interview in 1945, he had not seen him for fifteen years and was surprised how good he looked. "He is still slim, almost as young-looking as he was, still wisecracking one minute and sentimentalizing the next. Age has not withered New York's Peter Pan, nor have setbacks soured him."

But this was not the Jimmy Walker of old. He had drastically cut back his drinking and found his greatest enjoyment in speaking to Catholic groups. For most of his public life, his behavior had been, by his own admission, "in direct denial of the faith in which I believed," but lately he had returned to the Church, finding solace in prayer and the sacraments. Every night at bedtime he read a book of the saints to his children. "The glamour of other days I have found to be worthless tinsel, and all the allure of the world just so much seduction and deception," he told a gathering at a Communion breakfast.

Though his hair had not gone gray and his cheeks were still ruddy, he was in declining health, assaulted by paralyzing headaches that caused him to retire, alone, to a darkened bedroom for hours at a time. When he collapsed at home after a speech before a boys group in early November 1946, Nan summoned his doctor, and then a priest when he fell into a coma after a blood clot formed in his brain. He was rushed to the hospital and never regained consciousness. He left this world on November 18, 1946, at age sixty-five. Nan was at his side, holding his hand. He would have liked that. She was the living link to the days he had remembered most fondly: growing up in a lively, working-class neighborhood, protected and encouraged by a strong father and an indulgent mother, and feeling in his bones the energy and urgency of the larger city—its call to bigger things.

His youthful dream was to be a songwriter, a player on the Broadway scene, but the father he worshipped, a force in the local Democratic organization, had pushed him into law and politics. With Manhattan's Tammany Hall machine solidly behind him, the slim young dandy made a rocketlike ascent, becoming, in quick succession, a state assemblyman, a state senator, and president pro tempore of the Albany Senate, where he guided into law Governor Al Smith's progressive reforms.

When sworn in as the city's ninety-seventh mayor on January 1, 1926, he was one of the most popular figures ever to rise to that office; even some of Tammany's fiercest critics expected solid things from him. A little over six years later, on September 1, 1932, he was forced to resign, pushed out of office on suspicion of rank corruption by members of his own party, led by his political sponsor, ex-Governor Al Smith and current Governor Franklin Delano Roosevelt. Party leaders had no choice. A sweeping investigation launched by Republicans in the New York legislature, and conducted by Judge Samuel Seabury, counsel of a joint legislative committee formed to investigate corruption in New York City government, had unearthed massive graft and incompetence in the Walker administration and in the municipal courts it oversaw.

Yet even in his hour of disgrace, Walker had a large and loyal following in the city. Though emphatically competent, Seabury was a frigid inquisitor, pompous and forbiddingly distant, and under his scorching cross-examination, Walker had handled himself, if not with candor, with his usual wit and style. "You tell him Jimmy," supporters shouted the morning the smartly dressed mayor stepped out of a black city sedan to enter Seabury's packed hearing room. The feeling among many New Yorkers, including some hard-eyed pols like Edward J. Flynn, political boss of the Bronx and later a confidant of President Franklin Roosevelt, was that Walker "was never personally dishonest," that he had been done in by some of his more "superficial and rapacious" friends, rich and well-connected men he had unwisely trusted. In time, this became Walker's own professed version of reality. "No one can buy or sell me but friends sometimes have made a fool of me."

It is doubtful that Walker himself truly believed this. Years after Governor Roosevelt's own investigation made it impossible for him to stay in office, Walker confided to Gene Fowler, the city newsman who became his first biographer: "I knew how to say 'no,' but seldom could bring myself to say it. A woman and politician must say that word often, and mean it—or else." While Seabury had failed to trace a single "wrong dollar to Walker's pocket," Walker was too bright and knowing—contra Flynn—to be duped repeatedly by those close to him. He needed money, lots of it, to live the high life, and though there may never have been explicit quid pro quos—this gift for that favor from the city—he had egregiously violated the public trust. He did this through his moral carelessness and inattention to the details of governance—and his lack of vigilance over his own life and the lives of those officials he appointed or retained to do the city's business honestly and efficiently. This was inexcusable if not unlawful behavior. In the end, Mayor Walker slid his neck into a noose of his own making. The writer Ben Hecht had it right: "No man could have held life so carelessly without falling down a manhole before he was done."

Walker's amorality also prevented him from making the quick comeback his political friends had begun to plot on the eve of his resignation, just before he left with Betty Compton for Europe, where they were married. His die-hard supporters counted greatly on the fact that Walker had not been officially charged with a single crime. After returning from abroad, Walker should, they advised, call in reporters, insist he had received an unfair hearing from Roosevelt, and announce his candidacy for mayor in a special November election called to fill his vacated seat. He should leave it to the people of New York to decide if he had violated their trust.

It was an audacious gamble that might have worked. Walker had lost some of his luster but was still electable; in fact, he remained electable until the day he died. In a 1945 New York *Daily News* straw poll, 38 percent of New Yorkers wanted him to be the next mayor. He received more support than any other potential candidate, including La Guardia, who received only 25 percent of the votes cast. And Walker won in all five boroughs. This was a reprise of the 1929 election, when he defeated Congressman La Guardia's bid to unseat him, winning every election district in the city, an unprecedented feat.

Walker's style was undeniably a source of his popularity but in the month he resigned, many New Yorkers remembered the substance, as well. Jimmy Walker had gotten things done.

The sensationalism that has substituted for serious scholarship about Walker has obscured some of his solid accomplishments. While not a pugnacious reformer in the La Guardia mold, Walker made greatly needed improvements in the city's hospitals, struck down restrictions against African American doctors at Harlem Hospital, built new schools, parks, and playgrounds, established New York's first municipal sanitation department and the city's first planning commission, and pushed through tunnel, bridge, and highway projects to relieve vehicular congestion. He started or laid the groundwork for the West Side Highway, the FDR Drive, the Triborough Bridge, the Queens-Midtown Tunnel, and hundreds of miles of new subway lines. New York voters also associated him with two great civic accomplishments that he had nothing to do with: the completion of the Holland Tunnel—The Highway Under the Hudson, as it was called—in 1927, and the construction, beginning that same year, of the George Washington Bridge, spanning the Hudson a few miles north of the city's first automobile tunnel. To millions of city voters, he remained in 1932 "the living symbol of a glittering chapter in city history," said *The New York Times.*

The city never built more ambitiously or aggressively than it did during Walker's administration. Manhattan was turned into a gigantic construction site, with steel girders climbing into the clouds, rivet guns hammering away,

and mud-caked laborers digging up the streets and moving entire buildings to
make way for more underground trains. Most of the activity was in Midtown,
which experienced an epochal rebuilding process that began just before World
War I and reached full momentum in 1927, Walker's second year in office.
The changes were everywhere. The New York Central Railroad's hideously unsightly train yard, a scar on the land extending for entire city blocks north of
West Forty-second Street, was made over into an arrow-straight boulevard of
regal apartment houses: Park Avenue, "Street of Dreams." On Fifth Avenue, the
castellated mansions of the descendants of Gilded Age tycoons—the Vanderbilts, Huntingtons, and others—were torn down and replaced by fashionable
shops and department stores, among them Saks Fifth Avenue and Bergdorf
Goodman, making Fifth Avenue just below Central Park a Parisian-like shopping emporium. Much of this was the work of Jewish real estate kings, up from
the ghetto. Jewish entrepreneurs also moved the city's garment industry from
near Madison Square to just south of Times Square in Midtown, to be closer
to the out-of-town buyers of women's fashions who came streaming into the
city by train, debarking at one of its imperial rail stations—Grand Central Terminal or Pennsylvania Station—and staying at new, fashionably tall Midtown
hotels. In an astonishingly short span of time, the entire area around Grand
Central Terminal was turned into a new skyscraper city, a city within a city,
Terminal City, many of its office towers and hotels connected to one another,
and to the terminal, by underground passageways lined with smart shops and
restaurants.

These seismic changes in the cityscape were inspired and engineered
by businessmen of towering ambition, a number of whom, including Irwin
S. Chanin, Walter P. Chrysler, and Fred F. French, had risen from meager
circumstances. But they could not have been carried out without the active
encouragement of city government. Mayor Walker never tired of reminding
voters of this. He ran himself ragged attending the groundbreaking and ribbon cutting of almost every major civic improvement in his nearly seven years
in office, even the installation of traffic lights on Park Avenue. He was perpetually upbeat, reminding New Yorkers that they were living in the greatest city
in the world, at its maximum moment. "The great basis of Walker's popularity
was his passion for making everybody happy," wrote reporter Alva Johnston.
"In spurts he handled the city's business impressively, but his chief task was
that of spreading sunshine in the metropolis."

At cornerstone ceremonies and black-tie banquets, Walker displayed his
unerring ability to make people he had never seen before feel that there was
a special bond between them and him, a "bond of sympathy." Listening to
Walker, whether at a B'nai B'rith convention or a quilting party, people felt he

was speaking directing to them, "Hundreds of thousands, if not millions of New Yorkers, firmly believe that they are among Jimmy's closest friends," Alva Johnston noted in the year of Walker's resignation.

New Yorkers also remembered that Walker had been one of the only New York politicians to demand the repeal of Prohibition the very year it went into effect. In Albany, he had led the fight against the Eighteenth Amendment, and as mayor he became "the embodiment of New York's, and to some extent of the nation's dislike of Prohibition and Puritanism," wrote Johnston. "He became the foremost American champion of a man's right to be himself. His life was an antiseptic against hypocrisy; it was a standing rebuke to the Anti-Saloon League and the Methodist Board of Temperance, Prohibition and Public Morals; it was holy water to the devils of intolerance and persecution."

Thirty-three years after Walker's death a cabbie told the writer Thomas J. Fleming, "This town ain't been the same since we lost Jimmy Walker."

But in 1932, Walker had too much going against him to be given a second chance. Seabury's revelations, Smith's and Roosevelt's opposition, along with the Great Depression, which ended the biggest construction boom in the city's history, mortally wounded him. The Church finished him off.

The Catholic Church in New York City had for years been outraged by Walker's sexual escapades with actresses and chorus girls. During Walker's first term, the archbishop of New York, Patrick Joseph Cardinal Hayes, son of sternly orthodox immigrants from County Kerry, Ireland, sent a prominent layman to censure Walker for "bringing shame" on both his wife and the church of his ancestors. Walker—forever his own man, giving orders, rarely taking them—would not be lectured to; he named two esteemed Catholics, benefactors of the church, whose sexual conduct was no better than his own. "You go back and tell the cardinal to take care of his two altar boys and I'll take care of myself."

That was all Walker heard from the Church until late September 1932, when word got back to the cardinal that Walker was planning a political comeback. Not long after this, Monsignor John P. Chidwick, a representative of Cardinal Hayes, preached the funeral oration for Martin G. McCue, an East Side Tammany leader, at Manhattan's St. Agnes Church. Everyone of consequence in the city's Democratic Party was in the church that morning, including John McCooey, Brooklyn's political boss, and John Francis Curry, head of Tammany Hall—the two Democratic powerhouses behind the effort to reelect Walker. Curry, a devout Catholic who "would no more think of missing Mass in the morning than he would think of missing the race track in the afternoon," was a close friend of Monsignor Chidwick, who had performed his marriage ceremony.

In his funeral oration, the monsignor lauded McCue's deep religious faith and personal morality, offering his life as an example for all political officials. "Not only in official life, but in private life, should a man be clean and pure." To the Democratic chieftains in the pews that morning these words were "charged with meaning," wrote *New York Times* reporter William R. Conklin, who would write the inside story of Walker's failed comeback. It was high drama, "the spiritual government of the city arrayed against its temporal government." And it was virtually unprecedented. The Catholic Church of New York rarely intruded in politics.

Monsignor Chidwick spoke with cool deliberateness. He personally knew most of the Democratic district leaders who were at the funeral Mass, and settled his eyes on several of them as he preached. They knew he spoke for the cardinal, and that going against the Church was an unwinnable cause.

John Curry had an idea of what was coming even before he entered the church that morning. He had had dinner with Monsignor Chidwick earlier in the week. When he raised the prospect of Walker's bid for reelection, Chidwick told him that if that happened the Church would go after Walker hard. That meant a public rebuke of Walker's personal morality and an ecclesiastical censure of his relationship with Betty Compton.

Word may have reached Walker, who was still abroad when the Democrats met at Madison Square Garden to choose a candidate. His name was put into nomination as a formality, and he cabled the convention, declining the honor. Tammany's new choice was Surrogate Judge John P. O'Brien, a clean but colorless candidate. He won the special election for mayor in 1932, defeating Acting Mayor Joseph V. McKee, a write-in candidate. La Guardia, a Republican Party–City Fusion candidate, crushed O'Brien and third party candidate McKee the following year.

It was the end of the Jimmy Walker Era.

PART ONE

POWER AND POLITICS

CHAPTER ONE

A TEST FOR TAMMANY

*Tammany today stands higher in the respect of the com-
munity than it has ever stood before.*

NEW YORK *WORLD*, JANUARY 1, 1926

The Labors of Hercules

On the brisk Manhattan morning of his inauguration, New Year's Day 1926,
Jimmy Walker arrived at City Hall exactly on time, shocking nearly everyone
who had gathered to greet him. As he stepped out of his sleek gray town car,
he waved to the crowd, "a noisy, joyous gathering," many of the celebrators old
friends from his Greenwich Village neighborhood. Some of his loyalists had
just finished bringing in the New Year, the women's evening gowns showing
beneath their winter wraps. When the mayor-elect came into view, they blew
whistles and party horns, and some of them held up hip flasks to salute their
trim debonair hero as he swept past them and up the marble steps, acknowl-
edging a few old friends with a nod and a quick pull on the brim of his silk hat.
Shoulders hunched forward, eyes staring straight ahead, he spoke to no one in
the crowd. "Let me in. I want to work," he said to the policemen who opened a
wedge for him through a solid wall of reporters and photographers.

Every corridor and room in the stately building, the oldest city hall in continuous use in the country, was packed with Walker enthusiasts. Graybeards
at City Hall judged it the largest crowd ever to attend the swearing in of a New
York mayor. Nearly eight hundred people elbowed their way into the chambers
of the Board of Estimate, the principal governing body of the city, to witness
Jimmy Walker take the oath of office.

When Walker entered the chambers around noon the crowd broke into
wild applause, cheering him as if he were a "matinee idol." He was dressed like

13

a Broadway sport, in a tight-fitting double-breasted suit and black pointed patent leather shoes—"tooth-pick shoes"—shined to a gleam and encased in gray spats. As he approached the dais, he bowed to his wife, Janet, to other members of his family, and to the assembled leadership of Tammany Hall. After being sworn in by Justice Robert F. Wagner, Sr., an old friend, Walker approached the podium and adjusted the special microphone. This was the first inauguration of a New York City mayor to be broadcast on the new medium of radio.

In a brief, businesslike address, Walker vowed to rid city government of corruption and political favoritism and deliver greatly needed urban services—more schools, playgrounds, parks, and hospitals. He would ask the state legislative to increase the city's debt limit so that he could borrow money to build new subways, highways, tunnels, and bridges—and modern expressways along Manhattan's waterfront—to relieve mounting traffic congestion caused by the tremendous increase in the number of automobiles and trucks on city streets. Walker pledged as well to establish the city's first municipal bus line and its first garbage and sewage disposal system, the initial step in a long-overdue effort to clean up New York's dangerously polluted rivers, pestilence-breeding recipients of most of the city's raw sewage.

But the issues of most immediate importance to the new mayor were the expansion of the municipal subway system and the retention of the nickel subway fare, measures of immense consequence to hundreds of thousands of New Yorkers who commuted to their jobs on the city's scandalously overcrowded underground system, the world's largest rapid transit system. Walker had been swept into office on the promise to prevail against the two private corporations that operated the subway trains under a long-term lease with the city. These companies—the Interborough Rapid Transit Company (IRT) and the Brooklyn-Manhattan Transit Company (BMT)—were lobbying strenuously to raise the price of a ticket, which, by law, could not be increased except by mutual agreement between the city and the operators. Walker said he would "cut off his right arm" rather then increase the five-cent fare.*

Along with a number of prominent urban progressives, Walker saw sub-

---

* The city government built the original subway system at the turn of the century with public funds. A 1913 arrangement to more than double the mileage of the system, called the "dual contracts," granted the IRT and the Brooklyn Rapid Transit Company (BRT) a lease of forty-nine years to operate the city-owned subways. (The BRT went into bankruptcy in 1918 and was reorganized five years later as the BMT.) The companies paid part of the construction costs for expansion and the entire cost of equipment, and agreed to a five-cent fare for the duration of the operating leases. After ten years, the city had the right to terminate the leases, pay off the companies for their investments, and "recapture" the subway lines.

way construction as a form of urban planning. The expansion of the system would accelerate the exodus from the dismal tenements and rookeries of lower Manhattan, providing convenient linkages to downtown centers of employment and amusement for upward-bound families who could finally, in the prosperous 1920s, afford to move to green spaces in Queens, the Bronx, and the outer reaches of Brooklyn, where new housing was being built with furious energy by private contractors. Most of the great problems facing the City of New York, Walker insisted, arose from overcrowding at the center—the twenty-three-square-mile island of Manhattan, whose nearly two million residents made it one of the most congested urban places on earth. Once the slums of Manhattan's Lower East Side were thinned out, Walker believed the value of vacated real estate would fall, inducing private builders to construct affordable modern apartments for those residents who chose not to move. As a further inducement for developers, he proposed generous tax incentives and city assistance in tearing down disgracefully maintained tenement housing.

The mayor went further, sounding, unexpectedly, like a visionary. He would end the "haphazard and piecemeal" methods of dealing with city problems. "In the future," he said, "we must proceed to deal with them on a city-wide, comprehensive scale," recognizing that problems like congestion and substandard housing were closely interlinked. Before his administration could vigorously attack these problems, however, there would have to be "an accurate, scientific survey of the city." Walker pledged to assemble a team of experts from government and the private sector to identify New York's most pressing problems and suggest ways to deal with them in an integrated fashion. When the survey was completed, his administration would fashion a "City Plan"—the first in Gotham's history—to guide Greater New York's future development.

This was an audacious program of urban rehabilitation, yet Walker pledged to work for "the lowest tax rate possible." Could he balance his aggressive municipal agenda with fiscal restraint? "The labors of Hercules," said a skeptical *New York Times*, "would be nothing by comparison."

Walker had already made many of his municipal appointments. His administration would be "Tammany through and through," he openly admitted. Almost every appointed city official, including twenty of Walker's twenty-five city commissioners, was beholden to Tammany. A product of Tammany's political culture, Walker saw patronage and the merit system—what some considered fire and ice—perfectly compatible. He would reward loyal Democrats, but only those clearly qualified for their positions.

Walker was proud to be part of Tammany, proud of all it had done for his tribe—Irish Catholics who had begun arriving in the city in successive waves in the 1840s, escaping the ruinous Potato Famine. The Society of St. Tammany—named after Tamanend, a legendary chief of the Lenni-Lenape nation—had been formed in 1789 as a fraternal and patriotic organization with a set of pseudo–Native American rituals and titles. Headquarters was the "Wigwam," Tammany members were "braves," members of the governing board were "sachems," and the head of Tammany was the "grand sachem." The organization quickly evolved into the most powerful urban political machine in the country. Its sharp-witted early leaders, among them Aaron Burr and Martin Van Buren, went after the working man's vote, supporting universal male suffrage and the abolition of imprisonment for debt. With no effective city organization for public relief, Irish immigrants turned to Tammany's attentive ward leaders, who helped them find work and gain citizenship, and rallied to the relief of destitute and disoriented families, providing milk for their babies, coal to warm their rooms, and dollars to bury their dead with dignity.

The Irish were also drawn to Tammany out of sheer self-defense. It was a shield against the virulently anti-Catholic and nativist movements of the time, whose street gangs attacked their churches and assaulted their priests, and whose hate-filled demagogues lumped together all Irishman as "paddies"— coarse, loud, hard-drinking, and clannish, smelling of whiskey and boiled cabbage. The Irish found protection inside Tammany and eventually took it over. In the years after the Civil War, an organization that had originally excluded Catholics and the foreign-born became a disciplined political army dominated by first- and second-generation sons of Erin. Beginning in 1872 with John Kelly, the first of ten successive Irish American bosses, they turned Tammany into an instrument of Irish advancement, filling the police and fire departments with the children of the Famine Generation and elevating young countrymen of promise to political positions.

Tammany fished for votes among almost every ethnic group, opening opportunities on the bench and in city government for Germans and Russian Jews; but tens of thousands of Jewish voters in the city's Garment District remained loyal to their socialist parties and trade unions. Thousands of Italian immigrants, blocked by the Irish from holding positions of even small consequence in Tammany, turned in frustration to the Republican Party. New York's expanding African American population did not vote in great numbers until the 1930s; most of those who did vote remained loyal to the party of Lincoln and emancipation. The handful of Tammany clubhouses that recruited African American members maintained separate recreational facilities for them, with blacks in the basement and whites upstairs.

At times, Tammany ruled New York, but Tammany rule was never continuous. When Tammany went too far, when it stuffed too many ballot boxes, when its leaders stole from the city with reckless abandon, reform movements rose up and tossed it out of office. The election of Jimmy Walker was the first time Tammany "ruled supreme" since the thieving administration of Robert A. Van Wyck, defeated at the polls in 1901 by Republican reformer Seth Low. This ended the long rule of arrogantly corrupt Richard Croker as headman of Tammany Hall.

Walker's predecessor as mayor, John F. Hylan, a Brooklyn Democrat, had been backed initially by Tammany, out of expediency, but no one at the Wigwam considered him a blood brother. As mayor he had taken orders, not from Tammany, but from wily Brooklyn political boss John McCooey, whose allegiance to Tammany was never complete. Hylan was also closely aligned with newspaper publisher William Randolph Hearst, a sworn enemy of Tammany. An independent Democrat, active in New York politics for over two decades, Hearst owned two big New York dailies, the *American* and its evening edition, the *Journal*, papers that relentlessly attacked Governor Al Smith, a Tammany man to the core of his being.

Going back to the middle of the nineteenth century, to the scandalous rule of Boss William Magear Tweed, Tammany Hall had been linked in the public mind with colossal corruption. At the time of Jimmy Walker's inauguration, however, reporters, including prestigious Walter Lippmann, began writing about "A New Tammany," a chastened political organization led by clean-government progressives like Governor Smith, Justice Robert F. Wagner, Sr., and State Senator Jimmy Walker. These were new men who "have ideas of their own . . . and are not of the Old Tammany brew of hacks and tools of the boss," observed the *New York Post*. A number of them, including coolly self-possessed Edward J. Flynn, the boss of the Bronx, had been to college and law school and were "as much at home in dinner coats and plus-fours as their grandfathers were in red undershirts." In the years before World War I, these young insurgents had begun advancing an ambitious agenda of social and labor legislation at the state level, measures that were backed by Charles Francis Murphy, the shrewdest and most powerful overlord in Tammany history.

When Murphy died of a heart attack in 1924, Governor Smith stepped into the power vacuum at the Wigwam and handpicked Murphy's successor, Judge George Washington Olvany, a graduate of New York University Law School. The first Tammany leader to complete college, Olvany pledged to commit the organization—which was preeminently a municipal, not a statewide machine—to the reforms the governor was instituting in Albany.

The press was eager to give Tammany a chance. The *New York Herald Tribune*, the most respected Republican organ in the city, saw Walker's election as

Tammany's "greatest opportunity in its history." Mayor Walker "takes office with the good will of the entire people." The more liberal New York *World*, a longtime Tammany nemesis, was equally hopeful. "Tammany today stands higher in the respect of the community than it has ever stood before. . . . If it governs well it will deserve and will receive full credit. If it fails, it . . . will have no excuses." The Walker administration would tell if there was truly a New Tammany.

Walker did not shrink from the challenge. "I have determined to be the best mayor this city ever had," he told reporters who covered City Hall. But there were skeptics in the room. Everyone knew that Jimmy Walker had not been Al Smith's original choice for mayor, that the governor had questioned whether his old friend and political acolyte was suited for the job.

The Battle of the Boroughs

During the run-up to the city's 1925 Democratic mayoralty race all attention had been on Alfred Emanuel Smith. He had just begun his third term as governor and had come close to securing his party's nomination for president at its bitterly divided 1924 convention in Madison Square Garden. Smith was feeling his power, moving purposefully to prepare the ground for 1928, when he hoped to become America's first Roman Catholic president. Part of his plan, worked out in secret with George Olvany, was to prevent the re-nomination of Mayor John Hylan for a third term. Smith considered Hylan monumentally incompetent; just as critical, Smith could not control Hylan, a political creature of Hearst and McCooey, powerbrokers not known for their civic integrity. He wanted a confidant he could trust to govern honorably and competently. With anti-Tammany sentiment running strong in the rural districts of the country, a city scandal could ruin his run for the presidential nomination.

The Hylan-Hearst combination would be hard to beat. Cagey John McCooey was one of the toughest political in-fighters in urban politics; and he was gearing up for a fight. Brooklyn had recently overtaken Manhattan as the most populous borough in New York City, and a third Hylan term would make its political machine more powerful perhaps than Tammany and establish McCooey as the rightful political ruler of the city's Democratic Party. Tammany Hall had historically controlled only the Democratic politics of Manhattan, but during the twenty-two-year-long reign of Boss Murphy, from 1902 to 1924, it extended its sway over the Democratic organizations of the other four New York boroughs—Bronx, Queens, Brooklyn, and Staten Island whose leaders resented the encroachment of Tammany under imperious Boss Murphy.*

After Murphy's death, however, Tammany was reduced to controlling only Manhattan and the Bronx, and New York City returned to what it has been ever since, "not a city but a league of cities," each nearly autonomous city or borough having its own elected president, who governed like a "minor mayor." All the while, Queens, Brooklyn, and the Bronx—and even thinly populated Staten Island—were exploding with growth, making them stronger politically and more independent of Tammany. In the Bronx, Edward J. Flynn remained a staunch Tammany man out of an admixture of loyalty and self-interest. With Murphy's backing, he had recently become the Democratic boss of the Bronx, and he was a close friend of Al Smith, whom he vowed to stand behind in the approaching showdown with McCooey. But Maurice Connolly, the longtime borough president of Queens, and David S. Rendt, Staten Island's Democratic boss, aligned with Hylan and McCooey. So when Al Smith left Albany and de-camped in New York City in the summer of 1925 to unseat John Hylan he ran into a firestorm of opposition from three of New York's boroughs.

To prevail, Smith needed a masterful campaigner. After being turned down by his first two choices, Surrogate James A. Foley and State Supreme Court Justice Robert Wagner, he settled on Walker, the choice of Olvany and Flynn.

Forty-three-year-old Jimmy Walker was charming, fast on his feet, and a supremely skilled communicator. But he was a dangerous gamble—his careless personal life was an open book. Flynn and Olvany believed he could be reined in. Smith did not—at least not initially. The governor had other concerns. At a meeting of Democratic leaders in Smith's Albany office, Robert Moses, one of the governor's most trusted confidants, claimed that Walker was "incapable of sustained effort." That struck a chord with Smith, whose career was a pure product of sustained effort. On the other hand, everything seemed to come easily for light-spirited Jimmy Walker.

Jimmy and Al

No one in New York politics knew Senator Walker better than Al Smith. They first met on New Year's Eve 1895, at a party at the Walker home on St. Luke's Place, in Greenwich Village. Walker was only fifteen at the time, and Smith was a twenty-three-year-old politician of promise from a Lower East

---

* Each of the boroughs was also a county. Brooklyn was Kings County, Queens was Queens County, Staten Island was Richmond County, Manhattan was New York County, and the Bronx was Bronx County.

Side Tammany ward who had come to visit Jimmy's father, a former Tammany alderman. A bachelor who supported his widowed mother, Catherine Mulvihill Smith, the daughter of Irish immigrants, Smith lived with her in a railroad flat near the Manhattan anchorage tower of the Brooklyn Bridge. Though a pious Catholic, Smith had a racy vocabulary and was known to lift a glass or two.

They next met in 1910, just after Walker was elected to the Albany Assembly with the backing of the local Tammany boss. "My father went with me to Grand Central the day I was leaving, and Al was there to meet us," Walker recalled years later. "He practically took me aboard the train by the hand, and our rooms were in readiness for us when we reached Albany. He introduced me to all the people he thought I should know—and kept me away from those he thought I shouldn't."

This was Smith's sixth year in the Assembly and he and Walker were roommates for a time—part of the Tammany "buddy system"—at the Ten Eyck Hotel, the unofficial headquarters of Albany's insiders. Smith and Walker took the train to Albany together every Monday morning and returned to New York as seatmates on Friday afternoons. On Sunday evenings, Walker and his fiancée, Janet "Allie" Allen, a vaudeville performer, visited Al and his wife of nine years, Catherine "Katie" Dunn, at their new home at 25 Oliver Street, not far from where Smith was born. Allie sang and Jimmy played the piano for her.

The two young assemblymen shared a passion for theater and popular music, and Smith used these social occasions to school Walker in the intricacies of Albany politics. Al Smith was built for politics; from an early age he was determined to follow into power his Tammany sponsor and surrogate father, Thomas F. Foley. "Big Tom" Foley, an enormous red-faced Irishman with a black handlebar mustache and arms of iron, looked after the Democratic neighborhoods of his district "as English squires looked after the welfare of their country villages."

Foley's saloon at Water Street and James Slip was not far from where Smith was born, and Smith would spend his free evenings there, running errands for the organization and watching with pride as his mentor handed out coins to kids on the block and discreetly supported indigent Irish widows. In 1903, Foley pronounced Smith, a rapid riser in the organization, ready for the State Assembly, a nomination that guaranteed his election.

Jimmy Walker had also grown up in a Tammany neighborhood, one his father presided over; but from an early age he had set his sights on Broadway, not Albany, hoping to become a songwriter and a composer of musical comedies. An indifferent student, he spent his Saturdays at the vaudeville houses on Union Square, often lingering from eleven in the morning until closing at midnight. His father wanted him home, hitting the books, preparing for a career in law and politics. To appease him, Jimmy attended New York Law School, barely graduating. Then, claiming he was not yet ready for politics, he took a job writing lyrics for a music publishing house and began hanging around West Twenty-eighth Street, between Broadway and Sixth Avenue. This was New York's famous Tin Pan Alley, named for the cacophony of sounds—like the banging on tin pans—which dozens of song "pluggers" made on their upright pianos. Each plugger was squeezed into a cubbyhole in a music publisher's building, where he pounded away all day, trying out new tunes for vaudeville and the sensationally successful sheet music business.

Here on the street where American popular music was born, Walker met Jimmy Durante and Irving Berlin; and here, in 1908, at age twenty-eight, he made his first breakthrough as a songwriter with a sentimental ballad, "Will You Love Me in December as You Do in May?" Thousands of copies of sheet music were sold, bringing in royalties of over $10,000. Walker spent part of the windfall on a dozen custom-tailored suits, a stack of handmade silk shirts, three fedoras, and a walking stick—something no Broadway swell would be seen without. But there were no successful encores as a songwriter, and the following year Walker bowed to his father's wishes and ran for the State Assembly. He won handily and celebrated by buying an engagement ring for Allie, his steady date since his law school days.

Al Smith had started out slowly in Albany and urged Walker to do the same. On instructions from Foley, Smith had sat in the last row of the Assembly chamber and didn't utter a single word on the floor in his first year in office. He took orders from Tammany until he was powerful enough to give them.

Al Smith learned to be an effective legislator through painstaking research. After a simple dinner of corned beef and cabbage, he would head to the Capitol library, where he would pore over every bill that had been introduced that day in the legislature. In time, he became the most accomplished bill writer in the Assembly. Walker, by contrast, was a natural. "There's no smarter man I ever knew," said Joseph Proskauer, a Smith associate notoriously stingy with praise. Walker prepared for debates in the Assembly as he had studied for exams in law school: not by reading—he claimed to have read only six books from the time he entered law school until the year he ran for mayor—but by what he called aural intake. A classmate read aloud to him from the textbooks, recitations Walker put to memory. In Albany, an aide would read the essentials of a bill to him minutes before he was to appear on the floor of the Assembly. Walker would then stride into the chamber and argue for or against it with effortless ease. He was so good that New York producer David Belasco sent young actors to Albany to "learn something from the little master."

Walker became a force in the Assembly in his very first year, a self-assured speaker and a gifted debater. He advanced rapidly, becoming a senator in 1915 and floor leader of his party in 1920. His wit was so devastating he once helped kill an opposition measure with a wisecrack, a Clean Books Bill that would have censored sexually suggestive literary works on the argument that they offended young women's sensibilities. "No woman," Walker said, "has ever been ruined by a book."

Walker transformed politics into theater, becoming eventually a "gallery god." When he "was scheduled to speak the galleries were crowded and applause was almost continuous as he walked swiftly up and down the broad center aisle of the Assembly chamber, a slim, excited figure with his dark hair in disorder, dressed like a Broadway actor, relishing the laughter that his sallies earned," wrote reporter Henry Pringle.

Walker had real political courage. He took on the Ku Klux Klan when it was a force in the early 1920s in upstate New York, "unmasking" the organization by securing the passage of a bill, the Walker Law, that required it to file sworn copies of its constitution, membership rosters, oaths, and list of officers. "We see men of the mask attempting to dictate how we shall worship God, regardless of the conviction of our own consciences," he spoke with angry eloquence, glaring at senators known to be sympathetic to the Klan. "We see the immigrant excluded. We see everything and everybody threatened with censorship. We thank God that these are the characteristics of only a comparatively few fanatics but, few though they be, they are a menace to the Republic, and they must be obliterated."

Murphy's Young Men

Early in his Albany career Walker caught the eye of Boss Murphy, who saw him as a "comer," a young reformer who could help him change Tammany's public image in the aftermath of the public scandals that had undone Richard Croker. Politics had made Murphy immeasurably rich, master of a magnificent seaside hideaway on Long Island with its own private nine-hole golf course. But he coveted power even more than money. After defeating several challengers for his position, he vowed "to remain the leader of Tammany Hall as long as I live." He then gained near complete control of the entire state Democratic Party, becoming the first and last Tammany leader to accomplish this. Virtually invulnerable, Murphy called a halt to the strong-arm methods of the past—voter fraud and intimidation—methods he himself had used to climb to the top. In the future, Tammany would prevail by ballots, not bullying.

It was Murphy's pursuit of power—not just to have it but also to hold it in perpetuity—that turned him into a supporter of real political reform. Long before he secured Walker's election to the State Senate in 1915, he had begun working closely with Walker, Smith, and Wagner, progressives who were introducing legislation that would redound to Tammany's benefit, rehabilitating its image and broadening its electoral reach. The press called them Murphy's Young Men and they met with the boss on weekends at Delmonico's, Murphy's favorite Manhattan restaurant, where his private table in the opulent Scarlet Room rested on four carved Bengal Tigers, the mascot of Tammany. In Murphy's private salon on the second floor of Delmonico's, even convivial Jimmy Walker was reduced to silence in the boss's sphinxlike presence.

Murphy spoke only when necessary and then in short "jerky" sentences, punctuated by periods of silence that sometimes lasted for over a minute. "He looks dense," the reporter Lincoln Steffens described Murphy, "but he acts with force, decision, and skill." And he was a pillar of support for his Albany boys, whose reforms "make us many votes," he told social worker Frances Perkins, later President Franklin Roosevelt's secretary of labor. "Give the people everything they want," Murphy is said to have told Walker, his "boy."

But Al Smith, who know him better, saw a troublesome side of Jimmy Walker. The governor, a faithful husband and the solicitous father of five children, was worried about the midweek pleasure excursions Walker made from Albany to Manhattan, where he was seen conspicuously with Broadway actresses, bootleggers, and gold-digging chorus girls. Walker had also begun to drift apart from Smith. At informal social events he seemed embarrassed to be in the governor's company. It happened all too often. Jimmy would be sipping champagne and chatting amiably with a small circle of intimate friends when Al would roar in and take over the room, a cigar in one hand, a glass of beer in the other, wearing an outrageous tie, bright red suspenders, and a garish vest that didn't entirely cover his prominent paunch. Smith didn't speak—he shouted—his gravelly voice as loud as his clothing.

Now the leader of the Democrats in the State Senate, with a thriving Manhattan law office to support his lifestyle, Walker no longer jumped to Smith's commands and started seeing less of him socially. When Big Tom Foley died in January 1925, Smith took Walker aside at the funeral and lectured him for attending the opening performance of a Broadway show the previous evening, when the rest of Tammany was in full mourning. "Listen Al," Walker said sharply. "You're confused. It was Tom Foley who died, not I."

This sustained Smith's suspicion that Walker was not completely committed to politics. The governor was not mistaken. Long after he was forced from office, Walker would confide to his friend and biographer Gene Fowler: "The excitement of politics got into my veins. I had happy years in the Senate, but always my heart was in the theatre and in songs. I really was moving against my own desires most of the time, and the inner conflicts were great."

In the summer of 1925, on the eve of the Democratic primary for mayor, Al Smith saw his careless friend about to be consumed by a catastrophe of his own creation. Walker was being seen around town with Yvonne "Vonnie" Shelton, a sleek-bodied French-Canadian singer and dancer he had spotted years before in the Ziegfeld Follies. His wife, Allie, had put on weight, and although the couple had no children the former showgirl preferred to stay at home at night and wanted her husband beside her.

Walker may have been a time bomb, but with the fight with John Hylan fast approaching, and with Flynn and Olvany pressing for Walker, Al Smith, almost against reason, began to hope for a conversion, telling his Tammany golfing buddies that "if Walker . . . would rid himself of that certain party he has been going around with—which he won't—and go back to Mrs. Walker, then things might be different."

Word got back to Walker and for the next few weeks he was not seen at any of his favorite Manhattan nightspots. It was a ruse, however. Walker was partying in a penthouse rented by a friend from a dowager who was on holiday. In his complimentary biography of Walker, Gene Fowler makes light of this charade, but it is, in fact, a deeply revealing indicator of Walker's character. Jimmy Walker had a casual way of blurring the distinction between right and wrong, legal and illegal. For Walker, it "was a question of convenience rather than morality," the writer Peter Quinn shrewdly notes. "The unforgivable offense was to be boring or colorless."

In late July, Al Smith summoned Walker to the Half Moon Hotel on Coney Island, where he was spending the weekend with his family. When Walker arrived, the governor greeted him cordially and then cut straight to the point: How had he managed to keep away from Vonnie and the clubs? "We all grow up sometime," Walker reputedly replied. When Smith offered him a drink, Walker, suppressing a smile, asked for soda water. At the end of the conversation, Smith placed his hand on Walker's shoulder and told him he was his man to beat John Hylan. Later, Joseph Proskauer asked the governor incredulously, "Al, you believed him?" Smith replied, shaking his head, "Joe, the man swore to me on the memory of his sainted mother."

The following week, after an uninvited visit from several Tammany envoys, Vonnie Shelton left for Cuba. Her "vacation" lasted through the primary season.

It would be one of the most bruising political battles in the city's history. Smith's decision to back Walker split the Democratic Party along borough lines, Manhattan and the Bronx against Queens, Brooklyn, and Staten Island. This was more than a mayoralty election; it was a war for control of the future of the city's Democratic Party. The stakes were enormous. New York City had the biggest municipal patronage pot in the country.

What a Candidate!

On August 20, 1925, Jimmy Walker launched his campaign "among his own," in the Greenwich Village neighborhood he had never left, either physically or emotionally. He had been living there with Allie since their wedding day, April 11, 1912, in the house he had been raised in at 6 St. Luke's Place. In an emotional speech at a local schoolhouse, Walker paid tribute to his deceased parents, Ellen Ida Roon, the high-spirited daughter of a local saloonkeeper, and William Henry Walker, an immigrant carpenter from Castlecomer, County Kilkenny. William Walker had arrived in "The Village" at age eighteen, on his own, fresh off the boat, carrying a carpenter's toolbox on his back and a prayer book in his pocket. He rose to become the owner of a thriving lumberyard and the district's Tammany alderman. He served four terms and then a term in the State Assembly, from 1892 to 1893, before closing out his life in politics as superintendent of public buildings in Manhattan. Jimmy remembered him that evening as his old friends did, as provider of parks in the neighborhood and recreational piers for kids on the west bank of the Hudson River.

Walker worshipped his father, a big easygoing man whom he called "Boss." No matter how fast or high Jimmy Walker rose he never forgot that he was the son of a simple carpenter who had fled poverty and despair in the land of his birth. On Walker's first trip to Europe, in 1927, aboard the fabulous ocean liner *Berengaria*, he made an impromptu speech: "I am crossing the ocean tonight in the imperial suite of this wonderful ship, but I can't help but remember that there was a man, my father, who crossed this ocean with a coil of rope for his pillow."

Smooth Jimmy Walker could make blarney sound like Byron but in that opening speech of his mayoralty campaign, on that balmy August night in lower Manhattan, he spoke directly from the heart. This was, after all, the place where the part of him he treasured most still resided.

Of all his legislative accomplishments, he was proudest of his support for the Workman's Compensation Bill that provided long-overdue benefits for laboring people injured on the job. He had backed it, he told his followers that night, because that's what his father would have done; and because he had seen in his youth "the mangled forms come off the holds of ships down there on the [Chelsea docks]," the Hudson River piers just west of the Village, where men of the neighborhood worked as longshoremen, a job more dangerous than coal mining and without health or life insurance coverage. When he had risen in the Assembly to speak for that bill, he had spoken, he said, "from my heart. I was looking back with the eyes of my childhood." That was all he needed to say; he already had the support of these friends and kin.

When one of Walker's Broadway friends asked a Tammany chieftain what kind of mayor he would make, the answer came unhesitatingly: "Oh, he'll make a lousy mayor. But what a candidate!"

Walker had an excellent edge going into the campaign: the near complete support of the New York press corps. John Hylan was a public relations nightmare, loud, boorish, and harboring a paranoid suspicion of reporters. Journalists from the Manhattan dailies—though never the Hearst sheets—returned the compliment, characterizing Hylan as a "colorless bore" whose long-winded speeches put even his most devoted supporters to sleep. And being a family man who neither smoked nor drank hardly advantaged ponderous John Hylan with hard-living New York scribes.

The times were as right for a candidate like Jimmy Walker as they were wrong for John Hylan. Radio and the newsreels had just emerged and Walker was a tremendously more attractive campaigner than beefy, beetle-browed "Red Mike" Hylan, named for his crimson-colored hair and volcanic temper. Hylan was a stumbling, painfully awkward speaker, and was reflexively obstinate and entirely humorless.

Hylan appeared before campaign crowds "like a man on stilts," wrote one observer, "standing there, a bulky, seemingly inanimate figure, reading off in a singsong monotone the words that others have written for him." Walker, a much smaller man—only five-feet-eight-and-a-half inches tall and weighing no more than 130 pounds—had the lean lines of a cabaret dancer. But Red Mike Hylan would not be beaten on style points. His crusading support for the nickel subway fare gave him great pulling power in Queens and in the outer areas of Brooklyn, places like Canarsie and Bay Ridge that were fast filling up with families whose livelihoods depended on cheap and convenient mass transportation. And he was strongly backed by Boss McCooney.

The mayoralty race was largely a campaign of contrasting personalities.

Hylan and Walker were running on virtually the same issues: the preservation of the nickel fare and the building of a publicly owned and operated subway system to compete with the city's two older, privately run systems. The five-cent fare was politically sacrosanct. No viable candidate for mayor could support a plan to increase it, even though the transit companies, burdened by inflation during and immediately after World War I, were forced to cut services drastically after Hylan refused to allow them to raise the fare to eight cents.

Walker tried to separate himself from Hylan by emphasizing his reputation for getting things accomplished in Albany. He castigated Red Mike as a blundering obstructionist who pilloried all who challenged him, refusing to work with moderate Republicans and civic-spirited businessmen to get the transportation improvements the city desperately needed. Although Hylan had recently won approval of a municipally owned and operated subway line, the Independent Subway System (IND), the city lacked the revenue to build it. If elected, Walker promised to go immediately to Albany to try to persuade Republicans and upstate Democrats to draft an amendment to the state constitution allowing the city to raise its debt limit so that it could borrow the funds to begin constructing the new system.

Al Smith had more riding on this election than Jimmy Walker and he became Walker's bulldog, tearing into Hylan and Hearst without cease. It was "the most hotly contested primary campaign in the history of the City of New York," said *The New York Times*. "The Governor made war, real war," reported the New York *Sun*, his ardency intensified by his understanding that the whole country was watching this contest—that his presidential possibilities rested on its outcome. "This is a crisis," proclaimed the *Albany Knickerbocker*. "Either Al Smith wins and goes striding toward the national goal he has set for himself, or else he comes out of this thing a second-rater. It is big."

"The primary campaign of our opponents," said Norman Thomas, the Socialist Party candidate, "has been on the intellectual level of two angry neighbors calling each other names down the dumbwaiter shaft." Smith bore in on Hylan's connections with Hearst, "his blind, obedient subservience to a super-boss, who stood over him and was the keeper of his heart, the keeper of his conscience." Hylan shot back by reviving the old Brooklyn slogan that the Tammany tiger "must not cross the bridge." He hit equally hard on the moral issue. Nightclubbing Jimmy Walker would turn New York into a "wide-open town" of dope dens and gambling halls bankrolled by a mysterious Manhattan gangster whom Hylan never named, but who was recognizably Arnold Rothstein, the Broadway gambling king who had reputedly fixed the 1919 World Series.

While Hylan steered clear of Manhattan, Walker went directly into Hylan country, to Staten Island, Queens, and Brooklyn, where Flynn and Olvany had prepared the ground by building strong counter-organizations. Everywhere he spoke he made a strong pitch for women, pointing to his leadership in Albany for state ratification of the Nineteenth Amendment, which gave women the right to vote. Rushing from meeting to meeting, campaigning almost nonstop, he ended the primary race exhausted and weighing only 110 pounds.

On election evening, Smith and Olvany waited for the returns at Tammany headquarters on Fourteenth Street. Walker remained at his headquarters in Midtown until eleven o'clock and then took a car to the Wigwam, arriving just as the results were coming in from Brooklyn. "The Tammany Tiger," it soon became apparent, *had* "crossed the bridge." Walker won Brooklyn by five thousand votes and, as expected, swept Manhattan and the Bronx. He defeated Hylan by a margin of almost 100,000 votes. Walker's victory secured Smith's leadership of the state Democratic Party and made him the front-runner for the 1928 presidential nomination. In bringing down Hylan, Smith won an additional victory: Hearst was never again a major factor in New York City politics.

The "family quarrel is over," Smith announced hours after the results were tabulated. Two days later, John McCooey endorsed Walker in the general election against the Republican candidate, Frank D. Waterman, president of the Waterman Fountain Pen Company. Hylan and Hearst held off supporting Walker until the very end of the campaign, and then only halfheartedly. Walker would make Hylan wait four years for his reward: a seat on the bench of the city's Children's Court. "Now the children can be judged by one of their peers," Walker told friends.

The contest against Hylan had been a bare-knuckle affair, but Walker and Smith saw no need to draw blood from the amiable but colorless Fountain Pen King, who mounted a weak, one-issue campaign, vowing to run the city as efficiently as a business firm, a recurrent but rarely successful campaign strategy of Republican candidates for city office.

On election morning, the Tammany army—fifty thousand strong—mobilized and entered the field. The neighborhoods were their battle stations. Each smaller election district in the city's twenty-three Assembly districts (the jurisdictional successors to the nineteenth-century wards) had two captains, a man and a woman. They were charged with checking the registration lists to ensure that every Democratic voter made it to the polls; if necessary, makeshift ambulances were summoned to gather up the sick and the nearly dead. The jobs of the captains rode on their ability to bring in the numbers; those that failed were replaced soon after an election. The captains stood as sentinels at the polls. Registered Democrats who had not voted by mid-afternoon were sent written notices instructing them to report at once to their polling stations. Most voters did not have to be prodded. These same captains had been there for them year-round, helping them find work, steering them to citizenship classes, attending weddings, Communion breakfasts, and wakes, and getting wayward husbands and children out of minor scrapes with the law.

At ten o'clock on election night, Jimmy Walker left his political headquarters at the Commodore Hotel, just across from Grand Central Terminal, and went to the Wigwam to confer with Smith and Olvany. Walker found them in the executive room, smoking cigars and listening to radio reports of the election returns. It was all good news. When Walker went upstairs and entered the crowded ballroom the band struck up "Tammany," the anthem of "The Hall," and everyone joined in. When the music stopped, it was announced that Walker had won a smashing victory; late returns would give him 62 percent of the vote. Standing on the stage, a million-dollar smile on his face, Walker called for quiet. "It is very gratifying to know that the people of this great city have placed its affairs for the next four years in the hands of Tammany Hall."

In earlier days, a statement like this would have frozen the hearts of Tammany haters, yet even Frank Waterman did not appear alarmed. Jimmy Walker had made "some pretty strong promises" in the campaign, he said. "I hope that some of the excellent younger men who are now coming into control of Tammany Hall will see to it that these promises are performed." Norman Thomas, who liked Walker personally, was guardedly optimistic: "After the stupidities of the Hylan administration . . . a personable and plausible mayor [has] moved into City Hall."

Storm Clouds

Every public move Walker made in the weeks following his election was carefully crafted to bolster public trust in his administration. His appointments to positions in the upper bureaucracy—municipal offices exempt from civil service requirements—were largely men of character and ability. Edward Flynn was named city chamberlain, custodian of the municipality's public funds, a largely ceremonial sinecure. And in a move calculated to prove that his administration was "on the level," Walker offered the job of police commissioner, a position long coveted by Tammany, to George V. McLaughlin, state superintendent of banks and a close friend of Al Smith's, who had lobbied hard for his appointment.

Confident, aggressive, and just thirty-eight years old, McLaughlin informed Walker that he would take the job only if given "a free hand" in running the department. Under Hylan the police department had been controlled by political hacks that permitted Tammany district leaders to conduct illegal gaming operations in their clubhouses. McLaughlin demanded authority to mount aggressive raids on these vice dens—and without interference from Tammany honchos. Walker agreed. In the future the department would be run "from No. 210 Centre Street"—Police Headquarters—"not from City Hall," he assured McLaughlin.

For city health commissioner, the mayor-elect tapped Louis I. Harris, a long-serving civil servant who had courageously exposed corruption in Mayor Hylan's Health Department. Walker saved his biggest public relations splash for the week after his inauguration. In an open-door meeting with the heads of city departments and their deputies—and with dozens of reporters on hand— he announced that "all appointments and promotions must be made in the order in which names appear on Civil Service lists," a dramatic change from the long-standing Tammany policy of rewarding only its own. Any city official guilty of "irregularities" would be "dismissed without delay." Fiscal restraint would be a signature issue of his administration. Finally, every municipal employee would be obliged to give the taxpayers an honest day's work. "If I, who am no glutton for work, can come here each day and put in my time I must expect you to do your duty," Walker said sternly as he rose from his chair, abruptly ending the meeting.

It all played wonderfully in the press. "Not for many years has any Mayor of New York been able to feel that so large a part of the population liked him and supported him and wished him well," declared the New York *World*. After eight dull years of John Hylan, New Yorkers were hungry for change; and Jimmy Walker was an exhilarating alternative, a stylish boulevardier in line with the city's ultramodern culture and temperament. And this young mayor, like the great metropolis itself, was explosively alive and equally at home in its nightspots and neighborhoods, its ballparks and ballrooms, public places where he was seen and photographed with the headliners who gave 1920s New York its fabled reputation—Babe Ruth, Jack Dempsey, F. Scott Fitzgerald, Irving Berlin, Florenz Ziegfeld, and Damon Runyon. "The jazz age is in office in New York," wrote Henry Pringle.

"The contrast between the sober, plodding, heavy-handed Hylan and the gay, gloriously carefree 'Jimmy' is amazing," a Columbia University professor wrote at the time. "Each in his way stands for something essentially true about the people of New York. There are a million Hylans for every thousand Walkers, but every John has a conscious or subconscious longing to be a 'Jimmy.'

New York takes its fun vicariously with 'Jimmy.' Few New Yorkers ever see a 'first night' or get to a night club or know Gloria Swanson. 'Jimmy' does. They love him dearly for his very faults." The *Herald Tribune*'s Stanley Walker agreed: Jimmy Walker was "a symbol of release to millions of strap-hangers," ordinary folks who could only dream the life he lived.*

Walker could not have been elected in another era or another decade. When he was still working his way up in Albany, a crusty Tammany sachem pronounced him entirely unsuitable to become mayor of New York; to succeed in city politics you had to be either "Puritanical or cautious." The freewheeling 1920s put to ruin this hoary axiom. The attempt by prohibitionists to "legislate liberty out had legislated license in," wrote *New Yorker* reporter Alva Johnston. Sophisticated Manhattan "eloquence," he said, had been reduced to only two words: no—no to Prohibition; and yes—yes to living one's life by one's own rules. While Walker supported positive public intervention to improve the lives of the afflicted, he believed just as strongly that government should keep out of the private affairs of individuals. "Ninety-eight percent of the people want only to be let alone to enjoy freedom in safety," he said in the 1925 election campaign. "I maintain that a great majority of people want freedom to do as they like so long as they do not interfere with others." This was, as well, an expression of the new mayor's personal code. "My main idea has always been to be myself," he would tell friends. Along with his penchant for giving orders and not taking them, this would make him nearly impossible to control. Al Smith feared this, as few others did.

Very late on the evening he was elected, Walker had slipped reporters who were camped out in the lobby of his hotel room, and disappeared into the Manhattan night. When a correspondent for *The New York Times* knocked on his door and asked Allie where he was and when he might return, she replied with a shrug, "If I see him by about 5 o'clock in the morning, I will consider I am doing well."

Unknown to the press, Frank Farrell, an influential friend of Al Smith's, had, the next morning, gone to see the governor at his Manhattan hotel. He asked to speak to him privately and Smith steered him into the bathroom and shut the door. Farrell reported that Walker had spent the previous night at the apartment of his "reigning girlfriend," Vonnie Shelton, back from her sojourn in Cuba just in time for the celebration.

Another ominous omen was Walker's inability or unwillingness to honor his pledge to change Tammany policy on political patronage; counter pressure

---

* The *Herald* and the *Tribune* merged in 1924.

from district leaders, the real rulers of the city, was too strong. Three weeks after the election, *The New York Times* reported that George Olvany had spent four hours at his desk at the Wigwam "listening to suggestions and appeals on behalf of 'deserving' Democrats who his district leaders thought had earned rewards in the shape of municipal jobs." Olvany had called together the borough presidents—"the five little mayors," Walker called them—along with the other district leaders, and allotted each of them a generous share of the patronage pot. The district leaders snapped up for themselves most of the big clerkships and commissioner positions. In a closed meeting with Olvany following the election, Walker had allotted these choice appointments to Tammany, in clear violation of his public promise to adhere to the standard of merit. At this meeting, a deal had apparently been struck: Olvany would supply a list of names and Walker would rubber-stamp it. If Walker objected, he was too beholden to Tammany to stand on principle. And Al Smith was powerless to intervene.

Irony ruled. With the election of his handpicked candidate for mayor, Al Smith's influence over New York City politics actually diminished. It had been strong only in the one-year interregnum between Boss Murphy's death and the election of Jimmy Walker. After Walker's election, Tammany's district leaders moved aggressively to seize control of the Wigwam from the Smith contingent. It was from these political barons, each ruling over an Assembly electoral district, and almost all of them Irish, that Jimmy Walker could expect trouble in the days ahead.

Two Tammanys

The district leader "[is] the anode and the cathode of Tammany's political battery." He—there were no woman district leaders—"carried its power into the remotest corner of the city and to the humblest of its citizens. To the vast masses of the common people and most of the rest, the district leader is the chief point of contact with the organization, even with the government itself," wrote a close observer of New York politics in the 1920s. Almost every night of the week the people of his political province could find him in his clubhouse, meeting with aspirants for city jobs, and with neighbors who had been dealt some very bad cards.

In the daylight hours, the district leader was "at work in the city, seeing everyone that matters, pressing the needs of his constituents, arranging . . . excuses from jury duty, fixing traffic fines, seeing that men loyal to him are promoted to higher positions in the city government, revising assessments, [and] getting travelers passports." Not the least of his duties was securing permits for job seekers. New York City licensed 196 different occupations, and permits were required for every one of them. For doing the work of the people, the district leader expected iron loyalty and generous kickbacks—the sources of Tammany power. Everything had its price. Club members who received political jobs were expected to return the favor in hard cash; and all members paid monthly dues, part of which went directly into the pocket of the district leader. Then there was the so-called contract. If a person approached the district leader with a request—a traffic ticket to be fixed, a building code to be adjusted—payment was anticipated.

Before the rule of Boss Charles Murphy, district leaders had also resorted to petty thievery to build up their war chests: exacting "tribute" from prostitutes and bigger bribes from saloonkeepers who were allowed to run illegal gambling operations. This offended Murphy, who was, incongruously, both a moralist and a cheat. Although he stole from the city, he drank only sparingly, disapproved of profane language, and was in the pews every Sunday at the Church of the Epiphany. When he became master of Tammany, he had police crack down on brothels, streetwalkers, illegal gambling halls, and clip joints; even the Tenderloin, Manhattan's infamous vice district—Satan's Circus—was tamed. Murphy's "reign saw the disappearance of the old open alliances with vice and crime," wrote Milton MacKaye, an investigative reporter for the *New York Evening Post*. During the Boss's last years as leader, Tammany was "freer of political scandals than at any other time in its history," reported *The New York Times*.

Murphy had not undergone a spiritual conversion. He simply introduced new and more discreet ways for Tammany henchmen to defraud the city.

One of them was called "honest graft," an oxymoron that entered the language to describe Tammany's new style of making money, which included participating in, and profiting from, city contracts and buying land soon to rise in value because of municipal improvements.

Unlike the district leaders, Murphy's "Albany boys" were expected to keep their noses clean. That way they could protect the revamped reputation of Tammany, preventing it from ever again being overthrown by civil service reformers. And by keeping Al Smith clean, Boss Murphy had hoped to realize his final dream: placing a Tammany man in the White House.

A New Tammany had not replaced the old one. There were two Tammanys: the Tammany of the district leaders and the Tammany of the Albany progressives, operating in parallel, rarely intersecting, each with its own agenda and code of conduct. And Charles Francis Murphy, an amoral political genius, commanded both of them.

Under Murphy's tutelage, and with his full approval, Tammany's district leaders learned "that more money could be made by dealing with large corporations than by direct and unorganized pocket-picking," wrote Milton Mac-Kaye. Yet the greediest of the old chieftains grew unsatisfied with this. They saw Murphy's death, Smith's preoccupation with the 1928 presidential race, and the election of Jimmy Walker, known to be unconcerned with the details of governing, as an opportunity to flex their muscles, ruling their Assembly districts without interference from either the mayor or the governor.

As Jimmy Walker was settling into office, power inside Tammany was thus shifting dangerously from the Wigwam to the reinvigorated district club-houses. If Walker hoped to govern the city honestly and well, he would have to exert strong, Murphy-like control over them.

He would also need to constrain his reckless private life. When Boss Murphy was alive, Walker had been at least moderately discreet in his relationship with Vonnie Shelton. Now there was no one he feared and respected to place boundaries on his personal conduct.

There was another problem. Up to this time, Walker was solidly in the Smith camp, aligned with the Albany reformers. Changing his political address from Albany to money-driven Manhattan put Walker at greater peril, closer to opportunities for personal enrichment not available to him in the state legislature—and without Murphy to keep him honest. "Mr. Murphy would have nipped things in the bud," Allie Walker told Gene Fowler after her husband was driven from office, whereas Al Smith had tried and failed.

Murphy had also helped to discipline Tammany. After he passed from the scene and power began to flow back to the Tammany warhorses, a number of them reestablished their connections with big-time gamblers, inviting them into their clubhouses in return for a cut of the action. Some district leaders also became brazenly incautious. "It had been a rule for twenty years that necessary dirty work must be done behind drawn curtains and locked doors," wrote MacKaye in 1932, after nearly everything Murphy built had broken down. "Now all consideration of what the neighbors might think was abruptly abandoned."

Even before he became mayor, Jimmy Walker could see trouble ahead for himself and Tammany. After attending Charles Francis Murphy's Requiem Mass and interment, the largest New York City funeral since that of President Ulysses Grant, Walker confided to a friend, "The brains of Tammany Hall lie in Calvary Cemetery."

CHAPTER TWO

JIMMY WALKER'S NEW YORK

Young men and women in the 1920s had a sense of reckless confidence not only about money but about life in general.

MALCOLM COWLEY

The Job

"All my life I wanted a steady job," Jimmy Walker confided to a reporter a month after becoming mayor, "and it looks as if I have what I wanted." Never known for his work ethic, Walker maintained a furious pace in his first six weeks on the job, a sixteen-hour routine that would lead to a physical breakdown and a return, soon afterward, to his more scattered work habits.

In January 1925, Jimmy and Allie Walker were residing in a suite at the Commodore Hotel while their fifty-year-old house on St. Luke's Place was being renovated. Not until 1942 would the city provide its mayor with an official, municipally owned residence—Gracie Mansion, the former country home of Federalist merchant Archibald Gracie, situated splendidly in a park overlooking the East River at Eighty-eighth Street and East End Avenue. Until then, the mayors of the richest city in the world lived in their private residences, identified only by a pair of lanterns mounted on iron standards that flanked the front door, and a police booth near the sidewalk, with an officer on duty round-the-clock. The city did not even provide reimbursement for housing expenses or renovations. But Walker had no concerns on that count. When he casually mentioned to his friend Jules Mastbaum that his home improvements would cost $25,000, a sum equal to his yearly salary as mayor, the movie theater mogul told him to "fix up the house" and send him the bill. It was the first of the many unsolicited financial favors Walker received from wealthy friends.

Walker's mornings at the Commodore Hotel, and later at St. Luke's Place, began with a breakfast meeting with Edward Stanton, his chief secretary. While Eddie Stanton reviewed the mayor's schedule for that day, Walker would casually leaf through a newspaper and sip his tea. He usually read only the headlines, except for the sports page, which he devoured.

After a light breakfast, Walker would watch his personal valet, Sam Greenhaus, carefully place the mayor's business suit on a tailor's dummy built exactly to his size. Then Walker would slip out of his dressing gown—"silk in summer, camel's hair in winter"—and begin nervously pacing the room, suddenly fully awake, engaging in mock debate with Stanton over issues he expected to be confronted with that morning at City Hall. Greenhaus, a short, Gallic-featured man, would follow him around the room like the minion of some Oriental despot, handing him his wardrobe one item at a time. Fully dressed, Walker would turn slowly, in a full circle, for Greenhaus's final inspection. If a lapel was slightly curled or a wrinkle showed anywhere, Greenhaus would reach for a hot iron and "the defect would be pressed out right on the Mayor. Iron in hand, the valet sometimes would follow Walker to the front door to finish the job."

Outside, on the sidewalk, there were always a few hard-pressed souls waiting for a favor or a small "loan." Walker was always prepared for them. He regularly carried two rolls of bills, one in each pants pocket: a roll of dollars for the "moochers" and a roll of larger bills for his "special friends." He never kept track of these loans. "Why should I?" he explained. "Borrowers are short on memory as well as cash."

Walker cared for money but was careless with it. He would absentmindedly leave wads of hundred-dollar bills and un-cashed checks in pockets of pants he sent out to be cleaned and pressed. One honorable dry-cleaner returned a pair of trousers with $3,000 and a gold cigarette lighter in the pockets. "Money, to him, is entirely unimportant, a commodity made to be spent and utterly useless in the bank," wrote Henry Pringle. He was "invariably broke," but he had friends eager "to lend him more money than he could possibly use."

Walker and Stanton were driven to City Hall in the mayor's private town car, with a city employee at the wheel. The plan was to continue conducting business in the backseat, but Walker, who never learned to drive, was on edge traveling on Manhattan's densely packed streets, where most motorists treated newly installed traffic signals as courteous suggestions, not legal directives. Clutching the seat in a panic when another car cut in front of them, convinced at every intersection that a collision was imminent, he found it impossible to focus on the business of the city.

A siren was installed in his car when he became mayor, but the chauffeur was instructed never to sound it. The noise grated on Walker's fragile nerves and, he complained, "contradicted the atmosphere" of his $17,000 Duesenberg, the gift of another business benefactor. As much as Jimmy Walker loved that magnificent machine, he would have taken the subway if given the choice.

The mayor who loved crowds was secretly terrified of them. Even the few dozen reporters and favor-seekers that were invariably waiting for him at City Hall set his heart racing and turned his hands clammy. Walker hated to have people press in on him or lay their hands upon him. Much as he enjoyed going to big parties and being around lots of people, he "couldn't stand to be mauled," said Allie, "and very much disliked being slapped on the back." This made political campaigning emotionally difficult for him. He would reach out and shake hands with small groups of well-wishers and then furtively duck back behind a protective wall of policemen and political surrogates.

The mayor's mornings at City Hall were devoted to office business. Walker retained his personal staff from Albany, a small group of secretaries, stenographers, and aides who knew that the "path to his brain" was "through his ears, not through his eyes." Memos and policy papers were rarely exchanged, and Stanton, not Walker, attacked the piles of letters and documents on the mayor's desk. Walker preferred to conduct the city's business on the telephone or face-to-face. He was not even interested in dictating official letters. "You write them," he would tell his staff, "and I'll sign them." Yet his office was a place of considerable ferment. Walker was on the phone constantly, and he found it impossible to remain seated behind his desk during morning meetings with aides and city commissioners. Cigarette in hand, he would circle the room, firing off questions and absorbing information with his adhesive mind.

In those rare moments when he was alone in his office he had no inclination to keep a personal diary. The official papers he left behind are unrevealing of his private side and give no evidence of being vetted by Walker or his staff to enhance his place in history. Nor was Walker interested in self-scrutiny. Life was pleasant, he would tell friends, as long as one did not "analyze it too closely." And the mayor that some historians have lampooned as a publicity hound refused to have his name placed on buildings, parks, hospitals, or other public improvements he initiated. "The Mayor of New York," he said, "still believes himself to be a public servant and not a potentate."

At eleven o'clock, Walker would meet with reporters. He relished the give-and-take with the press, the jokes and easy banter. "He talks frankly and truthfully," said one reporter, "[and] has yet to have a confidence broken." The closeness had its cost. Reporters who covered City Hall rarely shined a harsh light on him. "Walker was a machine-made mayor, but almost equally he was a press-made mayor," Norman Thomas shrewdly pointed out. "He was good 'copy' for the 'boys.' . . . The reporters liked him because he was easy and warm-hearted and lent them money and thought of something to say that would fill an assignment. They swallowed his every utterance, for the most part uncritically, and gave him front-page headlines." Editors of the big New York dailies were often critical of Walker, but few subway straphangers read the editorials.

When Walker was finished with the press, he would break for lunch, and on his return—if the calendar called for it—presided over meetings of the Board of Estimate, his most important official duty as mayor, and the one he genuinely enjoyed. Established in 1901 under the charter of the newly consolidated City of Greater New York, the Board of Estimate and Apportionment, as it was formally known, was "a legislative, financial, and administrative agency unlike anything to be found in other American cities." It possessed virtually all the sovereign powers granted to the city, including the power to initiate the budget (the Board of Aldermen, whose members were elected from their legislative districts, could reduce or eliminate budget items, but not introduce them). Until 1938, when the board's name was shortened and its powers enhanced, it had eight members: three city officials elected at-large by the voters of New York— the mayor, the comptroller, and the president of the Board of Alderman—and the five borough presidents, elected locally. Each city-wide official had three votes; the presidents of Manhattan and Brooklyn, the largest boroughs, had two votes apiece; and the presidents of the other three boroughs one vote each. Citizens—up to three hundred at a time—were permitted to attend the sessions and bring complaints and petitions to the board. These were aired openly, if not always cordially, in a second-floor room at City Hall that "combined the simple dignity of a New England Church with the warmth of a town-meeting hall."

An irrepressible performer, Walker conducted these meetings with brio, alternately firm and witty. Here the Albany gallery god felt completely at home, fending off opponents with sharp retorts, promoting his agenda with energy and intelligence, and delighting spectators with his rapier-quick bons mots. But the audience had to wait for the performance. Not once was Mayor Walker on time for a meeting of the Board of Estimate. While this annoyed other members of the board, Walker brushed off their complaints, refusing, he said, "to live by the clock." When Walker finally appeared, an entourage of lobbyists and favor seekers trailed behind him as he swept into the chambers, nodding gravely to the audience and fellow members of the board, who had been irritatedly shuffling important-looking papers. As Walker sat down and called the meeting to order, he would look up from his agenda and smile at the citizens in their seats. Their spontaneous applause told him all was forgiven.

On one occasion, a bill before the board appropriated over $7 million for new schools. Walker opened the meeting by speaking to the measure with impressive eloquence. "He probably spent an hour studying the school problem before making that speech," a reporter said to a colleague after the meeting. "You could probably spend a year on it, and not make such a good speech." He loved repartee, but couldn't abide rudeness. At one board meeting an indignant petitioner shouted at Walker, "Liar!" Walker coolly scanned the audience, spotted the offending party, and shot back: "Now that you have identified yourself, we shall proceed."

At the conclusion of board meetings, Walker returned to his office for the remainder of the afternoon. Around five o'clock, Eddie Stanton would drop in and inform him that there would be a dinner somewhere in the city at seven o'clock, another one at eight, still another at nine, and that he was expected to speak at all of them. To prepare for the evening, his favorite time, Walker changed his clothing. He owned seventy suits, all of them designed by Jeann Friedman, an Austrian immigrant and former opera tenor whose shop was in Midtown, near the Ritz-Carlton Hotel. Walker spent $3,000 a year, roughly one-eighth of his salary, on his wardrobe, and never returned an item of clothing Friedman cut and sewed for him. If his tailor delivered a new suit or overcoat that was not to Walker's exacting taste, the mayor would tuck it away in a corner of his closet, not wanting to offend the adoring friend who had named his son after him.

The authors of an official biography of Walker described him as "the smartest dressed among all public men in the United States." Lucius Beebe, the arbiter of Manhattan sartorial taste, militantly disagreed. Walker, he said, with a whiff of superiority, was "a snappy . . . or sharp" dresser "in the Broadway mode." Beebe considered "extreme" Walker's form-fitted business jackets, broad-brimmed hats, pointy-toed shoes, and four-button gray spats. "I always felt a slight shudder at Mr. Walker's attire," he portentously told Gene Fowler.

Walker kept a dozen or so suits in Friedman's shop, and before heading out for the evening he would change his clothing there or in a private dressing room he had installed in the basement of City Hall. He changed outfits at least three times a day, five times in summer, the final time at the Manhattan penthouse of some wealthy benefactor. At the end of his evening, milk trucks were on the streets, beginning their early morning rounds. "When you know that if you don't go to bed you will go to sleep standing up, you can call it a day," Walker told reporter Thomas Hanley, who covered one of his whirlwind January days for the New York *World*.

Reporters were amazed by Walker's boiling energy. He was never at rest; he even slept fitfully. He ate irregularly and sparingly, only when he was hungry, and he had no recreations or hobbies. He did not golf or fish and only rarely played cards. He was born for the night and seemed to draw energy from the ceaseless round of banquets and dinners he felt obliged to attend. He would race from one to the other, never staying long, always arriving late and in high humor. One evening he showed up hours behind schedule at a Jewish fund-raiser. The crowd went wild when they saw he was wearing a yarmulke. One woman shouted: "Jimmy, circumcision next?"

"Madam, I prefer to wear it off."

In his first weeks in office, he rarely tired; when he did, he would lie down for twenty minutes "and be completely refreshed." He looked, wrote Hanley, "in splendid physical condition"; his steely blue eyes were clear, his cheeks had "the flush of health," and he walked with a spring in his step. What was the secret to his buoyancy? He relished his new job, he told Hanley, "nearly every minute of it." But Hanley worried that "his nerves would crack under the strain." Two weeks after Hanley filed his story Jimmy Walker broke down.

Speaking at an early February meeting of the Real Estate Board, the mayor grew faint and had to be helped to his seat. The following evening he collapsed, and doctors detected an accelerated heart rate. Walker was under mounting stress at the time, traveling back and forth to Albany, trying to get Republicans to agree to the constitutional amendment increasing the city's debt limit so contractors could begin work on the new independent subway system he had promised voters. His brother, Dr. William Walker, warned him that he was on the brink of a nervous breakdown and ordered complete bed rest. But the mayor was adamant. "I must go up, Bill. It is important for the city." After suffering another fainting spell the following morning, February 8, Walker took the afternoon train to Albany and appeared that evening in the chambers of the State Senate. On seeing him, ghostly white and perspiring, his friends escorted him to a committee room, where a physician examined him and said he was "suffering from overwork." William Walker had followed his brother to Albany and insisted he postpone his return to New York City and take a room at the Ten Eyck Hotel and rest for an entire week. But Walker stubbornly refused. That night, while he was on the train to the city, still weak and haggard-looking, Albany Republicans drafted a bond issue amendment extending the city's borrowing capacity for transit construction to $300 million. *The New York Times* called it a "brilliant victory for Walker," the first of his mayoralty. The transit referendum was not finally approved by the voters until November 1927, but well before then Walker began approving contracts for "one of the biggest engineering undertakings in history"—the construction of $700 million worth of underground trains.

When Walker arrived at Grand Central Terminal after his breakdown in Albany he was met at the platform by an old friend, Timothy A. Evans, an executive of the New York Central Railroad. Evans offered him a private railroad car for a weekend respite in Atlantic City. After Walker returned from the Jersey shore he made an unexpected announcement. His recent health scare, he told reporters, convinced him he must change his lifestyle. "One thing I have determined—the night engagements are off indefinitely. . . . The dinner coat is going on a long vacation."

It lasted less than a month. In mid-March, Walker returned to the banquet circuit and cut back on the part of the job he detested: the grind of morning office work. This carved out of his schedule what he considered the most terrible task of all—getting to work on time.

He would be awakened around ten by Sam Greenhaus, have a quick cup of tea, and then jump back into his soft, oversized bed. Propped up on pillows, he would make telephone calls while listening to the radio. After a light breakfast and a full hour in the bathroom, he would dress and prepare to meet the day. Unless there was a Board of Estimate meeting, he would arrive at City Hall as late as three in the afternoon "a couple of days a week," said reporter Warren Moscow, "and other days not at all."

When Walker was elected, there was speculation he would have to change his ways. "The prophets said that no man would operate a civic machine costing $1,300,000 a day without abandoning his night clubs, first nights, baseball games and prize fights. . . . Jimmy might start his term as 'The Jazz Mayor,' but the whine of the saxophone and the rattle of the traps would soon be stilled." This did not happen. "He finds time for all of his former diversions," Henry Pringle observed. Entirely without pretense, Walker shared with reporters his simple idea of the good life. "I would rather laugh than cry. I like the company of my fellow beings. I like the theatre and I am devoted to sports."

Against the advice of his family, he continued to drink, often to excess, but knew how to cover up the consequences. In the basement of City Hall, directly under his office, reached discreetly by a well-hidden circular staircase, was his "hangover room." It had a bed, which Walker used, and some exercise equipment, which he never touched.

As always, he was late for every appointment and every meeting, even one with the president of the United States, and he left City Hall early "on the slightest provocation." Members of the press warned him in private to be more regular in his habits; the public was beginning to notice. Walker would promise to change and blithely fall back on his profligate habits, grinning as he arrived, late as usual.

His wisecracking self-indulgence veered at times toward self-ruination. On one occasion, a rumor circulated through City Hall that he had been shot. He was reached by phone in a hotel room, still in bed with a hangover and a woman who was not his wife. "Shot?" he said, "I'm not even half-shot." Reporters printed the remark, but not where Walker was when he made it or whom he was with.

Walker's favorite excuses for dodging the responsibilities of governing were civic receptions and long vacations. Visiting dignitaries received highly publicized receptions on the steps of City Hall, or, if truly important, a ticker tape parade up Broadway. This was the province of Grover Whalen, the Wanamaker department store executive Walker hired as the city's official greeter. The flamboyant Whalen rarely appeared in public without a top hat, a gardenia, and a "dazzling, toothy smile." During his time in office, Walker gave nearly three hundred "open-air performances" outside City Hall, awarding the keys of the city to this or that celebrity.

Walker's therapeutic weekend in Atlantic City was the prelude to less essential sabbaticals. In the next two years, he would spend 143 days away from the city on excursions to exotic and historic places: Havana and Palm Springs, Paris and Rome. The thin historical record Mayor Walker left behind gives no hint of the reasons for his sudden and complete change of work habits, after barely six weeks in office. But surely the key to it was the breakdown he suffered in Albany. Walker had always been frail, was often ill, and was perpetually high-strung. He was also a hypochondriac. His brother William knew him well and refused his entreaties for prescriptions for this or that suspicious ailment. What Walker failed to get from his brother he got from other doctors, among them his first two health commissioners. Opening Walker's closet one afternoon for a secret peek at his fabled wardrobe, his niece, Rita Burke, discovered enough medicine bottles to stock a small pharmacy.

He had never in his life worked as hard as he had in the weeks before his breakdown in Albany; nor had he ever been as sick as he was at that time. This frightened him into believing he couldn't sustain the killing schedule that had brought on his collapse. Unwilling to surrender the parts of the job he loved most—meeting and greeting people and running sessions of the Board of Estimate—he became, in everything but name, a part-time mayor. It was not that he was overmatched by the job; he simply pulled away from it.

Jimmy Walker chose not to see it that way. He would rely upon his uncommon political aptitude—what Warren Moscow, fifty years later, described as "the quickest mind ever seen in politics, even to this day"—to get more done in two hours at his desk than John Hylan had been able to accomplish in two months. That presumption would turn out to be a calamitous mistake. In short bursts, Walker handled the job impressively. But without executive ability or experience, and with only a small, overworked staff to cover for his inattention to detail, Walker allowed much of the city's business to "drift along, or be attended to by incompetents and worse." This might have instantly ruined another mayor in another place and time, but "Father Knickerbocker, his pockets full of new money and his innards full of night club champagne, was more than tolerant to Jimmy," wrote city reporter Stanley Walker. Tolerant or not, what the city needed most from its new mayor was inspired and continuous executive direction, something Walker was suddenly either unwilling or temperamentally incapable of providing.

The City

Walker's responsibilities were staggering. The mayor who had most of all wanted to be a Broadway songwriter presided over the second largest government in the United States, next to the federal government. With a population of nearly six million, New York was about to pass London as the most populous city on earth, and its annual budget of roughly $500 million was nearly five times that of London's.

Walker entered office intent on being an urban builder, but merely maintaining New York's current level of services was itself a daunting financial undertaking. The city had 120,000 municipal employees, a labor force larger than the peacetime American Army. Twenty-five thousand public school teachers instructed over 800,000 pupils, and there were fourteen thousand policemen—a force larger than the standing army of Norway—six thousand full-time firemen, and nearly seven thousand miles of streets and sewers to be maintained by city workers. The publicly owned municipal water supply was secured from eight hundred or so square miles of watersheds, whose reservoirs and pipelines had to be monitored constantly. The largest public water network in the world, it delivered over 700 million gallons of pure water daily to the inhabitants of the city, approximately two and one half tons daily per household. It was a technological wonder, yet it was badly overextended; new pipelines had to be built and new sources of supply located. New York City had some of the best private hospitals on earth, but the burden of taking care of the unfortunate fell most heavily on abysmally maintained and administered city hospitals. And in the mid-1920s, over three-quarters of the public hospital system's patients were treated without charge, a near ruinous drain on the city budget.

The week Walker took office he was shocked to learn that he had inherited from the Hylan administration over $200 million worth of un-built but budgeted construction projects, a suspiciously large number of them in Brooklyn, Hylan's home borough. Walker announced an immediate policy of "rigid retrenchment"; he and Comptroller Charles Berry would block all "log-rolling" requests by borough presidents. But the new mayor was willing to spend lavishly on his own projects. "I would not keep a dog there," he muttered in disgust after an unannounced visit to Bellevue Hospital's medieval Psychopathic Ward facility. "If it takes the last dollar in the City Treasury to wipe out this disgrace . . . I'll do it."

Walker had the Board of Estimate appropriate $16 million for public hospital construction and set aside a special fund to modernize Bellevue's psychopathic division. Then he pushed through a bill consolidating the twenty-six municipal hospitals under a single commissioner, Dr. William Schroeder, Jr., a fellow of the American College of Surgeons, a World War I veteran, and a Tammany loyalist. "This is an outstanding event in the history of hospitals in New York," *The New York Times* reported; it ended decades of inefficiency, divided authority, and wasteful duplication of administration.

Walker enlisted the support of Comptroller Berry on this issue, but Berry, a tenacious fiscal conservative, kept a watchful eye on other spending initiatives, correctly convinced that the city was on a fast track to insolvency. New York's ballooning municipal debt was increasing by almost $100,000 a day in 1926 and was nearly equal to the combined debt of the forty-eight states of the union. New York City government was spending more money yearly than it cost to run the national government of Italy, a country of forty million people. Put another way, its annual budget was equal to the combined budgets of Chicago, San Francisco, Philadelphia, Boston, Detroit, and St. Louis.

This was doubly disconcerting to Charles Berry and other good-government progressives. With a $250 million payroll and $375 million worth of municipal contracts to award each year to private concerns, city government was an easy mark for Tammany thieves.

Berry and Walker warred continuously over the expanding size of city government, but Walker prevailed, spending lavishly on municipal improvements, schools, parks, and playgrounds, along with bridges, roads, docks, and subway lines. Walker insisted that as long as the city's private sector was prospering, municipal government could afford to expand. He had a point, but pursuing it as long-term fiscal policy was perilous.

Jimmy Walker's New York was the richest city in the richest country in all of history. World War I had drained Britain's capital resources, allowing New

York to displace London as the financial capital of the world, and the new center of world wealth. The financial fortunes of city government were closely tied to this robust urban economy. Unlike today, New York was almost entirely self-sufficient. It received no federal monies and only a small amount of state money for education. It derived its funding largely from real estate taxes, licenses and fees, and a personal property tax, which was rarely collected; there was no sales tax or city income tax.

Taxable real estate was New York City's principal source of revenue, and real estate speculation and the urban construction it stimulated—luxury apartment houses, palatial hotels, and gleaming skyscrapers—were the driving forces of the local economy. In the mid-1920s the value of New York City real estate was increasing almost as rapidly as the city budget. This put the Walker administration in the enviable position of expanding its budget yearly without having to raise real estate taxes markedly. Moderate tax rates, in turn, created a favorable business climate for additional private construction and more tax revenues. Why worry about overspending and looming indebtedness? Walker queried his comptroller. New York City government was the fortunate recipient of an ever-expanding pot of gold.

Jimmy Walker saw New York real estate as "the last Golconda," the ancient Indian city renowned for its unimagined quantities of diamonds. Known for taking long risks at the betting windows, Walker was staking his city's future, and his own political fortunes, on the health of the real estate market. If the value of taxable income leveled off or fell, city government would be in desperate trouble, unable to secure the loans to pay for its extravagance.

The city was a prodigious and irresponsible borrower, but the banks were partly to blame. They made no effort to compel the Walker administration to discipline its spending. Fiscal solvency did not become a matter of urgent importance to them as long as they could sell the city's obligations—its bonds—on the open market. That not being a problem in the 1920s, "the bankers were not greatly concerned over whether the city was living beyond its means and over whether expenditures must not be drastically curtailed," wrote Columbia University professor Lindsay Rogers after the real estate bubble burst in the 1930s.

Walker was even more sanguine than the banks that confidently backed him. The mayor who thought hard times was only the title of a novel peered into the future and saw growth without end, a continuation and expansion of what was already one of the greatest urban construction campaigns in the history of cities. "Nowhere in the world within a similar number of square miles can as much building progress be found," reported the New York *Daily News*.

It was easy to be an optimist in the new capital of world capitalism. The American economy had rebounded from a sharp post–World War I recession and was, when Mayor Walker was sworn in, entering its fifth consecutive year of growth, giving America the highest standard of living that any country had yet known. But prosperity was not evenly divided in this city of violent contrasts, imperial Fifth Avenue being only a short walk from the tenement squalor of Hell's Kitchen. Gotham had thousands of millionaires in 1928, yet a third of its families had yearly incomes of less than $1,500, $833 less than the "bottom level below which a family [of four] cannot go without danger of physical and moral deterioration," according to a United States Department of Labor study. Socialist Norman Thomas called for confiscatory taxes to spread the wealth more evenly, but Walker, like most politicians of the time—Democrat and Republican—counted on rising prosperity to lift all boats.

The economy of the Greater New York area was the largest regional economy in existence. The region extended beyond the city's borders into New Jersey, Connecticut, and areas of New York state north of the Bronx, a megacity four and a half times the size of Rhode Island, with a population of nearly ten million, more people than resided in any state in America except New York. The centerpiece of this regional economy was the Port of New York, the most prosperous commercial harbor in the world. It was a sustaining instrument of a bewilderingly diverse economy of sixty thousand manufacturing plants, producing everything from books to biscuits.

Throughout the 1920s, New York grew increasingly dependent on trucks to move its products, and cars to move its people, yet it was still a railroad city, served by thirteen major trunk lines that carried nearly 242 million passengers annually to and from its two great midtown terminals. It was also the greatest mass transit city in the world, with six hundred miles of subways and elevated railroads. Every day, nearly three million passengers traveled into and out of the area of Manhattan below Fifty-ninth Street, the southern boundary of Central Park.

Beginning around seven in the evening, the subways were packed to the doors with passengers headed for Times Square, the busiest transit station in existence. They came to see a Hollywood film, a Broadway show, or the Ringling Brothers Circus at Madison Square Garden. The more adventurous came to catch a risqué floor show at one of Midtown's swanky clubs or to listen to some hot jazz at a smoke-filled basement speakeasy. New York City made and distributed clothing and chemicals, beer and bread, but it also produced and transmitted—by print, radio, and rail—serious culture and mass entertainment, two of its core industries.

At a time when young American writers were escaping the country's culturally barren Main Streets for the temptations of Paris, European intellectuals were calling New York the city of tomorrow, a place bursting with exciting innovations in the arts of mass entertainment and communications. The "Futurist city," New York was in the vanguard of cultural, social, and technological transformations that would make the twentieth century the American Century: the rise of commercial radio and talking movies; the invention of television; the ascendancy of advertising; the beginnings of tabloid journalism; the spread, through radio and phonograph records, of a pulsating urban music called jazz; and the emergence of mass spectator sports—sold-out baseball and football stadiums and prizefights with million-dollar gates. The Manhattan skyline, the most tremendous in the world, symbolized the city's cultural and financial hegemony. "We beheld them with stupefaction in the moving pictures," the French philosopher Jean-Paul Sartre recalled his and other Europeans' fascination with Midtown's new Art Deco skyscrapers, chief among them the Chrysler Building. "They were the architecture of the future, just as the movie was the art of the future and jazz the music of the future."

New York had become, as the saying went, "the capital of everything"—America's financial, industrial, engineering, architectural, publishing, theatrical, musical, radio, advertising, opinion making, sports, fashion and gossip center. "The whole world revolves around New York," said jazz man Edward "Duke" Ellington, lured to the city in the early 1920s from the nation's capital. "Very little happens anywhere unless someone in New York presses a button!" As Thomas Wolfe wrote, "nowhere in the world can a young man [and he should have added woman] feel greater hope and expectancy than here."

A new capitalist culture gained dominance in America in the 1920s, one based on consumption, spending, and enjoyment, rather than production, savings, and self-denial. "Instead of being exhorted to save money, more and more of it, people were being exhorted in a thousand ways to buy, enjoy, use once and throwaway, in order to buy a later and more expensive model," the writer Malcolm Cowley described the new consumption ethic. New York was the source and center of this emergent culture of dream and desire. No world city was richer or more dedicated to money and material things than the fast-stepping town that young F. Scott Fitzgerald captured inimitably in his fiction. "There is little in New York that does not spring from money," wrote H. L. Mencken. "But what issues out of money is often extremely brilliant, and I believe that it is more brilliant in New York than it has been anywhere else."

Through its revolutionary system of mass communications—national network radio, the newsreels, talking movies, and Manhattan-centric magazines like *The New Yorker*, launched in the year Jimmy Walker became mayor—the city transmitted its image of modern culture and sophistication to the entire country, and to Europe as well. At no point in the nation's history has one city had such a decisive influence upon the rest of the country. But Jimmy Walker and his fellow Manhattan provincials found it difficult to admit that New York was, at the same time, the most desirable and the most hated city in America. "I find it an appalling place," wrote the Western journalist Earl Sparling, "rich for making money, poor for living. I despise its graft, its crime, its dirt, its accents, its utilitarian ugliness, its opportunistic cheapness, its parvenu swank, its swelling army of epicenes—even its philosophy of toleration, which is less a virtue than a confession of weakness, a lack of a way of life."

It was both a hard-hearted city and a hard city to break into. The young writer John Steinbeck arrived in New York from his native California in 1925 and left in despair a year later. "The city had beat the pants off me. Whatever it required to get ahead, I didn't have. I didn't leave the city in disgust—I left with the respect plain unadulterated fear gives," he wrote in 1943, two years after making New York his new home following the success of *The Grapes of Wrath*.

New York was an empire city, but like ancient Rome, a brawling, deeply divided one, with most of its recent arrivals living in tightly defined ethnic communities, where tribalism ran strong. Tens of thousands of these immigrants had yet to be assimilated, preferring to fall back on the languages and customs of their homelands. An astounding two million New Yorkers, over a third of the total population, were foreign born, and nearly three-quarters of all New Yorkers had at least one parent born abroad. Jimmy Walker's New York had more Italians than Rome, more Irish than Dublin, more Germans than Bremen, and more Jews than London, Paris, Berlin, Rome, and Leningrad combined.

In the 1920s, New York was becoming increasingly a Jewish town. By 1920, 30 percent of its population was Jewish, while the Irish percentage had dropped to 20 percent. But Tammany continued to take special care of its own kind, its Manhattan power base solidified temporarily by new and discriminatory immigration laws that favored peoples from Northern Europe. Despite the rapid movement of the Irish to the outer boroughs, Manhattan still contained 44 percent of the city's Irish immigrants, along with great numbers of second- and third-generation Irish Americans.

City government remained green to the gills. The great majority of appointed government officials, including most department heads, were Irish, as were six of the eight members of the Board of Estimate and most of Walker's personal staff.* Under Walker, the Irish would continue to dominate the police

---

* The elected borough presidents of Brooklyn, Queens, and Richmond were Irish. Julius Miller, the president of Manhattan, was Jewish, and Henry Bruckner, the president of the Bronx, was German American.

and fire departments, while the Board of Alderman, with jurisdiction over such weighty matters as parades, steamboat whistles, and circuses, was a kind of Hibernian social club. Only ten aldermen were German American, another ten were Jewish, and five were white Protestants. There was not a single Italian or African American alderman.

Jimmy Walker rejoiced in New York's cosmopolitanism, its widespread reputation as "The Gateway of America," and he was a strident opponent of federal laws restricting immigration from East Asia and from Southern and Eastern Europe. As mayor, he hoped to create more opportunities in city government for Jews, but also for Italians, who now comprised nearly 20 percent of New York's population. But Walker was also a political realist, unwilling to alienate Tammany sachems by reducing the numbers and power of the Irish in city government. This caused him to fall back on the animating principle of his economic program: expansion rather than fair division. Building more hospitals, parks, and subway lines would open up more city jobs for Italians and Jews, but only after the Irish received their full quota of the choice positions.

The major obstacle Walker would confront in governing New York was not its ethnic diversity. It was that New York was less a city than a loose federation of cities. While the mayor appointed the chiefs of the big city departments—fire, police, health, markets, and docks—the borough presidents were czars of their local streets and sewers and built all public works within their jurisdiction. They also had their own favorite contractors, engineers, and pools of laborers, giving them patronage power beyond the reach of the mayor. Next to the mayor, the four Democratic bosses of the four largest boroughs of New York were the most powerful figures in city government.

Though they possessed no constitutional authority, the district leaders—creatures of the political parties—formed yet another level of government. They handpicked candidates for election to the Board of Aldermen and closely controlled the votes of these "gentlemen of low intelligence and easy ethics." They also had a strong say in the nomination of county sheriffs and positions in the lower courts that were situated in their assembly districts. "New York City, with its thousands of police, has no more need of five sheriffs," wrote reporter Milton MacKaye, "than it has of a town crier or a dunking board for witches." These positions were purely political sinecures, preserved, as were a number of other redundant municipal jobs, to enhance the patronage power of the district leaders and borough presidents.

Democratic district leaders in Manhattan and the Bronx took direction from Tammany, but many of their compatriots in Queens, Brooklyn, and Staten Island were firmly under the control of their borough presidents. Neither George Olvany nor Jimmy Walker had much influence over them. When illegal behavior was traced to the district leaders, they were difficult to discipline or to bring to justice.

The Revolt of the Bosses

Although Walker would later be charged—justifiably—for accepting money and favors from his influential business friends, he began his term of office determined to root out corruption in the city's Health Department that had been unearthed by his crusading health commissioner, Louis Harris. Under pressure from key district leaders, however, Walker failed to pursue the investigation as aggressively as he might have.

Harris's first target was Harry Danziger, a shady milk dealer from Queens who had connections with officials inside former Mayor Hylan's Health Department. Harris had Danziger followed, and a city detective caught him extorting a group of legitimate milk dealers in the Bronx. Danziger had been running the scam for some time. Milk distributors had to pay him protection money or he would have hired thugs to spoil or steal their milk supply.

When Danziger was arrested for extortion, he confessed, turned state's evidence, and led prosecutors into deeper water. The entire city, he claimed, was "at the mercy of a huge milk combine" that was using "unscrupulous" methods to undersell legitimate milk suppliers and distribute tainted or adulterated milk. Big Midwestern milk dealers, working through Danziger, had been bribing city health officials to permit them to secretly ship to New York City great quantities of uninspected milk and cream. Some of these milk products had been adulterated—diluted by water or skim milk—to allow the conspirators to undersell local milk distributors.

It was the vilest form of corruption. Thousands of the "bootleg" milk cans were diluted by water from a "dirty stable hose." Commissioner Harris linked this contaminated milk with a recent outbreak of typhoid fever in the city that resulted in the deaths of dozens of children. Nearly a million quarts of the "doctored" milk had been sold in the city in 1925 and over a million dollars had been paid in graft to officials in Hylan's Health Department.

Danziger, it turned out, was merely a go-between in the "milk-graft ring." He confessed to funneling ninety of every hundred dollars he extorted or took as bribes—a total of nearly $1 million—to the "inside man" in the operation, Harry J. Clougher, a powerful official in Hylan's Health Department. Clougher was arrested on April 26, 1926, but Harris suspected the corruption went deeper, that Clougher was beholden to an unknown person of consequence in city government.

Clougher, a hard-as-nails Hylan loyalist, was convicted of accepting bribes to admit unlawful milk into the borough. Prosecutors had put pressure on him, threatening to request the maximum sentence of twenty years unless he revealed the others with whom, on Danziger's testimony, he had divided the graft money. But Clougher had been unshakable, knowing he would be taken care of by powerful persons higher up the chain of corruption. With Walker's support, Harris continued his investigation after Clougher was shipped off to Sing Sing prison in upstate New York. There were additional arrests of Clougher's former subordinates and Harris fired at least half a dozen other Health Department officials suspected of malfeasance. But he was unable to find evidence of higher-ups in the milk conspiracy. If there was a "master-mind" behind the milk scandal, that person was never found. Harris strongly suspected it was Charles L. Kohler, a prominent Democratic district leader who had worked in Hylan's Health Department. But obstructed by city prosecutors beholden to Kohler and other district leaders involved in the milk conspiracy, the commissioner was unable to accumulate enough evidence to charge him. And Mayor Walker, under heavy pressure from these same district leaders, ignored pleas by the Citizens Union, an influential civic watchdog organization, to appoint a special state prosecutor to take over the investigation. He did, however, later appoint Kohler as his budget director, a convenient position for political plunder.

Danziger avoided prison, his reward for cooperating with prosecutors. Clougher was released after serving only two years of his five-to-ten-year sentence. He left Sing Sing rich and unrepentant.

Powerful Democratic district leaders closed ranks to kill reforms initiated by another member of Walker's cabinet: police commissioner George McLaughlin. This was a battle royal, one that underscored, even more graphically than the milk scandal, the young mayor's high intentions and weak resolve.

District leaders had opposed putting McLaughlin, an independent Democrat, on the Tammany ticket in 1925; and from the day he took office, they obstructed his efforts to clean up a department "literally run by political bosses." McLaughlin transferred to active duty nearly a thousand politically connected policemen who had been holding cushy desk jobs. When district leaders showed up at Police Headquarters to protest, McLaughlin refused to meet with them.

A physically imposing man, broad-shouldered and over six feet tall, McLaughlin spoke in plain, hard-boiled language and was suspicious of back-slappers and bootlickers. Here was "a new racket" that old Tammany pols "couldn't fathom at all," wrote one reporter: a police commissioner who was "honest, direct, [and] forceful," one whose decisions "are always his own."

"He'll last three months," predicted a political reporter closely familiar with Tammany intrigue. Outraged district leaders mobilized to make sure of that, taking their complaints first to Governor Smith, then to Tammany leader George Olvany, and finally to Mayor Walker. All three of them sided with McLaughlin. "Favoritism, graft and corruption in the Department were to be stamped out," Walker declared.

The simmering confrontation exploded into full-scale warfare in the early summer of 1926, just as the milk scandal was heating up. The igniting incident was McLaughlin's decision to mount police raids on district clubhouses that were harboring illegal gambling operations.

The raids were led by Lewis J. Valentine, a tough and incorruptible detective who had been demoted to desk duty by Hylan's police commissioner after he persisted in raiding brothels and gambling joints protected by district leaders. McLaughlin promoted Lieutenant Valentine to deputy inspector and put him in charge of a newly formed Confidential Squad, a phalanx of fifty or so cops invested with power "to strike terror into the hearts of the crooked politicians and dishonest cops." There would be no interference from Tammany Hall. Mayor Walker had "promised."

Valentine first targeted the big-money games of the ruling chieftains of the New York gambling world: Arnold Rothstein, "Nick the Greek," Johnny Baker, and "Nigger Nate" Raymond—the "Broadway Crowd," they were called, because their customers were big-name entertainers, Wall Street tycoons, and society bluebloods. Rothstein and other princes of the trade ran floating crap games, moving the site every evening to a different hotel or penthouse, always under the protective eye of patrolmen paid handsomely by the gamblers.

Valentine planted men up and down Broadway and made dozens of raids, but was unable to secure a single conviction. The district leaders, many of them close associates of Rothstein and other big-time gamblers, controlled the lower courts and made certain that gambling charges were voided for insufficient evidence. Of the 514 persons arrested in gambling raids in 1926 and 1927, only five went to trial. But when McLaughlin convinced the Manhattan District Attorney's Office to issue subpoenas to prominent customers, simply to harass and frighten them, the pressure paid dividends; business fell off sharply. The gamblers then sought the protection of "the holy of holies," the district clubhouses, convinced they were as safe as churches. Rothstein opened operations in the clubhouse of city clerk Michael J. Cruise, who offered him immunity from arrest in return for a share of the profits. His fellow gamblers made similar arrangements with other district leaders.

When these district leaders approached the mayor, demanding that he harness his overzealous police commissioner, Walker flatly refused. But the pressure on him intensified when McLaughlin had Valentine raid the clubhouses of two of the most powerful New York political bosses, Thomas M. Farley, whose principality was Manhattan's Upper East Side, and alderman Peter J. McGuinness, a stalwart of John McCooey's Brooklyn machine. Both were harboring gambling operations in their political clubhouses, bleeding off some of the profits for their organizations.

At three o'clock in the morning, on May 29, 1926, Lewis Valentine's men entered Farley's clubhouse by force, without a warrant, and made mass arrests, but Farley used his clout to have all charges dismissed for insufficient evidence. Valentine's men had been unable to break down the tremendously thick steel door that guarded the room in which the gamblers ran their operation.

When the Confidential Squad broke through the doors of McGuiness's clubhouse in the Greenpoint section of Brooklyn the following March, they found receipts in a safe showing that $600,000 had been bet on horse races at the club, and that McGuinness himself had taken in profits of over $60,000. They arrested eight men, including McGuinness, on charges of bookmaking. Hours later, a friendly magistrate released McGuinness and the charges against him were dropped for lack of evidence.

Farley, who didn't want to bring attention to the profits, nearly $60,000 a year, he was making on other scams, did not seek revenge against McLaughlin, but McGuinness, a hot-tempered former longshoreman, did. He went straight to Walker, who he considered a friend, and demanded McLaughlin's resignation. Walker cut him short; he had no intention of meddling in police business. Nor could McGuinness get satisfaction from Olvany. "Gambling Raids Win Backing of Tammany Chiefs," ran a headline in the *Daily News*. "We are trying to run a clean town," Olvany was quoted as saying. "If district leaders think Tammany is going to support them in running gambling houses they are dead wrong." Olvany—Al Smith's man at Tammany Hall—realized that even the hint of a political scandal could ruin Smith's chances of becoming the Democratic Party's presidential nominee in 1928. George McLaughlin was clean, and Boss Murphy's Albany Boys—Walker, Flynn, and Wagner—stood squarely behind him, an act of allegiance primarily to Governor Smith.

Two weeks after the McGuinness raid, McLaughlin submitted his resignation to Mayor Walker after only one year and three months on the job. He was leaving his $10,000-a-year job for a $70,000 position as executive vice president of the Mackay Company, a telegraph and cable enterprise. McLaughlin released a letter thanking Walker for his unwavering support and "cooperation," and for allowing him a free hand in running the department. He and Walker emphatically denied that pressure from Tammany district leaders was behind his decision to step down, but *The New York Times* reported that there were "broad smiles" on the faces of Tammany officials when they talked to reporters about McLaughlin's resignation. "Hey, Pete, are the flags all out in Greenpoint?" a City Hall reporter asked McGuinness. "There's nothing unusual about it. I always win victories and am quite used to them."

Civic organizations and leading Republicans suspected that Tammany pressure had figured strongly in McLaughlin's resignation. If it did, hard evidence is lacking. A resignation under fire would have been out of character for flinty George McLaughlin, one of the most formidable police commissioners in the city's history. Nor is there a shred of evidence that Jimmy Walker, under heat from McGuinness and other district leaders, forced McLaughlin's resignation. McLaughlin probably acted out of a combination of frustration and disgust over his inability to get convictions, discontentment that came to a head when another lucrative opportunity became available.

Four years later, McLaughlin was called to testify in the Seabury investigation of municipal corruption. Asked if he had received the mayor's cooperation in his war on gambling, he replied: "Absolutely. . . . If co-operation was non-interference, I got 100 per cent cooperation." Judge Samuel Seabury then tried to get McLaughlin to admit that he had resigned as commissioner under pressure from the mayor. McLaughlin was adamant. "I left to make more money, putting it to you frankly." The *Times* ran the story under the headline, "McLaughlin Clears Mayor." But the unfounded rumor would not die: Walker and his Tammany cronies had undercut a cop who could not be corrupted.

Jimmy Walker prevailed upon his old schoolmate and former law associate Joseph A. Warren to become the next police commissioner. A loyal Tammany man, he came under immediate pressure from district leaders to disband the Confidential Squad and transfer Valentine to the other side of the moon. But thin, retiring Joe Warren had iron in his spine. The day he took over as commissioner he called Valentine into his office and ordered him to continue his raids.

Walker, however, was beginning to waver. In a private meeting, he told Warren about the "complaints" he was receiving "from some of the district leaders about the supervision their clubs were receiving [from the police]." Valentine's men "were a little harsh on them," Walker suggested, for it was only "petty gambling." This must have been an exceeding difficult struggle for the weak-willed mayor, "whose code," said his friend Edward Flynn, "was to support the organization."

For another year Warren was attacked ferociously by district leaders. He never faltered even though he was gravely ill, suffering from an undiagnosed nervous disorder. Nor did Walker interfere with the work of the Confidential Squad. But the district leaders, through their control of the lower courts that handled vice crimes, eventually won the war. Valentine's Confidential Squad would make over a thousand raids, but only one politician—a very small fish—was convicted, and his sentence was suspended.

The district leaders hoisted their glasses in celebration when Joseph Warren, in failing health, resigned as police commissioner on December 13, 1928. Warren had not wanted to resign; Walker forced his hand. That winter the mayor was looking into the core of a storm. The New York papers were assailing the police department for its failure to find the killer of gambling czar and drug kingpin Arnold Rothstein, who was shot and mortally wounded on November 3, 1928, after leaving a high-stakes Manhattan poker game. The police were suspected of stalling or sabotaging the investigation because of Rothstein's long association with Tammany Hall. Rothstein's business records had not been found, but if they were, and if they were made public, there were "going to be a lot of suicides in high places," Rothstein's lawyer informed District Attorney Joab Banton.

Walker would have to risk that. He was under too much pressure to find the killer; and his police commissioner was not moving with sufficient alacrity, he was convinced, because of his deteriorating health. After issuing an unfair ultimatum to Warren—solve the case in four days or retire—Walker demanded and accepted his resignation.

Warren's successor was Grover A. Whalen, chairman of the Mayor's Committee on Reception of Distinguished Guests, general manager of the John Wanamaker store in New York, and a steadfast Tammany man. Whalen vowed to wage war on organized crime, continue the raids on Tammany clubhouses, and bring to justice Rothstein's killer. He did none of these things, although he continued to do sterling work as the city's official greeter.

Grover Whalen, with his gorgeous striped suits and high silk hats, his military bearing and crisp directives, put on an impressive show as the new police commissioner, reorganizing the department along military lines. But as Mayor Fiorello La Guardia would later say: "It takes more than a silk hat and a pair of spats to make an efficient Police Commissioner." Instead of fighting Tammany thieves, Whalen fought communist trade unions, vagrants, and drunks. And in one of his first acts as a crime buster he fired the most fearless criminal fighter in the city. He did not even have the courage or decency to face Louis Valentine. Valentine was informed through departmental channels that he was being reduced in rank to captain and assigned to a precinct in Long Island City.

Whalen then abolished the Confidential Squad. Valentine's men had helped keep the district leaders from meddling in police business. Whalen was not strong enough, or willing enough, to do that.

Louis Valentine would have sweet revenge. In 1934, Mayor La Guardia appointed him police commissioner. He would serve until 1945, longer than any previous commissioner. La Guardia considered him "the best Police Commissioner New York ever had."

Jimmy Walker had held out against the district leaders for two conflict-filled years. But in hiring Grover Whalen and guaranteeing him the same freedom from mayoralty interference that McLaughlin and Warren had demanded, he provided the district leaders exactly what they were hungering for: virtual immunity from police harassment. McLaughlin and Warren had used their operational freedom to harass criminals harbored by Tammany insiders. Under Whalen—and a willfully blind mayor—the big games in the clubhouses flourished.

But Jimmy Walker was too proud to be a mere creature of the local Tammany bosses. On at least two occasions, he successfully fought both borough and district leaders, demonstrating a capacity to govern with resolve. Following his election in 1925, he had promised to create a city planning commission; to take strong measures to clean up New York's distressingly polluted harbor waters; and to give the city an improved bus system. Although hamstrung for a time by clubhouse and borough chieftains, he honored the first two of these pledges. He also brought several borough presidents into line on the bus issue, but here his slippery ethics and inattention to the details of governing hurt the city and opened up Walker for the first time to charges of corruption and cronyism. Just as there were two Tammanys, there were two Jimmy Walkers, the one a determined fighter for civic causes, the other a mayor lacking the steadfastness and moral courage to govern effectively.

Walker was "one of the best friends planning advocates ever had," writes historian Keith D. Revell. Early in his first term, he created the City Committee on Plan and Survey he had called for in his inaugural address. Its principal purpose was to prepare a master plan for New York, one that would suggest measures to restore order to the haphazard growth of the outer boroughs and promote citywide efforts to address problems that extended across borough boundaries. As Walker said when he formed the committee: "in the past we have provided most of our improvements with a view to the benefit of some particular locality. . . . We have not tried . . . to plan our improvements with a view to the best development of the city as a whole."

Implementation of the plan was to be in the hands of a yet to be created city planning commission, a permanent not an ad hoc body. Although the impossibly large (507 members) and hopelessly divided Committee on Plan and Survey—an unwieldy group of reformers and businessmen—never completed its survey, Walker went ahead and introduced a bill in Albany in 1928 to establish an official city planning commission invested with broad powers, an independent agency whose decisions could be reversed only by a three-fourths vote of the Board of Estimate.

The bill was soundly defeated in March 1929 by an unlikely coalition of conservative Republicans and Tammany legislators beholden to borough bosses who feared losing control over municipal construction projects in their jurisdictions—bridges, schools, tunnels, and sewers that were patronage boondoggles. When Walker reintroduced the bill the next year no action was taken on it. That July, he was forced to settle for what he could get: a pared down bill that gave the city its first ever planning department, but left borough presidents in control of public works in their jurisdictions. The newly created planning agency had a short life. Forced by the banks to make deep budget cuts in 1932, at the height of the Great Depression, and just after Walker resigned, the Board of Estimate eliminated it.

One year earlier, on July 7, 1931, Walker had broken ground on Wards Island, at the northern end of the East River, for the first unit of a $3 million sewage treatment facility said to be "the largest of its kind in the world." It was to have the capacity to remove from the harbor waters the polluting waste from 1,350,000 people, roughly one-fifth the population of Greater New York. And plans were on the drawing board to greatly enlarge the facility once funds became available.

When Walker took office, the city had no effective sewage disposal system; or rather it did, the waters around it, into which the city poured over 750,000,000 gallons of raw sewage every day (1.35 billion gallons by 1930), making its beaches unsafe for swimmers and its waters inhospitable to "the most edible" varieties of fish. The fact that this natural waste disposal system cost taxpayers almost nothing held back efforts to build a network of state-of-the-art treatment plants.

Comptroller Charles Berry, a former health department inspector, made construction of a centralized sewage treatment facility an administration priority. There was a scattering of sewage screening plants in the boroughs, all under the jurisdiction of borough presidents. But with a capacity to handle only 5 percent of the city's sewage, they were incapable of preventing daily discharges that piled up in harbor slips and under piers. "New York may be said to be situated on a group of islands surrounded by sewers," wrote a contemporary observer. "But for the rigor of the tides, pestilence would long since have decimated us."

Raising the issue of local autonomy, borough presidents coalesced to prevent Walker from transferring sanitation matters from their bailiwicks to city hall.

But Walker prevailed. He called for a referendum on his centralized sanitation program, mounted a publicity campaign around the slogan "partisan patronage versus the city's health," and won overwhelming approval for the measure at the polls in November 1929. Two years later, a new Department of Sanitation headed by Walker's friend and Tammany cohort Dr. William Schroeder, former commissioner of hospitals, awarded the contract for the Wards Island treatment plant. The funds to complete it, however, were hard to come by in the 1930s and construction ceased in 1933. Two years later, only 12 percent of the city's sewage was being treated, most of it inadequately. But conditions improved with the completion of the Wards Island sewage disposal plant in 1937, a La Guardia victory made possible by an infusion of federal funds. Additional treatment plants, most of them planned by the Walker administration, were built in the 1930s near the city's major beaches, but as Keith Revell notes, "real progress in water quality was delayed until the 1970s, when the federal Clean Water Act allowed cities to build long-overdue treatment facilities with 75 percent matching funds." Nonetheless, Mayor Walker had brought about the first major improvement in the city's sewage problem in its history.

Walker was less aggressive, and far less astute, in his effort to give the city better bus service. In 1926, New York had no citywide bus system similar in geographic reach and coordinated control to its magnificent subway system. In Manhattan and other boroughs the buses of wildcat companies, "emergency lines" operating without franchises and often with ramshackle equipment, were incapable of handling rapidly increasing ridership. On assuming office, Walker had promised to create an integrated, municipally controlled bus network serving all five boroughs. That year he found a firm eager to operate such a system. This was the Equitable Coach Company, a conglomerate of Ohio bus and tire manufacturers hastily organized by Walker's former Albany crony, State Senator John A. Hastings. The senator had assured the "Ohio boys," who cut him in for one-third of the company's common stock, that he had the mayor's ear, giving Equitable the "inside track" to a franchise valued at $100 million.

Initially, the borough presidents were unwilling to surrender control of transit matters in their jurisdictions to City Hall. Using the full powers of his office, including "hard threats" and under-the-table offers of political patronage, Walker got the presidents of Manhattan, Brooklyn, and Queens to come his way, and then compromised, allowing the Bronx and Staten Island to have their own borough-run companies. In late July 1927, over the opposition of Comptroller Berry, who warned that Equitable had no experience in running a large bus line, Walker rammed through the Board of Estimate a bill awarding a three-borough franchise to what the *Daily News* called his "Pet Bus Company." It was a company run by "financial adventurers" who expected to make profits from stock sales of $19 million over a period of ten years. But it turned out to be pathetically undercapitalized, without funds to put a single bus on the city's streets. It did, however, have capital on hand to purchase a $10,000 letter of credit for Jimmy Walker. Its New York agent delivered this to the mayor at City Hall two days before the franchise contract was signed and just as Walker was preparing to leave, with a hand-picked entourage, on a grand tour of Europe's capitals.

Years later, when the transaction was uncovered by Judge Samuel Seabury's investigators, Walker denied that he had been bribed. The letter of credit, he claimed, was for his traveling party as well for himself, and every member of the party had made a contribution to a common fund to pay for it. Walker also said he made good a $3,000 overdraft on the line of credit. And while Walker and Hastings admitted to having frequent discussions about Equitable, they denied that Hastings's association with the company had any part in the mayor's decision to back its bid for a franchise.

Embarrassed by his inexcusable failure to look into the financial state of a "fly-by-night" corporation, which did not own a single bus, Walker struggled unsuccessfully to find a bank or corporation willing to back Equitable. The straphanging public paid a steep price for Walker's astounding carelessness. How could the mayor even consider granting such a disreputable company the right to operate buses "in the largest city in the world . . . where adequate transportation is a necessity to the life of the community [?]," asked the *Daily News*. Equitable's charter was finally revoked in March 1929, and the city would not have a coherent surface transit policy until 1934, when Mayor La Guardia granted franchises to financially strong bus operators in each of the boroughs.

Was Walker guilty of accepting a bribe from Equitable? The circumstantial evidence suggests that he was, but Seabury's inquisitors, conducting the most thorough investigation of municipal corruption in the city's history, would fail to uncover evidence to recommend indicting Walker for malfeasance in the Equitable affair or in other instances in which he accepted far greater amounts of money from friends who had an interest in shaping some aspect of city policy. Under hammering questioning from Seabury, Walker admitted he had accepted and spent these gifts but he denied that they had been offered in return for preferential treatment.

Walker had always handled money cavalierly. "He didn't give a damn about money—who gave it to him, who got it, or where it came from," said Warren Moscow, "as long as he or a friend had it to spread around on a good trip, a good party, a not-so-good girl." But he had never, apparently, schemed to solicit funds for his own use. "You know that I am not a crook . . . ," he told a friend during the Seabury probe. "Had I been a grafter, it must be perfectly plain to everyone that I could have accumulated millions." But in secretly accepting money from rich friends, and spending it lavishly for personal expenses—money that would not have come his way had he not been mayor—he betrayed the trust of the people of New York and deserved to be removed from office. Jimmy Walker was no grafter; but this professed "son and servant of the city" had used his position to enrich himself.

That Walker saw nothing wrong with this is an indictment not only of him but of the Tammany ethos that sustained and sanctioned fraud, bribery, and outright municipal theft by district leaders, police, and municipal magistrates, unreported crimes that Walker disapproved of but was unwilling—and some cases unable—to stop. A Democratic mayor with more courage than Walker, or one less beholden to Tammany, "could have given the city better government," argues historian Charles Garrett, "but not substantially better government, unless [he] had been willing to rebel against the machine system—and even then it is not clear how much [he] could have accomplished." The 1920s were great times for Tammany, its power indivisibly linked to the general prosperity of the times. Jimmy Walker needed the machine even more than it needed him.

Walker rebounded nicely from the Equitable imbroglio. To quiet public criticism, he convinced the Board of Estimate in March 1929 to authorize $250 million for bridge and other transit improvements, with the bulk of the money earmarked for the Triborough Bridge, three steel spans that were to connect Manhattan, the Bronx, and Queens. This "epochal" project, as speakers at the shovel ceremony called it, along with a dose of good luck the next month, restored whatever lustre Walker had lost in the Equitable affair.* On April 8, the U.S. Supreme Court reversed a lower federal court's decision to permit the Interborough Rapid Transit Company (IRT) to raise its subway fare from five to seven cents. This all but assured Walker's reelection.

The Republicans, moreover, were unable to come up with a strong candidate. Party leaders were forced to hold their noses and put up progressive Congressman Fiorello La Guardia, a "dangerous radical" to some Republican higher-ups and "semi-Socialistic" to the conservative *Evening Post*. La Guardia had forced his candidacy on the party, threatening to wage an ugly, bloodletting primary battle if he was denied the nomination.

Confident he could easily defeat La Guardia, Walker, however, was taking

---

* Construction of the bridge began on October 25, 1929, just as the stock market crashed, and was soon halted when investors stopped buying municipal bonds. Designed by Othmar Ammann and completed by The Triborough Bridge Authority, the span was opened to traffic in July 1936.

no chances. He wanted a mandate, not simply a victory, and to get it he had to have the complete support of Tammany's election-day army. This meant an accommodation with the old guard, who were suddenly back on top at the Wigwam, having regained under Walker many of its former prerogatives.

The victory of the clubhouse leaders was secured in 1929 when George Olvany stepped down as head of Tammany after his patron, Al Smith, was decisively defeated by Herbert Hoover in the 1928 presidential race. Olvany's successor was fifty-five-year-old Irish immigrant John Francis Curry, long-time district leader of the West Side Manhattan neighborhood where he and his family resided, one block from the tenement in which he had been raised. "It is a fiction, this New Tammany," Curry announced on taking control. "I will carry out the politics in which I grew up." But would mercurial Jimmy Walker, the occasional reformer, go along? The sachems need not have worried. "I am the candidate of Tammany Hall . . . and when re-elected I will take my leadership and advice from John F. Curry," Walker told the press.

La Guardia, short, stocky, unkempt, and noisy, was a pugnacious and occasionally unscrupulous campaigner, striking hard at Walker's weaknesses, but stooping to innuendo and fabrication when he couldn't substantiate some of his sharpest charges of graft, waste, and neglect at City Hall, and rampaging corruption in the Tammany-controlled municipal courts. "[He] didn't have the proof," recalled Republican boss Stanley Isaacs. "What he said was probably true, but it didn't get under people's skin. They didn't believe him. They thought he was a little wild and reckless with his charges." On the other hand, prevailing sentiment in the neighborhoods about Walker was summed up in an oft-repeated remark. "One thing about Jimmy, he may steal a dime, but he'll always let you take a penny." And Tammany rule had been good for a lot of people—contractors, labor unions, businessmen, city employees, opponents of Prohibition, and ordinary citizens who rode the subway for a nickel. This was the "high noon of the power of the Democratic party in New York City . . ." wrote historian Richard C. Wade. "The voices of reform were overwhelmed by the sheer success of the system."

"We were too soon with the right man," said Samuel S. Koenig, chairman of the New York County Republican Committee, and one of the few party officials to enthusiastically endorse La Guardia.

The election was a Tammany sweep. Walker buried La Guardia in all sixty-two of the city's election districts; the Congressman pulled only 26 percent of the vote. It remains one of the worst defeats of a major political candidate in New York City history. "If ever there was a foregone conclusion it was this one," said *The New York Times*.

The *Times* was right about another thing. "[Mayor Walker] has given the majority of the people of New York about what they wanted"—most emphatically prosperity and jobs. The stock market collapsed less than two weeks before the election, but this was widely seen as a painful yet temporary economic panic, not the prelude to a decade-long depression. The economy never became an issue in La Guardia's campaign.

On election night, when Walker learned the results he summoned his official limousine and sped off to share the news with his new mistress, actress Betty Compton, in rehearsal at the Lyric Theatre for a Cole Porter musical. A policeman knocked on the stage door and asked for Miss Compton. When she appeared lightly clad in a dance costume, he wrapped her in a blanket, lifted her in his arms, and carried her through the snow to a beaming Jimmy Walker.

The election had consequences that only a few New Yorkers could fathom. With Walker aligned with Boss Curry, a man he was more at ease with than censorious Al Smith, it ensured that the organization's "powerful grafters" would be "without supervision or restriction," wrote Warren Moscow. "It was every man for himself."

"The mask is off Tammany," said Norman Thomas, a third-party candidate in the election. "A district leader of the old school sits in the seat of Tweed and Croker. Jimmy Walker is Mayor and Grover Whalen is Police Commissioner. The old gang is on the job."

PART TWO

CRIME AND PROHIBITION

CHAPTER THREE

TOO GOOD TO BE TRUE

*When I got into bootlegging I thought it was too good to
be true. . . . There was plenty of business for everyone. The
profits were tremendous. And let's face it, especially for a
young man, it was a lot of fun.*

JOSEPH BONANNO, BROOKLYN MAFIA BOSS

King of the Bootleggers

On December 4, 1925, New York newspapers reported the arrest of twenty
men, among them millionaire racetrack owner and Broadway personality
William Vincent Dwyer. The charges: smuggling illegal alcohol into the
country and "wholesale bribery and corruption of Government officials."
The Department of Justice called it the "greatest round-up in the history of
Prohibition."

Agents of the Prohibition Bureau in Washington, D.C., working hand in
glove with Emory Roy Buckner, the United States attorney for the Southern
District of New York, claimed to have smashed the "biggest rum ring" in the
country, "a gigantic liquor conspiracy" allegedly built and masterminded by
Dwyer. The international smuggling operation had offices in New York and
London, a fleet of twenty-one oceangoing ships, and a "secret service that rivaled our own," said Buckner.

Among the sixty other men arrested with Dwyer were his London purchasing agent, a federal Prohibition agent on his secret payroll, and over two
dozen members of the U.S. Coast Guard. The coastguardsmen were accused
of being bribed by Dwyer's cohorts with "money, wine, women, and song."
With their assistance, Dwyer's organization had smuggled into the Port of New
York the "greater part" of the illicit liquor brought into the city by sea over the

previous two years. Federal authorities had shut down "the most successful bootlegger in the history of Prohibition," said a triumphant Buckner.

One of the main offices of the syndicate's $40 million liquor operation was in the East River National Bank Building at 505 Lexington Avenue, in the heart of Midtown. There, federal agents had arrested one of Dwyer's associates, a dapper, gravelly voiced Italian immigrant with an Irish-sounding name. Said to be the syndicate's chief "purchasing agent," Frank Costello would later become one of the master criminals of the century, known as the "Prime Minister of the Underworld" for his skill in mediating Mafia disputes.

The government would try Dwyer and Costello separately and in that order, for Emory Buckner's attention was firmly fixed on "Big Bill" Dwyer, the kingpin of the liquor syndicate in which Frank Costello and his brother Eddie, who was arrested with him, were thought to be merely mid-level operatives. Costello was a shadowy figure who lived inconspicuously with his Jewish wife in a middle-class neighborhood in Queens, unlike the flamboyant Dwyer, a former Hell's Kitchen longshoreman who was in the news lately for bringing professional hockey to New York, with the support of the mayor elect.

Dwyer's New York Americans—formerly the Hamilton Tigers, the financially troubled Canadian team he had purchased for $80,000—were scheduled to open their season at the new Madison Square Garden on Eighth Avenue on December 15, two weeks after Dwyer's arrest. It was to be a social gala, a glittering charity affair attended by Mrs. Franklin Delano Roosevelt, Mrs. Vincent Astor, and Mrs. Charles L. Tiffany. Dwyer had looked forward to being the man of the hour, but George "Tex" Rickard, the Garden's publicity-conscious impresario, struck his name from the program, making Dwyer "the most silent owner in the history of professional sports."

Ruddy-faced Bill Dwyer entered the courtroom for his arraignment with a "broad smile and . . . an air of absolute confidence." He had arrived that morning in a chauffeur-driven limousine, dressed in an impressively tailored business suit and flashing three diamond rings, one of them with a ruby the size of his thumbnail as its center stone. New Yorkers knew him as the convivial owner of the Sea Grill Restaurant on West Forty-fifth Street, a popular watering hole for sportswriters, athletes, and politicians; and as he approached the bench he nodded knowingly to some of his Tammany friends in the courtroom.

Forty-two-year-old Bill Dwyer had no police record and had never carried a gun. A devoted family man, he lived in quiet comfort with his wife and five children at their seaside estate in Belle Harbor, Queens, entertaining only occasionally but splendidly, hosting Gatsby-like lawn parties on summer nights with white-coated waiters and vintage champagne. A subdued, soft-spoken host, he would glide past the lantern-lit tables, nodding cordially to his prosperous guests, new friends, and associates from Wall Street and Park Avenue.

At his busy Midtown restaurant, Dwyer was a different person, a grip-and-grin host, all flash and smiles, affable and easy with his money. Yet there was an air of mystery about him. Like F. Scott Fitzgerald's Gatsby, he had come out of nowhere. Customers wondered how he made his fortune, and made it so fast.

After his sensational arrest and arraignment, everyone knew. Bill Dwyer had for years been leading a second and secret life, unknown even to his close-knit family. He *was* a big man, a bigger bootlegger than Fitzgerald imagined Jay Gatsby to have been, bigger than any liquor smuggler in town. Big Bill Dwyer was "King of the Bootleggers."

William Vincent Dwyer grew up in a neighborhood ruled by some of the most violent youth gangs in the city. Somehow he had steered clear of them, attending public school and working as an usher in a vaudeville house near his home on Tenth Avenue and Twenty-third Street, deep inside an Irish-German enclave of grimy tenements, sprawling rail yards, and rotting coal piers. At an early age he took a job as a stevedore, a "dock walloper," on the Chelsea Piers, just south of Hell's Kitchen. He married a girl from the neighborhood, Agnes Frances Cassidy, and the couple began raising a family in a bleak four-room flat not far from where Dwyer had been baptized. A steady worker with a union card, reliable and sober, he gave little thought to rising higher in the world. That was before Prohibition became the law of the land.

Dwyer had a reputation for undeviating loyalty to the neighborhood boys he grew up with. One of his closest pals was George J. Shevlin, owner of a string of shabby saloons near the Chelsea Piers, where the federal government had recently leased warehouses to store the alcohol it had begun confiscating from distillers when Prohibition went into effect in January 1920. Dozens of the longshoremen who drank at Shevlin's saloon had spent their youth in local gangs that preyed on the storage warehouses along the Hudson River owned by the New York Central Railroad. Railroad police had hunted down these Hell's Kitchen thugs and destroyed their thieving gangs with chilling resolve. But here was an easier opportunity. Federal prohibition officials in New York lacked the funds to properly protect their warehouses, and the underpaid guards were irrepressibly corruptible. Shevlin told Dwyer he had formed a small gang of Chelsea roustabouts to rid government warehouses of their supplies of confiscated alcohol. Did Dwyer want in? He did; soon he and Shevlin were partners.

They preferred to operate nonviolently, using "grease," as the saying went, instead of muscle. Warehouse guards were bribed or deceived into accepting falsified permits allowing their holders to withdraw industrial alcohol intended for use in plants making chemicals, prescription drugs, and perfume. The pilfered alcohol was then sold to better-funded bootleggers who owned clandestine distilling plants where it was converted, with water and flavorings, into ersatz scotch, bourbon, and rye.

With the profits, the boyhood friends branched out, buying warehouses of their own, trucks to transport their illegal merchandise, and sluggers to guard it from competing liquor thieves. As their market expanded they began importing liquor by sea, purchasing it from international dealers, who helped them smuggle it into the country. When the business got too big and risky for Shevlin, he dropped out. In 1923 Dwyer found a new partner, an East Harlem bootlegger named Frank Costello.

It was an unlikely pairing—an Italian and an Irishman—but Costello and Dwyer were of a new generation of criminals; money mattered more to them than blood or heritage. Criminal visionaries, they saw the advantages of collaboration over tooth-and-claw competition. By combining their resources, they hoped to seize the lion's share of the liquor smuggling business in the biggest and thirstiest city in America.

As soon as they merged their smuggling operations, Costello and Dwyer began to rationalize and streamline their liquor syndicate, unconsciously mirroring the efforts of other service industries in America's new mass consumption society. They would become pacesetters in a sweeping transformation in the character and conduct of urban criminal enterprises, a movement from brutal, bare-knuckle competition to a higher degree of collaboration, coordination, and businesslike discipline. This mirrored a parallel organizational revolution well under way in American society. "As a society changes," wrote the eminent sociologist Daniel Bell, "so does, in lagging fashion, its type of crime. As American society became more 'organized,' as the American businessmen become more 'civilized' and less 'buccaneering,' so did the American racketeer."

Prohibition didn't create American organized crime but never in this country's history were criminals given a stronger incentive to enlarge and rationalize their illegal enterprises. It was a revolution in criminal practice that preceded and set the pattern for the much larger and more menacing criminal syndicates that came to dominate the fields of industrial racketeering, big-time gambling, and narcotics in the years after Prohibition. And it was a revolution in criminal enterprise set in motion, ironically, by a well-meaning effort to curb a potentially dangerous human appetite.

The Great Impossibility

At 12:01 A.M. on Saturday, January 17, 1920, National Prohibition—"the great impossibility," imbibing New Yorkers called it—took effect. At that moment the Eighteenth Amendment to the Constitution, ratified by the states the previous January, became the law of the land.*

Prohibition had been driven into national law by a bipartisan coalition of progressive reformers, industrialists, and temperance groups determined to make America "absolutely and permanently bone dry." They sanguinely expected that America would become a "saloonless land," a country cleansed of the vices associated with that supposedly pernicious institution, among them alcoholism, child and spousal abuse, broken families, and industrial accidents. Neighborhood saloons were also the headquarters of corrupt political bosses, whom reformers accused of rigging elections with paid and inebriated "repeaters." In New York City, Prohibition was seen by many Republican leaders as a way to break Tammany's grip on city government.

Optimism abounded; success seemed assured. Forty-six states had endorsed the Eighteenth Amendment, far more than needed for passage; and Prohibition had been ushered into law and would be vigilantly monitored by the Anti-Saloon League, one of the most formidable pressure groups ever to descend upon Congress. Headed by Ohio attorney Wayne B. Wheeler, it was America's first professional lobbying group and a propaganda engine unequalled in its day. With Prohibition, "a new nation will be born," declared a league spokesman, "[a] clean thinking and clean living" America.

The Eighteenth Amendment had no teeth until Wheeler, a masterful political strategist, prodded Congress to pass, over President Woodrow Wilson's veto, the Volstead Enforcement Act, named after its plain-living sponsor, Andrew J. Volstead, a Republican congressman from Minnesota. The Volstead Act made beverages containing 0.5 percent or more alcohol illegal and set up a mechanism for federal enforcement. The newly established Prohibition Bureau was put under the authority of the Treasury Department, not, as would have been more logical, the Justice Department; and the bureau en-

---

* Actually, large parts of the country had gone dry well before this, the result of local option legislation. By 1913, nine states had abolished the liquor trade; and over the course of the next six years voters in nineteen other states passed referendums approving anti-liquor laws, although none required complete and compulsory prohibition.

listed the United States Coast Guard, the Customs Service, and the Internal Revenue Service to assist its small, pathetically paid enforcement staff of 1,526 agents—roughly one agent for every 71,000 Americans. These agents were given the impossible task of preventing the importation of illegal liquor across the nineteen thousand miles of America's land and water borders. The New York City district, extending northward into Connecticut, was assigned only 129 agents. Most of them drew salaries of no more than $150 a month (equivalent to about $20,000 a year in 2014) and all were armed and untrained, a formula for failure.

At Wheeler's insistence, Congress had given the Treasury Department only a minuscule enforcement budget on the confident assumption that the great majority of Americans would dutifully obey a law that had been woven into the fabric of the Constitution. In a few years, he insisted, the budget for enforcement would be reduced even further; eventually full compliance would eliminate the need for any policing at all. It was the shallow reasoning of a blind believer.

Clear-thinking opponents of the new law, among them congressman Fiorello La Guardia, realized that reasonable levels of compliance could only be attained through a staggering monetary commitment to enforcement, a level of funding that a fiscally conservative Republican Congress would never approve.

The Eighteenth Amendment prohibited "the manufacture, sale, or transportation of intoxicating liquors," but was silent on the consumption of liquor in private homes. Few Americans knew exactly what was permissible or punishable under the new dictate. To assist them, the *New York Evening Post* provided a convenient list of "Don'ts for the Drinking Man."

UNDER CONSTITUTIONAL PROHIBITION
IT IS UNLAWFUL:

To buy or sell a drink anywhere except for sacramental or medicinal purposes.

To give or take a drink anywhere except in the home of the man who owns it.

To keep any liquor in storage anywhere but in your home.

To carry a pocket flask.

To restock your home supply when it runs out.

To manufacture anything above one-half of one percent [alcohol] in your home.

To make a present of a bottle of liquor to a friend.

To receive such a present from a friend.

To buy, sell, or use a home still or any other device for making liquor in the home.

Prohibition would be backed by the full force of the law, its adherents argued. "Any saloon man who attempts to sell liquor is foolish, for in doing so he will be guilty of a felony, punishable by sentence to Atlanta [Penitentiary]," declared the revenue agent in charge of enforcing the Volstead Act in New York City. Hardly anyone was listening. On the night Prohibition went into effect there were approximately sixteen thousand licensed saloons in New York City. At least two thousand speakeasies sprang up in the next few weeks. Seven years later the city had, by one estimate, over 32,000 of them.

A poll conducted in early 1920 by the *New York World* found "an overwhelming opposition to Prohibition by the man in the street." The law favored the "haves" over the "have-nots," said most respondents. The neighborhood saloon—the poor man's club—was padlocked, while the affluent continued to drink, without fear of legal infringement, in the leather and chrome bars of their exclusive clubs. The fortunate few had also lined up their own private bootleggers, in advance of Prohibition, ready on a phone call's notice to replenish their cellars.

Many New Yorkers sided with Jimmy Walker, who saw Prohibition as a tyrannical abridgement of personal freedom. Walker had said this, repeatedly and forcefully, on the floor of the New York Senate, beginning with his party's unsuccessful battle to prevent the Republican-controlled legislature from ratifying the Eighteenth Amendment. He was one of the few opponents of the Eighteenth Amendment who recognized Prohibition for what it truly was: a revolutionary measure, a law that would have a greater influence on the daily lives of Americans than any federal initiative since the Civil War.

Walker understood, furthermore, that Prohibition was unenforceable in New York City. The Eighteenth Amendment may have been broadly popular in other parts of the country, but not in Gotham, where social drinking was an integral part of the culture of both working-class people and society bluebloods—and was vehemently opposed by the leadership of Tammany Hall. "Even the Army and Navy of the United States are not large enough to enforce this unenforceable mockery," Walker declared. When the Supreme

Court struck down a Walker-sponsored state law making it legal to brew beer of moderate alcohol content, he led an all-out fight in the New York legislature—one of the most dramatic in the history of the state—to repeal the Mullan-Gage Act, the so-called baby Volstead Act, pledging New York state to support federal enforcement efforts. Walker insisted that Mullan-Gage was hopelessly ineffective; sympathetic juries were reluctant to convict even the most blatant violators of the Eighteenth Amendment. Bootleggers, jurors reasoned, were merely satisfying a powerful public demand for their product. In the first three years of Prohibition, police and federal Prohibition agents in New York state made seven thousand arrests for violations of the Volstead Act but obtained only twenty-seven convictions.

After five unsuccessful attempts to repeal Mullan-Gage, Walker and his coalition of "wets" finally prevailed in 1923 by a razor-thin one-vote margin, overcoming a heavily subsidized campaign by Wheeler's Anti-Saloon League, which had a sordid record of intimidating its opponents by digging into their personal lives and threatening to reveal any moral failings its investigators discovered. A senator hospitalized with pneumonia cast the deciding vote. On Walker's orders, he was put on a New York to Albany express train and carried into the chambers on a stretcher. "I'm dying, Jim," Senator John Hastings whispered to Walker as he was carried down the aisle. "But you're doing it on the battlefield, Jack," Walker responded. "Try to keep breathing—at least till they call your name."

After wavering for a time, Governor Al Smith signed the bill, an act of political courage that may have cost him his party's presidential nomination in 1924. All arrests for violating the Volstead Act now had to be made by federal agents, and all Prohibition cases were thrown into the federal courts, congesting the dockets and forcing judges to dismiss thousands of cases the courts had no hope of bringing to trial.

Frank Costello

Smugglers of illegal liquor operated with almost complete impunity in the first three years of Prohibition. Roughly two-thirds of the liquor smuggled into the country came overland from Canada, but most of the big bootleggers in New York City—the busiest and best ocean port in North America—preferred to bring in their supplies by sea. Freighters and schooners could carry more illegal contraband than trucks and were difficult for authorities to detect and intercept on the open Atlantic.

When Dwyer and Costello started out in the bootlegging business, independent of one another, they secured most of their liquor from Rum Row, a "ragtag armada" of booze-laden ships anchored in a long, discontinuous line off the Atlantic seaboard, from Maine to Miami. The self-proclaimed founder of Rum Row was William "Big Bill" McCoy, a Florida sea captain and boat builder who operated a small line of excursion boats and coastal freighters. In the early spring of 1921, McCoy ran 1,500 cases of liquor purchased legally in the British Bahamas into Savannah, Georgia, on the schooner *Henry L. Marshall.* On that single trip he cleared a profit of $20,000, more than he had made in any year in his legitimate business.

That May, McCoy began operating off the coast of Long Island, riding safely at anchor in international waters, just outside the U.S. territorial limit, which was then only three miles from shore. Here the Coast Guard couldn't touch him. McCoy, a nondrinker, sold his liquor to anyone with the means and the temerity to make the trip out to his two-masted schooner. The idea spread, and by 1922 the area of international waters off the tip of Montauk Point, with its proximity to the biggest illegal liquor market in the world, was the busiest of the so-called Rum Rows. It was a business dominated by small-time operators, most of them out to make a quick killing. In these bonanza years of rum-running, motorists parked along the New Jersey Highlands could peer out to sea and sight a dozen and more large ships "standing almost end to end, loaded with whisky and waiting for customers."

There was a pattern to the business. Every day near dusk, hundreds of small craft—the "Sunset Fleet"—set out from coves and inlets on the Long Island and Jersey shore and headed for Rum Row, hoping to evade, in the failing light, the half dozen or so Coast Guard vessels that patrolled these waters. The crews of these "contact boats" bought liquor on the spot from the "mother ships" and ferried it to shore, the modus operandi of both Costello and Dwyer when they first entered the seagoing smuggling trade sometime in 1922.

To keep the crews of the big mother ships from becoming bored and mutinous, their owners hired comedians and dance bands from Manhattan clubs, and allowed the mates to drink to stupefaction. Call girls were invited out to Rum Row. Hundreds of them came, a few "just for kicks," but most for the healthy "hazard" bonuses they were paid—prices double what they charged for their favors on land. Excursion boats packed with thrill-seeking sightseers sailed out to Rum Row on calm summer afternoons, their passengers "shouting good wishes and salutations at rummy crews."

The business was not without its risks. Prohibition pirates, called "go-through guys," plied the coastal waters in speedboats, hijacking the contact boats, and even occasionally a mother ship that might be drifting at anchor, its crew paralyzed by drink. Hijacking introduced a measure of uncertainty into the business of smuggling by sea, and mobsters on the make—venturesome criminals chasing the big money—deplore uncertainty. Dwyer and Costello, working separately at the time, moved to eliminate them.

Costello moved first and with ruthless resolve. He armed the hired guards on his contact boats with the new Thompson submachine gun, or tommy gun, a compact, handheld weapon designed in 1919—too late for the Great War— by General John T. Thompson. Invented to kill Germans, the Annihilator, as it was called, became the weapon of choice of Prohibition criminals and law enforcement officials, the gun that "made the twenties roar." After a few ugly incidents, sea pirates steered clear of Frank Costello's boats—and Dwyer's as well, after he placed orders for crates of tommy guns, available for sale on the open market.

Costello's resort to violence surprised no one who had known him when he was a neighborhood punk in East Harlem. He and his brother Eddie were both dangerous men, but Frank was more cunning and disciplined than his untamed older brother.

Frank Costello succumbed early to the lure of the bad life. Born on January 26, 1891, in the impoverished Calabria village of Lauropoli, Francesco Castiglia—his baptismal name—sailed for New York with his mother and a younger sister at age five. There they were reunited with Francesco's father and his older brothers and sisters, who had emigrated three years earlier to secure a place in the terrifyingly impersonal city.

The family began their new life in a three-story tenement on East 108th Street, in an Italian enclave in East Harlem where Francesco's parents opened a small grocery store. Working fourteen hours a day, the couple had little time for their children. Francesco was free to roam the streets, becoming in time a petty thief and pickpocket, stealing from pushcarts and preying on helpless old women. He later took perverse pride in the lesson he claimed he learned from his parents' unrewarded daily struggle: that hard work didn't pay, that crime was a smoother road to success.

In midlife, when Costello was a Mafia overlord, he would secretly begin seeing a Manhattan psychiatrist, Dr. Richard Hoffman. He wanted to unburden himself of the demons that had been tormenting him since he was a boy. He told Hoffman he hated his hardworking father for his fawning humility, for too readily accepting poverty as his ordained fate. And he confessed that he was never able to surmount his feelings of inferiority about being the son of a tradition-bound immigrant storekeeper. But his obsessive social insecurity, he failed to see, had fed his hunger for advancement, his penchant for grasping every opportunity that presented itself, legal or illegal, without conscience or afterthought. It had driven him to a life of crime and propelled him to the top of the criminal world.

At age thirteen, Francesco Castiglia quit school to join a gang of brawling hoodlums that included his brother Eduardo. Cocky, impulsive, and brazenly fearless, he was arrested three times for assault and robbery, and allowed to go free on each occasion by a lenient magistrate on insufficient evidence. His luck ran out in 1915. On a tip from an informer, police picked him up for carrying a concealed weapon, a felony in New York City. He was sentenced to a year in prison, but was released a month early for good behavior.

By this time, he was a married man and had begun calling himself Frank Costello, perhaps to further distance himself from the shuttered Calabria world of his parents. (Around the same time, his brother changed his name to Edward Costello.) His wife was Lauretta Giegerman, an attractive girl of fifteen from the German-Jewish quarter of upper Park Avenue that bordered East Harlem. Costello, a dark-eyed hellion with a pitted face and water-combed black hair, met her through her rebellious brother Dudley, one of his associates in crime. He and Lauretta were drawn together by feelings of social ostracism. "The Italians and the Jews, they stank in the nostrils of the Protestants," Costello would say later. "So when I met [Lauretta], I had the feeling she was like one of my own."

After leaving the city penitentiary on Welfare Island in 1916, Frank Costello vowed "never to pack a gun again," and he never did. Around this time he went into partnership with a hustler named Harry Horowitz. Their company made novelties and toys for children, but the real payoff came from punchboards, popular gambling games in New York saloons. Pulling down steady money as a businessman was a revelation for Costello. He discovered he had a head for figures; he could put to memory reams of information about sales, inventories, and suppliers. And he was a born-in-the-bones dealmaker—shrewd, imaginative, and coldly calculating. He expanded his reach, investing in real estate and other punchboard companies, and might have become a legitimate businessman had Prohibition not come along. With Dwyer and other incipient criminal entrepreneurs, many of them immigrants or sons of immigrants, Costello moved audaciously to seize and reshape a gigantic, federally suppressed industry. "Nothing like it had ever happened before," writes historian Mike Dash. "An entire American industry—one of the most important in the country—had been gifted by the government to gangsters." Frank Costello would put it succinctly: "it was a whole new ball game. And we owned the ball."

The Costello brothers entered the bootlegging business in 1920, the year the Horowitz Novelty Company went out of business when the punchboard craze suddenly fizzled out. Arnold Rothstein, "the Big Fixer," backed them, providing small loans, along with the protection of police, judges, and Tammany district leaders. He stayed in the background, bankrolling Costello and a host of other enterprising young bootleggers, most of them Italians and Jews from lower Manhattan, where Rothstein, the son of a rich Jewish businessman, had begun his life in crime as a pool shark and bookie. Bootlegging was a profitable but highly risky enterprise. The loss of a shipment of liquor to federal agents could cost as much as half a million dollars, and Rothstein was making far more money in his various other enterprises, most lucratively drug smuggling.

Costello revered Rothstein, his "tutor," the person who taught him that violence—the preferred Italian method of seizing a share of the New York liquor market—rarely paid. A sharp-witted bootlegger could make a fortune, and stay in business longer, by using force with discretion and by forming alliances of convenience with underworld confederates of other nationalities. The dollar, Rothstein believed, "had only one nationality, one religion—profit."

Rothstein had class, or at least coarsened Frank Costello thought so. He dressed stylishly—always looking "aces"—kept a low profile, and was seen in the best clubs with the money moguls of Manhattan. They placed their horse racing bets with him and he arranged to replenish their liquor supplies. Arnold Rothstein was the kind of underworld figure Frank Costello aspired to be, both feared and socially accepted; and he operated in Midtown, where Costello wanted to be, along the Great White Way. "All I know I stole," Costello would later describe his lifelong habit of adopting the mannerisms and ideas of persons he respected. "If I saw you hold a cigarette a certain way, and I liked it, I would hold it that way."

Costello began his rise to power as a bootleg king in lower Manhattan's Little Italy, territory controlled by Sicilian-born Giuseppe "Joe the Boss" Masseria, the stumpy, slit-eyed head of the Mafia in that unruly area of the city. Here Costello met and formed fast friendships with a trio of young Italian and Jewish gangsters, street hustlers as fearsomely ambitious as he was: Polish immigrant Meyer Lansky, "the Little Man," brilliant and preternaturally composed; Lansky's homicidal sidekick, Benjamin "Bugsy" Siegel, drawn irresistibly to guns and violence; and Siegel's and Lansky's Sicilian-born compatriot, Charles "Lucky" Luciano—born Salvatore Lucania. At the time, they were inconsequential neighborhood criminals, although vastly more enterprising than others of their kind. In 1931 the ruthlessly ambitious Luciano would arrange for the assassinations of Masseria, his godfather, and Salvatore Maranzano, Masseria's principal rival. He would then convene a gangland accord and set himself up as leader of New York's five Mafia families, with Lansky, "the Jewish Godfather," his principal partner.

Mobster legend has it that Costello, along with Lansky, considered violence "ignorance," and hence abjured it. That is pure myth. While preferring diplomacy, they reflexively hired "hit" squads when persuasion failed. "If you're writing a book about how nice a guy Frank was don't put too much in there about the Twenties," a friend of Costello's told the gangster's biographer some years later.

In 1921 Costello moved his bootlegging operation uptown to an office on Lexington Avenue, and looked to expand. Up until then, his liquor had come largely from Rum Row, government warehouses, and basement stills in East Harlem and Little Italy. At that time, most of the mother ships on Rum Row operated out of the Bahamas, but under pressure from the United States the British government moved to curtail the smugglers. The effort was not resolute enough to shut them down, but it did cause some bootleggers to look for safer, more reliable sources of supply. Frank Costello was one of them; he wanted a liquor pipeline he could control completely, from purchase to delivery.

That winter Costello set out on a journey that altered the direction of his life. Leaving Eddie to run the business, he booked passage on a freighter bound for a desolate island called Saint-Pierre, the capital of Saint-Pierre and Miquelon, a cluster of tiny French-controlled islands sixteen miles south of the Canadian province of Newfoundland. It was a journey that would catapult Costello from a small-time mobster to a major figure in the New York criminal world and would set in motion a great change in the business of smuggling by sea.

Costello's biographers make him out to be the founding father of the liquor trade on Saint-Pierre, another gangster myth. When Frank Costello first set foot on the island he was one of dozens of East Coast bootleggers following the scent of the money. Captain Bill McCoy was the first to run liquor out of Saint-Pierre, "a little squirt of a burg," Damon Runyon called it. The French-governed islands of Saint-Pierre and Miquelon—the sole remaining vestiges of France's vast North American Empire—had, for liquor smugglers, the unequaled advantage of being located outside both Canadian and American jurisdiction. They were isolated but not unknown. Steamers embarking from East Coast ports for Saint-Pierre "are carrying ever-increasing numbers of very busy American 'businessmen,'" menacing-looking characters wrapped in ankle-length overcoats and smoking long black cigars, reported *The New York Times* in December 1921. The island had become an instant boomtown, an urban offshoot of the Volstead Act. Schooners carrying cod netted in local waters filed false manifests claiming they were headed for the British Bahamas. Hidden in their holds were thousands of cases of Canadian liquor, bound for Rum Row.

Costello wanted in on the action. He loved the risk, the temptation of reaching for more than enough. And he had ideas. Instead of buying his liquor on Rum Row from middlemen in the pay of Canadian distillers, he would purchase it directly on Saint-Pierre and bring it to Rum Row on his own ships, ships he planned to lease and eventually buy. From drop points along the congested Rum Row off Montauk Point, his heavily armed speedboats would ferry it to shore. Bill Dwyer had the same idea, and his agents could well have been on Saint-Pierre when Costello first arrived there. New to the trade and without much capital, Dwyer and Costello were men of grasping ambition, restless and resourceful, up from the slums of Manhattan, driven by their recent taste of the good life.

Most of the alcohol for sale on the islands came from the Bronfman distilleries in Montreal, owned and operated by Samuel Bronfman, that liquor dynasty's directing force. Bootleggers could purchase their liquor supplies on Saint-Pierre and Miquelon, its smaller sister island, with ease and convenience at the waterfront offices of new export companies established by Bronfman and other Canadian distillers. These lords of the liquor trade built timbered waterfront warehouses to store their supplies and subsidized harbor improvements that allowed them to bring in larger ships. By late 1921, Canadian capital and American cupidity had turned Saint-Pierre into a frozen equivalent of a Wild West mining town. Incoming ships had lines of painted prostitutes hanging on the rails, their arrival announced boisterously by steam whistles and ships' bells. By then Saint-Pierre and Miquelon were the largest legal transshipment ports for Canadian and British liquor headed for the United States.

The Syndicate

In 1922, Costello and Dwyer, still working independently, set up permanent operations on the islands, hiring local agents to arrange for the purchase of their liquor. At this end of the transaction, there was absolutely no risk; everything they bought they knew they could sell. The risk resided in bringing the product to market through a hornet's nest of hijackers. The sea pirates had been effectively suppressed but land pirates proved tougher to deal with. In battling them, Costello and Dwyer came into direct and violent conflict, a rivalry that proved the prelude to a partnership.

To provide armed protection for his land convoys—the fleets of trucks that hauled his liquor from secluded beaches on Long Island to warehouses in New York City—Costello hired a gang headed by his new associates Meyer Lansky and Bugsy Siegel. When not fighting off hijackers with tommy guns the Bugs and Meyer Gang did some of its own hijacking, raiding the convoys of other smugglers. One of them was Bill Dwyer.

Dwyer had his own enforcers, but they were not nearly as formidable as Costello's Mafia-connected thugs. So Dwyer became a convert to cooperation. Sometime in 1923, he and Costello pooled their capital and connections and began building the syndicate that came to control the flow of liquor from Saint-Pierre to New York City. It was mutual opportunism. Costello had the muscle and Dwyer the political connections—Tammany district leaders who owned precinct captains, magistrates, and judges, along with a handful of federal customs agents stationed in New York Harbor. Costello may have seen another advantage in joining forces with Dwyer. The prominent sports promoter and restaurateur knew everybody who counted on Broadway—stars of the stage and the silent screen, the baseball diamond and the boxing ring. Partnering with him would give brooding, insecure Frank Costello the social validation he had been seeking.

Within a year after its formation, the Dwyer-Costello partnership was the biggest liquor smuggling syndicate in New York City. Federal investigators estimated that the "combine" imported $40 million worth of alcohol a year between 1923 and 1925, making it one of the largest service industries in Gotham. But in order to survive it had to surmount a crisis. In 1924, the newly formed combine encountered a threat to its very existence: a rearmed and resolute United States Coast Guard. In the first three and a half years of Prohibition the Coast Guard's small fleet of slow, poorly armed cutters—ships designed primarily for salvage and rescue operations—presented no threat to canny liquor smugglers. The Coast Guard was then intercepting, by one estimate, no more than 5 percent of the liquor smuggled into the cities of the Eastern seaboard.

This changed dramatically in 1924 when the Coast Guard leased from the Navy twenty-five World War I destroyers, equipped with batteries of high-caliber guns. The Coast Guard simultaneously began arming its crews with long-range rifles and Thompson submachine guns. It soon acquired hundreds of smaller ships: seagoing cutters, high-speed harbor "chasers," and small "picket boats" capable of operating close to shore and on inland waterways. In that same year, State Department negotiators reached an agreement with Great Britain, and soon afterward with other European nations, extending the United States territorial limit for liquor smuggling activities from three to twelve nautical miles, a decision that deeply offended one Colonial official, Winston Churchill, who considered Prohibition "an affront to the whole history of mankind."

In the spring of 1924, the Coast Guard's new "Dry Armada" took to sea with orders to wage full-out war on the smugglers along Rum Row. Target number one was the booze fleet operating off Montauk, Long Island. On spotting a suspicious-looking freighter anchored just beyond the twelve-mile limit, Coast Guard ships would set up a cordon in front of it to prevent any contact boats from making a rendezvous. "It soon became all but impossible, except in thick weather, for the [old] sunset fleet to venture out from shore," recalls coastguardsman Harold Waters. It was the end of the freewheeling days of independents like Bill McCoy, who had retired from the trade after his arrest and imprisonment the previous year.

Enforcement brought more arrests, but it also winnowed down the smugglers to a hard, determined core. There was too much money to be made for large operators like Dwyer and Costello to surrender to the Coast Guard. Enhanced enforcement opened the way not to the elimination of Rum Row, but to its control by the larger bootlegging syndicates—"the professionals," Waters called them—the only smugglers with the resources to outwit—not outgun— the United States Coast Guard. "The rules are changed," said *The New York Times*. "The amateur is no more."

The new day arrived when Costello and Dwyer commissioned the building of a fleet of high-speed contact boats, sleek, wooden-hulled "fliers" capable of carrying three hundred cases of liquor at speeds exceeding thirty knots. They were faster and more maneuverable than anything the Coast Guard could send against them. It became nearly impossible for the Coast Guard to stay ahead of the smugglers. Specifications of government craft were published, and when the Coast Guard commissioned to have faster boats developed, Dwyer sent these specifications to his associate in crime E. C. Cohron, owner of a marine garage and boatbuilding yard on the East River, by Hell Gate Bridge. In a matter of months, Cohron built eighteen speedboats and equipped them with powerful airplane engines purchased from the United States government. He mounted machine guns fore and aft and equipped most of the syndicate boats with high-frequency radio equipment. Working with electrical engineers hired on consignment, Frank Costello personally supervised the building of a network of clandestine ship-to-shore radio stations, most of them in weather-beaten seaside shacks. Using secret Morse codes devised by one of Britain's ace cryptanalysts, operators directed the movements of the syndicate's smuggling vessels, keeping them well clear of Coast Guard patrol boats and federal revenue ships. These stations were linked to the syndicate's nerve center: Costello's Midtown headquarters at 405 Lexington Avenue.

Costello hired a private pilot to further modernize smuggling operations. Every morning, the syndicate airman would board his small scout plane at a field near Mineola, Long Island, and fly out to Rum Row, directing vessels arriving from Saint-Pierre to spots where the organization's speedboats had been instructed to meet them. When federal agents eventually arrested the pilot, they publicized their catch as the first ever "air bootlegger."

Once the cargo was safely ashore, it passed through a security system that was a model of corporate efficiency. The Dwyer-Costello syndicate purchased police protection all the way from Montauk Point to Manhattan—a distance of 150 miles—and used every resource at its command to fend off hijackers. Scout cars—long black roadsters with bulletproof glass—rode ahead of the trucks, their occupants armed with double-barreled shotguns, tommy guns, pistols, and stilettos sharpened to a lethal edge, for some of the Sicilians preferred to kill by hand. Another car covered the rear of the convoy. There were wild shoot-outs between road gangs, and grisly murders. Later, members of the combine would claim that theirs was the only smuggling operation never to lose a truckload of whiskey.

In dealing with the law—Dwyer's specialty—the combine rarely resorted to violence. Policemen patrolling Long Island's narrow, lightly traveled roads were paid generously to steer clear of the convoys, whose itineraries they were provided in advance. If a Long Island cop who had not been paid off beforehand happened to stop a suspicious-looking convoy, the driver of the scout car would simply drop the "magic name" Bill Dwyer. The officer would then know to make a radio call to Dwyer's office in the Loew's Building, in Midtown. If everything checked out, the convoy was allowed to proceed, and the policeman would have his reward delivered within the week by one of Dwyer's smartly dressed representatives. Dwyer's brainchild, it was a credit system for paying off the police.

When a syndicate convoy reached the city limits, uniformed New York City patrolmen—Tammany boys on Dwyer's payroll—would occasionally ride on the running boards of the liquor trucks to ensure safe passage through their precincts. The drop-off points were neighborhood warehouses and garages located all over the city. Here the liquor was "cut"—diluted with distilled water, grain alcohol, coloring and flavoring agents. It was then rebottled, relabeled, and sold to speakeasies and private clubs.

It was in the cutting process that the easy money was made; doubling or tripling the amount of booze brought into the city meant doubling or tripling profits. Most of the industrial buildings that housed the syndicate's cutting plants were cleverly redesigned; a number of them had hidden sub-basements reached by concealed elevators, each elevator capable of carrying a fully loaded ten-ton truck. When shut, the elevator doors appeared to be brick walls.

"If any drinking men or women could see inside a cutting plant they would swear off drinking," said a Prohibition administrator. Chemicals capable of killing a person were used to make these spurious spirits. A New York investigative reporter estimated that only about 5 percent of the liquor in New York was "genuine stuff," brought into the country from England, France, Belgium, and other European countries. This high-quality hooch was hard to get and hugely expensive, but to please their more affluent customers, Dwyer and Costello made arrangements with their European suppliers to have it clandestinely imported in the holds of ocean liners.

When Dwyer and Costello first entered the bootlegging racket they had no intention of forming a large-scale organization to manage their operations. But international liquor smuggling was too lucrative and far-flung a business to run informally. Building and directing the syndicate became a "crash course" in management practices for Costello and Dwyer. They had to learn how to bargain for their products in regional and international markets, outfit and insure large oceangoing vessels against loss, secure hefty, short-term loans, and negotiate contracts with teamsters and boatbuilders. They had accountants, lawyers, navigators, marine engineers, boatbuilders, machinists, truck drivers, seamen, and gunmen on their payroll. Their syndicate—funded in part by a pool of secret investors, New York public officials and businessmen whose identities have never been uncovered—owned millions of dollars worth of boats, trucks, and warehouses, and had specialized departments to handle the myriad activities of the liquor trade. And it had, as Emory Buckner pointed out when he arrested Dwyer and Costello, its own counterespionage department, a "spy" system staffed by hardened criminals hired to ferret out and intimidate federal undercover agents investigating the combine's activities.

The partners divided their responsibilities. Costello—the inside man—recruited the gunmen who guarded the syndicate's liquor shipments and was the organization's principal purchasing agent. No longer did he need to make the difficult trip to Saint-Pierre; he stationed an agent on the island to handle his transactions and had one in London, as well, to manage the growing European side of the syndicate's smuggling operation. Dwyer—the organization's front man—hired trucking firms, leased or purchased warehouses and boatyards, handled political protection, and oversaw the syndicate's spy system. If one of the syndicate's men was arrested, Dwyer provided the services of his personal lawyer, Louis Halle, an able though entirely unscrupulous trial attorney who had offices in the Knickerbocker Building at Broadway and Forty-second

Street. Like thousands of other New York businesses, the syndicate found it convenient to operate out of a Midtown location. Here its leaders were close to their lawyers, their clandestine investors, their Hudson River warehouses and cutting plants, and the clubs and speakeasies that were the chief retail outlets for their bootleg whiskey. When Dwyer needed cheap labor—enforcers, seamen, teamsters—they were readily available locally in the seedy bars along the Hudson piers where he himself had gotten his start in the illegal liquor business. And Midtown was where Bill Dwyer had his restaurant, and where Frank Costello had long wanted to be.

By the summer of 1925, with the syndicate raking in enormous profits, Costello had finally become a "big cat" on Broadway, afforded regal treatment in its stylish night clubs, some of them his newly acquired investment properties. "Costello and [Lucky] Luciano were the only two Italian racket guys you'd see midtown," said the restaurateur Toots Shor, but they were rarely seen together, Costello preferring to keep his distance from Luciano to protect his new public image as a prosperous businessman and investor. An undercover policeman assigned to tail Costello in these years later said "all of his close associates were Jewish or Irish. You'd never see him with Italians. We had no idea he was involved with them."

In 1925, Costello became an American citizen and he and Bobbie, as he called Lauretta, moved out of East Harlem to a modest neighborhood in Bayside, Queens. Here, in an attempt to blend in, he began wearing conservative suits and custom-made white shirts. Suppressing his hair-trigger temper in polite company, he was an engaging conversationalist, knowledgeable about the theater and curious about world events. He was proud of his adopted country, he told his new friends, many of whom were surprised by his passionate patriotism.*

Costello never drew unnecessary attention to himself. He avoided reporters and gossip columnists, and paid bribes to ensure his name and face stayed out of the papers. To his neighbors in Queens he was a quiet-living Italian businessman, extravagantly proud of his backyard tomato garden.

The story of the Dwyer-Costello partnership has somehow escaped the scrutiny of serious scholars; even authors of sensationalized histories of organized

---

* In 1961, Costello's citizenship was revoked because he had concealed his bootlegging operations when he was naturalized in 1925.

crime give it only passing attention. Rising out of the slums of Manhattan, the fecund breeding grounds for some of the most successful entertainers and entrepreneurs of the 1920s, Dwyer and Costello established, in a mere two years, a criminal combine that was a forerunner of the big syndicates that came to dominate American organized crime after World War II.

Organized crime did not originate in the 1920s. Criminals began collaborating in this country as far back as the 1860s and 1870s, when owners of big gambling houses in New Orleans, Chicago, New York, and other large cities coalesced to battle moral crusaders intent on shutting them down. Years later, in the early 1900s, a small, tightly organized Sicilian Mafia arose in New York under the treacherous direction of a criminal genius named Giuseppe Morello. Before Morello's arrest and imprisonment in 1910, his syndicate gained control of the extortion rackets in the city's Italian community and built a major counterfeiting operation. But "before 1919, even the best organized and most efficient of the nation's criminals had controlled rackets worth no more than some thousands of dollars," writes Mafia historian Mike Dash.

Prohibition changed that. In the 1920s, bootlegging supplanted gambling as the underworld's biggest moneymaker, and the bootleggers who rose to the top of the criminal pyramid were those who formed powerful syndicates—empires of crime—the first of their kind in the gangster world.

The New York Mafia, which became the largest criminal syndicate in the country in the years after Prohibition, was largely unaffected by the centralization of crime brought about by Prohibition. Although the liquor trade was a source of revenue for New York's Mafia families, only a handful of local Mafiosi were interested in smuggling by sea; and the organizations they formed to manufacture illegal spirits in secret warehouses were mostly neighborhood and borough-wide concerns. "Prohibition did not lead to a higher degree of centralization . . . [of] enterprise [or] organization in the New York City Mafia," writes historian David Critchley.

When the New York Mafia became more centralized in the years after Prohibition, it followed—although perhaps not consciously—the precedent established by the Dwyer-Costello combine. Originally a locally based predatory organization, it was compelled to become more tightly organized and collaborative, forming loose alliances and market-sharing agreements with mobsters in other cities as it reached out to dominate illicit national and international enterprises such as narcotics, gambling, and labor racketeering. Even at the peak of its influence, however, the New York Mafia never achieved the level of organization and efficiency of a streamlined capitalist corporation; neither had its predecessor, the Dwyer-Costello syndicate. Dwyer and Costello ran their organization efficiently, but they were hardly buttoned-down corporate types.

Hustlers at heart, they moved from one illicit deal to another. Yet like corporate managers in the American service sector, they saw themselves—as did their customers—as servants of the marketplace, satisfying a lively demand for their product. This made it more difficult for the law to convict them. Prohibition created modern syndicate crime and gave it a halo of public protection.

As Easy as Tomatoes

The Dwyer-Costello combine had a decisive advantage in its ceaseless battle with the law. It "owned" dozens of coastguardsmen patrolling the waters off New York Harbor. This was Dwyer's work. Operating through his contacts on the Chelsea Docks, Dwyer began clandestinely buying Coast Guard captains and seamen sometime in 1923, placing them on his regular payroll. With this federal protection, his syndicate began taking longer chances. Dwyer instructed some of the combine's larger ships—seagoing schooners and freighters—to bring their liquor shipments directly from Saint-Pierre to piers in New York Harbor, bypassing Rum Row and thereby saving millions of dollars in trucking fees and in bribery money ordinarily earmarked for Long Island police.

These ships came through customs under false colors and registration papers, their decks stacked high with coal, cod, or Canadian iron ore. Buried underneath, or hidden in disguised lower decks, was the syndicate's illegal contraband. This type of smuggling became "as easy as tomatoes," in the words of one of Dwyer's harbor men. Coast Guard captains in Dwyer's employ tipped off the smugglers when the "coast was clear," and they then sailed with impunity into the harbor, off-loading their cargo at piers on both the East River and the Hudson River—sometimes with the help of New York City policemen, "regular callers" at Dwyer's office at 395 Broadway.

Bribing miserably paid coastguardsmen to stand patrol for his liquor ships had been surprisingly easy, but Dwyer went a step further, paying Coast Guard captains four and five times their monthly salary—per shipment—to smuggle his liquor shipments into the country on their government boats. Federal investigators would soon discover that "practically all boats in the Coast Guard service on Long Island Sound were engaged in bringing liquor ashore from ships on Rum Row off Montauk Point." Witnesses reported seeing coastguardsmen in full uniform and in the light of day helping Dwyer's teamsters unload dozens of cases of liquor from patrol boats with Coast Guard insignia.

Corruption spread to the highest levels of the Coast Guard. According to federal witnesses, Dwyer made regular visits to Washington, D.C., to meet with senior officials of the United States Coast Guard, delivering cash payments and

expensive gifts for their wives. One Coast Guard officer told federal investigators that he had been approached by Dwyer's agents and offered a new car, a
diamond ring, $25,000 in cash, a well-paying job in the Dwyer organization,
and a cottage on Long Island. He rejected the offer and reported it to his superiors, one of a small number of coastguardsmen to turn down the syndicate.

Bielaski and the Boy Scouts

In the late spring of 1925, retired army general Lincoln C. Andrews, head of
the federal government's Prohibition enforcement division, began receiving
disturbing reports from his field agents in the New York City region. Dozens of
coastguardsmen patrolling the waters off New York Harbor were taking bribes
from powerful but unidentified liquor smugglers. Suspecting that some of his
own agents were enmeshed in the scandal, Andrews called in a special investigator, A. Bruce Bielaski, a Manhattan attorney who had headed the Justice Department's anti-espionage efforts during World War I. Bielaski was to discover
who was accepting the bribes and trace the money to its source.

Burly, hard-eyed A. Bruce Bielaski was known in the federal service for his
inquisitional skills and penchant for operating outside the law to entrap his
suspects. The son of a Methodist minister of Polish ancestry, he was a blunt,
uncomplicated man with ruthless resolve. Before accepting the assignment,
he demanded from General Andrews the tools he needed to complete the job:
a secret fund of a quarter of a million dollars to pay informers and run scam
operations, and authorization to handpick a staff of thirty-five special agents.
Andrews agreed to these terms.

Bielaski would be working closely with U.S. Attorney Emory Roy Buckner
and his team of young, fiercely dedicated assistants—"Buckner's Boy Scouts"—
led by Buckner's protégé, John M. Harlan, a future justice of the United States
Supreme Court. Bielaski and his agents would collect the evidence; Buckner
and his Boy Scouts would put the bribe takers behind bars.

Forty-seven-year-old Emory Buckner was a legal luminary, a leading
member of the New York Bar for over a quarter of a century and a former
partner in a prestigious Wall Street firm headed by Elihu Root, secretary of
state under President Theodore Roosevelt. Courtly and silver-haired, with
sharply chiseled features, he lived stylishly with his youthful-looking wife in a
townhouse near Columbia University, hosting sparkling parties for his white
shoe associates.

Rich and respected, one of the finest trial lawyers of his time, Buckner was
at the pinnacle of his career in 1925, but was sailing into turbulent waters. That
February he had left his lucrative private practice to accept an appointment as

U.S. Attorney for the Southern District of New York. Enforcing Prohibition was his first major assignment, and it was an uncomfortably difficult one. He was charged with bringing to justice citizens who had broken a law he considered idiotic and unenforceable. The Volstead Act could be properly enforced in New York City, he believed, only if Congress appropriated massive funding to expand and reorganize the federal court system, hire hundreds of additional undercover agents, and pay them a living wage. "The zealots who created prohibition think the mere writing of the law on the statute books makes it a *fait accompli*. . . . They decline to know the truth," he told reporters in 1925. But Buckner considered it his sworn duty to enforce the law, and to do so "fearlessly." The day he became a U.S. attorney he went "on the wagon" and forbade his staff to drink.

Buckner disliked crude-edged Bruce Bielaski, but the inquisitor and his beefy undercover agents began to get results as soon as they set up covert operations in the city in the summer of 1925. Their methods—which Buckner blithely chose to ignore—were emphatically straightforward: track down suspects and get them to talk, using cash and legal immunity as inducements. If this failed, torture them. On July 27, with the help of a tip from a paid informer, they boarded the steamer *Augusta*, berthed in New York Harbor, and confiscated over four thousand cases of liquor hidden in its coal bunkers. Through another informer, they learned that Bill Dwyer owned the *Augusta*. This was the breakthrough that paved the way for the arrest, that December, of Dwyer, Costello, and their leading cohorts, along with the Coast Guard captains and seamen they had bribed.

At the government's request, the court divided the case into two parts. Dwyer and one group of defendants went before a federal jury the following July. Frank Costello, his brother Eddie, and the remainder of the alleged conspirators would be tried in January 1927. Buckner's main effort would be directed at Dwyer, the so-called Czar of Rum Row. Costello was thought to be merely one of Big Bill's minions.

The Trials

Dwyer was easy prey. The evidence against him—most of it provided by coast-guardsmen who had worked for him and were paid or coerced by Bielaski's men to turn against him—was overpowering. Midway through the trial, he realized he was "cooked." During a recess, he walked over to Buckner and whispered, "You know, while you were speaking, I thought to myself, I really should be convicted."

The jurors took only six hours to reach a verdict. It was not the decision Buckner expected. All the defendants except Dwyer and Edward Cohron, owner of the marine garage where the syndicate's speedboats were built, and where its crews were recruited and paid, were found not guilty. And Dwyer and Cohron were convicted on only one count of the indictment: conspiracy to violate the Volstead Act. Incensed by the jury's decision, Judge Julian W. Mack sentenced Dwyer and Cohron to two years in prison, the maximum under the law.

Frank Costello's attorneys took a lesson from the Dwyer trial. On several occasions Dwyer's attorneys had attacked Bielaski's methods—his "enforcement fanaticism" and bribery of witnesses with taxpayer money. Costello's legal team, led by Tammany district leader Nathan Burkan, would go one step further. If Judge Francis A. Winslow, a solid Tammany man, allowed it, they would turn the trial of their incontestably guilty client into a searing indictment of secret agent Bielaski. It was their only chance of avoiding a conviction.

Frank and Eddie Costello and sixteen other defendants were put on trial in U.S. District Court on January 4, 1927. The charges were bribery of United States Coast Guard officials and conspiracy to bring thousands of cases of Canadian liquor into the United States. Early in the trial, Burkan skillfully turned the testimony of Buckner's star witness, coastguardsman Nicolas Brown, against the government agents who were paying him to testify. When Burkan pressed Captain Brown to explain how he happened to become a federal witness, Brown rose to the bait with unexpected eagerness. In testimony the Tammany judge allowed, he told how he and three other coastguardsmen had been badly mistreated following their arrest back in December 1925. After being freed by Dwyer's bail bondsman, they were apprehended by Bielaski's agents and taken to the Coast Guard cutter *Seneca*, at anchor in New York Harbor. While Bielaski's men looked on, Coast Guard officials placed them in leg irons and put them in solitary confinement in the ship's filthy brig. They would remain there, they were told, until they agreed to plead guilty and become government witnesses. At the end of that week, Brown had agreed to sign a full confession, admitting he had been paid by Costello's agents to use the signaling system on his boat to steer other Coast Guard cutters away from the syndicate's rumrunners. Bielaski had then hired Brown as an undercover agent to gather evidence that led to the arrest of other coastguardsmen who had taken bribes from Costello and Dwyer.

After bringing forward additional evidence of Bielaski's strong-arm tactics, Burkan produced evidence of entrapment and wiretapping, exposing Bielaski's ownership of a Midtown speakeasy, where he ran a sting operation to try to entrap kingpins of the city's liquor trade. In his lacerating defense summation, Burkan called Bielaski a "mysterious and invisible power that employs as agents hijackers, pirates, crooks and bribe takers." Before sending the jury off to deliberate, Judge Winslow issued an order of direct acquittal, freeing Edward Costello on the basis of insufficient evidence. It was a promising portent for the other defendants. After deliberating for twenty-four hours, the jury acquitted eight of the defendants and could reach no agreement on six others, including Frank Costello. Costello had sat stone-faced throughout the trial, but when the verdict was read "a thin smile lifted the corner of his mouth."

The press placed the government's failure to convict Costello squarely on the "despicable" character of Bielaski's witnesses, "agent provocateurs," *The New York Times* called them. One juror said he would have held out "until Doomsday" before convicting anyone on the testimony of "such witnesses as the Government produced."

The Dwyer trial had received front-page coverage in the New York dailies. The Costello trial got less ink but was more significant: a full-out defeat for the "Dry Forces" in New York City. After two years of painstaking undercover work leading to the indictment of ninety-four "higher-ups" in the largest liquor smuggling operation on the East Coast, only two of the accused, William Dwyer and E. C. Cohron, had been convicted. This had as much to do with the law itself as with the underhanded methods the government had used to enforce it. It was sometimes the obligation of juries to acquit defendants accused of violating statutes "so severe or unreasonable as to work injustice," said *The New York Times*, and by their verdict of acquittal "virtually set aside a statute that never should have been enacted." Prohibition, in other words, called for Prohibition-style justice. It was one of the most controversial statements the sober *New York Times* would make in its long history.

Years later, in a private moment, Frank Costello boasted to his friend and biographer George Wolf that he had bought one of the jurors. The jury had voted eleven to one for conviction, Costello claimed, "but I owned the one." That is unlikely. Just after the verdict was read, one of the jurors confided to a *New York Times* reporter that the final ballot on Costello was six to six.

One month after the Costello verdict, the United States Court of Appeals upheld the convictions of Dwyer and Cohron. Before departing for Atlanta Penitentiary, Dwyer told reporters that he was not, as Buckner described him, "the richest of all bootleggers. I never was a millionaire. I was just the figurehead for a bunch of rich fellows who wanted to invest some money. . . . It may be that I have handled millions, but the money wasn't mine." And now, he said, he was deeply in debt, barely able to pay his attorneys.

Those who knew him found this impossible to believe. Seven years later the government would sue Dwyer to recover over $4 million in unpaid taxes on money he earned legitimately in the years 1922 to 1932; his illegal income vastly exceeded that. William Dwyer went to prison a rich man and emerged even richer, as money continued to pour in from his myriad business activities, legitimate and illegitimate. Nor was he, as he claimed, merely a front man for wealthier backers. While there were secret investors in the smuggling syndicate, Dwyer and Costello had built it and ruled it with resolve.

One of Dwyer's first visitors at Atlanta Penitentiary was an emissary from Frank Costello. The intermediary would arrive every month, like clockwork. Through him, Dwyer communicated with Costello, who managed their greatly reduced rum-running operations.

In August 1928, Bill Dwyer was released from prison early for good behavior. Calling his jail time "a little vacation," he returned to New York and was instantly in the news again as one of the city's premier sports promoters, devoting himself with enthusiasm to horse racing as well as ice hockey—and a few years later, professional football, as owner of the Brooklyn Dodgers football team. Less than a month after his release from prison, he convinced his friend and fellow sportsman Mayor Jimmy Walker to become one of the directors of the New York Americans, the hockey club he had brought to Madison Square Garden in the month he was arrested. Walker saw no shame in associating with someone who had broken a law that he himself was doing all in his power to undermine.

Dwyer reduced his smuggling operations after his return from prison—they had become too risky—but maintained an interest in several illegal breweries that enjoyed police protection, courtesy of his Tammany friends. In 1927, Frank Costello began drawing on the fortune he made as a bootlegger to move into safer illegal enterprises, eventually becoming the slot machine king of the entire East Coast. He also invested in a constellation of legitimate and semilegitimate enterprises, including real estate, an ice cream plant, a trucking firm, and an automobile dealership in the Bronx—the Frank Costello Auto Company. All the while, he kept in contact with his Italian friends in lower Manhattan. He was especially interested in strengthening his ties with Lucky Luciano, the furiously ambitious Sicilian who was on his way toward becoming the most powerful gangster in New York City. Costello would assume control of Luciano's Mafia "family" when Lucky was sent to prison in 1936 on a rigged-up charge of running a prostitution ring, perhaps the only major crime he never committed.

The New Pork Barrel

In the months following the Costello trial, congressional opponents of Prohibition, led by Congressman Fiorello La Guardia, stepped up their attacks on federal enforcement officials. The issue came to a head that June when Augustus Heise, Assistant Prohibition Administrator for the New York region, casually admitted in federal court that he had resorted to what he called "a Chinese method of torture" to obtain a confession from a Harlem bootlegger, winding a towel around the victim's head and twisting it tighter and tighter, painfully reducing the flow of blood to his brain. Heise also admitted that his agents had "accidentally" shoved another suspect through an upper-story window at Prohibition headquarters in downtown Manhattan.

Two days later, Heise and his superior, Major Chester P. Mills, Prohibition Administrator of the New York region, were forced to resign. Later that summer, the axe fell on General Lincoln Andrews, the national "Dry Czar" since 1925. His replacement, former New York lieutenant governor Seymour Lowman, announced that his office would no longer countenance torture as a means of eliciting confessions. "Enforcement fanaticism" must cease, declared Secretary of the Treasury Andrew Mellon.

As part of the purge, Mellon fired A. Bruce Bielaski and disbanded his undercover service. Bielaski joined nearly one thousand other Prohibition enforcement agents, nationwide, that had been dismissed from the federal service since 1920 for, among other things, bribery, extortion, embezzlement, perjury, and robbery. By then the corruption had crept deeply into the political system. "Prohibition . . . is a party-spoils system," said Chester Mills shortly after he was pressured to resign. At least three-quarters of the twenty-five hundred dry agents in the country were "ward heelers and sycophants," Mills wrote in *Collier's* magazine, friends and "henchmen" of Republican Party bosses, who had turned Prohibition into a Tammany-like patronage system for their own party, with the quiescent compliance of President Calvin Coolidge. Mills claimed that he had been under orders from Washington to seek the advice of state and city Republican leaders in all hiring decisions, and that he had complied, appointing only a dozen or so Democrats. Mills published the complete text of a letter he received from a Brooklyn Republican boss recommending a constituent for a job as a federal agent: "This is to certify that Samuel Gross is an enrolled Republican." Prohibition, said Mills, had become "the new pork barrel."

In the winter of 1927, the Coast Guard declared victory in its battle against Rum Row smugglers. Stepped-up federal enforcement had compelled New

York bootleggers to manufacture their supplies in hidden distilleries throughout the greater New York region, using alcohol seized from government warehouses, where it continued to be stored for industrial and medicinal purposes.
In December of that year, *The New Yorker*'s investigative reporter, Morris Markey, estimated that 95 percent of the liquor consumed in New York City was
made locally. That was a massively overinflated figure, but Markey had located
a major change that was occurring in both the New York and the national
bootlegging business. In manufacturing rather than importing their product,
illegal liquor dealers were following the lead of Bronx-based mobster Arthur
Flegenheimer, aka "Dutch" Schultz, and other illegal brewers of beer, the drink
of choice of most American consumers of alcohol.

In December 1927, with Bill Dwyer in jail and Frank Costello transferring
his interest to other illegal enterprises, the new king of the New York bootleggers was a beer baron: a convicted murderer named Owen Vincent "Owney"
Madden. Unknown to Buckner's investigators, Madden had been a partner
in the Dwyer-Costello syndicate since 1924, managing what eventually became the most profitable part of the syndicate's business: brewing a popular
local beer and purchasing clubs that served as retail outlets for it. A prominent
Broadway personality, Owney "the Killer" Madden could be seen nearly every
evening riding from speakeasy to speakeasy in his long Duesenberg roadster,
with his Hell's Kitchen pal—and later Hollywood star—George Raft, seated
beside him. Owney Madden, said Raft, "ran New York in those days."

CHAPTER FOUR

OWNEY MADDEN

I am in the land of ambition and success.

—F. SCOTT FITZGERALD TO ZELDA SAYRE,

NEW YORK CITY, 1919

Prince of the City

Owney Madden was a product of Prohibition. It transformed him as quickly and completely as it did the city he grew up in.

In February 1923, Madden was living with his widowed Irish mother, an immigrant scrubwoman, in a tenement in Hell's Kitchen, a region of lawlessness and despair that extended west of Eighth Avenue to the Hudson River from Thirtieth to Fifty-ninth Streets—a neighborhood so appallingly untamed it was known as "a frontier community."* Madden was thirty-one years old and had just been released from prison after serving eight years for ordering the execution-style murder of a gangland rival. He was broke and had no prospects, nor was he in good health. His body was horribly scarred by gunshot wounds that had never healed properly, and he was plagued by lung problems so acute he feared he would be in his grave before he was forty.

Four years later Owney Madden was the most formidable gangster in New

---

* No one is sure how the area acquired its name, although an equally vile slum called Hell's Kitchen existed in South London. The authors of *The WPA Guide to New York City* claim "its name, originally . . . came from the Hell's Kitchen Gang, organized in about 1868 by Dutch Heinrichs" (NY: Pantheon; originally published in 1939), 155. The exact southern and northern boundaries of Hell's Kitchen, now called Clinton by some of its upscale residents, are in dispute. Some local historians set the northern boundary at Fifty-seventh Street and the southern perimeter as far south as Twenty-third Street—others put the southern boundary at Thirty-fourth Street.

York City, the closest thing Manhattan has ever had to an Irish crime czar. Largely unknown today, without his own listing in the authoritative *Encyclopedia of New York City*, Madden "ruled the El Dorado that is Broadway" in the late 1920s, observed New York reporter Meyer Berger. He was that rare gangster, famous beyond the narrow confines of his world.

In 1927, Madden was running one of the largest illegal breweries in the country and was equal partners with Bill Dwyer and Frank Costello in their bootlegging syndicate. He also had a city-wide laundry business, was a major investor in Broadway stage productions, and owned interests in a number of Manhattan's swankiest nightspots, among them Harlem's fabled Cotton Club, where jazz great Duke Ellington would catapult to fame in late 1927. These illegal establishments were shielded by New York policemen loyal to Madden's other partner in crime: Tammany district leader James "Jimmy" Hines.

At the same time, Madden was clandestinely bankrolling the night club and stage careers of future Hollywood film stars George Raft, his boyhood buddy from the West Side, and Mae West, the wisecracking, whip-smart sex goddess with whom he was rumored to be having an affair. "He's a bad man but he treats me good," she described their relationship in a song from her 1934 film *Belle of the Nineties*.

Along with his business and golfing partner Frank Costello, Madden was an entrepreneur more than an executioner, a deskbound mobster who ordered the elimination of rivals only if deeply provoked. After his arrest for first-degree manslaughter in 1915, he was not incarcerated again until the summer of 1932, for violating his parole. Upon his release the following year, he left New York City for good. Prohibition was about to be repealed and the leaders of Italian Mafia families, more ruthless and rapacious than Madden, had superseded the Irish as the city's leading criminal entrepreneurs. Assessing the odds, Madden decided to flee rather than fight. He moved to the spa town of Hot Springs, Arkansas, married the daughter of the local postmaster, and built a new criminal empire founded on hot mineral baths and casino gambling. Everyone in town knew him, including the mother of future president William Jefferson Clinton. He became, in these years, a mobster elder statesman—the "Sage of Hot Springs"—counseling gangsters from all over the country, among them Mafia kingpin Meyer Lansky.

But his New York reputation lived on in the Broadway stories of his friend Damon Runyon. Dave the Dude, Runyon's romanticized Manhattan mobster, was inspired by Owney Madden. "Runyon made [Madden] the founder of organized crime in America," writes Runyon's biographer Jimmy Breslin. So too did dark, menacing-looking George Raft. The coolly composed tough guys Raft played in Hollywood films of the 1930s were modeled on the Manhattan gangsters he had worshipped in his youth, none of them more than Owney Madden. "My celluloid hoodlums," Raft recalled, "were always well-dressed, soft-voiced and underplayed," the characteristics Raft most admired in his old friend from "The Kitchen."

It had all come Madden's way—the money, the power, the reputation—with astonishing suddenness. It was a near perfect melding of the man and the moment. "The New York that Madden found when he got out of Sing Sing in 1923 was just about as well suited for his purposes as if he had created it all himself, for himself," wrote Stanley Walker, city editor of the *New York Herald Tribune*. The Prohibitionists had made it a markedly different city than the one Madden had left on a gray prison train in 1915. And like F. Scott Fitzgerald's James Gatz, son of "shiftless and unsuccessful farm people," Owney Madden, the issue of displaced Irish villagers, seized upon new opportunities created by Protestant purifiers and reinvented himself as a mysterious millionaire bootlegger. A feral street brawler and hard-eyed killer in his younger days, he packed away his revolver and safecracking tools, curbed his wild drinking and carousing, and transformed himself into a gangland organization man with a Broadway office and a bulletproof car.

As Madden saw it, he had no choice but to move in a new direction. The small slice of the New York criminal world he had ruled as "the Duke of the West Side" had disappeared by the time he left prison. The primordial skull-cracking gangs of pre-Prohibition New York had passed into extinction. In 1923, Madden was confronted with a Darwinian imperative: adapt or become extinct.

For over three decades, his old gang, the Gophers (pronounced Goofers), had ruled a large swath of the West Side, extending from Forty-second Street all the way down to Twenty-third Street, the extreme northern border of the territory of the rival Hudson Dusters, named for the river they lived near and the cocaine they put up their noses. In their glory days the Gophers could put over five hundred marauding thugs into the streets, armed with clubs, blackjacks, brass knuckles, slingshots, bricks, and pistols. They made Hell's Kitchen "one of the most dangerous areas on the American continent," wrote historian Herbert Asbury in *The Gangs of New York*. But by 1923, their power had been broken by a cold campaign of police suppression, and many of Madden's old associates were either dead or incarcerated. "A lesser man, a man of more limited imagination, or one who had been broken by prison, would have slipped back into the underworld as a mere punk, a nobody," wrote Stanley Walker, but Madden "had iron in his gizzard. . . . He had been cast down; the prohibitionists, unconscious of what they were doing, gave him a reason for being. The civilization that they had created welcomed him back, a frail and almost forgotten figure of legend, and made him master."

On the West Side streets Madden had ruled in his anarchic youth, a racket meant a benefit dance, a party to raise money for a neighborhood social organization. Now it meant a criminal syndicate. It was a new day of underworld mergers and combines. A supreme opportunist, Owney Madden grasped that fact; and by the sheer power of his reputation as an enforcer—"Owney the Killer"—worked his way into the biggest criminal syndicate in the city, becoming, for a time, more prosperous and powerful than his new underworld partners, Costello and Dwyer. In the days of his Manhattan ascendancy, Owney Madden was "as authentic a Big Shot as the underworld ever saw."

Owney the Killer

Owen Vincent Madden was born on December 18, 1891, in Leeds, England, to indigent but upward-striving Irish immigrants, Francis Madden and Mary Agnes O'Neil. The industrial Midlands was to be a way station for the bullish Maddens, a halfway point on their escape to America, but Francis had been unable to put aside the funds to get his growing family to the New World until he moved them to the booming port of Liverpool, where he found steady, slavish work as a cloth dresser in a sweatshop. When, in 1901, he died suddenly of unknown causes at age thirty-three, Mary placed her three children—Owney, his older brother, Martin, and his younger sister, Mary—in a children's home and went to live with her widowed sister on Tenth Avenue, in a predominantly Irish sector of Hell's Kitchen. She found a job scrubbing floors, surviving through prayer and hope, scraping together enough money to bring her children over within the year. She was there to meet them when they arrived in steerage in June 1902 on SS *Teutonic*, the newest ship of the White Star Line.

When the Madden children stepped off the streetcar that brought them to Tenth Avenue, their new American home, they entered a place more dispiriting than the Liverpool slum they had fled. Identical brick tenements formed solid walls on both sides of the avenue for as far as the eye could see, and the streets and sidewalks were unspeakably filthy. Dead cats and bloated brown rats lay rotting in the gutters; the streets were littered with garbage and steaming piles of horse manure; and nearby were the freight yards of the New York Central Railroad, set in the midst of stock pens and fat-rendering plants that gave off fumes "so intense at times as to be almost suffocating."

Menacing-looking men smelling of whiskey and cigar smoke lounged outside saloons and tobacco stores while plump housewives hung their wash out of the front windows of dismal flats, some chatting amiably, others hurling insults at one another. On the sidewalks and in the streets, there were gangs of skinny boys with dirt-smeared faces and green-stained teeth playing stickball, harassing pushcart peddlers, or racing about aimlessly. Hard-faced mothers and older sisters, perched on the stone steps of the five-story tenements, looked on sullenly.

A few blocks to the west, adjoining Twelfth Avenue, was the Hudson River—the North River, residents called it—its banks lined with warehouses, garbage dumps, and sprawling coal and lumber yards, its fast-flowing tide the color and consistency of discarded oil. Over Manhattan's East River "great bridges throw necklaces of light across the water; here the North River is dark and un-spanned," wrote a local social worker.

This neglected section of the city, its eastern border a few blocks from the Fifth Avenue mansions of the Vanderbilts, was "featureless and depressing." Its mostly second-generation Irish and Germans residents had been so beaten down by misfortunes they had "forgotten to be dissatisfied with their poverty." It was a place as poor as the Lower East Side but lacking its stubborn vitality. "There is something in the dullness of these West Side streets and the traditional apathy of their tenants that crushes the wish for anything better and kills the hope of change. It is as though decades of lawlessness and neglect have formed an atmospheric monster, beyond the power and understanding of its creators, overwhelming German and Irish alike."

But the middle West Side's outstanding characteristic was its anarchic lawlessness, not its poverty-induced lethargy. In *West Side Studies*, a sociological report published in 1914 by the philanthropic Russell Sage Foundation, the authors described the neighborhood boys as "incredibly vicious." Stabbings, assaults, and drunken street brawls were daily occurrences; "every crime, every villainy, every form of sexual indulgence and perversion is practiced in the district." Parents and children alike were virulent "cop-haters": "cop-fighting was the accepted sport." Fearing for their lives, police rarely patrolled the streets at night; when they did, it was always in pairs, particularly on Saturday nights, when every Gopher, it seemed, was fueled with bottled courage.

Eleven-year-old Owney Madden, small and scrawny but as tough as a dock rat, was pulled unresistingly into this whirlpool of crime and mayhem. He had been an incorrigible youth in Liverpool, skipping school to hang out in sweat-soaked gyms, where he cheered on his truculent uncle, who fought all comers for small purses. Shipped off to school at St. Michael's on West Thirty-fourth Street, he became in no time a truant and a neighborhood nuisance, drawn to the marauding life of the "semi-mythical" Gophers, who acquired their name from their fondness for hiding out in coal cellars and tenement basements. Madden had seen his father, his beloved "Da," broken by punishing labor in England's mills. In Hell's Kitchen, easier money could be made on the streets, traveling with the gang that ruled them with swaggering confidence. Gang life offered energy, excitement, and the prospect of advancement, if only by theft and thuggery. Almost instinctively Owney Madden began dressing like the cocky Gophers he admired from afar, wearing a cloth cap, a sweater with a roll-up collar, and high brown boots that laced up the front. Before he could become one of them, however, he had to prove himself in street combat. After holding up a fruit vendor, robbing a few drunks—"lush rolling," the boys called it—and winning a half dozen street fights with murderous determination, he was invited into their ranks.

As a Gopher, Madden was an ethnic outsider, more English than Irish. He was emphatically proud of his British accent and tough Midlands upbringing, and saved clippings from the sports pages of the *Yorkshire Post* until he died in 1965. He was also soft-spoken and well mannered, igniting suspicions that he might be a Momma's boy. Yet he proved to be as wild-spirited as any Gopher and shared the gang's lust for violent and gaudy entertainment: boxing matches, nickelodeons, and cheap dance halls. And along with most of his fellow gang members, he raised homing pigeons, caring for them in wooden and wire cages called lofts, stacked on top of one another on the roof of his Tenth Avenue tenement. In Hell's Kitchen, "pigeon flying is the chief sport," said a resident social worker.

Madden liked to watch his birds soar over the rooftops of the West Side, bank in tight formation to avoid the towering brick chimneys of slaughtering mills, and disappear into the gray haze over the Hudson. It was a simple pleasure he never surrendered. Later he would build pigeon lofts on top of the Cotton Club and other business buildings he owned. "Owney Madden is a connoisseur of fine pigeons of every description," a reporter for *The Washington Post* wrote years later. "Feeding, mating and studying them are his relaxations, and he has flocks scattered in various roosts about New Jersey, Brooklyn and Long Island. Lonely folk so often turn to pigeons somehow." So too do young folk eager to escape their constricting surroundings.

The boy who couldn't bear to see one of his birds suffer committed his first violent crime at age fourteen. Wanting to help his mother put a proper supper on the table, he waited in a darkened doorway and clubbed into unconsciousness a slickly dressed local hustler, whom he then relieved of $500. In his later years, Madden would tell this story often and always for the same reason: it showed he had cared for his family. Seen another way, it was a sign of an early contempt for human life.

By age sixteen, Madden was a ferocious street fighter, his signature weapon a length of lead pipe wrapped in an old newspaper. He also carried a .38 Smith & Wesson. He was someone to be feared, a crack shot and an "accomplished artist" with a pipe, a blackjack, and brass knuckles.

When the Gophers were not brawling with their tribal enemies, they were feasting on the freight cars of the New York Central Railroad, which had a large marshaling yard conveniently located for the youthful bandits on Eleventh Avenue and Thirtieth Street. The gang stole anything of value the cars carried—"swag," they called it—and fenced it to local businessmen. This ended abruptly in 1910 when the railroad company mobilized a private police brigade made up in part of former New York patrolmen eager to settle old scores with the Gophers. They clubbed the gang "from hell to breakfast," said a delighted local patrolman. The raids, accompanied by massive arrests and deadly shootouts, decimated the Gophers. The gang was reduced to three greatly weakened factions. The largest of them controlled that part of Hell's Kitchen below Forty-second Street. This gang came under the control of eighteen-year-old Owney Madden and was known to police as the Tenth Avenue, or Madden, Gang.

The year following the big police sweep, Madden married a local girl, Dorothy "Loretta" Rogers. Three months later, on the night of September 6, 1911, he murdered a member of the rival Hudson Dusters, for no other reason than to enhance his standing with fellow gang members. He was arrested, but police were unable to put together a case. "The witnesses left town," said a newspaper report. Henceforth Madden became known as "Owney the Killer." Every cop on the West Side wanted a piece of him.

Madden built up the size and resources of his Tenth Avenue Gang, the only Irish street gang of consequence left in the city. His boys specialized in shakedowns. Local merchants were compelled to pay protection money—guarantees that the gang would not set their property alight with firebombs. There were, as well, the standard sources of street gang revenue: stickups, lush rolling, safecracking, and second-story work. The Gophers also provided muscle for George Washington Plunkiett, a local Tammany district leader, and for other politicians who needed intimidators around election time to discourage opponents from voting. And in the warm-weather months, gang members blackjacked cops on the beat and stole their uniform coats, parading around in them to impress their lady friends.

Girlfriends of gang members belonged to the Battle Row Ladies' Social and Athletic Club, better known as the Lady Gophers. Led by a firebrand named Battle Annie, they were an auxiliary force in the Gophers' turf battles with rival gangs. There were also fellow travelers, boys in the neighborhood impressed by the exploits of the Gophers but lacking either the courage or the bad judgment to join the gang. One of them was Georgie Ranft, a pencil-thin prankster with sculpted features and jet-black hair combed straight back and heavily pomaded, a lady-killer in the making. Four years younger than Madden, he lived up the block from him with his stern German father, his protective Italian mother, and nine brothers and sisters. His father's violent beatings drove him out of the house when he was only thirteen. He lived hand-to-mouth and trained furiously in a local gym, hoping to make it as a professional boxer. Secretly, however, he dreamed of becoming a dancer in a Broadway club. Abandoned, lonely, and confused, he changed his family name to Raft. Madden took a brotherly interest in him. Raft would stand on tenement rooftops with the Tenth Avenue Gang, bombing cops with milk bottles, flowerpots, and bricks. Sometimes Madden would take him along on burglary jobs to keep an eye out for the "coppers."

On the night of February 3, 1912, one year after taking command of the Tenth Avenue Gang, Madden committed his second murder. Never loyal to his wife, whom he would abandon a year later after she gave birth to their daughter, Margaret, Madden was vying with William Henshaw, a dry goods clerk, for the attention of a local beauty. Madden and Henshaw got into an argument over her at a West Side dance hall. Hours later Madden shot him in the back of the head on a crowded trolley car. After ringing the trolley's brass bell to salute his victim's parting, he disappeared into the night. Before Henshaw bled to death he gave police the name of his assailant. Ten days later three detectives apprehended Madden after a furious chase through his neighborhood. Once again, witnesses refused to come forward. The charges were dropped and Madden was saved a second time from the electric chair.

The Henshaw murder swelled Madden's reputation on the streets of Hell's Kitchen, elevating him to a gangster monarch. Instead of sensibly lying low for a time, he brazenly established a clubhouse for his Tenth Avenue Gang in shabby rented rooms above the house of a local blacksmith. He called the second-floor dump the Winona Club. It had a bar, a punching bag, some threadbare couches, a piano, and a closet stocked with guns, ammunition, and burglary tools. Madden kept a small apartment there, hosting high-stakes poker games and furniture-smashing parties that lasted long into the night. "[We were] the wildest bunch of roosters you ever saw," he recalled with a tight smile some years later.

In the fall of 1912, Owney Madden made a pact with Jimmy Hines, an up-and-coming politician with ties to George Washington Plunkitt. It was the beginning of a long and mutually prosperous relationship.

Hines was running for alderman of the Eleventh Assembly District, on the West Side, north of Central Park, where he lived in the run-down neighborhood in which he grew up, near Eighth Avenue and 116th Street. A ham-fisted former blacksmith, he was running for the third successive time against the incumbent, James Ahearn, a rugged Irish plasterer. In the previous two elections, Ahearn had used street gangs to intimidate voters leaning toward the challenger. Hines had employed his own bruisers, including some Gophers, but in 1912 he arranged with Madden for the full services of his gang.

It was a riotous campaign, marked by character assassination and physical violence. The candidates behaved as badly as the thugs in their employ. At campaign rallies, Hines and Ahearn would stand on the backs of open delivery wagons, parked on opposite street corners, and hurl insults at one another. On one occasion, Hines, enraged by a piercing personal remark, marched across the street and felled Ahearn with a tremendous right hook, knocking him clear out of the wagon.

On election day Madden's "sluggers" formed protection squads that escorted Hines's supporters to the polls, where fellow Gophers stood watch to ensure that the other side cheated less efficiently than Hines's loyalists. When the votes were tallied, Hines won handily. An old-style Irishman, prizing loyalty above all other virtues, Jimmy Hines never forgot Madden's assistance.

On November 6, 1912, the day Jimmy Hines was elected, Owney Madden nearly met his creator. That evening he attended a "racket" at the Arbor Dance Hall on Fifty-second Street and Seventh Avenue, well out of Gopher territory. He made a reckless public entrance, striding to the middle of the dance floor, calling for the music to be stopped, and announcing, with arms folded, that he had come in peace and wouldn't "bump anybody off." He then retired to a table on the balcony, where he had a commanding view of the women on the dance floor. Sitting alone, sipping a whiskey, he was soon surrounded by eleven members of a rival gang. Rising to the challenge, Madden dared them to shoot. All eleven opened fire. Madden was rushed to Flower Hospital, where surgeons removed six slugs from his stomach; another five were buried too deep to be removed. At Madden's bedside, a detective asked him who had shot him, but the Gopher headman remained true to the code of the street. "The boys'll get 'em," he whispered. "It's nobody's business but mine who put these slugs into me." Within days, three of the eleven assailants were in the municipal morgue.

Three years later, Madden's string of luck with the law ran out. Up to then, he had been convicted four times for minor offenses but had managed to avoid prison. On June 2, 1915, he was sentenced to ten to twenty years in Sing Sing prison, in Ossining, New York.

Madden was convicted for ordering the execution-style murder of a rival for leadership of the Gophers, a homicidal punk named William Moore, who coveted Freda Horner, Madden's saucy nineteen-year-old girlfriend. "I didn't have it done," Madden told Stanley Walker fifteen years later, "but I have no kick coming. I believe in the law of compensation. All those times I was arrested . . . the cops had me right, but . . . they never had enough evidence."

Metamorphosis

Owney Madden was an exemplary prisoner. After undergoing a life-saving operation for his dangerously ulcerated bullet wounds, he befriended Warden Lewis E. Lawes, who had arranged the surgery, and worked with him to rehabilitate other convicts.* "He is a good influence upon the men," Lawes told reporters. Madden promised to help dozens of fellow inmates after they were released; years later, he would honor those pledges. "During the period of [Madden's] ascendency it would have been possible to pass an evening [on Broadway] having one's cab driven by a Madden man, the door of the night club opened by a Madden man, the food and drinks served by a Madden man, the clothes brushed by a Madden man back in the washroom," Stanley Walker recalled. These "graduates" of Sing Sing "college," as Madden called them, were under a strong admonition: "Don't go wrong."

It was advice Madden himself failed to follow. Within months of his early release on parole for good behavior, in February 1923, he returned to the criminal life. But it was with enlarged vision. Perhaps in his prison confinement he had glimpsed the future that awaited him if he failed to change: drab tenements smelling of garbage and boiled cabbage, and petty crimes with meager rewards. He was in frail health after his prison operation and several follow-up battles with pneumonia, but eager to pursue the matchless opportunities Prohibition presented for a man with his special skills. These prospects "made his blue eyes gleam."

But without money or solid connections, Madden would need a break to get started. This came in the form of tall, lantern-jawed Larry Fay, a former

---

* Many years later President Bill Clinton's mother, a nurse working at a Hot Springs, Arkansas, hospital, would put Owney Madden asleep for surgery. "She came home afterward," said Clinton, "and laughingly told me that looking at his X-ray was like visiting a planetarium: the twelve [sic] bullets still in his body reminded her of shooting stars." Bill Clinton, *My Life* (NY: Alfred A. Knopf, 2004), 25–26.

gang member from the West Side. He and Madden met at a floating craps game run by Arnold Rothstein in the basement garage of comedian Jimmy Durante's Club Durant on West Fifty-eighth Street. Madden had heard about the game from George Raft, who worked at the club as a dancer, a career he had turned to after failing to make it as a professional prizefighter. Fay was a well-connected, albeit minor, figure in the Manhattan underworld. He liked Madden and found a way to use him, exploiting his reputation as one of the most feared men in the city.

Larry Fay was one of New York City's first bootleggers. It was a racket he fell into almost accidentally, working the streets of Midtown as an independent cab driver. On an evening in early 1920, he picked up a customer along Broadway who asked to be taken all the way to Canada. Before Fay returned, he stuffed bottles of Canadian whiskey under the backseat of his cab. He sold his stash for nearly a thousand dollars, and began making regular runs to the border. When he had made a pile, he quit bootlegging and purchased his own fleet of cabs, fitting them out with attention-grabbing flashing lights, nickel trim, and musical horns.

The competition for cab customers was rough; dozens of New York hackies were washed-up boxers with crumpled ears and sour dispositions, men prepared to use their fists to secure the most profitable cab stands in the city. The best of them were in front of the city's main rail terminals: Grand Central, on East Forty-second Street, and Pennsylvania Station, on West Thirtieth Street. Fay needed an enforcer to secure these prime locations; Madden would be perfect for the job. So Owney Madden became a dispatcher, not of hackies, but of hard punchers, many of them former Gophers that he recommended for the position. He helped make flamboyant Larry Fay, with his purple shirts and cream-colored suits, a rich man.

When Fay sold his cab company for a small fortune, he put Madden in touch with George "Big Frenchy" DeMange, a former leader of the Hudson Dusters and one of the best-known safecrackers in the city. DeMange owned a small Manhattan nightspot, the Club Argonaut, and was looking for additional opportunities. Madden had made good money working for Fay, and he and Frenchy pooled their resources and opened a club. They were an oddly matched pair, the one bull-like and ponderous with a deliberative manner that strangers mistook for ineptitude; the other small, wiry, and wickedly intelligent. But they came to trust one another and joined their considerable criminal talents to make millions over the course of the next decade.

In 1923, the partners expanded, purchasing a struggling Harlem night-spot called the Club Deluxe from retired boxer Jack Johnson, the first African American heavyweight champion of the world. With backing from some of Madden's new associates, including Arnold Rothstein, they changed the name to the Cotton Club, installed a front man to manage it, and opened for business in September 1923, with black entertainers and a white-only clientele. It was soon Harlem's "gaudiest and best-known nightspot."

The following year, Madden became a partner in the Dwyer-Costello boot-legging syndicate. Eight years older than Dwyer, Madden knew Big Bill from Hell's Kitchen—both had been raised on Tenth Avenue—and Dwyer asked him to run a West Side cereal beverage company the syndicate had recently purchased and planned to convert into an illegal brewery. Under Prohibition law, breweries could obtain a government permit to make and sell "near beer," containing not more than one-half of one percent of alcohol. (Near beer was made by brewing regular beer and then reducing its alcohol content to the limit prescribed by the law.) Dwyer proposed that he and Madden use the syndicate's newly acquired Phoenix Cereal Beverage Company exclusively and clandestinely to make "high-powered" beer. Madden would oversee the syndicate's beer operations while Dwyer and Costello continued to run its seaborne smuggling ring.

Madden had come to Dwyer's attention in the same way that Frank Costello had: he and his hired thugs had begun hijacking Big Bill's liquor trucks. Knowing Madden's reputation, Dwyer thought it better to bring him into the organization than leave him outside it, a menacing rival.

The Phoenix Cereal Beverage Company was housed in a fortresslike red-brick building that occupied an entire city block on Tenth Avenue, from Twenty-fifth to Twenty-sixth Streets. It had been a legitimate brewery before Prohibition, and when Dwyer purchased it from the Clausen & Flanagan Brewing Company it had a government permit to make near beer, a product that had nearly bankrupted the company because hardly anyone would drink it. "After drinking a bottle of this near-beer," said humorist Will Rogers "you have to take a glass of water as a stimulant."

When Dwyer was sent to Atlanta Penitentiary in the summer of 1927, Madden assumed exclusive control of the brewery, although Dwyer continued to receive a share of the profits while he was in jail and for years afterward. The prize product of the Phoenix Brewery was Madden's No. 1, a smooth, creamy lager sold at the Cotton Club and all over Manhattan. Beer drinkers were appreciative. Before Madden went into the business, most of the brew sold in the city was needle beer, a vile-tasting cereal beverage to which bartenders added ether or bootleg alcohol, making it only mildly more palatable. Madden was a pioneer; New York's other Prohibition-era beer barons—Dutch Schultz and Irving Wexler, aka Waxey Gordon—did not become big-time producers until near the very end of the decade. Prior to 1929, the cruelly avaricious Schultz of criminal legend was "an ordinary punk in the Bronx," in the words of law enforcement officials—owner of a sleazy speakeasy and a small illegal beer business.

Madden took a paternal pride in his brewing enterprise; there was a demand for good beer in the city and he was supplying it. It wasn't that straightforward, however. If the owner of a club refused Madden's products, the Duke, as he was called, sent in his intimidators.

After taking control of the Phoenix Brewery, Madden purchased a penthouse that had a balcony overlooking the brewery, the largest in New York City. Damon Runyon and other Broadway personalities were regular visitors. "It's really better than killing somebody," Madden supposedly told Runyon, pointing proudly to his massive red-brick plant.

An illegal brewery of this magnitude could not have survived without police protection. District leader Hines took care of that.

Owney and Jimmy

By 1927, Jimmy Hines's sphere of operation extended beyond his Manhattanville political district all the way down to Midtown, where he had a separate office in Times Square. With the connivance of his old high school chum Joseph Shalleck, one of the shrewdest criminal lawyers in the city, Hines was the principal protector of liquor and gambling enterprise on the West Side, in the Broadway Theater District, and in West Harlem, which was part of his political district. Arnold Rothstein ran a gambling concession in Hines's Monongahela Club, and Hines was a friend and ally of Bill Dwyer, Frank Costello, Lucky Luciano, Meyer Lansky, and later Dutch Schultz. He played golf with Costello, attended fights at the Garden with Madden, and kept in touch with Dwyer while Big Bill was serving his term in Atlanta Penitentiary. All the while, he reached out to the children of the city, building a reputation—as did Owney Madden—as a public benefactor. The district leader hosted the annual Hines's June Walk in Central Park, an urban carnival for over 25,000 parents and children with ties to his Monongahela Club, while Madden gave generously to the Catholic Church and to charities entrusted with the care of disadvantaged children. Madden always carried a pocketful of nickels and would toss them to raggedly dressed kids who gathered around his highly polished Duesenberg, parked outside one of his clubs. To these street urchins, he was Uncle Owney, the big-hearted mobster.

Jimmy Hines cut a fine figure. He was solidly built, with arctic blue eyes and a full head of white hair, closely cut and plastered down. He was a superb athlete, one of the best infielders on the Monongahela Club's baseball team; and he had "muscles like the proverbial iron bands, and shoulders . . . like a blacksmith's," said *New Yorker* reporter Jack Alexander. Hines had the uncommon capacity to appear tough and charming simultaneously, a trait he shared with Madden; and while they rarely lifted their voices in anger, they had hair-trigger tempers. Each gave off a sense of power withheld, of rage kept in check. They looked like what they were—men you would not want to cross.

There were deep differences, however. "Madden looked and acted precisely as a racketeer should look and act," wrote Stanley Walker. "If a theatrical manager had put Owney on the stage, to act the part of Owney Madden, the critics would have said that it was a little too perfect for honest realism." His hair was black and sleek and combed straight back. In profile, his facial lines were like those of a falcon, his nose "a fierce beak," his eyes birdlike and mean. His slack chin fell away from his face and seemed to drop all the way to his neck, and his small mouth hardly moved when he talked, his speech studded with "deses," "dems," and "doses." And he had learned how to dress, unfortunately, from Larry Fay, preferring form-fitting, double-breasted suits with flaring lapels, silk shirts—purple or black—and white ties. "He wore fifty-buck shoes with pointy toes, shined so bright you could see your face in them," recalled an old friend, and he cocked his pearl-gray fedora menacingly over one eye. He was "always dolled-up," recalled Mae West, the perfect woman to have on his arm. With her impressive cleavage on display in skintight sequined dresses, she bore a deliberate resemblance to the proverbial gangster's moll.

The decor of Madden's two expensive Manhattan apartments was, however, tastefully avant-garde. He took advice on interior decoration from the illustrious Viennese designer Joseph Urban, and had the maestro remodel the Cotton Club, as well. Jimmy Hines, on the other hand, lived a private life of spartan simplicity. He took the subway to his Midtown office, and in the venerable Tammany tradition lived in a plain brick house in his boyhood neighborhood. There was not a single piece of furniture in the Hines household that could not have been purchased in a bargain basement; and the district leader's blue serge suits were bought off the rack. Rich beyond measure, Hines did not have a bank account and had no known investments. Until the time of his sensational trial and conviction in 1939 for protecting the Harlem numbers rackets of Dutch Schultz, Hines insisted that his principal income came from the modest insurance business he shared with his brother Phil.

Owney Madden protected his private affairs as guardedly as did Jimmy Hines. Unlike Al Capone, the bloated Windy City mobster he despised, Madden avoided the limelight and downplayed violence. "He was suspicious of the swaggering tough boys from Chicago, Philadelphia, and Boston," an acquaintance of his recalled. "He saw no reason for killing anyone. There was plenty of money for everybody." He remained inconspicuous at his Manhattan night clubs, where he could usually be found sitting at a back table drinking mineral water, or playing a two-handed card game in a cramped rear office with Big Frenchy DeMange.

Madden politely asked newspaper photographers not to take his picture. Mindful of his reputation, none did. The Manhattan gang chief never granted an interview and paid gossip columnist Walter Winchell to keep his name out of his column, a favor Madden returned by presenting Winchell with a Stutz Bearcat convertible. "All publicity, to Owney, was bad publicity," said Stanley Walker.

Jimmy Hines would have heartily agreed. He was a municipal pilferer with an honorable profile. A solicitous father and husband, he didn't drink; he smoked only rarely; and he was in the front pew of his parish church every Sunday morning. An expert on the writings of Thomas Jefferson, his favorite form of relaxation was a quiet evening at home with a scholarly book.

Owney Madden, by contrast, lived for the night. If he did have an affair with Mae West, as most of their friends suspected, it was hardly an exclusive arrangement. And he loved to mix with Broadway high-steppers: athletes, politicians, reporters, and show people—but only in places where he felt at ease. While he avoided publicity, he craved notoriety. At his clubs, he was thrilled when customers pointed him out and asked to meet him. "It was like knowing the mayor to know Madden," said entertainment columnist Ed Sullivan. Broadway denizens from tough urban backgrounds like Sullivan and Walter Winchell—Sullivan born in Harlem and Winchell raised there—were drawn into the force fields of New York's glamorously evil gangsters, men who had dominated their old neighborhoods and now commanded great parts of Manhattan.

Madden had his eccentricities and hidden fears, most of them arising from a near pathological concern about his health and personal safety. He wore white gloves in all seasons, and kept them on indoors; he was "sensitive to germs," he once confided to Mae West. Madden was noticeably on edge when in unfamiliar surroundings. "The least little thing," said a friend, "would make him jump," and when he went to dinner he insisted upon a table in the rear so he could have his back to the wall. He had been gunned down once and would

never again be so careless. Yet like most people who rise from lowly circumstances by force and deceit, his deepest fear was that he would fail in what he
had become, that he would be reduced—by the law or stronger rivals—to what
he had once been. In 1927, however, Madden was the unchallenged mob boss
on the Big Stem, the inside term for Broadway. His "reputation for revenge and
craftiness and his political influence at City Hall were so potent," writes Mafia
historian Selwyn Raab, "that even the Italian gangs stayed out of his territory."

Madden's territory was Midtown between Broadway and the Hudson River,
and he had offices in both Times Square and Hell's Kitchen, where he was still
a powerful presence, though now as a "businessman" and benefactor. "Around
the neighborhood, Madden was like the Democratic Party," recalls James "Bud"
Burns, one of the Duke's former truck drivers. "If you needed a favor, you went
to him. . . . Madden was worshipped around the neighborhood. He done a lot
of favors for the poor. A neighborhood guy died, he buried him. People around
Thirty-fourth Street that needed money for rent, he paid it. On Sunday, when
the guys in the bars played stickball for a barrel of beer, well, Madden paid for
that." Madden's henchmen "went after the guys they wanted, they didn't bother
the people in the neighborhood." And like Dwyer and Hines, Madden took
care of his loyalists. "When my brother got out of reform school, he got in with
Madden's gang," a Hell's Kitchen longshoreman reminisced years later. "He got
caught runnin' booze down to Philadelphia. I think he was in jail for about ten
minutes. He made a telephone call and they got him right out."

Madden and Hines worked out an elaborate system of police protection for
the Phoenix Brewery. It was not foolproof, however. Hines had little control
over federal undercover agents, most of them beholden to Republican political bosses. Under orders straight from Washington, they prowled the streets
and sidewalks around the big building night and day for signs of illicit activity: smoke rising from the chimneys or the smell of roasted barley wafting
through open windows on sultry summer days. One vigilant agent rented a
room directly across the street from the brewery. Late one afternoon he saw
three uniformed New York policemen on the street, signaling to someone inside the brewery. A few seconds later, the iron gates swung open and a line of
trucks came roaring out of the brewery, with "scout cars" taking positions in
front and back of the beer convoy. The agent called in for support but it arrived
too late.

Madden had government agents shadowed by former Gophers. These locals knew the neighborhood intimately—who belonged and who didn't. With
help from precinct cops beholden to Hines, they kept the federal spies under
round-the-clock surveillance. Uniformed patrolmen would stop Prohibition

agents riding near the brewery and cite them for bogus traffic violations; undercover operatives working on foot or sitting in parked cars were ordered to move on or face arrest for vagrancy. They had no choice but to comply, not wanting to publicly reveal their identities by showing their badges to officers known to be in the pay of the bootleggers they were pursuing. Men of patience as well as force, Madden and Hines were able, over time, to buy off a number of these federal agents.

The Phoenix Brewery was the target of several spectacular raids before a federal judge closed it for good in December 1932. When a raid appeared imminent, the police would alert workers inside the building. They would then bolt shut the brewery's castlelike double doors and begin sending a foaming river of Madden's No. 1 into the city's sewer system through hidden pipes connected to the storage and fermenting vats.

Madden and Dwyer also had influential friends in Washington, not all of them Tammany Democrats. When Maurice Campbell, prohibition director of New York, informed his superiors that he was planning to conduct a sweeping raid on the Phoenix Brewery sometime in late 1927, a prominent Republican politician—whose identity Campbell refused to reveal, then or later—called his office and offered big money to have Campbell pull in his horns. Days later, a written order arrived from Washington ordering the transfer to Long Island of the undercover men who were conducting the surveillance of the brewery.

But it took more than legal protection to keep Madden in the beer business. "There is nothing clandestine about a brewery," observed reporter Alva Johnston. Being a bulk commodity, beer "cannot flow . . . without gang protection extending all the way from hop poles to the throats of the masses. To ignore beer requires a conspiracy of the whole population." The lowliest of the paid conspirators were bluecoats patrolling the pavements in neighborhoods where speakeasies sold Madden's No. 1. Roughly half the beer purchased in New York was delivered in barrels; the local cops knew the schedules of the beer trucks and made sure not to be around when the trucks arrived. Only later would they stop by the "speak" for their reward. "Every cop was on the take," recalls a West Side club owner. "Owney Madden's beer would come, and the cop would get a dollar a barrel [from me]." But none of this would have been possible if the public had protested. No law is enforceable if there is widespread opposition to it.

For Owney Madden, Prohibition was the gift that kept giving. By 1927, he had a financial interest in over a dozen Midtown hot spots, among them the Silver

Slipper at Broadway and Forty-eighth Street, "*the* place to go" on the Great White Way," said a contemporary. "If one thing hallmarked Owney's clubs, it was absence of fear," recalled a well-heeled regular at the Silver Slipper. There was not "the slightest worry of violence or intimidation. Everything, from the show to the food and the quality of service, was of the highest standard. Believe me, there were other places you felt lucky to get out of alive."

Madden's clubs were part of an immense illegal organization that was "almost a model of business integration," said *The New York Times*. Madden also owned three New York laundry chains, businesses that provided excellent cover for his manifold bootlegging enterprises. When Big Frenchy DeMange, his partner in several enterprises, died peacefully in his bed in 1939 he left a fortune estimated at between $2 and $5 million. At the peak of his New York power, Owney Madden was worth greatly more than that. By 1927, his annual profits were in the range of $3 million.

Though they had long since parted on bitter terms, Madden owed a deep debt to Larry Fay. It was Fay who had hired Madden right out of prison and hooked him up with DeMange. When Madden and DeMange turned to hijacking, Fay provided start-up money. And when Larry Fay opened El Fey, a club on West Forty-fifth Street, Madden was invited in as a partner. It was the first Midtown club that Madden had a stake in, the beginning of his criminal career on Broadway.

Within weeks of its opening on May 1, 1924, El Fey was the swingingest spot in town. It wasn't New York's first night club, but it set the pattern, in its style and clientele, for almost every other Midtown night spot in those fast moving times Stanley Walker called "the Night Club Era."

CHAPTER FIVE

"THE NIGHT CLUB ERA"

Prohibition is better than no liquor at all.

WILL ROGERS

Larry Fay

Larry Fay was a small-time mobster who yearned for respectability. To mix with New Yorkers of wealth and fame—heiresses and actresses, bankers and boxers—was his keenest desire. And in the great Prohibition City there were people of prominence who thought it dangerously exciting be in the company of instantly rich bootleggers. This confluence of aspirations gave birth to the Jazz Age night club.

No one on Broadway was more fearsome-looking than hulking, hollow-eyed Larry Fay. When Fay began his career as a taxicab bootlegger in 1922 he would spend his idle evenings cruising Broadway in a long bulletproof sedan, flashing his money in speakeasies and bragging about his criminal exploits in Hell's Kitchen, where it was rumored he had been arrested forty-six times. But Larry Fay was not all that he appeared to be. Although he carried a long-barreled pistol, he had never fired it in anger, nor had he ever pulled off a major crime. His arrests were for minor offenses—pickpocketing, burglary, vandalism—punk stuff to men of harder temperament like Owney Madden. "Fay had neither the bold inclination nor the iron will to be an authentic Big Shot among the racketeers," wrote Stanley Walker.

It was Fay's urgent need "to hobnob with big names" that drove him from smuggling liquor to selling it. Slow-thinking Larry Fay wanted to own "the biggest cabaret in the world," but had neither the imagination nor the connections to open a classy club with top-shelf entertainment. By sheer coincidence he found the person who could help him in the Loew's State Theater Building at 1540 Broadway, the office complex that was the headquarters of the taxi business he put up for sale in late 1923.

Swedish-born Nils Thor Granlund—"Granny," to all who knew him—was a thirty-three-year-old press agent, radio broadcaster, and producer of live re-vues for the movie theaters of Marcus Loew. He was also a talent scout for Florenz Ziegfeld, Jr., helping the Broadway impresario recruit showgirls for the *Follies,* his annual Parisian-like revues. In 1923, Granlund was managing a small radio station that had a studio on the top floor of the Loew's State The-ater Building. One evening, Larry Fay heard him doing a benefit program and was instantly impressed. The following day, the stoop-shouldered, six-foot-three mobster showed up unannounced at Granlund's door. "I'm Larry Fay," he boomed. "I'm gonna build a [night] spot for high-class people and you're gonna be the emcee."

Granlund was not interested, but he suggested someone else, a washed-up silent film star named "Texas" Guinan, who was then working as the perfor-mance hostess at the Café des Beaux Arts. When Granlund mentioned that the Beaux Arts was one of Midtown's classiest speakeasies, attracting "the very best people in town," Fay's eyes lit up.

That evening, Granlund took Fay to the Beaux Arts to meet Guinan, whom he had known for years. The taxi magnate was impressed by her brassy style and slashing wit, the way she belted out her songs and pulled the custom-ers into the show, alternately cheering them on and playfully insulting them. Perched on a stool in the middle of a tiny dance floor, a tall, thickset peroxide blonde, she'd call out to the men in the audience, "Hello Sucker," and surpris-ingly, they seemed to like it.

Between acts, Fay invited Guinan to his table and sketched out his plans for a "joint" even more stylish than the Beaux Arts. When she showed some inter-est, Fay offered her half the profits. The deal was sealed with a handshake. Fay then turned to Granlund and offered him $150 a week to produce an "all-girl" show for his new hostess. Granny was interested and agreed to spice up the show with some of "Ziegfeld's prettiest." They would arrive around midnight, after appearing in the *Follies,* in time for the all-night club's first act. And they'd bring along some of the *Follies* audience, "the right people," Granlund assured Fay, "with money and social position."

With Granlund's help, Fay found a spot for his new establishment on Forty-sixth Street, east of Broadway, a former speakeasy that seated eighty customers, but only "if we hung some from the ceiling," Granny recalled. Fay had wanted a larger place. "I'm gonna beat Ziegfeld," he boasted, but Granlund counseled him to think small. Unlike Ziegfeld, he would be selling an illegal product; a large club would be an easy mark for federal agents. After bringing in Owney Madden and Arnold Rothstein as silent partners, Fay christened the place El Fey, never explaining to anyone why he chose to misspell his own name.

There were a few small cabarets in the city before El Fey opened, but most of them "were little more than market places for sex." It was a mobster's "second-story bandbox [that] got the night-spot trend started," Granlund wrote later. Imitators sprang up all over town, but none had a hostess as captivating as Texas Guinan, Manhattan's new "Queen of the Night."

Queen of the Night

Like Owney Madden, Texas Guinan was rescued from obscurity by the Eighteenth Amendment. Born in Waco, Texas, in 1884, Mary Louise Cecilia Guinan was America's first cowgirl movie star, "The Gun Woman," studio executives had dubbed her. But at the time she partnered with Larry Fay she was a Hollywood has-been, a thirty-nine-year-old actress struggling to support herself and her live-in parents with anything that came her way. She had also been unlucky in love, having fallen for and discarded at least three men. "It's having the same man around the house all the time that ruins matrimony," she wisecracked.

Her background was a mystery, even to her friends. In 1929, she sold her serialized autobiography to Hearst's *New York Journal*. Called "My Life—AND HOW!," it is a fabulous fiction, a wholly invented tale about her "Wild West" upbringing on her father's fifty-thousand-acre cattle ranch, where she had learned to shoot straight, ride bareback, and break a steer before she was ten years old. More than anything else she had wanted to be a rodeo rider, she said.

The truth was more prosaic. Her father was a wholesale grocer in Waco, a thriving cotton town where he lived with his wife and their three children, all of them Irish to the core and strict Catholics. In writing her own story Texas Guinan had heeded advice she offered readers of the column she wrote for a New York tabloid: "Exaggerate the world. Dress up your lives with imagination . . . don't lose that purple mantle of illusion."

Like other high-spirited Waco girls, Guinan learned to ride and handle a rope, but her consuming ambition was to be a Broadway actress, not a rodeo performer. She studied music at a convent school, played the organ at the local church, and "lived only for the day when I might have a chance to act before a packed house in a real theater." When she turned sixteen, her family moved to Denver, Colorado, where she performed in amateur and stock productions, mostly Wild West dramas. Soon promoters were calling her Tex.

She impressed everyone with her "live life to the limit" attitude. "She had a premonition that her life was going to be short and so she said she'd make it sweet too," said a cousin. But that exuberance masked a deep sadness she was never able to explain or expel.

In 1904, at age twenty, she eloped with John Moynahan, a cartoonist for *The Rocky Mountain News*. The newlyweds moved to Chicago, where Moynahan found work on a newspaper and Guinan studied music. Three years later she walked out on him and took an express train to New York, with dreams of becoming a Broadway headliner. Her solicitous parents joined her there and shared her disappointment at finding only minor roles in touring musical comedies and vaudeville productions.

She was going nowhere when she was discovered on the vaudeville circuit by a Hollywood talent scout. In 1917, she signed up with a production company and began appearing in low-budget, two-reel Hollywood Westerns, dressed in black chaps, swinging a lariat, and riding a snow-white charger. It was mostly hokum, but Texas Guinan did create a new role for women in films: the self-reliant heroine who can handle a six-shooter as well as a man. A gifted athlete, she did her own stunts and was wildly popular with silent film audiences. By 1922, she had made three dozen Westerns, one right after the other. "We never change plots," Guinan quipped, "only the horses."

But when "The Gun Woman" began to put on weight, the movie kings replaced her with slim, fresh-faced heroines. In 1922, she moved back to New York and it was there that she ran into her old friend Nils Granlund, who had previously done some publicity work for her. He helped her transition from horse operas to night clubs.

"You had to go there, damned near every night," playboy Ben Finney described the allure of El Fey. "You'd feel strange if you weren't at the El Fey." Larry Fay's club filled a vacuum in what comedian Jimmy Durante called Manhattan's "up-all-night racket." By 1923, Prohibition had killed most of the legendary drinking and eating establishments of Broadway's Edwardian Age, audaciously large, richly decorated restaurants, cabarets, and lobster palaces: Maxim's, Jack's, Delmonico's, Rector's, Reisenweber's, and others. The aristocracy of the "Gay White Way," the two-mile stretch of "din and dazzle" between Madison and Times Squares, had gathered in these temples of pleasure to dine, dance, and gossip with the leading lights of the theater world.

This entire social scene vanished with the Volstead Act. Without alcohol these cavernous eateries "felt like overupholstered mess halls," wrote historian James Traub. "Who would linger until the late hours over a carafe of ginger ale?"

By the time El Fey opened, Times Square had been transformed into what Herbert Asbury has described as "a raucous jungle of chop-suey restaurants, hot-dog and hamburger shops . . . radio and phonograph stores equipped with blaring loud-speakers, cheap haberdasheries, fruit juice stands, dime museums, candy and drug stores . . . flea circuses, penny arcades, and lunch counters which advertised EATS!" Some of these garish establishments "added to the noise and confusion by employing barkers and pullers-in." To complete the degradation, Hubert's Museum and Flea Circus superseded Murray's Roman Gardens, a fabled eatery with a revolving dance floor.

Most of Midtown's new illegal drinking establishments were on the narrow cross streets that led east and west off Fifth Avenue, in the Forties, Fifties, and Sixties, with the heaviest concentration in the East Fifties. "They preferred the retirement and inconspicuousness of the residential to the lights and prominence of Broadway," noted *The New York Times*.

There were two types of illicit drinking establishments on these side streets: speakeasies and clubs. Most speakeasies were well-hidden places without live entertainment, some of them no larger or more impressive than a cramped room in a fleabag hotel. Clubs were a different species. Initially, their owners advertised them as "intimate" social settings, turning that term into an oxymoron. Most were crowded and noisy, and featured live entertainment: comedians, jazz bands, and dance troupes. Bootleg liquor was sold with little discretion and patrons were usually permitted to bring their own bottles and flasks, provided they paid regally for setups: cracked ice and ginger ale. Only rich bootleggers and professional gamblers had the wherewithal—and the nerve—to invest in such risky enterprises. By 1925 mobsters had a stranglehold on the city's newest service industry.

Night Club Mad

The new night clubs were vastly different from the pre-Prohibition lobster palaces: smaller, livelier, and more risqué. The music was fast, one form or another of what everyone began calling jazz; and in places where food was served it was prepared indifferently. This suited the "new children of the night [who] wanted a gay show, swift music, and no curfew"—and who wanted their entertainment "hot."

The modern Manhattan night club was a creature of prosperity as well as Prohibition. Beginning in late 1922, the nation climbed out of a punishing postwar recession and went on a seven-year-long binge. New York City was awash with money and with consumers eager to spend after a long period of war-imposed rationing and postwar joblessness and labor unrest. By 1922, "the uncertainties of 1919 were over—There seemed little doubt about what was going to happen—America was going on the greatest, gaudiest spree in history. . . . The whole golden boom," wrote F. Scott Fitzgerald, "was in the air—its splendid generosities, its outrageous corruptions." To careless people in this new age of excess "frequenting a night club and throwing away money was a form of exhibitionism," said Stanley Walker. "Wealthy men from out of town visited the clubs for appalling orgies of spending and drinking."

The prices were brutal, especially at El Fey. A friend of Larry Fay's rounded up a group of friends and went to the club just after it opened. "We drank up everything—champagne at $20 a quart and all that. Larry sent me the bill the next day. It was $1,300 for the evening for me and my four or five friends. But I was glad to pay. It was worth it." When Texas Guinan called her customers "suckers," they proved it by paying a "couvert charge"—a new thing—of between five and twenty bucks, depending on the night of the week. The cover charge covered nothing; it merely guaranteed a customer a place to sit and get fleeced in a dozen other ways.

The rewards of running a club were as great as the risks. It was a setup ideally suited for suddenly prosperous mobsters who "would back anything, that had the element of chance in it," said Nils Granlund. The clubs also gave bootleggers like Owney Madden a convenient outlet for their product, as well as a place to hang out. "All dressed up, [the bootlegger] needed a place to glow. And the only place where he was welcome was Broadway," said night club impresario Billy Rose. Along the Broadway "belt" the bootlegger became the principal capitalist. No longer a highwayman, he was now a host.

As a supplier of entertainment to El Fey and dozens of other clubs, Nils Granlund bargained with mobsters on an everyday basis. He found them easy to transact business with—as long as one provided "good service." If a deal went sour, someone had to pay. Four owners of clubs for whom Granlund produced shows were found murdered.

Some New York City night clubs were "steer joints." Cruising taxi drivers, paid by the clubs' shady owners, directed unwary customers to them, promising easy women and lots of laughs. The patrons were swindled from the moment they checked their coats; if they objected too loudly it might result in a trip to the hospital. Larry Fay, on the other hand, allowed no rough stuff in his club. He had no choice, for he pulled in the clientele he had hoped to attract: "out-of-town buyers, theatrical celebrities, and a sprinkling of the social and under-world elite." His carefully coached doormen, waiters, and bouncers made the Social Register crowd feel both welcome and secure. Young society women—

Whitneys, Vanderbilts, and Astors—arrived in small groups and enjoyed the show without being pestered by sloppy drunks on the prowl; Larry Fay's tuxedoed gangsters were their guardian angels for the evening. "We go to cabarets," twenty-two-year-old socialite Ellin Mackay wrote in *The New Yorker*, "because we have privacy in a cabaret."

At El Fey, Broadway met Park Avenue. On any given evening one could find Gloria Swanson and Gertrude Vanderbilt Whitney, gossip columnist Walter Winchell and Cornelius Vanderbilt, IV, who had enraged his family by becoming a newspaperman. The merging of the two social strata was complete in January 1926, when celebrated songwriter Irving Berlin, a Russian-Jewish immigrant who grew up in a cold-water flat on the Lower East Side, married Ellin Mackay over the steaming objections of her father, Clarence, a telegraph mogul and member of the haughty northern Long Island country club set. The marriage occurred, not coincidentally, about the time "Cohen" replaced "Smith" as the most common surname in the Manhattan phone book.

"If you don't believe there is any such thing as democracy any more you should drop in on my gang some time," Texas Guinan told reporters. "That's real democracy, the odd assortment of people I entertain." Fifth Avenue debutantes and Paducah haberdashers, Wall Street princes and Jersey City paving contractors flocked to El Fey, where they rubbed elbows with mobsters "whether they liked it or not," said Nils Granlund.

"I found myself in a dazzling new world where millionaires and bluebloods mingled with well-dressed hoodlums who, not long before, had crawled out of holes in Brooklyn, Jersey, Harlem and the Lower East Side," recalled George Raft. Texas Guinan had hired Raft, on Madden's recommendation, as the club's only male dancer.

This fusion of social and ethnic groups was something new and liberating in New York nightlife. The pre-Prohibition Broadway aristocracy—the regulars at Rector's and Delmonico's—had tolerated the presence of a select group of Jewish entertainers and businessmen, but that was the limit of their social forbearance. El Fey changed the character and clientele of Midtown nightlife. "There are no social lines drawn in [my] night club," said Guinan. "I put dukes, princes, stage stars, society women and Wall Street millionaires next to movie extras, thirty-dollar-a-week clerks, traffic cops and ex-convicts. And they all love it."

El Fey was the trend-setter; competitors proliferated: Club Richman, the Embassy Club, the Regent Club, and Owney Madden's Silver Slipper, where the society crowd and the underworld paid to see some of the hottest night club acts of the 1920s. By 1927, there were at least seventy chic night clubs in Midtown, and dozens more in Harlem and Greenwich Village, the city's two other centers of fashionable club life. "Never before has there been such a meeting ground of the very highest and very lowest of human society," noted *Smart Set*, the literary sheet edited by H. L. Mencken and George Jean Nathan. Writing in Mencken's *The American Mercury*, Benjamin De Casseres called Joel's, a popular Midtown nightspot, "the melting pot of all nations and races . . . ultra-democratic, ultra-New York, ultra-cosmopolitan."

The new policy made excellent business sense. This was the historic moment when the children of New York immigrants began to move with vigor into show business, investment banking, and Midtown real estate. At the same time, striving second-generation immigrants began fleeing the Lower East Side for new middle-class housing in Brooklyn, Queens, and the Bronx. Every Saturday evening members of this incipient bourgeoisie packed the subway trains speeding toward Times Square, in search of a hot time. The women wore "evening dress of every range from grave to gay," wrote one observer, "and every origin from Paris to Podunk."

Night clubs became one of Manhattan's most lucrative businesses. In 1927, they employed twelve thousand waiters, nineteen thousand musicians, and eleven thousand entertainers; and they kept battalions of cab drivers on duty into the early hours of the morning. Twenty thousand out-of-town visitors frequented the clubs nightly and were joined by "a like number of native sons and daughters," said *The New York Times*. In one ten-month period, Larry Fay and Texas Guinan made a clear profit of nearly three-quarters of a million dollars.

"This town is nightclub mad," exclaimed *The New Yorker*. People from all over the world were streaming to Manhattan to see "the new American invention": the all-night club. "The town flocks to them," grumbled one disapproving writer, "fighting its way to pay five dollars couvert for the privilege of being a sucker." People came for the show, but also to be seen. "Exclusiveness is the night club's great and only stock in trade," said a club owner. "Take this away and the glamour and romance and mystery are gone. The night club manager realizes that he must pander to the hidden and unconscious snobbery of the great majorities. It is because they make it so difficult of access that everybody is fighting to get into them."

It was not exclusivity, however, but the illusion of it that made the clubs so alluring. Doormen were instructed to keep ordinary-looking customers—but never celebrities and millionaires—waiting in line on the sidewalk, even if tables were abundantly available. The secret to a club's success was its ability to maintain an aura of selectivity while still drawing on a broad cross section of society. Total exclusivity was a fast track to failure. It was a matter of numbers. Even in Manhattan, there were never enough rich and well-placed customers to fill all the clubs every evening. Quick learners like Texas Guinan realized that "Woolworth money is quite as good as Cartier's."

An Evening with Texas

"Texas Guinan of New York has emerged as a nationally known trade-mark for indoor fun after midnight," said *Vanity Fair.* "'Get hot!' is my slogan," said Guinan, "to encourage bedlam and get the crowd wild."

Staying hot—i.e., remaining in business—was a matter of avoiding the law. This took considerable ingenuity after Emory Buckner became U.S. Attorney for the Southern District of New York in early 1925, and launched an all-out campaign against the clubs, using a new instrument of enforcement: the padlock. This was an attempt to reverse the nearly impossible situation Buckner confronted when he took office. There were then at least two thousand Prohibition cases pending in the courts, with the number rising at a rate of two hundred a week. By law, every one of the defendants—bartenders and waiters, as well as club owners—had the right to a jury trial; but with only six federal judges in Buckner's jurisdiction, it would have taken at least ten years to settle the backlog of cases. In an effort to unclog the courts and speed up future cases against violators of the Volstead Act, Buckner instituted a policy called "prohibition by padlock."

The new strategy was ingeniously simple, if constitutionally suspect. A provision buried deep in the Volstead Act designated places selling illegal liquor as "public nuisances" and decreed that they could be shut down temporarily by court injunctions. Acting on the testimony of a single credible witness who had reputedly purchased liquor in a club, a federal judge was empowered to issue a restraining order. If the owner of the offending club failed to comply, the court could issue a civil injunction, padlocking his premises for up to one year. Under Buckner, court hearings replaced lengthy jury trials; federal judges issued decrees, not sentences; and the weight of the law fell squarely on owners, not employees.

At first, Buckner lacked the money and manpower to enforce the policy consistently and comprehensively. His resources were so meager he had to send four of his own attorneys, recent Ivy League graduates, to collect evidence against clubs; and he reached into his own pocket to set up an expense fund for them to purchase drinks. But with the backing of "Prohibition's Portia," U.S. assistant attorney general Mabel Walker Willebrandt, Buckner was soon allotted Treasury Department funds that enabled him to triple the size of his staff of lawyers and clerks and to create a separate Prohibition Division within his office to investigate and prosecute violators of the liquor laws, both retailers and smugglers. He also received permission from Willebrandt to establish special padlock courts to expedite his work. Operating without juries, judges were able to settle up to fifty cases a day, some of them in less than a minute.

Buckner began his padlocking campaign in the spring of 1925 by closing fourteen of the theatrical district's most fashionable clubs, among them El Fey and Madden's Silver Slipper. "New York's booze-bolstered night life is facing its greatest threat since the advent of Prohibition," reported one New York newspaper. By the end of his first year in office, Buckner had padlocked hundreds of clubs and speakeasies selling illegal liquor, most of them in Midtown.

But resourceful club owners nimbly evaded the law. When the courts shut down a club its proprietors simply changed addresses and reopened within weeks—often a few blocks from their padlocked premises. El Fey became the Texas Guinan Club, and then Del Fay, and, finally, in 1926, after Guinan split with Larry Fay, the 300 Club. Fay had gotten a little sloppy, allowing some of his mobster associates to lounge at the bar with their guns in full view. With that, Guinan ended the relationship.

The 300 Club, located at 151 West Fifty-fourth Street, opened on New Year's Eve 1925, with financial backing from Guinan's friends Owney Madden and Big Frenchy DeMange. One evening in late 1926, when Guinan was at the peak of her fame, the English writer Stephen Graham, in Manhattan to research a book on its surging nightlife, stopped by the 300 Club around midnight, before the hostess had arrived. The club, he recalled, was surprisingly small—a compact, windowless room with no more than thirty tables and a small open space in the corner for dancing. A quartet was playing soft jazz and the room was alive with anticipation. Around one o'clock Jimmy Walker showed up, his boyish face lit up by a smile as he moved from table to table, shaking hands and exchanging pleasantries. Moments later Texas Guinan made her entrance, as if on cue. "There she was like a queen," Graham wrote later. "The name was whispered from table to table, Texas, Texas." A buxom woman with a "magnetic" smile, she had on a rose-colored dress, rhinestone heels, and a triple necklace of pearls.

After making a courtesy call to the mayor's table, she climbed on a stool and "began to boss the company, the band, the waiters, and the dancers," her contralto voice "like the boom of a Texas tornado." Wooden clappers were on the tables, and on her command, everyone in the room began to bang them in unison, welcoming a line of "nearly naked girls" who came prancing onto the dance floor singing "a song about cherries. . . . At the chorus 'Cherries!' all the waiters shouted 'Cherries,'" and soon the entire room "resounded with hoarse cries as if had become a fruit market, 'Cherries!'" When the singing stopped Texas bellowed, "Where's the Butter and Egg Man?"—her mischievous term for any free-spending rube from west of the Hudson. (George S. Kaufman had borrowed the term, a year earlier, for the title of one his plays.) Eyeing her prey, a crimson-faced businessman who had been tipping the waiters fantastically, Texas shouted, "He'll be happy till he sees the check."

As the evening wore on the atmosphere became more Rotarian than Broadway. Leggy cigarette girls handed out snowballs made of felt and a full-scale snowball fight ensued; when it was over, Guinan encouraged everyone to play leapfrog on the dance floor. Tightly buttoned Stephen Graham found himself being pulled into the sophomoric revelry.

The solo performer of the evening was devastatingly handsome George Raft, sleekly attired, his pants creased so sharply you could cut your finger on them. "George did the fastest, and most exciting, Charleston I ever saw," recalled Fred Astaire. Raft doubled as the club's unpaid gigolo. "Because the customer was always right in Texas's place, like it or not, I became like a male whore," he said later. "These rich bitches, when they were feeling good, a little tight, they would have me. Then two nights later they might come in and never even say hello or let on that they knew me." Between acts, Raft ran the club's "drunk-rolling concession," splitting the proceeds with Texas Guinan's brother Tommy, the club's manager. When Raft spotted a well-oiled out-of-towner staggering toward the men's room, he'd follow him and lift his wallet while he stood at the urinal. It was a skill he had learned in Hell's Kitchen.

Fast with his fists, Raft also served as a bouncer. "As the night is stretched later and later [the] excitement becomes more and more violent," the writer Edmund Wilson described a typical evening at the 300 Club, "by four, there is likely to be a fight. . . . But Texas knows how to deal with them: the brawlers are summarily torn up by the roots and quietly put through into the streets, with the ruthlessness and dispatch of a Renaissance prince making away with a dangerous enemy."

Near six in the morning, the lights were turned down and a trio of young beauties lulled some of the remaining patrons to sleep in their seats with a soft rendition of "Bye-Bye Blackbird"—"Make my bed and light the light. I'll be home tonight." At this point, Stephen Graham joined Texas at a table in the back of the club, where she had her breakfast brought to her. She ate hastily and headed for the door. After leaving the club, she would take a hired car to her thirty-two-room townhouse in Greenwich Village, near Washington Square Park. She shared the place with her parents, brother Tommy, and a menagerie of dogs, cats, and parrots. Every room in this former hotel was stuffed with exotic antiques and bric-a-brac from around the world—and with memorabilia from her Hollywood days. A reporter from *Vanity Fair* cruelly described Guinan's living room as "a cross between a Hong Kong hop-joint and a pawn shop in Deauville."

The Guinan family remained resolutely Catholic—six of Guinan's uncles were priests—and she occasionally stopped at her parish church on her way home from the club for a moment of quiet prayer. Her brother and father were hard drinkers, but Texas never touched the stuff; she was, however, addicted to cigarettes, coffee, and poker. At closing time at the 300 Club, she would occasionally lock the doors, call for a deck of cards, and invite late-staying reporters Walter Winchell, Heywood Broun, Ed Sullivan, and Mark Hellinger to her table. Popular Broadway columnists, they used these occasions to mine Texas for juicy gossip about her in-the-news patrons. "Between 5 and tata time, Tex drank as many cups of java as she smoked cigarettes. And she kept up a running commentary about the people who jammed her night clubs," Winchell recalled.

Damon Runyon, whose mistress, Patrice Gridier, appeared in Guinan's chorus in 1925, savaged her role as a gossip queen in his story "Romance in the Roaring Forties." She appears there, thinly disguised, as Missouri Martin, "an old experienced doll . . . who tells everything she knows as soon as she knows it, which is very often before it happens."

The uproarious hostess was a recluse in her private moments. "Practically nobody saw her except in [her clubs]," said Ben Finney, one of her poker pals. "She wasn't what you'd call a round-the-town girl." Awaking around noon, she spent a good part of her afternoons with Tommy, going over the club's books. A heady businesswoman, earning over $4,000 a week in 1926, she invested her money shrewdly and gave generously to Catholic charities.

Speakeasy Days

Nighthawks preferring quiet evenings gravitated to the speakeasies, where the only entertainment was the other customers. Some speakeasies had an air of understated elegance; others were claustrophobic dungeons packed with deeply serious drinkers. "The cheap speakeasy has a Hogarthian degradation," said *The New York Times*. The gin was industrial alcohol, mixed with oil of juniper and glycerin, and the "scotch" was made from grain alcohol colored with prune juice and creosote, a syrupy greenish brown liquid obtained from the distillation of wood tar. If drunk in diluted form, this ersatz liquor could sear the throat; if improperly diluted, it could cause blindness, "delirium," and even brain damage.

The problem was made worse by the federal government's policy of putting highly potent "denaturants" like methanol—commonly called wood alcohol and used as antifreeze—into industrial alcohol to prevent liquor thieves from using it. Bootleggers set up "cleaning plants" to remove these foul-smelling chemicals through a process of "re-distillation," but it was nearly impossible to cleanse the product of all dangerous denaturants. Of the nearly half a million gallons of confiscated booze analyzed in New York City in 1927, 98 percent contained poisons. On New Year's Day 1927, New York newspapers reported scores of emergency admissions to local hospitals and at least fifty-nine deaths in the previous week from drinking "poison alcohol." That year, liquor made with dangerous denaturants killed nearly eight hundred persons in New York City.

By the late 1920s, most of the booze available in New York was made in the city from industrial alcohol, but a number of the higher-end speakeasies, located in baronial-looking townhouses off Fifth Avenue, served quality liquor "right off the boat." These places operated as if they were private clubs, with membership cards and pretentious names like the Bombay Bicycle Club or the Town and Country Club. Other "speaks" provided trusted customers with a password to be whispered to the bouncer through a sliding opening in the steel-reinforced entrance door. Taking their seats at the bar, gullible out-of-towners were instructed to speak softly—"easily"—because the law might be at the door.* Prohibition had turned drinking into an exhilarating act of civic defiance. The "big thrill was that we were all doing something unlawful," said columnist Louis Sobol.

Speakeasies democratized public drinking. Barred from pre-Prohibition saloons, women went to speakeasies in small groups and either sat at the bar with male customers or sipped highballs in discreetly curtained dining rooms. Some women arrived in sexually mixed parties, usually around the late afternoon cocktail hour, which became "a new American institution," according to social commentator Frederick Lewis Allen. But many came alone, or with a friend, without feeling conspicuous. "At noon and from the hour before dinner until late at night, [the more expensive speakeasies] are often filled with men and women, and the number of women who go together without feeling the need of masculine escort is astonishingly large," reported *The New York Times*. In destroying the old, exclusively male saloon, Prohibition had made one thing certain, added the *Times*: even if the Eighteenth Amendment were to be repealed, "the drinking place of the future will be co-educational."

"These were the speakeasy days," wrote novelist John Dos Passos, who lived in New York for part of the 1920s. A speakeasy was one of the easiest places to find in town. Corner newsstands sold elaborate guides to them, and cops

---

* No one knows for certain the exact derivation of the term speakeasy. Historian Michael A. Lerner argues that the term is "likely derived from the 'speak-softly shops'" of Victorian England, places where untaxed liquor was sold inexpensively. Michael A. Lerner, *Dry Manhattan: Prohibition in New York City* (Cambridge: Harvard University Press, 2007), 138.

on the beat would direct strangers to the nearest one; some obliging officers even provided the password. The New York police department estimated that there were more than five thousand illegal clubs and speakeasies in Manhattan in 1927—32,000 in the entire city. That was twice the number of legal bars, restaurants, and cabarets in the city before Prohibition.

"Speakeasies have been something more than a social institution in the last ten years of American life," *Fortune* observed in 1933. "They have been the leading retail outlets for one of the country's biggest industries. In the last ten years we have spent on drink almost as much as on meat, more than on shoes or tires or bread." The magazine's investigators reported that a prosperous New York speakeasy did a gross annual business of roughly half a million dollars. Its average proprietor earned an annual income of approximately $50,000.

In Manhattan, there were speakeasies "for every taste and purse." The best of them catered to the city's smart set. The headwaiters knew their customers' predilection for stone crabs or duck a l'orange, and "the doorman," said *Fortune*, "can always get you two or even four on the aisle if you feel like going to the theatre." Intimacy was the "great charm" of these elegant speakeasies, where women wore dresses by Chanel or Lanvin and men ordered their peach-colored scarves direct from Paris.

One of the most inviting speakeasies on Manhattan Island was The Puncheon, which opened for business in 1926 in a former townhouse on West Forty-ninth Street, just off Fifth Avenue. Formerly one of the most exclusive residential enclaves in the city, the neighborhood had recently succumbed to the assault of commerce. Its panicked owners fled to Park Avenue and leased their old five-story brownstones to owners of speakeasies, who were willing to pay higher rents than prospective apartment dwellers. By midsummer of the following year, The Puncheon was one of the most popular watering holes in the city.

Its regulars called the place Jack and Charlie's, after its co-founders, John Carl "Jack" Kriendler and Charles A. Berns, distant cousins whose struggling parents arrived in America at about the same time and from the same region of Austria. Two years later, The Puncheon would move three blocks north to 21 West Fifty-second Street, where it was rechristened "21," and where it still stands today, one of the most famous restaurants in the world, featured in novels, plays, and Hollywood films.*

---

* Although Jack and Charlie owned the building that housed their speakeasy, they leased the land from Columbia University. In 1928, they received $11,000 from Columbia to vacate No. 42 to make room for what became Rockefeller Center. Today, the GE Building

Jack Kriendler set out to make The Puncheon "a place where people of letters, social status, and wealth could feel comfortable," recalls his younger brother, H. Peter Kriendler. "No one was admitted who was not known, unless introduced by a regular." The Puncheon became a gathering spot for Park Avenue millionaires and their expensively educated sons, and for writers and theatrical figures from the Algonquin Round Table group, among them Robert Benchley, Dorothy Parker, Edna Ferber, George S. Kaufman, Harpo Marx, Heywood Broun, Alexander Woollcott, and Harold Ross, founder and editor of *The New Yorker*, the metropolitan weekly that published most of them.

Jack Kriendler and Charlie Berns grew up in tenement houses several miles from one another—Berns in a tough neighborhood on the West Side, just above Hell's Kitchen, and Kriendler in a Yiddish-speaking enclave on the Lower East Side. They were fractious street kids who settled arguments with their fists and stole what their parents couldn't afford to buy them: roller skates, baseball bats, footballs. After the death of her husband, a welder at the Brooklyn Navy Yard, Jack's mother, Sadie, worked as a midwife to support the family. She insisted that her boys stay in school. Charlie Berns's father, a tinsmith, preached the same sermon to his two sons.

While attending night school—Charlie at New York University to become an accountant, and later a lawyer, and Jack at Fordham to become a pharmacist—the cousins worked as salesmen for Sam Brenner, Jack's resourceful uncle, a shoe salesman who ran a thriving neighborhood speakeasy in the heart of the Jewish ghetto. With his polished old-world manners, hand-cut suits, and prominent diamond ring, he was one of the "spiffiest" purveyors of food and drink in that penurious part of town. "None of this was lost on Jack," said Peter Kriendler.

Two years into Prohibition, Jack suggested to Charlie that they open a speakeasy of their own to help pay their tuition. Charlie was not interested, but soon reconsidered and became "keeper of the till" at the Red Head, as the young partners dubbed their new place, a former tearoom in Greenwich

---

(formerly the RCA Building) at 30 Rockefeller Plaza, is on the site of the old Puncheon, which was located somewhere in between the *Today* show studios and Christie's auction house. Jack and Charlie opened their new speakeasy at 21 West Fifty-second Street on New York's Eve 1929. That evening, with the help of Robert Benchley and other regulars, they unhinged the wrought-iron gate that had been the portal to the Puncheon and installed it at "21." H. Peter Kriendler and H. Paul Jeffers, "21": *Every Day Was New Year's Eve: Memoir of a Saloon Keeper* (Dallas: Taylor, 1999).

Village, near New York University. The Red Head became a favorite drinking spot for the "flaming youth" made famous that year by F. Scott Fitzgerald, one of the club's regulars, in his book of short stories, *Tales of the Jazz Age*. The cousins sold their liquor in one-ounce flasks, "miniatures," they called them; and Jack Kriendler, who liked to fool around in the kitchen, prepared simple, affordable food.

The liquor was procured from Sam Brenner's bootlegger, who delivered it to the Kriendlers' five-room tenement flat on East Fourth Street, where Jack lived with his mother, three brothers, and four sisters. When the Red Head needed replenishment, Jack's three kid brothers would bring it over, a few flasks at a time, "in a little red wagon camouflaged with groceries." Police protection was provided, for a price, by the Lower East Side Tammany organization. "We would slip the [police] captain a $50 bill from time to time and a box of cigars to the cops on the beat," Charlie Burns recalled. "They could always count on us for free meals and drinks."

In 1923, Jack and Charlie sold the Red Head and bought a larger club—the Fronton—just across the street. Jack designed the club's "raid-proof" bar. It was built over a floor drain and consisted of several wooden planks that rested on two sawhorses. On it were pitchers filled with Scotch, rye, gin, and bourbon. "If any trouble came," Charlie remembered, "we could quickly pour the pitchers down the drain and scoot out the back through the coal cellar door and out onto Sixth Avenue."

In 1926, city condemnation proceedings for the construction of the Sixth Avenue subway forced the partners to close the Fronton and move uptown to a stately brownstone, with an iron gate in front, at 42 West Forty-ninth Street. By this time, Charlie had finished law school and passed his bar exam, while Jack had dropped out of college to give full attention to the business. Jack became The Puncheon's greeter and master-of-all-things, meeting prestigious "guests" at the door, escorting them to their tables, suggesting a wine, and joining them later for coffee and conversation. Smartly tailored, with a neatly trimmed mustache, he became an uptown Sam Brenner.

"Jack's dream," writes the club's historian Marilyn Kaytor, "was to give his speakeasy the ease and elegance of a European coffee-house with the overtone of an eighteenth-century English pub." But no one knew its lineage until the evening a Yale student named Ben Quinn walked into the bar, took a quick look around, and exclaimed, "I was born in this house. This is my old home. Martinis for everyone!"

With its unpretentious red-and-white-checked tablecloths, The Puncheon was a deceptively excellent eating place. Burgundies arrived at the table "lounging properly in silver baskets, and the pressed duck has a city-wide fame," wrote one food reporter. At a time when most of the best chefs in New York were working their miracles in the back kitchens of former townhouses, Jack hired Henri Geib, an internationally known Alsatian chef, and paid him an outrageous salary. In The Puncheon's two upstairs dining rooms, one floor above the bar, Geib served French wines, champagnes, and cognacs—from the club's independent bootlegger—and prepared a menu that included saddle of lamb, brook trout, fresh crab, Petite Marmite Henry IV, and Viennese coffee with whipped cream.

At the end of an evening at The Puncheon, a table of diners would be presented a bill "that would have rendered the average American breathless." Damon Runyon claimed that the Kriendler and Berns families had a secret "laughing room, well-insulated for sound, where [they] got together to plan the day's price list."

The entertainment at The Puncheon was Jack Kriendler, one of the great personalities of the Manhattan restaurant scene, alternately gracious and insolent, tyrannical and hospitable. Western outfits were his passion. One evening he would be wearing a silk suit designed by his personal tailor; the following night he'd be decked out in a cowboy suit of boots, chaps, holstered six-shooter, and Stetson hat, one of over one hundred Western outfits he had custom-made in his long career in the business. Charlie Berns was Jack's near opposite: plain-looking and pudgy, retiring and unassuming. Always in the background, he was, however, the club's "balance wheel." "Jack supplied all the looks and charm," Berns quipped, "while I supplied only brains."

Around ten o'clock most evenings, the legendary humorist Robert Benchley and a gang of his literary pals would encamp at the bar, or at a corner table next to it where they could count on running into two other stalwart imbibers: H. L. Mencken and his friend Frank Crowninshield, editor of *Vanity Fair*. Their wicked repartee was so entertaining that other patrons would gravitate to the barroom just to listen in.

Before the bill became outrageous, Benchley and his crowd would head across the street to Tony Soma's, where the booze was cheap and the food was barely edible. Tony provided the entertainment, singing operatic arias while standing on his head.

The Puncheon put its owners on a fast track to prosperity. One year after it opened, Jack moved his mother into an apartment on exclusive Riverside Drive and bought a box at the Metropolitan Opera House and a sable-lined coat. He and Charlie were convinced they were in the best business in creation. "The speakeasy makes money, and the customers and owners are happy," George Jean Nathan wrote of Jack and Charlie's. "In what other business is that true?"

To keep Prohibition enforcers off their backs, Jack and Charlie, along with

other speakeasy operators on the street, formed an association and contributed to a fund managed by a menacingly looking club owner named John Per-
ona, who in turn paid off easily corruptible federal agents. "It cost us about a
thousand a year," said Berns, "not including free meals and drinks." The Puncheon was raided only once during Prohibition and the place was quickly back
in business after Jack and Charlie paid a light fine. It was the prominent night
clubs that Emory Buckner had his sights set on, not discreetly run eateries like
The Puncheon.

Prohibition by Padlock

In December 1926, while Buckner and his staff were making final preparations
for the big liquor smuggling case against Frank Costello, Buckner was plotting
to move with determination against Texas Guinan, whose open defiance of the
Eighteenth Amendment had become an embarrassment to his office. By this
time, he had padlocked nearly 350 night clubs and speakeasies and was planning to shut down forty-three more. The 300 Club was at the head of the list.

Lately, Buckner had become increasingly intransigent in his battle against
the clubs. That summer he had formed his agents into "flying squadrons" and
had them smash through the locked doors of speakeasies with sledgehammers
and crowbars. "We have been ordered to make Broadway as dry as the Sahara,"
declared one of the agents, "and we're going to do it." But Buckner planned to
use legal subterfuge rather than naked force to move against Guinan and other
prominent violators of the law. The new tactic combined padlocking with the
added poison of a prison sentence.

In the past, whenever Buckner instituted padlock proceedings against a
club, the owners were given twenty days to answer the charges and were permitted to stay open in the interval. Henceforth, Buckner's agents would serve
proprietors with "personal" injunctions. If they were caught selling "forbidden
beverages" before their case came before a federal judge, they could be jailed
for contempt of court.

Buckner set his trap for Texas Guinan during the Christmas season of
1926, when the clubs were going full blast. At ten o'clock on the evening of
December 21, he launched "the most sweeping drive yet undertaken against
night clubs and restaurants." Seven "parties," each made up of assistant United
States attorneys general, federal Prohibition agents, and deputy marshals
armed with padlock complaint bills and temporary injunctions, spread out all
over Midtown to serve papers on the owners of fifty-eight of the city's most
"glittering" night clubs and "resorts," with Guinan's 300 Club the principal
target. Buckner had been secretly collecting evidence against these places for

the previous two weeks, using undercover agents posing as dissolute Russian aristocrats, Southern cotton brokers, and Florida land barons.

In the first hour of his huge holiday season raid, Captain John W. Inglesby, head of Buckner's special Padlock Division, posted an injunction notice on the door of the 300 Club. The charge: selling liquor to a customer. In four previous "padlock" proceedings against her clubs, Guinan had convinced the court that she was an "innocent" and "victimized" employee, not an owner or shareholder. This time she was named in the injunction as an owner, or "officer," of the 300 Club, a claim Buckner believed he could finally prove. His undercover agents had heard her telling friends that the club was her own venture. If the 300 Club continued to sell liquor in defiance of the injunction—as Buckner confidently anticipated it would—Texas Guinan would face a prison sentence, without benefit of a jury trial.

Having baited the trap, Buckner sprang it seven weeks later. In the early morning hours of February 16, he sent three young agents to Guinan's club posing as big spenders. One of them, Truman Fowler, a law school student, bought a pint of whiskey for ten dollars, sampled it, and then slipped out the door—the signal for the raid to begin. Eight Prohibition agents rushed into the club and made a hurried search of the premises. They found the injunction Inglesby had placed on the door back in December in the cuspidor, where Guinan had deposited it.

Inglesby then informed Guinan she was under arrest. "Play 'The Prisoner's Song'"—a popular Broadway tune—Texas called out to the orchestra. Escorted to the door by police, she hailed her brother Tommy and told him to take $5,000 from the register so she could hustle up a poker game at the station house. One of Buckner's agents who had posed as a customer asked Texas if he could drive her to the precinct station. He was "all apologies," said a *Daily News* reporter who had arrived at the scene with federal agents. As they left the club, the agent invited Guinan to have lunch with him at the Ritz later that day. At that point, the raid turned entirely farcical.

The club was filled that night with "famous people of the stage, literary celebrities, well known bankers and brokers and manufacturers." They gave Guinan a big hand as she exited, wearing a full-length fur coat. Two agents placed her in a paddy wagon, smiling on cue for a *Daily News* photographer before they closed the rear doors. She would not go unescorted. A hundred or so of her sodden patrons jumped into cabs and private cars, "giggling, screaming, roaring," and formed a caravan that made its way, twisting in and out of traffic, to the West Forty-seventh Street police station.

Guinan and the three others associated with the club were charged with selling liquor and with the more serious charge of contempt of court for disregarding a federal injunction. Buckner was sure he had finally nabbed the high priestess of Broadway. "This time it looks serious," agreed the *Daily News*. If Guinan was intimidated, she didn't show it. Before being released on bail, she treated the patrolmen at the station to a breakfast feast catered by the Waldorf Hotel.

Guinan's club would remain padlocked for six months, but over the course of the six weeks following her arrest the courts dismissed every charge leveled against her. In the three-hour federal hearing on the contempt charge, the judge ruled that the government failed to prove that Guinan had an ownership stake in the 300 Club. Long before Buckner's raid, she and her gangster partners had apparently expunged all evidence of their ownership.

Three weeks later, Buckner received word from Washington that his Prohibition enforcement unit was being disbanded. Shortly thereafter, Buckner resigned, turning the office over to Charles H. Tuttle, another prominent Republican. Buckner had finally become convinced, as his biographer notes, that Prohibition "could not be enforced in New York." He had been a deeply engaged but ineffective booze buster, outmaneuvered in the press and the courts by a brassy blonde.

Texas Guinan's highly publicized battle with Emory Buckner made her bigger than ever. After a vacation in Havana, a face-lift, and a strenuous diet that peeled off nearly forty pounds, she reopened the old Texas Guinan Club on Forty-eighth Street—the padlock decree had expired—and signed on to produce a big revue at the Shubert Theatre, *The Padlocks of 1927*, a stage version of her night club act. It opened that July and "her whole gang was there, the little girls prancing around with next to nothing on." The show, said one reviewer, was "loud, noisy, [and] unimaginative."

When *The Padlocks of 1927* closed at the end of the summer season, Guinan opened a rowdy club in the basement of the Century Theatre, on Sixty-second Street. She decorated it like a commingled circus and carnival, with a calliope, a shooting gallery, and an oversized fish tank stocked with trout; rods, reels, and bait were available on request. In the following two years, there were more clubs and more trouble with federal and local authorities: curfew violations, padlock proceedings, injunctions, and arrests, but not a single conviction. In summer 1927, the *Daily News*'s Broadway columnist wondered how long she would last as "an entertainer extraordinary. . . . Perhaps in a year, maybe two, she'll either burn out or people will tire of her." That was just about right.

After starring in the 1929 Hollywood film *Queen of the Night Clubs*, Guinan opened two clubs in quick succession, and then fell victim to the Stock Market Crash in October, which had a ruinous impact on Manhattan's night club trade. She moved to Chicago the following year and opened several clubs, but Prohibition officials shut down all of them. On November 5, 1933, Mary Louise Cecilia Guinan died of an intestinal illness—a perforation of the bowel—while touring the Pacific coast with one of her all-girl revues. She was forty-nine years old. (Earlier that year, Larry Fay had been shot and killed by the doorman of his new Casa Blanca Club, after Fay reduced his pay.)

Friends and family accompanied Texas Guinan's body from Vancouver to New York City for burial. She had been absent from Broadway for most of the last three years, but that's where she wanted to be put to rest. "I would rather have a square inch of New York than all the rest of the world," she had told her Manhattan friends before leaving for Chicago.

Texas Guinan deserves to be remembered as more than a night club headliner, a Prohibition Age flash in the pan. Almost singlehandedly, she changed the late night culture of New York, and she took on—if only for her personal benefit—powerful forces intent on enforcing the mores of a minority of New Yorkers. Along with Texas Guinan, millions of New Yorkers, said the *Daily News*, were convinced that the federal government was exacting "honest to God revenge on New Yorkers for being city people. . . . We do not want the dry laws enforced in New York City. . . . We think they represent an attempt by small town and country people, who cannot know metropolitan conditions, to tell us how we shall conduct our private and personal lives. We don't propose to take such dictation."

Guinan should also be remembered for altering entrenched ideas about American women and their position in the debate over Prohibition. She gave the lie to the idea that "*all* American women stood steadfastly behind the noble experiment," wrote one historian. Her headline-grabbing court battles gave encouragement to New York organizations like the Women's Committee for Modification of the Volstead Act, which in 1927 began lobbying strenuously against Prohibition. Led by M. Louise Gross, secretary to Tammany district leader Thomas F. Foley, and a close associate of Al Smith, this committee and other women's organizations Gross headed fought Prohibition under the argument that its enforcement emboldened federal officials to violate the Bill of Rights.

Testifying before the House Judiciary Committee in 1930, Gross said that unless the Volstead Act was repealed before her two young nieces grew older, she would send them "abroad where they can learn to drink like ladies."

On December 5, 1933, one month to the day after Texas Guinan died, Prohibition ended when Utah became the thirty-sixth state to ratify the Twenty-first Amendment to the Constitution. "It seemed almost a geologic epoch while it was going on," H. L. Mencken described Prohibition in sardonic language Guinan would have appreciated, "and the human suffering that it entailed must have been a fair match for that of the Black Death or the Thirty Years War."

CHAPTER SIX

"HE DID IT ALONE"

It was an age of miracles.

—F. SCOTT FITZGERALD

Lucky

It was a glorious June morning, blue skies and bright sunshine, as the city prepared to greet the heroic young flier from Little Falls, Minnesota. It would be the greatest celebration in New York history, a soul-stirring spectacle that would draw nearly four million people, four times more than watched any of the six great parades of veterans returning from the Great War.

Twenty-five-year-old Charles Augustus Lindbergh, Jr., had taken off from a grass airstrip on Long Island on May 22, 1927, in his single-engine monoplane, *Spirit of St. Louis*. Battling storms, freezing fog, and mind-numbing fatigue he reached Paris, a distance of 3,600 miles, thirty-three and one-half hours later. Others had crossed the Atlantic before him in dirigibles and lighter-than-air planes, but Lindbergh was the first to do it alone.* And he had done it as a virtual unknown, beating to the punch more famous and heavily financed competitors assembled at the same field from which he flew. "He left these shores a little more than three weeks ago an obscure air mail pilot, known only to those of his fraternity," the *Daily News* described his sudden acclaim. "He returns a national hero."

Lindbergh was flying from Washington, D.C., that morning, June 13, 1927, and was scheduled to land in New York Harbor in a seaplane, where Grover Whalen, chairman of the mayor's reception committee, would be waiting for

---

* In 1919, two British fliers, John W. Alcock and navigator Arthur W. Brown, flew the first nonstop transatlantic flight, from St. John's, Newfoundland, to Clifden, Ireland.

him on the *Macon*, the small craft Jimmy Walker reserved for visiting heroes and dignitaries. The *Macon* would dock at Battery Park, on the southern tip of Manhattan, and the slender, tousled-haired Swede would be driven in an open car through lower Broadway to City Hall. Following an official reception, he would ride with the mayor up Fifth Avenue, all the way to the Sheep Meadow in Central Park, where Governor Al Smith would bestow on him the State Medal of Valor.

That morning, sixty thousand people were waiting for Lindbergh at the Battery and along the narrow streets leading to City Hall. Thousands of them were out-of-towners who had arrived early on special excursion trains. Most of them would have to leave town that evening; there wasn't a single hotel room available in all of New York. "The crowds were grouped in thick masses upon window ledges, cornices and set-backs of the towering buildings of Lower Manhattan," reported *The New York Times*. "Every window was occupied along Broadway all the way to City Hall. Some of those windows were reported to have been rented for $1,000." Spectators clung to "all sorts of building projections like human flies." While on the curb-lines, over a thousand uniformed policemen, part of the 11,200 bluecoats assigned to guard the Lindbergh parade, struggled to hold back the crowds impatiently swaying and pushing behind them.

Couples postponed wedding plans to be part of "the greatest holiday in the history of the five boroughs." Only thirty-nine marriage licenses were issued at the Municipal Building that day, the lowest figure since the establishment of the city's license bureau.

Radio announcers were stationed at intervals along the line of the parade route, and at City Hall and in Central Park. They would describe the day's events to an estimated fifteen million listeners over an unprecedented fifty-station "hook-up" put together by a former telegraph operator named David Sarnoff, who had just founded the National Broadcasting Company (NBC), the nation's first national radio network. President Calvin Coolidge and tens of thousands of Washingtonians had greeted Lindbergh on his return from France on the U.S. Navy cruiser *Memphis*, but Mayor Walker vowed to outdo the reception in the nation's capital, appropriating the then staggering sum of $50,000 for the "Hail Lindbergh" celebration.

The Lindbergh parade would be merely the latest in a series of "triumphal marches through [our] streets," wrote *The New York Times*. "In recent years the celebrations accorded to returning heroes have taken place with such regularity that the stretch of Broadway from the Battery to City Hall has become America's Via Sacra, a triumphant line of march similar to that along which victorious Roman generals marched to receive their laurels." The previous summer, the city had put on a spectacular ticker tape parade for one of its own, Gertrude Ederle, daughter of an Amsterdam Avenue butcher, the first woman to swim across the English Channel. But the greatest reception New York had ever staged for a national hero was the "thunderous welcome" it had given Admiral George Dewey in September 1899 after he destroyed the Spanish fleet at Manila Bay. Asked to compare the Dewey reception to the one he was personally preparing for Lindbergh, Jimmy Walker said, "You ain't seen nothin' yet!"

Charles Lindbergh had become an adopted son of the city almost from the moment his silver-winged *Spirit of St. Louis* touched down at Curtiss Field on Long Island on May 12, 1927. Reporters stationed there to cover the "Race to Paris" took to him instantly, and turned him into a hero that only the stonehearted could resist. The story of Lindbergh's arrival, short stay, and return to New York in the late spring of 1927 reveals as much about the character and spirit of the city at that time as it does about the intrepid aviator it took to its heart.

That May, Lindbergh was a young man in a hurry, concerned that his rivals would set out for Paris before he was ready. Flying the *Spirit of St. Louis* directly from its small San Diego assembly plant to New York, with a brief stopover in St. Louis, his new home, he set two speed records: one for the Pacific to St. Louis "hop," the other for the entire cross-country flight—2,555 miles in twenty-one hours and twenty minutes of air time. He came to New York to lay claim to a prize offered by French-born New York hotelier and aviation enthusiast Raymond Orteig: $25,000 for the first nonstop flight, in either direction, between New York and Paris.

Lindbergh knew that disaster had opened an opportunity for him. France's dashing World War I ace Charles Nungesser, flying with his wartime comrade François Coli, had left Paris for New York on May 8 and mysteriously disappeared; an exhaustive sea search failed to locate them. Lindbergh's chief remaining rivals were American aviators Clarence D. Chamberlin and Richard E. Byrd. Chamberlin had set an endurance record the previous month in his single-engine monoplane *Columbia*, circling New York for over fifty-one hours; and Byrd, a Navy commander, had flown with his crew over the North Pole the previous year.* But that April, Byrd's trimotored Fokker, one of most expensive planes ever built, crash-landed on a test flight from Roosevelt Field, adjacent to Curtiss Field, badly injuring Floyd Bennett, Byrd's designated pilot for the At-

* A number of historians of polar exploration dispute Byrd's claim that he flew over the North Pole.

lantic crossing. Chamberlin was also temporarily grounded. His navigator had convinced a judge to issue a temporary injunction against Charles A. Levine, owner of *Columbia*, for a breach of contract, and the plane was impounded.

Even so, Lindbergh was the longest of long shots in a race in which the odds were stacked overwhelmingly against all the contestants. Lloyd's of London was offering odds of ten to one against any aviator flying the Atlantic in 1927. Charles Lindbergh was both green and fearless. Though fascinated with flight since he first set eyes on an airplane in 1912, he had not been close enough to even touch a plane until ten years later, when he enrolled in a private flying school in Nebraska; and he had not made his first solo flight until the following year, four years before he would set out for Paris. As a barnstorming pilot and wing walker, he was known for his wildly dangerous stunts, making low-level parachute jumps and standing on a wingtip of his partner's open cockpit biplane as it roared over the upraised heads of air enthusiasts in cow pastures all over the Midwest.

But Lindbergh was a natural, a supremely gifted pilot; and after his brief stint as a touring barnstormer, he had learned how to fly "modern and powerful planes," single-engine aircraft capable of speeds of over a hundred miles an hour, at an Army Air Service Training School. He graduated after one year with a commission in the Air Service Reserve, and became a mail pilot for a St. Louis aviation company. Carrying the federal mail between St. Louis and Chicago in World War I surplus planes, Lindbergh made four emergency parachute jumps, leaping from his aircraft in lightning storms and blinding fog. "Lucky," his fellow airmail pilots called him.

Lindbergh was virtually unknown in the East when he arrived at Curtiss Field. But his transcontinental flight from California to New York, which he plotted on fifty-cent road maps of the states he passed over, was a breathtaking feat, and newsmen covering the transatlantic race were eager to interview him. The "Flying Fool," they dubbed him: the only contestant who dared to challenge the Atlantic alone and in a single engine plane. "The sheer audacity and speed of the flier, who had already made two records in his flight from the Pacific, and his bashful and infectious smile won the heart of every one who saw him," wrote one New York reporter.

He was, said *The New York Times,* the "perfect picture of clean-cut youth": he did not drink, smoke, or chew, and he was unalterably dedicated to his craft. Lindbergh lived for little else but aviation, and the only person he was closely tied to was his mother, Evangeline, a schoolteacher in Detroit, where she had been living with her brother since the death in 1924 of her husband, Charles Lindbergh, Sr., a stormy progressive congressman from Minnesota.

In an age of ballyhoo and publicity mongering, the laconic aviator was refreshingly "a doer and not a talker." In the public mind, he stood in estimable contrast to swaggering newsmakers like Al Capone and F. Scott and Zelda Fitzgerald; and he made New Yorkers forget, if only for a fleeting moment, the criminal syndicates and scorching cultural battles spawned by Prohibition. Lindbergh arrived in New York four months after the shocking acquittal of mobster Frank Costello, one month after Emory Buckner left federal service following his unsuccessful campaign against Texas Guinan, and the very day the press headlined the dynamiting of a school by a demented anarchist, a senseless act that killed forty-two children. Charles Lindbergh seemed "the perfect antidote," writes biographer A. Scott Berg, "to toxic times."

"He stands out in a grubby world as an inspiration," said one newspaper account. But it was Lindbergh's steely self-assurance, not his moral bearing, that left the strongest impression on New York reporters. They wrote of his "fearless blue eyes," his unruffled composure, and his "all-pervading confidence in himself, and his engine. . . . No thought enters his head but that of success." And in a success-driven city, renowned for its risk takers in commerce and culture, these attributes resonated strongly with readers of the New York dailies.

New York to Paris

Grover Whalen happened to be sitting in the hangar at Roosevelt Field when Lucky Lindbergh first landed on Long Island on the afternoon of May 12, 1927. Whalen was there as the sole representative of a local promoter of aviation, Rodman Wanamaker, son of the merchant king John Wanamaker and head of the family's New York City department store. At the time, Whalen was holding down three positions simultaneously: chairman of the Mayor's Committee on Reception, general manager of Wanamaker's Manhattan emporium, and director of a million-dollar fund Rodman Wanamaker had established to support Richard Byrd, his champion in the competition for the Orteig Prize. Whalen had leased both Roosevelt and Curtiss Fields, and by combining the two had created a runway two miles long for Byrd's tremendously heavy trimotor, *America*.

When the sandy-haired stranger showed up unannounced at Roosevelt Field, he asked to see the boss. Whalen told him that he was in charge. "I'd like to use your two-mile runway," said Lindbergh. Whalen wanted to know where he was headed. "Paris," said Lindbergh unhesitatingly. Whalen smiled and asked the young man if he didn't know a better way to commit suicide.

Not taking Lindbergh and his hastily built, $10,000 plane as a serious threat, Whalen gave him permission to use the runway. For the next week, he saw no sign of him, even though they were both staying at the local Garden City Hotel. Lindbergh spent nearly every waking hour at Curtiss Field or in his hotel room, making last-minute preparations for his flight, while Whalen, who had recently found a pilot to replace the injured Floyd Bennett, focused on getting Byrd's plane ready to fly. With Chamberlin still held up by the courts and Byrd's plane repaired and seemingly ready, the contest came down to a battle of wills. When the weather was right, who would fly first, "America's King of the Sky," as the press called Commander Byrd, or the St. Louis mail pilot?

There was dense fog along the coast and a vile summer storm was hanging menacingly over the northern Atlantic, grounding all aircraft. "The fliers," wrote Berg, "were as excitable as thoroughbreds waiting in the paddock." On May 19, with light rain still falling and little prospect of the weather clearing for several days, Lindbergh and some technicians from the Wright Company, builders of his Wright Whirlwind engine, drove into Manhattan to see the new Florenz Ziegfeld musical, *Rio Rita*. As they approached the theater, Dick Blythe, one of the Wright engineers, asked the driver to stop at a downtown office building. He wanted to call in for the latest weather report. With thick fog blanketing Manhattan's skyscrapers, it seemed a fruitless exercise, but minutes later Blythe came racing back to the car shaking with excitement. There was a sudden change in the weather; the skies had begun to clear over the ocean. Lindbergh and his party sped back to Long Island, stopping only to pick up some sandwiches for Lucky's trip.

After hurrying to Curtiss Field to make arrangements for his plane to be serviced and checked, Lindbergh went back to his hotel to get some rest. Unable to sleep, he made last-minute preparations for his flight. Around 2 A.M. Grover Whalen's phone rang. It was "The Flying Fool." He was about to head to his hangar and wanted to be sure he had permission to have his plane towed by a truck from Curtiss Field to the longer Roosevelt Field. Whalen dressed and shaved in a flash. As he drove out to the field, he was shocked to find the local roads, ordinarily abandoned at that time of night, filling up with cars.

He would later learn why. Knowing that Whalen controlled Roosevelt Field, Phil Payne, city editor of the New York *Daily Mirror*, had promised to buy the telephone operators at the Garden City Hotel complete wardrobes—"coats, dresses, and lingerie"—if they would listen in on Whalen's line and inform him if either of the fliers began making preparations to take off. That night, Payne put the news flash in the early editions of his paper. He was able to act quickly because he had prepared in advance two headlines: "BYRD TAKES OFF TODAY," and "FLYING FOOL HOPS AT DAWN." He would need only one of them that morning. Rodman Wanamaker insisted that Byrd take his recently repaired plane through some additional tests.

Phil Payne's scoop "emptied out the speakeasies and night clubs of New York, Nassau, Westchester and Suffolk counties," Whalen wrote later. By six that morning, the roads leading to Roosevelt Field were jammed with "hundreds of cars full of men and women in evening clothes." Spectators sat on top of their cars in the dismal morning mist watching Lindbergh, dressed in his flying outfit—Army breeches and boots, a light jacket over a woolen shirt, and a red and blue diagonally striped tie—supervising the gassing of his plane, which had just received a fresh coat of silver paint. Although Lindbergh had flown the *Spirit of St. Louis* cross-country, the plane had never taken on a full load of gas. As the last five-gallon can was emptied into the plane, onlookers— among them Byrd and Chamberlin—noticed the tires sagging and making a noticeable indentation in the soft, rain-soaked field.

Lindbergh's only provisions were five sandwiches and two canteens of water. Any additional weight, even a parachute or a radio, would be a dangerous burden. Aviation experts urged him to take along a navigator, but he preferred, he said, "to replace the weight of the navigator with extra fuel," turning his small plane into a flying fuel tank. He had a compass. With any luck, that would get him to Paris.

After talking briefly with his chief engineer through the open door of his plane, Lindbergh gunned the engine, the most powerful machine of its kind. "As I stood by the *Spirit of St. Louis*," Grover Whalen recalled, "the only moment of hesitation I noticed was when he asked the Wright engineer, 'Shall I go?' The Wright engineer replied, 'Go on, kid' and turned away. I could see that he had tears in his eyes."

Seated in an open car with Phil Payne and five field mechanics carrying fire extinguishers, Whalen shadowed Lindbergh's plane as it taxied down the runway. The fragile, high-winged monoplane, weighed down by 2,750 pounds of gasoline and fighting a muddy field and an adverse tailwind, didn't take off until it reached the last quarter of the runway. Lindbergh cleared a tractor by about fifteen feet and a telephone line at the end of the field by barely twenty feet. "God be with him," said Byrd. "I think he has a 3-to-1 chance." It was 7:54, Friday, the 20th of May.

Lindbergh followed the Great Circle course from Nova Scotia to Newfoundland, then out across the Atlantic to the coast of Ireland, and then, southeasterly over Normandy to Paris. His plane was spotted over New England and Nova Scotia, but after fishermen saw him streak past St. John's, Newfoundland, Lindbergh was lost to the world until he reached the western shore of Ireland fifteen hours later. For those anxious hours, he was as alone as any human being had ever been. Flying low, dangerously close to the heaving sea, with the engine humming monotonously, he realized that he had not slept in the previous twenty-four hours. Staying awake, he suddenly discovered, would be even more difficult than finding his way to France.

That night there was a heavyweight bout at Yankee Stadium between Jim Maloney and his Boston rival Jack Sharkey. Before introducing the fighters, veteran announcer Joe Humphreys asked the forty thousand spectators to join him in silent prayer for the "Lone Eagle," who was somewhere over the Atlantic. The silence was broken, seconds later, by a "coarse voice" that "floated down from the dark, upper recesses of the stands—'That guy's got more guts than any fighter that ever lived!'" That sentiment "expressed elementally how all of us felt about the boy," wrote *Daily News* sports columnist Paul Gallico.

As Lindbergh sped toward Paris, a large, ever-changing crowd gathered in Times Square, where bulletins of his progress were pasted to a window high on the Broadway side of the New York Times Building. At 5:35 on Saturday afternoon, someone yelled, "He's arrived in Paris, boys." Seconds later, a "great spread of white paper marked up with black paint" told the crowd it was true: the kid had done it. A great cheer split the air.

Witnesses described the spontaneous demonstration that followed as second only to the excitement that had seized the city when the Armistice ending World War I was announced. Motorists laid on their horns; people shouted from windows of offices and apartment buildings; and movie theaters and Broadway matinees interrupted their shows to announce the electrifying news. In some theaters, the cheering lasted a full five minutes. Mayor Walker notified all city departments whose plants had steam whistles to sound them. "Within a few minutes sirens were shrieking, whistles were blowing, and ferryboats and tugboats were going full strong." Every fire station in the city's five boroughs sounded sirens at five-minute intervals. People gathered outside radio supply stores in Times Square, standing at "respectful attention . . . like soldiers on parade" as loudspeakers carried to them the radio announcement of Lindbergh's arrival at Le Bourget airport, followed by the playing of "La Marseillaise" and "The Star-Spangled Banner."

At the Roxy Theatre that night, patrons watched Fox Movietone footage of Lindbergh's plane taking off from Roosevelt Field, accompanied by a new sound system that captured the roar of the plane and the cheers of the spectators. As the *Spirit of St. Louis* struggled hesitantly into the air, "more than 6,000 persons arose and cheered," reported *The New York Times*, "drowning out the noise of the recording machine." Later that evening, at the Savoy Ballroom in Harlem, the club's feature dancer, George "Shorty" Snowden, watched some young high-steppers doing their own version of the Charleston, with wild breakaways and "swingouts," and reputedly said, "Look at them kids hoppin' over there. I guess they're doin' the Lindy hop." A new dance craze was born;

and so was a new hit song, "Lucky Lindy," completed by Tin Pan Alley composers just as news of Lindbergh's landing at Le Bourget came over the radio.
The following Monday, it was up in lights on the marquee of the Paramount
Theatre on Broadway, where it was played on the Wurlitzer between showings
of a silent film starring Clara Bow.

Over the next few days, New Yorkers devoured the news coming out of
Paris. People wanted to know every detail of the flight. "It wasn't easy going,"
Lindbergh told Carlyle MacDonald of *The New York Times*, the first reporter to
interview him. "I had sleet and snow for over 1,000 miles. Sometimes it was too
high to fly over and sometimes too low to fly under, so I just had to go through
it as best I could. . . . I flew as low as 10 feet [above the waves] in some places
and as high as 10,000 in others." Lindbergh admitted he had briefly nodded
off several times. "All I want[ed] in life was to throw myself down flat, stretch
out—and sleep," he described his feelings after his seventeenth hour in the air.

His control stick had to be in his grasp at all times, and because of the extra
gas tanks in the forward part of the plane, he could see ahead of him only with
the aid of a periscope, or by sticking his head out the side window. He became
so numb to hunger and cold that he ate only one of his sandwiches and drank
less than a pint of water. Before reaching the point of no return, flying into
absolute darkness, with no moon and with the weather desperately worse than
predicted, he had considered turning back, a thought that passed as quickly as
it came to him.

At nine that evening, an hour and a half after he was expected at Le Bourget airport, rumors had passed through the excited crowd of Frenchmen that
had gathered there that the amateur American had, like their own brave professionals, Nungesser and Coli, been swallowed by the sea. Then, an hour or
so later, a "gray-white airplane . . . slipped out of the darkness" and roared
over the field. At 10:24 P.M., Paris time, the *Spirit of St. Louis* touched down.
"A frenzied mob" of 100,000 Parisians smashed through a human barricade of
police and two companies of soldiers with fixed bayonets and made a "mad
rush" toward the plane, its propeller still spinning dangerously. Moments later,
Lindbergh was on the shoulders of half a dozen jubilant Frenchmen who were
spinning him around wildly. At that point, an alert French aviator pulled off
Lindbergh's leather helmet, placed it on a reporter's head, and shouted, "Here
he is." With the crowd distracted, he and some of his fellow fliers hustled Lindbergh to the safety of a nearby hangar, and from there, by car, to the American
embassy, where he became the guest of Ambassador Myron T. Herrick.

On first meeting the ambassador, Lindbergh presented him letters of introduction he had carried with him on the flight. "This is a new country to me
and nobody knows me here," he explained in his flat Midwestern accent. Re-

fusing to be examined by doctors, he said all he needed was a glass of milk and a long night's rest; he had been awake for almost sixty hours. The next morning, after calling his mother in Detroit, Lindbergh was a guest of the president of France, the beginning of a whirlwind week of welcoming festivities. Then it was off to London, where a crowd of nearly 150,000 people surged across the runway of Croydon Aerodrome and nearly damaged the *Spirit of St. Louis*.

Lindbergh was so besieged by mail that he had to hire the Bankers Trust company to handle it. Among the cables and letters were offers to promote a host of commercial products and to star in Hollywood films for over a quarter a million dollars a picture. "I have had suggestions to be a cowboy, sheik, robber and lots of other things—but I am an aviator. . . . I am not going to move to Hollywood," he told reporters. The only major offers he accepted were from *The New York Times*—$60,000 for exclusive stories on his flight—and from publisher George Palmer Putnam, who signed him to a book contract. Written in longhand, on white bond paper in an astonishing six weeks, the book would be published later that year, an acutely clear but strangely emotionless account of his life and flight.* It was called *"We,"* a term Lindbergh had begun using in Paris to describe what he saw as a collective achievement, "My ship and I."

"Where do you get that 'we' stuff?" a New York *Daily News* reporter had asked Lindbergh on his arrival at Le Bourget. "You were alone son." And that's how great numbers of New Yorkers saw his achievement. "Lindbergh Flies Alone," a misty-eyed editorial by Harold M. Anderson of the New York *Sun*, became one of the most popular newspaper pieces of the day.

Preachy celebrants of Lindbergh's achievement, from the pastors of Manhattan's most prominent churches to the editors of *The New York Times*, portrayed the clean-living Minnesotan as a luminous example of "youth and idealism." Ambassador Herrick, a bit awestruck, compared him to Joan of Arc, the young Lafayette, and the biblical David. But the New York tabloids, a truer indicator of the popular mind, saw Lindbergh as the perfect hero for a decade of outsized individual achievements, many of them by New York–based athletes like Babe Ruth and Jack Dempsey. Ruth and Dempsey were outsiders, non–New Yorkers who arrived in the city and raised its emotional temperature by thrilling individual feats on the diamond and in the ring, as Lindbergh had done in the sky. Courage and singular achievement, risk taking and individual

---

* The book sold more than 600,000 copies in its first year in print. Lindbergh's second memoir, *The Spirit of St. Louis*, sold nearly 200,000 copies and won the Pulitzer Prize for biography in 1924. In 1957, Warner Brothers film adaptation, starring World War II bomber pilot James Stewart, appeared in theaters, drawing big audiences.

effort, upstarts and underdogs surmounting surpassing odds—these were the attributes and individuals New Yorkers in the neighborhoods prized, as a flood of letters to the editors of the *Daily News* attested. And "remember, always remember, that Lucky Slim Lindbergh did his deed alone, with no living thing nearby to help him fight the terror of solitude," wrote Gallico in a column he titled, tellingly, "The Man Who Flew Alone."

Lindbergh's unaffected attitude during "the first wild sweep of fame" was a reminder to older Americans of a more innocent age they imagined they had once lived in and had lost irretrievably. Writing in the afterglow of the 1920s, F. Scott Fitzgerald captured precisely the surge of moral nostalgia Lindbergh evoked. "In the spring of '27, something bright and alien flashed across the sky. A young Minnesotan who seemed to have nothing to do with his generation did a heroic thing, and for a moment people set down their glasses in country clubs and speakeasies and thought of their old best dreams." But to countless New Yorkers in the year 1927, "the apex," in sportswriter John Lardner's, words, of a decade of "hero worship"—the "perfect year for the perfect feat"—it was what Charles Lindbergh did more than what he was that truly mattered.*

And now the man who flew alone was coming home. He wanted to see more of Europe and then return to America, alone again in the *Spirit of St. Louis*, but President Calvin Coolidge thought this too risky. In early June, Coolidge sent the cruiser *Memphis* to Cherbourg to pick up Lindbergh and his plane, which was dismantled and packed in crates. After being honored in the nation's capital, Lindbergh would fly to the city where he had begun his epochal flight. Looking ahead to his return to New York, he told reporters that after the tremendous receptions he had received in Paris and London "I find myself wondering what sort of reception I will get at New York. Perhaps my story will be an old one by the time I get back."†

---

* John Lardner was the son of the even more illustrious sportswriter, Ring Lardner.

† As Lindbergh sailed back to America, his ship passed within ten miles of Clarence Chamberlin in the single-engine *Columbia* as he pressed on to Berlin, with owner Charles Levine as a passenger and relief pilot. Although *Columbia* ran out of fuel and was forced down a hundred miles from the German capital, Chamberlin set a new nonstop transatlantic record, covering over 3,900 miles in forty-three hours and thirty-nine minutes. Later that month, Commander Richard Byrd and three other crew took off from Roosevelt Field and made it to Paris, through wicked weather, on the night of June 30. But with Le Bourget shrouded in fog, they had to touch down at sea, off the coast of Normandy. In a period of less than six weeks, three American planes had crossed the Atlantic, but only Lindbergh had done it alone.

Prince of the City

Lindbergh had intended to fly the *Spirit of St. Louis* from Washington to New York, but engine trouble forced him to revise his plans. On Monday morning, June 13, he set out for New York in an Army pursuit plane, escorted by a cavalcade of twenty-three other aircraft. As the planes passed over Baltimore, Wilmington, Philadelphia, and Trenton, tens of thousands of people waved from the streets and the rooftops of buildings. Lindbergh landed at Mitchel Field on Long Island and boarded a golden-winged amphibian, which took him to the waters off lower New York Harbor, near where the Verrazano Narrows opens to the Atlantic. A police boat picked him up and brought him to the *Macon*, where Whalen and dozens of dignitaries had been watching his progress with binoculars.

When Lindbergh was spotted boarding the mayor's reception vessel "bedlam broke loose in the harbor," Whalen recalled. An armada of some four hundred vessels accompanied the *Macon* up the bay, "screaming, honking, blowing off steam." There were ferryboats, tugs, tankers, steamships, motorboats, private yachts, and excursion craft, all of them festively decorated and "jammed to the rails," forming a jagged line of escort nearly four miles long. "Fireboats shot streams of water at the sun. River steamers staggered under the weight of passengers massed on one side. Smoke and steam from wide-open whistles clouded the sky," wrote *The New York Times*.

After hastily changing into a blue business suit, "the hero of the air" climbed to the bridge of the *Macon* and stood alone, his hands clasped behind his back, the wind whipping through his thick hair. On either side of him, in the distance, he could see part of the crowd of over 200,000 spectators on the shores and docks lining Bay Ridge, South Brooklyn, and Staten Island, waving American flags. "I didn't think it would be like this," he was heard to say.

At the Battery, an open limousine stood waiting as Lindbergh walked down the gangplank on Whalen's arm. Then there was a near calamity. With Lindbergh standing in the special rear compartment of the open-top touring car, the excited chauffer hit the accelerator too hard, the car lurched forward, and the hero of the hour was swept off his feet. "He might have done a somersault over the lowered top of the car and landed on the pavement had not Grover A. Whalen . . . caught him by the leg and hauled him back into the rear seat while the crowd gasped in fear of a tragedy," reported a correspondent who was standing a few feet away.

Led by marching bands and fifteen thousand soldiers and sailors, the car rolled regally up Broadway. A blizzard of paper fell from the skyscrapers that hugged the sidewalks of the narrow streets of lower Manhattan, from the Battery to City Hall—"the Canyon of Heroes," New Yorkers called it. It was the most spectacular ticker tape parade in the city that had only recently invented the phenomenon. "Ticker tape and torn fragments of newspapers, telephone books, disgorged files, confetti and every conceivable kind of paper were shaken out of skyscraper windows in such abundance that several times the hero of the reception was obscured to the spectators," wrote one reporter. The atmosphere was so thick with paper it was transformed "into a semi-solid," said a witness. High above the tallest buildings on earth, skywriters wrote and rewrote Lindbergh's name over the city "in letters a mile long."

As Lindbergh's car turned into the driveway leading to the mayor's reception stand at City Hall, "three white-robed women sounded their trumpets." Extending his hand to the boyish-looking aviator, Jimmy Walker smiled and said that if Lindbergh had brought any letters of introduction to New York City they were "not necessary . . . New York City is yours—I don't give it to you: you won it." Escorted to the microphones, Lindbergh spoke briefly, with ease and earnestness, thanking the city for its generosity and not once mentioning his flight. Then the mayor joined Lindbergh and Whalen in the touring car for the triumphant ascent up Fifth Avenue, through nearly four miles of massed humanity. People hung from trees; and in places where the crowd was thickest, police and firemen formed a solid line along the curb, hands clasped together, to keep Lindbergh worshippers from rushing his car.

Behind Lindbergh, in another open car, was his mother, the special guest of the mayor. She was as astonished as her son by the size and intensity of the spectacle. By the end of Lindbergh's stay in New York, he would receive nearly half a million letters and 75,000 telegrams. One enthusiast wrote to the *Times* and demanded that President Coolidge resign within the month and hand over the job to Lindbergh, a far greater man. In the coming months, Lindbergh would be unable to keep track of his bank balance; when he wrote checks, people would keep them instead of cashing them. He was perhaps the greatest instant celebrity in all of history.

After stopping in front of St. Patrick's Cathedral to allow Lindbergh to shake hands with red-robed Patrick Joseph Cardinal Hayes, the procession continued up the avenue to Central Park, where a crowd of over 200,000 watched Governor Al Smith pay the final tribute of the day to the tall, stately-looking flier. The weary mayor, badly in need of a bracer, looked on absently.

"There never was anything like it," said *The New York Times,* which devoted the first sixteen pages of its Tuesday edition to coverage of the Lindbergh reception.

From Central Park, Lindbergh and his mother were driven to 270 Park Avenue, the apartment of Walker's friend Harry H. Frazee, the Broadway producer and former baseball magnate who, as owner of the Boston Red Sox, had sold Babe Ruth to the Yankees.

The following evening, Lindbergh was feted by nearly four thousand dignitaries at a banquet at the Commodore Hotel, adjacent to Grand Central Terminal. It was promoted as the biggest dinner gathering in the history of the country; even Jack Dempsey couldn't get a ticket. There was such a "stampede" to shake Lindbergh's hand that a wall of six policemen had to be placed in front of his seat on the dais. Before the speeches began, the ballroom was darkened and a model of the *Spirit of St. Louis* appeared, set against a massive wall painting of the skyline of Manhattan. While a radio announcer read newspaper bulletins of Lindbergh's progress across the Atlantic, the miniature plane, its propeller whirling, moved across the room, where on the far wall there was a painting of Paris. With the room still darkened, the guests rose spontaneously and sang "The Star-Spangled Banner."

The following evening Lindbergh attended a special performance at the Ziegfeld Theatre of *Rio Rita*, the musical he had driven into Manhattan to see the night he received news that the weather had cleared. He had come full circle. It was time to pick up his plane in Washington and head back home to St. Louis. That Friday, after receiving his check for $25,000 from Raymond Orteig, he left the city that could not get enough of him.

Although Lindbergh would not have known it, his parade up Fifth Avenue traced Manhattan's relentless march northward, over three centuries, from the Battery, to Washington Square, to Herald Square, to Midtown—the area between Forty-Second Street and the southern border of Central Park—the expanding city's newest commercial and entertainment center. Nor would Lindbergh have known that the street of classically composed limestone buildings that Harry Frazee's apartment house stood on was "a recent and sudden phenomenon."

"The fame of Park Avenue is so great," wrote Hulbert Footner, author of a popular New York City travelogue, "that it has generally been forgotten how recent it is." In 1900, a gigantic railroad yard, thirty tracks wide, fanned out from Grand Central Terminal and stretched northward for nearly three-quarters of a mile, between Forty-second and Fifty-sixth Streets, obliterating vehicular cross streets and sending billowing clouds of black smoke into the Manhattan sky. Pedestrians crossed the marshaling yard on iron catwalks, braving the swirling smoke and ash. "It was a trip of daring for foot passengers," said one writer.

This enormous industrial ditch was "a veritable 'Chinese Wall,'" severing Park Avenue, a north–south thoroughfare, at Forty-second Street. Thirteen years later, when a new station was opened on the site of the old one—the original Grand Central Depot, built by Cornelius Vanderbilt, "the Commodore," in 1871—the avenue immediately north of it was transformed in little over a decade into a stately boulevard with a common cornice line and a park-like promenade running down the center of the roadway. In the month of the Lindbergh parade, work was being completed on the second of two elevated roadways that led around the terminal, like a collar, connecting upper and lower Park Avenue. From this "viaduct," the view north, wrote Footner, "presents the most majestic urban vista in the world."

In the area around Grand Central a miniature skyscraper city was being built in 1927, a Manhattan business district second in importance only to Wall Street. Called Terminal City, it was one of the boldest private construction projects in the history of cities, and would soon house the tallest building on earth—the dream project of a former railroad mechanic from Ellis, Kansas, named Walter Chrysler.

Fifth Avenue, from just below Forty-second Street to Fifty-ninth Street, was also undergoing a great change in 1927. This was symbolized by a scene Charles Lindbergh witnessed on his ride up Fifth Avenue. As his car reached the corner of Fifth and Fifty-seventh Street, Lindbergh noticed that riveters working high on the steel framework of a new commercial building had hung up a sign: "Welcome Home, Lindy." The building was being constructed on the site of the French renaissance palace built by Cornelius Vanderbilt II, the favorite grandson of the Commodore. The Cornelius Vanderbilt palace had recently fallen to the wrecker's ball. This was part of a commercial invasion of the avenue that transformed it in the 1920s from Vanderbilt Alley, a street lined with urban châteaus erected by the descendants of the Commodore, to the most expensive shopping street in the world. Its centerpiece would be the new Bergdorf Goodman department store, completed in 1928 on the spot where Cornelius Vanderbilt II's mansion, once the largest private residence in the city, had stood since 1883.

In 1927, New York's new street of millionaires was Park Avenue, and a number of old families from Fifth Avenue, including some Vanderbilts, had begun migrating there, abandoning their dark, cheerless mansions for brilliantly modern apartments, high-rise living quarters of a size and opulence not seen before anywhere.

This momentous mid-Manhattan transformation was set in motion by the plans of a largely forgotten transportation genius, William Wilgus, chief engineer of the New York Central Railroad. And it began with Wilgus's idea to have his railroad company move into the real estate business, starting on Park Avenue.

PART THREE

THE MAKING OF MODERN MANHATTAN

CHAPTER SEVEN

REVENUE PLUCKED FROM THE AIR

This beautiful street, with electrified trains whizzing through its bowels, is a spine of metropolitanism.

FORTUNE, JULY 1939

Park Avenue

In *The Great Gatsby*, F. Scott Fitzgerald gives a luminous picture of Manhattan from the Queensboro Bridge, spanning the East River at Fifty-ninth Street. Speeding toward the city in his cream-colored convertible, Long Island bootlegger Jay Gatsby passes "over the great bridge, with the sunlight through the girders making a constant flicker upon the moving cars, with the city rising up across the river in white heaps and sugar lumps all built with a wish out of non-olfactory money. The city seen from the Queensboro Bridge is always the city seen for the first time, in its first wild promise of all the mystery and the beauty in the world."

Coming off the Manhattan side of the bridge, Gatsby would have turned down Park Avenue to reach the Forty-second Street restaurant where he was meeting his gangster associate Meyer Wolfsheim, a character loosely based on Broadway big shot Arnold Rothstein.

Two years later, in 1927, Scott's wife, Zelda, set to work on an equally vivid portrait of that same stretch of Manhattan from a car traveling in the opposite direction, up Park Avenue, from Grand Central Terminal, toward the great steel span at Fifty-ninth Street. Ahead of her stretched a stately avenue "straight as a sunbeam."

"It is a street for satisfied eyes," Zelda writes in "The Changing Beauty of

Park Avenue," published a year later in *Harper's Bazaar*. "Through the arches and open gates [of tall apartment houses] one sees paved courtyards big enough to convey a cloistered, feudal feeling." And at places along the avenue there are restaurants with a taste of Paris and small, glittering shops where "shopping is pleasant and expensive and holy." It is a street for leisurely walk-ing—a European street—but also a street "to use when in a hurry." Along its smooth, level pavement, long gray limousines and stubby black cabs glide back and forth, avoiding the crush of Fifth Avenue, progressing from traffic signal to traffic signal "by a series of hundred yard dashes."

Coming from the south, after passing through exclusive Murray Hill, there is "even a drawbridge," an elevated roadway built over Forty-second Street and circling Grand Central Terminal, "so that sweeping off into the Avenue one experiences the emotion of entering a stronghold—the stronghold of easy wealth. . . .

"Such is this flaming street—widened now until it has become the most co-lossal thoroughfare in flaming Manhattan. It is known the world over. And yet we heard a well-groomed and cosmopolitan-looking young lady say one day, 'Oh yes, that's the street next to Madison, isn't it?' And she lived in New York!"

When journalist Will Irwin left for Europe in 1914 to cover the Great War, New York society was "ensconced" on Fifth Avenue, from Forty-second Street to the Metropolitan Museum of Art at the intersection of Eighty-second Street. "That thoroughfare and the cross streets which flanked it to the eastward, were the sole haunt of fashion," he recalls in his genial 1927 book, *Highlights of Manhattan*. "Returning in 1919, we heard for the first time the name of Park Avenue as a synonym for wealth, and walked round the station to behold this grandiose conception in the process of building." Only "the newly rich," Irwin thought at the time, would live "on apartment-house terms, like larvae in a honey-comb. And yet—every month some member of the 'exclusive set' was giving up his mansion on Fifth . . . and 'buying a duplex' in a Park Avenue apartment-house." In the "new strange Manhattan" that arose after the war, the "superbly wide" stretch of Park Avenue from Grand Central Terminal to Fifty-seventh Street superseded Fifth Avenue as the acme of exclusivity.

And where was that disfiguring feature of the old Park Avenue: the tre-mendous rail yard of the New York Central? It was "underfoot," wrote Irwin, "though you realize it only when a taxicab strikes one of the metal strips at the crossings and the pavement trembles as with the ghost of an earthquake." The roadway trembled ever so slightly because it was built on a steel platform that formed the roof of the rail yard.

Unmentioned in Irwin's portrait of transfigured Park Avenue is the engineer who buried the tracks out of sight. William Wilgus was the founder of this "new quarter of the very rich." But his ideas were turned into steel and stone only because of a calamity that shocked the entire city.

The Commodore's New York

It was the proverbial accident waiting to happen. After leaving the head of the station yard at Fifty-sixth Street, the New York Central's commuter and long-distance passenger trains descended into a dark, two-mile-long tunnel that ran down the center of Park Avenue to Ninety-sixth Street, where a masonry viaduct carried them across the Harlem Valley and the Harlem River to the Bronx. The tunnel had originally been an open, street-level cut, but in the mid-1870s municipal furor over the deafening noise, vibrations, and smoke of the trains compelled the Vanderbilt railroad to depress the tracks below street level. They were covered over, bridges were built connecting the two sides of Fourth Avenue, and large ventilation slots were placed in the roof of the tunnel to release the smoke and poisonous gases of coal-burning locomotives. Attractive fenced-in plots framed these smoke vents, creating a continuous boulevard strip that ran down the center of Park Avenue, literally on the lid of the tunnel. The center island dressed up the avenue, but smoke, gas, and hot cinders shot up through the ventilation openings in sudden, volcano-like eruptions, disfiguring adjoining properties and injuring pedestrians.

On January 8, 1902, at the peak of the morning rush, the smoke and steam inside the brick-lined tunnel was so thick that an engineer of a commuter train from White Plains, New York, failed to see a succession of stop lights and signals and slammed into the rear of a commuter train from Danbury, Connecticut, which was sitting at a red signal light at Fifty-eighth Street, waiting for traffic to clear in the congested rail yard. The onrushing locomotive failed to come to a full stop until it sliced, sickeningly, halfway through the wooden rear coach of the Danbury train. "The scene presented in the narrow passageway of the almost pitch-dark tunnel immediately following the crash was harrowing beyond description," wrote a city reporter. Rescue workers were "guided through the blackness by the groans and cries of the injured and dying." The engine of the White Plains train was jammed so far into the Danbury car that it was "almost completely buried out of sight." The bodies of the dead were mangled nearly beyond recognition and many of the living were "lying on top of the heated boiler and were in imminent peril of roasting to death." Fifteen people were killed instantly and two died later. Forty others were injured. It remains Manhattan's worst railroad disaster.

The accident occurred a few blocks from the Fifth Avenue mansions of the descendants of the late Cornelius Vanderbilt, founder of the family dynasty. The Commodore's grandson, William Kissam Vanderbilt, chairman of the New York Central Railroad, rushed to the scene minutes after news of the catastrophe spread. Approached by reporters, he refused to speak to them; after assessing the carnage, he headed straight to the railroad's headquarters at Grand Central Terminal.

Also at the scene was John D. Crimmins, a prominent member of a Park Avenue organization that had been waging a hard fight for the use of electric-powered trains in the tunnel. In the days after the tunnel disaster, the protest movement that Crimmins helped to organize turned into a city-wide crusade. The following year the New York legislature prohibited the use of steam-powered passenger locomotives in Manhattan after July 1, 1908. The New York Central had five years to electrify all trains operating out of its Forty-second Street station.

William Wilgus was eager to take on the challenge. Troubled by "the dangers and discomforts of the Park Avenue tunnel," he had, years earlier, formulated plans to electrify several of the Central's busiest suburban lines, but the railroad's directors had not yet authorized construction. Their caution was understandable. Although dozens of American cities had installed electric trolleys, and although New York planned to open the first segment of its electrically powered subway system in 1904, no railroad was then using electricity to power heavy trains for long distances at high speeds. But the mandate of the state legislature left the railroad no choice. Even before the final vote in the Assembly, Wilgus was called in and assigned a task "astonishing in its magnitude and its daring."

Thirty-eight-year-old William J. Wilgus, a lean, bearded outdoorsman, had been with the New York Central for only ten years. Born in Buffalo, New York, he graduated from a local high school but had no interest in extending his formal education. He would take only one college class in his life: a correspondence course in drafting through Cornell University. Wilgus learned his profession by practicing it, working in the field as a rodman, draftsman, and engineer with a succession of Midwestern railroads. In 1893, he became a lowly assistant engineer of one of the New York Central's branch lines. Tremendously bright, with a head for business as well as building, he rose rocketlike in the company. Six years later he was promoted to chief engineer of the entire railroad system and assigned the task of supervising the expansion and modernization of Commodore Vanderbilt's Forty-second Street station. Two years later, just months before the Park Avenue Tunnel accident, he was put in charge of yet another expansion of the overcrowded station.

Traffic was growing phenomenally, far beyond the redesigned station's ability to handle it effectively. In 1900, over five hundred trains entered the station daily, treble the traffic of 1871. "It is a remarkable fact," wrote the editors of *Scientific American,* "that although New York is the second largest city in the world, it has but one railroad terminal station within its boundaries, [and] . . . it is being overwhelmed by the increase of traffic."

Something had to be done, though no thought was given to changing the location of the station, one of the most propitious in the city. Commodore Vanderbilt's decision in 1869 to erect the largest railway station in America on Forty-second Street was a turning point in New York City history. When the station, with its immense iron-vaulted train shed, was formally opened on November 1, 1871, a "practically unsettled" industrial landscape of slaughter-houses, saloons, squatter's shanties, and smoke-scarred maintenance buildings of Vanderbilt's New York & Harlem Railroad—New York City's first railway— was transformed into one of the most prized real estate holdings on earth. Van-derbilt's early biographers have described his decision to build there, forty-five minutes by horse car from the beating heart of Manhattan, as prophetic, a sign of his intuitive commercial genius. But the sharp-dealing Dutchman had been forced by city government to locate his station there, next to rocky ground where an old woman raised goats, supplying her neighbors with milk.

From the time the New York & Harlem Railroad began steam-powered operations in 1835, from City Hall to Harlem, along Fourth Avenue—renamed Park Avenue in 1888—it had been the target of outraged residents who lived near its tracks. Pedestrians were killed and injured, sparks set wooden buildings on fire, and horse-drawn traffic was disrupted at grade-level crossings. Finally, in 1857 the city banned steam locomotives from operating below Forty-second Street, the far northern boundary of Manhattan's most densely settled areas. Incoming trains had to stop at Forty-second Street, where passengers transferred to horse-drawn rail cars that hauled them to the Harlem's main station on Madison Square at Fourth Avenue and Twenty-sixth Street, the future site of the first Madison Square Garden.

It was not Vanderbilt's decision to locate his station on Forty-second Street that showed uncommon foresight; rather it was his decision to place it on *East* Forty-second street, directly in the path of the main channels of Manhattan's inexorable march northward along three great avenues that ran up the center and east side of the island: Broadway, Fifth, and Park. Urban development was meager by comparison on the West Side for reasons related, as we shall see, to another of the Commodore's strategic decisions.

The comfortable classes followed the dispossessed in this great uptown movement that began to acquire momentum in the years immediately after the Civil War. They displaced a scattering of Irish tenants who had settled on the empty ground around St. Patrick's Cathedral when construction began in 1859. These upper-middle-class families, some of whom were descendants of city founders, were drawn to the area by the pleasant riding paths and promenades of Central Park, opened to the public in the same year work had begun on St. Patrick's; and they built their three-story brownstone houses and Protestant churches on or around Fifth Avenue, just to the south of Frederick Law Olmsted and Calvert Vaux's 843 acres of sylvan parkland.

Then came the really rich. Toward the end of the century, the descendants of the Commodore began building ponderous limestone mansions on Fifth Avenue, between Forty-second Street and the park. To build above Fifty-ninth Street, the southern boundary of Central Park, was seen at that time, writes Edith Wharton, as a "bold move which surprised and scandalized Society." Not until the opening years of the twentieth century would upper Fifth Avenue become "Millionaires' Row."

Cornelius Vanderbilt's decision to build his passenger depot on a five-block parcel on Forty-second Street was not an isolated act. It was the triumphant culmination of one of the greatest urban railroad reorganizations in history, one that indelibly reshaped the island of Manhattan.

When Vanderbilt, builder of the country's largest fleet of steamships, moved suddenly and spectacularly into railroading in 1863, at age sixty-nine, he first seized control of the nearly bankrupt New York & Harlem Railroad. He coveted the Harlem because it was one of only two steam railroads with a right of entry into Manhattan. The other was the Harlem's principal rival, the Hudson River Railroad, which also ran north to Albany, not inland like the Harlem, but along the east bank of the Hudson River from two decrepit stations in lower Manhattan.

One year after taking over the Harlem, Vanderbilt continued his "program of conquest" by gaining control of the Hudson River Railroad and merging it in 1869 with a much larger railroad he had acquired only two years earlier. This was the New York Central, a trunk line with continuous service from Albany to Buffalo—and direct connections from there with branch lines running all the way to Chicago.

Majority ownership of the New York Central & Hudson River Railroad, one of the greatest transportation systems in the world, gave America's new "Railroad King" control of a ribbon of iron extending from the Atlantic to the

Great Lakes, and made New York City, already a financial and shipping colossus, a rail capital as well.[*]

In 1869, the year of the great New York railroad combination, the Commodore built a short spur line north of the Harlem River, linking the tracks of the New York Central and the Harlem for the purpose of redirecting their traffic. Manhattan would be forever transformed. Henceforth, passenger trains of both busy railroads—along with the New York, New Haven & Hartford Railroad, which had purchased the rights to use the Harlem's tracks inside New York—were funneled to Forty-second Street. All freight traffic was routed to a new station Vanderbilt constructed that same year on the West Side of Manhattan, on the site of St. John's Park, close to the city's Hudson River piers and near where the Manhattan entrance of the Holland Tunnel is located today. A bronze statue of the buccaneering capitalist was unveiled at the terminal's opening ceremonies. Situated commandingly atop the entrance to the station, it paid tribute to him as an empire builder. It could just as appropriately have called him a city builder.

When Vanderbilt opened his new passenger depot on Forty-second Street he discontinued the Harlem's horse-drawn service down Fourth Avenue. The city would have to come to him, on Forty-second Street—and it soon did. Dozens of streetcar lines began converging at Grand Central Depot, offering service along a widened Forty-second Street to ferry piers located on both the Hudson and East Rivers. And when the Third Avenue elevated railroad went into operation in 1878 it built a spur right to the front doors of Vanderbilt's station house.

In gaining mastery of the only two rail lines penetrating Manhattan, and dividing and redirecting their traffic, Vanderbilt became a city shaper, sealing the fate of the West Side as Manhattan's paramount industrial area, and the area along Forty-second Street, from Times Square to the East River, as its new office, hotel, and entertainment district. No one has had a more far-reaching impact upon the economic geography of New York City.

St. John's Station—as it was called—radically transformed the lower West Side. It pulled the city's oceangoing businesses crosstown, from the East River seaport to deep-water slips on the wide, easier-to-navigate Hudson. The docks there were conveniently connected to a Vanderbilt railroad that linked New York with the expanding grain and meat markets of America's midland prairie.

---

[*] The new amalgamated company was called simply the New York Central. The Harlem remained an independent company in name only; Vanderbilt retained firm control of it. T. J. Stiles, *The First Tycoon: The Epic Life of Cornelius Vanderbilt* (New York: Alfred A. Knopf, 2009), 366, 439, 506.

On the East Side of the city, Vanderbilt's original passenger depot, and the one that replaced it in 1913, would function like gigantic urban magnets, drawing commerce and culture into their force field. Although the movement would be delayed for some time, downtown businesses, from publishing and advertising to fashion and theater, would eventually pull up stakes and migrate to what became known as Midtown.

The Wilgus Plan

When Grand Central Depot opened in 1871, Commodore Vanderbilt was confident it would proudly serve the city for at least a full century. Thirty years later, William Wilgus, along with a number of municipal reform groups, considered the station a great civic "blunder." The fanlike rail yard, the largest in the Western Hemisphere, separated "the city into two parts for fourteen blocks—nearly three quarters of a mile, between 42nd Street and 56th Street," Wilgus wrote. Municipal cross streets were severed and replaced by two vehicular bridges that traversed the rail yard, narrow iron catwalks incessantly jammed with commercial traffic. (There were also three pedestrian bridges.) For a long stretch above Forty-second Street, Park Avenue was a blighted industrial corridor lined with tenements, saloons, factories, stables, warehouses, a brewery, and the Steinway Piano Factory, a wasteland that looked like "a Midwestern cow town."

The electrification of the station would end the smoke menace, but Wilgus, a boldly imaginative risk taker, wanted to go even further. Instructed to expand the station to handle the increased traffic, he greatly exceeded his charge and ran straight into a storm of resistance from company directors.

The idea came to him sometime in September 1902, eight months after the accident in the Park Avenue Tunnel. It was late afternoon and he was standing at the northward-facing window of his third-floor office in the company's headquarters in Grand Central Depot, looking out at the "chaos of cars and locomotives" in the rail yard. Expansion of the present station, he ruminated, would be a "mere palliative measure." Instead, the company should turn necessity into opportunity. The switch to electricity mandated by the government opened the way for the total elimination of the rail yard, which was a criminal waste of valuable city land. Wilgus would replace it, along with the old station building, with a state-of-the-art terminal complex—a bonanza for the city and the railroad company. It was like a vision, he said later, and he went straight to his desk to sketch it out. "It was the most daring thing that had ever occurred to me."

That December Wilgus drafted a letter to William H. Newman, president of the New York Central, proposing that the company "tear down the old [station] building and train shed and in their place, and in the yard on the north, create a double-level, under-surface terminal on which to superimpose office quarters and revenue producing structures made possible by the intended use of electric power." Here in one sentence was the entire plan; it needed only elaboration.

Under the Wilgus plan, the New York Central would, in effect, be creating two terminals, one on top of the other, both of them underground. The station's sixty-seven tracks would be submerged forty feet and placed on a double-decked steel bridgework, an immensely strong structure that resembled a bunk bed. Commuter trains would use the lower level, long-distance trains the upper one. When the new track system was completed, steel bridges would be constructed at street level and their roadbeds paved with asphalt. The section of Park Avenue that had been abolished by the old steam yard would be restored, and municipal cross streets that had been closed for over half a century would be reopened. With smokeless electric power there would be no suffocating buildup of noxious gas, no flying cinders, and no need for an unsightly and dangerous ventilation system. Everything would be clean, efficient, and futuristic. After outgoing passengers dropped off their luggage at a conveniently located ground-level service area, they would descend from the main concourse to their gates, not on steep stairs, but on broad, gently sloped ramps. Additional passenger ramps in the virtually "stairless" building would lead to a separate suburban station; to a planned municipal subway station under Park Avenue; and to the sidewalks of Forty-second Street.

A revolutionary loop system would make the terminal a paragon of transportation efficiency.* Incoming trains would no longer have to back out of the station after discharging their passengers, a complex time-consuming operation. They would continue around a loop and "steal away" to the covered yards, where they would be "cleaned and made ready for the next trip." This loop system would allow the station to handle up to two hundred trains an hour, "gliding in and out" of long tunnels "as silently as ghosts."

The main station concourse would be a small skyscraper, fifteen stories high, providing office space for the company and additional space to rent out. In a March 1903 memo to President Newman, Wilgus argued that the company would reap even greater profits by building adjacent to the station a "first class hotel similar to the august Waldorf Astoria." An urban as well as a trans-

---

* It was a "terminal," not a "station," because the railroad's horse cars no longer carried passengers to destinations downtown.

The anatomy of Grand Central Terminal, a great "people-moving" machine—a
station virtually without stairs. (NEW YORK HISTORICAL SOCIETY)

portation visionary, Wilgus suggested further that the company build on the
roof of the underground terminal "a great civic center," a spacious and strikingly handsome plaza. This "would vastly strengthen the company's position
as regards to competitive traffic."

Here Wilgus was thinking of the Central's chief rival, the Pennsylvania
Railroad, the largest, most heavily capitalized transportation company in existence; and next to U.S. Steel, the most powerful corporation in America. In
early 1902, the New York Central's passenger trains still retained exclusive
rights to enter Manhattan overland. The trains of the other ten railroads serving New York had to stop at the New Jersey shore of the "un-bridged" Hudson
River. Passengers—nearly 140 million of them in 1902—then transferred to
crowded, uncomfortable ferries for the final leg of their journey, to docks in a
waterfront section of lower Manhattan "as squalid and dirty and ill smelling
as that of any Oriental port." This situation was galling to Alexander Cassatt,
president of the Pennsylvania Railroad. "I have never been able to reconcile
myself to the idea that a railroad system like the Pennsylvania should be prevented from entering the most important and populous city in the country by
a river less than a mile wide."

Shortly after the Park Avenue Tunnel accident, Cassatt obtained a franchise for his railroad to enter Manhattan through tunnels under the Hudson River; and the railroad began electrifying trains that would speed silently through these sub-aquatic passageways. It was no secret that the "Pennsy" planned to build a mammoth all-electric station on the West Side, at Thirty-third Street, near the southern border of Hell's Kitchen. And the architects, it was announced, would be McKim, Mead & White, the triumvirate of American design. But Wilgus knew that the Pennsy, a conservatively run, Philadelphia-based operation, had no interest in entering the volatile Manhattan real estate market in order to upgrade the shabby area around its new station. If the New York Central greatly improved land around the all-electric station he proposed, it would gain a competitive advantage over its main rival for the plum Chicago trade.

When presented with the Wilgus proposal, the New York Central's officials howled in protest; it was too audacious, too expensive. By this time, active leadership of the railroad had passed from the Vanderbilt family to a coterie of Wall Street lawyers and financiers, the most powerful among them J. Pierpont Morgan, and these captains of commerce ridiculed what they termed the "grocery store" idea of "lending the station to revenue producing purposes." The Wilgus plan was headed for the scrap heap unless the engineer could convince the board that the company could recoup, somehow, the staggering cost of implementing it.

Wilgus did this through patient explication, buttressed by hard economic data. The governing idea was to have the New York Central lease the "air rights" it owned over its electrified tracks. Once the underground track system was in place, there would be open rectangles between the newly restored cross streets, openings through which passersby would be able to see trains running along the upper-level track. Wilgus suggested that the company convert these open spaces into revenue-generating building sites. Under his plan, the Grand Central would form a real estate company to lease this "empty air" to private developers. These speculative builders would then fill the voids with apartments, hotels, stores, and offices, anchoring their buildings, not in soil—there would be none—but in Manhattan bedrock, reached by steel columns that straddled the railroad's subsurface tracks. The new civic structures would perform a double function: they would upgrade the neighborhood around the station and complete, at no cost to the railroad, the roofing over its underground tracks.

Finally, Wilgus suggested that the railroad build an "elevated driveway" around the station, a roadway linked to a new viaduct-like structure, or arch bridge, that would allow motorists on Park Avenue to leap over thickly congested Forty-second Street. (This would become Zelda Fitzgerald's "drawbridge" onto upper Park Avenue.) When the terminal and its neighboring hotels, office buildings, apartments, and high-end stores were in place, the Grand Central Zone, as Wilgus called the railroad's acreage north of the station, would be "the most attractive locality in New York City," the catalyst for a new Midtown.

Wilgus then prepared a "financial forecast," estimating—with dead-on accuracy, it turned out—that the revenue accruing from high-end apartments and hotels built on the Central's air rights holdings would "earn an income sufficient to pay the interest, not only on the cost of the terminal itself, but also on . . . our electrification schemes." As he would write later, "Thus from the air would be taken wealth with which to support obligatory vast changes otherwise non-productive."

In a matter of months, Wilgus had turned what was seen as a ruinously expensive civic enterprise into a seductive profit-generating scheme. The board was easily won over and approved the plan without a single dissenting vote. On June 30, 1903, Wilgus, to his "intense joy," was directed to begin the gigantic improvement he had suggested, a plan that would transform America's second largest railroad company into a master planner of Mid-Manhattan.

A Monument to Movement

Along with Pennsylvania Station, Grand Central Terminal was the largest building enterprise in the history of the republic; and at Grand Central, one of the busiest traffic points on the continent, work went forward with no interruption to existing service. When the old station was demolished, a temporary one was already in place, capable of handling more than six hundred trains daily.

Construction began only nine days after work commenced on Pennsylvania Station. "An army was set to work," wrote a reporter from *Munsey's Magazine,* "and it toiled night and day" for a full decade. The first order of business was the excavation of the gallery for the two tiers of tracks, a hole forty feet deep, two blocks wide, and half a mile long. The great dig was a sight to see. A New England merchant came down to New York one morning in 1906 to buy Christmas stock, peered out the window of his sleeping car, and exclaimed, "What are they doing here? . . . It looks like a mining camp."

It was, like Pennsylvania Station, a purely capitalist project, carried to completion without a cent of public funding, and it involved the near complete reconstruction of an entire urban precinct. Twenty-five miles of sewers, along with many more miles of gas and water lines, were removed or replaced, and nearly two hundred buildings demolished on additional land the railroad purchased for the project. Over a million and a half cubic yards of rock and granite were cut or blasted with dynamite, and enough earth was removed to fill the cars of a train extending from Manhattan to Omaha. At times, nearly ten thousand workers were on the construction site, toiling round-the-clock.

On September 30, 1906, while excavation was still proceeding, the first electric train ran into the Central's yards, with a beaming William Wilgus at the controls. It ran on a low-voltage third-rail system, with power supplied by two coal-fired plants. Scheduled train service with electric engines began that December. Wilgus had beaten by over a year the mandate for electrification imposed by the state legislature, a "miracle" engineering accomplishment, said the American Society of Civil Engineers.

Then, in Wilgus's moment of great triumph, disaster struck. On February 16, 1907, one of the Central's new electric trains, an express to White Plains, New York, rounded a curve at Woodlawn in the Bronx, and flew off the tracks. Twenty-five people were killed and at least 150 more suffered injuries. Once again the railroad was excoriated in the press and the district attorney's office launched an investigation. The *New York Evening Journal* blamed the accident on the flawed design of the new locomotives the railroad was using. They were "too heavy" for the rails, it correctly noted. Called before the State Railroad Commission, New York Central officials placed the blame squarely on Wilgus, who had worked with General Electric in developing the engines. His professional reputation at stake, Wilgus mounted a massively documented defense, but without informing him the company modified the design of the engines, eliminating excess weight over the driving wheels. Outraged by what he considered the company's treachery, Wilgus resigned in protest that September and went into private practice. By then the electrification of the lines had been virtually completed and the building of the underground terminal was proceeding according to his engineering blueprints. From this point forward the architects of the main Concourse Building made the major innovations.

The coveted architectural commission was awarded in 1904 to the little-known firm of Charles Reed and Allen Stem of St. Paul, Minnesota. Some suspected favoritism, and with good reason. At the time, Reed was collaborating with Wilgus on a rail station in Troy, New York, and also happened to be married to Wilgus's sister. These factors surely advanced his firm's chances against powerhouse outfits like McKim, Mead, & White and the Chicago firm of Daniel H. Burnham.

After winning one of the greatest commissions in the history of the building arts, Reed and Stem were informed by William K. Vanderbilt that they would be collaborating with another firm. Impressed by Charles McKim's preliminary designs for Penn Station and outraged by Reed and Stem's plans to build a twenty-story hotel over Grand Central, Vanderbilt had convinced the Wall Street financiers who ran the railroad to hire his cousin and closest friend, Beaux Arts architect Whitney Warren, a devotee of the subdued classicism of Charles McKim. Handsome, vainglorious, and extravagantly rich, Warren was as ferociously competitive in business as he was on the sportsfield. "The standard of success in this country is the making of money," he told a group of architectural students, "therefore the architect should [fight to] make money and be considered successful." He and his partner, Charles D. Wetmore, were forced to work together, always uneasily, with Reed and Stem, under the title Associated Architects. When Reed died in December 1911, William Newman severed ties with the St. Paul firm and made Warren and Wetmore sole architects of Grand Central. It was an unseemly timed separation. Newman and Wetmore worked out the arrangement as they traveled back to Manhattan together in Newman's private rail car after attending Charles Reed's funeral in Scarsdale, New York.*

Warren and Wetmore scrapped the plan for a high-rise, revenue-generating hotel and designed a low, classically inspired structure devoted almost exclusively to railroad-related operations. Ornament was applied sparingly but boldly. A massive sculptural group of the ancient gods Mercury, Minerva, and Hercules, designed by the Frenchman Jules-Félix Coutan, was placed on the great clock above the south facade's triumphal triple archway—Mercury symbolizing "the glory of commerce, supported by moral and mental energy—Hercules and Minerva." There was no sculptural tribute to the Commodore, but in 1929 his statue would be removed from the company's freight terminal in lower Manhattan and placed on the Park Avenue viaduct. Today, few people notice it. "With a smile forever fixed in bronze, [he] looks down upon the world he created," wrote the editors of *Fortune*.

The terminal's showpiece was—and still is—an illuminated mural of the constellations painted on the concave, Pantheon-like ceiling of the Grand Concourse, a chamber tall enough—120 feet—to hold a twelve-story building. Whitney Warren had Parisian artist Paul Helleu design this magnificent barrel-vaulted steel and plaster ceiling. The astrological mural impressed a

---

* With Wilgus's support, Allen Stem's and Charles Reed's attorneys sued Warren and Wetmore for their fair share of the architectural fees. In 1922, after lengthy litigation, the courts awarded Stem and the Reed estate nearly $500,000. The American Institute of Architects expelled Whitney Warren for unprofessional conduct. Undeterred, Warren and Wetmore continued their highly successful architectural practice.

contemporary critic as "bold and unique; a blue sky over which are spread figures, in delicate gold tracery, showing the signs of the zodiac, with hundreds of other stars, some of which are made real by little electric lights placed behind them. This feature alone would make the station one of the sights of the city."*

This great room that would soon echo with the announcement of arriving and departing trains was a monument to the romance of long-distance train travel. Thirty feet above the Tennessee marble floor, a balcony was carried along all but one wall of the building. At the west end, a grand staircase descended to the lower level and the station's soon to be famous Oyster Bar. At the center of the concourse, on top of the circular main information booth, was the terminal's signature gold clock, each of its four faces made from opal. "Nice city," says the actor Percy Kilbride as he enters the Main Concourse in the 1950 film *Ma and Pa Kettle Go to Town*. "Pa, this is the station," his daughter corrects him.

On the evening of November 26, 1911, the Pennsylvania Station began regular train service. The station was part of a massive and revolutionary transportation complex, the only one of its kind in the world. Its underground tunnels stretched from New Jersey to Manhattan and from there, eighty feet below the surface of the East River, to Long Island City in Queens, with connections to New England. The gigantic project, writes historian Hilary Ballon, "changed the law of nature; it annihilated the water barrier and reshaped the landscape of New York into a continuous network of rail connections."

Two years later, at midnight on February 1, Grand Central Terminal, the eastern terminus of the Vanderbilt railroads, was opened to the public. A crowd of three thousand New Yorkers rushed into the building, and sightseers continued to pour through its portals all through the following day. Designed to accommodate a hundred million people a year, the building handled the crowds with ease.

Some reporters, deservedly, gave credit to Wilgus as a modern "miracle-worker," but Grand Central officials failed even to mention him in their lavish brochure commemorating the opening of the terminal. It was as if he never existed. Reed and Stem received equally unfair treatment. Nor does the bro-

---

* The constellations are shown on the ceiling in reverse, as if viewed from the heavens above. Historians have been unable to determine if the design was taken from a medieval manuscript that presented the constellations as seen from above, or if this was a mistake made by Helleu or the painters. In March 1913 a commuter from New Rochelle first pointed out the apparent error. NYT, March 23, 1913.

chure mention that Warren and Wetmore had scrapped, but were forced to re-institute, Wilgus's ideas for a ramp system, a perimeter roadway, and a viaduct over Forty-second Street.

The Terminal Building, splendidly restored in the late 1990s, solely as a commuter station, remains a paradigm for architects and planners of large public spaces. It also exemplifies one of the axioms of urban design. Without "congestion," the massing of people at central points and along major transportation corridors, cities risk becoming dead places; but without "movement," the smooth circulation of people and products, congested cities stand the equal danger of death by suffocation. New York's principal contribution to "citycraft" is not congestion, writes architecture historian Douglas Haskell, "but congestion with movement." And New York's "most brilliant congestion with movement resolution" is Grand Central Terminal.

With New York City's historic transportation breakthroughs in oceanic shipping (the opening of regularly scheduled packet lines to Europe), inland transportation (the Erie Canal and the Vanderbilt railroads), high-speed intra-urban circulation (elevated rail lines, electric trolleys, and the country's first subway system), America's master metropolis demonstrated tellingly that commerce is mainly about movement. In Grand Central Terminal, writes Haskell, "New York brought her two major achievements—concentrated building and swift urban transportation—into a single, interrelated, planned operation. The event was majestically fantastic."

A "monument to movement," Grand Central Terminal became one of the great urban mixing machines in the world, taking people arriving by trains, taxis, trolleys, subways, elevated railroads, and on foot and delivering them with dispatch to their destinations. Charles Follen McKim designed Penn Station, his last major project, to facilitate movement but wanted passengers to proceed through its marble corridors almost reverentially, taking in the grandeur of the imperial architecture. At Grand Central, form follows function and nowhere supersedes it.

Arriving long-distance passengers exited, not at a cavernous train shed, but at separate, well-lighted gate areas, their platforms perfectly flush with the floors of the New York Central's luxurious sleeper cars. Stepping from an electrified train at the new Grand Central, said one traveler, "[was] like passing from one handsome apartment into the great corridor of another." By 1927, more than 43 million passengers would pass through Grand Central Terminal, a number close to one-third of the population of the United States. In the golden decades of rail travel, when railroads were integral to the survival of cities, Grand Central was perhaps the one building without which New York could not function.

Grand Central Terminal was also, as Wilgus had planned, a generator of "new urban energies," reviving run-down neighborhoods around it. In this regard, geography alone gave it a clear advantage over Penn Station. Grand Central, as we have seen, was situated on the main lines of commercial and residential advance up the island, and at the intersection of what were, in 1927, three of New York's busiest subway lines. Penn Station, by contrast, was on the industrial West Side, on the edge of Hell's Kitchen and hard by a decaying remnant of the Tenderloin, turn-of-the-century New York's vice district. And until the Eighth Avenue subway line was opened in 1932, the new station was directly served by only one subway: the Broadway–Seventh Avenue line.

But geography is not destiny; cities, as the writer Jane Jacobs argues, "are wholly existential." The New York Central Railroad, which allowed Manhattan to overcome its island isolation, is decisive testimony that cities are not ordained by geography. And being a local company, with large real estate holdings in Manhattan, it had a stake in urban improvement. As the predominant landlord in the Grand Central Zone, every investment it made or encouraged was money is its pocket. By contrast, the Pennsylvania Railroad, an out-of-town company, did nearly nothing to arrest the decline of the area around its Temple of Transportation. Years later, the editors of *Fortune* would deride the leadership of the Pennsy. "To sensitive New Yorkers the station's body is on Seventh Avenue, but its soul is in Philadelphia. . . . The New York Central, on the other hand, was put together in New York, and New Yorkers think of the Grand Central as a native."

The first big Grand Central Zone projects were built or begun before 1920. Many of them were designed by Warren and Wetmore and were constructed close to, or even directly connected to, the terminal: the Vanderbilt, Biltmore, Roosevelt, and Commodore Hotels; the Yale Club, right across the street on Vanderbilt Avenue; two large office buildings; a major exhibition hall; a U.S. Post Office building; and nearly a dozen high-rise apartment buildings, the most impressive of them Warren and Wetmore's majestic twelve-story Marguery.

Construction of a new Terminal City did not begin in earnest until the postwar recession had run its course in late 1921.* And it occurred with rapidity along three great axes: Park Avenue, from the terminal to Ninety-sixth Street, near the southern border of Harlem; Fifth Avenue, from Forty-second

---

* Terminal City refers to the entire rebuilt area around the terminal, including structures built on land not owned by the Grand Central Railroad. The Grand Central Zone refers to projects built on land owned by the New York Central Railroad.

Street to the upper reaches of Central Park; and East Forty-second Street, from the East River to Times Square, where a new skyscraper business and banking district—a little Wall Street—was created. "Ten years ago, 42nd Street gloried in its four 'towering' skyscrapers . . . beautiful structures [that] were the pride of all Midtown Manhattan," wrote New York booster W. Parker Chase in 1932. "Today, over 50 *new* skyscrapers pierce the sky in this pulsating Midtown district, which tower so far above these former spires of the air that they appear like small town buildings."

Although hardly anyone knew, the high rises on Park Avenue, some of them occupying entire city blocks, were without basements—buildings with railroad tunnels for cellars. Manhattan's Street of Dreams was built on steel stilts.

In 1927, the Grand Central bypass, as originally designed by Wilgus, was nearing completion. A viaduct bridging Forty-second Street and connected to an elevated roadway around one side of the terminal had been finished for some time. The second, or westerly part of the circular roadway, was opened to traffic in the fall of 1928. Park Avenue had been transformed from "an inconvenient local street to the most modern highway in New York," writes historian Christopher Gray. Unhindered by stoplights, motorists passed above the crosstown traffic at Forty-second Street and proceeded up the spine of New York's first planned residential precinct, a civic achievement masterminded and carried through not by municipal government, but by enlightened private enterprise.

William Wilgus had dreamed it; and in the tremendous Manhattan upsurge of the 1920s, he saw it come to fruition, exactly as he predicted: with "revenue plucked from the air."

CHAPTER EIGHT

STREET OF DREAMS

*Park Avenue on the island of Manhattan is the end of the
American ladder of success. Higher one cannot go.*

STUART CHASE, 1927

The Building Boom

It was the most spectacular decade of building in the city's history. During
World War I both commercial and housing construction declined sharply nationwide, with workers and building materials directed toward military mobi-
lization. But after a severe postwar recession, the economy rebounded robustly
in late 1921 and for the next eight years a new building went up in New York
City every fifty-one minutes, on average. Older buildings were demolished at
an equally rapid rate.

The Grand Central Terminal Zone was the eye of this hurricane of construction activity. In the years between the opening of Grand Central and the
Lindbergh parade, the assessed value of land in Terminal City shot up nearly
250 percent. "The city is being rebuilt," wrote *The New York Times* in late 1926.
"In not more than half a dozen years the skyline of midtown Manhattan . . .
[and] Park Avenue has been lifted a hundred feet."

The speculative fever was abetted by an acute postwar shortage of housing
and office space, and by new sources of investment capital available to real
estate developers. "The building orgy outlasted and outdid all others in New
York real estate history," explained historian Arthur Pound, "because ways
and means were found for getting the little fellow's money into big deals." The
commercial real estate business was no longer governed by transactions between one buyer and one seller. Large landholding companies emerged and
sold stock on the open market, making it easier to become a real estate investor

"than buying sugar." Small investors were also enticed into purchasing mortgage bonds. These were created by splitting up large mortgages into smaller, affordable parcels, a practice introduced years earlier by the New York Central and other big railroad companies. Mortgage companies pledged to safeguard the bond holdings of small investors, promising them that their money was more secure than it would be in the vaults of their neighborhood banks. "So assured, a public, ignorant of risk, was drawn into the risky game of real estate speculation," wrote Pound.

When the supply of housing and office space finally began to overtake demand in 1927, New York architects and real estate developers remained serenely confident that blue skies were in the financial forecast for years, perhaps decades, to come. After the speculative bubble burst in October 1929, the solemn guarantees of the bond hucksters proved worthless, and investors, small and large, were ruined. But in the buoyant 1920s, such a bleak scenario was beyond imagining for most New Yorkers.

The building boom fed on itself. Spiraling land values drove up taxes on older rental properties, providing incentive for owners of prime Manhattan real estate to build taller buildings, with more rental space, on their heavily taxed sites. City government poured oil on the fire. In 1921, in response to the housing shortage, it exempted new residential construction from real estate taxes for a period of ten years. No single piece of legislation in New York history gave a greater boost to the city's construction industry. In the 1920s, New York City would account for fully 20 percent of all new residential construction in the country. Builders of large apartment houses were the pacesetters. In 1926, 77 percent of all new residential construction was given over to apartment dwellings.

The following year only five new single-family houses were built in all of Manhattan; and for half of that year, the city's Building Department failed to receive a single application for a permit to put up a private house. Almost none of the new money available for housing went to the construction of apartments for the needy. The returns were vastly greater on high-end construction on Park Avenue than they would have been on modest apartments on the Lower East Side. Here, as in nearly every other sector of the city's commercial culture, profit ruled.

Development along Park Avenue was accelerated and given a distinctive cast by circumstances peculiar to its real estate market. In any large, thickly settled city, it is exceedingly difficult for a developer to acquire separate, but contiguous, parcels of real estate in order to assemble a building lot of sufficient size to put up a big revenue-generating building. This was the attraction of land leased from the New York Central's real estate company. The sole owner of a million square feet of prime Midtown land, the Central leased this land and the air rights over it in large, sometimes block-size, parcels. Urban land offered in this way—already assembled into big lots ready for development—was deeply attractive to speculative builders. But only to those with the means and incentive to construct the kind of housing that yielded the highest return on investment: apartments for the hugely rich.

By leasing rather than selling its air rights, the company was able to "exercise a strict supervision over the architectural features of the buildings." This was important to sharp-eyed capitalists like J. P. Morgan and John D. Rockefeller. Stockholders in the New York Central's real estate company, they also lived in the vicinity of the terminal and were interested in upgrading the area. Though unimaginatively similar in style, the buildings constructed on Grand Central property were among the most substantial and richly appointed in the city, establishing Park Avenue's reputation as the world's most fashionable apartment thoroughfare. "Windows and prim greenery and tall, graceful, white facades rise up from either side of the asphalt stream," wrote Zelda Fitzgerald, "while in the center floats . . . a thin series of watercolor squares of grass—suggesting the Queen's Croquet Ground in *Alice in Wonderland.*"

Mansions in the Sky

By 1927, the commanding apartment buildings along Park Avenue were not just tall; they were immensely tall, true towers, the first skyscrapers built for permanent living. The tallest of them was the Ritz Tower, shooting up from the pavement at the corner of Fifty-seventh Street and Park Avenue. Built for bluebloods and tycoons by Emery Roth, an immigrant Jew from Eastern Europe, it opened in October 1926 and was one of the first residential buildings in New York constructed in sympathy with the city's landmark zoning law of 1916.

Concerned about diminishing sunlight and fresh air in the canyonlike streets created by the closely massed skyscrapers of lower Manhattan, the city placed a limit on the maximum height and bulk of tall buildings. Height limits were based upon the width of the street a building faced; if a developer proposed to exceed the legal limit, the stories above it had to be set back, roughly one foot for each four feet of additional height. Skyscrapers could be of any height, provided they occupied no more than a quarter of their lot.

Forced to work within the confines of the so-called zoning envelope, architects began constructing "set-back" skyscrapers, with sections of the buildings set back further and further as they rose from their bases into the island's sky. "Wedding cake" architecture, some New Yorkers called it; others compared the new-style skyscrapers to the Hanging Gardens of Babylon with their ascending terraces. Great parts of Midtown were being transformed from "brownstone into Babylon," said *The New York Times*.

Unlike apartment houses built only five years earlier on Park and upper Fifth Avenues, most of them twelve to fifteen stories. The Ritz Tower, however, was forty-one stories high. The tallest inhabited building in the world, it dominated the skyline of Midtown Manhattan as the Woolworth Building did that of lower Manhattan. Residents of its upper stories had unobstructed views in all directions for a distance of twenty-five miles on clear days, "panorama[s] unexcelled in all New York," Emery Roth boasted.

It was a new way of living for the rich. They became sky dwellers, their "mansions in the clouds" higher than anyone had ever lived. In its architectural aspirations alone, the Ritz Tower expressed the shoot-for-the-moon spirit of the Jazz Age. Sculpted in rusticated limestone, it rose from its base "like a telescope," up through its set-back terraces to a square tower crowned by a glistening copper roof.

Arthur Brisbane, the internationally known newspaper mogul, had commissioned the building. He wanted to live in it and make money from it. The former editor of William Randolph Hearst's *New York Evening Journal*, flagship of the Hearst newspaper chain, Brisbane authored a column, "Today," that was syndicated in two hundred Hearst papers, and lately had become editor of Hearst's racy tabloid, the New York *Daily Mirror*. Both he and his boss, close friends who had flirted with socialism in their youth, were aggressive investors in Manhattan real estate, partners in Hearst-Brisbane Properties and developers of the Ziegfeld Theatre and the Warwick Hotel on the West Side.

The Ritz Tower was a residential hotel: a type of urban living that had arisen in America in the late nineteenth century and become increasingly popular in 1920s Manhattan. Property taxes, keyed to skyrocketing real estate values, made the urban palaces along Fifth Avenue, north of Forty-second Street, prohibitively expensive to maintain, even for the Vanderbilts. One by one, owners of these ponderous mansions, many of them widows, sold them to real estate speculators and moved to residence hotels along Park Avenue. But the very rich lived in their sky houses only part of the year. Wives, children, and grandchildren spent entire summers abroad or at waterfront "cottages" in Newport, Rhode Island, and newly fashionable Palm Beach, Florida. Working fathers and sons stayed in Manhattan and joined their families at their summer retreats for weekends and extended vacations. In September, families reunited on Park Avenue for the city's obligatory social season, either in residence hotels or in their elegant cousins that took in both resident and transient guests: the Barclay, the Park Lane, and the Drake, names associated with exclusivity and extravagance. "In town it is no longer quite in taste to build marble palaces, however much money one may have. Instead one lives in a hotel," said a Manhattan social arbiter. It was the height of convenience for those who could afford it. Families could close down their summer homes and arrive at their Park Avenue hotel an hour behind their moving truck and baggage. They could then dress for dinner "with a full complement of maids and valets—members of the house staff—and thereafter continue their accustomed mode of life without the slightest break in the calm course of their living. A pen and a check book," said one writer, "are the sole requisites of housekeeping or home making."

But the outstanding attraction of the luxury apartment was the merging of mansion and flat. As the editors of *Interior Architecture* explained, "The city dweller finds combined in the apartment hotel the quiet, the permanence, and, to a certain extent, at least, the personality, of his own house with the conveniences and freedom from responsibility supplied by hotel service, brought to its present perfection."

"This is the age of the apartment," declared Elsie de Wolfe, the city's foremost interior designer. "Modern women demand simplified living, and the apartment reduces the mechanical business of living to its lowest terms." Nowhere more than at the Ritz Tower. Arthur Brisbane hired the Ritz-Carlton Hotel Company, owners of Manhattan's ultra-exclusive Ritz-Carlton Hotel, to manage it. The company ran it like a luxury hostelry, providing residents with full hotel amenities, including maid service, barber and beauty shops, three first-class restaurants, and an Italian tea garden entered through a Florentine gateway. The suites ranged in size from one to eighteen rooms and had serving pantries rather than kitchens. Meals were prepared in a basement kitchen and sent up to the floors on swift, electrically heated dumbwaiters. Servants delivered them to the apartments. When residents desired a different dining experience, they had their chauffeurs drive them down the avenue to the Crillon Restaurant, in the McKim, Mead & White–designed Hecksher Apartments, or to the fashionable Marguery, just across the street.

The Ritz Tower commission was a career breakthrough for Emery Roth, a Hungarian Jew relatively unknown in Manhattan in 1925. Roth was entirely self-trained. In 1884, he arrived in America at age thirteen with only seven dollars in his pocket, a dreamy romantic who loved to paint and draw. His father had died suddenly that year, and his mother, burdened with seven other children, could no longer afford to support him at a Budapest gymnasium on the paltry salary she earned as a village innkeeper. He settled first in Chicago, where he supported himself as a shoeshine boy, and later as a barber's apprentice. Eventually, he found steady work as a draftsman in the office of the firm of Daniel H. Burnham and John Wellborn Root, principal designers of the White City for the World's Columbian Exposition of 1893. "No technical or art school could have afforded me greater opportunities for advancement in design than the two years I spent on that job," Roth wrote in his unpublished memoirs. He called the Chicago fair his "Alma Mater." The austere classicism of its exposition buildings had a lasting influence on him.

When the fair closed in the fall of 1893, Roth moved to New York and secured a minor position in the firm of Richard Morris Hunt, architect of one of the White City's exposition buildings. After Hunt died in 1895, Roth formed his own architectural firm. In 1900, after designing the ten-story Belleclaire apartments on upper Broadway—a jewel of a building—he began receiving commissions from the Bing brothers, Leo and Alexander, whose real estate firm, Bing & Bing, specialized in the construction of apartment buildings in New York's outer boroughs. When the building recession ended, Roth was one of the chief beneficiaries. "The construction boom is on," he wrote excitedly at the time. "God only knows when it will stop."

An aggressive self-promoter, Roth found himself awash in commissions— from Bing & Bing as well as other Jewish developers, many of them fellow émigrés from Eastern Europe. In 1924, he was actively seeking work in new territory—Midtown Manhattan—when he landed the Ritz commission. Two years later he collaborated with Bing & Bing on three impressive apartment hotels: the Dorset, at 30 West Fifty-fourth Street; the twenty-story Hotel Drake, a block south of the Ritz Tower; and the Hotel Alden on Central Park West. All bear the mark of Roth's reverence for the Italian Renaissance.

The Drake and the Dorset exemplify what Roth is best known for—not soaring originality but what has been called the "ensemble" effect. Along with J. E. R. Carpenter, Rosario Candela, and the firm of Schultz and Gross, Roth's chief competitors for luxury apartment house commissions, Roth insisted that a building fit in with its neighboring structures, complementing them rather than competing with them for attention. His still standing apartment hotels in central Manhattan "have a style, an aura to them," writes architectural historian Paul Goldberger, "a sense that a city is made well when the whole is greater than the parts."

The exception is the Ritz Tower, an exuberantly styled building that clashed with the subdued limestone blocks of Warren and Wetmore, the style setters on the avenue. "Monolithic packing cases," social critic Stuart Chase pilloried them in 1927, "structures almost as gaunt as factories," and with dark interior rooms without windows. But "monoliths" like the Marguery, contra Chase, were built around gardenlike interior courtyards, guarantees "made by realty barons that people under their protection will always have enough air—and always morning air," wrote Zelda Fitzgerald. The main rooms of the most expensive apartments were located on the outside walls, either facing the avenue or the courtyard, and had therefore plenty of light and air. And the rooms themselves had "individuality and warmth," observed reporter Will Irwin. Staggering budgets were set aside for interior decoration, money that supported an entire colony of craftsmen and decorators along Madison and Lexington Avenues. A number of apartments had walnut and brass bars imported from London; and one lord of the avenue had a steel safe seven feet high. When he turned the combination and swung open the heavy door there appeared "row upon row . . . a collection of rare old vintages and liqueurs, as dazzling as it [was] priceless."

But no one on the street outdid Arthur Brisbane. He supervised the design of his own aerie, an eighteen-room duplex on the nineteenth and twentieth floors of the Ritz Tower. Here he entertained guests in the princely splendor of his twenty-foot-high living room, modeled after the banquet halls of Florentine palazzos. Brisbane had enough reserves to sustain his lavish lifestyle, but not enough, it turned out, to keep up with the ruinously high mortgage payments on the building. Two years after the Ritz Tower was completed, he sold it, along with his apartment, to Hearst, who moved in with his mistress, actress Marion Davies.

The apartment hotels Roth designed in 1927 placed him in the front ranks of the city's architects and led to hundreds of prestigious commissions. Most of them were on upper Fifth Avenue and Central Park West. The best of them is the still elegant San Remo, completed in 1930, a high, two-towered beauty with captivating views of Central Park. Roth's sons and later partners, Julian and Richard, who wrote their own signatures on the skyline of post–World War II Manhattan, claim that their sensationally prolific father designed more than five hundred apartment buildings in New York. He remains the "unquestioned master of the luxury residential skyscraper," writes Goldberger.

The Ritz Tower, a precedent-shattering building, became the model for dozens of apartment houses and residential hotels suddenly favored by "sky-conscious" New Yorkers in the late 1920s. But even before it was on the drafting board, Alfred Stieglitz and Georgia O'Keeffe took a top-floor apartment at the thirty-four-story Shelton Hotel at Lexington Avenue and Forty-ninth Street. They spent hours gazing at the city's skyline from their windows. O'Keeffe painted skyscrapers that looked like treeless mountains, while Stieglitz photographed them just as they were.

In the more aristocratic parts of Park Avenue, a new type of masonry cliff, the cooperative apartment, became "the order of the day." The residents were the ostensible owners, although unlike the currently popular condominium model, they did not own the walls and floors of their apartments. They held stock in a corporation that owned the building, their number of shares keyed to the size and amenities of their apartments. Shareholders were assessed monthly maintenance fees and expected to behave according to "a set of commandments" set down in their "proprietary lease," strictures enforced by an elected board of directors. Some of the rules were outrageous: prohibitions against eating in the building's elevators or sitting on the furniture in the lobby while waiting for guests. Committees composed of powerful residents intrusively scrutinized the personal lives and bank accounts of prospective buyers. The tyrannical board of one super-exclusive cooperative had applicants write an essay on why they aspired to live at that august address. While money remained the key consideration for entering the gilded gates of a Manhattan cooperative, some boards excluded successful actors and musicians, Jews and African Americans. Occasionally, newly rich Italians and Irish were denied without explanation. Upward-striving New Yorkers seeking what F. Scott Fitzgerald called "the consoling proximity of millionaires" had to surrender their self-esteem for the privilege.

By the end of the 1920s, the cliff dwellers of Manhattan were beginning to appropriate for their own pleasure the once forlorn roofs of apartment buildings. The "Cinderella" of New York architecture, the "penthouse," or roof apartment, had for decades been considered the least attractive part of a high building, a boxlike residence for the servant class, set among soot-scarred chimneys and wooden water tanks. In the late 1920s, these cramped dormitories for the laboring class were torn down and replaced by new luxury quarters, some of them fronted by floral gardens "as impressive as the formal terraces of a Newport mansion," said reporter Virginia Pope.

Pope saw "a new chapter of New York's social history . . . being written above the roof line. Balls and dinners are given in the luminous apartments during the winter season. When warm weather comes 'garden parties' take place on the balustraded terraces and there are 'al fresco' lunches, teas and after-theatre suppers." In their roof houses, New Yorkers achieved "a detachment impossible to any dwelling set on earth," said Will Irwin. There were no neighbors in sight; "only the tainted air above Manhattan."

Up this high, "the noises of the city are but a gentle hum," observed a writer from *The New Yorker*. This gave pointed emphasis to the avenue's envious geographic advantage—a garden street close to the swirling center of Midtown, its corporate towers, theaters, stores, and restaurants. And if one wanted to go slumming, it was a quick taxi or limousine ride to Texas Guinan's 300 Club, or to Jack and Charlie's Puncheon, where Park Avenue bigwigs were treated like royalty.

Everything the rich needed to sustain their urban lifestyle was close at hand. After the completion of Grand Central Terminal, some of the most privileged social clubs of the city began migrating to Park Avenue. The impossibly restrictive Union Club, the oldest social club in the country, purchased a Park Avenue building site in 1927, nine years after the Racquet & Tennis Club's new McKim, Mead & White building was completed a few blocks north of Grand Central. Close by, on West Forty-fourth Street, was the clubhouse of the New York Yacht Club, the most exclusive sporting club in the world. Founded in 1844, it was the preserve of the Morgans, the Astors, and the Vanderbilts.

Melting Pot of the Rich

In 1927, the street of "stone canyons" made fair claim "to the most stupendous aggregation of multimillionaires which the world has ever seen." Compared with Park Avenue, "the Faubourg St. Germain is a beggar and Mayfair a barmaid," said Will Irwin. Unlike late-nineteenth-century Fifth Avenue, it was a melting pot of the rich, where new money mingled with old. Fortunes on Park Avenue were accumulated in countless ways: in the solid enterprises Gilded Age tycoons built and controlled—oil and steel, banking and railroads, tobacco and cotton—and in the adventurous enterprises of an emerging mass consumption economy—motion pictures, motor cars, radio, and the marketing of everything from toothpaste to toilet tissue. There were also "butter-and-egg" men on Park Avenue, as well as ravishing young women with no visible means of support, visited in the night, or around the lunch hour, by silver-haired gentlemen in limousines.

In a new departure, the "long arrived" and the "newly arrived" lived side by side, even if they didn't communicate with one another. Mixed in with them were "gold-seekers from across the ocean . . . dispossessed German princes, grand-dukes, Magi, outlandish diplomats, fashionable psycho-analysts, and mendicant ladies from the Old World masking their snares beneath their smiles," wrote visiting French novelist Paul Morand.

In 1927, there were approximately fifteen thousand millionaires in America. Of these, over three thousand resided in New York City, and more than half of them lived on Park Avenue. At least fifty certified millionaires lived in one apartment building on the avenue. Not even Fifth Avenue in its most opulent era could "boast such serried phalanxes of millionaires. More fashion it may have had, more individuality, more resplendent names bursting above the rooftops of an adolescent nation—Vanderbilts, Goulds, Astors . . . but never such solid, crushing and cascading wealth." If money was the sole measure of the good life, America truly had a heaven, said Stuart Chase, and Park Avenue was it.

The purchasing power of this privileged class was breathtaking, concentrated purchasing power that exceeded, in all probability, that of any large group of people living in any city, in any age. With only one-third of one percent of New York City's population, Park Avenue spent nearly three and a half times more for personal living expenses than the city allotted for education, and one-fifth of what the forty-eight states combined allocated for elementary and secondary public schools. "The man who earns only $50,000 a year is a poor man if he lives on Park Avenue," said H. Gordon Duval, president of the Park Avenue Association and the unofficial "paladin" of the avenue. This was in 1927, when a New York City industrial worker with a wife and four children was statistically living above the poverty line if he made $1,880 a year, or $36 a week.

Many members of the new money crowd, among them theater mogul Harry Frazee, were conspicuous in the nightlife of the city. The transplanted Fifth Avenue set, on the other hand, lived discreet and interior lives, their social circles confined to like-thinking families with "aged-in-the wood money": fortunes accumulated before the Great War and the bull market. This "distinguishes them," wrote family renegade Cornelius Vanderbilt, Jr., "from the [somewhat younger] Park Avenue set that acquired its pearls, chinchilla wraps and yachts only after Gavrilo Princip shot the Archduke." The old-money families "salted away the bulk of their inherited fortunes in government bonds and cash . . . they never gambled on margin," wrote Vanderbilt in his hilarious exposé, *Farewell to Fifth Avenue.* The general public saw the women—but only rarely—being helped into their limousines by uniformed doormen, and the men ascending the steps of the all-male Racquet & Tennis Club, with top hats and canes, and "the mustaches of British officers." More conspicuous were the residents' small and exotic dogs, out for a walk twice a day on the leashes of white-gloved "housemen."

On Park Avenue in the 1920s there could still be found "relics of the sow's ear age"—small brick grocery stores, butcher shops, real estate offices, a commercial garage, and even a tire shop. But heavy industrial traffic was prohibited and residents fought resolutely to keep their street free of "ribald commercialism." Several private bus lines applied unsuccessfully for franchises to operate on the avenue, but their bids were discouraged by, of all people, Mayor Walker, who promised its predominantly Republican residents he would do all in his power to preserve their street as "the last really residential avenue in the city."

Even the Metropolitan Opera House, searching for a site for its new and more magnificent home, was unwelcome. "In season, there would be disturbing noises and undue commotion," protested the Park Avenue Association.

Summer at Sea

"I love New York on summer afternoons when everyone's away," says Jordan Baker in *The Great Gatsby*. Come June, the residents of Park Avenue headed either for the cooling breezes of seaside resorts or for the grand hotels of the continent. "Park Avenue virtually commutes across the Atlantic," wrote social observer Maurice Mermey.

The transatlantic journey began the night before sailing, when the bags were sent ahead, mountains of them, delivered straight to ships' cabins by a special teamster service. A bon voyage dinner was held the next evening at a friend's apartment or at a chic Midtown speakeasy. Then the travelers would head off by taxi or limousine to the Chelsea Piers, accompanied by relatives and friends. Many of the major lines sailed at midnight, and approaching one of the long finger piers in a crowded car, the ship looked "incredibly romantic, floodlit and overrun with people in evening dress."

The great liners sailed for Europe from the Hudson River waterfront between Twenty-third and Twenty-ninth Streets, where in 1927 as many as a dozen ocean liners tied up or cast off every day. These floating communities, the largest moving objects built up to then, were virtually part of the city. Their bows hugged the shore so tightly they became "fragment[s] of Manhattan," wrote Paul Morand. In no other place in the world did ocean liners berth so near the pulsing life of the town.

In this city of the sea, with more deep-water frontage than any other harbor on earth, it was the custom to escort one's friends all the way to their cabins. Some well-wishers went to the piers so often they were on speaking terms with captains and pursers. While the crew of one of these monarchs of the sea made final preparations to sail there might be as many as five thousand visitors onboard, more of them than there were passengers. When the warning whistle blew, announcing that the ship was about to put out to sea, there were shouted conversations between the crowds on the pier and their departing friends, hanging on the ship's rails. After a final blast from the ship's whistle, the great ocean vessel stirred and moved with a silence that was "phantomlike." The well-wishers then scrambled for places at the river end of the pier, waving handkerchiefs and scarves. Out on the Hudson, the ship was swung around by a dozen furiously working tugs. Moving down the harbor, her broadside to the pier, the gleaming portholes resembled a giant necklace.

———————

Returning to New York by sea was as impressive, if not as uplifting, as leaving it. Incoming passengers, gazing at the city's serrated skyline, the mountains of Manhattan, could almost feel the beat of the city while still at steam in the harbor. In his lighthearted 1927 book, *The Frantic Atlantic*, Basil Woon wrote that Americans went to Europe in search of "drinks, divorces and dresses." But many privileged Americans found a kind of serenity abroad, even those who had endured forced marches through Europe's fabled resorts. "The leisurely pace they learned to savor over the summer was disrupted somewhere just south of the Battery," writes historian John Maxtone-Graham. "Like some infectious plague over the water came a compelling urge for haste. The familiar tempo was there, the race of traffic that swarmed and buzzed through fissures in Manhattan's concrete bluffs. Assembled aimlessly in shore suits and faces, none could resist that frenetic call."

When the docking hour was announced, passengers heading for points west would send a wireless to the maître d' of the Waldorf-Astoria at Thirty-third Street, asking him to secure space on "the only thinkable train," the Grand Central's 20th Century Limited.

The patricians of Park Avenue had their chauffeurs waiting for them at the pier to carry them crosstown as fast as traffic would allow, up grimy West Street, on the waterfront, through a "surging mass of back-firing, horn-blowing, gear-grinding trucks and taxies," insistent reminders of the call of commerce. Commerce—the force that had shaped their city, their destinies, and the curiously provincial precinct they called home.

CHAPTER NINE

VANISHING SOCIAL CITADELS

How this city marches northward!

—GEORGE TEMPLETON STRONG

Vanderbilt Country

The end of an era in New York history was foretold in May 1925 when local newspapers reported the sale of the Astor mansion at 840 Fifth Avenue, across from Central Park. It was one of the most famous addresses in the city, the white marble palace where the late Caroline Webster Schermerhorn Astor—"*The* Mrs. Astor" as she preferred to be called to set her apart from family rivals—entertained a select set of rich and well-born New Yorkers, known as the "Four Hundred," roughly the number of guests who could fit comfortably into Mrs. Astor's ballroom at her former residence at 350 Fifth Avenue. The sale signaled the transfer of property from old to emerging money and was engineered by the richest of all the Astors, and the one least respectful of the family's commercial and political lineage.

Young, devastatingly handsome Vincent Astor, an internationally known sportsman and philantropist, had inherited the bulk of his father's fortune in 1912 when he was a twenty-year-old student at Harvard and Colonel John Jacob Astor IV went down with the *Titanic*. The Colonel, son of "*The* Mrs. Astor," had left instructions in his will that Madeleine, the eighteen-year-old woman he had taken as his second wife only a year before sailing on the *Titanic*, could live in the Astor mansion provided she remained a widow. When she remarried in 1916, she was banished from the family seat. Nine years later Vincent, who felt no lingering allegiance to the place, sold it for $3 million.

And to the horror of his grandmother's haughty Protestant friends, he sold it to a recently rich Polish Jew.

Blazingly ambitious Benjamin Winter had arrived in New York virtually penniless at the turn of the century and risen rapidly to become one of the most successful real estate speculators in New York. A sharp-elbowed arriviste to residents of upper Fifth Avenue, Winter told reporters he planned to demolish the Astor residence and replace it with a high-rise apartment hotel, one of the first in that neighborhood of old townhouses and mansions. "The announcement," said *The New York Times,* "caused a sensation."

Surviving members of the Four Hundred considered the sale of the Astor home to an outsider an act of class betrayal. But Vincent and his radiant wife Helen Dinsmore Huntington had separated themselves from this stodgy crowd. In 1927, they bought a townhouse on upper Fifth Avenue. There and at their Long Island estate, they entertained writers, artists, and entertainers, a class of people Vincent's grandmother had looked upon with studied disdain.

The Astor mansion, at the corner of Fifth Avenue and Sixty-fifth Street, stood considerably north of the stretch of Fifth dominated by the Vanderbilts, whose continuous line of mansions was one of the spectacles of the city. But it was known that Benjamin Winter had that family's residential colony in his sights. In May 1925, two weeks after sealing the deal for the Astor mansion, Winter made his first incursion into Vanderbilt territory, purchasing the empty mansion of Anne Harriman Vanderbilt, on the northwest corner of Fifth Avenue and Fifty-second Street. Anne was the second wife of the late William Kissam Vanderbilt, the New York Central director who had hired Warren and Wetmore to complete Grand Central Terminal. When "William K." died in 1920, he left his widow their urban château on Fifth Avenue and a trust of $8 million. Unwilling to pay the heavy cost of upkeep, and uninterested in playing the role of a society hostess, Anne Vanderbilt had escaped to Sutton Place, a seedy area along the Midtown shoreline of the East River that she and a group of her wealthy friends hoped to revive. On the day Benjamin Winter purchased her vacated mansion, he announced plans to raze it and construct a twenty-story business building on the site. This presaged the end of the castlelike piles south of Central Park. It was a pivot point in the history of the city, the eclipse of a metropolitan era dominated by the Vanderbilts, successors to the Astors as New York's most powerful social clan. The family had built this neighborhood within walking distance of the Commodore's rail station and transformed it into a showcase of their staggering wealth and power. This had been Vanderbilt Country.

Beginning in the 1890s, the Vanderbilts were joined on Fifth Avenue by other "titans of new money." They comprised a veritable "who's who" of American economic might: Andrew Carnegie, Henry Clay Frick, Charles Schwab, Harry Payne Whitney, F. W. Woolworth, Charles T. Yerkes, Elbridge T. Gerry, Solomon Guggenheim, James B. Duke, Harry Flagler, and Collis P. Huntington. With the Vanderbilts dominating their own stretch of the avenue, these later arrivals built their urban fortresses on the blocks directly north of Vanderbilt Alley, on the shaded stretch of Fifth Avenue facing Central Park. "Two miles of millionaires," *Munsey's Magazine* called that part of Fifth Avenue above Forty-second Street. In this "plutocratic side of the metropolis, [there is] a concentration of wealth and splendor not equaled in any other capital of the world," it noted.

In the mid-1920s this tight little world came under direct assault. By then, Park Avenue had supplanted Fifth Avenue as the most fashionable address in the city; and commerce was driving headlong up Fifth Avenue, with real estate moguls like Benjamin Winter in the vanguard. Although Winter constructed apartment towers on upper Fifth Avenue, he and other developers were prevented by municipal zoning ordinances from constructing commercial office buildings, stores, and hotels on that part of Millionaires' Row. Winter knew that the big money was to be made south of Fifty-ninth Street. Here, as well, commerce had already begun to make deep incursions.

Since the turn of the century, the Vanderbilts had been battling to blunt the advance of trade into their "sacred precinct," buying underdeveloped lots near their urban estates and selling or leasing them to a select circle of friends. In 1901, when a syndicate of developers announced plans to build a high-rise hotel on the corner directly across from the home of William Kissam Vanderbilt, he and one of his brothers bought the lot for a million dollars and sold it to railroad financier Morton F. Plant, who constructed an attractive limestone townhouse. But Plant disappointed them. In 1917, he sold the property to Cartier, the Paris jewelry firm, which had opened its first Manhattan shop eight years earlier. Legend has it that Plant exchanged the building for a two-strand pearl necklace valued at $1 million, an item his wife coveted.

Around this time, city government ordered the removal of stoops, gardens, and bay windows along Vanderbilt Alley, claiming they impeded the movement of shoppers. The Vanderbilts were outraged, but powerless to turn back the future. The stab to the heart came in 1926 when a group of Fifth Avenue potentates tried to stop Benjamin Winter from erecting his skyscraper on the site of the recently demolished Anne Vanderbilt mansion at Fifth Avenue and Fifty-second. Their lawsuit hinged on a nineteenth-century covenant preventing the erection of commercial buildings on that block of Fifth Avenue.

In a surprisingly quick decision, the New York Supreme Court ruled in favor of Winter, arguing that the restrictions written into property transfers over a hundred years ago had become "extinct."

In the year of that watershed decision, Benjamin Winter found two other Vanderbilts eager to sell, which left only one Vanderbilt mansion out of the original seven on Fifth Avenue. The previous year, Alice Vanderbilt, widow of Cornelius II, the Commodore's grandson, had sold her gigantic urban château on Fifth Avenue and West Fifty-seventh Street to a syndicate headed by Frederick Brown, a German-Jewish immigrant with real estate holdings as extensive as Benjamin Winter's. Brown demolished Alice's turreted and castellated monstrosity, and by the end of 1927 every Vanderbilt palace on Fifth Avenue that had been sold had been torn down. Wrecking crews were also busy farther up the avenue, where the marble and stone mansions of some of the city's most prestigious merchant families—the Woolworths, the Guggenheims, the Goulds, and the Brokaws—were razed and replaced by apartment towers that continue to form the skyline of the East Fifties.

The lone Vanderbilt holdout was Alice's son, Brigadier General Cornelius Vanderbilt III, "Neily," as family members called him. He and his wife, Grace Wilson Vanderbilt, daughter of New York banker Richard T. Wilson, resided at 640 Fifth Avenue, the former home of the Commodore's successor, William Henry Vanderbilt, the founding father of Vanderbilt Alley. Grace spent a fortune transforming it into one of New York's most fashionable addresses. A steely-eyed martinet, she attended to nearly every detail and entertained lavishly while her husband—an inventor, engineer, and World War I combat veteran—spent great parts of the year on his yacht, or when in New York, reading military history and drinking prodigious quantities of beer in his leather-lined study. Besieged by Benjamin Winter, Frederick Brown, and other real estate speculators, Grace and her indifferent but obliging husband spurned all offers to sell the family's final stronghold on the avenue. Hemmed in by commerce, it became a "shrine dedicated to archaic rituals and fading splendor."

Although the Vanderbilts and other old New Yorker families continued to launch their daughters into New York society at debutante balls, they had become foreigners in their own city. In 1890, New York City was 48.8 percent Protestant, 39.2 percent Roman Catholic, and 12 percent Jewish. By 1920 the Protestant and Catholic percentages had dropped to 34.6 percent each, while the Jewish proportion had increased to 29.2 percent. "The changes involved more than numbers," writes historian Ben Yagoda. "Over that period the white Protestant aristocracy of New York was eclipsed in prominence and, to a measure, power—not simply by Jews and Catholics, but by an entire new class of New Yorkers who had earned rather than inherited their money and who expected to earn their way into society on their merits." Rather than competing with these fast-rising groups, respectable society treated them with "Jovian aloofness," as if they did not exist. A few chose to move permanently to Europe, or to travel incessantly, abandoning the surging city "where existence," wrote Paul Morand, "is meaningless for the idle."

"It must be tragic for the bearers of the great old names to discover (if they do discover) how completely they have been superseded," wrote Hulbert Footner. Grace Wilson Vanderbilt was one of few who would not concede defeat. Until her death in 1953, at age eighty-two, she continued to entertain in gilded splendor, with formal dinner parties and afternoon teas. Her resplendently uniformed servants rolled out a red velvet carpet from the entrance of her home to the curb for visiting kings and queens, presidents and princes. She was the last of the Fifth Avenue Vanderbilts, a woman of invincible resolve struggling to hold together the remnants of the city's Edwardian aristocracy.*

Some New Yorkers viewed these changes with profound regret. Lost forever, victims of the "march of business," were "New York's Social Citadels," said *Vanity Fair.* Editors at that smugly stylish sheet went further, placing the onus on "speculators and traders who only ten years ago boasted of no fortunes at all." These "operators" were charged with "driving the Vanderbilts and the Astors from Fifth Avenue."

Asked by *The New York Times* to comment on his conquest of Fifth Avenue, Benjamin Winter, a small, quick-witted man with flashing eyes, insisted he was performing a "civic service." It came down to "sentiment or progress, and I thought that progress should come first." Luxury apartment buildings were, he said, the avenue's new "commercial" palaces, and were a style of living more appropriate to changing times. And in any event, the owners of the "vanishing social citadels" had not sold them "unwillingly," as *Vanity Fair* claimed. The irony, Winter insinuated, was appropriate. Commerce had put the Vanderbilts on Fifth Avenue, and changing commercial conditions had driven them off it.

A capitalist with imperial designs, Winter saw the destiny of Fifth Avenue through the lens of his own recent accomplishments. A new generation of businessman was authoring a fresh chapter in the history of what had long been the city's choicest address. Like the Commodore in his prime, Winter saw himself as an urban builder whose private speculations were producing salubrious civic changes.

---

* Grace Wilson Vanderbilt finally moved out of her Fifth Avenue mansion after her husband's death in 1942. The house was torn down to make way for a skyscraper. She continued to host gatherings for the old guard in her new townhouse on upper Fifth Avenue. NYT, January 8, 1953.

"It was an exciting time to be a builder in New York City," writes a historian of New York City real estate. For immigrant entrepreneurs "nothing could be more American than to tame a plot of land and erect on it a pioneering structure, to take part in what America prided itself on doing best—inventing the future and making it solid." By 1927, 80 percent of the speculative builders in the city were Jewish, a great number of them immigrants. Some had gotten their start in the garment industry, making or selling clothing for pennies an hour, and had then moved into real estate, building industrial lofts for their own and other clothing enterprises. By the mid-1920s, a number of them had sufficient capital to erect grand hotels, department stores, and office blocks in the heart of Midtown.

One of the most successful of them was Frederick Brown, son of a successful Carlsbad, Germany, landlord. Set up for a comfortable life in his home city, he was drawn in another direction, captivated by Rose Levy, a dark-eyed American beauty visiting Germany with her mother. Arriving in New York on the same ship that carried Rose and her mother back home in 1905, Brown found employment with a clothing dealer in lower Manhattan, and within a few months established his own store in Paterson, New Jersey, not far from the home of the girl he would soon marry. But "the bigness and opportunities of New York never left my mind," he recalled years later, "and I determined to follow the bent of my forebears in real estate." He moved back to Manhattan with his new family and began buying and developing tenement properties on the Lower East Side. By the early 1920s he was purchasing for resale entire city blocks on Park and Fifth Avenues and helping to assemble the sites for Saks Fifth Avenue and the Savoy-Plaza and Sherry-Netherland Hotels, both hotels near the southern entrance to Central Park. An avid art collector, he owned works by Van Dyck, Rubens, and Gainsborough, along with two of the most valuable Rembrandts in existence. Eventually he would surpass Benjamin Winter as the largest individual real estate developer in the country. Operating out of a Manhattan office staffed by only five employees—a secretary, a stenographer, two bookkeepers, and a switchboard operator—he pulled in over $60 million a year.

Benjamin Winter's rise was even more astounding. A native of Lodz, Poland, he and his family booked passage to New York in 1901, when he was nineteen years old, with aspirations to be a portrait painter. While attending night school to learn English, he searched for employment. "I can paint," he told an inquiring uncle. "Good," said his uncle, who badly misunderstood him. "You can make $6 or $7 a week at that." A week later, with his uncle's intervention, he was employed in a paint plant on the Upper East Side. Toiling twelve hours a day, he put aside enough money to go into business for himself as a painting contractor. It took him twelve years to save his first thousand dollars. He used the money to buy a shabby house he remodeled and converted into apartments—his initial plunge into real estate. At first, he focused exclusively on the tenement house market of lower Manhattan. After the war he began investing heavily in mid-Manhattan properties, borrowing capital from fellow Polish Jews hungry to make a killing in the city's postwar land bonanza. By 1925, he was one of the most powerful land traders in Midtown; his real estate deals averaged $5 million weekly. Four years later, he would own over five hundred million dollars of Manhattan real estate.

Finding it increasingly difficult and expensive to raise capital for the big, venturesome deals he was making on Fifth Avenue, he formed his own real estate investment company in 1927. That year, Winter Incorporated began making public offerings of preferred and common stock through a Wall Street brokerage firm. He called this public financing of his operations "the most significant event in recent real estate history," far more consequential than the mortgage bonds that traders had been offering to individual investors for some time. Companies like his, linking real estate and Wall Street, proliferated in the late 1920s. They signified, said Winter, "the beginning of a new era in the development of real estate on an extensive scale . . . in which the public can now share . . . in the growth of the great [corporations] of the country." His company, he claimed, was opening opportunities for small traders to become part of "the romance of reality in New York."*

"The real estate market is becoming more and more a competitor of the stock market for the favor of investors," reported *The New York Times*. But by luring small investors into their operations, speculative land dealers were putting them at great risk. When Winter went bust during the Great Depression, he took down with him hundreds of modest coupon cutters.

Bankrupt in 1937, Winter would recoup most of his fortune before his death in 1944, unlike the Fifth Avenue Vanderbilts, who never recovered from their shockingly sudden loss of power and status.

Sutton Place

In January 1921, *The New York Times* reported that Anne Harriman Vanderbilt planned to "lead an exodus from Fifth Avenue . . . to Sutton Place," an area

---

* Mortgage bonds split large commercial mortgages into small units that were sold to thousands of investors. Winter took the next step, giving the public the opportunity to participate more directly in the real estate market through ownership of stock in a real estate corporation.

of decaying brownstones on a short extension of Avenue A known as Sutton Place, between Fifty-seventh and Fifty-eighth Streets. Situated on high ground along the East River, in the shadow of the Queensboro Bridge, this tiny urban precinct became a forerunner of modern-day gentrification.

Forty-eight-year-old Anne Morgan, daughter of J. P. Morgan, left her overbearing father's brownstone palace on Murray Hill, just east of Fifth Avenue, to join her friend and lover. Anne had become passionately attracted to tall, regal-looking Anne Vanderbilt. Although neither acknowledged the relationship publicly, the two famous heiresses lived side by side in adjoining townhouses: Vanderbilt at One Sutton Place, at the northeast corner of Fifty-seventh Street, and Morgan at 3 Sutton Place. Lounging in Adirondack chairs on Morgan's terraced rear garden, they could look out at "the eddying whirlpools of the river."

When Mrs. Vanderbilt moved from Fifth Avenue to One Sutton Place this isolated Midtown neighborhood had for decades been in steep decline, populated largely by bohemian artists and laborers attracted by its low rents. In 1920, a consortium of investors purchased a row of dilapidated brownstones on Sutton Place, fixed them up, and put them on the market. But it was not until Anne Vanderbilt and Anne Morgan moved to Sutton Place, as the entire "redeemed" riverfront community came to be called, that it began to attract residents with money to invest. Many of the pioneers were women of social standing, active in common philanthropic enterprises, widows and daughters of capitalist grandees who had lived on Fifth Avenue or downtown on Gramercy Square, home to some of New York's founding families. Sutton Place had suddenly become New York's newest "society colony," said *The New York Times* in 1921. "Rich Move Eastward," the paper headlined.*

In the early 1920s, Sutton Place was "the only cluster of homes in New York built largely by and for women," writes historian Alfred Allan Lewis—women of "independent means" and "independent minds." It was not long, however, before big investors and affluent married couples were drawn to the place. In 1924 the first cooperative apartment house went up, financed by the Phipps Corporation, a real estate company founded by Pittsburgh steel magnate Henry Phipps, Jr. It was called One Sutton Place South and was built on the site of an old coal storage facility. Opportunistically, the Phipps Corporation used the names of the neighborhood's "patrician pioneers" as "bait" to attract desirable tenants.

---

* Today, Anne Morgan's former home is the residence of the secretary-general of the United Nations.

Phipps commissioned a penthouse on the building's roof for his daughter Amy and her dashing aviator husband, Frederick E. Guest, the former private secretary of his cousin Winston Churchill. The showcase apartment had a wall of French doors that opened to river views and was surrounded by "voluptuous sky gardens and brick-and-tile patios." It was the talk of Manhattan. When Mrs. Vincent Astor came to visit, she said it made her Fifth Avenue townhouse "look like a pigsty."

In the 1920s, a Sutton Place address "placed you among the knowing who considered Fifth Avenue absurdly passé and Park Avenue vulgarly ostentatious," wrote one social commentator. By 1927, the riverfront gentrification had spread southward into neighboring Beekman Place, situated on a high river bluff, called Cannon Point, which extends from Forty-ninth to Fifty-first Streets. Once the summer estate of the descendants of eighteenth-century merchant prince James Beekman, it had become in the late nineteenth century an industrial slum, with cigar factories, cattle yards, fat-rendering plants, and a brewery, all of which used the river as a dump. In the 1920s, the area underwent a third transformation, becoming a select "colony of millionaires, people of the theater, [and] highly paid artists and writers."

The reconstituted Beekman Place was the work of two sharp-eyed urban visionaries: the developer Joseph G. Thomas and his wife, muralist Clara Fargo Thomas. Charmed by the location, the couple commissioned, as speculations, three luxurious apartments in 1924. The first was rented quickly, and other residents were soon attracted to the cliff-side colony's shaded streets, turning decaying brownstones into some of the handsomest townhouses in Manhattan.

An enlightened site planner, Thomas was decades ahead of his time. New Yorkers are "only just beginning to realize what our waterfronts might mean to us," Clara spoke for both of them. Thomas had his apartments built with a waterfront theme, a stab at re-creating an American Venice on the banks of the East River. Beekman Terrace, the first to be built, overlooked the water at Fifty-first Street. A lower garden descended to a small pier with bas-reliefs of St. Mark, the patron saint of Venice. Joseph Thomas planned to introduce gondolas, but was talked out of launching these unsteady craft on a greasy tidal stream crowded with tugs and coal barges. But a private boat service was provided for tenants and Thomas named the third of his Beekman Place apartments the Campanile. Completed in 1930 in Venetian Gothic style, it drew celebrity tenants, among them Noel Coward, Greta Garbo, and theater critic and "21" regular, Alexander Woollcott. "Beekman Place brings an exclamation of pleasure from all who see it for the first time," said roving reporter Hulbert Footner. "There is no traffic here. It could hardly be believed

that so quiet and secluded a spot could exist within a stone's throw of roaring
First Avenue."

By 1929, an unbroken line of exclusive apartment buildings and townhouses,
a mile long and less than a mile wide, extended along the rugged bluffs of
the East River. And from Sutton Place, two long rows of high-rise apartment
towers had been built, facing one another across Fifty-seventh Street, in the
direction of Grand Army Plaza at Fifth Avenue. This was one of the great attractions of sequestered Sutton Place: its proximity to Fifth Avenue, only a few
blocks away, up Fifty-seventh Street, past Emery Roth's Ritz Tower, on the corner of Park and Fifty-seventh. By 1927, Fifty-seventh Street, from the entrance
to the Queensboro Bridge to the Plaza Hotel, was Manhattan's most exclusive
crosstown shopping street, America's Rue de la Paix. Discriminating shoppers
favored this generously wide thoroughfare to the narrow, thickly congested
sidewalks around Herald Square, home to Macy's department store. "Milady
likes to spend her money without having to battle street crowds," wrote one
commentator.

By this time the former Vanderbilt Alley on Fifth Avenue had become the
city's most prestigious fashion center, "the aristocrat of shopping thoroughfares." Merchants and developers had come to consider this entire section of
Midtown, from the East River to Fifth Avenue, as a single, continuous region
of luxurious living and shopping. "Fifth Avenue has ceased to be merely the
name of a street," wrote a local business correspondent. "It now designates a
section embracing not only Fifth Avenue but neighboring Madison and Park
Avenues, and intersecting cross-streets in the heart of the metropolis. Its area
is one and one-half square miles—the richest and most desirable shopping
center in the United States, probably in the world."

By demolishing the Vanderbilt mansions, Benjamin Winter and Frederick
Brown had opened opportunities for new businesses on the cleared land, among
them high-fashion stores and beauty salons devoted to the "ultra-exquisite."
The finest of these soon-to-be legendary Fifth Avenue establishments were
born in the minds of a new breed of Manhattan millionaires, merchandising
visionaries—several of them women—who changed the consumption patterns
of twentieth-century Americans.

CHAPTER TEN

THE WOMAN'S CITY

Where are the men? A few representatives of the bullied sex
struggle for place, it is true; but their soberer garments and
apologetic mien seem to bury them.

WILL IRWIN, 1927

Prince of the Avenue

In March 1927, Frederick Brown was finalizing one of the biggest real estate transactions in the history of Fifth Avenue. Edwin Goodman, the Jewish clothing merchant, leased from Brown's real estate corporation part of the land cleared by the recent demolition of the Alice Vanderbilt mansion at Fifth Avenue and Fifty-seventh Street. It was one of the prize parcels in the city, large and splendidly situated, facing Grand Army Plaza and the Plaza Hotel. Goodman also leased part of the shell of a high-rise commercial building being constructed on the site. This was the uncompleted structure from which construction workers would salute Charles Lindbergh on the final leg of his parade up Fifth Avenue in June of that year.

The building site was to be the new location of Bergdorf Goodman, Edwin Goodman's sensationally successful women's clothing business, located just down the street at 616 Fifth Avenue. For Goodman, it was a risky move. The lease was $300,000 a year, more than his accountants said he could afford; and his competitors were certain he was overreaching, moving farther north than anyone in the retail clothing trade had ever ventured. For weeks before and after the deal was consummated, Goodman was physically ill with worry, his brittle nerves on edge. He had taken a step so "perilous" that he cautiously decided to divide his new store into shoplike sections that he could sublet should business at the new location falter or fail.

191

Goodman need not have worried. His timing was impeccable. The move up the avenue put him "close to the greatest buying power in the world." His new Bergdorf Goodman store would be in excellent proximity to upper Fifth Avenue, Park Avenue, Sutton Place, and Beekman Place—chic Midtown neighborhoods undergoing a high-rise building boom at precisely the time Goodman put ink on the real estate contract.

Goodman had been on Fifth Avenue for some time, only far less conspicuously. Unlike his current plain-faced shop, the new marble-fronted emporium that Brown's architects were designing would be "a mansion-style commercial building." Its green-tiled mansard roof and signature show windows would make it a beacon for upscale Manhattan shoppers and a Midtown landmark as distinctive in its own right as the Vanderbilt château.

When the nine-story building was completed in 1928, Goodman sold his brownstone home on the Upper West Side and moved his family into a penthouse he designed on the top floor of the store, with a panoramic view of upper Manhattan. When sales doubled the following year he doubled the size of the store's Fifth Avenue frontage by leasing the shops directly south of it. In less than a decade, he would own his store and the entire block between Fifty-seventh and Fifty-eighth Streets on his side of Fifth Avenue. His purchases reunited under his ownership the complete site of the old Vanderbilt mansion. This was supremely satisfying to Edwin Goodman. A former garment worker from Rochester, New York, he was the new prince of the avenue.

"On Manhattan, there are *couturier* houses as 'exclusive' as Bergdorf Goodman," said *Fortune* in 1931. "Yet the incomes of these houses are comparatively modest, their clienteles comparatively small. None of them has succeeded in clothing women in an exclusive way on so magnificent a scale as that which Mr. Goodman has achieved, with 18,000 customers on his books." Edwin Goodman was by then one of the preeminent figures in international haute couture, and he had ascended to this position "by a series of moves, each one more improbable than the last."

Born in Lockport, New York, and raised in nearby Rochester, the son and grandson of German-Jewish shopkeepers, Goodman took a job at a local tailoring business after dropping out of high school, work he embraced with a fervor that puzzled his parents. At age nineteen, he headed to New York City, the world center of the women's garment industry. After working for several years as a cutter and fitter of women's clothing, he partnered in 1901 with Herman Bergdorf, owner of a thriving gas-lit tailor shop at Fifth Avenue and Nineteenth Street.

Goodman was perfect for the position. Bergdorf catered to fashionable ladies from farther up Fifth Avenue, and slender, rakishly handsome Edwin Goodman was a painstakingly proficient fitter, popular with both society matrons and their impressionable daughters. The aging Bergdorf, a pleasure-loving immigrant from Alsace, worked slavishly in the mornings and spent his afternoons lounging in a neighborhood wine saloon getting pleasantly plastered. In his absence, newly married, twenty-five-year-old Edwin Goodman ran the shop with Prussian efficiency, supplying the business acumen his partner lacked. Two years later, Bergdorf retired to the cafés of Paris after selling his share of the business to his partner. Goodman kept the brand name but moved the salon farther up Fifth Avenue, first to Thirty-second Street, and then, in 1914, to a new five-story building directly across from St. Patrick's Cathedral, on the future site of Rockefeller Center.

Nine years later, he shocked and confounded his competitors in the trade. The punctilious master tailor who made or directed the making of every item in his store, and who catered almost exclusively to upscale clientele, opened a ready-to-wear department. His rivals raised their eyebrows and predicted failure. But this Rochester upstart had made the smartest business decision of his life, one that would bring sweeping changes to the women's clothing industry—and make him astoundingly rich.

Although a risk taker, Goodman was never known for his impulsiveness. His decision to become the first American couturier to offer ready-to-wear garments—along with, not in place of, his line of hand-tailored items—was solidly grounded. He had seen the world changing, taking note of his customers' complaints about spending hours being pinned up in the fitting rooms. "Women were no longer hothouse creatures with nothing better to do than be fitted," said a fashion reporter. Goodman was the first to introduce style in ready-to-wear garments, the first to insist that they could be "fashioned." He went to the manufacturers and demanded that they fashion the dresses he ordered. "He hammered quality down their throats," writes his biographer. What Goodman couldn't buy from the big shops, he had his team of designers make—near-perfect reproductions of Paris originals. And his customers began buying them. Goodman had defied the iron axiom of the industry. An exclusive merchant *could* standardize and survive, so long as his service remained polished and personalized.

Service had always been Edwin Goodman's forte. Courtly and courteous, he made every customer who walked through the door feel special. There were no big display cases or clothing racks in his salon opposite St. Patrick's Cathedral. A stylishly dressed saleswoman—a *vendeuse*—greeted each customer, bringing the merchandise out for "madam's" inspection, as if she were being shown a matchless work of art.

In the early 1920s, Goodman brought his son Andrew and his daughter Ann into the business, though he remained the all-controlling force. Young and pulsing with ideas, Andrew and Ann were soon known as *"les enfants terribles"* of the ready-to-wear trade. "We didn't know anything about ready-to-wear," recalled Andrew Goodman, a college dropout, "but . . . at that time nobody else did either. We were kids, but we were kids in an infant industry. We had freshness and enthusiasm. But most important of all was that we had Father behind us." By 1927, dozens of Bergdorf Goodman's customers were spending, individually, over $100,000 a year in the store. "We would talk to our customers," says Ann Goodman Farber, "learn their tastes and moods and desires, then find just what they wanted and see their eyes light up when we showed it to them."

The founder took paternal pride in his creation, and never considered opening a branch store. To duplicate in another city the service and fittings he provided in his New York establishment "would be impossible or impracticable," he claimed. When he leased his new store on Grand Army Plaza, he involved himself in every aspect of its design and layout. Its façade of South Dover marble was tinted with black, orange, yellow, and green; and the interior was finished in opulent Louis XV style, with the exception of one resolutely modern salon. On the fourth floor were the workrooms of his designers, whose originals were soon competing successfully with Dior and Balenciaga. There was a full-scale clothing mill on the floor above. Five hundred dressmakers working in front of big windows overlooking Central Park made nearly half of Bergdorf's ready-to-wear items.

But by the late 1920s, Goodman was no longer exclusively a dressmaker. He had greatly expanded his line of merchandise, offering a full line of women's apparel, from necklaces to lingerie. His staff became masters of "the ensemble," matching the sporty outfits of ridiculously rich clients to the wardrobes of their pet dogs, whose clothing was also purchased at Bergdorf Goodman. One customer ordered a custom-made navy blue suit and asked for a swatch of material so she could have her new touring car painted to match it. Another bought ermine ensembles for her child's dolls.

Edwin Goodman was on the floor for up to eight hours a day, his tailor's chalk and tape measure at the ready, "impeccably tailored, calm, [and] conversational." The wives and daughters of Manhattan's "nationally known tribes"—the Astors, Vanderbilts, Mellons, and du Ponts—wanted to be dressed by Goodman. If these pampered women didn't have time for a personal fitting, a good number of them were comfortable making their selection from Bergdorf Goodman's extensive line of ready-to-wear dresses. They were special. Goodman never offered for sale more than fifty of any particular design; and dozens of expensive dresses were sold exclusively to as few as two women.

Edwin Goodman kept financial control of the store firmly in his own and his family's hands; no stockholders would drive him in directions he didn't want to go. And as his store became bigger and more impersonal, he strove to give his workers the feeling that their opinions mattered—even if they were rarely consulted. It was a masterfully orchestrated facade by a benign autocrat. Twice a year, before the new designs were shown to the public, Goodman held a fashion show for his workers. Six hundred of them would gather in a salon on the fourth floor, while models paraded in front of them, aglitter in the season's new creations. "The atmosphere," wrote a reporter, "is that of a large family: there is criticism, applause, laughter." At the head of the room sat Goodman, on a long couch; on his right was his wife, Belle, the firm's honorary vice president. On her left sat Andrew and Ann; next to Ann was Ethel Frankau, Goodman's chief designer. This was "the court of last appeal." Designs that fell short of their exacting standards were scrapped; but no decision overrode the will of the founder.

Edwin Goodman's only relaxation was baseball. On summer afternoons, he would retire to a small guest room in the family penthouse, stretch out on the bed, and listen to a Yankee game on a tiny radio—only to be drawn back, after a few innings, to the business of the store. Although the penthouse had seventeen rooms and every convenience imaginable, it was built on top of a building that was—by city law—a factory; and only a janitor and his family were permitted to live within the walls of an industrial concern. With the compliance of Jimmy Walker's indulgent building code authorities, Goodman evaded the law by listing himself and his wife as Bergdorf Goodman's custodians. They were the richest janitors on earth.

Hattie Carnegie, Inc.

Fifth Avenue was also where the husbands of Bergdorf Goodman's customers went to be outfitted. "There are good custom tailors outside of New York," said a student of the trade. "But the industry's center unquestionably rests on Manhattan's Fifth Avenue, between Forty-second and Fifty-seventh Street." The flush years of the Fifth Avenue tailoring trade were the late 1920s, when stock prices were soaring and most masters of the trading floor had up to a dozen custom-fitted suits in their closets. A number of these recently rich brokers had reserved apartments at one or the other of the dazzling residence hotels— the Savoy Plaza and the Sherry-Netherland—that were nearing completion in

1927 on the easterly corners of Fifty-ninth and Fifth Avenue, across from the Plaza Hotel. Tall and exuberantly modern, they redefined the streetscape of old Vanderbilt Alley. When completed later that year, the Sherry-Netherland surpassed Emery Roth's Ritz Tower as New York's tallest residential hotel; it was taller than the Washington Monument. The "yearly transformation [of Fifth Avenue] has . . . reached full tide," wrote urban reporter James C. Young in 1927. "Even the shadows are different from those of other years. Where the blue sky used to hang like a canopy, there are towers and buttresses of new and strange buildings. The saunterer who once carried every chimney in his memory finds the avenue so altered that he can scarcely recognize a landmark." By this time, many of the avenue's venerable churches and private clubs had moved to new addresses, and the automobile traffic was growing "worse by the day." Fifth Avenue and Forty-second Street had become "the busiest corner in the world." Old Fifth Avenue was "a street of leisure," said Young. "The new avenue bustles and pushes and elbows."

At midday, the pavements of Fifth Avenue were even more densely packed than the roadway. At the noon hour in the fall season, women decked out in mink coats and cultured pearls headed for lunch at the St. Regis, at the corner of Fifty-fifth and Fifth, a pleasant prelude to an afternoon of leisurely shopping, capped off by tea and scones at the Plaza's Palm Court. "I liked to walk up Fifth Avenue and pick out romantic women from the crowd, and imagine that in a few minutes I was going to enter their lives, and no one would ever know or disapprove," says Gatsby's friend Nick Carraway. "Sometimes, in my mind, I followed them to their apartments on the corners of hidden streets, and they turned and smiled back at me before they faded through a door into warm darkness."

On any given day, socialites and movie stars could be seen crossing from Fifth to Park, to the plum-colored East Forty-ninth Street shop of fashion designer Hattie Carnegie. "Four feet, ten inches and 104 pounds of dynamic energy," as *The New York Times* described her, "she set the pace of United States dressmaking for a generation." Although she would never learn to sew and never made a dress herself, "she knew how to tell those who could how to make clothes that appeal to the wealthy and fashionable." Starting out as a thirteen-year-old messenger girl at Macy's, with a wardrobe of three blouses and a skirt, she would come to control an $8 million fashion empire. Custom dresses in her retail shop at 42 East Forty-ninth Street carried staggering price tags, but the "backbone" of her business was the building at 711 Fifth Avenue that housed her wholesale line. There she designed dresses that were sold in high-end stores across the country. And while these items were also expensive, she kept the prices within reason—as Edwin Goodman did—by manufacturing her own stock.

She had not always been Hattie Carnegie. Born in Vienna, Austria, in 1886, Henrietta Kanengeiser arrived in New York with her mother and six siblings in 1892, joining her father, who had gone ahead of the family after their house had burned to the ground. Growing up in an environment of stringency and constricted horizons, she dreamed of clawing her way to the top in this super-kinetic city, where every day, it seemed, ideas were being turned into fortunes. Perhaps to fortify her resolve, she changed her last name to Carnegie after learning that the Scottish-born steel king had started life in America as a bobbin boy, changing spools of thread in a cotton mill. In 1909, she and a seamstress named Rose Roth opened a custom dress and millinery shop on East Tenth Street. "Miss Roth made dresses, Miss Carnegie made hats, and they both made money," said *The New York Times*. There was more to it than that, however. A striking young woman with red-gold hair, ice-blue eyes, and a trim figure, Hattie modeled the wardrobes that Roth fashioned, drawing customers with money to the partners' showroom.

Four years later the partners moved their business to the Upper West Side, to an affluent settlement near Riverside Drive whose residents could comfortably afford their expensive in-house creations. With the shop located, inauspiciously, above a Chinese restaurant, a laundry, and a cheap delicatessen, Hattie herself became the business's sole advertisement, wearing the shop's designs in swanky restaurants and clubs, and occasionally at the opera. It was work she took to easily; her "Viennese soul adored rich surroundings, good food, and attractive people."

The shop prospered but the strong-willed partners feuded endlessly, and in 1919 Hattie bought out Rose Roth. She then shifted the business from the sale of original creations to the redesign of Parisian fashions, "modulated to the American spirit." In that year she sailed to Paris for the first time, "happy and excited as a child." Over the next decade she would make at least seven transatlantic crossings yearly, returning each time with over a hundred patterns.

In 1923, she used her savings of nearly half a million dollars to buy and luxuriantly decorate a stucco townhouse on East Forty-ninth Street, a new retail shop that would make her a fixture in the industry. By then a self-trained designer, she sold dresses trimmed with mink, velvet evening gowns, and her soon to be famous "little Carnegie suits." Two years later, while still designing custom clothing, she branched out into the wholesale trade, making women's garments in her own factories, under her own label, and selling them to retailers—stylishly understated creations with classic lines: "the Carnegie look," it was called. A parvenu and a public personality, Hattie Carnegie "captured the new spirit of democratic fashion by making high style available at a reasonable price."

She couldn't sew a straight seam or draw patterns, "but she had a feeling about clothes and a personality to convey her ideas to the people who were to work them out," said a fashion report. Petite and ultra-feminine, and an incurable flirt in mixed company, she was a completely different person in her shop, a steely taskmaster with no tolerance for error. Lording over her small staff of assistant designers and sketchers, "her near-sighted eyes [are] everywhere at once," said the reporter. And she had "the temper of a termagant," with the capacity to "reduce the strongest man to a pulp." The clothes that came out of her shop—three collections a year—were shown at her retail shop and also at her wholesale headquarters on Fifth Avenue, where there were cutting rooms, fitting rooms, shipping rooms, rows of sewing machines, and hundreds of workers. Buyers arrived at its brown-and-white-satin showroom from every major city in America and purchased for their country club clientele the same clothing that New Yorkers bought at Carnegie's retail shop near Park Avenue.

But Hattie Carnegie's favorite customers were women of wealth and fame, whom she treated ingratiatingly. The actress Joan Crawford would wire her: "Send me something I'd like." Others came from out of town, direct from the train station to her door. They raged about her prices but trusted her judgment, knowing she wouldn't sell anything that wasn't the best. One of her proudest accomplishments, she boasted, was to make pudgy and plain Allie Walker, the mayor's wife, "look very nice."

In 1927 she was selling, astonishingly, $3 million worth of clothing a year. In that year, after two failed marriages, she wed her childhood sweetheart, Major John Zanft, a high-powered motion picture executive. They moved into a duplex apartment at 1133 Fifth Avenue, with furnishings and wall hangings imported from Paris, "museum pieces [that] would make a curator's mouth water." With her husband spending most of his time in Hollywood, Hattie lived the life of the new 1920s-style Manhattan socialite: rich, indulgent, and high-spirited. She slept under silk sheets, had gold faucets in her bathroom, made the round of the night clubs, and played high-stakes poker, claiming it improved her concentration. Her card playing partners were, not surprisingly, the women she dressed: actresses and socialites—none of them women of her parents' faith. Henrietta Kanengeiser's youthful decision to change her last name may have been an effort, as well, to distance herself from her Jewish roots. Her blond hair and blue eyes also helped, as did her practice of hiring tall, fair-haired women in her shop. So did the type of clothing she designed. "In contrast to the stereotype of the flamboyant clothing worn by *nouveau riche* Jewish women, the classic Carnegie Look embodied [an] ideal: the wealthy American woman secure in her social and financial position," writes historian Virginia Drachman.

Hattie Carnegie expanded her empire in the 1930s and 1940s, offering cosmetics, fragrances, jewelry, and chocolates. In 1947, with more than a hundred stores selling Carnegie products, *Life* magazine anointed her the "undisputed leader" of American fashion, with a multifaceted business incorporated under her name. "Hattie Carnegie, Inc. is Hattie Carnegie," said the editors. But that was its unforeseen weakness. When Hattie Carnegie died in 1956, the business spun into decline and eventually closed in the 1970s.

Saks Fifth Avenue

Fifth Avenue, just south of the park, "has become 'The Woman's City,'" wrote Will Irwin in *Highlights of Manhattan*. Fashionably slender women in Hattie Carnegie suits filled its French-inspired shops and stores, most of them recently opened for business. In 1927, the newest big store on the avenue was Saks Fifth Avenue, occupying an entire block between Forty-ninth and Fiftieth. Here price was not preeminent as it was at Macy's and other big department stores around Herald Square. Adam Gimbel, the store's young president, had created a "super-Macy's" for the comfortable classes.

Saks Fifth Avenue was formed in 1923 by a merger of Saks & Company, a high-end specialty store founded by Andrew Saks, a former street peddler from Baltimore, and Gimbels, the Philadelphia-based retail empire that had a store on Herald Square. There it competed with Macy's, both emporiums specializing in cash sales, big volume, and good value. Saks & Company, located just across the street from Macy's and down the block from Gimbels, had no hope of competing with these merchandising colossi. But under the direction of Horace Saks, Andrew's Princeton-educated son and successor, it had prospered at this tremendously busy location, selling expensive men's and women's clothing and exotic, hard-to-find merchandise—safari tents, Persian rugs, and alligator-skin luggage—to a discerning clientele. But Horace Saks was not satisfied with solid success; it was he that brokered the deal that led to the creation of Saks Fifth Avenue.

Beginning In the early 1920s, Horace Saks began pressing his family to move its store farther up Fifth Avenue, closer to its customers, many of them young Park Avenue "sporting people" passionate about travel, racing cars, and big-game safaris. Cautious family members, however, were reluctant to surrender their store's profitable Herald Square location and move north of Forty-second

Street, where no big retail store had yet gone. But Saks found an ally in Bernard Gimbel, the young president of his family's New York department store, and the grandson of Adam Gimbel, the Bavarian immigrant who founded the retailing empire, selling merchandise out of an oilcloth pack in his antebellum travels along the Mississippi River.

Over the years, Horace Saks and Bernie Gimbel had formed a close friendship. They commuted to work together, their families vacationed together at the beach in Elberon, New Jersey, and they were avid golfers, forming a low-scoring pairing on Sunday mornings. In 1923, Saks worked out a deal with Gimbel that satisfied both families. Saks & Company merged with Gimbel Brothers, allowing the families to consolidate their Herald Square stores, an arrangement that would prove profitable to both parties. By the terms of the agreement, the Gimbel family, the controlling partners, allowed Saks to construct a new luxury emporium on Fifth Avenue, across the street from the shop Edwin Goodman occupied before moving to the Vanderbilt plot.

But the stars were not aligned for Horace Saks. In 1925, one year after Saks Fifth Avenue opened its doors, he went to his doctor to have a carbuncle on his cheek lanced. He died on the operating table of septic poisoning. He was only forty-three years old. One year later, Adam Gimbel took over Saks Fifth Avenue and made its name a "national adjective" for exclusiveness and style.

Raised in a wealthy Philadelphia neighborhood and educated at Yale, he had been a "reluctant recruit to business." In college, he read deeply in history, literature, and architecture with the intention of doing postgraduate work in one of these fields. But in 1916, when his father asked him to take a leave of absence from college and work in the store for a year, on a trial basis, he surrendered and signed on. "He put me to work cleaning the store, driving a truck, the usual initiation for beginners," Adam recalled, "but he made it so pleasant for me that I never went back to college." Eight years later, at age thirty, he was second in command at Horace Saks's new store.

When Adam succeeded his deceased friend he planned to stick to Saks's founding idea: to create under one roof a cluster of specialty shops that would compete with the small luxury stores that had begun to appear on Fifth Avenue. Like Saks, he had a weakness for "fancy," out-of-the-ordinary merchandise, some of it shockingly expensive. On display in his show windows, at one point, were a chauffeur's livery and an alligator-skin trunk. But Adam Gimbel didn't stick to Saks's formula for long. He was an idea man, a restless innovator quick to follow hunches and take long chances. He was also a close observer of mid-Manhattan's changing commercial geography. Adam Gimbel "was acutely conscious of something that Saks had failed to see," *Fortune* would later note. "A new society was rising on Park and Fifth Avenues—a society made up of women who were willing to pay well for things a cut or two above the ordinary." Eager to attract them, Gimbel remade his store. His inspiration was a tour of the Exposition Internationale des Arts Décoratifs et Industriels Modernes, the famous 1925 Parisian exhibition showcasing the newest ideas in the decorative arts, including fashion, jewelry, and interior decoration. Art Deco, or Art Moderne, as it was then called, replaced the flowing, organic forms of Art Nouveau with bold colors, sharp geometric lines, and the generous use of lacquer, chrome, and stainless steel. On his return from Paris, Adam Gimbel ripped out Saks's plain merchandise counters and redesigned the sales floor and show windows, putting his store in the vanguard of the new style *moderne.*

Within a year, Saks became a magnet for style-conscious shoppers. But Gimbel also wanted to develop "volume," and to couple it, as Edwin Goodman had, with luxury—only it would be "volume of a size that the luxury trade never even dreamed of." He did this by building his own workrooms in the upper stories of his Fifth Avenue store, creating an upscale emporium that doubled as a factory. This was the Saks formula: "elegance in volume at a price." No large specialty shop in the nation was doing this—"at least on the Saks scale." Edwin Goodman was also a manufacturer as well as a merchandiser, but Adam Gimbel was the first of the nation's high-end retailers to go full-scale into the business of mass production.

The Saks workrooms were hidden away on the store's ninth and tenth floors. "They hum with the sound of sewing machines," wrote a business reporter, "they are bursting with girls stitching diligently over long tables spread with rippling, exotic fabrics, with whacky designers, grave-faced fitters, blinking tailors, and mannequins lolling about waiting for fittings." During peak periods, Saks employed nearly one thousand skilled workers. The building could not hold them all, so Adam Gimbel outsourced some of the work to contract shops located all over the city. His workers made everything from wedding dresses to hunting vests, but the store's specialty was the elegant gowns designed by statuesque stylist Sophie Haas Rossbach, a rich Philadelphia divorcée Gimbel had personally recruited and would marry in 1931. He wanted her to make Saks attractive to the kind of women who shopped at Hattie Carnegie's boutique.

Adam Gimbel was a hopelessly sloppy dresser. He wore his rumpled sport coats until they had holes in the elbows, and had Sophie cover them with leather patches. Sophie—who would be inducted into the Fashion Hall of Fame—singled him out to friends as "an example of exactly what the well-dressed man shouldn't wear." As head of the store's ultra-exclusive Salon Moderne, created in 1927, Sophie became Saks's principal advisor on what was in vogue; almost on her own, she made Saks the most profitable fashion specialty store in the country. Her job, as she crisply described it, "was to assist the buyer in seeing that the store . . . met the needs of people who lived the sort of life I did."

Adam Gimbel called his store his "child." It was a loved one he couldn't let go of, remaining president until his retirement in 1969, just before his death. In another echo of Edwin Goodman, he wanted his store to have the welcoming atmosphere of a "home in which the customers are treated as guests." He lectured his stockholders: "We can borrow money but we can't borrow customers." Yet Adam Gimbel, the polished product of old money, was not as remorselessly driven as the self-created founder of Bergdorf Goodman. He traveled extensively, played polo as well as golf, and read at least one book a week. And in a brutally competitive business, one that had raised pugnacity to an attribute, he was soft-spoken and diplomatic. Yet in a battle of wills he could be as "hardheaded as a steel master."

Like Edwin Goodman, he had a fixed idea of the kind of clientele he hoped to recruit and retain. While thousands of Saks's customers lived in the vicinity of the store, most of them were women from the affluent suburbs of New York, Chicago, Boston, and other large cities. Saks was in the thick of Manhattan's hotel district and a short cab ride from both Grand Central Terminal and Penn Station. On average, 300,000 visitors a day arrived at these rail depots. "This floating population is a spending population par *excellence*," wrote the authors of a 1927 study of the city's retail shopping trends. "It is, from the point of view of the shopkeeper, the cream of the buying population of the whole United States." To make shopping more convenient for out-of-towners who preferred to travel without a lot of cash, Saks offered easy credit terms for solidly established customers. Unlike cash-only Macy's, 85 percent of Sak's sales were credit transactions; and nearly half the store's active accounts had addresses outside the New York City area. This encouraged Adam Gimbel to launch a national chain of Saks Fifth Avenue stores. The biggest and most impressive were in Chicago and Beverly Hills, but the mainstay of the Saks empire remained the Fifth Avenue store.

To add to its allure, Gimbel brought in a leading Parisian coiffeur in 1927 and opened a stylish beauty salon. It prospered, but was never able to compete on even terms with New York's two most famous beauty palaces, located a few blocks up the avenue. They were owned and imperiously operated by feuding rivals: Elizabeth Arden and Helena Rubinstein, two of the richest, most successful businesswomen in the world.

Every Woman Has a Right to Be Beautiful

In May 1927, forty-eight-year-old Helena Rubinstein leased the mansion of deceased railroad king Collis P. Huntington, a stately six-story structure at the southeast corner of Fifth Avenue and Fifty-seventh Street. There she planned to establish the newest and most stylish of her salons, with living quarters on the top floor. For over a decade, the Polish-Jewish beauty specialist had a thriving business directly across the street, on the west side of Fifth Avenue, but she wanted an even more sumptuous place. "She filled the new building . . . with modernist furniture, sculpture and ancient objects of art that come from all parts of the world," wrote Jo Swerling of *The New Yorker*. When the salon was completed the following year, Rubinstein spent the good part of a week in a sanatorium, recuperating. "Always after the opening of a new salon she has a nervous breakdown," wrote Swerling. "She expects it and looks forward to it. It is part of her schedule."

Thirty years before this, Helena Rubinstein was living on the margins of poverty in the Jewish quarter of Kraków, Poland, the eldest of eight daughters of a kerosene dealer. In 1927 she was a multimillionaire with dozens of salons worldwide and voluptuous private residences in New York, Vienna, Paris, and London. Eccentric and unpredictable, she was, by turns, impulsive and calculating, tightly disciplined and wildly erratic. She would go an entire year without buying a single hat or gown and then set out on a weeklong shopping spree. She spent a fortune on original works by Picasso, Matisse, and Dali but carried her lunch to work in a brown paper bag and would fly into a rage if one of her servants accidentally dropped a ten-cent plastic bowl. "Madame could never remember the names of her best friends," an associated noted, "but she never forgot the components of a single product that bore her name." Known in the beauty business for her reckless impulsiveness, she rarely made a major mistake of judgment or "instinct," instinct being the salient quality "upon which she depends," said Swerling, "with the faith of a zealot."

A tyrant in her business dealings, she lived in fear and loathing of only one person: Elizabeth Arden, whose salon, with its signature red door and gleaming brass nameplate, was only three blocks from Rubinstein's new shop. Arden despised Rubinstein with equal fervor. Though the two beauty divas attended the same parties and worked within blocks of one another for over six decades, they would never formally meet. Legend has it that neither of them ever mentioned her rival by name—"the Other One," Rubinstein called Arden. "No one had the courage," she hissed, "to bring us face to face."

Mutual acquaintances of these competing cosmetics tycoons were struck by their abundant similarities. Both lied brazenly and repeatedly about their past, claiming to be much younger than they were and to have suffered far less than they did in their earlier years. Self-punishing workaholics, they put career above all else, including friends and husbands. Autocratic employers, driving their workers to tears and firing them on a whim, they inspired reverential loyalty among some of their most trusted associates, often through acts of deep generosity. Arden's assistants never knew "from one hour to the next," wrote reporter Margaret Case Harriman, "whether to expect a calling down or a champagne party." In both her personal and public life, Madame Rubinstein, said Patrick O'Higgins, her longtime assistant, was as an unfathomable paradox, both a "benevolent empress" and a "greedy peasant."

But unconquerable willpower was the trait that Arden and Rubinstein most closely shared. Entering a "chancy field of enterprise, ruled by high price, high style, and high tension," they became the empresses of the American beauty business, sole owners and stockholders of their global companies—astonishing accomplishments for immigrants with little formal education and difficult early lives.

Helena Rubinstein was in declining health and in her early nineties in 1964 when she completed her autobiography, *My Life for Beauty*. It is an unreliable work, filled with gaping omissions and fabulous fabrications. She had been raised, she claimed, not in Kraków's Jewish ghetto, but in a large and comfortable house near the city's famed market square; and the foundation of her success, she said, was a magical face cream used by her mother and seven sisters, a concoction reputedly acquired from a Hungarian chemist, a certain Dr. Jacob Lykusky. A search by Rubinstein's most reliable biographer discovered no trace of a Dr. Lykusky or of a cream made from the "essence of almonds" and the bark of an evergreen tree that grows in the forests near Kraków. It was a homemade Polish skin cream, not an exotic treatment acquired from a mysterious physician, that launched Helena Rubinstein's career in the beauty business.

In her prime, Rubinstein was often photographed in a laboratory, a scientist dressed in a starched white smock, peering into beakers as she holds them up to the light, searching for yet another beauty elixir. This fit neatly with her claim to have studied medicine for a time at Kraków University. That was entirely apocryphal; but she had fallen in love with a student from the university, a Catholic boy she had planned to elope with until her devoutly religious father found out and ordered her out of the house. Banished to Vienna to live with her mother's sister, she rejected every Jewish suitor her Viennese relatives sent her way. In 1886, she set out, on her own, for Australia. She had an uncle who lived there with his family on a sheep ranch in the Outback town of Coleraine and needed help running his small general store. It was in that harsh, sun-scorched place that Rubinstein developed a special cream to protect her lustrous skin. Its base was lanolin, the oil that sheep secrete into their fleece. She mixed the lanolin into a pot of her mother's Kraków cream and began searching for ways to market it.

After a falling out with her abusive, hard-drinking uncle, she moved to Melbourne and opened a beauty shop—Australia's first—with a "loan" from an unknown person, most likely a married man who was pursuing her. By 1907, at age thirty-five, her salon, a "business tailor-made to a female population drying up in the sun," was booming. Rubinstein also established a thriving mail-order business for her Valaze skin softening cream. And she had discovered, by trial and error, the secret to financial success in the beauty business: the markup. A pot of Valaze sold for what a Melbourne dressmaker might make in a week, but Rubinstein found that high prices did not discourage sales. "On the contrary—if one of her lines failed to sell, Madame would raise the price, and sales would miraculously increase," writes historian Ruth Brandon.

In 1908, she turned her business over to her sister Ceska, whom she had lured to Australia, and returned to Europe. She set up a residence in London with her new husband, Edward Titus, a Polish American journalist who had handled her advertising in Melbourne. The marriage produced two sons, but with a new salon to oversee, Rubinstein had little time for them or Titus, who, it turned out, had a roving eye. Rubinstein soon found herself enmeshed in a dismal marriage with an unfaithful man whom she found infuriatingly attractive. "Edward Titus excited my imagination; he was an intellectual, interested in everything, and he had many friends in the literary and artistic world." They would live apart, with intermittent reconciliations, until their divorce in the 1930s freed her from the only person who had subjugated her.

In 1912, Rubinstein moved to Paris to open another salon, handing over management of the London establishment to her sister Manka. "The world's first self-made female tycoon," magazines described her. When war broke out in Europe in 1914, Rubinstein moved to New York with Manka, Titus (temporarily), and the children. But the Great War had only hastened a decision she had come to earlier. She was a beauty merchant, and America was a fresh field to conquer.

It was "a bitterly cold day," Rubinstein would later describe her arrival in New York. "The first thing I noticed was that . . . all the American women had purple noses and grey lips, and their faces were chalk white from terrible powder. . . . I recognized [at once] that the U.S. could be my life's work." She opened her first Salon de Beauté in a brownstone on Forty-ninth Street, just off Fifth Avenue, and expanded almost immediately, establishing salons in six other

American cities. In New York, her only serious rival, she soon discovered, was a Canadian farm girl who had recently changed her name.

Florence Nightingale Graham was born in the village of Woodbridge, outside Toronto, around 1878. (The date is in dispute; Arden later claimed she was born in 1884.) Her parents had emigrated from Britain and her father, an impoverished farmer, raised her and four brothers and sisters after his wife died of tuberculosis when Florence was only five years old. Bright and independent-minded, "Flo" Graham grew up with an overpowering desire to escape the grim rural world of her father and become a self-sufficient woman cradled in luxury. It was a passion fed by her reading of gauzy romantic novels about lowborn girls who surmount great obstacles. Forced to drop out of school in her teens to support her family, she moved to Toronto and drifted through a succession of unpromising jobs. Against her father's wishes, she moved to New York in 1908, where her brother had preceded her. For dreamy-eyed Florence Graham, Manhattan was an intoxicating place of wealth and possibility.

By sheer chance, she found work as a cashier in a Fifth Avenue salon managed by Eleanor Adair, a pioneering beauty culturist who specialized in facial treatments for society women. Graham had no knowledge of the beauty trade, but she was an attractive redhead with captivating blue eyes and flawless skin, and she made it known she was desperate to advance. Pulled off the cash register, she was taught how to do facial massages and mix Adair's popular moisturizing creams. Two years later, she left Adair's shop and opened a salon with a more experienced friend, Elizabeth Hubbard. It was located strategically at Fifth Avenue and Forty-second Street. Graham and Hubbard were emotionally mismatched, however, and Hubbard walked out six months later and opened her own shop just down the block. Flo Graham reopened for business at the original address, but under a different—and she thought, more attractive—name: Elizabeth Arden. She took her new first name from her former partner and her last name, in all likelihood, from Alfred Lord Tennyson's *Enoch Arden*, a poem she treasured. To make certain the name was exactly right, she mailed a letter to herself, addressed "Miss Elizabeth Arden." When the envelope arrived the next morning she knew she had made the right decision.

With a loan of $6,000 from a distant relative, she remodeled the studio, carving out a small laboratory and three treatment rooms decorated with oriental rugs and French antique furniture. Five years later, she opened a small wholesale department. It was the most important business decision she would ever make.

Convinced that the face creams women put on at night were "too hard and slippery," Arden had A. F. Swanson, the chemist who produced her supplies, come with up with a cream that was light and fluffy, "like whipped cream." She called it Venetian Cream Amoretta, and it became the source of her long-term success. The laboratory Swanson worked for was located far uptown. To save shipping costs, Arden carried the cream in a demijohn on the crowded El train to the new salon she opened at Fifth Avenue and Fifty-third Street, in the heart of Vanderbilt Country. When it began to sell, she hired Swanson as her personal chemist and set him up in a laboratory in the back of her flourishing wholesale offices. Soon she also selling eye shadow, lipstick, and other facial products produced on-site.

Helena Rubinstein had begun making and wholesaling these same products a year earlier, and the two became locked in an ever-escalating competition for dominance of the New York beauty business. But both evangelists for beauty had to break through lingering societal pressures against makeup. Around World War I, makeup was worn almost exclusively by actresses, prostitutes, and fast-living working-class girls. "The vilest rumor that could be circulated about a woman," said a journalist, "was 'she paints.'" The popularity of silent movies helped change this. Actresses wore heavy makeup to accentuate their eyes, cheekbones, and lips. Seeing starlets like Mary Pickford in long close-up shots helped to alter perceptions about cosmetics. Liberated women began putting on lipstick and eye shadow; and the more daring ones applied them in speakeasies and restaurants—at their tables, not in the privacy of the powder room. By the mid-1920s "powder and paint became essential signs of femininity," as well as badges of independence. By clever advertising campaigns, Arden and Rubinstein solidified these changes in the way women decorated themselves.

But they were not solely in the business of painting women and nourishing their skin. "[They] went to work on a face not so much to decorate it as to give it a workout," said *The New York Times*. "Don't work on the surface, but work from inside out," was the beauty gospel they preached; "build up the tissues to remove wrinkles." Arden called it "muscle strapping": patting the face vigorously to draw blood to the capillaries of the skin. Both of their Fifth Avenue salons specialized in full-treatment care, which included electrical massages and muscle-tightening physical exercise. Beauty, they commonly believed, "had a scientific base; it sprang from the food you eat, the exercises you perform, your state of mind. . . . All that must come first before you plucked and painted yourself." The salons of Rubinstein and Arden were super-garages and repair shops for feminine faces and bodies. Treatments included facials, manicures, pedicures, eyelash dying, paraffin waxing, yoga, and stretching—along with classes in social deportment and fencing.

The competing cosmetics queens went after the same customers: middle-aged women seeking to recapture their beauty, and plain-looking younger women who "hoped to find beauty in a bottle." Shrewdly linking the beauty business with women's rights, they insisted that every woman had a right to be beautiful.

Although Arden and Rubinstein lavished most of their attention on their Fifth Avenue salons, it was their wholesale trade that made them powerhouses in the beauty business. In 1915 Arden had married Thomas Jenkins Lewis, a handsome silk merchant with a pleasing personality, a marriage that made her an American citizen. Following his discharge from the Army in 1919, "Tommy" was put in charge of his wife's wholesale business and almost instantly made it the anchor of Arden enterprises. Out on the road, he also bedded every attractive female buyer he could.

Under Tommy Lewis's driving direction, high-end department stores like Saks Fifth Avenue and Neiman Marcus began selling Arden products, all of them beautifully packaged in a pale shade of pink, always pink, for Arden considered pink "the most flattering color in the spectrum." By 1927, nearly a hundred individual Arden products were on sale internationally, including a full line of negligees and evening dresses; and the wholesale business, once the smallest part of the Arden empire, had become the largest, grossing nearly $4 million, annually. Half a million of that went directly to Elizabeth Arden, who never stopped reminding scandalously unfaithful Tommy that he worked for, not with, her. With the added profits from her twenty-nine salons in Europe and America, Elizabeth Arden, the self-styled "czarina of the cosmetics business," cleared over a million dollars a year.

She had a well-oiled sales machine. "Arden Women," immaculately groomed and dressed in white uniforms with pink bows in their hair, toured the country, giving demonstrations at the cosmetics counters of exclusive shops and department stores.

Rubinstein was even more proactive. She and her sister Manka set out regularly on whirlwind promotional tours of the company's mini-salons in leading department stores, all of them staffed by smartly uniformed Rubinstein representatives. During the day, she and Manka were sales representatives; at night they trained the salons' assistants to be beauty consultants. "We lived out of our suitcases like actresses in a theatrical touring company," Rubenstein recalled. When Helena was on the road, Titus took care take of their boys, along with Manka's son. He soon tired of running "a little kindergarten class," however, and in 1924 he returned to Paris, where he opened a bookshop and started a small avant-garde publishing house. One of the first writers he secured was D. H. Lawrence.

In building a mass market for cosmetics, Arden and Rubinstein built a new American industry, centered in Midtown Manhattan. When Rubinstein first arrived in the city, women were spending an estimated $25 million a year on beauty products. By 1927, this had risen to nearly $2 billion, half a million more than Americans spent on electric power that year. Soon to be one of the ten largest industries in the country, the beauty business pumped life into a host of related industries: newspapers, magazines, department stores, and drugstores. By 1927, toiletries were the second most heavily advertised products in national magazines and had begun to be advertised on the radio. In that year there were over three thousand beauty establishments in New York City alone, up from three hundred in 1900; and the U.S. Department of Labor estimated that three-quarters of the women living in cities purchased beauty products regularly. Meanwhile, a new word crept into the English language: "cosmetician"—a person trained "to make faces please."

The beauty trade was a woman's industry, built largely by women and catering almost solely to them—and with a workforce dominated by women. "The cosmetics business is interesting among modern industries in its opportunities for women," Helena Rubinstein observed. "Here they have found a field that is their own province—working for women with women, and giving that which only women give—an intimate understanding of feminine needs and feminine desires." It was also a business that paid good wages. In the late 1920s, the average paycheck of an American working woman was just over seventeen dollars a week. An experienced graduate of one of the city's new beauty culture schools could make sixty dollars a week, plus tips and commissions. On Fifth Avenue, many of the big shops paid their beauty specialists up to $400 a week. There were also opportunities for entrepreneurship: opening salons, beauty schools, and mail-order concerns. Arden had decisively demonstrated this. In a mere twelve years, she had turned a business started with a $6,000 loan into a $15 million empire.

By the late 1920s, Arden and Rubenstein were international celebrities, photographed and interviewed by leading magazines. Built like an icebox, four-foot-ten inches tall and almost perfectly square, Rubinstein, nonetheless, had a genius for making herself look stylish. With her jet-black hair swept back in a chignon, and wearing bright red lipstick, spike heels, and loose-fitting silk gowns that partially hid her girth, she looked more chic and moderne than Arden, who favored pink outfits and lipstick and cultivated a soft, ultra-feminine look.

Watching Arden from afar, at a later date in their lives, Rubinstein made a cold appraisal: "Nice skin, good chin, but too much color in the hair for her age!" Rubenstein's own hair was rinsed blue-black at least every six weeks.*

Elizabeth Arden suffered few disappointments since leaving her father's farm. The greatest of them came after she and Tommy finally ended their stormy, childless marriage in 1934. They agreed on a settlement that Arden's lawyers stacked heavily in her favor. For a meager $25,000 settlement, Tommy agreed not to work in the cosmetics trade for five years. But he got his sweet revenge the very year the stipulation expired. Helena Rubinstein hired him, if only to wound her rival. Arden would consider that betrayal by Tommy more egregious than his serial infidelities.

When Arden died at age eighty-eight in 1966, she was, like Rubinstein— who had died one year earlier—in sole command of her beauty empire. Unremitting work, the scourge of their personal lives, had given them what they wanted even more than money: power, reputation, and influence. Once these fiery combatants were gone, control of the beauty business—which now included cosmetic surgery—passed to powerful men, and remains to this day a male preserve. But it was two willful immigrant women, starting with little more than vision and vigor, who first drew attention to the industries' bounteous possibilities.

The Metropolitanites

While their national marketing strategies differed greatly, five of the great merchants of Fifth Avenue—Rubinstein, Arden, Goodman, Gimbel, and Carnegie—appealed to the same slice of the market: "the upper spending group," the kinds of people who shopped regularly in Midtown and read *The New Yorker*. Founded in 1925 by Harold Ross, a tramp reporter from Salt Lake City, Utah, *The New Yorker* was predominantly a local magazine in its first years, one that "reflected the life and times of New York." But Ross's brainchild was even more specialized than that; it was a Manhattan magazine. Its coverage

---

* In late 1928, Rubinstein sold the American part of her business to Lehman Brothers for over $7 million (roughly $84 million today). Lehman's subsequent decision to enter the midlevel market infuriated her. Sales suffered in the early years of the Great Depression. When stock prices dropped through the floor, Rubinstein began quietly buying back shares until she was in a position of majority control. She bought back her business and returned to New York from Europe.

of the other boroughs was scanty and its most loyal cadre of readers resided in the high-rent districts of Midtown, a distinctive group of prosperous, educated, and worldly wise New Yorkers.

When Ross launched the magazine he seemed uniquely ill suited to reach this urbane readership. A disheveled-looking high school dropout, "impatient and noisy," he had never had money and knew no one who did. And he was a Westerner whose knowledge of New York was abysmal when he arrived in the city with his wife, Jane Grant—a former *New York Times* reporter—after working in Paris on the editorial board of the Army newspaper, *Stars and Stripes.* But Ross had recently secured the financial backing of his poker-pal Raoul Fleischmann, heir to a family fortune accumulated in the yeast and bread-baking business. "As polished as Ross was rough, as polite as Ross was profane," Fleischmann shared Ross's affliction for gambling, and both were members of the Algonquin Round Table group, regularly attending, with Woollcott, its luncheon gatherings and Saturday night poker games.

Bored with the baking business, Fleischmann agreed in 1924 to back Ross's plan to publish a magazine "built around New York" and pitched to a "highly selective audience." The magazine's sardonic wit and irony would be supplied by their Algonquin friends, most prominently Dorothy Parker and Alexander Woollcott, theater critic for the New York *World.* Woollcott lived next to Ross and his wife in two run-down Hell's Kitchen buildings that they had turned into a sort of literary commune. Drop-in guests included Robert Benchley, Edna St. Vincent Millay, and Scott and Zelda Fitzgerald, a party crowd that put Ross in touch with other top writing talent.

The New Yorker floundered and nearly folded in its first year of publication, unable to attract enough readers or advertising. In a long-shot effort to save his sinking enterprise, Ross hired Ralph Ingersoll, a twenty-four-year-old reporter from the *New York American.* A Yale graduate, Ingersoll was a rising talent, a promising writer and editor. "But all this meant little to his employer," writes James Thurber in his slyly satiric account of his years at *The New Yorker.* "What meant a lot was that Ingersoll was a grandnephew of Ward McAllister, [*The* Mrs. Astor's social advisor] and knew his way around Park Avenue and Long Island." Ingersoll "has entrée in the right places," Ross would later tell Thurber. "He knows who owns private Pullman cars, and he can have tea with all the little old women that still have coachmen or footmen. . . . It's damned important for a magazine called the *New Yorker* to have such a man around."

As Ross well knew, advertising follows circulation, not vice versa, in the magazine business. If *The New Yorker* became the magazine of choice of the Park Avenue set, Ross would be able to sell space to the Fifth Avenue stores that relied on their trade. Knowing his partner was a boneheaded businessman, Fleischmann hired John Hanrahan, "a hustling little Irishman," as the magazine's promotion manager and general advisor, promising him 10 percent of *The New Yorker*'s profits. Working out of an office building far from the magazine's headquarters on West Forty-fifth Street—Ross wouldn't allow him near his writers and editors, fearing he might influence the editorial content—Hanrahan developed an advertising campaign that pulled the magazine out of the red. He did this by translating Ross's editorial message into sales language appealing to potential advertisers.

Ross had outlined that message with cool clarity in the now famous prospectus he drafted in 1924.

> *The New Yorker* will be a reflection in word and picture of metropolitan life. . . . It will be what is commonly called sophisticated, in that it will assume a reasonable degree of enlightenment on the part of its readers. . . .
>
> *The New Yorker*'s conscientious guide will list each week all current amusement offerings worthwhile—theater, motion pictures, musical events, art exhibitions, sport and miscellaneous entertainment—providing an ever-ready answer to the prevalent query, 'What shall we do this evening?' . . . Readers will be kept apprised of what is going on in the public and semi-public smart gathering places—the clubs, hotels, cafes, supper clubs, cabarets and other resorts.
>
> There will be a personal mention column—a jotting down in the small town newspaper style of the comings, goings and doings in the village of New York. . . .
>
> *The New Yorker* will carry each week several pages of prose and verse, short and long, humorous, satirical and miscellaneous.
>
> *The New Yorker* expects to be distinguished for its illustrations, which will include caricatures, sketches, cartoons and humorous and satirical drawings in keeping with its purpose.
>
> *The New Yorker* will be the magazine which is not edited for the old lady in Dubuque. . . . *The New Yorker* is a magazine avowedly published for a metropolitan audience. . . . It expects a considerable national circulation, but this will come from persons who have a metropolitan interest.

Hanrahan married *The New Yorker*'s "commercial idea" to Ross's editorial program. By emphasizing Ross's appeal to a discriminating metropolitan readership, he convinced some of Midtown's leading merchants that *The New Yorker* "was uniquely positioned to help them." Advertising in a local magazine whose biggest chunk of circulation was in the neighborhoods where the preponderance of their clientele lived and congregated, Fifth Avenue department stores, beauty salons, and boutiques would be able to reach them far less expensively than by buying space in national publications like *Vanity Fair* and *Time*. The message resonated. In 1926, Elizabeth Arden and Helena Rubinstein bought full-page ads, and Adam Gimbel signed a yearlong contract, news that ignited a spontaneous celebration in Hanrahan's office.

The New Yorker had the extra advantage of having a reporter who covered the Fifth Avenue fashion scene with fairness and flair and had built up a ravenously loyal readership. Lois Long was a twenty-two-year-old Vassar graduate when Ross hired her away from *Vanity Fair* to cover, not fashion at first, but the city's boiling night club scene. The beautiful, high-spirited daughter of a Congregational minister, she was, Ross thought, ideally equipped for her new responsibilities: an unsuccessful Broadway actress with a reputation as a "girl about town," a standout at jazz clubs and penthouse parties. "Ross never doubted that the ideal *New Yorker* writer, to say nothing of the ideal *New Yorker* reader, would be someone as like Lois Long as possible," recalled longtime *New Yorker* staffer Brendan Gill. "He felt himself an outsider in New York, and in his eyes Miss Long was the embodiment of the glamorous insider." Under the pseudonym "Lipstick," she contributed a regular column on the city's nightlife, "Tables for Two," plunging "joyously into a New York that seemed to be always at play—a city of speakeasies, night clubs, tea dances, football weekends, and steamers sailing at midnight."

Tall and slender, her jet-black hair fashionably bobbed, a long string of thin pearls dangling from her neck, "she could have modeled for Miss Jazz Age." She smoked and drank prodigiously, told racy jokes, and threw all-night parties at her Murray Hill apartment. She knew where all the best clubs were, and would invite members of the staff to join her on her night club beat. They'd usually start their evening at Jack and Charlie's. When it closed, they'd hit the early morning spots. "You never knew what you were drinking or who you'd end up with," Long recalled. "We wore wishbone diaphragms that weren't always reliable. There was a woman doctor who handled abortions for our crowd. She would take a vacation at Christmastime to rest up for the rush after New Year's Eve."

Long would often show up at the office around noon on the day her column was due, bleary-eyed and hungover, praying she would be able to "make it to the ladies room before throwing up." But she never failed to meet her deadline. On some nights she would arrive at *The New Yorker*'s headquarters around three in the morning, dressed in her evening clothes. The handful of writers who were still laboring over their copy would look on in bemusement

as she kicked off her heels, stripped down to her slip, and began typing furiously, "a cigarette dangling from her mouth." Ross tolerated her behavior
because he considered her indispensable. "Ross actually liked us all to go on
binges," Long put her own interpretation on her editor's forbearance. "He had
a theory that we would be so remorseful afterwards that we would write especially well the next day."

In 1927 Lois Long was named the magazine's fashion editor and began
writing wickedly humorous criticism under the heading "On and Off the Avenue." "Lois Long invented fashion criticism," said William Shawn, who succeeded Ross as editor after Ross's death in 1951. "[She] was the first American
fashion critic to approach fashion as an art and to criticize women's clothes
with independence, intelligence, humor and literary style." Ralph Ingersoll
considered hers "the most important of all early *New Yorker* columns. . . . It
was," he said, "a magazine sensation [that] broke a fifty-year-old tradition that
commercial names—let alone addresses and prices—should never be mentioned in polite publishing."

Lois Long brought to her work "freshness and honesty, qualities hitherto
nonexistent" in that esoteric field of reporting, said Ingersoll. It was common
at that time for merchants to pay hefty bribes to reporters in return for puff
pieces, a nefarious practice that Long publicly exposed. Advertising "blackmail," she called it. Long wrote for women like herself, upper-middle-class
New Yorkers who wanted to look good without spending a fortune on hand-
tailored items, the kind of women who bought elegant ready-to-wear dresses
at Bergdorf Goodman. She excoriated the "fashion dictators," most of them
Parisians, who tried to enforce what women should wear, regardless of cost
or discomfort; and she was the only fashion columnist in the country to visit
ready-to-wear wholesalers and review their offerings. Her column, Ingersoll
claimed, brought *The New Yorker* "just the readership it needed to secure its
all important retail advertising." Beginning in 1927, and for the next thirteen
years, The *New Yorker* placed in the top three of American magazines in number of advertising pages sold.

Nineteen twenty-seven was the turning point in *The New Yorker*'s fortunes,
the most important year in the magazine's history. In that year it developed
its distinctive character and tone, the collective contribution of the illustrious writing and editorial talent Ross had recruited. By then, the regular staff
included older hands like Dorothy Parker, Morris Markey, E. B. White, and
White's future wife, managing editor Katharine Sergeant Angell. Robert Benchley and James Thurber came on board that year. Sharing an office "the size of a
hall bedroom," Thurber and White became "the wheel horses of the magazine's
humor" and collaborated on their first book, *Is Sex Necessary?* The Ohio-born

Thurber made "The Talk of the Town" column the decade's wittiest, most informative guide to what was happening in Manhattan. "It gave the reader the feeling" said Ingersoll, "that he had been everywhere, knew everyone, was up on everything."

Part of this solid nucleus was one of the most talented young artists in the country, Curtis Arnoux Peters, an arrogant, darkly handsome Yale graduate. He first arrived at the office in 1925 in sneakers, and had lately been leading a jazz band at a Manhattan night club. His cartoons, rendered mostly in charcoal and wash, poked fun at the customs of New Yorkers of every social station. To protect the name of his father, a New York children's court judge, he signed them "Peter Arno." Violating Ross's dictum that "there'll be no sex, by God, in the office," Arno and Lois Long fell into a hot public liaison, two nighthawks who loved liquor and the fast life. They married in 1927.

That year, Raoul Fleischmann, the magazine's publisher and chief stockholder, refused an offer of $3 million for *The New Yorker*. By this time the magazine had become what was known in the trade as "a good publishing property." Its circulation had grown from an anemic 1,500 copies in the crisis summer of 1925 to over 61,000. The largest concentration of regular subscribers lived in a Midtown area extending from Murray Hill to Central Park, and eastward to Sutton Place, with Park Avenue having the most readers.

By zeroing in on an upscale local audience, while slowly shoring up a national list of "New York–minded people," Ross and Fleischmann built a magazine with some of the most loyal subscribers in the trade: the Metropolitanites. As opposed to mere "city dwellers," of which there were millions in the five boroughs, "the Metropolitanites," wrote the *Fortune* editors who coined the term, "cannot imagine living in any U.S. city except New York. They like its swift tempo because they are hurrying to absorb more than anyone in a lifetime could touch, let alone understand." They were regulars at the theater and the opera; they shopped at Saks and drank at Jack and Charlie's; they were in the front rows of most big fights at the Garden; and on winter evenings, from the frosted windows of their lofty apartments, they looked out satisfyingly at floodlit skyscrapers and great liners setting out to sea. And they read *The New Yorker*, the only "institution" that had discovered "exactly who the Metropolitanites" were and how to appeal to their extravagant tastes.

CHAPTER ELEVEN

FRED FRENCH

Fred F. French is a big name in New York.

W. PARKER CHASE

A Daring Newcomer

In March 1925, the real estate tycoon Frederick Brown sold a prime piece of Fifth Avenue frontage to developer Fred F. French, a "daring newcomer" in the Manhattan construction business. The skyscraper that French planned to erect on the northeast corner of Fifth Avenue and Forty-fifth Street would be the headquarters of his recently assembled real estate empire. Excavation began the following year, and on October 24, 1927, the Fred F. French Building, one of the great "business palaces" of Midtown, opened its polished brass doors. At thirty-eight stories, it was one of the two tallest structures on the avenue, only slightly shorter than the new Delmonico Office Building, located one block south, on the former site of Delmonico's restaurant. These 1927 additions to the Midtown skyline were "veritable giants" among the low-rise buildings huddled around them, said one reporter.

They were also urban bellwethers. Since the early 1920s, businesses had been migrating at a rapid rate from downtown to Midtown, where land costs and rents were far cheaper. The best location was close to the stir and tumult of Grand Central Terminal, not far from the Fred French Building. By 1927, the Commodore's once remote rail station was hemmed in by "twenty of the most valuable blocks of real estate in the Western Hemisphere."

Up to this point, heavy development around Grand Central Terminal had occurred almost entirely to the north of it, on Park and Lexington Avenues and on the bluffs of the East River—and to the west of Grand Central, on old Vanderbilt Alley. Beginning in 1927 there was a second Midtown construction boom, this one directly centered on Forty-second Street, east and west of the terminal, down to the banks of the East River and westward to Times Square. By 1929, there was a long row of immensely tall towers, either completed or under construction, along East Forty-second Street and its tributaries. In that year, New York had 188 buildings twenty-one stories or more, approximately half of all buildings of that height in the country. Chicago lagged far behind with 65. And in New York, 60 percent of these tall buildings were located north of the downtown financial district, the city's first skyscraper center.

Between 1925 and 1929, there was nearly a 100 percent increase in Manhattan's office space, most of it in the Midtown region. Real estate gamblers like Fred French were almost singularly responsible for these new business towers. The modern metropolis "has created a new phenomenon—the speculative builder," wrote Colonel W. A. Starrett, brother of fellow skyscraper builder Theodore Starrett. "All cities have them, but only in New York and perhaps in Chicago do they deal regularly in sky-scrapers."

The "almost volcanic eruption" of skyscrapers along East Forty-second Street began with the fortresslike Graybar Building. Completed in 1927, this gigantic office complex was built so close to Grand Central Terminal that it was virtually an extension of it. Next came the Chanin Building, started that same year, a fifty-six-story Art Deco triumph that faced the entrance to the terminal. It was, briefly, the tallest building north of Wall Street until the Chrysler Building was completed on the eastern flank of the terminal in early 1930.

While Grand Central was the main draw, it was the instant success of the Fred F. French building—almost entirely rented before it was ready for occupancy—that gave other developers the courage to build tall and expensively on the southern rim of Terminal City. But the first big skyscraper project to be planned on East Forty-second Street was not a corporate tower. It was a Manhattan anomaly, a secluded garden community of shaded walkways and pocket parks situated on a rocky bluff that rises seventy feet at the eastern terminus of Forty-second Street. This was Tudor City, another dream project of Fred French.

The visionary real estate developer had begun secretly assembling the site in 1925, while the Graybar Building was still on the drafting table. By then he was a wealthy man, with holdings valued at nearly $80 million. It had been a fast rise to the top: fifteen years earlier, Fred French was peddling third-rate real estate out of a musty basement office in the Bronx and surviving on a pauper's diet of coffee and canned goods. Completed in 1930 at a cost of $100 million, Tudor City was the largest residential project in Manhattan. Its ten towers—

the highest of them thirty-two stories (and still standing)—contained 2,800 apartment units and six hundred hotel suites. A "pioneering effort" in private enterprise urban renewal, it remains one of the pleasantest and most affordable places to live in central Manhattan.

With capital raised by the French Plan, an innovative stock-sharing scheme he devised in 1921, Fred French transformed a blighted stretch of Midtown adjacent to a steam plant into an urban garden spot, a middle-class community with multiple metropolitan amenities, some of them unavailable to residents of the parvenu palaces of Park Avenue.

Tudor City virtually completed the transformation of Midtown's eastern riverfront begun by those millionaire reformers Anne Vanderbilt and Anne Morgan. At the same time, the new skyscraper district that grew up along East Forty-second Street indelibly stamped the character of that great metropolitan corridor. In the years between 1927 and 1930, this new mercantile and residential center achieved its mature form, and Forty-second Street became Manhattan's second central business district. A miniature Wall Street, it was markedly different in character and cachet from the closeted world of the Morgans and the Harrimans—rich yet uncompromisingly modern, a place where new blood and fresh ideas mattered.

The tremendous towers of East Forty-second Street, cities unto themselves, formed the turbulent center of "one of those inner cities that characterize a metropolis." This new Midtown was a tightly bound area of recently remade urban space, shaped in the form of a great rectangle. Sutton Place, Beekman Place, and Tudor City formed its eastern boundary; Park Avenue—from the terminal to Fifty-ninth Street—its axis; Fifty-ninth Street its northern perimeter; Fifth Avenue its western border; and Forty-second Street its southern boundary. It was, in the aggregate, the unplanned product of tens of thousands of individual business decisions. And one of its principal creators was Fred French.

Who on Earth Was Fred French?

"Who on earth was Fred F. French [?]," a mother and daughter from the tenements of the Bronx—characters in Don DeLillo's 1997 novel, *Underworld*—ask themselves as they enter the spectacular lobby of his Fifth Avenue skyscraper. The year is 1934, and though the real estate sultan was still alive and in the news, the average New Yorker "did not have a clue," DeLillo writes, "to the identity of Fred F. French." Had the women in DeLillo's novel inquired, they would have learned that he was, surprisingly, one of them, a deprived kid from the Bronx for whom majestic Manhattan had been very nearly a foreign country.

Frederick Fillmore French was born in 1883 and raised by a hovering mother and a hard-drinking father, a cigar salesman who wasted his days tinkering with unpromising inventions. "He failed because he neglected to apply himself," French pitilessly appraised him years later—and in so doing, revealed much about himself.

His father died when Fred was not yet ten years old, forcing the boy to take after-school work—peddling newspapers, washing windows, and mowing lawns—to keep his family of five afloat. On the pavement in front of his home on 162nd Street, he set up a "kids" circus, charged a penny a seat, and used the proceeds to buy a loaf of bread for his mother. All the while he harbored a secret dream: to have a great house on the Hudson surrounded by gardens and green lawns.

He wanted to work full-time, but his mother, a graduate of the University of Michigan and a distant niece of President Millard Fillmore, insisted he stay in school. It was an inspiring public school teacher—"the Great O'Reilly," worshipful students called him—who turned around Fred French's life. With O'Reilly's backing, the boy won a Pulitzer scholarship, providing four years of free tuition at New York's highly competitive Horace Mann School. After graduating with honors, he went on to Princeton, but left after one year, repelled by its club life and social snobbery. "The notion that one boy was . . . superior to another because his father was prominent or rich . . . disturbed and depressed me," French wrote in his unpublished autobiography.

Instead of returning to the Bronx, he headed west to Texas and New Mexico, in search of opportunity, hopping rides on freight trains, picking up odd jobs, and staying in a succession of dreary flophouses before signing on as a ship's helper on a steamer heading from Galveston to South Africa. Days before sailing a letter arrived from home. His sister was gravely ill; the next day he booked passage on a freighter bound for New York.

With money he had saved in his travels, he entered the engineering program at Columbia University, where his quick mind and bounding energy attracted the attention of a number of faculty members, one of whom he would hire years later. His sister recovered, but at the end of his first semester, the bank threatened to foreclose on his mother's home. He gave her the $400 he had put aside for his next semester's tuition and took work in an iron foundry, and later as timekeeper on a construction job in Midtown, just off Fifth Avenue. He was invariably broke and often hungry. While working in Manhattan, he rented a windowless, dollar-a-day hotel room; in the evenings, after a meal of canned corn and dry bread, he read Gorky, Chekhov, and Tolstoy, "believing a person should improve [himself] even when in difficulty."

Finally he decided to go into business for himself, even if it meant running "a peanut stand." In 1910, he formed his namesake company. Using his mother's house as collateral, he borrowed money and began selling real estate from the coal cellar of a neighboring building. When a partner he took in absconded with the company's money, French was hauled into bankruptcy court. He vowed to pay back his creditors and did, "to the penny," establishing a solid local reputation for integrity.

After marrying the girlfriend of his sister Hazel, he rebuilt his business with the help of a substantial trust fund that his wife, Cordelia, inherited. He began purchasing and improving undeveloped property in the Bronx and upper Manhattan. He constructed dozens of apartment houses and commercial buildings, using his own staff of architects and engineers. At this point, he made a gutsy, career-turning decision. Taking out a $250,000 loan, he constructed a sixteen-story office building at the corner of Forty-first Street and Madison Avenue, "in the heart of the action." When the building was completed in 1920, he moved his business there and began aggressively buying Midtown real estate.

His initial investments paid off handsomely, and he left the Bronx for good, moving with Cordelia and their two sons to the penthouse of an apartment building his company had erected at Fifth Avenue and Eighty-second Street, one of the premier addresses in the city. The glass doors of the living room opened on to a lushly landscaped garden, planted in three feet of transplanted soil. Off to one side was a handball court, where tall, athletic Fred French challenged and solidly drubbed business associates; around the perimeter of the roof was a low parapet, from which there was a panoramic view of Central Park. Leaning on the wall one morning, French noticed, "quite by accident," that if he looked across the Park "through a rift in the skyscrapers beyond" he could see "the waters of the Hudson." Alone with his diary that evening, the cigar salesman's son was drawn back to his earliest ambition: "the house on the Hudson." What he had seen that morning was, he wrote, a "sign . . . consecrating his success."

In that year, 1925, he purchased land at 551 Fifth Avenue, the future site of the Fred French Building. It was "just about the best corner for a high-class office building in all of New York," he believed, in the heart of a region that was being described as "the seventh wonder of twentieth-century commerce." And just around the corner, coincidentally, was the building on which he had labored as timekeeper for a construction crew back in 1905, one of the lowest moments of his life.

On September 17, 1927, construction gangs hoisted the Stars and Stripes from the culminating steel girder of the Fred French Building. The soon to be completed building was one of thirty tall office structures erected that year in Midtown, a number that has "not been matched since," according to the city's Landmarks Preservation Commission. With a boost from Tammany Hall, the building opened for occupancy just in time for the fall 1927 rental season. Earlier that year, French had paid a $30,000 "fee" to the law firm of Tammany chieftain George Olvany, who prevailed upon city officials to allow French's contractors to skirt a provision in the city's building code they had violated. French, a pliable Republican, would call on Olvany to secure a similar favor for his Tudor City project.

Mesopotamia in Manhattan

The Fred French Building was something new on the Manhattan skyline. The building's setback terraces form the base of a seventeen-story rectangular "slab" with a flat roof. The architects, H. Douglas Ives, the French Company's in-house designer, and the outside firm of John Sloan and Thomas Markoe Robertson, settled on this innovative design as a way of maximizing the amount of rentable space on a relatively small urban lot. This new "genre of tower" would lead to higher-density development in Midtown while "enlivening the skyline" with shapes both massive and slender. For the exterior of the French Building, Ives drew generously on the art and architecture of the ancient Middle East, using brilliant colors, polychrome terra cotta, and enameled brick, along with sharply defined setbacks in the style of Assyrian Ziggurats.

The Fred French Building is Manhattan's only Mesopotamian skyscraper, but the decorative scheme has strong references, as well, to French's character and career. The central symbol on the northern and southern facades of its slender slab is the rising sun, symbolizing renewal, which French saw as the dominating theme of his life. The golden bees emblazoned in the terra-cotta stand for "thrift and industry," values the Manhattan landlord prized, while the panels on the eastern and western sides of the rectangular tower contain the heads of Mercury: the ancient messenger spreading the ideas of the French Plan. Like Frank Woolworth's lower Manhattan tower, the Fred French skyscraper is architecture as autobiography.

Designed to be a "showplace" building, its central lobby featured soft gray marble walls and gleaming bronze lanterns and elevator doors. The elaborately carved doorways appear to be patterned after the Ishtar Gate, named for the Babylonian goddess—an evocation, perhaps, of Jazz Age Gotham as a modern Babylon.

The Fred French Building was not a Manhattan original. Dozens of set-back skyscrapers were built earlier in the decade. A clear standout was Ar-thur Loomis Harmon's thirty-four-story Shelton Hotel, the tallest hostelry in the world when it opened in 1924 on the corner of Lexington Avenue and Forty-ninth Street. (It is now the Marriott East Side Hotel.) A severely plain structure of brown, roughened brick with three dramatic setbacks, it was the first tall building in the city expressly designed to conform to the new zoning law of 1916. The architectural renderer Hugh Ferriss heralded it as a presen-timent of a new era in urban design. Beginning in 1922, Ferriss and archi-tect Harvey Wiley Corbett had begun to collaborate on futuristic articles and drawings showing Manhattan buildings "rising like mountains, huge masses slicing into the air." The zoning law's mandate that towers be set back from the street signaled the end, Ferriss wrote, "[of] terrific vertical towers [springing] from nothing but a sidewalk." Instead, "summits will have the composition of mountain ranges," their shape more important than their style.

The Fred French Building is an integral but little acknowledged contribu-tor to this aesthetic reorientation, a precursor of a new order of architecture, a "style so recent," wrote Will Irwin, "that we have not given it a name, but as distinctive as Gothic or Classic." Despite the extravagant decorative scheme at the top of its slab, the building relies for its effect primarily on mass, bulk, and silhouette, the idea championed by Hugh Ferriss. "Taller and more animated than the Shelton, it was," says the city's Landmarks Preservation Commission, "one of the boldest and most creative responses to the [Zoning] Code that had yet appeared."

By staying within the limitations imposed by the new zoning law, rather than trying to subtly subvert it, the architects of the French Building worked along parallel lines with more gifted New York architects. The most outstand-ing were Ely Jacques Kahn, creator of clean-lined 2 Park Avenue, a 1927 Art Deco masterwork; Raymond M. Hood, whose dark and powerful Radiator Building (1924), facing Bryant Park, set him on a course to become New York's greatest skyscraper architect; and Ralph Walker, designer of the Barclay-Vesey Building of 1926, a plain masonry mass that abjured fake classical and Gothic embellishments, adding a new look to the downtown skyline. Working inde-pendently, these young architects helped to fashion a distinctly New York style, one that emerged full-blown at the end of the decade with iconic structures like the Chrysler Building and the Empire State Building. It was a style "born of ne-cessity," wrote Kahn. "The New York laws protecting property rights, light and air, have encouraged a new art by reason of the very restrictions they contain." This "New York born architecture is an adaptation of no other," said Colonel W. A. Starrett. "It is our own, expressing ourselves. It is the sounder for having a reasoned motive rather than individual fancy behind it. Beauty of line and form, rather than beauty of ornamentation, distinguishes it."

Tudor City

In early 1925, while his Fifth Avenue headquarters was still in the planning stage, Fred French undertook an even more ambitious project: a skyscraper city for residential living. To make it happen, he had to execute—with the greatest secrecy—the biggest real estate transaction in recent Manhattan history.

Powerfully built Fred French took pride in his physical condition. Every business day he left the office at lunchtime and took vigorous walks in the Midtown area, his eyes open for promising real estate opportunities. On the advice of a company associate, he found himself returning repeatedly to a grubby area at the eastern end of Forty-second Street, where that street meets First Avenue and the East River by a tunnel under Prospect Hill. The hill used to be known as Corcoran's Roost, the former haunt of the nineteenth-century Irish cutthroat Paddy Corcoran and his Rag Gang, the scourge of the neighborhood. The adjacent streets, East Forty-first and East Forty-third, did not run through to First Avenue, but terminated at Prospect Hill, creating a natural cul-de-sac. Seventy feet below the crest of Prospect Hill was an unsightly stretch of First Avenue. Its cattle pens, slaughtering houses, packing plants, and smoke-belching Edison power plant occupied four full blocks of riverfront.* But where others saw squalor and smog, Fred French spotted opportunity. This four-block-square hillock, filled with crumbling brownstones and shabby commercial buildings, was ideally situated, French thought, for a Midtown community pitched to the middle class.

There were risks involved, but French knew he wouldn't be betting on a long shot. In 1925, he had his company conduct a business survey of Midtown. The results were unsurprising. East Forty-second Street, still a residential neighborhood in 1925, was about to undergo as sweeping a physical transformation as the one that was reconstituting Vanderbilt Alley. In 1910, there were 310,000 people living between Thirtieth Street and Sixtieth Street. By 1925, there were only 200,000; and that number would drop dramatically over the next few years as walk-up apartment houses and brownstones were razed to build corporate monoliths. In 1925, the area just to the west of Prospect Hill was poised to become "the greatest business neighborhood on Manhattan

---

* The old slaughterhouse district was demolished in the 1940s to make way for the United Nations Headquarters.

Island." In Terminal City alone there was fifty million square feet of occupied office space; and new construction on Forty-second Street and Lexington and Madison Avenues added a hundred thousand additional workers each year. The center of gravity of Manhattan Island was shifting and French was determined to cash in on the opportunities this presented for a sharp-witted land dealer.

The masters of enterprise who would rule in the new corporate towers would reside on Park Avenue and upper Fifth Avenue, but where would their middle managers and accountants live? With housing in the area being demolished at a rapid rate, they would head to the suburbs unless attractive and affordable apartments could be found "convenient to their work." This was the animating idea of Tudor City.

Red-hot to begin buying and building, Fred French turned the Tudor City project into a full-scale commercial crusade. Beginning in November 1925, his land agents purchased lots as fast as possible. They operated in complete secrecy. If word leaked out that a big player was "running wild" on the local real estate market, prices would skyrocket. The operation was "a realtor's epic," wrote *The New Yorker*'s Alva Johnston, "a Homeric tale of haggling, scheming, plotting, and counterplotting." In a mere thirty-five days Fred French's broker, Leonard S. Gans, oversaw the purchase of five acres of contiguous riverfront real estate, a herculean achievement in a clotted Midtown region at the peak of the city's building boom. "Only the refusal of the meat packers to sell their slaughterhouse properties prevented Tudor City from spreading out even further along the river," Gans noted later.

When the project was officially announced in December 1925, it became the talk of New York. A complex of ten tall buildings, it would be the largest residential development in the city and "the first residential skyscraper enclave in the world." Tudor City would also be New York's most ambitious urban renewal project of the 1920s, a privately funded venture that would complement the riverfront improvements begun further north by the privileged ladies of Sutton Place. City officials considered it the most important commercial development in that section of town since the building of the new Grand Central Terminal. The project would cost $100 million roughly $800 hundred million in today's dollars. Fred French would raise every cent of this through the French Plan, the financial scheme he created in 1921 to underwrite his expanding real estate investments.

Six years after Tudor City was completed, the editors of the *Real Estate Record* assessed Fred French's contribution as a Manhattan developer. "Other men have successfully applied the technique of assembling contiguous and adjacent holdings. . . . French's claim to a place in the history of real estate will rest . . . on . . . his financial genius."

Most speculative real estate investors hired Wall Street brokerage houses to market their securities. French eliminated the middleman, hiring his own sales force to sell stock in the company. By marketing its own securities, his company obtained a "never ending stream" of new capital for its building programs at much lower cost than if it had used the services of a brokerage concern or a bond house. To entice investors, French's sales force offered them the opportunity to own equity in a project, as well as a share in its profits; and unlike most real estate developers, French marketed his stock as aggressively to small investors as to large ones, and on the same terms. He had, he claimed, democratized real estate investment. "Never before," said this master pitchman, "have the public been permitted to participate in the erection and ownership of income producing buildings and obtain their rightful share of the profits. . . . Never before . . . has the man with $100 to invest been given the same terms as the man with $100,000."*

It was an ingenious plan, cutting-edge for its time, the antecedent of post–World War II mass real estate syndication schemes. The Fred F. French Companies used funds raised from its sale of long-term stock shares to pay for half the cost of acquiring a site and constructing a building on it. The other half was covered by a conventional mortgage. For each share of preferred stock the company sold, it gave the buyer one share of common stock, and kept one for the company as its profit.† French vowed to take no profits from the property until he had repaid the investors their original stake, plus 6 percent a year. When the mortgage was paid off, the investors owned the building jointly with the Fred F. French Companies and the profits were divided equally "in perpetuity."

French promoted the plan as a conservative investment, ideal for those willing to accept slower returns for a steadily growing equity value. Eventually over thirty thousand people from all walks of life invested in the plan, an "equity audience" that was nearly 2 percent of the customers of the New York Stock Exchange in 1929. This is an impressive figure when one considers that

---

* The investment syndicates formed later in the decade by Benjamin Winter and other big speculators also issued securities to small investors, but issued them through Wall Street brokerage houses, passing on the cost to investors.

† Preferred stock entitles the holder to a fixed dividend whose payment has priority over that of common stock dividends. Common stock entitles the holder to dividends that vary in amount depending on the fortunes of the company.

French stock was not listed on any exchange. Such a heavy influx of revenue allowed his company to finance over $100 million of New York City real estate.

The French organization retained complete control of its projects from inception to completion through a number of ancillary companies. The Fred F. French Investment Company sold stock and acquired the building site. Fred F. French, Architects and Designers, planned and built the project, using its own architects, engineers, and contractors; and another French company managed the properties. Costs were kept under control, and profits maximized for both investors and the company, by having the underwriter, architect, builder, and real estate manager working in harmony under clear central direction. French was the only land developer in New York City, perhaps in the country, to integrate every aspect of the real estate business into "one profitable whole."

The French Plan had the added advantage of encouraging sound construction practices. In conventional real estate financing there is pressure to build quickly so that the completed building can be resold at a big profit and impatient investors paid off. This often encourages shoddy construction. By contrast, French stock offered no opportunity for a quick kill. Investors were in for the long haul since no dividends were paid on the common stock until all the preferred stock was retired. Only then was their common stock converted to half ownership. Because of the long lives of the stock issues, the company had a powerful incentive to build properties that held their value. As one prominent real estate expert noted, the French Company shrewdly recognized that "sound architecture [gives] *investment values* to buildings, as distinguished from a *speculative status.*"

The survival of the company hinged on its ability to sell stock. Without sales there could be no construction. This impelled French to take direct responsibility for training and motivating his sales force. A Babbitt with brains, he styled himself an enlightened capitalist performing "one of the most important functions of mankind—the distribution of ideas and things among men."

His daily sales conferences were conducted with the fervor of a fundamentalist camp meeting. Every morning his phalanx of salesmen, 150 strong, gathered in the auditorium of the Fred French Building to listen to the preachments of the founder. At nine o'clock sharp the doors were locked; those arriving late had to listen through keyholes. His friend Kenneth Murchison, an architect and architecture critic, was at one of these meetings. "Fred French steps forth with fire in his eye and proceeds, with amazing eloquence and force, to instill a part of his great enthusiasm in these salesmen, sending them forth in flying squadrons to mop up the ready cash of those investors who are lying in wait for a good thing."

"He is . . . [the] Mark Antony of business," said Alva Johnston, the orator who "talked Tudor City into existence." His secular sermons were parables on the possibilities of self-improvement. Teach yourself to smile, "stand before your bathroom mirror and practice smiling for ten minutes in the morning and at night," he would plead. "Get smiling into your system." He spoke with "religio-commercial enthusiasm," translating "Scripture into go-getter dialect."

Three years before the Madison Avenue adman Bruce Barton published *The Man Nobody Knows*, his best-selling 1925 book depicting Jesus Christ as an inspiration for the modern businessman, Fred French was using the "Son of the Father" in the service of commercial gain. Follow the biblical advice of "the greatest salesman of all time," French implored his salesmen. "Knock and it shall be opened unto you." To which French added his own fillip: "Keep knocking until the door is opened, and, if it isn't opened pretty soon, kick [it] down."

Hard, persistent labor was the secret to success, he would thunder. At age thirty-two French wrote in his diary, "Still working like H—!" And he continued to work, nonstop, until his last breath. "He is a marvel of enthusiasm," said Murchison, "[but] he seems to do nothing but work." At home, he read inspirational literature and studied philosophy for clues to self-advancement. He handed out reprints of these essays and chapters to his sales force. If Fred French's son John is to be believed, his father's lectures had an "electrifying" effect on the sales force. On the other hand, their enthusiasm may have arisen from the fact that they were paid only if they produced. You are the "scouts," French told his "commission-only" sales force, "the adventurers who dare . . . to spurn a regular income." John French extolled his father's practice of dividing his sales force into "enthusiastic" competitive teams, but quietly conceded that only "sometimes" did the winners get a bonus.

Fred French also reached out directly to his thirty thousand stockholders with his monthly house organ, *The Voice*. He wrote most of the copy, a hodge-podge of homilies and pious stories of his early struggles as a Texas miner and an underpaid construction boss.

Like the fictional George F. Babbitt, French was socially intolerant and narrow-minded. He refused to hire women—"they can't hew to the line"—and his sales force was lily-white and prevailingly Protestant. His great hero was Theodore Roosevelt, exemplar of the strenuous life. French went on bear hunting trips to the North Woods "fully accoutered, his rifle and hunting clothes identical with Teddy's." But even on these escapes into the wild, he was ever on the lookout for ways to motivate his sales force. On his return from a hunting trip in Wyoming he wrote a banal effusion on how "Hard Work Brings Success in Hunting as Well as in Business."

A vehement man, he retained, said *The New York Times*, "something of that dominating power which stood him in good stead as a construction 'overseer.'" His voice could be soft and soothing, but he drove his managerial staff—which included his former engineering professor at Columbia—relentlessly. "Agents are sent out to buy sites as if to battle," wrote Robert M. Coates in his pitch-perfect *New Yorker* profile of French.

Away from the office, he was more relaxed. He liked to roughhouse with his boys in a playroom he had built for them; and he allowed them to poke fun at his perfectly bald dome. He loathed social occasions. When he and his wife entertained, it was mostly for clients. A teetotaler, he served grape juice in wineglasses; and though he loved gourmet food, he had no gift for informal conversation. For him, an excellent evening was an evening at home with the family. He thought the theater "a waste of time" and wouldn't own a car because he feared repairmen might cheat him.

French's greatest excitement was his mid-Manhattan housing project. Once the land was acquired, construction went forward at a furious pace, according to the designs of H. Douglas Ives, this time laboring alone. In the late summer of 1927, just as work was coming to a close on the Fred French Building on Fifth Avenue, the first two towers of the complex—an apartment building and an apartment hotel—were opened. Three years later, Tudor City was completed and more than 98 percent rented. The achievement was unprecedented: a shantytown transformed into a tower city "in the heart of everything," said one New York booster. Only a four-minute walk from Grand Central Terminal, Tudor City was "more secluded, more quiet, more remote from the disturbances of the city than many a suburban home," claimed an ad generated by the Fred F. French Management Company.

The site planning was inspired. No building faced the river and the abattoirs that defiled its banks. The back walls of the apartments were without windows, and the entrances were oriented inward, toward two landscaped parks with wooden benches, vine-draped gazebos, and gravel paths for dog walkers. Uniformed landscaping crews transported fully grown trees to the site and tended to the lawns and gardens.

Tudor City had a full slate of recreational and cultural amenities for its 4,500 residents: a gymnasium, bowling alleys, clay tennis courts, babysitting services, a library, and communal sundecks atop two of the towers. There was even a small eighteen-hole golf course with sand traps and a tricky water hazard; and the links were illuminated for night play. In foul weather residents could practice on an indoor miniature course, under the eye of the community's golf pro. "Live here," said Fred French with customary overkill, "and cut ten to fifteen strokes off your score."

Tudor City took its name from its architecture. With the single exception of the Art Deco hotel, the buildings are clad with rusticated reddish brown bricks and designed to suggest the towers and spires of Tudor castles and manor houses. The company settled on this style because of its proven marketability. It had already built a number of Tudor-style apartment complexes in the outer boroughs—all of them successful. But Ives was no mere copyist. He melded historic ornament with the decade's progressive penchant for mountainlike massing and composition.

Five of the buildings in Tudor City were apartment hotels equipped with restaurants, meeting rooms, lounges, telegraph offices, newsstands, theaters, valet services, and places to store luggage. Their studio units rented briskly to young, unmarried secretaries, bookkeepers, and salesmen—and to busy executives who lived in the far suburbs and needed to spend a night or two in the city, if only to see their mistresses. The other four apartment houses had three to seven-room suites. The last building to be constructed was the seventeen-story hotel.

With its quaint post office and specialty shops, Tudor City's small commercial strip resembled a Cotswold High Street, albeit one enclosed by formidable modern towers. And the community's luxurious appointments belie the fact that it was an emphatically affordable place. "Tudor City does not appeal to millionaires," proclaimed a French Company advertisement, "but to the better type of the 'middle classes.'"

In 1929, with his miniature city thriving, Fred French began work on an even bigger residential project, this one on New York's Lower East Side, between the Brooklyn and Manhattan Bridges. Over forty brokers, working through dummy corporations, spent $5 million buying fifteen acres of slum property for a "walk-to-work" white-collar community within easy reach of Wall Street. The brokers French hired were required to take oaths of secrecy and sign papers binding them not to discuss the project with "anyone." Few realized that French, known to them only by his code name "The Big Chief," was directing the operation. The great real estate raid was a masterwork of speed and sleuth, but it all appeared for naught when the Stock Market Crash compelled French to stop building.

The Great Depression cut off the flow of investment money, and French was forced to default on millions of dollars of preferred stock issued through the vehicle of his French Plan. In 1931 he suffered another public embarrassment. Hauled before the Seabury Committee investigating corruption in city government, he was questioned closely about the payments he had made to

George Olvany's law firm to secure favorable interpretations of the city's building code regulations, transactions for which he was never legally charged.

Two years later, French recovered his equilibrium and lined up support for his housing scheme from former Governor Al Smith, who had grown up in the slum French would demolish to make room for his new community. French then convinced the federal government's Reconstruction Finance Corporation to back a scaled-down version of his housing development, under the proviso that it operate as a limited dividend corporation. Knickerbocker Village, a middle-income community of two twelve-story apartment buildings managed by the Fred French Companies, became the country's first federally funded urban redevelopment project. It was not, however, the kind of community French had envisioned—smaller than originally planned and bereft of the community amenities of Tudor City. It was also beset with problems. The worst was an ugly rent strike triggered by the French Companies's failure to have the apartments fitted out in time with the household appliances and other conveniences the original tenants had been promised.

On August 30, 1936, two years after the strike was settled to the tenants' satisfaction, French suffered a massive heart attack in his sleep and was pronounced dead the next morning. He was fifty-three years old. He left this world with only $10,000 in personal property, a heavy mortgage on a vacation estate in the Berkshires, and stockholder lawsuits that would take decades to resolve. He left, as well, two landmark projects in his native city, a stately Fifth Avenue skyscraper and a skyscraper village that worked lasting changes in mid-Manhattan's cityscape. "He is a success," said Robert Coates, "and the record of his accomplishments is written in the blind magnificence of stone and steel."

CHAPTER TWELVE

MASTERS OF THE SKYLINE

By night the skyscraper looms in the smoke and the stars and has a soul.

CARL SANDBURG, "SKYSCRAPER"

Irwin Chanin

In 1927, four months before the official opening of the Fred F. French Building, Irwin S. Chanin announced plans for a "twelve million dollar tower" on the southwest corner of Lexington Avenue and Forty-second Street, directly across from Grand Central Terminal. At fifty-six stories—eighteen floors taller than the Fred French Building—it would be the first of the immensely tall skyscrapers on Forty-second Street and the fourth highest building on earth. Sloan and Robertson, collaborating architects on the Fred French Building, captured the commission. They had recently designed the Gray-bar Building, a bulky, thirty-one-story colossus, the largest office building in the world at that time, with 1.5 million square feet of space. Located on Lexington Avenue and East Forty-third Street, one block north of the Chanin site, this "Jazz Age ziggurat" hovered over Grand Central Terminal and was connected to it by a pedestrian passageway. But even with its strategic location, it was considered a risky investment. Would high-end commercial tenants be interested in locating on Lexington Avenue, in what was still considered a "quiet neighborhood"?

There was equal concern about the Chanin project. At least the Graybar Building had the backing of its heavily capitalized client: the Graybar Electric Company, a spin-off of the Western Electric Company.* Irwin Chanin, on the other hand, was a "Mysterious Stranger in [Manhattan] business affairs," a builder who lived across the river in Bensonhurst, the Brooklyn neighborhood where he was raised by hard-pressed Jewish immigrants from Ukraine. Chanin was a Manhattan arriviste, inadequately equipped—or it seemed—to take on a project of this magnitude. He was young—thirty-four years old—and had been in the real estate business only seven years.

Back in 1919 he had borrowed his fiancée's life's savings of $300 to form a family-run construction company. For the first few months it had no capital and only one project under contract, a pair of single-family houses in Brooklyn, where Chanin was living with his parents. Unable to afford the streetcar fare, he peddled out to the construction site every morning on a bicycle.

With the assistance of his brother Henry, his financial manager, Chanin managed his investments superbly, expanded the business, and built a solid reputation with the Wall Street bond houses that financed his first Manhattan projects: the Fur Center Building in the Garment District and a string of dazzlingly modern Broadway theaters. But in 1927, when the Chanin Construction Company planted its sign on the cleared Forty-second Street site of its projected skyscraper, "a good many people didn't know whether the Chanins were builders or, since the name was well known on Broadway, theatre-owners who had taken up building as a sideline."

Two years later, the great skyscraper was finished, and Irwin Chanin was being touted in print—along with real estate rival Fred French—as one of New York's "hundred wonder men." His "achievements," wrote *The New Yorker*'s Niven Busch, Jr., were staggering: "a whole city of scattered buildings, a hundred and forty-one of them in New York and Brooklyn." A small, dark-eyed man, as serious-looking as an undertaker, Chanin was "one of those amazing Jews who perform what seem to be miracles of achievement," wrote reporter Mary B. Mullet. And his crowning accomplishment was the Chanin Building, which was almost completely rented before its doors were opened. This, along with recent reports that the Graybar Building was fully rented, confirmed Irwin Chanin's conviction that the area around Forty-second Street and Lexington Avenue was poised to become the most impressive skyscraper district on earth.

A millionaire several times over, Chanin claimed to be unconcerned about money. "Money is the easiest thing in the world to get," he would say. "You just

---

* The Graybar Company was named after the founders of Western Electric: Elisha Gray and Enos Barton.

have to have ideas and it will come to you—why, it will pour in." Irwin Chanin saw buildings as "ideas," his ideas, extensions of himself in stone and steel. A self-trained architect, he placed his personal imprint on every one of his real estate projects, and contributed more to the distinctive design of the Chanin Building than the architects he hired. Although his brother Henry was listed as an equal partner in the firm, Irwin Chanin, "a master of the skyline," made all the big decisions. "He started things in the first place," said Niven Busch, "and the story of the Chanins' rise is really his story."

Irwin Salmon Chanin was born in Bensonhurst on October 29, 1891. His father, Simon, a general contractor, and his mother, Zenda, were natives of Poltava, in Ukraine. They had arrived in the United States in 1889 and settled in Brooklyn, but returned to Poltava with their three children when Irwin was eight years old. With a nest egg of $10,000, they had enough, they thought, to live comfortably back in the home country, which they missed desperately. Eight years later, in 1907, they were back in Bensonhurst after Simon, an impulsive dreamer, lost the family's savings on a succession of ill-advised investments.

Irwin had attended a private school in Russia, where he had developed an interest in architecture and engineering. In Bensonhurst, he worked for his father, plastering and painting for a dollar a week; and at age eighteen he was accepted at Cooper Union in downtown Manhattan, a tuition-free college that offered degrees in art, architecture, and engineering.* "I didn't waste time and strength in other ways: dancing and sports and just playing around," he later described his narrowly focused years at Cooper Union. "I wanted to learn all there was to be known about engineering."

After graduating at the top of his class in 1915, he worked for a subway contractor before enlisting in the wartime Army. He wanted to see combat, but spent most of his time locked inside a top secret barbed wire enclosure near Cleveland, building a poison gas plant. "Before going there, I never had put up a building of any sort," he recalled years later. Following his discharge, he returned to his parents' home in Bensonhurst and "tried to figure out some way to make a living."

At the time, all he had was $200 and what friends considered a "crazy idea." Contractors in Bensonhurst were making a killing buying land and putting up hastily built frame houses for upward-bound Jewish families fleeing the

---

* Its architecture school was later named after Irwin Chanin, a major benefactor.

Lower East Side. Chanin thought he could build better houses for the same price. With loans from his future wife and a trusting neighborhood banker, he bought a pair of vacant lots in Bensonhurst, built two cottages, and sold them for a tidy profit of $6,000. "I adopted the creed," he said later, "which I have clung to ever since: Give people something different, something better, and something *more* than they have a right to expect." A decade later, at the official opening of his Forty-second Street skyscraper, a beaming Irwin Chanin showed off a plaster model of the Bensonhurst cottages that were "the first step in his rise."

When his Bensonhurst business began to take off, Irwin brought in his brother Henry, an accountant, as secretary-treasurer. The first office of the Chanin Construction Company was a corner desk in their father's paint store. Orders for more houses came pouring in, and after the brothers built a tall office complex in downtown Brooklyn they were ready for the big move: "over the bridge," into Manhattan. In 1924, they built one of the first skyscraper lofts in the Garment District. The next year, operating out of their new Midtown headquarters, they began constructing Broadway theaters.

It was Irwin's idea. "I discovered that there wasn't a 'dark' theatre in the city. . . . Every one of them was open and making money for the owner. So I determined to build a theatre." This was the Forty-sixth Street Theatre; and it was followed by five more in quick succession, eight by 1928, including the Majestic, the largest legitimate theater in the Times Square district. Chanin's playhouses were "among the best equipped in the world," said *The New York Times*. They had state-of-the-art acoustics and stage equipment; and none of them had "cheap seats"—a gallery with a separate entrance on the side of the theater. Irwin Chanin had not forgotten an "old grievance." As a student at Cooper Union, the Broadway theater had been his sole diversion, but he had been able to afford only the fifty-cent seats in the top galleries. "I wasn't allowed to use the main entrance, and this always humiliated me. . . . At my theatres," he told a reporter, "the girl from the 'five-and ten' and the richest aristocrat in town enter by the same door."

Chanin hired his own play director and began backing Broadway productions, all the while looking for fresh real estate opportunities in Midtown. Late one evening, working well past closing in their Manhattan office, he and his brother decided to spend the night at a hotel rather than return by car to their Brooklyn homes. They called six of the biggest hotels in town; all were fully booked. The light went on: they would build a hotel, which Irwin would name after his "ideal of a man." The thirty-story Hotel Lincoln, the tallest in the Times Square district, occupied an entire block front on Eighth Avenue, next door to three Chanin theaters.* But as the 1,400-room hotel was nearing completion in the late spring of 1927—the eighth anniversary of the founding of the Chanin Construction Company—the brothers sold it for $9 million and turned their full attention to their new skyscraper project on Forty-second Street.

Sky Boys

Excavation began that spring, following the demolition of the fortresslike Manhattan Storage Warehouse—its five-foot-thick brick walls designed to withstand "burglary, fire, and assault." It was one of the most difficult and costly wrecking jobs undertaken in the city. When the dust cleared and the foundations of the new building were laid, tremendous derricks with hundred-foot-long booms appeared on the site. At this point, the steel gangs arrived to construct the skyscraper's imposing metal frame, a supporting skeleton designed to carry 200 million pounds.

Skyscrapers are the largest and costliest habitable structures on earth, some of them with daytime populations equal to that of small cities. By the 1920s, they had become too big and technologically complex for a single architect or a small architectural office to take on. Only corporate-like architecture offices staffed by teams of draftsmen, designers, and engineers, working hand in glove with highly specialized construction companies, could build them fast enough to satisfy financial backers. "The architect designing a big building today," said Raymond Hood, "is more like a Henry Ford than a Michelangelo."

As in assembly line construction, speed was the sine qua non: every hour lost to delay meant the loss of dollars and cents. This threw enormous responsibility on the builder, the "generalissimo" of the project. Once the plans were completed, it was his show. He oversaw the work of the fifty to sixty trades and the dozens of industrial concerns involved in the construction of a typical New York skyscraper, coordinating and supervising the work of electrical engineers, heating contractors, rivet crews, plumbers, bricklayers, carpenters, plasterers, and dozens of other highly specialized operatives. This is why all-controlling developers like Irwin Chanin and Fred French had their own construction companies: to ensure that every part of the builder's business, from the ordering of lightbulbs to the raising of thousand-pound beams, came under their exacting scrutiny.

----

* Its name was later changed to the Milford Plaza.

The skyscraper is an American original. Invented in late-nineteenth-century New York, and brought to full maturity in Chicago in the 1890s with the development of the self-supporting metal skeleton, it is the most remarkable single construction feat of a nation known the world over for its engineering achievements: roaring steel mills, long-reaching railroads, and wondrous suspension bridges. "The skyscraper is the most distinctly American thing in the world," said W. A. Starrett. "It is all American and all ours in its conception, [and] all-important in our metropolitan life." America's preeminent contribution to world architecture, it is a symbol of the ideas and aspirations of a new civic culture that appeared with its development, a culture whose main business was business itself.

Like the building of a medieval cathedral, the construction of the Chanin Building was a thrilling public spectacle, a technological show that took place out in the open, in the heart of town. As its spidery steel framework reached dizzying heights, some spectators arrived at the site with binoculars to spy "tiny ant-like men walking along the topmost girders, hopping from one to the other." These "sky boys" were being featured in dozens of full-length articles that appeared in New York newspapers and magazines during the Midtown building boom, "dashing and tragic figures who walked on air like supermen and dropped from the sky like stricken birds." As the Chanin Building reached for the clouds, a film called *Skyscraper* opened at the new Paramount Theatre at Forty-third and Broadway. It was crudely melodramatic, yet its depiction of "the heroes of the girders" was impressively realistic.

High steel construction had become popular Manhattan street theater. Bystanders who gathered around the construction site of the Chanin Building witnessed an operation that was conducted, amazingly, off the backs of trucks. In this densely crowded section of the city, a skyscraper had to be built this way; there was no vacant land to store building materials, neither bricks nor I-beams, neither wire nor wood; and contractors were forbidden to store anything on public sidewalks and streets. Construction trucks headed for the Chanin Building—as many as four hundred a day—had to keep moving, loading and unloading at breakneck speed so as not to impede traffic in the congested Grand Central Zone. Everything they carried, from structural steel to bathroom fixtures, had to be installed at once into the building.

This demanded near perfect timing. Eighty hours after beams were forged at Pittsburgh mills they arrived at the Chanin construction site within minutes of the time they were to be placed on the building's frame. Other materials, not just steel, arrived exactly on time after transport by rail, water, and highway from places thirty to three thousand miles away: brass pipe from Connecticut; asbestos from Quebec; insulating cork from Portugal; limestone from Indiana; travertine from Italy; granite from Vermont; zinc from Oklahoma. At the "end point" there was a "convergence of muscle and material and technology," men working as "hard as they could, moving ever higher."

Onlookers were treated to a construction ballet of intricate precision and synchronization, and the most fascinating street spectacle was aloft: the iron-men navigating "needle beams" four inches wide, a fifth of a mile above the pavement, without handholds or safety supports of any kind, their lives depen-dent on their uncanny sense of balance and seeming indifference to perilous heights.* Yet it wasn't quite as easy, or as natural, as it appeared. "I have seen men who had not had experience with height . . . get down and hug themselves around the beam, their eyes tightly shut, and gasping as though they were drowning," said W. A. Starrett.

Working in unison with the derrick operators, the "raising crews" met the long trucks carrying the steel columns, beams, and girders, each one with a code mark chalked or painted on it, indicating its assigned place on the great skeleton. The steel was warm to the touch, still holding heat from the forge. The raising gangs swung heavy cables around these bundles of steel and sig-naled to the derrick operator to lift them skyward to the "connecting" gangs, perched high up on the girders, where "even the birds don't fly." The "connec-tors," aerial artists working in teams of two, muscled these swinging beams into place and slipped bolts into precut holes to join them together temporar-ily. Then the riveters arrived and permanently sealed the connections.

The riveting gangs were "wondrous to watch." Crowds of pedestrians gathered on the sidewalk around the Chanin Building, craning their necks as the crews put on "the best open-air show in town," a "sky spectacle," wrote a *New York Times* reporter. There were four men in a riveting gang: a heater, a catcher, a bucker-up, and a gunman. The heater placed a few wooden planks across the widely spaced steel girders that formed the outline of part of one of the future floors of the building. These planks were the platform for the porta-ble, coal-burning forge in which he heated the rivets. The other three members of his crew placed a narrow plank scaffold on the steel on which they would be

---

* They called themselves ironworkers although they worked with steel. A steelworker, as the saying went, makes steel; an ironworker builds steel structures. All New York's skyscrap-ers of the 1920s had a steel skeleton. Today, reinforced concrete has replaced steel as the structural material of many tall hotels and apartment houses. It can be applied quicker than steel and is easier to mold and modify in the construction process. But steel is far stronger, and remains the structural material of many tall buildings.

working. There was "just room enough to work; one false step and its goodbye Charlie," wrote *New Yorker* reporter Joseph Mitchell.

Using long tongs, the heater pulled a cherry-red rivet—a small steel cylinder with no threads and one round head—out of the portable oven. He then tossed it underhand, "in a glowing arc," to the catcher, standing as far as seventy feet away, and sometimes on a floor above. The catcher snared it with his "glove"—a battered metal can—plucked it out of the can with a pair of tongs, and placed it in the hole of the two overlapping steel members to be riveted together. The bucker-up held the mushroomlike cap of the rivet in place with a short metal tool called a dolly bar. The gunner then pressed the head of his pneumatic hammer against the stem of the rivet and held it there, absorbing its bone-jarring concussive force until the stem of the still malleable rivet was smashed into a "cap," flush against the steel. The entire operation took less than a minute—"heat, toss, insert, smash, then move on across the steel to the next rivet hole." An experienced crew could pound in five hundred rivets a day—"muscle and steel and heat, working together to forge a skyscraper."

The operation looked effortless, but was highly dangerous. If the catcher missed a blazing rivet, it either hit him or fell below, a malevolent missile ca-

Ironworkers secure a rivet. (LEWIS WICKES HINE/NEW YORK PUBLIC LIBRARY)

pable of driving a steaming hole into a person's skull. A curious reporter asked a "catcher" if he was trained for his job, perhaps by catching cold rivets. "Naw. It's as easy as catching a baseball. It's the same thing. They just stick you in there—and you catch them or get burnt."

The work began at eight in the morning and the closing whistle blew at four-thirty sharp. Work stopped almost instantaneously. "Hundreds of men banging, tearing, hammering, drilling, raising a racket, and then—nothing, like a switch thrown, a stunned quiet that made the ears ache for sound." From high on the steel frame of the Chanin Building iron connectors shimmied down the columns "monkey fashion," their tool belts riding low on their waists. Other workers descended long ladders to the same place, the middle floors, where they boarded elevators that carried them to the street. They headed out together, a long, discontinuous line, the ironmen joined by carpenters, plasterers, electricians, tile men, steamfitters, plumbers, painters, and cement finishers.

It was a rare ironworker who headed home before stopping for a shot and a beer. Cheap speakeasies proliferated around the big construction sites in the city, the owners "protected"—for a price—by Tammany cops. The ironmen had money to spend; they were paid union scale, nearly two dollars an hour. Some men lingered into the night in the obliging company of a bought woman, but most preferred the raucous companionship of their fellow workers, a great many of them "cousins and brothers and fathers and sons." Whether joined by blood or not, an iron gang was a tight fraternity, a "family," the men called it. If one of them failed to show up at the job, the rest of the gang took the day off rather than work with a new man.

Steel erectors had the most dangerous job in construction; the third most dangerous job in existence, after logging and commercial fishing. Their accident rate was appalling. Each year, two out of every hundred ironworkers could expect to die at the worksite, and another two to be permanently disabled. In the 1920s, ironworkers suffered one violent death, on average, for every thirty-three hours on the job, with falls accounting for most fatalities and serious injuries. "We do not die. We are killed," ironworkers would say.

The men had no safety harnesses or hard hats, and only a modicum of accident insurance coverage if they happened to belong to a union. Later in the century, insurance companies and the federal government's Occupational Safety and Health Administration (OSHA) would force construction companies to institute stronger safety measures. This would cut down on injuries and fatalities, but in the 1920s a "bloodless building" was a rarity.

There were normal "annoyances" that ironworkers rarely complained about: showers of sparks that fell from acetylene torches, inflicting deep burns;

and the racket of the rivet hammers, which caused more than a few men to lose their hearing. But ironmen did complain—incessantly and intensely—about the weather. "When it rains, everything gets slippery. And when it gets cold, sometimes your hands get so stiff that you can't hang on to anything. That's bad."

Sidewalk spectators witnessed dozens of grisly accidents caused by weather, carelessness, or plain bad luck. Homebound workers hurrying along Fifth Avenue around five-thirty on August 3, 1926, paused to watch an ironworker riding a girder like a tightrope walker. There was applause and whistling. Just as the girder was about to be eased into position on the building's metal frame, it swung wildly out of control and smashed into another girder. The steel cable snapped, sending the rider to his death in a steep, headfirst descent. The errant girder nearly killed dozens of pedestrians.

The unfortunate ironworker had not been paying attention, but when an entire construction company was guilty of negligence the results could be catastrophic. Four workmen were killed instantly and eleven others injured when a six-ton bundle of steel plummeted twenty stories from a skyscraper frame on West Broadway. Witnesses said the steel fell with the speed of "a high explosive shell" and crushed the men "before they sensed its coming." Four employees of the construction company were arrested and charged with manslaughter. The brakes on the hoisting engine had malfunctioned and failed to halt the "avalanche of steel on its downward flight." Investigators found evidence of negligence. Unqualified superintendents had allowed the derrick cables that hoisted the steel to become dangerously overloaded.

A year earlier, a more deadly accident nearly occurred on the twentieth story of the Chanin Building's metal skeleton. The cables supporting a steel boom—the hoisting arm of the derrick—snapped as the boom was lifting a ten-ton girder from a loading truck. A large crowd on East Forty-first Street was watching when the boom began plummeting to the pavement, somersaulting as it fell three hundred feet. Pedestrians scurried for cover and were spared when it bounced off the framework of the building and broke into two parts. One part buried itself in the roof of a house across the street; the other struck the loading truck, nearly severing it in two. The operator of the boom was seated in his cab at the foot of the building, unaware that the boom had fallen. When it hit the loading truck, parked only a few feet behind him, he "sprang from his seat and ran away, thinking an explosion had occurred."

Irwin Chanin was in the office of his construction company, two blocks away, when word reached him. He rushed to the scene and was relieved to learn that no one had been hurt. No charges were filed against his powerfully influential company.

High-ironmen were recruited from all over the country. Some of the best were former square-rig sailors: Swedes, Danes, Finns, Norwegians, and Newfoundlanders, men with wind-lashed faces and gnarled hands. They were practiced seamen who had worked high in the rigging and on the tops of masts, and had been "driven ashore" when their sailing ships became obsolete. They had learned "equilibrium, agility, and sure-footedness in the shrouds," and how to "cling to life in howling gales." But like America itself, the profession drew men from nearly all walks of life and nearly every part of the globe. They traveled in gangs, and every gang had its "pusher," or boss, and its own customs and superstitions. Nomadic and fiercely independent, "there's not a job from Broadway to the moon they wouldn't jump at," wrote New York novelist Ernest Poole. "The higher it is, the windier, the more ticklish, the better."

"You get to love it and can't quit it," said one veteran ironman. "Who wants to be a pencil pusher after he's worked with steel." Ironmen didn't feel they were reckless, and didn't like being called "cowboys." It took steady nerves to work on high iron. And it was purposeful work, work they were proud of—building a skyline like none other on earth. "It's nice to point to a . . . towering building and say, 'I erected that,'" said a Manhattan ironman.

The Mohawks in High Steel

"In the New York gangs this year, two full-blooded Indians are at work: cool-headed and sure, a solid pair who have little to say," Ernest Poole wrote in 1908. By the 1920s there were hundreds of Mohawks climbing high steel in the city. They were converts to Catholicism from a small reservation of three thousand souls at the Lachine Rapids on the south shore of the St. Lawrence River, nine miles upriver from Montreal. They called their home Kahnawake, Mohawk for "at the rapids."*

The New York pioneers—John Diablo, their leader, and three other tribesmen—had arrived sometime in 1915 or 1916 to work on the Hell Gate railroad bridge, the longest steel arch span in the world when it was completed in 1917. When Diablo fell to his death, his compatriots took his body back to the reser-

---

* A small minority had converted to Protestantism and a few held fast to their ancient "longhouse" religious practices. In his classic essay on New York's Mohawk ironworkers, *New Yorker* reporter Joseph Mitchell called the reservation Caughnawaga and its people the Caughnawagas.

vation and never returned. But other Mohawks came after the war to work on the steel frameworks of the Fred French, the Graybar, and the Chanin Buildings. They found rooms in flophouses and walk-up hotels in North Gowanus, a Brooklyn neighborhood along the poisonously contaminated Gowanus Canal, close to their local union hall. From Brooklyn, the gangs rode the subway to the skyscraper canyons of Manhattan. At least one weekend a month they returned to the reservation. It was a draining, twelve-hour drive, and few made it without a bellyful of beer. Border agents harassed them, but after a contentious court fight, the U.S. government permitted them to cross the border freely. They had only to show a photo-ID card—a "passport," they called it—certifying that they were members of the tribe.

In the late 1920s some of the Mohawk wives made the move to Brooklyn to be with their husbands. They transformed a tight, ten-block area of North Gowanus into a real community, not simply a place to drink, eat, and sleep. They called it Little Caughnawaga, the white man's spelling of the name of their Canadian settlement. (This area is now known as Boerum Hill.) Married couples lived in rented houses the wives kept "sparklingly clean"; local Italian grocers carried the Mohawks' favorite cornmeal—fine ground and packaged; and Caughnawaga men drank imported Canadian beer at the Wigwam, a Nevins Street saloon with a framed picture of Jim Thorpe, the great Native American athlete, on the wall. Pasted on the barroom mirror were notes from widows of fallen ironworkers thanking the men for taking up a collection for their grieving families. "I enjoy New York," a Mohawk ironman told Joseph Mitchell. "The people are as high-strung as rats and the air is too gritty, but I enjoy it." But like most other Mohawks, he didn't love it enough to make it his permanent home. The Mohawks "think of their Brooklyn dwellings as secondary camping grounds," wrote *Times* reporter Meyer Berger. "When spring comes they send their families back to [Canada] . . . and see them only on weekends." The men who stayed in Brooklyn filled their vacant hours swapping stories and playing lacrosse, a game their ancient ancestors invented.*

---

* This community, whose population never exceeded nine hundred residents, began disappearing in the early 1960s, as crime and drug trafficking increased in the Gowanus area. It vanished around 1967, with the completion of the Northway, an extension of Interstate 87. The new road halved the commuting time to Montreal from twelve to six hours, allowing the men to move their families back to Kahnawake, where they could visit them nearly every weekend. During the week the men lived in rented rooms scattered around Brooklyn and the Bronx. When the New York construction boom went bust between 1985 and 1995, the Kahnawake ironmen drifted off to other cities or went back to the reservation, only to

The Kahnawake Mohawks were renowned for their skill and daring. Said to be "as agile as goats," they "walked the iron" with aplomb, at heights that would have made a circus performer cringe. It was in their blood. Their ancestors had been constructing high iron bridges since 1886. In that year the Dominion Bridge Company began building a cantilever railway bridge across the St. Lawrence River for the Canadian Pacific Railroad. Part of the bridge abutment rested on Kahnawake reservation property, and, as compensation, the railroad hired tribesmen as day laborers, unloading boxcars and hauling stones for the bridge's foundations. As the work progressed, the Mohawks "would climb up into the spans and walk around up there as cool and collected as the toughest of our riveters," said an official of the bridge company. They began to pester the foremen to give them a crack at riveting. "So we picked out some and gave them a little training, and it turned out that putting riveting tools in their hands was like putting ham with eggs. . . . They were natural-born bridgemen." There were twelve of them, all in their teens. "The Fearless Wonders," other villagers called them.

When the Canadian Pacific Bridge was completed, the men of the reservation began working on a number of other steel spans over the St. Lawrence. By 1907 there were seventy skilled bridgemen on the reservation. In late August of that year, thirty-three Kahnawake men were horribly crushed or drowned when an enormous span they were working on near Quebec City buckled and collapsed into the river. No one expected the Mohawks to return to bridge building. But the Quebec Bridge disaster made high steel "more interesting" to Kahnawake males, recalls a village patriarch. They were proud "that they could do such dangerous work." It made them "the most looked-up-to men on the reservation."

At this point, the women of the village intervened. If the men were going to continue to work on bridges the wives and mothers demanded that they split up and disperse. That way, if there were other disasters there would not be so many widows. Kahnawake gangs took jobs in Buffalo, Cleveland, and Detroit, and eventually New York, where it was an easy transition from bridge building to skyscraper work. "Booming Out," the men called their urban migrations; and in secret defiance of their wives' wishes, many of them stuck together as gangs.

Migratory work was consistent with their ancient warrior belief that taking care of the family and the settlement was women's work; and working on high iron enhanced their self-esteem in a female-dominated society where

---

return when construction picked up again in the late 1990s. By 2001 there were about 250 Mohawk ironworkers in the metropolitan region. Renee Valois, "The Mohawks Who Built Manhattan," The History Channel Club, History.com.

women—"progenitors of the nation"—had historically been the major decision makers. To this day, Mohawk women are forbidden to touch their husbands' leather work belts and tools, symbols of male sexual potency, particularly the bolt pin, a long, hard implement that fits into the belt directly over the crotch. Even young boys are enjoined not to handle their father's tools, many of them family heirlooms. When a Kahnawake boy puts on a belt and tools for the first time—a *rite de passage*—he becomes a man.

But did Mohawk ironmen go about their work without a quiver of fear, as Joseph Mitchell suggested in his famous 1949 essay "The Mohawks in High Steel"? This is unlikely.

This widely held idea actually predates Mitchell's essay. Mohawk ironmen "lack . . . any sense of height or fear of falling," a credulous *New York Times* reporter wrote in 1940. In an effort to explain Mohawk "fearlessness," another *Times* reporter, writing in 1927, offered this racialist explanation: "To an Indian death has no terrors; passing on to the happy hunting ground is merely shutting a door behind him."

In research conducted four years later, journalist Margaret Norris set the record straight, although hardly anyone was listening. Norris and a fellow investigative reporter talked to ironworkers of all nationalities who freely admitted that courage on the job was an acquired, not an inherited, trait; and that their disciplined intensity at extreme heights grew out of years of experience. "The strange sense of security these men feel while defying the law of gravity is really the outgrowth of caution so constant, so deeply ingrained that it has become unconscious—part and parcel of their beings."

Mohawk ironworkers "deny that they are biologically different from any other men," Meyer Berger wrote years later. "They say they don't think they're better on high steel because they have stronger nerves." Everyone in Little Caughnawaga knew the story of John Diablo; and the notes on the barroom mirror at the Wigwam suggest that Mohawks fell to their deaths with alarming regularity. Apprenticeship and rigorous training—cultural not biological factors—explain Mohawk skill on the girders.

"There's pride in walking iron," a Kahnawake Mohawk described the emotional draw of this perilous work. There was also good money in it. And that, emphatically, was the major reason it was so attractive to the community's first ironmen. The alternatives were bleak: become a "circus Indian," dancing in war paint for traveling American tent shows; sell moccasins to Montreal wholesalers; or travel in an old buggy from farmhouse to farmhouse, selling tonics and purges made of herbs, roots, and seeds.

For later Kahnawake Mohawks—like those who worked on the Chanin Building—ironwork continued to be a path to self-esteem and personal betterment. Furiously expanding Manhattan was a place of opportunity for them, a chance for a second, and better, life, just as it was for that Bensonhurst striver, Irwin Chanin. And this encouraged a sense of ownership. "I have a name for this town," said Danny Montour, a Mohawk ironworker. "I call it the City of Manmade Mountains. And we're all part of it, and it gives a feeling—you're . . . a mountain builder."

City of Opportunity

On July 2, 1928, Irwin and Henry Chanin were photographed driving two gold rivets—the final rivets—into a column on the top floor of the steel frame of their skyscraper. Less than one year later, the Grand Central Zone had its tallest completed skyscraper, the highest one built anywhere in the city in more than a decade. From the forty-eighth floor, where opening ceremonies were held, the Chanin tower dwarfed most of the surrounding structures. "There's no use in going any higher unless you want to see the gates of Paradise," said Mayor Jimmy Walker as he stood by one of the windows on that sunlit Manhattan morning.

The Chanin Construction Company moved into the building a few weeks later, taking all the space above the fiftieth floor. The move coincided with the tenth anniversary of the founding of the company, which now had real estate holdings worth nearly $100 million.

The building was designed with strong dramatic touches. Irwin Chanin, builder of Broadway playhouses, wanted it to be "part of the theatre of the city." At night, over two hundred powerful floodlights, built on a setback at the fifty-third floor, illuminated the crown of the tower. On cloudless evenings, the tower could be seen from communities forty miles away, "an architectural island floating . . . in the sky."

Terra-cotta arabesques are graven into the walls of the lower stories, and there is a frieze over the building's storefronts depicting the theory of evolution. But most of the building's massive base is of unadorned brickwork, and shoots straight upward, depending for effect on a succession of dramatic setbacks, culminating in a row of deep buttresses that give the pinnacle a "vigorous, toothed appearance." The building answered Hugh Ferriss's call for skyscrapers designed in "masses rather than in facades."

Restrained on the outside, the inside is exuberantly ornate. The profusion of Art Moderne decoration in the lobby makes the Chanin Building one of the city's Art Deco masterpieces. Like Adam Gimbel, Irwin Chanin had visited Paris's Art Moderne exposition in 1925 and returned under the spell of leading-edge French designers. American-born Rene Paul Chambellan, one of the foremost Art Deco sculptors in the world, did most of the work on the lobby, in collaboration with the Chanin Company's chief designer, Jacques Delamarre. But Irwin Chanin chose the theme: "New York—City of Opportunity"—with his own life as illustrative example.

The allegorical sculpture in the lobby depicts the story of New York as the "legendary beacon" for venturesome immigrants. Eight bronze panels, and the radiator grilles beneath them, symbolize Courage, Effort, Determination, and Vision—"the mental and physical processes," as the building's brochure didactically explains, "by which an individual in New York City may rise from a humble beginning to wealth and influence by the power of his own mind and hands." Chanin wanted his building to represent everything that New York had given him, and that he had given back to the city.

Chanin carried the City of Opportunity theme into the elaborate private office suites he and his brother occupied on the fifty-second floor. These offices were entered through a pair of bronze gates, whose cogs, gears, and stacks of coins represented Irwin Chanin's embrace of modern technology and the era of economic plenty it had ushered in, with New York City as a great generator of these beneficent transformations. On one of the shining bronze convector grilles in Irwin Chanin's office was a stylized depiction of downtown Manhattan—"a tribute to the age of the skyscraper." And there were drafting triangles and other tools of his multifaceted career as architect, engineer, and construction magnate.

Two floors above his offices, an open-air observation promenade, available to the public, encircled the building. Whenever Chanin was in need of a mental pickup, he would walk out on it for a matchless view of Manhattan and the parts of it his firm had built. Adjusting his gaze, he could make out in the distance the roofs of the Bensonhurst neighborhood where he had gotten his start.

Irwin Chanin was a descendant of poverty who lived lushly. The private bathroom in his suite of offices was suited for a Manhattan Medici. The judges at a building trades convention named it "America's finest bathroom." But in the Chanin Building, function was as important as form. It was one of the most efficiently organized business buildings in the world. A subterranean passageway under Forty-second Street linked it to Grand Central Terminal's subway arcade; and there was a bus station of the Baltimore & Ohio Railroad on the ground floor. Motor coaches providing service to and from the railroad's train shed in New Jersey pulled into the Chanin Building and revolved on a turntable that deposited passengers onto one platform, and received them on another. There was also a shopping arcade in the lobby and a theater on the fiftieth floor. Designed by Chanin, the theater would be used for business meetings and evening entertainment, including movie previews, radio shows, live dramatic presentations, and concerts conducted by Arturo Toscanini.

The year the Chanin brothers moved into their new offices they were living with their wives and children in the same apartment building on Ocean Avenue in Brooklyn. On workday mornings Irwin Chanin would drive across the Brooklyn Bridge in his magnificent Pierce-Arrow, a passage that traced his rise from obscurity. He and his wife had three children and a country estate in a wooded section of Westchester. On occasional weekends he would play a round of golf, although he preferred fishing and swimming. He drank sparingly, but was addicted to cigarettes and work. His standard workday was eighteen hours. When talking about things that interested him his eyes would glow and he would leap out of his chair and begin pacing the room, "illustrating his ideas with gestures and pantomime." He was a small man with a bald forehead, manicured mustache, and round glasses too large for his face; and enthusiasm was his commanding characteristic. "Even in his old age [he lived to be ninety-six], he was taut and full of nervous energy," one of his friends recalled. "You had the sense that behind those thick glasses were 150 good, new building ideas."

The developer who helped make East Forty-second Street a great street became its chief prophet and promoter. "The Grand Central zone soon will have a skyline which will eclipse in fame that of the original skyscraper zone," he had predicted at the opening ceremonies of his building. But his civic exuberance blinded him to the costs of overgrowth: traffic and crowding that would soon approach the stagnation point. The buildings at Forty-second Street and Park Avenue were so densely packed that cars had to be detoured above them, on the terminal's viaduct and circular roadway, and directly through one of them: Warren and Wetmore's thirty-four story New York Central Building, completed in 1929. Straddling Park Avenue just north of the terminal, the golden-domed headquarters of the New York Central Railroad had two arched tunnels that ran right through it, one for northbound, the other for southbound traffic entering or exiting the Grand Central Terminal viaduct, making it the only "drive through" building in the city.*

These roadway improvements, writes city historian Christopher Gray, created "a virtual express highway from 40th to 46th Street," but this inaptly named metropolitan throughway did little to alleviate traffic tie-ups around the station. As architecture critic Lewis Mumford predicted, better roads were like magnets, drawing ever-increasing numbers of cars to them.

---

* It is now the Helmsley Building.

In 1927, the year construction began on the New York Central Building, plans were announced for a new Forty-second Street skyscraper that would fantastically increase crowding in Terminal City—a business building capable of housing twelve thousand tenants and employees. It was the personal project of automobile magnate Walter Percy Chrysler, a humbly born Midwesterner who arrived in mid-Manhattan as suddenly and spectacularly as Irwin Salmon Chanin.

CHAPTER THIRTEEN

THE SILVER SPIRE

I like to build things.

—WALTER CHRYSLER

Motor Car Magnate

In 1925, Walter Chrysler began searching for a Manhattan site for the global headquarters of Chrysler Motors, the Detroit-based automobile company he had created that year. Two years later, he found a prime piece of real estate on the northeast corner of Forty-second Street and Lexington Avenue, just across Lexington Avenue from Grand Central Terminal. Sixty years earlier, this land had been grazing ground for a herd of scrawny goats. In 1927, it was one of the most prized pieces of urban real estate in existence. It was owned by Cooper Union and was currently leased by former Republican state senator William H. Reynolds, a flamboyant real estate developer who had built part of Coney Island amusement park. After drawn-out negotiations, Chrysler purchased the eighty-four-year lease from Reynolds for a reported $2 million.

Earlier that year, Reynolds had hired forty-year-old, Brooklyn-born William Van Alen to design a brazenly tall business building for the site, but had been unable to secure funding to begin construction. Chrysler retained Van Alen as his architect but altered his design, replacing his glass-domed rooftop observatory with a sleek silver tower to be made from highly polished steel.

Walter Chrysler would not simply build tall; he would shoot for the sky. On March 6, 1928, he announced plans for a sixty-eight-story tower of 809 feet—a "giant of giants," twelve stories higher than the Chanin Building. It would be the tallest habitable structure in the world, exceeding by seventeen feet the Woolworth Building in Lower Manhattan.

Van Alen, an avant-garde architect, had found the perfect client: a rich

and progressive businessman—creator of audaciously modern cars—who intended to build a skyscraper unlike any other on Manhattan Island. A graduate
of Paris's prestigious Ecole des Beaux-Arts, Van Alen had spurned the dogma
of that temple of Classicism for a style expressly his own, eclectic and adventurously modern. Almost everything he had done on his return from Paris had
a "tinge . . . of something different" and was self-consciously theatrical, said
architect Kenneth M. Murchison. His Childs Restaurant at Fifth Avenue and
Forty-ninth Street—which still stands—has a rounded corner of plate glass
that looks to be made of rock crystal. When first opened, the restaurant was
so smartly modern, so unlike other chain store diners, that fashionable ladies
from Park Avenue were unashamed to be seen there having coffee and cream
pie in the company of chorus girls and racketeers.

Before Chrysler hired Van Alen, the architect was practicing on his own,
having recently split with H. Craig Severance, his partner of ten years. Near
opposites in temperament and style, he and Severance had a stormy relationship. Polished and well spoken, Severance was a member of the exclusive Metropolitan Club, where he recruited clients over bootleg bourbon and Havana
cigars. Van Alen, by contrast, was gawky, withdrawn, and noticeably uneasy in
social company. The firm's chief designer, he was a committed iconoclast. "I
am not particularly interested in what my fellow men are doing," he declared.
He wanted to do "original" work, and not be "misled" by other architects. "To
my mind, Van Alen was the best of the modern architects of the period," said
Chesley Bonestell, the great architectural renderer who would work with him
on the Chrysler project.

Van Alen was excited by Walter Chrysler's resolve to construct the tallest
building on earth. "If this is to be a skyscraper," he proclaimed, "why not make
it scrape the sky." But there would be competition. In April 1928, one month
after Chrysler unveiled his plan, he learned that a syndicate headed by thirty-
three-year-old investment banker George L. Ohrstrom had commissioned
Van Alen's former partner to design "the tallest bank and office structure in
the world"—the 840-foot Bank of Manhattan Building at 40 Wall Street. It was
to be thirty-one feet higher than the Chrysler Building. Ohrstrom's challenge
triggered a sky race unprecedented in the history of New York real estate, a
highly publicized battle between two architects who had ended their relationship badly, and two capitalists who loathed one another from afar.

Brawny, square-jawed Walter Chrysler made the Forty-second Street skyscraper his personal project. He was building it, he announced, for his sons,
Walter Jr. and Jack; he had established generous trusts for them, but didn't want
them to become dissolute millionaires. "They had to work," he said, to learn
the joy of it, "the wild incentive that burned in me." The Chrysler Building was

also a personal investment. Chrysler paid for it with his own, not the company's, money, and he took an interest in every aspect of its design and construction. Although he claimed to be building it for his sons, it was his project in every way; it became, like the Midtown skyscrapers of Irwin Chanin and Fred French, a testament to the builder's business creed and to the company he had built from scratch. He wanted his headquarters building to be super-tall, he told a reporter, so he "could peer down over New York at the [thirty-six-story] General Motors building on Broadway," a scantling compared to the majestically tall Chrysler Building.

On November 11, 1928, four months after ironworkers completed the framework of the Chanin Building, diagonally across Forty-second Street, excavators began digging the foundation of Walter Chrysler's $20 million dream project. While steam shovels unearthed the foundations of the shabby retail stores William Reynolds had built on the site as placeholders, Chrysler and Van Alen put the finishing touches on the design, work that Chrysler found hugely pleasurable. He was "having a lot of fun going thoroughly into everything with the architects," he told a reporter. "I like to build things."

"The career of Walter Percy Chrysler would make a faultless model for a success story of the type Horatio Alger used to write," said *The New York Times*. It was a story of "insuperable obstacles" and "superhuman doggedness," as "dramatic a chapter of industrial history as has been written in our time," added *Fortune*.

Walter Chrysler was the third child of German American parents who had moved to the bleak prairie town of Ellis, Kansas, in 1878, when Walter was three years old. Located 170 miles west of Walter's birthplace, Wamego, Kansas, Ellis was home to large Union Pacific operations, and Walter's father found work there as a locomotive engineer. It was a lawless place. Cowboys "full of whiskey and the devil" would come stampeding through town on payday, shooting out the windows of stores and saloons; and hostile Indians raided the homes of outlying settlers. At the clapboard schoolhouse that Walter Chrysler attended there were at least half a dozen fistfights at every recess. "A kid who had a yellow streak would lead a dog's life," Chrysler remembered. Hot-tempered, Walter Chrysler had the sharpened instincts of a survivor; and as he notes proudly in his autobiography, he "raised his small share of hell."

There was another side of him, however. Shaped by strict parental oversight, he was disciplined, focused, and uncommonly energetic. He milked the family cows and trudged door-to-door selling cream and butter that his mother made every Monday morning in her rustic kitchen. After high school, he found work in the Union Pacific shops, sweeping floors and oiling machinery for five cents an hour—wildly curious about locomotives and wanting to be a railroad mechanic. Advancing rapidly to apprentice machinist, he forged and tempered steel to make his own tools. He would hold on to them for the rest of his life, along with a working model of a locomotive he built from scratch.

Restless and hungry to advance, he left Ellis at age twenty-two and became a journeyman machinist, moving from one Midwestern railroad town to another with his new bride, Della Forker, a childhood friend. "Give the boss a little more than he expects and he will see that you are rewarded. And if he doesn't—the best thing to do is to find another boss." In that crisp declaration, Walter Chrysler described both his philosophy of work and his roving disposition.

At age thirty-three, he landed a job as superintendent in charge of all locomotives on the Chicago & Great Western Railroad system, but after learning that no man in overalls had ever advanced to an executive position in the company, he quit after two years and took a job as plant superintendent of a locomotive manufacturing company in Pittsburgh. Then, in 1911, he abruptly changed careers, joining the Buick Motor Company. "To me, [the automobile] was the transportation of the future, and . . . I wanted to be a part of it."

His fascination with automobiles can be traced back to 1908, when he was still working for the Chicago & Great Western. In that year, he went into hock to purchase his first car at a Chicago auto show, an ivory white touring machine with red leather upholstery and trim. Unable to drive, he had the car shipped to his home in Oelwein, a small town in northeastern Iowa. Instead of taking it out for an experimental spin, he disassembled and reassembled it in his backyard barn, trembling with excitement to discover what made it run. He did this at least a half dozen times before finally pushing it out of the barn for its inaugural run. With bug-eyed neighbors looking on, he engaged the clutch and the car shot forward, sailed through a ditch, and wound up in a neighbor's garden patch. "After that initiation, I made swift progress," he recalled, "until the Chrysler family was riding . . . right through the bustling heart of Oelwein."

Three years later he was in Flint, Michigan, running the world's second largest automobile production plant. The job at Buick, a subsidiary of General Motors, paid only half the salary he was making in Pittsburgh, but "I was not prepared to let this chance get away from me," he said later. Walter Chrysler's entire career was distinguished by a willingness "to take risks to win distant rewards," said historian Thomas C. Cochran.

In 1916, after becoming the number two production man in the industry, next to Henry Ford, Chrysler was promoted to president of Buick and vice president of General Motors, at a salary of over half a million dollars a year. He took most of it in company stock, the foundation of a fortune. After a falling out with GM founder and president William Durant, he quit the company in 1919, sold his stock for $10 million, and moved with his family from Michigan to Manhattan, taking an apartment on Park Avenue. Four years later, he purchased a French Renaissance estate at Great Neck, on Long Island Sound, the setting for *The Great Gatsby*. It had sixteen acres of grounds and gardens, a carpet-like lawn that sloped down to the water's edge, and a boathouse and pier for his luxury yacht—"the typical residence," said a reporter, "of a leader in the Sanhedrin of the successful."

He had been lured to New York by Wall Street bankers to save a failing auto company, Willys-Overland, headquartered in New York with a small production plant in Elizabeth, New Jersey. After rescuing the firm from bankruptcy, he was asked to take over Maxwell Motors, another financially distressed enterprise. He salvaged that company too and assumed the presidency in 1923. But Chrysler wanted to be an automotive innovator, not just a savior of crippled companies. With this in mind, he put down $3 million of his own money, recruited three young production geniuses—his soon to be famous Three Musketeers, Fred M. Zeder, Owen R. Skelton, and Carl Breer—and had them develop the history-changing car that would bear his name, the Chrysler Six, a compact mechanical marvel with a high-performance engine and a smooth, effortless ride.

But Walter Chrysler aimed higher than this. He hoped to build on the anticipated success of the Chrysler Six to transform small, undercapitalized Maxwell Motors into the principal challenger of Ford and General Motors, the pillars of the industry. At the time, the obstacles seemed insuperable. To retool his plants to manufacture the prototype car in volume, the former roundhouse foreman needed at least $5 million in venture capital. He thought he had acquired it in early 1924, but the two New York banks that had offered to back his company abruptly changed course, convinced that a new medium-priced car could not compete successfully with the solidly established Buick. At this point, "we were pretty close to ruin," Chrysler admitted later.

A blizzard saved him. In the winter of 1924 Chrysler put his new model on display at Midtown's Grand Central Palace, as part of that year's New York Automobile Show, the largest auto show in the country. The main exhibit building, however, was in the Bronx, and that's where most spectators and investors planned to assemble. But on opening day, a paralyzing snowstorm and a succession of subway accidents diverted crowds from the big show in the Bronx to the Commodore Hotel, where Walter Chrysler was on the display floor with his new car. "We stole . . . the show," he proudly recalled. "From morning until late at night, a crowd was densely packed around us." Fast and stylish, with the silver cap of Mercury—its distinctive radiator ornament—mounted on the hood, the Chrysler Six came in a range of eye-catching "King Tut" colors aimed at the average middle-range pharaoh.

The following day, Edward R. Tinker of Chase Securities approached Chrysler in the lobby of the Commodore and announced that his banking house had reconsidered and was prepared to underwrite the manufacturing costs of the Chrysler Six. Fearing Tinker might change his mind, Chrysler followed him to his Wall Street office, and sent in B. E. Hutchinson, his vice president, with an ultimatum that was actually a reckless bluff: "it's now or never." Chrysler waited on the sidewalk on that wickedly cold afternoon while "Hutch" traced Tinker to his private barbershop in the building. With his face masked with lather, Tinker closed the deal. Blunt-speaking Walter Chrysler, who still wore the mismatched outfits of a mid-American Rotarian, had won over the pinstriped nabobs of Wall Street. We were "out of the woods. We had our money, we had our car."

The Chrysler Six sold phenomenally—32,000 in the first year of production—turning a company debt of $5 million into a profit of over $4 million. Like Henry Ford's Model T, it was a revolutionary machine, one that transformed the auto industry, along with the buying habits of the American car consumer. "This car stands alone as the dividing line between what may be termed 'old' and 'modern' cars," writes automobile historian Mark Howell. While the Chrysler Six had lots of innovative functional features, including four-wheel hydraulic brakes, it appealed to consumers primarily on the basis of form rather than function; it was instrumental in moving the American automotive industry from utility to style and speed. It was the car of its time—the extravagant 1920s—a period in which desires supplanted needs. At a sticker price of fifteen hundred dollars this "miniature masterpiece," as *Fortune* called it, gave consumers the "thrills" of a roadster costing over three times as much. New Yorkers by the hundreds bought it at showrooms along Automobile Row—on Broadway, above Fiftieth Street— the largest concentration of car dealerships in the world. On weekends they set out on excursions to new parks and beaches that Robert Moses, Governor Al Smith's parks commissioner, was building on Long Island. Hundreds of miles of beautifully paved and landscaped parkways would soon follow.*

---

* New York had approximately 600,000 motor vehicles in 1928. Martin Clary, *Mid-Manhattan* (NY: Forty-second Street Property Owners and Merchants Association, 1929), 160.

In June 1925, one year before Moses began acquiring barrier beaches and bay front for Jones Beach State Park, the crown jewel of his Long Island park system, Walter Chrysler discontinued the Maxwell line of cars and renamed his company the Chrysler Corporation. The following January he entered the luxury market with the Chrysler Imperial 80, an instant hit. The next year, after introducing the solidly practical Plymouth, a direct challenge to the new Model A Ford, unveiled in late 1927, he acquired Dodge Brothers, an old and respected company in America's newest powerhouse industry. It was "the biggest consolidation in the history of the automobile industry," and it transformed Chrysler Motors into a corporate behemoth. The dependable but gadget-less Dodge, along with the Plymouth coupé, put the master mechanic from Ellis, Kansas, within closing distance of Henry Ford, one of the idols of his youth. For the first time, the term "Big Three" was used to describe the commanding companies in the industry: General Motors, Ford, and Chrysler.

The New Yorker hailed Walter Chrysler as "the outstanding production genius in the [auto] industry." He was that rare businessman with a keen understanding of both production and finance, said *Time,* who named him its "Man of the Year" for 1928, the second to be so honored after Charles Lindbergh.

The former five-cent-an-hour oil boy was commander in chief of an enterprise with sixty thousand employees and resources of over $200 million; and Chrysler Company stock had become one of the hottest items on Wall Street. "No man has come so swiftly, so dazzlingly, so impressively to the front of American industry in the last three years," wrote *Forbes.* "His name, formerly unknown beyond motor circles, has been blazoned throughout the world. In America it has been on every tongue."*

Swaggering Walter Chrysler accepted his recent success without a modicum of modesty. Ordinary men achieve success by honesty and hard work, "but men who get very far ahead have some other qualities," he portentously lectured a reporter from *Time.* "Some are idea-resourceful. They possess imagination. They dare to take a chance and be different. They are willing to tackle anything."

"That," said *Time,* "explains Walter Chrysler."

A Heaven-Climbing Contest

Chrysler saw himself as an urban as well as an industrial visionary, a businessman with striking ideas about skyscrapers as well as automobiles, the two

---

* In 1933, Chrysler overtook Ford to become the second largest producer of cars in the world.

great shaping forces of the large American cities of his day. In 1928, the year
he introduced the moderately priced DeSoto, he turned his attention to his
Forty-second Street skyscraper. He wanted it to be stylish as well as tall, an
exemplar—like his Chrysler Six—of progressive industrial design.

It would also be a monument to his accomplishments, his meteoric rise
from mechanic to Manhattan mandarin. Before steel contractors began assembling the building's frame, Chrysler had Van Alen go back to the drawing
board and design a glassed-in observatory near the top of the tower. Here,
beneath a painting of the Chrysler Building, he would put on display, in a
handsome wooden box, his "fondest treasure[s]": the tools he had made by
hand as a seventeen-year-old apprentice mechanic, emblems of his advance.

Once construction started, it went like "a bat out of hell." The supervisor of
steel construction used two sets of derricks simultaneously: some exclusively
for hoisting steel, others solely for setting it in place. Steel was "in almost constant motion until its final placement," wrote Van Alen.

Walter Chrysler pushed the operation hard, augmenting his demands with
streams of profanity. He prodded both his architect and his engineers, pound-
ing his desk with his fist for emphasis, pushing a finger into their faces, and
when agreement was finally reached, cutting the tension with off-color jokes
and sharp slaps on the back. Yet he refused to press the project at the expense
of the workers' safety. Scaffolds were equipped with guardrails and tarpaulin-
covered roofs; large floor openings were boarded over; special wooden scaffolds, called aprons, were installed to capture hot rivets and other falling
objects; and there was a first-aid station on the ground floor, staffed by a doctor and a registered nurse. Between 2,500 and 3,000 workers were employed at
all times on the building, but not a single life was lost. (One seriously injured
worker died later.) While Chrysler genuinely cared about the men, he viewed
accident prevention as sound business practice: injuries and deaths were costly
to everyone involved with putting up a large building.

As his skyscraper went up, the still vigorously fit fifty-three-year-old auto
king would climb all over it, inside and out, barking orders and poking into everything. He got "the greatest thrill of his life," he said, watching his skyscraper
leap out of the ground. Throughout the construction process, he hosted a
number of Manhattan luncheons to honor his laborers and supervisor, who
developed a real affection for him. "Bluff, sanguine, gregarious, he commands
respect," said a writer for *The New Yorker*. "You cannot be with him and not
like him as a man." He was more distant in his dealings with William Van
Alen. Entirely different types of men, their relationship was uncomfortably
awkward.

To document the building's construction, step by step, Chrysler hired Margaret Bourke-White, a young industrial photographer who was then commuting between her residences in Cleveland and New York City, having recently taken a position with *Fortune*, Henry Luce's soon to be launched business monthly. In this "heaven-climbing contest . . . I was brought in as a sort of war correspondent on the Chrysler side," she recalled in her autobiography. "Mr. Walter Percy Chrysler was aware of the stupendous advertising value generated when the world's highest building bears the name of your product. And this is where I came in."

Dark-eyed and sensuous, Bourke-White had a reputation for parading her exquisite body. She wore low-cut blouses and hung over the desks of her prospective male clients to point out this or that photograph in her portfolio. "What a lucky lady I am," she wrote in her diary, "I can do anything I want to with these men." Chrysler, a notorious womanizer, was attracted to her, but there is no evidence of a romantic relationship.

She did, however, fall wildly in love with his building. She photographed the construction in the dead of winter in 1929–30, eight hundred feet above the street, working on an open scaffold "that swayed 8 feet in the wind." Heights, she said, held "no terrors" for her.

Never for a moment had Walter Chrysler believed he would lose the sky contest. But in early October 1929, the Bank of Manhattan appeared to be the clear winner.* That month, the owners of 40 Wall Street received permission from the city's Buildings Department to install a lantern story with a fifty-foot flagpole, taking their building to the lordly height of 925 feet, "dwarfing" the 845-foot Chrysler Building "triumphantly," reported the *New York Herald Tribune*.

But Walter Chrysler would not settle for second place. He instructed Van Alen and steel engineer Ralph Squire to begin secretly assembling "a high spire . . . with a needle-like termination" inside a large air shaft in the building's silver tower. Working at great speed and sworn to secrecy, ironmongers custom-built a 185-foot tall "vertex," as this latticed steel flagpole was called. They then waited for a clear, calm day. On the morning of October 23, 1929, "the signal was given," Van Alen recalled, and a gigantic derrick grabbed hold of the steel needle, which slowly emerged from the top of the dome "like a butterfly from its cocoon. . . . In about ninety minutes," said Van Alen, "[it] was securely riveted in position, the highest piece of stationary steel in the world."

---

* Today it is a Trump building.

On the day it went up, and for days afterward, not a single reporter wrote of "the cloud-piercing needle." They may have thought it was a tremendously tall construction derrick, for both structures had a steel-latticed design. Even the *Herald Tribune*'s correspondents, who followed the sky race more closely than other reporters, missed the raising of the vertex; nor had they known it was being built. There were no Chrysler press releases on the day the silver spire appeared on the Manhattan skyline. Perhaps Walter Chrysler feared the risky stunt would end calamitously, killing workers and pedestrians. Watching from Fifth Avenue and Forty-second Street, Van Alen and his chief engineer had "four sinking spells [and] continuous vertigo . . . during the raising of the vertex," Kenneth Murchison recalls, "and the architect is still a bit shaky when he thinks of what might have happened to innocent bystanders below."

The steel needle made the Chrysler Building—at 1,046 feet, 4.75 inches from pavement to pinnacle point—the highest structure ever built, 105 feet taller than its downtown rival, higher even than the Eiffel Tower. The process of building and raising the vertex was an unprecedented and wholly unexpected engineering feat, and a triumphant Walter Chrysler waited until November, when 40 Wall Street was completed, to proclaim his building the victor in the sky contest.

When Chrysler's seventy-seven-story "epic of publicity" was opened for tenants on April 1, 1930, eighteen months after construction commenced, a prominent architecture magazine awarded Van Alen a "Doctor of Altitude."

The Most Stunning Thing in Town

"They look like money," Andy Warhol would say of Gotham's Art Deco towers. But the Chrysler Building is less about money than it is about modernity, the new age of "metals and mass effort" that auto magnate Walter Chrysler helped to usher in. "It represents our modern life," Kenneth Murchison wrote, "its changing conditions and forces." Murchison anointed Van Alen "the Ziegfeld of his profession . . . glorifying American mechanical genius" the way the Broadway showman glorified the American girl. He loved the building that some critics derided as a "freak" and a "stunt"—a "shameless exhibition" of the colossal ego of its client, said an irritated Lewis Mumford.*

---

* In 2005, one hundred architects, developers, critics, and historians were asked by New York's Skyscraper Museum to choose their ten favorite Manhattan towers. Ninety of them named the Chrysler Building. The runner-up was Ludwig Mies van der Rohe's Seagram Building of 1958. David W. Dunlap, "In a City of Skyscrapers, Which is the Mightiest of the High? Experts Say It's No Contest," NYT, September 1, 2005.

The Chrysler Building was master of the Manhattan skyline for only one year. On May 1, 1931, the 1,250-foot-tall Empire State Building, designed by the architectural firm of Shreve, Lamb & Harmon, officially opened at the corner of Thirty-fourth Street and Fifth Avenue. Eighty-four thousand visitors paid admission to its rooftop observatory in the first month it opened; and many of them thought it "the eighth wonder of the world." The Chrysler Building is an equally satisfying Manhattan icon—"hot jazz in stone and steel," Le Corbusier called it. From a distance, its tower of polished steel, flashing in the sunlight or brilliantly illuminated at night, is the most stunning sight on the skyline.* To be tired of New York, said Cole Porter, was to be "tired of the Chrysler Building."

The building's lobby is nearly as impressive as its silver spire. This is entirely due to Walter Chrysler. When Van Alen first brought Chrysler a plaster model of the building, the lobby had four large columns. The automaker objected; the columns made the space looked cramped. "When people come into a big building, they should sense a change, get a mental lift," he said. That week the columns were scrapped in favor of an open, triangular-shaped floor plan. The completed lobby is a masterwork of dramatic design. Indirectly lit, its walls are of red, richly veined Moroccan marble. The floor is Sienna Travertine carved into patterns that point the way to the elevators. There are thirty-two of them, in four groups, each car with a different design and color, and each operator dressed—originally—in a different uniform "for each of the four seasons." The interior of the cabs are finished in exotic inlaid woods: Japanese ash and Oriental walnut, among them. Chrysler, however, wanted visitors to be as impressed with the speed as with the design of his elevator cabs. The fastest elevators on earth made the trip from the lobby to the top floor in sixty seconds flat.

Speed and movement, their representation in art and engineering, is the leitmotif of Chrysler's tower. The building's long, spacious lobby is a people-moving machine as impressive, in a smaller way, as the main concourse of Grand Central Terminal; and like the concourse, it has a dazzling ceiling. Chrysler commissioned the noted artist Edward Trumbull to paint one of the largest ceiling murals in existence, a celebration of the vision and human effort that went into the creation of the building and the machine age it exemplified. Silvery airplanes, blazing steel furnaces, and the Chrysler Building itself appear in Trumbull's mural. One panel is devoted entirely to the work of riveters, steel riggers, stonemasons, carpenters, plasterers, and brick masons. All fifty figures

---

* The tower was not illuminated until 1981, when Van Alen's original scheme for lighting its triangular windows was discovered and installed.

depicted in the mural are modeled on men who actually worked on the build-ing. It is New York City's commanding artistic testimony to the laborers who constructed its Art Deco towers.

There are other modern touches. Van Alen installed a futuristic digital clock in the lobby, and for the first time in America, Nirosta steel—a new alloy of chromium, iron, and nickel developed at Germany's Krupp Works—was used extensively on a large building. It has a lustrous surface and does not rust, tarnish, peel, or corrode. Van Alen used it on the tower—which extends from the sixty-first floor to the tip of the spire—the window frames, the re-volving doors, the lobby lighting and trim, and the gargoyles built onto the exterior walls of enameled gray, white, and black brick. On the lower floors, these gargoyles are fashioned in the form of the winged radiator caps of the Chrysler Six. Higher up—on the thirty-first floor—fearsome-looking eagles of polished metal stretch their long necks and peer down at the spreading city.

Like Irwin Chanin, Walter Chrysler had a poor boy's love of luxury. Chanin had his cloud theater; Chrysler his three-story Cloud Club, a male-only re-doubt for three hundred or so of the city's power brokers, many of them sportsmen like him, a wing shooter, yachtsman, and golfer. While Prohibi-tion lasted, the Cloud Club doubled as a speakeasy. Members were allocated wooden lockers to store their bottles; each locker had carved hydrographic symbols on its doors to prevent federal agents from identifying its millionaire lawbreaker. (Chrysler had concerns because he was caught bringing a few bot-tles of illegal liquor into the country.) And there was a cedar humidor stocked with cigars and a room with deep cushioned chairs where members could puff on their Montecristos while watching the progress of their investments on a stock ticker.

Chrysler had a secluded private dining room in the club with a glazed glass frieze ringed with life-sized figures of automobile workers, their tools engraved in black relief; but he was often seen in the main dining hall, which featured a panoramic painting of the city and its harbor, with futuristic air-planes soaring above them. Some of the top aviators in the world dined here at Chrysler's invitation.

The Cloud Club had an Old English Bar and Grill with pegged plank floors and wooden beams, a well-stocked library, a barbershop, an oyster bar, and a combination gymnasium and massage room. Not to be outdone by Irwin Chanin, Chrysler supervised the design of a men's room described as "one of the great lavatories of all time." His office, occupying the entire fifty-sixth floor, was as richly decorated as Chanin's; and when he occasionally stayed overnight in the building, he slept in splendor in a Tudor-style duplex apartment with leaden windows and heavy wooden doors, a space incongruously at variance—as were the faux medieval touches in the Cloud Club—with the building's resolute modernism.

Walter Chrysler was a reckless philanderer who enjoyed the company of what he called his "five o'clock girls"—actresses and chorus girls who dropped by his office at that hour for cocktails with him and his friends. He was more circumspect with his full-time mistress, the actress Peggy Hopkins Joyce, a former Ziegfeld Girl and onetime lover of Charlie Chaplin. After meeting her sometime in the late 1920s, Chrysler saw her, for a time, only behind closed doors. "I have a very ardent admirer just now who is showering me with gifts," Ms. Joyce noted in her diary. "He is quite prominent and I dare not write his name but will call him Mr. Z."

Chaplin described Peggy Joyce as "bright, immoral and intriguing," with "one single, fierce ambition—to become a millionairess [sic]." Nearly twenty years the actress's senior, Walter Chrysler bought her $2 million dollars worth of jewelry, including a 134-karat diamond—Peggy's "skating rink," gossip columnists called it. He hired a bodyguard and two secretaries to spy on her, and presented her with four sumptuous cars, one of them a canary yellow roadster with silver trim and black patent leather upholstery. None of them, tellingly, were Chrysler products. Even his high-end Imperials, which he gave as annual gifts to his wife, Della, and his four children, were not good enough for his blond temptress. But in the early 1930s, when he began conducting his affair with Peggy publicly—humiliating his staunchly loyal wife—he must have enjoyed showing her around his proudest Chrysler product: his silvery skyscraper.

If, as Lewis Mumford suggests, "each generation writes its biography in the buildings it creates," the Chrysler tower is the emblematic structure of Jazz Age New York, a symbol of its exuberant experimentalism, its embrace of speed and style, its romantic excess. The building is an expression, as well, of the brassy resolve of the prairie striver who dared to challenge GM and Ford, and who built in the world's skyscraper capital "the most stunning thing in town."

On May 27, 1930, the day the building formally opened, a beaming Walter Chrysler worked the room, dressed in a rumpled suit and shirt and a loud flowered necktie. The Cloud Club did not open until the following July. There is no record that William Van Alen was a member; if he was, "it must have presented seating difficulties for the maitre d'," writes historian Christopher Gray. That summer, Van Alen sued Walter Chrysler for most of his fee and put a mechanic's lien on the building to recover it. He had worked without a written contract for his services, and the two men had failed to settle their dispute about the size of his fee. Van Alen claimed he was owed a balance of $725,000 on a fee of $865,000. This was 6 percent of the cost of the skyscraper, the standard fee established by the American Institute of Architects. Chrysler stood firm with an offer of $175,000, an amount above the $8,000 a month he had already paid Van Alen.

The architect won his lawsuit in 1931, but never designed another building of consequence. The economic depression hurt his practice, but a more severe blow was his reputation as the man who had dared to sue powerful Walter Chrysler. Van Alen's "swan song" was his spectacular appearance in 1931 at the annual Society of Beaux-Arts Architects ball at the Hotel Astor. In a costume contest called "The Skyline of New York," he appeared with other prominent city architects dressed in fantastical representations of their best-known buildings. Van Alen's costume of silver metal cloth and pliable wood—its headpiece an exact reproduction of the spire of the Chrysler Building—stole the show. After this he passed into obscurity. He died in 1954, largely forgotten; his office records and correspondence are not known to have survived, further ensuring his obscurity. "It is perhaps inconsistent," wrote Cecil Beaton, the British photographer and designer, "that New Yorkers, who have such a love for celebrities, do not know the names of their most brilliant architects."

Months before his building was completed, Chrysler hired over four dozen brokers to promote it to prospective renters. It was an easy sell, even after the Stock Market Crash of 1929. The first fully air-conditioned building in the world, it had flexible office space, a sprinkler system, a centralized vacuum cleaning system, and a house staff of 350. And tenants didn't have to put up with thick black discharges from neighboring smokestacks, a problem in nearly every other sizable American downtown. Terminal City was a smokeless city. Many of its high-rise office buildings and apartment houses, erected on steel columns over the New York Central's submerged track system, had no space for steam or power plants. Steam heat was delivered, and still is, through underground conduits running from the coal-fired plants of the New York Steam Corporation, located along the East River.

By midsummer of 1930 the Chrysler Building was nearly 70 percent rented and turning a profit. One of the most satisfied tenants was Margaret Bourke-White, who had a studio on the sixty-first floor, with windows looking out on the building's tremendous steel eagles. She loved the view so much she asked the building manager to allow her to become the Chrysler tower's only permanent resident, with living quarters added onto her studio. But New York City law, as we have seen, forbade anyone from living in a business building except the janitor. "My first step, was to apply for the job as Chrysler Building janitor," Bourke-White described her determined campaign. Mayor Walker may have allowed Edwin Goodman and his family to become the "janitors" of the new Bergdorf Goodman store, but Bourke-White didn't have Goodman's political clout or the support of Chrysler officials in charge of the building. She had the compensation, nonetheless, of having one of the handsomest studios in the city, and surely the highest one in the world. Her friend John Vassos, the designer, decorated it with minimalist furniture and natural woods and aluminum. She had a large terrace for parties and it was there that she kept her two pet alligators, gifts from a friend in Florida. On clear Manhattan mornings, she'd crawl out on the shining gargoyles to "take pictures of the changing moods of the city." Her assistant took a now famous photograph of her precariously perched on one of the gleaming eagles, high above Gotham, camera at the ready. She loved her studio so much, she said, she "hated to go home at night."

Valley of Giants

The Chrysler Building was the epitome of commercial convenience. To catch a subway to any point in the city, Bourke-White did not need to step outdoors. Like a number of other Forty-second Street "perpendiculars," the Chrysler Building was connected to Grand Central Terminal and other buildings in its vicinity by a network of shop-lined underground passageways. The Grand Central Zone was a veritable "city under one roof," a place "unique in the world's history," wrote *New York Times* reporter Roy Mason. Inside this labyrinth, accessible from twenty-six entrances and exits, was "every kind of food and clothing a human being needs, great banks, restaurants, stores of all descriptions, gymnasiums and swimming pools"—and in the terminal, an art gallery, tennis courts, a movie theater, a police station, an emergency hospital, and a post office. Four of the hotels in this miniature metropolis—the Biltmore, the Commodore, the Belmont, and the Roosevelt, along with the Yale Club on Vanderbilt Avenue—contained rooms for over twelve thousand guests; and Grand Central's long-distance train platforms tied this roofed city to all of America.

On June 15, 1927, the 20th Century Limited, the New York Central's "flier" to Chicago, celebrated its twenty-fifth anniversary. It was "the fastest train traveling over the longest distance in the world." The 961 miles between

New York and Chicago were covered in less than twenty hours, and the train's observation, dining, club, and sleeping cars were the quintessence of quality travel. The Limited had private sleeping cars with chairs and sofas, maid and valet service, a beauty salon, double compartments with showers, and dining cars that served five-star dinners. "I take the Century," said novelist Michael Arlen, "because I want very little in this world, only the best."

Arriving in New York from the midland metropolis at precisely nine-thirty in the morning—"a moment of majestic finality," in writer Jan Morris's words—a passenger leaving Track 34 stepped into the rush and stir of the city; 130,000 passengers and 650 trains passed in and out of Grand Central daily in 1927. A passenger taking a subway to his or her next destination joined "a surging human mass" struggling to reach the platforms of the local trains.

Arriving passengers choosing to head out into the city on foot confronted a mass of humanity "so dense night and morning," wrote New York chronicler Hulbert Footner, "that it is difficult to make a way through it if you are traveling against the current." Even the passageways in the subterranean city under Forty-second Street were so congested, that pedestrians often had to walk lock-step, like the robotlike workers in *Metropolis*, Austrian filmmaker Fritz Lang's 1927 dystopian masterwork. In Terminal City, only those traveling vertically reached their destination with dispatch. Here, as in the rest of New York, the greatest traffic movers were elevators. Manhattan alone had nearly twenty thousand passenger elevators. They carried over twelve million people daily, more than were transported by the subway, surface, and elevated lines combined.

By 1930, the area around the terminal was a "Valley of Giants," home to three of New York's six tallest skyscrapers: the Chrysler and Chanin towers, along with J. E. R. Carpenter's fifty-three-story Lincoln Building on East Forty-second Street, between Madison and Park Avenues. These were free-standing towers—"cloud houses," Paul Morand called them—built further apart, and therefore more conspicuous than the bulky monoliths downtown, "huddled together in a massive range of manmade mountains." No longer the northern frontier of Manhattan's built-up area, Forty-second Street had become the commercial, hotel, and transportation hub of New York—"City of Incredible Towers," said Le Corbusier, province of "great masters of economic destiny . . . up there like eagles in the silence of their eminences." Here money was everything.

In 1927—eight years before Le Corbusier first landed in New York—East Forty-second Street was becoming to the American service industry what Detroit was to the country's auto industry. Its buildings and those of its commercial tributaries—Lexington and Madison Avenues—housed prestigious law firms, big advertising agencies, headquarters of national and international corporations, and branch offices of downtown banks and brokerage houses, most of whom had recently moved to Midtown to be near Grand Central Terminal and its unsurpassed subway connections. These were businesses in which "speed was the essential thing. . . . Swift movement, swifter thinking. . . . Ten thousand telephones whirring with words," wrote *The New Yorker*'s Morris Markey. "Ten thousand typewriters clattering breathlessly. Men and women leaning over desks, intent, eager, utterly forgetful of any world beyond their own vision. Business, business, business—the only end of living."

In the middle of the nineteenth century, things were made and moved on East Forty-second Street, an industrial corridor of factories, stockyards, and the Commodore's noisy steam trains. In the 1920s, the only things manufactured on the street were "spectacular quantities of tension."

Under the Asphalt

This new nexus of metropolitan life had exploded into existence, and large parts of it still had an unfinished look at the end of the 1920s. A great part of Forty-second Street, all the way westward to Eighth Avenue, where the city's new subway system—the Independent or IND—was being built, was an immense and thunderous construction site—a "thicket" of brand-new buildings "with ragged breaks where steel skeletons of new buildings are climbing up." By 1927, literally thousands of construction crews were at work on Midtown skyscrapers, and nearly ten thousand men were building, simultaneously, the IND, which included a new station in Times Square, from Fortieth to Forty-fourth Streets, the longest subway station in the world. The connection was not coincidental; in New York, subways and skyscrapers are inextricably interlinked. Along with Grand Central Terminal, the new Times Square subway station was one of the principal reasons skyscraper developers were busy on East Forty-second Street. Subways were the city's great people carriers; and the newest and largest buildings in Midtown were built close to the newest and largest subway stations.

"Never before in the history of the island has there been such a vast amount of tearing down and building up," declared *The New York Times*. The noise was earsplitting, the machine-gun staccato of rivet guns vying with the rumble of trucks, the squawking of automobile horns, the nerve-jarring cacophony of El trains, and the dynamiting and steam shoveling at building sites. "Civilization has never before been confronted with such a malignant plague," said an irate college professor.* In 1927, the mayor's health commissioner, Dr. Louis Harris, decided to do something about it, launching a greatly publicized "anti-noise campaign" to put an end to the "riveting din in the city." The racket from the riveting guns, said Harris, was jarring the nerves and menacing the health of city residents. Medical experts pointed to tests conducted at Colgate University, where white rats subjected to "duplicated city noises" ate less, grew more slowly, and were more "irritable" than lab rats kept in relative quiet. Harris brought in consulting engineers to testify to the feasibility of gas and electric welding, and called for a city ordinance banning rivet guns. But Mayor Walker was unwilling to challenge a building industry that was the most lucrative source of municipal tax revenue.

With the Midtown construction boom in full swing, with steam shovels and blasting crews digging deep foundations for the IND and the Chanin Building, local newspapers published a spate of articles about the underground complex of public and private utilities—the sub-city—that supported and sustained Manhattan's newest Vertical City.†

Much of Eighth Avenue was a gigantic gulch, ten miles long, with the roads decked over with sheets of steel or heavy wooden beams so that traffic could pass, a construction process known as "cut-and-cover." To keep traffic moving, only half of a street was dug up at a time, and most of the work was done at night. It was as if a "colossal knife" had descended on Manhattan Island and "cut it from end to end along the line of Eighth Avenue and Central Park West," wrote city reporter Waldemar Kaempffert.

New York's first subway was dug with pick and shovel; the new subway was "machine built," with mechanical excavators and gigantic cranes and power shovels. One of the great innovators on the project was Samuel Rufus Rosoff, a short, portly Jewish immigrant from Minsk who had arrived in New York, alone, in 1894, at age twelve, and peddled newspapers and slept under the Brooklyn Bridge until he found steady work. He skipped school entirely and failed at a dozen jobs before becoming owner of a handful of small construction companies, along with a sand and gravel pit along the Hudson River; and he wasted away much of the profits he made in these pursuits by shooting craps, playing the horses, and betting on prizefights. In 1925, he bid on a con-

---

* In the 1920s, Manhattan had four El lines. The Sixth Avenue El was torn down in 1939. The Ninth Avenue and Second Avenue lines were dismantled in 1940 and 1941. The Manhattan section of the Third Avenue El was not demolished until 1955.

† Construction of the municipally owned and operated IND began in 1925. The first section of the Eighth Avenue portion opened in September 1932. The line was not completed until 1940.

tract to build part of the Eighth Avenue subway. He knew nothing about subway construction, but he did know a few aldermen. They made sure he got the job. Ten years later, he was "Subway Sam," the biggest and richest subway contractor in the world.

Rosoff was the first subway contractor to put compact steam shovels, cranes, and compressed air jackhammers into the trenches—and to use underground conveyor belts, dump trucks, and earthen ramps to remove the dirt in record time. In 1927, he could be seen nearly every evening in the slime and muck of one of his ditches, sometimes in evening clothes, "bawling orders above the din of steam shovels and drills." A "lovable roughneck," he would often bring along guests he was dining with, the entire party "all togged out in dinner clothes," heading for the ditches after coffee and cognac.

One of his subway sidekicks was Jimmy Walker. The dapper mayor closely followed the construction of the subway, descending into ditches on a flat-bottomed excavation scoop, all the way to the floor of tunnels, eighty feet underground. Thousands of New Yorkers were as curious, although not nearly as adventurous, as their mayor. All along the line of construction there were open areas where pedestrians could look down into the "nether world" that was being laid open by excavators: a maze of pipes, conduits, wires, and cables "rising, dipping, crossing and interweaving like the exploring roots of some fantastic jungle." These were the guts, nerves, and arteries of a subterranean system for which there existed no master map.* It was a people-less region that New Yorkers took for granted until a water main broke, a steam pipe burst, or a power plant shut down, leaving large parts of New York without electricity.

Down in the subway ditches, power shovels and cranes encountered thick tangles of pipes and cables—fully 45,000 miles of them. There were pipes and tunnels for water, gas, sewage, and steam—and a bewildering tangle of cables for telephone, electric power, and telegraph service. "If these are cut," wrote Kaempffert, "New York is helpless." So contractors built entirely new systems of water and gas mains. Temporary sewer pipe flumes were installed while excavation went on, and electric light and telephone cables were laid bare and supported, above ground, on wooden stringers. Amazingly, not a single standing building was seriously damaged; not one vital utility line was ruptured.

Covering the progress of this stupendous excavation, more than one reporter was made aware of how vulnerable the city was to sabotage. Its unguarded subsurface of pipes, conduits, mains, and ducts was so congested

---

* Every public utility and city department with equipment underground had a map of its own system. During subway construction, the Board of Transportation relied on these maps to guide its construction crews.

under some streets that "it would be impossible to insert even so much as a lead pencil from curb to curb." With luck and cunning, "a small crew of hard-working saboteurs could probably make New York uninhabitable within seventy-two hours," wrote one reporter. "Their objectives would be few and easily located: the central power plants, the few important telephone and telegraph exchanges," and New York's great water carrier, City Tunnel No. 1, running nearly the full length of Manhattan. "Afterward the defenses of New York Harbor could be dismantled and moved away, because New York City wouldn't be worth defending."

To the average New Yorker such a scenario was too fantastic to take seriously. Digging and blasting, uncovering the innards of the city, meant only one thing: progress, progress measured not just in skyscrapers and corporate gain but also in new places and kinds of mass entertainment. While giants of construction and industry were reshaping the area around Grand Central Terminal, entertainment and communications impresarios, many of them as new to the city as Walter Chrysler, were remaking the Times Square district above Forty-second Street into the amusement and communications capital of the world, a place of light and spectacle where network radio and the modern movie palace were born.

Mayor Jimmy Walker, 1927.

The kingpins of New York's biggest bootlegging syndicate: William "Big Bill" Dwyer (top left), Owen "Owney" Madden (above), Frank Costello (bottom left).

Death Avenue, Hell's Kitchen. A New York Central train on Eleventh Avenue, near Owney Madden's home, led by a "cowboy" on horseback waving a red warning flag. Tenth and Eleventh Avenues were known collectively as "Death Avenue" because of the hundreds of people killed by what aroused residents called "treacherous freights." The tracks were elevated in the 1930s.

Huge beer vats, along with other brewing equipment valued at $2 million, seized by Prohibition agents in a raid on Owney Madden's Phoenix Brewery on Tenth Avenue between 25th and 26th Streets. Agents had to break through a concrete wall to get to the vats.

"Texas" Guinan, Manhattan's wildly popular nightclub hostess. Part owner of a number of her clubs, she reportedly earned a fortune, even while being raided repeatedly by Prohibition agents.

The Puncheon Club on West 49th Street. Cousins Jack Kriendler and Charlie Berns made it an expensive venue for writers and celebrities. Damon Runyon claimed that Jack and Charlie had a secret "laughing room" where they planned the day's price list. In 1929 the club moved to its present location at 21 West 52nd Street and was renamed "21."

9

Manhattan, June 13, 1927. Spectators, part of a crowd of four million, view the ticker tape parade on Broadway for Charles Lindbergh on his triumphant return to New York after his solo flight from Long Island to Paris.

Grand Central Terminal was the magnet project for the rebuilding of Midtown Manhattan. William J. Wilgus, the New York Central Railroad's chief engineer, masterminded the planning of the terminal and the miniature city—Terminal City—that was built around it on railroad company property. All but forgotten today, Wilgus was an inspired urban planner as well as an accomplished engineer.

In 1900, the area immediately north of the terminal was a gigantic rail yard. Beginning in 1903, Wilgus sank the tracks, electrified them, and decked them over, creating modern Park Avenue, which became in the 1920s the most exclusive residential street in America.

An elevated roadway, or viaduct, ran over East 42nd Street and connected with a "collar" road that ran around the terminal. When completed in 1927 the road carried both northbound and southbound traffic. Depending on direction, Park Avenue traffic passed through one of two portals built into the New York Central's new headquarters building (seen here, looming over the terminal).

Park Avenue looking south toward the New York Central Building, now the Helmsley Building.

Until the early 1920s, Vanderbilt family mansions dominated both sides of Fifth Avenue from 42nd Street to 59th Street, the southern entrance to Central Park, a concentration of wealth unequaled in any other American city. This picture, taken on Easter Morning 1900, shows a string of Vanderbilt mansions on one side of the avenue.

Vanishing social citadels. In the early 1920s, real estate moguls, led by immigrants Benjamin Winter and Frederick Brown, began buying Vanderbilt mansions, razing them, and constructing tall commercial buildings, turning Fifth Avenue north of 42nd Street into the "aristocrat of shopping thoroughfares."

In 1926, a syndicate headed by Frederick Brown purchased and demolished the urban château of Alice Vanderbilt, widow of Cornelius Vanderbilt II. Located at Fifth Avenue and 58th Street, it was the largest house in New York. Brown leased part of the property to Fifth Avenue tailor Edwin Goodman, who constructed a fabulously modern store, Bergdorf Goodman, to house his burgeoning business. It still stands on the site.

Cosmetics tycoons Helena Rubinstein (above), a Polish immigrant, and Elizabeth Arden (below), a former Canadian farm girl, built million-dollar beauty businesses in their Fifth Avenue salons. Bitter rivals, they never spoke, although their salons were only blocks apart.

The Fred F. French Building, an Art Deco masterwork completed in 1927, was one of the first skyscrapers built in Midtown. Located at Fifth Avenue and East 45th Street, it was the headquarters of the Fred French real estate empire.

20

Fred F. French.

21

French's next project, begun in 1927, was Tudor City, a secluded garden community with ten tall towers at 42nd Street and the East River, only a four-minute walk to Grand Central Terminal.

22

23

In 1919, Brooklyn's Irwin S. Chanin, son of Jewish immigrants from Ukraine, was jobless and broke. Ten years later, when his magnificent skyscraper headquarters on East 42nd Street was completed, his construction company was worth nearly $100 million. Appropriately, Chanin chose as the decorative theme of its lobby, "New York—City of Opportunity," with his own life as illustrative example.

24

In 1928, four years after introducing at the New York Auto Show the first car bearing his name, the Chrysler Six, Walter P. Chrysler began supervising the construction on East 42nd Street of what he boasted would be "the tallest building in the world"— the international headquarters of his Detroit-based auto company.

Post & Mc
Chrysler F
Lexington
& 43rd St:
October 18
Photo # 27

Chrysler's announcement set off a "sky race" with builders of an office tower at 40 Wall Street. As both buildings neared completion, newspapers declared the downtown challenger the winner. But Chrysler ordered the construction, in secret, of a 185-foot-high steel spire inside his building's uncompleted tower. When it was raised on October 23, 1929, the seventy-seven-story Chrysler Building, at 1,046 feet tall, was the highest structure ever built—but only for eleven months, until it was superseded by the Empire State Building.

By 1930, when the Raymond M. Hood–designed Daily News Building was completed, the area around Grand Central Terminal was a "Valley of Giants," home to four of New York's six tallest buildings: from right to left, the Daily News, Chrysler, Chanin, and Lincoln Buildings.

On New Year's Day 1905, Adolph Ochs, publisher of *The New York Times,* moved his paper's headquarters from Park Row downtown to Long Acre Square, which the city renamed Times Square, at the intersection of 42nd Street with Broadway and Seventh Avenue. The twenty-five-story Times Building and the subway station underneath it ignited commercial development of the area north of 42nd Street and turned Times Square into New York City's great "amusement center."

Times Square, New Year's Eve 1907, with the Times Tower crowned by a powerful searchlight. To celebrate the completion of the Times Building, Ochs organized a rooftop fireworks display on New Year's Eve 1904, attended by 200,000 revelers. Three years later, a blazing electric ball was lowered from the top of the tower at midnight, the beginning of a fabled New York tradition.

Times Square, brilliantly lit on a rainy night. A French visitor called the pageant of lights "a conspiracy of commerce against night."

March 11, 1927, opening night of the Roxy Theatre at 153 West 50th Street. Billed as "The Cathedral of the Motion Picture," its opening was the high-water mark of the Golden Age of the Movie Palace.

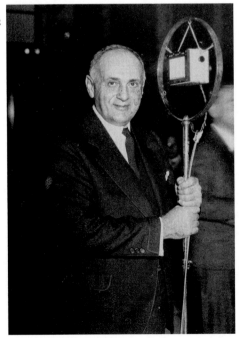

After arriving in New York in 1912, Samuel "Roxy" Rothafel became manager of several Broadway movie palaces, where he presented elaborate film "prologues" that included symphonic music, ballet, and vaudeville acts. In the early 1920s he began broadcasting these prologues and soon had his own variety show, the most popular on radio.

CHAPTER FOURTEEN

THE MAGIC CARPET

*Don't give the people what they want—give them something
better than they expect.*

—ROXY

The Cathedral of the Motion Picture

A guest at Terminal City's Commodore Hotel out for a stroll across town on
a winter afternoon in early 1927 would have noticed a change in the character of Forty-second Street as he crossed Sixth Avenue. This was the approach
to Manhattan's Theater District. Directly ahead was the triangular piece of
real estate where Broadway met Seventh Avenue at Forty-second Street. Here
stood the imposing New York Times Tower, which had stamped its name on a
place once known as Long Acre Square.

Along Forty-second Street, east of Times Square, were long rows of theaters featuring drama, musical comedy, and the shabby remains of vaudeville.
"Screamingly ugly by day," the street would be lit up fantastically at night,
its pavements packed to the curb, most of the crowds heading to a musical
comedy or a live revue. North of Times Square, at Fiftieth Street and Seventh Avenue, plasterers and carpenters were working furiously to complete
the Roxy Theatre in time for its highly publicized opening on March 11. The
largest, most elaborately equipped movie theater in existence, The Roxy bore
the name of its manager and promotional genius, Samuel L. "Roxy" Rothafel,
a friend of Irwin Chanin's, whose construction firm was building the movie
palace to the specifications of architect Walter W. Ahlschlager.

Roxy, like Chanin, had started out at the bottom, a traveling salesman,
bartender, and sandlot baseball player in the anthracite fields of northeastern Pennsylvania. Now the "leading motion picture showman in the country"

would have the largest, most architecturally interesting theater in the world, Chanin had told reporters.

On opening night, Roxy would present the silent film *The Love of Sunya*, starring Hollywood queen Gloria Swanson. His theater was already being billed as the "Cathedral of the Motion Picture," an art and entertainment form that had gotten its start with pioneers like him, in dingy backrooms with rented pianos and borrowed chairs. By 1927, the cinema houses had completed their "conquest" of the theatrical district, wrote reporter Will Irwin—sweeping the legitimate theaters off Broadway and onto its narrow side streets, running eastward toward Sixth Avenue and westward toward Eighth, on the border of Hell's Kitchen.

Roxy was the commanding figure in this transformation. The "Napoleon among exhibitors," he was the first promoter to attract large, enthusiastic audiences to New York's film theaters, pulling them in with added attractions: hundred-piece symphony orchestras, ballets, vaudeville skits, and thrilling light and color effects. "In America, one name before all others is identified with the presentation of moving pictures, the name of S. L. Rothafel, known as Roxy," wrote the cultural critic Gilbert Seldes.

The movies had become so popular that Roxy's financial backer, former film producer Herbert Lubin, had been unable to find a place for his new theater along the central stem of Broadway, from Times Square to Fifty-third Street. The lords of the silver screen had taken all the prime spots. Here stood the Loews, the Strand, the Capitol, the Rialto, the Paramount, and twenty smaller houses, all of them with marquees that extended out to the curb line. Roxy's theater was situated a little to the west of the flashing lights of Broadway, on the former site of an old horse-car barn. The location, he hoped, would not deter any of the thousands of working people—his kind of crowd—that poured into Times Square nightly on the subways—bricklayers and clerks, secretaries and housewives "well pressed and brushed." There were so many of them on weekend nights that special detachments of policemen were strategically positioned to herd them northward, across densely trafficked cross streets, to the brilliantly lit theaters that lined both sides of Broadway. "On they come as the police stop the traffic to let a new batch through," Will Irwin described this parade of moviegoers, "marching with the steadiness and solidity of a regiment. . . . Mankind is going to the magic carpet which carries it into enchanted lands where life is too wonderful for daily living. Humanity is seeking relief from the wheel."

The grand opening of the Roxy Theatre was the high water mark of the golden age of the American motion picture palace. The Paramount Theatre had opened in Times Square the previous November, and Roxy had vowed to surpass it in size, spectacle, and mechanical wizardry. The palatial 3,664-seat Paramount was filled to capacity every evening. But the wagering on Broadway was that Roxy would outshine Adolph Zukor, the Hungarian Jew who had founded Paramount Pictures and was the propelling force behind the company's combined New York theater and office skyscraper. This was, after all, Roxy—filmmaker, producer, composer, stage director, talent scout, musical arranger, and radio personality, star of his hugely popular variety show, *Roxy and His Gang*. Everyone in America who owned a radio knew him; and in New York he was almost as prominent a personality as Jimmy Walker. "His influence could be felt everywhere in the city," said *The New York Times*.

"I'll make a bet that in my time or yours you are never going to see this theatre equaled," Roxy told reporters shortly before opening night. But his bravado masked a deep unease. Construction costs for his new theater had driven Lubin, his original backer, deeply into debt and threatened to push back the opening by months. But help arrived in early March, days before the opening. Hungarian-born film mogul William Fox (born Wilhelm Fried), founder of the Fox Film Corporation, paid $5 million for a controlling interest in the Roxy Theatres Corporation and vowed to open on time. The deal got Lubin off the hook, for a tidy profit of $3 million, and gave Roxy the deep-pocketed patron he needed to support his excesses.

Tall, imperious William Fox had started out in life selling lozenges to passengers on New York Harbor excursion boats. The acquisition of the Roxy Theatre was, he said, "the supreme achievement" of his lifetime. It gave him his first "big capacity house" in the city, the perfect Broadway outlet for first-run Fox pictures. And in buying the theater, he was buying Samuel Rothafel. Fox knew that the powerful and profligate Roxy would be nearly impossible to rein in, but he considered his investment well worth the risk. Roxy "[is] the greatest genius of motion picture presentation," Fox told reporters. He sold seats, and Fox considered that the ultimate test of a theater manager.

Twice the size of the Paramount, the Roxy was erected at the then astounding cost of $10 million, half of what the Chrysler Building would cost. Yet it was, initially, a better investment than Walter Chrysler's. In its first year of operation, it would draw six and a half million patrons and gross more than $100,000 a week, unprecedented numbers for an American theater.

Opening night went off exactly as Roxy hoped it would. "[Rothafel] has conceived, laid out and built the largest theatre since Rome fell," said *The New Yorker*'s Kenneth Macgowan, "and he has equipped it more perfectly for its purposes than any in the world." Lubin and Fox had put up the money, but in style and spirit the theater was all Roxy. He was responsible for its ornate design and its ingenious mechanical features. "The great P. T. Barnum is not dead," said an opening night reviewer. "He lives and reigns once more in the form of Roxy."

The theater was outlandishly lavish, "swarming with marble statuary and French rock crystal chandeliers." A long foyer led to six sets of bronze-trimmed doors. Passing through them, patrons entered a grand rotunda. (Roxy threatened to fire any of his ushers who referred to it as "the lobby.") It was five stories tall, with green marble columns supporting a lofty dome, and was capable of accommodating over 2,500 ticket holders waiting for the next show.

Opening night patrons glided toward the auditorium, the theater's centerpiece, across a stretch of oval carpet "grand enough for a royal procession." Inside the auditorium, hidden in a chamber under the stage, was a Kimball pipe organ, advertised as one of the largest in existence. It had been placed there so that its sound would mingle with the music of Roxy's 110-piece orchestra, the largest standing orchestra in the world. Three organists, sitting at its separate consoles, "played the same piece of music simultaneously with such ferocity that it seemed as if the Apocalypse were descending," wrote Broadway critic Brooks Atkinson.

The theater was equipped with the most advanced entertainment technology, including "Vitaphone," a system introduced by Warner Brothers for synchronizing picture and sound. And the lighting was spectacular, colors from the entire spectrum and enough power to illuminate a town of 25,000 people.

The Moorish-inspired auditorium, which seated over six thousand patrons, was in a style that Roxy—unschooled in the finer points of architecture—called Spanish, "with a quick journey," as his equally clueless press agents put it, "into Africa." Most critics derided the theater as garish and overdone—"everything in excess, everything . . . suffocated in magnificence." But *The New Yorker*'s architecture writer, George Chappell, found "Roxy's new home . . . a truly fine expression of what a place of entertainment should be." Chappell read Roxy perfectly. His architectural opus, Chappell pointed out, was not built for audiences that frequented the legitimate theaters off Times Square. Its "architecture of fantasy" mirrored the taste of ordinary Americans who went to the movies and reveled in "luxury and beauty . . . beyond their means." While Roxy instructed his publicists to call him "The *Maestro*," he was first and last an entertainment merchant, whose supreme ambition was to "please his clients." For a dollar and fifty cents—the standard price for two tickets—a Bronx steamfitter and his wife would be able to take any available seat in the house—none were reserved—and enjoy a four-hour show in luxuriant comfort, a whisper away, perhaps, from a New York notable. And they would be treated like royalty by platoons of crisply courteous ushers.

On opening night, at the sound of a bugle blast, Roxy's ushers marched into the theater, outfitted in gold-braided uniforms and spotless white gloves, and under the disciplined direction of ex-Marine Sergeant Charles Griswold. They flew into action, opening doors, providing inside information on the theater, and escorting guests to their seats. Most were tall, handsome, and perfectly erect; and they bore themselves with decorum and solemnity, their faces as impassive as "well-trained morticians."

These young men, many of them New York City college students with ROTC training, were proud to be Roxy ushers. Sergeant Griswold had put them through a boot-camp-style training program, with some help from Roxy, a former Marine Corps drill sergeant; and they had been melded into a tight fraternity. They called each other "brother," and upon acceptance into the group, each new brother received a medallion and a kit that included a flashlight, a pencil and pad, breath mints, and smelling salts.

Griswold had polished his 120 young men "to a high luster of courtesy." They were forbidden to snap their fingers or to point; and all patrons, even children, were to be called "sir" or "madam." The ushers were so intimidatingly correct that some opening night guests lowered their voices in their presence.

The Roxy was more than a theater; it was a superbly equipped entertainment complex. Hidden away from the public areas were rehearsal halls for musicians and dancers, five floors of dressing rooms, dry-cleaning and laundry facilities, an ushers dressing room and lounge, a music library housing over fifty thousand orchestral scores, offices for two hundred Roxy employees, and a menagerie for show animals, which might include—depending on the acts on any given night—camels, bears, elephants, tigers, and seals. On one of the top floors there was a radio studio large enough to accommodate Roxy's entire symphony orchestra, the Roxy Chorus, various soloists, and another Kimball pipe organ. Roxy's performers had their own cafeteria, billiard room, nap room, gymnasium, and showers. There was even an infirmary equipped by a Mount Sinai physician for surgical emergencies.

Still a formidable athlete in his forties, Roxy had his own handball court and a fully equipped health club in his penthouse suite, which had a kitchen, a large dining room, and two bedrooms, one with cedar closets where he kept part of his wardrobe of eighty suits. Roxy planned to stay in his theater-apartment when he worked late into the night, attended by a uniformed butler and a chef. Close by was a winding staircase that led down to his private box. There he could watch shows with friends and dignitaries, as he anxiously did on opening night.

Opening night ticket holders had begun to stream into the theater around six o'clock, about the time the street in front of the theater began to fill up with celebrity watchers. By six-thirty, there were over ten thousand people jammed into the intersection of Seventh Avenue and Fiftieth Street, with thousands more on the way by subway and streetcar. Spotlights mounted on trucks lit up the Alhambra-like walls of the theater.

Around seven o'clock the luminaries began arriving, stepping out of long limousines. "There's Mayor Walker," someone would cry out. "That's Gloria Swanson and her husband," and "Charlie Chaplin"—and "Look at Irving Berlin." Even Texas Guinan was there. "They came—the Mayor, actors, chorines, bankers, merchants, lawyers," wrote *Time*. "They beheld a vast, bronzed, Spanish Renaissance structure imposing its Moorish splendor upon the corner of Seventh Ave. and Fiftieth Street, in the backyard neighborhood of Broadway, otherwise asprawl with garages, night clubs, hotdog stands, pawn-jewelers." Roxy's theater was actually an exercise in urban gentrification. Its opening, said one Broadway veteran, had discomforted the "lads who ordinarily foregather there of an evening to play 'craps,' shoot each other, stab one another and otherwise make merry."

As the invited guests pushed their way into the auditorium they spotted Samuel L. Rothafel, who had descended from his private perch to greet them. There he stood, "a poker-faced Buddha in a tuxedo, beneath an arrangement of red and white carnations that spelled out R-O-X-Y." His impassive face lit up—"almost as if a button had been pressed"—whenever he spotted someone special in the crowd. Beside him were his wife, Rosa, a shy woman in a velvet fur-trimmed cloak, and their teenage daughter, Beta, bright-faced and sparklingly personable. (Their son was away at Peekskill Military Academy on the Hudson.)

At eight-thirty sharp, three chime notes alerted the audience to move to its seats. The lights dimmed, and the great Kimball organ rose on an elevator platform from the orchestra pit. The organists, dressed in green velvet smoking jackets, "thundered" through the Pilgrims' Chorus. Then the instrument sank back into its chamber, the chimes rang again, and the theater went dark. An actor dressed as a hooded monk walked on stage under the cone of a spotlight and gravely read the invocation from a scroll—the "Roxology," the unimpressed would call it. "Ye portals bright, high and majestic, open to our gaze the path to Wonderland and show us the realm where fantasy reigns . . ." After yet more of this solemn tripe, he ended with, "Let there be light." At that moment, a flood of amber light spilled down onto the Roxy Symphony Orchestra, under the direction of Erno Rapée, the rigidly formal Hungarian conductor and classical composer. Maestro Rapée signaled for silence and opened the program with a symphonic verse depicting the events surrounding the writing of "The Star Spangled Banner." At this point, the golden curtains on the stage were drawn, revealing an image of Fort McHenry being bombarded by artillery fire. The audience rose as one for the playing of the National Anthem.

From there on it was entirely Roxy's show. He had created the "tableau" or pre-film entertainment, which lasted far longer than the feature film. There was a grand ballet, a performance by Roxy's hundred-member choral ensemble, and a musical drama, "A Fantasy of the South," followed, incongruously, by the "Roxy Pictorial Review," a selection of the most popular newsreels of the week, among them a mini-documentary of the construction of the Roxy Theatre. Baritone Douglas Stanbury then appeared on stage and belted out "A Russian Lullaby," the song Roxy had commissioned Irving Berlin to write for the opening. The prologue concluded with Rapée leading the Roxy Symphony Orchestra in a stirring rendition of the overture to *Carmen*, accompanied by the screening of a Vitaphone reproduction of Bizet's opera. Then, finally, there was the showing of *The Love of Sunya*.

Attending a similar Roxy extravaganza later that year, the French writer Paul Morand pronounced it a "profanation" of music, art, color, and film, but at the conclusion of opening night, Roxy could not have been more pleased. As the bleary-eyed crowd filed out of the theater well past midnight, Roxy stood on his private balcony with his wife, a barkeeper's daughter, looking down at the emptying rotunda. Roxy and Rosa had exchanged vows, eighteen years ago, in tiny Forest City, Pennsylvania. Now he was, said *The New Yorker*, "the Jehovah of a theatre that could seat that whole town."

"It's the Roxy and I'm Roxy." He turned to Rosa, unable to contain his excitement. "I'd rather be Roxy than John D. Rockefeller or Henry Ford."

The evening had been vintage Roxy, the music and theatrics overwhelming the feature film. Gilbert Seldes wrote of Roxy: "Nothing he ever said or did gave the slightest indication that he had any interest in the moving picture whatever—that is except as an element in entertainment." Roxy was the originator of what he called, pretentiously, the art of film presentation. This was his pride and passion. He was a showman, not a serious promoter of films, and this fact hastened his rapid rise and his equally swift demise.

They Never Did Anything

Little is known of Samuel Lionel Rothapfel's first years but he was probably born in Bromberg, Germany (now part of Poland), in 1882, the first son of a German-Jewish shoemaker and a Polish farmwomen (Roxy dropped the "p" in his last name sometime during World War I, when anti-Germany senti-ment ran strong in the United States). Three years later his father, Gustave, immigrated to America, and brought his family over the next year after he set-tled in Stillwater, Minnesota, a grim Scandinavian lumbering town on the St. Croix River. His father, known locally as "the little Jew," was a frustrated man, shamed by his inability to climb out of poverty. "My ancestors were peasants," Roxy told an interviewer years later. "They never did anything."

Unable to support his family in timber country, Gustave Rothapfel brought them to Brooklyn in 1894, when Roxy was thirteen. "I was the black sheep of our small family," Roxy said later. "I . . . was always moping about, dreaming, dreaming." Forced to quit school to help support his family, he took a job as a cash boy in a department store in lower Manhattan. When he quit after a few days, his father threw him out of the house. At fourteen years old he had to learn to live on his own. Over the next several years he had "so many jobs" it would have taken him "an hour just to name them all," he said years later. "I could not hold one more than two weeks." More out of confusion than com-mitment, he joined the Marine Corps at age eighteen and was sent to China during the Boxer Rebellion, where he served on a gunboat. In 1905, he ended his military service back in the States as a drill sergeant.

After his discharge, he returned to New York, jobless but with a fresh out-look on life. He took a job as a traveling book salesman, selling cheap paper-bound books door-to-door. He had tried and failed at a job similar to this before joining the Marines, "but this time . . . I *sold* the books! I had got a grip on two things: the needs of discipline and the power of imagination. I used the discipline on myself, and the imagination on my customers." His work took him to northeastern Pennsylvania's coal country, where he also played minor league baseball and picked up the nickname Roxy, easier for fans to pronounce than Rothapfel. Selling illustrated travel lectures to coal-mining families taught him a life-changing lesson: "people will respond to the fine things of life, if you give them a chance."

One December afternoon, while knocking on doors in Forest City, just north of Scranton, he stopped for a hot dog at a family-run tavern. Sitting at the bar, he spotted the owner's attractive daughter, Rosa Freeman, working in the kitchen. He would return again, nearly every day, the beginning of a ro-mance. They wanted to get married, but Rosa's father, Julius, didn't think Roxy was "steady" enough for his daughter. "He thought I was a rover and a good-for-nothing. He didn't believe I would stick to anything." If Roxy wanted her hand in marriage, he would have to prove his dependability by tending bar for Julius for at least a year. Eighteen months later he married Rosa. They would soon have two children.

Rosa's father had a large back room that he rented out for sauerkraut dinners and dances, boozy affairs punctuated by brawls between warring mining clans. Roxy wanted to turn it into a roller rink but changed his mind after seeing how popular one-reel movies were becoming in hard-pinched coals towns like Scranton. He persuaded Julius to turn the dance hall into a motion picture theater. "I bought a second-hand screen and projection machine, hired a pianist and charged 5 cents admission. In that little dance-hall theatre I started in a crude way to do what I am doing now," he told a reporter years later.

The theater was slated to open on New Year's Day 1908. Roxy walked seven miles in deep snow to the Carbondale rail depot to pick up his rented three-reel films; he then borrowed two hundred chairs from a local undertaker. The chair situation created a problem. Every time there was a big wake he had to close the theater. Later, he bought his own secondhand chairs.

It was a one-man operation. Roxy hand-painted the posters, distributed the handbills door-to-door, ran the projector, picked the music, and hired a local woman to play the piano. Roxy stood at the door collecting nickels and was the master of ceremonies. He showed silent films on a hand-cranked projector and introduced, and regularly interrupted them with lugubrious lectures on the mechanics of his miracle-like imaging system, knowledge he had picked up through reading that very month. "Pearls of wisdom," he called these impromptu talks.

When the audiences got larger, he hired a violinist and a baritone singer. To make the shows distinctive, he experimented with colored lights that played on the screen, which added, Roxy thought, a "sensual richness" to the black-and-white "flickers." During a showing of the Pasadena Rose Festival, Roxy tied sponges dipped in rosewater to a couple of cheap electric fans. When the parade's rose floats came on the screen he turned on the fans. Smell-O-Vision, Roxy called it.

"The surroundings were poor and mean and ugly," Roxy would later describe that back room theater. "But perhaps for that very reason I saw more clearly, at last, what it was that I wanted to do. I was still only dimly conscious of it. But I can say now, without affectation, that I began trying even then to create something beautiful for people who have an unsatisfied longing for beauty." Gustave Rothapfel's prodigal son had finally found a way to advance in the world, and he would pursue his dream with terrible intensity, determined never again to fail.

On a visit to New York, he so impressed the editors of a film magazine that they commissioned him to write a series of articles. "Motion pictures are no longer a fad—they are here to stay, and are sure to become the greatest source of amusement in this country," he predicted. S. L. Rothafel "was one of the first to see in our primitive moving pictures the beginning of a new and powerful world industry," a reporter would later identify Roxy's principal contribution to film history.

Three years before Roxy opened his coal miners theater, two partners living in McKeesport, Pennsylvania, Harry Davis and John Harris, had converted a local store into a makeshift movie house and begun charging a nickel for admission. Searching for a name for their venue, they added the Greek word for theater to the word nickel. The name caught on, and when Roxy got started in the business the "nickelodeons" dominated the emergent movie business. By 1911 there were nearly five hundred of them in New York City alone. The audiences were largely the working poor, a part of the population "to whom ten cents a week constitutes a real dissipation," wrote a critic who predicted that movies would never appeal to any but this class of people. Roxy demurred. After his Forest City success, he reached out to the middle class.

The year Roxy opened his tavern-theater, B. F. Keith, "grand vizier" of American vaudeville, hired him to improve the motion picture showings in his nationwide chain of vaudeville houses. Keith loathed motion pictures, using them, at first, to drive out audiences, clearing the house for the next vaudeville performance. He had recently noticed, however, that people were remaining in their seats to watch the one-reel films. Rothafel became B. F. Keith's "Johnny Appleseed," writes historian Daniel Okrent, "spreading his notions of motion picture presentation across the country." Traveling in luxuriously appointed Pullman cars, sad-eyed Samuel Rothafel could hardly believe his good fortune—astonished that he had advanced so far so rapidly.

On a train trip in 1911, Roxy fell into a conversation with Herman Fehr, owner of a dying vaudeville theater in Milwaukee. After a short visit to Chicago, he returned to Milwaukee and accompanied Fehr to his "white elephant." Sitting with Fehr in the empty auditorium, he told him that there was only one way to make it pay: movies. "He threw up his hands at that idea," Roxy recalled. Roxy was hired on the spot and given an advance of $5,000 to convert Fehr's Alhambra Theatre into a motion picture house. Less than a month later, the theater was packed to capacity at every performance.

After reversing the plunging fortunes of two other Midwestern theaters Roxy became the most sought after theater exhibitor in the country, master of "atmospheric prologue," the capstone of which was an hour and more of live classical music, followed by synchronized music to accompany the silent film.

Before Roxy's innovations, music was considered a standard but unimportant part of the cinematic experience. There might be a single piano player or a small third-rate orchestra, but that was it. Roxy broke tradition by hiring professional musicians and installing enormous pipe organs in his theaters. He also hired, and personally trained, staffs of uniformed ushers. The middle class, as well as the factory class, he believed, deserved courtesies ordinarily reserved for the rich, and cultural performances equal in excellence to grand opera—and at affordable prices. "I want to make the truck driver and his wife feel like a king and queen."

In 1913, Roxy was called to New York, back to the city in which he had failed at everything he tried. He was to manage the Regent Theatre on upper Broadway, which was in parlous financial shape. Roxy closed the theater temporarily and revamped it, adding plush carpets and seating, a primitive air-cooling system, and a sixteen-piece orchestra. In another innovation, he put the musicians on stage, behind potted palms and a bubbling fountain— uniting music and motion picture in a gardenlike tableau.

Roxy selected the score for every film; and for one of the first times ever the music was thematically merged with the action on the screen. Sound and motion were synthesized, an important contribution to the burgeoning film industry. "The presentation was . . . the best that has been seen in this city," wrote one opening night reviewer. "Such a production should be on Broad-way." It would be, six months later.

When Roxy took over the Regent there were no movie houses in Times Square; live theater reigned on Broadway. The Regent, located roughly seventy blocks away, on 116th Street, in the prosperous German-Jewish section of Harlem, became, under Roxy's direction, a smashing success. This did not go unnoticed by the new breed of entertainment entrepreneurs who were planning to build film theaters in and around Times Square, success-hungry Jews, like Roxy, who had grown up in extreme poverty and advanced rapidly in an industry in which there were few social or ethnic barriers. Not long after the Regent reopened, Roxy was stolen away to run Times Square's first movie palace: the spectacular Strand Theatre, under construction in 1914 on the site of an old carriage factory at Broadway and Forty-seventh Street. Roxy was exultant; he was paid the highest salary of any film presenter in the country.

At that time there were almost a thousand movie houses in New York City, but they were scattered over the five boroughs and almost all of them were small, makeshift operations with tiny screens, primitive projection equipment, and stiff wooden chairs. The larger, more elaborate theaters that showed films were designed originally for live presentations. The Strand was the first New

York theater built expressly for showing films. Opening night drew the city's society crowd, including Vincent Astor and his fiancée, Helen Dinsmore Huntington. This was unprecedented for a film premiere. "Going to the new Strand Theatre last night was very much like going to a Presidential reception, a first night at the opera or the opening of the horse show," wrote *The New York Times*'s drama critic. "It seemed that everyone in town had simultaneously arrived at the conclusion that a visit to the magnificent new movie playhouse was necessary." In its initial year, the Strand drew over ten thousand patrons a day. They were treated to Roxy's unprecedented use of four projectors, which allowed him to show nine-reel movies without a single break.

The nickelodeons were still hanging on in 1914. Roxy-style theaters, imitating nearly everything the Stand offered, from carpets to courtesy, killed them off. Vaudeville suffered an even swifter demise. A decade later the Palace was the only major vaudeville house left in New York City.

From the Strand, Roxy moved on to the Rialto and the Rivoli, Broadway's newest film basilicas. He managed the two theaters simultaneously, both of them in the beating heart of Times Square. The Rialto was another step forward in movie house architecture: a theater without a stage. Even the Strand had a stage so that the theater could be converted, on a moment's notice, for drama or opera. "The Rialto is a motion picture house pure and simple," wrote one critic. "It is stageless, the screen being placed boldly against the back wall of the theater. It is built in the conviction that the American passion [for] the movies is here to stay."

The Rialto and Rivoli were first-run theaters, film palaces that specialized in premiering expensively promoted Hollywood creations. By 1920, movie grandees like Kiev-born Lewis J. Selznick would not dare risk introducing a feature film anywhere but in New York; and if at all possible, at a Roxy-run theater, where, using banks of lights with dimmers, Rothafel gave each scene its own color scheme, along with its own music. This came at a price: musical and vaudeville-style programs that often overshadowed the films. But Roxy knew how to fill the seats. And he was firmly convinced—as were with the owners of the major theater chains—that it "made absolutely no difference at the box office whether the feature was any good or not." Marcus Loew, builder of one of the country's largest theater chains, summed up prevailing sentiment in the trade: "We sell tickets to theaters, not movies."

Theater owners who employed Roxy found him difficult to deal with. Petulant and autocratic, ignoring entreaties for financial restraint, he poured sensational amounts of money into the theaters he managed but never owned. "His forte," said *Variety,* "was in selling his dreams to people who had the capital to make them come true."

Roxy himself was an expensive item. In addition to his hefty salary, he cut a chunk out of a theater's profits to create his own unauthorized expense account. He needed money because he lived big. He had a sumptuous suite at the Rivoli, attended by a Japanese houseboy, whose chief responsibility was to preside over an electric hot dog boiler in a dressing room adjacent to the impresario's office. Roxy could not go more than a few hours without a frank-furter smothered with sauerkraut and mustard. A heavy gambler, he ran up staggering phone bills placing wagers at horse tracks all over the country. In 1919, in a fit of pique, he left both the Rialto and the Rivoli when questioned about long-distance phone calls he had placed to a Maryland racetrack and charged to his budget.

He would not be out of work for long. The next year, he began his famous run as head of "presentations" at the then nearly bankrupt Capitol, a 5,300-seat theater on Fifty-first Street, the largest, most ornate movie house in the world. Almost immediately, Roxy introduced a dozen and more improvements. He scrapped the owner's disastrous policy of selling high-priced reserved seats, and lowered the ticket prices to thirty cents for a matinee—and no more than a dollar for an evening performance. And in what became a Roxy trademark, he made a special appeal to women, installing a nursery to park the children and a cafeteria that became a hangout for young working girls. They, along with housewives, could drop by the Capitol after a rough day and be com-pletely pampered. Doormen would tip their hats, ushers would bow to them, and maids in the ladies' room would curtsy when they entered. "She bathes in elegance and dignity; she satisfies her yearning for a 'cultured' atmosphere," reporter Lloyd Lewis described the appeal of a "De Luxe Picture Palace."

The Capitol was yet another Roxy miracle. Almost singlehandedly he turned a failing enterprise into a Broadway sensation. When Roxy took over the Capitol, Goldwyn Pictures made it its Broadway premiere house; and Roxy, in turn, made it the country's highest-grossing movie theater. While continu-ing to emphasize music over movies, Roxy took great care to book quality films, including *Nanook of the North*, the first feature-length documentary, and *The Cabinet of Dr. Caligari*, the new classic German Expressionist film. But Roxy was not opposed to performing surgery on even the most esteemed films. He smoothed out some of the more complex psychological themes of mental derangement in *The Cabinet of Dr. Caligari* and gave the gloomy film an uplifting ending. It was an act of cultural desecration, bowdlerizing one of the great horror films of all time so as not to offend the sensibilities of his middle-class audience.

Brooks Atkinson derided Roxy as a "showman with the vision of a de-mented prophet," a promoter who turned the Capitol Theatre into a "cultural orgy"—Swiss lullabies preceding performances of Beethoven and Brahms. But Roxy gave his audiences superb music—Debussy, Tchaikovsky, Stravinsky, Strauss—the only classical compositions most of his patrons would ever hear. In addition to the "Roxyettes," the long-legged, high-kicking dance troupe he brought in from St. Louis, Roxy presented first-rate ballet and choral performances, and hired some of the finest musical talent in the city, including Maestro Rapée, a virtuoso pianist and later conductor of the Radio City Symphony Orchestra.

Robert E. Sherwood, one of the country's leading playwrights, appreciated what Roxy was accomplishing. "Although movie audiences were supposed to be composed entirely of incurable lowbrows, Roxy gave them highbrow entertainment and made them like it." This was the genius of Roxy's approach. Before he appeared, there was no public demand for what he offered. "Don't give the people what they want," Roxy explained his formula. "Give them something better than they expect."

Roxy was an easy mark for cultural critics, "a leatherneck putting on culture . . . the king of kitsch." Largely misunderstand was the depth of his convictions. However thin his credentials (he couldn't read a note of music), Roxy saw himself as a cultural missionary to the common crowd. "It has been a long cherished dream of mine," he once said, "to give the masses the highest possible type of music for the lowest price of admission." He hated sneering references to the herd, the hoi polloi; these were curious people who could be made to appreciate fine music and dance. The bigger the crowds he drew to the Capitol, the more he became convinced they were there mainly for the classical performances. He may have been right, but the key component of the Roxy method would turn out to be its fatal weakness.

Roxy shrewdly understood that while early silent films sold seats, they did not, on their own, sell enough seats to make his business profitable. Audiences flocked to biblical epics like *The Ten Commandants* and *Quo Vadis*, and to Rudolph Valentino's desert dramas, but there were never enough customers sufficiently interested in the more mundane fare that Hollywood served up to fill theaters as capacious as the Capitol, the Rivoli, and the Strand. Roxy had discovered a way to bring in the crowds and keep them coming back. This would begin to change, however, after the premiere of the first talking picture, *The Jazz Singer*, in October 1927, seven months after Roxy opened his Cathedral of the Motion Picture. The first "talkies" were crudely produced. But when they improved they would kill interest in Roxy's interminable prologues and put an end to his fabulous run of success. That would not happen until the Depression years, however. Until then, Roxy and his musical prologues continued to be popular. In 1922, *Motion Picture News* honored Roxy, along with Thomas Edison, Charlie Chaplin, and D. W. Griffith, as one of the dozen individuals who had contributed most to the advancement of the silent film industry. Two years later, on the fifth anniversary of the Capitol, an industry trade paper estimated that 26 million people, a number equal to one-fifth of the American population, had paid admission to the theater since its opening. "So successful were his methods, so magical his name," wrote Gilbert Seldes in 1937, one year after Roxy's death, "that you may still find Roxy theaters in the West Indies and in the Far East."

Roxy and Radio

Since the first regularly scheduled radio broadcast in 1920, Roxy had been closely considering the new medium's entertainment potential. Most theater owners viewed radio as "a menace to the movies." Not Roxy. Broadcasting could bring attention to his Capitol Theatre—and to himself—if only he could find a way. He eventually did, although entirely by accident. In the summer of 1922, the electronics giant American Telephone & Telegraph launched WEAF, New York's first radio station with a transmitter powerful enough to reach an audience beyond the metropolitan region. At the same time, AT&T's engineers, working out of laboratories in lower Manhattan, were trying to develop better public address systems. To test their ideas, they persuaded a skeptical Roxy to discard the megaphone he used to direct musical rehearsals and substitute a microphone hooked up to an amplifier and loudspeaker. Roxy was delighted with the results. He could sit at a desk attached to a seat in the auditorium and direct the entire show without racing all over his theater.

AT&T executives next convinced Roxy to broadcast the musical portions of his shows on WEAF. On Sunday evening, November 19, 1922, two weeks after Roxy first put on earphones and heard voices carried over the air, the station aired an orchestral performance, with ballet, of Richard Strauss's *Ein Heldenleben*. It was a radio revolution: the first full broadcast sent out live from the stage of a theater. Standing in the wings behind a microphone Roxy described the entire show for the radio audience—the conductor, the scenery, the lighting, the costumes, and the pinpoint pirouettes of his prima ballerina, Maria Gambarelli, his "beloved Gamby." Roxy later admitted that his knees "knocked together" as he stepped to the mike for first time, but he quickly gained his bearings. "My friends call me by my nickname, Roxy, and when you write you can call me that, too." His unrehearsed sign-off, "Good night, pleasant dreams, God bless you," became his trademark farewell.

It was another radio first, the beginning of the variety show format, a program presided over by a host who is not a performer. And it was the start of

Roxy's meteoric career as a national entertainer. The next day, fans lined up four abreast and far down the block to get into the Capitol; and that week Roxy received thousands of letters. "I nationalized the Capitol Theatre in one day!" he boasted.

On February 4, 1923, Roxy broadcast from a new studio inside the Capitol Theatre, and with a new format he had cooked up. He put together an ensemble of Capitol headliners—singers, ballerinas, and musicians, including Gamby and Eugene Ormandy—and chatted amiably with them after their performances, allowing his audience to get to know them, their likes and dislikes, even their romantic involvements. Roxy had succeeded in bringing the Capitol Theatre "into the family life of America." Radio, he said, "has brought me into the homes of my Public. We are in touch."

Roxy changed American radio, transforming it from a form of communication into a form of entertainment. His primary variety show format would remain a radio standard well into the future. Roxy, the cultural evangel, also saw radio as an extension of his mission to enhance the musical aptitude of ordinary Americans. Every household, he said, ought to have a "fine radio set," as well as a phonograph and a piano. These are "as necessary in the modern home as the chairs, beds, knives and forks."

Roxy's studio show became a national sensation. Listeners loved Roxy's personal touch. He read letters from his "children" out there in radio land. Sometimes he would choke up in the middle of one of them and break into tears. His priestly earnestness and his empathy with his audience made him "one of the most beloved . . . personalities in the public eye today," said a reporter for *Radio News*. Some critics derided his "drooling sentimentality," but they had no impact on his loyal audience.

No one will ever know "whether Roxy actually believes in the tonic qualities of the milk toast he hands out so lavishly," wrote Broadway writer Allene Talmey. An outgoing man—flashy and exuberant, handing out "nicknames on five minutes' acquaintanceship"—he was, at core, a deeply secretive person who kept his inner thoughts to himself. Whatever his true feelings, he struck his listeners as someone who was trying to reach out to them and enhance their lives, a beloved uncle dishing out down-home advice. By 1924, some five million people were tuning in every Sunday evening to *Roxy and His Gang*, and Roxy received as many as ten thousand letters a week, many of them "misspelled and poorly expressed, but filled," said Mary Mullett—the only reporter Roxy ever allowed to read them—"with touching gratitude and affection."

One letter from an older married couple whose children had left home demonstrates how strongly Roxy touched the lives of his listeners. "We are lonely. But our Sunday nights are not lonely, for we have you! Tonight you told us to put out the lights, so that we might enjoy the music better. Well, we did. And then—we didn't turn them on again, but found ourselves sitting together, holding each other's hands *à la* thirty-two years ago!"

Roxy, the former Marine, was especially popular with families of wounded and sick veterans. From his Capitol studio, he launched a campaign to provide every patient in a veterans hospital with a small radio receiving set and earphones. Roxy and other members of the Gang went on the road with regularity to present them to the "battle-stricken boys of our land."

Roxy soon had competitors. Other big film theaters in New York began broadcasting their own stage programs and music, and Warner Brothers created its own New York station, WBPI. But in those early days of radio no one could successfully compete with Roxy, a master showman who enhanced his popularity by going on promotional tours to places within reach of AT&T's new "chain" of radio stations, connected by its phone wires. On his visit to Boston in 1925, over fifty thousand people showed up to greet Roxy and His Gang when they arrived at the train terminal. They packed the streets "from curb to curb, struggling to get near enough to see [Roxy]."

But Roxy, curiously, had few supporters at AT&T. Its board members insisted that his soupy monologues about "the condition of Aunt Matilda's health" weren't "dignified enough" for a station that was trying to attract high-powered corporate sponsors. It was a major miscalculation. In early 1925, AT&T ordered Roxy "to conduct himself after the fashion of the usual Sabbath announcer." Roxy promised to change, but cagily turned the tables on his censors. The following Sunday he gave what one commentator called the "most stilted introduction known to radio." Listeners noticed, and wondered what was the matter with him. The next day they learned in the papers that Roxy had been "edited." Letters of protest flooded the station. It was "the greatest expression of opinion ever drawn from a radio audience," said one reporter. AT&T backed off.

That year Roxy began writing a nationally syndicated newspaper column and produced a book, *Broadcasting: Its New Day*. He had become "a one-man multi-media empire," reaching an audience of eight million listeners a week. "He is the stellar god of a new force—a 'Big Timer' of the ether," a reporter described his mass appeal.

Those who met Roxy for the first time were invariably unimpressed; he seemed anything but a Broadway powerhouse. Balding and thickset, with a middle-age paunch, he had a high-pitched voice and was mawkishly ingratiating. "When Roxy thanks a friend," said Allene Talmey, "God and Love and the Sermon on the Mount are all inextricably mixed." Behind his enormous glass-topped desk, slouched in a chair, chewing on a pipe, he was the very picture of repose. But he was, in truth, a human dynamo, almost impossible to keep up with as he tended to every detail of his theater, from the buttons on the ushers' caps to the hairstyles of the ticket sellers in the booths. Work was his life, and he went at it with furious resolve. His doctors warned him to slow down, but success had made him "hyperactive and desperately needful of attention." He worked up to eighteen hours a day, a habitual self-improver who learned everything he knew by close study.

Three hours before a stage performance, he was at his specially installed portable desk, in the eighth row of the Capitol Theatre, in shirtsleeves and with his green eyeshade pulled low on his forehead, a microphone in front of him. One minute he was raising the platform of the orchestra to improve its tone, the next he was rushing on stage to rearrange a ballet performance—jovial and sternly imperious by turns but alert to every nuance of the performance. "He was almost superhuman!" said Mary Mullet, who watched him conduct a rehearsal. "He seemed to have a hundred eyes, alert to see every flaw, every possibility of improvement."

Roxy found it impossible to relax. He had pastimes—poker, handball, and golf—but he played them with steely determination, wagering heavily on every hand, every hole, every game. Guilty that he was not spending enough time with his family, he began holding his regular Sunday night card games at his apartment on Riverside Drive; but the games extended deep into the night, in a thick cloud of cigar smoke and profanity, disturbing the sleep of Rosa and the children.

Newspaper reporters were invited to play. They became his friends, and during the day Roxy would occasionally skip away with one of them to the racetrack in his high-powered sports car, which he drove like a demon. He was always available to the press, and would have his favorite reporters over for breakfast, with Rosa making ham and eggs and staying in the shadows. She remained steadfastly loyal through widely circulated rumors that he was having serial affairs with his female performers.

Roxy's syrupy congeniality masked a deep-seated power complex. He needed to be in control—the absolute dictator of things—and that meant having a theater of his own. It was in 1925 that Broadway promoter Herbert Lubin first approached him with just such an opportunity. Lubin had recently purchased a property just north of Times Square and had hired the Chanin brothers to begin building "the greatest film theatre ever dreamed of." Lubin wanted Roxy to run it. He was offered a big salary, a block of stock, and a percentage of the profits; and the theater would bear his name. But he needed

Lubin's assurance that he would have authority "to spend any amount" on his stage spectacles. When Lubin surrendered, Roxy signed the papers. That July, Roxy's Gang went on the air from the Capitol Theatre for the final time, and Roxy cleaned out his desk.

Excavation work on the Roxy Theatre began that December. "I will be the absolute despot of it," Roxy told reporters. After the theater opened, *The New Yorker* ran a cartoon showing a little girl standing in its towering rotunda and asking: "Mama, does God live here?"

Times Square

The opening of the Roxy Theatre marked an important shift in the character and culture of Broadway. The movies had taken New York and the country by storm. In 1927, there were 21,000 motion picture theaters in America, and only five hundred or so theaters putting on live drama and musical comedy. Taxis and limousines still crowded the narrow streets off Times Square on gala theater nights, delivering smartly dressed patrons to the dozens of legitimate theaters located there, but the subway crowd had taken over Times Square. "Now Broadway at the theater-hour belongs to the people," wrote Will Irwin.

Theaters in great numbers had begun moving north of Forty-second Street only after 1904, when the new subway station opened on what had been Long Acre Square. In 1896, Adolph Ochs, a fast-rising thirty-eight-year-old Chattanooga, Tennessee, newspaper publisher, borrowed money to purchase the financially troubled *New York Times*. Eight years later, after putting the paper on solid financial footing, he moved its offices from Park Row, near City Hall—"Newspaper Alley"—to a new skyscraper he had commissioned on Long Acre Square. His oblong tower was built on the site of the old Pabst Hotel and directly over the subway station. "It is telling," writes entertainment historian Ken Bloom, "that the entrance of the Pabst Hotel faced downtown while the new Times Tower faced uptown."

Ochs's newspaper staff took possession of the tower on January 1, 1905. It was the second tallest building in the city, next to the Park Row Building, headquarters of Joseph Pulitzer's New York *World*.

When Adolph Ochs had first announced plans to move to Long Acre critics complained, "Too far uptown." "Who'll take the offices?" By the end of 1905, the building was nearly fully rented and the square was being described as a burgeoning business, hotel, and entertainment center, "the Piccadilly of New York—the very heart and centre of the city." The Astor family built the twelve-story Hotel Astor, and just after that, the Hotel Knickerbocker, both in the shadow of the Times Building. Just to the north, theaters began slowly moving in.

Shortly before the *Times* moved into its new publishing plant, the city had changed the name of Long Acre Square to Times Square, and officially designated the square—actually a trapezoid—as "the open space formed by the intersection of Broadway and Seventh Avenue and extending from Forty-second to Forty-seventh Street."

To mark his paper's move, Ochs planned a grand celebration. On New Year's Day 1905, a photograph on the front page of his newspaper showed Times Square packed with hundreds of thousands of revelers, most of them carrying noisemakers of every variety, with cowbells predominating. People had begun to gather on the square around six o'clock the previous evening. By that hour, the Times Building was lit from pavement to peak with fantastic colored lights. "It seemed almost as if the building were aflame." At the stroke of midnight, fireworks, "bombs," and "skyrockets" were shot from the roof of the building. "A great shout went up and an ear-splitting blast was sounded from the horns of merrymakers on the streets below." Their noisemaking melded with the steam whistles of factories, locomotives, and tugboats. "Never was a New Year's more joyously celebrated," said the *Times*.

Two years later, on New Year's Eve 1907, a "blazing electric ball" made of 350 lights was lowered from the top of the Times Tower, the beginning of a fabled New York tradition. In that year, five million subway riders passed through Times Square station, which was "astir at all hours of the day and night." Most of the evening arrivals came to play; this had become the city's great "amusement center." Here was the largest concentration of legitimate theaters and vaudeville halls in the country. As Times Square flourished, Broadway below Forty-second Street became an entertainment backwater, much of it eventually taken over by the city's northward-moving garment industry.

When Prohibition brought down the big elegant restaurants and cabarets—their owners unable to survive on the sale of food alone—the area of Broadway north of Times Square was, as we have seen, cheapened significantly. Yet Broadway remained "the street that never sleeps," and real estate values continued to soar, as movie palaces competed for space with legitimate theaters in what was manifestly an unfair fight. With their small playhouses, ten-month seasons, and nine-plays-a-week schedule, owners of legitimate theaters couldn't afford the exorbitant taxes on the "main stem" of Broadway. Owners of movie houses could. They fit larger audiences into their theaters, charged far less for admission, and put on as many as four shows a day. Even so, New York's legitimate theaters showed remarkable resiliency. While the number of legitimate theaters in the country declined from 1,549 to 674 in the years between 1915 and 1925, the number of theaters in New York City actually grew during this period and into the 1927–28 theater season, when more plays opened on Broadway than at any time in its history, before or since. That season, a playgoer had 268 shows to choose from at a never equaled sixty playhouses. The city's large and increasingly prosperous population and its robust tourist trade kept legitimate theater thriving until the Stock Market Crash of '29, but only because of the speculative daring of New York's theater entrepreneurs, who were willing to chance the abysmal odds—about six to one—against a play becoming a "hit."

The Great Depression would deal a heavy but hardly fatal blow to the New York theater industry. In the entire United States there were two hundred theaters in the mid-1930s, and forty-four of them were in the Times Square district, but there were fewer of them every year. Many of the survivors were kept alive, as they had been for years, by movie money. It was Hollywood—"the archangel of Broadway"—that kept dozens of New York theaters in business in the late 1920s and into the 1930s. In these years, Hollywood money backed as many as a quarter of all shows on Broadway. West Coast producers used the New York stage as a "testing ground" for plays with film potential. Theater-derived films would then come back to Broadway as major motion pictures, packing the movie palaces that were the legitimate theaters' greatest competitors. As early as 1927, there really was no American Theater. There was only "a New York Theater," and Hollywood had a direct hand in it, both as principal supporter and damaging competitor.

Hollywood also helped to destroy New York City's indigenous film industry. Gotham was an important filmmaking center up to the late 1920s, with Paramount Pictures producing over a hundred silent movies at its Astoria Studio in Long Island City, Queens. But the drift was strongly westward to Southern California, with its perpetual sunshine and spacious production lots. Four days away from New York by fast train, Hollywood was making most of the country's commercial films by 1927. But "to Broadway first come all important motion pictures," said Adolph Zukor, head of Paramount. "If Broadway approves, the chances are that the rest of the country will also approve." As with plays, New York set "the pace for success in the back country."

Although Hollywood became the film industry's dominant production center, skyscrapers on Times Square and East Forty-second Street became the corporate headquarters of many of the country's major motion picture companies. "Show me any other industry," said Zukor, "that has done so much for Broadway." It went both ways, however. Hollywood could not have come into being without New York money and talent. As historian Neal Gabler has pointed out, the American film industry "was founded and for more than thirty years operated by Eastern Europeans," many of whom, like Zukor and William Fox, first settled in New York, grew up in crushing poverty, and worked their way into the film industry after starting out as furriers, upholsterers, or street peddlers. Hundreds of stars of the silver screen, including Hell's Kitchen's Mae West and George Raft, also got their start in New York. And without New York's unrivaled subway system, the great movie palaces of Times Square, most of them owned by Hollywood satraps, would have remained half empty.

In 1927, the recently enlarged Times Square station, four levels deep and handling nearly a quarter of a million riders a day, became the biggest, most heavily used tube station in the world. It was the "pivotal point in the entire subway system of the city," and the main portal, said Stanley Walker, to "the capital of America's amusement world." Times Square "is the spirit of New York," the "carnival supernal," wrote the author of a popular city guidebook.

New York's "subway crush" was "unmatched anywhere," and it was at its worst on Times Square. Contemporary writers pointed to it as "a spectacle" to behold, its "dense moving masses of humanity swamping the sidewalks for blocks north of Forty-second Street and requiring four or five stout cops to a corner to keep the cross streets occasionally clear for the motors to get through." These massed urban crowds were unprecedented in the modern Western world. "Parisian boulevards are pale and meager by comparison," wrote visiting English writer Stephen Graham.

The crowds streaming out of the Times Square subway station every evening walked through a living museum of architectural styles. "Nothing whatever in Times Square matches anything else," which was part of its "charm," wrote Will Irwin. Still standing in 1927 were rows of broken-down brownstone houses and ramshack rooming houses. Built among them were clamorous public dancing palaces. The most popular was Roseland Ballroom, a "whites only" dancing hall on Fifty-first and Broadway, which featured African American jazz bands and was considered safer and classier than the notorious "taxi" dance halls: rowdy rip-off joints where patrons paid a dime for each dance and pickpockets did a bonanza business. Eating places abounded on Times Square, from the Automat to the Astor, from Lindy's at Broadway and Fifty-first—Damon Runyon's hangout—to Sardi's on Forty-fourth Street, where Jack Dempsey held court at the bar.

"Mildly insane by day, the square goes divinely mad by night," wrote Will Irwin in 1927. "For then on every wall, above every cornice, in every nook and cranny, blossom and dance the electric advertising signs." When New York's main entertainment district was located at Herald Square, the buildings were splendidly lit, making that stretch of Broadway "The Great White Way," but it was only after Broadway moved to Times Square, in a sense, that these advertising signs took on motion and burst into nearly every color of the spectrum, creating a pageant of moving, rolling, zigzagging light. The square was lighter by night than by day, said Stephen Graham. "The blind are aware of some extra luminosity when they are taken along it." It was so light one could recognize the face of a friend across the street. Paul Morand called it "a conspiracy of commerce against night."

There were small signs, but it was the spectacularly large ones that caught the eye. Broadway was the "apotheosis of electricity," wrote French visitor Odette Keun. "Bottles of beer appear on the firmament and transform themselves into dwarfs drinking; showers of gold peanuts fall from the skies; dragons breathing smoke become a film title; cigarettes are ignited; automobiles materialize." It was the most brazen form of advertising in the world, a merchandisers' show that cost millions to put on. The rental value of some of the buildings on this "flaming avenue" exceeded that of the buildings themselves; one of the largest electric signs on Broadway contained nineteen thousand lamps and twenty-one miles of electrical wiring. Mesmerized by this "long kaleidoscope of colored lights" arranged to sell everything "from pork to pianos," the English writer G. K. Chesterton remarked to his American friends: "What a glorious garden of wonder this would be, to any one who was lucky enough to be unable to read."

This nocturnal advertising was smart, available to the eyes of the estimated million people who poured into Times Square nightly in 1927. Even Le Corbusier, that somber critic of American commercialism, was impressed by "the luminous advertising on Broadway . . . exploding, moving, sparkling, with lights turning white, blue, red, green, yellow."

"Here is our poetry," wrote Ezra Pound, "for we have pulled down the stars to our will." Other cities, even London, tried to imitate the Great White Way, "but none gets this massed effect of tremendous jazz interpreted in light," wrote Will Irwin.

Times Square was never empty, even in the early morning hours, after the white-coated street sweepers had finished their work. By nine o'clock hawkers were already out on the sidewalks trying to talk tourists into their stores with "unbeatable" bargains. And the street reverberated with the sounds of radio. Every other store, it seemed, sold either radios or phonographs, and most of these shops had large speakers that blasted music into the street. The racket was tremendous. As part of his anti-noise campaign, city health commissioner Louis Harris tried to get these stores to lower the decibels, but to no avail. This was the radio age; everybody wanted a radio set, and it had to be the latest model. The new ones were coming out at such a rapid rate that a smart consumer frequented a radio store almost weekly. The stores with the largest inventories and the latest sets were on Times Square, where they competed fiercely.

Most of them stayed open well into the night. It was not unusual to see people standing in line for a movie at the Paramount Theatre holding in their arms, in large wooden boxes, new desktop radios they had purchased down the street. In 1927, radio was New York's biggest new industry and radio stock was flying high on Wall Street. In that year, Roxy was still the biggest attraction on commercial radio. He had moved his weekly variety show from the Capitol Theatre to a studio in his own theater and had signed a contract with the National Broadcasting Company.* NBC was America's first national radio network, founded in late 1926, but not an emergent force in American culture until the following year when it expanded and tried to drive out of business a far smaller network, the immediate predecessor of CBS, the Columbia Broadcasting System.

Nineteen twenty-seven and twenty-eight are the two most important years in the history of commercial radio. In those years two young, fantastically creative entertainment entrepreneurs took hold of the industry, one a Jew from Belarus, the other the descendant of Ukranian Jewish immigrants. David Sarnoff and William Paley, the founders, respectively, of NBC and CBS, transformed the entertainment culture of their adopted city, and eventually of the entire country. They made New York America's "Radio City." Later they would move into television, solidifying their status as the century's communication kings.

---

* In 1931, Roxy left the theater named for him to design and manage two new theaters in Rockefeller Center: Radio City Music Hall, which featured live presentations, and the RKO Theatre, which showed films. Most of his performers moved with him, including the Roxyettes, who became the Rockettes, the dance troupe that still performs at Radio City Music Hall. Roxy's outdated vaudeville-style performances were a disaster and he was forced to resign from Rockefeller Center, his last theater project, in January 1934, "heartbroken," said his friends. His last hurrah came in 1935 when William Paley hired him for a twenty-six-week engagement of *Roxy and His Gang* on the CBS network. He was attempting to return as managing director of the original Roxy Theatre when he died in his sleep on January 13, 1936. The Roxy Theatre at 153 West Fiftieth Street, between Sixth and Seventh Avenues, was closed in 1960 and demolished. NYT, April 10, 1931; Ross Melnick, "Rethinking Rothafel," *The Moving Image* (Fall 2003), 88.

PART FOUR

BRINGING IN THE FUTURE

CHAPTER FIFTEEN

SARNOFF

*In a big ship sailing in an uncharted sea, one fellow needs
to be on the bridge. I happen to be that fellow.*

DAVID SARNOFF

The Boy from Minsk

The visionary who brought radio into the American home was born in a foreign village so backward it was nearly medieval. The story of his rise in a new industry of global dimensions is a stirring commercial saga. Interwoven with it is the story of New York's emergence as the radio capital of the world.

David Sarnoff was born on February 27, 1891 in Uzlyany, a desolate shtetl in Belarus twenty miles south of Minsk. The village had no telephone, telegraph, electricity, or gas; and most of its hard-pinched residents had never seen a ship or a train, or a place much larger than their own hamlet of some two hundred souls. "I had not even seen a picture of a ship," Sarnoff described the bleak isolation of his upbringing. His father, Abraham, was a small-time trader and house painter who was never in sound health; his strong-willed mother, Leah Privin, was a seamstress from a long line of rabbis. Unable to properly support his wife and three young sons, Abraham set out for America on his own when David was five; he would call for his family when he had established himself in the Land of Hope. While they waited for word, David was placed in the care of his mother's uncle, a rigidly Orthodox rabbi from a distant village. His mother's family had marked him to be a Talmudic scholar, the highest calling available to a boy in the village.

Living in his grand-uncle's household, he was forced to follow a strict religious regimen. Every day, from morning till dusk, he studied and chanted the Torah and the Psalms. He was also required to put to memory two thousand words of the Talmud a day. If he failed his daily assignment, he was sent to bed without supper. In the summer of 1900, he was released from his uncle's tyrannical grip. A letter from his father, with money for passage to New York, had arrived in Uzlyany, and nine-year-old David was reunited with his family for the long-awaited journey. Leah packed a large straw hamper filled with dried breads and smoked fish. This would be her family's sole source of sustenance on the journey. They then set out on foot for Minsk, the largest place David had ever seen; from there they traveled by train to the port of Libau on the Baltic Sea.

They were frightened to their marrow, and none of them had great hopes for success in America. They knew nothing about New York, nor could they speak a word of English. And Abraham had glumly informed them that he was having difficulty eking out a living as an itinerant painter and paperhanger.

When they arrived in New York, Abraham was not there to meet them. Through a mix-up, he was waiting on the wrong dock. Burdened with heavy bundles of clothing and bedding, his bewildered family wandered through the city's streets, tired and hungry, until they finally found him at the home of former neighbors from Uzlyany with whom he had been boarding. Leah had fortunately remembered to take the address with her. Looking much older and wearier than David had remembered him, Abraham took them to their new home—a three-room cold-water flat in a tenement on the Lower East Side.

Two days after arriving in New York, David went to work to help support his family. Rising at four in the morning, he hawked Yiddish newspapers on the streets and ran errands for a local butcher. Around eight o'clock, he would head off to school at the Educational Alliance, one of the first social settlements in New York City. In the evening, he sharpened his English by reading newspapers plucked out of garbage cans. In time, the Educational Alliance became his intellectual refuge. There he learned the art of public speaking and became a member of the debating club—anything to advance himself. Uncommonly ambitious, he became a budding businessman at fourteen. With money borrowed from neighbors, he purchased a newsstand in Hell's Kitchen and moved his family—which now included a sister and another brother—into a brick walk-up in that prevailingly Irish-German ghetto. He and two of his brothers worked the stand, fighting off gangs of toughs intent on stealing their money. David, who had an excellent voice, earned additional money singing solo soprano in a synagogue in lower Manhattan. His father had come down with tuberculosis and was terminally ill, and the family needed every penny the brothers could bring home.

In 1906, David graduated from the eighth grade and promptly quit school to look for full-time work. It was the end of his formal education. Like scores of other New York newsboys, he dreamed of becoming a reporter. Dressed in his only suit and tie, his hair plastered down to make him look older, he headed out on a June morning for Thirty-fifth and Broadway, headquarters of *The New York Herald*, a paper he had been reading regularly. He wanted to be a copy boy, but resigned himself to take any job he was offered. "More than anything in the world, I wanted to rise above that ghetto background," he said later.

Entering the building's lobby, he walked through the first door he saw and boldly announced that he'd come for a job on the *Herald*. He was told he was on the wrong floor; this was the office of the Commercial Cable Company, an underseas cable firm that handled the dispatches of the *Herald*'s foreign correspondents. But the company could use another messenger boy. He was hired on the spot at five dollars a week and given a uniform and a bicycle.

It was in the cable company's riotously busy office that he first saw telegraph operators at work. He was enthralled by the miracle of wireless telegraphy, its ability to communicate in an instant with Tokyo, London, and Johannesburg. He saved two dollars of his first month's wages, bought a dummy telegraph key, and taught himself to send and receive signals in Morse code, tapping out messages in short furious bursts.

The job at the cable company didn't last long, however. Assigned to work on the High Holy Days of Rosh Hashanah and Yom Kippur, he flatly refused—not for religious reasons but because he wouldn't be able to sing for a fee at the synagogue. He was told to hand in his uniform and bicycle; it was the first and last job David Sarnoff would ever lose.

That September, he found work as an office boy with the British-owned Marconi Wireless Telegraph Company of America, located at 27 William Street in downtown Manhattan. Founded by the inventor of wireless, Guglielmo Marconi, it was the most powerful wireless company in the country. He would work there and at its American successor, the Radio Corporation of America, RCA, until 1970, one year before he died at the age of eighty—a multimillionaire communications tycoon.

Desperate to advance, Sarnoff would head for the settlement house library after work to read about Marconi and learn all he could about the new field of wireless communication. It was, he discovered, changing the world, and he wanted to be part of the effort.

The scientific founder of radio—a term that had begun to replace "wireless" in popular usage—was the nineteenth century German physicist Heinrich Hertz. In 1887, Hertz became the first scientist to prove the existence of electromagnetic "waves," invisible wavelike energy that traveled through a mysterious space called the "ether" at the speed of light—186,000 miles per second—and could penetrate solid objects. But Hertz, a pure scientist, was uninterested in exploiting the commercial potential of his sensational discovery. That would be left to Marconi, a reclusive young inventor who resided with his parents on their majestic estate near Bologna after failing to qualify for admission to the local university. Marconi was the first to put Hertz's ideas to practical and commercial use, liberating telegraphy from the wires and submarine cables that constrained its use. Working in a cluttered attic laboratory, he used a spark-producing transmitter, or oscillator, and a Morse key to send messages—dots and dashes—through the air on electromagnetic waves. He then captured them with a primitive receiver. When the Italian government showed no interest in his invention, his mother, Annie Jameson, the Scotch-Irish granddaughter of the founder of the Jameson whiskey empire, moved with her son to London, the center of world communications, hoping to get his invention funded, patented, and on the market. Marconi, who spoke flawless English, was flooded with invitations to demonstrate his device, whose transmitting power he improved steadily in experiments over both land and water. In 1897 he received his patent; months later a small group of powerfully placed investors aligned with him to form the Wireless Telegraph and Signal Co., or British Marconi, as it came to be called. The first electronic communications company in the world, it would dominate wireless telegraphy in Britain and everywhere else for the next two decades.

In 1901, Marconi accomplished the seemingly impossible, transmitting a barely audible Morse code signal—the letter S—across the Atlantic Ocean to the company's new American subsidiary, the Marconi Wireless Company of America. Transatlantic stations were built and would eventually replace undersea telegraph cables, but initially wireless was used almost exclusively for ship-to-ship and ship-to-shore communication, ending the perilous isolation of large vessels at sea. This was where the contracts and the money were, and this was the consuming concern of Marconi's British and American companies: supplying and installing wireless sets for ships and coastal stations.

If young David Sarnoff were to advance in Marconi's American company, he would need to establish a niche for himself in this business. At the same time, however, he began following with avidity developments in wireless that went beyond the immediate concerns of the Marconi Company. It was his eventual exploitation of these breakthroughs in wireless technology that propelled him to the top of the radio and telecommunications industry.

While Marconi was flinging his coded wireless signals across the Atlantic, North American scientists and engineers were demonstrating that radio could send the human voice through the air. On Christmas Eve 1906, Reginald Fessenden, a Canadian inventor, transmitted human voices as well as music—including a solo rendition of "O Holy Night" on his violin—to ships at sea from his experimental station at Brant Rock, Massachusetts. He accomplished this with the help of an alternating current generator, or alternator, built for him by Ernst F. W. Alexanderson, a Swedish immigrant who worked in the laboratories of GE, the General Electric Corporation, formed in 1892.

Fessenden's transmission system worked in an altogether different way than Marconi's. The Italian's was based on sudden bursts of electric impulses; Fessenden sent out a continuous wave that carried the human voice on it, a breakthrough that established him as the founder of radio broadcasting.

That same year, 1906, Lee de Forest, an American scientist, patented a revolutionary invention: the audion, an oscillating vacuum tube that made it possible to carry music and human voices over considerable distances. "I discovered," he said, "an Invisible Empire of the Air." When AT&T acquired rights to the audion, it would begin transcontinental wire telephony in 1915. De Forest, like Fessenden, was obsessed with radio broadcasting, and both would attempt, with only limited success, to increase its range and quality. Their listening audience was composed entirely of radio hobbyists—"hams"—using crystal set receivers increasingly available in stores and mail order catalogues. A ham maneuvered a wire, called a "cat's whisker," across a quartz crystal detector to capture radio waves with the help of a small antenna connected to a pair of earphones. But the poor quality of the reception raised doubts about the future of radio broadcasting. "The 'homeless' sound waves often lost their way, causing the signal to fade to nearly nothing," said *The New York Times.*

Only true believers and eccentrics thought radio's future lay in broadcasting: sending voices out over the air, not from one point to another, but to millions of homes. (The word "radio" derives from the fact that signals from transmitters radiate in all directions.) The hard-boiled businessmen and engineers that ran the world's wireless companies, led by British Marconi, were fixated on gaining control of patents and making equipment for station-to-station transmission. And for a time, that's where David Sarnoff staked his destiny: in wireless communication, not broadcasting.

In 1906, the year Fessenden and de Forest made their initial broadcasting breakthroughs, "Davey" Sarnoff met his new hero. When Marconi came over from England that summer, Sarnoff cleverly positioned himself to meet him and relate his life story. Impressed with the boy's get-go, the dashing young Italian made him his personal messenger boy. "I carried his bag, delivered candy and flowers to his girl friends."

The following year, with a boost from Marconi, Sarnoff became a junior wireless operator, with a salary that allowed him to sell his newsstand and move his family from Hell's Kitchen to a slightly better flat in the Brownsville section of Brooklyn, one year before his father's death. He was fast establishing himself as one of the company's most valued wireless operators. His expert "fist" could tap out forty-five words a minute for eight hours, almost without stopping. Working at the company's remote North American land station on Nantucket Island, he used his free evenings to read "with eager absorption" accounts of Fessenden's and de Forest's efforts to transmit speech and music "on the wings of the electromagnetic wave."

Promoted to full operator, he was back in New York in 1910 as the new night manager of the Marconi station on the roof of Wanamaker's department store, at Ninth Street and Broadway. There, two years later, at age twenty-one, he became entwined in an international tragedy that altered the direction of his life.

On Sunday evening, April 14, 1912, the newly christened British liner RMS *Titanic*, the largest, fastest, and most luxurious passenger ship ever built, struck an iceberg in the North Atlantic on its maiden voyage to New York and sank, taking down 1,517 passengers and crew with it. Sarnoff and his official biographer—his cousin Eugene Lyons—vastly inflated the part he played in the rescue operation. Sarnoff claimed that he alone had received the first message from *Titanic*'s sister ship, RMS *Olympic*, 1,400 miles out at sea—the wireless ship-to-shore communication that conveyed word that the luxury liner was sinking fast and that another ship in the vicinity, SS *Carpathia*, was heeding *Titanic*'s distress call and steaming toward her. Sarnoff said he notified the press immediately and stayed at his post for the next seventy-two hours, round-the-clock, without sleep, taking messages from *Carpathia* until the list of survivors was complete. When the ordeal was over, "I was whisked in a taxicab to the old Astor House on Broadway and given a Turkish rub," he wrote years later.

This became the Sarnoff legend, reported as fact by reputable newspaper and magazine writers, historians and biographers—and further embellished by Sarnoff's publicists. While less dramatic, the real story is still compelling.

Sarnoff could not have been at his telegraph key the Sunday evening *Titanic* sank. The Marconi station kept store hours and Wanamaker's was closed that night. Nor could Sarnoff have stayed at his equipment, unrelieved, for the entire time it took for all passengers to be accounted for. On the Wednesday following the first reports of the disaster, interference with wireless traffic was so great that the Marconi Company closed down most of its stations, including its Wanamaker post. But one part of Sarnoff's tale stands up to scrutiny. Soon after news of the sinking arrived in the States, William Randolph Hearst's *New York American* struck a deal with Wanamaker's to have news of the disaster passed along to the paper. Assisted by two other operators, Sarnoff kept a long vigil, sitting with earphones stuck to his head, taking down the names of survivors that *Carpathia* wired to American marine stations. It was a moment of high drama. "Word spread swiftly that a list of survivors was being received at Wanamaker's and the station was quickly stormed by the grief-stricken and curious," Sarnoff recalled with fidelity.

"The *Titanic* disaster brought radio to the front, and incidentally me," Sarnoff would say later. The sinking of the *Titanic* catapulted wireless communications into international prominence. The 705 passengers who survived would have perished from exposure had not *Titanic* and other vessels in the vicinity been equipped with Marconi wireless. Company stock skyrocketed when President William Howard Taft signed into law a measure requiring all large oceangoing vessels to have at least two radio operators on board; and Sarnoff, one of the heroes of the hour, was promoted to chief inspector of the radio equipment for ships entering New York Harbor.

At this point in his career, Sarnoff could have branched off into engineering or even invention, but his place, he decided, was with the managers. "An engineer or a scientific experimenter is at the place where the money is going out," he explained. A manager is at a place where money is coming in through "the sale of contracts and service." This is where he would make his mark: as a corporate in-fighter with a close understanding of the fast-developing state of wireless technology, a salesman with the sensibility of a scientist. He was sui generis; no one else in the company hierarchy had his kind of professional range.

The following year, Sarnoff was elevated to an executive position in Marconi's company. Not long after this, he called a family conference and announced that they were moving to the Bronx, to a brand-new furnished apartment he had just rented, with hot water, electric lights, and steam heat. He instructed his mother to give away or destroy every piece of furniture, bedding, and kitchenware from their Brownsville flat. He didn't want a single reminder of their previous struggles.

The Radio Music Box

In September 1915, Sarnoff sent a memorandum to company vice president Edward J. Nally. It recommended that American Marconi make a bold move into the entertainment business. Here, said Sarnoff, was where the future of radio resided. "I have in mind a plan of development which would make radio a 'household utility' in the same sense as the piano or phonograph. The idea is to bring music into the home by wireless." Sarnoff envisioned a receiver—a "Radio Music Box"—equipped with amplifying tubes and a loudspeaker that would eliminate the need for earphones. "The box can be placed on a table in the parlor or living room, the switch set accordingly and the transmitted music received. There should be no difficulty in receiving music perfectly when transmitted within a radius of 25 to 50 miles."

Sarnoff went on to forecast with impressive accuracy the future of modern broadcasting. "Hundreds of thousands of families" could "simultaneously receive from a single transmitter" concerts, recitals, lectures, and even baseball scores sent directly from ballparks as games were in progress. If mass-produced "in quantities of 100,000 or so" the Radio Music Box could be priced at an affordable seventy-five dollars. Furthermore, by putting on interesting programs the company could create demand for the music boxes it would manufacture in its plants. In this prophetic memo, Sarnoff was suggesting the "electronic equivalent of the Model T," writes one historian, an item middle-class consumers could afford and that would eventually transform society.

Sarnoff, whose ego was as large as his ambition, would later call his memo the most important idea in the history of commercial radio. It proposed to advance wireless from "point-to-point" to "point-to-mass" transmission, from an audience of one listener, to an audience of millions. But the memo was shelved; Nally never answered it. He and other company officials considered it "a harebrained scheme," as Sarnoff caustically described their response years later. But this is unfair. With the approach of World War I, the Marconi Company was understandably channeling its efforts to fill lucrative wireless contracts for the United States Navy. It was in no position to act on Sarnoff's memo, which called for a massive shift in the company's production and marketing program from maritime wireless to radio broadcasting at a time when one field was hugely profitable, the other entirely unexplored. And Sarnoff was proposing something quite chancy, expecting consumers to buy radio sets at a time when there was nothing of interest to listen to on the radio, there being not a single broadcasting station in the entire country. Even Thomas Edison belittled commercial radio in these years. "It will die out in time so far as music is concerned," he told a colleague. "But it may continue for business purposes."

When the United States declared war on Germany on April 6, 1917, President Woodrow Wilson closed down all nonessential radio stations in the country, freezing technical advances in home broadcasting. By government fiat, the military became radio's only customer during the war. When German submarines cut the Allies' underwater cables, radio traffic replaced them. Sarnoff, an ardent patriot, volunteered for military service, but was turned down because his work at Marconi was deemed essential to the war effort.

With her son making a cushy wartime salary, Sarnoff's mother, Leah, decided it was time for him to marry. She picked the bride, Lizette Hermant, a captivating French-born girl she had met at the family's Bronx synagogue. She then arranged the marriage with Lizette's mother, who had only one concern: David's wild talk about "voices in the air." After an arranged "accidental" meeting and a tightly supervised courtship, during which the young couple fell deeply in love—though neither spoke the other's language—they were married in July 1917. They found a home in suburban Mount Vernon, and one year later Robert W. Sarnoff, the first of their three sons, was born. The following year David Sarnoff found himself working for a new company, a spin-off of American Marconi.

In 1919, American Marconi broke with its parent company, British Marconi, and was swallowed up by General Electric. Under the terms of a historic agreement worked out by GE vice president Owen Young and Assistant Secretary of the Navy Franklin Delano Roosevelt, American Marconi became the Radio Corporation of America, which was essentially the old Marconi Company under American control. GE would manufacture radio equipment; RCA—its subsidiary—would market it.

The Navy had engineered the deal in an effort to end British Marconi's supremacy in telegraphic communications. General Electric controlled the rights to Ernst Alexanderson's alternator, the high-frequency transmitter that Fessenden had used to send out music and voices over the air, a device powerful enough to transmit the human voice across the Atlantic. As part of the arrangement, GE was prevented from leasing the device to a foreign company. This gave the United States an insuperable advantage in the field of global wireless communication, and New York City soon replaced London as the world center of radiotelegraphy.

It was an enormous and unexpected opportunity for twenty-eight-year-old Sarnoff. He was named RCA's commercial manager, which put him third in line in the company's hierarchy, behind chairman Owen Young and president Edward J. Nally. But with Young and Nally still heavily involved with GE, Sarnoff practically "ran [RCA] almost from the beginning," recalled one of his associates. "With the possible exception of the Ford Motor Company, no gigantic American corporation is to a comparable degree the creation of one man," writes biographer Eugene Lyons. "He visualized the organization as it was to become—strong, integrated, independent of outside control—from the beginning, when others saw it only as a limited accessory to the electric industry."

Sarnoff's enhanced power put him in a position, finally, to make RCA a broadcasting powerhouse, and he was uniquely equipped to do this. Both a dreamer and a pragmatist, he had "that rare combination of permitting his head to be in the clouds and keeping his feet on the ground," said Owen Young. And he welcomed challenges; loved a good fight. "Driving through obstacles is his habit, his joy," said a reporter. "I realized that I couldn't compete with gentiles in a gentile industry if I were merely as good as they were," Sarnoff confided to an associate some years later. "But if I were, say, twice as good, they couldn't hold me down. So I decided to be twice as good."

Even in his youth Sarnoff was a forbidding figure. "His chill blue eyes shine with impatient energy, his boyish, scrubbed-pink face radiates cockiness," a reporter described him. He was short—only five-feet-six-inches tall—but his bull-necked, barrel-chested body bristled with authority, and he walked with quick, determined steps. By this time in his career he had begun to dress fastidiously in hand-made, conservative suits. He didn't drink, but was rarely seen without a long Havana cigar in his mouth. And he had almost no sense of humor, unsurprising for someone who had had to fight for nearly everything that came his way. He could be coldly formal, governing his emotions guardedly. He spoke the King's English beautifully, pointedly corrected friends who didn't, and he spent hours poring over drafts of his running river of public pronouncements, many of them models of clarity and concision. But away from the podium and the clawing scrutiny of corporate rivals, he was able to relax and tell earthy stories. He would later have extramarital affairs, but was otherwise a considerate and indulgent husband and father; and he never forgot where he came from, or the people he had passed by on the way up. His lifelong habit was to help friends and relatives who had fallen upon bad times, and he took an interest in the youngest members of the company. When he rose to the presidency of RCA, he would host an annual luncheon for its messengers on September 30, the date he joined the Marconi Company.

Work was his ruling obsession. He loved classical music and opera and was a devoted reader of history and biography, but had almost no other leisure time interests. He rarely went to the theater or the movies and he dreaded the idle conversation of cocktail parties. He played no sports and never exercised. "There are," he once said, "three drives that rule most men: money, sex, and power." Power was what he most wanted, the power to turn promising ideas into products and enterprises.

Less than a year after RCA was formed, Sarnoff sent a memo to GE executives resurrecting his music box idea. Owen Young, his strongest ally in the company, was intrigued, but not sufficiently to allow RCA to branch out into radio broadcasting. But as a concession, Young set aside $2,500 for Sarnoff to develop a sample radio music box. Within a decade, Sarnoff would turn this meager investment into a clear profit of nearly $16 million.

Having gained Young's tentative approval, Sarnoff moved like a man possessed, drafting plans for an RCA-sponsored radio station and outlining a research and marketing scheme for his "radiola." The station and the radiola were interlinked. Without a broadcasting station the radiola was "just a refrigerator without any ice in it," he told GE executives. On his own, he took his radio box idea to Dr. Alfred Goldsmith, RCA's director of research. To Sarnoff's surprise, Goldsmith had already developed a battery-powered receiver similar to the one he had been proposing. Sarnoff told Goldsmith to press ahead and adapt his radiola for the market, but in November 1920, RCA suffered a near-lethal setback when its competitor, Westinghouse, backed the creation of the world's first commercial radio station, KDKA, in Pittsburgh, Pennsylvania.

Unlike the hundreds of experimental stations that had been established before it, KDKA broadcast regularly scheduled programs, with its popular host, Frank Conrad, transmitting directly from his garage in Wilkinsburg, just outside Pittsburgh. Westinghouse's business plan mirrored the one Sarnoff had presented to Marconi executives in his 1915 memo. The programs generated by KDKA and other stations Westinghouse planned to establish were intended to create demand for the new receivers it had begun to put on the market at an affordable twenty-five dollars. This is how American radio broadcasting began: as a "marketing tool" of manufacturers eager to sell the receivers they produced.

With the beginning of regular broadcasting, "home radio"—once the exclusive province of hobbyists plucking voices out of the air with their crystal sets—became a national sensation. The early programming was crudely amateurish: volunteers playing phonographic records, local bands appearing live in the studio, and storytelling for children. But it was free, and public demand seemed insatiable. "Radio was destined . . . to alter the daily habits of Americans as profoundly as anything that the decade produced," said historian Frederick Lewis Allen.

Radio sales boomed and stations appeared in every state in the country; RCA and GE, with their almost exclusive commitment to wireless communication, were in danger of being left in the dust. But in 1921, Sarnoff's cause got a boost when, at his initiative, RCA greatly expanded its control of patents, patents he required to produce an up-to-date version of his radiola. In that year,

Owen Young negotiated a patent-sharing agreement with RCA's chief competitors: AT&T, Westinghouse, and United Fruit, which controlled wireless
operations in the Caribbean. The "patent pool" gave Young's company access
to all major radio patents in the country. This was a huge victory for Sarnoff,
whom Young promoted to general manager of RCA. It gave him independent
authority, direct from the chief, to market his music box and begin moving the
company into broadcasting—although considerably behind its rivals.

Sarnoff dreamed up a bold publicity stunt to announce RCA's entrance into
commercial radio. Although his company had no broadcasting station, equipment, or personnel, and Sarnoff had no interest in sports, he would attempt
an exclusive broadcast of the ballyhooed heavyweight championship fight between Jack Dempsey and French challenger and war hero Georges Carpentier,
scheduled for July 2, 1921, at Boyle's Thirty Acres, near Jersey City.

Working with New York City boxing promoter Tex Rickard, he received
permission to have a microphone placed at ringside. And with the help of
his friend Franklin Roosevelt, Sarnoff persuaded the Navy to allow him to
borrow a radiotelephone transmitter, the largest one in the world. Sarnoff had
it shipped to a Lackawanna Railroad shed near the site of the fight and had
RCA engineers build a makeshift antenna and string a telephone line from the
ringside microphone to the transmitter. Drawing on funds he discovered in a
moribund RCA account, Sarnoff orchestrated the entire technical setup for a
mere fifteen hundred dollars. Then he went back to Rickard and worked with
him to place radio sets with big amplifying speakers in school auditoriums,
movie theaters, and barns throughout the Northeast. Finally, he and Rickard
convinced J. P. Morgan's daughter Anne, head of the Committee for Devas-
tated France, to promote the fight as a charity benefit, with a share of the gate
receipts going to her organization. Sarnoff persuaded one of his employees,
Major J. Andrew White, editor of the RCA-owned magazine *Wireless Age*, to
give the blow-by-blow account at ringside. Sarnoff sat at White's right elbow,
prepared to take over should White succumb to either the withering heat or
the excitement. "We were tired and bleary-eyed," White recalled, "but in our
minds' eyes, Sarnoff and I were seeing the crowds that were pouring out of the
theaters and halls in Pittsburgh and St. Augustine, Boston and Washington,
Albany, Philadelphia, and Akron, their ears full of a modern miracle. We knew
then that the era of radio for millions had begun."

Luckily for Sarnoff, Dempsey knocked out Carpentier in the second minute of the fourth round. The transmitter overheated and turned into a "molten
mass" seconds after Carpentier hit the canvas. It was the first sports event car-

ried by radio in the New York metropolitan region, and it reached an estimated 400,000 listeners. In Manhattan, a crowd of a hundred thousand gathered around loudspeakers attached to the *New York Times* building. RCA president Edward Nally wired Sarnoff: "You have made history." After the broadcast, Sarnoff received permission to have RCA operate its own broadcasting station in New York City and begin aggressively marketing his radiola. He celebrated by buying a new Lincoln touring car and moving his family from Mount Vernon to a plush Manhattan apartment. His New York office was in the Woolworth Building, where he was close to fast-breaking developments in the radio industry, whose big New York laboratories were located nearby.

Sarnoff suddenly found himself in great demand as a public speaker. Never one to undervalue his own accomplishments, he used RCA's publicity machine to promote his image as the "prophet of the radio age." If not a prophet, he was surely a visionary. His true genius was his ability to get scientists and capitalists to collaborate, turning promise into performance. "He was not so much an originator," a colleague pointed out, "as a bold and discriminating selector of partially developed ideas already floating around. Having made his selections, he pressed them hard."

RCA's new broadcasting station was in the twenty-one-story Aeolian Hall, on West Forty-second Street, just off Fifth Avenue, opposite the New York Public Library. It was the beginning of a great shift in the broadcasting business from downtown, in the vicinity of the Woolworth Building, to Midtown, where the talent for the shows was to be found. Two huge towers, each 115 feet tall, were placed on the roof of what was then one of the tallest buildings in Midtown. The towers transmitted signals from RCA's twin stations, WJZ, formerly in Newark, and WJY. The first performers were embarrassingly unprofessional: church choir singers, washed-up musicians, just about anybody who could fill the air with music or talk. But established performers were brought in the next year. Paul Whiteman, the "King of Jazz," gave a concert that included George Gershwin playing his now legendary *Rhapsody in Blue*. At Sarnoff's insistence, classical music ruled, and artists were not paid for their performances.

An idealist as well as a capitalist, Sarnoff wanted to make radio a "public service." In his image of the broadcasting industry, RCA and its competing companies would reap most of their profits not directly from programming, but from the sale of their radio sets. This ruled out advertising on the air. On this point, Sarnoff appeared to have the support of Secretary of Commerce Herbert Hoover, the "tsar" of American radio. "I believe that the quickest way to kill broadcasting," Hoover proclaimed in 1924, "would be to use it for direct advertising. The reader of the newspaper has an option whether he will read an ad or not, but if a speech by the President is to be used as the meat in a sandwich of two patent medicine advertisements, there will be no radio left." Hoover's lofty public pronouncements, however, collided with his policies as commerce secretary. A strong defender of free markets, he proved unwilling to regulate advertising on the air.

Sarnoff, too, believed that "free enterprise must rule in the world of communications," that federal ownership or overregulation "would effectively stifle inventive efforts" by industry scientists and entrepreneurs. But he hoped to achieve his reforms through corporate voluntarism, with each network agreeing to keep marketing off the airwaves. This proposal got nowhere, however; and with the scent of money in the air, advertisers began moving into commercial radio. It became a contest to see which stations could recruit the best talent and the most powerful advertisers. AT&T, with its flagship Manhattan station, WEAF, was the national leader in broadcasting, and its corporate board was determined not only to best RCA but to destroy it, establishing itself as the incontestable leader of the approaching Radio Age.

The industry's outstanding commercial and technological innovator, AT&T was positioned to accomplish this. A telephone as well as a radio conglomerate, it fed its programs over its wide-flung phone lines. This allowed it to send its signals at the speed of light—like a long-distance phone call—to affiliated stations across the country, which it strung together into a "chain"— the world's first rudimentary radio network. The company's phone lines also connected its nationwide system of stations with racetracks, baseball fields, and boxing arenas. Originally, AT&T had leased its lines to rival broadcasters; that practice would cease in 1924, part of its campaign to obliterate RCA.

Under an arrangement called toll broadcasting, AT&T itself provided no programs. It sold radio time to "anyone who had a message for the world or wished to entertain." They were "to come in and pay their money as they would upon coming into a telephone booth, address the world, and go out." On August 28, 1922, a Queens real estate company paid WEAF fifty dollars to broadcast a ten-minute message announcing the availability of cooperative apartments in Jackson Heights, Queens. It was a history-making event: the world's first radio commercial. Several apartments were sold, and soon other New York businesses, among them Gimbels and Macy's, purchased time on WEAF.

Initially, AT&T placed tight guidelines on advertisers. Their products were not to be described in detail and there was to be no mention of price. The rough consensus at AT&T, and in the industry in general, was that if radio stations allowed advertising, it should be done tastefully. "Handled with tact and discretion, radio advertising might become effective and profitable," said the advertising industry's trade paper, *Printer's Ink*, but it strongly opposed efforts "to make radio an advertising medium. . . . The family circle is not a public place, and advertising has no business intruding there unless it is invited."

Some radio executives suspected that invasive and annoying commercial announcements might backfire on both the clients who paid for them and the radio stations that aired them. A former vice president of AT&T remembers how the first sponsored program by a toothpaste company was delayed for weeks while higher-ups at WEAF debated the propriety of mentioning on the air such an "intimate" topic as dental hygiene. By the end of 1923, however, WEAF was proving decisively that advertising paid. Presented with the spreadsheets, AT&T executives relaxed their restrictions on advertising. The door had been kicked open; by the end of the decade, radio would be the only major American industry supported entirely by advertising. This made it an international anomaly. In Western European countries, the national governments would make radio a nonprofit public monopoly, beginning in 1927 when the BBC, British Broadcasting Corporation, originally privately owned, went public. Although WEAF carried public service programs, including parts of the 1924 Republican National Convention, it left no doubt that it was in broadcasting to make money, not to provide a public service.

In 1923, AT&T took a giant step toward full-scale commercial broadcasting. Sponsors were henceforth permitted to put on variety programs under their product's trade name, provided the sponsor did not "directly" advertise its product. *The Eveready Hour,* sponsored by the National Carbon Company, makers of Eveready batteries, went on the air that December. The Eveready Company, not the station, organized the series, but it didn't put the show together. Its powerful Chicago advertising firm, N. W. Ayer & Son, did that. Ayer's representatives hired the orchestra and performers, among them George Gershwin and Will Rogers, paying Rogers the then unprecedented fee of a thousand dollars to appear for one evening on WEAF.

By this time, Sarnoff had conceded defeat in his fight to keep the airwaves free of advertising. His most pressing concern in 1924 was not the intrusion of advertisers into radio—a battle he had lost—but AT&T's refusal to rent its landlines to RCA. This was the final obstacle in his effort to build a true national broadcasting network with strongly affiliated stations, something AT&T was dangerously close to accomplishing with its chain system. Denied access to these lines, RCA was forced to broadcast entirely from a New York studio and was unable to produce programs from concert stages, athletic arenas, or big theaters like the Capitol, where, beginning in 1922, *Roxy and His Gang* went out to the nation every Sunday night on WEAF.

The breakthrough for Sarnoff came in 1925 when AT&T lawyers became convinced that the telephone company's aggressive expansion into radio was likely to provoke the Federal Trade Commission to declare the company a conspiracy in restraint of trade and begin legal proceedings to dismantle it. AT&T had another problem: it didn't have enough stations to create a true national wired network. It needed stations controlled by RCA, and Sarnoff was unwilling to surrender them. The company with imperial aspirations was suddenly willing to arbitrate its differences with RCA, despite the fact that one of its executives considered Sarnoff an "abrasive Jew" and had pressed Owen Young to remove him.

In 1926, Young, working closely with Sarnoff, hammered out an agreement that permanently ended AT&T's involvement with broadcasting and opened the way for RCA to become the commanding player in the industry. AT&T sold WEAF to RCA, and RCA took over AT&T's toll network. Most significantly, AT&T leased the wires of its Bell System to RCA for a minimum annual fee of $1 million. The principal architect of the leasing arrangement, Sarnoff had convinced his corporate board to take a long risk. RCA did not yet have enough revenue-producing stations to pay its mountainous rental fee to AT&T. Within five years, however, RCA was the Bell System's largest single customer and easily able to afford the highest telephone bill in existence. By that time, commercial radio, an enterprise that did not exist in 1919, was one of the emergent industries of Western capitalism.

Radio's Wonder Boy

As Sarnoff had predicted, radio became a "household utility," as indispensable to many families as a telephone and a vacuum cleaner. By 1923, commercial radio was the fastest growing industry in the United States, with New York City the capital not just of radio broadcasting but of the manufacture and retail sale of radio equipment. RCA aggressively promoted and sold three of the technical devices that fueled the ever-accelerating demand for home radios: a vacuum tube that could pluck signals out of the air from hundreds of miles away; a vacuum tube amplifier that made possible the loudspeaker system that did away with the need for earphones; and sophisticated receiving sets that could be tuned easily and sharply, eliminating cumbersome controls and much of the annoying interference from competing radio traffic. The new tuning systems also helped to cut down static, "a weird aerial visitor," said one writer, "which ranges between the hiss of frying bacon and the wail of a cat in purgatory."

Almost singlehandedly Sarnoff had steered RCA into the radio business, but had there not been an unexpected and continuing upsurge in consumer demand, the company would not have radically altered its corporate priorities from ship-to-shore to station-to-home transmission. "Demand developed with an intensity that industrial America had never before experienced," wrote an RCA official. "No other new product in the nation's history—not railroads, automobiles, motion pictures, or personal computers—has ever experienced the kind of demand that there was for radio receivers and broadcasting in 1922–23, a phenomenon that established RCA as the most glamorous and fastest growing corporation of the decade," writes historian Robert Sobel. From 1922 to the end of the decade, radio sales increased by over 1,400 percent. In 1922, the United States produced barely sixty thousand radio receiving sets, and radio had an audience of only about 75,000 listeners. Eight years later, radio was a billion-dollar industry—one of New York City's largest—with over six hundred stations broadcasting to more than twelve million American homes, approximately 40 percent of American families. "Radio was . . . the *first* modern mass medium," writes historian Tom Lewis. "Radio made America into a land of listeners." No one had done more to bring about that transformation than David Sarnoff, radio's "wonder boy."

In 1926, with one-fifth of American homes owning a radio, Sarnoff made his boldest move yet. That September he created, under RCA Auspices, the National Broadcasting Company, the world's first true radio network, a chain of stations—unlike AT&T's earlier one—with strong ties to the mother organization. Owen Young named Merlin Hall Aylesworth, an attorney heavily involved with electric utilities, NBC's first president. Tall, charming, and well connected, he was the perfect public figurehead for a new company that aroused government suspicions that it was a monopoly. Sarnoff, the real power at the network, was appointed to the board and told his time would come.

NBC was actually two networks in one. The main network, called Red, had WEAF as its principal station. The Blue network had WJZ. The names came from the color of the grease pencils RCA engineers used to draw the lines on the map connecting stations as far west as Kansas City, Missouri, to their two New York super stations. These Gotham stations sent out programs to the affiliates; the affiliates also generated some of their own programming, mostly local news and sporting events.

On November 15, 1926, the Red and Blue networks were launched simultaneously with a greatly ballyhooed four-hour broadcast from the old Waldorf-Astoria Hotel at Thirty-fourth and Fifth Avenue. A thousand guests were in attendance, big names in the worlds of finance, advertising, theater, politics, and sports. Silver-throated Graham McNamee, New York radio's premier announcer, was the master of ceremonies. Speaking from a microphone that hung from the ceiling of the hotel's Grand Ballroom, he introduced the glittering array of talent that Sarnoff had recruited. Walter Damrosch conducted the New York Symphony Orchestra; Metropolitan Opera star Titta Ruffo sang arias; and the comedy team of Weber and Fields performed a skit. Leaving the ballroom at the end of the evening, a Fifth Avenue dowager was heard to declaim to her husband, "My dear, I had no idea! We simply must get one of these radios."

To reach the five to six million radio sets in American homes, Sarnoff added seven Pacific stations to the network in January 1927, making NBC, with thirty-five stations coast to coast, a bona-fide national network. The following month, NBC aired President Coolidge's address to the joint session of Congress. Dour, monosyllabic Calvin Coolidge, arguably the worst public speaker in the history of the presidency, had the largest listening audience of anyone up to that time.

RCA was one of the hottest stocks on Wall Street, although Sarnoff himself did not profit greatly from the company's bonanza performance. He had only a modest stock portfolio, and in June 1929, four months before the Crash, he sold all his RCA shares. He did it on a hunch.

Communications Colossus

David Sarnoff was as interested in making things as in making money. "Of all RCA's activities, research is nearest his heart," a contemporary described him. A company had to innovate untiringly in order to survive.

Whenever Sarnoff settled on an idea for a new RCA product or service, he set a deadline for its implementation and challenged his scientists and engineers to meet it, putting the whip to them. His wrath could strike as suddenly as a thunderbolt. "I don't get ulcers," he barked. "I give them." But Sarnoff also possessed an admirable ability to assemble and work with teams of technical experts, and give them considerable latitude. He was "a type seldom found in industrial life, a good leader who had confidence both in himself and in his troops," said one of his scientists.

In January 1927, RCA was a young, aggressive company headed by a combative thirty-six-year-old immigrant who had clawed his way to the top, a risk taker who had shaped a corporate culture that closely paralleled his personality. At that time it was solely a radio company; by the end of the year, it was a multidimensional corporation, poised to become a communications colossus.

Nineteen twenty-seven was a milestone year for Sarnoff and RCA. "The first months of NBC were among the most frantic in radio history," writes historian Erik Barnouw. On June 11, when a triumphant Charles Lindbergh returned to New York, NBC set up the world's first multiple-announcer broadcast. "Spaced along the ticker-tape route, with a background of screaming throngs, famous announcers passed the air spotlight to each other like a flaming torch." It was the highpoint of the year in radio broadcasting, drawing an audience of nearly sixty million out of a national population of 119 million.

Earlier that year, President Coolidge signed into law a landmark Federal Radio Act. It brought a semblance of order out of the chaos created by too many stations attempting to be heard on too few frequencies. The government created the Federal Radio Commission (FRC), the predecessor of the far stronger Federal Communications Commission of 1934, and it began assigning each station a designated frequency and power level, eliminating overlap and giving listeners, finally, unimpeded reception.

By this time the technology of radio broadcasting was almost complete, its "bone structure" securely formed. Henceforth, RCA's efforts were directed toward the improvement of the product for home use. In September 1927, Sarnoff introduced the revolutionary Radiola 17, a "plug-in" radio that ran on electrical current instead of batteries—the first nonbattery receiver for home use. Models with wood-trim cabinets and stylishly lit consoles became part of the American family's living room furniture. But Sarnoff was not content to be merely a radio innovator. In 1927, he was poised to move RCA into a host of new fields, among them motion pictures, phonographs, and television.

He began negotiations to purchase the Victor Talking Machine Company of Camden, New Jersey, the country's largest manufacturer of phonographic records and phonographs, including a combined radio and record player—a complete home entertainment center, with the radios provided by RCA. The deal was finalized two years later. It created the RCA Victor Company, with Sarnoff as chairman of the board. Company products and advertising continued to bear the Victor trademark, one of the most famous in the industry—a curious terrier listening to "His Master's Voice" coming out of a gramophone. Only now the little mutt had a new master.

RCA acquired Victor's mammouth redbrick plant in Camden and converted it into a world-class research and development laboratory for communications technology, including transatlantic facsimile transmission. RCA had opened a primitive wireless facsimile service between New York and London in 1926, and it expanded and improved this service the next year, transmitting news photographs, architect's drawings, and legal documents. It took forty minutes to send a photograph from London to New York in 1926. The following year RCA was sending them twice as fast. RCA was in the news constantly in 1927, New York's most forward-looking corporation—an engine of innovation like the city itself. In February, while negotiations with the Victor Company were in their preliminary stage, Sarnoff staged a private demonstration at New York's Rivoli Theatre of an innovation that would make RCA a major player in the American movie industry. Developed by GE engineers, drawing on the pioneering ideas of Alexander Graham Bell, Photophone was a mechanism for synchronizing sound and images on a theater screen. "It is now practical," Sarnoff announced, "to photograph the President of the United States—voice as well as action—and to quickly distribute films reproducing the event in all parts of the country."

But Sarnoff was a year behind the competition. Vitaphone, a similar sound-on-film system, had already been introduced by Western Electric, the manufacturing arm of AT&T. Roxy purchased it for the gala opening of his Cathedral of the Motion Picture on March 11, and it was, as well, the enabling technology for *The Jazz Singer*, starring vaudeville legend Al Jolson. The film premiered on Broadway on October 6, 1927. Seventeen minutes into the production, when Jolson spoke the first words ever uttered in a feature film—"Wait a minute! You ain't seen nothin' yet"—the audience stood up and cheered lustily. The film broke box office records, and every major production company in Hollywood was now interested in making talkies, creating a market David Sarnoff was determined to conquer with Photophone, an improvement upon Vitaphone.

In 1928, he created a new company, RCA Photophone, to market the device to movie theaters. He then partnered with Boston's Joseph Kennedy to form a motion picture production company called Radio-Keith-Orpheum—RKO—and had RKO buy its "talking mechanisms" exclusively from RCA. This gave him a strong foothold in the new industry of "talking cinema." "Among great film companies must be ranked Radio Corp.," said *Time*, "and to the list of cinema tycoons must be added the name of short, stocky David Sarnoff." In a decade-long internal struggle, he had turned RCA, originally a communications company, into what was now being called—to his great satisfaction—an "entertainment company."*

---

* In 1932, two years after the federal government initiated antitrust action against GE, along with Westinghouse and AT&T, RCA was set up as an independent entity, separate from GE. This had long been Sarnoff's supreme ambition. "The Department of Justice handed me a lemon," he said, "and I made lemonade out of it." H. W. Brands, *Masters of Enterprise* (NY: Free Press, 1999), 177.

But the most promising development in mass entertainment, Sarnoff believed, was not talking films but television, which he had described in 1923 as "seeing . . . by radio." In April of that year he had sent a memorandum to RCA's board of directors envisioning a time in the "near future," probably "within the next decade," when radio cabinets would be equipped with television sets, turning the American living room into a home theater. Unlike his Radio Box Memorandum, this communiqué was merely "informational," not a summons to action. At the time, Sarnoff had too much on his plate to become absorbed with research on early forms of television. But in 1927, his interest in television's commercial feasibility was freshly aroused by major breakthroughs by GE and AT&T scientists. Most noteworthy was the first convincing demonstration of the possibilities of television by a Bell Labs research team headed by Herbert E. Ives. That April, Ives used Ma Bell's cables to send moving pictures from Washington, D.C., to a postcard-size screen—two by three inches—at a Bell Telephone laboratory in lower Manhattan. The images of Secretary of Commerce Hoover talking to an executive of AT&T were slightly blurred, but clear enough to impress the fifty reporters invited to the demonstration. "Television Triumphs," *The New York Times* announced the next morning. "It was as if a photograph had suddenly come to life and begun to talk, smile and nod its head."

AT&T did not think "Telephonic Television" was commercially feasible because of the expense and the complexity of the equipment, but it continued to push ahead with research, hoping for a breakthrough. GE scientists were also attempting to develop their own television cameras and receiving sets. While encouraged by these developments, Sarnoff believed that engineers at both GE and AT&T were working with the wrong base technology. They were using a mechanical scanner: a whirling metal disc—punctured with holes—that converted visual images into a stream of electromagnetic waves that were sent through space to a receiver, which converted them back to visual images. This cumbersome system, with its large rotating parts, powered by a motor, required constant adjustment to prevent the picture from becoming distorted. Sarnoff, by contrast, believed that clear picture transmission could only be achieved through an all-electric system, with the scanning done electronically, not mechanically. And unlike AT&T executives, he never doubted television's commercial feasibility. Television, he predicted, would become "the next great industrial development," and a more powerful instrument of social change than radio.

In 1927, he began fashioning plans to mobilize scientific talent to make RCA the leading force in television research. It did not take him long to discover Vladimir T. Zworykin, electronic television's Guglielmo Marconi. In

1923, this visionary Russian immigrant had developed a primitive version of an iconoscope, an electronic camera eye for scanning pictures. It was a crude but workable television system that would eventually consign to the junk heap sets equipped with mechanical scanners. At the time, Zworykin was working at Westinghouse, which ordered him to focus on more practical inventions. Frustrated, he began looking for other companies to sponsor his research. Sarnoff agreed to meet with him sometime in 1929, and the two émigrés, with their common interest in electronics, hit it off immediately. That year Zworykin was sent to RCA's research laboratories in Camden to head the company's campaign to develop commercial television.

It was an ideal match: an adventurous scientist and a corporate titan with massive resources to underwrite his research. In the coming decade, the partnership paid off magnificently for RCA. Under Sarnoff's direction, RCA became the world leader in the development of both black-and-white and color television. Expending millions on research, and conducting a bruising legal battle with Philo T. Farnsworth, a young, independent Idaho inventor who had filed a patent application for his own electronic television system in January 1927, Sarnoff finally prevailed.* On April 20, 1939, he appeared before

---

* Unknown to Sarnoff, Farnsworth first demonstrated his television system to his wife, her brother, and one of his investors in a San Francisco loft in 1927—five months to the day after Herbert Ives conducted his highly publicized experiment in New York City. One of the first images he projected onto a screen was a dollar sign.

In 1930, when Farnsworth, aged twenty-four, applied for a patent for his all-electronic television, it took Sarnoff by surprise. Sarnoff had his lawyers contest his claim. The next year Farnsworth obtained his patent. Fearing that the upstart Farnsworth, whose work was now being financed by Philco, might win the race to develop commercial television, Sarnoff offered Farnsworth the opportunity to join his research team in 1931. There was one proviso: anything he invented at RCA would belong to RCA, a standard restriction that Sarnoff placed on his researchers. Farnsworth refused; he would go it alone. Erratic and almost impossible to get along with, he fell out with Philco and was never able to get the backing he needed to put his invention into production.

In April 1939, when Sarnoff used the occasion of the opening of the New York World's Fair to launch RCA's first commercial telecasting service, Farnsworth, who happened to be in New York, watched the ceremony on a television displayed in a department store window. He felt as if a building had fallen on him. Later that summer, after Sarnoff failed to prove—in a drawn-out litigation—that Zworykin, not Farnsworth, had invented electronic television, he capitulated, paying Farnsworth $1 million for the rights to his patents, along with royalties on every television he sold in the near future. Sarnoff then filed the patents away; he had no intention of undermining or challenging Zworykin's work. In 1939, publicists at RCA celebrated Sarnoff and Zworykin as the founders of television. Farnsworth, who died in 1971 after a long battle with depression and alcoholism, has more than an equal claim to that title.

a television camera at the opening of the New York World's Fair. It was the first publicly conducted television broadcast in the country. "And now we add radio sight to sound," Sarnoff proclaimed.

Commercial television would have a longer gestation period than commercial radio, which had burst into being with great suddenness. Network television would not overtake radio and rule the air until the 1950s, when reliable and affordable sets became readily available. In 1927, when Sarnoff's interest in television was reinvigorated, radio was just entering its so-called golden age, developing, finally, a range of interesting programs to fill the daytime and evening hours. Here also, Sarnoff was a dominating, though, initially, uninspiring force. The NBC network was his creation, and he patterned its early programming after his own personal interests—his ideas about proper public entertainment. He and Lizette regularly attended operatic and symphonic performances and he continued to be a voracious reader, despite the accumulating burdens of power. Friends marveled at the range of his intellectual interests, from the Talmud to Tchaikovsky, from electronics to military strategy. And this is how he structured his programming: a steady diet of uplifting classical music, along with other cultural offerings. To pay the bills, there were variety shows sponsored and produced by the advertising people he loathed.

In 1927, Sarnoff moved NBC's entertainment operations from Aeolian Hall to a new fifteen-story office building at Fifth Avenue and Fifty-fifth Street, across the way from the stately St. Regis Hotel. Designed by avant-garde architect Raymond Hood, it was an ultramodern broadcasting center, the best in the country and Hood designed it to entice the top talent in New York.

A number of performing artists were, at first, reluctant to appear on radio, fearing that their voices and music would be horribly distorted. But when Italian operatic sensation Amelita Galli-Curci and band conductor John Philip Sousa, "The American March King," performed in Sarnoff's new studios, opinion changed—although the extravagant fees Sarnoff paid prominent performers surely contributed to this: Sousa received $50,000 for his appearance.

NBC's early broadcasts were nearly prevailingly highbrow: classical and pops concerts were featured on *The Maxwell House Hour, The Palmolive Hour, The General Motors Family Party,* and Dr. Walter Damrosch's weekly *Music Appreciation Hour.* And the network's *Eveready Hour* featured serious drama, all part of Sarnoff's mission to provide listeners not just a dose of culture but what he called, sententiously, a liberal arts education.

Initially, advertisements on NBC shows were brief, "well mannered," and strictly controlled. Sponsors were told to announce the trade names of their products only at the beginning and conclusion of the shows. This rule proved impossible to enforce, however. Advertisers brought in the money Sarnoff needed to pay his musical artists and AT&T's exorbitant phone bills; and power, as is usually the case, followed money: the power of "outsiders" to dictate programming.

But in 1927, NBC's commanding problem was not controlling advertisers, a battle Sarnoff was resigned to losing. Rather it was Sarnoff's flat and uninspiring programming: concerts by the Chicago Civic Opera followed by inane lighter fare sponsored by makers of popular brands of toothpaste and ginger ale. Unable to evolve a successful formula for "radio amusement," Sarnoff and his NBC subordinates fell back on "a churchly dignity. This saves them, frequently, from being banal or ridiculous," said *The New Yorker*'s Morris Markey, "but it does not save them from being rather dull."

Young William Paley was anything but dull. The playboy son of a rich Philadelphia cigar maker, he knew what he was up against when he purchased the New York–based network that had been formed in 1927 as a rival of NBC. Paley's Columbia Broadcasting System was a struggling, shoestring operation pitted against a behemoth backed by RCA, the nation's most powerful mass communications company. But Paley spotted Sarnoff's weakness and set out to exploit it. Although he knew virtually nothing about radio technology, he had audacious ideas about programming and promotion, and his family's money to gamble on them. To meet Paley's challenge, iron-willed David Sarnoff would be forced to change.

CHAPTER SIXTEEN

PALEY

Bill Paley plays to win, and he wins in great style.

—FELIX ROHATYN

The Kid

Speaking at a 1966 banquet honoring David Sarnoff, William Paley paid his bitterest rival the highest compliment. "To all of us, David will always be broadcasting's Man of the Future . . . [its] most imaginative prophet." For forty years Paley had battled Sarnoff for broadcasting supremacy and he had the "scars to prove [it]," he said.

It was a rivalry that increased the range and quality of American radio, and later of television. Sarnoff, the engineer-manager, put his radio box into the American home, and Paley, more than anyone else, determined what came out of those boxes. He did this by linking radio firmly and permanently to advertising, making advertising the "life-blood of American broadcasting." Radio's super-salesman, "he merchandised more products for more different companies, and sent out more different entertainers on more different programs, than anyone in the history of mankind," wrote journalist David Halberstam.

In 1927, William Paley began making regular trips to New York to oversee the production of a radio variety show his father had underwritten to merchandise his cigars. Tall and strikingly handsome, a jocular twenty-six-year-old man-about-town, Paley couldn't replace a radio tube if his life depended upon it, and the barely solvent network that put on the show had only sixteen regular employees—and sponsors for fewer than one in five of its shows. One year later, Paley purchased the network outright and took on David Sarnoff and NBC. "His was one of the most staggering success stories of the American twentieth century," wrote Halberstam, "a century whose early genius seemed to flower in production and whose later genius emerged in sales and promotion."

William Samuel Paley was born on September 28, 1901, in a Jewish ghetto on Chicago's West Side, its high-rise rookeries stacked next to one another in long, dismal rows. His father, Samuel, had arrived in America with his family in the late 1880s, at age fourteen, escaping the explosive anti-Semitism of the villages around Kiev. Samuel's father, Isaac, a prosperous lumber dealer in the old country had lost his savings in the New York stock market, forcing his son to quit school and apprentice with a cigar maker to help support their large, tightly pinched family. By 1896, the year he became a naturalized citizen, Samuel owned his own cigar store. Two years later, he married Goldie Drell, the earthy sixteen-year-old daughter of struggling Ukrainian parents. Together, they rolled cigars in the small family factory behind their house; their uncle, Jacob Paley, handled sales and kept the books. By age twenty, Sam Paley was a wealthy man.

In 1919, he moved his family to Philadelphia—known to cigar makers as "the graveyard of unionism"—to avoid yet another crippling strike waged against his company by Samuel Gompers's powerful American Federation of Labor. Within six years, he was a millionaire, owner of Congress Cigar, with seven factories in four states. His company's La Palina brand was the best-selling high-grade cigar in America, with sales close to 1.5 million a day.

William, an indifferent student, started college at the University of Chicago and graduated from the University of Pennsylvania's Wharton School of Finance in 1922. That summer he went to work for his father, doing everything from sweeping floors to supervising the building of an eight-story plant. A natural salesman, sharp-witted and coolly persuasive, he was expected to succeed Samuel as head of the family business. By 1926, he was vice president of the company and had already made his first million.

Bill Paley played as hard as he worked. "I lived a two-sided life, industrious and fun-loving," he wrote in his exuberant, if occasionally unreliable, autobiography. He was "a good time Charlie," recalls one of his fraternity brothers. "He chased the girls." He was especially attracted to the long-legged showgirls he met backstage at theater openings in Philadelphia. He bought them roses and champagne, and when the shows moved on to New York he followed a number of them there, disappearing from his job for days at a time, conduct his indulgent father tolerated.

A hot-blooded thrill seeker, he lost piles of money at Philadelphia's illegal

gambling clubs. He had a studio apartment in the Warwick Hotel on fashionable Rittenhouse Square, and "felt truly independent and free to dance, drink,
and gamble and enjoy the night life—just so long as I got to the office on time
the next morning. . . . My friends and I wined, dined and danced our way
through nightclubs, speakeasies and restaurants and somehow survived the
bootleg booze."

In his quiet moments, late in the evening, he listened to the radio, which
seemed to him a magical instrument, pulling sound out of the air in a way he
could not quite fathom. "I never got over the surprise and the fascination. I
often sat up all night, glued to my set, listening and marveling at the voices
and music which came into my ears from distant places." One of his favorite
stations was WCAU, a small Philadelphia operation owned by two radio enthusiasts, the brothers Isaac and Leon Levy, close friends of his family. It was
his family's association with the Levy brothers that brought William Paley into
the world of radio.

Isaac Levy was a brash young lawyer and a reckless poker player, a nighthawk
who loved the fast life as much as Bill Paley. Leon was a quiet, clean-living
dentist. In 1927, their station was barely surviving against the competition of
two local stations affiliated with newly formed NBC. That spring, George A.
Coats, a fast-talking promoter—and sometime paving machine salesman—
approached them about signing up with a new network he had just formed
with his partners, Arthur Judson, a New York talent agent, and Major J. Andrew White, the former RCA employee who had helped David Sarnoff stage
the broadcast of the Dempsey-Carpentier fight in 1921. The Levys were interested, but wanted to know more about the network, United Independent
Broadcasters, Inc. Coats filled them in.

The new network, he told them, owed its origin to David Sarnoff's duplic-
ity. The previous summer, Judson had heard rumors that Sarnoff was preparing to launch America's first national radio network. When he approached
Sarnoff and asked for an exclusive contract to supply talent for NBC broadcasts, with Coats as his partner, Sarnoff showed some interest. Less than a
month later, Sarnoff changed his mind and established his own talent bureau.
At a contentious meeting in Sarnoff's office, Judson tried to get Sarnoff to
reconsider, threatening to form a rival "chain" and do battle with NBC. Sarnoff was sharply dismissive. He had just paid $1 million to acquire access to
AT&T's phone lines. Where would Judson, a small-time operator, get that kind
of money? And with that, hard-eyed David Sarnoff showed Judson the door
with a jab of his long cigar.

Judson and Coats then hooked up with Major White, by then a noted radio broadcaster and Manhattan character, a natty dresser who wore a white carnation in his lapel and pince-nez on a thin black ribbon. White wanted to run a major network; Judson wanted a radio market for his orchestral and operatic artists; and George Coats just wanted to make money.

The partners—all of them—were nearly broke. Coats freely admitted this to the Levy brothers when he first met them in their station's cramped studio, a single room in an alley next to the boiler facilities of a West Philadelphia hotel. But the network, he insisted, had promise; it was the only competitor of NBC for the allegiance of what would soon be, he believed, a vast national radio audience.

Isaac Levy was a tenacious bargainer. He had United Independent guarantee his station $500 a week—fifty dollars an hour—to carry ten hours of the chain's prime programs, to be sent out from studios in New York. In return, the network could sell advertising during these ten hours and keep the profits. Coats agreed, and with contacts supplied by the Levy brothers, went on the road and signed up fifteen other stations on the same terms. When word got back to Major White, he flew into a rage. The fledgling network couldn't afford to pay what amounted to a total guarantee of $8,000 a week to sixteen stations, a crushing burden for the flimsily financed company to take on.

In the summer of 1927, staggering under the load of these contracts, United Independent was perilously close to bankruptcy when it was saved by the Columbia Phonograph Company. Columbia had become alarmed at the growing popularity of radio, and rumors that its rival, the Victor Talking Machine Company, was about to fall into David Sarnoff's lap, creating a conglomerate that Columbia would be hard pressed to compete with. George Coats convinced Columbia that an investment in United Independent would allow it to profitably promote its records and record players on the new network. Columbia bought the operating rights of United Independent and renamed the network the Columbia Phonograph Broadcasting System. With Columbia's money, the fledging network accomplished what Sarnoff had thought impossible, signing a contract with AT&T to lease some of its newest phone lines. On September 18, 1927, it made its debut with a performance by artists from the Metropolitan Opera Company, all of them Judson's clients. It was a disaster. Stations west of the Alleghenies received no sound for fifteen minutes when a thunderstorm downed the company's new AT&T wires. There was also annoying static throughout the entire program, which ran an hour and a quarter beyond schedule.

Things only got worse. After losing $100,000 a month for the next three months, and with no other sponsors in sight, Columbia threw in the towel.

At this point, the network dropped the word "Phonograph" and became simply the Columbia Broadcasting System. Unable to meet their payroll, Judson, Coats, and White went back to the Levy brothers, but they lacked the capital to keep Columbia afloat. Two of their friends, however, were interested in the new network: Jerome Louchheim, a local construction tycoon, and Sam Paley, the Quaker City cigar king.

Fascinated by radio's commercial possibilities, Louchheim bought a controlling share of the network. Paley wasn't interested in getting into the radio business, but signed a contract with the network to have it pick up a local variety show—a Levy brothers production—called *The La Palina Smoker*. As part of the arrangement, his son Bill agreed to produce the show. It was originally to feature a host called the La Palina Boy, but Bill—already an astute advertiser—replaced him with Miss La Palina, a "sultry voiced" woman who played the part of a guest at an all-male smoker. Surrounded by a group of wisecracking admirers, she sang to the accompaniment of a small orchestra and joined in the fun with the boys and a host comedian. The show was an instant hit, one of radio's first successful dramatizations. The Congress Cigar Company had been losing ground against cigarettes, but the show increased sales from 400,000 cigars a day to a million in twenty-six weeks. "It was one of radio's earliest spectacular achievements," said *Fortune*.

Producing the show brought Bill Paley to New York at least once a week for the next six months. There he met Judson and White, reviewed the operation, and "felt the excitement of this new enterprise, however shaky it might be from a financial standpoint." Paley watched the network fall deeper into debt, despite continued infusions of cash from Louchheim, the Levys, and other investors in Philadelphia's tightly bound Ukrainian-Jewish community. When Louchheim was injured in an accident in the fall of 1928 and unable to travel to New York, Paley bought him out. The price was half a million dollars, which gave him ownership of just over half the network's stock. "The network's shaky condition did not deter me," he wrote later. "It was the great promise of radio itself that impelled me to act and to act immediately." It was a new, exciting industry ideally suited for a young man of means and ambition. "I had about a million dollars of my own and I was willing to risk any or all of it in radio." He didn't go into it alone, however. His father agreed to throw in $100,000 of his own money to take some of the burden off his son.

A long-simmering desire to get out of the cigar trade—something he doesn't mention in his autobiography—figured in Paley's decision. "Bill didn't like the tobacco business," recalls a family friend. "It wasn't glamorous enough for him. He didn't like looking at tobacco and didn't like smelling tobacco. The only part he liked was the advertising end." He wanted to get into a business he could start himself, preferably in New York. He had been snubbed by the sons of Philadelphia's insular, deeply entrenched German-Jewish community. His father was from a Ukrainian shtetl and made cigars; their fathers were bankers and department store kings from great continental cities like Hamburg and Berlin. "I think Paley longed to show them that he could and would make good in New York, not in Philadelphia," said a business associate of his father's.

On September 26, 1928—two days before his twenty-seventh birthday—William Paley officially became president of a small network that was a big money pit. "My friends thought I was crazy to quit a sure-fire thing with my father," he recalled.* That week he took the train to New York. "I left Philadelphia for New York unaware that I was starting a new life. I moved into an apartment in the Elysée, a smart little hotel on Fifty-fourth Street between Madison and Park, which had one of the best French restaurants in town. The economy was booming, the stock market had begun its last wild rise before the crash, and the theatrical district, through which I passed on the way to work, was in its glory."

The network had its headquarters in a suite of offices in the tower of the new Paramount Building on Times Square. When Paley arrived for work, the employee in charge of the door—mistaking him for a callow kid looking for a job—wouldn't let him in. Paley had to produce identification to gain entry to Major White's outer office.

A strutting peacock in his hometown, Paley was intimidated by New York. "Bill Paley was like a polite Fuller Brush salesman. He was actually bashful meeting people of intellectual prominence. . . . In a roomful of people he would appear to be . . . inarticulate," recalls Edward Bernays, the public relations guru whose services Paley would later retain. Bernays, along with Judson and White, saw Paley as a spoiled rich kid who had come to the big town to take over a "plaything his father had bought him." The "great, tall city was frightening, terrifying," Paley would write in his autobiography. To make himself look older and more distinguished, he had a Fifth Avenue tailor fashion him a closetful of conservative double-breasted business suits, and he ordered dozens of custom-made high-collar shirts. To complete the look, he combed his jet-black hair straight back from his forehead, like a Wall Street mandarin.

Paley's office on top of the Paramount Building was the largest in the

---

* By the time of his death in 1990, Paley's initial investment in Columbia had ballooned into a fortune of $356 million.

company's suite and had been expensively decorated by his predecessors. It had handsome dark paneling, a stone fireplace, and a decorative grille that concealed a radio. Working late into the evening, Paley would look out over "the glittering sweep of Broadway, bathed in the glow of one million electric lights," writes biographer Sally Bedell Smith. "Enormous signs blazed their white letters: advertisements for Lucky Strike, Squibb's Dental Cream, Maxwell House Coffee, Chevrolet. . . . Everywhere he looked he saw reminders of the commerce he sought to exploit with his tiny network." But the brightly lit marquees of Times Square were also reminders that America's "play land" was dominated by movies and the theater. "In comparison with stage and screen, radio then ranked nowhere in show business," Paley wrote later. "In the twenties, movie stars disdained the upstart medium. Only musicians took to it. Radio was for music, popular and classical, along with bits of news, talks, vaudeville-like skits and, on occasion, the broadcasting of big events such as political conventions." An American "radio art had not yet been created. But I had the gut feeling that radio was on the threshold of a great awakening, that marvelous things were about to happen and that I had come to a medium at the right moment."

Paley threw himself into his new job, "trying to cash in on the radio boom." He had to raise money quickly or his rickety network would surely collapse. His first move was to combine United Independent and Columbia into one corporation. Major White, who had done more than anyone else to keep Columbia alive in its first year, was demoted to managing director and his responsibilities were greatly reduced. Coats was shunted aside, and although Judson remained for a time as the chief talent scout, this would be Bill Paley's network; he would be its battlefront commander. From the start, CBS was a "one-man show, of which Paley was ship and captain and crew," said Bernays.

Paley was able to make his mark quickly—as Sarnoff had—because the broadcasting business was still new, with no established elders controlling it. "As in the case of all the great doers of the earth, [Paley] is shot with luck," said a New York business writer. "At the age of twenty-seven he tumbled unexpectedly into the one business that lacked an older generation." Paley's only competition was Sarnoff and NBC. That was formidable enough, but catching up with and overtaking NBC became William Paley's commanding obsession.

"Compared with NBC, [CBS] was not much of a network," Paley observed later. It had only sixteen wobbly station affiliates; Sarnoff had more than fifty. And Sarnoff had behind him the enormous resources of the Radio Corporation of America. RCA used NBC's programs to incite demand for the radio sets it manufactured. If Sarnoff's network fell into trouble, RCA would bail it out. Bill Paley was performing a high-wire act without a safety net.

Initially, Sarnoff refused to recognize CBS as a serious rival. "Not long after I came to New York, I asked somebody to arrange a meeting for me with Merlin H. Aylesworth, then president of NBC, so that we could know each other and talk about the future of radio," Paley observed in his autobiography. "My friend came back two days later, ashamed, and reported he could not arrange the meeting." After finally meeting Paley for the first time, thirty-six-year-old David Sarnoff began calling him "kid" behind his back. The task Paley had taken on would soon overwhelm him, he said. Differences in class and culture fueled Sarnoff's enmity. He, an immigrant messenger boy, had built NBC; Paley, a child of privilege, had inherited CBS. Although not a religious man, Sarnoff would also come to resent Paley's late night antics and preference for dating, and later marrying, Protestant women.

But the reigning emperor of network radio underestimated the pretender to the throne. Boyishly charming Bill Paley was as ferocious a corporate warrior as David Sarnoff. He had cut his teeth in the tobacco trade, one of the most ruthlessly competitive enterprises on earth, an industry dominated by mavericks who took possessive pride in the concerns they had built. Sarnoff was in for the fight of his life.

From the time he took over CBS, Paley operated almost in defiance of the way Sarnoff ran NBC. Unlike Sarnoff, he didn't charge his affiliated stations for unsponsored programs sent to them in the daytime hours. In return, however, stations were required to broadcast CBS's evening shows, which had sponsors. This gave Paley control over the affiliates' prime-time schedules, an inducement for advertisers, whose messages were sent out over the air at peak listening hours, when the entire family gathered around the living room radio set. With Paley and Major White working the phones up to ten hours a day, dozens of stations joined the chain, and advertisers signed on, slowly at first and then by the dozens. CBS grew furiously, tripling its number of stations by the end of 1929, its first full year of operations. By then it had forty-nine stations in forty-two cities, from New York to Seattle. That first year under Paley, the network lost nearly $400,000; it would never again have a losing year.

But Sarnoff had more stations and a fuller slate of sponsored programs, among them *Amos 'n' Andy*, far and away the most popular show on American radio. This African American situation comedy, voiced and written by two white vaudeville performers, Charles Correll and Freeman Gosden, originated on Chicago's WMAQ station in 1926, and featured the fictional characters

Amos Jones and Andy Brown, proprietors of the Fresh Air Taxi Company.*
Sarnoff had purchased it, along with *Roxy and His Gang*, to widen his listening
audience. At the peak of the show's popularity on NBC's Red network, it drew
60 percent of radio listeners, and there were Amos 'n' Andy candy bars, toys,
comics, and records. A frustrated William Paley didn't even bother to put a
sponsored show up against it. He didn't yet have the kind of talent to challenge
Amos 'n' Andy.

"Quite early in the game, I . . . came to believe that the crux of this business
was programming—i.e., what went on the air," Paley described his strategy
for overtaking NBC. "It seemed logical to me that those who put on the most
appealing shows won the widest audiences, which in turn attracted the most
advertisers and led to the greatest revenues, profits, and success." To accomplish this, CBS "had an urgent need for more and larger studios from which
we could originate better shows for our own local station and for the network."

In 1928, CBS's production studios were in a penthouse in Steinway Hall,
on Fifty-seventh Street and Sixth Avenue. One year later, Paley moved them
to a new office building on Madison Avenue and Fifty-second Street. The location excited him. It put CBS at the epicenter of the New York advertising
world, and advertising, he was convinced, was the future of American radio.
But to attract more advertising CBS would need more attractive programming.
Arthur Judson's broadcasting schedules were heavily weighted toward classical
music and music appreciation. They "lacked variety," Paley recalled after he
fired Judson, "and . . . were a drag on our future expansion."†

While eager to hold on to the more prestigious of Judson's high-toned
programs, Paley was more interested in popular entertainment; he wanted to
reach people that read the tabloids and listened to *Roxy and His Gang* and
Amos 'n' Andy on NBC. To help him accomplish this, he brought in Edward
Bernays. A small man with a big ego, Bernays was the founder of the new field
of public relations, and the nephew of Sigmund Freud. Among his clients were

---

* In 1948, Paley acquired the *Amos 'n' Andy* show, the keystone of NBC's broadcasting
schedule. Beginning in 1950 it became an equally successful CBS television series. Three
years later, protests by the NAACP forced CBS to cancel it. The show lived on in syndicated
reruns until 1966, when CBS, under mounting pressure from civil rights groups, withdrew
it. The final *Amos 'n' Andy* radio show was broadcast on November 25, 1960.

† Years later, Judson reflected on his displacement by the son of a cigar maker, whose publicists would later anoint the "Founding Chairman" of CBS. "He would never have had the
courage to found the network; I would never have had the means to build it." *New York Post*,
March 2, 1984.

powerhouses like Procter & Gamble, the U.S. War Department, and Chrysler Motors; and his 1923 book, *Crystallizing Public Opinion*, was already a classic in the field. Paley had read it and was excited about retaining the services of the most respected figure in public relations. "I thought, my God, to be important enough to have a public relations man. Somebody who could tell you what to do and what not to do."

Bernays had Paley take out ads in top advertising journals and conduct surveys of his listening audience to find out what people wanted from a radio network. Radio excited Bernays's imagination. "It made a bigger impression on me than the first motion pictures. . . . Sound came out of a box . . . without wires . . . it seemed miraculous." But when Paley hired Bernays, radio was "still unproven as to its effectiveness as a social, educational, political or economic force," and, initially, Bernays had misgivings about his new client, "a soft-sell salesman, a rarity in those days of go-getter salesmen."

He need not have worried. In no time, Bill Paley became "the idol of the stockholders" and a prime player in the Midtown social scene, selling radio as he drank and caroused with Manhattan notables. Six feet tall, with piercing brown eyes and a winning smile, he radiated confidence and avidly sought stunning actresses and wealthy socialites, preferably WASPs. Blind with excitement, part of the social whirl in "the most sinful city in the world," he felt his life was just beginning. Though he worked up to sixteen hours a day, he became a fixture in the "magical" nightlife that he had lived vicariously back in Philadelphia through the pages of *The New Yorker* and *Vanity Fair*. He was a regular at "21" and a popular guest at parties on Long Island's Gold Coast, invariably arriving with a dazzling "Jazz Baby" on his arm.

In 1929, Paley was conducting a torrid affair with one of the most sensual women in the world, dangerous-living Louise Brooks, movie actress and fashion model. Brooks was a twenty-two-year-old former Ziegfeld Girl, brilliant and beautiful, impulsive and amoral, and impossible to control. "As an emblematic figure of the twenties, epitomizing the flappers, jazz babies, and dancing daughters of the boom years, Brooks has few rivals, living or dead," wrote British theater critic Kenneth Tynan. *Photoplay*, whose reporter Brooks received lying seductively in bed, described her: "She is so very Manhattan. Very young. Exquisitely hard-boiled. Her black eyes and sleek black hair are as brilliant as Chinese lacquer. Her skin is white as a camellia. Her legs are lyrical." And she dressed to kill, wearing—in her words—"sleek suits and half-naked beaded gowns and piles and piles of furs." She ran up clothing bills that staggered even free-spending Bill Paley.

He was totally captivated by her, though unable to pull her away from her full-time lover, George Marshall, a boorish millionaire (and later owner of the

Washington Redskins) who made his money in the laundry business." "I knew all sorts of actresses, but she was a different kind of girl," Paley wistfully recalled their relationship sixty years later. "I wasn't the least bit sophisticated in those days. She was. She took me by the hand, took me around, told me what to do."*

She knew almost everyone of importance on Broadway and had slept with dozens of powerful men in the entertainment and financial worlds, including Charlie Chaplin and Otto Kahn, legendary Wall Street banker and patron of the arts. She introduced Paley to prospective advertising clients and to hot young comedians, singers, and musicians—a nearly limitless pool of talent that he would draw upon for his network shows.

Selling Radio

Unlike Sarnoff, Paley had no illusions about making radio a public service; for him, broadcasting was first and last a business—and an entirely new kind of business. "Almost every move anyone made in this fantastic beginning business, amounted to crossing a new frontier," he noted in his autobiography. "There really were no precedents and no limits to what you could do or try to do. It was a business of ideas." And that was Paley's forte: he was first and last an idea man. No one could produce and sell radios like David Sarnoff, but no one could produce and sell programming like William Paley. From the day Paley took command of his new network, he was its chief program director—its "talent scout," in his own words. He had "a natural feel for entertainment. He both loved it and could judge it." He was "born," he would tell friends, "with a sense of what was important to the American public."

Sarnoff avoided meeting with advertising executives, delegating the task to subordinates. Paley relished it. He entered meetings with them charged with purpose, his eyes radiating alertness, but his manner understated and urbane, never loud or insistent. With his instincts for salesmanship and his keen comprehension of popular taste, he turned radio "from an advertising sensation" into an "advertising success."

When Paley took control of CBS only a few dozen advertisers had fully grasped the commercial potential of radio. Most advertisers had to be "wooed to CBS," Paley recalled years later, and the strategy he used "was to entice them with good ideas. In our offices, my associates and I would dream

---

* Paley would secretly support her, his first dream woman, after her movie career went aground in the 1930s and she became, years later, an alcohol-drenched recluse, living, as she said, in "self-imposed ruin," in a two-bedroom flat in Rochester, New York. Barry Paris, *Louise Brooks* (NY: Alfred A. Knopf, 1989), 444, 521.

up radio shows of all types. I would take our best ideas to an advertiser and say, 'If I could get you so-and-so, would you agree to give serious consideration to that program?' If there seemed to be some real interest, I would then approach the entertainer and say, 'What if I could get you so much money for a weekly show, would you . . . ?' I would then bring the sponsor and the artist together in a studio for a live audition. If it clicked, a new CBS program was born"—a program produced by the sponsor's advertising agency and named after the sponsor's product. So CBS had *The Listerine Program* and NBC—not to be left behind—had *The A&P Gypsies*; and both networks began allowing their star comedians to humorously weave the sponsor's name into their performances: "This is Bob 'Pepsodent' Hope," or "Jello-O again, this is Jack Benny."

Attracting the stars—this became both networks' commanding concern, their very means of survival. In preparing his 1929 winter schedule it occurred to Paley that if CBS aspired to be the number-one network, it ought to have top popular orchestra in the country. Unarguably, this was the Paul Whiteman Orchestra. Whiteman's "White Jazz," a soft-sounding amalgam of light jazz and concert music, was an attempt, said historian Ann Douglas, "to make jazz respectable and classical music popular." It was music exactly congruent with the middlebrow programming philosophy of William Paley: family-oriented entertainment, lively and appealing to young and old alike, but not salacious or unconventional. "From the beginning I saw that the business side of broadcasting required us to reflect in our programming the taste of the majority," Paley wrote unashamedly in his autobiography.

Paley took his Whiteman idea to the advertising agency that represented the Lorillard Tobacco Company, makers of Old Gold cigarettes. "Get Paul Whiteman and you have a deal," the company's account executive told him. The next morning Paley boarded the 20th Century Limited for Chicago, where Whiteman was playing at the exclusive Drake Hotel, on Lake Michigan. During a break, he approached Whiteman and introduced himself. "A portly man with great presence, Whiteman looked at me and laughed," Paley recalls. "'Young man, you don't think I'm going to do a regular program on *radio,* do you?'" Whiteman had made spot appearances before, but Paley tried to persuade him to do a regular weekly program. "He thought it would debase his reputation." By the end of the evening, however, Whiteman had agreed to give it a try. Paley was a smooth salesman, but the real persuader was the $35,000 a week he offered the band. Whiteman's weekly *Old Gold Program* premiered on February 5, 1929, with the comedian Eddie Cantor as the guest star.

Paley also landed crooner Bing Crosby, a rising star on Decca Records. Crosby was a binge drinker noted for his unreliability, but Paley took a chance on him and paid him astoundingly well. Crosby promised to change, but failed to show up for his first broadcast. Days later, he gave a hideously drunken performance on his first night on the air. Two studio employees had to hold him up as he tried to sing. Paley was listening to the program at a vacation cottage on Long Island. He raced to the phone, called the station, and had Crosby pulled off the air in mid-performance. He stayed with him, however, and hired a guard, on duty twenty-four hours a day, to prevent him from drinking. "It worked," said Paley. "He knew his job was at stake."

Paley put Crosby in the same time slot as *Amos 'n' Andy*—his first direct programming challenge to David Sarnoff—and went on to recruit a sensational array of talent, including singers Kate Smith and Morton Downey; the Mills Brothers, one of the top jazz ensembles in the country; and comedians Will Rogers, Jack Benny, and the marital team of George Burns and Gracie Allen. "He had the tenacity and charisma of an empire builder," a *New York Times* reporter said of Paley, "attracting the best people to work for him."

Paley balanced lowbrow soap operas and light entertainment with cultural programs of distinction. The cultural programming appeared in what were called "throwaway" slots, so named because no advertiser in his right mind would challenge the NBC juggernaut. Paley's Sunday afternoon broadcasts of the New York Philharmonic Orchestra, conducted by Arturo Toscanini, became the most popular music program on national radio. In 1936, CBS introduced *The Columbia Workshop*, a series of exciting experimental radio dramas by aspiring as well as established writers, among them Dorothy Parker, William Saroyan, Irwin Shaw, James Thurber, Archibald MacLeish, Stephen Vincent Benét, Aldous Huxley, and W. H. Auden. And CBS's *Mercury Theatre of the Air*, developed by Orson Welles and John Houseman, put on a succession of impressive productions.

Paley was eager to erase his image as a former "cigar salesman" and "do something with meaning," said one of his CBS associates. But his laudable dose of cultural programming can be more accurately attributed to his inability to fill his entire schedule with sponsored programs. As he knew, it was better to put on an unsponsored cultural program than no program at all, silence being the only kind of noise that a radio station was "ashamed of."

But it was the commercial success of shows like *Amos 'n' Andy*, not Paley's or Sarnoff's cultural offerings, that transformed the character of American radio, turning it into a true medium of mass entertainment, with advertising at the forefront. Advertising executives no longer had to be convinced of the opportunity radio provided to spread their message. Radio gave advertisers, as one of them noted, "a latch key to nearly every home in the United States." Using the very air people breathed, it allowed them to do what they had been "dreaming of" for years, said an NBC executive: enter the sanctity of the "family circle" in the evening hours. Far from being annoyed by strident merchandising "most of the audience seems actually to like it," said *Fortune*. "Curious is the fact that the sponsor is likely to lose more listeners by adding a symphony than by adding a sales talk."

Radio opened up to advertisers the largest captive audience in history, nearly 52 million people by the early 1930s. And shows were sent out to them free of charge, leaving many listeners grateful but confused. "I certainly appreciate your wonderful entertainment," a Milwaukee man wrote to CBS headquarters. "Why don't we have to pay for this? I can't believe that it's given to us."

David Sarnoff, who had originally seen advertising as "a new and noisy method of letting peddlers into your home," no longer "sniffed at" the money advertisers were bringing in. Sarnoff hated comedy and would leave the room in disgust when his wife turned on *Amos 'n' Andy*. But to stay ahead of hard-charging Bill Paley, he aired more situation comedies than CBS. The dollar was driving radio, shaping its character and content, and Sarnoff held his nose and pocketed millions. By 1932, the average radio program on both networks was "about one-fifth sales and about four-fifths entertainment." Three years later, a handful of advertising agencies would control more than a third of the airtime on both CBS and NBC—and nearly all their time in the prime evening hours.

Most listeners were heedless of the social consequences: shows that were censored—flattened out—so as not to offend anyone. Neither network wanted to risk losing a sizable part of its broad national audience, which cut across class, occupational, and ethnic lines. Homogenized programming guaranteed that they wouldn't. "Radio has been extremely timid about permitting the broadcasting of anything that contravenes the established order," radio commentator Hans von Kaltenborn noted. "Its influence has gone to stabilization rather than change." Its corporate sponsors, said Kaltenborn, objected to anything that "provokes and stimulates independent thinking."

"We have a certain responsibility for creating programs, but basically we're the delivery boys," Sarnoff lamely tried to explain his abdication to the advertisers. Paley, by comparison, was proud of his network's growing reliance on advertising. It paid dividends. By 1931, CBS's net profits were roughly $2.25 million, almost exactly the same as those of NBC.

Radio made William Paley, an already rich man, far wealthier. In 1929 he had taken an apartment at 480 Park Avenue. His triplex was all opulence and excess, the city's finest bachelor quarters. Furnished and fitted out by Lee Simonson, Broadway's most celebrated theater designer, it occupied the top three floors of a new building at the corner of Park and Fifty-eighth Street. Paley's custom-built bed had remote controls for radio and lighting; behind it were built-in shelves for hundreds of books, more than sufficient for the literary appetite of a philanderer and workaholic who read infrequently. Adjoining the bedroom was a dressing room of African walnut with a Gatsby-like closet for three hundred suits and special racks for over a hundred handmade India-cotton shirts. The second floor—reached by a winding aluminum staircase—had a living room and dining room; and the top floor was designed exclusively for parties, with a semicircular bar stocked with bootleg liquor. A stand-up piano was built into the wall, with only the keyboard showing, and French doors opened onto a terrace and roof garden, a quiet spot with an enviable view of Manhattan.

Paley hosted boisterous cocktail parties as well as quiet, formal dinners prepared by his personal chef, reputedly the finest in the city. Watts, his English butler-valet, managed these affairs. Another hired hand was given the unenviable task of getting his boss out of bed in the morning—always, Paley admitted, a "terrible struggle." Feeling as if an axe had split his head, Paley would be hauled out of bed and led through a rigorous round of calisthenics. "Every morning I fired him," Paley said—only to rehire him after he had showered and was given a massage.

In 1931, after Louise Brooks went off to Hollywood, Paley began sleeping with alluring Dorothy Hart Hearst, wife of John Randolph Hearst, the hard-drinking son of newspaper kingpin William Randolph Hearst. Paley had "maleness, an animal component, a sexual vitality," she would later describe her attraction to him. One year into the relationship Dorothy divorced her husband and married her lover.

This was the end of Paley's triplex apartment and of his butler-valet. No longer "boss of the house," Watts left in disgust. At Dorothy's insistence, the couple moved to a townhouse in Beekman Place, the rebuilt East River community of refined millionaires. They loved the neighborhood so much they tore down their townhouse and built a splendid six-story home in its place.

Thirty-year-old Bill Paley, married and seemingly settled down, was still exciting to be around, with his money, his ideas, his boyish enthusiasm, and his multiplying hobbies, which included international travel, motorboating, airplanes, and—with Dorothy's assertive encouragement—watercolor and oil painting, and collecting works by Matisse, Gauguin, and Picasso. He and Dorothy were at Midtown clubs three or four nights a week, and after midnight, their limousine driver would ferry them up to Harlem to hear Duke Ellington. They opened their house to the Algonquin Round Table crowd, and Paley took a liking to Alexander Woollcott, a fantastic storyteller, and gave him his own radio show, *The Town Crier*. Dorothy introduced her husband to *New Yorker* editor Harold Ross. Years later, Paley tried to buy the magazine.

Bill and Dorothy Paley settled into a comfortable routine; weekdays in the city, and weekends at their eighty-five-acre estate—Kiluna Farm—in Manhasset, on Long Island's North Shore. Though they adopted a boy and girl, marriage and fatherhood failed to tame Bill Paley. He was never faithful. Most of his transgressions were one-night stands with actresses, chorus girls, and secretaries, but while married to Dorothy he impulsively proposed to at least two women: seventeen-year-old Hungarian actress Zsa Zsa Gabor and Lady Mary Dunn, the wife of a British aristocrat. "Let's run away together," he suggested to Lady Mary three days after they met.*

More than his off-hour pleasures, Bill Paley relished the challenge of being the co-leader—with Sarnoff—of a breakthrough industry with its uniquely modern rules for survival. Radio stations "sell time, an invisible commodity, to fictitious beings called corporations for the purpose of influencing an audience that no one can see," a writer accurately described America's broadcasting industry. The broadcasting business was both financially alluring and dangerously risky. A network could cover the entire country for a fixed investment that was "ridiculously small." But "with the turn of a dial we can be obliterated," said Paley.

To stay on top, Paley surrounded himself with talented people and gave them freedom to run their own departments. In 1930, on Edward Bernays's recommendation, he hired Edward Klauber, former night editor at *The New York Times*, who was then serving on Bernays's staff. He quickly became Paley's most valued associate.

One of Klauber's first decisions was to invite Bernays to lunch and fire him. It was too expensive, he told him, for CBS to have two public relations men, himself and his former boss. Klauber then turned around and hired another prominent public relations consultant, Ivy Lee, Princeton-educated and a representative of the Rockefeller family—just the person to enhance Paley's standing with Manhattan's old Protestant families.

---

* In 1940, one of Paley's lovers committed suicide by leaping from the window of a Detroit hotel. She left behind a note to Paley saying she still loved him. The affair and the publicity that came in the wake of the suicide cast a pall over the marriage, which ended in 1947. That same year Paley married Barbara Cushing Mortimer—known as Babe—the ravishingly beautiful daughter of Boston's great neurosurgeon Harvey Cushing. She died of lung cancer in 1978.

Paley's brain trust was more youthful and aggressive, "quicker to capitalize on breaks" than Sarnoff's top managers. Paley also ruled with a lighter hand than Sarnoff, building a stronger esprit de corps among his top people, eliciting their advice and often heeding it. "There was no mistaking what David Sarnoff wanted," said an NBC executive familiar with his boss's forbidding glower. "He was very lucid and direct. There was no bullshit." Paley professed to manage by committee, to be a team player, yet it was an unambiguously manipulative form of consensus building. "Mr. Paley doesn't dictate," said one of his chief executives. "He leads by persuasion. If you differ with him, by the time you're through talking with him he has indicated how his point of view had more to recommend it than yours." While he listened patiently to the ideas of others, once his mind was made up he acted on his own, and with imperial dispatch. And when provoked or rudely challenged, he could be tyrannical. While he rarely shouted and pounded the desk, "he took his dominance matter-of-factly," said a journalist who knew him well.

Paley prevailed upon his staff to move "with unholy speed" to make CBS the world's largest commercial network. In the early 1930s, however, CBS was unable to beat NBC in the ratings war, a competition begun in 1930 when the Association of National Advertisers established the Crossley Report, the first audience rating system, a survey based on telephone calls to nearly half a million listeners. In 1935, NBC had the five most popular shows on radio, but the next year CBS shocked the radio world by briefly overtaking NBC in the ratings. In the 1936–37 season, four of the top five radio programs were on CBS. Paley pulled this off by robbing Sarnoff's talent bank, paying head-turning sums to steal three of NBC's most popular entertainers: former vaudeville kings Al Jolson and Eddie Cantor, and Major Edward Bowes, the avuncular host of *The Original Amateur Hour*, the top-rated show on radio in 1935. That year, Paley also landed NBC's *The Rise of the Goldbergs*. Of all of radio's comedy shows, only *Amos 'n' Andy* would enjoy a longer life than this saga of Jewish family life in a Bronx tenement written and directed by Gertrude Berg, who also starred as the prying matriarch Molly Goldberg, "a woman," as the show's byline went, "with a place in every heart and a finger in every pie."

Up to this point, the competing networks had been abiding by a gentleman's agreement not to poach each other's talent. Paley had violated it out of a sense of frustration; Sarnoff had proven to be a far sharper rival in programming than he had anticipated. Forced to play CBS's game, Sarnoff had done it with panache and with deeper resources than Paley could call upon in the 1930s. "No one can speak with greater authority of his strength and perseverance as a competitor," Paley would acknowledge Sarnoff's tenacity at that 1966 gala honoring Sarnoff's sixty years in the communications industry. "He never relaxed in his efforts."

By that time, the long battle between them for broadcasting supremacy, first in radio, later in television, had been won. CBS was the most powerful communications organization on earth, and had been since the late 1940s, when Paley conducted further and more sweeping talent raids on NBC, "Paley's Raids," as they were known in the industry. But it was William Paley's "sure sense of how to entertain the American public," not his lawless audacity, that was "the rock upon which . . . he had built [a broadcasting] empire," said *The New York Times*. "He is to the medium as Carnegie was to steel, Ford to automobiles, Luce to publishing, and Ruth to baseball. None has yet been succeeded in kind."

CHAPTER SEVENTEEN

JAZZ AGE BABY

The News for years has been accepted as the phenomenon of twentieth-century journalism.

—NEWSWEEK, JULY 3, 1944

Vox Populi

In the late 1920s, New Yorkers got their news almost exclusively from their daily papers. Neither NBC nor CBS had a news bureau to capture the news and broadcast it at regularly scheduled times, and no radio station in the country had a news-gathering department. In 1928, CBS "had only a single teletype machine bringing us the news from the United Press," William Paley recalled, "and we announced any big breaking stories from time to time."

Radio coverage of the inauguration of President Herbert Hoover in March 1929, a lengthy broadcast that reached an audience estimated at 63 million, convinced both Paley and Sarnoff to expand their news and public affairs offerings. Later that year, CBS launched its first regularly scheduled news program—a five-minute segment in the morning. It was a meager beginning. In 1931, Paley was publicly calling CBS "The News Network," but he had yet to hire a single correspondent or news editor; neither had David Sarnoff, whose network paid even less attention to the news. Not until 1937, when Paley sent Edward R. Murrow to London to cover Hitler, did CBS begin broadcasting live, on-the-spot news and became an aggressive news-gathering operation. Along with his soon to be famous "Murrow Boys"—William L. Shirer, Eric Sevareid, Howard K. Smith, Richard C. Hottelet, and Charles Collingwood—Murrow made *CBS World News* a national sensation.

It was in this tense prewar atmosphere that radio finally became a major competitor of newspapers. By 1938, more than a quarter of the American pub-

lic turned on the radio to get most of its news. And with the face of the globe
changing almost weekly, radio got the news to people faster than print journalism, and with exemplary fidelity and objectivity. This inaugurated a long,
fiercely fought battle between radio and newspapers for the public's allegiance.

But a decade earlier, newspaper publishers saw print and broadcast news
as complementary, not competing, public services. As *The New York Times*
explained in 1927: "People get the news as it happens, over the air, and then
start talking about it and want to read about it in print, comparing the official
report with what they have heard."

In that year, the newspaper publisher that worried least about the threat of
radio was Joseph Medill Patterson, founder of the *Daily News*, whose electrifying success was "the most significant trend in American journalism since the
war," said Stanley Walker, city editor of the *New York Herald Tribune*. When
Patterson launched his paper in 1919, rival editors predicted it would disappear within a year. For a time, it looked like they were right. In 1919 it had
an anemic daily circulation of just over 57,000. But four years later it had the
largest daily circulation in New York City, double that of *The New York Times*.
Its 633,000 readers made it the most widely circulated daily newspaper in the
country. In 1926, its weekday circulation reached one million; and its Sunday
edition exceeded that, making the *News* the largest-selling paper in the country's history and the third most widely read newspaper in the world, behind
two London tabloids. "No newspaper in all history has piled up such a record
in so short a period," the *News* boasted when its Sunday circulation reached the
four million mark in 1944, twice that of any other daily in the United States. By
that time, Patterson was widely regarded as a publishing revolutionary, one of
the geniuses of modern mass journalism, along with those nineteenth-century
giants James Gordon Bennett, Horace Greeley, Joseph Pulitzer, and still active
William Randolph Hearst.

Patterson rose to prominence by creating and bringing to a high pitch of
enticement the American tabloid, this country's most original contribution to
daily journalism in the first half of the twentieth century. Tabloid journalism
was invented in England in the 1890s when Alfred Harmsworth, 1st Viscount
Northcliffe, began building a newspaper empire of halfpenny papers featuring
sex and scandal, papers printed on sheets about half the size of a regular newspaper broadsheet. (The term "tabloid" is derived from a nineteenth-century
medicine sold in small tablets.)

This was not an entirely new development, however. Nineteenth-century
American mass circulation papers published by Hearst and Pulitzer, and even

earlier by James Gordon Bennett, editor of the *New York Herald*, the first of the successful "penny" papers, had employed sensationalist news coverage, much of it of dubious credibility, to appeal to the common crowd. And like Hearst's two New York papers, the *Journal* and the *American*, Pulitzer used screaming headlines and mounted noisy crusades for war, reform, or whatever else happened to sell papers.

In launching his tabloid—the first ever published in the United States—Joseph Patterson employed a number of the circulation-boosting techniques of his legendary New York predecessors. What set his paper apart was its crisply abbreviated presentation of the news, its fulsome use of photographs, its massive coverage of Broadway gossip and mass spectacle sports, and its compact size, which made it easy to read on a crowded subway car or sitting at the packed counter of a Chelsea hash house.

It was an unabashed picture paper, with photographs on every page, and entire sections devoted entirely to photographs, making it a pioneer of photojournalism. Joseph Pulitzer's *World* had used photographs to tell stories, but photographs dominated Patterson's paper, which was initially called the *Illustrated Daily News*, with a camera with wings as its logo. "Think in terms of pictures," Patterson told his staff in the paper's first year of operation. When the king of England visited New York, Patterson deployed twenty-five freelance and twenty-eight staff photographers along the motor route the monarch and his queen took through the city. He wanted to be sure "to have a picture if any nut took a pot shot" at them.

The *Daily News* was distinctive in other ways. This "Jazz-age baby" caught the flavor and character of New York in the "wacky twenties" better than any of its competitors. An emphatically local paper—almost all its readers and advertising dollars came from the greater New York City region—it was a mirror of its time and place: Gotham in the most dazzling decade in its history, its people bewitched by film and radio, flappers and financiers, sports and speculation. It was a new kind of paper designed to capture a new kind of news. The paper's "phenomenal success," said one observer, "is easily explained: it played up the gaudiness of the post-war period, purveying the forbidden thrills of sex and homicide, squeezing the last drop of scandal from every divorce, murder, [and] kidnapping." Born at the opening of the Jazz Age, it was the outstanding example of what has been called Jazz Journalism. Like jazz, it was bold, brassy, and experimental—and widely vilified as vulgar and prurient by churchmen and moralists. "Gutter" journalism, an outraged critic called it.

The 1920s was also the Age of Personalities, with the public as interested in the private lives of athletes and Broadway highlighters as they were in their public lives. The *News* accommodated them. In 1925, Patterson made Mark

Hellinger, a skinny, black-haired kid who wore pin-striped suits, dark blue shirts, and white ties, the paper's entertainment reporter, assigning him a Sunday column, "About Broadway." Hellinger's best friend and constant companion was Walter Winchell, whose *New York Evening Graphic* column, "Your Broadway and Mine," was a feedbox of juicy gossip. Following Winchell's precedent, Hellinger made Broadway his "exclusive domain" and wrote in a "confidential tone," revealing deep secrets about people's lives. But whereas Winchell trafficked in raw gossip, brutally exposing the extramarital affairs and family tragedies of the beautiful people—"no one was safe" from his Monday column—Hellinger wrote in short story form, with humor and heartache. He rarely used his column "to hurt anyone," said his *Daily News* colleague and biographer, Jim Bishop.

"There are only two simple aims in the successful operation of any newspaper," said John Arthur Chapman, one of the *News's* first writers and later its drama critic and historian: "Try to give the reader what you think he wants and try to make him want what you've got." Published to the exactness of that observation, no other paper in New York had a closer relationship to its readers. People went to *The New York Times* and the *New York Herald Tribune* for exhaustive coverage of national and international news, but thousands of *Daily News* readers had never picked up a copy of either of these papers. By 1927, the *Daily News* and its two local imitators, William Randolph Hearst's *Daily Mirror* and Bernarr Macfadden's *New York Evening Graphic*, had captured over 40 percent of the readership of New York newspapers.

The *Daily News* was the paper that plumbers and plasterers, secretaries and stenographers went to for entertainment, gossip, and useful information about navigating the metropolis. Its "A Friend in Need" column helped people exchange toys, musical instruments, and clothing—and find tutors, babysitters, and lost pets. There was advice on "how to become beautiful or cultured, develop a correct posture, use the right knife or fork, and achieve health and love." A special department sold horoscopes and handwriting analysis for a nickel. Late at night, impatient lovers telephoned the *News* to inquire where they could get married right away. "Despondent men and women telephone for a last bit of human contact before turning on the gas," reported *The New Yorker*. "Sometimes they talk so long there is time to send the police around and thwart their plans."

Patterson's writers covered the news with concision and clarity, and their editorials were "simple, unaffected, friendly, as if the paper were saying, 'Well, pal, I'll tell you how we feel about things.'" The writing was never condescending. "The *News* writes up, not down, to its readers," said Stanley Walker. Disparaged by mainstream media as a "sewer-rag" and "an unholy blot on the fourth estate," the *News* had, Walker claimed, "one of the liveliest and best-paid staffs ever put together in New York." It was read in Midtown as well as downtown; and in mid-Manhattan it was read not only in the tenements of Hell's Kitchen but also on Park Avenue, where it regularly outsold the stately *New York Times*. On any given morning, bankers and brokers could be seen leaving Times Square newsstands with a copy of the *News* tucked discreetly inside their *Wall Street Journal*. "I never liked the *Daily News*," said humorist H. Allen Smith, "because it pandered, in a blatant and unashamed way, to the basic instincts and vulgar tastes of the lower orders—the same as I do." For readers like Smith, the *News was* New York, seen from the bottom up, though its founder was a massively rich Chicagoan, part of a newspaper dynasty founded in the Age of Lincoln.

The Captain

Joseph Medill Patterson is one of the most infuriatingly complex figures in newspaper publishing history. Before launching the *Daily News*, he was a novelist, playwright, legislator, farmer, socialist, feminist, war correspondent, soldier, and blazingly creative editor and copublisher, with his cousin Robert Rutherford McCormick, of the *Chicago Tribune*. This was the paper that Joseph Medill, their Canadian-born grandfather, had taken command of in 1855 and used to champion the presidential candidacy of Abraham Lincoln.

Joseph Patterson, born on January 6, 1879, was the son of Joseph Medill's daughter Elinor (Nellie) and Robert W. Patterson, Jr., who became general manager of the *Tribune* in Medill's declining years and editor in chief after his death in 1899. Elinor inherited—with her older sister, Katherine (Kate)—Medill's $4.5 million estate and became an insufferable society queen, a snob and a flaming bigot like her father, who once said that the only solution to the Irish problem in Chicago was to put arsenic in their food. She and her husband had come to loathe one another, lived apart, and coldly addressed each other as Mr. and Mrs. Patterson. Joseph Paterson rebelled early and conspicuously against the privileged world in which he and his younger sister, Eleanor (Cissy), were raised.* As a young blade he would defiantly show up at the opera "slightly drunk" and smelling of the polo stables, wearing mud-caked tan shoes, a wrinkled tailcoat, and a lumberjack shirt. To prove to his mates that he was neither soft nor coddled, he'd head downtown to the spit-and-sawdust bars

---

* Eleanor Medill "Cissy" Patterson became an international socialite and, in 1931, publisher of the *Washington Times-Herald*, the best-selling paper in the city.

of the Levee, the city's infamous red-light district, and pick fights with the meanest-looking drunks at the bar. He was a match for the roughest of them: "a natural athlete . . . a breakneck Polo player . . . square jawed . . . straight as a lance, sinewy, wide of shoulder, knit like a boxer."

After attending boarding schools in Chicago and Paris, he went east, to Groton and then Yale, where he rowed crew and played football, and where his immoderate drinking—a family scourge—earned him the sobriquet "Bourbon Joe." In the summer before his senior year at Yale, he joined Hearst's *New York Evening Journal* and was sent to China, where he ran dispatches for reporters covering the Boxer Rebellion. After graduating in 1901, he returned to Chicago to work as a reporter on the family's newspaper. Shortly thereafter, the rebellious roughneck shocked and delighted his parents by marrying within their privileged social circle. His bride was petite, emotionally fragile Alice Higinbotham, the pampered daughter of Harlow Higinbotham, a partner of department store mogul Marshall Field.

Patterson found work at the *Tribune* uninspiring; he despised its stale Republican editorials and its "tediously dull" handling of the news. He much preferred Hearst's approach of giving the people what they wanted, "good and hot." In 1903, at age twenty-four, he began a lifelong, never resolved search for a political identity. He switched parties from Republican to Democrat and became immersed in Chicago's progressive movement, whose middle-class leaders were clamoring for municipal ownership of the city's shockingly corrupt public utilities. In that year he was elected to the Illinois House of Representatives, the beneficiary of a secret deal, unknown to him at the time, between his father and the state's Republican bosses—an arrangement Robert Patterson would soon regret. During a tumultuous legislative debate over public ownership of Chicago's streetcar companies, Joseph Patterson and his fellow insurgents "started a demonstration in which books and inkstands were hurled and the Speaker of the House sought safety in the cloakroom."

Patterson then made headlines in every Chicago paper except his family's by stumping for Judge Edward F. Dunne, a reformer whose Republican opponent was supported by the *Tribune*. "Capitalism has seen the end of its days as we have known it," Patterson bellowed at a Dunne rally. His horrified father was in Washington at the time, attending Theodore Roosevelt's inauguration. He raced home and presented his son's resignation, in absentia, to the *Tribune*'s board of directors. When Dunne was elected, he rewarded Patterson with the post of commissioner of public works, and Patterson immediately went after his father-in-law's State Street department store for violations of the city's health code for workers. A year later, Patterson stepped down, disillusioned with Dunne's "skin deep" reformism. In an open letter of resignation to Mayor

Dunne, he declared himself a socialist, without ever having read Marx or Engels. He then published an autobiographical essay, "Confessions of a Drone," in which he confessed to receiving an annual living allowance from his mother. "I spend all of it. I produce nothing—am doing no work. I (the type) can keep on doing this all my life unless the present social system is changed." Proud to have a prominent plutocrat in its ranks, the American Socialist Party placed him on its national executive committee.

When his irate mother trimmed his allowance, he announced plans to "go to work and try to produce at least a portion of the wealth which I consume." He left Chicago with his wife and two young daughters—a third would arrive in 1913—and bought "Westwood," a farm near Lake Forest, Illinois, the privileged North Shore suburb that his family had helped to establish. His neighbor was utilities magnate Samuel Insull, whose hobby was raising pheasants, prize birds that Patterson took delight in shooting when they crossed onto his land.

His bewildered wife, Alice, put up a good show. "I don't know what being a socialist is," she told reporters, "but if that is what my husband is, I'm for it." In truth, she hated the farm even more than socialism, and let her husband know it, with the encouragement of her outraged family. Patterson's only income was an occasional "begrudging check" from his "highly irritated mother," recalled his daughter Alicia (later the founder and publisher of *Newsday,* a tamer tabloid than the *News*). "Father was nearly broke when I was born, in 1906, and we were living on a basic income of thirty-five dollars a week. . . . His family had cut him off." Joseph Patterson "was quite happy there with his family, his books, and his black loam soil," Alicia recalled. "Plowing is better exercise than polo," he told a visiting reporter. He raised pigs and cows and wrote proletarian essays, novels, and plays. Two of the novels were published, and three of the plays appeared on Broadway. His writings dealt unflinchingly with drug abuse, divorce, and big-city political corruption; and his autobiographical novel, *A Little Brother of the Rich,* excoriated Windy City high society, depicting the women of his mother's social set as clawing gossips and closet alcoholics. The book sold over a hundred thousand copies and received strong reviews. A critic called Patterson "an unpolished Galsworthy."

Pulled deeper into socialist politics, Patterson became disillusioned with the party's dogmatism and sectarian infighting. This opened him up for a dramatic personal change, a return to "the greener capitalist paradise of the *Tribune.*" The precipitant was a family tragedy. In 1910, his clinically depressed, alcoholic father committed suicide, alone in the room of a Philadelphia hotel. This left the paper without a publisher. Joseph Patterson's cousin, Robert Rutherford McCormick, was the likely successor. The son of Medill's other daughter, Katherine, and diplomat Robert Sanderson McCormick, the nephew of

Cyrus McCormick, the Reaper King—"Bertie," as the family called him—was a prominent Republican attorney, cofounder of the firm that became Kirkland & Ellis. But Elinor Patterson, refusing to be upstaged by her equally power-hungry sister, convinced her wayward son to quit full-time farming and return to Chicago to help Bertie run the paper. The cousins agreed to share management of the *Tribune*. Patterson took over the daily features and the popular Sunday edition, "the flagship of the fleet," while McCormick ran the business side of things. "The family knew I didn't know anything about the newspaper business," McCormick said later, "but they also knew I wasn't a Socialist."

The cousins, otherwise good friends, feuded heatedly over politics and social issues, one an arrogant aristocrat outfitted by London tailors and boot-makers, the other a tribune of the people who showed up at the office in work shirts, cloth cap, and baggy pants. But they did agree that the *Tribune* needed to become livelier. Patterson took the lead, introducing ideas lifted from the British scandal sheets he admired. He ran crime news on the front page, hired actress Lillian Russell to give beauty advice, launched a lovelorn column, and ran a regular feature on the movies. "He was the first to see the motion picture as an expanding industry in which the readers of newspapers would have a lively interest—in news and gossip about the stars," recalled his friend Burton Roscoe, the paper's cultural reporter.

As editor of the *Tribune*'s Sunday edition, Patterson developed a passion for comic strips, and he ran the Sunday supplement in tabloid form—yet another effort to appeal to a mass audience. But he was as interested in elevating his readers as he was in titillating them. He handpicked masterworks from the Chicago Art Institute and reproduced them in full color on the front page of the Sunday supplement, using a new rotogravure press he imported from Germany to print multicolored photographs in sepia tone. And he published fiction from distinguished writers: H. G. Wells, George Bernard Shaw, Joseph Conrad, Theodore Dreiser, Sherwood Anderson, H. L. Mencken.

By 1917, Patterson and McCormick had turned a paper that had ranked third in Chicago circulation when they took it over into the most widely read daily in the country. "Joe Patterson had an almost mystical sense of what ordinary people wanted to read," writes the *Tribune*'s historian. He was a forerunner, in print journalism, of radio mogul William Paley, both of them masters of mass entertainment.

Patterson's deputy in running the Sunday edition was his lover, Mary King. The devoutly Catholic daughter of a New York City doctor, she would become in 1923 the mother of Patterson's son James, secretly raising him in a Manhattan apartment with her two sisters until he moved in with his father when he was seven years old. Eight years later, in 1938, Patterson married Mary King after his estranged wife finally granted him a divorce. "I never had a good idea in my life that she wasn't at least the first half of it," he said of Mary King.

He and King were strong supporters of women's suffrage and aggressively pushed women's causes in the paper—to cousin Bertie's displeasure. But Bertie had only to wait to have his say. In an unusual arrangement, the two iron-willed cousins shared control of editorial policy, McCormick shaping it one month, Patterson the next.

When war broke out in Europe in 1914, Patterson hurried to the front and spent three months as the paper's combat correspondent. An isolationist, like Bertie, but a proponent of military preparedness, he enlisted in the Illinois National Guard the following year. When his country joined the fight in April 1917, he volunteered for service and became a second lieutenant of artillery in the 42nd Division, the famed Rainbow Division. He saw action in five of the most savage campaigns of the war, was gassed, slightly wounded, and promoted to captain. An inspiring leader, he was deeply attached to his men, who affectionately called him "Aunty Joe."

On the evening of July 20, 1918, during the Second Battle of the Marne, he and Bertie met in a village near Paris, where Patterson's artillery regiment was headquartered in a ruined farmhouse. McCormick had been heading a field artillery unit of the 1st Division—later named the Big Red One in honor of its shoulder patches—and had advanced to full colonel, which he took as his title for the remainder of his life. Recovering from an attack of Spanish influenza he suffered in a tough fight to capture the German-held hamlet of Cantigny, Colonel McCormick wanted to visit his cousin before returning home. To escape the echoing thunder of distant artillery fire, the cousins retired to a local barn with a bottle of scotch. Sitting in a haystack, they discussed future plans. Earlier in the war, while on furlough, Patterson had traveled to London to consult with Lord Northcliffe, a close friend of the family's, about launching a tabloid in New York City. The British press lord, whose London *Daily Mirror* was selling 800,000 copies a day, was enthusiastic. Tabloids, he told Patterson, were the "newspapers of the future. . . . New York's got to have a picture tabloid. . . . If the rest of you don't see the light soon, I'll start one myself."

It was to be a joint venture, with both cousins returning to their jobs at the *Tribune* and running the tabloid from Chicago, drawing on that paper's deep talent pool. It would have to be run on a shoestring, however. The cousins' dominating mothers controlled the *Tribune*'s finances and didn't want the paper closely associated with the unseemly tabloid trade. They would only allow "the boys" to borrow modest sums from the Tribune Trust. So the paper was underfunded in its first years; and the icily aloof Colonel, who had already begun his drift from Teddy Roosevelt progressivism to Andrew Mellon conservatism, soon lost interest in a financially dubious project appealing to the common crowd. This suited Joseph Patterson. From the opening issue, the *Daily News* was his product.

The News

In the spring of 1919, Patterson began setting up operations in New York City, the biggest, most competitive newspaper market in the country. There were seven other morning newspapers and ten afternoon papers, led by Hearst's *New York Journal*, which had over 687,000 daily sales, followed far behind by the *Times, The Evening World, The World*, and the *New York American*, the next four largest-selling city papers. Breaking into this crowded field would be difficult, especially with an absentee publisher. Although Patterson made regular trips to New York, he continued to reside in Chicago, running his tabloid largely through a flood of phone calls, letters, and telegrams.

The *News* started with a staff of nine loyalists who set up shop in a cramped room of the decrepit Evening Mail Building, at 25 City Hall Place, in an area known as Printing House Square, the center of the city's newspaper industry. Initially, Patterson relied heavily on two transplanted Chicagoans: Roy C. Hollis, head of the *Tribune*'s New York advertising department, and William H. Field, the former business manager of the *Tribune*. They were tasked with creating what would become "the most turbulent and profitable venture in journalism in modern times."

The first issue of the *Illustrated Daily News* hit the newsstands on June 26, 1919. People noticed it instantly—it stood out on the racks, only fifteen inches by eleven, half the size of the standard American broadsheet. The initial press run of 150,000 copies sold out, mostly out of curiosity. While rival papers were giving front-page coverage to the titanic postwar strikes that were shutting down sizable sections of the New York economy, the *News* featured a beauty contest, with a prize of $10,000 to be awarded to "the most beautiful girl in New York City."

"The *Illustrated Daily News*," Patterson announced in its lead editorial, "is going to be your newspaper. Its interests will be your interests. . . . It will be aggressively for America and for the people of New York." Although Patterson would soon drop the word "Illustrated" from the masthead, convinced it was a "rotten" name for a paper, photographs were, from the beginning, the backbone of the *Daily News*. "The story that can be told by a picture can be grasped instantly," Patterson noted in that initial editorial.

In a confidential telegram to Field, Patterson spelled out the paper's editorial intent more candidly. "Remember always take the side of the people in controversies provided people are not asking the impossible." This demanded close knowledge of the city and its citizens. On long visits to New York to oversee the paper, Patterson roamed the streets of lower Manhattan, dropping in at basement speakeasies, cheap coffeehouses, and shelters for the homeless. "He was not just an onlooker," said a *New York Times* reporter, "but lived among the down-and-outers, ate and drank with them, and panhandled coins." His "sojourns in Bowery flophouses and two-bit movie theaters were not eccentricities," *The New Yorker's* A. J. Liebling would write. "He studied people as closely as the Plains Indians studied the buffalo herds—and for much the same reason." His staff claimed he was a greater newspaperman than Lord Northcliffe because his mind was really "the public's mind," while Northcliffe's "was what he thought the public's mind ought to be."

But something had changed. His empathy with the common people was no longer conjoined with radical politics. His brief immersion in partisan politics had made him suspicious of moral crusaders, their sectarianism and eagerness to place "restraints upon the enjoyment of life," a suspicion shared by many of his readers, who had just had Prohibition shoved down their throats. Until 1933, when he began vigorously supporting President Franklin Roosevelt, "a fellow aristocrat with a kindred spirit," he and his tabloid remained politically independent. The paper campaigned with state senator Jimmy Walker for an aggressive school and park building program and for more subways, bridges, and tunnels. Prohibition was as anathema to Patterson as it was to Walker, and his paper also supported Walker's successful campaigns in the state legislature for Sunday baseball and movies. Otherwise, there was "little trumpeting for a cause." The politically chastened Joseph Patterson was driven by a single idea: to publish a paper that New Yorkers by the millions read and enjoyed. Although that often meant reaching into the gutter for stories on sex and scandal, the former barroom brawler did hold his reporters to a moral code, laying down guidelines for coverage of prominent figures caught in compromising situations. "There should be some hesitancy about breaking up a home, particularly if there are children," he instructed William Field in 1921. "In general matters of private scandal, private love affairs outside the law, I think we should be chary, provided there has not been a . . . court record."

A New York tabloid would succeed, Lord Northcliffe had told Patterson, if it were "kept simple and bright enough for the masses to understand and enjoy." Keeping it simple was no problem; it was strapped for cash. This "brash, sickly child" of the *Tribune* was a mere twenty pages long in its first year on the newsstands and had only three pages of advertising. Nor did it have its own printing plant, newsgathering staff, or photographers. The paper was made up in the *Evening Mail's* composing room and printed on that paper's obsolete presses. Its coverage of national news was taken directly from the *Tribune*, and it purchased photographs from "picture chasers," wannabe journalists who begged, borrowed, or stole pictures from photographers at other papers. "All of us city-side staffers became expert beggars and thieves," John Chapman recalled.

Under pressure from Patterson, the editors began squeezing funds out of their starved budgets to build a photographic staff with the capability of serving a "picture-hungry" public. "It is essential to get more news pictures," Patterson ordered. "That is our life blood, and if we do not excel in that we are done for." Initially, the paper could afford to hire only one full-time photographer, but he was a gem. Edward Norman Jackson, a former Army war photographer on the front lines in France, would remain with the paper until his retirement in 1958, at age seventy-three. "Jackson is a bloodhound when he sets out for a picture," said the editor of a rival paper.

Patterson's paper hemorrhaged money in its first two months of operation, with circulation ranging from eleven thousand to thirty thousand. Despairing staff members told Patterson it had no chance of surviving, but the founder was obdurately committed to its success. The afternoon the first issue appeared, Arthur Brisbane, Hearst's legendary editor, showed up at the offices of the *Daily News* and offered to buy out the paper for $50,000 in an effort to clear the field for Hearst to start his own tabloid. Patterson spurned the offer without a second thought and rejected another bid from Brisbane later that year. The final offer carried a threat. If Patterson refused to change his mind, Brisbane said his "ruthless boss" would start up his own tabloid and drive Patterson back to Chicago.

Five years later, in June 1924, Hearst launched his New York *Daily Mirror*, a picture paper with a layout similar to the *News*. Unlike the *News*, however, it was unashamedly vulgar. It once ran a contest to pick the ugliest woman in New York: the prize—free plastic surgery. That same year, Bernarr Macfadden, an eccentric diet and exercise guru with bulging muscles, launched the *New York Evening Graphic*, the third and most lurid of the city's tabloids. Published on faded pink paper, it ran headlines about sex orgies, "love nests," torture, and suicide. In its resolve to shock, the "Porno-Graphic," as reporter Henry Pringle called it, catered "to a class other newspapers had ignored, those with twisted mentalities the world calls perverts." Typical headlines were "Tots Tortured by Cult to Drive Out the Devil," and "I Did Not Marry My Brother." This tasteless tripe ran beside Walter Winchell's venomous gossip column and Macfadden's advice page, wherein the "great muscle-flexer and carrot eater" preached clean living, exercise, and diet—and offered guidelines for satisfying sex, illustrated by scantily clad models. The paper's first editor, investigative reporter Emile Gauvreau, holds the unwanted distinction of inventing the composograph, a fake photograph in which two or more photos are blended together and airbrushed for a uniform look. Readers were treated to doctored pictures of "husbands in pajamas shooting wives in their underwear" and "wives in their underwear stabbing husbands in pajamas." When the *Evening Graphic* folded in 1932, a writer offered its collapse as evidence that there was "such a thing as restraint . . . in tabloid journalism."

Neither the *Daily Mirror* nor the *Evening Graphic* became a serious competitor to the *News*. The *Mirror* sold better than the *Graphic*. In its first year, circulation shot up to 300,000, but by that time the *News* had a daily circulation of over 820,000, and far more advertising than either of its more excessive rivals. But success had not come easily.

Tell It to Sweeney

The breakthrough occurred in the fall of 1920, when circulation passed the one hundred thousand mark. The following year the *News* moved to roomier quarters in a renovated building on Park Place, across from the Woolworth Building, and purchased its own modern presses. In May of that year Patterson put out the first Sunday edition. It sold for a nickel—three cents more than the daily edition—and was an instant success, reaching a circulation of over 300,000 a year later. Some staff members attributed the paper's sudden spurt to a wildly popular contest it ran in its first year. The editors published four lines of limerick, and offered a daily prize of $100 for the best fifth line. The contest ran a hundred days and there were over 1.2 million respondents. Many readers bought the *News* just to keep up with the limericks.

Sex and sensationalism, personalities and pictures, remained, however, the paper's priorities. "The things people were most interested in," Patterson believed, "were, and in order, (1) Love or Sex, (2) Money, (3) Murder. They were especially interested in any situation which involved all three." Writing to William Field during the paper's starving time, Patterson reminded him "to lay emphasis on romantic happenings and print pictures of girls who are concerned in romances, preferably New York girls. Also, one or more pictures every day with reference to a crime committed the previous day in New York."

Along with his editor in chief, Philip A. Payne, Patterson continued to see pictures as the main attraction of the *News*. But pictures alone fail to explain a spike in circulation to over 800,000 by 1924. "Brevity, next to pictures" was the principal attraction of the tabloid, Payne told an interviewer that year. The *News,* he said, covered roughly the same stories found in *The New York Times,* but it was news "briefed to the bone."* The tabloid's brevity was "harmonious with the period," its passion for speed and simplicity—"quick lunch" in drugstores and automat cafeterias, fast trains, planes, and automobiles. In the rollicking 1920s, "anything modern had to be brief—whether skirts, songs, or media forms," writers one historian. "Radio and movies were fast and pleasant. So were new magazines such as *Reader's Digest* and *Time.* The new tabloid newspapers were even less demanding." They gave readers "all the news of the day in such form that can be assimilated hurriedly," said Payne, "without causing mental indigestion."

In its coverage of world affairs, "the *News* could tell in two columns most of what *The New York Times* took eight to tell," said *Time.* That's a stretch. More accurately, it excelled at what the "Gray Lady" considered unfit to print. In 1925, when movie queen Gloria Swanson was planning her marriage to a French marquis, her third trip to the altar, the *Times* gave all the facts except the one that mattered most to readers: her age. The *News* spent weeks getting that top secret information and played it up in its lead stories of the wedding.

An aggressive circulation strategy also contributed to the furious growth of the *News.* This was partly the work of Max Annenberg, the tough-as-nails circulation manager Patterson brought in from the *Tribune.* German-born Max and his younger brother Moses were gangland-style enforcers who had a hand in the murder of at least a dozen news dealers in Chicago's newspaper wars of the first decade of the century. Max Annenberg came to New York prepared for conflict. He urged Patterson to use sluggers and gunmen to intimidate rival distributors, but Patterson was firm: "No more killing." Instead, Annenberg stacked foreign-language newsstands with copies of the *News,* in the expectation that a picture paper would appeal to immigrants who had not yet mastered English.

Joseph Patterson also knew how to move papers. When he was in New York, he'd have his circulation staff report for work at 4 A.M. and he'd ride with them on the distribution trucks to the corner newsstands. "Then we'd hang about and see who bought these papers and get an idea of our audience"— what kind of clothes they were wearing, what brand of cigarettes they bought,

---

* In 1925, Patterson's tabloid published more than three-quarters of the news stories that received major coverage in the *Times.* John D. Stevens, *Sensationalism and the New York Press* (NY: Columbia University Press, 1991), 122.

recalled staffer Paul Gallico. When one of his editors complained about these early morning tours, Patterson exploded. "The idea of these tours is to make you fellows realize that every line you put in the paper ought to be aimed directly at these people. You can't publish a successful paper by ear."

After scouting the newsstands, Patterson would hop on a subway train, "a prime research laboratory," and patrol the cars looking over people's shoulders and into their laps to see what part of the *News* they were reading. His on-the-spot research convinced him that his most loyal readers were "not the proletariat . . . but the lower bourgeoisie": clerks, garment workers, salesmen, "machinists, druggists, delicatessen owners, chain-grocery employees, the small home owner and buyer on the installment plan." With this information in hand, he put together features directed to their interests. There was a regular *Daily News* "Straw Poll" and a "Voice of the People" column, which drew an astonishing fifty thousand letters a year. Following the success of the first limerick contest, there were dozens of other contests. Readers were invited to pick the "The Ideal Mate" or "The Most Beautiful Child in the City."

Stealing a trick from Tammany's district leaders, Patterson made the entire family feel part of the enterprise. He wanted schoolchildren to read the paper; to make it attractive to them he launched essay contests geared to different grade levels. Prizes included group trips to Yankee Stadium, Coney Island, and the Barnum & Bailey Circus at Madison Square Garden—*Daily News* variants of Tammany's popular boating excursions and clam bakes. The paper sponsored skating and swimming parties, diving meets, and, beginning in 1927, the *Daily News* Golden Gloves boxing tournament, the largest national amateur boxing contest in the world. But the paper's biggest attraction and publicity gambit was the Harvest Moon Ball, the most popular amateur dance contest in the country. The finals, running for several days, were held at Madison Square Garden, with music by some of the top bands and singers in the city. Up to twenty thousand persons were turned away every night.

The *News* continued to sponsor beauty contests. Mark Hellinger was a judge of one of them. The winner was a Ziegfeld Girl named Gladys Glad (her real name). She was awarded a car but was too young to drive it. Three years later, Hellinger married her.

Patterson's tabloid was unabashedly sexist, exhibiting pictures of leggy showgirls in swimming suits and less. But with Mary King as the driving force, it actively recruited women reporters and columnists and paid them equitable salaries and benefits. It also specialized in services for women, offering features on cooking, beauty, child care, health, fashion, interior decoration, and etiquette—"The Correct Thing." In a direct appeal to younger, liberated readers—many of them flappers—Patterson published excerpts from F. Scott Fitzgerald's Jazz Age novels, *This Side of Paradise* and *The Beautiful and the Damned.* By 1925, women composed nearly a third of the paper's readership.

The *News* had many of the best cartoonists in the business, some doing double duty for the *Tribune's* Sunday supplement. Newspapers had been running comics since the end of the nineteenth century, but not until the *News* appeared did they become a fixture in the dailies. Patterson's surveys showed that many readers bought the paper mainly to keep up with *The Gumps, Moon Mullins, Gasoline Alley,* and *Little Orphan Annie,* the phenomenally successful Harold Lincoln Gray series that made its debut in 1924 and later became a weekly radio series. Gray had intended the strip to be about an orphan boy named Otto, but Patterson, the father of three girls, told him there were enough comic strips about boys and suggested the name Gray adopted.

Patterson spent more time with his cartoonists than he did with his reporters and came up with the names for a number of the paper's comic strips. When a young Oklahoman named Chester Gould approached him about running a comic strip with a feature character called "Plainclothes Tracy," Patterson suggested a better name. "Let's call this man Dick Tracy. They call cops Dicks." It became one of the most popular comic strips in newspaper history. To keep it current, Patterson advised Gould to take college classes in criminology and learn all he could about blood analysis, lie detector tests, and fingerprinting. He wanted the series to have "authenticity."

Patterson insisted that his comics depict the lives and everyday dramas of ordinary people. *Winnie Winkle, the Breadwinner,* the story of a young working-class woman, emerged from his informal study of New York stenographers. While Patterson's staff was one of the best paid in the business—"it doesn't pay," he told his businesspeople, "to underpay your staff"—he was especially generous to his cartoon artists. He paid Sidney Smith, creator of *The Gumps,* one of his most popular comics, over a $100,000 a year, and once presented him with a Rolls-Royce as a bonus. The cartoonists, he believed, were the ones who brought in readers and kept them loyal to the paper.

Second in his hierarchy were his photographers, for the *News* was to be viewed as well as read. Getting high-quality photographs was difficult because the synchronized flashbulb had not yet been developed in the 1920s. *Daily News* photographers carried a bulky camera, a heavy case of glass plates, a flash pan, and a few bottles of magnesium powder. "Making a flashlight picture was a noisy, smoky nuisance objected to by almost everybody," recalled John Chapman, who occasionally doubled as one of the paper's photographers. An ounce of powder sprinkled on the flash pan made "a violent explosion when set off by a flint-and-steel spark, and many a *News* staffer suffered severe burns of the face or hand."

The job was made more burdensome by the fact that many people of prominence were, for varying reasons, camera shy. Edward N. Jackson recalls a time when ladies of social standing would scream for the police whenever a photographer came into view, fearing that the ensuing publicity would make their families targets for thieves and kidnappers. Mobsters had their own reasons for staying out of the news, but they had gorillas on hand to rough up pestering paparazzi. Jackson, however, had "remarkable bargaining, conciliating, and negotiating powers," said *New Yorker* writer Alva Johnston. "He won diplomatic victories over foreign potentates and New York City magistrates and gunmen." Covering the trial of beer baron Waxey Gordon, he got the famous bootlegger to agree to pose in return for a promise not to photograph him while he was in handcuffs. Soon afterward, Waxey developed a deep interest in cameras. After being sentenced, he asked to be allowed to take up the study of photography in prison. "I'll have a new vocation when my term expires," he told an incredulous judge.

Jackson saw himself as "a historian of manners and of social change," capturing his age with searing still images. He respected writers and artists but claimed to feel sorry for them because they used such imprecise "implements as pens and brushes"; with these, they could get only "loose approximations" of events.

By 1927, the *News* had twenty-three staff photographers fitted out with excellent Speed Graphic cameras, which began to be equipped with flash bulbs that year. Some photographers also carried small cameras on shoulder straps, using them for quick, candid shots. Patterson eagerly published these grainy photographs, selecting them "with an eye to dramatic or human appeal." The success of the *News* caused other New York papers, including the *Times*, to give more space to photographs. The *Times* also increased the size of its sports page and began using bolder headlines. *Times* owner and publisher Adolph Ochs considered the *News* anything but a real newspaper, but conceded that Joseph Patterson had found "the magic formula for mass appeal."

To survive, the *News* needed more than good copy, comics, and pictures—or even robust circulation. It needed advertising, which comprised two-thirds of a successful daily newspaper's income, circulation making up only one-third. Advertisers were hard to come by at first because Madison Avenue executives, particularly those representing shops and department stores along Fifth Avenue, were convinced that a picture paper pitched to the common crowd was an imprudent allocation of their clients' capital. When Patterson's surveys of New York newsstands demonstrated that a good percentage of the people who bought the *News* dressed in suits and ties and fur coats, he hired a movie cameraman to photograph them; he and his staff showed the films to skeptical admen. This stratagem, along with a small bump in circulation, worked wonderfully. In 1921, a handful of big Midtown stores took out ads in the paper, but this was not nearly enough to put the *News* in the black. The real turnaround came the following year when a young staffer named Leo E. McGivena coined a slogan that became the foundation for one of the most successful advertising campaigns of the decade: "Tell it to Sweeney! The Stuyvesants will understand."

Working from the United States government census of 1920, McGivena challenged the "snobbish assumption" that the typical working-class New Yorker, the archetypical reader of the *Daily News*, was primarily a "subsistence" customer who confined his or her purchases overwhelmingly to "necessities." McGivena and the small research team he put together dug up facts and statistics that substantiated the conclusions Patterson had arrived at in his informal surveys of the newsstands. Readers of the *News*, McGivena argued, were "a new kind of market" for savvy city merchandisers.

The "Sweeney" campaign debuted in *Printer's Ink*, "the bible" of the advertising industry, and continued into the 1930s. "Sweeney lives in an apartment in Brooklyn, on Upper Manhattan, in the Bronx, or has a house on Staten Island," read a typical ad. He has kids and they need "baby carriages, foods, medicines, shoes, clothing, books, pianos, bathing suits, Christmas trees . . . tuition . . . in fact, everything. . . .

"Sweeney and Mrs. Sweeney are ambitious and expectant of Life. . . . They look forward to grapefruit for breakfast, their own homes, a little car, money in the bank and a better future for the Sweeney juniors. . . .

"There are millions of families of Sweeneys in and around New York, with incomes from $6,000 down. . . . You men who aspire to sell large bills of goods in New York, remember the Sweeneys. They comprise 75% of any large city's population." The message ended with this line: "Tell it to Sweeney—in the *News*, bought by more than *two-fifths* of all the people of New York City who buy an English language morning newspaper."

The *News*'s advertising accounts increased dramatically when the Sweeney ads appeared, and Patterson had McGivena's staff conduct marketing surveys of selected geographical areas of Manhattan to substantiate their preliminary findings. The casework was under the direction of a short, pencil-thin young woman named Sinclair Dakin. Work began with a two-month study of the

Lower East Side, a tightly congested, heavily Jewish area of less than two square miles with a population equivalent to that of Cincinnati. "Slumland," its status as a market was considered "zero" by advertisers.

Dakin found a neighborhood in the process of furious and salutary change, with a good measure of upward mobility. Great numbers of the area's Jewish, Italian, Spanish, Greek, and Chinese residents were still horrifyingly poor, but Dakin also found "buying power . . . beyond any economist's imagination." Unionization had brought higher wages for garment workers, and many of the children of clothing workers had begun to move into entrepreneurial positions both inside and outside the ghetto. Savings rates were high, especially among Jews; and families put their earnings in local banks or used them to buy real estate. Young people married early and moved out to better neighborhoods in Brooklyn, Queens, and the Bronx, and "introduced their parents to washing machines, vacuum cleaners and other appliances." Many returned to the old neighborhood on weekends to buy clothing and furniture because "the values were better." In "Slumland" the per capita sale of pianos, imported English baby carriages, and Russian caviar was, amazingly, the highest in New York.

McGivena had Dakin conduct similar sociological surveys of Greenwich Village, Battery Park, and the East Side of Midtown, where there were still large pockets of poverty. She proved that the Sweeneys of New York "were worthwhile customers for any advertiser."

The field studies of Dakin and her associates established the *News* as one of the leading marketing authorities in New York, and got McGivena's salesmen past the receptionists and into the suites of the account executives of leading Madison Avenue firms. By 1927, the *Daily News* had more lines of advertising than any other city paper.

Behind the roaring success of the *News* was a publisher willing to go to unseemly extremes to increase circulation. In 1928, the *Daily News* defied law enforcement authorities and common decency by featuring on the front page one of the most grisly photographs ever to appear in an American newspaper. It was published at the conclusion of one of the most sensationalized murder trials of the decade, a trial that provides revealing insight into the decade's newspaper ethics and the mind-set of its newspaper readers.

Dead!

Around three o'clock in the morning on Sunday, March 20, 1927, Ruth Snyder, a young Queens Village housewife, and H. Judd Gray, her married lover, brutally murdered Ruth's husband, Albert, the art editor of a motorboating magazine. They beat and strangled him in his bed, using a heavy window sash weight, some chloroform-soaked rags, and a double piece of picture wire.*

At 1:30 A.M., Monday morning, under aggressive questioning at the Jamaica precinct house, Ruth Snyder confessed and named Gray, a thirty-four-year-old corset salesman from East Orange, New Jersey, as her accomplice. That afternoon detectives picked up the dapper traveling salesman at the Onondaga Hotel in Syracuse, New York, where he said he had been staying for the past few days on business. Unknown to Gray, a hotel cleaning woman had already turned over to his pursuers the stub of a Pullman ticket she had found in the wastepaper basket of his room. It was for the 8:45 A.M. New York City to Syracuse train on Sunday, March 20. The police had their man.

On the train ride back to New York, detectives showed Gray the ticket stub. Yes, he told them, he was in the Snyder house that Sunday morning. Later that day he signed a full confession.

After conferring with her lawyers, thirty-two-year-old Ruth Snyder, a buxom blonde described by her sister-in-law and neighbor as "man-crazy," recanted, claiming her confession had been made under duress. Gray stuck to his story. On March 23, a grand jury indicted the pair for murder in the first degree. They were taken to Queens County Prison, where they would be confined during the trial. Since they had conspired to commit murder, they would be tried jointly, not separately, as their lawyers requested. They would be in the courtroom at the same time, with different stories and different lawyers, testifying against each another. Trial was set for April 18 in Long Island City, "just across the river from the roar of New York." Sixty-one-year-old Supreme Court Justice Townsend Scudder, one of the state's most distinguished jurists, would preside. He was an outspoken opponent of capital punishment. First-degree murder carried a penalty of death by electrocution.

In his written confession, Gray named Ruth Brown Snyder, whom he had been seeing for nearly two years, as the one who had conceived and plotted the crime. He had reluctantly helped her murder her husband and conceal the evidence.

On the evening of the murder, Ruth Snyder and her husband, accompanied by their nine-year-old daughter, Lorraine, had gone to a neighborhood bridge

---

* The sash weight, or counterweight, used in the Snyder murder was a heavy, six-inch-long metal bar that was designed to be concealed in a widow frame and connected to the window by a sash cord or chain that ran over a pulley at the top the fame. There were two of them in typical double-hung windows and their purpose was to make the window easier to open and close.

party. Before leaving, Mrs. Snyder secretly left the door to the kitchen open so that Gray, who would be arriving from Syracuse, could enter the house. Earlier that evening, she had placed a sash weight that Gray had given to her weeks earlier, along with a pint of whiskey, under the pillow in her live-in mother's bedroom. Josephine "Granny" Brown was away from the house on a nursing assignment and would be gone all evening.

When the Snyder family returned home, Ruth Snyder put Lorraine to bed, changed into her nightclothes, and slipped into bed with her heavily inebriated husband. When he began snoring, she sneaked down the hall and met Gray in her mother's room. He was hiding on the floor, perspiring heavily and had drunk the entire pint of whiskey. "You are going to do it, aren't you," Ruth confronted him. "I said, 'I think I can,'" Gray hesitatingly replied. He was having second thoughts; he had never set eyes on the man he was about to murder in his sleep, with his daughter down the hallway. He felt trapped, however. Ruth Snyder, he told police, had made "veiled threats" to tell his wife and young daughter about their affair "unless I helped her with this plan."

A few minutes later Ruth Snyder took Judd Gray by the hand and led him down the hall to the master bedroom. They entered together and murdered Albert Snyder. Gray struck first, smashing his skull with the sash weight. Snyder, a burly man in his mid-forties, fought back violently, thrashing wildly and causing Gray to drop the weight. Gray screamed for help, using the revealing name he called his all-controlling lover. "Mommy, Mommy, for God's sake, help me." Ruth Snyder then "took up the weight," according to Gray's confession, "and hit him over the head." Gray claimed to know nothing about the picture wire wound tightly around Albert Snyder's neck with a gold mechanical pencil marked, revealingly, with the initials "JG." Nor, according to his confession, did he know about the chloroform-soaked rags that had been stuffed in Albert Snyder's nose and mouth. He had brought chloroform and strips of cotton cloth with him that night, but said he had not used them.

In his "alcoholic haze," he had lost track of events for a minute or so after his struggle with Ruth Snyder's husband. He did remember this, however. When he and Ruth left the bedroom, she asked him if her husband was dead. Judd said he was not. "This thing has absolutely got to go through," she reputedly said in a panic, and disappeared into the room, where the bottle of chloroform and the wire were still on the bed. "I am pretty sure that [the] wire about his neck . . . must have been tied by her," Gray had written in his confession.

To cover their tracks, the murderers had ransacked the house, trying to make it look like burglars had broken in and looted the place. But they did such a bumbling job that police knew at once that it wasn't the work of intruders. (A mink coat was left hanging in a closet, untouched, and Ruth Snyder's jewelry was found hidden under her mattress.) Gray then gagged Ruth Snyder loosely with some gauze and tied her up with clothesline—stupidly not tight enough to leave marks. When he finished, he took a taxi to Grand Central Terminal and boarded the Empire State Express to Syracuse and the Hotel Onondaga.

Lorraine Snyder found her mother the next morning, and telephoned their next-door neighbors, who notified the police. Snyder told detectives that she had been knocked unconscious for five hours by a blow to the head delivered by a large, Italian-looking man with a thick black mustache. There were no signs of forced entry, however, and the Queens County forensic pathologist could find no bruises on Ruth Snyder's body. The pathologist laughed out loud when a detective told him that Mrs. Snyder said she had been senseless for five hours: "Five *hours*! Five *minutes* would be more like it!" Detectives then found the sash weight in a toolbox in the basement; it was flecked with what appeared to be blood. It was soon discovered that in November 1925, Ruth Snyder had forged her husband's signature in order to increase his life insurance from $20,000 to nearly $50,000. The policy had a double indemnity clause. If Albert Snyder were to die accidentally his wife would receive $96,000. Murder was considered an accident.

Ruth Snyder had told this to Judd Gray, and at her urging the couple had begun planning the murder in ardent letters to one another and on frequent occasions when they shared a bed at Manhattan's Waldorf-Astoria Hotel. On days when Ruth Snyder could not find a child-sitter, she brought Lorraine along and left her alone in the hotel lobby. "A more cold-blooded crime has never been conceived," the Queens district attorney told the press.

"I thought everything was perfect," Judd described his feelings hours after the murder. Damon Runyon, who would cover the trial for Hearst's *New York American*, was in a state of disbelief. "For want of a better name, it might be called 'The Dumbbell Murder.' It was so dumb." A circus atmosphere prevailed in one of the largest, most impressive courtrooms in the country. Tremendous crowds gathered in front of the old building every morning of the eighteen-day-long trial, and people came to blows in their determined struggle to gain entry. At least thirty uniformed policemen were posted at the doors, and every morning over two thousand spectators packed themselves into a courtroom designed to seat two hundred. A great number of them were women; Park Avenue matrons decked out in diamonds and mink sat next to Queens Village housewives in cotton dresses and cloth wraps. Counterfeit tickets were printed and snapped up for fifty dollars apiece.

One hundred and twenty reporters were on hand, "more than represented all the American newspapers and news agencies in the Far East," said British author Silas Bent. Also in the press benches were hired celebrities, on special assignment for tabloids and pulp magazines. Hearst's *Daily Mirror* hired Peggy Hopkins Joyce, the former showgirl and future lover of Walter Chrysler. She sat within whispering distance of historian Will Durant, author of the surprise bestseller *The Story of Philosophy*. Durant was on special assignment for the *New York Telegram*. Sultry Mae West, recently released from prison for staging *Sex*, a risqué farce, covered the case for the *National Police Gazette*. The comedian Jimmy Durante was given a column in Bernarr Macfadden's *Evening Graphic*, as was evangelist Aimee Semple McPherson, who used the example of Judd Gray to prevail upon young men to pursue a "girl like Mother . . . not a red-hot cutie."

Among the interested spectators were composer Irving Berlin, short story writer Fannie Hurst, the Marquis and Marchioness of Queensbury, film-maker D. W. Griffith, hellfire-and-brimstone preacher Billy Sunday, and the renowned dramatist and producer David Belasco, who didn't miss a day of the trial. "I thought it a matter of public duty to attend," the "Bishop of Broadway" declared on the opening day of testimony. "I think it will prove to be one of the most dramatic trials in history."

"Never has such a barrage of nonsense and bromide . . . appeared in the public prints on any one subject as has streamed from the pens and pencils of the Noted Authors giving the Olympian eye to the doings in the Queens County courtroom," wrote novelist and playwright Ben Hecht. He was one to know; he was there nearly every day.

Newspapers hyped the case because a woman—and a young mother, at that—was on trial for her life. Thousands of American women were put on trial yearly for murder, but only eight women residents of New York State had been legally executed, all of them before 1900; and none had been sentenced by a Queens County court. Only one woman in the entire country, Mary Rogers of Vermont, had been put to death in the twentieth century.*

Every New York newspaper placed the story on its front page, ran it under blazing headlines, and devoted pages to it. Patterson assigned courtroom coverage to one of his ace investigative reporters, Grace Robinson. She was accompanied by three of the paper's most senior writers. Photographers were banned from the courtroom, but both defendants were photographed as they entered and left the courtroom. In a *Daily News* exclusive, Ruth Snyder was photographed behind bars. There were also dozens of pictures of the murder-

---

* Rogers was hanged in Vermont in 1905 for killing her husband for a $200 insurance policy. New York state had last executed a woman—Mrs. Martha Place—in 1899. She was electrocuted in Sing Sing Prison. By 1927, many Western states had abolished the death penalty.

ers' families, including, appallingly, Ruth Snyder's daughter, who in one shot was seen sending a card to her mother.

The *News* treated the trial like a serial soap opera. "Follow the next act in this smashing drama of love and murder in tomorrow's . . . editions of *THE NEWS*." Reading the *Times*, one got all the facts of the trial; in the *News* one got to know the defendants intimately, wondering—with the paper's reporters—whether Ruth Snyder was a peroxide blonde.

Most reporters paid little attention to the evidence. "Even before the jury was selected Ruth Snyder and Judd Gray had been tried, convicted, electrocuted and buried by every paper in town," recalled a *Daily News* writer. Ruth Snyder came under unusually harsh censure. "The defiant blonde" faced "as hostile an audience as ever gloated over a slow death in a Roman arena," wrote Grace Robinson. Early in the trial, the crowd in the courtroom had turned strongly against her. Part of it was her demeanor. The "Iron Widow," as reporters began calling her, sat stone-faced through some of the most emotional moments of the proceedings.

Under friendly questioning by his lawyers, Judd Gray revealed that his lover had tried to kill her husband at least half a dozen times over the past year and a half. "Mrs. Snyder's favorite pastime," wrote Damon Runyon, "was trying to knock her husband off." She was desperate to be free of him, she had told Gray when she hatched the murder plot; and it wasn't just about the insurance money. Albert Snyder had an uncontrollable temper, treated their daughter contemptuously, and had begun to drink heavily. He was cold and distant, and preferred "to stick around the house" on evenings. She, on the other hand, liked "to have a good time and go out to parties and dance," she told the court.

Ruth Snyder would surely have preferred divorce to murder, but to get a divorce, along with alimony and custody of her daughter, New York law mandated that she prove depraved cruelty or adultery. She could do neither. After ten years of marriage, "Ruth Snyder was going a bit crazy," writes historian Landis MacKellar in his close history of the case. "She suffered fainting spells, palpitations of the heart, hot flashes, headaches, and abdominal pains. Her menstrual periods were a misery." This was in 1925, the year she met Judd Gray, a friend of a friend, at a Midtown restaurant. They began their affair that summer. Red-hot in love, Gray found her "the most exciting, uninhibited woman" he had ever encountered. She, in turn, found a soul mate and an appealing sexual partner to whom she could spill out her problems and act out her erotic fantasies. But as much as Ruth Snyder hated her husband, she refused to admit it in open court. When called to the stand, dressed in black, with a rosary hanging around her neck—a sign of her recent decision to convert to Catholicism—she did confess to having originally plotted the crime with her lover. But, at the last minute, she had changed her mind, she testified, and tried to prevent Gray from carrying it out, "wrestling" with him as he clubbed her husband until he pushed her to the floor and she fainted. "He murdered my poor, dear husband in a cruel and barbarous manner, despite all I did to prevent him."

Caught, under cross-examination, in a blaze of inconsistencies and lies, and stumbling lamely and repeatedly to amend her testimony, Ruth Snyder fatally damaged her own case. When one of her lawyers pictured her as a "helpless frightened tool of her lover," a devoted housewife until she had met him, the audience laughed aloud and the judge threatened to clear the courtroom.

To pump up the story for their readers, reporters had originally glamorized the attractive but far from beautiful Ruth Snyder as a curvaceous Scandinavian seductress. She was, said Runyon, "a chilly looking blonde with frosty eyes and one of those marble, you-bet-you-will chins." Others reporters described her as a sex-crazed seductress. A quack phrenologist hired by Hearst's *Daily Mirror* said Ruth Snyder had "the character of a shallow-brained pleasure seeker, accustomed to unlimited self-indulgence, which at last ends in an orgy of murderous passion and lust."

Reporters characterized Judd Gray, by contrast, as a timid-looking little man—"a dead setup for a blonde," wrote Runyon. Asked point-blank why he had committed the murder, Gray said he had been manipulated by "veiled threats and intensive lovemaking." After bouts of uninhibited sex, "she got me in such a whirl that I didn't know where I was at." This fit squarely with his attorneys' portrayal of him as a "love slave," a "hapless" victim of a "designing, deadly . . . [sexually] abnormal women, a human serpent, a human fiend in the guise of a woman." He was a victim, moreover, who was ready to die for his sins. "Judd is not interested in the outcome," his mother told the *Daily News* in an exclusive interview. "The only judgment he fears is the one in the hereafter."

Gray was entirely convincing on the stand. "He was smartly dressed and well barbered" and wore round tortoiseshell glasses that made him look like a college professor, wrote reporter Milton MacKaye. "His manner with both judge and attorneys was ingratiating and almost painfully courteous." He offered no defense and constructed a wholly plausible case against himself and his lover; he even admitted to getting drunk to give himself courage for the crime. Under twelve hours of scorching cross-examination, he remained unshaken.

Throughout his testimony, his eyes never met Ruth Snyder's, "though she fixed him with a gaze of withering, unutterable malice." With her thin lips "curled to a distinct snarl at some passages in the statement," she reminded Damon Runyon of "a wildcat and a female cat, at that, on a leash."

The courtroom had remained dead calm during Gray's testimony. When he stepped from the stand, Ruth Snyder began sobbing. "The drab, factually mundane narrative of her lover had broken her as had nothing else in the hearing," wrote British author Nigel Morland. "The man told a good story," David Belasco remarked to friends at the recess that followed Gray's searing testimony.

As the evidence mounted against Ruth Snyder, the striking blonde with ice-blue eyes became, in reporter's descriptions, "a commonplace woman" whose "irresistible charm is visible only to Judd Gray." Sophie Treadwell of the *Herald Tribune* described her as "fattish"; and reporters for the *Daily News* suddenly noticed that she had a "cruel mouth" and "cold eyes. . . . You can see behind those eyes the beginning of a great fear," the fear of being "burned alive on the electric chair."

On May 9 the case went to jury. The jurors had scarcely retired when "curiosity caused a near riot in the courtroom." Great numbers of the two thousand spectators rushed forward, knocked aside six bailiffs, and swarmed around the counsel table. "Staring as though at a couple of animals, the crowd milled about Mrs. Snyder and Gray," wrote Grace Robinson. "It was," she said, "one of the . . . most disgraceful scenes any courtroom has ever witnessed."

Would the jurors send a woman to the electric chair? Damon Runyon thought not. "I couldn't condemn a woman to death no matter what she had done. . . . It is all very well for the rest of us to say what *ought* to be done to . . . Mrs. Ruth Brown Snyder, but when you get in the jury room and start thinking about going home to tell the neighbors that you have voted to burn a woman . . . I imagine the situation has a different aspect."

He couldn't have been more wrong. The all-male jury took only an hour and eleven minutes to find both defendants guilty of first-degree murder.* On hearing the verdict, the "Marble Woman" dropped into her chair sobbing and cupped her face with her hands. Judd Gray wobbled slightly, sat down, and "pulled a prayer book out of his pocket and began reading it." Four days later, Judge Scudder sentenced both defendants to die in the electric chair. As two black Cadillacs pulled away from the Long Island City jail to take the prisoners up the Hudson to the Death House at Sing Sing, an unruly crowd of thousands swarmed around them. People shook their fists and hurled insults at Ruth Snyder. "Hel-lo, Ruthie," one person yelled. "How do you feel now?"

That November, the Court of Appeals affirmed the convictions and defense lawyers for both parties petitioned Governor Al Smith to commute the

---

* New York law prevented women from serving on juries in murder trials.

death sentence. At this point, all attention focused on the "self-made widow," the mother of a child condemned by the court to be an orphan.

On January 10, 1928, Smith announced his decision. He would not intervene; Ruth Snyder and Judd Gray would die, as scheduled, two days later. Ruth Snyder "will ride a thunderbolt to eternity," the *News* commented crudely.

Around eleven o'clock on January 12 witnesses to the execution filed into the death chamber and took their seats in wooden, churchlike pews. The tall yellow electric chair was just in front of them, in the middle of the room, a few feet from the back wall.

Ruth Snyder would die first, for she was the less composed of the two. Judd Gray had prepared for his death calmly, as if it were divinely ordained, but in the days leading up to the execution Snyder had begun "to scream all night and almost every night" and was taken to the electric chair "in a state of horror-stricken misery that appalled those who attended her." She entered the death room holding a crucifix and accompanied by a Catholic priest who was whispering the prayer for the dying.

Two female attendants fastened her legs and arms, another secured a strap across her chest, and a fourth placed cathodes on her bare right leg. The state's gaunt executioner, Robert Elliott, placed a helmet fitted with electrodes on her head and tightly fastened the chin strap. He then slipped a black leather mask over her face. The priest gave her the Last Rites and took the crucifix from her. She was trembling violently. A prison doctor stood a few feet away and to the right of the chair. He nodded to Elliott, who pulled a switch. A "distinct click-click" was heard; then a low, ominous "humming sound" filled the room. "It was the 2,000 volts and 10 amperes of alternating current ebbing and flowing its disintegrating, jelling way through [Ruth Snyder's] veins and arteries and nerve tissues." Her chest expanded and she shot bolt upright against the leather straps, "chin thrust forward, muscles tense, stiff."

The doctor nodded again, the signal for the executioner to throw the switch a second time, just to be sure. As Ruth Snyder's body strained against the straps, her hair caught fire. There was a third surge of electricity—two thousand volts—then her body slumped down, "limp again." At 11:06 the doctor turned to the witnesses and said in a low voice: "I pronounce this woman dead."

After Ruth Snyder's body was wheeled into the autopsy room, Judd Gray, closely shaved and dressed in a gray pin-striped suit, was brought into the death chamber. It was 11:08 P.M. At 11:11 the current was turned on and blasted through his body for nearly four minutes. In his death agony, his hair began to smolder and give off smoke, his right sock caught fire, and sparks flew about his legs. His face and neck turned "horribly red then white" and his mouth was still wide open as he was unstrapped from the chair, lifted onto a gurney, and taken from the room.

"In the autopsy room the two lovers shared their last intimacy—on a pair of stone slabs," wrote reporter John Kobler.

"Gathered outside the prison, an enthusiastic crowd made holiday, as if for a medieval burning or a breaking on the wheel," wrote literary critic Edmund Wilson. Looking on, the prison warden, Lewis E. Lawes, told reporters he no longer believed in the death penalty. "Whether or not one believed that the culprits deserved what the law was giving them, one could not help thinking of their children, their parents and Judd Gray's wife," said Wilson. "Who, indeed, will believe that electrocution is not a method of inflicting death horrible out of all proportion to any possible deterrent effect."*

Early in the trial, Joseph Patterson had told his staff: "If this woman dies I want a picture of her."

Twenty of the twenty-four legal witnesses to the execution were newspaper reporters. By order of Warden Lawes, neither photographers nor cameras were permitted in the death chamber. This did not stop Joseph Patterson, who brought in a former *Tribune* photographer named Thomas Howard, a wartime buddy of his who was working in Washington, D.C. None of the witnesses to the execution knew him by face or name. Howard entered the room as a *News* reporter, but had a tiny camera strapped to his ankle. It was equipped with only one exposure. There would be no second chance if anything went wrong.

The camera was attached to a long, thin cable that ran up the inside of Howard's leg and through a hole in his trouser pocket. In his pocket, connected to the wire, was a bulblike shutter release. This was essential to the deception. The clicking of an ordinary camera shutter "would have sounded like a cannon in the stillness of the execution chamber." Howard took a front seat in the death chamber, twelve feet from the electric chair. The lighted room would provide good illumination. As the current surged through Ruth Sny-

---

* The electric chair was invented by associates of Thomas Edison. In 1890, New York became the first state to electrocute a prisoner. Electrocution was seen at the time as a more humane alternative to what *The New York Times* called "the barbarities, the inhumanities of hanging." NYT, August 7, 1890.

der's body, Howard hitched up his cuff far enough to clear the lens and pressed the shutter release in his pocket.

The next day's edition of the *News* carried the grainy, slightly blurred photograph on the front page. Above it, in bold, was a one-word headline, "DEAD!" "This is perhaps the most remarkable exclusive picture in the history of criminology," the paper boasted. For his vulgar violation of common decency, Howard received a bonus of $100.

Patterson happened to be in Chicago the Saturday afternoon the picture arrived at the Manhattan office of the *News*. When managing editor Frank. J. Hause showed up for work he was greeted with howls of disapproval from the staff in the business department. "What the hell are you trying to do to this newspaper," one executive demanded. Shown the photograph in advance of publication, outraged advertisers had threatened to cancel their ads; the

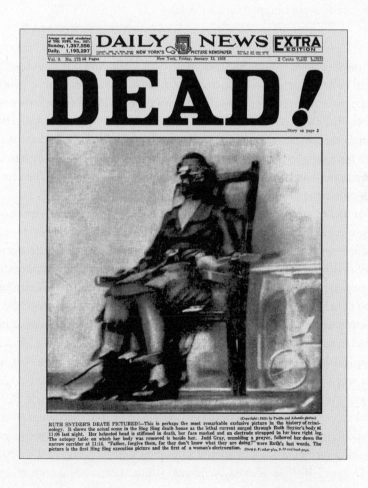

picture was "too revolting." Hause said he had merely acted under orders, but Patterson had not seen the picture and Hause had not wired him to get permission to run it, or to order it rerun the following Sunday. The "stunt" caused a furor. A few publishers and reporters saw it as a "great journalistic feat," others as "a reprehensible breach of civilized taste." None of the city's sober papers "would have printed the picture if they had got it," said Stanley Walker. He saw it for what it was: an "obvious pandering to the morbid mind."

A week or so after the picture was first published, Patterson returned from Chicago and took Hause aside. If he had been in his shoes he would not have known whether or not to run the photograph, he told Hause; he had no idea it would be so ghastly. "But since you ran the picture, okay."

Patterson could not have been unhappy with the sales the picture generated. A quarter of a million extra copies of the execution edition sold out within hours after it hit the newsstands, and three-quarters of a million copies of the reprint were snapped up a week later.

Why did the Snyder-Gray murder hold New York, and the country, "spellbound"? The entire episode, from indictment to execution, was in good part a press-generated phenomenon, "vastly-overplayed by all New York papers," admitted the *Daily News*'s Arthur Mefford, a respected journalist who covered the trial. "At best, it was nothing but a cheap, sordid murder," Mefford told a writer for *Editor & Publisher*, the trade weekly. "Never, in my opinion, was there another story in which so much bunk got into print. . . . The reporters themselves were to blame for this."

But there is more to it than that, as the editors of Mefford's paper pointed out in a perceptive postmortem assessment of reader interest in the case. A suburban mother was on trial for her life, an inherently dramatic story. But Ruth Snyder was fascinating to readers not because she was extraordinary, "but because she wasn't." That was also true of Judd Gray and Albert Snyder. It was their "lack of distinction" wrote Alexander Woollcott, that held people's attention. "They were just average folk—the ordinary suburban people in moderate circumstances that you jostle every day in Grand Central, the Pennsylvania station, or on the Jersey ferries," the *News* editorialized. "Ruth was a rather good-looking housewife in the editor's modest home in Queens Village. Albert Snyder . . . liked to sit around the house evenings, with a pipe and a book. . . . It might have been the household of your next door neighbor."

Judd Gray was "equally obscure and average. He was a traveling salesman, a church member, a lodge man and known as a good father and husband in East Orange." If these seemingly normal suburbanites could commit such a ghastly crime, nearly anyone could. So nearly everyone was interested. And the *News* and other papers fed on and fueled their curiosity with the preposterous idea that this was "one of the greatest dramas in criminal history."*

There was something else at play. Newspapers traditionally gave most of their coverage to the rich and the poor. "The middle class rarely makes the front page," said *The New Yorker*'s Elmer Davis. In the Snyder-Gray case "you had hundred-dollar-a-week people figuring as principals in a crime of passion; small commuters, members of a class which has received perhaps less attention than any other group in the country. Fiction and news alike had neglected them." This was not completely correct. Joseph Patterson had always favored them, fed their appetite for sensationalism; and now for the first time he had a big story that featured them. It was a natural for his readers, and he exploited it eagerly.

The idea of the "hundred-dollar-a-week people," the idea "that we are all potentially, if not actually, Grays and Snyders," described the moral code of Joseph Patterson, who believed that we are governed by our emotions, not by our reasoning powers. The superego was not strong enough to contain the id. Patterson had built his tabloid on this principle.

The Mainspring

Living in Manhattan had done little to change Joseph Patterson. "He is probably the worst-dressed man of means in New York," said Jack Alexander, who profiled him for *The New Yorker* some years after he moved to the city in 1925 to take direct control of his tabloid and be close to Mary King and their son. "Many of his friends consider it a great trial to be seen on the street with him." Even so, he cut an impressive figure, a six-footer who carried his sturdy two hundred pounds with the confidence of an athlete. He had a strong jaw, blazing brown eyes, a deeply lined face, and neatly trimmed graying hair. And although he walked with a military bearing, he rarely talked about his war service and preferred that staff call him Mr. Patterson, not Captain. Only two or three friends from his early days with the *Tribune* called him Joe.

---

* The case would inspire a Sophie Treadwell play, *Machinal: A Tragedy in Ten Episodes*, which appeared on Broadway in the 1928–29 season and was both a commercial and critical success. A young upstart named Hal Dawson, later known as Clark Gable, played Judd Gray. Tangentially based on the Snyder-Gray case are a 1935 novella by James M. Cain, *Double Indemnity*, and the 1944 film of the same title, directed by Billy Wilder, written by Raymond Chandler, and starring Barbara Stanwyck as a sultry housewife who, with her lover, carries out a plot to kill her husband. The 1981 film *Body Heat* is another loose adaptation of the case.

He was unknowable, a man of irresoluble contradictions—amiable and approachable one moment, icily distant the next. He would go out on assignments with young reporters and treat them to drinks afterward. Passing them in the newsroom the next day, he wouldn't give them the courtesy of a nod. A loner, he kept even his top editors at a "majestic distance." He didn't even like shaking hands with people.

Patterson ran his paper as if it were a frontline artillery battery, with the staff loading and firing without cease, yet he rarely summoned his editors to his office; he considered that demeaning. He would converse with them informally at their desks in his regular walks through the newsroom. He never barked orders, or "chewed out anybody in private or in public," said John Chapman. "His approach was 'Let's try this,' or 'Don't you think it would be a good idea if we.'" But all but the most obtuse understood that he was issuing mandates, not suggestions. Patterson left no doubt he was the mainspring of the machine, a kindly "tyrant," said Burton Roscoe, "who had been subjected to the tyranny of his mother."

Behind his back, his staffers called him "God." Somebody would say, "God's in the building," recalled Paul Gallico. "His word was law . . . but he was a benevolent God. He . . . was fair and just . . . wonderful to work for." The paper, said Gallico, "reflected Patterson, his toughness and . . . his understanding of his audience." He understood them because he continued to mingle with them, even after the paper became hugely successful in the late 1920s. On summer afternoons, he'd sometimes leave the office early, buy a popsicle, and catch a subway to Coney Island, where he'd soak up "the nickel thrills." He rarely ate in expensive restaurants, preferring lunch stands and basement speakeasies, where he could mix with his readers. He was known to ask taxi drivers, complete strangers, to join him. Originator of the paper's "Straw Poll," he would go out onto the streets with the poll's team of reporters to take "the public sampling." One day, a coworker found him in a tenement, perched on a stool in the kitchen, listening to a black woman's opinion of FDR.

His eccentricities were legion. He dreaded ostentation and show, and had an almost paranoid preference for privacy. His penthouse apartment on East Eighty-fourth Street, designed by Raymond Hood, architect of the *Tribune*'s splendid tower on Michigan Avenue, had a private entrance on the ground floor and its own elevator. Later, when Patterson hired Hood to design a mansion for him on a secluded piece of wooded land overlooking the Hudson at Ossining, New York, he laid down two unalterable demands: make it look "very ugly," and "make it look as if I didn't have any money." Hood fashioned a plain, boxlike mass and had it painted to resemble a camouflaged military bunker.

One afternoon, while accompanying circulation inspector Joseph Gold-stein on his visits to news dealers, Patterson asked Goldstein to help him buy a car so he could commute from Ossining without being a prisoner to the train schedule. The following afternoon Goldstein took him to the showrooms of Isotta Fraschini, Cadillac, and Lincoln. Patterson, he noticed, looked ill at ease. They ended up on a tawdry stretch of upper Broadway, where the boss bought a stripped-down Studebaker for $540.

Patterson framed but did not compose the paper's editorials. Beginning in 1926, they were written by twenty-seven-year-old Reuben Maury, a strong writer with no newspaper experience. Patterson would tell Maury what to write, and Maury would put the chief's ideas into his own language. It was an unenviable task. Pacing the floor, thick clouds of cigarette smoke hanging above him, Patterson dictated to Maury but forbade him from taking notes— that "made him nervous." After Patterson was finished dictating, he'd leave the building to catch an afternoon movie. When he returned around four o'clock a neatly typed draft would be on his desk, ready for his scrutiny. He made his changes with a dull pencil stub. "He would have no truck with mechanical pencils or pencil sharpeners," said Chapman. Nobody knew why.

By the summer of 1927, the *News* had grown so lustily it needed more space, and Patterson began to search for a Midtown building site, preferably close to Grand Central Terminal. "If I can be on a cross-town street to Times Square," he told his real estate scouts, "I'll get my tabloids on the sidewalks in the morn-ing ahead of any of my competitors." His land agents assembled in secret an L-shaped parcel on the south side of East Forty-second Street, just down the street from the terminal, and one block the other direction from Fred French's Tudor City.

After wrecking crews demolished a row of undistinguished low buildings, ironworkers began assembling the frame of a square silver tower designed by Raymond Hood and his partner, John Mead Howells, a building that com-pleted the skyscraper transformation of the area around the terminal. The building was divided in two. The *News* was composed, edited, and printed in a nine-story plant on the long Forty-first Street part of the parcel. Most of the rest of the thirty-six-story tower was profit-making rental space. The first uptown issue of the *News* rolled off the presses on the evening of George Washington's birthday, February 22, 1930.

The freestanding slab—still there, but no longer occupied by the *News*— is nearly "destitute of ornament." Bands of white brick line the solid walls, and the windows are linked vertically by alternating reddish brown and black stripes of polychrome patterned brick. *The New Yorker* pronounced the design "simplicity itself. Nothing quite so unadorned has met our eye before." The main lobby is another story. It has a high dome of black onyx, inspired by Patterson's visit to Les Invalides, Napoleon's Paris tomb; and in a partially sunken pit in the center of the main floor is an enormous, handpainted revolving globe—"eerily lit from below." The terrazzo floor is laid out like a giant compass. Inlaid bronze lines indicate the distances of fifty-eight world cities from New York, and maps and weather charts in glass showcases line the room.

The weather charts were Hood's idea, and when he first suggested them, Patterson objected. "Weather charts!" he exploded, "What the people want are 'murder charts,'" living maps of the metropolitan area indicating where the latest crimes had been committed. But he bowed to Raymond Hood and agreed to turn over the meteorological project to Dr. James Henry Scarr of the United States Weather Bureau. The immodest weather scientist called his creation "the most unique and most elaborate collection of geographical, astronomical and meteorological data gathered in one place anywhere in the world." It had a weather observation center, with dials and maps connected with instruments on the roof. Complete weather reports and forecasts were posted every hour. Patterson called it "popular science" for the people.

There is the same union of form and function in the Daily News Building as in its near neighbor, Walter Chrysler's silver spire. One is a brash symbol of automobile culture; the other, with its stripped-down simplicity, is a tabloid in white brick and glass, a building calculated, wrote Douglas Haskell, to make "its impact at once, before you turn the page."

Except for the brick patterns, the building's only ornament is a polished granite plaque above the Forty-second Street entrance. On it Patterson had artisans chisel the last six words of a remark attributed to Abraham Lincoln: "God must have loved the common people because HE MADE SO MANY OF THEM." They ought to have been honored. Patterson was making nearly $5 million a year on them.

The construction of the Daily News Building was a Depression-era project, and not long after moving in Patterson made "an abrupt shift," in A. J. Liebling's words, "from sexual buffoonery to earnest plugging for the New Deal." The *News* supported Roosevelt over Hoover in the 1932 election in the hope that he would repeal Prohibition and institute a more equitable distribution of national wealth. After Roosevelt's inauguration, Patterson assembled his editors and announced: "We're missing the bus. People don't care as much about playboys, Broadway, and divorce. They want to know how they're going to eat."*

"The *Daily News* was built on legs," Patterson said later, "but when we got enough circulation we draped them." Although there would be less crime and sex, the *News* retained its circulation bedrocks: advice columns, radio and movie news, comics, and Broadway gossip.

Joseph Patterson had always been a heavy drinker; during World War II the drinking got out of control. Mary King, whom he married in 1938, the year of his divorce from Alice Higinbotham, tried to rein him in but that proved impossible. In the spring of 1946, Patterson was admitted to Doctors Hospital in Manhattan. He died there of cirrhosis of the liver on May 26, at age sixty-seven. The burial, with full military honors, was at Arlington National Cemetery. It was a Catholic ceremony. In his final weeks on earth he had converted to the faith of his wife.

Before the coffin was transported to Washington, Patterson lay in repose in the library of his estate in Ossining. Over a hundred employees at the *News* chartered a train to go up the Hudson to pay a final farewell to the publishing titan many of them had only half jokingly called God. At the time, no one was sure what would happen to the *News* or where it would stand on the issues of the day. "Since he had carefully discouraged independence of expression among his subordinates," wrote A. J. Liebling, "nobody outside the News Building can even suspect what *their ideas* may be."

---

* Patterson, an isolationist, backed Roosevelt until March 11, 1941, when he angrily broke with him over his signing of the Lend-Lease Act, which provided U.S. military aid to the United Kingdom, the Soviet Union, and other nations at war with the Axis powers.

CHAPTER EIGHTEEN

SLUGGERS

New York is a "home run town."

—MILLER HUGGINS

Golden People

On a September afternoon in 1923, Paul Gallico stepped into the ring to fight Jack Dempsey, heavyweight champion of the world. A rookie sports writer for the *Daily News*, Gallico had been sent to Dempsey's training camp in Saratoga Springs, New York, to do some color pieces on the champ's preparation for his upcoming title defense against a giant Argentine named Luis Angel Firpo, a "furious wild-eyed ring monster," reporters called him.

Earlier that week, Gallico had asked Dempsey to spar a round with him. He wanted to write a story about how it felt to be hit by the hardest puncher on earth. His hope was to write an "exclusive" that would impress his boss, Joseph Patterson, who was trying to get rid of him. Dempsey was incredulous. "Do you want to be killed?" he asked Gallico, but the likable young writer brought him around. At six-foot-three and two hundred pounds, Gallico was a few inches taller and almost ten pounds heavier than Dempsey, and had been an athlete at Columbia, where he played football and basketball and captained the varsity crew team. He could handle himself, he told the menacing-looking slugger with the battered nose and the four-day growth of beard.

"We're just going to sort of fool around and take it easy," Gallico told Hype Igoe, boxing writer for the *New York Evening Journal*. Looking up at him skeptically from his typewriter, Igoe said, "Son, don't you know that man can't take it easy."

There were three thousand spectators at ringside when a ghost-white Gallico, wearing headgear, swimming trunks, and a rowing shirt from college, stepped through the ropes and took his corner. At that moment, Dempsey's handlers were carrying from the ring the third sparring partner the champ had knocked out that day. When the bell sounded, Gallico grazed his opponent with a light jab. Seconds later, he was on the deck, leveled by a shot to the left eye that "would have busted down a brick wall," said Dempsey's manager, Jack "Doc" Kearns. A sensible man would have stayed down, but Gallico got up. Dempsey pulled him into a clinch and whispered, "Hang on kid till your head clears." Then the champion instinctively let loose six sharp rabbit chops to the back of Gallico's neck and it was over. It had lasted one minute and thirty-seven seconds.

Grantland Rice, the dean of American sportswriters, happened to be in the Dempsey camp that afternoon. "At the end, the head of young Mr. Gallico was attached to his body by a shred," he wrote. "We only hope he is not asked next to cover an electrocution."

Less than an hour after pulling himself off the deck, Gallico was in his cabin writing his story of what a knockout felt like. "The ten seconds I spent unconscious on the canvas were the turning point of my career," he said later. When he called in the story, Patterson "laughed his head off" and gave him the byline. Two months later, he promoted Gallico to sports editor.

Gallico was at ringside when Dempsey met Firpo, "The Wild Bull of the Pampas," at the Polo Grounds on September 14, 1923, before a crowd of ninety thousand. It was Dempsey's fifth defense of the crown he had taken from another giant of a man, Jess Willard, in Toledo, Ohio, on Independence Day 1919. That afternoon he crushed his six-foot-six, 245-pound opponent into "a shapeless mass of gore and battered flesh," wrote Grantland Rice.

The Firpo bout was the first time Gallico had seen Dempsey fight, and it left a lifelong impression. Lasting only three minutes and fifty-eight seconds, nothing like it had ever been seen for "pure animal savagery," Gallico wrote. It was like "a slashing, death struggle of wild beasts." In less than four minutes, Firpo was felled ten times and Dempsey twice. "Half-maddened by battle lust, [Dempsey] stood over the fallen challenger when he knocked him down,* instead of retiring

---

* In his excellent biography of Dempsey, Randy Roberts challenges the idea that it was unfair, but not illegal, for a fighter to stand over his fallen opponent. "Even before the Dempsey-Firpo bout such a tactic was illegal. The rule was quite clear. . . . 'When a contestant is down, his opponent shall retire to the farthest corner and remain there until the count is completed. Should he fail to do so, the referee and timekeeper may cease counting until he has so retired.'" After the Dempsey-Firpo fight, the rule was reworded and "may" was changed to "must," a change that would cost Dempsey the championship four years later in his fight with Gene Tunney. Randy Roberts, *Jack Dempsey: The Manassa Mauler* (Baton Rouge: Louisiana State University Press, 2003), 191.

to a corner for the count, and slugged him again when he had barely regained his feet," wrote Gallico. "And once even stood behind him and hit him on the rise."

"This isn't a boxing match," said ringside reporter W. O. McGeehan. "This is a fight." From the opening seconds, when the awkward, six-foot-three, 216-pound challenger landed a short uppercut that knocked Dempsey to one knee, the crowd rose to its feet and remained standing for the remainder of the fight, shouting hysterically. Temporary seats set up in the Polo Grounds' infield toppled over when fans stood on them to catch the instantaneous eruption of violence. One of the spectators threw a punch at welterweight champion Mickey Walker after Walker landed on him accidentally. "I was gonna deck the stupid, fat son of a bitch who swung at me," Walker remembered. "But when I saw his face I pulled my punch. Hell, I was a Yankee fan and I wasn't about to bust up Babe Ruth."

After Dempsey floored Firpo a seventh time in the first round, trying, he said later, to put out the "lust to kill" he saw burning in the Argentine's eyes, Firpo charged him in a "blind rage" and landed a right to the jaw that knocked Dempsey backward through the ropes, head over heels. He landed among the typewriters of the boxing reporters at ringside. Dempsey yelled for help—"Push me back. I gotta get back." Two writers gave him a heave, and he was back in the ring before the count of ten.

At this point, the fight should have been stopped, with Firpo declared the winner by a disqualification. The Marquis of Queensberry rules clearly state that a fighter who falls "through weakness or otherwise . . . must get up unassisted." But referee Jack Gallagher allowed the fight to resume. The crowd was "almost 100 per cent American," with only a sprinkling of Hispanics, observed The New York Times, "and not one spectator in every ten wanted to see the world's title pass to South America." A disqualification would have ignited a riot.

Back on his feet, a semiconscious Dempsey pressed the fight, though everyone at ringside could see he was glassy-eyed and on rubbery legs at the end of the round. "In his corner Dempsey was still half out," Gallico reported; "he didn't know what round it was, what day of the week, or what town he was in." Every punch Firpo landed "staggered me," Dempsey said afterward, yet he answered the bell, and floored Firpo three times with an explosion of crushing blows. The last combination, a left uppercut to the jaw followed by a straight right to the heart, left the Argentine senseless, stretched out on the canvas floor near his own corner, where he was counted out. As Firpo struggled to stand, Dempsey, in an unexpected display of sportsmanship, rushed over and picked him up.

After the fight, Dempsey said he had no memory of being knocked out of the ring. He had only regained full consciousness in his corner, asking his handlers, "Which round was I knocked out in?"

At ringside that evening was the noted Ashcan School painter George Bellows, commissioned by the New York *Evening Journal* to make sketches of the fight. The painting he executed later of Dempsey being knocked through the ropes hangs in the Whitney Museum of American Art. Bellows has Dempsey being felled by a roundhouse left, not, as happened, by a sweeping right to the jaw.

The Firpo fight, and Dempsey's preparation for it, took twenty-six-year-old Paul Gallico's career in an unexpected direction. At the time, he had no interest in professional boxing. Widely read in the classics and fluent in French and German, he wanted to be a novelist, an aspiration encouraged by his immigrant parents, Hortense Ehrlich, a Viennese-trained singer, and Paolo Gallico, a tempestuous Italian who played piano in the New York Philharmonic Orchestra. Gallico had joined the *Daily News* in 1922, one year after graduating from Columbia following military service during the war, and had landed the job through the intervention of his wife's father, a Chicago *Tribune* columnist. Gallico enjoyed movies, so Patterson made him the paper's film editor, only to replace him shortly thereafter for criticizing films Patterson thought his readers might enjoy. But Philip Payne, the *News*'s recently appointed managing editor, saw Gallico's promise and hid him "out of sight" in the sports department. It was Payne who had assigned Gallico to cover the Dempsey camp; Patterson thought he had fired him.

Over the next thirteen years—before leaving to become a prolific novelist and children's author—Gallico covered the national sporting scene with energy and empathy. The George Plimpton of his day, his strong suit was participatory journalism. He batted against Lefty Grove, swam against Johnny Weissmuller, golfed against Bobby Jones, played tennis against Wimbledon champion Helen Wills, skied on an Olympic course, drove laps at the Indianapolis speedway, and performed aerial acrobatics with a noted stunt flier. He also founded the *Daily News* Golden Gloves tournament and promoted dozens of sporting events for the paper's readers—golf-driving contests, roller-skating derbies, water circuses, and a canoe race around Manhattan Island.

With Grantland Rice, he belonged to what he called, unapologetically, the Gee Whiz School of sportswriters, the mordant Ring Lardner being the monarch of the more skeptical "Aw Nuts School." Writing with fire and enthusiasm, he built up the drama for every heavyweight championship fight, every World Series, every major college football game, and helped turn at least half a dozen athletes—his "Golden People"—into sports legends. "I contributed . . . tremendously . . . to this innocence, this naïveté," Gallico recalled his years on the *Daily News* sports desk. But in the Golden Age of American Sport, when at least a dozen transcendent athletic performers arose contemporaneously—

Babe Ruth in baseball, "Red" Grange in football, Bobby Jones in golf, Man o' War in thoroughbred racing, Bill Tilden in tennis—hero worship came easily, he said, and without shame.

Gallico was impressed most of all with Jack Dempsey, drawn to him more by his color and crowd appeal than his ring record, which was decidedly mixed. "During my thirteen-year tenure at the sports desk of the *Daily News*, I saw Jack Dempsey fight only four times. In those four bouts he was defeated twice and in the other two, which he won by knockouts, each time he came close to being knocked out. . . . Yet, of all the fighters I have ever known . . . Dempsey still rules over my imagination as the greatest, most exciting and dramatic."

It is difficult to understand today why so many millions of Americans were enthralled by Dempsey's pantherlike ferocity. "Prize fighting is popular because, watching it, civilized people are vicariously purged of their primitive inclinations," opined *Time* in 1927. Perhaps, but there is more to it than that. In tough working-class communities, "a punch on the nose" was "a settler of arguments," the "accepted method of replying to an insult," or dealing with a bully or an intruder, said Gallico. And Dempsey's following was overpoweringly blue-collar. "Jack Dempsey, he was our man," recalled Chicago writer Studs Terkel, son of struggling Russian-Jewish parents, who was eleven years old when Dempsey met Firpo. "He came out of the Wild West, its logging and mining camps, and he came up the hard way, just like we did. He was tough and unrefined, and that's how he fought. Dempsey wasn't a boxer; he was a slugger like Babe Ruth, another wild kid who was brought up on the streets and lived by his instincts. We listened to his fights on the radio and fired fake punches at each other when he scored a knockdown."

Dockworkers in Chelsea and Hell's Kitchen, required every morning to bow to the hiring boss, were delighted when Dempsey, in his "zeal to conquer," defied the rules of the ring, punching below the belt or standing over a downed opponent and smashing him the instant he rose to his feet. But that kind of behavior alienated the society crowd that boxing promoter Tex Rickard, "Master of Ballyhoo," lured to the heavyweight contests he sponsored. Notables like Elihu Root and Anne Morgan bought ringside seats to Dempsey's fights to see him lose, outraged by his lawless fistic behavior and his failure to serve in the military in World War I, when he had gained an exemption to support his impoverished family in Colorado. Adding to the outrage, Dempsey had posed for a news photograph, reputedly doing war work in a Philadelphia shipyard, dressed in overalls but with shining patent-leather shoes. "The fancy footgear," said sportswriter Red Smith, "raised noisy doubts about his contribution to the war effort."

It was impossible to be neutral about Jack Dempsey. You either loved or detested him, and that was exactly his appeal to newspaper publishers like Joseph

Patterson. Every time Dempsey went into battle it was high drama, and people followed him as they followed no other champion, except, perhaps, Muhammad Ali. Dempsey drew the greatest crowds in the history of boxing—five of his fights in the 1920s were million-dollar gates.* All of them were covered on the front page of every major American paper.

Joseph Patterson and other big-city newspaper publishers put some of their finest writers on the sports desk, and for good reason: the sports section sold newspapers. Beginning in the early 1920s, with a rising standard of living and a shortened workweek that freed up Saturday afternoons and Sundays for leisure pursuits, the sports sections of American newspapers grew phenomenally. Once read almost exclusively in barbershops and barrooms, the previously skimpy sports page became "second only to the general news pages in importance," said *New York Herald Tribune* city editor Stanley Walker. By 1927, New York's major newspapers were devoting between 40 and 60 percent of their local coverage to sports, with the Sunday sports section often running to twelve pages. In that year, the average urban American newspaper was giving twice as much space to the sports section as it had ten years earlier. When Dempsey fought Firpo there were over eight hundred sportswriters in the Polo Grounds, and from ringside they filed nearly a quarter of a million words by Western Union. This new fascination with organized sport elevated the prestige and living standards of a class of writers that had previously been considered "one grade above the office cat."

In the 1920s, sportswriters became among the best-paid reporters on New York dailies; and not a few of them supplemented their salaries with under-the-table handouts from boxing promoters and club owners eager to have them write puffs about their athletes and teams. The reporters who made New York the sportswriting capital of the world were the "elite" of their papers, often to the despair of their colleagues in the newsroom. They traveled all over the country in deluxe accommodations and on lavish expense accounts. Grantland Rice, whose syndicated column ran in more than 250 newspapers, pulled in over $100,000 a year, more than the Yankees paid Babe Ruth.

A number of these celebrity makers became celebrities themselves. Joining veteran Grantland Rice and upstart Paul Gallico were James P. Dawson and John Kieran of the *New York Times*, W. O. McGeehan, Heywood Broun, Frederick G. Lieb, Allison Danzig, Ring Lardner, and Damon Runyon, the "min-

---

* The next one came in 1935, when Joe Louis fought Max Baer.

nesinger of the Golden Decade." On the sports page could be found some of the best—along with some of the worst—newspaper writing of the decade. Runyon and Lardner, Gallico and Kieran, McGeehan and Broun were story-tellers in the great national tradition. They conveyed the excitement of a major athletic event with wit and style—and occasionally, as with Lardner, stinging acerbity. "They know that the qualities which vitalize all writing—irony, re-straint, accuracy, illuminating detail and humor . . . [are] . . . possible, even necessary in sports writing," wrote Stanley Walker, who considered Gallico one of the finest sports columnists in the city.

Unlike Rice, a student of the classics who liked to show off his erudition, often with lamentable results, Gallico wrote in down-to-earth prose perfect for *Daily News* readers: knowledgeable sports enthusiasts unlikely to be hood-winked by luxuriant verbiage. And he could be witheringly critical—even of his Golden People. But whereas McGeehan and fellow sportswriters at the *Herald Tribune* were under strict orders to avoid "godding up" professional athletes, Gallico promoted his sporting heroes for Joseph Patterson as aggres-sively as Madison Avenue promoted beer and bananas for its clients.

There is no better illustration of professional writing as personal promotion than Marshall Hunt's coverage of Babe Ruth for the *Daily News*. Hunt was the *News*'s first sports editor, hired at the age of twenty-four after serving as an Army pilot in France during the war. Patterson devoted the entire back page to sports coverage, which put heavy pressure on Hunt, who was the paper's entire sports department and was operating without a wire service. At the end of the day he'd write his baseball stories after reading the play-by-play accounts in other New York dailies, work he considered "the greatest larceny in the world."

Hunt's "salvation" was Paul Gallico. His promotion to sports editor allowed Hunt to become what he really wanted to be: a full-time sportswriter. Hunt, a great talker, convinced Patterson to allow him to take a radically new approach to covering baseball. "I wasn't there to cover the Yankees or the games," he later explained. "I was there to cover the Babe."

The Babe

The Yankees acquired George Herman Ruth from the Boston Red Sox on De-cember 26, 1919. He had been a full-time pitcher, the best left-hander in the American League, before being converted to an everyday outfielder in 1919 because of his prowess at the plate. That year he had batted .322 and hit 29 home runs, a total that surpassed by two the record set in 1884 by Ned Williamson of the Chicago White Stockings. (The Philadelphia Athletics Frank "Home Run" Baker, the leading home run hitter in the American League in 1914, hit eight round-trippers.) Since acquiring Ruth in 1914 from the minor league Baltimore Orioles, the Red Sox had won three World Series, but were stuck with a New York–based owner indifferent to their success. Harry Frazee's true passion was producing Broadway plays, and in 1919 he was strapped for cash—several of his recent shows had flopped. He sold Ruth to the Yankees for $125,000 and a $300,000 personal loan from Colonel Jacob Ruppert, co-owner of the Yankees with the spectacularly named Tillinghast L'Hommedieu Huston, an engineer and self-made millionaire.*

In his first year with the Yankees, the twenty-five-year-old sensation surpassed all expectations. Although the Yankees finished third, they won 95 games, a club record, and Ruth cracked an unheard-of 54 home runs, more than were hit by fourteen of the other fifteen major league teams. The next year he hit 59, drove in 171 runs, and batted .378, leading the Yankees to their first American League championship in the club's history.

In these two seasons, Babe Ruth singlehandedly transformed organized baseball. Up to then, it had been a game of "small ball," pitching, fielding, squeeze plays, and placement hitting, a strategy honed to a sharp point by New York Giants manager and part-owner John McGraw. Ordering his pitchers to either walk Ruth or throw him nothing but slow curveballs, McGraw piloted his team to victory over the Yankees in the Polo Grounds, the park the Yankees rented from the Giants, in the first two subway World Series in 1921 and 1922. But the long ball, aided by a livelier ball—the yarn wound more tightly around its cork center by improved machines—was the future of the game, and it became, with Ruth, "the people's choice."†

Before Ruth, most of the great hitters, typified by Detroit's Ty Cobb, used the bat like an axe, standing near the front of the plate and chopping at the

---

* The sale helped pull Frazee out of debt, and in 1925 he produced *No, No, Nanette*, a box office sensation.

† Baseball manufacturers denied any deliberate effort to make the ball livelier. They attributed the increase in home runs to their use, after 1919, of a higher-quality yarn and to tighter winding. New restrictions on pitchers, instituted in February 1920, also played a part. It was henceforth illegal for a pitcher to tamper with a ball or treat it with a foreign substance—spit, gum, mud, licorice, whatever. And after the Cleveland Indians Ray Chapman was killed in August of that year by a pitch that hit him in the head, a new, easier-to-see ball was substituted whenever the one in play became scuffed or dirty. Harold Seymour, *Baseball: The Golden Age* (NY: Oxford University Press, 1971), 423–24.

ball with a short, sharp swing, trying to place it for a hit. Babe Ruth, with his abnormally acute eyesight, timing, and muscular reactions, changed this. He stood deep in the batter's box, in a closed stance, and took a long, sweeping cut, smashing the ball with power and precision. He was so good at it some people thought he was a "freak."

Shutouts and one-run games had been standard before 1920, but "the booming bat of the Babe," wrote sportswriter John Daley, "demonstrated that runs could be gathered like bananas—in bunches. He soon had everyone swinging from his heels, shooting for the fences and trying to follow his lead." In 1922, major league teams hit 1,055 home runs, over three times as many as they had five years earlier. Yet no one approached Ruth's home run output until the emergence of teammate Lou Gehrig as another long-ball sensation in 1927.

People flocked to the Polo Grounds to see "Big Bam" (short for "Big Bambino") swing for the seats. In 1920 the Yankees broke all major league attendance records, becoming the first team to attract more than a million fans at home, outdrawing their landlords by over 359,000 in their own ballpark. This incensed McGraw, who had the Giants' principal owner, Charles A. Stoneham, inform Ruppert and Huston that he "would be pleased if they would make plans to build a ballpark of their own as quickly as possible." In May 1922, Ruppert began building the largest stadium in baseball on the site of an old lumberyard in the Bronx, just across the Harlem River from the Polo Grounds, fifteen minutes by subway from Times Square. "Yankee Stadium was a mistake," said Ruppert. "Not mine, but the Giants."

Completed in an amazing 284 days, the stadium was ready for opening day of the 1923 season. Governor Al Smith threw out the first pitch and the Yankees beat the Red Sox 4–1. Ruth baptized the new park with a three-run shot into the short right field "porch," to the delight of a standing-room crowd of 62,000. "As Ruth circled the bases . . . the biggest crowd in baseball history rose to its feet and let loose the biggest shout in baseball history," reported *The New York Times*. Reporter Fred Lieb dubbed Yankee Stadium "the house that Ruth built," and the right-field bleachers became "Ruthville." One month later, Huston, who never got along with Ruppert, ended the partnership, leaving Ruppert as sole owner. That year, after winning their third pennant in a row, with Ruth batting .393, the highest of his career, and hitting 41 home runs, the Yanks finally beat the Giants in the "Broadway Series," securing their first world championship. The Giants' pitchers walked Ruth eight times, but he still hit three home runs.

For the second time, the World Series was broadcast on radio, with the announcer sitting in a box seat, close to the field, speaking into large microphones to an estimated five million listeners. As "wireless" coverage of games increased dramatically in succeeding years, along with movie house newsreels, so too did the popularity of Ruth. Because of Ruth, a "new type of fan" began to come to the ballpark—"the fan who didn't know where first base was but had heard of Ruth and wanted to see him hit a home run." Ruth's titanic drives were as dramatic as Dempsey's knockout blows. Yankee manager Miller Huggins said it all: the fans love the guy "who carries the wallop."

Ruth also changed the game as "spectacle," altering the way fans watched it. When he stepped to the plate, peering at the mound and trying to intimidate the pitcher with a few waves of his bat, the "combat zone" shrank to the sixty feet and six inches between the pitcher's rubber and home plate. Fans became aware of a private war between pitcher and hitter; for a few tense moments it became a contest between two, not eighteen, men, one of them possessing the power "to wreck the game."

Baseball had needed a superman in the year following the 1919 "Black Sox" scandal, which resulted in eight Chicago White Sox players being banned from major league baseball for life for accepting money from gamblers to throw the series to the Cincinnati Reds. Word of the scandal began to appear in newspapers late in the 1920 season, and people worried about the future of the game. A magnificent prodigy led baseball "out of the wilderness and back into the aura of respectability," wrote Grantland Rice.

Off the field, Ruth himself was a spectacle. A man of "measureless lust," he lived big and openly, drawn to the bottle, the flesh, and the dinner plate. He and his wife, Helen Woodford, whom he had met and married in 1914 when she was an eighteen-year-old waitress in a Boston coffee shop, lived in an eight-room suite in the plush Ansonia Hotel on upper Broadway. In the evenings, when the Yankees were in town, Ruth prowled the clubs and speakeasies of Manhattan and northern New Jersey, almost always without companions, preferring out-of-the-way places where he knew the owners, who protected his privacy. "He runs alone," wrote reporter Westbrook Pegler. Baseball historian Lee Allen memorably described Ruth as "a large man in a camel's hair coat and camel's hair cap, standing in front of a hotel, his broad nostrils sniffing at the promise of the night." It was as if he were inhaling the city, claiming it as his own.

He had a voracious appetite for food and beer. "I've seen him at midnight," said Ty Cobb, "propped up in bed, order six huge club sandwiches and put them away, along with a platter of pig's knuckles, and a pitcher of beer. And all the time, he'd be puffing on big black cigars." When traveling with the team, he'd rent a large hotel suite, stock it with bootleg whiskey, and place a keg of beer in the bathtub. The women would begin arriving about nine, and by midnight the Sultan of Swat, dressed in a red robe and Moroccan slippers, had made his selection. "Good night," he'd announce in his booming voice, the signal for everyone to leave, including the "rejected applicants." He may have wanted privacy because he grunted and groaned in bed, "the noisiest fucker in North America," said a friend.

Ruth's exploits with women were kept out of the news by obliging sports reporters. They concealed his extramarital dalliances as accommodatingly as their colleagues at City Hall did Jimmy Walker's. In Ruth's second year with the Yankees, the team was taking a train from its training camp in Shreveport to New Orleans when the train stopped at Baton Rouge. Reporter Fred Lieb was playing poker when "suddenly the front door of our car opened violently," he later related, "and a panting Babe Ruth came rushing through. He was being pursued by a dark-haired, dark-eyed woman carrying a knife pointed at Babe's back. . . . Babe got off at the rear end of the train and ran up the platform the full length of the train." He managed to elude his irate pursuer, double back through the station, and leap onto the first car just as the train began steaming out of the station. "I still wonder why we newsmen acted as we did," Lieb wrote in 1977. "There were eleven of us sitting there and no one said a word. We just went on typing, reading magazines, and playing cards. . . . Later I was told the woman was the wife of a Louisiana legislator."

He was the most storied and publicized baseball player in history, and one of the most photographed figures of the decade. Southern communities on the Yankees' spring training schedule mandated in their contracts that Ruth play and declared half day holidays when he roared into town. Banks and stores closed, the local ballpark was sold out, and boys sat on tree limbs and tied themselves to telephone poles to watch him hit. When the Yankees' train pulled out of the local station, women lined the tracks and passed their telephone numbers to the Babe through the open window of his Pullman car.

This "rage for Ruth" was part of the national, certainly an urban, shift from puritanical values; the unrestrained Bambino was the perfect hero for a people casting off encrusted moral restraints. Even his brazen defiance of club rules—breaking curfew and showing up at the ballpark late and hungover—endeared him to fans in an emerging corporate society that was producing faceless company sycophants. White-collar workers fearful of flouting authority and telling the boss to go straight to hell could take vicarious pleasure in Ruth's insubordination.

He was the most human of heroes. "Affable, boisterous and good-natured to a fault, he was always as accessible to the newsboy on the corner as to the most dignified personage in worldly affairs," wrote *The New York Times* after his death from throat cancer on August 16, 1948. And he was, said the *Times*, "intensely real and 'regular.'" He cried in public when he let down his fans, and his misses at the plate were as "prodigious," wrote Paul Gallico, "as his hits. At the end of a swing his legs would be braided like a barroom pretzel, and he would be facing three-quarters of the compass around from where he had started."

Yet this maker of "sport miracles" was no modern Adonis. He had round shoulders, a torso like a beer barrel, and spindly legs; and there was that "pudding face." Even in peak condition he had a paunch, and he talked loudly and crudely. Welders from Weehawken could look up from their beer and spot more ideal specimens at the bar.

Ruth appealed to ordinary people who had known failure but lived in hope. He had grown up in a South Baltimore neighborhood called Pigtown because of its proximity to the city's slaughterhouses. His German American father, George Senior, was a hot-tempered saloonkeeper who lived above his combination bar and grocery store with his family: his wife, Kate Schamberger, and their two children, George Herman and his younger sister, Mary Margaret or "Mamie." With his parents working up to twenty hours a day in the saloon, George Junior lived on the streets, a foul-mouthed truant who was pilfering whiskey and chewing tobacco as a child. Frequent and vicious beatings by his drunken father failed to tame him. When he was only seven years old, his Lutheran parents had a justice of the peace declare him "incorrigible" and commit him to St. Mary's Industrial School for Boys, a grim gated enclosure that looked like a penitentiary. "Against his will, young Ruth had found a refuge from the kind of neglect that could have killed him," writes one of his biographers.

Run by the Xaverian Brothers, a lay branch of the Jesuit order, St. Mary's was a reform school for orphans, delinquents, and boys from broken homes. Years later, Ruth would look back on his twelve years there as a liberating experience. He became a practicing Catholic, learned a trade—shirtmaking and tailoring—and was encouraged to play baseball by the school's director of discipline, Brother Matthias, a six-foot-six bear of a man who became his surrogate father, "the greatest man I've ever known," said Ruth. By 1914, he was a rawboned six-foot-two, 150-pound pitcher and catcher on the school's best team (it had forty-four of them), a fearsome hitter who was also undefeated on the mound.

His parents never saw him play. His mother came to visit him once a month until her death in 1912; his father didn't come at all. During his last two years at St. Mary's, Ruth received no visitors until the early winter of 1914, when Jack Dunn, owner of the Baltimore Orioles, showed up in the schoolyard one afternoon with Brother Matthias. Dunn had a contract in hand, offering Ruth $600 a year to join the team. That was "my first knowledge," Ruth said later, "that I was going to be a professional ballplayer instead of a tailor."

Years later, in his talks to children, Ruth would offer his personal history as evidence that "whether you're homeless or homely or friendless . . . the chance is still there. I know." Never mentioned was his unequaled talent. Paul Gallico called Ruth, with his innocent belief in progress, "the messiah of the under-privileged and wretched young."

Ruth sold newspapers, just as the newspapers sold him. When he first arrived in New York Joseph Patterson had recognized him at once as a "circulation builder." And he saw Hunt, a storyteller who loved golf and fishing, as a perfect sidekick for Ruth. "I would . . . take him fishing, hunting, anything. . . . So the Babe became sort of a *Daily News* man. . . . We covered him twelve months of the year." When the team moved its training camp from Louisiana to St. Petersburg, Florida, in 1925, Ruth and his newspaper shadow would "sneak away at night. . . . I was a born fisherman. So was he," Hunt remembers. "I had a boat tied up four or five miles from the hotel. We'd hang a lantern and fish until midnight."

They got along wonderfully. "I never had a cross word with the Big Ba-boon. He was no intellectual . . . but he . . . liked people . . . and was an agree-able guy," recalls Hunt. He was polite in social company although he could never remember anyone's name, even those of his teammates. To Ruth, ev-eryone under thirty-five was "kid," everyone older was "Doc." His teammates called him Jidge, a contraction of George, or "Bam" or "Big Fellow," but never Babe, the nickname given to him by his Baltimore Orioles teammates—one of Jack Dunn's *"babes."*

Assigned to cover Ruth, beginning in 1923, Hunt followed him year-round for nearly the remainder of the decade, a new practice for baseball reporters. He covered his off-season barnstorming tours, his vaudeville gigs, his work-outs, his trips to hospitals to visit sick children, and his storm-tossed marital life. And though he never reported it, he followed him into gambling dens and whorehouses as well. Marshall Hunt was bound by a code of silence, a code of his own creation. If a scandal arose, he called the editor of the *Daily News* and asked that another reporter be sent to cover it.

The Comeback

In the winter of 1927, Marshall Hunt was with the Babe in Hollywood, where Ruth was making a movie and getting in shape for the upcoming season. Ruth was on the comeback trail, still trying to rebuild his reputation and career, which were nearly ruined during the 1925 season. That year the Yanks finished in seventh place, thirty games behind the Washington Senators. "I ... [was] the big bust of 1925," Ruth conceded.

The batting champion in 1924, Ruth's average caved to .290 the next year, with a mere 25 home runs; and suspensions and bad health brought on by his gargantuan appetite for food and fortified drink kept him out of the lineup for over a third of the season. "I was young and healthy and saw no reason why I could not play both day and night." It was more than that, however. His marriage was disintegrating and his wife, Helen, was hospitalized with a nervous breakdown, brought on by his relationship with a full-time mistress.

Claire Merritt Hodgson, a young Georgia-born widow with a baby daughter, was a professional model and part-time actress. The affair had begun in 1923 and Ruth conducted it so openly—parking his fire-engine-red Packard roadster in front of Claire's apartment overnight—that even his most diligent protectors in the press corps found it impossible to conceal. Then there were his health problems. Coming north from spring training, Ruth collapsed at a railroad station and was hospitalized with what reporters called "the bellyache heard round the world," an intestinal abscess brought on by excessive eating and drinking. On June 1, Ruth returned to the team after surgery, "gaunt and wobbly-legged," with a long scar across his abdomen. When he recovered, he returned to his old ways, out on the town nearly every night, in restaurants, bars, and houses of ill repute. It got so bad that manager Miller Huggins hired a private detective to trail him when the team was on the road. In Chicago, Ruth was seen with six different women on the same night.

The axe fell in St. Louis, the team's next stop. After twice ignoring Huggins's 1 A.M. curfew, Ruth arrived late for the opening game with the Browns. Huggins told him not to bother to put on his uniform. He was suspended and fined $5,000, the highest fine imposed on a baseball player up to that time. Ruth called it "a joke," but Huggins stood firm.

When Ruth returned to New York he found reporters and photographers from the *Daily News* camped outside Claire Hodgson's apartment on West Seventy-ninth Street. Joseph Patterson had lifted the protection the paper had been providing him. Pictures of Claire and Helen appeared on the same page of the *News*. After visiting his bedridden wife at their apartment, allowing photographers to photograph them together, in tears, he took a cab to Ruppert's office to plead his case and have the suspension lifted. Ruppert got along splendidly with his players, but Ruth found him coldly unsympathetic; the decision to reinstate rested entirely with Huggins, said the Colonel. After apologizing to Huggins and the team, Ruth was back in the lineup nine days later; but he had fallen "from king to jester," said *Sporting News*.

Many of his fans believed that Ruth, at age thirty, was washed up as a player. He needed to change, and he did. His comeback was one of the greatest in sports history.

It began in December in a gym on the corner of Madison Avenue and East Forty-second Street. Ruth weighed over 250 pounds and "was as near to being a total loss as anyone I have ever had under my care," said the gym's owner and presiding presence, Arthur A. McGovern, a former flyweight boxer from Hell's Kitchen. McGovern put Ruth on a strict exercise and nutrition program. Within months he was in the best shape of his life.

Ruth also began to live his life more discreetly, if not more responsibly. The raucous hotel parties gave way to quiet dinners in the back rooms of speakeasies. "Sporting girls," as Babe called his playmates, were often there, but were handpicked by the owners and paid to keep quiet.

Claire Merritt Hodgson, however, changed him in fundamental ways. She shared her apartment on West Seventy-ninth Street with her daughter, Julia, her mother, and two brothers, and Ruth became warmly attached to the entire family, virtually living with them in the years before he and Claire were married in April 1929, three months after Helen was fatally burned in a house fire in Watertown, Massachusetts, where she had been living with a local dentist. Marshall Hunt considered Claire "a gold digger" and a home breaker. "I was not breaking up a home," she would later defend her honor. "It was broken." First as Ruth's mistress, then as his wife, Claire kept an ever-tightening rein on his social life and helped Christy Walsh, his business agent, bring his finances into order. She kept him away from the racetracks and even managed to improve his grammar and table manners. "Christy Walsh and I talked the Babe into making as certain as possible that the disaster of 1925 was not repeated," Claire said later.

Next to Claire and his illegitimate daughter, Dorothy—four years old in 1925—Christy Walsh was the most important person in Ruth's adult life.*

---

* Dorothy Ruth Pirone did not learn the identity of her birth mother until she was fifty-nine years old. For most of her life she had been led to believe her mother was Helen Ruth. Only in 1980 did she learn that her birth mother was Juanita Jennings, her father's mistress, whom Dorothy had known all her life as a close family friend. When Ruth married Claire

They had been together since the spring of 1921, when twenty-nine-year-old Walsh, a former sports page cartoonist in Los Angeles, arrived in New York with the idea of forming a syndicate of sports reporters to ghostwrite stories for famous athletes. A self-described "happy hustler," Walsh could not believe that Ruth, "a gift from the gods of exploitation," was "on the loose," unsigned by any big syndicate.

Walsh "camped" on the doorstep of the Ansonia for days, a contract in his pocket, but Ruth eluded him by sneaking in through the janitor's entrance. One evening, Walsh happened to be talking to a neighborhood beer dealer when Ruth called in and ordered a case. The delivery boys were gone for the day, so Walsh offered to take the beer to Ruth. Ten minutes later he was in Ruth's kitchenette, "counting bottles with the Babe." They got along instantly and Walsh signed him to a contract the next day, guaranteeing him $1,000 for every newspaper article published under his name.

Walsh placed Ruth's articles in Hearst's New York papers, the *American* and the *Journal.* Sportswriter Bill Slocum, "the Number One man of all the homerun ghosters," in Walsh's description, wrote most of them. Sometimes Slocum would stay overnight in Ruth's guest room and drink beer with him into the early hours. The next morning he'd write his ghosted stories at Ruth's breakfast table. "He writes more like I do," Ruth said, "than anyone I know"— which has to be one of the Babe's most priceless literary orchids.

By the mid-1920s, Christy Walsh had built a syndicate of thirty-four newspaper writers, among them Hype Igoe, Damon Runyon (briefly), Runyon's Colorado friend Gene Fowler, and Ford Frick, one of Babe's ghostwriters and later commissioner of baseball in the 1950s and early 1960s. Under contract were dozens of athletes, coaches, and trainers, including Lou Gehrig, John McGraw, Dizzy Dean, Rogers Hornsby, Ty Cobb, Walter Johnson, and Miller Huggins; and outside baseball, Alonzo Stagg, Bill Tilden, and Knute Rockne. Walsh estimated that his syndicate's total output for sixteen seasons would have covered over 5,600 solid newspaper pages, nice work for "a green punk from the west coast who in the beginning didn't know a syndicate from a night club," he boasted in his privately printed memoir.

In Ruth's first year with Walsh his newspaper earnings jumped from $500 to $15,000. Publishing articles containing statements falsely attributed to the supposed author was "deceitful," Walsh later admitted. It turned respected reporters into merchandisers and propagandists. But only one writer that Walsh

---

in 1929 he adopted her daughter, Julia, who was twelve years old at the time. She remembers him as a "loving father" and later devoted much of her life to his memory. (NYT, May 20, 1989; *Nashua Telegram,* June 6, 2010.)

recruited—the universally respected columnist W. O. McGeehan—refused to join his syndicate.

In late 1925, with his career unraveling, Ruth depended on Walsh for more than an occasional check. That winter, he entrusted his finances and all his business dealings to him, making Walsh America's first full-time sports agent. It was a prudent decision. The California flimflam artist had a doglike devotion to Ruth and handled his off-the-field transactions shrewdly and prudently, investing his earnings in untouchable annuities that would guarantee him a comfortable retirement. He had a free hand because his famous client was uninterested in his investment portfolio. On one occasion Walsh tried to get Ruth excited about what appeared to be a sure deal. "It means at least $100,000," he pleaded. The Babe cut him off: "Talk to Claire . . . *The Lone Ranger* is on."

"Hard as nails and . . . in wonderful condition," Ruth recovered splendidly in the 1926 season. He focused almost entirely on baseball and mended his relationships with teammates and Miller Huggins. The Yankees won the pennant by three games and Ruth hit .372, with 47 home runs and 153 RBIs. His stirring performance inspired the popular song "Along Came Ruth," written by Christy Walsh with music by Irving Berlin: "He's the King of Swat/He's the big shot/The idol of the day."

The idol of the day made the final out of the seventh and deciding game of the World Series with the underdog St. Louis Cardinals. With hard-drinking forty-year-old Grover Cleveland Alexander pitching flawlessly in relief into the ninth inning, after shutting down the Yankees in the previous game, Ruth worked the count and drew a walk with two outs and the Yanks down 3–2. Up to this point he had been the outstanding player of the game, making a sensational diving catch on the warning track and hitting his fourth home run of the series. With Yankee slugger Bob Meusel at the plate, Ruth took off on the first pitch and was gunned down by a perfect throw from catcher Bob O'Farrell. It was a close play, with the Rogers Hornsby, "The Rajah," applying the tag as Ruth executed a hook slide into second base.

The previous year, he would have been singled out as the goat of the game, but this was the remade Ruth, the darling once more of New York sportswriters. Even Miller Huggins sprang to his defense. "We needed an unexpected move. Had Ruth made the steal, it would have been declared the smartest piece of baseball in the history of World Series play."

Ruth had a great season, but felt his comeback was incomplete. The Yankees had fallen one game short of a world championship, and his home run total had fallen far short of his expectations. Yet he had done well enough, he thought, to merit a sizable raise; and he counted on Marshall Hunt to help him get it.

While he and Hunt were in Hollywood together in the early winter of 1927, with Ruth making a movie called *Babe Comes Home*, Hunt wrote an exclusive *Daily News* series on the "new Bambino": sharply focused and in peak condition at 218 pounds, almost forty pounds lighter than at the end of the disastrous 1925 season. "He plays tennis, fishes, hunts, swims, and does other sports. There is a clause in the movie contract stipulating the establishment of a gymnasium and handball court for Babe." And he had brought Artie McGovern with him to Hollywood to supervise his workouts, and to make sure, said Hunt incredulously, that he was in bed by nine. But the "'Sultan of Swat,' . . . [is] telling the world he'll never, never renew his allegiance to the Yankees at the terms offered by Col. Ruppert—a mere $52,000 a year," wrote Hunt. The Babe would sign for nothing less than $100,000. Would he retire if he were offered less? Hunt, disingenuously, hinted that he might. A grateful Ruth rewarded him with a job as a technical advisor on his film.

In late February Ruth headed back to New York to meet with Ruppert, who personally conducted the contract negotiations with his players. When Ruth arrived at Grand Central he was met by reporters and photographers. He pushed through them, jumped into a black limousine, and headed to Ruppert's private office in his brewery building on Ninety-first Street and Third Avenue, confident that "Uncle Jake" would meet his terms. But Jacob Ruppert was not one to succumb to ultimatums.

Ruppert was sixty years old in 1927, a lifelong bachelor who was born and brought up in Yorkville, a Manhattan neighborhood "as Teutonic as the Black Forest." Though both he and his parents were native New Yorkers, he spoke, when excited or angered, in a heavy German accent.

He began his adult life working for fifteen cents an hour in his father's Yorkville brewery, washing kegs and carrying one-hundred-pound sacks of barley. He was given more responsibility and at twenty-nine was handed the reins of the company. In succeeding years he served four consecutive terms in the House of Representatives, a solid Tammany man in an overwhelmingly Republican district. With the passage of the Volstead Act, he turned his Upper East Side brewery into a profitable supplier of near beer and malt extract.

He was proud of the title "Colonel." As a young man, he had joined the Seventh Regiment of the New York National Guard, a "silk stocking" brigade, and at age twenty-two had become an aide-de-camp, with the rank of colonel, on the staff of Governor David B. Hill. He had interests, however, beyond beer and baseball, politics and military affairs. He collected first editions and Chinese porcelains, bred trotting horses, sailed his yacht on Long Island Sound, and maintained a private zoo at his summer estate on the Hudson. One of the biggest real estate holders in New York City, he owned a number of Midtown skyscrapers.

As owner of the Yankees, he lived alone in a twelve-room townhouse on upper Fifth Avenue, and had a succession of stunning lovers. A fastidious dresser, he put pinstripes on the Yankee uniforms, partly to make Ruth look thinner, and insisted that his players have two sets of uniforms, one for home games, the other for away games, so they would always look sharp. He wanted the Yankees to be the class of baseball, proud, even arrogant; and he wanted them to become a dynasty. Re-signing Ruth in 1927 was his highest priority, but he would not bow to his dictated terms.

In a closed-door negotiations that lasted less than an hour, the greatest celebrity in baseball history emerged with a "record-setting" three-year deal paying him $70,000 a year, a salary only $5,000 less than that of President Coolidge. He remained the highest-paid player in baseball, and was making, in addition, over $150,000 a year from appearances in movies, postseason exhibition games, and vaudeville shows—and from ghostwritten articles and endorsements of commercial products. The total package was nearly as much as Ruppert had paid in 1914 for his share of the Yankee franchise. The only athlete who made more money was Jack Dempsey. "I'll earn every cent of my salary," Ruth told reporters gathered outside Ruppert's office on the day he signed his contact. "There'll be no more monkey business for me." Hours later he was on the night train to St. Petersburg to begin spring training.

In the privacy of his cabin, Ruth read reports in the *Daily News* of Jack Dempsey. There were rumors that the former champ, defeated the previous September in Philadelphia by Gene Tunney, a ruggedly handsome Marine Corps veteran from Greenwich Village, was considering a comeback. A gifted fighter—a boxer not a big puncher—Tunney had won by a unanimous decision, turning the man killer's face to pulp by short, sharp shots, and deftly fending off his bull-like charges. Humiliated by a fighter he had expected to destroy, Dempsey had announced his retirement and returned to his home in Los Angeles.

Ruth had seen all of Dempsey's big fights, knew him and liked him, and had visited him at his Los Angeles home a few weeks earlier, after finishing his Hollywood movie. The greatest athletic heroes of the 1920s, they were products of bleak beginnings whose fortunes became forever connected to New York in the same year: 1920. That was when Ruth signed with the Yankees and

Dempsey fought for the first time at the Garden, the arena in Madison Square that Tex Rickard had leased that same year.

Ruth was angry with Dempsey for retiring. He thought he owed himself, his fans, and friends "one more crack"; and he had told him this—pointedly, repeatedly—when they met in the living room of Dempsey's home. But Dempsey had been immovable. Ruth left before dark, still "glaring at me," Dempsey recalled, "in case I hadn't heard him loud and clear."

And now, on a train speeding south, Babe Ruth read that his friend, recently recovered from a monthlong battle with blood poisoning that required six surgeries, had gone to the mountains above Los Angeles to train. There was an offer on the table from Tex Rickard, a person more important to Dempsey's career than Christy Walsh was to the Babe's. Come back to New York, to Yankee Stadium, and fight another challenger, to be determined that spring. The winner would take on Tunney. Rickard was sure it would be Dempsey, and that the rematch with Tunney would be the most anticipated fight in the history of pugilism.

CHAPTER NINETEEN

TEX

Each boxing match is a story—a unique and highly con-
densed drama without words.

JOYCE CAROL OATES

The Babe and the Buster

Babe Ruth arrived in St. Petersburg on the morning of March 8, 1927, accompanied by Marshall Hunt. That afternoon he and Hunt went golfing and
the Babe smashed a drive 365 yards, a hundred yards farther than most tour
professionals were hitting the ball. He then went over to the Yankees' training
field and, dressed in a white sweater, casual slacks, and dress shoes, cracked
four balls out of the park. He was ready to play baseball.

That year the Philadelphia Athletics, managed by Connie Mack, were
heavily favored to unseat the Yankees as American League champions, but the
Yankees were also loaded, with strong pitching and hitting, and an emerging rival to Ruth, twenty-three-year-old Lou Gehrig, "Columbia Lou," a shy
working-class kid from upper Manhattan who had quit Columbia University
in 1923, after his sophomore year, to sign with the Yanks. He hit .313 with 16
home runs and 109 RBIs in 1926, and seemed marked for greatness.

The Yankees opened the season with a four-game sweep of the Athletics
and remained in first place from wire to wire. The only suspense was who
would hit more home runs, Ruth or Gehrig. As the team entered the last week
of April, Marshall Hunt began giving as much coverage to Gehrig as to Ruth.
By then the two were locked in a thrilling home run contest. Ruth had hit 59
in 1921, and that record suddenly seemed in jeopardy.

On June 13, the day of the Lindbergh parade, Gehrig hit his fourteenth
home run and Ruth cracked his twenty-first. By July 3, "The Babe and the

Buster," as Christy Walsh christened them, were tied with 26 home runs each. With the American League race virtually decided by then—the Yanks were in first place by eleven and a half games—all attention swung to what sportswriters were calling the Great American Home Run Handicap. For the first time ever, someone was challenging a healthy Bambino for long-ball dominance.

The Babe and the Buster could not have been more unalike, but that summer their destinies were entwined, and to gild the story, reporters made them out to be closer than they actually were.

Henry Louis Gehrig grew up in crippling poverty in a tenement in Washington Heights, the sole surviving child—three died in infancy—of German immigrant parents. A retiring, unconfident boy, large for his age, but chubby and soft, he was taunted and bullied by neighborhood toughs, who nicknamed him "Fat." At his mother's urging, he attended the High School of Commerce, on West Sixty-fifth Street, where he kept to himself, an awkward loner who "lacked the courage," he said later, to try out for the baseball team until his junior year. Months of rigorous training at a German sporting society hardened his body and lifted his confidence. The next year, sheer bone and muscle, he was the strongest hitter in the city's public school leagues.

After graduating in 1921, he entered Columbia University, where he had previously helped his mother, a cook for one of the fraternities. Good-looking, with wavy hair and shining blue eyes, he lived at home and never dated. "Handsome as he was, the campus flames simply couldn't afford to be seen with a boy who didn't even have decent clothes," wrote Paul Gallico, a Columbia graduate who would write a biography of Gehrig.

In the spring of 1923, his coach took him to Yankee Stadium to see Babe Ruth play. "When I saw the way he swung, watched the perfect rhythm and timing, I made up my mind that there was one man to pattern after." A few weeks later, Paul Krichell, a Yankee scout, watched Gehrig hit two home runs in three at-bats and reported back that he had "discovered the next Babe Ruth." Four days later Gehrig signed with the Yankees for $8,000. After playing sparingly, he was sent down to the minors until the final week of the season. In the first inning of his first start he hit his first big-league home run, driving in Ruth, who had hit a triple. No one marked it as a harbinger.

On June 2, 1925, in his first full season with the big club, he replaced first baseman Wally Pipp, who was having a miserable year. That season Gehrig hit .295, with 20 home runs. He would be a fixture at first base for nearly fourteen years, not missing a single start, a record for consecutive games played that would stand for fifty-six years.

Gehrig "hero-worshipped" Ruth as a player, but none of the Babe's "vulgar-ities and animal-like crudities rubbed off on [him]," said Fred Lieb. "Rarely did he use a cuss word in daily conversation. Nor did he attend the sex parties Ruth hosted in his hotel room when the Yanks were on the road." He didn't smoke or drink, and his idea of a good time was an early morning fishing trip on the Harlem River with his father, a janitor. He remained modest and self-effacing; he made $26,000 in 1927 and considered himself satisfyingly compensated. "If Ruth wins the home run contest," wrote Paul Gallico, "it will come as a great blow to the pure."

Ruth understood Gehrig and watched him grow into his greatness without a hint of jealousy. "More power to him," he told a reporter. "It helps me to have a tough hitter coming up right after me." They roomed together on the road during the 1927 season, and Ruth taught Gehrig to play bridge, put him in touch with Christy Walsh, who signed him to his escalating roster of ghosted clients, and regularly dropped by the Gehrig residence near Columbia University for some of Lou's mother's old-country cooking. Marshall Hunt called them a "brother act," and Christy Walsh staged hundreds of photo ops of the two relaxing together, but Ruth was close with none of his teammates. "The Babe liked Lou, insofar as he was capable of loving anyone," said Gallico.

Jack and Tex

Babe Ruth, a national sensation, was never as popular as Jack Dempsey was in 1927, the year of the ex-champ's comeback. That June, just as the home run race between the Babe and Buster began to burn up the news wires, public in-terest shifted to Dempsey's tremendously anticipated fight with Jack Sharkey, a hard hitting braggart from Boston, scheduled for July at Yankee Stadium. The winner would meet Gene Tunney in September at a site still to be decided.

Dempsey's return to the ring after the battering he took in Philadelphia was the most difficult decision of his life. Some of his doctors feared he would suffer permanent brain damage if he fought again. And at age thirty-one, Dempsey himself wondered if he was past his prime. Tex Rickard assured him he wasn't, that he simply had a bad night in Philadelphia. But it wasn't Tex's intervention that decided the issue, nor was it the money. It was Dempsey's thirst for revenge.

In the late winter of 1927, Dempsey had gone into training at a secluded spot in the Ventura Mountains, north of Los Angeles. He put himself though a grueling regimen and emerged tanned and fit, confident he had the legs and heart to regain his title. In early June, he had broken the suspense and returned to New York to sign with Rickard to meet Sharkey, a young and hungry fighter who had fought his way to Dempsey by winning an elimination contest staged by Rickard in the spring of 1927. At the signing, Rickard predicted a gate in excess of a million dollars, unprecedented for a nonchampionship fight, and announced that Dempsey would begin training that week at his old camp near Saratoga Springs. So the two men who had transformed boxing as thoroughly as Babe Ruth had transformed baseball were partners once more—the world's greatest boxing promoter and its greatest ring attraction. Together—and with Ruth—they would create modern mass spectator sport.

Professional boxing in New York State had been dead in 1919, and Rickard and Dempsey revived it, turning it into a multimillion-dollar business centered in Rickard's Madison Square Garden offices. They made heavyweight championship fights, battles once held before all-male crowds in Western mining towns, into urban spectacles, staged in big metropolitan arenas, with ringside seats reserved for the rich and the notable, male and female. "The one could scarcely survive without the other," *New York Times* reporter James Dawson described the partnership that gave boxing "a tone and affluence hitherto unknown." They had arrived at the precipice of success independently. Only when they met and combined did they become truly transformative.

"He began as a rough, tough nobody, a hard, mean, life battered hobo," wrote Paul Gallico. William Harrison Dempsey was born in a log cabin in Manassa, Colorado, on June 24, 1895, the ninth of eleven children of Hyrum Dempsey, an itinerant railroad worker and farmhand, and Mary Celia Smoot, a boardinghouse matron. "I am basically Irish," Dempsey noted in his autobiography, "with Cherokee blood from both parents." His parents had become Mormons not long after they arrived in the Western mountains, but while Celia, a tiny, deceptively tough woman, lived by the Book of Mormon till her last hour, her husband was a "Jack Mormon," drinking, smoking, and violating "most of the laws of the faith he believed in fundamentally." The boys in the family followed his lead, but without holding to the faith.

Hyrum moved his family across Colorado and Utah, from job to job, never able to adequately support them. William Harrison, called Harry by the family, dropped out of school in the eighth grade and left home at sixteen. For the next five years he lived the life of a nomad, riding "the rods"—the slender steel break beams underneath freight cars, only inches above the tracks—and sleeping in hobo jungles and whorehouses, every day a battle. He took any work that came his way: mining coal, washing dishes, digging ditches, punching cattle, and shining shoes. Whenever he hit bottom, he would stand on street corners in dismal mountain towns and beg for meal money. But soon he was earning enough to support himself as a saloon fighter, his only available escape from poverty and despair.

He fought under the name Kid Blackie in barrooms and mining camps, sometimes walking fifty miles to find a fight. He'd brazenly swing into a saloon and announce that he could lick "anybody in the house . . . for a buck." A skinny 130-pounder with a screechy, high-pitched voice, he seemed laughably beatable, but his wicked left hook put plenty of his larger challengers on the floor. Whenever he met his match, a barfly who could hit, he'd "run like hell," he admitted later.

By age nineteen he was a professional prizefighter with his own manager, Jack Price, a Salt Lake City pal, and a new name, "Jack" Dempsey," the name of his hero, "The Nonpareil," a retired Irish middleweight who won his first sixty-two fights. By the end of the next year Dempsey had defeated most of the toughest fighters in the mountain states, annihilating, not just defeating them, standing over them when they fell, and blasting them as they tried to rise.

For Dempsey, boxing was a meal ticket, not a sport; one played baseball; one didn't "play" boxing. And he never stepped into the ring without the utter ruin of his opponent as his aim. In June 1906, with no one left to fight, he and Price headed for New York City, where "the *real* fighters" were.

They shared a narrow upper berth on the train ride east, using their cardboard suitcases as pillows, and arrived at Penn Station with less than thirty dollars between them. No one had heard of Jack Dempsey, the "Salt Lake City Tiger," and it was hard to get fights. "I was skinny . . . had a broken nose, no clothes, and was scared stiff. I talked with a Western accent. . . . My grammar was brutal." Walking aimlessly through the city one evening, he reached Forty-second and Broadway and asked a stranger where he could find the Great White Way. The man burst out laughing.

The only sports reporter that took an interest in him was Damon Runyon, who knew Dempsey's boyhood friend, Gene Fowler of the *Denver Post*. Price got his 160-pound wonder some fights at Grubbs Gym, on 116th Street, but the purses were not big enough to support them. They slept in Central Park and showered in local gyms before finding a cheap room near the Polo Grounds. When Price got word his mother was dying, he returned to Salt Lake City. Dempsey soon followed him after being mauled by a much bigger fighter who broke three of his ribs. His plan to "conquer" New York had lasted exactly a month. "Only later did I realize that New York never wants you—it's you that wants New York."

Back in Salt Lake City, Dempsey married Maxine Cates, a dark-eyed seductress fifteen years older. She played the piano in a saloon on the non-Mormon side of town and did tricks on the side. When she wouldn't stop selling her flesh, Dempsey renewed his career as a peripatetic fighter, on the road constantly, seeing her only when he returned to Salt Lake City. They argued fiercely and frequently, and she soon left him, never to return. Dempsey was granted a divorce on grounds of desertion.

If he was to be a successful fighter, he realized, he would need a professional manager. In 1917, he signed with John "Doc" Kearns (formerly Philip Leo McKernan), an ex-welterweight boxer and Oakland, California, fight promoter. They met in a bar close to where Dempsey was fighting that week; Kearns started a brawl, and he and Dempsey cleaned out the place.

Kearns led a life "so fantastic," said a *Los Angeles Times* reporter, "that a Hollywood movie writer would blush if he had to put it down on paper. No one would believe it." The son of a Waterloo, Michigan, miner, he left home at age fourteen and went bust prospecting for gold in the frozen Klondike, where he ran into a gambler and saloonkeeper named Tex Rickard. At various times in his life, Kearns had been a boxer, a bartender, a whaler, a lumberjack, a baseball pitcher, a smuggler of illegal Chinese immigrants, and a salesman hawking cemetery lots. He was a friend of the novelist Jack London, who had given him the name Jack Kearns after one of his fictional characters.

A honey-tongued charmer, he and Dempsey became fast friends, although two men could not have been more different. Dempsey was shut-in, shabbily dressed, and scrupulously careful with his earnings. Kearns was a braggart, a perfumed dandy, and a spendthrift "whose ability to make money disappear . . . approximated genius." And while Dempsey was entirely trustworthy, Kearns was a liar and a cheat. "I've told so many lies . . . that sometimes I don't know myself when the lies end and truth begins," he once admitted. But "we trusted each other enough," said Dempsey, "to form the basis of a more or less stable relationship." Dempsey needed Kearns because he could get him good fights. Kearns needed Dempsey because he could "hit like a mule's kick."

Kearns convinced Dempsey to move to Oakland, luring him there with a free train ticket and a fresh five-dollar bill. He put him up in his mother's home and helped him perfect the left hook that became the most feared punch in existence. Dempsey became a local legend, scoring eleven first-round knockouts against top-shelf competition. This attracted promoter Tex Rickard, who, as we have seen, signed him to fight in Toledo in July 1919 against heavyweight champion Jess Willard. When the scowling challenger, weighing a lean 187 pounds, slaughtered the much larger—though out of shape—Willard in three rounds, fracturing his cheekbone and several of his ribs, it was the wider public's first glimpse of the ring style that would change American boxing—"swift, pitiless, always direct and percussive."

Rickard would have preferred to stage the Willard fight at the Polo Grounds, but boxing had been outlawed in New York state in 1917. The Battle of Toledo drew only nineteen thousand spectators in a makeshift wooden arena that seated eighty thousand. One of only a handful of Rickard's fights to lose money, it was, nonetheless, a bonanza for the cunning Texan. He had found a fighter who could make him millions.

After the fight, Rickard promoted the new champion as a model American, "modest, with boyish simplicity," a clean liver who "refuses to indulge in braggadocio." This was part of a calculated campaign to deflect attention from Dempsey's reputation as a draft dodger, a "slacker," in the language of the time, a legal charge brought against him by his vindictive ex-wife, who claimed he had falsified his draft records.* The next year, a federal jury exonerated Dempsey on the grounds that he was, as he claimed, the sole supporter of his mother and his seriously ill father, and had tried, without success, to join the Navy near the end of the war. But the charge stuck. "Our greatest fighter sidestepped our greatest fight," said *The New York Times*. Some super-patriots would not forgive Dempsey until April 1945, when, as a forty-nine-year-old U.S. Coast Guard commander, he landed the men he had trained on the invasion beaches of Okinawa.

The Battle of the Century

"What's most beautiful about boxing," writes novelist Colum McCann, "are the lives behind it." And Tex Rickard, a hustler with "Shylock on his shoulder," lived one of the fullest and most fascinating lives of the early century. He was a complex, even contradictory, man. A hayseed who didn't live in a city until he was forty, he arrived in New York, a battlefield of wits, and fashioned an organization composed of six hundred millionaires. But this quick-witted Westerner was, inexplicably, an easy mark for hucksters selling worthless inventions and stock in nonexistent companies. Never accused of being principled, he remained true to his word in two of the world's most larcenous professions: gambling and boxing promotion. A fighter didn't need a contract with Tex; a handshake was sufficient.

---

* Babe Ruth had avoided active duty during the war by joining the Massachusetts Home Guard.

George L. "Tex" Rickard was born in Wyandotte County, Kansas, on January 2, 1870, but grew up in north-central Texas cattle country, where he worked as a range hand and became, at age twenty-four, marshal of the local town of Henrietta, an easy job that allowed him to sneak away to play poker and drink whiskey. In 1894, he married the daughter of the town's doctor, and when both she and their infant son died within two months of the birth, he headed, in black despair, to Alaska. Gold was discovered in the Klondike, and after reaching the area by foot over perilous mountain passes, Rickard began making money from the prospectors, buying and selling mining claims and running a seedy saloon. He then headed to Nome, Alaska, a jumping-off place to the Klondike, where he became part owner of the Northern, the biggest, gaudiest gambling house in the North American Arctic. Rickard ran a "square house." Local miners trusted the tall, thin-lipped Texan with the steely-eyed stare and stowed their earnings in his massive steel safe. He made nearly half a million dollars in four years, but lost nearly all of it at his own gambling tables and in wild speculations.

After mining for diamonds in South Africa, he settled briefly in California, where he married Edith Mae Haig in 1902. The couple had a daughter, and, in 1905, hearing that gold had been struck in Nevada's alkali desert, Tex moved his family to the instant town of Goldfield, where he opened yet another Northern, this one with a sixty-foot-long mahogany bar. Within a year Rickard was one of the wealthiest men in Goldfield, and the town's biggest booster.

To put the town on the map, drawing more suckers to his saloon, Rickard promoted a world lightweight title fight in 1906 between "Battling" Nelson (Oscar Mathaeus Nielsen), the most popular white fighter in the country—a vicious, dirty brawler who was almost impossible to knock out—and Joe Gans of Baltimore, a consummately skilled fighter who was boxing's first African American champion. To draw such prominent fighters to this unpromising place Rickard raised a record purse of $30,000, stacking all of it, in glittering twenty-dollar gold pieces, in the window of the town's principal bank. It was the largest guaranteed purse in the history of boxing, and pictures of the columns of coins appeared in newspapers all over the country. Rickard announced that the fight would be filmed, and shown in theaters across the country.

It would be "The Battle of the Century," said the *Goldfield Daily Sun*. It would be more than that. Rickard sold it, obliquely, as a battle for racial superiority. Gans was a gentleman who mixed easily with whites; Nelson was a virulent racist who referred to blacks as "coons."

There had been a few mixed-race boxing matches before this, but never with fighters of this stature. Rickard took extraordinary measures to maintain order, posting three hundred armed private police at ringside, and barring liquor inside the arena. This was also for the benefit of women spectators. At that time, it was considered scandalous for respectable women to be seen at a boxing contest. "I will expel any woman who attends this prize fight from my flock," said a prominent Goldfield pastor. Rickard urged local women to openly defy the pastor, promising he could provide for their "protection and comfort." On Rickard's orders, local carpenters built screened-in boxes at the rim of his green pine amphitheater, far from ringside so that the three hundred gowned and veiled ladies in attendance wouldn't be offended by the violence and low language of the combatants. Gans won the fight on a Nelson foul—an intentional low blow—in the forty-second round before a crowd of more than eight thousand. The fight had lasted nearly three hours, and when the referee announced the disqualification the crowd cheered him. They also cheered Gans, booed Nelson, and filed out in an orderly manner. Tex Rickard, cardsharp and saloonkeeper, was America's new "fight king."

When the local gold boom collapsed, Rickard sold the Northern and moved on to Reno, where he promoted another "battle of the races": the now legendary 1910 fight between black heavyweight champion Jack Johnson and America's "Great White Hope," ex-champion James J. Jeffries. Johnson won by a knockout in the fifteenth round, an outcome that ignited race riots in Chicago and Savannah.

Rickard pocketed the proceeds of the Johnson-Jeffries fight and left with his family for Paraguay, where he set himself up as a beef baron on 350,000 acres of untamed land in the interior of the country. On the side, he ran a traveling circus. Five years later, after selling his herd of 35,000 cattle, he returned to the United States and the boxing business. His next big promotion was the Dempsey-Willard fight in 1919.

Dempsey defended his title twice the next year, knocking out Billy Miske in the third round at Benton Harbor, Michigan, and aging Bill Brennan in the twelfth round at Madison Square Garden. Brennan had fought gamely and was ahead on points when Dempsey put him away with a left to the chest. The *Times* called it "one of the most vicious and closely-contested fights in history," a fight that showed Dempsey to be vulnerable.

The Brennan battle was staged just after Senator Jimmy Walker piloted a bill through state legislature legalizing professional prizefighting in New York. That same year, Rickard and John Ringling, his new partner and financial backer, took out a ten-year lease, for $200,000 a year, on the old Madison Square Garden on Twenty-sixth Street, between Madison and Fourth Avenues. Ringling would continue to hold his circuses there, while Rickard set out to make it the epicenter of world boxing. As he told his wife, "the man who controlled the largest arena in the east would control the promotion of every great sporting spectacle to come."

The Garden's most recent mortgage holder, the New York Life Insurance Company, had allowed the Stanford White building to fall into disrepair, and it had been losing money since it was built. Rickard would be the first of its caretakers to make it pay. The Dempsey-Brennan fight, which drew a sell-out crowd of over sixteen thousand, was a promising start. The following year, after putting on an incredible one hundred boxing contests at the Garden, Rickard staged his first million-dollar fight—not in the Garden, however, but in a gigantic wooden bowl he built on a dreary mudflat in Jersey City, New Jersey. This is the spectacle that established him as a true master of ballyhoo, the Roxy of the boxing business.

"If you want to select an exact date when it was proven publicly that American sports had become big business, July 2, 1921, certainly makes sense," wrote Dempsey biographer Roger Kahn. That was the date of the Dempsey-Carpentier fight.

After defending his crown against two journeymen opponents, Dempsey needed a match with an exciting, popular challenger if Rickard was to deliver the big gate he had been promising him. The handsome Frenchman Georges Carpentier, a decorated World War I flier and the European heavyweight champion, fit the bill. It would be the first large-scale international heavyweight bout; and to heighten interest, Rickard worked behind the scenes to have Dempsey, whom he had cast as a giant killer against Willard, seen as the villain. It would be Slacker Jack against the War Hero.

Tex Rickard's master idea, the idea that made him the greatest boxing promoter of all time, was that each fight must be a story, a drama heightened by a blaze of publicity. "We got to dramatize this one for the newspaper boys," he told Dempsey and Kearns at a prefight meeting in his Madison Square Garden office. It would not just be the draft dodger against the war hero; it would be "the boxer" against the "brute."

"And to make this good, we're goin' to wrap this foreign invader in mystery." Carpentier was small for a heavyweight. Seeing him train, people would get the idea that the fight was going to be "one-sided," Tex sermonized. "So we're goin' to lock him up in a barn and have him do all his trainin' in secret under a heavy guard. 'Course, we'll let the newspaper boys take a peek at him once in a while, as a special favor.

"You fellers seen that million-dollar gate, yet?" he asked Dempsey and Kearns. They looked at him blank-eyed and confused, but would soon get the idea.

The match was an international sensation, one of the top stories in the world. London newspapers recruited former war correspondents to help their sports desks cover the fight, and Paris papers gave it more space than they had America's entrance into World War I. It was Rickard's biggest promotion thus far, and it stamped him "as one of the great showmen of all time," said *The New York Times.*

The fight would draw too big a crowd to fit in the Garden, and Republican governor Nathan L. Miller, who had defeated Al Smith in the Warren Harding sweep of 1920, prevented it from being staged anywhere else in the city. Miller viewed boxing as "a threat to good morals." If Rickard put on the fight at the Polo Grounds, then the largest outdoor stadium in the city, he would lead a full-out battle to repeal the Walker Law, he warned the promoter. So Rickard began working with Jersey City political boss Frank Hague, paying him, reportedly, $80,000 for his services. After touring several sites with Hague, Rickard agreed on Boyle's Thirty Acres, an empty marsh in Jersey City owned by Hague crony John F. Boyle. Trolley lines ran past the site, and it was a short walk from the Manhattan ferries, the Hudson Tube, and the terminals of three major railroads.

Dempsey would pocket $300,000, an amount roughly equal to what Charlie Chaplin received for a film. Carpentier's payout would be $200,000. By inking their contracts, the combatants transformed professional boxing, once considered so morally repugnant that fights had to be staged on river barges and in cattle stockades, into a lucrative capitalist enterprise. And Rickard had set a precedent. Beginning with this fight, championship boxers became the world's highest-paid athletes.

That spring Rickard began constructing a temporary arena seating ninety thousand spectators. A new man in the metropolis, he was pulling off a miracle. "It has remained for this man from Texas, Alaska, and Nevada," wrote the *New-York Tribune*, "to show the wiseacres of the world's greatest amusement center just how to make a successful study of crowd psychology—to figure out just what sort of an entertainment a man will travel half-way around the world to see, and then to go ahead and provide that entertainment on a scale of breath-taking lines of magnificence."

New York City was not the venue of the fight, but that's where the customers congregated. "[It is] the greatest crowd that has ever invaded New York for a sporting event," said the *Times*. "Army and navy football games of the past and world's series . . . dwindle into insignificance as attractions when compared with the Dempsey-Carpentier wrangle." An estimated thirty thousand out-of-towners, some of them from places as distant as China and South Africa, booked hotel rooms, and New York papers took special notice that many men brought their wives and daughters.

The fight drew a full house, and gate receipts reached $1.6 million, a new record. In the choice seats were members of the New York society crowd Rickard had been cultivating, drawn to this Jersey fen by the master promoter's support for a committee, headed by Anne Morgan, daughter of the capitalist corsair, to aid the war-torn regions of France. The previous December, Rickard had donated to Morgan's charity the profits from a lightweight championship bout at Madison Square Garden featuring Manhattan's Benny Leonard, the Jewish "ghetto wizard." Among the spectators were more women than had ever witnessed a boxing contest. This same crowd arrived in Hoboken in limousines, yachts, private rail cars, and chartered tugboats to root on their Gallic Galahad—slim, blond, and debonair—against the black-visaged Coloradan. "Gorgeous Georges," wrote Paul Gallico, "was the bait."

"I have never been in a great crowd that was more orderly, or that had less to complain of in the way of avoidable discomforts," said H. L. Mencken. Rickard hired hundreds of well-drilled ushers and special police to make sure that rowdies didn't rush down the aisles in groups, as was then common, and seize the seats of paying customers before they arrived. The cognoscenti were escorted to their numbered and reserved seats with the utmost decorum, as though they were at the opera, and were shielded from hecklers and hellions by a human wall of enforcers. Even the tickets had class; they were embossed and gold-backed, and looked like Treasury certificates.

It was a parade of notables. Joining Henry Ford, John D. Rockefeller, Jr., and three of President Theodore Roosevelt's children at ringside were delegations from New York's Fifth Avenue clans: Vanderbilts, Goulds, Harrimans, Whitneys, Baruchs, and Astors. Al Jolson headed up the Broadway contingent, which included David Belasco, George M. Cohan, and Colonel Jacob Ruppert. Rickard said that escorting Rockefeller to his seat was the "very greatest moment" of his life.

The U.S. Senate and the House of Representatives adjourned early that day, in time for over a hundred lawmakers to take special trains to Jersey City. "All the leaders of fashionable and theatrical society were on hand, most of them in checkerboard suits and smoking excellent cigars, or, if female, in new hats and pretty frocks," noted Mencken.

Just in front of Mencken sat Tex Rickard, alongside his partner, John Ringling, and within hailing distance of Frank Hague and his cohort in corruption, Atlantic City boss Enoch "Nucky" Johnson. High above them, on a specially constructed tower, cameramen prepared to film the bout for distribution to theaters. In Times Square, a crowd estimated at a hundred thousand gathered to receive bulletins transmitted from New Jersey. An announcer, speaking through three large amplifiers, would give a blow-by-blow account of the fight, and written bulletins were to be posted on the Times Building on three large boards. More than 300,000 Americans prepared to listen to the fight on the radio, over that special hookup David Sarnoff had installed.

Those arriving early caught the fifth of six preliminary bouts between Soldier Jones, a washed-up Canadian pug, and Greenwich Village's Gene Tunney. Tunney prevailed in the seventh round of a sloppy fight.

The writer George Bernard Shaw, hired by Hearst's *New York American* to cover the main bout, pronounced Carpentier "the most formidable boxer in the world," and predicted he would "knock Dempsey into the Hudson River." The Frenchman was a stylish fighter with a good right hand, but at 170 pounds, he wasn't a real heavyweight. When Tex Rickard "first cast a professional eye on Carpentier he saw not a great fighter [but] a business revolution," said sportswriter John Lardner.

Much of the crowd, buoyed by the buildup and Dempsey's lackluster performance against Brennan, cheered confidently as the clean-shaven Frenchman approached the ring to the sounds of "La Marseillaise." As the unshaven Dempsey disrobed, he heard thunderous cheers from deep in the stands—his working-class supporters—mingled with cries of "slacker" and "bum" from the front rows, which grew harsher when people saw the American flag sewn on the waistband of his white trunks. Several ringside spectators screamed that he was disgracing their country.

It was over in a flash. Dempsey went into his famous bobbing crouch and his "killer instinct was not satisfied," said James Dawson, "until he had battered Carpentier helpless with vicious short-arm body blows at short quarters and set up the knockout punch," a right hook that dropped Carpentier to the canvas with such violent force that his feet flew straight up into the air. Dempsey rushed over and helped his senseless and bleeding victim to his feet. From ringside, someone sent a cable to all French ships at sea: "Your Frog flattened in the fourth." Dempsey was more gracious. He leaned over the ropes and told reporters he was "sorry" he had to "knock out such a good man."

The next morning, *The New York Times* gave most of the paper's first thirteen pages to the fight. Mencken could have saved the *Times* some ink. "It was simply," he said, "a brief and hopeless struggle between a man full of romantic courage and one overwhelmingly superior in every way."

The Grecian Nose

In the five years leading up to the Carpentier bout, Dempsey had beaten every respectable heavyweight except Harry Wills, "the Brown Panther," a powerful but awkward African American fighter from New Orleans. Dempsey wanted to fight Wills. "Harry Wills . . . was made for me," he said later. "I could always lick those big slow guys." But Rickard was insistent. "We can't have a nigger heavyweight champion." With no other strong contender in sight, Dempsey stayed away from the ring for two years and became the most sought after commercial athlete in the world. He and Doc Kearns went on vaudeville tours; Dempsey sparred and Doc told colorful lies. And a Hollywood studio signed Dempsey to star in an embarrassingly bad serial called *Daredevil Jack*.

All the while Tex Rickard stayed back in New York and fought the biggest battle of his life. In January 21, 1922, he was arrested for having "immoral relations" with seven underage girls. They swam regularly in the enormous public pool—the largest in the world—he had built in Madison Square Garden in 1921, and he was accused of inducing one of them, a fifteen-year-old, to perform sexual acts "too vulgar to detail," said *The New York Times*. The court considered the charges serious enough to have Rickard incarcerated in the Tombs while awaiting trial. In court, eight days after his arrest, Rickard's lawyer exposed the questionable character of his oldest accusers—one of them an admitted thief and check forger. The jury, deliberating for only an hour and a half, acquitted the fifty-year-old promoter of all charges. The courtroom, filled with Rickard's loyal supporters, erupted in cheers, but as one of his attorneys told the Texan before the verdict: "You may get acquitted of the charge of child abuse, but you can never really be exonerated. Patches of doubt always remain. Your reputation is permanently stained." Rickard's biographers give no credence to the sexual charges, but he was known to be attracted to very young women.

In 1923, while Rickard struggled to recover from this ugly scandal, a rusty Jack Dempsey defeated Tommy Gibbons, a skillful defensive fighter, in a closely contested fifteen-round decision staged in Shelby, Montana. Dempsey considered Gibbons his toughest opponent since Willard. It prepared him for his meeting with Luis Firpo two months later. For this memorable fight in mid-September 1923 Rickard reversed himself, casting Dempsey as the hero, the hundred-percent American battling to keep the heavyweight crown in the homeland against the foreigner. In promoting the fight, Rickard, as was his custom, paid for the cooperation of reporters whose identities have never been revealed. "The big New York City boxing writers came to Rickard's office once a week, usually on a Friday, and I gave them their ice—seventy-five dollars," recalls Dick Fuchs, Rickard's payoff man. "They took the money and they wrote what we told them to write. Rickard always said, 'Buy me the writers. Pay them whatever it takes. I'll get my money back at the gate.'" Rickard considered this "sugaring" of sportswriters "advertising," and paid up to $25,000 a fight for the publicity, shrugging it off as a routine business expense. One reporter called the "ungodly union" of promoters and press men "the rottenest condition in American journalism."

After the Firpo bout, Rickard advised Dempsey to fight more sparingly. Rickard needed time, he said, "to prepare for another ballyhoo buildup." So Dempsey went into temporary retirement. Universal Studios signed him to a long-term film contract for $1 million, work that kept him in Los Angeles. New York remained his "shining city," but the big money—the "non-fight money"—was in Hollywood.

Dempsey was no actor. "When I started I was really bad and I never got any better." Yet this man with "the will to do hurt," as the writer Joyce Carol Oates described Dempsey, liked the soft life in Hollywood. Estelle Taylor, the actress he married in 1925, put him "into another world," a world that changed him fundamentally. He began to spend money lavishly and had his battered snout rearranged by a plastic surgeon. A new Grecian nose, slicked-back hair, and plucked eyebrows "[have] transformed . . . one of our foremost demonstrators of modified murder" into a "somewhat sheepish and harmless-looking young man," wrote the *Herald*'s W. O. McGeehan, one of Dempsey's harshest critics. "The 'movies' seem to have softened our champion where Mr. Gibbons and Senor Luis Angel Firpo failed."

When Dempsey wasn't in Los Angeles he was usually in New York, signing up for a vaudeville tour, meeting with advertising executives eager to recruit him, or hanging out with old friends. "I found New York in the twenties the greatest place on earth," he wrote later. "Jimmy Walker was the mayor, and he resembled a burning stick of dynamite." With Walker and his other late night companions—Ring Lardner, Claudette Colbert, Mark Hellinger, and Fred Astaire—he dropped in at El Morocco, the Silver Slipper, and one or another of Texas Guinan's clubs. His favorite spot, though, was Billy LaHiff's Tavern on West Forty-eighth Street, a raucous British-style tavern popularized by Runyon and Walter Winchell.

Winchell, Hellinger, and other gossip columnists covered Dempsey's every move—he was never out of the public eye—but by 1926, the beginning of the third year of his boxing hiatus, his fans had begun to complain about his inactivity, and he had lost the loyal support of dozens of sportswriters. "We stepped into one of the largest Broadway motion picture houses," wrote Grantland Rice, "where a moment later Jack Dempsey was shown in a newsreel. There was first dead silence—followed a second later by a salvo of hisses. . . . [Dempsey] now ranks with Jack Johnson as being the most unpopular of heavyweight champions."

Compounding Dempsey's problems was his deteriorating relationship with Doc Kearns. Estelle considered Kearns vulgar and unscrupulous and insisted that her husband find a new manager. It was not a hard sell. Dempsey had long suspected that Kearns had been taking a larger cut of his purses than he was owed. When Dempsey ended the partnership in 1925, Kearns began pummeling him with lawsuits. Dempsey became anxious and irritable, angry with himself for allowing Kearns to cheat him. At this point, Dempsey phoned Rickard to say he was ready to reenter the ring. The promoter urged him to come east and meet him in his offices in the new Madison Square Garden, just completed that year. He had an idea.

The House That Tex Built

The new Garden was a testimony to Rickard's tenacity. The very year he took over the old Garden he had begun laying plans for its replacement, a larger and more modern building, closer to New York's amusement center, which had gravitated to Midtown, an area, Rickard believed, "worthy of the big business that boxing had become." It was a move he had to make. His lease with the New York Life Insurance Company expired in 1925, at which point the company planned to tear down the Garden and erect an office tower, which it eventually did. But building a new Garden would require more money than Rickard had or his partner, John Ringling, was prepared to risk. To cover the cost of purchasing the land and constructing the arena, a total of $5.6 million, Rickard assembled a syndicate of Manhattan financiers, among them Walter Chrysler. The syndicate paid for 90 percent of the construction costs; Rickard raised his share by selling stock in an organization he named the Madison Square Garden Club. Its members—six hundred of them said to be millionaires—enjoyed exclusive seating privileges. Ringling was chairman of the corporation that ran the building, and Rickard was its president and de facto managing director, at a salary of $30,000 a year. Like Roxy, Rickard would not own the great structure associated with his name.

Construction commenced in 1924 at a site on Eighth Avenue, between Forty-ninth and Fiftieth Streets, one block west of Broadway. "When the new Garden was under construction, Rickard was like a child with a new toy," recalled the *Times*'s James Dawson. Wearing his soft, snap-brim Stetson and puffing a long Perfecto, he was at the construction site every morning, "stumbling around the mass of planks, pipes, steel, brick and mortar, stargazing there in the vast, gaunt, naked structure, impeding the progress of the skilled workers." As his dream project took form, "a palace for sports like the world's never known," he would take guests on inspection tours, pointing his gold-headed

Malacca cane toward some new building improvement. "This is something new, it's terrazzo," he would say. Tex didn't know terrazzo from gabardine, but he believed in miracles because he had seen them happen. "I've never wanted to do anythin' more in my life," he told his wife, Edith Mae, who died the year the Garden was completed.

Designed by Thomas W. Lamb, architect of some of Broadway's most opulent movie palaces, Rickard's Garden opened on November 28, 1925. It was a strickly utilitarian structure with a capacity of 18,500 for fights, but the first event was a six-day bicycle race. The races would be one of the arena's popular attractions, along with hockey, circuses, mass meetings, dog shows, rodeos, track meets, car shows, radio exhibits, and beginning in 1927—the year Rickard took over the champion New York Celtics of the recently formed American Basketball League—professional basketball. (College basketball would come later.) "If New York has a heart," said a local writer, "it might be the Garden. Almost everyone goes there, for one purpose or another." Standing on the corner of Forty-ninth Street and Eighth Avenue after the Garden was completed, Rickard told a reporter. "That is my monument. That is the biggest thing in my life."

Rickard's mission as manager of the new Garden was, predictably, "the improvement of the customer." Paul Gallico remembers him standing in the Garden's lobby before one of his Friday night fight cards, an erect man with alert eyes and an impish smile, watching the crowds pour in, some of the women dressed in ermine, hanging on the arms of escorts in dinner jackets. Jimmy Walker, a stockholder in the new Garden, made his entrance a little before ten o'clock almost every Friday, just as ring announcer Joe Humphreys began announcing the main event. A squad of policemen led him down the aisle.

Walker had been a regular at the old Garden. It was the new Garden that really brought in the new crowd. It began with the gala formal opening on December 15, 1925. "Society Out in Full Force," read the headline in next morning's *Times*. Seventeen thousand spectators, including "many society matrons of this city and Canada," gathered to watch the first professional hockcy game played on New York City ice. It was the Montreal Canadiens against the New York Americans, the expansion club—the former Hamilton Tigers—lured to Manhattan by a group of businessmen headed by bootlegger Big Bill Dwyer, arrested two weeks before the event by federal Prohibition agents.*

Rickard drew in polite society, as he had for the Carpentier fight, by pro-

---

* A month after Dwyer's early release from federal prison in August 1928, he was elected to the Board of Governors of the National Hockey League.

moting an athletic event as a charity affair. This one was for the benefit of the Neurological Institute Society of New York. Seated in special boxes decorated with colorful bunting were bejeweled women from the Astor, Warburg, Whitney, and Rothschild clans, some of them wearing galoshes over their opera slippers. It would be fantastic to suppose that even one of these grande dames set foot in the Garden for another hockey game, but they came—and in great numbers—for equestrian shows and flower exhibits. It was the "lovers of the game perched high in the galleries" that would make professional hockey "New York's newest pastime." In 1926, Rickard formed a team of his own, the red-white-and-blue-clad New York Rangers, or Tex's Rangers, as they were often called. Perennial winners, they competed with the "Amazin' Amerks," longtime losers, for the loyalty of fans in this, the largest arena in the National Hockey League.

The new Garden was on the edge of unruly Hell's Kitchen, and when "sluggers" wielding blackjacks and brass knuckles began rushing the turnstiles and seizing the reserved seats of late-arriving paying customers, Rickard hired hulking guards, equally armed, to cure the West Side boys of their "bad manners." In Rickard's reign the Garden became one of the most profitable and civilly run "sports organizations the world has ever known," said the editors of the boxing magazine *The Ring*. Making attendance at sporting events safe for women and their escorts made excellent financial sense. Two tickets were sold instead of one. By 1927, the Garden was clearing a profit of $1.4 million a year.

Rickard made his own private profits by entering into a sub rosa arrangement with ticket speculators, chief among them his old friend Mike Jacobs, "ruler of the Broadway ticket business." Jacobs, who ran a dingy ticket concession across the street from the Garden, would buy blocks of seats for a fight and hold them until Rickard's paid reporters pumped up the contest to the point where they could be sold for up to 500 percent over their original price. Rickard, who had an "easygoing approach to ethics," made his money by selling the speculators his own tickets at a premium above the box office price. He pocketed the profits; the Garden didn't receive a penny. Rickard covered his hide by donating a small portion of the Garden's profits to William Randolph Hearst's fund to purchase unadulterated milk for babies, prompting reporter Westbrook Pegler to comment, "The babies get the milk—but who gets the cream."

"He could be . . . almost ruthless in his manipulations," boxing writer Mel Heimer described Rickard, "but he also had a seemingly deserved reputation for directness and honesty." He was generous to former fighters, trainers, and corner men who had fallen upon bad times. Groups of these broken men waited for Tex outside his Garden office almost every afternoon. The tall, narrow-eyed promoter, dressed in a sharp three-piece suit, his shirt collar perfectly white and highly starched, would pull out a thick roll of bills and freely hand out fives and tens. He could afford to be generous. In transforming an ostracized sport into a lucrative industry he was amassing a personal fortune of well over $2 million, $1 million of it in cash. And what was "fascinating," said Jack Kofoed, one of the writers who covered him, is that he lacked the commanding trait of the true con artist: "He never caught the public imagination. He was too cold, too self-centered, for that."

In 1926 Tex Rickard was planning his biggest fight yet, a match between Dempsey and fast-rising Gene Tunney. It would be a fight that would draw too big a crowd for the Garden. Only the Yankee Stadium would do, he told Dempsey when the ring-rusty champ arrived back in New York from Los Angeles.

But the public wanted another fight: Dempsey against Harry Wills, and Wills's camp was pressing hard for it. At age thirty-three, their fighter was running out of time. Rickard, knew the fight would draw a million-dollar gate, but remained strongly opposed to it. Pressured, he lied to the press, claiming that powerful but unnamed Washington officials had warned him not to promote an interracial bout, that it would be bad for race relations. More likely, Rickard's own views on race figured in his decision. As an old fight professional remarked, "There was a lot of the hookworm belt [the racist South] in Tex."

It had to be Tunney, Rickard insisted, but the three-person New York State Athletic Commission, controlled by Democratic powerhouse James Farley and Tammany loyalist, John Brower, refused to issue Dempsey a license to fight in the state unless he was matched against Wills. It was a decision backed by Tammany and Mayor Walker. The Wigwam was eager to turn Harlem's African American Republican voters into steadfast Democrats.

The issue became more perplexing when Brower changed his mind, not wanting New York City to lose a fantastically lucrative Dempsey-Tunney fight. Farley remained firm, however, and issued a strongly worded minority report, which carried weight with the New York State License Commission, the body that had the final voice in these matters. In mid-August, the License Commission issued a decision: Dempsey had to fight Wills next, or he couldn't fight in New York state.

That week Rickard made a stunning announcement. He was taking the Dempsey-Tunney fight out of town. Philadelphia had just built an enormous concrete stadium on the south side of the city for the celebration of the Sesquicentennial, the 150th anniversary of the signing of the Declaration of Independence. The fight would take place there on the evening of September 23, 1926.

Tunney had been preparing for Dempsey since 1920, when he watched him defeat Billy Brennan at the Garden, studying his every move. Boxing experts, however, didn't give him a chance against the champion's crushing power. Rickard was undeterred. It would be, he told reporters, a battle for the ages. Secretly, he believed Tunney would be slugged into submission.

CHAPTER TWENTY

PURSUITS

Losing was the making of me.

JACK DEMPSEY

Tunney

The Fighting Marine, the first native-born New Yorker to contend for the heavyweight crown, should have been the pride of Manhattan. But New York fight fans outside Tunney's neighborhood had a hard time warming up to this son of the city. "The Greenwich Village Folly," critics called him.

He was born James Joseph Tunney on May 25, 1897, on the Hudson River side of Greenwich Village, one of seven children of Irish immigrants John Tunney, a longshoreman on the nearby Chelsea docks, and Mary Lydon, his sweetheart from a neighboring village in County Mayo. The youngest of his four sisters dubbed him Gene, unable, as a child, to pronounce Jim correctly.

As a rail-thin boy attending St. Veronica's School and later De LaSalle Academy in the Village, he was a superb all-around athlete, but turned almost exclusively to boxing in order to defend himself against the street thugs who ruled the waterfront area around his gloomy Perry Street tenement. Although a promising student—an avid reader of ancient history and a participant in theatrical productions—he dropped out of school at age fifteen to help support his family, taking a job as an eleven-dollar-a-week mail clerk at the Ocean Steamship Company.

At sixteen he began fighting professional boxers at local athletic clubs. He was six feet tall and only 135 pounds, but had diamond-hard discipline and nerves of steel—and he was fast, with his hands and on his feet. At home he followed a strenuous program of self-improvement, pushing himself from a wall, one finger at a time, for a hundred times a day to strengthen his chronically fragile hands.

In 1918, he joined the Marine Corps and was shipped to France, although
not to the front. Filled out and fit, blond, square-jawed, and good-looking,
he became the base heavyweight champion and went on to win the American Expeditionary Forces light heavyweight crown. After the war, his first
feature bout was his appearance on the undercard of the Dempsey-Carpentier
fight against overmatched Soldier Jones. In January 1922 he defeated Battling
Levinsky to win the light heavyweight championship of America, but was de-
throned later that year by Harry Greb, the "Pittsburgh Windmill," a fighter
"with the instinct of a jungle beast."

"Greb handled Tunney like a butcher hammering a Swiss steak," wrote
Grantland Rice. "By the third round Gene was literally wading in his own
blood." In a demonstration of stubborn courage, he was still standing at the
final bell, barely conscious after losing two quarts of blood. Tunney remained
in bed for a week with a fractured nose and deep cuts around his eyes, but
returned to the ring and put on weight. He defeated Greb twice in 1923 and
scored a technical knockout over Georges Carpentier the following year at the
Polo Grounds. In June 1925, he knocked out heavyweight Tommy Gibbons,
the fighter who had taken Dempsey the distance in Shelby, Montana. This put
him in the running for a shot at Dempsey's crown, a fight he was convinced
he could win. He would "thwart the murder in Dempsey's fists" with precision
punching and defense, pugilism's equivalent of the "small ball" strategy of New
York Giants manager John McGraw, the master of dead ball–era baseball. "A
good boxer," Tunney was convinced, "can always lick a good fighter."

Tunney had been studying the champion since his return from France. In
1920, he met him on a commercial ferryboat crossing the Hudson. During the
twenty-minute ride, Dempsey was friendly and forthcoming, showing a genuine interest in Tunney's career. Yet as they spoke, Tunney kept thinking: "one
day [I will] fight this man and beat him."

Tunney was ringside for all of Dempsey's title defenses in New York; and
he studied films of his other fights. He even hired a few of his former sparring partners. In the Carpentier and Firpo fights, Tunney discovered what he
believed to be Dempsey's fatal weakness: a wild right hand that often missed
badly, leaving him wide open for a straight right to the jaw. After Tunney's
preliminary bout with Soldier Jones, Grantland Rice asked him: "What are
your plans?"

"My plans are all Dempsey," Tunney replied.

Outwardly, he was fire and confidence, but there were moments when he
feared the "Man Killer" would "murder" him. "One night at the beginning of a
long training period, I awakened suddenly and felt my bed shaking," he unbur-
dened himself years later. "Ghosts or what? Then I understood. It was I who

was shaking, trembling so hard that I made the bed tremble. I was that much afraid . . . afraid of what the great Dempsey would do to me. . . . Right there, I had already lost the Dempsey fight before it was even fought. . . . What could I do about this terror?"

For one thing, he ceased reading the newspapers. This helped him to stop obsessing over the "Dempsey menace." He disciplined himself not even to think of losing. And he prayed. He got down on his knees every night and asked God "not that I might win. I just asked that I might not embarrass myself."

Just before the Dempsey fight, Tunney played a round of golf in Florida with Grantland Rice and Tommy Armour, the great Scottish American professional. On every hole he would hit his drive, toss the club to his caddie, and run down the fairway, throwing phantom punches and muttering, "Dempsey, Dempsey, Dempsey."

"In blind and stubborn defense of the Dempsey image," Paul Gallico wrote years later, "I took sides, picked up the wrong story, and missed out on the far more thrilling one that was being enacted under my nose. This was the stalking of Dempsey for six long years and the patient, painstaking preparation to defeat him."

Tunney was aloof, bookish, and pedantic, and this caused Gallico and other boxing writers to undervalue his ability and trivialize his record, which was undeniably strong: he had never been knocked off his feet and had beaten a string of solid fighters. One incident, in particular, set reporters against Tunney. At his training camp in East Stroudsburg, Pennsylvania, the challenger was spotted carrying around a copy of the *Rubáiyát* by Persian poet Omar Khayyám. When word reached one of Dempsey's camp followers, he hurried to Dempsey: "It's in the bag, Champ. [He's] up there reading a book!"

Tunney spoke to reporters formally and didactically, in stilted "phrases that might have been remembered out of some book," said the *New Yorker*'s Morris Markey. When pressed about his polysyllabic vocabulary and showy display of erudition, the challenger shot back, "I don't think you have to be illiterate to be a boxing champion," a remark that further alienated hard-shelled boxing aficionados like Gallico, Runyon, and Ring Lardner. We took "an almost perverse joy in hounding" this athlete whose cardinal sin was being "caught with a book in his hands," recalled Gallico.

In assailing Tunney, Gallico and his crowd failed to catch his resemblance to their own hobo hero. Tunney and Dempsey had risen in life by dedication and discipline, and a determination never to lose. Both had started out thin and vulnerable and had become formidable only through grueling practice and preparation. Tagged early in his career as a "feather duster" puncher, Tunney spent a winter in a lumber camp in Canada, working as a woodsman, chopping trees to strengthen his hands. What he lacked—and what Dempsey had—was "the killer instinct . . . I found no joy in knocking people unconscious or battering their faces," he said after his retirement from the ring. "The lust for battle and massacre was missing." "You will search pugilism and not find a champion with as little desire to kill, or even injure," said writer Walter Davenport, who titled his *New Yorker* piece on Tunney "Gene the Genteel."

This is misleading. Hard punching was part of his strategy. He would knock out forty-eight of sixty-five opponents in his career.

Although Dempsey had not defended his title in three years, he went into the Philadelphia fight a prohibitive three-to-one favorite. He was not, however, the people's choice. Neither was Tunney. Dempsey's long absence from the ring, and his avoidance of Harry Wills had damaged his reputation and cut deeply into his fan support. In this fight, Tunney was insignificant. Many of Dempsey's disgruntled followers would have pulled for anyone Tex put in the ring against him.

That sat well with Rickard. "Tex . . . found the bout the easiest to ballyhoo of any in his experience," recalled his new wife, Maxine Hodges, a twenty-three-year-old former showgirl he would marry two weeks after the Philadelphia fight. "They want to see the champ's head knocked," Tex told friends. "I guess I don't have to worry about this one."

The Fight

"An army bigger than all of Caesar's legions poured out of New York . . . bound for the Dempsey-Tunney fight," wrote *The New York Times.* On the day of the fight, passenger trains left Pennsylvania Station every half hour, carrying fifty thousand New Yorkers to Philadelphia; another 25,000 came by car. The official attendance was 120,757, but most likely it reached 130,000 with gate-crashers; an estimated two thousand of those with tickets were millionaires. Gate receipts were an unprecedented $1,895,733, Rickard's third million-dollar gate. Tunney collected $200,000, more than double Babe Ruth's salary for that year; Dempsey earned three-quarters of a million dollars.

When Tunney entered the ring, with the Marine Corps emblem emblazoned on the back of his robe, most of the crowd rose and cheered. Dempsey was greeted by "a roar of boos that rocked the entire amphitheatre." Then the skies opened up; the rain came in sheets and didn't stop until after the fight.

From the opening bell, Dempsey looked slow and ungainly against the back-pedaling Tunney, who thwarted his charges with whiplash counter-punches. Things went exactly as Tunney had planned in his prefight study of Dempsey's ring strategy. "I feinted Dempsey a couple of times, and then lashed out with the right-hand punch, the hardest blow I ever deliberately struck. . . . I hit him high on the cheek. He was shaken, dazed. His strength, speed, and accuracy were reduced. Thereafter it was a methodical matter of out-boxing him, foiling his rushes, piling up points, clipping him with repeated, damaging blows, correct sparring."

Tunney cut Dempsey to pieces, closing his left eye, opening deep gashes over his other eye, and bloodying his mouth and nose. In the tenth and final round the crowd began screaming for him to finish off the champion, reduced now almost to helplessness.

It was a unanimous decision, the first time ever that the world heavyweight crown changed hands on points. When the decision was announced, "a roar of satisfaction" spread from ringside to the most distant seats, "until the whole stadium was saluting the new champion," wrote Elmer Davis. Sitting in his corner, the nearly blinded Dempsey grabbed his trainer and said, "Lead me out there. I want to shake his hand."

"You were too good for me," Dempsey said, putting an arm around Tunney. Then, as Dempsey was led from the rain-soaked ring he heard cheers of support, a steady chant, rising in volume: "Champ, Champ!" The cheering, said one observer, was "deafening," a homage to Dempsey's unyielding resolve, the beaten warrior who refused to go down. He heard it until he reached his dressing room. Then he collapsed and cried.

When the former champion returned to his hotel suite, Estelle, who could not bear to see him fight, was waiting for him. "What happened?" she asked as she examined his battered face. "Honey, I forgot to duck." One of the newsmen in the room picked this up, and sent it out over the wire. That single comment was the beginning of Jack Dempsey's rapprochement with his public.

The Comeback

Dempsey in defeat was more popular than he had ever been, and New York sportswriters were strongly behind him as he prepared for his comeback fight with Jack Sharkey at Yankee Stadium on July 22, 1927. History was against him, however; no heavyweight champion had ever regained his title.

It was the biggest fight day in New York history. Eighty thousand paying customers, the largest crowd ever to see a prizefight in the city, packed Yankee Stadium, making it the only non-title fight ever to draw a million-dollar gate.

Sharkey predicted he'd knock out Dempsey, and he nearly did in the first round. He tore into him and staggered him twice. When the bell rang, Dempsey was barely able to make it back to his corner. "Here's your bum champion!" Sharkey shouted to the crowd. "How d'ya like him now?"

But Dempsey recovered in the sixth round, and in the seventh, he closed in and the two fighters became locked in a clinch. Struggling to free himself, Dempsey hit Sharkey with a succession of low, hard shots to the body. Sharkey dropped his arms, turned his head to the referee, and yelled, "He's hitting me low!" At that moment, Dempsey connected with a left hook to Sharkey's chin, and the challenger collapsed to the canvas and was counted out. "It was one of the last good punches of my life," Dempsey said years later. "It was everything I could throw." Dempsey left the ring to thunderous applause; now it was Tunney and sweet revenge.

Dempsey wanted Rickard to stage the rematch in New York. "Did you hear the way the New York people cheered me, Tex . . . this is my town." But when the New York Boxing Commission refused to budge on the $27.50 ceiling it had established for ringside seats, Rickard settled on Chicago, where he could get up to forty dollars for a ringside seat. And the Windy City had an outdoor stadium that could hold over one hundred thousand people. "It's economics Jack," Rickard told a disappointed Dempsey. It would be Soldier Field on September 22.

On July 24, two days after Dempsey knocked out Sharkey, Babe Ruth hit his thirty-first home run, putting him even with Gehrig. The two sluggers battled neck and neck into the first week of September, when they were tied at forty-four. Then, just as the great home run race reached its crescendo, it was over. The turning point was a doubleheader against the Red Sox at Fenway Park on September 7. Gehrig hit his forty-fifth, but Ruth put three into the seats. In the final twenty-two games, Gehrig would hit only two more, while Ruth went on an unprecedented tear.

On September 13, the Yankees clinched the pennant, Huggins's fifth in nine years, by taking a doubleheader from Cleveland, and the Big Bam hit his fifty-first and fifty-second. But with the Dempsey-Tunney rematch only nine days away, the Yankees and Babe Ruth became a backstory. As big as Ruth was, Dempsey was even bigger, and nothing excited the city like a heavyweight fight with Dempsey in one corner.

The Chicago Count

As early as mid-August, every newspaper editor in New York had reassigned its top sportswriters to Chicago to cover the buildup to the fight; history had shown that a Dempsey fight meant a 50 percent increase in readership. Earlier that year the business managers of New York newspapers had named Dempsey the century's "greatest stimulus to circulation."

"Dempsey descended on Chicago a short time ago and took the town by storm," wrote John Kieran in the last week of August. "Everywhere he went he was followed by admiring thousands. He blocked traffic when he appeared in the street." To avoid the crowds, Dempsey put Estelle in a downtown hotel and went into training at Lincoln Fields Race Track, forty miles south of the city. But his fans followed him there; on one weekend there were eight thousand paid spectators in his camp.

This being Chicago, the local papers were filled with reports about a fix. The city's hotel lobbies and speakeasies, as well as the training camps of both fighters, had "their quota of hard-looking men," gamblers and "slit-eyed [thugs] who wear their rods on hip or shoulder," wrote Gallico. Al Capone boasted to reporters he had bet $50,000 on Dempsey and hinted that the fix was in—that he would ensure that the referee was a Dempsey man. Hearing this, Dempsey sent Capone a handwritten note asking him to "lay off and let the fight go on in true sportsmanship." The next day Estelle received enough flowers to fill her entire hotel suite.

Rumors of a fix increased interest in the fight, and so did renewed charges that Tunney was a "would-be highbrow." This time the igniting factor was Tunney's ill-disguised distaste for the fight crowd, including many of his fellow boxers. Before beginning training, he had been spending time with the polo and golfing set from Greenwich, Connecticut, friends and family of the woman he was dating, Mary Josephine "Polly" Lauder, an heiress of the Andrew Carnegie fortune. Tunney's unofficial spokesperson, the reporter W. O. McGeehan, fanned the flames, saying he found nothing wrong with being "addicted" to books or preferring the company of "nice" people, "in preference to the manly and wholesome company of gamblers, gunmen, and gorillas."

Tunney's own public statements alienated hardened fight fans. He had come to Chicago, he told a gathering of his local supporters, for "a boxing match with Mr. Dempsey," not a "fight. . . . I am a boxing enthusiast, but I do not believe in fighting."

"There is greater interest around the globe in this fight than in any other sporting event in history," said *The New York Times*. The lobbies of the big hotels in the Loop were so jammed it was hard to gain entry. Special trains arrived hourly from all over the country; the 20th Century Limited reported that for the first time ever all its private cars had been placed in operation.

New York "daredevils" flew to Chicago by private plane from Roosevelt Field, where Lindbergh had left for Paris; and the travel agents Thomas Cook and Sons chartered thirty planes to accommodate its moneyed clientele. People arrived by ship and train from Madrid and Melbourne, Sydney, and Singapore. "A changed world has taken pugilism to its bosom," wrote *The Literary Digest*. " 'Big Business,' aided by the sedulous art of publicity, has boosted it to the dimensions of a stabilized and standardized industry."

It was the biggest fight crowd of all time, and the combatants would share the richest purse in the history of the sport. Gate receipts rose to $2.6 million on the eve of the fight, and ticket sales exceeded 100,000. Tunney's check for nearly a million dollars would be the largest ever collected for a single sporting event before the days of closed-circuit television. Dempsey's cut would be nearly half a million, the biggest purse ever awarded to a challenger.

Rickard's ticket headquarters at Chicago's Congress Hotel "was like the bonanza days in the rich mining camps," said Gallico. "In and out of the doors . . . wandered men with money in their fists . . . There was money crammed into safes, stuffed into desk drawers, laying around loose in wire baskets. . . . Plainclothesmen and coppers with guns and cartridge bandoliers worn outside stood guard at the doors and watched the never thinning crowd of thugs, politicians, fight managers, society men, plain and fancy whores, gang leaders, bootleggers, actors, newspapermen, bankers and brokers, mingling in the corridors waiting to get into the sacred chambers." They were there to see Rickard, to explain to him why it was imperative that they have the best seats available. In the midst of this chaos, the preternaturally calm Texan sat behind his desk, chewing a cigar and reminiscing about his first promotion, when Joe Gans and Battling Nelson fought in Goldfield, Nevada, for the then fabulous sum of $30,000.

"It [is] the spectacle of spectacle," James Harrison of *The New York Times* described Soldier Field the night of the fight, "the veil of darkness over it all; the rippling sea of humanity stretching out as far as the eye [can] see." In the hundred or so front-row seats were nine governors, a dozen mayors, over twenty Broadway stars, members of European royalty, congressmen and senators, capitalist titans Bernard Baruch, Charles M. Schwab, and Otto Kahn, and radio mogul David Sarnoff. But the very best seats were set aside for Chicago's own, Robert McCormick and Joseph Patterson, the most famous cousins in the country. Surveying the crowd at ringside, Tex Rickard turned to sportswriter Hype Igoe and supposedly said: "Kid, if the earth came up and the sky came down and wiped out my first ten rows it would be the end of everything.

Because I've got in those ten rows all the world's wealth, all the world's big men, all the world's brains and production talent." A Westerner to his very marrow, Rickard never aspired to be blueblood, but he yearned for the acceptance and patronage of polite society. This was his moment.

At ringside were nearly four hundred newspapermen, part of the 1,200 who had been issued press tickets, the largest number of reporters ever to attend an American athletic contest. At one corner of the ring sat Graham McNamee of NBC. Radio's outstanding announcer, he would describe the fight to fifty million American listeners, and millions more in the fifty-seven countries within range of Sarnoff's radio signal. Eight hundred miles to the east, great crowds gathered along Broadway, near the Times Building. Hundreds of them climbed into sightseeing buses equipped with radios, heeding the cries of barkers: "Hear the fight for fifty cents." Broadway's theaters and movie palaces were half empty, and at the 71st Regimental Armory, two boxers, one dressed in black trunks, like Dempsey, the other dressed in white trunks, like Tunney, prepared to re-enact the fight, blow by blow, as reports came in over the telegraph wire. In a poll taken of 122 prominent athletes, seventy picked Dempsey to win. Among them were Babe Ruth and Lou Gehrig. Somehow Arnold Rothstein was included in the poll, perhaps as a sportsman. "Tunney is a cinch," he said. "I bet on him last year and I'll bet on him this time."

From Paris, one of the stops on his whirlwind European tour, Mayor Walker sent word: "Dempsey will win."

He didn't care who won, Tex Rickard lied to reporters. A Dempsey defeat would, in truth, be calamitous for him. "There was never a bigger crowd magnet in any sport in the world than Dempsey," the *Daily News* caught Rickard's real feelings. "If he's licked, it will be many days before there is another. . . . Tunney will never be a greater card than Dempsey NO MATTER WHO HE LICKS."

On the morning of the fight, Dempsey had told reporters at his camp that he would "knock that big bookworm out inside of eight rounds."

The ex-champ, wrapped in a white robe, marched down the long aisle to the ring, greeted by thunderous applause. This was Soldier Field, a memorial to American fighting men who had died in past wars, but, unlike Philadelphia, there were no audible shouts of "slacker" or "draft dodger."

The cheers for Tunney were less enthusiastic. When he entered the ring, Dempsey went over to him and asked him how he was doing. "Quite well Jack, and you?" The gloves were then brought into the ring in boxes, tied with blue ribbon. At 10:07 the fighters were called to the center of the ring for their instructions. "In the event of a knockdown," said referee Dave Barry, a silver-haired ring veteran, "the man scoring the knockdown will go to the farthest neutral corner. . . . Unless the boy scoring it goes to the farthest neutral corner, I will not begin the count. . . . Do you understand, Jack? Do you understand Champ?" Both fighters nodded. Incredibly, it was the first time, Tunney said later, that anyone had called him champ.

From the opening bell, Tunney began scoring virtually at will. "He had me staggering and leaning against the ropes by the second round," Dempsey said after the fight. "By the third and fourth rounds I was in a bad way, weary and bleeding." In the seventh round, Tunney continued to pepper Dempsey with left jabs and hooks, mixing in an occasional right cross. Then Dempsey charged recklessly and connected with a roundhouse right to Tunney's head, followed by a shattering left hook to the jaw. Dempsey closed fast, landing five quick shots to the head. "Like a tiger, Dempsey was upon his foe, vicious, savage, a man berserk," wrote John Kieran from ringside.

Tunney went down like a falling tree and landed on his back near Dempsey's corner, his left hand reaching blindly for the ropes, one leg crumpled beneath him. "His handsome, expressive face turned blank, almost idiotic," said his friend W. O. McGeehan. "Tunney is down!" screamed Graham McNamee. "Tunney is down from a barrage of lefts and rights to the face!" Dempsey enthusiasts were on their feet, screaming for the kill. Across the country, eleven people died of heart failure listening to McNamee's near-hysterical account of the knockdown.

The moment Tunney hit the canvas, Paul Beeler, the knockdown time-keeper, leaped to his feet, stopwatch in hand, but seeing Dempsey in his own corner, which was the nearest corner, he stopped his count. Referee Barry never started a count. "Go to a neutral corner, Jack," Barry commanded, but Dempsey growled, "I stay here." Reporters at ringside were shouting themselves hoarse for Dempsey to move when Barry took him by the arm and pointed emphatically toward the corner diagonally across the ring. "I forgot the rules," Dempsey would explain the defiance that cost him the championship. "I was the jungle fighter . . . used to standing over my opponents to make sure that when I pounded them down, they stayed down."

Only when Dempsey reached the neutral corner did Barry move toward Tunney and start counting. Paul Beeler shouted "five," for he had already counted "four" when Tunney went down, but Barry refused to pick up the count there, and began, "one!" By the time Barry got to five, Tunney had revived to the point where he was counting with the "tolling seconds" as he sat holding the middle rope with his left hand. He struggled to his feet at the count of nine. He had been down for at least fourteen seconds, probably more, and should have been counted out.

Sitting next to Paul Gallico, a little man with a smashed-in nose and cauliflower ears was looking with astonishment at a stopwatch he had clicked on the moment Tunney hit the canvas. "Why, he's been down for sixteen seconds!" he said. The little fellow was Battling Nelson.

When he got up, Tunney began backpedaling. It was the first time in his twelve-year professional career he had been knocked down, but he rallied gamely, moving backward faster than the leg-weary challenger could move forward. Unable to catch him, Dempsey made little pawing motions with his gloves and mumbled scornfully, "Come on and fight." On Dempsey's face was "such a glance of bitter, biting contempt for his opponent," said Gallico, "that for the moment I felt ashamed for the man who was running away."

Tunney was too smart to take the bait. As he told a reporter after the fight, "I honestly thought Dempsey was going to kill me."

The Jack Dempsey of Boyle's Thirty Acres would have, but this was not that man. Sensing Dempsey's frustration, the crowd became enraged with Tunney's desperate defense. People began screaming at him, calling him a coward.

"Fight, you son of a bitch," one ringsider bellowed.

In the next round, a fully revived Tunney knocked Dempsey to one knee with a right to the jaw. Even before his knee hit the canvas, Barry rushed in, with his arm raised high in the count of one, with Tunney standing in the middle of the ring, not in a neutral corner. Dempsey was up and fighting before Barry could raise his hand aloft for the two count. As Dempsey biographer Roger Kahn wrote, "Watching this moment on videotape, one is consumed by outrage. Two knockdowns, one round apart, and two different sets of rules. The explanation, I believe, is not complicated. In my tape of the [fight] I am looking at a crooked referee."

At the end of the fight the "Terror of Toledo" was a wreck, cut, bleeding, and barely able to stand. "He was almost helpless when the final bell rang," Tunney said later. It was a unanimous decision, with Tunney winning seven of ten rounds. Gene Tunney was the first fighter to get off the floor and beat the great Dempsey. And Dempsey, who had stood over Firpo and battered him every time he got up, was the fatal victim of a rule his actions had caused boxing officials to put in the books.

"I was robbed of the championship," Dempsey said in his dressing room after the fight. Interviewed by reporters, timekeeper Beeler said that when Tunney got to his feet, "I . . . took a look at my counting watch, which I had started the instant Tunney hit the canvas, and stopped the instant he got off the floor. The watch said seventeen seconds."

Was the fight fixed? The mobsters had tried, but failed, to influence the decision. Capone had pressed to get Dave Miller, the top referee in Chicago, and a man reputedly beholden to Capone, assigned to the fight. If he had been in the ring, he probably would have counted out Tunney, but the boxing commission had defied Capone and picked Barry.

Hank Greenspun, a Las Vegas reporter who knew his mobsters, later told Kahn that the Philadelphia Jewish mob, led by Boo Boo Hoff and Abe Attell, had bought Dave Barry. There is not a shred of evidence to support this assertion; and in any event, if Barry was crooked he could easily have disqualified Dempsey for numerous low blows. "Dempsey should have been thrown out of the ring before that seventh round ever happened," Gallico told his *Daily News* readers. Some of his punches "looked deliberately low and struck with intent." Tunney claimed Dempsey hit him with three foul punches in the third round, and repeatedly clubbed him with illegal rabbit punches, short, choppy blows to the nape of the neck. In his dressing room after the fight, Tunney showed reporters a black-and-blue mark on his groin, five inches in diameter, where Dempsey had landed a left hook. Never once, however, did Tunney complain to the referee.

The Dempsey camp appealed, unsuccessfully, to state and regional boxing commissions to reverse the decision of the referee and two judges. The controversy has persisted, and the question is still asked: could Tunney have gotten up and defended himself in the seventh round without those extra seconds? Gallico thought not. "Tunney lay crumpled on the canvas in front of me. I looked into his face; he was stunned and glassy-eyed. He never would have made it to his feet before 'ten,' I'll swear." Tunney was forthright: "I don't know," he admitted twenty years later; but he was quick to add that he was fully conscious at the count of two, and "could have jumped up immediately and matched my legs against Jack's, just as I did."

In no way was Tunney fresh and ready to resume at the count of two, as he claims; five perhaps, but even then he would have been in no condition to defend himself. A careful review of the fight film tells this writer that Dempsey knocked out Tunney, but by his inattention to the rules, gave him time to get back into the fight.

If the Chicago fight had been held under New York rules, Dempsey would probably have won. In New York, only the timekeeper, stationed outside the ring, kept the count. The fighter scoring the knockdown was required to go to a neutral corner, but while he did, the timekeeper was to proceed, uninterrupted, with his count. When the referee went to the side of the fallen boxer, he was to pick up the count of the timekeeper, not start a new count, as Dave Barry did.

It is a controversy that will never be settled. Writing many years later, Gene Tunney said his only disappointment was that he and Dempsey had not met when they were both at their "unquestionable best," when Dempsey was, as Tunney acknowledged, "possibly the greatest fighter that ever entered a ring. . . . We could have decided many questions, to me the most important of which is whether 'a good boxer can always lick a good fighter.'

"I still say yes."

Dempsey and Rickard were equally eager for a rematch, but a specialist who assessed the damage to Dempsey's eyes warned him that he risked permanent impairment, possibly blindness, if he returned to the ring. That week, Dempsey announced his retirement and signed a contract with David Belasco to star with Estelle in a Broadway play called *The Big Fight*. With Dempsey out of boxing, New York sportswriters turned their full attention to the Big Bam's pursuit of sixty.

Heavenly Days!

Entering the final days of the season Ruth faced a daunting challenge. On September 26, four days after Tunney beat Dempsey, his home run total stood at fifty-six, but the Yanks had only four games to play. The most Ruth could hope for, Marshall Hunt wrote despairingly, was to tie his 1921 record of fifty-nine home runs, and even that was a long shot.

The following day Ruth began his furious drive for the record with a grand slam against Lefty Grove; Gehrig also hit a home run, his first since September 6. Two days later, Ruth hit his fifty-eighth and fifty-ninth against the Washington Senators, and narrowly missed two more by a few feet. The home run that tied his record was a grand slam. "Heavenly days!" Marshall Hunt wrote the next morning.

That afternoon, the next-to-last day of the season, Ruth came to bat in the eighth inning at Yankee Stadium against southpaw Tom Zachary of the Senators. The score was tied, and the Yankees had a runner on third. Ruth took three pitches and then hit a slow curve down the right field line and into the stands, just fair. Zachary shouted, "Foul ball! Foul ball!" and began arguing with the umpire. Ignoring him, Ruth "made [a] triumphant, almost regal tour of the paths. He jogged around slowly," said the *Times*, "touched each bag firmly and carefully and when he imbedded his spikes in the rubber disk to record officially Homer 60, hats were tossed into the air, papers were torn up and tossed liberally and the spirit of celebration permeated the place."

"Sixty, count 'em, sixty. Let's see some other son of a bitch match that," Ruth shouted in the clubhouse after the game. A few days later a humbler Bambino confessed to Gallico that he "never dreamed it was possible. I never thought I could do it."

He didn't credit Gehrig, but Gallico did. His "devastating clouting" had "forced the pitchers to throw strikes at Ruth. To pass Ruth to get at Gehrig was plumb suicide in mid-season." The next day, Lou Gehrig Day, at the stadium, the big first baseman celebrated by hitting number 47, and the Yankees secured their 110th win, finishing in first place by nineteen games over the second-place Athletics.

Gehrig hit .373, knocked in 175 runs—breaking Ruth's 1921 record of 170—and won the American League's Most Valuable Player award. Ruth hit .356, had 164 RBIs, and would have beat out Gehrig for the MVP award had he been eligible. In that era, a player could win it only once in his career.

That October the New York baseball writers honored the Babe as the player of the year. "They didn't give it to me because I had hit 60 home runs," Ruth recalled. "They told me they were giving it to me because of the comeback I had made after my terrible season of 1925, when a lot of them figured, and wrote, that I was all washed up." While this surely figured in the balloting, it was Ruth's September surge that counted for more. He hit an astounding sixteen home runs in twenty-one games, putting a notch in his bat for each of them. And over the course of the season he hit home runs in every ballpark in the league and at least six against all seven opposing teams. He hit more home runs than any *team* in the American League except his own, and he had fourteen sacrifice bunts.

At that time, a player was awarded a home run if his hit bounced into the stands. No Ruth home run bounced into the stands. And while Yankee Stadium's short right field porch benefited Ruth, he hit thirty-two of his home runs on the road. Together, he and Gehrig accounted for a quarter of the home runs hit in the American League.

On the evening of October 1, the Yankees left Penn Station for Pittsburgh to meet the Pirates in the first two games of the World Series. "We won the 1927 World Series the day before it started," Ruth would say later. In batting practice that afternoon the Yankees put on an eye-popping display of long ball power, while the Pirates, who had finished their workout, watched in silent awe from the empty grandstand as Ruth and Gehrig hit balls to parts of the spacious park that had never been reached. With one of his final swings, the Babe hit one completely out of Forbes Field. "You could actually hear them gulp while they watched us," Ruth said of the Pirates.

The Bronx Bombers swept the opposition in four games, winning, surprisingly, in the old McGraw way—with solid pitching, aggressive base running, and airtight fielding. Ruth clubbed two home runs—the only ones hit by either team—and batted .400. That winter, a nationwide poll named Ruth and Gehrig the second and fourth, in that order, most popular athletes in America. Jack Dempsey was first and Gene Tunney third. Coming off the greatest years of their careers, Gehrig and Tunney, hometown boys, continued to live in the shadows of two heavy hitters from the other side of the Hudson.

End Game

That winter, Tex Rickard tried to get Dempsey to come out of retirement. "With Jack in action," he told friends, "the boxing game was fun. Now it's just a business." After the Battle of the Long Count, as it was being called, Tex had been invited to a victory party thrown by Tunney's friend Bernard Gimbel at the Hotel Sherman. The boxer Benny Leonard spotted him, sitting alone in the lobby of the Sherman. "Tex, why don't you go upstairs? They're all celebrating."

"Celebrating what?" he said sourly, as he turned and left the hotel.

The next year Rickard put on a match at Yankee Stadium between Tunney and Tom Heeney, a lightly regarded New Zealander, Tunney having no desire to fight the more formidable Jack Sharkey. For the first time since Toledo, there was no stirring story, nothing to play up. The fight was stopped in the eleventh round with Heeney a bloody mess, but "the man who really took the count," said one writer, "was Tex Rickard."

The fight drew 46,000 fans, only half the capacity of the stadium. "Dempsey drew more gate-crashers than that," wrote W. O. McGeehan. Rickard and his Madison Square Garden Corporation, which had guaranteed Tunney half a million dollars, took a punishing loss, in the area of $400,000.

That July, Tunney announced his retirement. In his last three bouts, he had earned approximately $2 million, and he would make millions more as a successful businessman. He also had a formidably rich partner. He and Polly Lauder were married that October in Rome, before a small gathering of relatives and friends.

On the way to his rendezvous in Europe with Polly for the wedding, Tunney finally received the acclaim he deserved: a gala neighborhood send-off. As "Tooney," as he was known to his Irish neighbors, prepared to board the *Mauretania* at the Chelsea Docks, longshoremen with hooks stuck in their belts were there to cheer him and slap his back. The children from St. Veronica were also there, and "giggling girls" from nearby factories slipped out to catch a glimpse of the nattily dressed champion. Recording the scene were more cameramen than had met President Wilson when he returned from Versailles.

When the crowd "surged in at him," police escorted him to the balcony of the upper floor of a pier building, where he turned and stared down at the crowd, a Panama hat on his head and a vivid summer tie flapping over one shoulder.

"He was the best advertisement the sport ever had," the *Los Angeles Times* sports columnist Jim Murray would write decades later. "He was like no other Irishman you ever saw, but he was the greatest Irish athlete who ever lived. If you don't think so, tell me who was."

Tex Rickard had lost, for good, both of his million-dollar fighters. After 1929, "our stream of super-champions ran dry, replaced," said one boxing observer, "by a turgid brook. The champions were now just ordinary mortals, good players but nothing more." That would not change until the emergence of a black heavyweight far superior to Dempsey: Joe Louis, the "Brown Bomber" from Detroit.

In the years before Louis's hegemony, Jack Dempsey hit the skids, losing $3 million—nearly everything he had—in the Stock Market Crash. In 1931, a year after he and Estelle went through a messy divorce, the Manassa Mauler put on the gloves again and fought exhibition bouts, beating some 175 opponents over the course of the next year. He knocked out over a hundred of them, sometimes two or three in an evening. "He found fighting chumps undignified," wrote Roger Kahn, "but he needed cash."

He earned over a quarter of a million dollars fighting, and occasionally refereeing boxing and wrestling matches, and in 1935 he opened Jack Dempsey's Restaurant at Eighth Avenue and Fiftieth Street, across the street from Madison Square Garden.* He was usually there, greeting friends and strangers at the door with a high-pitched "Hiya, pal." (He wasn't much better at remembering names than Babe Ruth.) If he spotted someone from his past, he would sweep aside the rope and instruct his headwaiter to find him a choice table. "You march in proudly," said Paul Gallico. "It feels like being present in court."

After their retirements, Dempsey and Tunney, whom history would always link together, became loyal friends and worked together to promote Roosevelt's New Deal. In 1965, they were in the nation's capital to witness Tunney's son, Congressman John V. Tunney, Jr., of California, take the oath of office. "I feel like part of me is gone," Dempsey said after Gene Tunney's death in 1978. "I feel alone."

Dempsey scored the final knockouts of his career in his late sixties. He was in a cab headed from his restaurant to the Central Park West apartment he shared with his fourth wife, Deanna Piattelli. The cab stopped at a red light

---

* After World War II, the restaurant moved to 1619 Broadway. It closed in 1974.

and two young muggers, spotting a well-dressed elderly gentleman—an easy mark—approached and pulled open the rear doors. The driver froze, but Dempsey reacted. "I took care of the situation. I belted one with a right and the other with a left. I flattened 'em both."

In a final tribute to Dempsey, sixteen thousand fans packed Madison Square Garden in 1970 to celebrate his seventy-fifth birthday. He lived for thirteen more years, and whenever he appeared in public he was "the main event," said *New York Times* sportswriter Dave Anderson.

To the end, which came on May 31, 1983, he continued to attribute much of his success to Tex Rickard, his second father.

Rickard had not been himself after the Chicago fight. In a panicky effort to recoup his losses from the Tunney-Heeney fight, he invested, disastrously, in motion pictures, schemed to build a vast outdoor arena in New York, and hatched a plan—a "new dream"—to turn Miami into an "American Monte Carlo," with a dog racing track, a grand hotel, a boxing arena, and one of the largest gambling palaces in existence.

While in Miami with Dempsey on New Year's Eve 1929, he complained of stomach pain and was taken to the hospital. An emergency operation for an infection of the appendix was unsuccessful, and he died on January 6, four days after his fifty-eighth birthday. At the end, Jack Dempsey was holding his hand.

George Lewis Rickard, the man who made millions selling violence, squandered the bulk of his fortune in wild speculations, most of them unknown to his surviving family. Still, he had done what only a few entrepreneurs have accomplished. He transformed the culture of his trade and the city in which he practiced it. "Luck gave him the cards," said W. O. McGeehan, "and he knew how to play them."

A train bearing Rickard's body, his widow, and Jack Dempsey left Miami for New York just before midnight on the day he died. Dempsey looked dazed and bewildered. "I've lost the best pal a man could have," he told reporters.

The day Rickard died the main entrance to Madison Square Garden was draped in dark bunting and a flag flew at half-staff atop the building. When his body arrived at Penn Station, a crowd of several thousand assembled outside, braving the intense cold. One hundred uniformed policemen escorted the elaborate bronze coffin to the Garden. Before the motorcade pulled out, an old fellow pushed through the crowd to get a glimpse of the cortege. "Egad," he said, "he *was* a showman; even his funeral is a sellout."

Tex Rickard's body was placed in state at the center of the Garden's main floor. A double line of blue-clad police formed a corridor from the building's entrance to the bier. Paul Gallico was there, as the mourners passed in solemn file before the coffin. "There was no light in the Garden," he recalled, "except for a row of slanting shafts of late sun that cut down through the narrow clerestory windows just beneath the roof of the building. Two of these fell athwart the bier." The only noises in that hushed hall were the sounds of shuffling feet on the terrazzo floor and the whispered goodbyes of the fifteen thousand people who came to see him off.

The Barnum of boxing would not have minded that his final show was free.

CHAPTER TWENTY-ONE

VISIONS

Men, thinly scattered, make a shift, but a bad shift. . . . It is
being concentrated which produces convenience.

SAMUEL JOHNSON

Car Crazy

In December 1927, two months after the second Dempsey-Tunney fight, Madison Square Garden hosted the largest public event in its history: the unveiling of a revolutionary automobile from Henry Ford. "No introduction of a commercial product ever has attracted more interest," wrote the New York *World*.

Since 1908, the Ford Motor Company had been making only one car, the iconic Model T, and it had made over fifteen million of them. The Tin Lizzie remained inexpensive and reliable, and still came mostly in only one color: black. But times were changing. The American motorcar was fast becoming a style statement as well as a means of transportation, and the Ford Motor Company had begun to lose sales to sportier, more richly appointed models produced by General Motors and Chrysler, cars that were "low, sleek, and gleaming."

In 1921, every second car made in the United States was a boxy-looking Model T, a machine whose very lack of style was one of its original selling points. By 1926, however, Ford's market share was down to 34 percent, only slightly ahead of fast-closing GM, producer of the smartly equipped and affordable Chevrolet. Henry Ford's beloved "flivver" had outlived its time, but its stubborn creator was reluctant to admit it. Finally, his son Edsel and other company officials convinced him to begin developing an "entirely new Ford car" to meet the company's surging competition. In June 1927, the last Model T rolled off the assembly line and the company shut down its auto factories.

For the next five months, the Ford Motor Company made no cars, devoting itself entirely to the massive challenge of retooling plants and equipment that had been dedicated for fifteen years to the sole purpose of making Model T's.

The first Model A, as the new car was known, was completed at Ford's immense River Rouge plant on October 21, 1927, but Henry Ford announced that it wouldn't be unveiled until December 2. This was a cleverly calculated move, part of one of the most brilliant public relations campaigns in the history of capitalist enterprise, an exhibition of salesmanship founded on secrecy and the anticipation it incited. For months, no information was released about the new model. Then, in late November, tantalizing facts about the "car-that-is-to-be" were released for five consecutive days in full-page advertisements in over two thousand newspapers—virtually every daily in the United States and Canada. By December 1, nearly half a million Americans were prepared to place orders for the car, sight unseen, a testament to the faith people had in Henry Ford, a hero of the age of invention.

"Today will be remembered as one of the greatest days in the entire history of the automobile industry," the Ford Motor Company announced on December 2, 1927. In New York City, crowds started gathering outside the main Ford showroom on Broadway and Fifty-fourth Street at three in the morning, in the freezing rain; by late evening, forty thousand people had passed through the doors of the "salon," and another 65,000 viewed the new Ford at a showroom at 60 Broad Street, where a dozen policemen maintained order. "The new Ford was introduced in New York City yesterday like a world celebrity," *The New York Times* reported. "A quarter of a million persons saw it in the showrooms of seventy-six dealers in the metropolitan district and gave it their approval by signing 50,000 orders."

It went on like this for a month and more, in New York and everywhere else in the country. Twenty-five million Americans visited Ford salesrooms in one week in December 1927. Ford officials in New York hired Madison Square Garden for a full week to ease the crush on their showrooms. More than one million New Yorkers viewed the Model A at this special Ford exhibition, breaking attendance records for the arena.

The Model A did not disappoint. The engineering was state-of-the-art; the car was easy to steer, shift, and brake; and it "went like a rocket," reaching a cruising speed of sixty-five miles per hour. It came in a variety of color combinations, had low-slung, sweeping lines, and was affordable, costing only a few dollars more than the previous year's Model T, and less than the Chevrolet. "How can Ford make this for $385?" marveled one of the car's New York admirers.

The subway remained the principal people carrier in motor-age New York City, but by 1927 thousands of local families that didn't own a car eagerly looked forward to the day when they could afford one. In 1918, there were roughly 125,000 motor vehicles registered in the city; ten years later there were 700,000—and nearly a quarter of a million additional vehicles from outside the city poured into it every business day, creating snarling congestion on narrow, gridded cross streets designed for horse-drawn vehicles.

The congestion was at its worst on the island of Manhattan, but motor traffic was stacked up and stalled in all places in a city that had 4,145 miles of streets but not a single mile of arterial highway. "The vaunted American imagination has never in the quarter-century of the automobile's existence devised an adequate motor highway about our greatest metropolis," said *The New York Times*. At rush hour, a car on Fifth Avenue was limited to an average speed of less than three miles per hour, no faster than a pedestrian walking at a brisk pace. "Metropolitan misery," Frank Lloyd Wright called Manhattan's super-congestion. "The only way to cross the street in New York City now," he quipped, "is to be born on the other side."

The city's subways were as crowded as its streets. In 1927, the subway system carried nearly two billion riders, "the most stupendous volume of traffic ever known in the world," said the *Daily News*. The crowding in the subway cars was distressing—"metropolitan man-sewers," Lewis Mumford called them—but the system carried nearly two-thirds of metropolitan travelers in 1927. Without it, New York would have been paralyzed.

Yet the subway was also a primary cause of congestion. Almost everywhere new lines were built in Manhattan they encouraged business concentration and high rise development. One of the enduring myths of New York City history is that the city's main skyscraper zones—one in lower Manhattan and the other in Midtown—emerged because bedrock in these areas was close to the surface, making it easier and less expensive to sink foundations than in the deep bedrock valley between them. A recent study has shown, however, that Manhattan real estate developers preferred to build skyscrapers in commercial zones with excellent rapid transit service, and that "depth to bedrock . . . had relatively little influence" on their decisions about where to build. These findings would not have surprised William Barclay Parsons, chief engineer of New York's first subway system. "The spectacular consequence of the subway," he wrote in 1929, "has been the skyscraper." It was a "vicious circle": subway lines built to alleviate congestion produced even greater congestion.

Privately owned bus lines began to compete with subways and taxicabs in the 1920s, and city officials hoped that buses would reduce the wildly increasing number of cabs on the city's streets. But without proper terminals, the suburban buses especially were forced to park for long intervals at the curb, tying up traffic. Nothing, however, blocked traffic more than trucks loading and unloading merchandise at stores and small factories. In 1927, less than 3 percent of Manhattan's business buildings had any type of truck loading or unloading facility, leaving merchandise to be transferred by hand between the back of the vehicle and the receiving room.

Manhattan's commercial streets, to be sure, had been chaotically packed in the age of the horse, but the car and the truck compounded the problem enormously on a narrow island that had a permanent population of 100,000 to the square mile, making it the most densely populated commercial core in the world. A "crisis is now . . . upon us," warned William Wilgus, master builder of Grand Central Terminal, and it demanded "quick relief," for both concentration and movement—the guiding ideas behind the design of Grand Central Terminal—were essential to a healthy functioning urban organism.

Wilgus would unveil plans of his own to relieve congestion. They were part of a great civic discussion among architects, planners, businessmen, and public officials over the root causes of New York's mounting congestion problem. It was one of pivotal public debates in the history of the city, and it produced a cascade of proposals—some purely practical, others daringly visionary—to alleviate the crowding that jeopardized New York's standing as the global capital of commerce and light industry.

The principal point of contention was whether the skyscraper or the automobile—the major shaping forces of the modern American city—was the dominant cause of congestion.

Just Imagine

In 1927, just as mid-Manhattan's skyscraper building campaign began to accelerate with the completion of the French Building and municipal approval of architect John A. Larkin's planned 110-story "super-skyscraper" near Times Square, the tall business building came under withering public assault.* *The New York Times* was "horrified" by Larkin's proposal to concentrate thirty thousand office workers in a building that made "the tower of Babel look like a child's toy." Skyscrapers would be the ruination of New York unless strong measures were taken to rein in their immense size and proliferation, said Henry H. Curran, former borough president of Manhattan.

In 1927, Curran engaged in a series of widely publicized debates with ar-

---

* The Larkin project died and Raymond Hood's McGraw-Hill Building was built on the site.

chitect Harvey Wiley Corbett, artist Hugh Ferriss's collaborator and, with him, a passionate proponent of high-rise development. Curran was pressing for a statute limiting the height of new buildings to ten stories. "The worst enemy of the American city today is the skyscraper," he thundered. In New York, it "has already become a plague that may well range alongside our ancient city scourges of cholera, yellow fever, tuberculosis and slums."*

"Nonsense," replied Corbett. The automobile, not the skyscraper, was the principal cause of New York's traffic problems. London, Paris, and Los Angeles had no skyscrapers, yet all of them had "extreme" traffic congestion. "London is a seven-story city, and those of us who have tried to do business there . . . spend most of our day in taxicabs and buses." The skyscraper, Corbett insisted, was actually an instrument of de-congestion, taking "horizontal" traffic off the city's subways, streets, and sidewalks and on to its high-speed elevators—its unrivaled "vertical" transportation system. "In downtown New York, a businessman consults his broker, eats his lunch, sees his lawyer, buys his wife a box of candy, gets a shave, all in the same building. At most he walks a few blocks. Most of the time he travels up and down instead of to and fro."

Corbett's answer to the congestion generated by the automobile was a city of stupendously tall towers and high-speed expressways. In artist's sketches of his reimagined New York, the streets belong exclusively to motorized traffic. Above them are arcaded walkways, "embedded" into shops and restaurants. Pedestrian bridges span intersections, creating an interlinked network of skyways. This system would promote the uninterrupted movement of traffic that Corbett considered "as essential to the life of the city as the movement of the blood is to the life of the body."

Corbett's hypothetical skyscrapers were greater in height and mass than any yet built, and were communities unto themselves, designed for work, living, recreation, and culture, with apartments, shops, gymnasiums, and theaters. To relieve congestion, they were widely spaced, with low-level buildings razed to make room for parks and sunken boulevards. Corbett's New York was an Americanized version of Le Corbusier's 1923 Voisin Plan, by which the Swiss architect proposed to raze the run-down historic Right Bank of Paris, preserving only the central monuments, and replace it with a city of gleam-

---

* Whatever the merits of Curran's argument, he was spitting into the wind. It was unrealistic to expect the city's commercial community to stop building skyscrapers. Both Wall Street and City Hall had a financial stake in skyscraper development. Tall buildings were cash registers on the land, raising the value of urban real estate and thereby increasing real estate taxes, city government's chief source of revenue.

ing skyscraper offices and apartments, spaced far apart so that each glass-enshrouded tower would be surrounded by green space and would have wide and fine views. Rendered in luminous black-and-white drawings and murals by Ferriss and decorative artist Robert W. Chandler, Corbett's city of the future was put on display at gallery exhibits, and in one instance—the Titan City Exhibition of 1925—at Wanamaker's Department Store, part of the tricentennial celebration of the founding of New York City. The Titan City show drew big, enthusiastic crowds and was heavily covered in the press. "The future of architecture has become a matter of public concern," wrote one critic.

Corbett did more than depict his Pinnacle City, as he called it; he advanced a plan to bring it to life. At first, a number of temporary covered walkways would be constructed above street level in the most densely packed areas of Midtown. As further blocks were redeveloped, arcaded sidewalks, reached by footbridges, would be built into every new building. Corbett described his idealized Manhattan as a "modernized Venice, a city of arcades, piazzas, and [pedestrian] bridges, with canals for streets, only the canals will not be filled with water but with freely flowing motor traffic." The idea would spread and New York would "become a model for all the world."*

To humanist Lewis Mumford, Corbett's "titanic dream city" was a "project from Cloudcuckooland. . . . Only a megalomaniac imagines that life in a two-hundred-story building is in any way better or greater than life in a two-story building," he wrote after viewing the Titan City exhibit. "We are dealing here . . . with a religion, with a deep mystical impulse, a hierarchy and a theology. . . . Traffic and Commerce are the names of the presiding deities." There was not a single human being in the sketches Ferriss made for the Wanamaker display. Mumford found this telling; Pinnacle City was designed for the care and convenience of automobiles, and for the requirements of New York's high-rise developers. It discouraged the kind of social interaction that made city streets and sidewalks public theater, sealing people off from one another in "coffins in the sky."

There were, of course, those who found living up in the clouds enchanting; among them were Mumford's friends, the photographer Alfred Stieglitz and his

---

* The entire country would get a glimpse of Corbett's City of the Future in the popular musical comedy *Just Imagine*, released in 1930. Ferriss's drawings were the model for the Hollywood movie set built by a team of 250 artists and assistants employed by Fox Films. New York City was depicted with towers 250 stories high, futuristic airplanes directed by policemen in balloons, and a sunken eight-lane central boulevard for "terrestrial traffic." "The Cinematic City of the Future," *Fortune* 2 (October 1930): 129.

artist wife, Georgia O'Keeffe. "New York is madder than ever," Stieglitz wrote to Sherwood Anderson in 1925. "The pace is ever increasing. But Georgia and I somehow don't seem to be of New York—not of anywhere. We live up in the Shelton [Hotel]. . . . All is so quiet except the wind—& the trembling of steel in which we live. It's a wonderful place." For Stieglitz and O'Keeffe—as for Corbett and Ferriss—New York was, above all, a compelling visual spectacle, not as it was for Mumford, a place of homes and families, neighborhoods and street life.

Titan

In the mid-1920s, architect Raymond Hood joined the debate on congestion, proposing a more imaginative variant of Corbett's Pinnacle City. Hood's ideas were noticed. He was one of the most sensational figures in the city and another of its Alger-like success stories.

"Raymond Hood . . . is [the] brilliant bad boy" of architecture, tied to no style, unconventional and experimental, wrote *The New Yorker*'s Allene Talmey. Consistency was his bête noire; each of his buildings was decisively different from the others. "A style is developed by copying and repetition," he declared, "both destructive to creation." Beginning as a traditionalist, Hood became a "strict functionalist"—a functionalist, however, who happened to be an urban dreamer.

Hood lived fully and exuberantly, a solid family man who drank too much, drove too fast, and worked too hard. "His life was a joy ride in which everybody got a thrill including the client," wrote architect Thomas E. Tallmadge on the occasion of Hood's untimely death in 1934 of rheumatoid arthritis, at age fifty-three.

Raymond Mathewson Hood had moved from famine to fame in an astonishingly short time. In 1921, he was a thirty-nine-year-old New York architect with no clients—unemployed, heavily in debt, and struggling to support a wife and newborn child. In a moment of despair, he considered leaving the profession and applied for a job at a Rhode Island bank.

This was his second failed effort to make it in New York City. Born and raised in Pawtucket, Rhode Island, the son of a prosperous manufacturer of boxes and crates, and the great-grandson of the first Baptist Sunday School teacher in town, he had come to New York after graduating from MIT in 1903 to work as a draftsman in the office of Cram, Goodhue & Ferguson, solidly successful Gothic designers. He lived frugally at a local YMCA and evinced a dislike of "uproarious" New York and its dark skyscraper canyons. "Downtown . . . is a place in which the sun never penetrates, except by reflection," he wrote in one of his gloomier letters.

After six months, he departed for Paris, hoping to be admitted to the Ecole des Beaux-Arts. "Hood alighted at the *Gare du Nord*, a bright Pawtucket child with three bags and a full set of objections," wrote Allene Talmey. An unbending Baptist, "he objected to Notre Dame, refusing to enter or admire it on the grounds that it was Catholic. He objected to the eternal hugging and kissing on the boulevards, and to the Continental Sunday with open theatres and open cafés." Denied admission to the Ecole after receiving a zero in freehand drawing, he tacked a small crucifix over his bed for luck and passed the entrance exams three months later. He was soon drinking, smoking, and cavorting with Parisian women—and he visited Notre Dame and came away humbled and impressed. Six years later, after a brief return to America, he received his diploma and took a job with a prominent Pittsburgh architect. Bored after three years in the Steel City, he headed east in 1914, determined, he told a friend, to become the "greatest architect in New York."

Hood rented two rooms in a dingy brownstone walk-up on West Forty-second Street, using the front room as an office that he shared with young architect Rayne Adams, and the back room for sleeping and eating. So little work came to either of them that they hung up a sign: Adams & Hood, Fumeurs. While renovating Mori's Restaurant, a bohemian hangout on Bleecker Street in Greenwich Village, Hood was provided free meals and an apartment upstairs. The owner, Placido Mori, enjoyed his company—a vehement young man engrossed every evening at the tables "in violent discussions."

While living at Mori's, Hood married his secretary of a few months: Elsie Schmidt, as quick-witted and alive as her husband. One year into the marriage—in 1921—he and Elsie were nearly dead broke and residing in a cramped apartment on Washington Square. Elsie was pregnant and he had no architecture commissions. His only steady income came from designing radiator covers for the American Radiator Company, but he lost that job the day he and Elsie's first child, Raymond Jr., was born. He was ready, he despairingly told Elsie, to quit architecture. "And then," said a friend, "he got lucky."

That year, Chicago's dynastic cousins, Robert McCormick and Joseph Patterson, decided to build a new headquarters building for their newspaper on North Michigan Avenue. The following June they announced an international competition for its design, and invited ten leading architects to submit drawings and plans. The prize was $50,000 and the commission to build the Tribune Tower. The competition was open to other architects, but the invitees were given a clear edge: $2,000 each to support work on their submissions.

John Mead Howells was one of the privileged ten. The son of the novelist

William Dean Howells, he was a bright but derivative designer, with plenty of other work to occupy him. To have a fair chance at the prize he needed a creative partner with time on his hands. Hood was innovative and available, and they had been classmates at the Beaux-Arts. They entered the competition as a team. Howells did a preliminary drawing and Hood supervised the drafting work, which yielded a design dramatically different from Howells's original conception: a tall, rounded shaft that culminated in a slender tower, with decorative flying buttresses modeled on those of a medieval cathedral. In an excruciatingly close vote, the neo-Gothic design of Howells and Hood won out over the stylishly unornamented submission of Finnish architect Eliel Saarinen—more a sublime piece of urban sculpture than a building fitted out for newspaper work. "Real beauty in design is achieved," Hood would write later, "when utility is your goal."

When Hood heard that he'd won the competition he sat "stunned at the telephone, immovable for an hour," he told friends. He then began drinking and didn't stop for twenty-four hours. The unemployed designer of radiator covers had become, in a single day in December 1922, one of the notable architects in the world. After he sobered up he realized he had only eleven dollars to his name. He approached Placido Mori and borrowed money to buy a suit and a train ticket to Chicago to accept the award. Howells kept $40,000 of the prize money and gave Hood the remaining $10,000. When Hood returned from the awards ceremony, Elsie commandeered a cab and went around to each of their creditors to show them the check.

After work began on the thirty-six-story Tribune Tower, Hood was commissioned by the American Radiator Company, his former employer, to design its new Manhattan headquarters on a mid-block site on West Fortieth Street, facing north, toward the New York Public Library and the "open expanse" of Bryant Park. Only twenty-one stories tall, the black brick Radiator Building, completed in 1924, melded into the fabric of the city and had a pronounced though not overpowering street presence. It was a design, however, that Hood would unfortunately move away from, both in his architecture practice and his musing about the city of tomorrow.*

The American Radiator Building launched Hood's career as a celebrity Manhattan architect, although he surely didn't look like one. "His clothes," said Talmey, "are ugly in a gloomy brown way, and his friends say that he does

---

* Georgia O'Keeffe painted the building in 1927—at night, with the interior lights turned on.

not care for display in dress." He received clients in his office in the Radiator Building in casual slacks and an open shirt, sitting in a Windsor chair with his feet propped up on a stool. A small, compact man, he had quick eyes and a shock of short-cropped, gray-black hair that stuck straight up in the air like porcupine bristles.

Though commissions came pouring into his office, feeding his boundless capacity for work, Raymond Hood also liked to play. On Friday afternoons he'd meet for drinks with his three best friends: Ely Jacques Kahn, builder of impressive loft buildings in the Garment District; Ralph Walker, architect of the style-setting Barclay-Vesey Building; and Joseph Urban, the Austrian-born designer of productions for the Ziegfeld Follies and the Metropolitan Opera. They called it their "Four Hour Lunch Club." Most of the time they gathered at Mori's, but any comfortable Midtown watering hole would do, except the Century Club, the preserve of old-family gentleman-architects whose tradition-bound work they detested. The Century Club's Ivy League architects were in the Social Register. Hood and his luncheon companions were "only in the telephone book."

Hood's favorite cocktail was a high-octane concoction of applejack, absinthe, and lemon juice, and he would usually have more than a few. At large social gatherings, with other architects, his voice would rise with every round, and he would aggressively challenge the ideas of everyone at the table and go off on tangents, sketching on the tablecloth with a thick pencil as he spun ideas for fresh projects. "When Hood has . . . the floor . . . he has it for keeps," said a colleague.

He'd usually stay in the city on Friday night, but occasionally he'd risk it, driving furiously, fueled by alcohol, through dozens of red lights to the ocean-front home he had built in 1925 in Stamford, Connecticut. It was "a simple English house," Talmey described it, with lots of antique furniture, a place jarringly dissimilar to the stripped-down, modernist buildings he came to favor. It was, as well, an unlikely place of repose for a man who had once claimed that Central Park was "country enough" for him. There was a tennis court out back, and on sunlit summer weekends Ray Hood would play tennis with his houseguests—ending the afternoon with a swim in Long Island Sound, joined by Elsie, their three young children, and the family's collection of dogs.

On a visit to Hood's Connecticut home, a friend noticed that the white pillars on the front porch were covered with architectural sketches. Nothing in the house was "sacred," Elsie explained. "My tablecloths are all covered with pencil marks. It is impossible to keep a laundress." Waiters at Mori's would have understood. They regularly added the cost of their tablecloths onto Hood's cover charge.

Hood's next big commission was the Daily News Building, but before he began serious work on it he was in the news with his bold designs for a futuristic Manhattan. "There never was an architect who loved his art who did not love to pipe dream," he once said. "It is almost an essential part of his temperament."

Elaborate drawings of Hood's City of Towers were presented at exhibition at Manhattan's Grand Central Palace in the summer of 1927. As in Corbett's plan, New York is transformed into a city of freestanding towers, miniature towns under one roof, each of them with apartments, offices, and a host of recreational and commercial facilities. But there are no pedestrian skywalks in Hood's metropolitan model, only greatly widened avenues to increase circulation, with pavements running alongside them. And his towers, unlike Corbett's, are shaped like trees, built from the ground up on long columns—tree trunks—with no livable space below the tenth or eleventh floors. Only staircases and elevators reach down to the ground level. This was to give all tenants, not just those on the upper floors, pleasant views and plenty of sunlight. "Our much maligned skyscraper," Hood wrote, "is providing space up in its towers where a huge part of the population may work free of the dust, noise and gasoline fumes of the street, in a much brighter atmosphere than is evident in the low cities of London and Paris."

In a later version of Tower City, Hood suggested that Manhattan's towers be organized into self-contained superblocks—skyscraper parks—each occupying an entire city block. Individual parks would be organized around a common economic interest, such as publishing, advertising, the clothing trades, or radio. Radio would be the organizing idea for Rockefeller Center—Radio City—Hood's last important commission. Beginning in 1929, the year he unveiled his superblock plan, his architecture firm began collaborating with a Rockefeller Center design team that included Harvey Wiley Corbett. This was how Hood proposed that Tower City be built: by visionary architects working hand-in-glove with civic-spirited capitalists on skyscraper superblocks that would gradually replace outmoded, low-rise structures—over decades—not, as in Le Corbusier's plan for Paris, in one shockingly sudden bulldozing and rebuilding process. Manhattan's ceaseless process of building up and tearing down would create opportunities to assemble the land and construct these highly specialized business centers. "It is safe to say," Hood told a reporter, "that there is hardly a block in the center of New York that will not be torn down and rebuilt within the next 20 years." This excited him; "it gave the architect a chance to experiment."

Instead of having dozens of competing speculators rebuild downtown neighborhoods, Hood suggested that each project be guided by "a single directing intelligence" with the power and money to purchase the land and oversee its development, as the New York Central Railroad had done in the area of its old rail yards, and the Rockefeller family was planning to do at Rockefeller Center. While master builders like Fred French favored market-driven urban growth, and reformers like Lewis Mumford favored government planning, Raymond Hood placed his faith in a union of government and business, an alliance based on mutual self-interest. Only enlightened capitalists, working with architects and city authorities, could, he believed, provide the foresight and funds "to prevent New York from strangling itself by its own growth," while, at the same time, increasing human congestion—"the best thing we have in New York."

Hood's skyscraper parks were the pivotal points of concentration in his Tower City, places where much of the city's business could be conducted face-to-face. "What we want is congestion and more congestion," he told a group of his colleagues over coffee and cigars at the Architectural League. "Wall Street for the bankers; the garment centers for the cloak-and-suiters. The concentration of trades in different districts, and so on, and then shoot them up in the air in hundred-story buildings. In this way you can pay a dozen calls in the morning, all within easy reach. . . . New York has the right idea—a busy bee hive with bees swarming all over; just a fine big ant hill with ants everywhere, that's my idea of what a city should be." The antithesis, he said, was Paris, "a dead city. . . . Try to get from one place of business to another; you might just as well take a day off to transact a single affair." Paris, he claimed, was "badly planned," badly planned, that is, for business, unlike Hood's ideal city, a place built "solid" for business.

Raymond Hood's "paradoxical" idea was "to solve congestion by creating more congestion," writes Dutch architect Rem Koolhaas. "The wonder of New York," said Hood, "is that . . . a man can work within a ten-minute walk of a quarter of a million people." The skyscraper had created this condition; and by concentrating people and business, it made it possible to carve out additional space for motor vehicles and outdoor recreation. But while there are spacious parks in Hood's plan, it is, as Koolhaas writes, a city primarily of "interior pleasures" and indoor encounters, many of them close to the clouds. In his 1978 manifesto, *Delirious New York*, Koolhaas embraced Hood's ultramodern culture of congestion; but Mumford, who admired Hood's individual buildings, found his Tower City chillingly dehumanizing. Its super-skyscrapers were freestanding monoliths, isolated from the city around them, like the gigantic underground buildings that housed the Helot-like workers of German filmmaker Fritz Lang's dystopia *Metropolis*, which appeared in theaters the year Hood unveiled his City of Towers.*

Hood's City of Towers was also a City of Bridges, tremendous river spans lined with exclusive apartment houses. Imagine the island of Manhattan, circa 1950, as a giant "tarantula," he wrote, its legs spreading over the city's waterways, one leg extending all the way to Staten Island, the other to New Jersey. Imagine, further, these legs as bridges, as many as a hundred of them, with roadways as wide as Park Avenue. On the flanks of the bridges are skyscraping apartments for millionaires and "near millionaires," and every bridge spills into Midtown Manhattan. Captivated by Hood's visionary scheme, a *New York Times* reporter imagined a day when the bridge communities would sponsor "great annual regattas and water contests, participated in by picked champions from all the bridges."

Where are the common laborers in Hood's "Manhattan 1950"? There is no room for them on an island given over completely to commerce, consumption, and communications—and Park Avenue–style living. Hood predicted that escalating land values and the onrush of commerce would eventually "wash off the island" all but the city's capitalist mandarins, and deposit the laborers and clerks, along with many of the industries that employed them, in the outlying boroughs, where they were increasingly headed anyway in 1927, Manhattan having lost over half a million residents in the previous seven years.

The eminent Italian architect and historian Manfredo Tafuri claims it was not Hood's intention "to furnish solutions. His aim, rather, was to offer an ideal image of the metropolis." Hood would have disagreed. The only part of his hypothetical city he considered "utopian" was the bridge communities. The remainder of the plan was "practical rather than visionary," and could be in place, he said, by 1950. Manhattan would become a city of mega-towers in the 1960s, a decade or so later than Hood predicted, although, thankfully, not nearly on the scale he envisioned.

Raymond Hood had launched his career as a Manhattan architect with a better idea. His Radiator Building, built to human scale, open to sun and air, with a small municipal park and a neoclassical public library across the street, would have been a preferable template for a reconstituted New York.

---

* Hood's self-sufficient skyscrapers are harbingers of huge, multipurpose complexes such as Detroit's Renaissance Center and Atlanta's CNN Center, entirely "internalized environments" whose "distinguishing characteristic is self-containment," wrote the urban visionary William H. Whyte. "Intended for the salvation of the downtown, they tend to be independent of it and the design proclaims them so." William H. Whyte, *City: Rediscovering the Center* (NY: Doubleday, Doran, 1988), 206.

The Regional City

Into the 1930s, Lewis Mumford remained the principal opponent of Hood's and Corbett's plans for a skyscraper megalopolis. But Mumford was a dreamer as well as a critic. "In a world of words Mumford is a master builder," his friend Mark Van Doren described his special genius. "He builds cities, societies, civilizations, cultures—truly builds them, with the most durable stuff available to man: ideas." Mumford's urban plan took in the entire metropolitan region, not just Manhattan. A decentralist, he proposed a wholly new settlement pattern for the region, one that led to the creation of two experimental communities— one in New York City, the other in one of its suburbs.

A native New Yorker, the illegitimate and only child of Elvina Mumford, a German American boardinghouse matron, Lewis Mumford grew up in a lower-middle-class neighborhood of brownstones bounded on the east by Central Park and on the west by the Hudson River. After attending Stuyvesant High School, the finest science school in the city, he enrolled in the tuition-free City College of New York—the immigrants' Harvard—but dropped out after a year, dissatisfied with the type of formal education that substituted knowledge about life for direct experience with it.

New York, which he called his Walden Pond, shaped his life and his work. "I was a child of the city," he opens his luminous autobiography, *Sketches from Life*. "New York exerted a greater and more constant influence on me than did my family." Under the influence of his distant mentor Patrick Geddes, the Scottish botanist and town planner, whose motto was *Vivendo discimus* ("By living we learn"), he began exploring Manhattan's streets and buildings and neighborhoods with the same keen-eyed curiosity that Thoreau brought to his exploration of the rural scene, doing pen and ink drawings of buildings, painting watercolors of river scenes, and conducting amateur geological surveys.

Over a lifetime of steady effort—he died in 1990—this furiously productive autodidact produced a body of writing that for its range and richness is unmatched in modern American letters. "Our century has no other figure like Lewis Mumford," Paul Goldberger observed: essayist, social philosopher, historian of the city and civilization, urban planner, literary critic, biographer of Herman Melville, and "surely the greatest architecture critic of our age." The writer Malcolm Cowley called him "the last of the great humanists."

In 1927, Mumford was living with his beautiful, dark-eyed wife, Sophia, and their two-year-old son Geddes in Sunnyside Gardens, Queens, a small residential community that he and his associates in a group called the Regional

Planning Association of America (RPAA) had recently designed and built. A solidly set man with flashing brown eyes and a closely trimmed mustache, Mumford had joined the RPAA in 1923, the year it was founded by three of the outstanding figures in American regional planning: architects Clarence Stein and Henry Wright and environmentalist Benton MacKaye, founder of the Appalachian Trail. Within a year after joining the RPAA at age twenty-nine, Mumford was its leading theoretician, proposing ideas that would exert a powerful hold on the American city planning fraternity for the next three decades.

He and his small group of kindred thinkers had come under the spell of Ebenezer Howard, the court reporter turned urban visionary who founded England's Garden City movement. In *Garden Cities of To-morrow,* published in 1898, Howard outlined a plan to stop the unbounded growth of industrial London and restore the city to human scale by relocating its excess population in new medium-sized towns situated in the outlying countryside. These self-sufficient garden communities, with their own businesses and industries, were to be ringed by greenbelts of farm and parkland, placed so as to prevent urban sprawl. Land was to be communally owned and the towns controlled by public authorities to prevent speculation and keep the population to a manageable number—around thirty thousand. In the decade before World War I, Howard supervised the building of two garden cities just north of London—Letchworth and Welwyn Garden City. Inspired by his ideas and example, the RPAA drafted plans and programs that challenged prevailing trends in American city planning.

Mayor Walker and his urban strategists saw New York City's growth as both inevitable and salutary, and proposed to alleviate the city's congestion by building additional roads, bridges, tunnels, and subways. The RPAA, by contrast, proposed to depopulate New York City and resettle hundreds of thousands of its people in new regional communities. The garden city was to be the alternative to the bloated metropolis; it would also be its salvation, Mumford argued. By siphoning off population, it would drive down urban land prices artificially inflated by skyscraper congestion, allowing New York to build more parks, playgrounds, museums, and intimate neighborhoods of two- and three-story houses, apartments, and shops.

Mumford was one of the first modern writers to question the widely held assumption that rising land prices and physical expansion were unassailable signs of urban progress. The real losers in Midtown's surging commercial growth, he argued in his 1926 essay "The Intolerable City," were the citizens themselves. Exorbitantly high rents made it virtually impossible for parks, museums, civic centers, art galleries, and other less profitable or nonprofit cultural institutions—along with small stores, community swimming pools, and playgrounds—to compete for urban space with skyscrapers and other lavishly financed commercial projects.

Mumford was equally concerned with the ecological impact of explosive urban growth. His essays for the RPAA contain the kernel of what is perhaps the first environmental argument in urban literature against the metropolis. Comparing New York City to a living biological organism, he argued that when it grew too large it disrupted its symbiotic relationship with its surrounding territory, destroying the ecological balance between city and country. Growth overtaxed local resources, forcing the ravenous megacity to reach out further and further for water, fuel, food, building materials, and sewage disposal areas. At this point, its relationship with its region became parasitic and a cycle of ecological imbalance began. The metropolis merged into its contiguous communities, consuming farmland and the forests and creating a continuous belt of settlement—a megalopolis, an ecological disaster area.

But for Mumford, trend was not destiny. The automobile, the telephone, the radio, and long-distance electric power transmission promised to bring about a new age of industrial and residential decentralization—and with it, environmentally balanced communities. To hasten this movement and give it direction, Mumford and his colleagues in the RPAA proposed a network of regional cities for the New York metropolitan area, each with its own industries and housing for a full range of income groups. These were to be real cities, not income-segregated dormitory suburbs. For this reason, Mumford preferred the term "regional city" to Howard's "garden city"; garden city connoted a leafy suburban enclave, not the kind of lively and diverse small city the RPAA favored.

In 1923, Clarence Stein persuaded his friend Alexander Bing, a civic-conscious New York real estate developer, to back the building of the first American regional city. The following year the RPAA formed the City Housing Corporation, a limited-dividend company with a ceiling on profits, and began building Sunnyside Gardens on an undeveloped waste site in Queens that it purchased from the Pennsylvania Railroad. Completed four years later, it became, almost instantly, a thriving community of nonprofessional workers—mechanics, office workers, and tradesmen, along with Mumford, Wright, and a number of other young New York writers and artists who, on becoming parents, fled bohemia for the outer boroughs. The affordable houses were oriented for maximum sunlight and breezes; and clusters of them faced inward toward common lawns and gardens designed "for restful gatherings or for quiet play." It was an ideal place to start a family, and was only a ten-minute subway ride from central Manhattan.

The City Housing Corporation made a profit on Sunnyside Gardens, and the RPAA used these funds to begin work in 1928 on Radburn, a far larger community, intended for 25,000 residents, on undeveloped farmland in Fair Lawn, New Jersey, sixteen miles from New York City. Radburn was never completed—it became a victim of the Great Depression, which bankrupted the City Housing Corporation—but two large neighborhoods that were built—"superblocks" sealed off from motor traffic—housed a total of one thousand residents by 1931.

Mumford realized that the RPAA would need help from the private sector and heavy government subsidies to build full-scale regional cities in other locations in the New York region. But New York City businesses had a direct stake in congestion, and even the progressive Smith Administration—a national leader in housing reform—had no interest in the program: it would be prohibitively expensive, and it called for government seizure of private land, a socialist idea. An appeal to the Republican dominated federal government would have been an empty exercise. This lack of public and private support made Mumford's regional towns of villagelike superblocks even more unrealistic than Hood's central city of skyscraper superblocks. In denouncing Hood's plan in 1927, Mumford identified, inadvertently, a fatal flaw in his own urban program. "No one has suggested where the funds for [Tower City] reconstruction are to come from."

But perhaps a small beginning could be made in, of all places, the central city. While Mumford was convinced that the kind of neighborhood planning he favored could be carried out best in thinly settled areas far from the city, where the land was inexpensive and the entire site could be laid out, he believed that a variant of the neighborhood unit could work in the clotted heart of New York City. By blocking off some streets to vehicular traffic and relocating schools, branch libraries, small health clinics, shops, movie theaters, and pocket parks within the new superblocks, New York City officials could relieve the urban transit system of some of its burdensome load and provide secure and healthy environments for raising children.

Impossible? Strangely unmentioned in Mumford's writing is Fred French's Tudor City, a self-enclosed superblock in the heart of the Grand Central District, an affordable pedestrian-centered community within blocks of everything Midtown Manhattan offered. But as we have seen, the Great Depression ruined Fred French and his idea died with him. More tragically, when well-intentioned city planners created urban redevelopment districts for the economically disadvantaged in the 1950s, they turned to Mumford's superblock idea and created self-enclosed projects that banished what Mumford considered the most valuable of the city's features—its teeming streets. Instead of lively cities within cities, housing experts, with funds extracted from state and federal government by New York City building czar Robert Moses, erected bleak high-rise projects—super-slums—sealed off from the city that surrounded them.

Although Mumford denied it, there was an undercurrent of anti-urbanism in his writings, "powerful and city destroying ideas," Jane Jacobs called them in her seminal 1961 book, *The Death and Life of Great American Cities.* Mumford directed his fire not at the small and medium-size historic cities he favored in his travels, places like Salzburg, Edinburgh, and Oxford, but at large metropolitan concentrations—conurbations, Ebenezer Howard called them. Over the course of the 1920s he grew progressively disenchanted with New York, the center "of a furious decay, which [is] called growth, enterprise, and greatness." When he could finally afford it, he moved his family in 1936 to Leedsville, New York, a hamlet of a dozen or so houses in rural Dutchess County. Working out of a study no larger than a monastic cell, he continued to write on architecture and art for *The New Yorker*, commuting to New York by train—he never learned to drive—once a week to explore its museums and galleries, its new buildings and bridges. And from Leedsville, with the fury of an Old Testament prophet, he excoriated the skyscraper and the automobile for ruining the New York of his youth, where the automobile was a curiosity and most of the skyscrapers were well spaced, sticking out like so many pins in a pincushion.

The ideals Mumford prized in cities were community and sociability, order and stability—village values, he called them. In his haste to condemn, however, he failed to see that New York in the 1920s was—and still is—a city of neighborhoods, thousands of them, each nearly self-sufficient. "No matter where you live in New York," wrote essayist E. B. White, "you will find within a block or two" nearly everything you need: a grocery store, a barbershop, a newsstand, a dry cleaner, a laundry, a delicatessen, a flower shop, an undertaker's parlor, a movie house, a tailor, a drugstore, and a shoe repair shop. Mumford rarely ventured into these urban villages; his abhorrence of the size and furious pace of Manhattan drove him to focus almost solely on the city's failures, most of them center city failures. Midtown, America's greatest opportunity center, was, for him, "solidified chaos"—noisy, filthy, and filled with beggars, souvenir salesmen, and garish advertising.

In his repugnance, Mumford had turned to a placid alternative: cities that would have been devoid of Manhattan's messy vitality. Somehow he failed to see that the very things he liked most about New York—its theater life, museums, libraries, and galleries—were, in E. B. White's words, the "by-products" of the congestion he abhorred. "I have . . . to confess shamefacedly . . . I like life enormously as it is . . . lived in New York," wrote critic Henry McBride. "The congestion that so disturbs Mr. Mumford seems . . . much to the taste of average New Yorkers. They particularly like to go where they think everybody is going and if a percentage of them get killed in the effort to see Mr. Babe Ruth play baseball, why it is apt to be considered a more than usually successful afternoon. As for the looks of the place, that suits me too. Of course it is anarchic. . . . But it has a wild and curious beauty."

The skyscrapers Mumford detested were for White—raised in suburban Mount Vernon, New York—visible symbols of "aspiration and faith, the white plume saying that the way is up." The city's energy added to its allure—that and New Yorkers' superhuman adaptability. "Mass hysteria is a terrible force," White wrote in *Here Is New York*, his paean to his adopted city, "yet New Yorkers seem always to escape it by some tiny margin: they sit in stalled subways without claustrophobia, they extricate themselves from panic situations by some lucky wisecrack, they meet confusion and congestion with patience and grit—a sort of perpetual muddling through."

"It is a miracle that New York works at all," said White. "The whole thing is implausible." And the thing that made it work—that has always made it work—was concentration and diversity. This made it fertile ground for the exchange of information and the cultivation of new ideas—new ways of building, selling, communicating, and entertaining. Walter Chrysler discovered this, and so did Roxy, Texas Guinan, Fred French, Irwin Chanin, Tex Rickard, Helena Rubinstein, Hattie Carnegie, David Sarnoff, Bill Paley, and, yes, Raymond Hood, whose ideas on congestion and concentration—stripped of their skyscraper ecstasy—are richly suggestive. No new town, or town planner, could possibly replicate what New York provided. It was a city so spontaneously alive it contained "the seeds of [its] own regeneration."

To Master a Metropolis

In 1927, the Russell Sage Foundation published the first volumes of its twelve-volume survey and blueprint for the New York metropolitan area: The Regional Plan of New York and Its Environs. It was the most ambitious plan ever put forward for a major American city, and Mumford should have been hopeful. Urban experts of unimpeachable authority had drafted the plan, and their recommendations were based on the kind of exhaustive regional survey Patrick Geddes considered the sine qua non of proper planning. The plan's director, moreover, was Scotsman Thomas Adams, who had worked with Ebenezer Howard to develop England's Garden City movement and had served as manager of Letchworth, the first garden city. But Mumford had seen parts of the plan in draft form as early as 1925 and was greatly disappointed.

"I would like to register my dissent . . . before a spade of earth has been turned over or a block of schist dynamited," he wrote in *The New Yorker* in 1932, after the final volume was published. The Adams plan ran counter to the guiding principle of the RPAA, accepting as "automatic" and "inevitable" the continued growth of the New York metropolitan area and mid-Manhattan's dominance of that explosively expanding region. A friend and old ally had become, in Mumford's view, a saboteur of the very urban ideas he had once championed. With this plan, the determined decentralist had become a leader of the forces of metropolitan concentration.

A month after *The New Yorker* piece appeared, Mumford tore into Adams with full fury in a two-part essay in *The New Republic*, pronouncing the Russell Sage plan "a monumental failure," "a warning rather than a good example." Adams answered in kind, and he and Mumford went at each other like two scorpions in a bottle.

The Regional Plan put New York City at the forefront of urban design, worldwide. It had a bolder social agenda than Daniel Burnham's famous 1909 Plan for Chicago, with its narrowly aesthetic and architectural orientation. And it embraced a much wider area: New York City and its encircling suburbs, towns, and farmland, an area covering three states and 436 local and municipal governments, with a combined population of nearly nine million. Its eight volumes of exhaustive research and analysis, a number of them classics of planning literature, fed into two culminating volumes filled with recommendations for virtually every department of metropolitan life: housing, industry, trade, transportation, recreation, land use, and architecture. The implementation of the plan, however, was left to municipal and regional authorities. The planners themselves had no power to carry out their agenda; their proposals were purely advisory. Even so, the plan became highly influential, in part because the Regional Plan Association, the independent body created by the Russell Sage Foundation in 1922 to draft the master document, remained in existence beyond 1932 and lobbied strenuously and often effectively for its proposals.*

---

* The Regional Plan Association had far greater weight and authority than the Department of City Planning that Jimmy Walker's administration created in 1930.

Reaching four decades into the future, the Russell Sage planners projected that Manhattan would be in the 1960s what it was fast becoming in the 1920s: an international center of finance, communications, entertainment, shopping, and advertising—the world's first postindustrial city, with its supreme downtown. But this was not to be Harvey Wiley Corbett's Brobdingnagian metropolis of colossal towers and spacious greenery. It was to be a commercial island, purged of its slums and unsightly industrial areas, and its new skyscrapers would look strikingly like the Empire State Building—freestanding towers resting on narrow bases that didn't crowd the land. There would be no Corbusier-like purging of old skyscrapers; the Chrysler, French, Chanin, and Daily News Buildings would stand, proud urban monuments refitted to new uses. Adams insisted that tearing down older and smaller buildings and erecting towers of far greater height and volume would not alleviate congestion.

In Adams's *Regional Plan*, Manhattan's linear avenues were to be widened and there was to be an expressway along the East River shoreline, the precursor to Robert Moses's FDR Drive. Adams and his fellow planners also suggested a parkway and major beautification program for the Hudson shoreline north of the main dockage and rail facilities of the New York Central Railroad, a project Moses had unveiled in 1930. Harvey Wiley Corbett was on one of the key committees that created the *Regional Plan*, and he snuck in a proposal for elevated and arcaded walkways in the downtown, but Adams limited them to only a few highly congested Midtown streets.

The Russell Sage planners proposed to relocate almost all of Manhattan's industries, along with their workers, to Brooklyn, Queens, the Bronx, and those parts of New Jersey along the Hudson River. This would bring into being a vast factory and blue-collar housing zone within a twenty-mile radius of Midtown. Only light industries that had to be in or near Midtown, near buyers and suppliers, would remain there. In their new locations, the diffused industries would have plenty of space for expansion and for loft and loading facilities, space hard to come by in clotted Manhattan. This was roughly the program of industrial decentralization proposed by Raymond Hood, although Adams and his regional planners hoped that private developers could be encouraged to build modern and affordable apartments for working-class families on handsomely landscaped boulevards and cross streets. And unlike Hood's City of Bridges, no attention was given to the housing requirements of the wealthy; Manhattan's moguls were already regally situated.

Outside the factory zone, undeveloped land would be reserved for farming, recreation, and large private homes. This was Thomas Adams's idea. The master planner was convinced that substantial houses on lots of an acre or more would prevent the land from being subdivided into tacky suburban developments. Although there were no plans for fully formed garden cities with greenbelts and superblocks, it was suggested that the New Jersey's Hackensack Meadows, only five miles from Midtown, be transformed into a model industrial community, with shops and theaters, playgrounds and parks.

New rapid transit lines and arterial highways would tie together the entire region; and a high-speed electric freight and passenger system devised by William Wilgus would alleviate much of Manhattan's congestion. Under Wilgus's system, vehicular and rail traffic headed to destinations beyond Manhattan was to be detoured around it on "by-passes or belt lines," a metropolitan beltway for cars running adjacent to a rail "loop." Tunnels under the Hudson would connect rail terminals in New Jersey with new freight terminals in Manhattan and Brooklyn, thinning out economically injurious crowding in New York Harbor.

Outside the city, a network of landscaped parkways—restricted to private automobiles—would connect New York City to unspoiled nature: mountains, lakes, and seashore. In their enthusiasm for parkways, however, the Russell Sage planners made the same mistake that Lewis Mumford made. Seeing the automobile as a useful instrument of economic decentralization, they badly miscalculating its city-killing potential. "No profound changes in the densities and general structure of cities are in sight as a result of the motor vehicle," Adams wrote in a 1931 postscript to the plan, a prophecy that echoed falsely the very moment he advanced it. The parkways that Robert Moses was furiously building in the very year the *Regional Plan* was published were already becoming escape roads to suburbia, not just access ways to nature. And they would be augmented in the 1930s by ambitious federal and state highway systems. The New Deal program of federally guaranteed mortgages for single-family houses, and New York City government's refusal to build new subway lines outside city limits—on the understandable argument that they would pull people away from the city, not closer to it—were the final and fatal hammer blows to the *Regional Plan*'s "dream of a dense, efficient, prosperous industrial zone" tied to Manhattan by mass transit.

The Manhattan that the *Regional Plan* envisioned, on the other hand, was largely realized, with one profound exception. Adams and his colleagues failed to anticipate the massive role the federal government would take after World War II in building and subsidizing housing for the needy. This oversight had more to do with policy than prophecy. Adams, who had spurned many of Howard's garden city ideas, was philosophically opposed to public housing, as were most other planners on his committee. The Russell Sage Foundation, moreover, was made up largely of local titans of industry and commerce, capitalists unalterably opposed to federal meddling in the marketplace.

This was Mumford's most telling criticism of the *Regional Plan.* "No comprehensive planning for the improvement of living conditions can be done," he wrote, "as long as property values and private enterprise are looked upon as sacred." With the plan committed to the idea that "all housing should yield a fair return on the investment," there was little hope, Mumford argued, that the needs of the two-thirds of New York City's population that couldn't afford decent housing would be met.

Thomas Adams, Mumford fulminated, had been turned into a puppet of New York's financial interests. Deeply offended, Adams responded with an equally wounding remark, one that forever ended their friendship. "I am sorry we cannot count on support from your able pen," he wrote Mumford, "because, with all deference, your duty to the public is more important than your intellectual enjoyment as a critic."

As Mumford despondently expected, it was the *Regional Plan*, not his own organization's ideas, that set the agenda for collective action in the New York metropolitan area. By 1932, over one hundred of its nearly five hundred specific recommendations had been implemented. But that impressive record is deceptive. Many of the proposals woven into the plan had been conceived or partially built before the final plan was published. Most of the parkway and park programs recommended by the regional planners were the work of Robert Moses, an administrator of broad vision and vehement resolve. Neither a professional planner nor a politician, he would become the greatest master builder in New York history, shaping post-1927 New York for four decades through his monarchial control over public works and public housing. His would be the largest road-and-bridge-building program since the Roman Empire.

But the master builder's influence was not as encompassing as Robert Caro suggests in his magisterial biography *The Power Broker.* Another metropolitan power broker, the Port of New York Authority, first suggested highway and parkway programs that Moses carried through; and it conceived and constructed massive regional projects of its own.* Created in 1921 by the states

---

* In 1972, the Port of New York Authority was renamed the Port Authority of New York and New Jersey "in deference to that smaller state's political power and sensitivities." Jameson W. Doig, *Empire on the Hudson: Entrepreneurial Vision and Political Power at the Port of New York Authority* (NY: Columbia University Press, 2001).

of New York and New Jersey, the Port Authority was ineffectual at first, with little power or public support to carry out the transportation improvements its founders proposed. But over the course of the 1920s and early 1930s, it learned how to accrue independent authority by issuing bonds to undertake great public works, building them, as Moses's projects were built, "with unexpected speed and without direct burden to the taxpayer."

In November 1927, two of the most stupendous public works projects in the history of New York City were in the news: the Holland Tunnel, which was opened to traffic that month, and the George Washington Bridge, whose groundbreaking was a great civic event. The world's longest vehicular tunnel was the work of a joint commission formed in 1919 by the states of New York and New Jersey, but when completed it was taken over by the Port Authority. The world's longest suspension bridge was the first great project of the Port Authority. These two titanic physical structures are testaments to a time when America's greatest city not only planned big, but built big, as well.

CHAPTER TWENTY-TWO

HIGHWAY UNDER THE HUDSON

*The automobile had a greater spatial and social impact
on cities than any other technological innovation since the
development of the wheel.*

KENNETH T. JACKSON

Tunnel Day

In November 1927, Manhattan Island was "connected with the United States,"
wrote *The New York Times*. "Instead of standing in line at the entrances of fifteen ferries that now serve as the physical means of communication between
New Jersey and New York City, fifteen million automobiles and motor trucks
will drive every year into the twin tubes of the Holland Tunnel under the Hudson River and speed from shore to shore in a few minutes."

A joint project of the states of New York and New Jersey, the tunnel cost
$48 million and took seven years to build, seven years of contentious politi-
cal infighting and fractious labor disputes that drove up the cost by $20 mil-
lion and caused the project to fall more than three years behind schedule. But
the vehicular tunnel was an engineering triumph, the Eighth Wonder of the
World, contemporaries called it.

Before it was built, the only tunnels under the Hudson River between New
York City and New Jersey were rail tubes for passenger service; and not a single
bridge spanned the river, nearly a mile wide in places. Cars, trucks, horse-
drawn wagons, and pedestrians jammed the ferryboats that plied the Hudson
between Manhattan and New Jersey. Most "walk-on" passengers were New
Jersey commuters employed in Manhattan, and travelers headed to and from

454

the castellated rail terminals that lined the New Jersey shore. Only two national railroads had passenger stations in the city: the New York Central and the Pennsylvania, forcing tens of thousands of New Yorkers daily to depend on the unreliable ferries to get to their trains on time. In 1926, 120 million people used the Hudson River ferries. When there was impenetrable morning fog, it was said that half the employees in the city were late for work and thousands of travelers missed their trains.

The ferries were steam-driven and immensely old, great turtlelike creatures that thrashed their way through the oily black waters. Heavy fog, high winds, and occasional ice jams meant long interruptions in service—as did frequent labor disputes. At rush hour and on holiday weekends cars, buses, and trucks—an average of fifty thousand daily in 1926—were delayed for up to four hours, forming lines that extended for miles into downtown Jersey City. And on every crossing—fair weather or foul, night or day—ferry captains had to fight their way through the most densely crowded harbor in the world, dodging thick swarms of barges and freighters and steering for their slips almost by instinct.

The Holland Tunnel would reduce, but not end ferry service on the Hudson; it alone could not handle the ever-increasing number of cars and trucks in the New York area. But with the tunnel completed, and a bridge at Washington Heights under construction, "every blast of the ferry hooter had a dying ring."

The Holland Tunnel—two separate, parallel tunnels, one for eastbound, the other for westbound traffic—was dedicated on November 12, 1927, at 4:55 P.M. At that moment, President Calvin Coolidge, aboard his yacht in the Potomac River, pressed the golden telegraph key that President Woodrow Wilson had used to set off the detonation that opened the Panama Canal. An electrical charge pulled back two enormous American flags covering the openings of the tunnel on the New York side, and thousands of pedestrians surged into the white-tiled, brightly lit passageway and began walking from "shore to shore," singing as they strolled and playfully shouting to hear the echo of their voices. Within an hour, an estimated 25,000 people had covered the 9,250 feet from entrance to exit. Another fifty thousand walked through the tunnel from New Jersey to Manhattan. Along the way, groups of celebrators paused at the brightly painted blue line on the wall marking the boundary between the states joined by the revolutionary under-river road. Manhattan families stood in New York state and reached out, across the line, to grip the hands of Bayonne families standing in New Jersey. At 7 P.M. the tunnel was closed for a final inspection, to reopen at 12:01 A.M., the time set for vehicular traffic to begin its "regular, paid passage."

The first car to enter the tunnel carried General George R. Dyer, chairman of the New York State Bridge and Tunnel Commission. In the second car was Mrs. Clifford M. Holland, widow of the first chief engineer of the tunnel, whose death was hastened by unrelenting work on the great civic project that bore his name. Seated next to her was Mrs. Milton H. Freeman, widow of the chief engineer who succeeded Holland and had also died while the tunnel was under construction. The third vehicle was a delivery truck from Bloomingdale Brothers department store. This was the start of something. The payoff would be enormous for Midtown businesses that relied on trucks.

On the New Jersey side more than one thousand cars were massed at the tunnel plaza, awaiting the thrill of driving under a tremendous American river. They were seven abreast for four blocks, and the line was even longer on the New York side. Drivers leaned on their horns, and passengers hung out of the windows blowing horns and setting off sirens, creating a din reporters compared to New Year's Eve in Times Square. On a signal, they entered the tunnel, paying a fifty-cent toll. Over fifty thousand vehicles passed through the tubes that day, carrying nearly a quarter of a million passengers. "I'm going through again," shouted one motorist who had already made the round-trip. A taxi driver claimed he was making his eighth trip with passengers. New York City sightseeing buses became "tunnel excursionists," their Times Square hawkers charging a dollar for round-trips. No other public work since the opening of the Brooklyn Bridge "had so touched the imagination of the people," said tunnel administrators.

In an informal 1929 poll, Manhattan officials were asked to pick the greatest "wonders" of the city. The subway system and the Holland Tunnel tied for first place.

Pedestrians who passed through the tunnel on dedication day reported that the air was far fresher than the air they breathed on the streets of Manhattan. That was the accomplishment of Clifford Holland and his associate Ole Singstad, codesigners of the world's first ventilation system for vehicular tunnels. When work began on the Holland Tunnel there were half a dozen other vehicular tunnels in the world, but none was nearly as long as the Hudson tubes, and therefore did not require state-of-the-art ventilation systems. When New York and New Jersey formed a joint commission in 1919 to construct the Holland Tunnel, no one knew if a subaqueous roadway over nine thousand feet long could be purged—consistently and completely—of the poisonous carbon monoxide discharged by gasoline-powered vehicles. It was one of history's great construction gambles.

The risk was taken because the demand was acute. Speaking at the tunnel's dedication ceremonies, Governor Al Smith reminded people of the crisis that had stung the rival states into concerted action. "In 1918 . . . we had an ice jam in the Hudson River and Manhattan Island was threatened with a coal famine while hundreds of thousands of tons of coal, lying in the Jersey break-up yards, were visible from the tall buildings in Lower Manhattan. We were, nevertheless, unable to get it across the river. That can never happen again."

That crisis was a product of the thickening congestion in the Port of New York, congestion more damaging to the city's commercial life than the traffic bottlenecks on its streets. With only the New York Central Railroad having overland access to the docks and piers of Manhattan, the national railroads that serviced the port had to float their cargo to Manhattan and Brooklyn in six thousand and more tugs and barges. Harbor delays were so frequent by 1917 that some shippers began switching to other ports. Grain shipments, once the maritime metropolis's greatest export, began migrating to Canada. Great quantities of cotton went to Galveston; sugar and coal to Newport; cocoa beans to Philadelphia; and coffee and sugar to New Orleans.

But the port problem was more complex than this. The Port of New York was, at the same time, the most prosperous and prodigal shipping center on earth, enormously rich yet disastrously wasteful, essential to New York's well-being yet the chief source of its vulnerability. New York City could not have survived for a week without the complex waterborne shipping system the railroads assembled to surmount the Hudson River barrier, yet this maritime system was "inefficient and disorganized to the point of chaos," writes port historian Carl Condit, "vulnerable to natural and human events of a destructive character." Only when chaos led to catastrophe was action taken to tunnel and later bridge the North River.

The Port of New York

"New York City owes its location, its growth, its prosperity, and even its very existence, to its port," writes historian Kenneth Jackson. It was the port, primarily—not the big banks on Wall Street—that made New York City the metropolitan powerhouse of the 1920s. Historically, the port preceded Wall Street and made it possible, drawing in the capital that was traded on its floor; and it was the port that gave New York its core character and its first burst of prosperity.

From the time of the Dutch settlement in the early seventeenth century, New York's location on a wide and deep harbor at the mouth of a inland-reaching river had made it a volatile and cosmopolitan place, a greedy, thriving city of the sea. For over a century it had been the gateway for people and products flowing into the country and the major shipping point for all that American farms and factories sent out to the world. In the 1920s, 42 percent of the country's foreign trade, by value, came over New York's wharves, and more than one-fifth of the foreign commerce of the United States passed through its port. This made it first in the world in shipping, and one of the greatest man-made spectacles on earth.

"The view is properly considered to be the most significant panorama that modern civilization offers and is fit to inspire the most profound musings of statesmen and poets," wrote the editors of *Fortune*. "Where the yards, docks, and factories line the waterfronts, puffs of smoke and steam rise in the air on a grander scale than in any region of volcanic springs. Back of these busy rims, vast acres of dwellings stretch almost to the horizons. And at the center, as if all these people and their activities had constituted a geologic force, the buildings of Manhattan are thrust toward the sky."

In 1927, New York was one of only a handful of the international cities built upon a great harbor. Of the twelve cities of the world with a population of two million or more, only four were located upon large harbors with deep-water channels to the sea: Buenos Aires, Leningrad, Shanghai, and New York. Like all essential ports, it was a place where rails met water—an industrial port, in fact, the "world's greatest industrial aggregate." On its shoreline were nearly thirty thousand places of production, along with rail terminals that connected the port with every part of the country. The Port of New York was the city's basic industry, giving employment to a quarter of a million workers, among them sailors, longshoremen, truck drivers, tugboat pilots, customs officials, brokers, and clerks. Another three million men and women worked in shipyards, assembly plants, oil refineries, or other enterprises directly dependent on the commerce of the port. New Yorkers think of Nantucket and Provincetown "as towns with a nautical atmosphere," wrote reporter A. J. Liebling, but fail to realize that "the fellow standing next to them in the subway is just as likely to be a second engineer off a freighter as a certified public accountant."

New York Harbor is enormous, capable, in 1927, of holding all the navies of the world. Located at the mouths of four rivers—the Raritan, Passaic, Hackensack, and Hudson—it has four estuaries and seven major bays, most of them larger than a good-size European harbor. Its 771-mile waterfront covers 1,500 square miles, making it larger than the state of Rhode Island. The harbor is connected by the Hudson River with inland waterways that put its tugs and barges in touch with the Great Lakes; and coastal freighters have access to

New England via the East River and Long Island Sound. And though the port has easy access to the open Atlantic, only seventeen miles away, it is protected from ocean storms and wave action, and its brackish tidal water rarely freezes, except, on occasion, in January.

That's fortunate, for 1920s New York could not have survived without shipping. "New York is more completely dependent upon water for survival than any other port city in the world," said noted poet and *Fortune* writer Archibald MacLeish. A city of stone, it grew nothing and had no industrial raw materials. Over 80 percent of what it needed came to it by water and rail. "Blot out" its two railroad stations and its piers and Midtown "would be in shambles in a week—a desolation in thirty days," wrote reporter Martin Clary in 1929.

The Hudson Piers

From Midtown, the port would have seemed a hard place not to notice; it was so big and noisy, belching smoke by day and "troubled at night by the clank of freighter-car couplings and the obscene bombilations of trucks." But almost all of Manhattan was cut off from it by the tracks of the New York Central, which ran along Manhattan's West Side, and by the dreary and dangerous neighborhoods that had grown up in Chelsea and Hell's Kitchen, their rows of tenements forming what novelist Mario Puzo called "the western wall of the great city." From a Midtown skyscraper one could gaze at smutty-nosed tugs pushing coal barges across the glistening sheet of New York Bay, but hidden from view were the guts and grit of the port—the freight facilities that hugged its Hudson River shoreline, piers handling everything from coal to coffee. If a curious New Yorker had wanted to go there, it was forbidden, blocked off by sheet iron fences and vigilant watchmen—and with good reason: theft was prevalent and thousands of tons of freight swinging precariously from cranes made it one of the most dangerous work sites on earth.

In 1927, more than half of all shipping in New York Harbor was concentrated along the Hudson and on the East River docks of Brooklyn. The Brooklyn piers handled most of the port's heavy international freight. Some seven miles of piers, grain elevators, freight terminals, and high brick warehouses extended in a solid line from Red Hook—a peninsula that opened onto Upper New York Bay—northward to Greenpoint, just below the Queensboro Bridge. But the Hudson shoreline, from the Battery to the northern reaches of Hell's Kitchen, a distance of some five miles, was the hub of the port. At the Chelsea Piers, running from Twelfth to Twenty-second Streets, fast-running ocean liners—the greyhounds of the sea—were berthed next to ponderous steam freighters that carried cargo and produce that was consumed in the city, along with freight arriving by rail from the rest of the country for transshipment to nearly every harbor on earth. Directly north of the Chelsea piers were additional docks and piers, and at Sixtieth Street—at the bottom of a bluff—the sprawling freight and harbor facilities of the New York Central, a clamorous industrial site only a short walk from Broadway.

Night and day, long trains arrived at the Central's yards: refrigerator cars stocked with beef, pork, lamb, and fresh milk; and cars carrying chickens and eggs, and livestock for slaughter (fish arrived on the other side of Manhattan, near the Fulton Fish market on the East River). The incoming freight cars were hooked up to smaller locomotives and sent as far as four miles south to St. John's Park Terminal, built by Commodore Vanderbilt just below Canal Street, where today stand the exit ramps of the Holland Tunnel. The New York Central's West Side Freight Line, known as the "Life Line of New York," carried three million tons of food into the city annually, but in the cruelest of ironies, the Life Line was a killer of children. Tenth and Eleventh Avenues, the cobblestone thoroughfares on which trains ran at street level, became known collectively as Death Avenue for the number of people killed and maimed by "treacherous freights." Many of the dead were schoolchildren, "ground to death," said the *Times*, some of them decapitated. In an early-twentieth-century report, the Bureau of Municipal Research claimed that over the course of nearly sixty years, New York Central engines killed 436 people. Outraged residents called one of the engines "The Butcher," and mounted periodic protests to have the tracks removed.

Beginning in the late nineteenth century, the city required the railroad to send a man or boy ahead of the locomotives on horseback, waving a red warning flag or a lantern—the West Side Cowboys, they called themselves. "Larry Angeluzzi spurred his jet-black horse proudly through a canyon formed by two great walls of tenements, and at the foot of each wall, marooned on their separate blue-slate sidewalks, little children stopped their games to watch him with silent admiration," wrote Mario Puzo in *The Fortunate Pilgrim*, his autobiographical novel of life in Hell's Kitchen in the 1920s and 1930s. "He swung his red lantern in a great arc; sparks flew from the iron hoofs of his horse as they rang on railroad tracks, set flush in the stones of Tenth Avenue, and slowly following horse, rider and lantern came the long freight train . . . heading for the open railroad yards that formed a great spark-filled plain down to the Hudson River."*

---

* The original St. John's Park Freight Terminal was demolished in 1936. A new terminal of the same name, on another site, was dedicated in 1934.

Merchant Armadas

Ten national railroads dominated the New Jersey shoreline directly across the Hudson from Manhattan's West Side. They were masters of an industrial barony that ran from Edgewater to Bayonne. Of the thirteen Class I roads that served New York City, all but three, the old Vanderbilt lines—the New York Central, the New Haven, and the Long Island—had facilities on the crowded Jersey shoreline. They brought into the harbor coal and cars, sand and cement, bricks and beef—and nearly everything else that New York urgently needed or wanted. "Shipping in the port constitutes the right arm of the giant organism and railroad transport the left," wrote one authority. "Deprived of one or the other, the organism would be disastrously crippled."

But these powerful railroads had been stopped from crossing the Hudson, first by the government of New York City, and later by the cost and difficulty of driving freight tunnels under the river or throwing bridges over it. They found it less costly to make the final leg of their run into New York by water, carrying their cargo to various points in the harbor. Even the mighty Pennsylvania, the only trunk line to burrow under the Hudson, could use its tubes for passenger trains only. It depended on its industrial navy of port vessels to send its freight into Gotham, turning the harbor into a "giant floating railroad yard."

Each railroad had its own merchant armada, and they competed fiercely, by speed and quality of service rather than cost. The railroads covertly agreed not to compete in any other way; that would have been ruinously expensive. As it was, the investment in terminals, classification yards, towing vessels, and specially equipped barges and car floats ran into the hundreds of millions of dollars. This was the disadvantage of operating in "the only seaport in the world divided into two parts by an un-bridged and un-tunneled waterway."

The railroads stubbornly resisted efforts by city officials to have them pool overlapping resources and establish central control over their harbor fleets. Instead, each built and maintained its own harbor hauling, or "lighterage," system. Bulk freight was brought to New Jersey's Hudson River shoreline from rail centers as far west as Omaha. It was then carried to New York City docks and cargo terminals by "lighters"—uncovered, flat-bottomed barges pushed or towed by tugboats—or by "car floats"—unpowered barges with standard rail tracks mounted on their decks. Between three thousand and five thousand railroad cars daily crossed the densely packed harbor in long lines of barges that were hard for tugboat captains to maneuver and impossible to stop if they ran into fast-approaching trouble. "In their heyday," observes Phillip Lopate, the modern prose-poet of the New York waterfront, "the barges were almost as synonymous with New York's iconography as its skyscrapers."

The haulage of the lighters and car floats was unloaded at Manhattan's docks and sent out on trucks to points in the city and beyond, or loaded onto ships headed for other coastal and international ports. Perishable fruits and vegetables were auctioned off to wholesalers right at the piers. Almost all the city's food and fuel came by water, the rest of it on the cars of the New York Central. With over 1,500 car floats and lighters and some 150 tugboats in the railroad companies' nautical empire, New York was the largest lighterage harbor in the world.

Even the New York Central, with its direct freight line into Manhattan, relied on the lighterage system, establishing a maritime line between its Weehawken, New Jersey, terminal and its rail yards in the West Sixties. From there cargo destined for transshipment by sea to other ports was floated directly to the piers of waiting ocean freighters. Its Manhattan tracks, laying several blocks inland, were cut off from these steamship piers by thickly settled neighborhoods and industrial districts that had grown up along the shoreline after the tracks had been laid in the mid-nineteenth century.

In the absence of sound railroad planning, the cumbersome and financially wasteful lighterage system—with two competing barges frequently doing the work of one—remained virtually unchanged from World War I to the 1960s, until the development of containerized shipping. Port authorities estimated the annual loss from preventable waste in the harbor at $2 billion a year around World War I. Even so, the railroads made money, and this prevented them from cooperating—that and the hope that the states of New York and New Jersey would soon build at least one vehicular tunnel under the river, allowing them to ship perishable items to Manhattan by truck.

On the Waterfront

Men who almost never stepped onto a moving ship were an integral part of the harbor's immense exchange engine. A veritable army of longshoremen, approximately fifty thousand strong, loaded and unloaded the cargo of lighters, car floats, and freighters berthed at the docks. Speed was the ruling principle on the docks; for the lighterage system to remain profitable cargoes had to be loaded and unloaded at breakneck pace, forcing some longshoremen to work for long stretches without interruption, sometimes for up to forty hours. With the docks packed tightly together on the crowded Manhattan shoreline, the work was deadly dangerous. Huge loads of cargo, jerked from the holds of ships, swung through the air, swaying and twirling as they narrowly missed the heads of working men. On the decks of ships "the whistles and calls of command, the rattle and whir of winches, the creaking of booms and drafts, the noise of chains are confusing to ear and brain," wrote Charles Barnes in his classic 1915 study, *The Longshoremen*. At night the dangers were far greater. Hand signals were hard to see; bone-weary men found it impossible to concentrate; and workers long accustomed to the job became—like high ironmen on the frames of skyscrapers—"indifferent to the dangers around them," even after seeing friends fall into the holds of ships, breaking legs, arms, and necks, and having their skulls smashed.

The men were fatalistic to an extreme. "When you go to work in the morning you never know what hour you are going to be carried out. Somebody's got to get hurt, and that's all there is to it." When men were mangled they were removed from the work site as quickly and quietly as possible so as not to "rattle" or distract the others. It was a frequent occurrence. A longshoreman had one chance in five hundred of being killed or permanently disabled.

Job security was nonexistent. Longshoremen were recruited for work through a corrupt and archaic system known as the shape-up. It cruelly played on the men's insecurities, their desperate desire for work. There was no guarantee that a "dock walloper" who worked on Monday would be employed on Tuesday, or that one who worked in the morning would have his job that afternoon. Longshoremen had to "shape up" twice a day, in the morning and at noon. At the sound of a whistle, they gathered outside the locked gates of the pier and formed a semicircle around the hiring boss, who picked out the men who were going to work that shift. Longshoremen fortunate enough to be chosen received numbered metal tags, their admission cards to a shift on the pier. The power of the hiring boss was "absolute. Upon his nod depends the longshoreman's bread and butter," wrote a New York reporter. He had his favorites—"boys" from his neighborhood, church, or saloon—but he could easily be bribed with a pint of whiskey or a ten-dollar bill. Longshoremen willing to pay for work placed toothpicks behind their ears. The hiring boss passed these men through the gate with an imperial wave of the hand. He collected his kickbacks hours later in a local gin joint.

The oversupply of labor—two or three times the number of men needed for work—was the "central pillar" of the shape-up system, the key to keeping the men compliant and underpaid, easy to dominate and humiliate. The discards hung around outside the pier "like sheep in droves," wrote Theodore Dreiser, awaiting the noontime shape-up. No one went home; no one gave up. Despair could break a dockhand's family. If a man complained about the money or the work, there was always a desperate fellow at the gate ready to replace him. Persistent troublemakers were likely to leave the docks "in a barrel of cement," said one longshoreman. Dreiser wrote of the men's condition: "I have sometimes thought that cattle are better provided for, or at least as well."

The longshoreman was "the forgotten man in the great city of New York, the forgotten man of American labor," said novelist Budd Schulberg, screenwriter for *On the Waterfront.* Their own union, the International Longshoremen's Association, afforded them no protection. Its leaders were in bed with the stevedoring companies that the railroads contracted to employ them. Union leaders negotiated labor agreements with no input from the rank and file. The leaders, in turn, were paid off for agreeing not to order strikes. After an unsuccessful wildcat strike in 1919, vehemently opposed by the union's power structure, it would be another twenty-six years before the men walked off the job. In that protracted period of labor peace, Joseph Patrick Ryan, a former dockworker who grew up in Chelsea, took control of the union and got himself elected president in 1927, and, years later, "president for life." A large man, "solid as a river barge, bull-necked, heavy-fisted," he was a steadfast Tammany man. Mayors and governors, cardinals and crime overlords, attended the annual banquet given by the Joseph P. Ryan Association, an affair whose single purpose was to honor Joseph Patrick Ryan. All the while, Ryan—who wore expensive suits, drove long cars, and favored gaudy painted ties—kept the men he claimed to love poor and powerless. In the 1920s, an average longshoreman made between $200 and $300 less than a New York family of four needed "to maintain itself in health and decency."

The shape-up allowed Ryan to keep tight control over his men; the "withheld job" was a club to coerce workers to join the union and keep their dues current. These funds found their way, circuitously and secretly, into the pockets of Joe Ryan.*

Ryan's boyhood friend was waterfront tycoon William J. "Big Bill" McCormack, the perennial chairman of the arrangements committee for Ryan's annual dinners. By 1930, this former vegetable truck driver was a multimillionaire, a Knight of Malta, and "Mr. Big" in the port—a secretive man who owned Joe Ryan and practically ran the port. According to federal investigators, he controlled key union locals and dozens of the businesses the unions serviced. Among his good friends was Governor Al Smith, whom

---

* When federal prosecutors finally caught up with Ryan in the early 1950s, he was forced from the union presidency and sentenced to six months in prison for accepting an annual gratuity from a shipping executive. His sentence was suspended due to bad health.

he had hired to run his trucking companies when Smith lost his reelection bid in 1920. Smith repaid the favor after the next election, installing this former "Chelsea boy" as chairman of the New York State Boxing Commission's License Commission.*

With Ryan in league with McCormack and other powerful shippers, the shape-up remained in force until the 1950s, when it was exposed by courageous parish priests and reporters, and outlawed by the states of New York and New Jersey. (This is the story depicted in *On the Waterfront*.) Until then, it kept the longshoremen compliant and quiescent, underpaid and afraid. It remained an essential part of the port's lighterage system—keeping it competitive by ensuring labor stability and speedy turnarounds.

On one occasion in 1927, the luxury liner *Berengaria* "docked, disposed of all her passengers, unloaded and distributed a few thousand tons of miscellaneous freight, took on thirty-six thousand gallons of oil, eight hundred thousand gallons of water, took on food and mail, reloaded her freight and passengers, and was off again in fourteen hours." Feats like that can only be accomplished with slave labor, a rarely mentioned but integral component of the lighterage system.

All this happened within a short walk from Times Square, but nobody paid attention to it in the 1920s. Tourists didn't know about it, New Yorkers didn't seem to care about it, and the Tammany-controlled government didn't interfere. Ryan was left alone because he kept the peace. A long labor strike would have paralyzed great parts of New York City's economy, particularly the Midtown building industry, and would have left residents dangerously short of food and fuel.

The corruption and congestion, mayhem and wastage were as just as great on the streets near the Manhattan piers as they were on the piers themselves. If a driver needed a loader to help him get his shipments from the pier-shed floor onto his truck he had to pay a bribe to a gang of thugs. In the 1920s, "Boss" Ryan used his muscle to replace these small-time criminals with union men. Truck drivers had no choice but to comply with the system. Refusal brought an unwelcome visit from one of Ryan's "private storm troopers." If a trucker didn't need a loader, he got one anyway, and was forced to pay him. And if a trucker wanted to move to the head of the line, he had to pay a "hurry-up" charge. Gangs controlled entire piers, protecting their loading concessions through "a

---

* Ryan died in 1963; McCormack lived for two more years, and was never charged with or convicted of a crime.

process of conquest and military occupation," wrote reporter Alva Johnston. Murder was not uncommon.

The loading racket was unique to the Port of New York, and it persisted into the 1950s, another baleful consequence of the port not having direct rail connections to its piers, or sufficient space on its docks for the efficient transfer of cargo.

More Than I'll Ever Be Paid For

"New York has done less to develop its port along modern lines than any other important shipping center in the world," said the editors of a leading railroad journal just before World War I. "The present congestion of traffic," they predicted, was a prelude to catastrophe.

When the crisis came in the furious January of 1918, with the frozen harbor clogged with wartime shipping, the port was almost totally immobilized. The coal that managed to reach the harbor through blizzard conditions extending all the way to Chicago was piled up in snow-covered mountains on the Jersey shore, or in barges immobilized by high winds and vast fields of ice. It was a veritable blockade, and it pushed the city "to the point of desperation."

Hundreds of schools and industrial plants were forced to close; department stores and other retail establishments were ordered not to use power or light; stores and theaters were forbidden to use lights for decorative or display purposes, darkening Broadway; and the federal government instituted a policy of "workless Mondays" in all the boroughs of New York. William McAdoo, the wartime director general of railroads, ordered the Pennsylvania Railroad to open its passenger tunnels under the Hudson to coal trains, but this measure fell far short of alleviating the city's fuel famine. Riots broke out in the poorer districts of the city. In upper Manhattan, a crowd of a thousand men, women, and children, "carrying all sorts of receptacles," broke into a local coal yard and began plundering wagons about to deliver fuel to city hospitals. The police were called in to disperse the mob, which then moved on to attack another fuel yard blocks away.

The weather finally broke in mid-February, and heating fuel began arriving in the city. Shaken by what they had witnessed, the governors of New York and New Jersey vowed it would never happen again. With the railroads opposed to comprehensive planning, the adjoining states had to act on their own to relieve the "the excessive costs and delays caused by the river barrier." In 1919, they established independent state commissions to work in unison to construct a vehicular tunnel under the Hudson. The commissioners had been considering a bridge extending from lower Manhattan to New Jersey, but the deciding factors were practicality and cost-effectiveness. Tunnels had already been dug under the Hudson and East Rivers, while a bridge of such great length had not yet been built anywhere in the world, and would have been, it was argued, an exorbitantly expensive and risky project.

In June of that year, Clifford M. Holland was named chief engineer of the tunnel project. Born in Somerset, Massachusetts, in 1883, he was "probably the youngest engineer ever entrusted with an undertaking technically so difficult and economically so momentous," said the *Times*. At the time of his appointment, he was supervising the construction of four subway tubes under the East River. He had begun work on the tunnels in 1906, in a subordinate position, days after graduating from Harvard with a degree in civil engineering. Two years later, the scholarly-looking engineer married Anna Coolidge Davenport of Watertown, Massachusetts, a wife willing to tolerate his complete devotion to his work.

By early 1920, Holland and his staff—some of them nearly twice his age— had fashioned plans for twin cast-iron-lined tubes; their entrances and exits were separated by two city blocks so that traffic didn't converge and cause undue congestion. Work on the ventilation system began in 1920, and digging operations commenced two years later, the crews boring out "a Highway under the Hudson," as newspapers called it.

Crews of sandhogs and engineers operated under the riverbed in claustrophobic compartments whose compressed air counterbalanced the pressure of river water bearing down on them. These work areas were built behind imposing tunneling shields, steel plate cylinders whose forward edges acted as cutting instruments. The shields contained doors through which immigrants from Ireland, Italy, and the West Indies assaulted the face of the tunnel with shovels and picks. Powerful hydraulic jacks pushed the shield forward after the sandhogs had removed the soft earth within reach. The mud, sand, and stone were hauled out in small rail cars—enough debris to nearly fill the Woolworth Building. Workers then bolted together iron rings to line the tunnel. Cement grout was pumped behind the rings to reinforce them.

In October 1924, tunneling crews working toward one another from Manhattan and New Jersey met at mid-river. After the last deposit of silt was blasted away and the tunnel was "holed through," engineers announced that the two ends of the tube were aligned within a fraction of an inch of one another. Clifford Holland's mathematical calculations had been spot on.

He would never know this. Two days before the historic hook-up, Holland died of heart failure at a sanatorium in Battle Creek, Michigan, where he had been recovering from a nervous breakdown brought on by the pressures of the job.* He was only forty-one years old.

Holland's body arrived in New York City for burial at almost the very instant the final blast was set off to clear the way to connect the two parts of the tunnel. It was "a salute," said *The New York Times*, "at once ironic and fitting."

Work continued under Holland's chief lieutenant, Milton H. Freeman, but five months later he died of pneumonia, a condition brought on, his doctors surmised, by "work" and "worry." The task of completing the tunnel fell to Norwegian-born Ole Singstad.

What had originally been the Hudson River Vehicular Tunnel was renamed the Holland Tunnel shortly after the chief engineer's death. In honoring Holland, reporters and eulogists focused on the monumental scale of the digging operations he had overseen, overlooking his principal engineering legacy: the tunnel's revolutionary ventilation system. Had it not worked, the tunnel would have been useless.

Wind Factories

Nothing remotely like it had ever been attempted. The vehicular tunnels recently built in Europe were much shorter, had less traffic capacity, and handled a large number of horse-drawn wagons. They were ventilated by a natural draft through the tunnel openings, the kind of draft that sweeps through a long corridor of a house when the windows are open. The building of a tunnel in car-crazy America called for an entirely new approach. With each tube expected to receive the exhaust emissions of nearly two thousand vehicles per hour, the Holland tubes would have become lethal gas chambers had they been ventilated by natural draft. Public concern about the tunnel's ventilation system was heightened in 1924 when a much shorter vehicular tunnel in Pittsburgh had to be closed temporarily because of perilously high concentrations of carbon monoxide.

Holland and Singstad had taken on this challenge the day they were hired. To support their efforts, they commissioned ancillary research projects at Yale University, the University of Illinois, and the Bureau of Mines in Pittsburgh, which had its own experimental underground tunnels. A number of prestigious engineers suggested that huge fans ventilate the tunnel, one fan blowing clean air into the tunnel, the other fan sucking foul air out. Holland and Sing-

---

* There is a small bust of Clifford Holland hidden behind a Port Authority booth at the Manhattan entrance to the tunnel.

stad protested. The amount and velocity of air needed to clear out the high volume of poisonous gases would have generated winds of up to eighty miles per hour. Were a fire to break out, winds of this force would turn the tunnel into a raging inferno. Yet a man-made hurricane was exactly what was needed to clear the tunnel of carbon monoxide. To tame this hurricane, Holland and Singstad devised a system that relied upon a transverse, instead of a longitudinal, movement of air, a system widely assailed as unworkable by expert tunnel engineers.

When the new ventilation system was up and working, a seventy-two-mile-an-hour storm raged in a long air duct built under the tunnel's roadway. This stream of fresh air was released through curbside vents, and came out "so gently," said a reporter for *Scientific American*, "that five feet away your hand cannot feel the movement." The fresh air mixed with noxious gases and was sucked out by exhaust fans through vents in the ceiling. In this way, the air inside the tunnels was changed every ninety seconds. "The air will be just as pure under the middle of the river as it will be near the entrances," Holland assured tunnel commissioners. And it was.

This ventilation system—the taming of the hurricane—continues to work today exactly as it did in 1927. Air is pumped into the tunnels and sucked out by eighty-four enormous fans located in four ventilating buildings, two on each side of the Hudson. They are as high as ten-story office buildings, and were seen by Lewis Mumford as important contributions to machine age architecture. Two of them rise out of the water, about one thousand feet from either shore—yellow-brick river towers that are half submerged. The other two are a block or so inland: one in Jersey City, the other at Washington and Canal Streets in Manhattan. These "storm factories" produce nothing but wind, the tamed and tempered cyclones that clean out the killing gases. Fresh air—the only raw material required by the storm factories—is captured through louvered openings in their walls, openings that look like Venetian blinds. When the gales have purged the tunnel of gas, the foul air is channeled to the storm factories and emitted into the atmosphere though stacks in their roofs. If this system ever broke down, the Holland tubes would become gas-saturated chambers "in which life could not be sustained."

Two weeks before the Holland Tunnel was opened, a *New York Times* reporter was permitted to drive through it. "The first thing that strikes one upon entering the tunnel, especially on a hot day, is a rush of cool, well-ventilated air, as on walking into a 'refrigerated' moving-picture theatre," he wrote. The tunnel was "as light as day," the artificial light brilliantly reflected off its walls of vitreous white tile. "Along the left-hand side of the tube, for the entire length of the tunnel, runs an elevated walk with a white metal railing. Traffic policemen in blue uniforms, employed by the New York–New Jersey Tunnel Commissions, will be stationed at intervals of 250 feet. A telephone and signal light system, with stations at every police post, will enable the guards to spread information instantly from one end of the tunnel to the other in case of an accident or traffic jam." After exiting in Jersey City, the reporter swung his car onto a recently widened street that led to the Lincoln Highway. Dedicated in 1913, it was the country's first transcontinental auto road. With the completion of the Holland Tunnel, it reached from Times Square to Lincoln Park in San Francisco. Manhattan was now connected by a ribbon of paving to all of America, not just New Jersey.

The tunnel was an instant sensation. Eight and a half million vehicles passed through it in the first year of operation; the figure would reach 35 million by 1931, when the tunnel was well on its way toward paying for itself with tolls. Along with Chinatown and Grant's Tomb, it became "one of the metropolitan spectacles that must not be missed," said reporters. Barkers for the tourist buses parked around Times Square had a new spiel: "See the Holland Tunnel! Round trip through the new tubes now starting!" The "rubberneck" buses were packed for months following the opening of the tunnel. Some native New Yorkers, hardened by the metropolitan grind, were more relieved than exhalant. They now had built-in "insurance" against the danger of another food and fuel blockade caused by ice jams in the Hudson.

The tunnel came to be regarded as an "economic necessity." In 1927 it cost more to transport a bale of cotton from a pier in New Jersey to a warehouse in Manhattan than it did to carry that same item from Hoboken to Savannah. The Holland Tunnel did not, as New York merchants hoped, lead to the gradual elimination of this expensive lighterage service. Not even an additional under-river crossing, the Lincoln Tunnel—opened to traffic in 1937 between West Thirty-ninth Street in Manhattan and Weehawken—did that.* There was far too much cargo in the harbor in the 1920s and 1930s to be handled by trucks and tunnels. Nor did the Holland Tunnel relieve auto congestion in Midtown Manhattan. It did exactly the opposite, encouraging more people to come into the city by car. Thousands of commuters and tourists who had previously relied on the trains and the ferries now drove into Manhattan in the family car, creating a new local industry—the building of parking lots and garages.

The most important long-range impact of the tunnel was a rapid increase

---

* The Lincoln Tunnel's third and final tube was not completed until 1947.

in truck traffic in and around Manhattan. "The tunnel," the *Times* had correctly predicted in 1922, "will mean the triumph of the truck for short hauls hereabout." Less than one year after the Holland Tunnel opened, nearly six thousand trucks a day were using it. They carried fresh fruit and vegetables that had previously been floated to market, and indispensable parts and raw materials for Manhattan's thousands of small, highly specialized businesses. And out of the city, on the backs of trucks, went the products these businesses made or merchandised—women's suits by Hattie Carnegie, dresses by Edwin Goodman, and makeup by Helena Rubinstein and Elizabeth Arden.

Soon, garment firms with mid-Manhattan addresses began relocating their factories on cheaper land in Jersey City, near the tunnel plazas; and later, as roads improved, in more distant locations. The opening of the Holland Tunnel was the beginning of the decentralization of Manhattan industry, an epochal metropolitan transformation.

The George Washington Bridge accelerated this historic process. Pressure from underdeveloped New Jersey towns and townships upriver from the Holland Tunnel led to the decision to bridge the Hudson, and to do it at 178th Street, connecting Manhattan with New Jersey's growth-hungry Bergen County. And the engineer who designed the bridge—one of the immortals of his profession—was greatly responsible for mobilizing and channeling political support. Had Othmar Hermann Ammann, an indrawn Swiss immigrant, not been a surprisingly savvy political operator, his unrivaled bridge—poetry in steel—might have remained a distant dream.

CHAPTER TWENTY-THREE

POET IN STEEL

*The George Washington Bridge over the Hudson is the
most beautiful bridge in the world.*

LE CORBUSIER

Ammann

In 1904, twenty-five-year-old Othmar Ammann, a recent graduate of the prestigious Swiss Federal Institute of Technology in Zurich, arrived in New York City. He had come to America on the advice of his favorite professor, Karl Emil Hilgard, who had worked for three years as a bridge engineer for the Northern Pacific Railroad. Hilgard wanted Ammann—small, slender, and reserved—to gain experience working on one or another of the staggering engineering works Americans were constructing to link together their continent-wide country. "In the U.S. I have seen youngsters in charge of work which in Europe only graybeards would be allowed to perform," the professor had told his protégé. Ammann planned to stay only a year or two, but after returning to Switzerland briefly to marry Lilly Wehrli, a young woman he grew up with, he would remain in the United States for the rest of his life.

He was hired at the first door he knocked on, the Broadway office of Joseph Mayer, a prominent consulting engineer. Mayer had made preliminary sketches for a rail bridge across the Hudson at Seventieth Street, and "his ideas influenced me a lot when it came to planning the George Washington Bridge," Ammann recalled years later.

Ammann had grown up in Feuerthalen, a picturesque Rhine River town of old wooden bridges, masterfully designed structures that had first inspired him to become an engineer. Working for Mayer, he dreamed of spanning the fast-running Hudson. "My first serious interest in the problem of bridging the

472

Hudson was awakened shortly after my arrival in New York on a visit to the top of the Palisades Cliffs from where I obtained a splendid view of the majestic river. For the first time I could envisage the bold undertaking, the spanning of the broad waterway with a single leap of three thousand feet from shore to shore, nearly twice the longest span in existence. . . . From that moment as my interest in great bridges grew I followed all developments with respect to the bridging of the Hudson River with keenest interest."

A rare combination of artist and realist, Ammann was a young man of fixed purpose. "Get all the experience you can," he wrote in his notebook. "Learn from those who mastered your trade or profession before you. . . . If the experience you need isn't thrown in your way, you must move heaven and earth to get it." Not satisfied to stay with one firm, he left Mayer's employ after six months and moved through a succession of jobs that gave him the field experience he was seeking. He worked for the Pennsylvania Steel Company, in Steelton, Pennsylvania, the second largest bridge construction firm in America, and in that capacity served with one of the chief construction engineers of New York's Queensboro Bridge. And in 1907, at age twenty-eight, he headed an investigation of the collapse of a cantilever bridge across the St. Lawrence River near Quebec, an accident that took the lives of seventy-nine workers, among them (as we have seen) thirty-three Mohawk high ironworkers. These apprenticeships prepared Ammann in 1912 for what he considered the job of his dreams: chief assistant to the great Austro-Hungarian engineer Gustav Lindenthal, designer of the Queensboro Bridge. Lindenthal—brilliant, impulsive, and full of Wagnerian aspiration—was working on the world's longest steel arch span, Hell Gate Bridge, a railroad crossing over the East River at its most treacherous point.

But the flamboyant Lindenthal had an even greater project in mind, one he had been pursuing for thirty years: to span the Hudson with a monumentally large bridge. He had initially proposed a rail bridge stretching from Hoboken to lower Manhattan, but now, at age seventy-one, he was urging a Weehawken to Manhattan connection, a "double decked titan" for railroad and vehicular traffic that would bring cars, trucks, rail passengers, and freight into the city at West Fifty-seventh Street, in the heart of Midtown. The bridge was to be financed by a private company the engineer had founded with several of his wealthy backers.

Ammann eagerly looked forward to working on that project, but when World War I stopped all bridge building in the country, Lindenthal was forced to lay off his young Swiss collaborator. With no prospects in sight, Ammann considered returning to Switzerland with Lilly and their two small children. Lindenthal, however, found work for him managing a floundering New Jersey clay mining operation in which he had invested heavily. Ammann took the position only because of Lindenthal's promise to put him to work on the Hudson River project as soon as the war ended. It was Othmar Ammann's emotional break, clean and forever, with his home country.

As promised, Ammann was invited back to Lindenthal's office in 1920. By this time he had turned around the financially troubled clay company, deeply impressing one of its chief investors, George Silzer, a fast-rising New Jersey politician. They developed a friendship that would alter the arc of Ammann's career.

"The new project brings me great satisfaction, it is a great noble structure," Ammann described his initial enthusiasm for Lindenthal's bridge to his family back in Switzerland. The bridge's clear span was projected to be more than one and a half miles long, and its two land anchorages were each wider than the main branch of the New York Public Library. "The towers will be as high as the tallest skyscraper in New York," Ammann excitedly told his family.

Lindenthal's stupendous bridge project had the support of William Randolph Hearst. The newspaper publisher had heavy real estate investments in the Columbus Circle neighborhood and hoped the bridge would make this area a new center of mercantile development, but Lindenthal's scheme ran into a storm of opposition from other leading Midtown businessmen. It would congest an already overcrowded area of the city, they argued, and its tremendously long approach ramps, extending all the way to Broadway, would require the demolition of established businesses in the area. Nor were most of the railroad companies who would be expected to use the bridge willing to invest in such an extravagant enterprise.

By 1922, Ammann had begun to voice his own objections to the "stupendous scope of the plan." Lindenthal's company was by then in parlous financial condition, incapable, Ammann thought, of taking on this vastly expensive project. Lindenthal—tall and barrel-chested, with a loud, slicing voice and an explosive temper—was a fearsome person to confront, but Ammann had quiet courage belied by his appearance. In March of 1923, he wrote in his diary: "Submitted memo to G.L., urging reduction of H. R. BR. Program . . . G.L. rebuked me severely for my 'timidity' and 'shortsightedness' in not looking far enough ahead. He stated that he was looking ahead for 1,000 years."

It was the most difficult time in Ammann's professional life and he spilled out his frustration in a letter to his mother back in Switzerland, "The giant project for which I have been sacrificing time and money for the past three years lies in ruins. In vain, I as well as others have been fighting against the unlimited ambition of a genius . . . obsessed with illusions of grandeur. He has the power in his hands and refuses to bring moderation into his gigantic plans."

That June, Ammann wrote to his friend Samuel Rae, president of the Pennsylvania Railroad. Lindenthal's bridge, he told Rae, would take up to a dozen years to build. In the meantime, highway congestion was becoming "calamitous" in the upper part of Manhattan. One way to relieve it, Ammann believed, was to build a vehicular bridge at Washington Heights, around 178th Street, directly across the river from Fort Lee and the New Jersey Palisades. The two rocky bluffs that bracketed this narrow opening in the river valley would provide secure anchorage for the bridge's towers.

Historical trends, Ammann believed, argued for a vehicular bridge; the future belonged to the car and the truck, not the train. "Today, any bridge across the Hudson River at New York must be viewed primarily as a highway structure, only incidentally accommodating rail traffic."

Ammann had begun secretly designing his bridge while working for Lindenthal. "At an opportune moment," he told Rae, "I shall present this proposition before Mr. Lindenthal." Ammann did this with all the delicacy he could muster, but Lindenthal was intractable. He would not reduce the scale of his project, and he accused Ammann of disloyalty for suggesting that he should. Unable to reconcile their differences, Ammann and Lindenthal parted company. The two old friends would meet cordially at formal occasions, but the breach was permanent.

Lindenthal continued to lobby for his colossal bridge even after the War Department, which had jurisdiction over bridges in tidal water, rejected his plan in 1929 because it failed to meet the department requirement for clear height for ships. Until his death in 1935, Lindenthal waged a contentious campaign to have the federal government approve his "titan" at West Fifty-ninth Street. It was a futile exercise. The money and political support were unavailable, even had he gotten the clearance.

With Fresh Hope and Courage

After splitting with Lindenthal, Ammann opened a small Manhattan office, where he planned to work "on my own initiative and with my own plans." With no salary, he supported his family in the town of Boonton, in Morris County, New Jersey, with the help of loans from family in Switzerland.

Months before this, George Silzer, elected governor of New Jersey in 1922, had urged Ammann to put aside his pencils and calipers and begin lobbying for his bridge in Bergen County, a heavily rural district likely to profit from a bridge in upper Manhattan, just across the river. Bergen County was solidly Republican territory, and Silzer—a Wilsonian Democrat—thought Ammann would be a more effective advocate for the bridge than a left-leaning governor.

If it were seen as Ammann's, not Silzer's, bridge it would also stand a better chance of being approved by the Republican state legislature.

Over the course of the next two years, Ammann stepped outside his rules and the regular tempo of his life, meeting with dozens of small citizens organizations, chambers of commerce, and governing boards in Bergen, Passaic, and Morris Counties. He also spoke with organizations on the other side of the river: in Washington Heights, the Bronx, Harlem, Yonkers, and Westchester County, the engineer in the role of "political entrepreneur."

Ammann looked more like a Scandinavian sea captain than a political operator. His face was "weather-beaten" and "deeply lined from eye to jaw"; he wore old-fashioned stiff collars; and he carried an out-of-date hunting case watch. But he was a resolutely modern man, capable of pressing his point with lean logic. His bridge, he insisted, would pay for itself with tolls, not tax money; and it would open up northern New Jersey to rapid economic development. Modern highways, housing developments, and industrial parks would fill out the landscape, and the suburban pioneers, he predicted, would come from the overpriced apartment communities of upper Manhattan.

Ammann lobbied for his bridge by day and worked on its design late into the night. He drove himself furiously, a man possessed. To relieve the tension, he gardened, rode horses, and played the violin. He and Lilly were also patrons of the Metropolitan Opera and the New York Philharmonic.

In early 1924, Ammann unveiled his proposal for bridging the Hudson. "By the degree to which Lindenthal's scheme seemed overambitious and overblown, Ammann's seemed disarmingly restrained and eminently doable," writes his biographer. The engineer envisioned a wide aerial roadway of eight lanes, with pedestrian walkways on the upper deck and four light-rail lines on the lower deck. (The lower deck was to be constructed at a later date, when the need arose.) The estimated cost was $30 million, one-tenth the cost of Lindenthal's dream bridge. (The final construction cost would double, to $60 million.) The bridge was to span the river in one "gigantic" leap of 3,500 feet. That was nearly double the length of the largest existing suspension bridge: the Benjamin Franklin Bridge between Philadelphia and Camden, New Jersey. It was daunting but feasible, Ammann believed.

Ammann's bridge was designed with a severe sense of control, a delicate balancing of power and restraint, unsurprising for an engineer endowed with the sensibilities of an artist. Public structures "should please the eye," he told a colleague. "Many people will have to look at [this] bridge for the rest of their lives."

After Ammann showed his drawings and draft proposal to Silzer, the governor submitted them to the Port of New York Authority, formed in 1921 by the states of New York and New Jersey to develop common transportation projects, chiefly projects to alleviate harbor congestion. Along with Governor Al Smith, Silzer wanted the Port Authority, an independent, quasi-governmental body, to fund a Hudson River bridge in order to keep it free from the pull of local politics. They also wanted to pay for it with revenue bonds issued by the authority, not by city or state taxes.

If Silzer had presented a bridge proposal to the authority four years earlier it would almost certainly have been rejected. At that time, and for years afterward, the Port Authority was trying to convince the railroads that serviced the harbor to eliminate most of their expensive tug and lighterage system, pool their resources, and build two immense freight-carrying tunnels under the harbor. But by 1925, the authority had made no progress in its negotiations with the recalcitrant railroads and was prepared to swing its support to a vehicular bridge, even while continuing to negotiate, with diminished hope, with railroad officials. In March 1925, the legislatures of New York and New Jersey approved the construction of a bridge at Fort Lee and turned over the job to the Port of New York Authority. State loans were provided to begin the project. In this way, a public authority created to pursue railroad reform was suddenly "swept into the automotive age."

But who would design the bridge? The Port Authority originally intended to award the job to "an engineer of long established reputation," but Silzer made a convincing case for his Swiss friend. That year Ammann was hired and given power over the project. He was also charged with designing the Bayonne Bridge, connecting that city with Staten Island, and supervising the construction of two other Staten Island bridges: the Goethals Bridge, named after General George Washington Goethals, builder of the Panama Canal, and the Outerbridge Crossing, named after Eugenius H. Outerbridge, the Port Authority's first chairman. Ammann's authority was enhanced the following year when Silzer, after completing his term as governor, became chairman of the Port Authority.

Knowledge

Groundbreaking for the Hudson River bridge took place on September 27, 1927. Construction began the following month and proceeded exactly on schedule. By June 1929, the two steel towers were completed, and ironworkers began spinning the high-strength wire suspension cables over the river chasm, cables made by John A. Roebling & Sons, the New Jersey firm founded by the designer of the Brooklyn Bridge. As the work neared completion—eight months ahead of schedule and $1 million under budget—the great bridge was finally given a name.

The Port Authority elicited suggestions. "I would prefer the name Bergen," said the secretary of the Bergen County Chamber of Commerce; other Bergen County officials proposed that the bridge be named after William B. MacKay, the leading sponsor of the bridge bill in the New Jersey legislature. Thankfully, the Port Authority board had a more developed sense of history. On this majestic site the Continental Army had built, on opposite sides of the river, Fort Washington and Fort Lee, strongholds that General Washington lost to the British in November 1776, before leading his battered troops into the heart of New Jersey, a strategic retreat that saved the young nation.

On October 24, 1931, the George Washington Bridge was dedicated. Governor Franklin D. Roosevelt and ex-Governor Al Smith arrived together and received a warm welcome, but the "greatest and most enthusiastic greeting" was for Ammann, riding in an open car to the grandstand, constructed at the center of the bridge. Beside him sat his estranged master, Gustav Lindenthal. Ammann had appointed Lindenthal a design consultant on the bridge, a gracious salute to the willful engineer who still refused to forgive his former protégé for contributing to "the death of his dream."

Governor Roosevelt gave passing credit to Ammann in his dedication speech, but Ammann was not asked to approach the podium, and the elaborate program prepared for the occasion, with its history of the genesis of the project, failed to mention him. It was as if the bridge had been built—as the program had been put together—by a faceless committee. At one point in the ceremonies, a photographer approached Ammann—not knowing who he was—and asked him to step aside so he could get a shot of the governor. "Oh, I'm sorry," said Ammann as he politely moved out of the way.

The next morning the "George," as it was already being called, was opened to traffic. Over 56,000 cars and 33,000 pedestrians crossed the span that first day. Where there had been an empty chasm five years before stood a soaring structure of steel and cement, standing two hundred feet over two-thirds of a mile of water, a channel George Washington and his generals had tried to block against a hostile foe with the sunken hulls of ships. It was the first over-water connection between Manhattan and the rest of North America—a bridge twelve men died building.

Less than one month later, the Port Authority opened the Bayonne Bridge across the Kill Van Kull. It was the world's longest steel arch bridge, six hundred feet longer than Hell Gate Bridge, the supreme work of Amman's former master. On the advice of architect Raymond Hood, the American Institute of Steel Construction's award for that year's most beautiful bridge went to the Bayonne Bridge. It was an unpopular decision. "The most impressive as well as the greatest engineering structure of his generation," the *Engineering News-Record* called the GW Bridge.

"The George Washington Bridge is now the best around the waters of New York," said Lewis Mumford, high praise from the cultural critic who considered the Brooklyn Bridge "the most satisfactory example of American art in the nineteenth century." Ammann's bridge "is a delight to the eye: a piece of harmonious and imaginative engineering, the like of which is not yet to be found in any of our skyscrapers," wrote Mumford. But it was Ammann's fellow countryman, Le Corbusier, who offered the most memorable homage. "The George Washington Bridge over the Hudson is the most beautiful bridge in the world," the visiting Swiss designer wrote after seeing it in 1935. "Made of cables and steel beams, it gleams in the sky like a reversed arch. It is blessed. It is the only seat of grace in the disordered city."

Le Corbusier's eye was drawn to the two soaring steel towers, with their distinctive crisscrossed bracing, standing up "in the sky with a striking nobility," higher than the Washington Monument. "Here, finally, steel architecture seems to laugh." Impressed with the square-shouldered granite towers of the Brooklyn Bridge, Ammann had hoped to encase the towers of his bridge in decorative granite and concrete, according to plans fashioned by Cass Gilbert, architect of the Gothic revival Woolworth Building, but with the economic depression deepening, the Port Authority refused to release funds for the work. Ammann was disappointed, considering his bridge bare and unfinished. Others disagreed. "Happily for the aesthetic success of the bridge, the stonework . . . was suspended," wrote Mumford. Unlike John and Washington Roebling's bridge, the stone would have been entirely ornamental, not an integral part of the structural system that supported the bridge's apron; there would have been no union of art and utility, the bridge's outstanding artistic achievement.

In a speech at Columbia University, Le Corbusier gave thanks to the "unknown man" who had made the decision that "saved" the bridge. "The two towers and the mathematical play of the cables make a splendid unity," he said. "It is one. That is the new beauty": fire-forged steel elevated to art.

Over time, Ammann grew to love his accidental art, and the towers of every other bridge he designed are clad in steel, although none of them reveals, as the GW does, its structural skeleton. "A dreamer in steel," Robert Moses called Ammann.

The GW Bridge's most daring engineering achievement, and one of its most pleasing aesthetic aspects, is its unusually slender deck. Before construction began many engineers doubted the safety of a deck this thin and long—the equivalent of fifteen city blocks. "To grasp the breathtaking magnitude of this engineering feat," writes biographer Darl Rastorfer, "imagine New York's Fifth

Avenue between Forty-second and Fifty-seventh Streets lifted and suspended in air six stories above a river. You must also imagine Fifth Avenue to be twice its width and thronged curb-to-curb with automobiles, buses, and trucks." The wafer-thin deck that Ammann designed to carry such heavy loads is a throw-back to the very first vehicular suspension bridges, whose decks were made as light as possible in order to reduce costs. But ten of these nineteenth-century suspension bridges either collapsed or suffered severe damage in windstorms. The problem became so widespread that the French government outlawed for twenty years the construction of suspension bridges.

"Engineers have had a tendency to make suspension bridges more and more rigid in order to eliminate the wave-like motion due to flexibility," Am-mann explained the corrections his nineteenth- and early-twentieth-century predecessors made to give their bridges greater stability. This rigidity was accomplished by what was known as "stiffening": that is, by the use of great trusses and other devices that are heavy, unsightly, and expensive.

Ammann's research convinced him that an unusually long bridge "did not require this excessive amount of metal to make it stiff." His study of what is known as "deflection theory," taught him—seemingly against common sense—that the heavier a bridge was, the lighter its deck could be. Latvian engineer-mathematician Leon Moisseiff, designer of the Manhattan Bridge (1909), was the first to apply deflection theory to a lengthy, all-steel suspen-sion span. The central idea of deflection theory, as formulated by the Austrian Joseph Melan, is that the heavy stiffening trusses applied to the bottom of the deck are unnecessary. In designing his GW Bridge, Ammann reasoned that the great weight of the deck and cables alone would provide sufficient structural strength against the effects of wind and traffic. A suspension bridge could be both light and strong; and making it light would reduce its cost. The problem was that Ammann's bridge was more than twice as long as Mois-seiff's, and its deck design was strikingly thinner, with "comparatively light, shallow, stiffing trusses instead of heavy, rigid trusses." Although convinced of the soundness of his theoretical work, Ammann would be the first to test it on an unprecedentedly long and light center span. This was "untried territory."

Not even Ammann could be certain his bridge deck could stand up under powerful winds, or the load of stalled, bumper-to-bumper traffic on its origi-nal six lanes (two more were added in 1946). Othmar Ammann's bridge deck was as much a "leap of faith" as Clifford Holland's ventilation system.*

---

* The lower level of the bridge, also designed by Ammann was added in 1962. It supports a six-lane road, not the four electric railway tracks Ammann originally envisioned.

On dedication day, when long columns of soldiers, sailors, and Marines came swinging down from the Manhattan plaza and marched out onto the bridge, spectators "felt the gigantic span vibrate as if shaken by earth tremors," said *The New York Times*. Military commanders had been told for over a century to have their troops march at "route step"—a more relaxed form of marching where they were not required to stay in step—when crossing a suspension bridge for fear that rhythmic marching in heavy boots would set in motion harmonic vibrations that would destabilize the bridge and cause it to collapse. But that day on the George Washington Bridge there was no panic, no signs of concern. "The crowds were only amused at the strange sensation."

There is no record of Ammann's reaction. We do know, however, that the night before the dedication he had assured the concerned commander of the parade that his troops need not "break step" when they reached the cable-supported central span. The bridge "would stand up if an army of elephants marched over it."

"What made you so sure that it would hold up?" his wife asked him years later. "Knowledge," he calmly replied.

"He is a lean elderly man in a high starched collar. Briefly he sits at the window of his apartment, 32 stories up in the Carlyle Hotel, and he seems restless," wrote Gay Talese in March 1964. Then the limber eighty-five-year-old engineer fetched a telescope and pointed it out the window at the Verrazano-Narrows Bridge, the subject of Talese's most recent book. Ammann did this often from the bedroom window of the apartment he and his second wife, Klary (Lilly died of cancer in 1933), had taken when the commute from New Jersey had become too much for him. From there, and from another window, he could see every one of the bridges he had designed in this city of bridges: the Bayonne Bridge (1931), the Triborough Bridge (1936), the Bronx-Whitestone Bridge (1939), the Throgs Neck Bridge (1961), and the Verrazano-Narrows Bridge (1964), the longest suspension span in the world when it opened to traffic. In the near distance, Ammann could see his self-acknowledged masterwork, the George Washington Bridge. Every time he and Klary drove past it they bowed and gently saluted. "That bridge was his first," explained a friend of Ammann's, "and it was a difficult birth. And he'll always love it best."

"No twentieth-century engineer had left more of a mark on steel bridge design than Othmar Ammann," writes David P. Billington, the world's outstanding historian of the art of structural engineering. But Ammann would surely have been disappointed had he lived into the next century. New York has not built a major bridge since the Verrazano, completed a year before Othmar Ammann died.

Pathway to Midtown

Ammann's first bridge was a history changer. The structural lightness of the George Washington Bridge is socially significant; it represented the shift in transportation that occurred in the 1920s from the heavy locomotive to the lighter automobile. And it had as great an impact on the New York metropolitan region as Holland's tunnel, giving impetus to a momentous social and economic transformation, one foreseen but not shaped by New York's regional planners. It was New York's builders, not its dreamers, who brought in the future.

When the GW Bridge was completed, the great arches were "a gateway," in Paul Goldberger's words, "from city to country." But not for long. As Ammann had anticipated, apartment house dwellers in the congested, high-rent districts of the Bronx and Washington Heights—along with factories and warehouses on Manhattan's West Side—began migrating to thinly populated Bergen County. Even before the bridge was opened, county officials began improving their highway and road systems and expanding bus service to and from Manhattan. Seeing the future, Henry Ford announced plans to open a plant in Bergen County. But it was the developers who spearheaded the movement. Dr. Joseph V. Paterno, a Manhattan real estate king who had made his fortune buying land and building apartments in advance of transportation improvements, purchased vast tracts of prime real estate in the area of Englewood Cliffs, within sight of the bridge, and began selling it at auction in 1927. This set off what newspapers called a "Palisades Boom." "Bergen County Should Be Part of New York, Just as Queens County Really Is Part of New York," ran a line from a Paterno advertisement. Soon it was, in a practical sense.

Before the opening, in 1909, of the Queensboro Bridge, the population of Queens was only 284,000. By 1930 it was over one million. Bergen County would experience a similar growth surge immediately following the groundbreaking ceremonies for Ammann's bridge. In 1910, it had 138,000 residents; by 1940, population had leaped to 400,000. Today, with a million residents, it's the most populous county in New Jersey, and the GW, with its additional upper lanes and lower deck, is "the busiest bridge in the world." Over a hundred million vehicles cross it annually.

A parallel pattern occurred in the counties just west of the Holland Tunnel. Tax valuations for the five New Jersey counties nearest the tunnel, including Bergen County, increased by over $2.2 billion from 1916 to 1929, giving these five counties tax valuations that were two-thirds of the total tax valuations of the entire state in 1929. "This connecting highway between the two States has had a greater influence upon the development of the metropolitan area located in New Jersey than any other single factor," said a New Jersey tunnel commissioner in 1930.

Like the Holland Tunnel, the GW Bridge gave powerful impetus to the trucking industry in its escalating battle with the railroads. Truckers moving goods in and out of New York City could now reach destinations in the Bronx and northern Manhattan without having to use the Holland Tunnel; and when New Jersey completed an express highway it had begun building in the mid-1920s, trucks coming out of Manhattan over the GW Bridge were able to more easily reach the densely packed industrial zone around Newark—along with points west as far as Detroit and Chicago. Carried for five miles on viaducts, this highway formed "an over-land bridge directly to the heart of Manhattan."

Thus, beginning in the 1920s, the Northeast's greatest rail center built vital infrastructure that greatly aided the trucking industry, "a mortal competitor" with rails "in the shipment of general freight," wrote Carl Condit. By 1930, the Port Authority had shifted its emphasis conclusively from "rails to rubber," abandoning its lingering hopes for a rail tunnel system in the harbor. In that year, the authority took over the operation of the Holland Tunnel and put Ammann in charge of designing the Lincoln Tunnel. When it was completed, Ammann supervised the construction of the Queens-Midtown Tunnel under the East River between Thirty-sixth Street in Manhattan and Long Island City in Queens. Clifford Holland's former partner Ole Singstad designed it, using the same ventilation system he and Holland had developed for the Holland Tunnel. The project, which Mayor Jimmy Walker and Midtown merchants had been urgently pushing since 1927, was finally begun in 1936 and finished in four quick years.

Othmar Ammann was as avid an advocate of the New York region's new road-net as Robert Moses. The GW Bridge and New Jersey's new highways became a greatly needed bypass, taking that state's northbound and southbound traffic around rather than through Manhattan. "The city must have more and more of these roundabout ways," said The New York Times, "if it would avoid the fate of downtown Rome in the days when there was so great a thronging in the thoroughfares that Caesar found it necessary to forbid the passage of wagons through the streets." But in eliminating one source of congestion, the GW Bridge created another one when it was linked directly to Midtown by Robert Moses's Henry Hudson Parkway, the most ambitious intercity transportation initiative of the interwar years.

When opened in 1936, the parkway ran from the GW Bridge to Seventy-second Street, where it tied into the recently constructed West Side Highway, an elevated roadway that ran all the way to the Holland Tunnel, and eventually to the southern tip of Manhattan. In effect, the two highways were one continuous expressway that hugged the Hudson shore of the city. It was "a veritable motorist's dream," said an enthusiastic reporter for the New York *Journal American*, who, with other reporters, was given a chauffeured ride on the interlinked river road before it was opened to the public.

Moses confidently predicted that his Henry Hudson Parkway—one of the most beautiful drives in the world—would forever "eliminate" the West Side's north–south traffic tie-ups. Commuters from the city's exploding trans-Hudson suburbs quickly put the lie to that. From the time it was opened, rush hour traffic on the new roadway—and its West Side extension—was bumper-to-bumper from the bridge to the Battery—a sluggish river of steel and rubber. It was even worse on weekends, "eager citizens enjoying the scenery, but not getting anywhere." Traffic on the new roadway was "a monstrous force," wrote a reporter in the summer of 1936.

Moses, Ammann, and the Port Authority were not to blame. They confronted a nearly intractable dilemma. In 1930, 85 percent of those employed in Manhattan lived outside it; and the preponderance of these commuters loved their cars and preferred to drive to work. Without new bridges, tunnels, and roads to move these cars New York City would have been virtually immobilized for great parts of the day and evening. It is hard to envision the city functioning in the auto age without the Holland, Lincoln, and Midtown Tunnels, Ammann's bridges, and Moses's parkways. And in any event, New York never became an auto-centered city like Los Angeles and Atlanta. Its visionary builders gave the city a highway, bridge, and tunnel network that complemented, but did not supplant, its rail-based mass transit system. "The resultant balanced transport system, combining extensive subway and commuter rail lines with a far-flung web of major roads, enabled the city to grow and thrive in the auto age," noted a historian writing in 2007.

But undeniably—and sometimes avoidably—many New York residents became casualties of new measures to cut down congestion. The Henry Hudson Parkway wound through a new lushly landscaped park carved out of six miles of "muddy wasteland," with the New York Central's tracks roofed over, out of sight. Those living in the vicinity of the park profited from this tremendous civic improvement, but the parkway ran directly into the West Side Highway, a hideously ugly and unnecessary structure. The editors of *The New Republic* had warned Manhattan borough president Julius Miller, its chief proponent, of the probable consequences of his inaptly named West Side "boulevard." It will dump its thousands of south-bound vehicles into a district which is already near the saturation point. . . . An overhead road reduces the value of adjoining property, cuts off light and air, and is a monstrosity which should be contemplated only under the most desperate necessity."

While the Henry Hudson Parkway offered majestic river and skyscraper perspectives, the West Side Highway—begun in 1929 and not completed until 1948—ran above the streets, cutting off light and air and subjecting residents of Hell's Kitchen to continuous noise and pollution. Clouds of carbon dioxide bombarded them day and night, and they knew exactly whom to blame. The borough president had insisted that it be called the Miller Highway.*

At least one salutary social policy came out of this so-called West Side Improvement: the elimination of Death Avenue. In 1929, the city and the New York Central reached an agreement to have the railroad remove its tracks on Eleventh Avenue and elevate part of its West Side freight line—the future High Line—and depress other parts in walled and enclosed cuts. The railroad also built new factory lofts and warehouses and constructed them so that its trains ran directly through them, an effort to increase the efficiency of port-front operations. Jimmy Walker, who had been pressing for such an agreement since his days in Albany, called the elimination of Death Avenue "probably the greatest industrial or commercial improvement that the Borough of Manhattan or the City of New York has ever known." But in succeeding years, truck traffic increased phenomenally in the Hell's Kitchen and Chelsea neighborhoods that bordered the port; and residents now had a railroad, as well as a highway, running directly over their streets, homes, and markets.

With the completion of the Holland Tunnel, the narrow streets along the piers were more packed than ever with trucks, as were the streets of Midtown's Garment District. Many clothing firms had already begun to move the manufacturing part of their businesses to New Jersey, Pennsylvania, and New York City's outer boroughs, places with convenient access to the country's fast-developing highway system. The Holland Tunnel greatly accelerated this exodus. Garment makers were joined by meat, dairy, wood, heavy machinery, and precious metal industries, all increasingly dependent on truck transportation. "And because trucks could haul beer and liquor as easily as they could move machinery, even speakeasies, gambling dens, and houses of ill fame moved toward the roadhouses on the fringes," writes Kenneth Jackson.

---

* Most of the West Side Highway was demolished, piecemeal, in the 1970s and 1980s. The north section, from Fifty-ninth to Seventy-second Streets, was repaired and remains in use. The current West Side Highway, officially the Joe DiMaggio Highway, is overwhelmingly a surface road, a wide urban throughway completed in 2001.

This was the start of the deindustrialization of Manhattan foreseen and promoted by Thomas Adams and his fellow regional planners. But it occurred in a haphazard, wholly unplanned manner. Northern New Jersey became the sight of a furious rural land grab. Hastily built middle-income housing communities—"motor slums," critics called them—decimated farmlands and forests and were built inconveniently far from stores, theaters, and the ordinary amenities of urban life, creating an automobile-dependent lifestyle. "The real process now underway [in the New York suburbs] is not urbanization, but suburbanization," *The New York Times* editorialized in 1929.

But thousands of small businesses remained in Manhattan. They stayed because to move would have been financially ruinous. Most of these businesses are still in the city, contributing to its character and cachet. These businesses are there because of the density and propinquity that central city advocates like Raymond Hood and Harvey Wiley Corbett celebrated. In Midtown, as opposed to suburbia, the free market worked in harmony with the visions of the regional planners, keeping Manhattan the country's theater, music, publishing, communications, and fashion center, a downtown with only one great industry, aside from the port: the manufacture and sale of high-fashion women's clothing.

CHAPTER TWENTY-FOUR

A SCHOOL OF MINNOWS

Talented people want to be near other talented people, and the miracle of New York is that it has the physical compactness to make that possible.

PETER D. SALINS

Seventh Avenue

"Straight, wide, and uncompromising, Seventh Avenue emerges from the southern border of the Park and pierces the heart of Greenwich Village," wrote city observer Will Irwin in his 1927 book, *Highlights of Manhattan*. On its way southward from Central Park, the avenue passed through the Broadway Theater District, skirted Times Square, and then became, for a dozen blocks, a "high-walled" city canyon formed by stone skyscrapers as plain-faced as any in Manhattan.

It was the noon hour on a sparkling spring day when Irwin sauntered down Seventh Avenue, notebook in hand, conducting field research for his Manhattan panorama. Just ahead, as he crossed Forty-second Street, great crowds of men packed the sidewalks, nearly all of them wearing gray fedoras and smoking long, black cigars. They were dressed like big-town Babbitts, in conventional ready-made suits and white shirts with high starched collars, but the faces were "all foreign: not a single lean Yankee countenance." Most of these "schmoozers" were Russian Jews, but there were also a large number of "classical Italian faces" in the crowd. These were the city's garment workers "getting their noonday breath of fresh air." And the "windowed walls" above them housed much of New York City's clothing industry, an industry in which these two ethnic groups formed nearly 90 percent of the labor force.

At the lunch hour, the upper blocks of Seventh Avenue were an entirely

487

male province, but as Irwin pushed southward "the girls of the needle trades surge[d] into this sober current like the overflow from the dye factory into a sluggish river." Most of them were dressed in the latest styles. No working girls, except those on Paris's exclusive boulevards "are more chic," Irwin wrote.

The streets were jammed with trucks loading and unloading thick stacks of women's garments—so many trucks that traffic failed to move "an inch in twenty minutes." "Push boys" were everywhere, recklessly maneuvering swaying racks of dresses across Seventh Avenue, between buildings and into and out of narrow elevator cars. "It's a beehive of workers," wrote *Fortune*, "the one place in America where the elevators never seem to catch up with the traffic." There were no smoke stacks or "clanging machinery," but the noise was deafening—the shrieking horns of trucks, the booming voices of the loft bosses, and the whirring of thousands of electrically driven sewing machines, a buzzing sound that could be heard on the street below through the open windows that lined the workrooms of the prodigious loft buildings that formed the sunless corridor Will Irwin descended.

"I know of no parallel situation in any great city of Europe or interior America," Irwin wrote in *Highlights of Manhattan*, "the manufacturing district lying tight against the pleasure-district and a few hundred yards from the fashionable shopping district." He was speaking, of course, of Times Square, and just south of it, Herald Square, home to Macy's and Gimbels, and hundreds of smaller merchandising establishments. "And what massing of industry it is. . . . Seventh Avenue stands as important in the clothing industry as Wall Street in finance. . . . No one man built it up, no super-industrialist like Ford. It is the accumulation and creation of a thousand expert and enterprising master tailors," refugees from Teutonic militarism and czarist oppression.

In 1927, the women's wear section of Manhattan's Garment District extended from Forty-second Street to Thirtieth Street, between Sixth and Ninth Avenues, with Seventh Avenue—Fashion Avenue—forming its spine. This compacted industrial zone, less than a mile long and half a mile wide, housed the world's heaviest concentration of clothing manufacturers, nearly seven thousand shops employing some 200,000 workers.

It was "a school of minnows," not whales. Unlike Chicago's garment industry, there were no gigantic factories employing eight to ten thousand workers; only small, highly specialized shops. Nearly half of them employed fewer than five workers and only two hundred out of a total of four thousand had more than fifty workers. In output and number of workers employed, however, these shops comprised the biggest manufacturing industry in the biggest industrial city on the planet.

Midtown Manhattan was the center of one of America's "billion dollar industries," and in the 1920s the growth sector of that industry was women's clothing. In 1925, 78 percent of the total value of American-made women's wear came from New York City shops. It was an industry dominated but not controlled by women. Men owned the shops and performed the skilled work; women did nearly 90 percent of the unskilled work. Only as high-fashion designers and out-of-town buyers were women paramount.

By 1927, most firms in Midtown's Garment District were making only women's clothing: coats, suits, and skirts—but predominantly dresses. Over half of the dresses made in America were made in New York City. The dress business was sovereign on Seventh Avenue, but its reign had begun only recently, at the end of World War I, when women of all ages, not just flappers, began abandoning the "constricting" corset and wearing loose-fitting dresses.

It was this sudden change in women's fashion—as much as anything else—that brought the garment industry into the heart of Midtown in the 1920s. Two decades earlier, the men's clothing trade was dominant in the city, and almost all clothing that came out of New York was made on the Lower East Side. "The story behind this concentration of the clothing trade between the Pennsylvania Station and Times Square, this amassing of wealth in real estate, buildings, and plants," wrote Will Irwin, "is material for an epic of business."

Lefcourt

One of the central figures in this urban transformation was Abraham E. Lefcourt, a sharp-dealing dynamo who had started out in life as an immigrant newsboy and bootblack. His rise to respectability is the story of the migration of the needle trades from downtown to Midtown.

When A. E. Lefcourt died of heart failure in 1932, at age fifty-five, he had built more skyscrapers than any other Manhattan developer, twenty-four of them in twenty years. In 1927, his real estate holdings were estimated at over $100 million, and the following year alone he built $50 million worth of construction. "No other single individual or building organization has constructed in its own behalf as many buildings as are in the Lefcourt group," said *The New York Times*. If placed end to end, his buildings would have covered a distance of a mile in length, and if stacked one on top of the other would have formed a super-skyscraper eight times the height of the Woolworth Building.

Abraham Lefcourt began his career as a developer in the Garment District during World War I, and in fewer than ten years he became the largest individual owner of property in that area, its most powerful industrial leader, and the person most responsible for its relocation to Midtown. "If something should happen tomorrow to sweep away every dollar I have in the world, I don't believe I would be frightened . . . ," he had boasted in 1924. "I could rebuild my fortune in half the time it has taken me to make it." He was, said a reporter, "the man who has never failed."

Five years later, A. E. Lefcourt's real estate empire was in ruins, a casualty of the stock market collapse. Unable to rebound, he died bankrupt, with less than $3,000 in his estate. Few important capitalists have risen so quickly and collapsed so swiftly and completely.

Abraham Lefcourt earned his first dollar at the age of twelve, when he quit school to help support his family—"poor as temple mice"—by selling newspapers and running a bootblack stand on Grand Avenue, on Manhattan's Lower East Side. He had been raised on nearby Henry Street, the son of Russian-Jewish parents who had arrived in New York from Birmingham, England, in 1882, when he was five years old. When the bootblack stand began to prosper, he hired two neighborhood boys to run it during the day and took a sales position with a large Manhattan retail store specializing in women's dresses. Working in retail convinced him that better opportunities resided in wholesale. At age sixteen, he landed a job with a women's apparel firm and stayed there for more than half his lifetime, progressing from clerk, to bookkeeper, to buyer, to traveling salesman, and eventually, at age twenty-five, to head of the business after the owner retired. This completed what Lefcourt called his "college education in business."

He had only $200 when he started out on his own in a cutthroat business whose failure rate was distressingly high. He purchased the plant and his cloth on credit, paid his workers with borrowed money, and was off, he recalled years later, "to a flying start." In 1910, he used every penny he had amassed—just over $200,000—to build a twelve-story loft building for his flourishing firm on West Twenty-fifth Street, between Broadway and Sixth Avenue. At that time, his office staff consisted of himself, a boyhood friend, and a faithful stenographer. Within a year he was one of the leaders of New York's women's wear business—a cofounder of the Cloak, Suit, and Skirt Manufacturers' Protective Association, an organization of needle trade employers formed to present a united front in the industry's fractious relations with the International Ladies' Garment Workers' Union.

In 1912, Lefcourt moved his business to another loft he constructed on West Thirty-seventh Street, farther north than anyone in the industry had yet ventured. Other garment makers warned him—as fellow tailors would warn Edwin Goodman when he moved his shop to Midtown two years later—that he was "facing certain failure." But this proved to be the start of a vast geographic shift of New York City's principal industry.

In 1900, almost the entire women's apparel industry was concentrated south of Fourteenth Street, in the Jewish ghetto in which David Sarnoff and Irving Berlin had been raised. A decade later, the industry began its northward march, from Lower East Side tenement shops that were being pressured out of existence by state laws outlawing home production, to boxlike factory buildings in the area around Madison Square. In the streets branching out from this posh shopping triangle, wedged between Broadway, Fifth Avenue, and Madison Avenue, immigrant capitalists set up ground-floor showrooms catering to women of means interested in purchasing fashionable ready-made dresses, barely discernible knockoffs of originals by Parisian designers.

Problems soon arose, however. At noontime, tens of thousands of garment workers paraded up and down Fifth Avenue, blocking the sidewalks and the storefronts of retail establishments from Thirtieth to Forty-second Streets. These were foreign-looking workers, intimidating by their mere presence to the socially closeted uptown women who shopped in the stores along Fifth Avenue. In 1914, the owners of the big department stores on Thirty-fourth Street, backed by the leading banks of the area, formed the Save New York Committee, an organization mobilized to rid Fifth Avenue of its garment firms. The fear was that they would move farther up Fifth Avenue, close to the big stores on Herald Square, eight blocks north of Madison Square. "Being the most important body of consumers for the women's ready-to-wear," these stores "had the whip-hand," wrote Will Irwin. Working hand-in-glove with powerful mercantile families who lived on the avenue, they pressured banks to stop lending money to developers of lofts north of Thirty-fourth Street along Fifth Avenue. They also threatened a boycott of garment makers who refused to comply with their demands. This was the stick; the carrot was an offer to help finance the relocation of the industry.

In 1921, Fifth Avenue merchants and leaders of the women's clothing trade, Lefcourt among them, reached a city-shaping agreement: Seventh Avenue between Thirty-second Street—site of Pennsylvania Station—and Times Square, would be the new center for the women's clothing trade. The industry would move uptown, but west of Fifth Avenue. This was an official endorsement of a decision Abraham Lefcourt had made on his own nine years earlier.

With the exception of Pennsylvania Station, the Pennsylvania Hotel, and the new federal post office headquarters in Manhattan, most of the area was, in 1921, a bleak commercial desert, a stretch of shabby three- and four-story brick residences, along with seedy hotels and taverns that had been part of the city's old Tenderloin vice district. "The wrecker tore into them," said Will

Irwin. "Twenty-story [steel] skeletons became in a few magical weeks the workshops of a thousand operatives." From Seventh Avenue, the industry spread eastward, toward Broadway, and westward, into Hell's Kitchen, but not as far as the Hudson docks. The city's furiously growing fur business followed women's wear northward, relocating just south of it, along three blocks of Seventh Avenue. There, "terraced skyscrapers" pierced the sky. The transformation was virtually complete by the summer of 1926, when A. E. Lefcourt began constructing his block-long Lefcourt Clothing Center on Seventh Avenue, a magnet building that started the relocation of what remained of New York's declining men's clothing industry to the stretch on Seventh Avenue between Twenty-second and Twenty-sixth Streets.

By this time, Lefcourt had been dabbling in real estate for three years. In 1923, on his forty-sixth birthday, he retired from the clothing business and formed his own construction and real estate company, devoting himself entirely to the lucrative task of relocating New York's needle trades. He bought property in the new garment zone, erected factory lofts on it, and drew tenants to his modern, solidly constructed buildings. On the eve of the Stock Market Crash, there was not a single vacancy in any of the twenty-four Midtown buildings he constructed, a number of them office towers located above Forty-second Street.

Proud, vain and boastful, Abraham Lefcourt closely protected his reputation and was not averse to inflating it. Like Fred French, he styled himself a city builder, not an urban land gambler. "I buy and keep," was his business maxim. He also cast himself as a friend of labor, a more dubious claim. In 1919, he had tried, unsuccessfully, to coerce the unions to return to the oppressive sweatshop practice of having workers paid by the number of garments they produced—piecework—instead of the hours they put in weekly. Then this union buster boasted that he had, almost singlehandedly, eliminated the garment industry's sweatshops, the exploitive subcontracting system whereby a middleman, or "sweater," directed the work of garment makers, many of them working in their squalid tenements. Lefcourt's clothing mills, designed by some of the finest architects in the city, including Ely Jacques Kahn, were spacious and brightly lit; and among the first fireproof buildings in the new Garment Center. But Lefcourt's intentions were purely pecuniary. Loft space in these skyscraper factories, with their adaptable space, rented easily, and for a good price; he had begun constructing them only after sweatshop working conditions had been alleviated—although certainly not eliminated—by state legislation sponsored by Al Smith, Robert Wagner, Jimmy Walker, and other Tammany reformers, long-overdue changes Lefcourt had opposed.

A driven man, Lefcourt never took a vacation and his sole recreation was swimming. Money, he told a reporter in the late 1920s, was no longer his main motivation. He worked for the "thrill of accomplishment. . . . I had all the money I needed long ago." He named most of his buildings after himself, and topped them with distinctive towers. He would stand by the window of his office on the highest floor of the Lefcourt-Marlborough Building at 1359 Broadway and gaze at these dazzling towers. His proudest accomplish was writing his name on the Manhattan skyline.

His conceit about his rapid rise soon became a joke. Every time he opened a new building he would announce that it stood on the very spot where, decades before, he had sold newspapers and shined shoes. Soon there were more Lefcourt skyscrapers than there could possibly have been Lefcourt bootblack stands.

Fashion Avenue

The new Midtown Garment District was largely a creature of coercion. Forced to move off lower Fifth Avenue by established merchants, the industry wound up exactly where it had to be. It needed to be there, on the southern rim of Times Square, because the business had changed fundamentally.

By the mid-1920s, Manhattan's garment trade had become predominantly a fashion trade, with merchandising taking precedence over manufacturing. The mass production side of the business had begun to relocate to the outer boroughs and across the Hudson to New Jersey and Pennsylvania. Most of the sewing shops that remained on Seventh Avenue made high-fashion dresses that could not have been profitably or properly produced anywhere else.

The clothing firms that ruled Seventh Avenue had classy showrooms close to their major customers—out-of-town buyers in the city for only a few days at a time, four times a year, to purchase dresses from the seasonal offerings of the big dress houses. The overwhelming majority of these buyers disembarked at one of the two Midtown train stations, stayed in a Midtown hotel, ate in Midtown restaurants, and spent their evenings at Midtown clubs, speakeasies, theaters, and movie palaces.

Mid-Manhattan was an ideal location for the industry for other reasons. When the Holland Tunnel was completed in 1927, trucks had easier access to Seventh Avenue. Subway service was also excellent on Seventh Avenue, making it convenient for garment workers—most of them first- and second-generation Jewish and Italian unmarried women—to commute to work from places as distant as the Bronx and Brownsville, Coney Island and Queens—and as close as Little Italy in lower Manhattan. Few who worked in the industry in the 1920s—male or female—lived near the point of production; home and work had become separate spheres. By 1925, an estimated 40 percent of women's garment workers employed in Manhattan lived in Brooklyn and the Bronx, and another fifteen thousand or so had moved from lower to upper Manhattan. By then, only 15 percent of New York Jews lived on the Lower East Side; and this number would continue to decline for the remainder of the decade.

This dispersal of the industry's workforce occurred simultaneously with its physical relocation, and the subway ensured that there was no concurrent disruption in production. It would have been nearly impossible for the women's garment industry to be located anywhere else but in Midtown, with its unrivaled mass transit connections. The work was seasonal and a central location made it feasible to expand and contract the labor force with a minimum of cost or effort.

The new Independent Subway System, with its main line along Eighth Avenue, made it easier for the bosses to get to and from work. Real estate developers followed the line of the new subway northward. In 1923, only 3 percent of Manhattan's Jews lived on the middle and Upper West Side, most of them German Jews. In the mid-1920s, Emery Roth and other developers began building towering Art Deco apartment houses on the West Side for the new grandees of the garment trade, the great majority of them from Russia and Eastern Europe.

This was not the same industry that Abraham Lefcourt had started out in. Women's clothing was made and sold differently in the 1920s, and this transformation made it possible for clothing entrepreneurs to operate small shops on Seventh Avenue without installing factory-scale manufacturing facilities that would have been prohibitively expensive in this high-rent district. The new production arrangement was called the "jobber-subcontractor system." It was unique to New York, and gave the city a decisive advantage over other industrial centers that produced women's clothing. Its salient characteristic was the separation of making and marketing. The jobber, or contractor, concentrated on merchandising, and the subcontractor on production. To survive, the jobber had to be in Midtown, near his customers, whereas the subcontractor had to be outside Midtown, where labor costs and rents were vastly lower. The jobber-subcontractor system, more than any other factor, explains why some parts of New York's garment business remained in Midtown while others seceded to the suburbs.

In the decade before World War I, New York's garment industry was highly centralized, an industry of whales not minnows. Manufacturers, operating out of a single plant, assumed every aspect of production, from design to cutting, sewing, finishing, and sales; and the industry was concentrated in large shops, most of them located in ponderous cast iron buildings near Madison Square. Beginning around 1920, the owners of these large shops broke them up and created a highly decentralized system of independent shops. This reduced production costs and made it possible for clothing capitalists to nimbly respond to fast-changing women's fashions, a system ideally suited to a cutthroat, rough-and-tumble business. Firms that failed to adapt swiftly to changing styles became extinct.

It was an exploitive three-tiered system, with the jobbers—the former manufacturers—on top, the subcontractors in the middle, and the workers on the bottom. The jobbers were independent, highly specialized contractors who supervised the cutting, and sometimes the finishing, of fashionable women's dresses in their small combination shops and showrooms on or near Fashion Avenue. Theirs were the thousands of sewing machines—no more than a few dozen in most shops—that Will Irwin heard on the pavements of Seventh Avenue.

The jobbers also sold casual wear—housedresses, undergarments, and skirts—but these items were mass-produced in sewing shops run by subcontractors, shops that were located on the Lower East Side, in the city's outer boroughs, in industrial cities like Newark and Bayonne, and in the coal fields of northeastern Pennsylvania—places where labor was cheap, safety standards lax, and unions weak or nonexistent.

The Holland Tunnel and, later, the GW Bridge made the system profitable. Trucks were the lifeline between Seventh Avenue and the scattered subcontracting plants. They linked the center of the industry to its periphery, and allowed the jobber to have "the best of two possible worlds": a design headquarters and impressive showroom in Midtown, and access to production shops outside the city, shops he didn't own and workers he didn't pay, but shops and workers he ruled over autocratically.

The jobbers were the clothing industry's venture capitalists: they put up the money, arranged for the production of ready-to-wear items, displayed them in their showrooms, and sold them to retail buyers. The subcontractor was the manufacturer, but the skirts and dresses he made were designed by the jobber and made from materials sent to him on consignment by the jobber. The subcontracting plants handled only mass-produced items, and in these shops there was an unbridgeable division of labor based on gender; women did the mind-numbing machine work, men did the skilled cutting and pressing.

The New York garment business was pure tooth-and-claw capitalism, a throwback to the nineteenth century. The jobbers imposed upon their subcontractors Darwinian conditions, pitting them against each other for survival. Jobbers dealt with only those firms that met their nonnegotiable demands for maximum speed and cost cutting. This forced subcontractors to drive down wages and suppress unions, often with the help of hired thugs, hundreds of them employed by master criminal Arnold Rothstein, who also worked, on occasion, for the unions.

Hundreds of these small production plants were driven out of business every year. In a three-year period in the 1920s, over two-thirds of New York City's contract shops were forced to close down, unable to keep up with the competition. In slack periods, even the most prosperous subcontractors fired their entire workforce and moved out of the plant to avoid paying rent on an idle production facility. When fresh orders came pouring in, the subcontractor rented a new shop, hired a new workforce, and went back into business. The worst of these plants were, in the words of a union investigator, "rat-holes"; work was carried on under medieval-like conditions. But this exploitive subcontracting system gave New York an enormous competitive advantage over cities like Chicago, which continued to produce clothing in large plants in which union shop stewards prevented the most egregious forms of exploitation.

Even unionized workers in some shops were compelled by the sharp competition between subcontractors to accept substandard wages and working conditions. If their boss didn't lower his overhead sufficiently to land a contract, he would be out of business and they would be out of work—perhaps permanently. This system shifted the heaviest burden incurred by fluctuations in production from the subcontractors to the workers, the great majority of them young Italian women.* By 1925, unmarried Italian women had replaced Jewish women as the largest ethnic and gender group in the New York City needle trades. But throughout the 1920s, Jews retained a stranglehold on the highest-paying positions. Almost all jobbers and subcontractors were Jews. The jobbers tended to be second- and third-generation Jews; the subcontractors were almost entirely immigrants from Russia and Poland.

It would have been feasible to make all women's clothing like the New York

---

* Irish and German women living in Hell's Kitchen worked in small factories in their immediate neighborhood, plants that made a baffling array of products: neckties, tin cans, candy, biscuits, paper products, and cigarettes. Garment manufacturers on Seventh Avenue and elsewhere in the city preferred to stick with Italian and Jewish women whose extended families had some experience in the trade. Ruth S. True, *West Side Studies: The Neglected Girl* (New York: Russell Sage Foundation, 1914), 43–44.

subcontractors did—mass-producing them under assembly line conditions—but discriminating women consumers demanded "a maximum of style." The "style" part of the industry was centered on Seventh Avenue, where fashion ruled supreme and jobbers had to adapt to wildly fluctuating demand. This required that they be in or near the turbulent center of the city. Rent and labor may have been expensive, but it would have been suicidal to move elsewhere. Jobbers produced high-fashion silk dresses made from Parisian patterns and could not risk ruining the product by slipshod supervision or careless high-speed production. Making these dresses called for highly skilled tailoring and intense scrutiny by hard-eyed spotters with long experience in the business. So these high-fashion items were made right on Seventh Avenue, where designers and cutters also enjoyed the advantages of concentration: a supply of skilled labor and proximity to subsidiary industries that supported the making and merchandising of fashionable clothing: button-making shops, sewing machine repairmen, modeling agencies, advertising firms, and fashion magazines.

High-fashion women's garments were also creatures of caprice, sensitive to fluctuating trends in women's taste. Only "inside shops" on Seventh Avenue, with short production schedules and highly experienced workers, could respond rapidly to fast-changing consumer trends. So while sewing was still done in Midtown in the 1920s it was confined almost exclusively to expensive, à la mode items. Only one in five of New York–made dresses were sewn in "close-in shops." Once the national production center for men's and women's garments of all types, most of them mass-produced, Jazz Age Manhattan became America's exclusive design and sales center for high-fashion women's clothing.

America Comes to Seventh Avenue

It was to the Seventh Avenue showrooms that out-of-town buyers congregated after they arrived in the city and checked into their hotels. The designers were the stars of a Seventh Avenue fashion show, but it was the jobbers who took the risks and creamed the profits. "If you're a [jobber] teamed with a good designer it's hard for you not to make money," wrote a reporter who covered the industry. But the risks were tremendous. A jobber had his designers build a "line" of dresses and then gambled on their success four seasons a year. It was a business as highly speculative as the stock market.

Running a fashion studio and specialty shop also demanded a lot of upfront money; there were few young Abraham Lefcourts in this altered industry—

expectant capitalists with thin to nonexistent resources. A hefty slice of a job-ber's budget went to entertaining writers and photographers from *Vogue* and *Harper's Bazaar*, and having his own designers dine at the Plaza and the St. Regis, surveying the crowd to see what fashionable women who sailed every spring to Milan and Rome were wearing. And at least once a year, he sent a design team to the big style shows in Paris, for most New York dressmakers were brilliant adaptors of Parisian styles, not striking originators. Even so, the best of them had to be pampered lest they be stolen away.

Most of the buyers worked exclusively for one or another big depart-ment store chain, although some were resident buyers representing a hun-dred and more independent stores. There were "no shrinking violets" among them, wrote a fashion reporter. "They are usually ladies who have fought their way through the stock rooms or sales floor of a store and have hearts of polished granite. But let them show compassion and the merchandise managers quickly find buyers who are not softies." It was the high-fashion women's garments they purchased in bulk, after days of close scrutiny and bare-knuckle haggling, that established Seventh Avenue's reputation as a style center second only to Paris, and that kept the ascendant capitalists of the industry huddled together near the urban core. For them, Midtown was the center of the earth.

The city's biggest industry was also the one that best captured its tempo and temperament: fast moving, cynical, adaptive, resourceful, competitive, and highly ethnic. In New York "survival depends upon ingenuity, 'shmearing,' cut-ting a corner, trimming a margin, finding some other way to make a fast buck in a swift race," wrote sociologist Daniel Bell, the son of immigrant Jewish garment workers from the Lower East Side. "This is what has given New York its particular beat and distinctive character."

The dress industry also fueled the city's prosperity, a prosperity that made possible New York's richly diverse cultural life. The wealth generated by the garment industry's small unit, single-plant firms, along with other small, highly competitive firms in industries like printing, plastics, and radio tech-nology, produced a tremendously large middle class, probably the largest middle class of any city in the country. And because so many sharp-elbowed entrepreneurs were Jewish, "it was a middle class," said Bell, "that hungered for culture and improvement." In the 1920s, the Jews were the city's most ag-gressive "consumers of culture," in Nathan Glazer's words, reading books and cosmopolitan magazines, frequenting the city's theaters and film palaces, and buying the recordings of jazz artists promoted by firms on Tin Pan Alley, the center of New York's thriving music publishing business, a business, like dress-making, dominated by small entrepreneurial firms, most of them owned by Jews. New York became a jazz capital in the 1920s, in part because risk takers on Tin Pan Alley were willing to gamble on upcoming African American musicians, selling their music to big record companies, booking them at hip clubs, and promoting them as cultural revolutionaries.

PART FIVE

JAZZ AGE ICONS

MUSIC IS MY MISTRESS

*No figure in jazz history could surpass Ellington in creating
a completely satisfying and self-sufficient musical mood.*

TED GIOIA

The Duke

Tin Pan Alley—the place Jimmy Walker had gone in 1908 to try to make it as a
songwriter—was a short walk up Seventh Avenue from the Garment District.
In Walker's youth, it was concentrated around West Twenty-eighth Street, but
by the mid-1920s most of the big music publishers, booking agencies, and recording studios had migrated to the mid-Forties and lower Fifties, between
Broadway and Eighth Avenue, close to the concentration of clubs, dance halls,
and radio studios around Times Square, their talent bank. Like the women's
clothing industry, whose uptown migration it mirrored, the city's music business had to be in Midtown, America's entertainment epicenter.

The most resourceful entrepreneur on Tin Pan Alley was Irving Mills, a
short, dapper Jewish promoter who, with his brother Jack, had opened a small
music publishing business in 1919. Forever looking for fresh talent, he was
especially interested in African American jazz performers, artists shunned by
the big music publishers. "Everybody [in the business] looked down on me,"
Mills recalled years later. "They said, 'Geez, he fools around with niggers. Nigger bands.'"

Born on the Lower East Side in 1894, Mills began his musical career as a
"song demonstrator," belting out the new tunes of the day in grubby downtown
dance halls, with the assistance of a megaphone. He was a slick, fast-talking
hustler, but had undeniable qualities: a wonderful ear for music and iron loyalty
to his clients, many of them rapidly rising songwriters and composers—black

as well as white—that he had discovered. In November 1926, Mills signed to a recording contract a tall, smoothly polished African American bandleader and composer from Washington, D.C. His friends called Edward Kennedy Ellington "Duke" for his courtly bearing and stylish wardrobe. He brushed his hair straight back and had a meticulously trimmed, pencil-thin mustache. The creases in his pants were pressed to a sharp edge, his shirts and ties were beautifully matched, and he walked deliberately, with his shoulders thrown back, regally self-assured. "Make way, here comes the Duke," his high school mates would playfully announce when he entered a room.

Mills had discovered Ellington playing at a basement dive called the Club Kentucky, a rowdy interracial club in the Broadway Theater District. Ellington had been in town for two years, unable to break through to the big time, but two months after signing with Mills he was a rising sensation in the recording business. For the next thirteen years, Mills handled almost everything Ellington did in the music industry. It was a partnership similar to the one that Jack Dempsey had with Tex Rickard, and Babe Ruth had with Christy Walsh.

Nineteen twenty-seven was Duke Ellington's breakout year, an epochal moment in his transcendent career as a jazz artist and composer. In that year, he and his band, the Washingtonians, recorded a series of hard-swinging hits, among them "Birmingham Breakout," "Creole Love Call," and "Black and Tan Fantasy," wax discs that led in December of that year to a career-making engagement at Owney Madden's Cotton Club, Harlem's hottest nightspot. Soon after this, Ellington signed a radio contract with Bill Paley. Paley's new CBS network carried Ellington's music to the entire nation, bringing him recognition from distinguished historians of music as one of this country's greatest composers, maker of music that was authentically American.

Jazz was born in New Orleans and Chicago in the first two decades of the twentieth century, but not until the pioneers of this syncopated music "converged in New York," as Ellington said, and "blended together" did jazz emerge as a popular art form. It was then, in the mid-1920s, that Ellington began creating a unique form of big-city jazz. And he first experimented with it, not in Harlem—his new Manhattan home—but in Midtown, in that smoky basement speakeasy where Irving Mills had first heard him play.

"Elegant, reserved without being stiff, articulate even in his evasions, well mannered to the point of ostentation, elitist despite his populist tendencies . . . Edward Kennedy Ellington would have been a striking man even if he had never played a note of music," writes jazz historian and composer Ted Gioia.

He was born on April 29, 1899, the son of James Edward Ellington, a butler for a rich Washington physician, and Daisy Kennedy, the stunning daughter of a local police captain. The Ellington family lived in an all-black neighborhood on the fringes of the downtown, and Duke's father served as a caterer at the White House on at least one occasion before taking a job as a printmaker in the Washington Navy Yard. Daisy Ellington doted on her only son and made him feel "blessed," privileged, with his younger sister, Ruth, to be part of north-west Washington's light-skinned African American achievers—schoolteach-ers, clerks, and government workers who established, in that rigidly segregated city, their own network of solidly based churches, schools, civic organizations, choral societies, orchestras, and theaters.

Duke worshipped his genteel, devoutly religious mother. "There is no place I would rather be tonight, except in my mother's arms," he said years later at a White House reception in his honor. But growing up, he wanted to be like his father, J. E. to his friends, and Uncle Ed to his children and the dozen or so cousins who descended on the Ellington residence—a family gathering place—every Sunday afternoon. "J. E. always acted as though he had money, whether he had it or not," his son described him in *Music Is My Mistress,* his elusive autobiography. "He spent and lived . . . as though he were a million-aire." Ellington wanted to be like his "pappy": "a party man," a great ballroom dancer, and "a connoisseur of vintages." But raising Edward Ellington was a joint enterprise, and both parents instilled in him strong racial pride and soar-ing self-assurance. No unconquerable barriers stood in his way, his parents reminded him: life can be shaped by one's own inclinations and achievements.

The Ellingtons were a music-loving family, owners of two treasured up-right pianos. Daisy played parlor songs and light ragtime, and J. E. played operatic arias at family gatherings. When Edward's feet could barely touch the pedals, his mother signed him up for piano lessons, but his interests lay elsewhere. "My piano teacher, Mrs. Clinkscales (that was really her name), got paid several times a week for many weeks for these lessons, but I missed more than I took, because of my enthusiasm for playing ball, and running and racing through the street." He was a dutiful child but had a well-masked streak of rebelliousness, sneaking away in his teens to Frank Holliday's pool room, at Seventh and T Streets, a gathering place for rag pianists; and to the Gayety burlesque house, to see the high-kicking chorus girls.

An indifferent student, he took an interest in only one subject, commer-cial art, and entered Samuel H. Armstrong Technical High School to study it. About this time, his passion for music was awakened when he began attending "rent parties," or "shouts," as they were called locally, rollicking, all-night gath-erings open to anyone willing to pay the fifteen cent admission fee, money the host used to keep the landlord at bay. The ragtime musicians he met at these gatherings became his models and mentors. "Those ragtime pianists sounded *so* good to me! And they looked so good! Particularly when they flashed their left hands. I noticed that the left hand was the trick of it and that audiences were most impressed by a showy left hand. So I developed a showy left hand."

Ellington cut classes to play the piano in the school gym; other kids joined him and danced to his propulsive music. He played so fast and enthusiastically, with rag music's exaggerated syncopation, that the piano appeared to shake. He was soon playing for money at dances and parties, and filling in at Washington clubs and cafés, where he performed for both white and black audiences. "I learned that when you were playing piano there was always a pretty girl standing down at the bass clef end of the piano," he said later. "I ain't been no athlete since."

He started composing his own songs at age fifteen, but in his senior year, when he received a scholarship to study commercial art at Pratt Institute in Brooklyn, he was faced with the most important decision of his young life: art or music. Three months before graduation, he quit school to become a sign painter by day and a professional musician at night. "I never took up the scholarship to Pratt because by playing piano, and by booking bands for dances, I was making a lot of money." He would need it; at age nineteen he married his neighborhood sweetheart, Edna Thompson. Less than nine months later their son Mercer was born. Later Mercer would say that the only reason his mother and father married was to legitimize their son. (Ellington would live with other women, but never divorce Edna.)

Ellington was the feature performer in a local dance band called the Duke's Serenaders. The group included future Ellington highlighters Sonny Greer, a hip New Jersey drummer, and Otto "Toby" Hardwick, a saxophonist who was Duke's former schoolmate. They didn't play jazz, which was not recorded until 1917; they called their music "sweet"—a pleasing blend of ragtime and conventional popular tunes. For Duke, everything changed in 1921 when he went to see a traveling vaudeville revue featuring wild-living saxophonist Sidney Bechet, one of the originators of New Orleans jazz. "I had never heard anything like it. It was a completely new sound and conception to me."

Ellington knew about the blues—Southern folk music that had been popularized and commercialized more than a decade earlier by black bandleader and composer W. C. Handy, the self-described "Father of the Blues." But it wasn't until he heard the incomparable Sidney Bechet at Washington's Howard Theatre that he began to incorporate the blues, however subtly, into his music.

———

The next year, Sonny Greer was invited to New York to play drums in the band of vaudeville clarinetist Wilbur Sweatman. "If you want me," said Sonny, "you gotta take Duke and Otto, too." The three young musicians had long dreamed of playing in Harlem, which had recently eclipsed Washington as the cultural capital of black America. "Harlem, to our minds, [had] the world's most glamorous atmosphere. We had to go there," Ellington recalled.

They arrived in March 1923, and Sweatman's band opened the next night at Harlem's prestigious Lafayette Theatre. "It is impossible to enter New York," Ellington remembered his thoughts at the time, "without feeling that something wonderful is about to happen. Whether you arrive by plane, ship, train, car or bus, bridge or tunnel, you feel the immediate excitement of starshine." The young poet Arna Bontemps, who arrived in Harlem from California the very next year, described his first night in the "Negro Capital of the World." The words could easily have come from the pen of Edward Kennedy Ellington. "From a window of a small room in an apartment on Fifty and 129th Street I looked over the rooftops of Negrodom and tried to believe my eyes. What a city! What a world! And what a year for a colored boy to be leaving home for the first time . . . full of golden hopes and romantic dreams."

But Ellington, who left Edna and Mercer behind in Washington, met nothing but disappointment in his effort to break into this place where life woke up at night. After the band's weeklong run, Sweatman moved on, and Ellington and his friends were out of work, and soon out of money. On some nights, they split a nickel hot dog three ways. Hustling food money in pool halls and cadging drinks in local speakeasies, they managed to land a handful of minor engagements in Harlem clubs; most evenings they slept in the apartment of one of Sonny Greer's aunts. They were nighthawks, cruising Harlem's pulsating cabarets; and on Saturday evenings Ellington would play for a dollar at house rent parties, where, between acts, he and Sonny would gorge themselves on fried chicken and biscuits and sip corn whiskey in quarter pint portions called shorties.

At these all-night "jumps" they encountered the robust music Ellington had first discovered back in Washington: Harlem stride piano. This was a "bravura keyboard style" that emerged from ragtime and called for "rapid tempos, virtuosic devices borrowed from classical musical, and the use of the piano's full register." It was called "stride" for the "large strides or leaps in the left hand," a flashy, purely improvisational style that had "tremendous rhythmic propulsion." Duke would watch the local stride pianists, called "ticklers," engage in wickedly contested "cutting battles," trying to outperform one another. "Sometimes we got carving battles going that would last for four or five hours," and "hard cash was bet on the outcome," said Willie "The Lion" Smith, one of the kings of stride. It wasn't long before Ellington began integrating stronger elements of stride into his own music.

After three months without steady work, Ellington and his homesick friends were ready to call it quits. One evening Duke found fifteen dollars on the street. He and the boys raced to a restaurant, had a quick meal, and then took the subway to Penn Station. They were off to Washington for some home cooking and "to get ourselves together," Ellington recalled, "before we tried it again."

Otto Hardwick went to his parents' home and Sonny Greer stayed with the Ellington family. "I still remember the smell of hot biscuits when we walked in," Duke said later. "There was butter and honey. My mother broiled six mackerel. There was lots of coffee. Uncle Ed got out the old decanter and we lay there drinking corn [whiskey] in the sunshine. It was nice."

They were back in New York in June, this time with their trumpet-playing friend, Arthur Whetsol. The leader of their new five-piece group, called the Washington Black Sox Orchestra, was a Baltimore banjo player named Elmer Snowden. On a visit to Washington, "Fats" Waller, the celebrated jazz pianist they had met in Harlem, promised them a job, but it vanished by the time the Snowden band arrived in New York. That September, Leonard Harper, a Harlem-based producer for shows in Midtown nightspots, got the band an engagement at the Hollywood Club, a new basement speakeasy run by a silent syndicate of gangsters. This was it; this was Broadway. "We do it, Daddy," Sonny said; but even serenely confident Ellington wondered if they could.

The Club Kentucky

The Hollywood Club, soon renamed the Club Kentucky, became the band's New York base for the next four years. It was in Midtown, not Harlem, that Duke Ellington first became a musical notable. "The 'real New Yorker' is not always born in New York," he wrote in *Music Is My Mistress*. "He becomes one at the very instant when he discovers that his own ingredients are completely compatible with the city's soups and salads."

Before the war, mid-Manhattan's white clubs were largely closed to black musicians, but by the early 1920s African American jazz and blues performers were beginning to break through the color barrier. Fletcher Henderson, a flamboyant young pianist and orchestra leader from Georgia, opened at the famed Roseland Ballroom on Broadway and Fifty-first Street, where flashy New Orleans–born Louis "Satchmo" Armstrong played trumpet briefly with the Henderson Orchestra before returning to Chicago, his home city, in 1925. Black revues and floor shows were becoming increasingly popular in Times Square clubs and cabarets; and there were at least a dozen Broadway imitators of Florence Mills, the sensational black cabaret singer and comedian whose career was launched when she appeared with the songwriting team of Noble Sissle and Eubie Blake in *Shuffle Along* (1921), Broadway's first successful black musical comedy. One of its innumerable knockoffs, James P. Johnson's *Runnin' Wild* (1923), featured sultry jazz singer Adelaide Hall, who would later hook up with the Ellington band.

In 1923, nineteen black floor shows were produced on Broadway, and Manhattan had over two hundred public dance halls. They drew six million paid customers, a bonanza for black musicians. This wasn't integration; the performers were black, the audiences white, but a few Midtown nightspots—among them the Hollywood Club—welcomed both black and white patrons. "It was at the [Hollywood] Club" Ellington said later, "that our music acquired new colors and characteristics." At the time, Ellington was moving beyond creative renditions of ragtime to a looser, more spontaneous style known as jazz, or jass, as it was originally spelled, a type of music impossible to precisely define but characterized by improvisation, syncopation, and a regular or forceful rhythm. This uniquely American musical style had originated in New Orleans, spread to Chicago, and begun to sweep New York just before Ellington arrived in the city.*

For most Caucasian pleasure seekers, jazz was merely "dance music played with a little 'pep'" and some "snappy" rhythm. But even close students of jazz couldn't agree on what it was. As George Gershwin said: "the word has been used for so many different things that it has ceased to have any definite meaning." If it had one agreed-upon meaning it was rebellion. "The word supposedly derived from black slang for the central appetitive act," writes Broadway historian Ethan Mordden, "which tells us how forward and defiant the jazz 'movement' intended to be. It was like saying 'fuck' to your father."

His entire life, Duke Ellington refused to use the word "jazz" to describe his music. "I don't write jazz," he told a reporter. "I write Negro folk music."

The Ellington band began to take on permanent form at the Hollywood Club. Freddie Guy, a slim, light-skinned guitarist, joined the group. He was inarguably good, but it was the new cornet player who decisively transformed the band's sound. James "Bubber" Miley was a slim, moon-faced South Carolinian who had been raised in New York City. He was "a character," said Otto Hardwick, "with laughing eyes and mouth full of gold teeth," and he could make his horn "growl" like a human voice. Ellington and Hardwick considered him

---

* The first jazz recordings were made in 1917 by the Original Dixieland Jazz Band, an all-white group headed by D. J. LaRocca. The group appeared in New York that year at the Paradise Ballroom and started a dance craze.

"the epitome of soul" and had recruited him by going up to Harlem after work and getting him "stiff. . . . When he came to he was in a tuxedo growling at the Hollywood, on Broadway!" said Hardwick.

"Our band changed character when Bubber came in," Ellington recalled. "He used to growl all night long, playing gutbucket on his horn. That was when we decided to forget all about the sweet music." To create his characteristic "wah-wah" sound, Miley placed the rubber cup from the end of a plumber's plunger into the trumpet's bell and pulled it in and out. But there was more to it than that. The "growl," Mercer Ellington explained in his memoirs, was composed of "three basic elements . . . the sound of the horn, a guttural gargling in the throat, and the actual note that is hummed." Miley used his guttural growls "to intone the tragic sounds of graveyard cities, the late night calls of slow freight trains or the simple crying of a deserted woman."

It was Miley, along with Charlie Irvis, a new trombonist and fellow growler, that transformed the group from "a polite dance band" to a hot jazz ensemble. Hot jazz bore no resemblance to symphonic jazz, the highly stylized, elaborately scored "white jazz" of Paul Whiteman, the musician credited with making "a lady out of jazz." Spontaneity and improvisation, sessions in which individual musicians are free to exercise their freedom in unrehearsed solos, became part of the Ellington band's repertoire. So did the New Orleans sound when soprano saxophonist Sidney Bechet joined the band. "Often, when Bechet was blowing, he would say, 'I'm going to call Goola this time!'" Ellington recalled. "Goola was his dog, a big German shepherd. Goola wasn't always there, but he was calling him anyway with a kind of throaty growl."*

"Call" came from the blues and was an essential component of Ellington's music in those early days. Musicians would call out to somebody, tell a quick, poignant story, or release some pain. "The audience didn't know anything about it, but the cats in the band did," said Ellington. Elmer Snowden was the only band member who continued to prefer "sweet" music, but he was soon forced out by the group when he was found pocketing an inordinate share of the nightly take. Ellington took over and renamed the band the Washingtonians.

The Hollywood Club was a cramped, dingy cellar café with tables for only a hundred or so customers, but Ellington's band made it a Broadway hotspot, a

---

* Although Ellington idolized Bechet, he had to let him go after his uncontrolled drinking and volatile temper made him "too hard to handle." Barney Bigard, *With Louis and the Duke: The Autobiography of a Jazz Clarinetist*, ed. Barry Martyn (NY: Oxford University Press, 1985), 72.

hangout for actors, athletes, bootleggers, drug pushers, chorus girls, and prostitutes—and an after-hours spot for musicians who played the posh Broadway
clubs. On any given night, the crowd might include Bix Beiderbecke, Eddie
Duchin, Tommy Dorsey, and Paul Whiteman, whose band had a long run
at the Palais Royale, a classy club nearby. Whiteman would bring along his
arrangers and other members of his orchestra, and more than once George
Gershwin accompanied him. The two of them had written the jazz symphonic
classic *Rhapsody in Blue* that Whiteman played as part of "an experiment in
music" at Manhattan Aeolian Hall on the afternoon of February 12, 1924. It
was the first time jazz was played on the concert stage, and the performance
was "an uproarious success," said the New York *Herald*.

Whiteman loved Ellington's music and praised it loudly in the club; Ellington, for his part, felt Whiteman and his "cats . . . blew up a storm." But
Whiteman, as he himself admitted, had "toned down" the "demonic energy" of
hot jazz, but without, he hoped, taking "the life out of the music."

Black entertainers frequented the Hollywood Club and spread the word
that Ellington was making a new kind of music. This drew in Fats Waller, Willy
"The Lion" Smith, and other Harlem headliners, who would drop by late in the
evening after they finished their uptown engagements. On some nights, the
floor was "so crowded," said Sonny Greer, "you couldn't dance." Closing time
was when the cash register stopped ringing.

It was a loose-living, big-spending crowd. "The money was flying," said
Greer. With tips, Ellington cleared as much as a hundred dollars a night. He
spent most of it on booze. "Everybody in our band . . . became a juice hound,
juice meaning any kind of firewater," he later admitted. "Liquor drinking
among the musicians was done from the gladiator perspective, in just the same
way as when they challenged each other on their instruments." Ellington quit
drinking later in life, claiming he retired as the "undefeated champ . . . I drank
more booze than anybody ever."

Alcohol was the drug of choice for Ellington and the other Washingtonians, but there was a thriving narcotics traffic on Broadway, run by Arnold
Rothstein. He found the heroin trade more profitable—and far less risky—
than bootlegging. If Ellington partook, there is no record of it. He lived on the
edge, however—wildly, recklessly. Some nights he would send the band home
early and he and Sonny would "work the floor. I had one of those little studio
upright pianos on wheels that you could push around from table to table, and
Sonny would carry his sticks and sing. Answering requests, we sang anything
and everything—pop songs, jazz songs, dirty songs, torch songs, Jewish songs.
Sometimes, the customer would respond by throwing twenty-dollar bills."
Leaving the club flush, he and Sonny would blow it all by the time they got

back to their apartments in Harlem, where Duke was now living with Edna in a rented room on Seventh Avenue, while his parents took care of Mercer back in Washington. "We had to go from joint to joint to be received, and to find out what was happening." Almost everywhere they went they bought a drink for the house and found friendly female companionship.

In early 1925, there was a fire at the Hollywood Club, probably set by its mobster owners to collect the insurance money. (Greer claimed that when "business would get slack . . . the boss Leo Bernstein [would] . . . say, 'You all take your horns home, we're going to have an accident down there tonight.'") The club closed for repairs and the Ellington band took an engagement in Massachusetts. When the group returned in March, the Hollywood Club had been renamed the Club Kentucky and the Washingtonians were being advertised by ownership as "probably the hottest band this side of the equator."

That year, the band was featured on a weekly afternoon radio broadcast, recorded in the studios of station WHN. Ellington also cut seven records with small outfits that specialized in music for black people. His career was on the uptake, but he was dissatisfied. The Club Kentucky was not a top-shelf venue, and the band had no other prospects. He wanted to be like Fletcher Henderson, who was cutting records with big-time companies, not the "small fry" Ellington was working with. Duke was good, but he needed exposure.

Things changed in 1926 when he signed with brash, richly connected Irving Mills. At that time, jazz, in its myriad variations, was becoming, like boxing, a big business. A jazz orchestra, like a good fighter, could not rise on its own merits. Most orchestra leaders were unqualified to deal with the details of booking, finance, and hiring. Agents like Mills filled the void, and became czars of the music business, the Tex Rickards of their trade.

"It was imperative that we have a man like [Mills], a front man," said Sonny Greer, "because I don't think we could have done it alone without his guidance." Mills was never immodest about his part in bringing Ellington forward. "If I hadn't raved about him when I heard him the first night, he might have just been . . . another one of the bandleaders working in the café. I was very fortunate, Duke was very fortunate."

Mills knew that the big money in the music business came from recording songs, not playing in clubs; and that recordings were becoming a new performance medium, not simply a promotion for live appearances. Under his direction, Duke and the Washingtonians began recording for Vocalion, a subsidiary of the Brunswick record company, a firm that was developing a new line of "race" recordings by black performers. Mills also signed the band to record for Victor and its rival, Columbia, the number one and two recording companies in the world. This increased Ellington's visibility and made his music available for the first time to large numbers of whites as well as blacks. In 1927, Ellington and Mills entered into a corporate partnership that gave Mills exclusive publication rights to Duke's music. Mills managed the band as well, and supervised every orchestration and arrangement it played. And he put his name, unethically, on dozens of Ellington compositions that were entirely Ellington's. Duke was annoyed but avoided a confrontation. Mills was doing a lot for him, and he was appreciative. "This was . . . the beginning of a long and wonderful association," Ellington said later. Mills "was the first to demand that [Ellington] get the same [financial] consideration as the big white acts," Mercer Ellington described Mills's importance to his father's career. "[He was] energetic, astute, enterprising, imaginative . . . and one of the greatest showmen of his time."

"Nobody compared to Irving Mills," said legendary recording mogul John Hammond. "He was the best. And he just broke his back for Duke, he really did." He made a ton of money doing it—more, probably, than he deserved.

In 1927, Mills arranged for station WHN to broadcast live from the Club Kentucky, beginning at 2 A.M. A young announcer introduced the Ellington band and hosted the show. Mills also insisted that Ellington record only the music he had written. This was important to Ellington, who wanted to be known as a composer as well as a bandleader. In late 1926 and early 1927, Ellington composed and recorded three jazz classics: "East Saint Louis Toodle-Oo," "Black and Tan Fantasy," and "Creole Love Call." Bubber Miley performed one of the greatest trumpet solos in recording history on "Black and Tan Fantasy," and "Creole Love Call" was hauntingly enhanced by Adelaide Hall's wailing and humming. Her vocal obbligatos became distinctive instrumental components of the orchestra. "The record sessions were Mills's greatest achievements for Duke," wrote biographer Barry Ulanov. "They put Ellington within reach of everybody with a phonograph."

Ellington tailored each of his compositions to the three minutes allowed him on a wax disc, and painstakingly arranged the seating of his players and the position of the microphones to get the richest possible sound. "Records became Duke's greatest means of expression," writes Ulanov, "the medium in which his band was always at its best." They were his greatest gift to music, a legacy made possible by his working in mid-Manhattan, the recording center of the world, and being discovered by one of the outstanding impresarios of Tin Pan Alley.

The Cotton Club

In the summer of 1927, Duke and the Washingtonians made another of their New England tours, drawing enthusiastic crowds wherever they appeared. The contract with the Club Kentucky expired that year, and when the band returned to New York, Mills began looking for additional ways to promote Ellington's music nationally. At that point, an opening appeared, unexpectedly, at Harlem's Cotton Club, at the corner of Lenox Avenue and 142nd Street.*

This was the place that Owney Madden and a consortium of hoodlums had purchased in 1923, when it was called the Club Deluxe. Madden had Joseph Urban, Florenz Ziegfeld's set designer, turn a second-story hang-out into a swanky seven-hundred-seat supper club with an antebellum plantation motif. Band leader Cab Calloway described the room: "The bandstand was a replica of a southern mansion, with large white columns and a backdrop painted with weeping willows and slave quarters. The band played on the veranda of the mansion, and in front of the veranda, down a few steps, was the dance floor, which was also used for the shows. The waiters wore red tuxedoes, like butlers in the southern mansions . . . and there were huge cut-crystal chandeliers."

In early December 1927, on the eve of the big holiday season, the owners found themselves in a quandary. Andy Preer, the leader of the house band, had died suddenly that May, and Joe "King" Oliver had turned down the job as his replacement. There are several versions of what happened next, but apparently songwriter Jimmy McHugh, who had written the score for the club's new winter revue and whose songs Irving Mills published, convinced stage manager Herman Stark and Madden partner Big Frenchy DeMange to contact Mills. Stark and club manager Harry Block went to hear the Ellington band play at Harlem's Lafayette Theater on the last day of the New York run of *Dance Mania*, a vaudeville revue that was scheduled to appear in Philadelphia the next day. After the show they came to an agreement with Ellington and Mills. Mills delivered the contract to Ellington in Philadelphia a few days later.

There was a problem, however. Ellington was under contract with *Dance Mania*'s producer, Clarence Robinson, to complete his two-week engagement, and Robinson would not release him. Word reached Madden and he got in touch with Philadelphia gang boss Boo Boo Hoff. Hoff sent one of his emissaries to speak to Robinson. "Be big," he mumbled, "or you'll be dead." Robinson was "big," and on December 3 the Ellington band took the midnight train to New York, "an inauspicious start to an unimagined rise to fame," writes Ellington's friend and biographer A. H. Lawrence.

The next night Ellington's dance band opened at the Cotton Club, playing background music for the club's revues and dance music between acts. The revues

---

* Lenox Avenue is now Adam Clayton Powell, Jr., Boulevard.

featured gorgeous, café-au-lait-colored singers and dancers; none could be over twenty-one, and some of them, like Lena Horne—who would join the chorus years later at age sixteen—were in their mid-teens. Every girl had to be at least five-foot-six: "Tall, Tan, and Terrific." Unlike Small's Paradise, a competing club whose waiters danced the Charleston while balancing trays of drinks on their fingertips, or the Savoy, Harlem's "Ballroom Deluxe," where Fletcher Henderson's Rainbow Orchestra held sway, the Cotton Club was "a white sanctuary." The entertainers and waiters were black, the customers and owners white. "There were brutes at the door to enforce the Cotton Club's policy," said novelist Carl Van Vechten, a noted white champion of black culture. The gangster owners knew that their white clientele wanted to be entertained by blacks, not to mix with them. Ellington found this policy demeaning and later used his influence to have the owners admit light-complexioned blacks, local black entertainers, and his own mother and father, after they moved to Harlem. Most of Harlem's social and intellectual elite stayed away, not wanting to patronize a Jim Crow establishment.

Owney Madden was at the club frequently, but was rarely seen at the tables. He would play cards in a back room with Big Frenchy and some of the staff; Ellington would sometimes join them after the club closed. Madden liked him and treated him as an equal. The other performers were treated "with a kind of surface respect," recalled Howard "Stretch" Johnson, a dancer in the chorus. "They recognized us as . . . a more talented group of blacks, but generally they thought of us as niggers, like everybody else. They were a bunch of hoods, and they were using the club as a moneymaking operation, so rapport between the performers and the club management was rather distant. They would befriend a few Uncle Tom individuals, and rub their head in typical racist patronizing fashion."

"Cotton Club shows were Ziegfeldian in their gaudiness," writes historian David Levering Lewis, "and almost too athletic to be sensuous, with feathers, fans and legs flying in time to Ellington's tornado rendition of compositions like house songwriter Jimmy McHugh's 'When My Sugar Walks Down the Street.'" But discriminating patrons favored Ellington's own compositions to the ones he played for the club's "panting, jumping spectaculars of costume and cacophony."

"Sunday night in the Cotton Club was *the* night," Ellington recalled. "All the big New York stars in town, no matter where they were playing, showed up at the Cotton Club to take bows": Texas Guinan, Jimmy Durante, Fred Astaire, George Raft, Paul Whiteman, Al Jolson, George Gershwin. Ellington, whose contract was stretched out to four years, made it the most exclusive club in Harlem, with a special "Royal Box" reserved for "The Nighttime Mayor," Jimmy Walker. "At this time Harlem was as white as it was black," said tap dancer "Honi" Coles. "At night everybody from downtown came up, after everything closed downtown. Diamonds and minks and furs."

The Cotton Club supposedly attracted the after-theater crowd, but, as Coles intimated, most of the customers arrived in exuberant spirits, and with fresh supplies, after closing their favorite Midtown watering holes. Madden's No. 1 beer and bottles of scotch and champagne were available for customers who had forgotten their flasks. Rowdiness, however, was not tolerated in the club that Britain's Lady Mountbatten dubbed the "Aristocrat of Harlem." "Impeccable behavior was demanded in the room while the show was on," said Ellington.

Harlem had become the nightclub capital of the world, and it was a spectacle. "You saw throngs on Lenox and Seventh Avenues, ceaselessly moving from one pleasure resort to another," wrote social chronicler Lloyd Morris. "Long after the cascading lights of Times Square had flickered out, these boulevards were ablaze. Lines of taxis and private cars kept driving up to the glaring entrances of the night clubs. Until nearly dawn the subway kiosks poured crowds on the sidewalks. The legend of Harlem by night—exhilarating and sensuous, throbbing to the beating of drums and the waling of saxophones, cosmopolitan in its peculiar sophistications—crossed the continent and the ocean." Returning in 1927 to the cabarets he had frequented years earlier, Harlem-based writer Rudolph Fischer was amazed and aghast that they had suddenly "turned white. . . . These places therefore are no longer mine but theirs."

At the Cotton Club, Ellington played the music he had been developing during his four years at the Club Kentucky, a propulsive synthesis of Tin Pan Alley, hot jazz, Harlem stride, the blues, and traditional African American folk music. He became, said Ted Gioia, a "painter of musical landscapes, the poet of jazz."

But the owners and the audiences forced some compromises. The Midtown crowd wanted to hear the slick commercial music of the Broadway revues; and the mobsters were eager to please them. "They put pressure on," said Sonny Greer. "When the Syndicate say they want something, they got it or you wasn't in business." Many of the acts had a jungle setting, with the dancers shaking and shimmying in skimpy, feathered outfits, barely held together by string. "The shows had a primitive naked quality that was supposed to make a civilized audience lose its inhibitions," wrote Mercer Ellington. This called for a special kind of accompaniment; Ellington called it "jungle style jazz," and its most characteristic sounds were Bubber Miley's lionlike growls.*

For years, Ellington had been moving his band in this direction—away from ragtime to something hotter and more fervid. At the Cotton Club, he

---

* Bubber Miley was forced to leave the band in 1929, after his unreliability and alcohol abuse got out of control.

added new and audacious flourishes: "bursts of dissonant chords, whole tone scales, unexpected percussive attack, or querulous arpeggios," writes Gioia. In this hokey plantation setting, Ellington's orchestra became "the most dazzling band jazz had yet seen."

Ellington's driving, rhythmic music pulled audiences out of their seats to do the Shimmy, the Shuffle, the Black-Bottom, the Turkey Trot, and the Charleston. "Maybe these Nordics, at last, have tuned in our wave-length," wrote Rudolph Fischer. "Maybe they are at last learning to speak our language."

In late 1927, Ellington was the "greatest" black bandleader in New York— after Fletcher Henderson—said the *New York Age*. He would soon sweep past Henderson, aided by the new medium of network radio. The Ellington band first broadcast from the Cotton Club on local station WHW, but in 1928 Bill Paley signed him to a CBS contract and put him on the air nationwide several times a week, sometimes at the dinner hour, other times at midnight. Before this, the music of black bands had been broadcast locally and regionally, never nationally. This was the first time most white Americans heard black music. "The world was waiting for that," said Sonny Greer.

"We'd play a set, people would come up to the bandstand and tell us they heard us on the air, in Walla Walla, Washington; Elko, Nevada; Boise, Idaho; Austin, Texas, and places like that," said band member Harry Carney. "After a while I got a little book and began writing in it the names of the towns people said they were from." The music of New York became America's music.

Duke Ellington was no longer just "an idol of the jazz cult," as one writer called him. He was a national figure. Although history has not judged him as such, he was as important a part of Harlem's cultural renaissance as any of the writers and professors of W. E. B. Du Bois's celebrated Talented Tenth, elitists who excoriated jazz and the blues as degrading and vulgar. Howard University professor Alain Locke, a pillar of the Harlem intellectual community, urged African American composers to create "jazz classics," not the "trashy type" of jazz played in clubs and cabarets. Hot jazz and blues would never be viewed as "great Negro music," he confidently predicted.

In 1920s Harlem, there were two cultural revolutions occurring simultaneously: one in music, the other in literature and painting, but there was little communication between the community's writers and its musicians. "Those of us in the music and entertainment business were vaguely aware that something exciting was happening," recalled Cab Calloway, "but we weren't directly involved . . . the two worlds, literature and entertainment, rarely crossed. We were working hard on our thing and they were working hard on theirs."

In the spring of 1930, Ellington took a large apartment on Harlem's Sugar Hill, described by David Levering Lewis as "a citadel of stately apartment buildings and liveried doormen on a rock, [a citadel that] soared above the Polo Grounds and the rest of Harlem like a city of the Incas." The call went out to Washington, and Ellington's mother and father, along with his sister, Ruth, moved in with him, Mercer, and Mildred Dixon, a petite, dark-eyed dancer at the Cotton Club. Sometime in 1929, Ellington had started seeing Dixon, right about the time he and Edna sent for Mercer to join them. "I came home from school one day," Mercer recalled, "and there was a strange woman living with my father and taking care of me and Ruth. My mother, it turned out, had moved. . . . They had separated without telling us. Nobody in my family liked to be the bearer of bad news." In a stormy exchange just before they separated, Edna had slashed her husband's cheek with a knife. "People were curious about that scar for the rest of his life," said Mercer.

Mildred—"Sweet Babe," Duke called her—had finely chiseled features and wore her long hair in a bun, like a ballerina. "She had innate class comparable to Ellington's own," Mercer recalled, "and he showed her great courtesy, attention, and affection." They never married, however. He would leave her in 1938 for Beatrice "Evie" Ellis, another Cotton Club entertainer. He was never a loyal partner to anyone, nor did he want "the role of a parent," according to Mercer. It is no coincidence that he titled his memoirs *Music Is My Mistress*.

In 1931, Duke Ellington left the Cotton Club and began touring nationally and internationally with his band. He continued to live in New York, and returned periodically to the club for short engagements.* In Europe and in his own country, students of classical music began comparing him, in his range and originality, to Mozart, Bach, and Schubert; "one of the world's immortals," a continental scholar called him. But the plaudit that touched him most deeply came from the editors of the *Pittsburgh Courier*, the highly respected African American newspaper. "He is declared to be 'The King of Jazz' in America today. Long live the Duke and may he reign upon the throne for many years."†

---

* In 1936, after a race riot in Harlem, the Cotton Club moved to Broadway and Forty-eighth Street, the site of the old Palais Royal. It closed for good on June 10, 1940.

† In 1939, Duke Ellington and Irving Mills parted ways. Ellington would never explain publicly why they split, only that they ended their financial partnership without rancor. There are, however, indications that Ellington was becoming growingly displeased with Mills's opposition to his efforts to compose and perform concert jazz, and with Mills's handling of his finances. "In spite of how much he had made on me, I respected the way he had operated," Ellington wrote in *Music Is My Mistress*. "He had always preserved the dignity of my name." Edward Kennedy Ellington, *Music Is My Mistress* (Garden City, NY: Doubleday, 1973), 89.

CHAPTER TWENTY-SIX

MASTER OF ALLURE

Inch too large around the hips.

—FLORENZ ZIEGFELD

The Great Ziegfeld

In 1929, Duke Ellington and his Cotton Club Band landed a coveted spot in Florenz Ziegfeld's costume musical *Show Girl*, which opened on Broadway that summer. The impresario wanted to pack his show with headline talent from vaudeville and cabaret, and his African American musical director, Will Vodery, recommended Ellington. George Gershwin wrote the music and the show starred *Follies* regulars Ruby Keeler and Jimmy Durante.

It wasn't the first time Ziegfeld had crossed Broadway's unstated but rigidly enforced color line. He had hired black singer and comedian Bert Williams to appear with white performers in the *Follies of 1910*. It was the first time a black entertainer had a lead role in a big Broadway show. White entertainers in blackface makeup played African American characters in all-white shows, a practice that continued into the 1930s.

Williams appeared on stage solo at first, or with white male singers and comedians, but never with a white woman. Two years later, when he performed with a long line of Ziegfeld chorus girls, the powerful Shubert syndicate, which had begun to take control of almost all Broadway theaters, took note: "White people even in the north are revolted by the commingling of negro men and white women on stage. The idea certainly is revolting to self-respecting Caucasians and its continuance will undoubtedly bring widespread discredit upon the theatre. No one is astonished, however, that Ziegfeld is the one manager who exploits this condition on Broadway. It is in line with his policy of going to lengths to which no others would demean themselves."

Ziegfeld continued to showcase Williams as one of the *Follies'* feature performers, although he had him wear burnt-cork blackface, an indignity Williams silently resented. Like Duke Ellington, courtly, soft-spoken Bert Williams challenged racial barriers not by blunt outrage, but by the incontestable power of his talent. In 1940, Ellington composed and recorded a moving tribute to him: "A Portrait of Bert Williams."

"He was the finest comedian I have ever had," Ziegfeld wrote after Williams's death in 1922, at age forty-seven. When David Belasco had tried to steal him away to appear in a play he was producing, Williams turned him down. "[Ziegfeld] took me out of a nigger show and gave me my chance," he told Belasco. "As long as he wants me, I'll stay with him."

Show Girl was a critical and commercial flop, but Ellington was a sensation. At Ziegfeld's insistence, his entire band appeared, not in the orchestra pit, but prominently on stage with forty-five Ziegfeld Girls in minstrel costume. Ziegfeld could risk putting Ellington's orchestra on stage with his chorus girls because he was the most powerful producer on Broadway, "perhaps the greatest music-show producer that the world theatre has thus far known," said critic George Jean Nathan. During the 1927–28 Broadway season he mounted six blockbuster shows. Four of them ran concurrently, and one of them, *Show Boat*, was a theater classic, the first Broadway musical to feature a racially integrated cast and to deal sensitively with the explosive issue of miscegenation.

Nineteen twenty-seven—a breakthrough year for Duke Ellington—was the year Florenz Ziegfeld, Jr., startled the theater world, making an improbable comeback after his detractors were sure he was through. No Broadway producer would have a run of success like the one Ziegfeld enjoyed that year, beginning in February, when he opened his magnificent new theater.

For years Ziegfeld had wanted his own theater, a place where he could have complete control over his productions and reap the full profits from them. His annual *Follies* were held at the New Amsterdam Theatre on West Forty-second Street, just off Times Square, where he paid exorbitant monthly rent to its owners, theater moguls Marc Klaw and his cold-blooded partner, Abraham Lincoln Erlanger—"Dishonest Abe," as he was known on Broadway.* Ziegfeld

---

* At the turn of the century, Erlanger and Klaw had built a large chain of theaters and vaudeville playhouses and formed, with producer Charles Frohman and others, the Theatrical Syndicate, a monopoly that controlled nearly every operational detail of five hundred and more theaters nationwide until the late 1910s, when the Shubert Brothers, Sam, Lee, and Jacob, arrived in New York City from Syracuse and built their own theatrical empire. After

finally got his wish in 1925, when his friend William Randolph Hearst approached him with a proposal to finance the building of an enormous Ziegfeld Theatre across the street from the Hotel Warwick, a luxury residential hotel Hearst was erecting on Sixth Avenue and West Fifty-fourth Street for his lover, actress Marion Davies, so they could host their Hollywood friends.* The area was a Broadway backwater, blighted by decaying buildings and the half-demolished Sixth Avenue El, but Hearst and his partner, Arthur Brisbane, hoped to create a Sixth Avenue real estate empire, with the hotel and theater as centerpieces. Both Hearst and Ziegfeld stood to benefit: Ziegfeld was given total control over the construction, decoration, and running of the theater, and Hearst would have an attraction to draw resident tenants to his posh, out-of-the-way hotel. (Ziegfeld retained his minority financial stake in the New Amsterdam.)

When the Warwick opened, Ziegfeld rented a suite. He would stay there after rehearsals, sometimes with one of his showgirls, rather than driving back to Burkeley Crest, the estate in Hastings-on-Hudson, where he resided with his wife, actress Billie Burke, and their only child, Patricia, eleven years old in 1927.

The architect of Ziegfeld's theater was Austrian-born Joseph Urban, the designer of Owney Madden's Cotton Club and creator of sumptuous stage sets for the *Follies* since 1915. Urban designed the first playhouse in America expressly built for modern musical extravaganzas, perhaps the finest theater ever built in New York. "A theater is more than a stage and auditorium," Urban explained his intentions. "It is a place to experience a heightened sense of life." The auditorium, shaped like the inside of an empty eggshell, brought together players and patrons. Seating over 1,600, it was extravagant without being overwhelming. There were no boxes for "grandees," no "antiqued paintings that equated theatre with Western power structures. . . . For once," said Ziegfeld biographer Ethan Mordden, "an auditorium actually looked like a place of magic. Not a home for Shakespeare. . . . A place of musical comedy: of Ziegfeld."†

---

breaking the syndicate's stranglehold on the nation's theater industry, the Shuberts turned out to be even more controlling and Machiavellian than Abe Erlanger. In 1925, the Shuberts controlled nearly every legitimate theater in Manhattan, while Erlanger and Klaw held on to a scattering of playhouses, among them the New Amsterdam, the jewel in their crown.

* Renamed the Warwick New York Hotel, it remains one of Manhattan's finest hotels. When the Beatles first came to New York they stayed at the Warwick.

† The Ziegfeld Theatre was torn down in 1967 to make way for an office skyscraper. A movie theater was built down the street at 141 West Fifty-fourth Street and named the Ziegfeld.

Ziegfeld had an office suite on the seventh floor, equipped with a private balcony that commanded a view of the entire auditorium. "The suite," said Ziegfeld's press agent, Bernard Sobel, "was crowded with beautiful furniture, modern electrical conveniences, and a great refectory table laden with objets d'art, silver cigar boxes, Tiffany glass vases and a collection of . . . jade, silver and gold elephants, all with the trunks up." Since childhood, Flo, or Ziggy, as almost everyone alternately called him, loved elephants and considered them good luck. A large outer office was reserved for Ziegfeld's loyal secretary, Matilda Golden (later Matilda Clough), whom Ziegfeld renamed Goldie. "God Almighty, who would name a kid Matilda?"

On February 2, the playhouse opened with *Rio Rita*, a south-of-the-border musical comedy that was one of Ziegfeld's most opulently stayed extravanzas. The story follows a Texas Ranger in pursuit of a notorious bandit who gets sidelined by Rita, a Mexican temptress. The leaden plot was overshadowed by Urban's stage sets; the luxurious costumes created by longtime *Follies* designer John Harkrider; and the stirring music and dancing. *Rio Rita* had a Broadway run of sixty weeks and earned more than any show up to that time. It exemplifies Ziegfeld's genius for turning lowbrow dramatic forms like musical comedy into art without diminishing their mass appeal. This became known as the "Ziegfeld touch," and it was "inimitable," said *The New York Times*.

While *Rio Rita* was still in rehearsal, Ziegfeld had decided to produce one more *Follies*, to be presented at the New Amsterdam while *Rio Rita* continued its long run at his new theater. It was to be a show that would outdo the *Follies'* most impressive imitator, the *Scandals*, a "thrill-a-second" revue created in 1919 by former Ziegfeld hoofer George White—less sumptuous than the *Follies* but with jazzier music and sensual dancing by barely dressed chorus girls. White had hired Gershwin for some of his earlier shows; Ziegfeld countered by bringing in his friend Irving Berlin to write the score for the *Follies of 1927*. Berlin would work with perennial Ziegfeld headliner Eddie Cantor, whose "clap-hands . . . bursting-with-energy" style made him the most sought-after comic artist on the Broadway stage.

Ziegfeld worked himself to a state of nervous exhaustion putting together the show. Yet sitting in the office suite of his new theater, with phones ringing off the hook, typewriters clicking, and messenger boys rushing in and out, he seemed "the personification of utter calm" to interviewer Walter Tittle. The great showman spoke in a low-pitched voice, slowly and courteously, and seemed entirely at ease, said Tittle. "Laconic, slow to anger, ice-water calm in the midst of chaos," his daughter, Patricia, remembered him in her memoir.

"He always gave you all of his attention," recalled J. P. McEvoy, one of his writers. "If you ever did get into his office you could stay there for the rest of the day." The problem was getting in. The outer office was crowded beyond belief with some the world's most beautiful women "and some of its ugliest songwriters. Important names! Famous faces! Gorgeous bodies! Scintillating minds! They could all sit there, overflow the corridors, jam the elevators, stew in their juices—and wait."

"The Great Ziegfeld" was fifty-eight years old, a tall, striking-looking man who brushed his thick hair tight, close to his head, and parted it in the middle, giving him a "Mephistophelian look." His features were immobile, and he almost never laughed aloud. "His entire staff of comics—and he employed the greatest in the world—couldn't make him laugh," Eddie Cantor recalled.

He was athletic, with broad shoulders and muscular arms, and he had an avid interest in outdoor sports. A horseman, ice-skater, big-game hunter, and deep-sea fisherman, he also boxed, lifted weights, and drove racing cars. Yet he was every inch the Broadway dandy. His shoes were handmade; he had his nails manicured twice a week; and "he took as much care of his hair as any debutante," claimed his wife.

He loved luxury. An exacting valet took care of his every need. At his disposal were three limousines; and he traveled in private railroad cars, and made passage to Europe in a suite on the SS *Majestic*. When traveling across the country by train he brought along his own chef. On the other hand, he so hated personal luggage that he packed his toilet articles in a folded-up newspaper.

Ziegfeld had great personal charm and a commanding presence. When he entered a room "the Red Sea parted," said a friend. In his dealings with his chorus girls, stage stars, and newspapermen he was patient, courtly, and courteous, but composers, choreographers, costume designers, and some members of his staff found him unreasonably demanding, seldom satisfied, and "frequently cruel." Artists as prestigious as Gershwin were ordered to deliver entire scores in three weeks to the day. Back in 1919, Ziegfeld had Irving Berlin compose the hauntingly beautiful "A Pretty Girl Is Like a Melody," which became the anthem of the *Follies*. He had instructed Berlin to produce it in a single night.

At his office, Ziegfeld lived in a cocoon, protected by dark-eyed Goldie. "Keeper of the key," she controlled access to Ziegfeld and uncomplainingly tolerated his erratic work habits. An insomniac who didn't arrive at the office some days until well past noon, he would think nothing of calling Goldie—or one of his actors—in the middle of the night. He had three gold-plated phones in his bedroom and was usually on all of them at the same time; but his favorite means of communication was the telegram. He sent as many as a hundred a day, some of them to staff members right across the hall. And he'd send thousand-word telegrams to actors in their dressing rooms, only several floors below. To underscore a point, he'd send the same person up to a dozen "missiles" in the same day. "If Ziegfeld dies," a friend joked, "sell Western Union short."

To guard his privacy, he devised a secret system for locking his office door. He could open it from inside the office, but only Goldie could open it from the outside. On one occasion, when Goldie forgot to lock the door, a telegram messenger barged into the office and ran out, shouting, "He's laying a girl on the desk!"

A risk taker and a rule breaker, he lived for his work. Producing the *Follies of 1927*, he put in furious eighteen-hour shifts, carrying on the work at home, where from "the eminence of his massive bed," beginning around six in the morning, he would badger press agents, costume designers, actors, writers, musicians, and the eternally accommodating Goldie with phone calls and telegrams. In the privacy of his home, the composed public pose vanished completely.

At rehearsals, however, he was patient, even patronizing, shaping the show with tempered equanimity. Though he could barely carry a tune, he was familiar with nearly every phase of stagecraft. Seated in one of the front rows at rehearsal, he knew exactly what effect he wanted to achieve with each song, set, prop, and costume. "And in pursuit of that objective" wrote a theater critic, "he was more than willing to exhort, harass, cajole, and bedevil the best talent that guile and money could buy." Headline actors and actresses are notoriously temperamental, and Ziegfeld fed their egos and showered them with expensive gifts: diamond bracelets, Swiss watches, and little bags filled with gold coins. Yet this self-enclosed theatrical genius would not allow them, or even his closest friends, into his private life. "He embodied more than any other Broadway leader the idea that commercial success in American culture is built on an imposing public profile with no personal content whatsoever," Mordden writes. "Everybody has heard of you, but no one knows who you are."

He was one of the most contradictory characters on Broadway: "worker and playboy, patrician and vulgarian, alternately cruel, gentle, pestiferous and lovable," in Bernard Sobel's words. Even his wife found him impossible to peg. Everyone on Broadway knew he had risen from mid-American obscurity, and that he was a habitual gambler, winning and losing hundreds of thousands of dollars, millions in today's money, at the gaming tables of Monte Carlo, Biarritz, and Palm Beach. But almost no one knew, except by rumor and innuendo, how often Ziegfeld had gambled in life, risking his reputation and his ties to those he loved to get what he wanted, only to discover that he wanted

Opening night on Broadway, 1930. In the 1920s, the movie palaces pushed the legitimate theaters off Broadway and onto the narrow streets that fed Times Square. While most films were made in Hollywood, most big premieres were on Broadway. "If Broadway approves, the chances are the rest of the country will also approve," said movie mogul Adolph Zukor.

RCA executive David Sarnoff in 1927, the first year of operation of his Midtown-based NBC network, the world's first national radio hookup. Behind Sarnoff's leadership, Manhattan solidified its position as the capital of American radio, its center of innovation, and the source of most of its advertising money and studio talent.

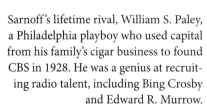

Sarnoff's lifetime rival, William S. Paley, a Philadelphia playboy who used capital from his family's cigar business to found CBS in 1928. He was a genius at recruiting radio talent, including Bing Crosby and Edward R. Murrow.

Chicago publisher Joseph Medill Patterson came to New York in 1919 and launched the *Daily News,* America's first tabloid newspaper. By the mid-1920s it was the most widely read daily in the country. It specialized in sex, sports, and crime—and photojournalism.

The *Daily News* gave lurid coverage to the Snyder-Gray trial of 1927, the most sensationalized murder trial of the decade. Ruth Snyder, a Queens housewife, and her married lover, Judd Gray, brutally murdered Snyder's husband in his bed and were convicted and sentenced to death. This photo shows Snyder in the witness stand.

Heavyweight champion Jack Dempsey is knocked out of the ring by Luis Firpo at the Polo Grounds on September 14, 1923, in what *Daily News* reporter Paul Gallico called a "death struggle of wild beasts." The painter George Bellows captured the moment Firpo sent Dempsey through the ropes and into the ringside press section, after Dempsey had floored Firpo seven times in that savage first round. Reporters pushed Dempsey back into the ring and he knocked out Firpo in the next round. Bellows has Dempsey being felled by a left, not, as happened, by a right to the jaw.

The Firpo fight was promoted by Madison Square Garden impresario "Tex" Rickard, who almost singlehandedly revived professional boxing in New York and made Dempsey's fights lavishly publicized spectacles with million-dollar gates. Here Rickard (right) is with Dempsey in New York in June 1927 after he coaxed Dempsey out of retirement to fight Jack Sharkey at Yankee Stadium.

Clean-living Gene Tunney, born and raised in an Irish neighborhood near Manhattan's Chelsea docks, training for his first fight with Dempsey. New York fight fans favored hard-living, hard-punching Dempsey over Tunney, a "scientific" boxer who read British poetry, just as they favored home run king Babe Ruth, with his voracious appetite for women, food, and drink, over Lou Gehrig, another straight-arrow native son.

Baseball historian Lee Allen described Babe Ruth memorably as "a large man in a camel's hair coat and camel's hair cap, standing in front of a hotel, his broad nostrils sniffing at the promise of the night."

Begun in 1920 and opened in November 1927, the Holland Tunnel, under the Hudson River between Manhattan and Jersey City, was the longest vehicular tunnel in the world. It was designed and named after Chief Engineer Clifford M. Holland, who died of a heart attack during construction, at age forty-one.

Enormous fans in four of these ventilation buildings, two on each side of the Hudson, create a constant airflow in the tunnel through ducts beneath and above the roadway. Without this ventilation system, the first of its kind in the world, poisonous carbon monoxide from the exhaust of cars, buses, and trucks would quickly reach lethal levels.

Begun in October 1927, one month after the opening of the Holland Tunnel, the George Washington Bridge connected Manhattan and Bergen County, N.J. Swiss-born Othmar Ammann, "A Poet in Steel," designed this and five other New York City bridges. When completed in 1931, the GW was the longest span on earth. Le Corbusier called it "the most beautiful bridge in the world."

Courtly Duke Ellington and his locally popular dance band left Washington, D.C., for New York in 1922, around the time this picture was taken. The group had its first sustained engagement—four years—at the Hollywood Club, a Midtown basement café later renamed the Club Kentucky. In December 1927 Ellington's jazz band opened at Harlem's Cotton Club, where its performances were soon broadcast to the nation on Paley's CBS network.

Best known for his *Ziegfeld Follies,* extravagant costume revues to "glorify the American girl," Chicago-born Florenz Ziegfeld stunned his critics in 1927 by producing *Show Boat* at his Ziegfeld Theatre, which opened that year. A musical set on a Mississippi River showboat, the play dealt sensitively with the explosive issue of miscegenation, had a mixed black and white cast, and songs that grew directly out of plot and dialogue. It revolutionized American musical theater.

Book publisher and Broadway producer Horace Liveright in 1924 in his office at Boni & Liveright, the firm he moved a year earlier from downtown to the heart of Midtown's speakeasy district. The hard-drinking former stockbroker gambled on books and plays, publishing early work by Hemingway, Faulkner, and Eugene O'Neill, along with Freud, Dreiser, and T. S. Eliot. His insistence that publishers aggressively market books like Hollywood films changed American publishing.

yet more. In his excess and energy, his dissipation and daring—and, above all, his improbable success—he embodied Jazz Age New York better than F. Scott Fitzgerald, the writer who named the era.

"He loved to gamble and usually lost," Bernie Sobel wrote of the pull of the casino, not appreciating that almost all of his boss's life was a gamble.

The Gambler

From the time he was very young, Ziegfeld was convinced that "life," as Fitzgerald once wrote, "was something you dominated if you were any good." For Ziegfeld, domination was the child of rebellion, a rebellion against his father's unyielding campaign to control his life.

German-born Dr. Florenz Ziegfeld, Sr., had studied at the prestigious Leipzig Conservatory before sailing to America. After serving as a colonel in the Union Army in the Civil War, he founded the Chicago Musical College, one of the most esteemed music schools in the country. His Chicago-born wife, Rosalie de Hez, great-granddaughter of one of Napoleon's commanders, raised Florenz in the Catholic faith, over the fuming protests of her devoutly Lutheran husband. On one thing, however, they were united: their son was to succeed his father as head of the conservatory. Florenz Sr. pushed his son relentlessly, putting him through grueling lessons and punishing him for playing popular tunes on the family piano. But Florenz Jr. had not the slightest interest in classical music. He craved excitement, and became, for a time, a huckster and a charlatan.

At age sixteen, he won a marksmanship contest and an invitation to join Buffalo Bill's Wild West Show, then appearing in Chicago. He didn't last long; his father tracked him down and hauled him home. His next stab at show business was an act featuring "The Dancing Ducks of Denmark," performed in a Windy City park. It was closed down by the Society for the Prevention of Cruelty to Animals when it was discovered that Ziggy got his locally grown birds to dance by putting gas jets under the iron stage on which they performed.

Ziegfeld's first triumph as a promoter came in 1893. The year before, his father had established a nightclub—The Trocadero—in a downtown armory. It featured European orchestras and popular acts and was to run for the duration of the Chicago World's Fair of 1893, when the city was thronged with tourists. Attendance was dismal, however, and Ziegfeld, acting as his father's business manager, was sent to New York to procure livelier musical and variety acts. To his father's horror, he returned with Eugene Sandow, a twenty-three-year-old European strongman. Ziegfeld dressed the painfully shy Austrian in leopard-skin tights and sandals and had him lift "human dumbbells"—an iron bar with a basket on each end containing a male volunteer from the audience. On opening night Ziegfeld persuaded some the city's leading ladies, including Bertha Palmer, the doyenne of Chicago society, to come backstage after Sandow's act for the "exciting privilege" of touching his bulging muscles. The papers picked up the story and "The Great Sandow" became an instant sensation. "He was my first star attraction," said Ziegfeld.

When the fair closed, Ziegfeld resigned from his father's musical college and took Sandow on the road, packing theaters from New York to San Francisco. The act ran its course in San Francisco when Ziegfeld arranged for the strongman to fight a lion named Commodore with his bare hands. Three thousand suckers bought tickets to see the match, held in a small circus tent. When Commodore was pushed into the cage with Sandow he seemed dazed and confused and backed sheepishly into a corner. Suspecting, correctly, that the animal had been drugged, the crowd began screaming, "Fake!" "Fraud!" and "swarmed out of their seats and started to tear down the place. I did not see any of this," Ziegfeld recalled. "I was in Oakland with the money. Some subtle sense had warned me not to linger for the denouement."

Ziegfeld made over a quarter of a million dollars (about $6 million today) on Sandow, but lost most of it at the gaming tables, "beginning a lifelong pattern of tumultuous swings between wealth and insolvency." In 1896, as a talent scout for the Broadway comedy *A Parlor Match*, he prowled the theaters of Europe searching for an actress to appear in the leading role. At London's Palace Theatre he found his starlet: twenty-three-year-old Anna Held, a petite vaudeville singer with an hourglass figure and blazing brown eyes. Billed as a French-born sensation—"five feet of sizzling personality"—she was, in truth, Annhaline Held, born in Warsaw, the daughter of Polish-Jewish parents. Ziegfeld was broke at the time and Anna was separated from her husband and was raising a young daughter, Liane. Flo persuaded her to place Liane in a French convent and return with him to New York. A cable to Manhattan-based railroad tycoon James "Diamond Jim" Brady, the first of Ziegfeld's millionaire backers, produced the funds that allowed him to bring Anna to Broadway on a fabulous salary of fifteen hundred dollars a week. The next year, she obtained a divorce and she and Ziegfeld began living together in a common law marriage.

A Parlor Match got off to a sluggish start but rocketed to success when a press agent Ziegfeld hired told reporters that Anna took a daily beauty bath in milk to preserve her silky skin. To give the shaky story credibility, the agent paid a Brooklyn milkman to claim that he had sued Ziegfeld for an unpaid bill for sixty-four quarts of milk. Anna did her best to enhance her saucy reputation with a teasing rendition, in her thick Parisian accent, of the popular song "Won't You Come and Play Wiz Me?" The name of the young actress with the "misbehaving" eyes "became as well known in this country as the name of the President," said the *New York World*.

Over the next seven years, Anna Held had the leading roles in a succession of musical comedy hits on Broadway—all of them backed by her husband's brassy publicity and lavish stage sets. When Anna's act got stale and the critics began to carp, the couple took off, in 1906, for Europe, where Ziegfeld won $1.5 million at the gambling tables in Biarritz, $100,000 of it in a single game of baccarat. Four months later he and Anna returned to New York, flat broke. The next year, he produced his first *Follies*.

It was actually Anna's idea: a revue mimicking Paris's "Folies Bergère." Harry B. Smith, author of the Broadway column "Follies of the Day," suggested the name, and Abe Erlanger put up the money. Ziegfeld had begun producing vaudeville acts for Erlanger and Klaw after his return to New York and they needed a summer show to put on at the rooftop garden of the New York Theatre, at Broadway and Forty-fourth Street. The inaptly named Jardin de Paris was a dingy theater with rows of folding chairs, a corrugated steel roof, and open sides, but Ziegfeld's shows brought in the crowds. Comedians W. C. Fields and Charlie Chaplin starred in the first revues, fast-paced productions that featured singing and dancing, along with slapstick humor drawn from contemporary news stories. Gradually, however, the chorus girls took center stage in what became a rapid-fire four-hour variety show that took New York by storm. The *Follies* played on Broadway in the summer season, and then went on the road to nearly every sizable city in America.

Prior to Ziegfeld, chorus girls were known for their "bulk" rather than their beauty. A popular burlesque act was called the Billy Watson Beef Trust. Ziegfeld, a more sophisticated flesh peddler, used sexy young women in precision-like ensembles. By 1911, the press had begun referring to the *Follies* as Ziegfeld's "girl show . . . girls, girls and then more girls, with comedians galore." But Ziegfeld presented his female acts with such exquisite taste that they appealed to mixed-sex audiences. He "brought the female body out of its associations with low, all-male burlesque and beer halls," notes one historian.

Ziegfeld called his stately performers showgirls, not chorus girls. Chorus girls danced and kicked; Ziegfeld Girls "glided and posed." It was as if they were in a luxurious brothel, showing off their wares. Ziegfeld pulled this off without crossing the line between desire and debauchery. The stately showgirls, with their exotic costumes, topped by fantastically elaborate headdresses, were presented as objects of desire, commodities to be seen but not touched. They didn't sing, dance, or speak; they were little more than striking scenery.

In the summer of 1913, Erlanger sanctified the success of the *Follies* by moving it to his New Amsterdam Theatre, which would be the home of the *Follies* for the next fifteen years.* The years 1915–16 were crucial ones for Ziegfeld. This is when he first hired Joseph Urban as his stage designer and brought in a number of future stars, including Will Rogers, Fanny Brice, and Eddie Cantor, a talented trio that joined Bert Williams—hired earlier—as the *Follies'* chief comedic attractions. Cantor became Ziegfeld's dearest friend, the son he never had, but he had a near equal affection for Fanny Brice. He discovered her in 1910, at age eighteen, singing "Sadie Salome," in a Yiddish accent, in a Broadway burlesque. When she showed up for work the following day, she was handed a telegram signed "Florenz Ziegfeld." She thought it a joke, but on a hunch made a phone call. "A moment later she was whooping down Broadway."

Florenz Ziegfeld was a star maker. With the exception of Bert Williams, most of his major comedy stars were unknowns when he hired them: Cantor, Rogers, Brice, Ed Wynn, W. C. Fields. And in coming years, soon-to-be legendary actors, lyricists, and composers—a veritable who's-who of American popular theater—joined the *Follies*. Along with Gershwin and Berlin there were Noël Coward, Jerome Kern, P. G. Wodehouse, Mae West, Bert Lahr, Fred and Adele Astaire, Ruby Keeler, Marilyn Miller, Ruth Etting, Helen Morgan, Louise Brooks, Peggy Hopkins Joyce, Sophie Tucker. All would achieve fame in the 1920s, and many of the *Follies* songs of that time became classics: "Shine on Harvest Moon," "A Pretty Girl Is Like a Melody," and "By the Light of the Silvery Moon."

By 1920, critics were calling the *Follies* "the most glamorous series of shows that Broadway has ever had." The audiences on opening nights included "practically everybody known on Broadway who is not in Europe or in a hospital," said one wag. Excellent imitators arose: besides *George White's Scandals*, there were Irving Berlin's *Music Box Revue* and *Earl Carroll's Vanities*. "But none of them could compare with the *Ziegfeld Follies* for taste, abundance, sensuousness and splendor," in the opinion of *New York Times* critic Brooks Atkinson.

---

* Between 1913 and 1927, thirteen editions of the *Follies*, 1913–20, 1922–25, and 1927 opened at the New Amsterdam. Beginning in 1915, the theater's roof garden—a dance and supper club called the Danse de Follies—also hosted over a dozen editions of the Ziegfeld *Midnight Frolic*. The club offered up dinner, drinks, and the *Frolic* floor show after the *Follies* ended around midnight. The club stayed open year-round and was a gathering place for Manhattan high society. In 1922, it closed its doors, a victim of Prohibition. Richard Ziegfeld and Paulette Ziegfeld, *The Ziegfeld Touch: The Life and Times of Florenz Ziegfeld, Jr.* (NY: Harry N. Abrams, 1993), 54, 62.

By this time, Ziegfeld had split with Anna Held. In 1910, he fell in love with seventeen-year-old Lillian Lorraine, a sensuous, self-destructive *Follies* starlet given to binge drinking and jealous rage. When Ziegfeld installed Lillian in a suite in the Ansonia, the same apartment-hotel in which he and Anna resided, Anna divorced him in 1913 on grounds of adultery.*

The following year, Ziegfeld met sparkling Mary William Burke, the daughter of a Southern society belle and a popular circus clown—Billy Burke. She was one of the biggest stars on Broadway, with success on the London stage, but she and Flo had never set eyes on one another until they met at a New Year's Eve costume ball at the Hotel Astor. Burke made a grand entrance on the arm of the writer Somerset Maugham, in whose play, *The Land of Promise*, she was starring. Ziegfeld had come to the event with Lillian Lorraine, but she had stormed out earlier, after one of their explosive arguments. "I had never met Flo Ziegfeld, but I knew all about him. Everyone in New York knew about him," Burke recalled. "His reputation with women was extremely dangerous." They danced together that evening, and were drawn to each other, despite the difference in their ages: he was forty-six and she was thirty. That April, after the Saturday matinee of her show, they drove over to Hoboken and were married in the tiny back room of a parsonage.

It was a difficult marriage, but one that held. They became one of the city's most famous Jazz Age couples—indulgent, irreverent, and arrogantly irresponsible. "There were no tedious reformers in our circle to remind us that in China thousands of human beings were struggling for a handful of rice a week . . . or—or even to suggest to us that some of our American notions of grab and exploit were based on shaky logic. We would not have believed it anyway," Billie Burke wrote with unapologetic candor in her memoirs. "But I cannot truthfully say that I am sorry I was there. The Roaring Twenties were very pleasant if you did not stop to think."

Flo and Billie entertained like Ancient Romans at Burkeley Crest, the country estate on the Hudson that Billie had purchased for herself and her mother before she was married. Their gabled mansion sat on an incline surrounded by two dozen acres of fenced-in parkland.

When Flo moved in with Billie, so did the animals. He found animals more comfortable to be around than people, and turned Burkeley Crest into a menag-

---

* Though Ziegfeld and Held were never formally wed, their common law marriage was legal in New York state.

erie. At one time, there were fifteen dogs, along with donkeys, parrots, pheasants, dwarf ponies, horses, chimpanzees, lambs, buffalo, a herd of deer, two lion cubs, and a pair of Canadian bears named Tunney and Dempsey. There was also a baby elephant called Ziggy, which roamed the grounds at will and once stormed into the kitchen in search of biscuits, almost crushing the family cook. Ziegfeld's friend, circus owner John Ringling, would invite him to come down to the Manhattan docks when new shipments of animals arrived and have any of them he wanted; Ziegfeld also brought home animals he used in his Broadway shows. The elephant, complete with a keeper, was a present for his daughter, Patricia, on her sixth birthday. Flo had Joseph Urban design a glass-jeweled howdah for Ziggy, and another designer build a playhouse for Patty that was a perfect replica of Mount Vernon, right down to the candles and crockery.

With a full-time staff of sixteen, Flo and Billie were able to host parties for up to sixty guests, but they preferred smaller get-togethers of a dozen or so theater people—authors, composers, and designers, but almost never entertainers from the *Follies*. On summer Sundays, guests roamed the lawns and gardens at leisure, pitching horseshoes or playing tennis on the rose-bordered courts. There was a swimming pool and Japanese teahouses in which to relax and enjoy Chardonnay from Flo's excellent cellar. Flo "produced those Sunday dinners the way he produced the *Follies*," recalled Patty, "and he could not bear a false note in either the dinners or the shows."

The Ziegfelds also had an island retreat, "Camp Patricia," in the Laurentian Mountains, north of Montreal. "Daddy's version of Walden-in-Canada included a main house, a guest lodge, a dining room and kitchen under their own separate roof, a storehouse, a dormitory for the guides, and a house built especially for Mother, with its own boat landing," wrote Patty. Astonishingly, there was no telephone; it was the only place Ziegfeld could relax, although never without company—dozens of summer guests who would dine with the family on quail, salmon, and hot blueberry pie. Here, hundreds of miles from Broadway, he appeared "ambitionless," said Billie.

It cost $10,000 a year to maintain Camp Patricia and Burkeley Crest, but Billie and Flo spent without a care. They had four cars between them, including two Rolls-Royces, and Billie expended a small fortune on furniture. "Neither of them was capable of thrift, or cared a fig about it," Patty described her parents. Ziegfeld was incapable of passing a show window with an enticing display, according to Eddie Cantor. "Whether it was an automobile or a yacht, if it struck his fancy, he went in and bought it as casually as if he were buying a necktie." As Billie was to write years later, "The world was a place created just for fun, and Flo Ziegfeld of all people was the man best equipped for having that fun."

The dark clouds were Flo's unfaithfulness and his chronic gambling addiction. The gambling scared Billie because he did it alone and with heedless abandon. In the 1920s, he did his serious gambling in Palm Beach, where the family vacationed in winter. It was a place more sinfully rich—and pretentiously proud of it—than Newport or Southampton. The millionaire bachelor Alexander Phillips, a popular regular at other exclusive vacation spots, never felt at home in Palm Beach. "I did not drink and I had no wife to exchange."

The Ziegfelds rented the Moorish palace of Colonel Edward R. Bradley, owner of Bradley's Beach Club, an illegal gambling resort made safe from the law by the fact that most of its members, among them Joseph P. Kennedy, were rich as Croesus. After visiting the local stock market exchange in the morning, Flo would fish for tarpon and marlin in his boat *Sally,* named after his successful 1920 musical comedy, or play a round of golf with friends, betting big on every hole. After dinner, he would head off to Bradley's Beach Club, the place that nearly killed his marriage.*

"Flo gambled at night. All night." And he gambled for "the most spectacular stakes. He would win or lose fifty thousand dollars in an evening, sitting dour-faced and silent at the roulette wheel hours after everyone else had gone home determined to break the bank, determined to be the best," said Billie. He would gamble even if they had guests at the house, and over his wife's tearful objections. Late at night, she would ride over to the club on her bike and stand inside the door until she caught his attention, and then, in whispers, she'd plead for him to come home. "Usually he did not come," Billie recalled, and she would pedal back home, sobbing as she tried to keep her balance.

She suffered alone, without support, alternating between torpor and tornado-like bursts of anger. "Everyone except Mother . . . took the whole thing lightly," Patty remembered. Irving Berlin, a frequent guest, wrote a comic poem, "The Gambler's Bride," about Billie's travails. When he read it aloud at a party the company "howled."

"I wanted to be an artist then," Billie was to write later, "but in those years I had another job. It was simply to hold my husband." Flo promised to change, and sometimes did for a short time, but he was in the grip of an addiction he would never shake. He gambled on nearly everything: tennis, croquet, the Harvard-Yale game, and "whether the next man who walked down the street would have blue eyes or brown." Billie thought of leaving him over this, as well as his flagrant unfaithfulness, but she stayed. "One of the things I knew," she described her feelings at the time, "was that Flo loved me, and that he loved his

---

* Ziegfeld invested money in Palm Beach. In 1926, he opened the Club de Montmartre, a chic restaurant-theater, and the following year he built the town's famous Paramount Theatre.

home and his family." Enraptured with him, yet pathetically in thrall to him, she couldn't cut loose.

He, in turn, needed Billie and Patty. Without their love and support he feared he'd succumb to devastating dissipation.

The Great Glorifier

Nineteen twenty-five was a crisis year for Florenz Ziegfeld. He had not produced a hit play since *Sally,* and although no *Follies* in his lifetime lost money, critics began complaining that the shows had become "something of a windup toy, autonomous once the plans were set in motion." Ziegfeld was also strapped for cash; the average Broadway show cost around $25,000. He spent at least $170,000 on his revue—and he was, in addition, losing irreplaceable stars. Bert Williams made his final *Follies* appearance in 1919. Fanny Brice left in 1923. Will Rogers, Eddie Cantor, and W. C. Fields went to Hollywood. After a bruising legal dispute with Abe Erlanger and Marc Klaw over the division of proceeds for the *Follies,* Ziegfeld was not permitted to use his name to promote the revue. In 1926, he was forced to move the *Follies* to Palm Beach, under the name *Palm Beach Nights.*

It was at this point that William Randolph Hearst offered to build him his own theater. Shortly afterward, he settled his dispute with Erlanger and Klaw and made arrangements to have the *Ziegfeld Follies of 1927* appear at the New Amsterdam Theatre. Reinvigorated, he began assembling talent for the show.

Over the years, "the master of allure" had handpicked nearly three thousand girls for his revues. He used this time-tested procedure for the *Follies of 1927.* Alice Poole, another of his faithful secretaries, kept his Book of Girls, containing the names, addresses, phone numbers, and descriptions of thousands of "beauties" who had appeared in previous *Follies* or been recommended by talent scouts. She would invite a large group of these women to Ziegfeld's office each day. They stood in long lines outside the theater, "flocks of girls of all sizes and shapes, weights and ages . . . For every girl in the show business or out wanted to be known as a *Follies* girl," said J. P. McEvoy.

Goldie interviewed them and made the first cut. The winners were sent directly from her desk into Ziegfeld's office. "Most of them entered frightened and trembling," by one account. "But he set them quickly at ease. . . . His eye though, was that of an eagle and in one second he sized them up from head to toe," picking out the ones who would be granted auditions. He could look at them in street clothes and pick "the firecrackers."

At the auditions, groups of forty girls, one at time, strolled across the stage of the darkened theater and then stood under the floodlights. Ziegfeld sat in the front row of the orchestra, with Goldie on one side of him and his stage director on the other. The atmosphere in the theater became tense when the three of them began quietly discussing the qualifications of each candidate. Ziegfeld then called over his assistant stage manager and, in a whisper, identified the girls he wanted. After the girls had been told to step down from the stage, the assistant stage manager approached each one individually with the good, or bad, news. "This is done in a low tone," Ziegfeld told a reporter, "so that only the girl herself can hear. . . . In this way we try to save the rejected ones from any embarrassment, or feeling of humiliation."

The auditions went on for weeks. Out of a pool of over a thousand women, Ziegfeld picked just over a hundred for the 1927 *Follies*. "His eye for beauty, as precise as a sextant, included his own family as well as his shows," Billie remembered. "A friend once complimented him on his daughter's beauty. Flo answered in his small voice: 'Inch too large around the hips.'"

Ziegfeld, or his ghostwriting press agents, published articles explaining the "picking" process. "Vivacity must be a girl's outstanding characteristic. . . . She must be intelligent. . . . Her figure must be almost perfect"; she had to be young, preferably between eighteen and twenty-two; and she had to have great ankles. "No matter how perfect her dimensions may be, if her ankles are bad," Ziegfeld declared, "the whole effect is lost because the first feature that the audience sees when the curtain rises is the ankles."

If she couldn't dance—and most of the girls were merely figurines, eye-candy for the men in the audience—she must "carry herself gracefully." The "secret" of selecting girls, Ziegfeld added, "is merely a question of variety—that is, having enough different types to satisfy all opinions." This did not, however, include women of color. Like the dancers at the Cotton Club, the Ziegfeld Girls were all of one race.

The girls were generously paid, making more than twice what chorus girls in other shows received. And each girl received a twenty-dollar gold piece at the end of every week of rehearsal.* They saw themselves as successful working women, and while preparing for the *Follies of 1927* they formed themselves into a small and interdependent community, gathering for lunch or after rehearsals at a corner drugstore only a few blocks from the New Amsterdam.

Most members of the chorus lived alone or with other showgirls in afford-

---

* Marilyn Miller, Ann Pennington, and other featured girls made fabulous salaries, and had privileges that included maid service, a car, and a chauffeur.

able hotels and apartments on the fringes of Broadway. Some of them married stagehands and moved to the outer boroughs. A select few married affluent bachelors, or became, like Jimmy Walker's Betty Compton and William Randolph Hearst's Marion Davies, sexual companions of prominent and powerful married men; but no sugar daddy ever got backstage. Ziegfeld made sure of that. Inside his theater, his girls remained "forbidden" fruit—but not to him. "He was the perpetual predatory male," claimed Sobel. "A glimpse of a beautiful woman transfixed his attention: made him forget home and family."

"What the girls do outside of the theatre is none of my affair," Ziegfeld told reporters. That was not true. "No seminary students were ever under closer surveillance," said Eddie Cantor. Ziegfeld Girls were expected to wear hats, dresses, and heels in public, and not to overdo the rouge, mascara, and lipstick. "A Ziegfeld Girl had to be a lady at all times," one former *Follies* girl recalled. "She must do noting to disgrace the name of Ziegfeld." It was rumored that Ziegfeld arranged abortions for a number of his most popular showgirls. A pregnancy could be excused. The capital sin was to put on weight.

The world inside the New Amsterdam was an unsubtle tyranny. Billie remembers her husband standing in the back of the theater, leaning against a wall, his cigar "tilted upward," watching a performance. "He would detect it instantly if any one girl in the line had varied her costume or tilted her hat. If he discovered such a calamity, he would hurry back to his office and dictate a telegram to the company manager: ANY GIRL WHO CHANGES OR TWISTS HER HAT WILL BE FIRED."

For the 1927 *Follies*, as for all previous *Follies* Ziegfeld spent as much time on the girls' costumes as he did on the songs and skits. He personally selected and purchased every outfit. When his handpicked designers delivered the finished costumes "the first thing he did was turn them inside out," said Eddie Cantor. It was "the quality of the lining against the bodies of the girls which made them act and feel more feminine," Ziegfeld explained, "and enhanced their grace and movements on the stage."

At dress rehearsals Ziegfeld would call out in the middle of a comedy skit, "That's enough. Bring on the girls." He continued to insist that men came to the *Follies* for the legs, not the laughs. "He has no idea that . . . playgoers have patronized the *Follies* . . . because they were spirited and funny," wrote Gilbert Seldes. "To him they are still girl shows."

And as always, he proudly professed that his aim was to "glorify the American girl." Seldes wasn't the only critic who found Ziegfeld strangely unaware of how silly that idea had become. In Ziegfeld's office, "glorified" remained the preferred synonym for "in the chorus." People said "she was glorified in 1921" or "she hasn't been glorified since 1924," and there was neither "self-consciousness nor irony in the expression." Nor was there even a veiled admission that "glorifying" a girl meant displaying her like a commodity, turning a stage filled with beauties into a sexually charged shop window.

The writer Edmund Wilson, who frequented the *Follies*, complained that Ziegfeld's "American Beauties" looked regimented and controlled as rows of them descended a grand staircase in "a deliberate and rigid goose-step." Their "Anglo-Saxon straightness—straight backs, straight brows and straight noses . . . their peculiar frigidity and purity," was, he wrote, an expression of the "peculiar frigidity and purity, the frank high-school girlishness that Americans like." Seldes, a champion of the popular arts, disagreed. The girls were admittedly stately and haughty—even mechanical in their movements, but that was part of Ziegfeld's plan. By making them "appear slightly inaccessible" they became "a little more desirable."

The twenty-first edition of the *Ziegfeld Follies* opened at the New Amsterdam on August 16, 1927. "He has been at it in New York for more than a quarter of a century," Alexander Woollcott wrote of Ziegfeld, "and yet, when the night comes for one of his curtains to rise for the first time, a kind of frenzy seizes Manhattan. The price of tickets rises to dizzying heights. . . . Traffic for blocks around [the] theater ties itself into nervous, anticipatory knots. The police reserves are called out to keep the restive citizens in order. . . . This infectious notion that something prodigious is under way, is no accidental by-product, no touching public recognition of sheer merit, but the direct result of canny showmanship," tricks of a "master showman" who learned them not in the "capitals of Europe," but "in the midways and side shows of his youth."

The *1927 Follies* lacked the punch and originality of earlier editions, but were unequaled for splendor and showmanship. And with Eddie Cantor appearing in nearly every act—singing, strutting, and doing his double takes— they recaptured some of the old magic. The *Ingénues*, ninety girls in white dresses at the keyboards of ivory white pianos, were a bright new edition, and honey-haired Ruth Etting was captivating in her *Follies* debut. "The curtain opened," said Mae West, "and here was this girl. Not what you'd call a classic beauty—but unusual. She had a sex quality that seemed to mesmerize the audience. And when she finished singing, they just kind of went crazy."

The reviews were mixed. It had its "stirring and glamorous moments," said the *Daily News*. "In fact, as 'Follies' go, it had everything—except the faintest glimmer of imagination." Brooks Atkinson disagreed, arguing that Ziegfeld had "mounted a completely satisfying production." Even Edmund Wilson conceded there was "splendor about the Follies," a "glittering vision which rises straight out of the soul of New York." Elaborate, luxurious, and expensive, the *Follies* had in them something of the Plaza and of the Jazz Age tales of F. Scott Fitzgerald. And they moved, like Manhattan, "with the speed of an express train."

George Jean Nathan went further, insisting that the *Follies* were an art form, one that appealed to the "aesthetic" rather than the "intellectual" sense, teaching audiences not to understand life but to enjoy it. Ziegfeld's art, "the art of gaiety . . . is an art no less than the art of gloom," he wrote. "The Great Glorifier" was as fully an artist, in Nathan's eyes, as Constantin Stanislavski, the legendary Russian actor and theater director.

Jimmy Walker, a *Follies* regular, was in Europe on a publicity and pleasure tour when the 1927 edition opened. He showed up at the New Amsterdam in late September to see himself impersonated by his friend Eddie Cantor, who handed out keys to the city to actors playing Charles Lindbergh, Gertrude Ederle, and other luminaries. Next came a song, "My New York," written expressly for the mayor by Irving Berlin, who had organized Broadway for him in the elections of 1925. Then Walker stood and delivered one of those "rambling, sparkling speeches that make the hearers forget the Mayor and love the man," said the New York *World*. Leaving the theater, Walker was asked if he thought Prohibition would last. "Perhaps it will," he replied, "if it ever gets started."

The 1927 *Follies* ended abruptly when Eddie Cantor came down with pleurisy and was ordered to bed by his doctors. Hearing reports that Cantor had been seen around town convinced Ziegfeld that he was well enough to go on, and in a long rambling telegram he reprimanded him, telling him he needed "a good spanking" and had to return to the show. With Cantor unable to return, the *Follies'* road show closed on January 6, 1928. When a contrite Ziegfeld discovered that Cantor really had pleurisy, he wired him from Camp Patricia. "Caught a little bear at six this morning. Shall I bring him for your kids? Love and kisses, your father, Flo." Sometime later, Ziegfeld invited Cantor to Dinty Moore's, his favorite Manhattan eatery, and casually presented him with a Rolls-Royce convertible.

When working on a show, Ziegfeld's energy, said a friend, was superhuman. After the New York debut of the *Follies of 1927*, he suffered an attack of nausea and vomiting, brought on by exhaustion and anxiety, eating at odd hours, and not getting enough sleep. It was a regular occurrence, forcing him to be bedridden for two or three days at a time. In the late summer of 1927, Ziegfeld rebounded in less than a week, excited by another big production that was simmering on the back burner. It would be the capstone of his career.

Show Boat

"The history of the American Musical Theatre, quite simply, is divided into two eras: everything before *Show Boat*, and everything after *Show Boat*," writes Miles Kreuger, the outstanding authority on the production. "This seminal work revealed that a Broadway musical was free to embrace any kind of theme, however controversial, [and] could deal with serious issues in a suitably mature fashion."

The play is based on the best-selling 1926 novel of the same title by Pulitzer Prize–winning author Edna Ferber, an episodic, cross-generational tale about life on a floating theater that plies the Mississippi from 1880 to the 1920s—a story rich in color and historical authenticity, and dealing head-on with the wounding impact of racial prejudice, along with a number of other social issues: alcoholism, gambling addiction, spousal desertion, and miscegenation.

Theater composer Jerome Kern read the book as soon as it came out and called his friend, thirty-one-year-old lyricist Oscar Hammerstein II, grandson of the legendary Broadway theater builder and opera impresario Oscar Hammerstein. Ferber's novel, he said, would make a terrific show for them to work on together. "It's got a million dollar title and I think it's wonderful." Hammerstein rushed out and bought a copy, read it in a flash, and set to work at once on a stage adaptation. Here was an opportunity to take the American musical in an entirely new direction.

That November, Ferber signed a contract giving Kern and Hammerstein the musical-dramatic rights to her novel. They then took the score they were working on to Ziegfeld. The Great Glorifier seemed the producer least likely to put on a successful musical production dealing with serious social issues. But Kern had collaborated with Ziegfeld on the runaway hit *Sally*, and was convinced that only he—with his power, money, and eye for detail—could mount *Show Boat* with a star-filled cast and the appropriate costumes and set. (Hammerstein would say later that Ziegfeld's lavish production was "as essential to the play as the words and music.") Kern also knew that Ziegfeld was the only producer in New York who had put black and white entertainers—male and female—on stage together.

Ziegfeld loved Kern and Hammerstein's script outline and signed a contract with them on December 11. Writing to a friend after Kern and Hammerstein performed part of the score for him, he couldn't contain his enthusiasm:

"It is the best musical comedy I have ever been fortunate to get hold of; it looks wonderful and there are two of the greatest parts that have ever been written"—Gaylord Ravenal, a flamboyant, loose-living riverboat gambler, and his wife, Magnolia, the ravishing daughter of Captain Andy Hawkes and his spouse, Parthy, owners of the *Cotton Blossom Floating Palace Theatre*.

That week, Kern visited African American singer Paul Robeson at his Harlem apartment and persuaded him to take on a major role in the show, performing as a kind of "one-man Greek chorus." Ziegfeld had initially agreed to stage the show no later than April 1, 1927, but the year-long delay in producing *Show Boat* forced Robeson to cancel in order to fulfill a previous commitment.

In the spring of 1927, Kern and Hammerstein began to worry that Ziegfeld, after spending extravagantly on his palatial theater and *Rio Rita*, might not have sufficient capital to properly put on *Show Boat*. One Sunday afternoon they decided to drive up the Hudson to Burkeley Crest and pin him down. They called Ziegfeld in advance, and on arriving were met at the door by a butler who looked like a "bank president." Another officious servant escorted them upstairs to Ziegfeld's bedroom suite, with its kingly four-poster bed. Entering, they spotted the showman in the adjoining bathroom—as big as a drawing room—being shaved by a distinguished-looking gentleman with a flowing white beard. Hammerstein said later it was "the most impressive production he had ever seen, on or off the stage."

Minutes later, Ziegfeld appeared in a brocade dressing gown, and asked them to join him for a "pot luck" lunch. Footmen stood behind every chair as black-coated waiters served five gourmet courses. Late that afternoon Kern and Hammerstein headed back to New York, their mission unaccomplished. "We had the turtles imported up from Florida," Hammerstein recalled. "We had all the delicacies in the world. How could you ask a man like that if he had money enough to put on a show?"

That summer, Kern and Hammerstein spent long hours at Kern's house in Bronxville working on characters and scenes, plotting how the songs would flow naturally from the story and characters. "We had fallen hopelessly in love with it," recalled Hammerstein, who wrote the book and lyrics. "We couldn't keep our hands off it. We acted out the scenes together and planned the actual direction. We sang to each other. We had ourselves swooning."

One afternoon Kern showed up at Edna Ferber's Manhattan apartment "with a look of quiet exaltation in his eye." He sat down at her piano and played and sang "Ol' Man River." "I give you my word," Ferber wrote in her memoirs, "my hair stood on end, the tears came to my eyes. . . . This was music that would outlast Jerome Kern's day and mine."

When Ziegfeld read the first draft of Hammerstein's script he thought it promising but ponderous. "That's the gloomiest story I've ever read. That will die on Broadway. It has to have humor in it." But he liked the music, and gave Hammerstein a free hand in developing the story. When Ziegfeld suggested fantastic costumes and *Follies*-style stage scenery, Kern, with the helpful backing of Joseph Urban, convinced him to use realistic effects. The costumes were faithful reproductions of time and place, as was the scenery.

When the show went into rehearsal in the early fall of 1927, Ferber would occasionally sneak into the back of the Ziegfeld Theatre to watch. One afternoon, just as the entire cast seemed ready to drop from exhaustion, Ziegfeld emerged from his office and walked quietly down the aisle, "an imposing figure, handsome, erect, broad-shouldered. Instinctively all on stage turned their faces toward the dim auditorium. You sensed that an electric personality had entered the house," Ferber recalls.

One had. A flat voice came through the floodlights. "What the hell's this? You're dragging around like a lot of corpses. This is a rehearsal. You're supposed to play as if you were giving the performance. . . . Any of you boys and girls too tired to go please get out. Go home! And stay there."

Everyone in the theater knew he didn't mean it, said Ferber. "It was the showman cracking the whip. . . . The speech wasn't as brutal as it sounds. He served as astringent." The performers needed it; toward the end, rehearsals were running to twenty hours a day.

At the time, Ziegfeld was working simultaneously on two other shows, scheduled for early 1928, *Rosalie* and *The Three Musketeers*. Overwork sometimes drew down his spirits and it was in a gloomy mood that he telegraphed playwright and producer William Anthony McGuire: "Why did I ever undertake so many shows? I am in the worst predicament of my life. I've got three flops on my hands." McGuire wired back: "Please accept my condolences in this, your darkest hour of success."

Ziegfeld was with Kern, Hammerstein, and Ferber when *Show Boat* had its first out-of-town tryout in November at the National Theatre in Washington. By this time, he had convinced himself that the show was a flop, and he cried when there was so little applause for the big numbers. "They don't like it. I knew they wouldn't," he sobbed.

Legend has it that the audience was so stunned by the socially controversial subject matter that they filed out in silence. "On the contrary," writes Ethan Mordden, "it took a good ten minutes to clear the house after the final chorus of 'Ol' Man River,' at a time when ovations were uncommon and standing ones occurred at most two or three times a decade, at New York premieres only." The reviews in the morning papers were impressive, but even then Ziegfeld had his doubts. It wasn't until he arrived at the theater later in the day and saw a long line extending from the box office for several city blocks that he realized the show had "made it." But this was Washington. "New York," he said, "would tell the story."

The following month, Ziegfeld moved *Rio Rita* to the Lyric Theatre on Forty-second Street to make room for *Show Boat* in his new Joseph Urban playhouse. Ferber did not attend the opening performance. "I couldn't bring myself to go . . . I suppose I cared too deeply." Ziegfeld was in the theater but couldn't watch. He spent the entire show on the staircase leading to his private balcony with his secretary Goldie. When the curtain came down after the final act, there was a five-second pause, and then "thunderous applause."

Robert Coleman of the *Daily Mirror* declared it "a work of genius," a production that demonstrated that "managers have not until now realized the tremendous possibilities of the musical comedy as an art form." It was that rare theater classic whose greatness was recognized instantly. New York critics agreed that it was "the best musical show ever written," said Brooks Atkinson. At least half a dozen of its songs, including "Can't Help Lovin' Dat Man," would enjoy wide popularity for over half a century and more.

Show Boat was the first Broadway musical to have both a black and a white chorus and black and white characters on stage at the same time. Black performers had major roles—baritone Jules Bledsoe most memorably as Joe, the ship's hand, who gives several haunting renditions of "Ol' Man River." For the first time in an American musical, a black man was portrayed as a dignified human being, an old stevedore "tired of livin' an' skeered of dyin'."

In perhaps the most radical departure of all, a white woman in blackface, Tess Gardella, played Joe's wife, Queenie, the ship's cook. The cast of ninety-six chorus members included sixteen black male singers, sixteen black female singers, and twelve black female dancers. The white and black women in the chorus were, said Robert Coleman, "the most beautiful girls ever glorified by Ziegfeld." Staged at a time when the Ku Klux Klan was a powerful force in American society, in the North as well as the South, *Show Boat* was a daring leap by the past master of "light, escapist fare."

The cast was racially integrated, but so, too, artistically, were the story and the music, a marked departure from standard musicals by Kern, Berlin, and others. The songs grew directly out of the plot and dialogue, and the characters were realistic and fully developed, a rarity in musical theater and a bold breakthrough for Broadway's consummate fabulist. And Kern brilliantly blended black spirituals of cotton country with ragtime and modern jazz.

The most emotionally charged moment in *Show Boat* occurs when a sexually jealous member of the troupe exposes light-skinned Julie Dozier as a mulatto. Julie, played by torch singer Helen Morgan, is married to a white man and racially mixed marriages are unlawful in Natchez, Mississippi, where the showboat is docked. When the local sheriff boards the *Cotton Blossom*, Julie's husband, Steve Baker, the leading man of the troupe, whips a snap knife out of his pocket, grabs Julie's hand, and runs the blade across the tip of her finger. Pressing his lips to the open cut, he sucks the blood, mingling it with his own. As the sheriff is about to arrest the couple, Steve asks if he would consider a man white "that's got Negro blood in him." No, says the sheriff, "one drop of nigger blood makes you a nigger in these parts." Steve then reveals that he has more than one drop of Negro blood in him—a fact testified to by members of the boat's company, who had watched him swallow his wife's blood. The sullenly defeated sheriff leaves, but ominously warns the troupe to be careful: the townsfolk would not tolerate a racially mixed cast. As the black chorus sings "Mis'ry's Comin' Aroun'," Steve tells Captain Andy that he and ill-fated Julie will be leaving the company.

A former chorus girl and friend of Texas Guinan's, this was Morgan's first dramatic role, and it launched her meteoric theater career. Jerome Kern had seen her perform in a minor revue, perched on a piano and singing in a voice that artist James Montgomery Flagg called "a composite of all the ruined women in the world." In *Show Boat*, she sang "Bill," the mournful ballad that served as the presentiment for a life, in succeeding scenes, of drink and despair.

The only serious flaw in the original production is the ending. Hammerstein kept all the characters alive to the end and arranged a joyful reunion for the long-parted lovers, Magnolia and Ravenal, decisions he "came to regret," he said later.

It was the longest running of Ziegfeld's shows, with 572 performances in New York. Shortly after the original company reassembled for a post-Broadway tour, the stock market crashed and the tour ended disappointingly in March 1930. But *Show Boat* was revived five times on Broadway and three times in London, and was made into three Hollywood films. No similar work—combining emotional depth with soaring music—appeared until the 1943 opening of Richard Rodgers and Oscar Hammerstein's *Oklahoma!*

Show Boat was a "unique breakaway . . . the first truly, totally American operetta," writes theater historian Gerald Bordman. "[It] took a piece of beloved Americana and treated it with appropriate romanticism and yet with a theatrical seriousness. . . . Identifiable American types—the river gambler, the showboat crew, the black workhand—sang American sentiments in an American musical idiom."

Around this time a story about Ziegfeld—surely apocryphal, yet revealing—began to circulate around Broadway. It has him, sometime in 1925, sitting in a barber chair being prepared for a shave, his face covered by a hot towel. Unaware that he is in the shop, a group of customers is gossiping about him, claiming he's finished, that he'll never produce another hit. Hearing this, Ziegfeld rips the towel off his face, jumps out of the chair, and proclaims he'll stage not one but four hits on Broadway simultaneously.

He actually put on six hit shows in a row, an unequaled feat of theatrical bravura. *Rosalie*, a hugely expensive musical comedy starring Ziegfeld's old flame and *Follies* star Marilyn Miller opened in early January 1928 at the New Amsterdam. *The Three Musketeers*, a musical adaptation of Alexandre Dumas' novel, opened at another venue three months later. All four productions—*Rio Rita, Show Boat, Rosalie,* and *The Three Musketeers*—played to capacity houses in the winter of 1928, and revealed Ziegfeld "as something more than a ballyhooer of legs and knees," wrote Brooks Atkinson. In December, Ziegfeld rounded out his fabulous year with *Whoopee!*, a resounding critical and financial success starring *Follies* highlighters Eddie Cantor and Ruth Etting. Ziegfeld was exultant. With his six box office hits in succession—including the 1927 *Follies*—he was a millionaire again. But there would be ruinous consequences. In the following year, money and fame—more than he ever had—would lead this heedless risk taker to excesses that would bring him down.

CHAPTER TWENTY-SEVEN

A BAG OF PLUMS

*I pray to God to send me temptation and to give me not
the strength to resist it.*

—HORACE LIVERIGHT

Jazz Age Publisher

He was the Ziegfeld of his profession, a gambler and a showman, uncommon
characteristics for a publisher of deeply serious books. Horace Liveright, a
former Wall Street bond salesman, transformed American publishing as fundamentally as Florenz Ziegfeld transformed American musical theater. "He
was doing books that the old staid publishers wouldn't touch. And he was
doing advertising that old publishers wouldn't do," recalled Bennett Cerf, the
publishing giant whose first job in the business was with Boni & Liveright,
Liveright's Manhattan-based firm. "With a silk hat on, he would have been a
perfect Mississippi River boat gambler."

A showoff and charlatan, he was, as well, a publisher with principles, willing
to take long chances on obscure works of literary merit and to fight for worthy
causes. With Jimmy Walker as his attorney, he led a successful battle against
literary censorship in New York state; and with an idealistic socialist named
Albert Boni, he founded the Modern Library, affordable reproductions of the
classics of world literature—one of the most successful publishing ventures in
the history of the trade, and a godsend to college professors and students at a
time before paperback books. With the profits from these moderately priced
masterworks, he produced a succession of financial risky Broadway plays, one
of them a 1926 stage adaptation of Theodore Dreiser's novel about abortion,
murder, and social hypocrisy, *An American Tragedy.* But while Broadway seduced him as strongly as books, he was for a time, in Sherwood Anderson's

543

words, "the outstanding figure in the American publishing world," gifted with an uncanny ability to find and retain extraordinary authors, titans of the trade as well as unknowns with breakthrough talent. Endowed with "the persuasive powers of a Svengali," he lured to his firm Ernest Hemingway, William Faulkner, Sherwood Anderson, Theodore Dreiser, e.e. cummings, T. S. Eliot, Ezra Pound, Waldo Frank, Sigmund Freud, George Moore, Eugene O'Neill, Bertrand Russell, Liam O'Flaherty, Robinson Jeffers, Lewis Mumford, and Hart Crane. In one sensational year, 1922, he published three incontestable literary classics: e.e. cummings's *The Enormous Room*, T. S. Eliot's *The Waste Land*, and Eugene O'Neill's *The Hairy Ape*. In the space of a decade, he published seven Nobel Prize winners.

A high school dropout, Liveright had an inborn intuition about books. He took on titles that other publishers considered too radical—Michael Gold's *Jews Without Money*—or sexually controversial—Bertrand Russell's *Marriage and Morals*. Several were crushing failures, but in the 1920s his firm published more living writers of enduring reputation than any other New York publisher. And his editorial staff was one of the finest ever assembled. It included playwright Lillian Hellman; Edward Weeks, later the editor of *The Atlantic Monthly*; and Louis Kronenberger, who went on to become drama critic and editor at *Time* and *Fortune*. "A job with any publishing house was a plum," Hellman wrote in her memoirs, "but a job with Horace Liveright was a bag of plums."

Two members of Liveright's staff, book salesman extraordinaire Richard Simon and his Columbia classmate Bennett Cerf, went on to form—with partners Max Schuster and Donald S. Klopfer, respectively—their own publishing firms: Simon & Schuster and Random House. Liveright and these younger brothers in spirit were brash, adventurous Jews who challenged the trade's Anglo-Saxon old guard. "Most publishers were stodgy old poops who had no imagination at all," said Cerf. "They had inherited the business or they had built it up the way a banker would build a business in a small town. They had no imagination. Their advertising was dusty. The books themselves were ugly. There was no attempt to dress them up." Liveright, by contrast, attractively packaged his books and aggressively promoted them with "Hollywood-style" advertising. "The other publishers hated him" said Cerf, "because he broke every known rule in the publishing business and got away with it," turning his flimsily financed firm into "a roaring success."

None of the young publishing rebels, not even high-living Bennett Cerf, had Liveright's flamboyance and commanding presence. A frustrated thespian, he idolized the legendary figures of the stage. "He'd ask the girls, 'Do I remind you of anybody?' and if they said John Barrymore, he would be particularly pleased," Cerf described his mentor. "He was a kind of matinée idol in his own way, very handsome, smoked cigarettes in a long holder." While he wasn't Barrymore, he had one of the inexplicable qualities of a star of the stage or screen: when he was in the room people couldn't take their eyes off him. In his prime, at age forty, he had "an unforgettable look," wrote Kronenberger, "graying hair, a beaked nose, and piercing black eyes; a face so riveting as to obscure his body, which . . . was lean and fairly tall."

Though he started in the publishing business in 1917, his period of ascendancy exactly paralleled the frantic 1920s. His firm was "the Jazz Age in microcosm, with all its hysteria and cynicism, of Carpe Diem, of decadent thriftlessness, and of creative vitality," writes novelist Edith M. Stern, a young editor at Boni & Liveright in its halcyon days. In 1923, Liveright moved his firm from cramped downtown quarters to a spacious brownstone on West Forty-eighth Street, just off Sixth Avenue, in the heart of Midtown's speakeasy district. The speakeasies on that block became "branch offices" of Boni & Liveright. On some days there were as many bootleggers in the office as there were Liveright authors.

Liveright's impromptu publishing parties were "full of lush girls and good liquor," Hellman wrote. They drew a crowd that on any given afternoon might include Ira and George Gershwin, Dorothy Parker, Paul Robeson, Alexander Woollcott, George Jean Nathan, Walter Chrysler, Florenz Ziegfeld, Herbert Bayard Swope, and Wall Street wizard Otto Kahn, a senior partner of Kuhn, Loeb & Company, the nation's second most powerful private bankers after J. P. Morgan & Company. Kahn, the city's greatest patron of the arts, "Manhattan's Maecenas," was a great friend of Liveright's; he loaned him money he needed to keep his chaotically run publishing house financially afloat, and passed along tips on hot stocks, which Liveright gambled on more adventurously than the more prudent German-Jewish financier. The capitalist titan was the unlikely benefactor of three of Liveright's most controversial authors: Eugene O'Neill, a raging alcoholic; Michael Gold, a dedicated communist; and Hart Crane, a gay poet who drank ruinously and had sex with waterfront sailors. Liveright's friendship with Kahn epitomized the socially volatile world that Liveright both inhabited and helped to create, filled with people of every political stripe and social station. At his parties, one could find squat, silver-haired "Otto the Magnificent," dressed in his Savile Row suits, his mustache "waxed to fine points," flirting, scotch in hand, with a terrifically tall Ziegfeld Girl.

A married man, Liveright would sit in the corner at these parties with a wannabe starlet on his lap, openly fondling her breasts. "Horace . . . had a compulsion for making a pass at every girl the first time he met her." He had to test himself, to prove that he was irresistible to women. "That was his game,"

Cerf reported years later. "He was John Barrymore. He wasn't a sex fiend. He was showing off."

Liveright's peak years as publisher were 1926 and 1927, the firm's annus mirabilis, but the beginning, as well, of his sad and steep decline. In 1926, sales from Dreiser's *An American Tragedy* and Anita Loos's *Gentlemen Prefer Blondes* were booming, and these blockbusters were soon followed by Eugene O'Neill's *Lazarus Laughed*, Dorothy Parker's *Enough Rope*, Lewis Mumford's *The Golden Day*, e.e. cummings's *Is 5*, Sherwood Anderson's *Tar*, Ezra Pound's *Personae,* Hart Crane's *White Buildings*, William Faulkner's *Mosquitoes*, Waldo Frank's *Virgin Spring*, and Hendrik Willem van Loon's *America*, a historical saga from the pen of the affable Dutchman who was the best-selling author of nonfiction in the 1920s. "Never before, and possibly never since," Hellman claimed, "has an American publishing house had so great a record."

Liveright captured and cultivated these authors with generous advances, heavy advertising, and close personal attention. When he lavishly promoted Sherwood Anderson's novel *Dark Laughter*, the author was thrilled to see his face staring at him from the advertising pages of newspapers and "on the walls of buses and subways. . . . I was as excited as a young girl about to go to her first dance," Anderson remembered. "The sympathy and attention given to writers, young or old, was more generous than had been known before," said Hellman.

In 1927, Horace Liveright was at his apogee, living high and spending fantastically on books and plays. Three years later he was finished as a producer and banished from the publishing company he had founded in a coup led by Arthur Pell, a tight-buttoned accountant he had hired eleven years earlier, fresh out of City College of New York. This jarring reversal occurred a year after Liveright lost nearly every cent he had in the Stock Market Crash of 1929. Three years after Pell took over the firm, Horace Liveright died of pneumonia at the age of forty-nine. He passed his last hours in a cheap Manhattan rooming house, bankrupt and broken in spirit. "Most of the authors he had started on the road to success . . . were far too busy to spare the few moments necessary to pay him a last tribute," wrote Bennett Cerf. "It was a dismal last curtain to a spectacular career."

The Gambler

Horace Brisbin Liveright was born in the stark western Pennsylvania mining town of Osceola Mills, the son of Henry Leibrecht, a German-Jewish mine owner and dry goods merchant from Würzburg. Leibrecht had emigrated with his parents in 1857, at age sixteen, and immediately anglicized his name to

Liveright.* His wife, Henrietta Fleisher, was also the child of German-Jewish immigrants, although her family was solidly established in Philadelphia society. The young couple met and married in Philadelphia in 1872 and moved shortly thereafter to the Pittsburgh area coalfields, where Henry was intent on making a fortune. In 1893, under pressure from his wife, he moved the family back to Philadelphia when Horace was nine years old. For the remainder of Horace's time at home, his father, a kindly patriarch with a flowing beard, commuted between Philadelphia and Osceola Mills, where he attended to his mining properties.

Horace was the most spirited of the five Liveright children—the family rebel, a heavy drinker in his teens with a lively sexual appetite and an avid interest in socialism. A voracious reader, he had limitless academic promise, but took little interest in his formal studies, arrogantly insisting he knew more than his teachers. At the end of his first year of high school, he dropped out to take a job as an office boy in a local banking and brokerage firm, where his oldest brother, Otto, had established himself. Rising rapidly to margin clerk, he played the stock market actively, frequented drinking parties at Philadelphia hotels, and dressed like a dandy, sporting a flower in his lapel and beginning his lifelong habit of carrying a walking stick—anomalous behavior for a professed socialist.†

Like Jimmy Walker in his youth, Horace Liveright aspired to be a songwriter, but unlike Walker he had real talent. In his spare evenings he worked on a comic opera, *John Smith*, which he sold to Broadway musical producer Edward E. Rice. It looked like the start of a promising career, but Rice went bankrupt while the play was in rehearsal, and Liveright went back to selling bonds, this time in New York City. After losing one job because he refused to temper his alcohol-fueled socialist diatribes around the office, he landed a position with one of the commanding firms on Wall Street. He had a stunningly successful first year; "by a succession of speculations," he ran a few hundred dollars into $100,000, a windfall that convinced him to resign and open his own investment firm. He made a quick million, in today's money, but lost all of it almost immediately when the market turned decisively against him. Chastened by failure, he would not purchase a stock certificate again until 1925,

---

* It is pronounced Live-right, not Liver-right.

† Liveright never joined the Socialist Party, or read Marx or Lenin, although he did publish Leon Trotsky. His inchoate radicalism was rooted in an emotional sympathy for the underdog. See Edward L. Bernays, *Biography of an Idea: Memoirs of Public Relations Counsel Edward L. Bernays* (NY: Simon & Schuster, 1965), 277.

though he continued to play high-stakes poker recklessly and drink to stupe-faction, passing out at parties and on dinner dates. If he died young, his only regret, he declared at the time, would be that he "didn't drink enough."

In 1911, he married Lucille Elsas, the raven-haired daughter of German-born industrialist Hermann Elsas, a cotton and paper products mogul. The couple had met in Manhattan and Liveright won her away from the writer Walter Lippmann. He and Lucille had two children, a boy and a girl, but father-hood failed to tame him.

Over the next four years, Hermann Elsas supported his profligate son-in-law in a succession of business ventures, one of them selling toilet paper. Every enterprise ended in failure, but the last one led to a career-changing meeting with Albert Boni, a young unemployed socialist. They met at the advertising firm of Liveright's cousin Alfred Wallerstein, where Horace had been provided free office space to merchandise a line of cheap household gadgets, one of them a self-sealing jar. Boni had rented a desk on the same floor to plan his next business venture.

Albert Boni and his brother Charles had recently sold their Washington Square Bookstore, a famous meeting place for Greenwich Village radicals. At that same time, they sold the rights to a mass-market scheme called the Lit-tle Leather Library. The small, imitation leather books, most of them classics by British and continental writers, were priced at ten cents and sold over a million copies in the first year, mostly in Woolworth five-and-dime stores; bookstores refused to carry them because of the slim profit margin. When Liveright happened to pick up one of the Little Leather books lying on Boni's desk, Boni excitedly described his scheme to market them in a larger format and at a higher price—sixty cents—in order to expand the profit margin. The series would comprise a library, a modern library of recognized classics and of contemporary books of established worth. It was a sure-fire scheme, he be-lieved; all he needed was the capital to underwrite it. That night, he took the idea to his father-in-law. With the greatest reluctance, Hermann Elsas loaned him $12,000, the onset of a plague of problems for the paper products prince and his devoted daughter.

A partnership was formed in 1917 under the name Boni & Liveright, but the partners argued often and ardently. Albert Boni was devoting more time to radical politics, Liveright complained, than to the grind of launching an undercapitalized business. When the partners decided to split after only one year together, they flipped a coin to determine who would take sole owner-ship. Liveright won the coin toss, but left Boni's name on his reorganized firm, which also began publishing original works of literature, history, philosophy, and poetry. To oversee this side of the operation Liveright hired as editor in chief T. R. Smith, a highly respected magazine editor with a flashing mind and one of the finest collections of exotic pornographic literature in existence. Short, round-faced Tommy Smith was a legendary drinker and bon vivant who seemed to know everyone of importance on the New York and London literary scene. Yet this cherubic-looking fellow with the pince-nez was one of the most ruthless editors in the business. Tommy Smith "gave the impression that he considered associating with most of our authors a form of slumming," said one of Liveright's staff.

Liveright brought in Julian Messner, an old Wall Street buddy, and gave him near total control of sales and manufacturing, a decision that allowed Horace to concentrate on building a list of outstanding works, many of them by up-and-coming authors that established houses avoided. Liveright reached many of his publishing decisions by an unfathomable process of intuition. He would meet unknown writers, chat for less than hour, and sign them to sizable advances, often over the sound business objections of Messner. And he was eager to take chances on established but controversial writers, among them Upton Sinclair, author of searing anticapitalist exposés; Theodore Dreiser, who was searching for a firm willing to republish *Sister Carrie*, his partially suppressed novel about a promiscuous Chicago woman; and socialist John Reed, author of *Ten Days That Shook the World*, a stirring eyewitness account of the opening moments of the Bolshevik Revolution.

In 1919, Liveright published *The Moon of the Caribbees and Six Other Plays of the Sea* by then obscure Eugene O'Neill, a Provincetown friend of John Reed's. Liveright advanced the New York–born playwright a measly $125. O'Neill was grateful rather than insulted; it was unheard of for a publisher to try to sell unproduced plays. The next year, O'Neill won a Pulitzer Prize for *Beyond the Horizon*, a Liveright publication.

Liveright knew he was facing long odds when he expanded into the trade book business. He had entered a prevailingly Christian industry. The established houses, among them Harper & Brothers, Charles Scribner's Sons, Houghton Mifflin, and Little, Brown, regularly turned away young Jews interested in careers in publishing; the few that were hired found advancement difficult to near impossible. Many of the established firms were also rigidly conservative, unreceptive to experimental or politically radical literature. "Most of the older and richer houses are run by old women in pantaloons; there is no great trade in America, indeed, which shows a vaster imbecility," wrote H. L. Mencken at the time. "Some of the largest houses in the country devote themselves chiefly to merchandising garbage that should make any self-respecting publisher blush."

The first Jew to enter New York's book publishing business was the gifted amateur B. W. Huebsch, a talented musician and lithographer. Beginning his second career at the turn of the century he published in 1916 James Joyce's *Portrait of the Artist as a Young Man*; in the early 1920s, before merging with the Viking Press, he was still putting out a small list of distinguished work.

Alfred A. Knopf, fresh out of Columbia, was next. In 1915, at age twenty-two, with less than $5,000 in the bank, he set up shop in a one-room office on Forty-second Street. The only other occupant of the solitary room was his fiancée, Blanche Wolf. They married the following April and remained inseparable lifelong collaborators. Within seven years, Alfred Knopf was one of the most respected publishers in New York, with an office in the Heckscher Building on Fifth Avenue and Fifty-seventh Street, one of the most prestigious addresses in the city. "I love books physically," Knopf announced in his 1917 fall catalogue, "and I want to make them beautifully." During his first three years in business, he published two dozen or so books, all of them wrapped in striking dust jackets.

Knopf broke tradition with his innovative advertising, using his name— "Mr. Alfred A. Knopf"—to "announce" the appearance of a new book, a practice older publishers considered excessive showmanship by a brash upstart. Without funds to hire a sales force, Knopf became his own book agent, and grew "a fierce mustache that enabled him to get by office boys and approach book buyers." Yet he was never seduced into believing that advertising or salesmanship alone could put a book across. "Getting talked about," he claimed, is what made a book sell.

In Knopf's first years in the trade, his list was stacked with outstanding European writers, most of them Russians—living and dead—inspiring Blanche Wolf to make the borzoi, a Russian wolfhound, the firm's trademark, a decision she came to regret. "I bought a couple of the [dogs] later and grew to hate them," she told a writer from *The New Yorker*. "They were cowardly, stupid, disloyal, and full of self-pity, and they kept running away. One died and I gave the other to a kennel. I wish I'd picked a better dog for our imprint."

Beginning in 1917, Alfred Knopf broadened his list and began publishing American writers of imperishable renown—H. L. Mencken, Willa Cather, Langston Hughes, and Wallace Stevens—promoting them with energy and élan. The "old boys" began to pair him with Liveright, mercantile interlopers in a gentleman's trade. Knopf, however, resented the comparison: Liveright was too flashy, too much the libertine, and far too idiosyncratic in his literary proclivities. "Alfred Knopf had the one thing Liveright lacked: he had class," Cerf would say later. Liveright was intensely jealous of him, and desperately "wanted to beat him. He didn't care about the old fogies he was competing with. It was Knopf he had his sights set on."

In the spring of 1919, Liveright hired Edward L. Bernays, the young public relations whiz, to "puff" his catalogue. Earlier that year, Vienna-born Bernays had approached the publisher with an irresistible proposal. He was the nephew of Sigmund Freud and wanted Liveright to put out an American translation of his uncle's *General Introduction to Psychoanalysis*, Freud's most accessible work. Liveright leapt at the opportunity. He and Bernays arranged for the book to be translated and Liveright published it the next year, pricing it high so that it would be presented for what it was: a serious work of observational science, not a book promoting sexual license, as crusading moralists charged. The book was a solid seller and made Freud the subject of Manhattan cocktail party conversation.

Liveright then hired Bernays to a one-year contract. Most established publishing firms "were run like conservative Wall Street banks," Bernays wrote of his time with Liveright. "Books were handled in the same way they had been published—for a select audience and not for the larger public." With the exception of Knopf, most publishers, after "announcing" a book, left it to make its own way on the basis of merit, reviewers' opinions, or word of mouth. With Bernays's counsel, Liveright set out to change that, creating a show business approach to book publishing. The boy wonders—Bernays younger by a few years than thirty-one-year-old Liveright—settled into a comfortable working relationship, both of them hucksters at heart. Unlike most publishing executives, Liveright made decisions almost instantaneously, the way he had operated on Wall Street; and Bernays found that "exhilarating." When Bernays suggested that the firm's books be promoted as unabashedly as Wrigley's hawked its chewing gum, Liveright agreed wholeheartedly.

Publishing a book, Bernays believed, should be as much "an event" as the opening of a Broadway play or a Hollywood film. Up to then, it was the practice in book promotion to simply mail out the author's biography and photograph, along with a terse description of the book, to literary editors. Bernays went directly into the marketplace to increase sales, offering at no cost to newspapers well-written articles on Liveright's books. Dozens of newspaper editors, eager for attractive space fillers written by others, requested copies. After Bernays's contract expired, Liveright used this and other unconventional approaches to change the way books were sold, determined never to allow a book to languish because the pubic didn't know it existed.

Liveright's highly publicized battles against literary censorship also helped him sell books, putting him on the front page of newspapers in every major American city. In 1923, he led a fight to defeat the Clean Books Bill sponsored by reactionaries in the New York state legislature. The proposal would have given the state virtual carte blanche to bring an indictment against a book if even a single passage was judged "filthy or disgusting" by the New York Society for the Suppression of Vice and its unmovable organizer, John S. Sumner. Only two New York publishing houses, Harcourt Brace and Putnam's, openly supported Liveright's position. This made Liveright's stand more estimable to young writers like Waldo Frank. "He is a crusader," Frank wrote, "a romantic champion of good books. He stands, first and last, for the Revolt of our misled youth against every proper tradition of the land." And Liveright was fighting the good fight with his own money, and with none of his books currently under attack by the moral guardians. Other publishers stayed on the sidelines either because they supported the Clean Books Bill, or, more likely, feared alienating the state's powerful moral arbiters.

Liveright's most powerful allies were his firm's lawyer, Arthur Garfield Hays, a noted champion of free speech, and Garfield's legal partner, Senator Jimmy Walker, who led the fight in the Albany Senate to defeat the Clean Books Bill, which had passed the Assembly by a large majority. At Walker's behest, Liveright went up to the state capital to play poker at the Ten Eyck Hotel with undecided senators whose votes they would need. The game went on for days, and it was patently rigged. Liveright lost all his money, purposely, and had to call Arthur Pell to dispatch additional funds daily by messenger. On the eve of the vote, he brought to Albany a group of his disheveled writers to bolster his cause. Walker told him to send "these nuts" home; he would handle things.

Under the proposed law, even the Bible and Shakespeare could be censored, Walker told legislators in his silky Hibernian tones. They were the only two books, he said, his sainted mother kept in her home. To pass this bill would be to defile her memory, "God rest her soul." After Walker ceded the floor, the bill was defeated.

On Liveright's return to Manhattan, the city's literary community gathered to honor him at a gala banquet at the old Hotel Brevoort. He would be their champion for the remainder of the decade, fighting every major city and state effort to impose censorship on books as well as theater productions. "I can say without fear of denial that outside of the active offices of the Civil Liberties Union, I have for the past ten years in my publishing, in my speeches and in the amount of time and money I have expended done more to oppose all sorts of censorships than almost anyone else in this country," Liveright wrote Bertrand Russell in 1929.

The year the censorship bill was defeated Liveright moved his firm uptown, from a sterile business building on West Fortieth Street to the comfortable four-story brownstone in Manhattan's speakeasy district, defying the publishing axiom that "dignity and dust were the mark of a successful publisher." Liveright's second-story office had its own bar, and he decorated the large reception room on that floor with Italian Renaissance furniture and Oriental rugs; a large wood-burning fireplace made it seem like the smoking room of an English squire. When Liveright went into show business the next year, producing *Firebrand*, a successful Broadway play based on the amatory adventures of the Renaissance sculptor Benvenuto Cellini, carpenters cut a hole through a wall in the reception room to the house next door, which Liveright had rented. A movable bookcase served as the entrance to this, his new theatrical office. "It was for us, a never-ending source of amusement to watch the expressions on the faces of the people in the waiting-room when the bookcase would suddenly swing into the room and a startlingly beautiful secretary would glide out to summon an equally beautiful actress to her interview in the theatrical offices," said Liveright's new partner, Donald Friede.

Friede had become first vice president of the firm in 1925, at age twenty-four, with six months experience in publishing—"first" because there were already three vice presidents. Whenever Liveright sailed into financial trouble he brought in a bright young man with money as a vice president. In exchange for their lofty positions, they were required to buy shares in the firm, funds Liveright used to support his Broadway productions and his Wall Street speculations, which resumed with vigor the year Friede joined Boni & Liveright. Friede's contribution—$110,000—came from a trust his deceased father had left him; it gained him a half interest in the company. "I have every reason to be grateful," Friede would write in his memoirs. "I got a ringside seat at a show that has never been equaled."*

The Boni & Liveright building was "a rambling hive," said Friede. Situated between the shipping room in the basement and the tiny rooms in the attic, where the advertising department was housed, were the executive offices, each

---

* Friede left Liveright in 1928 to form Covici, Friede, in partnership with Pascal Covici. His final position in publishing was as senior editor at Doubleday.

of them "looking as much as possible, like comfortable living rooms, with not a single conventional desk in evidence." Leading off the reception room was a canopied terrace, reached through three French doors. Furnished in summer with lounge chairs, it was a "favorite resting place for hot and thirsty authors," and the scene of memorable Liveright cocktail parties, with music provided by Harlem jazz ensembles.

In 1923, the staff was extraordinary, even by the elevated standards of that decade. Julian Messner continued to run the sales department, which still included Richard Simon, a towering young man with a winning smile. Simon was serving his last months before departing to form his own firm with his friend Max Schuster. Simon's successor, whom he had agreed to train, was his twenty-five-year-old Columbia College classmate, Bennett Alfred Cerf, "sleek and dark, with very bright eyes and a ready laugh," a prankster whose fondness for inane practical jokes masked a razor-sharp intellect.

A graduate of Columbia University's School of Journalism and editor in chief of *The Jester*, the student humor magazine, Cerf had been plucked from his uncle's Wall Street brokerage firm, where he was writing, on the side, a financial column for the *New-York Tribune*. The only child of Frederika Wise, daughter of Nathan Wise, a wealthy German American tobacco merchant, and Gustave Cerf, a lithographer of Alsatian-Jewish heritage, Cerf was raised in a spacious apartment on Riverside Drive. A natural charmer with a slight lisp and a devastating wit, he had been following Simon's career with envy and astonishment after they graduated from Columbia. Cerf was bored with Wall Street, and Simon's "superior career infuriated me," he recalled. "Every time I met him, I would rage at him and say, 'You dumb cluck, you don't open three books a year and *you're* working for a publisher! That was *my* dream.'"

In the early fall of 1923, Simon had recommended Cerf to Horace Liveright as his replacement and arranged a meeting between the two in Liveright's office. Liveright, the first publisher Cerf ever met, took him to the Algonquin and "charmed the hell out of me," Cerf recalled. Liveright told him he "needed money very much," and that if Cerf put "a little money into the business"—$25,000—he could "start with style" as a vice president. When Cerf agreed to consider the offer, Liveright asked him to take Theodore Dreiser to a baseball game. "I'm bored to death by baseball," Liveright complained. Cerf was awestruck. "Dreiser was a giant." After lunch, he went straight to a telephone booth and called his uncle and employer, Herbert Wise. He wouldn't be returning to the office that afternoon—probably never.

He withdrew the money from a $100,000 trust fund left him by his deceased maternal grandfather, and the next day he took the position, at fifty dollars a week, and went on the road with Simon to learn how to sell books. "[Dick] was a superb salesman, and the very fact that he hadn't read the books made him able to sell them that much better." To him, they were all sensational.

In Boston, the book manager of the Jordan Marsh department store gave Simon and Cerf, stylishly dressed out-of-towners, a difficult time. On their way back to the hotel, Cerf stopped suddenly and announced, "Dick, within ten years, I hope I may become one of the best publishers of the country. And if I do I'll never forget how that s.o.b. behaved this afternoon." A decade later, Cerf would be cofounder (with Donald Klopfer) of Random House, a firm he built to greatness.

When Cerf returned from Boston in the fall of 1923, he discovered that he had joined a most unusual publishing house. Almost every afternoon there was a cocktail party in Liveright's combination office and reception room, with devilish Tommy Smith mixing the drinks, adding a dash of a bootlegger's supplement that was very nearly ether. "Just two sips were enough to send you reeling," said Cerf. Herbert Bayard Swope, playboy publisher of the New York *World*, was a regular at these impromptu gatherings that might include Paul Morand, Paul Robeson, Sinclair Lewis, Edna Ferber, and Sherwood Anderson—with George Gershwin on the piano. Liveright had a well-used casting couch, and his office parties "could involve stained and ripped garments, periodical passing out in public, disappearing couples, maudlin recitals, unmanageable guests, and almost as much spilled liquor as swilled, almost as many gate-crashers as guests," recalled Louis Kronenberger, a young man too timid to partake.

On Friday evenings part of the party crowd would reconvene at Swope's estate in Great Neck, Long Island, thought to be F. Scott Fitzgerald's model for Gatsby's estate. Swope and his wife, Margaret, would serve supper "at three o'clock in the morning and champagne nearly all the time." With two shifts of servants attending to his guests, parties sometimes lasted for two to three days. "Mr. Swope of the *World* lives across the way, and he conducts an almost continuous house party," wrote Swope's neighbor Ring Lardner.

Harlem was another of Liveright's favorite end-of-the-evening spots. At one of these uptown gatherings, his guest was British philosopher and socialist Bertrand Russell, in New York to celebrate the publication of his first book with the firm, *Education and the Good Life*. The great humanitarian had a bad time. "[Liveright and his friends] insisted on taking me to Harlem where the rich niggers live," Russell described his night at the "black and white" Ebony

Club in a letter to his wife. "I wanted to enjoy myself, but when we got there they invited black ladies to our table & one was expected to dance & flirt with them. To my surprise, the mere idea was unspeakably revolting to me, & and I left the place and went home."

The "ladies" in question were not, as Russell intimated, women of the night, but two tastefully dressed members of "the very upper crust of Harlem's social and intellectual set," recalled Sherwood Anderson, who was at the table that evening. "They were very quiet but took part in the dinner conversation and it was evident that they were what is called 'well read.'"

Liveright also hosted parties at his Manhattan apartment when his wife was out of town with the children. "Any writer on a New York visit, any new book, any birthday," Lillian Hellman remembered, "was an excuse for what he called an A party or a B party. (Liveright was possibly the first publisher to understand that writers care less for dollars than for attention.) The A parties were respectable and high-class chatty. The B parties were drunk, cutup sex stuff and often lasted into another day and night with replacements. I was invited to both the A and B parties, maybe because I was young and thought to be unjudging, maybe for reasons not so good. . . .

"The respectable parties were filled with wives, single or divorced ladies, and a few well born Lesbians. . . . The B parties were filled with pretty ladies, semi-ins, almost-actresses or newspaper girls, and they slept quite openly with the gentlemen guests, or executives of Liveright's, or the bankers Horace so often had at his parties because he so often needed their money."

Even during business hours, the brownstone on Forty-eighth Street was a raucous place. Hellman, a vivacious office factotum, would sprint, rather than walk up the stairs to her attic desk to avoid being pinched. "All the men at the office made routine passes at the girls who worked there—one would have had to be hunchbacked to be an exception."*

Horace advertised his sexual flings to everyone but his wife, Lucille, and his children. Lucille knew about them but had not caught him red-handed until the day she walked into his office when he was reading, for the adolescent amusement of his editors, a love letter from another woman. "She sailed in ignoring us," recalls Bennett Cerf, and said, "This time I caught you. . . . What was that letter you were reading, a letter from one of your girls?" Liveright stuffed the letter into the top drawer of his desk, rose to his full height, and "in his best Barrymore manner" said: "Lucille, you have insulted me in front of my staff. . . . I demand that you open that drawer and read aloud to my staff the

---

* Hellman quit her job in late 1925 to marry Arthur Kober.

letter you just saw me put in that drawer." She wilted and apologized. "We were absolutely swept by admiration, a performance by a master mountebank!" said Cerf, a comment as reflective of his boyish immaturity as Liveright's.

There was almost no recognition of rank in the office. Gum-chewing telephone girls loudly announced into their mouthpieces, "Your sweetie's calling"; and seventeen-year-old office boys hailed visiting authors by their first names. Stenographers and shipping clerks wandered about the building reading manuscripts, "offering opinions," said Hellman, "about how to advertise or sell a book." Kronenberger thought the office "resembled a gossipy Alpine village"; Anderson called it a "madhouse."

What discipline that prevailed was provided by Arthur Pell, the coldly reserved accountant Liveright had hired in 1919 at the insistence of his father-in-law. Pell's unenviable task was to control Liveright's improvident spending and watch over Hermann Elsas's investments in the firm.

Pell and Liveright never got along: opposing personalities and business philosophies. The way to sell books, Liveright believed, was to spend heavily on advertising and advances; Pell, by contrast, was a ruthless cost cutter and budget balancer whose "harrowing duty," said Friede, was to make sure the bills got paid. Liveright spent lavishly on advertising—big, splashy ads, most of them from the attic desk of Marxist Isidor Schneider, a gifted poet who would join the Communist Party in the 1930s. From the time Liveright hired Bernays until the mid-1920s, he continued to increase the firm's advertising budget, in defiance of the evidence directly in front of him: the books he barely advertised—the standards in the Modern Library—were his strongest sellers, generating a steady quarter of a million sales a year. Yet no matter how many books Boni & Liveright sold—contemporary novels, histories, biographies, plays, collections of poetry, or classics—the firm was never solvent. In 1925, a booming year for Liveright trade books, the auditor's statement showed a net profit of less than $9,000. "Actually nobody cared very much," said Friede. "Certainly I didn't." It was "much too exciting" to read Faulkner's *Soldier's Pay* in manuscript, or to throw a dinner for Dreiser, O'Neill, and Anderson, literary giants who had never spent an evening together. "With all this going on . . . [who] could bother about making money? Publishing was for fun, and so was the publisher's life."

Liveright's was an anomalous enterprise—a marketing success that was a financial calamity. That was, in large part, because Liveright used it to underwrite his other interests. The enormous sums he spent for his parties were drops in the bucket compared to the money he gambled and lost on Broadway plays and Wall Street long shots. Otto Kahn, his stock market tipster, was on the inside, where split-second decisions had to be made. "But Liveright would necessarily always be a little behind him, and that was usually fatal," said Friede.

Pell fumed and complained, but did not yet have the clout to rein in his boss. Their relationship was strained, but this failed to affect the social atmosphere in the office. The brownstone on Forty-eighth Street was "wonderfully free from tension, or a sense of insecurity, or a Fear of the Boss," recalls Kronenberger. The staff was well paid, raises were frequent, and the vacations grew annually longer. It was, Liveright boasted, "the one real socialist publishing house in New York." All employees shared in its prosperity.

Perhaps because Liveright wasn't a model boss, he didn't expect model employees. If he arrived late for work, why shouldn't they? No one was told when to show up in the morning and when to leave at night. No one was a "slave of the clock."

Editorial meetings were informal, convened on a moment's notice and with no set agenda. "There'd be a call: 'Come down to Horace's office,'" Cerf remembered. "We never knew whether it was to have an editorial meeting or hear him boast about his latest conquest." Liveright wanted editors "who would inflate his ego and echo his judgments"; editorial meetings were "one-man shows"; few "dared dispute his edicts," Cerf asserted. This doesn't square with the memories of other Liveright editors. They remember a publisher who listened to their advice and gave them wide latitude. If an editor felt strongly about a book, Liveright would tell him to sign it up, so long as the advance wasn't staggering. "The employees he chose had vivid personalities, keen minds," wrote former staffer Edith Stern. "They . . . stayed with him, because for all his trying unpredictability and exhibitionism he had the heroic quality, rare in both publishers and employers, of encouraging you to be yourself."

Liveright's editors, in turn, learned to respect his hunches, what Stern called his instincts or "flairs"—for as she said, "they transcended judgment." He had an uncommon ability to discover good books. And if a book was morally or politically controversial, it only whetted his appetite. "Horace relished the scandal," said Stern. "It brought publicity, and sales . . . but behind the posturings and sensationalism lay Horace's passionate conviction that literature must be fresh and free, that if a book was vital it must be published, whether or not it would sell." He was, she said, "a man who was not afraid."

Liveright stuck by his authors as well as his editors, and counted on his top writers to bring fresh talent into the firm. He "had a way of trusting his authors," said Sherwood Anderson. Through Anderson's intercession, Hemingway and Faulkner published their first books with Liveright. "He took your word for it" when you recommended a writer, said Anderson. "He'd say, 'Send them to me,'" and there on his desk, beside a bottle of whiskey, would be his checkbook.

Although Anderson had steered *In Our Time*, Hemingway's book of short stories, to Boni & Liveright, Liveright turned down the expatriate writer's second submission, *The Torrents of Spring*. This was a vicious, black humor parody of Anderson, whom Hemingway now considered a competitor, not a patron. The manuscript arrived at Boni & Liveright with a glowing recommendation from F. Scott Fitzgerald, and Liveright's editors wanted to publish it. Liveright also knew that Max Perkins at Scribner's—just around the corner—was trying to capture Hemingway, and that refusing to publish *Torrents* would make Hemingway available to him. Caught in a quandary, Liveright consulted Anderson. "I won't stand for it," said Anderson. So Liveright turned it down and lost Hemingway to Perkins. "It would be in extremely rotten taste, to say nothing of being horribly cruel, should we want to publish it," Liveright wrote Hemingway in Paris.*

When Perkins published Hemingway's first novel, *The Sun Also Rises*, in 1926, Anderson told Liveright, "You should have printed [*Torrents of Spring*] without saying anything to me."

That kind of integrity kept authors loyal to Liveright. Just as he trusted them, they trusted him. The exception was Theodore Dreiser, his "flagship" author after the sensational success of *An American Tragedy*, published in 1925. Loyal to no one, suspicious of everyone, Dreiser negotiated with other publishers behind Liveright's back and was convinced Liveright was cheating him. Every few months he would stop by Liveright's office and demand to scrutinize the ledger to see if his royalty statements were correct. A virulent anti-Semite, the novelist hated the fact that his publisher was a Jew, and "a crooked one at that."† He stayed with Liveright because he considered this "Jew" the finest publisher in New York.

---

* There is solid evidence that Hemingway wrote *The Torrents of Springs* confident that Liveright would reject it, allowing him to move to Scribner's. While Hemingway thought Liveright was "a damn good publisher," he was angry with him for printing only 1,335 copies of *In Our Time*. Michael Reynolds, *Hemingway: The Paris Years* (NY: W.W. Norton, 1999 edition; first published in 1989), 330–40.

† T. S. Eliot also thought Liveright was cheating him. In 1923, Eliot wrote to his American literary agent: "I wish I could find a decent Christian publisher in New York who could be trusted not to slip and slide at every opportunity." Ezra Pound, another anti-Semite, remained on cordial terms with Liveright, and scoured Europe for literary talent for Boni & Liveright. Tom Dardis, *Firebrand: The Life of Horace Liveright* (NY: Random House, 1995), 98.

There was no pleasing Dreiser. In 1926, Liveright commissioned a writer to turn *An American Tragedy* into a Broadway play, which Liveright successfully produced. When he lined up a Hollywood producer to make the novel into a feature film, Liveright scheduled a lunch with Dreiser and Paramount movie mogul Jesse L. Lasky at the Ritz-Carlton Hotel to hammer out the terms of the contract. After talking with Dreiser beforehand over drinks, Liveright entered the restaurant confident he would receive 30 percent of the purchase price. At a sensitive point in the negotiations, Liveright excused himself to allow Dreiser and Lasky to confer in private. When he returned to the table, he discovered that Dreiser had worked out a final arrangement that reduced Liveright's cut to 11 percent. Liveright was incensed. When he called Dreiser a liar, the tall, heavy-set writer rose to his full height, shouted an oath, and challenged the bone-thin publisher to a fight. Thunderstruck, Liveright remained frozen in his seat. Dreiser threw a cup of hot coffee in his face and stormed out of the restaurant.

Later, Dreiser had the temerity to demand a written apology. Liveright capitulated. "I should not have said what I did. One gentleman should not talk this way to another, particularly in front of comparative strangers." In another craven surrender, Liveright sweetened Dreiser's contract with Boni & Liveright and made him a member of the firm's board of directors. Liveright stuck with Dreiser though the fading titan failed to publish another original novel for Boni & Liveright. Losing him, Liveright believed, would fatally damage his reputation as a publisher, despite the fact that he had what Donald Friede considered "the most phenomenal list ever assembled by a publisher." Few people so successful were so insecure.

Horace Liveright was stagestruck. For a time—in the mid to late 1920s—he seemed more interested in the theater than in publishing. In 1925, he produced *Hamlet in Modern Clothes*, an American version of a successful London play. Liveright asked Friede to invest in it, and Friede eagerly came up with $25,000. The things that excited Liveright excited Friede: to go backstage "at will, to sit in empty theaters watching rehearsals, to go to the first night feeling that I had a part in bringing all those people in the audience into the theater." The play flopped: the reviews were lukewarm and the public stayed away.

The next year, Liveright put on two productions: the immensely successful *An American Tragedy*, and *Black Boy*, a drama about a young African American boxer in the grip of crooked fight promoters. *Black Boy*, also backed by Friede, was written expressly for Paul Robeson, two years out of law school. When the former Rutgers football star showed up one morning at Liveright's office to sign a contract to star in the production, Liveright invited Robeson and his wife to join him and Friede for a celebratory lunch at a local speakeasy. They would meet in Liveright's office at noon. When Robeson left the building, Friede suggested that the publisher call ahead to see if the owners would accept an African American couple. "Nonsense," said Liveright. "They [will] be proud to serve him." Friede persisted and Liveright made the call. The manager told him that he would not seat or serve the Robesons, as did the owners of every other place Liveright called. Friede then arranged for his domestic cook to prepare a lunch for the Robesons at his Manhattan townhouse.

Liveright was livid, literally shaking with rage for the remainder of the afternoon. The incident made him all the more determined to make *Black Boy* a hit. But the play ran for only thirty-seven performances; and Liveright's other 1925 play, a modern-dress adaptation of *Hamlet,* also flopped.

Two years later, Liveright produced his biggest Broadway success, *Dracula,* based on Bram Stoker's Victorian horror novel. Dorothy Peterson, Liveright's dark-eyed mistress, costarred with Bela Lugosi, the Hungarian actor, in the role of the vampire, a part he would become identified with for the remainder of his life. (Liveright's marriage was effectively over by 1926, although Lucille did not divorce him until 1928.) The reviews were mixed, but the play was a box office smash, running for 241 performances, its macabre allure enhanced by the publicity surrounding Liveright's announcement that he had hired a uniformed nurse to be in the theater for every performance.

At age forty-three, Liveright was at the top of life, one of his biggest years as a publisher crowned by success on Broadway. And two of his close friends and former staffers, Richard Simon and Bennett Cerf, were enjoying their best year thus far as publishers. But they were making money, while Liveright was nearly broke—and, more worrisome, didn't seem to care.

Simon and Schuster

"That brownstone house at 61 West 48th Street . . . was a hatchery of talent: obscure youngsters who worked there at run-of-the-mill jobs have since become Names," Edith Stern wrote in 1941.

Richard Leo Simon was twenty-one and M. Lincoln "Max" Schuster twenty-four—both graduates of Columbia—when they met for the first time in 1921. Simon was selling pianos for the Aeolian Company on West Forty-second Street, and Schuster was editing a trade magazine for an automobile association whose offices were in the same building. Simon had heard that Schuster loved music and dropped by his office one afternoon to try to sell him a piano. He couldn't make the sale, but as he was leaving he spotted a copy of Romain Rolland's *Jean-Christophe* on Schuster's desk. They were both great fans of the French novelist, and their discussion led to a fast friendship. Both were unhappy in their work, but aside from this, and their common interest in Rolland, there seemed little else to draw them together. They came from dissimilar backgrounds and had different tastes and interests.

Simon, the eldest of five children of Anna Meier and Leo Simon, a rich feather-and-silk manufacturer, grew up in a large brownstone on fashionable East Fifty-ninth Street, not far from Sutton Place. Surrounded by an intensely musical family, he became an accomplished pianist, able to play Mozart as expertly as he could Scott Joplin. Attending Manhattan's Ethical Culture School, he picked up pocket money providing piano accompaniment for opera singers who were preparing for performances. At Columbia, where he would graduate in 1920 after serving briefly in the Army, he led the glee club and was one of the most popular men on campus—handsome and rakishly slim with a "careless, engaging manner." He was physically fit, played tennis, said Schuster colleague Michael Korda, "with a terrifying will to win," and was an amateur photographer and a superb bridge player.

Max Schuster, by contrast, was reclusive, disheveled, and looked far older than his years; his only leisure pursuits were book collecting and playing the violin. Born in Kalusz, Austria, in 1897, he had been brought to New York when he was seven weeks old. His father, Barnet, ran a stationery and cigar store in Washington Heights, and Max attended DeWitt Clinton High School, where he developed a deep interest in Abraham Lincoln, adopting Lincoln as his middle name and signing himself "M. Lincoln Schuster." Unusually precocious, he hoped to start out in life as a newspaper reporter and move eventually into publishing. The day after graduation, he landed a summer job as a copy boy for the New York *World*.

That September, he entered Columbia University's Pulitzer School of Journalism. He was only sixteen and "ridiculously small for his age," the sole student in his class in short pants. A classmate who had looked forward to college as a maturing experience would say later that the very sight of little Max Schuster in his short pants disgusted him and made him want to transfer. When Schuster matriculated, he was only four-feet-eleven-inches tall and weighed eighty-nine pounds, but at age eighteen he suddenly shot up eleven inches and gained over seventy pounds, a growth spurt he would attribute, quite seriously, to "sheer will power."

At Columbia, he supported himself by writing articles for magazines and serving as the college correspondent for the *Boston Evening Transcript*. After graduating in 1917, he worked for the administration of President Woodrow

Wilson, writing pamphlets to support the country's war bonds drive. After the war, he returned to New York.

When he first met Richard Simon, his new friend was about to take a position as a book salesman for Boni & Liveright. Within a year Simon moved up to sales manager. At the time, Schuster and Simon had fallen into the habit of having lunch together and began discussing plans to establish their own publishing house. Simon's well-positioned family was eager to back the new enterprise, but the two friends wanted to start out on their own. In December 1924, they combined their savings—less than $8,000—rented a one-room office at 37 West Fifty-seventh Street, and painted on the door "Simon & Schuster, Publishers." They moved in on January 2. Having nothing else to do, they went out for lunch. When they returned they saw that someone had scrawled a message underneath their sign—"Of what?"

Their publishing plan was risky in the extreme. They had not a single book or author under contract. Instead of signing up writers, they would come up with ideas and "find people to carry them out." This became the governing philosophy of their firm; they would adhere to it unvaryingly for nearly a decade. Simon called it "planned publishing." They would exploit current fads and trends and publish books with a straightforward commercial appeal, combining these, whenever possible, with works of literary merit. "Made" books, they called them.

Their first publication was a book of crossword puzzles. It wasn't their idea; it was the suggestion of Richard Simon's aunt, who had become interested in the crossword puzzles published in the Sunday *World* and wished there was an entire book devoted to them. Simon warmed to the idea, but everyone he approached thought it a harebrained scheme. His friend Franklin P. Adams, a feature columnist at the *World*, dismissed it as "a suicidal notion" and implored him to bury it. "If you must publish," a prominent bookseller told Simon, "keep your name off it, or you're dead in the publishing business." But with no other prospects on the horizon, Simon met with the *World*'s three crossword editors and paid them advance royalties of twenty-five dollars each to produce what he and Schuster published as *The Crossword Puzzle Book*. It appeared on April 10, three months after they had formed their firm. It was released under the imprint of the Plaza Publishing Company, a dummy corporation. "We . . . did not want to be typed as game-book publishers at the start," Simon said years later.

Priced at $1.35, with an eraser-topped pencil attached to each copy, the book was launched with a tiny ad on the *World*'s crossword puzzle page— "Ready at Last! The first Crossword Puzzle Book! Why Wait! Order Today!" Purchases were by mail only, and customers were guaranteed their money back "if not 100% satisfied." Orders poured in and three more editions were published within months, these later editions proudly bearing the imprint of Simon & Schuster. By mid-October, four of the country's top five best-selling works of nonfiction were Simon & Schuster crossword puzzle books. On a single December day in 1924 the firm sold nearly 150,000 copies; by Christmas sales had climbed to nearly half a million. Office space was expanded from one room to an entire floor, and then a second floor; and twenty clerks were hired to handle the orders. Thirty more were put on the payroll the next year.

The crossword puzzle became a national mania. A traveler arriving from Europe by sea in 1924 said that nearly every person in a deck chair was busily working on a Simon & Schuster puzzle book. At the end of 1924, the three editors of the first crossword book divided $25,000 in royalties, and Richard Simon and Max Schuster cleared a profit of $100,000. No new publishing house, then or later, started out with such a blaze of success. Max Schuster, who had never done a crossword puzzle in his life, bought a country home. Richard Simon, who enjoyed crossword puzzles but played them poorly, ordered a rack of custom-made suits.

The crossword puzzle craze ended as abruptly as it had begun. While the puzzle books continued to sell steadily, accounting for a million and a half sales by 1934, the "great boom" was over by early 1925. The fifty clerical employees had to be let go and the payroll was cut back to three people: Richard Simon, Max Schuster, and Leon Shimkin, a seventeen-year-old assistant hired in the midst of the crossword frenzy. In 1925, the firm sustained a loss of $25,000 and had acquired the disparaging reputation as a publisher of novelty items. It was also saddled with a sales incentive policy Simon had recently instituted: allowing bookstores to return unsold copies for credit. "Here today, back tomorrow," Alfred Knopf would mordantly describe the new practice that other publishers were forced to adopt to remain competitive.

"In April 1925 the fortunes of the year-old firm of Simon & Schuster were at low ebb," Simon would write decades later. "We were selling practically no books at all, [and] no good manuscripts were coming into the house." The firm was saved, and its image recast, by an obscure professor of philosophy. Sometime in 1925, Max Schuster had come upon a series of *Little Blue Books* on the history of philosophy by Dr. Will Durant, a freelance writer who did double duty as an instructor at Columbia University. Selling for a nickel apiece, the books were published by a tiny press in Girard, Kansas. Schuster secured the copyright to the series and hired Durant to bring the booklets together in a single volume called *The Story of Philosophy*—a "made" book of a very high order. Durant produced a doorstopper of a manuscript, but both Dick Simon and Max Schuster read it with relish. They priced it at a substantial five dollars, and launched it in the spring of 1926 with a high-powered advertising campaign. It was an immediate best-seller, and it had "legs," becoming the third most popular nonfiction title published in the 1920s. Durant followed it with *The Mansions of Philosophy*. With his wife, Ariel, as collaborator, he would devote the remainder of his career as a Simon & Schuster author to an eleven-volume *The Story of Civilization*, one of the most popular works of history ever published.

The ads for Durant's first book were unlike any the industry had yet seen. Most of them covered a full page in newspapers and magazines, and had screaming, tabloid-style headlines. "Richard Simon was one of the first to revolutionize bookselling by employing modern methods of promoting, advertising, merchandizing and marketing literary productions," said *The New York Times*.

Nervous and high-strung, Dick Simon remained the master salesman, while ponderous Max Schuster generated ideas for books, spending hours each day clipping and indexing interesting stories and quotes he came upon in newspapers and magazines, which he filed in a byzantine system only he could fathom. Schuster had a strongly held belief that "you could learn anything, change anything, help yourself ahead in any way merely by reading the right book." This was exhibited in the kind of books he imagined and got others to write—books on how to play tennis, raise a dog, become a dancer, read a book, and stop worrying. The Common Sense Library, it was called. Its running river of self-help volumes sold furiously. "Nobody was ever better at inventing books that filled a *need*," wrote Korda, later editor in chief at Simon & Schuster.

Schuster, whose favorite expression was "I'll give you a definite maybe on that," had a hard time making up his mind, and would run his ideas for books past Simon, a more decisive, if less reflective man. Schuster's insistent question was "Is there a book in it?" Simon's was "Will it sell?" Max is the "spark plug" and Dick the "brake," said a mutual friend.

The partners sold books and recruited writing talent without holding cocktail parties during office hours or treating prospective authors to lunch at the Ritz. Simon did, however, continue the Liveright practice of hiring gorgeous young women as secretaries. In the evenings, Schuster, a bachelor, read at home or dined with friends. Hard-drinking, chain-smoking Simon played contract bridge for high stakes and frequented Manhattan watering holes with his fast-living friends, habits that not even Andrea Louise Heineman, his strong-willed former secretary, could curb after they were married in 1934 and had the first of their four children.*

---

* One of their children is singer Carly Simon.

During business hours, Schuster rarely ventured from the office, even for lunch, while Simon continued to go into the field to test the market. "The best way for anyone to learn the publishing business is to sell books on the road to booksellers," he would tell his staff. He visited bookstores incessantly, seeking advice about what to publish and how to package the product. Carl A. Kroch, president of Kroch's and Brentano's, the largest privately owned bookstore chain in the country in the 1920s, considered Simon "the most innovative publisher" he had ever known. "He had a tremendous influence on the entire industry. It was he who experimented, so successfully, with the odd price for books," selling them, say, for $4.95 and not five dollars, creating the impression that the buyer was getting a bargain. And Simon gave Kroch, the "Baron of Books," advice that he took to heart. People, he claimed, were afraid to go into bookstores, fearing they might say something to a haughty salesman that would make them appear ignorant. "Make them want to come into your store," he told Kroch, "make them feel at ease and welcome."

His concern for the reader carried over into the way he produced books. Simon had bronze desk plaques made for all editors and assistants. Embossed on them were these words: "Give the reader a break." This meant ensuring that every page of every book was written with clarity and concision and had a typeface that made it easy to read. He put postcards in books to elicit responses from readers.

Toward the end of the 1920s the partners began supplementing their Common Sense Library with serious works of fiction and nonfiction, signing up respected writers like John Cowper Powys, Edward Dahlberg, and Alice Duer Miller, and hiring Clifton Fadiman, later head of *The New Yorker*'s book review section, as editor in chief. Unlike Liveright, they kept the list small and treated each title as "a separate business venture." Their advertising budget per book was five to ten times that of most other publishers, but if a book failed to gain traction, they stopped promoting it, never—as the military saying went—reinforcing defeat.

Books with broad popular appeal, however, continued to be the firm's mainstay. "Max and Dick were mercurial geniuses who . . . sensed the emergence of a new audience composed of people who hadn't bought books in the past," Fadiman wrote years later. And they went aggressively after this potential audience with how-to books, as well as vividly written works on travel and adventure. The most controversial of them was *Trader Horn: Being the Life and Works of Alfred Aloysius Horn*. This was a South African ivory trader's tale of dubious reliability that Simon & Schuster published in 1927, only to suffer ridicule when Horn (whose real name was Smith) was brought from Johannesburg to Manhattan to promote the book. A sodden stumblebum with an unruly white beard and Kiplingesque ideas on empire and race, he remained dreadfully drunk the entire time he was in the country. (Ethelreda Lewis, a South African novelist, actually wrote the book.)

Praised in *The New York Times* but lambasted elsewhere as "senile drivel," *Trader Horn* sold 170,000 copies and was made into a feature film that was nominated for the Academy Award for Best Picture in 1931. The book was not one of Schuster's ideas; he and Simon had purchased it on the strength of an enthusiastic foreword by John Galsworthy, who would win the Nobel Prize in Literature in 1932. An embarrassing misstep, it made a fortune for the firm.

"There was electricity in the air," a staffer recalled the atmosphere at Simon & Schuster in those years, "it was fun to come to work, fun to be in the office, and we hated to leave at the end of the day." Max Schuster, a tormented workaholic, was rarely seen in the corridors and hardly knew his own sales staff. Most days, he worked in seclusion in his office, meeting only with Simon, Fadiman, and a few other top staffers. He and Simon collaborated on an advertising column called "From the Inner Sanctum." Appearing twice weekly in *The New York Times*, under Schuster's name, and in *Publishers Weekly*, under Simon's name, it was packed with uncensored inside information on the state of their publishing house, including lists of the firm's worst-selling books. It was one of the most successful advertising and public relations coups in the history of the book trade, one that avoided "blurb-infested" promotional language. "We write as we would talk to friends and acquaintances," said Simon. There was a marked difference, however, between Simon's copy, which was breezy and informal, and Schuster's, which was far more sober. For Max Schuster, all of life was serious business. "He read even the most innocuous memo," writes Korda, "as if it were a fragment of the Dead Sea Scrolls, his lips moving as he mumbled it aloud to himself, his eyes behind thick, old-fashioned, perfectly round horn-rimmed glasses, giving him a certain owl-like look as he searched for hidden meanings, ballpoint pen at the ready, twitching in his right hand ready to scrawl corrections, emendations, and second thoughts in the margin."

Simon kept the office atmosphere light and playful, hiring staff with little or no publishing background, "congenial spirits who knew how to sell books (without necessarily having any inclination to read them)," in Korda's words. He was a risk taker who boldly introduced promotional practices that horrified gray beards at established houses. In 1925, he had put together one of the most sensational promotional campaigns ever mounted for a book. The volume was *Barber Shop Ballads*, edited by an amateur author named Sigmund Spaeth.

Simon had used every medium and outlet available to him: radio, newspapers, magazines, theater, motion pictures, school groups, glee clubs, Rotary, Kiwanis, and Lions clubs. The climactic event was a nationwide contest to determine the champion barbershop quartet. The finals were held at New York's Hippodrome and first prize was a vaudeville contract on the Keith-Orpheum circuit. Gimbels had a big window display of Spaeth's book, and inside the store the author signed copies, along with the jacket of a recording, an "Hour of Barber Shop Ballads," produced and put on the air by WGBS, the radio station owned by Gimbels.

Two years later, Simon used billboards in cities across the country to advertise Will Durant's *The Story of Philosophy.* They were almost as large as the billboard at Fifth Avenue and Forty-second Street that Horace Liveright mounted to promote Emil Ludwig's best-selling biography of Napoleon. Not to be outdone, Alfred Knopf hired a battalion of sandwich-advertising men to hawk his firm's books on Broadway; and in 1928, when Donald Friede left Boni & Liveright to cofound Covici-Friede, with night club–hopping Romanian partner Pascal Covici, he used skywriting to promote a book called *Murder,* sending open-cockpit planes over Manhattan, Brooklyn, and the Bronx.

In 1926, Simon & Schuster, along with other commercial publishers, was provided a vehicle for selling books that involved no financial outlay. In that year, the Book-of-the-Month Club was established, and began the practice of sending members a dozen books a year. Membership increased to over fifty thousand in six months, and the rival Literary Guild was formed the following year. Booksellers screamed in protest, but the bait of a "lump order" of tens of thousands of volumes was too tempting for publishers to refuse.

The two-year period before the Stock Market Crash was a strong time for Simon & Schuster, but it ended in near calamity when it was discovered that one of the firm's top sellers of 1929 was a fraud. Joan Lowell's *The Cradle of the Deep,* promoted in the firm's catalogue as an "unghost-written autobiography" of the beautiful young author's adventures aboard a four-masted schooner, was a nautical hoax. The ship that Joan Lowell had supposedly sailed on had sunk long before she could possibly have set foot on it; and Joan Lowell, purportedly a descendant of the famous Boston Lowells, turned out to be Helen Joan Wagner, a Hollywood bit actress with a lively imagination. The Lowell fiasco, coming on the heels of the *Trader Horn* incident, made Simon & Schuster the "laughing stock of the trade," and briefly took the edge off the partner's "confidence in themselves," wrote *The New Yorker's* Geoffrey T. Hellman. Simon had a nervous breakdown, and the firm lost money in 1930 for the first time in five years.

After publicly admitting they had been "completely taken in," the partners recovered their balance, and had the firm back on solid footing by the end of the year with three sensational sellers: Robert Ripley's *Believe It or Not!*; the English translation of the Austrian author Felix Salten's *Bambi*; and Ernest Dimnet's *The Art of Thinking*—yet another of Max Schuster's self-improvement manuals. But Simon & Schuster kept in print and promoted *The Cradle of the Deep*, this time as a novel, and it continued to sell. "The people who had handed over their money under the impression they were buying the truth remained to cheer the fiction," said one writer.*

In 1930, Richard Simon and Max Schuster relocated their firm to larger quarters at 386 Fourth Avenue, in a Midtown area known as "Publisher's Row," where over 70 percent of all new books in the United States were published. In this tight cultural precinct on or near Fourth Avenue, all but four of the country's twenty or so major trade book publishers had established their headquarters.† Trade book publishers were—as most still are—dependent on the "economies of communication" that went with a Midtown address. As publishing houses became commercial and competitive, they needed to be near the literary agents, advertising agencies, book clubs, magazine and newspaper publishers, radio stations, photographers, manuscript readers, commercial artists, and other enterprises and vendors they depended upon to purchase and promote their products. "The whole publishing business," writes an economic historian, "is one which depends to an extraordinary degree on personal contact and personal acquaintance with the people involved. Contacts of this sort would be difficult to maintain without location in New York." Indeed, it would have been abnormal for an American industry such as this to locate anywhere else but in the idea and media center of the country. But as was the case with the city's garment industry, the production plants and storage houses of the final product—the printing plants and warehouses—came to be located outside the city, where land and labor costs were less expensive than in Manhattan.

---

* In 1957, Richard Simon suffered two heart attacks and resigned from the firm. He sold his stock to Leon Shimkin and Schuster. That same year, Shimkin and Schuster repurchased Simon & Schuster from Marshall Field Enterprises, which had bought it in 1944. In 1966, Schuster sold his half interest in the company to Shimkin and retired to become an independent author and editor. Simon died in 1960, Schuster in 1970.

† The four exceptions were Little, Brown; Houghton Mifflin (Boston); Lippincott (Philadelphia); and Bobbs-Merrill (Indianapolis).

John Tierney of *The New York Times* offers yet another reason why book publishers kept their offices in Midtown Manhattan. "They could have economized long ago," he writes, "by moving their headquarters and letting editors rely on a perfectly adequate information highway for transmitting manuscripts: the postal service." But that would have put them, in the 1920s, far from The Puncheon, the Ritz, and other popular Midtown restaurants and speakeasies where editors and publishers had lunch with literary agents, authors, and movie producers—and where deals were negotiated and made. Men of the world like Simon, Knopf, Cerf, and Liveright wanted to do more than process manuscripts. They wanted "to gossip and hear new ideas," and convince agents and authors that they had the wherewithal to publish their books in style. "New York is the capital of lunch," says Tierney, "and leaving the capital can be risky."

When Richard Simon and Max Schuster moved to their new Midtown address, they were each drawing $60,000 in yearly salary out of the business. This was at a time when few top executives at other publishing houses were making more than $10,000 a year. The partners had accomplished the nearly impossible, becoming personally prosperous in a business in which profits were slim, the market was slight, and the producer had to deal with booksellers, among the most anxious, uncertain, and debt-ridden of American retailers.

Quality was often a casualty. Unlike Horace Liveright in his "days of splendor," Richard Simon and Max Schuster treated most of their books as "pieces of merchandise that can be sold with profit."* By 1934, the tenth anniversary of the firm, the partners had published 251 books, 80 percent of them "made" books. "Out of politeness and a forlorn hope," wrote Geoffrey Hellman, the founding partners assigned a junior editor and a handful of outside assistants to read four thousand unsolicited manuscripts a year. Of these, they "rarely bought more than one."

At Random

By this time, the publishing house Richard Simon's Columbia College contemporary Bennett Cerf had formed with Donald Klopfer was on solid ground. He and Klopfer had an easier time entering the business than Simon and Schuster,

---

* The Simon & Schuster Building, in Rockefeller Center, sits today on the site to which Horace Liveright moved his firm in 1924.

and for a single reason: Horace Liveright's ill-advised decision to sell the Modern Library to Cerf. It was the most catastrophic of a succession of misjudgments that would cause Liveright to lose control of his firm to bean counter Arthur Pell.

"And so I'm off for bed after the most eventful day of my life," Cerf wrote from his cabin on the SS *Aquitania* on the evening of May 20, 1925, bound for Southampton and a restful English vacation after taking "a step that will alter my entire career," he confidently told his diary. That morning Liveright had invited Cerf—tall, bespectacled, and perfectly tailored—to a bon voyage luncheon at Jack & Charlie's Puncheon on West Forty-ninth Street. "My father-in-law is driving me crazy," Liveright confided to Cerf over cocktails. Hermann Elsas wanted an accounting of the money he had loaned his son-in-law to establish himself in the publishing business, and Liveright said he had no idea "where it is. Oh, how I'd like to pay him off and get rid of him," he told Cerf. At this point, Cerf said blandly, "One very easy way to pay him off, Horace, is to sell me the Modern Library."

The Modern Library served as Boni & Liveright's backlist, as enduring titles are called; and with sales of the firm's trade books fluctuating wildly, Liveright needed the financial stability that steady sales of the classics—over 300,000 copies a year—provided. Liveright was perfectly aware of this, and knew full well that the Modern Library was "one of the great properties in the whole publishing business," but, impulsively, he asked Cerf what he would be willing to pay for it. Before the second round of drinks arrived, they had agreed on a price: $210,000. And with that, Cerf set off for home to pack for his trip; the papers would be signed when he returned from abroad.

When business manager Julian Messner learned what Liveright had done, he pleaded with him not to sign the contract. But Liveright was adamant. Cerf's offer would get him out of the financial "hole" he had dug for himself with his improvident spending on Broadway productions. Besides, he had given his word to Cerf, and a handshake for Liveright was as good as a signed agreement. Messner's only hope was that Cerf would be unable to raise the money.

But Cerf came from a wealthy family. With funds from his own trust fund and a loan from his uncle, Herbert Wise, a Wall Street plunger, he knew he could come up with half of Liveright's asking price. To raise the other half he counted on Klopfer, a twenty-three-year-old Williams College dropout he had met while both of them were working on Wall Street. Klopfer was treasurer of his stepfather's big diamond-cutting business, work he loathed. He and Cerf had been dreaming about getting into the book business for over a year. The night Cerf left for Europe, Klopfer came down to the Chelsea piers to see him off. Here was the opportunity they had been waiting for, Cerf excitedly told him; $100,000 would make Klopfer an equal partner in the venture. Three weeks later, when Cerf returned from England, Klopfer informed him he had sold his interest in the United Diamond Works and was eager to make the leap into publishing.

On August 1, 1925, the partners—with Cerf as president and Klopfer as vice president—set up their new business, Modern Library, Inc., in two rooms on the ninth floor of a loft building on West Forty-fifth Street. In their first year they sold 385,000 copies of the Modern Library volumes, more than in any year under Liveright's indifferent management of the series. The bulk of the sales was to the college market, but occasionally they'd get big orders from department stores like Macy's, prompting them "to dance around with glee." They expanded the series, and by 1927 they had recouped their entire investment and repaid Uncle Herbert's loan. "The minute we gave our full attention to it, the series simply boomed," said Cerf, who had an unusual talent for both commerce and culture.

Like Simon and Schuster, Cerf and Klopfer were opposites who complemented one another. Cerf was a pleasure-loving bon vivant; Klopfer was quiet and deliberative, as "diffident of the limelight" as Cerf was partial to it. Cerf collected jokes, played silly tricks on Klopfer and other friends, and was given to outlandish statements. "Everyone has a streak of pure unadulterated ham," he said on one occasion. "Many won't admit it. I revel in it." He and Klopfer sat at desks facing each other and had only three employees: a secretary-bookkeeper and two shipping clerks. In their three decades together, they would never have a serious disagreement about policy, or "anything else of importance," Klopfer would write later. Initially they did their own selling. "When we went into a store . . . the bookseller knew he was meeting the actual publishers. They liked that," said Cerf, who drew "his nourishment from human contacts." They also got their books into chain stores, which Liveright never bothered with, and even supermarkets. Aside from selling and overseeing production, there was "very little work to do," Cerf said later. Most of the time they were finished by noon. In the afternoon they'd play backgammon or golf, or go to baseball games. After dark, Cerf hit the town, known everywhere in Manhattan for his expensive table tastes.

With the business almost running itself, Cerf saw no reason why he and Klopfer should not enjoy themselves more on the job. He purchased a wine-making machine and had it installed in the office on a Friday afternoon. It was a wickedly hot weekend, and when the partners returned to work on Monday they found the office covered with grape juice. The machine had exploded.

Publishing the Modern Library "was a joy ride," Cerf recalled, "easy living," but it began to pall. "There was no great excitement, and I had inherited some of this restless excitement from Horace Liveright, the excitement of publishing original works. In 1927, he and Klopfer set out in this direction, cautiously, tentatively. Both were collectors of posh limited editions and admired the handsomely packaged books of England's Nonesuch Press. On one of his regular trips to Britain, Cerf charmed Sir Francis Meynell, editor of Nonesuch Press, to hand over to him, for a price, the American rights to his books. Cerf and Klopfer then chose "at random" the volumes they planned to publish in limited editions. And that's how Cerf came up with a name for the partners' new publishing concern: Random House. The commercial artist Rockwell Kent was in the office the day Cerf first suggested the name, and offered to draw what became the firm's famous trademark, which he executed in five minutes flat. The colophon—a large English-style cottage—debuted in January 1927 on the cover of an advertising broadside listing the first seven limited editions to be published that year under the Random House imprint. The first of them was a beautifully bound edition of Voltaire's *Candide*, illustrated by Kent. It was soon followed by other limited editions acquired from small American presses, among them Melville's *Benito Cereno* and Whitman's *Leaves of Grass*. Random House, today the world's largest trade book publisher, was launched without a single original title on its list, or a single living author.*

By 1928, the firm had outgrown its Forty-fifth Street office and moved that year to larger, freshly designed quarters at 20 East Fifty-seventh Street. It was there, in 1929, that Sir Francis Meynell visited Cerf and Klopfer. Both partners played the stock market, and did their trading through an office located on the floor below them. On their way to lunch one day, they took Meynell down to the trading room and convinced him to buy two hundred shares of a promising-looking stock. A few hours later, Meynell sold his shares at a profit of $2,000. "Can one do this during the lunch hour every day?" he asked.

When the stock market collapsed, so did the market for Random House's deluxe collector's editions. But the partners had the Modern Library, "so even during the Depression, we were sitting in clover," Cerf recalls. "We had cheap books." This wasn't enough, however. In 1933, Random House had to turn from rare books to trade books in order to survive. "It was," said Richard Simon, "quite a debut." In 1933, Cerf and Klopfer published a volume of poems by Robinson Jeffers, along with the plays of Eugene O'Neill, a friend of Cerf's who was anxious to switch publishers after Horace Liveright died earlier that

---

* Random House is today Penguin Random House.

year. That same year, Cerf concocted a plan to make James Joyce's *Ulysses* publishable in the United States. He imported a copy and notified federal authorities. When U.S. customs officials seized the novel, he brought action in federal court. His attorney, Morris Ernst, won a landmark decision in December 1933. The sympathetic judge, who read the novel twice, lifted the ban on it. That week, Random House published an unexpurgated *Ulysses* in a Modern Library edition, gaining Cerf a reputation in the industry—with Horace Liveright—as a guardian of free speech.

Cerf was a publicity hound the equal of Liveright, but he was more attentive to the market than his mentor. While cultivating illustrious authors like William Faulkner, another Boni & Liveright breakaway, he signed up dozens of writers who appealed to transient public taste. And he brought in authors slowly, mindful of expanding too aggressively during the Depression years. Until the 1940s, Random House remained a conservatively run operation sustained by the continued success and phenomenal expansion in the 1930s—to 550 volumes—of the series Horace Liveright had handed Bennett Cerf on a platter.[*]

---

[*] Cerf remained president of Random House until 1965 and served as its chairman from then to 1970. He died on August 27, 1971, at his home in Mount Kisco, New York. At the time of his death he was the best-known American publisher, his public visibility enhanced by his best-selling joke books and literary anthologies; his joke column, syndicated to 660 newspapers; his popular lectures; and, above all, by his sixteen years—beginning in 1951—as a regular panelist on the weekly television quiz show *What's My Line?* At times, he said, "I have to *remind* people that I'm a publisher." Geoffrey T. Hellman, "Publisher—II: Big Day for Random," TNY 35 (May 16, 1959): 62.

BLUE SKIES

Blue skies
Smiling at me
Nothing but blue skies
Do I see

—IRVING BERLIN, 1926

The Avalanche

Bennett Cerf remained close to Liveright after he left his firm. "I was sort of his Boswell—I followed him around everywhere," Cerf recalled toward the end of his own life. "He was so amusing and . . . was one of the most colorful people in the world." As the decade came to a close, however, Liveright began to change, growing more irritable, anxious, and insecure. He knew Arthur Pell was conspiring in the shadows to take over his publishing house, yet he was too preoccupied with the theater and the stock market to mount a sustained counteroffensive.

For Horace Liveright, publishing and market speculation were interlinked, as theater and stock gambling were for Florenz Ziegfeld. Both played the market to fund their extravagant artistic enterprises, winning and losing with astounding nonchalance, their irrational exuberance sustained by an inner voice that said blue skies were just ahead. As a publisher, Liveright operated like a "pyramiding speculator," wrote Donald Friede. "Tomorrow would be bonanza day. So why not spend today?"

"What brought Horace low," said Louis Kronenberger, "was not women [or] drink"—or even his "theatrical enterprises." He would probably have survived failure in all these facets of his unruly life had it not been for the Stock Market Crash.

Up to early 1929, Liveright had made some money on the market, small, spirit-lifting gains that were outbalanced by larger loses. Then, in midsummer 1929, the market turned permanently against him. He remained a bullish player, however, for stock prices reached new highs in those months, giving him hope that his own portfolio would rise with the tide. "I'm a stubborn fool and realize it," he wrote a business acquaintance on August 29, two months, to the day, before the great October collapse wiped him out.

Florenz Ziegfeld, with more money to put at risk, was a far bigger stock plunger than Liveright. In the summer of 1927, with *Rio Rita* selling out the house every night, he began speculating heavily in the market, eventually buying over $2 million of stock. Ziegfeld concealed these transactions from his wife. By this time, Billie Burke had gotten her husband out of his Palm Beach gambling club by "strategy and tears, but Wall Street was something I knew utterly nothing about," she admitted some time later. "Flo was in it far deeper than I had any idea."

What hurt Ziegfeld was *how* he played the market: "Flo never, to my knowledge, *invested* in anything, was never concerned with *yield*. He was interested only in *coups*," wrote Billie. This was in character and easily understandable. Like Liveright, his shoot-for-the-moon attitude was behind nearly every one of his great leaps in life. For Florenz Ziegfeld, as for Horace Liveright, not to gamble was to lose.

Ziegfeld began to get nervous about his Wall Street holdings at exactly the time Liveright did: in the summer of 1929. While vacationing at Camp Patricia, his Canadian getaway, he sent one of his employees in an old motorboat to the local telegraph office with a message addressed to E. F. Hutton, instructing his brokers to sell all his holdings. Minutes after the boat left the dock, Ziegfeld's visiting friend, newspaper publisher Paul Block, who was making a killing on the market, talked him out of it. Ziegfeld sent a messenger in a speedboat to intercept the telegram.

On the morning of October 29—Black Tuesday—Hutton tried to get in touch with Ziegfeld and urge him to sell when stock prices began plummeting uncontrollably, but he was in small claims court, contesting a bill for an advertising signboard he had found unsatisfactory. To solidify his case, he had brought along his entire office retinue to testify, everyone who would have been available to take the call back at the theater except the telephone operator—and she was sick and had failed to report for work. When Ziegfeld came home to Burkeley Crest that evening, after losing over a million dollars in the time it took him to dispute a $1,600 bill, he sat on the edge of Billie's bed and began to sob uncontrollably. "I'm through," he moaned, "Nothing can save me."

Days later, his spirits improved. He had lost a fortune several times at the gambling tables; this setback was simply "another turn of the wheel." He would roll up his sleeves and start anew. "This trait," said Eddie Cantor, "stayed with him till the end."

The Broadway musicals he continued to produce were failures, every one of them. So he tried Hollywood. After overseeing the film rendition of *Whoopee!*, he wanted to stay in California and break into movies, but even his close friends in the film business, chief among them Samuel Goldwyn, were wary of his reputation for putting on prohibitively costly productions. "Daddy and Mr. Goldwyn would talk for hours . . ." Patty recalled in her memoirs, "but they were worlds apart in their outlooks. Mr. Goldwyn had his eye on the penny, Daddy on the effect."

Whoopee!, filmed in early Technicolor, made millions, but Ziegfeld's creditors swept in and seized the proceeds. "Up to then, his millionaire friends had come to his aid," recalled Bernard Sobel, "but this time they also went down with the avalanche." Back in New York, the theater business was so bad that, at one point, the Ziegfeld Theatre was without a show. "Snow covered the roof, and the windows were white with frost," reported Sobel. "The glorifier walked into his office wearing his handsome beaver-lined coat, still an impressive picture of prosperity. Yet, oddly enough, instead of removing the heavy coat, he kept it on all day long. He had to do so . . . to keep warm, for there was no fire in the furnace and he didn't have enough money to buy coal."

Billie handed over her savings to her husband, but it wasn't enough to keep the wolves at bay. He and Billie were forced to mortgage Burkeley Crest, release all but two of the staff, and surrender part of their personal possessions to the courts. (Camp Patricia was later sold at a sheriff's sale for $2,500. With help from friends, Billie held on to Burkeley Crest until 1940.) To keep the family afloat, Billie went back to work full-time, on the stage and in Hollywood, in talking pictures. When she went to the West Coast, she took fourteen-year-old Patty with her and rented a modest house in Santa Monica.

For a teasing moment, Ziegfeld seemed to be on the rebound. He decided to revive the *Follies,* and found a financial backer, the brother of his old partner and nemesis Abe Erlanger. The show opened in July 1931 at the Ziegfeld Theatre—the only *Follies* to ever play there—but it was slammed by critics and played to half-empty houses. About this time, Ziegfeld began dodging process servers by sneaking out of the back exits of his theater.

The next year, at age sixty-five, living alone at Burkeley Crest, and occasionally at the Warwick Hotel, entertained by prostitutes and chorus girls,

Ziegfeld borrowed $100,000 from Eddie Cantor, and even more, perhaps, from mobsters Dutch Schultz and Waxey Gordon. He invested everything in *Hot-Cha!*, another lavish musical comedy. When the show failed, Ziegfeld's mental bank was empty; he had run out of ideas. He blamed his demise, fairly enough, on the Depression and competition from radio and movies, but there was also his sudden inability to connect with audiences. Exhausted mentally and physically, he came down with a debilitating respiratory virus. When his costume designer stopped by the Warwick to collect a loan, he was shocked to see the Great Glorifier propped up on pillows, his "smile wan . . . his voice weak."

That April, Ziegfeld made his radio debut, starring in an embarrassingly weak show called *The Follies of the Air*, and while still in precarious health, he staged a revival of *Show Boat*, this time with Paul Robeson as Joe, singing "Ol' Man River."* The show, featuring most of the original cast and subsidized by Ziegfeld's rich and generous friend A. C. Blumenthal, played to sold-out houses. "Ziegfeld finally had a hit," writes Ethan Mordden, "even if it was the same one he'd had before." But again, the creditors came calling, demanding an accounting. Defeated, but with the embers still glowing faintly, Ziegfeld wrote from his sickbed to Eddie Cantor. "Would like to do another show with you before I pass on."

In June, Ziegfeld's lung condition grew worse, and he was confined to Burkeley Crest, in the care of nurses. "Doctor claims it's life or death for me," he wrote his business manager. Alarmed, Billie came east and brought him back with her to California in a private rail car paid for by his sister Louise. In excruciating pain from the advanced stages of pleurisy, he was only partly conscious most of the way.

His California doctors ordered complete rest, but that July he ran up a telegraph bill of $6,000 (more than $75,000 today). He was most interested in keeping in touch with his friend David Sarnoff, who had shown him an early version of television. Television, he told Patty, would reduce his casting costs, allowing him to review future Ziegfeld Girls on a home screen. It was painful for his wife and daughter to watch his unavailing efforts to hold on to all he had been. "The élan was gone. . . . It was as if a great tree were toppling," Billie recalled, "and I was counting stray leaves."

On July 17, 1932, Billie admitted him, in gravely weakened condition, to Cedars of Lebanon Hospital in Los Angeles. Four days later, she received word that the phone company was about to cut off service in the Ziegfeld Theatre.

---

* In 1929, Universal Studios had made a film version of *Show Boat*.

The next evening, while she was working late at the sound studio, a call came in. She was to come to the hospital at once. Billie reached his bedside two minutes too late. The time of death was 10:31 P.M.—almost exactly the moment that a Broadway audience was rising from its seats to give *Show Boat* a tremendous ovation.

While Billie and Patricia were in seclusion at Will Rogers's ranch outside Los Angeles, Mayor Jimmy Walker, with his political career about to end that summer, reached them by telephone. He wanted to stage a city ceremony for Flo, a day of remembrance for the master of spectacle. Billie politely declined. Nor would there be a big Manhattan funeral. There was a small, private ceremony in the chapel of a North Hollywood mortuary. Will Rogers delivered the eulogy. What he failed to say—what he knew was true—was more important than what he actually said. Florenz Ziegfeld, like so many others of that tumultuous time, had been inspired by his adopted city to test the limits of the possible. "Anything can happen now . . . anything at all," Gatsby's friend Nick Carraway thinks on crossing into Manhattan over the Queensboro Bridge.

After the burial, Billie hired a private policeman to guard her husband's office in the Ziegfeld Theatre. He was stationed there so that creditors would not seize the glass elephants Ziegfeld kept on a prominent table—their trunks raised high, a sign of life and hope.

The Great Ziegfeld, once master of his world, had no physical assets: no real estate, stock, jewelry, or automobiles. His estate yielded less than $13,000 in cash; Billie was left with over $280,000 in unpaid debts.

A few weeks after the funeral, Billie showed up on the set of the movie she had been making. "This seemed like a hard and bitter thing to do at the time," she wrote later. "It was not, though, a matter of 'the show must go on.' . . . I was enormously fortunate that I had a job."*

Heartbreak

Horace Liveright's decline was more precipitous than Ziegfeld's. He had driven his publishing firm to the brink of bankruptcy before the market collapse. After that hard blow, drink and dissipation did him in.

Liveright's profligacy made it easy for Arthur Pell to gain control of the firm. While Liveright was on the slide, beginning, most seriously, in 1928, when his

---

* Ziegfeld was buried at Forest Lawn in Los Angeles. In 1974, his daughter, Patty, transferred his remains to Kensico Cemetery in Valhalla, New York, not far from Burkeley Crest, and next to Billie, who died in 1970 at the age of eighty-five. Patricia, married with children, died in 2008 at the age of ninety-one.

musical comedy *The Dagger and the Rose* closed before reaching Broadway, a setback that cost Liveright nearly $100,000, Pell had begun buying Liveright's shares in the company. This kept some of Liveright's creditors at bay, but at a steep personal cost: Pell soon owned the business, and Liveright was reduced to a mere figurehead. A spent force, he didn't even control his salary.

Liveright was forced to lay off his Japanese cook and move from his Midtown penthouse to a cramped suite in a nondescript hotel on West Fifty-eighth Street. His children, Herman, a student at the University of Wisconsin, and Lucy, who was residing with her mother in Westchester, continued to visit him regularly, painful exposure to their father's radically reduced circumstances. With his mistress, Dorothy Peterson, in Hollywood making pictures, his new apartment became a catch basin for a group of alcohol-soaked acquaintances, "non-paying lodgers and boarders," Liveright called these parasites.

After two more of his plays failed to make it to Broadway, Liveright tried to begin anew in Hollywood. He and Jessie Lasky, head of production at Paramount, had remained friends after Lasky purchased the film rights to *An American Tragedy*, and in the summer of 1930 Lasky hired him as an advisor on the film. When Lasky decided to scrap the project, considering Dreiser's novel too critical of conventional morality, Liveright was let go. He was picked up, but only for six months, by Pathé Studios "to assist in the production of films," an interesting job description but a position that put him in a "cubbyhole on the back lot," where he was ignominiously ignored. Lillian Hellman, a reader for Sam Goldwyn, occasionally ran into Liveright at Hollywood parties. "Some of the old glamour was there," she wrote in her memoirs. "But . . . the pride was breaking."

After being released by Pathé, Liveright returned to New York. He wanted Dorothy to accompany him, but she refused, sensing that he had no future. "As I held Dorothy in my arms and kissed her good-bye, it seemed to be a good-bye indeed, and not merely *au revoir*. Of course, one never knows." It was the last time they would set eyes on each other.

While Liveright was in Hollywood, Arthur Pell had moved Boni & Liveright from West Forty-eighth Street to a sterile new office building just off Fifth Avenue. The old brownstone, along with its neighbors, was marked for demolition, to create space for Rockefeller Center. "Moving to Forty-seventh Street," wrote Louis Kronenberger, "inaugurated the Pell regime—practical, prosaic, no-nonsense, quite unsuited to party-giving. . . . I remember Pell's telling me soon after we moved that I should be in the office by ten o'clock, and my thinking this sheer despotism."

With little else to do, Liveright would stop by the new office to visit Kronenberger, Julian Messner, and other friends from better times. On one of his visits, he looked unusually "tired and worn." The friend he had come to see had stepped out, and he waited patiently in the crowded reception room. Pell spotted him and said in a harsh voice that carried, "Horace, I don't think you'd better come in anymore; it doesn't look well for business." The man who had once ruled the place like a rajah didn't even answer.

But on other occasions, he "played . . . out his string like a gentleman," Bennett Cerf recalled. At the lunch hour, he could be found at the Algonquin, nervously tapping his long cigarette holder on the table, "a mere shadow of his former jaunty self, announcing ambitious theatrical projects," while everyone knew it was "a heartbreaking farce." With Dorothy lost to him, he found another woman, wildly seductive Elise Bartlett, a divorced actress who had appeared in a minor role in the Universal production of Ziegfeld's *Show Boat*. They married in haste in December 1931, and divorced five months later.

Broke and alone, Liveright tried to keep up pretenses. He had only a single, dark blue suit, which he wore every day. Manuel Komroff, a former Boni & Liveright editor, and presently a budding novelist and playwright, found him in his apartment one day—the door had been left half open—sitting with his blue serge jacket on the desk in front of him, a bottle of fountain pen ink and a rag in hand, trying to cover a tiny spot on the sleeve. The landlord of an apartment hotel he had been evicted from for failure to pay rent had confiscated most of his wardrobe. Tommy Smith and others offered to help with small loans, but Liveright proudly resisted, insisting he was on the rebound.

In January 1933, at age forty-nine, he came down with pneumonia and was hospitalized. It was only then that doctors discovered that he was suffering from emphysema. When Liveright was released from the hospital, Komroff convinced him to write his autobiography, which Richard Simon bought for $2,000 without reading a word, a splendid gesture by a lasting friend.* That July, Liveright began dictating the book to a stenographer provided by Messner. Late one morning, Sherwood Anderson paid a visit. Liveright was still in his pajamas, and sprawled all over the apartment were partygoers from the night before, still drinking. "Horace was sitting on a couch and the morning sun was streaming through a window." He was "very pale and very thin," and his eyes no longer glistened like black diamonds. "He was I think a little ashamed of his surroundings," Anderson recalled. "He arose and went with me into a hallway." Then, unexpectedly, he put his arm around Anderson's shoulders and said in a barely audible voice, "Well, what the hell, Sherwood, I've sunk."

---

* Liveright's autobiography, "The Turbulent Years," was never published. Along with Komroff's unpublished essay, "The Liveright Story," it is in the Manuel Komroff Papers at Columbia University.

A week later, he was hospitalized to have his lungs drained; when he was released, he resumed work on the book. "If I get well and strong pronto the book will be absolutely finished on contract time," he bravely wrote a friend.

Horace Liveright died three days later, on September 24, 1933. His daughter, Lucy, was with him at the end; Herman was away at school.* Liveright left an estate "not worth more than five hundred dollars," according to Herman Liveright, all of it in personal property. There was no will.

A scattering of his former friends and authors gathered a few days later in a nondenominational chapel to honor the man who had transformed American publishing, dead at forty-nine. Otto Kahn was conspicuously missing. Upton Sinclair delivered an unmemorable eulogy in a low, stumbling voice. It was Bennett Cerf's farewell, circulated later in *Publishers Weekly*, which would be remembered. It was in places harsh and unfairly cruel, but showed a deep appreciation of Liveright's legacy. Cerf had resented his mentor's extreme self-absorption. Liveright was, he said, ungrateful to "the people who really cared for him. All he wanted around him was people who would inflate his ego and echo his judgments." Yet Cerf professed "a deep love for this man" whose "reckless generosity" he, for one, "could not resist." The single voice of a firm that was both a "madhouse" and a focus of excellence, a million-dollar concern that was everlastingly insolvent, Horace Liveright was "a publisher whose like will never be seen again."

"It was all rather crazy, rather splendid," Sherwood Anderson wrote of Liveright and his times. "I have always thought, since the man's death, that too much emphasis has been put on the reckless splendor of the man rather than on his never failing generosity and his real belief in men of talent."

The forces that brought down Horace Liveright were those that brought the Jazz Age to "a spectacular death in October, 1929," in F. Scott Fitzgerald's words. Liveright and Ziegfeld, along with Fitzgerald, contributed greatly to the unrestrained extravagance of that age, with its near complete disregard of inhibitions. But the 1920s were, in Manhattan, far more than the "bleary-eyed" spree Fitzgerald chronicled in "The Crack-Up," his sullen "self-autopsy." No other decade in the life of that city was more exuberantly alive or enduringly creative.

---

* Bennett Cerf tried to buy the firm's assets for Random House, but Arthur Pell refused and sold the rights to dozens of Liveright's authors. In the 1960s, W. W. Norton took over what remained of the list. The Liveright imprint was recently revived there.

ACKNOWLEDGMENTS

The inspiration for this book, along with its title, came from a special edition of *American Heritage*, "Supreme City: New York in the 1920s," created and edited in 1988 by my old friend and editor at the magazine, Richard F. Snow. "The editors hope this record of a lost city will remind those who were there how good it was," Snow wrote in his captivating introduction to that edition, "and suggest to those who have come after what it was like to be part of that hectic, crowded decade when the blazing towers of the Manhattan skyline were a beacon signaling the world that America had come of age."

When I read those words I had just completed a biography of a great New Yorker, Lewis Mumford, who suggested that I write a biography of a city. My next book, *City of the Century*, was a prose portrait of nineteenth-century Chicago, and it was to be the first volume of a "tale of three cities" at pivotal moments in their development: Chicago in the 1890s, New York in the 1920s, and Los Angeles in the 1950s. Perhaps someday I'll complete the trilogy.

This book is based primarily on records from the period: newspaper and magazine accounts, autobiographies, memoirs, oral histories, published and unpublished letters, and myriad manuscript collections. But I had at my elbow the entire time I wrote it two indispensable contemporary volumes: *The Encyclopedia of New York City*, edited by the city's outstanding historian, Kenneth T. Jackson, and *New York, 1930: Architecture and Urbanism Between the Two World Wars*, an exhaustively researched, beautifully composed work by Robert A. M. Stern, Gregory Gilmartin, and Thomas Mellins. No author taking on New York in these years could have better sources at hand.

Ken Jackson got me started on this book by inviting me to join his stimulating seminar on New York City at Columbia University. Distance and a tight schedule prevented me from becoming a regular participant, but I profited immensely from the sessions I was able to attend.

I am fortunate to teach at a liberal arts college that prizes research as well as teaching. The reference librarians at Lafayette College's Skillman Library— especially Terese Heidenwolf, Lujuan Xu, and Kylie Bailin—helped me track down obscure books and articles and fact-check countless sources. No one at Skillman was more helpful than Karen Haduck, who searched and ordered more than 3,000 books and articles I either needed or thought I needed in my research.

Lafayette College, through a program called Excel, headed by Dean John Meier, provided me with a passel of excellent student researchers, chief among them: Margarita Karasoulas, Christy Fic, Hannah Finegold, Meredith Castor, Caroline Bailey, Emily Caracandas, Megan Tuttle, Tyler Bamford, Sara Nusbaum, Sam Griffith, Sean Grim, and Adam Rabin. Margarita, Christy, and Hannah were there at the start, and were inspirational; Tyler and Adam were tremendously committed group leaders from the midpoint to the end of the project. After going on to graduate work in history, Meredith Castor continued as my principal copy editor. Her knowledge of grammar is unassailable. Amazingly proficient Sean Grim was a great assistance with the photographs, helping me to find them, chose them, and order them.

I am grateful for the assistance and generosity of colleagues and staff at a number of archives, museums, and libraries, including the New York Public Library; Columbia University's Oral History Collection; the Rare Books and Manuscripts Library at Columbia University; the Manuscript Division of the Library of Congress; the National Archives in College Park, Maryland; the New-York Historical Society; the Skyscraper Museum; the Donnelly Library at Lake Forest College; the New York City Municipal Archives; the David Sarnoff Library; and the Rare Book and Manuscript Library, University of Pennsylvania. Special thanks to Ken Cobb at the Municipal Archives and Marilyn Kushner at the New-York Historical Society.

My son Greg, a New York enthusiast, helped with the research, and my granddaughter, Alyssa Miller, of Moravian College, provided expert clerical assistance.

Gina Maccoby, my longtime friend and literary agent, read the book from its inception and offered searching criticism and greatly appreciated encouragement. She is a big mind, with a big heart.

Bob Bender has been my editor since the mid-1990s. I have published five books with him, but he was never more helpful than with this one. He had the terrifying advantage of being a native New Yorker and a lifetime student of his city's history. But he never lorded it over me.

Bob's assistant, Johanna Li, was my lifeline. She had her hand in every aspect of this project and handled everything, every petty detail, every major crisis, with immeasurable competence and composure. My copy editors Fred Chase and Lisa Healy are as good as they get in their trade. I owe a special debt to Fred, whom I have worked with before. He is a master, incomparably good.

My wife, Rose, a terrific copy editor herself, read the book and offered sharply observant suggestions. She was there at every stage of this project—a book eight years in the making—keeping me grounded and providing emotional support. She is my anchor.

NOTES

Abbreviations Used in Notes

NYT   *New York Times*

NYW   *New York World*

NYP   *New York Post*

DN   *New York Daily News*

HT   *New York Herald Tribune*

TNY   *The New Yorker*

ENYC   *The Encyclopedia of New York City*, edited by Kenneth T. Jackson

NR   *The New Republic*

CCOH   Columbia Center for Oral History, Columbia University Libraries

PREFACE

PAGE

  xi   *"the tempo"*: F. Scott Fitzgerald, *The Crack-Up,* edited by Edmund Wilson (NY: New Directions, 1993), 18, 30.

PROLOGUE: THE JIMMY WALKER ERA

1   *"Jimmy Walker somehow"*: Gene Fowler, *Beau James: The Life and Times of Jimmy Walker* (NY: Viking, 1949), 354.

1   *"loved so well"*: NYT, November 21, 1946.

1   *The Great Altar*: NYT, November 19, 1946.

2   *"were people of importance"*: NYT, November 22, 1946.

2   *"New York is the hub"*: Arthur Daley, "Sport Loses a Firm Friend," NYT, November 20, 1946.

2   *"He'd duck"*: Ibid.

2   *"a sport in which"*: Fowler, *Beau James*, 180.

3   *"never did he deliver"*: Daley, "Sport Loses," NYT.

3   *"Joe, you have laid"*: Ibid.

3   *"[To] we hicks"*: Red Smith, "As He Seemed to a Hick," in Phillip Lopate, ed., *Writing New York: A Literary Anthology* (NY: Library of America, 1998), 687–88.

3   *Walker's "virtues"*: Milton MacKaye, *The Tin Box Parade* (NY: McBride, 1934), 3–4.

4   *"few men"*: NYT, November 19, 1946.

4 *People pressed in close:* NYT, November 22, 1946.

4 *"beneficences":* George Walsh, *Gentleman Jimmy Walker: Mayor of the Jazz Age* (NY: Praeger, 1974), 341.

5 *"the greatest mayor":* Quoted in ibid., 339.

5 *"He is still slim":* S. J. Woolf, "Jimmy Walker: Toastmaster to Our Town," NYT, April 8, 1945.

5 *"in direct denial":* Walsh, *Gentleman,* 340.

6 *"You tell him Jimmy":* NYT, May 26, 1932; DN, May 26–27, 1932.

6 *"was never personally dishonest":* Edward J. Flynn, *You're the Boss* (NY: Viking, 1947), 52–53.

6 *"No one can buy or sell":* NYT, November 24, 1946.

6 *"I knew how to say 'no'":* Fowler, *Beau James,* 92.

6 *"wrong dollar to":* William R. Conklin, "Manhattan Machine," in *We Saw It Happen: The News Behind the News That's Fit to Print; Thirteens Correspondent of the New York Times,* edited by Hanson W. Baldwin and Shepard Stone (NY: Simon & Schuster, 1938), 271.

6 *"No man could have":* Fowler, *Beau James,* 91.

7 *they advised:* Conklin, "Manhattan Machine," in Baldwin and Stone, eds., *We Saw,* 271.

7 Daily News *straw poll:* DN, May 20–22, 1945; NYT, May 22, 1945.

7 *"the living symbol":* NYT, November 20, 1946; Warren Moscow, *What Have You Done for Me Lately? The Ins and Outs of New York City Politics* (Englewood Cliffs, NJ: Prentice Hall, 1967), 23.

8 *"The great basis":* Alva Johnston, "The Jimmy Walker Era," *Vanity Fair* (December 1932): 41.

8 *"bond of sympathy":* Ibid.

9 *"the embodiment of New York's":* Ibid., 68.

9 *"This town ain't":* Thomas J. Fleming, "Was It Ever Fun Being Mayor?," *New York* (November 10, 1969): 37.

9 *"bringing shame":* Moscow, *What,* 24.

9 *"would no more":* Conklin, "Manhattan Machine," in Baldwin and Stone, eds., *We Saw,* 273.

10 *"Not only in official life":* Quoted in Walsh, *Gentleman,* 331.

10 *"charged with meaning":* Conklin, "Manhattan Machine," in Baldwin and Stone, eds., *We Saw,* 273.

10 *John Curry had an idea:* Ibid., 273–74; Moscow, *What,* 24–25.

CHAPTER ONE: A TEST FOR TAMMANY

PAGE

13 "Tammany today stands": NYW, January 1, 1926.

13 *"a noisy, joyous gathering":* HT, January 2, 1926.

13 *"matinee idol":* Fowler, *Beau James,* 19.

14 *Walker vowed:* NYT, August 19, September 22, 1925, January 22, 1926.

14 *world's largest rapid transit system:* Clifton Hood, *722 Miles: The Building of the Subways and How They Transformed New York* (Baltimore: Johns Hopkins University Press edition, 2004; originally published by Simon & Schuster, 1993), 114–15.

14 *"cut off his right arm"*: NYT, August 8, 1925.

15 *form of urban planning*: Adna F. Weber, "Rapid Transit and the Housing Problem," *Municipal Affairs* 6 (Fall 1902): 408–17.

15 *most congested urban places*: Nathan Kantrowitz, "Population," in ENYC, 920–23.

15 *"haphazard and piecemeal"*: NYW, December 11, 1925, January 8, 1926.

15 *"City Plan"*: NYT, November 2, 1925.

15 *"the lowest tax rate possible"*: NYT, August 19, 1925.

15 *"The labors of Hercules"*: NYT, August 20, 1925.

15 *"Tammany through and through"*: "Jimmy Walker," *Time* (January 11, 1926): 10.

15 *Almost every appointed city official*: Joseph McGoldrick, "Our American Mayors, XII: 'Jimmy' Walker," *National Municipal Review* 17 (October 1928): 569.

16 *The Society of St. Tammany*: For the history of Tammany, see especially Alfred Connable and Edward Silberfarb, *Tigers of Tamanny: Nine Men Who Ran New York* (NY: Holt, Rinehart & Winston, 1967); and Martin Shefter, "The Emergence of the Political Machine: An Alternative View," in *Theoretical Perspectives on Urban Politics*, edited by Willis D. Hawley and Michael Lipsky (Englewood Cliffs, NJ: Prentice Hall, 1976).

16 *Tammany fished for votes*: Robert Pecorella, *Community Power in a Postreform City: Politics in New York City* (Armonk, NY: M. E. Sharpe, 1994), 39.

16 *African American members*: Warren Moscow, *What*, 134.

17 *"ruled supreme"*: NYW, January 2, 1926.

17 *"A New Tammany"*: NYW, November 1, 1925.

17 *"have ideas of their own"*: Nancy Joan Weiss, *Charles Francis Murphy, 1858–1924: Respectability and Responsibility in Tammany Politics* (Northampton, MA: Smith College, 1968), 76.

17 *"as much at home"*: Joseph McGoldrick, "The New Tammany," *The American Mercury* 15 (September 1928): 3.

18 *"greatest opportunity in its history"*: HT, January 2, 2008.

18 *"Tammany today stands"*: NYW, January 1, 1926.

18 *"I have determined"*: NYT, April 26, 1926.

18 *a city scandal*: HT, January 2, 1926.

19 *"not a city but a league of cities"*: MacKaye, *Tin Box*, 15.

19 *exploding with growth*: Ira Rosenwaike, *Population History of New York City* (Syracuse, NY: Syracuse University Press, 1972), 90–133.

19 *Edward J. Flynn*: Flynn, *Boss*, 47–48.

19 *"incapable of sustained effort"*: Robert Moses, *Working for the People* (New York: Harper & Row, 1956), 29.

19 *Al Smith*: Robert L. Duffus, "Al Smith: An East Side Portrait," *Harper's Magazine* 152 (February 1926): 326; Robert Moses, *A Tribute to Governor Smith* (New York: Simon & Schuster, 1962), 39.

20 *"My father went with me"*: Frank Graham, *Al Smith, American: An Informal Biography* (NY: G. P. Putnam's Sons, 1945), 55–56.

20 *"buddy system"*: Emily Smith Warner, with Hawthorne Daniel, *The Happy Warrior: A Biography of My Father, Alfred E. Smith* (Garden City, NY: Doubleday, 1956), 60.

20 *"as English squires"*: Robert A. Caro, *The Power Broker: Robert Moses and the Fall of New York* (New York: Vintage edition, 1975; originally published in 1974), 116.

21 *no Broadway swell:* Fowler, *Beau James*, 41–48.

21 *He took orders:* Henry Fowles Pringle, *Alfred E. Smith: A Critical Study* (NY: Macy-Masius, 1927), 129.

21 *the most accomplished bill writer:* Caro, *Power Broker*, 119.

21 *"There's no smarter man":* Joseph Proskauer Interview, CCOH.

21 *aural intake:* O. H. P. Garrett, "Profiles: Fourteenth Street and Broadway," TNY 1 (August 29, 1925): 9–10; McGoldrick, "Our American Mayors," 568.

22 *"learn something from the little master":* Fowler, *Beau James*, 74.

22 *"No woman":* NYT, May 3, 1923.

22 *"gallery god":* Garrett, "Fourteenth Street," 10.

22 *"was scheduled to speak":* Henry Fowles Pringle, "Mayor at Large," in Henry Fowles Pringle, *Big Frogs* (New York: Vanguard, 1928), 48.

22 *"unmasking":* NYT, February 23, 1923, May 19, 1925.

22 *"We see men of the mask":* Quoted in Fowler, *Beau James*, 41–48.

22 *Boss Murphy:* Howard Zink, *City Bosses in the United States: A Study of Twenty Municipal Bosses* (Durham, NC: Duke University Press, 1930), 148.

22 *"to remain the leader of Tammany":* Ibid.

23 *Murphy's Young Men:* Henry F. Pringle, "Profiles: the Janitor's Boy," TNY 3 (March 5, 1927): 24; J. Joseph Huthmacher, "Charles Evans Hughes and Charles Francis Murphy: The Metamorphosis of Progressivism," *New York History* 46 (January 1965).

23 *"He looks dense":* Connable and Silberfarb, *Tigers of Tammany*, 240.

23 *"make us many votes":* Oliver E. Allen, *The Tiger: The Rise and Fall of Tammany Hall* (Reading, MA: Addison-Wesley, 1993), 226.

23 *"Give the people everything they want":* NYT, December 10, 1913; James A. Farley Interview, CCOH.

23 *his "boy":* Fowler, *Beau James*, 72.

24 *"Listen Al":* Ibid., 119.

24 *"The excitement of politics":* Ibid., 91–92.

24 *"if Walker . . . would rid himself":* Ibid., 142.

24 *"We all grow up sometime":* Richard O'Connor, *The First Hurrah: A Biography of Alfred E. Smith* (NY: G. P. Putnam's Sons, 1970), 41.

24 *"Al, you believed him?":* Joseph Proskauer Interview, CCOH.

25 *"among his own":* NYT, August 21, 1925.

25 *his deceased parents:* NYW, November 1, 1925.

25 *"I am crossing the ocean tonight":* Fleming, "Being Mayor," 40.

26 *"the mangled forms":* NYT, August 21, 1925.

26 *"Oh, he'll make a lousy mayor":* Fleming, "Being Mayor," 40.

26 *public relations nightmare:* Scrapbooks, John Hylan Papers, New York City Municipal Archives.

26 *"colorless bore":* Norman Thomas and Paul Blanshard, "Jimmy Walker," *The Nation* 135 (October 5, 1932): 300.

26 *"like a man on stilts":* William Bullock, "Hylan," *The American Mercury* 1 (April 1924): 444.

27 *The five-cent fare:* Hood, *722 Miles*, 197; Peter Derrick, "The N.Y.C. Mess: Legacy of the 5¢ Fare," *Mass Transit* 8 (July 1981): 121–13, 26.

27 *If elected:* NYT, November 2, 1925.

27 *"the most hotly contested"*: NYT, September 15, 1925.

27 *"The Governor made war"*: Norman Hapgood and Henry Moskowitz, *Up from the City Streets: Alfred E. Smith, a Biographical Study in Contemporary Politics* (New York: Grosset & Dunlap, 1927), 207.

27 *"This is a crisis"*: "Smith-Hylan Battle," *The Literary Digest* 86 (September 12, 1925): 8.

27 *"The primary campaign"*: NYT, August 24, 1925.

27 *"his blind, obedient subservience to"*: Ibid.

27 *"must not cross the bridge"*: Walsh, *Gentleman*, 48.

27 *"wide-open town"*: NYT, August 24, 1925.

28 *strong pitch for women*: Flynn, *Boss*, 54.

28 *Walker won*: NYT, September 15, 17, 1925.

28 *The "family quarrel is over"*: NYT, September 15, 1925.

28 *Hylan and Hearst held off supporting Walker*: NYW, October 30, 1925.

28 *"Now the children"*: Walsh, *Gentleman*, 54.

28 *the Tammany army*: James A. Hagerty, "Tammany Hall: Its Structure and Its Rule," *NYT*, October 5, 1930.

29 *The captains*: Robert A. Slayton, *Empire Statesman: The Rise and Redemption of Al Smith* (New York: Free Press, 2001), 43; Conklin, "Manhattan Machine," M Baldwin and Stone, eds., *We Saw*, 278–79.

29 *62 percent of the vote*: NYT, November 6, 22, 1925.

29 *"It is very gratifying"*: NYT, November 4, 1925.

29 *"some pretty strong promises"*: Ibid.

29 *"After the stupidities of the Hylan administration"*: Thomas and Blanshard, "Walker," 300.

29 *George V. McLaughlin*: NYW, December 23, 1925.

30 *"from No. 210 Centre Street"*: Ibid.

30 *"all appointments and promotions"*: NYW, January 6, 1926.

30 *"If I, who am no glutton"*: HT, January 6, 1926.

30 *"Not for many years"*: Editorial, NYW, January 1, 1926.

30 *"The jazz age is in office"*: Henry F. Pringle, "Jimmy Walker," *The American Mercury* 9 (November 1926): 273.

30 *"The contrast between"*: McGoldrick, "Our American Mayors," 577.

31 *"a symbol of release"*: Stanley Walker, "Jimmy Walker: The Dream Prince," in *The Empire City: A Treasury of New York,* Alexander Klein, ed., (New York: Rinehart, 1955), 271.

31 *"Puritanical or cautious"; "legislate liberty"; "eloquence"*: Johnston, "Walker Era," 68.

31 *"Ninety-eight percent of the people"*: Fowler, *Beau James*, 152.

31 *"My main idea"*: Hector Fuller, *Abroad with Mayor Walker* (NY: Shields Publishing, 1928), 249.

31 *"If I see him by about 5 o'clock"*: NYT, November 4, 1925.

31 *"reigning girlfriend"*: Warner, *Happy Warrior,* 172.

32 *"listening to suggestions"*: NYT, November 25, 1925.

32 *"the five little mayors"*: Moscow, *What,* 3, 14; NYW, January 1, 1926.

32 *"[is] the anode and the cathode"*: McGoldrick, "New Tammany," 5.

33 *"at work in the city"; the so-called contract*: Conklin, "Manhattan Machine," in Baldwin and Stone, eds, *We Saw,* 283.

33 *"tribute"*: Ibid.

33 *"reign saw the disappearance"*: MacKaye, *Tin Box*, 9.

33 *"freer of political scandals"*: NYT, April 26, 1924.

33 *"honest graft"*: William L. Riordon, *Plunkitt of Tammany Hall: A Series of Very Plain Talks on Very Practical Politics*, Terrence J. McDonald, ed. (New York: St. Martin's, 1994), 49.

33 *"that more money could be made"*: MacKaye, *Tin Box*, 9.

34 *"Mr. Murphy would have nipped things in the bud"*: Fowler, *Beau James*, 110.

34 *"It had been a rule for twenty years"*: MacKaye, *Tin Box*, 13.

34 *"The brains of Tammany Hall"*: Weiss, *Murphy*, 92.

CHAPTER TWO: JIMMY WALKER'S NEW YORK

PAGE

35 "Young men and women": Malcolm Cowley, "The Romance of Money," in Harold Bloom, *Bloom's BioCritiques: F. Scott Fitzgerald* (NY: Infobase Publishing, 2002), 81.

35 *"All my life"*: Thomas B. Hanley, "Mayor Walker Settles Down to His Sixteen-Hour-a-Day Job," NYW, January 31, 1926.

35 *Gracie Mansion*: For a history of Gracie Mansion, see Mary C. Black, *New York City's Gracie Mansion: A History of the Mayor's House* (NY: J. M. Kaplan Fund, 1984).

35 *"fix up the house"*: Fowler, *Beau James*, 168.

36 *"silk in summer"*; *"the defect"*: Ibid., 172.

36 *"moochers"*: Ibid., 164.

36 *Walker cared for money*: Ibid., 171.

36 *"Money, to him"*: Pringle, "Jimmy Walker," 278.

37 *"contradicted the atmosphere"*: Fowler, *Beau James*, 87.

37 *"couldn't stand to be mauled"*: Ibid., 86.

37 *"path to his brain"*: Pringle, "Jimmy Walker," 274.

37 *"You write them"*: Fowler, *Beau James*, 173. See also Pringle, "Jimmy Walker," 274.

37 *"analyze it too closely"*: Pringle, *Big Frogs*, 56.

37 "The Mayor of New York": Fowler, *Beau James*, 185.

37 *"He talks frankly"*: Hanley, "Mayor Walker."

38 *"Walker was a machine-made mayor"*: Thomas and Blanshard, "Walker," 300.

38 *"a legislative, financial, and administrative agency"*: Charles A. Beard, "New York, the Metropolis of To-Day," *The American Review of Reviews* 69 (June 1924): 613.

38 *"combined the simple dignity"*: Warren Moscow, "Jimmy Walker's City Hall," NYT *Magazine* (August 22, 1976): 31.

38 *"to live by the clock"*: NYT, November 19, 1946.

39 *"He probably spent an hour"*: Morris Markey, "A Reporter at Large: Deus ex Machine," TNY (April 17, 1926): 25–26.

39 *"Liar!"*: Fowler, *Beau James*, 184.

39 *Jeann Friedman*: "Jean and Jimmy," TNY 10 (May 5, 1934): 19–20.

39 *not to Walker's exacting taste*: Louis J. Gribetz and Joseph Kaye, *Jimmie Walker: The Story of a Personality* (New York: Dial, 1932), 279.

39 *"the smartest dressed"*: Ibid., 277.

39 *"a snappy . . . or sharp" dresser*: Fowler, *Beau James*, 166.

39   *"When you know"*: Hanley, "Mayor Walker."

40   *"Jimmy, circumcision next?"*: Moscow, "City Hall," 33.

40   *"and be completely refreshed"*: Hanley, "Mayor Walker."

40   *Speaking at:* NYT, January 6, 1926; NYW, December 8, 1925.

40   *"I must go up, Bill"*: NYT, February 12, 1926.

40   *"suffering from overwork"*: NYW, February 9, 1926.

40   *"brilliant victory for Walker"*: NYT, February 11, 1926.

41   *"one of the biggest"*: NYT, December 13, 1927, November 19, 1946.

41   *"One thing I have determined"*: NYW, February 12, 1926.

41   *"a couple of days a week"*: Moscow, "City Hall," 32.

41   *"The prophets"*: Pringle, *Frogs*, 38–39.

41   *"I would rather laugh"*: Pringle, "Jimmy Walker," 279.

41   *"hangover room"*: Moscow, "City Hall," 31.

41   *"on the slightest provocation"*: Pringle, *Frogs*, 50–51.

42   *"Shot?"*: Moscow, "City Hall," 33.

42   *"dazzling, toothy smile"*: MacKaye, *Tin Box*, 21.

42   *"open-air performances"*: Fowler, *Beau James*, 185; McGoldrick, "Jimmy Walker," 573–74.

42   *his niece, Rita Burke:* Fowler, *Beau James*, 176.

43   *"the quickest mind"*: Moscow, "City Hall," 33.

43   *"drift along"; "Father Knickerbocker"*: Stanley Walker, "Jimmy Walker, The Dream Prince," in Klein, ed., *Empire City*, 271.

43   *its annual budget:* DN, October 2, 1927. New York's population in 1926 was 5,873,356.

43   *New York's current level of services:* Beard, "New York," 613–14.

44   *"rigid retrenchment"; "log-rolling"*: NYT, January 12, 1926; HT, January 12, 1926.

44   *"I would not keep a dog there"*: Gribetz and Kaye, *Walker*, 169.

44   *"If it takes the last dollar"*: NYT, April 8, 1926, March 2, 1926.

44   *Walker had the Board of Estimate appropriate:* NYT, May 12, 1927, May 4, 1928, February 1, 1929.

44   *"This is an outstanding event"*: NYT, February 1, 1929.

44   *New York's ballooning municipal debt:* NYW, January 11, 1928.

44   *its annual budget:* Beard, "New York," 618.

44   *a $250 million payroll:* McGoldrick, "New Tammy," 1–5; Caro, *Power Broker*, 325–26.

44   *New York to displace London:* "Where Is the World Metropolis?," *Review of Reviewers* 60 (September 1919): 317; Paul Morand, *New York* (NY: Henry Holt, 1930), 313.

45   *It derived its funding:* Moscow, "City Hall," 32.

45   *"the last Golconda"*: Johnston, "Jimmy Walker Era," 41.

45   *"the bankers were not"*: Lindsay Rogers, "Fiscal Crisis of the World's Largest City," *New Outlook* (January 1933), 24.

45   *"Nowhere in the world"*: DN, October 2, 1927.

46   *"bottom level below which"*: Norman Thomas and Paul Blanchard, *What's the Matter with New York: A National Problem* (NY: Macmillan, 1932), 284.

46   *nearly three million passengers:* Robert Murray Haig, *Major Economic Factors in Metropolitan Growth and Arrangement: Regional Survey*, vol. 1 (NY: Arno, 1974; originally published in 1927), xii–xiii.

47   *the city of tomorrow:* Mark Sullivan, "Why the West Dislikes New York," *World's Work* 51 (February 1926): 406; Morand, *New York*, 305.

47 *"We beheld them with stupefaction"*: John-Paul Sartre, "Manhattan: The Great American Desert" (1946), in Klein, ed., *Empire City*, 455–57.

47 *"The whole world revolves around New York"*: Edward Kennedy Ellington, *Music Is My Mistress* (Garden City, NY: Doubleday, 1973), 65.

47 *"nowhere in the world"*: Thomas Wolfe, *The Web and the Rock: A Selection from The Web and the Rock* (NY: Harper Perennial, 2009), 273.

47 *"Instead of being exhorted"*: Cowley, "Romance of Money," in Bloom, *F. Scott Fitzgerald*, 81.

47 *"There is little in New York"*: H. L. Mencken, *A Second Mencken Chrestomathy* (NY: Alfred A. Knopf, 1998).

48 *"I find it an appalling place"*: Earl Sparling, "Is New York American?," *Scribner's Magazine* 90 (August 1931): 165.

48 *"The city had"*: John Steinbeck, "The Making of a New Yorker," in Kenneth T. Jackson and David Dunbar, eds., *Empire City: New York Through the Centuries* (NY: Columbia University Press, 2002), 669.

48 *two million New Yorkers*: Kantrowitz, "Population," in *ENYC*, 921. In 1930, 34.3 percent of New York's population was foreign born; Bureau of Census, Fifteenth Census of the United States Population, vol. III, pt. 2 (Washington, DC, 1932): 302–3.

48 *a Jewish town*: Chris McNickle, "When New York Was Irish, and After," in Ronald H. Bayor and Timothy J. Meagher, eds., *The New York Irish* (Baltimore: Johns Hopkins University Press, 1996), 339.

48 *Manhattan still contained 44 percent*: Marion R. Casey, " 'From the East Side to the Seaside': Irish Americans on the Move in New York City," in Bayor and Meagher, eds., *New York Irish*, 402.

49 *aldermen*: Moscow, "City Hall," 34.

49 *Jimmy Walker rejoiced in New York's cosmopolitanism*: Fuller, *Abroad with Mayor Walker*, 131, 211.

49 *the borough presidents were czars*: Moscow, *What*, 10; Beard, "New York," 613.

49 *"gentlemen of low intelligence"*: MacKaye, *Tin Box*, 15.

49 *"New York City, with its thousands"*: Ibid., 17.

50 *Harris's first target was Harry Danziger*: NYT, May 15, 1926, January 25, 1927.

50 *"at the mercy of"; "unscrupulous"*: NYT, May 1, 15, 1926.

50 *"dirty stable hose"*: NYT, May 1, 1926.

50 *"doctored" milk*: NYT, May 15, 1926.

50 *"milk-graft ring"*: NYT, May 1, 1926.

50 *"inside man"*: NYT, April 27, June 11, 16, 1926.

50 *Harris suspected*: NYT, April 26–27, 1926.

51 *But Clougher had been unshakable*: NYT, June 16, July 6, 1926.

51 *There were additional arrests*: NYT, June 2, 1926.

51 *"master-mind"*: NYT, May 19, 20, June 2, 1926.

51 *Danziger avoided prison*: NYT, January 25, 1927.

51 *"literally run by political bosses"*: "Nineteen Thousand Cops," *Fortune* 20 (July 1939): 167–68.

51 *"a new racket"*: "Tammany in Modern Clothes," TNY (January 16, 1926): 11–12.

51 *"He'll last three"*: Ibid., 11.

52 *"Favoritism, graft and corruption"*: Lewis J. Valentine, *Night Stick* (NY: Dial, 1947), 103.

52 *"to strike terror"*: Ibid., 104.

52 *"promised"*: Ibid., 17.

52 *the "Broadway Crowd"*: Ibid., 104–5.

52 *only five went to trial:* Charles Garrett, *The La Guardia Years: Machine and Reform Politics in New York* (New Brunswick, NJ: Rutgers University Press, 1961), 73.

52 *"the holy of holies"*: Valentine, *Night Stick,* 117.

52 *Walker flatly refused:* "Tammany in Modern Clothes," 11.

53 *Valentine's men entered Farley's clubhouse:* MacKaye, *Tin Box,* 192–93; William B. Northrop and John B. Northrop, *The Insolence of Office: The Story of the Seabury Investigations* (NY: G. P. Putnam's Sons, 1932), 162.

53 *McGuiness's clubhouse:* NYT, March 13, 30, 1927, October 4, 1931.

53 *"Gambling Raids Win Backing"*: DN, March 8, 1927.

53 *"We are trying to run"*: DN, March 18, 1927.

53 *Albany Boys:* "Tammany in modern clothes," 11.

53 *McLaughlin submitted his resignation:* NYT, March 30, 1927.

53 *"cooperation"; "broad smiles"; "Hey, Pete"*: Ibid.

54 *hard evidence is lacking:* Ibid.

54 *"Absolutely"*: NYT, October 15, 1931.

54 *he called Valentine into his office:* NYT, September 24–25, 30, 1931.

54 *"complaints"*: Valentine, *Night Stick,* 108.

54 *"whose code"*: Flynn, *Boss,* 139.

55 *only one politician:* Valentine, *Night Stick,* 108.

55 *Walker forced his hand:* NYT, December 12, 1928.

55 *"going to be a lot of suicides"*: Walsh, *Gentleman,* 171.

55 *Walker demanded and accepted his resignation:* NYT, November 6, December 14, 1928.

55 *Grover A. Whalen:* NYT, December 18, 1928.

55 *"It takes more"*: Walsh, *Gentleman,* 204.

55 *abolished the Confidential Squad:* NYT, December 18, 1928, October 13, 1931.

56 *"the best Police Commissioner"*: NYT, December 17, 1946.

56 *"one of the best"*: Keith D. Revell, *Building Gotham: Civic Culture and Public Policy in New York City, 1898–1938* (Baltimore: Johns Hopkins University Press, 2003), 247.

56 *"in the past"*: "Remarks of the Mayor on Organization of the City Committee on Plan and Survey," June 21, 1926, James J. Walker Papers, Municipal Archives, New York, New York. Hereafter cited as JJWP.

57 *never completed its survey: Report of the City Committee on Plan and Survey* (NY, 1928), 3–16, JJWP.

57 *soundly defeated:* Revell, *Building Gotham,* 250.

57 *eliminated it:* NYT, December 5, 1932, January 21, 1933.

57 *"the largest of its kind"*: Walter J. Schroeder, "New York Starts $300,000,000 Sewage Treatment Program," *The American City* 45 (August 1931): 11.

57 *750,000,000 gallons; "most edible"*: Kenneth Allen, "The Pollution of Tidal Harbors by Sewage with Especial Reference to New York Harbor," *Transactions of the American Society of Civil Engineers,* 85 (1922): 436; NYT, August 11, 1930; Revell, *Building Gotham,* 127.

57 *handle only 5 percent:* Allen, "Pollution," 435; George W. Fuller, "Sewage Disposal

Trends in the New York City Region," *Sewage Works Journal 4* (July 1932): 435.

57 *"New York may be said"*: McGoldrich, "Our American Mayor," 570.

58 *"partisan patronage"*: NYT, January 2, December 1, 1929; Revell, *Building Gotham,* 135.

58 *only 12 percent*: McGoldrick, "Our American Mayors," 569–70

58 *conditions improved*: Wellington Donaldson, "First Year of Operation of Wards Island Sewage Treatment Works," *Sewage Works Journal* 11 (January 1939): 100–116.

58 *"real progress"*: Revell, *Building Gotham,* 138.

58 *"emergency lines"*: NYT, January 10, 1927.

58 *"Ohio boys"; "inside track"*: William B. Northrop and John B. Northrop, *The Insolence of Office: The Story of the Seabury Investigation* (NY: G. P. Putnam Sons, 1932), 249.

58 *"hard threats"*: McGoldrick, "Our American Mayors," 522

58 *"Pet Bus Company"*: DN, January 23, 1927.

58 *"financial adventurers"*: Thomas and Blanshard, *What's the Matter,* 168.

59 *letter of credit*: Northrop and Northrop, *Insolence.*

59 *denied that he had been bribed*: Ibid., 249–64: [State of New York] Joint Legislative Committee to Investigate the Administration of The Various Departments of the Government of New York, *Hearing[s], July 21, 1931 to December 8, 1932* (NY: 1931–32), Municipal Archives, NY, NY.

59 *"fly-by-night"*: Norman Thomas and Thomas Blanshard, "Walker," *The Nation* 135 (October 5, 1932): 302.

59 *"in the largest city"*: DN, January 25, 1927.

59 *revoked*: NYT, March 26, 1929.

59 *Walker admitted*: Joint Legislative Committee . . . *Hearings,* passim; NYT, May 26–28, 1932.

59 *"He didn't give a damn"*: Moscow, *What,* 151.

59 *"You know"*: Fowler, *Beau James,* 323.

60 *"son and servant"*: NYT, November 6, 1929.

60 *"could have given"*: Garrett, *The La Guardia Years*, 55.

60 *authorize $250 million*: NYT, March 13, 1929.

60 *"epochal"*: NYT, October 26, 1929

60 *Supreme Court reversed*: NYT, April 8–9, 1929.

60 *"dangerous radical"; "semi-Socialistic"*: M. R. Weiner, "Fiorello's Finest Hour," *American Heritage 12* (October 1961), 38, 40.

61 *"It is a fiction"*: Walsh, *Gentleman,* 185

61 *"I am the candidate"*: Garrett, *La Guardia,* 63.

61 *"[He] didn't have the proof"*: Reminiscences of Stanley Isaacs, CCOH

61 *"One thing about Jimmy"*: Walsh, *Gentleman,* 199.

61 *"high noon"*: Richard C. Wade, "The Withering Away of the Party System," in Jewell Bellush and Dick Netzer, eds., *Urban Politics, New York Style* (Armonk, NY: M. E. Sharpe, 1990), 276.

61 *"We were too soon"*: Thomas Kessner, *Fiorello H. La Guardia and the Making of Modern New York* (NY: McGraw Hill, 1989), 164.

61 *"If ever"*: NYT, November 6, 1929; Walker received 62 percent of the vote; La Guardia 26 percent, and Norman Thomas 12 percent.

61 *"has given the majority"*: Ibid.

62 *Betty Compton*: Fowler, *Beau James,* 257.

62 *"powerful grafters"; "without supervision"*: Moscow, *What,* 151.

62 *"The mask"*: Walsh, *Gentleman,* 187.

CHAPTER THREE: TOO GOOD TO BE TRUE

PAGE

65 "When I got into bootlegging": Joseph Bonanno with Sergio Lalli, *A Man of Honor: The Autobiography of Joseph Bonanno* (NY: Simon & Schuster, 1983), 65.

65 *"wholesale bribery and corruption"; "biggest rum ring"*: NYT, December 4–5, 1925.

66 *"money, wine, women"; "the most successful"*: NYT, December 4–6, 1925, December 11, 1946; NYW, June 9, 1927.

66 *"purchasing agent"*: NYT, July 7, 1926, December 11, 1946, February 19, 1973; Bonanno, *Man of Honor,* 165–66.

66 *mid-level operatives*: NYT, November 19, 1926.

66 *former Hell's Kitchen longshoreman*: NYT, December 4, 1925.

66 *"the most silent owner"*: Trent Frayne, *The Mad Men of Hockey* (NY: Dodd, Mead, 1974), 58.

66 *"broad smile"*: NYT, December 4, 1925.

66 *owner of the Sea Grill Restaurant*: NYT, December 11, 1946.

67 *"King of the Bootleggers"*: Ibid.

67 *William Vincent Dwyer grew up*: Ibid.; Craig Thompson and Allen Raymond, *Gang Rule in New York: The Story of a Lawless Era* (NY: Dial, 1940), 80. Dwyer was born on February 23, 1883.

68 *The pilfered alcohol*: Thompson and Raymond, *Gang Rule,* 80–81.

68 *"As a society changes"*: Daniel Bell, *The End of Ideology: On the Exhaustion of Political Ideas in the Fifties* (Glencoe, Ill: Free Press, 1960), 117. See also Humbert S. Nelli, *The Business of Crime* (NY: Oxford University Press, 1976), 103.

68 *revolution in criminal practice*: Bell, *End of Ideology,* 116.

69 *"the great impossibility"*: The Prohibition commissioner in Washington announced on January 15, 1920, that constitutional prohibition would become effective "immediately after midnight of January Sixteenth, Nineteen Twenty: that is, effective January Seventeenth, Nineteenth Twenty." NYP, January 15, 1920.

69 *"absolutely and permanently bone dry"; "saloonless land"*: Quoted in David E. Kyvig, "Sober Thoughts: Myths and Realities of National Prohibition After Fifty Years," in David E. Kyvig, ed., *Law, Alcohol, and Order: Perspectives on National Prohibition* (Westport, CT: Greenwood, 1985), 10.

69 *"a new nation will be born"*: Humbert S. Nelli, "American Syndicate Crime: A Legacy of Prohibition," in Kyvig, ed., *Law,* 125.

69 *Volstead Act*: NYP, January 16, 1920; NYW, January 18–19, 1920.

69 *Prohibition Bureau*: Mark Edward Lender and James Kirby Martin, *Drinking in America: A History* (NY: Free Press, 1982), 149.

70 *America's land and water borders*: Charles Merz, *The Dry Decade* (NY: Doubleday, Doran, 1931), 52.

70 *The New York City district*: Norman H. Clark, *Deliver Us from Evil: An Interpretation of American Prohibition* (NY: W. W. Norton, 1976), 162.

70 *the budget for enforcement*: Lender and Martin, *Drinking,* 150.

70 *"Don'ts for the Drinking Man"*: NYP, January 15, 1920.

71 *"Any saloon man"*: NYW, January 18, 1920.

71 *speakeasies*: Warren Sloat, "Prohibition," ENYC, 944.

71 *"an overwhelming opposition"*: NYW, January 18, 1920.

71 *Jimmy Walker, who saw Prohibition*: Burton W. Peretti, *Nightclub City: Politics and Amusement in Manhattan* (Philadelphia: University of Pennsylvania Press, 2007), 73.

71 *unenforceable in New York City*: Michael A. Lerner, *Dry Manhattan: Prohibition in New York City* (Cambridge: Harvard University Press, 2007), 286.

71 *"Even the Army and Navy"*: Fowler, *Beau James*, 93.

72 *only twenty-seven convictions*: Lender and Martin, *Drinking*, 154.

72 *After five unsuccessful attempts*: NYP, May 5, 1923.

72 *"I'm dying, Jim"*: Fowler, *Beau James*, 106.

72 *Smith signed the bill*: Robert A. Slayton, *Empire Statesman: The Rise and Redemption of Al Smith* (NY: Free Press, 2001), 196–7, 201.

73 *"ragtag armada"*: Harold Waters, *Smugglers of Spirits: Prohibition and the Coast Guard Patrol* (NY: Hastings House, 1971), 49.

73 *William "Big Bill" McCoy*: Ibid., 50. For McCoy, see Daniel Okrent, *Last Call: The Rise and Fall of Prohibition* (NY: Charles Scribner's Sons, 2010), 161–68.

73 *began operating off the coast of Long Island*: Waters, *Smugglers*, 50.

73 *dominated by small-time operators*: Malcolm F. Willoughby, *Rum War at Sea* (Washington, DC: U.S. Government Printing Office, 1964), 22–25.

73 *"standing almost end to end"*: William G. Shepherd, "At the Rum Row War," *Collier's* (May 30, 1925): 8.

73 *"just for kicks"; "shouting good wishes"*: Waters, *Smugglers*, 53.

73 *"go-through guys"*: Peter Charles Newman, *King of the Castle: The Making of a Dynasty—Seagram's and the Bronfman Empire* (NY: Atheneum, 1979), 105.

74 *"made the twenties roar"*: "Thompson Model 1928 Submachine Gun," National Museum of American History, Smithsonian Institution.

74 *Francesco Castiglia*: NYT, February 19, 1973; George Wolf, with Joseph DiMona, *Frank Costello: Prime Minister of the Underworld* (NY: William Morrow, 1974), 18–96.

74 *they were reunited*: Leonard Katz, *Uncle Frank: The Biography of Frank Costello* (NY: Drake, 1973), 33–35.

74 *Dr. Richard Hoffman*: Ibid., 39, 154.

75 *arrested three times*: Nelli, *Business of Crime*, 103.

75 *sentenced to a year in prison*: NYT, February 19, 1973.

75 *"The Italians and the Jews"*: Giuseppe Selvaggi, *The Rise of the Mafia in New York* (NY: Bobbs-Merrill, 1978), 91.

75 *"never to pack a gun again"*: Wolf with DiMona, *Costello*, 32.

75 *"Nothing like it"*: Mike Dash, *The First Family: Terror, Extortion, Murder, and the Birth of the American Mafia* (NY: Random House, 2009), 268.

75 *"it was a whole new ball game"*: Wolf, with DiMona, *Costello*, 33.

76 *Arnold Rothstein*: Leo Katcher, *The Big Bankroll: The Life and Times of Arnold Rothstein* (NY: Da Capo, 1994), 236.

76 *"had only one nationality"*: Carl Sifakis, *The Mafia Encyclopedia* (NY: Checkmark, 2005 edition), 393.

76 *"All I know I stole"*: George Walsh, *Public Enemies: The Mayor, the Mob, and the Crime*

That Was (NY: W. W. Norton, 1980), 48.

76 *controlled by Sicilian-born Giuseppe "Joe the Boss" Masseria*: Dash, *First Family*, 270.

77 *Lansky, "the Jewish Godfather"*: The most authoritative biography of Lansky is Robert Lacey, *Little Man: Meyer Lansky and the Gangster Life* (Boston: Little, Brown, 1991).

77 *"ignorance"*: Katz, *Uncle Frank*, 8.

77 *"If you're writing a book"*: Wolf with DiMona, *Costello*, 39.

77 *more reliable sources of supply*: Katz, *Uncle Frank*, 61.

77 *"a little squirt of a burg"*: Okrent, *Last Call*, 167.

77 *"are carrying ever-increasing numbers"*: NYT, December 3, 1921.

78 *Bill Dwyer had the same idea*: Ibid.

78 *Samuel Bronfman*: Newman, *King of the Castle*, 52.

78 *equivalent of a Wild West mining town*: NYT, December 3, 1921.

78 *largest legal transshipment ports*: Newman, *King of the Castle*, 52–53.

79 *hijacking*: NYW, January 7, 1927.

79 *the "combine"*: NYT, December 4–14, 1925.

79 *presented no threat to canny liquor smugglers*: Waters, *Smugglers*, 56.

79 *Coast Guard was then intercepting*: Willoughby, *Rum War*, 161.

79 *This changed dramatically in 1924*: Ibid., 50.

79 *"an affront"*: Okrent, *Last Call*, 172.

80 *"Dry Armada"*: Waters, *Smugglers*, 56–59; Shepherd, "Rum Row War," 8–9.

80 *"It soon became all but impossible"*: Waters, *Smugglers*, 73.

80 *Bill McCoy, who had retired from the trade*: On his release from jail, McCoy sold his three schooners and returned to Florida, where he died in his bed in 1948. Willoughby, *Rum War*, 18.

80 *"the professionals"*: Waters, *Smugglers*, 103.

80 *"The rules are changed"*: NYT, December 14, 1924.

80 *powerful airplane engines*: John Kobler, *Ardent Spirits: The Rise and Fall of Prohibition* (NY: G. P. Putnam's Sons, 1973), 262.

80 *mounted machine guns*: Waters, *Smugglers*, 114, 134.

80 *secret Morse codes*: Willoughby, *Rum War*, 72.

81 *"air bootlegger"*: NYT, January 27, April 8, 1926.

81 *never to lose a truckload of whiskey*: Katz, *Uncle Frank*, 63.

81 *Policemen patrolling*: Ibid., 61–62.

81 *a credit system*: Thompson and Raymond, *Gang Rule*, 87.

81 *uniformed New York City patrolmen*: NYT, September 6, 1926.

81 *the syndicate's cutting plants*: Thompson and Raymond, *Gang Rule*, 92.

81 *"If any drinking men"*: Chester P. Mills, "Where the Booze Begins," *Collier's* (October 15, 1927): 8.

82 *"genuine stuff"*: Morris Markey, "A Reporter at Large: Conversations on Bootlegging—II," TNY 4 (May 12, 1928): 34.

82 *"crash course"*: Mark H. Haller, "Bootleggers as Businessmen: From City Slums to City Builders," in Kyvig, ed., *Law*, 140–41.

82 *a "spy" system*: DN, January 6, 1927; NYT, December 4, 1925.

82 *Louis Halle*: Thompson and Raymond, *Gang Rule*, 90.

83 *"Costello and [Lucky] Luciano"*: Katz, *Uncle Frank*, 116.

83 *"all of his close associates"*: Ibid., 77.

83 *He was proud of his adopted country:* Ibid., 8.

84 *a forerunner of the big syndicates:* Nelli, "American Syndicate Crime," in Kyvig, ed., *Law,* 123.

84 *"before 1919":* Dash, *First Family,* 267–68.

84 *"Prohibition did not lead":* David Critchley, *The Origin of Organized Crime in America: The New York City Mafia, 1891–1931* (NY: Routledge, 2009), 138.

84 *never achieved the level of organization:* Mark H. Haller, "Illegal Enterprise: A Theoretical and Historical Interpretation," *Criminology* 28, no. 2 (1990): 222.

85 *"as easy as tomatoes":* NYT, December 5, 1925.

85 *"coast was clear"; "regular callers":* NYT, December 6, 1925, July 13, 1926.

85 *"practically all boats":* NYW, January 7, 1927.

85 *Witnesses reported:* NYT, December 5–6, 1925, January 27, 1926.

85 *Dwyer made regular visits to Washington, D.C.:* NYT, July 17, 1926.

86 *One Coast Guard officer told federal investigators:* NYT, July 15, 1926.

86 *called in a special investigator, A. Bruce Bielaski:* John B. Kennedy, "Under Cover: An Interview with A. Bruce Bielaski," *Collier's* (August 13, 1927): 14.

86 *Burly, hard-eyed A. Bruce Bielaski:* NYT, December 21, 1926, January 9, 1927.

86 *"Buckner's Boy Scouts":* Martin Mayer, *Emory Buckner: A Biography* (NY: Harper & Row, 1968), 182.

87 *expand and reorganize the federal court system:* NYW, June 27, 1927.

87 *"The zealots":* Morris Markey, "Mr. Buckner Explains," TNY 1 (November 14, 1925): 8. See also Mayer, *Buckner,* 166.

87 *"fearlessly":* NYT, July 3, 1925; "To Dry New York with Padlocks," *The Literary Digest* 84 (March 21, 1925): 9.

87 *"on the wagon":* Mayer, *Buckner,* 184–85.

87 *they boarded the steamer* Augusta*:* NYT, December 9, 1925, October 8, 1927.

87 *arrest, that December, of Dwyer, Costello:* NYT, December 9, 1925.

87 *Czar of Rum Row:* NYT, December 4–5, 1925.

87 *"You know":* Mayer, *Buckner,* 205.

87 *The jurors:* NYT, July 10, 1926.

88 *Judge Julian W. Mack sentenced:* NYT, July 27, 1926.

88 *"enforcement fanaticism":* NYT, July 21, 1926.

88 *The charges:* NYT, January 4, 1927.

88 *paid by Costello's agents:* NYT, January 8, 1927.

88 *entrapment and wiretapping:* NYT, January 19, 1927.

88 *"mysterious and invisible power":* NYT, January 20, 1927.

89 *acquitted eight of the defendants:* NYT, January 21, 1927.

89 *"a thin smile":* Bill Brennan, *The Frank Costello Story: The True Story of the Underworld's Prime Minister* (Derby, CT: Monarch, 1962), 75.

89 *"despicable" character:* NYT, January 21, 1927.

89 *"until Doomsday":* Ibid.

89 *a full-out defeat for the "Dry Forces":* NYT, January 22, 1927.

89 *"so severe or unreasonable":* Ibid.

89 *"but I owned the one":* Wolf with DiMona, *Costello,* 72.

89 *the final ballot on Costello:* NYT, January 21, 1927.

89 *One month after the Costello verdict:* NYT, February 8, 1927.

89 *"the richest of all bootleggers":* NYW, June 9, 1927.

90 *Seven years later:* NYT, December 11, 1946.

90 *One of Dwyer's first visitors:* DN, July 19, 1927; Kobler, *Ardent,* 266.

90 *"a little vacation":* NYT, December 11, 1946.

90 *Less than a month after his release:* Thompson and Raymond, *Gang Rule,* 97.

90 *the slot machine king:* NYT, January 20, 1927.

91 *"a Chinese method of torture":* Chester P. Mills, "Dry Rot," *Collier's* 80 (September 17, 1927): 48; NYW, June 26, 1927; NYW, June 24, 26, 1927.

91 *Two days later:* NYW, June 26–28, 1927. Heise was later cleared by a grand jury and reinstated to the Prohibition Service.

91 *the axe fell on General Lincoln Andrews:* DN, July 31, 1927; NYW, May 21, June 25, 1927.

91 *"Enforcement fanaticism":* NYW, May 23, 1927.

91 *As part of the purge:* DN, September 28, 1927.

91 *one thousand other Prohibition enforcement agents:* NYW, September 12, 1927.

91 *"Prohibition . . . is a party-spoils system":* Mills, "Dry Rot," 48.

91 *"This is to certify"; "the new pork barrel":* Ibid., 5–6, 46, 48.

91 *Coast Guard declared victory:* DN, December 4, 9, 1927.

92 *95 percent of the liquor consumed in New York City:* Morris Markey, "A Reporter at Large: Booze," TNY 3 (December 31, 1927): 31.

92 *Markey had located a major change:* Nelli, *Business of Crime,* 161–62.

92 *"ran New York in those days":* Graham Nown, *The English Godfather* (London: Ward Lock, 1987), 74.

CHAPTER FOUR: OWNEY MADDEN

PAGE

93 "I am in the land": F. Scott Fitzgerald to Zelda Sayre, February 22, 1919, in Matthew J. Bruccoli and Margaret M. Dugan, *Correspondence of F. Scott Fitzgerald* (New York: Random House, 1980), 38.

93 *"a frontier community":* John Lardner, *White Hopes and Other Tigers* (Philadelphia: J. B. Lippincott, 1951), 119.

93 *the most formidable gangster:* Jerome Charyn, *Gangsters and Gold Diggers: Old New York, the Jazz Age, and the Birth of Broadway* (NY: Thunder's Mouth Press, 2003), 97.

94 *"ruled the El Dorado":* Meyer Berger, "Exploded 'Big Shots,'" NYT, January 4, 1942.

94 *"He's a bad man":* Charlotte Chandler, *She Always Knew How: Mae West, A Personal Biography* (NY: Simon & Schuster, 2009), 112.

94 *"Sage of Hot Springs":* Thomas A. Repetto, *American Mafia: A History of Its Rise to Power* (NY: Henry Holt, 2004), 155.

94 *"Runyon made [Madden]":* Jimmy Breslin, *Damon Runyon* (NY: Ticknor & Fields, 1991), 107. Pete Hamill claims that Dave the Dude was "probably" based on Frank Costello. See Hamill's introduction to Damon Runyon, *Guys and Dolls and Other Writings* (NY: Penguin, 2008), x.

95 *"My celluloid hoodlums":* NYT, November 25, 1980.

95 *"The New York that Madden found":* Stanley Walker, *The Night Club Era* (Baltimore: Johns Hopkins University Press, 1999), 112–13.

95 *"shiftless and unsuccessful farm people"*: F. Scott Fitzgerald, *The Great Gatsby* (NY: Charles Scribner's Sons, 1925), 104.

95 *"one of the most dangerous areas"*: Herbert Asbury, *The Gangs of New York: An Informal History of the Underworld* (NY: Thunder's Mouth Press edition, 2001; originally published in 1928), 236.

95 *"A lesser man"*: Walker, *Night Club,* 103–5.

96 *"as authentic a Big Shot"*: Ibid., 122.

96 *Owen Vincent Madden was born*: Nown, *English Godfather,* 16.

96 *She was there to meet them:* "Owney Vincent 'Owney' Madden," Arkansas Grave stones.org, Greenwood Cemetery, Garland County, AK, Shirley Tomkievicz, "Owney Vincent Madden, *The Encyclopedia of Arkansas History and Culture,* www.encyclo pediaofarkansas.net.

96 *"so intense at times"*: Otho G. Cartwright, *West Side Studies: The Middle West Side, A Historical Sketch* (NY: Russell Sage Foundation, 1914), 4.

97 *"great bridges throw necklaces"; "featureless and depressing"; "forgotten to be dissatisfied"; "There is something"*: Pauline Goldmark, ed., *West Side Studies: Boyhood and Lawlessness* (NY: Russell Sage Foundation, 1914), 3, 6, 8.

97 *"incredibly vicious"; "cop-fighting was the accepted sport"*: Ibid., 13, 21, 44.

97 *all comers; "semi-mythical"*: Ibid., 42.

98 *"pigeon flying is the chief sport"*: Ibid., 28.

98 *"Owney Madden is a connoisseur"*: Quoted in Nown, *English Godfather,* 17.

99 *"accomplished artist"*: Asbury, *Gangs,* 323.

99 *"from hell to breakfast"*: Ibid., 322.

99 *the Tenth Avenue, or Madden, Gang*: NYT, May 27, 1915.

99 *"The witnesses left town"*: Quoted in Denis Tilden Lynch, *Criminals and Politicians* (NY: Macmillan, 1932), 76.

99 *the only Irish street gang of consequence*: Lynch, *Criminals,* 76.

99 *gang members blackjacked cops*: Asbury, *Gangs,* 235.

99 *the Lady Gophers*: Ibid., 236; Ruth S. True, *West Side Studies: The Neglected Girl* (NY: Russell Sage Foundation, 1914), 10.

100 *Georgie Ranft*: Lewis Yablonsky, *George Raft* (NY: McGraw-Hill, 1974), 3–4.

100 *Never loyal to his wife*: The couple did not get a divorce until 1934, the year Madden married Agnes Demby, of Hot Springs, Arkansas.

100 *three detectives apprehended Madden*: NYT, February 13, 1912.

100 *"[We were] the wildest bunch of roosters"*: Walker, *Night Club,* 117.

101 *Hines was running for alderman*: NYT, March 26, 1957.

101 *On election day*: Jack Alexander, "District Leader—III," TNY 12 (August 8, 1936): 19.

101 *"bump anybody off"*: Asbury, *Gangs,* 330.

101 *"The boys'll get 'em"*: Ibid.

101 *he had been convicted four times*: NYT, June 3, 1915.

102 *ordering the execution-style murder*: NYT, May 28, 1915. Moore went by the alias "Little Patsy" Doyle.

102 *"I didn't have it done"*: Walker, *Night Club,* 117.

102 *an exemplary prisoner*: NYT, April 24, 1965.

102 *"He is a good influence"*: Walker, *Night Club,* 126.

102 *"During the period of [Madden's] ascendency"*: Ibid., 122–23.

102 *"made his blue eyes gleam"*: Ibid., 113.

102 *Larry Fay*: NYT, January 2, 1933.

103 *George "Big Frenchy" DeMange*: NYT, September 20, 1939.

104 *the Cotton Club*: Jim Haskins, *The Cotton Club* (NY: Random House, 1977), 30. Haskins says that Madden's men bought the club while Madden was in prison. This seems unlikely.

104 *"gaudiest and best-known nightspot"*: David Levering Lewis, *When Harlem Was in Vogue* (NY: Oxford University Press, paperback edition, 1989), 209.

104 *Dwyer asked him to run a West Side cereal beverage company*: NYT, July 22, 1931.

104 *"high-powered" beer*: Mabel Walker Willebrandt, *The Inside of Prohibition* (Indianapolis: Bobbs-Merril, 1929), 78.

104 *Dwyer thought it better to bring him into the organization*: Thompson and Raymond, *Gang Rule*, 47.

104 *"After drinking a bottle"*: Nown, *English Godfather*, 79.

104 *Madden assumed exclusive control of the brewery*: NYT, August 15, 1930, September 13, 1931; Lynch, *Criminals*, 73.

105 *Dutch Schultz*: NYT, August 18, 1938; "Breweries Operated by Jewish Syndicate," Municipal Archives, N.Y., N.Y.; Alan Block, *East Side–West Side: Organizing Crime in New York, 1930–1950* (New Brunswick, NJ: Transaction, 1983), 135. Most of Wexler's beer was brought into the city from breweries he controlled in New Jersey.

105 *"It's really better"*: Breslin, *Runyon*, 206.

105 *Jimmy Hines's sphere of operation*: NYT, April 24, 1965; John Morahan in Jeff Kisseloff, *You Must Remember This: An Oral History of Manhattan from the 1890s to World War II* (New York: Harcourt Brace Jovanovich, 1989), 593.

106 *"muscles like the proverbial iron bands"*: Alexander, "District Leader—III," 18; NYT, March 26, 1957.

106 *"Madden looked and acted"*: Walker, *Night Club*, 105–6.

106 *"He wore fifty-buck shoes"*: Quoted in Nown, *English Godfather*, 68.

106 *He was "always dolled-up"*: Chandler, *She Always Knew How*, 112.

106 *Jimmy Hines, on the other hand*: NYT, March 26, 1957.

107 *Hines insisted that his principal income*: Alexander, "District Leader—II," TNY 14 (August 1, 1936): 22; see also James Hines File, Municipal Archives, N.Y., N.Y.

107 *"He was suspicious"*: Quoted in Nown, *English Godfather*, 52.

107 *a Stutz Bearcat convertible*: Neal Gabler says that Winchell insisted on sending Madden a check for the car. See Neal Gabler, *Winchell: Gossip, Power and the Culture of Celebrity* (NY: Vintage edition, 1995; originally published in 1994), 155.

107 *"All publicity, to Owney"*: Walker, *Night Club*, 107.

107 *A solicitous father and husband*: Alexander, "District Leader—III."

107 *"It was like knowing the mayor"*: Stone Wallace, *George Raft: The Man Who Would Be Bogart* (Albany, GA, BearManor Media: 2008), 37.

107 *"sensitive to germs"*: Chandler, *She Always Knew How*, 112.

107 *"The least little thing"*: Quoted in Nown, *English Godfather*, 52.

108 *His "reputation for revenge"*: Selwyn Raab, *Five Families: The Rise, Decline, and Resurgence of America's Most Powerful Mafia Empires* (NY: St. Martin's, 2006), 41.

108 *"Around the neighborhood"*: James "Bud" Burns in Kisseloff, *You Must Remember This*, 592–93.

108 *"When my brother got out of reform school"*: Bill Bailey in Kisseloff, *You Must Remember This*, 586.

108 *police protection for the Phoenix Brewery*: NYT, November 30, 1932.

108 *Madden had government agents shadowed*: NYT, December 16, 1932; Lynch, *Criminals*, 66–67.

109 *several spectacular raids*: NYT, September 12, 1931, December 16, 1932.

109 *influential friends in Washington; Maurice Campbell*: Lynch, *Criminals*, 68.

109 *"There is nothing clandestine about a brewery"*: Alva Johnston, "A Reporter at Large: Gangs 'A La Mode,' " TNY 4 (August 25, 1928): 34.

109 *Roughly half the beer purchased in New York*: Lynch, *Criminals*, 46.

109 *"Every cop was on the take"*: John Morahan in Kisseloff, *You Must Remember This*, 588; James Hines Files, Municipal Archives, N.Y., N.Y.

110 *"the place to go"*: Nils Thor Granlund, *Blondes, Brunettes, and Bullets* (NY: David McKay, 1957), 150.

110 *"If one thing hallmarked Owney's clubs"*: Nown, *English Godfather*, 64.

110 *"almost a model of business integration"*: NYT, September 20, 1939.

110 *his annual profits*: Ibid.

CHAPTER FIVE: "THE NIGHT CLUB ERA"

PAGE

111 "Prohibition is better": Behr, *Prohibition*, 172.

111 *"Fay had neither the bold inclination"*: Walker, *Night Club*, 246.

111 *"to hobnob with big names"*: Nils Thor Granlund, *Blondes, Brunettes, and Bullets* (NY: David McKay, 1957), 118. See also NYT, January 2, 1933.

111 *"the biggest cabaret in the world"*: Granlund, *Blondes*, 176.

112 *"I'm Larry Fay"*: Ibid., 118.

112 *"the very best people in town"*: Ibid., 122.

112 *"Hello Sucker"*: Louise Berliner, *Texas Guinan: Queen of the Night Clubs* (Austin: University of Texas Press, 1993), 98.

112 *a "joint"; "Ziegfeld's prettiest"; "the right people"*: Granlund, *Blondes*, 122–24.

112 *"if we hung some from the ceiling"*: Ibid., 124.

112 *"I'm gonna beat Ziegfeld"*: Ibid., 6, 176.

113 *Fay christened the place El Fey*: David Pietrusza, *Rothstein: The Life, Times, and Murder of the Criminal Genius Who Fixed the 1919 World Series* (NY: Carroll & Graf, 2003), 206.

113 *"were little more than market places for sex"; "second-story bandbox"*: Granlund, *Blondes*, 127, 137.

113 *"It's having the same man around"*: Luke Warm, "Texas Guinan," Texasescapes.com. Guinan was legally married only once.

113 *her serialized autobiography*: Texas Guinan, "My Life—AND HOW!," *New York Evening Journal*, May 1–2 1929, April 29–30. An earlier version of her autobiography appeared in 1927 in the *New York Evening Graphic*. The only reliable biography of Guinan is Berliner, *Texas*.

113 *"Exaggerate the world"*: Texas Guinan, "Texas Guinan Says," *New York Evening Graphic*, May 6, 1931. A number of Guinan's columns are in a scrapbook in the Billy

Rose Theatre Collection, Library for the Performing Arts, New York Public Library, New York, NY.

113 *"lived only for the day"*: Guinan, "My Life," April 30, May 6, 1929.

114 *"live life to the limit"*; *"She had a premonition"*: Interview with Katy Hoban, *Rocky Mountain News,* October 5, 1945.

114 *she eloped with John Moynahan*: Guinan, "My Life," May 11, 1929.

114 *"We never change plots"*: Charles K. Stumpf, "Rootin', Tootin', 'Two-Gun Shootin' Texas Guinan," *Under Western Skies* 9 (January 1980): 10.

114 *"You had to go there"*: Berliner, *Texas,* 97.

114 *"din and dazzle"*: Lloyd Morris, *Incredible New York: High Life and Low Life from 1850 to 1950* (NY: Random House, 1951), 273.

114 *"felt like overupholstered mess halls"*: James Traub, *The Devil's Playground: A Century of Pleasure and Profit in Times Square* (NY: Random House, 2004), 29.

115 *"a raucous jungle"*: Herbert Asbury, *The Great Illusion: An Informal History of Prohibition* (NY: Doubleday, Dorav 1950), 190–91.

115 *Hubert's Museum and Flea Circus*: Christopher Gray, "Streetscapes," NYT, June 16, 1996.

115 *"They preferred the retirement"*: NYT, January 2, 1927.

115 *By 1925 mobsters had a stranglehold*: Granlund, *Blondes,* 137–38.

115 *"new children of the night"*: Walker, *Night Club,* 78.

116 *"the uncertainties of 1919 were over"*: F. Scott Fitzgerald, "Early Success," in Edmund Wilson, ed., *The Crack-Up* (NY: New Directions, 1993), 41.

116 *"frequenting a night club"*: Walker, *Night Club,* 78.

116 *"We drank up everything"*: Quoted in ibid., 84.

116 *"couvert charge"*: Ben Finney, *Feet First* (NY: Crown, 1971), 150.

116 *"would back anything"*: Granlund, *Blondes,* 138.

116 *"All dressed up"*: Charyn, *Gangsters,* 60, 66.

116 *"good service"*: Granlund, *Blondes,* 139–40.

116 *a trip to the hospital*: Charles G. Shaw, *Nightlife: Vanity Fair's Intimate Guide to New York After Dark* (NY: John Day, 1931), 20–21.

116 *"out-of-town buyers"*: NYT, quoted in Morris, *Incredible,* 327.

117 *"We go to cabarets"*: Ellin Mackay, "Why We Go to Cabarets: A Post-Debutante Explains," TNY 1 (November 28, 1925): 7–8.

117 *"Cohen" replaced "Smith"*: Geoffrey Perret, *America in the Twenties: A History* (NY: Simon & Schuster, 1982), 17.

117 *"If you don't believe"*: Guinan, "My Life," May 21, 1929.

117 *"whether they liked it or not"*: Granlund, *Blondes,* 139.

117 *"I found myself"*: James Robert Parish, *The George Raft File: The Unauthorized Biography* (NY: Drake, 1973), 59.

117 *"There are no social lines"*: Guinan, "My Life," May 21, 1929.

117 *"Never before has there been"*: Quoted in Lerner, *Dry,* 143.

118 *"the melting pot of all nations"*: Benjamin De Casseres, "Joel's," *The American Mercury* 26 (July 1932): 361.

118 *"evening dress of every range"*: Henry Irving Brock and J. W. Golinkin, *New York Is Like This* (NY: Dodd, Mead, 1929), 16.

118 *"a like number of native sons"*: NYT, January 2, 1927.

118 *a clear profit*: Lothrop Stoddard, *Luck, Your Silent Partner* (NY: Horace Liveright, 1929), 11.

118   *"This town is nightclub mad"*: TNY, June 13, 1925.

118   *"the new American invention"*: Susan Waggoner, *Nightclub Nights: Art, Legend, and Style, 1920–1960* (NY: Rizzoli, 2001), 7.

118   *"The town flocks to them"*: Shaw, *Nightlife*, 23.

118   *"Exclusiveness is the night club's"*: Barney Gallant quoted in Mark Caldwell, *New York Night: The Mystique and Its History* (NY: Charles Scribner's Sons, 2005), 225.

118   *"Woolworth money"*: Helen Bullit Lowry, "New York's After Midnight Clubs," NYT, February 5, 1922).

119   *"Texas Guinan of New York"*: Charles G. Shaw, "Three Americans," in *Vanity Fair: Selections from America's Most Memorable Magazine,* Cleveland Amory and Frederic Bradlee, eds., (NY: Viking, 1960), 142.

119   *"'Get hot!'"*: Guinan, "My Life," May 21, 1929.

119   *"prohibition by padlock"*: "To Dry New York with Padlocks," *Literary Digest* 84 (March 21, 1925): 8.

119   *court hearings replaced lengthy jury trials*: NYT, March 4, 1925; "I Shall Keep My Oath," *Success, The Human Magazine* 9 (July 1925): 66.

119   *Buckner lacked the money and manpower*: "The Talk of the Town: The Key to the Padlocks," TNY (March 21, 1925): 1.

119   *Buckner was soon allotted Treasury Department funds*: Emory R. Buckner testimony, U.S. Congress, Senate Committee on the Judiciary, *The National Prohibition Law: Hearings Before the Subcommittee,* 69th Cong. 1st sess., April 1926, 96–115.

119   *Operating without juries*: "To Dry," 9.

120   *Buckner began his padlocking campaign*: NYT, April 17, 1925.

120   *"New York's booze-bolstered night life"*: "To Dry," 8.

120   *Buckner had padlocked hundreds of clubs*: NYT, November 21, 1925.

120   *El Fey became the Texas Guinan Club*: Ibid.

120   *Fay had gotten a little sloppy*: Yablonsky, *George Raft,* 48.

120   *the English writer Stephen Graham*: Stephen Graham, *New York Nights* (NY: George H. Doran, 1927), 84, 87.

120   *"There she was like a queen"; "began to boss"*: All quotes in ibid., 93, 95, 178; and Will Irwin, *Highlights of Manhattan* (NY: D. Appleton-Century, 1937, Revised edition. Originally published in 1927), 347.

120   *George S. Kaufman had borrowed*: Howard Teichmann, *George S. Kaufman: An Intimate Portrait* (NY: Atheneum, 1972), 93.

121   *"He'll be happy"*: Irwin, *Highlights,* 347.

121   *The solo performer*: Yablonsky, George *Raft,* 37.

121   *"George did the fastest"*: Ibid., 40.

121   *"Because the customer was always right"*: Ibid., 43.

121   *"drunk-rolling concession"*: Parish, *Raft File,* 62.

121   *"As the night is stretched later and later"*: Edmund Wilson, *The American Earthquake: A Documentary of the Twenties and Thirties* (NY: Octagon, 1971 edition, originally published 1958), 32–33.

121   *"Bye-Bye Blackbird"*: Graham, *New York Nights,* 100–101.

121   *"a cross between a Hong Kong hop-joint"*: Shaw, "Three Americans," in Amory and Bradlee, eds., *Vanity Fair,* 142.

122 *a moment of quiet prayer*: Ibid., 141.

122 *"Between 5 and tata time"*: Walter Winchell, *Winchell Exclusive: "Things That Happened to Me—And Me to Them"* (Englewood Cliffs, NJ: Prentice Hall, 1975), 51.

122 *"an old experienced doll"*: Damon Runyon, *The Damon Runyon Omnibus* (NY: Blue Ribbon, 1939), 123, 127.

122 *"Practically nobody saw her"*: Berliner, *Texas*, 99.

122 *A heady businesswoman*: DN, February 19, 1927.

122 *"The cheap speakeasy"*: NYT, January 22, 1933.

122 *"delirium," and even brain damage*: NYW, February 6, 1927.

123 *Of the nearly half a million gallons*: Asbury, *Great Illusion*, 280.

123 *drinking "poison alcohol"*: NYW, January 1–4, February 6, 1927. There are no accurate nationwide statistics on deaths by poisoned alcohol, but one historian argues that "it is probable" that by 1927 over fifty thousand Americans died as a result of drinking liquor made from alcohol containing dangerous denaturants. See Edward Behr, *Prohibition: Thirteen Years That Changed America* (New York: Arcade, 1996), 221.

123 *killed nearly eight hundred persons*: NYW, January 4, 5, 1928.

123 *most of the booze available*: Markey, "Booze," 31.

123 *The "big thrill"*: Arnold Shaw, *52nd Street: The Street of Jazz* (NY: Da Capo, 1971), 13.

123 *"a new American institution"*: Frederick Lewis Allen, *Only Yesterday: An Informal History of the 1920's* (NY: Harper & Row, 1931), 95.

123 *"At noon and from the hour before dinner"*: NYT, January 22, 1933.

123 *"These were the speakeasy days"*: John Dos Passos, *The Best Times: An Informal Memoir* (NY: New American Library, 1966), 138.

124 *more than five thousand illegal clubs*: Lynch, *Criminals*, 48.

124 *"Speakeasies have been something more"*: "Manhattan Speakeasies," *Fortune* 7 (June 1933): 53.

124 *"for every taste and purse"*: Ibid.

124 *"the doorman"*: Ibid., 56.

125 *"a place where people of letters"*: Kriendler with Jeffers, *"21,"* 17–18.

125 *Jack Kriendler and Charlie Berns grew up*: Marilyn Kaytor, *"21": The Life and Times of New York's Favorite Club* (NY: Viking, 1975), 7–8.

125 *"spiffiest"*; *"None of this was lost"*: H. Peter Kriendler with Paul Jeffers, *"21": Every Day Was New Year's Eve: Memoirs of a Saloon Keeper* (Dallas: Taylor, 1999), 4.

125 *"keeper of the till"*: Ibid., 8.

126 *"miniatures"*: Berns in Kobler, *Ardent*, 226–27; Kaytor, *"21,"* 11.

126 *"in a little red wagon"*; *"We would slip"*: Berns in Kobler, *Ardent*, 227.

126 *"If any trouble came"*: Kaytor, *"21,"* 13.

126 *"Jack's dream"*: Ibid., 23.

126 *"I was born in this house"*: Ibid., 22.

126 *"lounging properly in silver baskets"*: "Manhattan Speakeasies," 54.

127 *Geib served French wines*: Kriendler with Jeffers, *"21,"* 22.

127 *"that would have rendered"*: Ibid.

127 *"laughing room"*: Daniel Okrent, *Great Fortune: The Epic of Rockefeller Center* (NY: Penguin, 2004), 380.

127 *"balance wheel"*: Kriendler with Jeffers, *"21,"* 77–79.

127 *"Jack supplied"*: Ibid., 23.

127 *Tony Soma's*: Billy Altman, Laughter's *Gentle Soul: The Life of Robert Benchley* (NY: W. W. Norton, 1997), 221–22.

127 *One year after it opened*: Kriendler with Jeffers, *"21,"* 22.

127 *"The speakeasy makes money"*: Ibid., 44.

128 *"It cost us about"*: Kobler, *Ardent*, 228–29.

128 *The 300 Club was at the head of the list*: NYT, January 2, 1926.

128 *"flying squadrons"; "We have been ordered"*: NYT, August 1, 1926.

128 *"personal" injunctions*: NYT, January 2, 1927.

128 *"the most sweeping drive yet"; Seven "parties"; secretly collecting evidence*: NYT, December 22, 1926.

129 *"innocent" and "victimized" employee*: NYT, February 17, 19, 1927.

129 *His undercover agents had heard her*: NYT, February 17–20, 1927.

129 *Truman Fowler; They found the injunction; "Play 'The Prisoner's Song'"*: NYT, March 31, 1927.

129 *He was "all apologies"; "famous people of the stage"*: DN, February 18, 1927.

129 *"giggling, screaming, roaring"*: DN, February 17, 1927.

130 *"This time it looks serious"*: Ibid.

130 *a breakfast feast*: Berliner, *Texas*, 120.

130 *dismissed every charge*: NYT, February 26, March 22, 1927.

130 *three-hour federal hearing*: DN, March 31, 1927; NYT, March 31, 1927.

130 *Prohibition enforcement unit was being disbanded*: NYT, March 25, 1927.

130 *"could not be enforced in New York"*: Mayer, *Buckner*, 194.

130 *The Padlocks of 1927*: NYT, April 5, 1927.

130 *"her whole gang was there"*: Walker, *Night Club*, 243.

130 *"loud, noisy, [and] unimaginative"*: NYT, July 6, 1927.

130 *"an entertainer extraordinary"*: DN, June 24, 1927.

131 *"I would rather have a square inch"*: Luke Warm, "Texas Guinan," TexasEscapes.com.

131 *"honest to God revenge on New Yorkers"*: Lerner, *Dry*, 265.

131 *"all American women stood steadfastly"*: Ibid., 189.

131 *the Women's Committee for Modification*: Asbury, *Illusion*, 315.

131 *M. Louise Gross*: Lerner, *Dry*, 191.

131 *"abroad where"*: "M. Louise Gross," www.2.potsdam.edu.

132 *"It seemed almost a geologic epoch"*: H. L. Mencken, *A Choice of Days* (NY: Alfred A. Knopf, 1980), 307.

CHAPTER SIX: "HE DID IT ALONE"

PAGE

133 *"It was an age of miracles"*: F. Scott Fitzgerald, "Echoes of the Jazz Age," in Wilson, ed., *Crack-Up*, 14.

133 *would draw nearly four million people*: NYT, June 14, 1927.

133 *"He left these shores"*: DN, June 13, 1927.

134 *sixty thousand people*: NYT, June 13, 1927.

134 *"The crowds were grouped"*: Ibid.

134 *"the greatest holiday"*: DN, June 13–14, 1927.

134 *Only thirty-nine marriage licenses:* NYT, June 14, 1927.

134 *Radio announcers:* NYT, June 12, 14, 1927.

134 *"Hail Lindbergh" celebration:* DN, June 12, 1927.

134 *"triumphal marches":* NYT, June 14, 1927.

135 *"thunderous welcome":* NYT, June 14, 1927.

135 *"You ain't seen nothin' yet!":* DN, June 12, 1927.

135 *he set two speed records; "hop":* NYT, May 13, 1927.

136 *Lloyd's of London:* A. Scott Berg, *Lindbergh* (NY: G. P. Putnam's Sons, 1998), 106.

136 *fascinated with flight:* Charles A. Lindbergh, *"We"* (NY: G. P. Putnam's Sons, 1928 edition; originally published in 1927), 23, 28–29.

136 *"modern and powerful planes"; "Lucky":* Ibid., 78, 187.

136 *"The sheer audacity":* NYT, May 13, 1927.

136 *"perfect picture":* NYT, May 21–22, 1927.

137 *"a doer and not a talker":* NYT, May 22, 1927.

137 *"the perfect antidote":* Berg, *Lindbergh,* 112.

137 *"He stands out":* Quoted in John W. Ward, "The Meaning of Lindbergh's Flight," *American Quarterly* 10 (Spring 1958): 6.

137 *"fearless blue eyes":* NYT, May 21, 1927.

137 *"I'd like to use":* Grover A. Whalen, *Mr. New York: The Autobiography of Grover A. Whalen* (NY: G. P. Putnam's Sons, 1955), 107–10.

138 *"The fliers":* Berg, *Lindbergh,* 110.

138 *There was a sudden change in the weather:* Ibid.

138 *Unable to sleep:* Lindbergh, *"We,"* 215.

138 *It was "The Flying Fool"; "coats, dresses, and lingerie":* NYT, May 13, 1927; Whalen, *Mr. New York,* 112.

138 *"BYRD TAKES OFF TODAY":* Whalen, *Mr. New York,* 112.

138 *"emptied out the speakeasies":* Ibid.

139 *noticed the tires sagging:* Berg, *Lindbergh,* 113.

139 *Lindbergh's only provisions:* NYT, May 21, 1927.

139 *"to replace the weight":* Lindbergh, *"We,"* 202.

139 *"As I stood by the* Spirit of St. Louis*":* Whalen, *Mr. New York,* 113.

139 *Whalen shadowed Lindbergh's plane:* Ibid.; NYT, May 23, 1927.

139 *"God be with him":* Berg, *Lindbergh,* 117.

139 *he realized:* NYT, May 21, 1927.

140 *"coarse voice"; "expressed elementally":* Paul Gallico, "The Man Who Flew Alone," DN, May 23, 1927.

140 *"He's arrived in Paris, boys":* NYT, May 22, 1927.

140 *second only to the excitement; "Within a few minutes":* Whalen, *Mr. New York,* 115.

140 *Every fire station:* NYT, May 22, 1927.

140 *"respectful attention":* Ibid.; Whalen, *Mr. New York,* 115.

140 *"more than 6,000 persons":* NYT, May 22, 1927.

140 *"Look at them kids hoppin'":* Berg, *Lindbergh,* 151.

141 *it was played on the Wurlitzer:* "Charles Lindbergh Music," www.charleslindbergh .com/music/index.asp.

141 *"It wasn't easy going"; briefly nodded off several times:* Carlyle MacDonald, "Could Have Gone 500 Miles Further," NYT, May 22, 1927.

141 *"All I want[ed] in life"*: Berg, *Lindbergh*, 124.

141 *He became so numb to hunger*: MacDonald, "Could Have."

141 *he had considered turning back*: NYT, May 22–23, 1927.

141 *"gray-white airplane"*: Edwin L. James, "Crowd Roars Thunderous welcome," NYT, May 22, 1927.

141 *"A frenzied mob"*: Ibid.

141 *"Here he is"*: Lindbergh, *"We,"* 225–26. See also NYT, May 23, 1927.

141 *"This is a new country"*: NYT, May 23, 1927.

142 *he had been awake for almost sixty hours*: James, "Crowd Roars," NYT; Lindbergh, *"We,"* 238.

142 *a whirlwind week*: NYT, May 23, 1927.

142 *Croydon Aerodrome*: NYT, May 30, 1927.

142 *"I have had suggestions"*: NYT, May 31, 1927.

142 *"My ship and I"*: NYT, May 23, 1927. See also Walter S. Ross, *The Last Hero: Charles A. Lindbergh* (NY: Harper & Row, 1968), 140.

142 *"Where do you get"*: DN, May 23, 1927.

142 *"Lindbergh Flies Alone"*: New York *Sun*, May 22, 1927.

142 *"youth and idealism"*: Myron Herrick, Foreword, *"We,"* 5.

143 *a flood of letters*: Letters to the Editor, 1927, William Patterson Papers, Lake Forest College, Lake Forest, Illinois.

143 *"remember, always remember"*: Gallico, "Man Who Flew Alone."

143 *"the first wild sweep"*: NYT, June 13, 1927; John Lardner, "The Lindbergh Legends," in Roger Kahn, ed., *Lardner: The World of John Lardner* (NY: Simon & Schuster, 1961), 30.

143 *"In the spring of '27"*: Fitzgerald, "Echoes of the Jazz Age," in Wilson, ed., *Crack-Up*, 20.

143 *"the apex"*: John Lardner, "The Lindbergh Legends," in Kahn, ed. *Word*, 30.

143 *"I find myself wondering"*: NYT, June 1, 1927.

144 *"bedlam broke loose in the harbor"*: Whalen, *Mr. New York*, 17.

144 *"screaming, honking"*: DN, June 14, 1927.

144 *"jammed to the rails"; "Fireboats shot streams"*: Ibid.

144 *"I didn't think"*: Russell Owen, "A Boy's Day in a Big City," NYT, June 14, 1927.

144 *"He might have done a somersault"*: NYT, June 14, 1927.

145 *"Ticker tape and torn fragments"; "into a semi-solid"; "in letters a mile long"*: Ibid.

145 *"three white-robed women"; "not necessary"; People hung from trees*: Ibid.

145 *One enthusiast*: NYT, June 18, 1927.

145 *unable to keep track of his bank balance*: Lardner, "Lindbergh Legends," in Kahn, ed., *World*, 40.

145 *"There was never anything like it"*: NYT, June 14, 1927.

146 *"stampede"; a model of the* Spirit of St. Louis: NYW, June 15, 1927.

146 *"a recent and sudden phenomenon"*: Irwin, *Highlights*, 221.

146 *"The fame of Park Avenue"*: Hulbert Footner, *New York: City of Cities* (NY: J. B. Lippincott, 1937), 226.

146 *"It was a trip of daring"*: *Engineering News* 69 (May 1, 1913): 1886.

146 *"a veritable 'Chinese Wall'"*: William J. Wilgus, "The Grand Central Terminal in Perspective," *American Society of Civil Engineers, Transactions, Paper No. 2119* 106 (October 1940): 997.

147   *"presents the most majestic":* Footner, *New York,* 226.

147   *"Welcome home, Lindy":* NYT, June 14, 1927.

CHAPTER SEVEN: REVENUE PLUCKED FROM THE AIR

PAGE

151   "This beautiful street": *Fortune* 19 (July 1939).

151   *"over the great bridge":* F. Scott Fitzgerald, *Gatsby,* 73.

151   *"straight as a sunbeam"; "It is a street":* Zelda Fitzgerald, "The Changing Beauty of
       Park Avenue," in Matthew J. Bruccoli, ed., *Zelda Fitzgerald: The Collected Writings*
       (NY: Charles Scribner's Sons, 1991), 403–5. Written in 1927, the piece was first pub-
       lished in *Harper's Bazaar* in January 1928. Bruccoli writes: "Published as by Zelda
       and F. Scott Fitzgerald, but credited to Zelda in his *Ledger."*

152   *"ensconced":* Irwin, *Highlights,* 221.

152   *It was "underfoot"; "new quarter":* Ibid., 219.

153   *a dark, two-mile-long tunnel:* William D. Middleton, *Grand Central: The World's
       Greatest Railway Terminal* (San Marino, CA: Golden West, 1977), 32–34.

153   *"The scene presented"; Approached by reporters:* NYT, January 9, 1902; Kurt C.
       Schlichting, *Grand Central Terminal: Railroads, Engineering and Architecture in New
       York City* (Baltimore: Johns Hopkins University Press, 2001), 55. Schlichting's is the
       most comprehensive history of the terminal. Two excellent histories of the termi-
       nal have appeared recently: Sam Roberts, *Grand Central: How a Train Station Trans-
       formed America* (NY: Grand Central, 2013); and Anthony W. Robins, *Grand Central
       Terminal: 100 Years of a New York Landmark* (NY: Stewart, Tabori & Chang, 2013).

154   *John D. Crimmins:* NYT, January 9, 1902.

154   *the New York legislature prohibited:* David Marshall, *Grand Central* (NY: McGraw-
       Hill, 1946), 237.

154   *"the dangers and discomforts":* Wilgus, "Grand Central Terminal in Perspective,"
       1002; William J. Wilgus to Joseph Gilder, November 14, 1926, William J. Wilgus Pa-
       pers, Manuscripts and Archives Division New York Public Library, New York, NY.
       Hereafter Wilgus Mss.

154   *no railroad was then using electricity:* Wilgus to Gilder, November 14, 1926, Wilgus
       Mss. Work on the Paris Metro had begun in 1898 and one line had opened in 1900.

154   *"astonishing in its magnitude and its daring":* Carl W. Condit, *The Port of New York: A
       History of the Rail and Terminal System from the Grand Central Electrification to the
       Present,* vol. 2 of *The Port of New York* (Chicago: University of Chicago Press, 1981), 1.

154   *Thirty-eight-year-old William J. Wilgus:* NYT, February 1, 1903; Marshall, *Grand Cen-
       tral,* 250. Wilgus has finally gotten his biography: Kurt C. Schlichting, *Grand Central's
       Engineer: William J. Wilgus and the Planning of Modern Manhattan* (Baltimore: Johns
       Hopkins University Press, 2012).

155   *"It is a remarkable fact":* "Congestion of Traffic at the Grand Central Station and Its
       Remedy," *Scientific American* 183 (December 1, 1900): 338.

155   *"practically unsettled":* NYT, February 2, 1913.

155   *prophetic:* Edward Hungerford, "The Greatest Railway Terminal in the World," *The
       Outlook* 102 (December 28, 1912): 902–4.

155   *the city banned steam locomotives:* James Marston Fitch and Diana S. Waite, *Grand*

Central Terminal and Rockefeller Center: A Historic-critical Estimate of Their Significance (NY: New York State Parks and Recreation, Division for Historic Preservation, 1974), 2.

155 *the Harlem's main station:* NYT, February 2, 1913.

156 *"bold move":* Federal Writers' Project, *The WPA Guide to New York City: The Federal Writers' Project Guide to 1930s New York* (NY: Pantheon Books edition, 1980; originally published in 1939), 233.

156 *"program of conquest":* Condit, *Port of New York,* vol. 2, 175. See also Robert Sobel, *The Fallen Colossus* (NY: Weybright & Talley, 1977), 56–57.

158 *Commodore Vanderbilt was confident:* Edward Hungerford, *Men and Iron: The History of the New York Central* (NY: Thomas Y. Crowell, 1938), 904.

158 *a great civic "blunder"; "the city into two parts":* Wilgus, "Perspective," 997.

158 *wasteland:* F. A. Collins, *The Romance of Park Avenue* (NY: Park Avenue Association, 1930), 65.

158 *"a Midwestern cow town":* James Trager, *Park Avenue: Street of Dreams* (NY: Atheneum, 1990), 26.

158 *"chaos of cars":* Hungerford, "Greatest Railway Terminal," 905.

158 *"mere palliative measure":* Wilgus to Gilder, November 14, 1926, Wilgus Mss.

158 *a state-of-the-art terminal complex:* Wilgus to W. H. Newman, March 19, 1903, Wilgus Mss.

158 *"It was the most daring thing":* Marshall, *Grand Central,* 239–40. See also *New York Telegram,* February 22, 1929.

159 *"tear down the old [station] building":* Wilgus to Newman, December 22, 1902, Wilgus Mss.

159 *would, in effect, be creating two terminals:* William J. Wilgus, "An Account of the Inception and Creation of the New Grand Central Terminal," Wilgus Mss.

159 *virtually "stairless" building:* NYT, February 2, 1913.

159 *"steal away":* Ibid.

159 *"gliding in and out"; "as silently as ghosts":* William Inglis, "New York's New Gateway," *Harper's Magazine 57* (February 1, 1913): 20; "The New Grand Central Terminal in New York City," *Engineering News* 69, no. 18 (May 1, 1913): 884. The upper-level loop system was completed in 1917. The lower-level loop system did not become operational until 1927.

159 *"first class hotel":* Wilgus to Newman, March 19, 1903, Wilgus Mss.

160 *"a great civic center":* Ibid.

160 *"would vastly strengthen":* Wilgus, "An Account," 1, Wilgus Mss.

160 *"as squalid and dirty":* Quoted in Jill Jonnes, *Conquering Gotham: Building Penn Station and Its Tunnels* (NY: Penguin, 2008), 11. See also Hilary Ballon, *New York's Pennsylvania Stations* (NY: W. W. Norton, 2002), 21.

160 *"I have never been able to":* Jonnes, *Conquering,* 14.

161 *gain a competitive advantage:* Wilgus, "Perspectives," 1003.

161 *active leadership of the railroad:* T. J. Stiles, *The First Tycoon: The Epic Life of Cornelius Vanderbilt* (NY: Alfred A. Knopf, 2009), 570.

161 *"grocery store" idea:* Wilgus to Gilder, November 14, 1926, Wilgus Mss.

161 *lease this "empty air":* Wilgus, "An Account," Wilgus Mss; Marshall, *Grand Central,* 240–43, 264.

161 *"elevated driveway"*: Wilgus to Newman, March 19, 1903, Wilgus Mss; Marshall, *Grand Central*, 241.

162 *"the most attractive locality"*: Wilgus to Newman, March 19, 1903, Wilgus Mss.

162 *"financial forecast"; "earn an income"*: Ibid.

162 *"Thus from the air"*: Wilgus, "Perspectives," 1003.

162 *"intense joy"*: Wilgus to Gilder, November 14, 1926, Wilgus Mss.

162 *handling more than six hundred trains daily*: Wilgus, "Perspective," 1010.

162 *"An army was set to work"*: Hugh Thompson, "The Greatest Railroad Terminal in the World," *Munsey's Magazine* 11 (April 1911): 35.

162 *"What are they doing here?"*: Hungerford, "Greatest Railway Terminal," 901.

162 *Twenty-five miles of sewers*: "Opening of the New Grand Central Terminal, New York," *Railway Age Gazette* 54 (February 7, 1913): 259.

162 *Over a million and a half cubic yards of rock*: Hungerford, "Greatest Railway Terminal," 906; Condit, *Port of New York,* vol. 2, 85.

163 *a "miracle" engineering accomplishment*: Schlichting, *Grand Central,* 99. Electrification was eventually extended to Harmon, New York, on the Albany line, and to Boston on the New York and New Haven line. William D. Middleton, *When the Steam Railroads Electrified* (Milwaukee: Kalmbach, 1974), 44.

163 *They were "too heavy"*: *New York Evening Journal,* February 19, 1907, 11.

163 *the company modified the design of the engines*: Schlichting, *Grand Central,* 99–105.

163 *Wilgus resigned in protest*: Wilgus to Gilder, November 14, 1925, Wilgus Mss.

163 *Charles Reed and Allen Stem*: Condit, *Port of New York,* vol. 2, 66.

164 *"The standard of success"*: Marshall, *Grand Central,* 260.

164 *Newman and Wetmore worked out the arrangement*: Condit, *Port of New York,* vol. 2, 69.

164 *"the glory of commerce"*: NYT, February 2, 1913.

164 *"With a smile forever fixed"*: "The Grand Central Terminal," *Fortune* 3 (February 1931): 99.

164 *a chamber tall enough*: John Steele Gordon, "An Immense and Distant Roof," *American Heritage* 48 (February–March 1997): 18.

165 *"bold and unique"*: "Opening of New Grand Central Terminal, NY," *Railway Age Gazette* (February 7, 1913): 235.

165 *"Nice city"*: Roberts, *Grand Central,* 129.

165 *"changed the law"*: Ballon, *New York's Pennsylvania Stations,* 18.

165 *A crowd of three thousand New Yorkers*: NYT, February 2, 1913.

165 *"miracle-worker"*: Inglis, "New York's New Gateway," 13.

165 *was as if he never existed*: John Belle and Maxine R. Leighton, *Grand Central: Gateway to a Million Lives* (NY: W. W. Norton, 2000), 54.

166 *"but congestion with movement"*: Douglas Haskell, "The Lost New York of the Pan American Airways Building," *Architectural Forum* 119 (November 1963): 108.

166 *"New York brought her two major achievements"*: Ibid.

166 *A "monument to movement"*: Herbert Muschamp, "Restoration Liberates Grand Vistas, and Ideas: An Appraisal," NYT, October 2, 1998. Grand Central still handles nearly 150,000 commuters a day, making it one of the world's busiest train stations.

166 *Charles Follen McKim designed Penn Station*: Ballon, *New York's Pennsylvania Stations,* 74.

166 *"[was] like passing"*: Robert Anderson Pope, "Grand Central Terminal Station," *The Town-Planning Review* 2 (April 1911): 59–60.

166 *more than 43 million passengers:* NYT, December 4, 1927 The U.S. population in 1927 was 119,035,000.

166 *without which New York could not function:* Kenneth Powell, *Grand Central Terminal* (London: Phaidon, 1996), 25.

167 *"new urban energies":* Fitch and Waite, *Grand Central Terminal,* 1.

167 *"are wholly existential":* Jane Jacobs, *The Economy of Cities* (NY: Vintage, 1970), 141–42, 144.

167 *"To sensitive New Yorkers":* "The Pennsylvania Station," *Fortune* 19 (July 1939): 157.

168 *"Ten years ago":* W. Parker Chase, *New York: The Wonder City* (NY: Wonder City Publishing, 1931), 230–31.

168 *"an inconvenient local street":* Christopher Gray, "Streetscapes: The Grand Central Viaduct," NYT, October 29, 1989.

168 *first planned residential precinct:* "New Roadways Around Grand Central Terminal Formally Opened," *The Real Estate Record and Builders' Guide* (September 15, 1928): 6; NYT, September 2, 1928.

168 *"plucked from the air":* Wilgus, "Perspective," 1023.

CHAPTER EIGHT: STREET OF DREAMS

PAGE

169 "Park Avenue on the island": Stuart Chase, "Park Avenue," NR 51 (May 25, 1927): 9.

169 *shot up nearly 250 percent:* Edwin H. Spengler, "Land Values in New York in Relation to Transit Facilities," *Studies in History, Economics and Public Law,* ed. by Faculty of Political Science, Columbia University (No. 33, 1930): 57.

169 *"The city is being rebuilt":* NYT, October 26, 1926.

169 *"The building orgy":* Arthur Pound, *The Golden Earth: The Story of Manhattan's Landed Wealth* (NY: Arno, 1975; originally published in 1935), 223–24.

170 *New York City would account for fully 20 percent:* L. Seth Schnitman, "Statistical Analysis of New York City Construction—1919 to 1930," *Real Estate Record and Builders Guide* 126 (October 11, 1930): 6–7.

170 *77 percent of all new residential construction:* Ibid. See also Tom Shachtman, *Skyscraper Dreams: The Great Real Estate Dynasties of New York* (Boston: Little, Brown, 1991), 111.

170 *five new single-family houses:* Elizabeth Hawes, *New York, New York: How the Apartment House Transformed the Life of the City, 1869–1930* (NY: Alfred A. Knopf, 1993), 237.

171 *was deeply attractive to speculative builders:* Joshua D'Esposito, "Some of the Fundamental Principles of Air Rights," *Railway Age* 83 (October 1927): 759.

171 *"exercise a strict supervision":* Walter Bernard, "The World's Greatest Railway Terminal," *Scientific American* 104 (June 17, 1911): 505.

171 *"Windows and prim greenery":* Zelda Fitzgerald, "Changing Beauty," 403–5.

171 *architects began constructing "set-back" skyscrapers:* Marc A. Weiss, "Skyscraper Zoning: New York's Pioneering Role," *Journal of the American Planning Association* 58 (Spring 1992): 204; Carol Willis, "Zoning and Zeitgeist: The Skyscraper City in the 1920s," *Journal of the Society of Architectural Historians* 95 (March 1986): 48.

172 *"brownstone into Babylon":* NYT, October 26, 1926.

172 *"panorama[s] unexcelled"*: Steven Ruttenbaum, *Mansions in the Clouds: The Sky-scraper Palazzi of Emery Roth* (NY: Balsam, 1986), 95.

172 *"mansions in the clouds"*: Steven Ruttenbaum, "Visible City, The Ritz Tower," *Metropolis* 4 (May 1985): 40.

172 *"like a telescope"*: Hawes, *New York, New York,* 231.

172 Arthur Brisbane: "Today," *Time* 8 (August 16, 1926): 24.

173 *"In town"; "with a full complement"*: Both quotes in Ruttenbaum, *Mansions,* 99.

173 *"The city dweller finds"*: "The Modern Apartment Hotel," *The American Architect* 131 (January 1927): 37.

173 *"This is the age of the apartment"*: Hawes, *New York, New York,* 213.

174 *"No technical or art school"*: Ruttenbaum, *Mansions,* 23.

174 *"The construction boom is on"*: Ibid., 67.

174 *"have a style"*: Paul Goldberger, "Foreword" to Ruttenbaum, *Mansions,* 11.

174 *"Monolithic packing cases"*: Chase, "Park Avenue," 9.

174 *"made by realty barons"*: Zelda Fitzgerald, "Changing Beauty," 403–5.

175 *"individuality and warmth"*: Irwin, *Highlights,* 217, 223.

175 *"row upon row"*: Chase, "Park Avenue," 10.

175 *entertained guests in the princely splendor:* "Brisbane Building Will Dominate Upper New York Skyline," *The Real Estate Record and Builders' Guide* 114 (September 13, 1924): 7–8.

175 *Roth's sons and later partners:* NYT, August 21, 1948.

175 *"unquestioned master"*: Robert A. M. Stern, Gregory F. Gilmartin, and Thomas Mellins, *New York 1930* (NY: Rizzoli, 2009), 21.

175 *"sky-conscious"*: Hawes, *New York, New York,* 231.

176 *"the order of the day"*: Chase, "Park Avenue," 10.

176 *"a set of commandments"; The tyrannical board of one super-exclusive cooperative:* This was 755 Park Avenue, built in 1930 by James T. Lee, a grandfather of Jacqueline Kennedy Onassis. See Steven Gaines, *The Sky's the Limit: Passion and Property in Manhattan* (NY: Back Bay, 2005), 46–51.

176 *"the consoling proximity of millionaires"*: F. Scott Fitzgerald, *Gatsby,* 10.

176 *The "Cinderella"; "as impressive"*: Virginia Pope, "Now the Penthouse Palace Is Evolving," NYT, March 23, 1930.

176 *"a detachment impossible"*: Irwin, *Highlights,* 223.

176 *"the noises of the city"*: "Ritz Tower," TNY 2 (May 15, 1926): 13.

177 *some of the most privileged social clubs:* NYT, June 21, 1927; "The Union: Mother of Clubs," *Fortune* 6 (December 1932): 45.

177 *"stone canyons"*: Chase, "Park Avenue," 9.

177 *"the Faubourg St. Germain"*: Irwin, *Highlights,* 220.

177 *ravishing young women:* Chase, "Park Avenue," 10.

177 *"long arrived"*: Irwin, *Highlights,* 224.

177 *"gold-seekers from across the ocean"*: Morand, *New York,* 250.

177 *fifteen thousand millionaires:* DN, May 1, 1927; Chase, "Park Avenue," 10.

177 *fifty certified millionaires lived:* NYW, January 28, 1927.

177 *"boast such serried phalanxes"*: Chase, "Park Avenue," 9.

178 *Park Avenue spent:* Maurice Mermey, "Croesus's Sixty Acres," *The North American Review* 227 (January 1929): 2.

178 *"The man who earns"*: NYW, January 28, 1927.

178 *"paladin"*: Mermey, "Croesus's," 4.

178 *a New York City industrial worker*: NYT, February 13, 1927.

178 *"distinguishes them"*: Cornelius Vanderbilt, Jr., *Farewell to Fifth Avenue* (NY: Simon & Schuster, 1935), 83–4.

178 *"the mustaches of British officers"*: Chase, "Park Avenue," 9.

178 *"housemen"*: Federal Writer's Project, *WPA Guide to New York City*, 234.

178 *"relics of the sow's ear age"; "ribald commercialism"*: Mermey, "Croesus's," 5–6.

178 *"the last really residential avenue in the city"*: NYT, May 21, 1927, September 23, 1930.

179 *"In season"*: Mermey, "Croesus's," 3–4.

179 *"I love New York on summer afternoons"*: F. Scott Fitzgerald, *Gatsby*, 132.

179 *"Park Avenue virtually commutes"*: Mermey, "Croesus's," 7.

179 *"incredibly romantic"*: John Maxtone-Graham, *The Only Way to Cross* (NY: Macmillan, 1972), 193.

179 *as many as a dozen ocean liners*: NYT, November 19, 1927.

179 *the largest moving objects*: Francis J. Duffy and William H. Miller, *The New York Harbor Book* (Falmouth, ME: TBW Books, 1986), 71.

179 *"fragment[s] of Manhattan"*: Morand, *New York*, 231.

179 *as many as five thousand visitors onboard*: Maxtone-Graham, *Only Way*, 178.

179 *"phantomlike"*: Bertram Reinitz, "Night Sailings Are Now Events," NYT, April 1, 1928.

180 *"drinks, divorces and dresses"*: Basil Woon, *The Frantic Atlantic* (NY: Alfred A. Knopf, 1927), 3.

180 *"The leisurely pace"*: Maxtone-Graham, *Only Way*, 334.

180 *"the only thinkable train"*: Lucius Beebe, *20th Century: The Greatest Train in the World*, (Berkeley, CA: Howell-North Books 1962), 140.

180 *"surging mass of back-firing"*: Federal Writers' Project, *WPA Guide to New York City*, 69.

CHAPTER NINE: VANISHING SOCIAL CITADELS

PAGE

181 "How this city": Philip Lopate, ed., *Writing New York: A Literary Anthology* (NY: Library of America, 1998), 191.

182 *"The announcement"*: NYT, June 17, 1944.

182 *Benjamin Winter had that family's residential colony*: NYT, May 6, 1925.

182 *Benjamin Winter purchased her vacated mansion*: NYT, May 20, 1925.

183 *"titans of new money"*: Allen Churchill, *The Upper Crust: An Informal History of New York's Highest Society* (Englewood Cliffs, NJ: Prentice Hall, 1970), 141.

183 *"Two miles of millionaires"*: "Two Miles of Millionaires," *Munsey's Magazine* 19 (June 1898): 352.

183 *"sacred precinct"*: New York Times, quoted in Christopher Gray, *New York Streetscapes: Tales of Manhattan's Significant Buildings and Landmarks* (NY: Harry N. Abrams, 2003), 173.

184 *had become "extinct"*: NYT, May 21, 1926.

184 *Benjamin Winter found*: NYT, January 6, 1927.

184 *Alice Vanderbilt; Frederick Brown*: NYT, January 3, 1926, July 17, 1927.

184 *"shrine dedicated to archaic rituals"*: Morris, *Incredible*, 297.

184   *"The changes involved more than numbers"*: Ben Yagoda, *About Town: The New Yorker and the World It Made* (NY: Da Capo, 2001), 59.

185   *"Jovian aloofness"; "where existence"*: Morand, *New York,* 253.

185   *"It must be tragic"*: Footner, *New York,* 233–34.

185   *with profound regret*: NYT, September 16, 1928.

185   *the "march of business"*: NYT, April 21, 1940.

185   *"New York's Social Citadels"*: "The Vanishing of New York Social Citadels: Four Great Establishments on Fifth Avenue That Have Unwillingly Given Up the Ghost," *Vanity Fair* 25 (October 1925): 51.

185   *"speculators and traders"*: Ibid. See also NYT, April 17, 1924, September 16, 1928.

185   *insisted he was performing a "civic service"*: NYT, September 16, 1928.

186   *"It was an exciting time"*: Tom Shachtman, *The Great Real Estate Dynasties of New York* (Boston: Little, Brown, 1991), 83.

186   *80 percent of the speculative builders*: Ibid., 111–12.

186   *"the bigness and opportunities of New York"*: "Skyscrapers: Pyramids in Steel and Stock," *Fortune* 2 (August 1930): 74.

186   *"I can paint"*: NYT, June 17, 1944.

187   *his real estate deals averaged $5 million weekly*: NYT, November 15, 1925.

187   *formed his own real estate investment company*: NYT, October 7, 1927.

187   *"the most significant event"; "the beginning of a new era"*: NYT, September 16, 1928; NYW, November 20, 1927.

187   *"the romance of reality"*: NYT, February 24, 1924.

187   *"The real estate market is becoming"*: NYT, July 31, 1927.

187   *"lead an exodus"*: NYT, January 9, 1921.

188   *Anne had become passionately attracted*: Alfred Allan Lewis, *Ladies and Not-So-Gentle Women* (NY: Penguin, 2001), xv.

188   *"the eddying whirlpools"*: Christopher Gray, "Streetscapes: A Prestigious Enclave with a Name in Question," NYT, September 21, 2003.

188   *populated largely by bohemian artists*: Christopher Gray, "Neighborhood: East Fifty-seventh Street," Part 3, *Avenue* 9 (June–July 1985): 73.

188   *newest "society colony"*: NYT, October 23, 1921.

188   *"Rich Move Eastward"*: Gray, "East Fifty-seventh Street," Part 3, 74.

188   *"the only cluster of homes"*: Lewis, *Ladies,* xvi, 362.

188   *"patrician pioneers"*: Block and Golinkin, *New York,* 118.

189   *"voluptuous sky gardens"; "look like a pigsty"*: Gaines, *Sky's the Limit,* 105.

189   *"placed you among the knowing"*: Morris, *Incredible,* 298.

189   *"colony of millionaires"*: Ibid. The Beekman mansion, built in 1766, was demolished in 1874.

189   *"only just beginning to realize"*: Gray, *New York Streetscapes,* 177.

189   *built with a waterfront theme*: Gaines, *Sky's the Limit,* 97.

189   *"Beekman Place brings an exclamation"*: Footner, *New York,* 241–42.

190   *America's Rue de la Paix*: NYT, May 20, 1928; Christopher Gray, "Neighborhood: East Fifty-seventh Street," Part 1, *Avenue* 9 (April 1985): 98.

190   *"Milady likes to spend"*: Quoted in Gray, "East Fifty-seventh," Part 1, 98.

190   *"the aristocrat"*: WPA Guide, 216.

190   *"Fifth Avenue has ceased to be merely"*: Captain William J. Pedrick, "The Story of Fifth Avenue," *The Magazine of Business* 53 (February 1928): 154.

190   *"ultra-exquisite"*: Chase, "Park Avenue," 9.

CHAPTER TEN: THE WOMAN'S CITY

PAGE

191   "Where are the men?": Irwin, *Highlights,* 183.

191   *The lease was $300,000 a year:* "Mr. Goodman's 18,000 Exclusives," *Fortune* 3 (June 1931): 62–63.

191   *"perilous"*: NYT, March 12, 1927.

192   *"close to the greatest buying power"*: NYT, May 20, 1928.

192   *"a mansion-style commercial building"*: Christopher Gray, "Streetscapes: The Bergdorf Goodman Building on Fifth Avenue," NYT, August 30, 1998.

192   *he doubled the size of the store's Fifth Avenue frontage:* NYT, May 1929.

192   *"On Manhattan"*: "Mr. Goodman's," 63.

192   *Goodman was perfect for the position:* Ibid., 62.

193   *first American couturier to offer ready-to-wear garments:* Booton Herndon, *Bergdorf's on the Plaza: The Story of Bergdorf Goodman and a Half-Century of American Fashion* (NY: Alfred A. Knopf, 1956), 4–5.

193   *"Women were no longer hothouse creatures"*: Quoted in ibid., 5.

193   *"He hammered quality"*: Herndon, *Bergdorf,* 5.

194   "les enfants terribles": Herndon, *Bergdorf,* 78–83.

194   *"We didn't know anything"*: Ibid., 78.

194   *dozens of Bergdorf Goodman's customers:* "Mr. Goodman's," 63–65.

194   *"We would talk to our customers"*: Herndon, *Bergdorf,* 86.

194   *"would be impossible"*: Ibid., 13.

194   *masters of "the ensemble"*: "Fifth Avenue's Finest," 78; "Mr. Goodman's," 63; NYT, August 20, 1953.

194   *"impeccably tailored"*: "Mr. Goodman's," 65.

194   *"nationally known tribes"*: Ibid., 100.

195   *"The atmosphere"*: Ibid., 105.

195   *"the court of last appeal"*: Ibid.

195   *only relaxation was baseball:* Ibid., 65; Herndon, *Bergdorf,* 100.

195   *the richest janitors on earth:* NYT, August 29, 1953; "Mr. Goodman's," 100.

195   *"There are good custom tailors"*: "Fifth Avenue Tailors," *Fortune* 6 (November 1932): 67.

196   *The "yearly transformation"*: James C. Young, "Fifth Avenue's Changing Tides," NYT, July 17, 1927.

196   *"I liked to walk up Fifth Avenue"*: F. Scott Fitzgerald, *Gatsby,* 61.

196   *"Four feet, ten inches"*: NYT, February 23, 1956.

196   *control an $8 million fashion empire:* NYT, February 2, 1956.

196   *the "backbone" of her business:* "Cloak and Suit," *Fortune* 1 (June 1930): 96.

197   *"Miss Roth made dresses"*: NYT, February 23, 1956.

197   *"Viennese soul adored rich surroundings"*: Nancy Hardin and Lois Long, "Profiles; Luxury, Inc.," TNY 10 (March 31, 1934): 24.

197   *"modulated to the American spirit"*: Richard Martin, "Hattie Carnegie," *American National Bibliography*, eds. Mark C. Carnes and John A. Garraty, vol. 4 (NY: Oxford University Press, 1999), 417.

197   *"happy and excited"*: Harden and Long, "Luxury, Inc.," 24.

197   *"little Carnegie suits"*: Virginia G. Drachman, *Enterprising Women: 250 Years of American Business* (Chapel Hill: University of North Carolina Press, 2002), 98.

197   *"the Carnegie look"*: Carol H. Krismann, *Encyclopedia of American Women in Business*, vol. 1 (Westport, CT: Greenwood, 2005), 109. For a history of New York fashion, see Caroline Rennolds Milbank, *New York Fashion: The Evolution of American Style* (NY: Harry N. Abrams, 1989).

197   *"captured the new spirit"*: Martin, "Carnegie," in *American National Biography*, 417.

198   *"but she had a feeling about clothes"; "the temper of a termagant"*: Harden and Long, "Luxury, Inc.," 23–24.

198   *"Send me something I'd like"; "look very nice"*: Ibid., 27.

198   *$3 million worth of clothing a year*: Ibid., 26.

198   *"museum pieces"*: Ibid.

198   *"In contrast to the stereotype"*: Drachman, *Enterprising*, 101.

199   *"undisputed leader"*: Ibid.

199   *"has become 'The Woman's City'"*: Irwin, *Highlights*, 183.

199   *"super-Macy's"*: "Saks Fifth Avenue," *Fortune* 18 (November 1938): 57.

199   *Saks Fifth Avenue was formed*: Tom Mahoney and Leonard Sloane, *The Great Merchants: America's Foremost Retail Institutions and the People Who Made Them Great* (NY: Harper & Row, 1966), 150.

200   *"national adjective"*: "Saks," 57.

200   *"reluctant recruit to business"*: NYT, September 10, 1969.

200   *"He put me to work"*: Ibid.

200   *On display in his show windows*: "Saks," 126.

200   *"was acutely conscious"; "volume of a size"; "elegance in volume at a price"*: Ibid., 128–30.

201   *"They hum with the sound"*: Ibid., 130.

201   *"an example of exactly what"*: Leon Harris, *Merchant Princes* (NY: Harper & Row, 1977), 80.

202   *"was to assist the buyer"*: NYT, September 10, 1969.

202   *his "child"*: Ibid.

202   *"home in which the customers"*: Ibid.

202   *"hardheaded as a steel master"*: "Saks," 57.

202   *"This floating population"*: Donald H. Davenport, with Lawrence M. Orton and Ralph W. Roby, *The Retail Shopping and Financial Districts in New York and Its Environs* (NY: Regional Plan of New York and Its Environs, 1927), Davenport et al., *Retail Shopping*, 27.

203   *"She filled the new building"*: Jo Swerling, "Profiles: Beauty in Jars and Vials," TNY 4 (June 30, 1928): 20.

203   *"Madame could never remember"*: NYT, April 2, 1965.

203   *"instinct"*: Swerling, "Beauty," 20.

203   *"the Other One"*: Patrick O'Higgins, *Madame: An Intimate Biography of Helena Rubinstein* (NY: Dell, 1972), 65.

203 *"No one had the courage"*: NYT, April 2, 1965.

204 *"from one hour to the next"*: Margaret Case Harriman, "Profiles: Glamour Inc.: Elizabeth Arden," TNY 11 (April 6, 1935): 27.

204 *"benevolent empress"*: O'Higgins, *Madame,* 367.

204 *"chancy field of enterprise"*: "I Am a Famous Woman in This Industry," *Fortune* 18 (October 1938): 58–60.

204 *"essence of almonds"*: Lindy Woodhead, *War Paint: Madame Helena Rubinstein and Miss Elizabeth Arden, Their Lives, Their Times, Their Rivalry* (NY: John Wiley & Sons, 2003), 25. See also O'Higgins, *Madame,* 191.

205 *"business tailor-made to a female population"*: Penelope Gree, book review, "The Rivals: A Joint Biography of Helena Rubinstein and Elizabeth Arden," review of Lindy Woodhead, *War Paint* NYT, February 15, 2004.

205 *her Valaze skin softening cream*: Elaine Brown Keiffer, "Madame Rubinstein," *Life* 11 (July 21, 1941): 37.

205 *"On the contrary"*: Ruth Brandon, *Ugly Beauty: Helena Rubinstein, L'Oréal, and the Blemished History of Looking Good* (NY: HarperCollins, 2011), 13.

205 *In 1908, she turned her business over*: Ibid.

205 *"Edward Titus excited my imagination"*: Ibid., 18.

205 *"The world's first self-made female tycoon"*: "The Beauty Merchant," *Time* 85 (April 1965): 98.

205 *"a bitterly cold day"*: Helena Rubinstein, *My Life for Beauty* (New York: Simon & Schuster, 1966), 57.

206 *Florence Nightingale Graham was born*: NYT, October 19, 1966.

206 *she mailed a letter to herself*: Harriman, "Profiles," 25; "I Am a Famous Woman," 62.

206 *With a loan of $6,000*: Woodhouse, *War Paint,* 95. Woodhouse dispels the myth that the loan came from her brother William, a china salesman who simply would not have had that kind of money. The loan probably came from an uncle in Philadelphia.

206 *she opened a small wholesale department*: "I Am a Famous Woman," 62; Carol P. Harvey, "Elizabeth Arden," in Frank N. Magill, ed., *Great Lives from History: American Women Series,* vol. 1 (Pasadena, CA: Salem, 1995), 78–82.

206 *"too hard and slippery"*: Harriman, "Profiles," 25–26.

207 *societal pressures against makeup*: Kathy Peiss, *Hope in a Jar: The Making of America's Beauty Culture* (NY: Metropolitan, 1998), 54.

207 *"The vilest rumor"*: "I Am a Famous Woman," 62. See also Woodhead, *War Paint,* 101.

207 *"powder and paint"*: Kathy Peiss, "Making Faces: The Cosmetics Industry and the Cultural Construction of Gender, 1890–1930," *Genders* 7 (Spring 1990): 143, 155.

207 *"[They] went to work on a face"*: NYT, November 20, 1927.

207 *"muscle strapping"*: "I Am a Famous Woman," 62.

207 *"had a scientific base"*: Maxene Fabe, *Beauty Millionaire: The Life of Helena Rubinstein* (NY: Thomas Y. Crowell, 1972), x.

207 *super-garages and repair shops*: Woodhead, *War Paint,* 7.

208 *"hoped to find beauty in a bottle"*: Drachman, *Enterprising Women,* 88.

208 *"the most flattering color"*: NYT, December 19, 1956

208 *"czarina of the cosmetics business"*: "I Am a Famous Woman," 63–64.

209 *one of the ten largest industries:* Nancy F. Koehn, *Brand New: How Entrepreneurs Earned Consumers' Trust from Wedgwood to Dell* (Boston: Harvard Business School Press, 2001), 149.

209 *over three thousand beauty establishments; "cosmetician":* NYT, November 20, 1927.

209 *a business that paid good wages:* NYT, November 4, 1927.

210 *"Nice skin":* O'Higgins, *Madame,* 66.

210 *"the upper spending group":* "The New Yorker," *Fortune* 10 (August 1934): 73.

210 *"reflected the life and times":* Stanley Edgar Hyman, "The Urban New Yorker," *NR* 107 (July 20, 1942): 92.

211 *its most loyal cadre of readers:* "The Metropolitanites," *Fortune* 20 (July 1939): 84, 217.

211 *"impatient and noisy":* E. B. White quoted in Yagoda, *About Town,* 79.

211 *"As polished as Ross was rough":* Thomas Kunkel, *Genius in Disguise: Harold Ross of The New Yorker* (NY: Carroll & Graf, 1995), 78.

211 *"built around New York":* Yagoda, *About Town,* 33.

211 *"highly selective audience":* "The New Yorker," 74.

211 *"But all this meant little"; "has entrée in the right places":* Jamers Thurber, *The Years with Ross* (Boston: Little, Brown, 1957), 118.

212 *"a hustling little Irishman":* "The New Yorker," 92.

212 *Ross wouldn't allow him near his writers and editors:* Ibid. Ingersoll wrote this piece for *Fortune,* which had a policy of not naming the authors of its featured essays.

212 *"The New Yorker will be a reflection":* Yagoda, *About Town,* 38–39.

212 *"commercial idea":* "The New Yorker," 74.

212 *"was uniquely positioned":* Kunkel, *Genius,* 102.

212 *Advertising in:* Scott Elledge, *E.B. White: A Biography* (NY: W. W. Norton, 1984), 122, 147; Yagoda, *About Town,* 98; Roy Hoopes, *Ralph Ingersoll: A Biography* (NY: Atheneum, 1985), 64.

213 *a spontaneous celebration:* "The New Yorker," 92; Kunkel, *Genius,* 131.

213 *"girl about town":* Matthew R. Connor, "Lois Long," John A. Garraty and Mark C. Carnes, eds., *American National Dictionary,* vol. 13 (NY: Oxford University Press, 1999), 879.

213 *"Ross never doubted"; "joyously into a New York":* "Lois Long," *TNY* 50 (August 12, 1974), 100. Gill wrote this *New Yorker* tribute to Long on the occasion of her death and repeated it almost verbatim in his memoir, *Here at the New Yorker* (NY: Random House, 1975), 203, 206.

213 *"she could have modeled":* Dale Kramer, *Ross and The New Yorker* (Garden City: Doubleday, Doran, 1951), 83. For Long as a typical 1920s flapper, see Joshua Zeitz, *Flapper: A Madcap Story of Sex, Style, Celebrity and the Women Who Made America Modern* (NY: Crown, 2006), 89.

213 *"You never knew":* All Long quotes from Harrison Kinney, *James Thurber: His Life and Times* (NY: Henry Holt, 1995), 378–79.

214 *"a cigarette dangling from her mouth":* Kennedy Fraser, *Ornament and Silence: Essays on Women's Lives* (NY: Alfred A. Knopf, 1996), 234. See also Kramer, *Ross,* 82–83.

214 *"Ross actually liked us all":* Kinney, *Thurber,* 378, 380.

214 *"Lois Long invented":* NYT, July 31, 1974.

214 *"the most important"; Advertising "blackmail"; "fashion dictators":* "The New Yorker," 90; Connor, "Long," in Garraty and Carnes, eds., *American National Biography,* 880.

214 *"just the readership"*: "The New Yorker," 76.

214 *placed in the top three*: Yagoda, *About Town*, 97.

214 *"the size of a hall bedroom"*: "E. B. White," "James Thurber," in E. B. White, *Writings from The New Yorker: 1927–1976*, edited by Rebecca M. Dale (NY: HarperCollins, Perennial, 1990), 223.

214 *"the wheel horses"*: "The New Yorker," 88.

215 *"It gave the reader"*: Kunkel, *Genius*, 123.

215 *"Peter Arno"*: Yagoda, *About Town*, 64.

215 *"there'll be no sex"*: Kunkel, *Genius*, 124. Arno and Long divorced in 1931.

215 *"a good publishing property"*: "The New Yorker," 73.

215 *The largest concentration of regular subscribers*: Yagoda, *About Town*, 96; "The Metropolitanites," 217. By 1951, *The New Yorker* had a circulation of 325,000, two-thirds of which was out of town.

215 *"New York–minded people"*: Quoted in Yagoda, *About Town*, 59.

215 *"city dwellers"; "the Metropolitanites"*: "The Metropolitanites," 84–85, 217.

CHAPTER ELEVEN: FRED FRENCH

PAGE

216 "Fred F. French is": Chase, *Wonder City*, 270.

216 *"daring newcomer"*: Pond, *Golden Earth*, 223, 2237; *NYT*, March 20, 1925.

216 *"business palaces"*: Chase, *Wonder City*, 245.

216 *"veritable giants"*: "10,000,000 French Projects to be Ready March, 1927," *Real Estate Record and Guide* (July 17, 1926): 7; Landmarks Preservation Commission, "Fred F. French Building," Landmarks Preservation Commission Designation Report, March 18, 1986, New York Public Library; 9. The Delmonico Building, as it was popularly known, was originally the headquarters of the Central Mercantile Bank.

216 *"twenty of the most valuable blocks"*: NYT, May 29, 1927.

217 *188 buildings*: "A Census of Skyscrapers," *The American City* 41 (September 1929): 130.

217 *"has created a new phenomenon"*: Colonel W. A. Starrett, *Skyscrapers and the Men Who Build Them* (NY: Charles Scribner's Sons, 1928), 109.

217 *"almost volcanic eruption"*: Federal Writers' Project, *New York Panorama: A Companion to the WPA Guide to New York City* (NY: Pantheon, 1989; originally published 1938), 203.

218 *"pioneering effort"*: Paul Goldberger, *The City Observed: New York, A Guide to the Architecture of Manhattan* (NY: Vintage, 1979), 133.

218 *"one of those inner cities"*: Federal Writers' Project, *WPA Guide to New York City*, 221.

218 *"Who on earth was Fred F. French [?]"*: Don DeLillo, *Underworld* (NY: Charles Scribner's Sons, 1997), 398.

219 *"He failed because"*: Robert M. Coates, "Profiles: Realtor," TNY 5 (June 1, 1929), 22.

219 *forcing the boy to take after-school work*: John W. French and Fred F. French, *A Vigorous Life: The Story of Fred F. French, Builder of Skyscrapers* (NY: Vantage, 1993), 6. This biography was written by French's son John, who drew liberally upon his father's unpublished autobiography.

219 *he set up a "kids" circus*: Coates, "Realtor," 22.

219 *"the Great O'Reilly"*: NYT, August 31, 1936.

219 *"The notion that"*: French and French, *Vigorous,* 16.

219 *"believing a person"*: Ibid., 75.

220 *"a peanut stand"; "to the penny"*: Ibid., 68.

220 *"in the heart of the action"*: Ibid., 123. See also *NYT,* April 4, 1920.

220 *"quite by accident"*: Coates, "Realtor," 23–24.

220 *"just about the best corner"; "the seventh wonder"*: French and French, *Vigorous,* 173.

221 *"not been matched since"*: Landmarks Preservation Commission, "French Building," 3–4.

221 *$30,000 "fee"*: Walsh, *Gentleman,* 282.

221 *"genre of tower"*: Stern et al., *New York 1930,* 595–97.

221 *in the style of Assyrian Ziggurats*: H. Douglas Ives, *The Voice,* February 1927, Fred F. French Companies Records, 1902–1966, New York Public Library hereafter cited as FFFCR; Carol Herselle Krinsky, "The Fred F. French Building: Mesopotamia in Manhattan," *Antiques* (January 1982): 284.

221 *"thrift and industry"*: *The Voice* (February 1927), FFFCR.

221 *"showplace" building*: Chase, *Wonder City,* 245.

221 *a modern Babylon*: Stern et al. *New York 1930,* 597.

222 *"rising like mountains"*: Paul Goldberger, *The Skyscraper* (NY: Alfred A. Knopf, 1982), 57.

222 *"[of] terrific vertical towers"*: Hugh Ferriss, "The New Architecture," *NYT Book Review and Magazine* (March 19, 1922): 8–27. See also Goldberger, *Skyscraper,* 58.

222 *a "style so recent"*: Irwin, *Highlights* 18.

222 *"Taller and more animated"*: Landmarks Preservation Commission, "French Building," 11.

222 *Barclay-Vesey Building*: Lewis Mumford, "The Barclay-Vesey Building," *NR* 51 (July 6, 1927): 176–77.

222 *"born of necessity"*: Ely Jacques Kahn, "Our Skyscrapers Take Simple Forms," *NYT,* May 2, 1926.

222 *"New York born architecture"*: Starrett, *Skyscrapers,* 101.

223 *Corcoran's Roost*: NYT, July 26, 1942.

223 *occupied four full blocks of riverfront*: NYT, January 24, 1926.

223 *creating a natural*: French and French, *Vigorous,* 177.

223 *"the greatest business neighborhood"*: NYT, March 4, 1928.

224 *"convenient to their work"*: French and French, *Vigorous,* 177.

224 *"running wild"; "a realtor's epic"*: Alva Johnston, "Knickerbocker Village—I," *TNY* 8 (August 6, 1932): 26. Johnston was referring to a later, similarly secret French Company project, Knickerbocker Village. See also French and French, *Vigorous,* 214.

224 *Fred French's broker*: NYT, December 19, 1925.

224 *"Only the refusal"*: Eugene Rachlis and John E. Marqusee, *The Land Lords* (NY: Random House, 1963), 171.

224 *"the first residential skyscraper enclave"*: Eric P. Nash, *Manhattan Skyscrapers* (NY: Princeton Architectural Press, 1999), 43.

224 *City officials considered it*: NYT, December 19, 1925.

224 *Fred French would raise every cent*: French and French, *Vigorous,* 179.

224 *"Other men"*: "Builder of Knickerbocker Village Dies," *The Real Estate Record and Builders' Guide* 138 (September 5, 1936): 2.

225 *"never ending stream"*: John Taylor Boyd, Jr., "Wall Street Enters the Building Field 11," *Architectural Engineering and Business* (June 1929): 119.

225 *"Never before"*: Fred F. French, *The Real Estate Investment of the Future* (NY: Fred F. French Investing Co., 1927), 9; advertisement for the French Plan, FFFCR.

225 *It was an ingenious plan*: Alexander Rayden, *The People's City: A History of the Influence and Contribution of Mass Real Estate Syndication in the Development of New York City* (Charleston, SC: BookSurge Publishing, 2007), 60–61.

225 *"in perpetuity"*: French, *Real Estate Investment,* 5, 9–10.

225 *"equity audience"*: Rayden, *People's City,* 93.

226 *allowed his company to finance*: French and French, *Vigorous,* 131; Rayden, *People's City,* 77.

226 *"one profitable whole"*: Coates, "Realtor," 22.

226 *"sound architecture [gives]* investment values: Boyd, "Wall Street" (May 1929): 769.

226 *"one of the most important functions"*: French and French, *Vigorous,* 132.

226 *fervor of a fundamentalist camp meeting*: Alva Johnston, "Knickerbocker Village—II," TNY 8 (August 13, 1932): 24.

226 *"Fred French steps forth"*: Kenneth M. Murchison, "Mr. Murchison of New York Says—Architect Tolerates French and His Building," *The Architect* 7 (January 1927): 505.

226 *"He is . . . [the] Mark Antony of business"*: Johnston, "Knickerbocker Village—II," 24.

227 *"stand before your bathroom mirror"*: Coates, "Realtor," 23.

227 *"religio-commercial enthusiasm"*: Johnston, "Knickerbocker Village—II," 24.

227 *"Son of the Father"; "the greatest salesman"*: French and French, *Vigorous,* 133.

227 *"Still working like H—!"*: Ibid., 131.

227 *"He is a marvel"*: Murchison, "Mr. Murchison of New York Says—Architect Tolerates," 505.

227 *"electrifying" effect; You are the "scouts"; "enthusiastic" competitive teams*: Ibid., 132.

227 *"they can't hew to the line"*: Coates, "Realtor," 24.

227 *"fully accoutered"*: Ibid., 25.

227 *"Hard Work Brings Success"*: Fred F. French, "Hard Work Brings Success in Hunting as well as in Business," *The Voice* (December 1926), FFFCR.

227 *"something of that dominating power"*: NYT, September 6, 1936.

228 *"Agents are sent out"*: Coates, "Realtor," 23–24.

228 *"a waste of time"*: "Skyscrapers: Pyramids," 75.

228 *Tudor City was completed*: NYT, August 19, 1928; French and French, *Vigorous,* 182.

228 *"more secluded"*: NYW, advertisement, Clip File, FFFCR.

228 *a full slate of recreational and cultural amenities*: NYT, March 1, 1930, July 26, 1942.

228 *"Live here"*: Advertisement for Tudor City, NYW, September 26, 1927. FFFCR.

229 *its proven marketability*: French, *Real Estate Investment* Landmarks Preservation Commission, "Tudor City Historic Designation Report," 1988, 18, New York Public Library.

229 *"Tudor City does not appeal to millionaires"*: Chase, *Wonder City,* 271.

229 *"walk-to-work"; "anyone"; "The Big Chief"*: Johnston, "Knickerbocker Village—II," 28, 32.

230 *Knickerbocker Village*: Alberta Williams, "White-Collar Neighbors," TNY 10 (November 24, 1934): 48–51.

230 *He left this world with only $10,000*: French and French, *Vigorous*, 248, 252.

230 *"He is a success"*: Coates, "Realtor," 25.

CHAPTER TWELVE: MASTERS OF THE SKYLINE

PAGE

231 "By night": Carl Sandburg, *Chicago Poems* (NY: Henry Holt, 1916), 67.

231 *"twelve million dollar tower"*: NYT, June 23, 1927.

231 *"immensely tall skyscrapers"*: NYW, September 11, 1927; Chase, *Wonder City*, 235. The Chanin Building was exceeded in height by the Woolworth Building, the Cleveland Terminal, and New York's Metropolitan Life Insurance Tower.

231 *"Jazz Age ziggurat"*: NYT, April 1, 1998.

231 *"quiet neighborhood"*: T-Square, "The Sky Line," TNY3 (May 21, 1927): 81.

232 *"Mysterious Stranger"*: Mary B. Mullett, "The Chanin's of Broadway," *The American Magazine* 106 (August 1928): 22.

232 *"a good many people"*: Niven Busch, Jr., "Skybinder," TNY 4 (January 26, 1929): 20. Chanin died in 1988 at the age of ninety-six.

232 *"hundred wonder men"*: Chase, *Wonder City*, 109.

232 *His "achievements"*: Busch, "Skybinder," 20.

232 *"one of those amazing Jews"*: Mullett, "Chanin's," 23.

232 *poised to become*: NYT, June 22, 1927, January 27, 1929.

232 *"Money is the easiest thing"*: Busch, "Skybinder," 23.

233 *saw buildings as "ideas"*: Ibid., 24.

233 *"a master of the skyline"*: Paul Goldberger, "Architecture: Chanin, a Master of the Skyline," NYT, December 7, 1982.

233 *"He started things"*: Busch, "Skybinder," 20.

233 *"I didn't waste time"*: Mullett, "Chanin's," 122.

233 *"Before going there"*: Ibid.

233 *"tried to figure out"*: Busch, "Skybinder," 20.

233 *"crazy idea"*: Mullett, "Chanin's," 125.

234 *Chanin thought he could build better houses*: Cameron Rogers, "Youth at the Top," *World's Work* 58 (January 1929): 59.

234 *"I adopted the creed"*: Mullett, "Chanin's," 125.

234 *"the first step in his rise"*: Busch, "Skybinder," 21.

234 *they built one of the first skyscraper lofts*: NYT, January 24, 1926.

234 *"I discovered"*: Mullett, "Chanin's," 126.

234 *"among the best equipped"*: NYT, January 24, 1926.

234 *"old grievance"; "I wasn't allowed"*: Mullett, "Chanin's," 126.

234 *"ideal of a man"*: Quoted in Mullett, "Chanin's," 127.

235 *the brothers sold it for $9 million*: NYT, June 8, 1927.

235 *"burglary, fire, and assault"*: NYT, June 22, 1927.

235 *"The architect designing"*: Henry H. Saylor, "The Editor's Diary," *Architecture* 63 (June 1931): 365.

235 *"generalissimo"*: NYT, March 2, 1930.

236 *"The skyscraper is the most distinctly American"*: Starrett, *Skyscrapers*, 1.

236 *"tiny ant-like men"*: Lowell Thomas, *Men of Danger* (NY: Frederick A. Stokes, 1936), 31.

236 *"sky boys"; "dashing and tragic figures"*: Jim Rasenberger, *High Steel: The Daring Men Who Built the World's Greatest Skyline, 1881 to the Present* (NY: Perennial, 2005; first published in 2004), 173.

236 *"the heroes of the girders"*: Mordaunt Hall, "Iron Workers Aloft," NYT, April 9, 1928. See also Edmund M. Littell, "Men Wanted," *The American Magazine* (April 1930): 46; and NYT, April 8, 1928.

237 *"end point"*: Thomas Kelly, *Empire Rising* (NY: Farrar, Straus & Giroux, 2005), 83. Kelly's novel is one of the best books available about skyscraper construction.

237 *ironmen navigating "needle beams"*: Margaret Norris and Brenda Ueland, "Riding the Girders," *The Saturday Evening Post* (April 11, 1931): 97.

237 *"I have seen men"*: Starrett, *Skyscrapers*, 183.

237 *"raising crews"; "even the birds don't fly"*: Littell, "Men Wanted," 46, 51.

237 *"wondrous to watch"*: Gay Talese, *The Bridge: The Building of the Verrazano-Narrows Bridge* (NY: Harper & Row, 1964), 49.

237 *"the best open-air show"*: C. G. Poore, "The Riveter's Panorama of New York," *NYT Magazine* (January 5, 1930): SM5.

238 *"just room enough"*: Joseph Mitchell, "The Mohawks in High Steel," TNY 25 (September 17, 1949): 43.

238 *"in a glowing arc"; "heat, toss, insert"*: Rasenberger, *High Steel*, 56.

238 *"muscle and steel"*: Kelly, *Empire*, 37.

239 *"Naw. It's as easy"*: Poore, "Riveters," SN5.

239 *"Hundreds of men banging"*: Kelly, *Empire*, 38.

239 *"monkey fashion"*: Norris and Ueland, "Riding," 101.

239 *"cousins and brothers"; "family"*: Rasenberger, *High Steel*, 243–44.

239 *Their accident rate*: Richard Hill, *Skywalkers: A History of Indian Ironworkers* (Brantford, Ontario: Woodland Indian Cultural Education Centre, 1987), 19.

239 *ironworkers suffered one violent death*: Starrett, *Skyscrapers*, 300.

239 *"We do not die"*: Rasenberger, *High Steel*, 57.

239 *"bloodless building"*: "Skyscrapers: Builders and Their Tools," *Fortune* 2 (October 1930): 91–92.

240 *"annoyances"; "When it rains"*: Poore, "Riveter's," 9.

240 *Homebound workers*: NYT, August 4, 1926.

240 *"a high explosive shell"; "avalanche of steel"*: NYT, April 21, 1929; NYW, April 21, 1929.

240 *"sprang from his seat"*: NYT, May 4, 1928.

241 *"driven ashore"*: Thomas, *Men of Danger*, 34.

241 *"equilibrium, agility"; "pusher"*: Walter Davenport, "High and Mighty," *Collier's* 85 (March 1, 1930): 13, 63.

241 *"there's not a job from Broadway"*: Ernest Poole, "Cowboys of the Skies," *Everybody's Magazine* 19 (November 1908): 642, 649.

241 *"You get to love it"*: Margaret Norris, *Heroes and Hazards: True Stories of the Careers of the Men Who Make Our Modern World Safe by Their Courage* (NY: Junior Literary Guild, 1932), 26–27.

241 *"It's nice to point to a"*: Ibid.

241 *"In the New York gangs"*: Poole, "Cowboys," 648–49.

241 *"at the rapids"*: Mitchell, "Mohawks," 38–39.

242 *But other Mohawks came after the war:* David Blanchard, "High Steel! The Kahnawake Mohawk and the High Construction Trade," *Journal of Ethnic Studies* 11 (Summer 1983): 49.

242 *U.S. government permitted them to cross the border:* Mitchell, "Mohawks," 47; NYT, December 29, 1926.

242 *"sparklingly clean":* NYT, November 4, 1957. See also Mitchell, "Mohawks," 50. The Kahnawake filmmaker Reaghan Tarbell tells the story of Little Caughnawaga in the film *To Brooklyn and Back: A Mohawk Journey,* produced by Mushkeg Media Inc., 2009.

242 *"I enjoy New York":* Mitchell, "Mohawks," 49.

242 *"think of their Brooklyn dwellings":* NYT, November 4, 1957.

243 *"as agile as goats":* Mitchell, "Mohawks," 42.

243 *"would climb up into the spans":* Ibid., 42–43. See also "Mohawks Like High Steel," *Bethlehem Review* (July 1954): 24.

243 *thirty-three Kahnawake men were horribly crushed:* Hill, *Skywalkers,* 21.

243 *"more interesting":* Mitchell, "Mohawks," 41–42. See also Hill, *Skywalkers,* 16.

243 *"Booming Out":* "Booming Out: Mohawk Ironworkers Build New York," a touring exhibition of photographs developed by the Smithsonian National Museum of American Indians.

244 *"progenitors of the nation":* Blanchard, "High Steel!" 59.

244 a rite de passage: Morris Freilich, "Mohawk Heroes and Trinidadian Peasants," in Morris Freilich, ed., *Marginal Natives at Work: Anthropologists in the Field* (NY: Schenkman, 1977), 169.

244 *"lack . . . any sense of height":* NYT, May 20, 1940. For the same mistaken idea, see Robert L. Conly, "The Mohawks Scrape the Sky," *National Geographic Magazine* 102 (July 1952): 134. This nurtured a related myth—that Mohawk Indians built nearly all of New York's City's skyscrapers. Actually Brooklyn Mohawks never comprised more than 15 percent of the city's ironworking force. Of the 150,000 ironworkers in the International Union of Ironworkers in 1987, approximately 7,500 were Native Americans. See Hill, *Skywalkers,* 10; and Rasenberger, *High Steel,* 161.

244 *Mohawk "fearlessness":* NYT, February 6, 1927.

244 *"The strange sense of security":* Norris and Ueland, "Riding," 97.

244 *"deny that they are biologically different":* NYT, November 4, 1957.

244 *Apprenticeship and rigorous training:* David Grant Noble, "Mohawk Steelworkers of Manhattan," *Four Winds* 2 (Spring 1982): 36.

244 *"There's pride in walking iron":* "Booming Out."

244 *"circus Indian":* Mitchell, "Mohawks," 174.

245 *"I have a name for this town":* Hill, *Skywalkers,* 30.

245 *On July 2, 1928:* NYT, June 29, 1928.

245 *"There's no use in going any higher":* NYT, January 30, 1929.

245 *real estate holdings:* NYT, January 17, 20, 1929.

245 *"part of the theatre":* Diana Agrest, ed., *A Romance with the City: Irwin S. Chanin* (NY: Cooper Union Press, 1982), 10.

245 *"an architectural island floating":* Matlack Price, "Chanin Building," *Architectural Forum* 50 (May 1929): 699.

245   *"vigorous, toothed appearance"*: T-Square, "The Sky Line: Some New Giants," TNY 4 (November 3, 1928), 92.

245   *"masses rather than in facades"*: Price, "Chanin Building," 699–700.

246   *"legendary beacon"*: Herbert Muschamp, "Architecture View: For All the Star Power, a Mixed Performance" NYT, July 12, 1992.

246   *"the mental and physical processes"*: "Chanin Building Brochure," New York Public Library. See also "The Chanin Building, New York City," *Architecture and Building* 61 (February 1929): 40; and Jim Patterson with Bob Perrone, "Rene Paul Chambellan—One of Art Deco's Greatest Sculptors," www.louisvilleartdeco.com/feature/RenePaulChambellan.

246   *"a tribute to"*: Donald Martin Reynolds, *The Architecture of New York City: Histories and Views of Important Structures. Sites, and Symbols* (NY: Macmillan, 1984), 234. Chanin eventually became a registered architect.

246   *"America's finest bathroom"*: Reynolds, *Architecture*, 231.

247   *"illustrating his ideas"*: Busch, "Skybinder," 20, 23.

247   *"Even in his old age"*: Quoted in David W. Dunlap, "Irwin Chanin, Builder of Theaters and Art Deco Towers, Dies at 96," NYT, February 26, 1988.

247   *"The Grand Central zone"*: NYT, January 6, 1929.

247   *"drive through"*: Hawes, *New York, New York,* 207.

247   *"a virtual express highway"*: Gray, *New York Streetscapes,* 134.

CHAPTER THIRTEEN: THE SILVER SPIRE

PAGE

249   "I like to build things": "Chrysler Motors," *Time* 13 (January 7, 1929): 37.

249   *Walter Chrysler began searching*: Vincent Curcio, *Chrysler: The Life and Times of an Automobile Genius* (NY: Oxford University Press, 2000).

249   *Chrysler purchased the eighty-four-year lease*: NYT, February 2, July 29, 1928, October 14, 1931.

249   *Reynolds had hired forty-year-old, Brooklyn-born William Van Alen*: "Final Sketch of the Reynolds Building, New York," *American Architect* 135 (August 1928): 269.

249   *"giant of giants"*: New York Sun, March 7, 1929. See also NYT, March 9, 1929.

249   *Van Alen, an avant-garde architect, had found the perfect client*: William Van Alen, "Architect Finds New Designs in Frame of Steel," HT, September 7, 1930.

250   *"tinge . . . of something different"*: Kenneth M. Murchison, "The Chrysler Building, as I See It," *The American Architect* 138 (September 1930): 26.

250   *His Childs Restaurant*: Christopher Gray, "Streetscapes: William Van Alen," NYT, March 22, 1998. For Van Alen's body of early work, see Francis S. Swales, "Draftsmanship and Architecture, V: As Exemplified by the Work of William Van Alen," *Pencil Points* 10 (August 1929): 526.

250   *"I am not particularly interested"*: Neal Bascomb, "For the Architect, a Height Never Again to Be Scaled," NYT, May 26, 2005. See also NYT, May 25, 1954.

250   *"To my mind"*: Ron Miller and Frederick C. Durant III, with Melvin H. Schuetz, *The Art of Chesley Bonestell* (London: Collins & Brown, 2001), 28.

250   *"If this is to be a skyscraper"*: Neal Bascomb, *Higher: A Historic Race to the Sky and the Making of a City* (NY: Broadway edition, 2004; originally published in 2003), 129.

250 *"the tallest bank and office structure in the world"*: NYT, April 10, 1929.

250 *"They had to work"*: Curcio, *Chrysler*, 406–7.

251 *"could peer down over"*: "Chrysler Motors," 37.

251 *"I like to build things"*: Ibid.

251 *"The career of Walter Percy Chrysler"*: NYT, August 19, 1940.

251 *"insuperable obstacles"*: "Chrysler," *Fortune* 12 (August 1935): 32, 34.

251 *"full of whiskey"; "A kid"; "raised his small share"*: Walter P. Chrysler, *Life of an American Workman* (NY: Dodd, Mead, 1937), 26–27.

252 *to make his own tools*: B. C. Forbes, "Chrysler Tells How He Did It," *Forbes* (January 1, 1929): 16; NYT, August 19, 1940.

252 *"Give the boss"*: S. J. Woolf, "A Motor Car Magnate's Rise to Power," NYT, August 19, 1928.

252 *"To me"*: Curcio, *Chrysler*, 124.

252 *to purchase his first car*: Forbes, "Chrysler Tells," 17. See also Theodore F. MacManus and Norman Beasley, *Men, Money and Motors* (NY: Harper & Brothers, 1929), 47; Chrysler, *Life*, 106.

252 *"After that initiation"*: Chrysler, *Life*, 108–9.

252 *"I was not prepared"*: Ibid., 127.

252 *"to take risks"*: Thomas C. Cochran, "Walter Percy Chrysler," *Dictionary of American Biography*, vol. 22, Supplement 2 (NY: Charles Scribner's Sons, 1955), 103.

253 *he quit the company in 1919*: NYT, June 2, 1929; Chrysler, *Life*, 163.

253 *"the typical residence"*: Lurton Blassingame, "Type Model," TNY 2 (January 8, 1927): 23.

253 *"we were pretty close to ruin"*: Chrysler, *Life*, 183.

254 *Walter Chrysler was on the display floor*: NYT, January 6, 1924.

254 *"We stole . . . the show"*: Chrysler, *Life*, 184.

254 *"King Tut" colors*: Claudia Roth Pierpont, "The Silver Spire," TNY 78 (November 18, 2002): 77.

254 *"it's now or never"; "out of the woods"*: Chrysler, *Life*, 186–88.

254 *The Chrysler Six sold phenomenally*: Ibid., 189.

254 *"This car stands alone"*: Mark Howell, "The Chrysler Six, America's First Modern Automobile," *Antique Automobile* 36 (January–February, 1972): 16.

254 *"miniature masterpiece"*: "Chrysler," *Fortune*, 31, 36.

254 *the largest concentration of car dealerships*: Martin Clary, *Mid-Manhattan* (NY: Forty-second Street Property Owners and Merchants Association, 1929), 160.

255 *solidly practical Plymouth*: NYT, July 5, 1928.

255 *"the biggest consolidation"*: NYT, May 30, 1928. The deal was negotiated with the Wall Street banking house that had purchased the company from the widows of the Dodge brothers.

255 *"the outstanding production genius"*: Blassingame, "Type Model," 24.

255 *named him its "Man of the Year"*: "Chrysler Motors," 32.

255 *commander in chief*: NYT, March 23, 1929.

255 *"No man"*: Forbes, "Chrysler Tells," 15, 32.

255 *"but men who get"*: "World's Record," *Time* 5 (April 20, 1925): 25.

256 *"fondest treasure[s]"*: Chrysler Tower Corporation, *The Chrysler Building* (NY: Chrysler Tower Corporation, 1930), 25. See also Phil Patton, "For Chrysler, a Tribute to His Own Rise," NYT, May 26, 2008. The observation tower was opened on August 4, 1930. NYT, August 5, 1930.

256 *"a bat out of hell"*: Curcio, *Chrysler,* 420. The building's construction is vividly documented in David Stravitz's collection of rare images, *The Chrysler Building: Creating a New York Icon, Day by Day* (NY: Princeton Architectural Press, 2002).

256 *"in almost constant motion"*: William Van Alen, "The Structure and Metal Work of the Chrysler Building," *The Architectural Forum* 53 (October 1930): 493.

256 *refused to press the project at the expense of the workers' safety*: William G. Wheeler, "Safeguarding Construction Crews in a Great Skyscraper," *Buildings and Building Management* 29 (December 2, 1929): 25–26.

256 *he viewed accident prevention*: Walter P. Chrysler, "Is Carelessness on Your Payroll?," *Building Age* 52 (March 1930): 41; NYT, January 19, 1930; F. D. McHugh, "Manhattan's Mightiest 'Minaret,'" *Scientific American* 142 (April 1930): 266.

256 *"the greatest thrill"*: NYT, January 21, 1930.

256 *to honor his laborers and supervisor*: NYT, September 11, 1929, January 21, 1930.

256 *"Bluff, sanguine"*: Blassingame, "Type Model," 23.

257 *"heaven-climbing contest"*: Margaret Bourke-White, *Portrait of Myself* (NY: Simon & Schuster, 1963), 76.

257 *"What a lucky lady I am"*: Vicki Goldberg, *Margaret Bourke-White: A Biography* (NY: Harper & Row, 1987), 93.

257 *"that swayed 8 feet in the wind"*: Bourke-White, *Portrait,* 77–78.

257 *the Bank of Manhattan appeared to be the clear winner*: NYT, April 10, 1929.

257 *"dwarfing"*: HT, November 18, 1929.

257 *"a high spire"*: Van Alen, "Structure and Metal Work," 493.

257 *"vertex"*: Murchison, "Chrysler Building," 30.

257 *"the signal was given"; "like a butterfly"*: Van Alen, "Structure and Metal Work," 494. There is no agreement among historians on the day, or even the month, the vertex was lifted into place. I have used the date for which there is the most reliable documentation. Curcio (*Chrysler,* 426) puts the date as September 28, 1929, and the *Scientific American* issue of April 1930 says it appeared suddenly "on a day in November, 1929" (McHugh, "Manhattan's Mightiest," 267). In his exhaustively researched study of the Chrysler Building, Neal Bascomb says it was raised on October 23, 1929 (Bascomb, *Higher,* 207).

258 *"the cloud-piercing needle"*: Van Alen, "Structure and Metal Work," 494.

258 *"four sinking spells"*: Murchison, "Chrysler Building," 30.

258 *the highest structure ever built*: HT, November 18, 1929; NYT, December 9, 1929.

258 *"epic of publicity"; "Doctor of Altitude"*: Kenneth Murchison, "The Spires of Manhattan," *Architectural Forum* 53 (June 1930): 878. See also Christopher Gray, "Streetscapes: William Van Alen," NYT, March 22, 1998; and NYT, February 8, 1931.

258 *"They look like money"*: Nash, *Manhattan's Skyscrapers,* 65.

258 *"metals and mass effort"*: "Our Modern Architecture," NYT, May 29, 1930.

258 *"It represents our modern life"*: Murchison, "Chrysler Building," 24, 78.

258 *"the Ziegfeld of his profession"*: Ibid., 24.

258 *"freak" and a "stunt"*: Ibid.

258 *"shameless exhibition"*: Lewis Mumford, "Notes on Modern Architecture," NR 66 (March 18, 1931): 120–21. See also Douglas Haskell, "Architecture: Chrysler's Pretty Bauble," *The Nation* 131 (October 22, 1930): 450.

259 *"the eighth wonder of the world"*: Bascomb, *Higher,* 271.

259 *"hot jazz in stone and steel"*: Le Corbusier, *When the Cathedrals Were White: A Journey to the Country of Timid People* (NY: Reynal & Hitchcock, 1947), 158–60.

259 *"tired of the Chrysler Building"*: Paul Goldberger, "The Chrysler Building at 50," NYT, August 18, 1980.

259 *"When people come into"*: Curcio, *Chrysler,* 419.

259 *"for each of the four seasons"*: Murchison, "Chrysler Building," 78. See also Paul Goldberger, "Perfect Space: The Chrysler Building Lobby, New York," *Travel & Leisure* 19 (June 1989): 126.

259 *One panel is devoted:* Edward Trumbull, Clipping File, New York Public Library.

260 *Nirosta steel:* NYT, July 9, 1929.

260 *Van Alen used it:* William Van Alen, "The Chrysler Building, New York," *Architecture and Building* 62 (August 1930): 223.

260 *three-story Cloud Club:* Charles McGrath, "A Lunch Club for the Higher-Ups," NYT, May 26, 2005. The club was permanently closed in 1979.

260 *"one of the great lavatories of all time"*: Tracie Rozhon, "A Scalloped Dream, a Hotelier's Fantasy," NYT, July 24, 1997.

261 *"five o'clock girls"*: Curcio, *Chrysler,* 639.

261 *"I have a very ardent admirer"*: Constance Rosenblum, *Gold Digger: The Outrageous Life and Times of Peggy Hopkins Joyce* (NY: Henry Holt, 2000), 184–85.

261 *"bright, immoral"*: Curcio, *Chrysler,* 640.

261 *Peggy's "skating rink"*: Ibid., 641.

261 *Even his high-end Imperials:* Rosenblum, *Gold Digger,* 185.

261 *"each generation writes its biography"*: Lewis Mumford, *Architecture: Reading with a Purpose, No. 23* (Chicago: American Library Association, 1926), 9, 25; Mumford, "The Modern City," in Talbot Hamlin, ed., *Forms and Functions of Twentieth-Century Architecture,* vol. 4, *Building Types* (NY: Columbia University Press, 1952), 802.

261 *"the most stunning thing in town"*: Murchison, "Spires," 878.

261 *building formally opened:* NYT, May 28, 1930.

262 *"it must have presented seating difficulties"*: Gray, *New York Streetscapes,* 140.

262 *Van Alen sued Walter Chrysler:* NYT, June 18, 1930; Bascomb, *Higher,* 261.

262 *The architect won his lawsuit:* NYT, August 22, 1931; HT, May 25, 1954.

262 *"swan song"*: Rem Koolhass, *Delirious New York: A Retroactive Manifesto for Manhattan* (NY: Monacelli, 1994), 130.

262 *"The Skyline of New York"*: NYT, January 18, 1931.

262 *"It is perhaps inconsistent"*: Cecil Beaton, *Cecil Beaton's New York* (Philadelphia: J. B. Lippincott, 1938), 125.

262 *Chrysler hired over four dozen brokers:* David Michaelis, "77 Stories: The Secret Life of a Skyscraper," *Manhattan Inc.* (June 1986): 122.

262 *nearly 70 percent rented:* NYT, June 15, 1930.

263 *"My first step"*: Bourke-White, *Portrait,* 78.

263 *"take pictures"; "hated to go home"*: Ibid., 76–78, 87–88.

263 *"perpendiculars"*: Morris Markey, "Night: Downtown," TNY 3 (November 19, 1927): 47.

263 *"city under one roof"*: Roy Mason, "City Under One Roof Extends Borders," NYT, August 29, 1926.

263 *"the fastest train traveling"*: NYT, June 12, 16, 1927.

264 *"I take the Century"*: Beebe, *20th Century,* 9.

264 *"a moment of majestic finality"*: Jan Morris, *Manhattan '45* (New York: Oxford University Press, 1986), 171–72; NYT, February 17, 1929.

264 *"a surging human mass"*: NYT, February 17, 1929.

264 *"so dense night and morning"*: Footner, *New York,* 165.

264 *nearly twenty thousand passenger elevators:* "Under the Asphalt," *Fortune* 20 (July 1939): 199.

264 *"Valley of Giants"*: NYT, July 13, 1930.

264 *"cloud houses"*: Morand, *New York,* 46.

264 *"huddled together"*: Charles Phelps Cushing, "Where Our City Soars and Dives," NYT, July 13, 1930.

264 *"City of Incredible Towers"*: Le Corbusier, *Cathedrals,* 42–43, 55–56.

264 *what Detroit was:* Belle and Leighton, *Grand Central,* 70; NYT, May 29, 1927.

265 *"speed was the essential thing"*: Markey, "Night," 46.

265 *"spectacular quantities of tension"*: Michaelis, "77," 106.

265 *"thicket"*: H. I. Brock and J. W. Golinkin, *New York Is Like This* (NY: Dodd, Mead, 1989), 11.

265 *"Never before"*: NYT, December 23, 1928.

265 *"Civilization has never before"*: NYT, November 4, 1928.

266 *"anti-noise campaign"*: NYW, May 27, 29, June 18, 1927. By the 1960s rivets would be largely replaced by high-strength steel bolts.

266 *"duplicated city noises"*: NYT, November 4, 1928.

266 *"colossal knife"*: Waldemar Kaempffert, "Burrowing into the Roots of the City," NYT, July 17, 1927.

266 *"machine built"*: Ibid. See also Frederick A. Kramer, *Building the Independent Subway* (NY: Quadrant, 1990), 16.

267 *"Subway Sam"*: "Construction: The Big Digger," *Time* 49 (April 7, 1947): 90, 92.

267 *"bawling orders"*: Russell Owen, "A Master Ditch Digger," TNY 3 (June 4, 1927): 19–21.

267 *The dapper mayor:* Walsh, *Gentleman,* 157–58.

267 *"nether world"; "rising, dipping"*: R. L. Duffus, "Metal Roots That Feed the Living City," NYT, April 13, 1930; "Under the Asphalt," 126, 128.

267 *45,000 miles:* "Under the Asphalt," 126.

267 *"If these are cut"*: Kaempffert, "Burrowing."

268 *"it would be impossible"*: "Under the Asphalt," 126.

268 *"a small crew of hard-working saboteurs"*: Ibid.

CHAPTER FOURTEEN: THE MAGIC CARPET

PAGE

269 "Don't give the people": Walter Reynolds, "Don't Give the People What They Want," *The Green Book Magazine* 12 (August 1914): 226.

269 *"Screamingly ugly"*: Footner, *New York,* 168.

269 *Roxy Theatre:* T-Square, "The Sky Line, Roxy to the Fore," TNY 3 (March 19, 1927): 75. T-Square is the pseudonym used by architecture critic George Chappell.

269 *a friend of Irwin Chanin's:* NYT, January 28, 1929.

269 *"leading motion picture showman"*: DN, February 21, 1927; "Who Are the Chanins?" NYT, January 24, 1926.

270 *"Cathedral of the Motion Picture"*: Mordaunt Hall, "New Roxy Theatre Has Gala Opening," NYT, March 12, 1927.

270 *"conquest"*: Irwin, *Highlights,* 326.

270 *"Napoleon among exhibitors"*: Ibid., 327.

270 *"In America"*: Gilbert Seldes, *The Movies Come from America* (NY: Charles Scribner's Sons, 1937), 104.

270 *"well pressed and brushed"; "On they come"*: Irwin, *Highlights,* 329.

271 *"His influence could be felt"*: NYT, January 14, 1936.

271 *"I'll make a bet"*: NYT, February 27, 1927.

271 William Fox: Benjamin B. Hampton, *History of the American Film Industry: From Its Beginnings to 1931* (NY: Dover, 1970 edition; originally published in 1931 under the title *A History of the Movies*), 334.

271 *"the supreme achievement"*: NYT, March 26, 1927. For Fox, see Neal Gabler, *An Empire of Their Own: How the Jews Invented Hollywood* (NY: Anchor, 1989), 64–72.

271 *"[is] the greatest genius"*: NYT, April 3, 1927.

271 In its first year of operation: NYT, March 12, 1927; Hampton, *History,* 334.

271 *"[Rothafel] has conceived"*: Kenneth Macgowan, "Profiles: Deus Ex Cinema," TNY 3 (May 28, 1927): 20.

272 *"The great P. T. Barnum"*: "Roxy's Cathedral," *Outlook* (March 23, 1927): 361–62.

272 *"swarming with marble statuary"*: Brooks Atkinson, *Broadway* (NY: Macmillan, revised edition, 1974), 183; NYT, February 27, 1927.

272 *"the lobby"*: Ken Bloom, "Roxy Theatre," in *Broadway: Its History, People, and Places: An Encyclopedia,* 2nd ed. (NY: Routledge, 2003), 463.

272 *"grand enough for a royal procession"*: Atkinson, *Broadway,* 183.

272 *"played the same piece of music simultaneously"*: Ibid.

272 equipped with the most advanced entertainment technology: "The Roxy Theatre, New York City," *Architecture and Building* 59 (April 1927): 109–10.

272 *"with a quick journey"*: NYT, February 27, 1927; Hall, "New Roxy Theatre."

272 *"everything in excess"*: Atkinson, *Broadway,* 182.

272 *"Roxy's new home"; "architecture of fantasy"*: T-Square, "Roxy," 75.

272 *"please his clients"*: Advertisement for Roxy Theatre, NYT, March 27, 1927; "The Roxy," *The Decorative Furnisher* 52 (April 1927): 83; "Modern Tendencies in Theatre Design," *The American Architect* 131 (May 20, 1927): 681; David Naylor, *Great American Movie Theaters* (Washington, DC: Preservation Press, 1987), 23.

273 *"well-trained morticians"*: Atkinson, *Broadway,* 83.

273 *"to a high luster of courtesy"*: Hampton, *History,* 333.

273 superbly equipped entertainment complex: "The Music That Is in Every Man: An Interview with the World's Most Remarkable Entertainer, 'Roxy,'" *The Etude* (December 1927): 903.

273 penthouse suite: Allene Talmey, *Doug and Mary and Others: A Book* (NY: Macy-Masius, 1927), 174–75.

274 *"There's Mayor Walker"*: NYT, March 12, 1927.

274 *"They came"*: "New Pictures," *Time* 9 (March 21, 1927), 38.

274 *"lads who ordinarily"*: Quoted in Bloom, "Roxy Theatre," in *Broadway*, 464.

274 *"a poker-faced Buddha"*: Ben M. Hall, *The Best Remaining Seats: The Story of the Golden Age of the Movie Palace* (NY: Clarkson N. Potter, 1961), 7.

274 *"thundered"*: Ibid., 8.

274 the *"Roxology"*: Stern et al., *New York 1930*, 257.

274 *"Ye portals bright"*: Hall, *Best Seats*, 8.

275 *"profanation"*: Morand, *New York*, 210.

275 *"the Jehovah"*: Macgowan, "Deus," 20.

275 *"It's the Roxy"*: Ross Melnick, "Station R-O-X-Y," *Film History* 17 (2005). Melnick has written the only biography of Roxy: Ross Melnick, *American Showman: Samuel "Roxy" Rothafel and the Birth of the Entertainment Industry, 1908–1935* (NY: Columbia University Press, 2012).

275 *"Nothing he ever said"*: Seldes, *Movies*, 105.

275 *Little is known*: Melnick, *American Showman*, 30.

276 *"the little Jew"*: Melnick, "Station," 218.

276 *"My ancestors"*: HT, February 17, 1918.

276 *"I was the black sheep"*: Brooklyn *Daily Eagle*, January 13, 1936.

276 *"I . . . was always moping about"*: Gabler, *Empire*, 95.

276 *a cash boy*: Mary B. Mullett, "Roxy and His Gang," *The American Magazine* 99 (March 1925): 34.

276 *"so many jobs"*: NYT, January 14, 1936.

276 *"but this time"*; *"people will respond"*: Mullett, "Roxy," 156.

276 *"steady" enough*: NYT, January 14, 1936.

276 *"He thought I was a rover"*: Mullett, "Roxy," 156.

277 *"I bought a second-hand screen"*: NYT, January 14, 1936.

277 *"Pearls of wisdom"*: Gabler, *Empire*, 96.

277 *he hired a violinist*: "The Music That Is," 903.

277 *"sensual richness"*: Bloom, "Roxy Theatre," in *Broadway*, 461. See also William Stephenson, "Rothafel, Roxy," *American National Biography Online*, www.anb.org.

277 *"The surroundings were poor"*: Mullett, "Roxy," 156.

277 *"Motion pictures are no longer"*: Ross Melnick, "Rethinking Rothafel: Roxy's Forgotten Legacy," *The Moving Image* (Fall 2003): 64–65.

278 *"was one of the first to see"*: Lucille Husting, " 'Hello, Everybody!': A Trip 'Back Stage' Elicits 'Roxy's' Personal Story," *Radio News* (December 1927): 604.

278 *Harry Davis and John Harris*: Ave Pildas, text by Lucinda Smith, *Movie Palaces* (NY: Clarkson N. Potter, 1980), 10.

278 *"to whom ten cents a week"*: Quoted in Stern et al., *New York 1930*, 246.

278 *"grand vizier"*: Hall, *Best Seats*, 29.

278 *Keith loathed motion pictures*: Bloom, "Roxy Theatre," in *Broadway*, 461.

278 *"Johnny Appleseed"*: Daniel Okrent, *Great Fortune: The Epic of Rockefeller Center* (NY: Penguin, 2004 edition; first published in 2003), 204.

278 *"He threw up his hands"*: Mullett, "Roxy," 158.

278 *"atmospheric prologue"*: Macgowan, "Deus," 20.

279 *"I want to make the truck driver"*: David Robinson, *From Peep Show to Palace: The Birth of American Film* (NY: Columbia University Press, 1996), 149.

279 *to manage the Regent Theatre*: Reynolds, "Don't Give the People," 226.

279 *music was thematically merged:* Stephen W. Bush, "The Theatre of Realization," *Moving Picture World* 18 (November 15, 1913): 714.

279 *"The presentation was":* Quoted in Hall, *Best Seats,* 35.

279 *the highest salary of any film presenter:* Melnick, "Rethinking," 68.

280 *"Going to the new Strand Theatre":* NYT, April 11, 1914.

280 *the Strand drew over ten thousand patrons:* "A Theatre with Four Million Patrons a Year," *Photoplay Magazine* (April 1915): 84.

280 *"The Rialto is a motion picture house":* Quoted in Hall, *Best Seats,* 51.

280 *"made absolutely no difference":* David Nasaw, *Going Out: The Rise and Fall of Public Amusements* (NY: Basic, 1993), 225.

280 *"We sell tickets":* Naylor, *Movie Theaters,* 16, 21.

280 *"His forte":* Joe Bigelow, "Roxy," *Variety* (January 15, 1936): 4.

281 *nearly bankrupt Capitol:* Melnick, "Station," 219.

281 *"She bathes in elegance":* Lloyd Lewis, "The De Luxe Picture Palace," NR 58 (March 27, 1929): 176–77.

281 *highest-grossing movie theater:* Melnick, "Station," 219.

281 *gave the gloomy film an uplifting ending:* Mike Budd, "The Cabinet of Dr. Caligari: Conditions of Reception," *Cine-Tracts* 3 (Winter 1981), 47.

281 *"showman with the vision":* Atkinson, *Broadway,* 182.

282 *"Although movie audiences":* Maggie Valentine, *The Show Starts on the Sidewalk: An Architectural History of the Movie Theatre, Starring S. Charles Lee* (New Haven: Yale University Press, 1994), 36.

282 *"Don't give the people what they want":* Reynolds, "Don't Give," 230.

282 *"a leatherneck putting on culture":* Gabler, *Empire,* 99.

282 *"It has been a long cherished dream":* Melnick, "Rethinking," 73.

282 Motion Picture News *honored Roxy:* "Screen—The Greatest," NYT, December 31, 1922.

283 *26 million people:* Gabler, *Empire,* 99–100.

283 *"So successful":* Seldes, *Movies,* 105–6.

283 *"a menace to the movies":* Hampton, *History,* 331.

283 *a radio revolution:* HT, January 14, 1936.

283 *"knocked together":* Ibid.

283 *"My friends call me by my nickname":* Melnick, "Station," 220.

284 *"I nationalized the Capitol Theatre":* William Peck Banning, *Commercial Broadcasting Pioneer: The WEAF Experiment, 1982–1926* (Cambridge: Harvard University Press, 1946), 114.

284 *"into the family life of America":* Gladys Hall, "He Makes the World at Home," *Classic* (August 1923): 25.

284 *"fine radio set":* "The Music That Is," 904.

284 *"one of the most beloved":* Lucille Husting, " 'Hello, Everybody!,' " 604.

284 *"drooling sentimentality":* Michele Hilmes, *Radio Voices: American Broadcasting, 1922–1952* (Minneapolis: University of Minnesota Press, 1997), 63.

284 *"whether Roxy actually believes"; "nicknames on five minutes' acquaintanceship":* Talmey, *Doug and Mary,* 173, 178.

284 *"misspelled and poorly expressed":* Mullett, "Roxy," 34. See also Melnick, "Station," 221; and James C. Young, "Broadcasting Personality," *Radio Broadcast* (July 1924): 248, 250.

284 *"We are lonely":* Mullett, "Roxy," 162.

285 *"battle-stricken boys of our land"*: Quoted in Hall, *Best Seats,* 75.

285 *"from curb to curb"*: "Roxy and His Gang," *The American Magazine* (March 1925): 34.

285 *"the condition of Aunt Matilda's health"*: HT, January 14, 1936.

285 *"to conduct himself"*; *"most stilted introduction known to radio"*; *"the greatest expression of opinion"*: Hilmes, *Radio Voices,* 62–63.

285 *"a one-man multi-media empire"*; *"He is the stellar god of a new force"*: Hall, *Best Seats,* 71.

285 *"When Roxy thanks a friend"*: Talmey, *Doug and Mary,* 174.

286 *"hyperactive and desperately needful"*: Okrent, *Great Fortune,* 210.

286 *"He was almost superhuman!"*: Mullett, "Roxy," 161.

286 *"the greatest film theatre"*: HT, January 14, 1936.

287 *"to spend any amount"*: Hampton, *History,* 331.

287 *"I will be the absolute despot"*: New York *Morning Telegraph,* December 20, 1926.

287 *"Mama, does God"*: Roxy File, Billy Rose Theatre Collection, New York Public Library for the Performing Arts, New York, NY.

287 *21,000 motion picture theaters:* Melnick, "Rethinking," 79.

287 *"Now Broadway at the theater-hour"*: Irwin, *Highlights,* 329.

287 *"It is telling"*: Ken Bloom, *The Routledge Guide to Broadway* (NY: Routledge, 2007), x.

287 *"Too far uptown"*; *"the Piccadilly of New York"*: NYT, January 1, 1906, April 12, 1904.

288 *"the open space"*: NYT, April 9, 1904.

288 *"It seemed almost as if"*: NYT, January 1, 1905. The *Times* outgrew the building and in 1913 moved to an annex on West Forty-third Street, where it remained until it built a prodigious tower on Eighth Avenue in 2007. The paper kept ownership of the old building until 1961.

288 *"blazing electric ball"*: NYT, January 1, 1908.

288 *"astir at all hours"*: NYT, December 31, 1905.

288 *"amusement center"*: Quoted in David W. Dunlap, *On Broadway: A Journey Uptown over Time* (NY: Rizzoli, 1990), 167, 175.

289 *the number of theaters in New York City actually grew:* NYT, October 19, 1930; Churchill, "Recalling."

289 *"the archangel of Broadway"*; *"testing ground"*: "The Theatre-Business," *Fortune* 17 (February 1938): 66–70. See also David C. Hammack, "Developing for Commercial Culture," in William R. Taylor, ed., *Inventing Times Square: Commerce and Culture at the Crossroads of the World* (NY: Russell Sage Foundation, 1991), 48; and Traub, *Devil's Playground,* 86.

289 *Astoria Studio:* Richard Koszarski, *The Astoria Studio and Its Fabulous Films* (NY: Dover, 1983). Famous Players-Lasky was renamed Paramount Pictures in 1927.

289 *"to Broadway first come all"*: Dunlap, *On Broadway,* 178.

289 *"the pace for success"*: Irwin, *Highlights,* 327.

289 *"Show me any other industry"*: Jill Stone, *Times Square: A Pictorial History* (NY: Collier, 1982), 83.

290 *"was founded and for more than thirty years"*: Gabler, *Empire,* 1.

290 *"pivotal point in the entire subway system"*: NYT, March 13, 1927.

290 *"the capital"*: Walker, *Night Club Era,* 199.

290 *"is the spirit of New York"*: Quoted in Anthony Bianco, *Ghosts of 42nd Street: A History of New York's Most Infamous Block* (NY: William Morrow, 2004), 81.

290   *"subway crush"*: Brock and Golinkin, *New York Is Like This,* 76–77.

290   *"Parisian boulevards"*: Graham, *New York Nights,* 13.

290   *"Nothing whatever in Times Square"*: Irwin, *Highlights,* 324–25.

290   *Roseland Ballroom*: Kathy J. Ogren, "Roseland Ballroom," *ENYC,* 1022.

290   *"Mildly insane by day"*: Irwin, *Highlights,* 324–25.

291   *"The blind are aware"*: Graham, *New York Nights,* 13.

291   *"a conspiracy of commerce"*: Morand, *New York,* 192.

291   *"apotheosis of electricity"*: Quoted in Bayrd Still, *Mirror for Gotham* (NY: New York University Press, 1956), 323.

291   *"flaming avenue"*: "Economics of the Great White Way," *Literary Digest* 86 (September 12, 1925): 23.

291   *"long kaleidoscope"*: Mike Marqusee and Bill Harris, eds., *New York* (Boston: Little, Brown, 1985), 140–41.

291   *"the luminous advertising"*: Le Corbusier, *Cathedrals,* 102.

291   *"Here is our poetry"*: William Leach, "Introductory Essay," in Taylor, ed., *Inventing,* 241.

291   *"but none gets this massed effect"*: Irwin, *Highlights,* 325.

CHAPTER FIFTEEN: SARNOFF

PAGE

295   "In a big ship": "The Fellow on the Bridge," *Time* 98 (December 27, 1971): 57.

295   *"I had not even seen"*: "The General," *Time* 58 (July 23, 1951): 75. See also Eugene Lyons, *David Sarnoff* (NY: Harper & Row, 1966), 26–28; and Carl Dreher, *Sarnoff: An American Success* (NY: Quadrangle, 1977), 10.

296   *When they arrived in New York*: Tom Lewis, *Empire of the Air: The Men Who Made Radio* (NY: Harper Perennial, 1993; first published in 1991), 92; Thomas Whiteside, "David Sarnoff's Fifty Fabulous Years," *Collier's* (October 12, 1956): 42.

296   *he became a budding businessman at fourteen*: Kenneth Bilby, *The General: David Sarnoff and the Rise of the Communications Industry* (NY: Harper & Row, 1986), 17. Bilby was an RCA executive; Whiteside, "Sarnoff's Fifty," 42.

297   *"More than anything"*: Ibid., 19.

297   *he was on the wrong floor*: David Sarnoff, as told to Mary Margaret McBride, "Radio," *The Saturday Evening Post* (August 7, 1926): 8.

297   *bought a dummy telegraph key*: Bilby, *General,* 20.

298   *Marconi was the first*: T. James Rybak, "Guglielmo Marconi," *Popular Electronics* 9, no. 4 (April 1992): 43–44; Hugh G. H. Aitken, *Sytony and Spark: The Origins of Radio* (Princeton: Princeton University Press, 1992).

299   *Reginald Fessenden*: Erik Barnouw, *A Tower in Babel: A History of Broadcasting in the United States to 1933* (NY: Oxford University Press, 1966), 19.

299   *Lee de Forest*: Lewis, *Empire,* 2.

299   *"I discovered"*: Barnouw, *Tower,* 25. See also Lawrence Bergreen, *Look Now, Pay Later: The Rise of Network Broadcasting* (Garden City, NY: Doubleday, Doran, 1980), 19.

299   *"The 'homeless' sound waves"*: NYT, January 14, 1910.

299   *"I carried his bag"*: "The General," 75.

300   *His expert "fist"*: Ibid.

300   *"with eager absorption"*: Sarnoff, "Radio," 8–9.

300 *"I was whisked in a taxicab"*: Ibid., 141–42; Lyons, *Sarnoff,* 59–60.

300 *Sarnoff's tale*: Dreher, *Sarnoff,* 29. A few historians question whether Sarnoff was even at the telegraph key. In 1912, he was in management and no longer a telegrapher; see Alexander B. Magoun, "Pushing Technology: David Sarnoff and Wireless Communications, 1911–1921," conference presentation, July 26, 2001. I find this argument unconvincing.

301 *"Word spread swiftly"*: Sarnoff, "Radio," 141–42.

301 *"The* Titanic *disaster"*: Lyons, *Sarnoff,* 60. See also Sarnoff, "Radio," 141–42.

301 *promoted to chief inspector of the radio equipment*: Bilby, *General,* 35.

301 *"An engineer or a scientific experimenter"*: Bergreen, *Look Now,* 17.

301 *He instructed his mother*: Lyons, *Sarnoff,* 68.

301 *Sarnoff sent a memorandum*: The original memo has never been found, and this has given rise to disputes about when it was written. Edward Dreher claimed that Sarnoff wrote the memo in November 1916 and backdated a copy of it to September 30, 1915, when he was preparing a 1968 collection of his writing, called *Looking Ahead,* perhaps to make it appear that he came up with the idea of a radio box before de Forest introduced the audion; see *Looking Ahead: The Papers of David Sarnoff* (NY: McGraw-Hill, 1968), 31. There is plenty of evidence, however, that Sarnoff wrote the memo in 1915. In a number of interviews and public statements he made in the 1920s, he consistently claimed that he submitted the memo in 1915; see Allan Harding, "What Radio Has Done and What It Will Do Next," *The American Magazine* (March 1926), 38. The Sarnoff Papers provide additional evidence. In November 1916, Sarnoff reminded Nally of an earlier discussion they had about radio. There is another reference to the 1915 memo in a letter from Sarnoff to Alfred Goldsmith, August 2, 1922; see the David Sarnoff Library, which was moved to the Hagley Library and Archive in Wilmington, Delaware, after the David Sarnoff Library and Museum in Princeton, New Jersey, closed its door in 2009. Hereafter cited as Sarnoff Mss.

301 *"I have in mind"*: Sarnoff Memorandum to Edward J. Nally, September 30, 1915, in Sarnoff, *Looking Ahead,* 31–32.

302 *"electronic equivalent of the Model T"*: Bergreen, *Look Now,* 21.

302 *"point-to-point"*: Bilby, *General,* 38–39.

302 *"a harebrained scheme"*: NYT, December 17, 1971.

302 *"It will die out in time"*: Robert Sobel, *RCA* (NY: Stein & Day, 1984), 37.

303 *"voices in the air"*: Lyons, *Sarnoff,* 76–77.

303 *a historic agreement worked out by GE*: Bilby, *General,* 46.

303 *This gave the United States an insuperable advantage*: Barnouw, *Tower,* 59–60.

303 *"ran [RCA] almost from the beginning"*: Quoted in Dreher, *Sarnoff,* 52.

303 *"With the possible exception"; "He visualized"*: Lyons, *Sarnoff,* 6–7.

304 *"that rare combination"*: Ibid., 4.

304 *"Driving through obstacles"*: "The General," 75.

304 *"I realized that"*: Bergreen, *Look Now,* 22.

304 *"His chill blue eyes"*: "The General," 78.

304 *tell earthy stories*: Gould, "Sarnoff," 43.

304 *never forgot where he came from*: NYT, December 13, 1971.

304 *"There are"*: "The General," 75.

305 *to develop a sample radio music box*: Lyons, *Sarnoff,* 97.

305 *"just a refrigerator without any ice in it"*: Sarnoff, "Why Super-Broadcasting Means Better Service," press release, October 26, 1924, Sarnoff Mss.

305 *KDKA, in Pittsburgh*: Susan J. Douglas, *Listening In: Radio and the American Imagination* (NY: Times Books 1999), 64.

305 *"marketing tool"*: Daniel J. Czitrom, *Media and the American Mind: From Morse to McLuhan* (Chapel Hill: University of North Carolina Press, 1982), 60.

305 *"Radio was destined"*: Allen, *Only Yesterday*, 67.

306 *Owen Young negotiated a patent-sharing agreement*: Dreher, *Sarnoff*, 58.

306 *Sarnoff orchestrated the entire technical setup*: J. Andrew White, "Report: Radiophone Broadcast of Dempsey-Carpentier Fight on July 2, 1921," Sarnoff Mss. In an August 1921 article in *Wireless Age*, Julius Hopp, a manager for concerts at Madison Square Garden, claimed that he, not Sarnoff, was the mastermind behind the broadcast. See Evan I. Schwartz, *The Last Lone Inventor: A Tale of Genius, Deceit, and the Birth of Television* (NY: Perennial, 2002). There is no available evidence to verify Hopp's account.

306 *"We were tired"*: J. Andrew White, "The Big Radio Broadcast," *Reader's Digest*, December 1953, copy in Sarnoff Mss.

306 *"molten mass"*: Dreher, *Sarnoff*, 72.

307 *reached an estimated 400,000 listeners*: Lewis, *Empire*, 158.

307 *"You have made history"*: Lyons, *Sarnoff*, 101.

307 *Sarnoff received permission*: Elmer B. Butcher, "Radio and David Sarnoff," part 2, 336, Sarnoff Mss. Butcher was a longtime associate of Sarnoff's at RCA and author of a forty-six-volume unpublished history of the company.

307 *"prophet of the radio age"*: Bilby, *General*, 61.

307 *"He was not so much an originator"*: Dreher, *Sarnoff*, 40.

307 *make radio a "public service"*: Sarnoff to E. W. Rice, June 17, 1922, Sarnoff Mss.

307 *"I believe that the quickest way"*: "Radio Congress," *Time* (October 20, 1924), 22.

308 *"free enterprise must rule"*: Sarnoff, Statement Before Interdepartmental Committee on Radio Legislation of Congress, Washington, DC, November 21, 1916, Sarnoff Mss.

308 *that practice would cease in 1924*: Susan Smulyan, *Selling Radio: The Commercialization of American Broadcasting 1920–1934* (Washington, DC: Smithsonian Institution Press, 1994), 47, 57.

308 *"anyone who had a message"*: Quoted in Barnouw, *Tower*, 106.

308 *the world's first radio commercial*: Bilby, *General*, 74.

308 *"Handled with tact and discretion"*: Quoted in Banning, *Commercial Broadcasting Pioneer*, 92.

309 *an "intimate" topic*: Bilby, *Sarnoff*, 97.

309 *AT&T took a giant step*: Banner, *Pioneer*, 153–54.

309 *AT&T lawyers*: Smulyan, *Selling Radio*, 56–59.

310 *"abrasive Jew"*: Daniel Stashower, *The Boy Genius and the Mogul: The Untold Story of Television* (NY: Broadway, 2002), 120.

310 *RCA was the Bell System's largest single customer*: Sobel, *RCA*, 68.

310 *RCA aggressively promoted*: Sarnoff, "Radio, Part Two," *The Saturday Evening Post* (August 14, 1926): 24.

310 *"a weird aerial visitor"*: Bruce Bliven, "How Radio Is Remaking Our World," *The Century Magazine* 108 (June 1924).

311 *"Demand developed with an intensity":* Bilby, *General,* 58.

311 *"No other new product":* Sobel, *RCA,* 36–37.

311 *increased by over 1,400 percent:* Allen, *Only Yesterday,* 142.

311 *billion-dollar industry:* Czitrom, *Media,* 79; Sarnoff, "The Rising Tide of a New Art," address at the University Club, Boston, January 28, 1928, Sarnoff Mss.; Sarnoff, "The Development of the Radio Art and Radio Industry Since 1920," lecture before the Harvard Business School, April 16, 1928, Sarnoff Mss.

311 *"Radio was":* Lewis, *Empire,* 2.

311 *he created, under RCA Auspices:* Barnouw, *Tower,* 189–91.

311 *two networks in one:* Dreher, *Sarnoff,* 102.

311 *four-hour broadcast:* Leonard Maltin, *The Great American Broadcast: A Celebration of Radio's Golden Age* (NY: Dutton, 1997), 15.

312 *"My dear":* Barnouw, *Tower,* 191.

312 *Sarnoff added seven Pacific stations:* NYT, January 31, 1927.

312 *largest listening audience:* NYT, February 20, 1927.

312 *one of the hottest stocks:* John Cassidy, "Wall Street Follies," TNY 75 (August 9, 1999), 29.

312 *he sold all his RCA shares:* Bilby, *General,* 91.

312 *"Of all RCA's activities":* Quoted in "The General," 78.

312 *"I don't get ulcers":* Stashower, *Boy Genius,* 154.

312 *"a type seldom found":* Quoted in Alex McKenzie, "Sarnoff: Controversial Pioneer," *IEEE Spectrum* 9, no. 1 (January 1972), 41.

313 *"The first months of NBC"; "Spaced along":* Barnouw, *Tower,* 192.

313 *Federal Radio Act:* David Sarnoff, "Radio Progress Passes in Review," NYT, September 18, 1927.

313 *"bone structure":* Bergreen, *Look Now,* 6.

313 *a "plug-in" radio:* Bucher, "Radio and David Sarnoff," 387, Sarnoff Mss.

313 *purchase the Victor Talking Machine Company:* Barnouw, *Tower,* 201.

313 *It created the RCA Victor Company:* Bucher, "Radio and David Sarnoff," 713, Sarnoff Mss.; Bilby, *General,* 92–101.

313 *transatlantic facsimile transmission:* "The New Age of Radio," address by David Sarnoff before the Economic Club of New York, November 27, 1928, Sarnoff Mss.

313 *facsimile service between New York and London:* Sarnoff, press release, September 18, 1927, Sarnoff Mss.; DN, January 8, 1927.

314 *"It is now practical":* Sarnoff, press release, February 11, 1927, Sarnoff Mss.

314 *a year behind the competition:* Ibid.

314 *"Wait a minute!":* Mordaunt Hall, "The Screen: Al Jolson and the Vitaphone," NYT, October 7, 1927.

314 *"Among great film companies":* "Radio into Talkies," *Time* (July 15, 1929): 48.

315 *"seeing . . . by radio"; "near future":* Memorandum, "Radio Broadcasting Activities," to RCA Board of Directors, April 5, 1923, Sarnoff Mss.

315 *"informational":* Bilby, *General,* 118.

315 *"Television Triumphs":* NYT, April 8, 1927.

315 *complexity of the equipment:* Ibid.

315 *working with the wrong base technology:* NYT, November 8, 1928.

315 *"the next great industrial development":* "Television," *Time,* 17 (May 18, 1931): 54.

315 *discover Vladimir T. Zworykin:* Bilby, *General,* 120–22. In 1936, RCA demonstrated a working iconoscope camera tube and kinescope receiver tube to the press.

316 *legal battle with Philo T. Farnsworth:* Schwartz, *Last Lone Inventor,* 122.

317 *"And now":* Sarnoff, Broadcast Speech, April 20, 1939, Sarnoff Ms.

317 *Sousa received $50,000:* Christopher Gray, "Where the Orchestras Played and the Mice Presided," NYT, February 18, 2010.

317 *"well mannered":* Morris Markey, "The Broadcasting Industry," TNY 4 (March 3, 1928), 42.

318 *"radio amusement"; "a churchly dignity":* Ibid., 46.

CHAPTER SIXTEEN: PALEY

PAGE

319 "Bill Paley plays": David McClintick, "What Hath William Paley Wrought?," *Esquire* 100 (December 1983): 299.

319 *"To all of us":* "Man of the Future," *Time* 88 (October 7, 1966): 106.

319 *"life-blood":* Federal Writers' Project, *New York Panorama,* 297.

319 *"he merchandised":* David Halberstam, *The Powers That Be* (NY: Alfred A. Knopf, 1979), 23.

320 *"His was one of ":* Ibid.

320 *"the graveyard of unionism":* Lewis J. Paper, *Empire: William S. Paley and the Making of CBS* (NY: St. Martin's, 1987), 10.

320 *La Palina brand:* William S. Paley, *As It Happened: A Memoir* (Garden City, NY: Doubleday, Doran, 1979), 16, 22.

320 *"I lived a two-sided life":* Ibid., 23.

320 *"a good time Charlie":* Quoted in Sally Bedell Smith, *In All His Glory: The Life of William S. Paley* (NY: Simon & Schuster, 1990), 37.

321 *"felt truly independent":* Paley, *Happened,* 23.

321 *"I never got over":* Ibid., 32.

321 *his family's association with the Levy brothers:* Robert Metz, *CBS: Reflections in a Bloodshot Eye* (Chicago: Playboy, 1975), 14–16.

322 *hooked up with Major White:* Paley, *Happened,* 38.

322 *Columbia bought the operating rights of United Independent:* "And All Because They're Smart," *Fortune* 11 (June 1935): 148.

322 *Columbia threw in the towel:* Ibid.

323 *became simply the Columbia Broadcasting System:* Barnouw, *Tower,* 223.

323 *Louchheim bought a controlling share of the network:* Paley, *Happened,* 33–34.

323 *"sultry voiced":* Smith, *Glory,* 59.

323 *"It was one of radio's":* "Smart," 148.

323 *"felt the excitement":* Paper, *Empire,* 22.

323 *Paley bought him out:* Paley, *Happened,* 34.

323 *"The network's shaky condition":* Ibid., 34–35.

323 *His father agreed to throw in:* Ibid., 37.

323 *"Bill didn't like the tobacco business":* Quoted in Paper, *Empire,* 22.

324 *"I think Paley":* Quoted in Edward L. Bernays, *Biography of an Idea: Memoirs of Public Relations Counsel Edward L. Bernays* (NY: Simon & Schuster, 1965), 426.

324 *"My friends thought"*: Jeremy Gerard, "William S. Paley," Builder of CBS, Dies at 89, NYT, October 27, 1990.

324 *"I left Philadelphia"*: Paley, *Happened*, 37–38.

324 *Paley had to produce identification*: Ibid., 38.

324 *"Bill Paley was like"*: Smith, *Glory*, 65–66.

324 *"plaything his father"*: Bernays, *Biography*, 426.

324 *"great, tall city"*: Paley, *Happened*, 38; Smith, *Glory*, 66.

325 *"the glittering sweep"*: Smith, *Glory*, 65.

325 *"In comparison with"*: Paley, *Happened*, 38.

325 *"trying to cash in on"*: Bergreen, *Look*, 44.

325 *"one-man show"*: Bernays, *Biography*, 427.

325 *"As in the case"*: "All Because They're Smart," 151.

325 *Paley's commanding obsession*: Ibid., 152.

325 *"Compared with NBC"*: Paley, *Happened*, 41. See also H. V. Kaltenborn, Reminiscences, CCOC, 16–19.

326 *"Not long after I came to New York"*: Paley, *Happened*, 41.

326 *began calling him "kid"*: Smith, *Glory*, 66.

326 *Paley operated almost in defiance of the way Sarnoff ran NBC*: Erik Barnouw, *The Golden Web: A History of Broadcasting in the United States, 1933–1953* (NY: Oxford University Press, 1968), 57–58.

326 *it would never again have a losing year*: Paley, *Happened*, 46.

327 *drew 60 percent of radio listeners*: Smulyan, *Selling*, 114–15.

327 *"Quite early in the game"*: Paley, *Happened*, 63.

327 *"lacked variety"*: Ibid., 47.

328 *"I thought, my God"*: Paper, *Empire*, 24.

328 *"It made a bigger impression"*: Bernays, *Biography*, 426–28.

328 *"the most sinful city"*: Paley, *Happened*, 17.

328 *dangerous-living Louise Brooks*: Louise Brooks, *Lulu in Hollywood* (NY: Alfred A. Knopf, 1982), 48; Barry Paris, *Louise Brooks* (NY: Alfred A. Knopf, 1989), 347.

328 *"As an emblematic figure"*: Kenneth Tynan, "Profiles: The Girl in the Black Helmet," TNY 55 (June 11, 1979): 68.

328 *"She is so very Manhattan"*: Ibid., 48.

328 *"sleek suits"*: Paris, *Brooks*, 514.

329 *"I knew all sorts of actresses"*: Ibid., 348.

329 *"Almost every move"*; *"talent scout"*: Ibid., 61–62.

329 *"a natural feel for entertainment"*: Halberstam, *Powers*, 24.

329 *He was "born"*: Gerard, "Paley."

329 *"from an advertising sensation"*: "An Appraisal," *Fortune* 6 (September 1932): 98.

329 *"wooed to CBS"*: Paley, *Happened*, 65–66.

330 *"This is Bob 'Pepsodent' Hope"*: Bergreen, *Look*, 58.

330 *"to make jazz respectable"*: Ann Douglas, *Terrible Honesty: Mongrel Manhattan in the 1920s* (NY: Farrar, Straus & Giroux, 1995), 350.

330 *"From the beginning"*: Paley, *Happened*, 112.

330 *"Get Paul Whiteman"*; *"A portly man"*: Ibid., 66–67.

330 *landed crooner Bing Crosby*: Ibid., 75.

331 *"It worked"*: Smith, *Glory,* 91–92.

331 *"He had the tenacity"*: Gerard, "Paley."

331 *"cigar salesman"; "do something"*: Quoted in Smith, *Glory,* 136, 141.

331 *"ashamed of"*: "An Appraisal," 44.

332 *"a latch key"; "dreaming of"*: Quoted in Czitrom, *Media,* 77.

332 *"most of the audience"*: "An Appraisal," 37.

332 *nearly 52 million people*: Ibid., 94.

332 *"I certainly appreciate"*: Quoted in Metz, *CBS,* xix.

332 *"a new and noisy method"*: Lewis, *Empire,* 235.

332 *"sniffed at"*: "Blue Chip," *Fortune* 2 (September 1932): 45.

332 *"about one-fifth sales"*: "An Appraisal," 37.

332 *control more than a third of the airtime*: Smith, *Glory,* 132–33, 137, 146.

332 *"Radio has been extremely"*: Czitrom, *Media,* 81–82.

332 *"We have a certain responsibility"*: "Sarnoff," *Newsweek* 78 (November 27, 1971): 47.

332 *CBS's net profits*: Barnouw, *Tower,* 250; Paper, *Empire,* 2, 28.

332 *His triplex*: NYW, January 14, 1930.

333 *"terrible struggle"*: Paley, *Happened,* 87.

333 *"maleness"*: Smith, *Glory,* 97–98.

333 *"boss of the house"*: Paley, *Happened,* 92.

333 *built a splendid six-story home*: Paley never liked 29 Beekman Place, and in 1940, he and Dorothy moved to the Waldorf, until they found a suitable house on East Seventy-fourth Street.

334 *"Let's run away together"*: Smith, *Glory,* 178–85.

334 *"sell time"; "ridiculously small"*: "Smart," 92.

334 *"with the turn of a dial"*: Quoted in Bernays, *Biography,* 432.

334 *invite Bernays to lunch and fire him*: Bernays, *Biography,* 424, 434.

335 *"quicker to capitalize on breaks"*: "Smart," 151.

335 *"There was no mistaking"*: Smith, *Glory,* 145.

335 *"Mr. Paley doesn't dictate"*: "Mr. CBS," *Time* 83 (January 31, 1964): 57.

335 *"he took his dominance"*: Quoted in Gerard, "Paley."

335 *"with unholy speed"*: "Smart," 152.

335 *robbing Sarnoff's talent bank*: Paley, *Happened,* 108.

335 *"No one can speak"*: Paper, *Empire,* 16.

336 *"Paley's Raids"*: Gerard, "Paley."

336 *"sure sense"*: Donald West, "Spotlight: The House That Paley Built—And Keeps," NYT, October 24, 1976.

CHAPTER SEVENTEEN: JAZZ AGE BABY

PAGE

337 The *News* for years: "Jazz-Age Baby, Patterson's Tabloid Tops Them on Its 25th Birthday," *Newsweek,* July 3, 1944, 60.

337 *"had only a single teletype"*: Paley, *Happened,* 118–20.

337 *sent Edward R. Murrow*: Ibid., 131.

338 *"People get the news"*: NYT, August 31, 1927.

338 *"the most significant trend"*: Stanley Walker, *City Editor* (Frederick A. Stokes Co., 1934), 65.

338 *an anemic daily circulation*: Leo McGivena, and Others, *The News: The First Fifty Years of New York's Picture Newspaper* (NY: News Syndicate Co., 1969), 106.

338 *largest-selling paper in the country's history*: Walter E. Schneider, "Fabulous Rise of N.Y. Daily News," *Editor & Publisher* (June 24, 1939); John D. Stevens, *Sensationalism and the New York Press* (NY: Columbia University Press, 1991), 112.

338 *"No newspaper in all history"*: DN, May 27, 1946.

339 *"Think in terms of pictures"*: Joseph Patterson to S. H. Bloomer, September 9, 1922, Joseph Medill Patterson Papers, Donnelley Library, Lake Forest College, Lake Forest, IL, hereafter cited as JMP Mss.

339 *"to have a picture"*: Quoted in Schneider, "Fabulous," 45.

339 *"Jazz-age baby"*: "Jazz-Age Baby."

339 *"phenomenal success"*: Quoted in A. J. Liebling, "The Wayward Press, Mamie and Mr. O'Donnell Carry On," TNY 22 (June 8, 1946): 95.

339 *Jazz Journalism*: Simon Michael Bessie, *Jazz Journalism: The Story of the Tabloid Newspapers* (NY: E. P. Dutton, 1938).

339 *"Gutter" journalism*: O. G. Villard, "Tabloid Offenses," *The Forum* 77 (March 1927): 487, 491, 486.

339 *Mark Hellinger*: Jim Bishop, *The Mark Hellinger Story: A Biography of Broadway and Hollywood* (NY: Appleton-Century-Crofts, 1952), 93–94.

340 *"exclusive domain"*: Gabler, *Winchell*, xii. 64. See also Bishop, *Hellinger*, 66.

340 *"no one was safe"*: Gabler, *Winchell*, 81.

340 *"to hurt anyone"*: Bishop, *Hellinger*, 69, 86.

340 *"There are only two simple aims"*: John Chapman, *Tell It to Sweeney: The Informal History of the New York Daily News* (Garden City, NY: Doubleday, Doran, 1961), 179.

340 *"how to become beautiful"*; *"Despondent men"*: Jack Alexander, "Profiles: Vox Populi—II," TNY 14 (August 13, 1938): 22.

340 *"simple, unaffected"*: Richard G. de Rochemont, "The Tabloids," *The American Mercury* 9 (October 1926): 192.

340 *"The* News *writes up"*: Walker, *City Editor*, 68–69.

340 *"sewer rag"*; *"an unholy blot"*: De Casseres, "Broadway Mind," 181; Bessie, *Jazz Journalism*, 19.

341 *"one of the liveliest"*: Walker, *City Editor*, 68.

341 *bankers and brokers*: George Y. Wells, "Patterson and the *Daily News*," *The American Mercury* 59 (December 9, 1944), 672.

341 *"I never liked"*: H. Allen Smith, *To Hell in a Handbasket* (NY: Doubleday, 1962), 276.

341 *Joseph Medill Patterson*: Megan McKinney, *The Magnificent Medills: America's Royal Family of Journalism During a Century of Turbulent Splendor* (NY: HarperCollins, 2011), 43–58.

341 *"slightly drunk"*: Burton Roscoe, *Before I Forget* (Garden City, NY: Doubleday, Doran, 1937), 39.

342 *"a natural athlete"*: Alfred Henry Lewis, "Joseph Medill Patterson: An Apostle of Hope," *The Saturday Evening Post* (September 15, 1906): 3.

342 *"Bourbon Joe"*: Robert Keeler, *Newsday: A Candid History of the Respectable Tabloid* (NY: William Morrow, 1997), 11.

342 *After graduating:* Richard Norton Smith, *The Colonel: The Life and Legend of Robert R. McCormick, 1880–1955* (Boston: Houghton Mifflin, 1997): 103.

342 *"tediously dull":* Alexander, "Vox Populi—II," 20.

342 *search for a political identity:* Frank Waldrop, *McCormick of Chicago: An Unconventional Portrait of a Controversial Figure* (Englewood Cliffs, NJ: Prentice Hall, 1966), 68.

342 *"started a demonstration":* NYT, May 27, 1946.

342 *"Capitalism has seen":* Lloyd Wendt, *Chicago Tribune: The Rise of a Great American Newspaper* (Chicago: Rand McNally, 1984), 376.

342 *"skin deep":* Ibid., 377.

343 *"I spend all of it":* John Tebbel, *An American Dynasty* (Garden City, NY: Doubleday, Doran, 1947), 282–83.

343 *"go to work":* "Joseph M. Patterson Dies," *Editor & Publisher* (June 1, 1946): 9.

343 *"I don't know":* Quoted in Alicia Patterson, as told to Hal Burton, "This Is the Life I Love," *The Saturday Evening Post* 231 (February 21, 1959): 44.

343 *"begrudging check":* Ibid.

343 *"Plowing is better exercise than polo":* Wendt, *Tribune,* 377.

343 *"an unpolished Galsworthy":* Quoted in Alexander, "Vox Populi—II," 21.

343 *"the greener capitalist paradise":* Wells, "Patterson," 676.

344 *"The family knew":* Wendt, *Tribune,* 400.

344 *"He was the first to see":* Roscoe, *Before,* 250.

344 *the most widely read daily in the country:* Wells, "Patterson," 675.

344 *"Joe Patterson had an almost mystical sense":* Wendt, *Tribune,* 378.

345 *"I never had a good idea":* Keeler, *Newsday,* 19.

345 *called him "Aunty Joe":* NYT, May 27, 1946.

345 *"newspapers of the future":* Chicago Tribune, May 27, 1946.

345 *"If the rest of you":* Bessie, *Jazz,* 78.

345 *allow "the boys" to borrow:* Chapman, *Sweeney,* 20.

346 *most competitive newspaper market:* Chapman, *Sweeney,* 59; Stevens, *Sensationalism,* 111.

346 *"the most turbulent":* Quoted in Chapman, *Sweeney,* 63. Field retired as general manager of the *News* in 1927. Roy Hollis, his assistant business manager, succeeded him and remained at the helm until 1946.

346 *The initial press run:* McGivena et al., *News,* 52, 83.

346 *"the most beautiful girl":* DN, June 26, 1919. See also NYT, June 23, 1919.

346 *"The* Illustrated Daily News*":* DN, June 26, 1919.

346 *"rotten" name:* Patterson to William H. Field, November 6, 1919, Field to Patterson, December 10, 1919, JMP Mss.

347 *"The story that can be told by a picture":* DN, June 26, 1919.

347 *"Remember always":* Patterson to Field, January 28, 1921, JMP Mss.

347 *"He was not just an onlooker":* NYT, May 27, 1946.

347 *"sojourns in Bowery flophouses":* Liebling, "Wayward," 97.

347 *"the public's mind":* Walker, *City Editor,* 69.

347 *"restraints upon the enjoyment of life":* Alexander, "Vox Populi—II," 19.

347 *"a fellow aristocrat":* Wells, "Patterson," 677.

347 *"little trumpeting for a cause":* Walker, *City Editor,* 69.

347 *"There should be some hesitancy":* Patterson to Field, March 11, 1921, JMP Mss.

347 *"kept simple and bright"*: Alexander, "Vox Populi—II," 19.

347 *"brash, sickly child"*: Walker, *City Editor*, 66.

348 *"All of us city-side staffers"*: Chapman, *Sweeney*, 96.

348 *"picture-hungry"*: Ibid., 116.

348 *"It is essential"*: Ibid., 70.

348 *"is a bloodhound"*: Walker, *City Editor*, 113.

348 *"ruthless boss"*: Chapman, *Sweeney*, 21–23; Patterson to Max Annenberg, May 7, 1921, JMP Mss.

348 *the prize: Mirror*, April 7, 1925.

348 *"love nests"; "Porno-Graphic"*: Pringle, *Big Frogs*, 133–34. For Macfadden, see Robert Ernst, *Weakness Is a Crime: The Life of Bernarr Macfadden* (Syracuse, NY: Syracuse University Press); and Mary W. Macfadden and Emile Gauvreau, *Dumbbells and Carrot Strips: The Story of Bernarr Macfadden* (NY: Henry Holt, 1953).

349 *"great muscle-flexer and carrot eater"*: Walker, *City Editor*, 71; *New York Evening Graphic*, September 10, 1925.

349 *"husbands in pajamas"*: Pringle, *Big Frogs*, 118.

349 *"such a thing as restraint"*: Alexander, "Vox Populi—II," 19. The Hearst tabloid did not cease publication until 1972.

349 *a circulation of over 300,000*: McGivena et al., *News*, 92.

349 *"The things people were most interested in"*: Roscoe, *Before*, 277.

349 *"to lay emphasis on"*: Patterson to Field, July 8, 1919, JMP Mss.

350 *"Brevity, next to pictures"; "briefed to the bone"*: Payne "What Is the Lure of the Tabloid Press?", *Editor & Publisher* (July 26, 1924): 7.

350 *"anything modern had"*: Stevens, *Sensationalism*, 118.

350 *"all the news of the day"*: "What Is the Lure?", 7.

350 *"the News could tell"*: "Passing of a Giant," *Time* (June 3, 1946), 88.

350 *Gloria Swanson*: Stevens, *Sensationalism*, 122.

350 *Max Annenberg*: Annenberg to Patterson, November 25, 1919, JMP Mss.

350 *"No more killing"*: Keeler, *Newsday*, 21.

350 *"Then we'd hang about"*: Paul Gallico, in Jerome Holtzman, ed., *No Cheering In the Press Box* (NY: Holt, Rinehart & Winston, 1974), 70.

351 *"The idea of these tours"*: Roscoe, *Before*, 277.

351 *"a prime research laboratory"*: Chapman, *Sweeney*, 87.

351 *"not the proletariat"*: Roscoe, *Before*, 277.

351 *fifty thousand letters a year*: "Passing of a Giant," 88.

351 *The winner was a Ziegfeld Girl*: Bishop, *Hellinger*, 150–51.

352 *nearly a third of the paper's readership*: "Circulation," file in JMP Mss.

352 *"Let's call this man Dick Tracy"*: Smith, *Colonel*, 247–49. The strip did not run in the *News* until 1931.

352 *"it doesn't pay"*: Patterson to Field, December 15, 1920, JMP Mss.

352 *a Rolls-Royce as a bonus*: Jack Alexander, "Profiles: Vox Populi—I," TNY 14 (August 6, 1938): 19.

352 *"Making a flashlight picture"*: Chapman, *Sweeney*, 92.

353 *"remarkable bargaining"; "I'll have"*: Alva Johnston, "Profiles: News Photographer—I," TNY 10 (December 1, 1934): 28.

353 *"a historian of manners"*: Ibid.

353 *Speed Graphic cameras:* M. C. Feenor to Patterson, July 1, 1927, JMP Mss.

353 *"with an eye to dramatic":* Walker, *City Editor,* 70.

353 *"the magic formula":* Wells, "Patterson," 675.

353 *It needed advertising:* "Personalities of the Day," JMP Mss.

354 *he hired a movie cameraman:* Alexander, "Vox Populi—II," 24.

354 *Midtown stores took out ads:* Roy C. Hollins to Patterson, May 16, 1921, JMP Mss.

354 *"Tell it to Sweeney!":* McGivena et al., *News,* 3.

354 *"snobbish assumption":* Ibid., 149.

354 *"a new kind of market":* Chapman, *Sweeney,* 133.

354 *"the bible":* McGivena et al., *News,* 150.

354 *"Sweeney lives in":* Chapman, *Sweeney,* 141–42.

355 *"Slumland":* McGivena et al., *News,* 165.

355 *"buying power"; "introduced their parents"; "were worthwhile customers":* McGivena et al., *News,* 167. Chapman, Sweeney, 165.

355 *had more lines of advertising:* Alexander, "Vox Populi—II," 19. Patterson was far less successful in drawing advertisers to *Liberty,* the general interest magazine he founded in New York in 1925 as a rival of *The Saturday Evening Post.* It folded in 1931, a victim of the Great Depression.

356 *"man-crazy":* Landis MacKellar, *The "Double Indemnity" Murder: Ruth Snyder, Judd Gray and New York's Crime of the Century* (Syracuse, NY: Syracuse University Press, 2006), 29. MacKellar argues that Judd Gray "essentially told the truth." See p. 337. Ron Hanson has written an arresting novel of the crime, *A Wild Surge of Guilty Passion* (NY: Scribner, 2011).

356 *a grand jury indicted the pair:* NYT, March 23–24, 1927.

356 *"just across the river":* Damon Runyon, *Trials and Other Tribulations* (Philadelphia: J. B. Lippincott, 1933), 1991.

357 *"You are going to do it"; "veiled threats":* NYT, April 28, 1927. The *Times* and most other New York papers published the full text of Gray's confession.

357 *"Mommy, Mommy":* DN, May 5, 1927.

357 *"alcoholic haze"; "This thing has absolutely got to go through"; "I am pretty sure":* NYT, April 28, 1927.

358 *"Five hours!":* MacKellar, *Murder,* 6.

358 *"A more cold-blooded crime":* NYT, March 22, 1927.

358 *"I thought everything was perfect":* DN, March 22, 1927.

358 *"For want of a better name":* Runyon, *Trials,* 139.

358 *"more than represented":* Silas Bent, *Ballyhoo: The Voice of the Press* (NY: Boni & Liveright, 1927), 194.

359 *"girl like Mother":* MacKellar, *Murder,* 114.

359 *"I think it will prove to be":* Ibid., 112.

359 *"Never has such a barrage":* Ben Hecht, "A Reporter at Large: The Olympian Eye," TNY 3 (April 30, 1927): 36.

359 *only eight women residents of New York state had been legally executed:* DN, January 12, 1928.

359 *Every New York newspaper:* Hearst's *Journal* and *Mirror,* Macfadden's *Graphic,* and Patterson's *Daily News* devoted between 4 and 5 percent of their papers' daily coverage, about eight to ten pages a day to the case, Stevens, *Sensationalism,* 154.

359   *Snyder was photographed:* DN, March 24, 1927.

360   *"Follow the next act":* DN, March 22, 1927.

360   *"Even before the jury was selected":* "Editors Analyze Selling Elements of Snyder-Gray Murder Story," *Editor & Publisher* (May 14, 1927): 49.

360   *"The defiant blonde":* DN, May 3, 1927.

360   *"Mrs. Snyder's favorite pastime":* Runyon, *Trials,* 185.

360   *"to stick around the house":* NYT, March 21, 24, 1927.

360   *"Ruth Snyder was going a bit crazy":* MacKellar, *Murder,* 31.

360   *"the most exciting":* Ibid., 40.

361   *"wrestling" with him:* DN, April 30, 1927.

361   *"He murdered my poor":* DN March 25, 1927. Snyder said this to reporters after his indictment.

361   *"helpless frightened tool":* Elmer Davis, "Clytemnestra: Long Island Style," TNY 3 (May 7, 1927): 36. See also NYT, April 30, 1927; and DN, April 30, 1927. The *Times* published a running transcript of the trial.

361   *"a chilly looking blonde":* Runyon, *Trials,* 139.

361   *"the character of a shallow-brained pleasure seeker":* Leslie Margolin, *Murderess!: The Chilling True Story of the Most Infamous Woman Ever Electrocuted* (NY: Pinnacle, 1999), 74.

361   *"a dead setup for a blonde":* Runyon, *Trials,* 172.

361   *"veiled threats"; "she got me in":* NYT, March 23, April 28, 1927.

361   *"love slave":* Quoted in MacKellar, *Murder,* 137.

361   *"Judd is not interested":* DN, May 7, 1927.

361   *"He was smartly dressed":* Quoted in John Kobler, *The Trial of Ruth Snyder and Judd Gray* (Garden City, NY: Doubleday, Doran, 1938), 52.

361   *"though she fixed him":* Kobler, *Trial,* 52.

361   *"curled to a distinct snarl":* Runyon, *Trials,* 152–53.

362   *"The drab, factually mundane":* Nigel Morland, *Background to Murder* (London: Werner Laurie, 1955), 131, 136, 139.

362   *"The man told":* Runyon, *Trials,* 183.

362   *"a commonplace woman":* Davis, "Clytemnestra," 36.

362   *"fattish":* MacKellar, *Murder,* 103; DN, March 24, 1927.

362   *"cruel mouth":* DN, March 24, 1927; MacKellar, *Murder,* 103.

362   *"curiosity caused a near riot":* DN, May 10, 1927.

362   *"I couldn't condemn":* Runyon, *Trials,* 198.

362   *jury took:* DN, May 10, 1927.

362   *dropped into her chair sobbing:* Morland, *Background,* 131, 137, 139.

362   *"pulled a prayer book":* Runyon, *Trials,* 200.

362   *"Hel-lo, Ruthie":* DN, May 17, 1927.

363   *"self-made widow":* DN, May 10, 1927.

363   *"will ride a thunderbolt":* DN, January 12, 1927. She was the twenty-fourth woman in the United States to be legally put to death.

363   *"to scream all night":* Morland, *Background,* 139.

363   *"distinct click-click":* DN, January 12–13, 1928.

364   *"horribly red then white":* DN, January 13, 1928.

364   *"In the autopsy room":* Kobler, *Trial,* 64.

364 *"Gathered outside"*: Wilson, *American Earthquake*, 161–62.

364 *"If this woman dies"*: Schneider, "Fabulous Rise," 46.

364 *had a tiny camera*: McKinney, *Medills*, 196–97.

364 *"would have sounded"*: Dana L. Thomas, *The Media Moguls: From Joseph Pulitzer to William S. Paley: Their Lives and Boisterous Times* (NY: G. P. Putnam's Sons, 1981), 47.

365 *"This is perhaps"*: DN, January 13, 1928.

365 *Howard received a bonus*: Kobler, *Trial*, 64.

365 *"What the hell are you trying"; "too revolting"; a "great journalistic feat"; "a reprehensible breach"*: All quotes in Chapman, *Sweeney*, 99.

366 *"would have printed"*: Walker, *City Editor*, 112.

366 *"But since you ran"*: Schneider, "Fabulous," 546.

366 *A quarter of a million extra copies*: Ibid., 46.

366 *"spellbound"*: Alexander Woollcott, *Long, Long Ago* (NY: Viking, 1943), 122.

366 *"vastly-overplayed"*: "Editors Analyze," 4, 49.

366 *"but because she wasn't"*: Woollcott, *Long*, 122.

366 *"They were just average folk"*: DN, January 13, 1928.

367 *"one of the greatest dramas"*: Ibid.

367 *"The middle class rarely"*: Davis, "Clytemnestra," 34.

367 *"that we are"*: "Editors Analyze," 4.

367 *"He is probably"*: Alexander, "Vox Populi—I," 16.

368 *"majestic distance"*: Wells, "Patterson," 679.

368 *shaking hands*: McGivena et al., *News*, 25.

368 *"chewed out anybody"*: Chapman, *Sweeney*, 42–43.

368 *"tyrant"*: Roscoe, *Before*, 249.

368 *"God"*: Gallico, in Holtzman, ed., *No Cheering*, 68–70.

368 *"the nickel thrills"*: Alexander, "Vox Populi—I," 17.

368 *"the public sampling"*: "Staff Tells Patterson's Concern for Masses," *Editor & Publisher* (June 1, 1946), 60.

368 *"very ugly"*: Alexander, "Vox Populi—I," 20; Chapman, *Sweeney*, 27.

368 *resemble a camouflaged military bunker*: Christopher Gray, "An Art Deco Precursor of the Daily News Building," NYT, November 12, 1995.

369 *Patterson asked Goldstein*: McGivena et al., *News*, 26.

369 *"made him nervous"*: Chapman, *Sweeney*, 52.

369 *"He would have no truck"*: Ibid.

369 *"If I can be on a cross-town"*: Walter H. Kilham, Jr., *Raymond Hood, Architect: Form Through Function in the American Skyscraper* (NY: Architectural Book Publishing, 1973), 19.

369 *"destitute of ornament"*: Claude Bragdon, *The Frozen Fountain* (NY: Alfred A. Knopf, 1932), 31–32; Landmarks Preservation Commission, "Daily News Building," March 10, 1998, New York Public Library.

370 *"simplicity itself"*: T-Square, "The Skyline: A Midwinter Renaissance," TNY 5 (January 18, 1930): 63–64.

370 *"eerily lit from below"*: Stern et al., *New York 1930*, 578.

370 *"Weather charts!"*: Kilham, *Hood*, 25.

370 *"the most unique"*: DN, July 23, 1930; "The Lobby of the News Building," brochure, JMP Mss.

370 *"popular science"*: Landmarks Preservation Commission, "Daily News Building," 5.

370 *"its impact at once"*: Douglas Haskell, "The Stripes of the News," *The Nation* 131 (December 24, 1930): 713. See also Mumford, "Notes on Modern Architecture," 119.

370 *nearly $5 million*: Liebling, "Wayward," 97.

370 *"an abrupt shift"*: Ibid., 90.

371 *"We're missing the bus"*: *Chicago Tribune,* May 27, 1946.

371 *"The* Daily News *was built on legs"*: Alexander, "Vox Populi—II," 24.

371 *"Since he"*: Liebling, "Wayward," 90.

CHAPTER EIGHTEEN: SLUGGERS

PAGE

372 "home run town": Leigh Montville, *The Big Bam: The Life and Times of Babe Ruth* (NY: Doubleday, 2006), 107.

372 *"furious wild-eyed"*: NYT, September 15, 1927.

372 *an "exclusive"*: Jack Dempsey with Barbara Piatelli Dempsey, *Dempsey* (NY: Harper & Row, 1977), 157; Jack "Doc" Kearns and Oscar Fraley, *The Million Dollar Gate* (NY: Macmillan, 1966), 183.

372 *"Do you want"*: Paul Gallico, "New Sports Writer Tests His Punch," DN, September 10, 1923.

372 *"We're just going"*: Gallico, in Holtzman, ed., *No Cheering,* 62; Dempsey with Dempsey, *Dempsey,* 158–59.

373 *"would have busted"*: Kearns, and Fraley *Million,* 184.

373 *"Hang on kid"*: Gallico, in Holtzman, ed., *No Cheering,* 64.

373 *"At the end"*: Quoted in Roger Kahn, *A Flame of Pure Fire: Jack Dempsey and the Roaring '20s* (Orlando, FL: Harcourt Harvest, 1999), 337.

373 *"The ten seconds"*: Gallico, in Holtzman, ed., *No Cheering,* 64.

373 *"a shapeless mass"*: Quoted in Mark Inabinett, *Grantland Rice and His Heroes: The Sportswriter as Mythmaker in the 1920s* (Knoxville: University of Tennessee Press, 1994), 25.

373 *"pure animal savagery"*; *"a slashing"*: Paul Gallico, *The Golden People* (Garden City, NY: Doubleday, Doran, 1965), 84–85; James P. Dawson, "Boxing," in Allison Danzig and Peter Brandwein, eds., *Sport's Golden Age: A Close-up of the Fabulous Twenties* (NY: Harper & Brothers, 1948), 61.

373 *"Half-maddened"*: Gallico, *Golden,* 85.

374 *"This isn't"*: Kahn, *Flame,* 343.

374 *"I was gonna deck"*: Ibid.

374 *"lust to kill"*; *"blind rage"*: NYT, September 15, 1923; Kahn, *Flame,* 344.

374 *"Push me back"*: Kahn, *Flame,* 346.

374 *"through weakness"*: Quoted in ibid.

374 *"almost 100 per cent American"*: NYT, September 15, 1923.

374 *"In his corner"*: Gallico, *Golden,* 85.

374 *"staggered me"*: Dempsey with Dempsey, *Dempsey,* 160.

374 *he was counted out*: Paul Gallico, "Dempsey Knocks Out Firpo," DN, September 15, 1923.

374 *"Which round"*: Dempsey with Dempsey, *Dempsey,* 148.

375 *Paul Gallico's career:* Paul Gallico, *Confessions of a Story Writer* (NY: Alfred A. Knopf, 1946), 5.

375 *"out of sight":* "Gallico," in Holtzman, ed., *No Cheering,* 62, 66.

375 *"Aw Nuts School":* Walker, *City Editor,* 123.

376 *"I contributed"; without shame:* Molly Ivins, "Paul Gallico," NYT, July 17, 1976.

376 *"During my thirteen-year tenure":* Gallico, *Golden,* 69.

376 *"Prize fighting is popular":* "A Matter of Opinion," *Time* (August 1, 1927): 23.

376 *"a punch on the nose":* Gallico, *Golden,* 71–72.

376 *"Jack Dempsey":* Author interview with Louis "Studs" Terkel, December 11, 1993, Chicago, IL.

376 *"zeal to conquer":* Rex Lardner, *The Legendary Champions* (NY: American Heritage, 1972), 217–18.

376 *"The fancy footgear":* Rod Smith, "Jack Dempsey Is Dead Here at 87," NYT, June 1, 1983.

377 *"second only to":* Walker, *City Editor,* 116.

377 *devoting between 40 and 60 percent:* William Henry Nugent, "The Sport's Section," *The American Mercury* (March 1929): 338–39.

377 *over eight hundred sportswriters:* Frederick W. Cozens and Florence Scovil Stumpf, "The Sports Page," in John T. Talamini and Charles O. Page, eds., *Sport and Society: An Anthology* (Boston: Little, Brown, 1973), 423–27.

377 *"one grade":* Gallico, *Golden,* 292.

377 *Grantland Rice:* Inabinett, *Rice,* 7–8.

377 *"minnesinger":* Gallico, *Golden,* 294.

378 *"They know":* Walker, *City Editor,* 117.

378 *"godding up":* Ibid., 131. See also Bruce J. Evensen, *When Dempsey Fought Tunney: Heroes, Hokum, and Storytelling in the Jazz Age* (Knoxville: University of Tennessee Press, 1996), 49.

378 *"the greatest larceny":* Montville, 166.

378 *"salvation":* Ibid., 167.

378 *the best left-hander:* Murray Schumach, "Babe Ruth," obituary, NYT, August 17, 1948.

379 *"the people's choice":* Marshall Smelser, *The Life That Ruth Built: A Biography* (NY: Quadrangle, 1975), 170, 189.

380 *"freak":* Ibid., 179.

380 *"the bombing bat":* John Daley, "Last Out for the Babe," NYT, August 17, 1948.

380 *"would be pleased":* Frank Graham, *The New York Yankees: An Informal History* (NY: Putnam's, 1943), 75.

380 *"Yankee Stadium":* Patrick A. Trimble, "Jacob Ruppert," *The Scribner Encyclopedia of American Lives: Sports Figures,* vol. 2 (NY: Charles Scribner's Sons, 2002): 315–15. See also Henry F. Graff, "Jacob Ruppert," *Dictionary of American Biography,* vol. 22, 589–90.

380 *284 days:* Robert W. Creamer, *Babe: The Legend Comes to Life* (NY: Simon & Schuster, 1992), 277–78.

380 *"As Ruth circled":* NYT, April 19, 1923.

380 *"Ruthville":* Babe Ruth, as told to Bob Considine, *The Babe Ruth Story* (NY: E. P. Dutton, 1948), 51.

381 *five million listeners:* Joseph Durso, *Yankee Stadium: Fifty Years of Drama* (Boston: Houghton Mifflin, 1972), 35.

381 *"new type of fan":* Graham, *Yankees,* 52.

381 *"who carries":* David Quentin Voigt, *American Baseball: From the Commissioners to Continental Expansion* (Norman: University of Oklahoma Press, 1970), 150.

381 *"combat zone"; "to wreck the game":* Smelser, *Life,* 179.

381 *"out of the wilderness":* Grantland Rice, *The Tumult and the Shouting: My Life in Sport* (NY: A. S. Barnes, 1966), 106.

381 *"measureless lust":* Roger Kahn, "The Real Babe Ruth," *Esquire* (August 1959): 29.

381 *"He runs alone":* Montville, *Bam,* 273.

381 *"a large man":* Creamer, *Babe,* 221.

381 *"I've seen him":* Richard C. Crepeau, *Baseball: America's Diamond Mind, 1919–1941* (Lincoln: University of Nebraska Press, 2000), 89.

382 *"Good night":* Kahn, "Real," 30.

382 *"the noisiest fucker":* Quoted in Creamer, *Babe,* 321.

382 *"suddenly the front door":* Fred Lieb, *Baseball as I Have Known It* (NY: Coward, Mc-Cann & Geoghegan, 1977), 159.

382 *"rage for Ruth":* Smelser, *Life,* 170.

382 *"Affable, boisterous":* Schumach, "Babe Ruth."

383 *"prodigious":* Gallico, *Golden,* 38.

383 *"sport miracles"; "pudding face":* Ibid., 37, 40; Paul Gallico, "The Golden Decade," *The Saturday Evening Post* (September 5, 1931): 13, 113.

383 *"incorrigible"; "Against his will":* Smelser, *Life,* 11.

383 *"the greatest man":* Ruth, *Story,* 11.

383 *undefeated on the mound:* Babe Ruth, *Playing the Game: My Early Years in Baseball* (Mineola, NY: Dover, 2011) 5. This ghostwritten book was based on conversations with Ruth.

384 *"my first knowledge":* Ruth as told to Considine, *My Story,* 13.

384 *"whether you're homeless":* Ruth as told to Considine, *My Story,* 9.

384 *"the messiah":* Gallico, *Golden,* 44.

384 *"I would":* Ibid., 18.

384 *"babes":* Montville, *Bam,* 36.

385 *"I . . . [was] the big bust":* Ruth as told to Considine, *My Story,* 55.

385 *"I was young":* Ibid.

385 *"the bellyache":* Creamer, *Babe,* 289.

385 *"gaunt and wobbly-legged":* Johnathan Eig, *Luckiest Man: The Life and Death of Lou Gehrig* (NY: Simon & Schuster, 2006 edition; originally published in 2005), 64.

385 *In Chicago:* Lieb, *Baseball,* 157.

385 *"a joke":* Seymour, *Baseball,* 432.

386 *"from king to jester":* Voigt, *Baseball,* 156.

386 *"was as near to being":* Smelser, *Life,* 326.

386 *"Sporting girls":* Lieb, *Baseball,* 160.

386 *"a gold digger"; "I was not breaking up":* Montville, *Bam,* 180.

386 *"Christy Walsh and I talked":* Mrs. Babe Ruth with Bill Slocum, *The Babe and I* (Englewood Cliffs, NJ: Prentice Hall, 1959), 90.

387 *"happy hustler":* Christy Walsh, *Adios to Ghosts!* (Self-published, 1937), 11.

387 "camped": Ruth as told to Considine, *My Story,* 42.

387 "counting bottles": Walsh, *Adios,* 12, 26.

387 "the Number One man"; "He writes more like I do": Ibid., 22, 25.

387 Ford Frick: Ford Frick, in Holtzman, ed., *No Cheering,* 210.

387 "a green punk": Walsh, *Adios,* 4.

387 his newspaper earnings: Ruth as told to Considine, *My Story,* 42.

387 "deceitful": Walsh, *Adios,* 14.

388 entrusted his finances: Ruth as told to Considine, *My Story,* 43.

388 "It means at least": Mrs. Babe Ruth with Slocum, *Babe,* 136.

388 "Hard as nails": Ruth as told to Considine, *My Story,* 59.

388 "We needed": Ibid., 236.

389 "He plays tennis": DN, January 23, 1927.

389 "'Sultan of Swat'": DN, February 11, March 4, 1927.

389 The Babe would sign for nothing less: DN, March 8, 1927.

389 "as Teutonic": Alva Johnston, "Beer and Baseball," TNY 8 (September 24, 1932): 23.

390 He collected: Smelser, *Life,* 125.

390 "record-setting": DN, March 5, 8, 1927.

390 highest-paid player: DN, March 8, 1927.

390 Jack Dempsey: NYT, March 6, 1927.

390 "I'll earn": Eig, *Luckiest,* 84–85.

390 visited him at his Los Angeles home: Dempsey with Dempsey, *Dempsey,* 207.

391 "one more crack": Ibid., 207–8.

CHAPTER NINETEEN: TEX

PAGE

392 "Each boxing match": Joyce Carol Oates, *On Boxing* (Garden City, NY: Dolphin/Doubleday, 1987), 8.

392 Babe Ruth arrived in St. Petersburg: DN, March 27, 1927.

392 Yankees were also loaded: John Mosedale, *The Greatest of All: The 1927 New York Yankees* (NY: Dial, 1975).

393 "lacked the courage": Harry T. Brundidge, "Lou Gehrig Gives Baseball Full Credit for Rescuing Parents and Self from New York Tenement District," *Sporting News* (December 25, 1930), 3.

393 his mother: Niven Busch, Jr., "The Little Heinie," *Twenty-one Americans: Being Profiles of Some People Famous in Our Time* (Garden City, NY: Doubleday, Doran, 1930), 324–25.

393 "Handsome as he was": Paul Gallico, *Lou Gehrig: Pride of the Yankees* (NY: Grosset & Dunlap, 1942), 66.

393 "When I saw": Eig, *Luckiest,* 38.

393 "discovered the next Babe Ruth": Ibid., 39.

394 "hero-worshipped": Lieb, *Baseball,* 176.

394 "If Ruth wins": DN, September 3, 1927.

394 "More power to him": DN, July 26, 1927.

394 "brother act": DN, May 24, 1927.

394 "The Babe liked Lou": Gallico, *Gehrig,* 95.

394 *feared he would suffer permanent brain damage*: Dempsey with Dempsey, *Dempsey*, 206.

394 *Rickard predicted*: NYT, June 23, 1927.

395 *"The one could scarcely survive"*: Dawson, "Boxing," in Danzig and Brandein, eds., *Sport's Golden Age*, 38–42; "Yes, 'Tex' Gave Them a Great Show in the End," *The Literary Digest* 100 (January 26, 1929): 32.

395 *"He began as"*: Gallico, *Farewell*, 26.

395 *"I am basically Irish"*: Jack Dempsey, *Jack Dempsey: By the Man Himself* (NY: Simon & Schuster, 1960), 11.

395 *"most of the laws"*: Ibid., 13.

396 *"anybody in the house"*: Ibid., 34.

396 *"run like hell"*: Dempsey in Peter Heller, *"In This Corner . . . !": Fifty World Champions Tell Their Stories* (NY: Simon & Schuster, 1973), 57.

396 *"the* real *fighters"*: Dempsey, *Dempsey*, 55.

396 *"I was skinny"*: Ibid., 57.

396 *"Only later did I realize"*: Ibid., 39–41.

397 *"so fantastic"*: Los Angeles Times, July 8, 1963.

397 *"whose ability to make money disappear"*: Charles Samuels, *The Magnificent Rube: The Life and Gaudy Times of Tex Rickard* (NY: McGraw-Hill, 1957), 188.

397 *"I've told so many lies"*: Los Angeles Times, July 8, 1963.

397 *"we trusted each other"*: Dempsey with Dempsey, *Dempsey*, 65.

397 *"hit like a mule's kick"*: Roberts, *Dempsey*, 45.

398 *"swift, pitiless"*: Oates, *On Boxing*, 88.

398 *"modest, with boyish simplicity"*: NYT, July 5, 1919. See also Randy Roberts, "Jack Dempsey: An American Hero in the 1920s," *Journal of Popular Culture* 8 (1974): 414.

398 *"Our greatest fighter"*: NYT, January 26, 1927.

398 *"What's most beautiful"*: Colum McCann, "Foreword," to George Kimball and John Schulian, eds., *At the Fights: American Writers on Boxing* (NY: Library of America, 2001), x.

399 *Rickard was born*: Colleen Aycock and Mark Scott, *Tex Rickard: Boxing's Greatest Promoter* (Jefferson, NC: McFarland, 2012), 24.

399 *part owner of the Northern*: W. O. McGeehan, "Rickard Rounds Up the Rubes," TNY 1 (December 12, 1925): 17.

399 *Local miners trusted*: Jack Kofoed, "The Master of Ballyhoo," *The North American Review* 227 (March 1929): 285.

399 *a record purse*: Kofoed, "Ballyhoo," 282; "Madison Square Garden," *Fortune* 12 (October 1935): 87.

399 *"The Battle of the Century"*: Quoted in William Gildea, *The Longest Fight: In the Ring with Joe Gans, Boxing's First African American Champion* (NY: Farrar, Straus & Giroux, 2012), 25.

399 *a battle for racial superiority*: Geoffrey C. Ward, *Unforgivable Blackness: The Rise and Fall of Jack Johnson* (NY: Alfred A. Knopf, 2004), 169. This is one of the best boxing books ever written.

400 *"I will expel any woman"*: Aycock and Scott, *Rickard*, 66.

400 *"protection and comfort"*: Ibid., 67.

400 *built screened-in boxes*: NYT, September 18, 1927.

400 *"fight king"*: Aycock and Scott, *Rickard*, 68.

400 *"battle of the races"*: Ward, *Unforgivable,* 197–201.

400 *he returned to the United States:* NYT, January 7, 1929. In 1916, he promoted the Jess Willard–Frank Moran fight at Madison Square Garden. It was a no decision.

400 *"one of the most vicious"*: Kahn, *Flame,* 217–19.

400 *"the man who controlled"*: Maxine Elliott Hodges Rickard, with Arch Oboler, *Everything Happened to Him: The Story of Tex Rickard* (NY: Frederick A. Stokes, 1936), 274.

401 *The Dempsey-Brennan fight*: Joseph Durso, *Madison Square Garden: 100 Years of History* (NY: Simon & Schuster, 1979), 137. It was actually the second Garden. In 1879, William Vanderbilt built the first Garden at Twenty-sixth Street and Madison Avenue. It was torn down in 1889 and replaced by the one designed by Stanford White.

401 *"If you want to select"*: Kahn, *Flame,* 231.

401 *"We got to dramatize"*: Jack Dempsey with Charles J. McGuirk, "The Golden Gates," *The Saturday Evening Post* 207 (October 20, 1934): 11, 73.

402 *Paris papers gave it more space:* NYT, June 29–30, 1921.

402 *"as one of the great"*: NYT, January 7, 1929.

402 *"a threat to good morals"*: Lardner, *White Hopes,* 78.

402 *Frank Hague: Jersey City Reporter,* July 16, 2001; NYT, April 14, 1921.

402 *"It has remained"*: "Barnum Was Great, but 'Tex' Rickard Gets More Money," *The Literary Digest* 69 (June 25, 1921): 38.

402 *"[It is] the greatest crowd"*: NYT, July 2, 1921.

403 *"ghetto wizard"*: NYT, December 16, 1920.

403 *"Gorgeous Georges"*: Gallico, *Farewell,* 95.

403 *"I have never been"*: H. L. Mencken, "Dempsey vs. Carpentier," in Kimball and Schulian, eds., *Fights,* 24.

403 *"very greatest moment"*: Kahn, *Flame,* 263.

403 *"All the leaders"*: Mencken, "Dempsey vs. Carpentier," in Kimball and Schulian, eds., *Fights,* 24.

404 *posted on the Times Building:* NYT, July 2, 1921.

404 *"the most formidable boxer"*: Kahn, *Flame,* 249, 259.

404 *"first cast a professional eye"*: Lardner, *White,* 76.

404 *disgracing their country:* Dempsey with Dempsey, *Dempsey,* 145–46.

404 *"killer instinct"*: Dawson, "Boxing," in Danzig and Branwein, eds., *Golden Age,* 57.

404 *"Your Frog"*: William Harper, *How You Played the Game: The Life of Grantland Rice* (Columbia: University of Missouri Press, 1999), 308.

404 *"sorry"*: Kahn, *Flame,* 266.

404 *"It was simply"*: Mencken, "Dempsey vs. Carpentier," in Kimball and Schulian, eds., *Fights,* 20.

405 *"Harry Wills . . . was made"*: Dempsey with Dempsey, *Dempsey,* 178.

405 *"We can't have"*: Kahn, *Flame,* 269.

405 *"immoral relations"; "too vulgar"*: NYT, January 22–24, 1922; Kahn, *Flame,* 272.

405 *"You may get acquitted"*: Kahn, *Flame,* 274.

405 *Dempsey as the hero:* NYT, January 7, 1929.

405 *"The big New York City"*: Kahn, *Flame,* 37–38.

406 *"ungodly union"*: Evensen, *When Demspsey,* 49–50.

406 *"to prepare"*: Dempsey with Dempsey, *Dempsey,* 147.

406 *"shining city"*: Kahn, *Flame,* 354.

406 *"When I started"*: Roberts, *Dempsey,* 73.

406 *"will to do hurt"*: Oates, *On Boxing,* 63, 86–87.

406 *"into another world"*: Dempsey, *Dempsey,* 154.

406 *"[have] transformed"*: "Dempsey as a Movie Hero," *The Literary Digest* 81 (June 21, 1924): 61–63.

406 *"I found New York"*: Dempsey with Dempsey, *Dempsey,* 180–81.

406 *"We stepped into"*: Kahn, *Flame,* 381.

407 *angry with himself:* Dempsey, *Dempsey,* 187, 189.

407 *"worthy of the big business"*: "Madison Square Garden," 102.

407 *"When the new Garden"*: Dawson, "Boxing," in Danzig and Brandwein, eds., *Golden Age,* 64; Rickard and Oboler, *Everything Happened,* 296.

408 *"I've never wanted"*: Rickard and Oboler, *Everything Happened,* 296.

408 *"If New York has"*: Federal Writers' Project, *New York Panorama,* 314.

408 *"That is my monument"*: *New York American,* June 5, 1928.

408 *"the improvement"*: NYT, September 18, 1927.

408 *Paul Gallico remembers:* Gallico, *Golden,* 188.

408 *"Society Out in Full Force"*: NYT, December 16, 1925.

409 *Seated in special boxes:* Ibid.

409 *"lovers of the game"*: NYT, December 15, 1925.

409 *New York Rangers:* NYT, December 16, 1926. The New York Americans changed their name to the Brooklyn Americans in 1941 and went out of existence after the 1941–42 season. The Rangers finished atop the American division in their first season and remained a winning franchise for many years.

409 *"bad manners"*: Samuels, *Rube,* 278–79.

409 *"sports organizations"*: "The Ring Editor, Six Years Ago," *The Ring* (February 1935): 41.

409 *clearing a profit:* NYT, May 19, 1927.

409 *"ruler of"; "easygoing"*: Gallico, *Golden,* 188; "Madison Square Garden," 85–86.

409 *He pocketed the profits:* "Madison Square Garden," 102.

409 *"The babies get the milk"*: Ibid., 86.

409 *"He could be"*: Mel Heimer, *The Long Count* (NY: Atheneum, 1969), 103–4.

409 *Groups of these broken men:* NYT, January 7, 1929.

410 *"fascinating"*: Kofoed, "Ballyhoo," 286.

410 *he lied to the press:* Dawson, "Boxing," in Danzig and Brandwein, eds., *Golden Age,* 64.

410 *"There was a lot"*: Quoted in Kahn, *Flame,* 385.

410 *Democratic powerhouse James Farley:* James A. Farley, *Behind the Ballots: The Personal History of a Politician* (NY: Harcourt Brace, 1972), 46–47.

CHAPTER TWENTY: PURSUITS

PAGE

412 *"Losing was"*: Kahn, *Flame,* 400.

412 *"The Greenwich Village Folly"*: John D. McCallum, *The World Heavyweight Boxing Championship: A History* (Radnor, PA: Chilton, 1974).

412 *program of self-improvement:* Gene Tunney, "My Fights with Jack Dempsey," in Isabel Leighton, ed., *The Aspirin Age, 1919–1941* (NY: Simon & Schuster, 1976), 154, 162.

413 *"with the instinct"*: McCallum, *World Heavyweight,* 128.

413 *"Greb handled Tunney"*: Jack Cavanaugh, *Tunney: Boxing's Brainiest Champ and His Upset of the Great Jack Dempsey* (NY: Random House, 2006), 140–41.

413 *"thwart the murder"; "A good boxer"*: Tunney, "My Fights," in Leighton, ed., *Aspirin*, 155, 168.

413 *"one day"*: Heimer, *Long Count*, 9.

413 *"What are your plans?"*: McCallum, *World Heavyweight*, 125.

413 *"murder" him; "One night"; "Dempsey menace"*: Quoted in ibid., 130–31.

414 *"Dempsey, Dempsey"*: McCallum, *World Heavyweight*, 128.

414 *"In blind and stubborn"*: Gallico, *Golden People*, 108.

414 *spotted carrying around*: Grantland Rice, "Boxing for a Million Dollars," *American Review of Reviews* (October 1926): 73–74; Gallico, *Farewell*, 86.

414 *"It's in the bag"*: Tunney, "My Fights," in Leighton, ed., *Aspirin*, 161.

414 *"phrases that might"*: Morris Markey and Johan Bull, *That's New York!* (NY: Macy-Massius, 1927), 79.

414 *"I don't think you have"*: Cavanaugh, *Tunney*, 269.

414 *"feather duster"*: Tunney, "My Fights," in Leighton, ed., *Aspirin*, 157.

415 *"the killer instinct"*: Ibid., 158.

415 *"You will search pugilism"*: Walter Davenport, "Gene the Genteel," TNY 3 (August 20, 1927).

415 *three-to-one favorite*: NYT, September 23, 1926.

415 *"Tex . . . found"; "They want"*: Maxine Elliot Hodges Rickard and Arch Obaler, *Everything*, 325.

415 *"An army"*: NYT, September 24, 1927.

415 *"a roar of boos"*: NYT, September 24, 1926.

416 *"I feinted Dempsey"*: Tunney, "My Fights," in Leighton, ed., *Aspirin*, 162.

416 *"a roar of satisfaction"*: Elmer Davis "Ex-Marine Gets Ovations as He Enters Ring," NYT, September 24, 1926.

416 *"Lead me out there"*: Red Smith, "Dempsey Is Dead."

416 *"You were too good for me"*: Cavanaugh, *Tunney*, 299.

416 *"Champ, Champ!"*: Dempsey with Dempsey, *Dempsey*, 201–2.

416 *"deafening"*: Philadelphia Inquirer, September 24, 1926.

416 *"What happened?"*: Dempsey, *Dempsey*, 195.

416 *Eighty thousand paying customers*: Nat Fleischer, *Jack Dempsey: The Idol of Fistiana* (NY: C.J. O'Brien, 1936), 128; Dempsey earned $317,000 of the official gross receipts of $1,083,529.

417 *"Here's your bum"*: Quoted in McCallum, *Heavyweight Boxing*, 152.

417 *"He's hitting me low!"*: Dempsey, *Dempsey*, 197–98.

417 *"Did you hear"*: Kahn, *Flame*, 410.

417 *"It's economics Jack"*: Both quotes in Kahn, *Flame*, 410.

418 *"greatest stimulus"*: Evensen, *When Dempsey*, x.

418 *"Dempsey descended"*: John Kieran, "Sports of the Times," NYT, August 26, 1927.

418 *"their quota"*: DN, September 22, 1927.

418 *Al Capone boasted*: Chicago Tribune, September 9–11, 1927.

418 *"lay off"*: Dempsey with Dempsey, *Dempsey*, 217.

418 *"would-be highbrow"*: DN, August 31, 1927.

418 *"addicted" to books*: W. O. McGeehan, "The Social Life of an Athlete," *Vanity Fair* 29

(August 1927): 63.

418 *"a boxing match"*: DN, September 3, 1927.

418 *"There is greater interest"*: NYT, September 22, 1927.

419 *"daredevils"*: Lardner, *Legendary*, 269.

419 *"A changed world"*: "Dempsey-Tunney Fight: A World Spectacle," *The Literary Digest* 92 (September 17, 1927): 40.

419 *Gate receipts*: This stood as a record gate until 1978, when it was broken by the Muhammad Ali–Leon Spinks fight in the New Orleans Superdome, which drew around $5 million. Joe Lee, "Gene Tunney, 1897–1978," *The Ring* (February 1979): 24.

419 *biggest purse ever awarded to a challenger*: Heimer, *Long Count*, 239; Smith, "Dempsey."

419 *"was like the bonanza days"*: Gallico, *Farewell*, 106.

419 *"It [is] the spectacle"*: James R. Harrison, "Greatest Ring Spectacle," NYT, September 23, 1927.

419 *"Kid, if the earth"*: Samuels, *Rube*, 289.

420 *the largest number of reporters*: NYT, September 23, 1927.

420 *"Hear the fight"*: Heimer, *Long Count*, 235.

420 *"Tunney is a cinch"*: Ibid., 214.

420 *"Dempsey will win"*: NYT, September 19, 1927.

420 *"There was never a bigger"*: DN, September 11, 1927.

420 *"knock that big bookworm"*: *Chicago Tribune*, September 23, 1927.

420 *"Quite well Jack"*: Heimer, *Long Count*, 243.

421 *"In the event of a knockdown"*: Dempsey with Dempsey, *Dempsey*, 218–19; McCallum, *Heavyweight Boxing*, 131.

421 *"He had me staggering"*: Dempsey with Dempsey, *Dempsey*, 219.

421 *"His handsome"*: W. O. McGeehan, "Condition," *The Saturday Evening Post* 201 (September 22, 1928).

421 *"Tunney is down!"*: NYT, September 23, 1927.

421 *eleven people*: Paul Gallico, DN, September 23, 1927; "Curiosities and Calamities of the Big Scrap," *The Literary Digest* 95 (October 8, 1927): 65.

421 *"Go to a neutral corner"*: Fleischer, *Dempsey*, 134.

421 *"I forgot the rules"*: Dempsey with Dempsey, *Dempsey*, 219.

421 *"tolling seconds"*: NYT, September 23, 1927.

422 *"Why, he's been down"*: Gallico, *Golden People*, 109.

422 *"Come on and fight"*: McGeehan, "Condition," 13.

422 *"such a glance"*: Gallico, *Farewell*, 22.

422 *"I honestly thought"*: Kahn, *Flame*, 421.

422 *"Fight, you son of a bitch!"* Cavanaugh, *Tunney*, 359.

422 *"Watching this moment"*: Kahn, *Flame*, 422.

422 *"He was almost helpless"*: Tunney, "My Fights," in Leighton, ed., *Aspirin*, 167.

422 *"I . . . took a look"*: McCallum, *Heavyweight Championship*, 115.

423 *Capone had pressed to get Dave Miller*: Gallico, *Farewell*, 84; Heimer, *Long Count*, 229.

423 *Hank Greenspun*: Kahn, *Flame*, 417–19.

423 *"Dempsey should have"*: DN, September 23, 1927.

423 *Tunney showed reporters*: Ibid.; NYT, September 24, 1927.

423 *"Tunney lay crumpled"*: Gallico, *Golden People*, 109.

423 *"I don't know"*: Tunney, "My Fights," in Leighton, ed., *Aspirin*, 166–67.

423 *New York rules*: NYT, September 27, 1927.

424 *"unquestionable best"; "possibly the greatest"; "I still say yes"*: Tunney, "My Fights," in Leighton, ed., *Aspirin*, 168. See also Arthur Daley, "The Dempsey-Tunney Long Count . . . A Living Legend," *The American Legion Magazine* (April 1965): 47.

424 *risked permanent impairment*: NYT, September 23, 1927; McCallum, *Heavyweight Championship*, 116.

424 *Marshall Hunt wrote despairingly*: DN, September 25, 1927.

424 *"Heavenly days!"*: DN, September 30, 1927.

424 *"made [a] triumphant"*: NYT, October 1, 1927.

424 *"Sixty, count 'em"*: Creamer, *Babe*, 309.

425 *"never dreamed"*: DN, October 3, 1927.

425 *"devastating clouting"*: DN, October 1, 1927.

425 *"They didn't give it to me"*: Ruth as told to Considine, *My Story*, 64.

425 *putting a notch*: DN, October 3, 1927.

425 *accounted for a quarter of the home runs*: John G. Robertson, *The Babe Chases 60* (Jefferson, NC: McFarland, 1998), 163.

425 *"We won"; "You could actually"*: Ruth as told to Considine, *My Story*, 64.

426 *a nationwide poll*: Eig, *Luckiest*, 121.

426 *"With Jack in action"*: Samuels, *Rube*, 290.

426 *"Tex, why don't you"*: Ibid.

426 *"the man who really took the count"*: "Tunney and the Boxing Business," 608.

426 *"Dempsey"*: Kahn, *Flame*, 428.

426 *"giggling girls"; "surged in at him"*: NYT, August 17, 1928.

427 *"He was the best advertisement"*: Jim Murray, "A Son of St. Patrick," *Los Angeles Times*, March 17, 1971.

427 *"our stream of super-champions"*: John Tunis, "Changing Trends in Sport," *Harper's Magazine* 170 (December 1934): 78.

427 *beating some 175 opponents*: Gallico, *Golden People*, 87.

427 *"He found fighting chumps undignified"*: Kahn, *Flame*, 431.

427 *"Hiya, pal"*: Red Smith, "Jack Dempsey Is Dead Here at 87," NYT, June 1, 1983.

427 *"You march in proudly"*: Kahn, *Flame*, 432.

427 *"I feel like part of me"*: Dave Anderson, "Sports of the Times: The Legendary Champion," NYT, June 2, 1983.

428 *"I took care"*: Ibid.

428 *"the main event"*: Ibid.

428 *"new dream"*: "Madison Square Garden," 102.

428 *Dempsey was holding his hand*: NYT, January 8, 1929.

428 *"Luck gave him"*: Samuels, *Rube*, 296.

428 *"I've lost"*: NYT, January 7–9, 1929.

428 *One hundred uniformed policemen*: NYT, January 9, 1929.

428 *"Egad"*: Hype Igoe, quoted in "Yes, 'Tex' Gave Them a Great Show to the End," *The Literary Digest* 100 (January 26, 1929), 44.

429 *"There was no light"*: Gallico, *Farewell*, 107.

CHAPTER TWENTY-ONE: VISIONS

PAGE

430   "Men, thinly scattered": James Boswell, *Journal of a Tour to the Hebrides* with Samuel Johnson LL.D. (Philadelphia: John F. Watson, 1810 edition), 14.

430   *"No introduction"*: NYW, November 28, 1927.

430   *"low, sleek"*: NYW, January 9, 1927.

430   *Ford's market share*: Robert Lacey, *Ford: The Man and the Machine* (Boston: Little Brown, 1986), 286.

430   *"entirely new Ford car"*: Steven Watts, *The People's Tycoon: Henry Ford and the American Century* (New York: Alfred A. Knopf, 2005), 372.

431   *"car-that-is-to-be"*: Ibid., 373.

431   *"Today will be"*: NYW, December 2, 1927.

431   *"The new Ford"*: NYT, December 3, 1927.

431   *It went on like this*: NYT, December 7, 1927; Douglas Brinkley, *Wheels for the World: Henry Ford, His Company, and a Century of Progress, 1903–2003* (New York: Viking, 2003), 357.

431   *breaking attendance records*: NYT, December 3, 1927; January 11, 1928.

431   *"went like a rocket"*: Lacey, *Ford,* 300.

431   *"How can Ford"*: NYW, December 3, 1927.

432   *In 1918*: R. L. Duffus, "A Rising of Traffic Rolls over New York," NYT, February 9, 1930.

432   *4,145 miles of streets*: NYT, January 9, 1927. For more on the impact of the automobile on New York City, see Harold M. Lewis, William J. Wilgus, and Daniel M. Turner, *Transit and Transportation*, vol. 4 of *Regional Survey of New York and Its Environs* (NY: Regional Plan of New York and Its Environs, 1928); and R. L. Duffus, *Mastering the Metropolis: Planning the Future of the New York Region* (NY: Harper & Brothers, 1930).

432   *"The vaunted"*: NYT, April 1, 1928.

432   *"Metropolitan misery"*: Frank Lloyd Wright, "The Tyranny of the Skyscraper," in Frank Lloyd Wright, *Modern Architecture, Being the Kahn Lectures for 1930* (Princeton: Princeton University Press, 1931), 87.

432   *"the most stupendous"*: DN, November 25, 1927.

432   *"metropolitan man-sewers"*: Lewis Mumford, *The Culture of Cities* (NY: Harcourt Brace, 1938), 242; Duffus, *Mastering,* 72, 74–75.

432   *"depth to bedrock"*: Jason Barr, Troy Tassier, and Rossen Trendafilov, "Depth of Bedrock and the Formation of the Manhattan Skyline, 1890–1915," *The Journal of Economic History* 71 (December 2011): 1060–61.

432   *"The spectacular"*: William Barclay Parsons, "Twenty-five Years of the New York Subway," NYT, October 27, 1929.

432   *"vicious circle"*: Daniel L. Turner, "Is There a Vicious Circle of Transit Development and City Congestion?" *National Municipal Review* 15 (June 1926): 321.

432   *Privately owned bus lines; less than 3 percent*: NYT, April 1, 1928; Lewis et al., *Transit and Transportation,* 18.

433   *the most densely populated*: John Bakeless, "The City of Dreadful Waste," *The Forum* 80 (1928): 730.

433 *"crisis is now"*: William J. Wilgus, "Transportation in the New York Region," supplement, in Lewis et al., *Transit and Transportation,* 161; for New York Skyscraper development see Carol Willis, *Form Follows Finance: Skyscrapers in New York and Chicago* (NY: Princeton Architectural Press, 1995).

433 *"super-skyscraper"*: "Designer of World's Tallest Building Answers Critics," *Real Estate Record and Builders' Guide* 118 (December 25, 1926): 7.

433 *"horrified"*: Stern et al., *New York 1930,* 603.

433 *the ruination of New York*: NYT, June 17, October 3, 1926.

434 *"The worst enemy"*: NYT, December 9, 1928.

434 *"extreme" traffic congestion*: NYT, February 23, 1930.

434 *"London is a seven-story city"*: "Skyscrapers and Traffic Congestion," *The American Architect* 131 (March 1927): 386.

434 *"horizontal" traffic*: NYT, September 13, 1931.

434 *"In downtown New York"*: NYT, February 23, 1927. See also "Defends Skyscraper as Builders' Greatest Asset to Municipality," *Real Estate Record and Guide* (November 27, 1926): 6.

434 *"embedded"*: Koolhaas, *Delirious New York,* 121.

434 *"as essential"*: Harvey Wiley Corbett, "New Heights in American Architecture," *Yale Review* 17 (July 1928): 697; Harvey Wiley Corbett, "The Problem of Traffic Congestion and a Solution," *Architectural Forum* 46 (March 1927): 201.

435 *"The future of architecture"*: Leon V. Solon, "The Titan City Exhibition," *The Architectural Record* 59 (January 1926): 92; Carol Willis, "The Titan City: Forgotten Episodes in American Architecture," *Skyline* (October 1982): 26–27.

435 *"modernized Venice"*: Corbett, "Problem of Traffic Congestion," 203–4.

435 *"become a model"*: Ibid., 204; Harvey Wiley Corbett, "The Separation of Vehicular and Pedestrian Traffic," *Creative Art* 9 (August 1931): 162; "Photographs," in Harvey Wiley Corbett Architectural Photographs and Papers, Avery Architectural and Fine Arts Library, Columbia University, New York, NY; "The Cinematic City of the Future," *Fortune* 2 (October 1930): 129.

435 *"titanic dream city"; "project from Cloudcuckooland"; "Only a megalomaniac"*: Lewis Mumford, "The Intolerable City: Must It Keep on Growing?" *Harper's Magazine* 157 (February 11, 1926), 289.

435 *"We are dealing here"*: Lewis Mumford, "The Sacred City," NR 45 (January 27, 1926): 270–71.

435 *"coffins in the sky"*: Lewis Mumford, "Culture of Cities," *Journal of the American Institute of Architects* 35 (June 1961): 54–60.

436 *"New York is madder"*: Thomas Bender and William Taylor, "Skyscraper and Skyline," in Bender, *The Unfinished City: New York and the Metropolitan Idea* (NY: New Press, 2002), 122.

436 *"Raymond Hood . . . is [the] brilliant"*: Allene Talmey, "Profiles: Man Against the Sky," TNY 7 (April 11, 1931): 24, 26.

436 *"A style is developed"*: Raymond M. Hood, *Contemporary American Architects* (New York: Whittlesey House, 1931), 15–16.

436 *"His life was a joy ride"*: Robert A. M. Stern and Thomas P. Catalano, *Raymond Hood* (New York: Rizzoli, 1982), 2.

437 *"uproarious" New York; "Downtown"*: Quoted in Kilham, *Raymond Hood,* 37.

437 *"Hood alighted"*: Talmey, "Man Against the Sky," 25.

437 *"greatest architect"*: Kilham, *Hood,* 50.

437 *"in violent discussions"*: *The Washington Post,* August 26, 1934.

437 *"And then . . . he got lucky"*: "Raymond Mathewson Hood," *Architectural Forum* 62 (1935): 130.

438 *"Real beauty"*: Raymond M. Hood, "Architecture," NYW, May 13, 1930.

438 *"stunned at the telephone"*: Talmey, "Man Against the Sky," 26.

438 *He approached Placido Mori:* Kilham, *Hood,* 56.

438 *"open expanse"*: Raymond M. Hood, "The American Radiator Company Building, New York," *The American Architect* 126 (November 19, 1924): 470; see also Raymond M. Hood, "Attempting to Build with Black Brick," *Contacts* 56 (July 1927): n.p; and Stern and Catalano, *Raymond Hood,* 9. The building is now the American Standard Building and houses the Bryant Park Hotel.

438 *"His clothes"*: Talmey, "Man Against the Sky," 24.

439 *"only in the telephone book"*: Ibid., 27.

439 *"When Hood has"*: Harry Allan Jacobs, "Architects Discuss Future Building," NYT, December 13, 1931.

439 *"a simple English house"; "country enough"*: Talmey, "Man Against the Sky," 27; "Hood," *Architectural Forum,* 133.

439 *"sacred"*: Harry Allan Jacobs, "Raymond Hood Uses Tablecloths and Pillars in Planning Modern Skyscrapers," NYT, December 7, 1930.

440 *"There never was"*: Stern and Catalano, *Hood,* 19.

440 *City of Towers:* "Tower Buildings and Wider Streets: A Suggested Relief for Traffic Congestion," *The American Architect* 132 (July 1927): 67–8.

440 *New York is transformed:* NYT, February 13, 1927. See also DN, February 20, 1927.

440 *"Our much maligned skyscraper"*: NYT, November 10, 1931.

440 *"It is safe to say"*: Raymond M. Hood, as told to F. S. Tisdale, "A City Under a Single Roof," *Nation's Business* 17 (November 1929): 28.

440 *"it gave the architect"*: "Hood," *Architectural Forum,* 133.

441 *"a single directing intelligence"*: Hood, "City Under a Single Roof," 208–9.

441 *"to prevent New York"; "the best thing we have in New York"*: Ibid.; "In Praise of Congestion," *Time* 18 (December 14, 1931): 16–17. See also Raymond M. Hood, "New York's Skyline Will Climb Much Higher," *Liberty* 2 (April 1926), 19–23.

441 *"What we want is congestion"*: Jacobs, "Architects."

441 *"paradoxical"*: Koolhaas, *Delirious New York,* 177.

441 *"The wonder of New York"*: Hood, "City Under a Single Roof," 208–9; see also "In Praise of Congestion," *Time,* 16–17.

441 *"interior pleasures"*: Koolhaas, *Delirious New York,* 177.

441 *found his Tower City chillingly dehumanizing:* Author interview with Lewis Mumford, June 8, 1984; Mordaunt Hall, "A Technical Marvel," NYT, May 7, 1927.

442 *"tarantula"; "near millionaires"*: "Three Visions of New York: Raymond Hood," *Creative Art* 9 (August 1931): 160; one part of this ensemble essay is written by Hood.

442 *"great annual regattas"*: Orrick Johns, "Bridge Homes—A New Vision of the City," NYT, February 22, 1925.

442 *"wash off the island"*: "Three Visions of New York," 160–61.

442 *lost over half a million residents:* "The Ever-Narrowing Home," in *Housing* 18 (NY: June 1929), 102.

442 *"to furnish solutions":* Manfredo Tafuri, "The Disenchanted Mountain: The Skyscraper and the City," in Giorgio Ciucci *et al., The American City: From the Civil War to the New Deal* (Cambridge: MIT Press, 1979), 458.

442 *"utopian":* Hood, "Three Visions of New York," 161.

443 *"In a world of words":* Harcourt Brace Jovanovich publicity pamphlet, no date, Lewis Mumford Papers, Rare Book and Manuscript Library, Van Pelt-Dietrich Library, University of Pennsylvania, Philadelphia, PA, hereafter cited as LMP.

443 *"I was a child of the city":* Lewis Mumford, *Sketches from Life: The Autobiography of Lewis Mumford* (NY: Dial, 1982), 3, 25.

443 *"Our century":* Paul Goldberger, "A Steely Humanist," *The Atlantic Monthly* 264 (July 1989), 88–91 (review of Miller, *Mumford*).

443 *"the last of the great humanists":* Malcolm Cowley to Julian Muller, October 19, 1978, LMC.

444 *Garden City movement:* For Howard and his influence on the RPAA, see Donald L. Miller, *Lewis Mumford, A Life* (NY: Weidenfeld & Nicolson, 1989), chapter 11; for the RPAA, see Carl Sussman, ed., *Planning the Fourth Migration: The Neglected Vision of the Regional Planning Association of America* (Cambridge: MIT Press, 1976); and Daniel Schaffer, "New York and the Garden City Movement Between the Wars," in Josef Paul Kleihues and Christina Rathgeber, eds., *Berlin–New York: Like and Unlike: Essays on Architecture and Art from 1870 to Present* (New York: Rizzoli International Publications, 1994). The minutes of the RPAA meetings are in LMC.

444 *"The Intolerable City":* Mumford, "Intolerable City," 286–87.

445 *ecological impact of explosive urban growth:* Lewis Mumford, "The Theory and Practice of Regionalism," *Sociological Review* 29 (January 1928): 24.

445 *"for restful gatherings":* Clarence Stein, *Toward New Towns for America* (Cambridge: MIT Press, 1966), 24.

446 *heavy government subsidies:* Lewis Mumford, "Cities Fit to Live In," *The Nation* 167 (May 15, 1948): 530–33.

446 *"No one has suggested":* Lewis Mumford, "Is the Skyscraper Tolerable?," *Architecture* 55 (February 1927): 69.

446 *within the new superblocks:* Author interview with Lewis Mumford, August 9, 1983.

446 *well-intentioned city planners:* For a searing critique of Mumford's superblock ideas, see William H. Whyte, ed., *The Exploding Metropolis* (Berkeley: University of California Press, 1993 edition; originally published in 1957), 10.

447 *"powerful and city destroying ideas":* Jane Jacobs, *The Death and Life of Great American Cities* (NY: Vintage edition, 1992; originally published in 1961), 18–20.

447 *"of a furious decay":* Mumford, "The Metropolitan Milieu," in Waldo Frank, Lewis Mumford, Dorothy Norman, Paul Rosenfeld, and Harold Rugg, eds., *America and Alfred Stieglitz: A Collective Portrait* (Garden City, NY: Doubleday, Doran, 1934), 40.

447 *"No matter where you live":* White, *Here Is New York*, 28–29.

447 *"solidified chaos":* Jacobs, *Death and Life*, 21.

448 *"by-products":* E. B. White, "You Can't Resettle Me!," *The Saturday Evening Post* 209 (October 10, 1936): 89, 91–92.

448 *"I have . . . to confess"*: Stern et al., *New York 1930*, 38.

448 *"aspiration and faith"*: White, *Here Is New York*, 23–24.

448 *"Mass hysteria"*: Ibid., 26.

448 *"It is a miracle"*: Ibid., 24.

448 *"the seeds of"*: Jacobs, *Death and Life*, 448.

449 *"I would like to register"*: Lewis Mumford, "The Sky Line: The Regional Plan," *TNY* 8 (May 21, 1932): 64.

449 *"automatic" and "inevitable"*: Lewis Mumford, "The Plan of New York: I," *NR* 71 (June 15, 1932): 123.

449 *"a monumental failure"*: Lewis Mumford, "The Plan of New York: II" *NR* 71 (June 22, 1932): 152, 154.

449 *forefront of urban design:* For *The Regional Plan*, see especially Robert Fishman, "The Regional Plan and the Transformation of the Industrial Metropolis," in David Ward and Olivier Zunz, eds., *The Landscape of Modernity: Essays on New York City, 1900–1940* (New York: Russell Sage Foundation, 1992); Fishman, "The Metropolitan Tradition in American Planning," in Robert Fishman, ed., *The American Planning Tradition: Culture and Policy* (Washington, DC: Woodrow Wilson Center Press, 2000); David A. Johnson, *Planning the Great Metropolis: The 1929 Regional Plan of New York and Its Environs* (London: E & FN Spon, 1996); and Andrew A. Meyers, "Invisible Cities: Lewis Mumford, Thomas Adams, and the Invention of the Regional City, 1923–1929," *Business and Economic History* 27 (Winter 1998).

450 *the world's first postindustrial city:* Fishman, "Regional Plan," in Ward and Zunz, eds., *Landscape*, 106.

450 *It was to be a commercial island:* Committee on the Regional Plan of New York and Its Environs, *Buildings: Their Uses and the Spaces About Them,* vol. 6 of the Regional Plan of New York and Its Environs (NY: Regional Plan of New York and Its Environs, 1931), 94. Adams was the principal author of this volume.

450 *precursor to Robert Moses's FDR Drive:* Caro, *Power Broker*, 342.

450 *Adams limited them:* Thomas Adams, *Regional Plan of New York and Its Environs, The Building of the City*, vol 2, (NY: Regional Plan of New York and Its Environs, 1931).

450 *factory and blue-collar housing zone:* Thomas Adams, "New York Blazes a National Trail," *Survey* 23 (October 15, 1929), 151.

451 *"by-passes or belt lines"*: William J. Wilgus, "Transportation in the New York Region," supplement, in Lewis, *Transit and Transportation*. See also Harold M. Lewis, "Motorways Proposed for New York Region," NYT, January 5, 1930.

451 *"No profound changes"*: Adams, *Building*, parts 2 and 3.

451 *"dream of a dense"*: Fishman, "Regional Plan," in Ward and Zunz, eds., *Landscape*, 123.

452 *"No comprehensive planning"*: Mumford, "Plan of New York: II," 124.

452 *"all housing should yield"*: Mumford, "Plan of New York: I," 149.

452 *"I am sorry"*: Adams to Mumford, January 9, 1930, Regional Plan Papers, Cornell University Library, Ithaca, NY.

452 *over one hundred of its nearly five hundred:* Regional Plan Association, *From Plan to Reality* (NY: Regional Plan Association, 1933), 14–16, 69.

453 *"with unexpected speed"*: Doig, *Empire*, 2.

CHAPTER TWENTY-TWO: HIGHWAY UNDER THE HUDSON

PAGE

454 "The automobile had": Kenneth T. Jackson, *Crabgrass Frontier: The Suburbanization of the United States* (NY: Oxford University Press, 1985), 188.

454 "connected with": NYT, October 9, 1927.

454 *Eighth Wonder of the World:* Carl C. Gray, *The Eighth Wonder* (Hyde Park, NY: B. F. Sturtevant, 1927).

455 *In 1926, 120 million people:* NYT, June 20, 1926.

455 *fifty thousand daily in 1926:* Ibid.

455 "every blast": Morris, *Manhattan,* 187.

455 *25,000 people:* Robert W. Jackson, *Highway Under the Hudson: A History of the Holland Tunnel* (NY: New York University Press, 2011), 182.

455 "regular, paid passage": NYT, November 13, 1927.

456 *The first car:* Ibid.

456 *reporters compared to:* Ibid.

456 "I'm going through again"; "tunnel excursionists"; "had so touched": NYT, November 14, 1927.

456 *greatest "wonders":* NYT, July 23, 1929.

457 "In 1918": NYT, November 13, 1927.

457 *Harbor delays:* C. G. Poore, "Program for a Greater Port of New York," NYT, April 13, 1930.

457 *migrating to Canada:* "On the Beach," *Fortune* 15 (February 1937): 140.

457 "inefficient and disorganized": Condit, *Port of New York,* vol. 2, 107.

457 "New York City owes": Kenneth Jackson, "Foreword" to Jameson W. Doig, *Empire on the Hudson: Entrepreunerial Vision and Political Power at the Port of New York Authority* (NY: Columbia University Press, 2001), xv.

458 *42 percent of the country's foreign trade:* Condit, *Port of New York,* vol. 2, 108–9.

458 "The view": "A Baedeker of Business in New York," *Fortune* 20 (July 1939): 109–10.

458 "world's greatest industrial aggregate": "On the Beach," 73.

458 *thirty thousand places of production:* Alexander Rogers Smith, "Greatest Shipping Port in the World," *Review of Reviews* 72 (October 1925): 374, 375; Edward E. Swantstrom, *The Waterfront Labor Problem: A Study of Decasualization and Unemployment Insurance* (New York: Fordham University Press, 1938), 1–2.

458 *a quarter of a million workers:* Swantstrom, *Waterfront,* 7.

458 "as towns with": A. J. Liebling, *Back Where I Came From* (San Francisco: North Point, 1990; originally published in 1938), 25.

459 "New York is more completely dependent": "On the Beach," 140.

459 "Blot out": Clary, *Mid-Manhattan,* 107.

459 "troubled at night": "On the Beach," 74.

459 "the western wall": Mario Puzo, *The Fortunate Pilgrim* (NY: Random House, 1997, originally published in 1965), 5.

459 *it was forbidden:* Phillip Lopate, *Waterfront: A Walk Around Manhattan* (NY: Anchor edition, 2005; originally published in 2004), 61.

459 *more than half of all shipping:* Josef W. Konvitz, "William J. Wilgus and Engineering Projects to Improve the Port of New York, 1900–1930," *Technology & Culture* 30 (1989): 401.

460 *West Side Freight Line:* "West Side Improvement," 1934 pamphlet, New York Public Library; Christopher Gray, "When a Monster Plied the West Side," NYT, December 22, 2011.

460 *"treacherous freights":* NYT, November 12, 1939.

460 *"ground to death"; "The Butcher":* Gray, "Monster."

460 *"Larry Angeluzzi":* Puzo, *Pilgrim,* 4.

461 *"Shipping in the port":* Federal Writers' Project, *New York Panorama,* 328.

461 *"giant floating railroad yard":* Keith D. Revell, *Building Gotham: Civic Culture and Public Policy in New York City, 1898–1938* (Baltimore: Johns Hopkins University Press, 2003), 61.

461 *railroads covertly agreed:* Erwin Wilkie Bard, *The Port of New York Authority* (NY: AMS, 1968), 23.

461 *investment in terminals:* George Matteson, *Tugboats of New York: An Illustrated History* (NY: New York University Press, 2005), 149; Benjamin Chinitz, *Freight and the Metropolis: The Impact of America's Transport Revolutions on the New York Region* (Cambridge: Harvard University Press, 1960), 38.

461 *"the only seaport in the world":* Calvin Tomkins, New York dock commissioner, quoted in Angus Kress Gillespie, *Crossing Under the Hudson: The Story of the Holland and Lincoln Tunnels* (New Brunswick, NJ: Rutgers University Press, 2011), 9.

461 *"lighterage":* Bard, *Authority,* 7.

461 *"In their heyday":* Lopate, *Waterfront,* 143.

462 *railroad companies' nautical empire:* Matteson, *Tugboats,* 143, 147.

462 *remained virtually unchanged:* Condit, *Port of New York,* vol. 2, 103.

462 *annual loss from preventable waste:* Bakeless, "Dreadful Waste," 728.

462 *army of longshoremen:* Swantstrom, *Waterfront,* 8.

462 *"the whistles and calls":* Charles B. Barnes, *The Longshoremen* (NY: Arno, 1977; originally published in 1915), 131, 137.

463 *"When you go to work":* Quoted in ibid., 133.

463 *one chance in five hundred:* Mary Heaton Vorse, "The Pirates' Nest of New York," *Harper's Magazine* 204 (April 1952): 30.

463 *"shape up":* Budd Schulberg, "Joe Docks, Forgotten Man of the Waterfront," NYT, December 28, 1952.

463 *"absolute":* Maurice Rosenblatt, "The Scandal of the Waterfront," *The Nation,* 161 (November 17, 1945): 516.

463 *He collected his kickbacks:* Testimony of Bresci Thompson, in Kisseloff, *You Must Remember This,* 490.

463 *"central pillar":* Barnes, *Longshoremen,* 72.

463 *"like sheep in droves":* Theodore Dreiser, *The Color of a Great City* (NY: Boni & Liveright, 1923), 11.

464 *"in a barrel of cement":* Quoted in Vorse, "Pirates' Nest," 29.

464 *"I have sometimes":* Dreiser, *Color,* 12.

464 *"the forgotten man":* Schulberg, "Joe Docks."

464 *afforded them no protection:* Chinitz, *Freight,* 43–44.

464 *"president for life":* Nathan Ward, *Dark Harbor: The War for the New York Waterfront* (NY: Farrar, Straus & Giroux, 2010), 59.

464 *"solid as a river barge"; "to maintain itself"*: Barnes, *Longshoremen,* 92. For Ryan, see also Maud Russell, *Men Along the Shore* (NY: Brussel & Brussel, 1966).

464 *"withheld job"*: Malcolm Johnson, *Crime on the Labor Front* (NY: McGraw-Hill, 1950), 133–49.

464 *William J. "Big Bill" McCormack*: Ward, *Dark Harbor,* 158.

465 *this former "Chelsea boy"*: Maurice Rosenblatt, "Joe Ryan and His Kingdom," *The Nation* 161 (November 24, 1945): 548.

465 *"docked, disposed"*: "On the Beach," 142.

465 *If a driver needed*: NYT, November 13, 1930.

465 *"private storm troopers"*: Felice Swados, "Waterfront," NR 93 (February 2, 1938): 263.

465 *"a process of conquest"*: Johnston quoted in Bell, *End of Ideology,* 167–68.

466 *Murder*: Johnson, *Crime,* 129.

466 *persisted into the 1950s*: NYT, January 12, 1952.

466 *"New York has done less"*: Condit, *Port of New York,* vol. 2, 109.

466 *"to the point of desperation"*: Condit, *Port of New York,* vol. 2, 118. See also John G. Bunker, *Harbor and Haven* (Woodland Hills, CA: Windsor, 1979), 194.

466 *"workless Mondays"*: NYT, January 21, 1918.

466 *"carrying all sorts of receptacles"*: NYT, January 2, 1918.

466 *"the excessive costs"*: NYT, December 10, 1922.

467 *"probably the youngest engineer"*: NYT, June 15, 1919, October 9, 1927.

467 *fashioned plans for*: Clifford M. Holland, "Linking New York and New Jersey," *The American City* 14 (March 1921): 231–32.

467 *"a Highway under the Hudson"*: Jerome W. Howe, "Boring Out a Highway Under the Hudson," NYT, September 14, 1924.

467 *nearly fill the Woolworth Building*: NYT, April 9, 1922.

467 *"holed through"*: NYT, November 12, 1927.

467 *Holland died of heart failure*: NYT, October 28, 1924.

468 *"a salute"*: NYT, November 13, 1927.

468 *"work" and "worry"*: NYT, March 26, 1925.

468 *would have become lethal gas chambers*: J. Bernard Walker, "The Hudson River Vehicular Tunnel," *Scientific American* 137 (September 1927): 201; "Holland Tunnel," in Stephen Johnson and Robert T. Leo, eds., *Encyclopedia of Bridge and Tunnels* (NY: Facts on File, 2002), 149.

469 *would have generated winds*: NYT, October 9, 1927.

469 *"so gently"*: Walker, "Vehicular Tunnel," 203.

469 *changed every ninety seconds*: NYT, November 28, 1926.

469 *"The air will be"*: NYT, October 2, 1927.

469 *seen by Lewis Mumford*: Lewis Mumford, "The Drama of the Machines," *Scribner's Magazine* 88 (August 1930): 157.

469 *"storm factories"*: NYT, October 9, 1927.

469 *"in which life"*: NYT, February 17, 1924.

469 *"The first thing"*: NYT, October 2, 1927.

470 *Eight and a half million vehicles*: NYT, November 11, 1928; Jackson, *Highway,* 188.

470 *"one of the metropolitan spectacles"*: NYT, February 5, 1928.

470 *built-in "insurance"*: NYT, November 20, 1927.

470 *"economic necessity"*: NYT, October 9, 1927.

470 *creating a new local industry*: NYT, May 28, 1928.

471 *"The tunnel"*: NYT, December 10, 1922.

471 *nearly six thousand trucks a day*: NYT, May 13, 1928.

CHAPTER TWENTY-THREE: POET IN STEEL

PAGE

472 "The George Washington Bridge": Le Corbusier, *Cathedrals,* 75.

472 *"In the U.S."*: Leon Katz, "A Poet in Steel," *Portfolio* 1 (Summer 1988): 31. For a history of the bridge, see Michael Aaron Rockland, *The George Washington Bridge: Poetry in Steel* (New Brunswick, NJ: Rutgers University Press, 2008), 41; and Henry Petroski, *Engineers of Dreams: Great Bridge Builders and the Spanning of America* (New York: Alfred A. Knopf, 1995).

472 *"his ideas influenced me"*: Louis A. Volse, "An Artist in Steel Design," *Engineering News-Record* 160 (May 15, 1958): 139.

472 *"My first serious interest"*: Urs C. Widmer, "Othmar Hermann Ammann, 1879–1965: His Way to Great Bridges," *Review* 15 (June 1979): 5.

473 *"Get all the experience"*: M. K. Wisehart, "The Greatest Bridge in the World and the Man Who Is Building It," *The American Magazine* 34 (June 1928): 183.

473 *"double decked titan"*: Rebecca Read Shanor, *The City That Never Was: Two Hundred Years of Fantastic and Fascinating Plans That Might Have Changed the Face of New York City* (NY: Viking, 1991), 142.

474 *"The new project"*: Jameson W. Doig, "Politics and the Engineering Mind: O. H. Ammann and the Hidden Story of the George Washington Bridge," in David C. Perry ed., *Building the Public City: The Politics, Governance, and Finance of Public Infrastructure* (Thousand Oaks, CA: Sage, 1994), 162.

474 *wider than the main branch*: Shanor, *Never Was,* 142.

474 *"The towers"*: Doig, "Politics," 162–63.

474 *require the demolition*: NYT, October 9, 1927.

474 *"stupendous scope"*: Ammann to Samuel Rae, June 12, 1923, in Widmer, "Ammann," 12.

474 *"Submitted memo"*: Widmer, "Ammann," 11.

474 *"The giant project"*: Rockland, *George Washington,* 45.

475 *"calamitous"*: Ammann to Rae, June 12, in Widmer, "Ammann," 11.

475 *"Today, any bridge"*: O. H. Ammann, "General Conception and Development of Design," *Transactions of the American Society of Civil Engineers* 97, (October 1933): 2.

475 *"At an opportune moment"*: Ammann to Rae, June 12, 1923, in Widmer, "Ammann," 13.

475 *Lindenthal continued to lobby*: Shanor, *Never Was,* 147.

475 *"on my own initiative"*: Darl Rastorfer, *Six Bridges: The Legacy of Othmar H. Ammann* (New Haven: Yale University Press, 2000), 15.

475 *George Silzer*: Doig, "Politics," 166, 172.

476 *"political entrepreneur"*: Jameson W. Doig and David Billington, "Ammann's First Bridge: A Study in Engineering, Politics and Entrepreneurial Behavior," *Technology and Culture* 35 (July 1994): 538.

476 *"weather-beaten"*: Milton MacKaye, "Poet in Steel," TNY 10 (June 2, 1934): 32.

476 *"By the degree"*: Rastorfer, *Six Bridges,* 15–16.

476 *The engineer envisioned:* O. H. Ammann, "General Conception," in Widmer, "Ammann," 25.

476 *"gigantic" leap:* Ibid., 23.

476 *"should please the eye"*: Volse, "Artist," 139. See also Ammann, "The Hell Gate Arch Bridge and Approaches of the New York Connecting Railroad over the East River," research paper published in the American Society of Civil Engineering, *Transactions* (1918): 863.

477 *In March 1925:* Hon. John F. Gavlin, "George Washington Bridge: Over the Hudson River Between New York and New Jersey," speech presented at the dedication ceremony, New York, October 24, 1931. Author's copy.

477 *"swept into the automotive age"*: Doig, *Empire on the Hudson,* 111.

477 *"an engineer"*: Othmar Ammann to George Silzer, April 17, 1925; Silzer to the Port Authority Commissioners, December 17, 1923, Governor George S. Silzer Files, New Jersey State Archives, Trenton, NJ.

477 *By June 1929:* Edward Cohen, "The Engineer and His Works: A Tribute to Othmar Hermann Ammann, P.E. (1879–1965)," *Annals of the New York Academy of Sciences* 136 (1967): 739.

477 *eight months ahead of schedule:* Rastorfer, *Six Bridges,* 39.

477 *"I would prefer the name Bergen"*: NYT, October 19, 26, 1930.

478 *"greatest and most enthusiastic"; "the death of his dream"*: MacKaye, "Poet," 25.

478 *"Oh, I'm sorry"*: Volse, "Artist," 138.

478 *opened to traffic:* NYT, October 25, 1931.

478 *"The most impressive"*: *Engineering News-Record* (October 22, 1931): 637.

479 *"The George Washington Bridge is"*: Lewis Mumford, "The Sky Line: Bridges and Buildings," TNY 7 (November 21, 1931): 82.

479 *"The George Washington Bridge over the Hudson"*: Le Corbusier, *Cathedrals,* 75.

479 *Ammann had hoped to encase:* Rockland, *George Washington,* 69.

479 *"Happily for the aesthetic success"*: Mumford, "Bridges," 82.

479 *"unknown man"*: Le Corbusier, *Cathedrals,* 75–76.

479 *"A dreamer in steel"*: Doig, "Politics," 151.

479 *"To grasp"*: Rastorfer, *Six Bridges,* 39.

480 *French government outlawed:* Ibid., 16–17.

480 *"Engineers have had"*: Othmar H. Ammann, "Brobdingnagian Bridges," *Technological Review* 33 (July 1931), 573.

480 *"did not require"*: Wisehart, "Greatest Bridge," 186.

480 *"deflection theory"*: Doig and Billington, "Ammann's First Bridge," 556.

480 *"comparatively light"*: Wisehart, "Greatest Bridge," 189.

480 *"untried territory"*: Doig and Billington, "Ammann's First Bridge," 550.

480 *"leap of faith"*: Ibid., 545.

481 *"felt the gigantic span"; "The crowds were only amused"*: NYT, October 25, 1931.

481 *"would stand up"*: Durrer, "Memories," 6–7. See also Sharon Reier, *The Bridges of New York* (NY: Quadrant, 1977), 105.

481 *"What made you so sure"*: Durrer, "Memories," 6–7.

481 *"He is a lean elderly man"; "That bridge"*: Gay Talese, "City Bridge Creator, 85, Keeps Watchful Eye on His Landmarks," NYT, March 26, 1964.

481 *"No twentieth-century engineer"*: David P. Billington, *The Tower and the Bridge: The New Art of Structural Engineering* (NY: Basic, 1983), 129.

482 *it represented the shift in transportation:* Ibid., 131.

482 *"a gateway"*: Goldberger, *City Observed,* 326.

482 *"Palisades Boom"*: NYW, May 15, 1927; NYT, January 19, February 9, 1930.

482 *"Bergen County Should Be"*: NYW, May, 15, 1927.

482 *over one million:* ENYC, 921.

482 *In 1910:* "Population of Counties by Decennial Census, 1900 to 1990," United States Bureau of the Census, National Archives, Washington, DC.

482 *"the busiest bridge"*: Rockland, *George Washington,* 3.

483 *"This connecting highway"*: Quoted in Jackson, *Highway,* 214.

483 *"an over-land bridge"*: Waldo Walker, "Great Express Highways for New York Zone," NYT, November 21, 1926.

483 *"a mortal competitor"*: Condit, *Port of New York,* vol. 2, 110.

483 *"rails to rubber"*: Bard, *Authority,* 177.

483 *Lincoln Tunnel:* NYT, January 26, 1930.

483 *as avid an advocate:* Ammann, "George Washington Bridge," 18.

483 *"The city must have"*: NYT, September 22, 1927.

484 *"a veritable motorist's dream"*: Robert A. Caro, *The Power Broker: Robert Moses and the Fall of New York* (NY: Vintage, 1975), 556. See also *Opening of the Henry Hudson Parkway and Progress on the West Side Improvement* (NY: Henry Hudson Parkway Authority, 1936), 7–10.

484 *forever "eliminate"*: Caro, *Power Broker,* 556.

484 *"eager citizens"*: NYT, November 2, 1937.

484 *"a monstrous force"*: "Unfit for Modern Motor Traffic," *Fortune* 14 (August 1936): 85.

484 *85 percent:* NYT, November 16, 1930.

484 *"The resultant balanced transport system"*: Owen D. Gutfreund, "Rebuilding New York in the Auto Age: Robert Moses and His Highways," in Hilary Ballon and Kenneth T. Jackson, eds., *Robert Moses and the Modern City: The Transformation of New York* (NY: W. W. Norton, 2007), 86.

484 *"muddy wasteland"*: Quoted in Caro, *Power Broker,* 555.

484 *"boulevard"*: NYT, November 21, 1926.

484 *will dump:* "Congested Traffic," NR 57 (November 28, 1928): 29–31.

485 *"probably the greatest"*: Gribetz and Kaye, *Walker,* 162.

485 *"And because trucks"*: Jackson, *Crabgrass,* 184.

486 *"motor slums"; "The real process"*: NYT, February 21, 1929.

CHAPTER TWENTY-FOUR: A SCHOOL OF MINNOWS

PAGE

487 "Talented people": Quoted in John Tierney, "What's New York the Capital of Now?," *The New York Times Magazine,* November 20, 1994.

487 *"Straight, wide"; "all foreign"; "windowed walls"*: Irwin, *Highlights,* 312–14.

487 *nearly 90 percent of the labor force:* Ben Morris Selekman, Henriette Rose Walter, and Walter J. Couper, "The Clothing and Textile Industries," in *Food, Clothing and Textile Industries, Wholesale Markets and Retail Shopping and Financial Districts,*

Present Trends and Probable Future Developments, vol. 1B of *The Regional Survey of New York and Its Environs* (New York: Regional Plan of New York and Its Environs, 1928), 57.

488 *"the girls"*: Irwin, *Highlights,* 315.

488 *"an inch"*: "America Comes to Seventh Avenue," *Fortune* 20 (July 1939), 183.

488 *"It's a beehive"*: Ibid.

488 *"clanging machinery"*: Irwin, *Highlights,* 315.

488 *"I know of no"*: Ibid., 319–20.

488 *"a school of minnows"*: "America Comes," 181.

488 *no gigantic factories*: Selekman et al., "Clothing and Textile Industries," in *Clothing,* 34.

488 *"billion dollar industries"*: Mabel A. Magee, *Trends in Location of the Women's Clothing Industry* (Chicago: University of Chicago Press, 1930), 1.

489 *78 percent of the total value*: Nancy L. Green, "From Downtown Tenements to Midtown Lofts," in David Soyer, ed., *A Coat of Many Colors: Immigration, Globalization, and Reform in the New York City Garment Industry* (New York: Fordham University Press, 2005), 28.

489 *nearly 90 percent*: Selekman et al., "Clothing and Textile Industries," in *Clothing,* 17, 24.

489 *Over half of the dresses*: Nancy L. Green, "Sweatshop Migrations: The Garment Industry Between Home and Shop," in David Ward and Olivier Zunz, eds. *The Landscape of Modernity: New York, 1910–1940* (NY: Russell Sage Foundation, 1992), 213–32.

489 *"constricting" corset*: "America Comes," 181, 183.

489 *"The story behind"*: Ibid.

489 *built more skyscrapers*: C. G. Poore, "A Skyscraper Builder Began as a Newsboy," NYT, January 20, 1929.

489 *"No other single individual"*: NYT, May 18, 1930.

489 *eight times the height*: NYT, November 20, 1932.

489 *largest individual owner of property*: NYT, November 14, 1932.

489 *"If something"; "I could rebuild"*: Harry A. Stewart, "Don't Keep Half Your Brain Busy Trying to Hide Something," *The American Magazine* 97 (April 1924): 67.

490 *Abraham Lefcourt earned*: Shachtman, *Skyscraper Dreams,* 67; Poore, "Skyscraper Builder."

490 *"college education"*: Stewart, "Don't Keep," 210.

490 *"to a flying start"*: Poore, "Skyscraper Builder."

490 *build a twelve-story loft building*: NYT, May, 18, 1930; Stewart, "Don't Keep," 211.

491 *"facing a certain failure"*: Stewart, "Don't Keep," 213.

491 *Save New York Committee*: Selekman et al., "Clothing and Textile Industries," in *Clothing,* 76.

491 *"Being the most important body"*: Ibid.

491 *"The wrecker tore"*: Ibid.

492 *"terraced skyscrapers"*: Ibid., 320–22.

492 *Lefcourt Clothing Center*: DN, August 11, 1927.

492 *"I buy and keep"*: Poore, "Skyscraper Builder."

492 *as a friend of labor*: NYT, November 14, 1932.

492 *Ely Jacques Kahn*: Jewel Stern and John A. Stuart, *Ely Jacques Kahn, Architect: Beaux-Arts to Modernism in New York* (NY: W. W. Norton, 2006), 80.

493 *"thrill of accomplishment"*: Poore, "Skyscraper Builder."

493 *Lefcourt-Marlborough Building*: Ibid.

493 *he would announce*: Shachtman, *Skyscraper Dreams*, 124–25.

493 *classy showrooms*: Magee, *Trends*, 114.

494 *an estimated 40 percent*: Green, "Downtown," in Soyer, ed., *Coat*, 41; Miriam Cohen, *Workshop to Office: Two Generations of Italian Women in New York City, 1900–1950* (Ithaca, NY: Cornell University Press, 1992), 60.

494 *only 15 percent*: Selma C. Berrol, "Manhattan's Jewish West Side," *New York Affairs* 10 (Winter 1987): 13–32.

494 *only 3 percent of Manhattan's Jews:* For the geographic migration of second-generation Jews, see Deborah Dash Moore, *At Home in America: Second Generation New York Jews* (NY: Columbia University Press, 1981).

495 *"the best of two possible worlds"*: Roy B. Helfgott, "Women's and Children's Apparel," in Max Hall, ed., *Made in New York: Case Studies in Metropolitan Manufacturing* (Cambridge: Harvard University Press, 1959), 114; Green, "Downtown," in Soyer, ed., *Coat*, 39, 42. In the 1920s, approximately one-fifth of women's garment firms sent their production work out of state. See Nancy L. Green, *Ready-to-Wear: A Century of Industry and Immigrants in Paris and New York* (Durham, NC: Duke University Press, 1997), 151.

495 *clothing industry's venture capitalists:* Louis Levine, *The Women's Garment Workers* (NY: B. W. Huebsch, 1924), 398–99.

495 *The subcontractor was the manufacturer:* Ibid., 400.

496 *over two-thirds of New York City's contract shops:* Green, *Ready-to-Wear*, 148.

496 *"rat-holes"*: Selekman et al., "Clothing and Textile Industries," in *Clothing*, 52.

496 *gave New York an enormous competitive advantage:* Magee, *Trends*, 68.

496 *to accept substandard wages:* Ibid.

496 *unmarried Italian women:* Green, *Ready-to-Wear*, 48, 224–27.

496 *Jews retained a stranglehold:* Selekman et al., "Clothing and Textile Industries," in *Clothing*, 24.

497 *"a maximum of style"*: Magee, *Trends*, 20.

497 *"close-in shops"*: Green, *Ready-to-Wear*, 148.

497 *America's exclusive design and sales center:* Helfgott, "Women's," in Hall, ed., *Made in New York*, 66.

497 *"If you're"*: "America Comes to Seventh Avenue," 187.

497 *as highly speculative:* Selekman et al., "Clothing and Textile Industries," in *Clothing*, 19.

498 *"no shrinking violets"*: Ibid., 187.

498 *"survival depends"*: Daniel Bell, "The Three Faces of New York," *Dissent* (July 1961): 225.

498 *"it was a middle class"*: Ibid., 226.

498 *"consumers of culture"*: Quotes in Ibid.

CHAPTER TWENTY-FIVE: MUSIC IS MY MISTRESS

PAGE

503 "No figure in jazz history": Ted Gioia, *The History of Jazz* (NY: Oxford University Press, 1997), 116.

503 *"Everybody [in the business]"*: Harvey G. Cohen, *Duke Ellington's America* (Chicago: University of Chicago Press, 2010), 48.

503 *Mills began his musical career:* A. H. Lawrence, *Duke Ellington and His World* (NY: Routledge & Kegan Paul, 2001), 33–34; John Edward Hasse, *Beyond Category: The Life and Genius of Duke Ellington* (NY: Simon & Schuster, 1995), 88–89; Samuel B. Charters and Leonard Kunstadt, *Jazz: A History of the New York Scene* (NY: Da Capo, 1981; first published in 1962), 208.

504 *"Make way":* Barry Ulanov, *Duke Ellington* (NY: Da Capo, 1975; first published in 1947), 12.

504 *"converged in New York":* Douglas, *Terrible Honesty,* 15.

504 *"Elegant, reserved":* Gioia, *History of Jazz,* 117.

505 *"blessed":* Hasse, *Category,* 21.

505 *"There is no place":* Warrick L. Carter, "Edward Kennedy Ellington," in Kenneth T. Jackson, ed., *Dictionary of American Biography,* Supplement 9, 1971–75 (NY: Charles Scribner's Sons, 1994), 259.

505 *"E.G. always acted":* Ellington, *Mistress,* 10, 12.

505 *a music-loving family:* Hasse, *Category,* 24.

505 *"My piano teacher":* Ellington, *Mistress,* 9.

506 *"Those ragtime pianists":* Ulanov, *Ellington,* 14.

506 *Ellington cut classes:* Mark Tucker, *Ellington: The Early Years* (Urbana: University of Illinois Press, 1995), 41. This is the standard account of Ellington's early years.

506 *"I learned":* Ellington, *Mistress,* 22.

506 *"I never took up the scholarship":* Ibid., 32.

506 *Mercer would say:* Hasse, *Category,* 49.

506 *they called their music "sweet":* James Lincoln Collier, *Duke Ellington* (NY: Oxford University Press, 1987), 33.

506 *"I had never heard":* Ellington, *Mistress,* 47.

506 *Sidney Bechet:* Hasse, *Category,* 67–68.

507 *"If you want me":* Studs Terkel, *Giants of Jazz* (NY: New Press, 1975), 79.

507 *"Harlem, to our minds":* Ellington, *Mistress,* 36.

507 *"It is impossible":* Ibid., 66.

507 *"From a window":* Arna Bontemps, "The Two Harlems," *American Scholar* 14 (Spring 1945): 167.

507 *"bravura keyboard style":* Hasse, *Category,* 71.

507 *"Sometimes we got carving battles":* Jervis Anderson, *This Was Harlem: A Cultural Portrait, 1900–1950* (NY: Farrar, Straus & Giroux, 1981), 156.

508 *"to get ourselves together":* Ellington, *Mistress,* 37.

508 *"I still remember":* Richard O. Boyer, "The Hot Bach, III," TNY 20 (July 8, 1944): 28–29.

508 *"We do it":* Ulanov, *Ellington,* 35.

508 *"The 'real New Yorker'":* Ellington, *Mistress,* 66.

509 *nineteen black floor shows:* Hasse, *Category,* 66; Tucker, *Ellington,* 91.

509 *"It was at the [Hollywood] Club":* Ellington, *Mistress,* 71.

509 *"dance music played":* Charters and Kunstadt, *Jazz,* 121.

509 *"the word":* "Mr. Gershwin Replies to Mr. Kramer, *Singing 1,* no. 10 (October 1926): 17.

509 *"The word supposedly":* Ethan Mordden, *Ziegfeld: The Man Who Invented Show Business* (NY: St. Martin's, 2008), 208.

509 *"I don't write jazz":* Boyer, "The Hot Bach, I," TNY 20 (June 24, 1944): 33.

509 *"a character"*: Tucker, *Ellington,* 101.

510 *"Our band changed character"*: Nat Shapiro and Nat Hentoff, eds., *Hear Me Talkin' to Ya': The Story of Jazz as Told by the Men Who Made It* (NY: Dover, 1955), 231.

510 *characteristic "wah-wah"*: Collier, *Ellington,* 46.

510 *"three basic elements"*: Mercer Ellington, with Stanley Dance, *Duke Ellington in Person: An Intimate Memoir* (Boston: Houghton Mifflin, 1978), 25.

510 *"to intone"*: Ulanov, *Ellington,* 49.

510 *"a polite dance band"*: Hasse, *Category,* 76; Ellington, *Mistress,* 72.

510 *"a lady out of jazz"*: Ellington, *Mistress,* 419.

510 *"Often, when Bechet"; "The audience"*: Ibid., 47.

510 *he was soon forced out*: Tucker, *Ellington,* 109.

511 *"an uproarious success"*: Geoffrey C. Ward and Ken Burns, *Jazz: A History of America's Music* (NY: Alfred A. Knopf, 2000), 100.

511 *"cats . . . blew up a storm"*: Ellington, *Mistress,* 103.

511 *"toned down"*: Ward and Burns, *Jazz,* 100.

511 *"so crowded"*: Hasse, *Category,* 80–81.

511 *Closing time*: Ellington, *Mistress,* 103.

511 *"The money"*: Collier, *Ellington,* 45.

511 *"Everybody in our band"*: Boyer, "Hot Bach, III," 28.

511 *"Liquor drinking among the musicians"*: Ellington, *Mistress,* 73–75.

511 *run by Arnold Rothstein*: Leo Katcher, *Big Bankroll,* 120.

511 *"work the floor"*: Ellington, *Mistress,* 72.

512 *Duke was now living with Edna*: Ellington with Dance, *In Person,* 16.

512 *"We had to go"*: Ellington, *Mistress,* 72.

512 *"business would get slack"*: Hasse, *Category,* 79.

512 *"probably the hottest band"*: Quoted in Charters and Kunstadt, *Jazz,* 213.

512 *"small fry"*: Lawrence, *His World,* 78–79.

512 *Agents like Mills*: Ruth Millard, "Jazz Is Now Big Business," *The World Magazine* (May 22, 1927): 3.

512 *"It was imperative"*: Collier, *Ellington,* 69.

512 *the big money*: Hasse, *Category,* 92.

513 *"This was . . . the beginning"*: Ellington, *Mistress,* 73.

513 *"was the first to demand"*: Cohen, *Ellington's America,* 52.

513 *"[He was] energetic"*: Ellington with Dance, *In Person,* 33.

513 *"Nobody compared"*: John Hammond interview, April 3, 1978, Oral History, American Music, Yale University Library, Special Collections, New Haven, CT.

513 *WHN to broadcast live*: Lawrence, *His World,* 79–81.

513 *"The record sessions"*: Ulanov, *Ellington,* 64–65.

513 *"Records became"*: Ibid., 65.

514 *"The bandstand"*: Cab Calloway and Bryant Rollins, *Of Minnie the Moocher and Me* (NY: Thomas Y. Crowell, 1976), 88.

514 *songwriter Jimmy McHugh*: Lawrence, *His World,* 110.

514 *"Be big"*: Boyer, "Hot Bach, III," 29.

514 *"an inauspicious start"*: Lawrence, *His World,* 111.

515 *none could be over twenty-one*: Jonathan Gill, *Harlem: The Four Hundred Year History from Dutch Village to Capital of Black America* (NY: Grove, 2011), 268.

515 *"a white sanctuary"*: Lewis, *Harlem*, 209. See also Morris, *Incredible*, 334.

515 *"There were brutes"*: Haskins, *Cotton Club*, 36.

515 *Ellington found this policy demeaning*: Ellington with Dance, *In Person*, 45.

515 *"with a kind of"*: Kisseloff, *You Must Remember This*, 311–12.

515 *"Cotton Club shows"*: Lewis, *Harlem*, 210.

515 *"Sunday night in the Cotton Club"*: Ellington, *Mistress*, 80.

515 *"Royal Box"*: Gill, *Harlem*, 269.

515 *"At this time Harlem"*: Ward and Burns, *Jazz*, 145.

516 *"Aristocrat of Harlem"*: Haskins, *Cotton Club*, 37.

516 *"Impeccable behavior was demanded"*: Ellington, *Mistress*, 80.

516 *"You saw throngs"*: Morris, *Incredible*, 333.

516 *"turned white"*: Rudolph Fischer, "The Caucasian Storms Harlem," in David Levering Lewis, ed., *The Portable Harlem Renaissance Reader* (NY: Penguin, 1995), 111, 115.

516 *a "painter"*: Gioia, *Jazz*, 116.

516 *"They put pressure on"*: Ibid., 126.

516 *"The shows"*: Anderson, *Harlem*, 175.

516 *"jungle style" jazz*: Ellington, *Mistress*, 419.

517 *"bursts of"*: Gioia, *Jazz*, 128.

517 *"the most dazzling"*: Charters and Kunstadt, *Jazz*, 218.

517 *"Maybe these Nordics"*: Quoted in Ward and Burns, *Jazz*, 145.

517 *"greatest" black bandleader*: Charters and Kunstadt, *Jazz*, 218.

517 *"The world"*: Hasse, *Category*, 112. See also Philip K. Eberly, *Music in the Air: America's Changing Tastes in Popular Music, 1920–1980* (NY: Hastings House, 1982), 43–49.

517 *"We'd play"*: Lawrence, *His World*, 155–56.

517 *"an idol of the jazz cult"*: "Introducing Duke Ellington," *Fortune* 3 (August 1933): 47.

517 *"jazz classics"; "great Negro music"*: Quoted in Cohen, *Ellington's America*, 29.

517 *"Those of us"*: Calloway and Rollins, *Minnie*, 105–6.

517 *"a citadel"*: Lewis, *Harlem*, 217. For the black elite on jazz, see p. 173.

518 *Ellington had started seeing Dixon*: Haskins, *Cotton Club*, 53.

518 *"I came home"*: Hasse, *Category*, 131.

518 *"People were curious"*: Ellington with Dance, *In Person*, 18.

518 *"She had innate class"*: Ibid., 48.

518 *"the role of a parent"*: Ibid., 18.

518 *"one of the world's immortals"*: Boyer, "Hot Bach, I," 30. See also R. D. Durrell, "Black Beauty," in Mark Tucker, ed., *The Duke Ellington Reader* (NY: Oxford University Press, 1993), 57–65.

518 *"He is declared"*: Tucker, *Early Years*, xi.

CHAPTER TWENTY-SIX: MASTER OF ALLURE

PAGE

519 *"Inch too large"*: Billie Burke, *With a Feather on My Nose* (NY: Appleton-Century-Crofts, 1949), 159.

519 *"White people"*: Quoted in Mordden, *Ziegfeld*, 114–15.

520 *"He was the finest comedian"; "[Ziegfeld] took me"*: Florenz Ziegfeld, Jr., "The Showman's Shifting Sands," *The Ladies' Home Journal* 11 (June 1923): 172.

520 *"perhaps the greatest"*: George Jean Nathan, "Ziegfeld," in Nathan, *The Magic Mirror: Selected Writings on the Theatre* (NY: Alfred A. Knopf, 1960), 86.

520 *paid exorbitant monthly rent*: Richard Ziegfeld and Paulette Ziegfeld, *The Ziegfeld Touch: The Life and Times of Florenz Ziegfeld, Jr.* (NY: Harry N. Abrams, 1993), 120.

521 *"A theater"*: Stern et al., *New York 1930*, 235–36.

521 *"grandees"; "antiquated paintings"*: Mordden, *Ziegfeld*, 235, 241.

522 *"The suite"*: Bernard Sobel, *Broadway Heartbeat: Memoirs of a Press Agent* (NY: Hermitage House, 1953), 179.

522 *"God Almighty"*: *Los Angeles Times*, April 12, 1989.

522 *earned more than any show*: NYT, March 12, 1928.

522 *"Ziegfeld touch"*: Ziegfeld and Ziegfeld, *Touch*, 12.

522 *"inimitable"*: NYT, July 25, 1932.

522 *"thrill-a-second"*: Mordden, *Ziegfeld*, 189.

522 *"clap-hands"*: Sobel, *Broadway Heartbeat*, 149.

522 *"the personification"*: Walter Tittle, "Ziegfeld of the Follies," *World's Work* 53 (March 1927): 563–64.

522 *"Laconic"*: Patricia Ziegfeld, *The Ziegfeld's Girl: Confessions of an Abnormally Happy Child* (Boston: Little, Brown, 1964), 18.

523 *"He always gave"*: J. P. McEvoy, "He Knew What They Wanted," *The Saturday Evening Post* (September 10, 1932): 10.

523 *"Mephistophelian look"*: Morris, *Incredible*, 266. See also, Burke, *Feather*, 148.

523 *almost never laughed aloud*: Gilbert Seldes, "The Great Glorifier," TNY 69 (May 31, 1993): 61. Originally published in 1931.

523 *"His entire staff"*: Eddie Cantor and David Freeman, *Ziegfeld: The Great Glorifier* (NY: Alfred H. King, 1934), 108.

523 *"he took as much care"*: Burke, *Feather*, 148–50.

523 *He loved luxury*: Sobel, *Heartbeat*, 103.

523 *When traveling across the country*: Marjorie Farnsworth, *The Ziegfeld Follies* (London: Peter Davies, 1956), 12.

523 *"the Red Sea parted"*: Quoted in Ziegfeld and Ziegfeld, *Touch*, 95.

523 *"frequently cruel"*: Sobel, *Heartbeat*, 106.

523 *Irving Berlin compose*: Randolph Carter, *The World of Flo Ziegfeld* (NY: Praeger, 1974), 83–84.

523 *"Keeper of the key"*: Ziegfeld and Ziegfeld, *Touch*, 109.

524 *"missiles"*: Ibid., 111.

524 *"If Ziegfeld dies"*: Quoted in Title, "Ziegfeld," 568.

524 *"He's laying"*: Quoted in Laurence Bergreen, *As Thousands Cheer: The Life of Irving Berlin* (NY: Da Capo, 1996; first published in 1990): 65.

524 *"the eminence"*: Carter, *Ziegfeld*, 91.

524 *"And in pursuit"*: Nathan Teitel, "The Man Who Invented Women," *The Saturday Review* 55 (November 4, 1972): 86.

524 *"He embodied"*: Mordden, *Ziegfeld*, 293.

524 *"worker and playboy"*: Bernard Sobel, "This Was Ziegfeld," *The American Mercury* 60 (January 1945): 96.

525 *"He loved to gamble"*: Sobel, *Heartbeat*, 106.

525 *"life"*: F. Scott Fitzgerald, "The Crack-Up," in Edmund Wilson, ed., *The Crack-Up* (NY: New Directions, 1993), 69.

525 *"The Dancing Ducks of Denmark"*: Robert C. Toll, *On with the Show! The First Century of Show Business in America* (NY: Oxford University Press, 1976), 297.

526 *"exciting privilege"*: Alexander Woollcott, "The Invisible Fish," in *The Portable Woollcott,* edited by Joseph Hennessey (NY: Viking, 1946), 448.

526 *"He was my first star attraction"*: Ziegfeld, "Shifting Sands," 172.

526 *"Fake!" "Fraud!"*: Ibid., 23, 171–72.

526 *"beginning a lifelong pattern"*: Ziegfeld and Ziegfeld, *Touch,* 28.

526 *"five feet of sizzling personality"*: Atkinson, *Broadway,* 114.

526 *Annhaline Held:* Burke, *Feather,* 140–41.

526 *A cable to Manhattan-based railroad tycoon:* Eve Golden, *Anna Held and the Birth of Ziegfeld's Broadway* (Lexington: University of Kentucky Press, 2000), 24.

526 *a daily beauty bath:* NYT, July 23, 1932.

526 *the agent paid:* Golden, *Anna Held,* 31.

527 *"misbehaving" eyes:* Linda Mizejewski, *Ziegfeld Girl: Image and Icon in Culture and Cinema* (Durham, NC: Duke University Press, 1999), 17, 41.

527 *Ziegfeld won $1.5 million:* Seldes, "Glorifier," 60.

527 *flat broke:* Tittle, "Ziegfeld," 566.

527 *"bulk"; the Billy Watson Beef Trust:* Lewis A. Erenburg, *Steppin' Out: New York Nightlife and the Transformation of American Culture, 1890–1930* (Westport, CT: Greenwood, 1981), 215.

527 *"girl show"*: Mizejewski, *Ziegfeld Girl,* 19.

527 *"brought the female body"*: Erenburg, *Steppin' Out,* 214.

527 *"glided and posed"*: Mizejewski, *Ziegfeld Girl,* 21.

528 *"A moment later"*: Nancy Caldwell Sorel, "First Encounters: Fanny Brice and Florenz Ziegfeld," *The Atlantic Monthly* 257 (January 1986): 81.

528 *"the most glamorous"*: Atkinson, *Broadway,* 115.

528 *"practically everybody"*: Quoted in Mizejewski, *Ziegfeld Girl,* 159.

528 *"But none of them"*: Atkinson, *Broadway,* 118.

529 *fell in love with seventeen-year-old Lillian Lorraine:* Nils Hanson, *Lillian Lorraine: The Life and Times of a Ziegfeld Diva* (Jefferson, NC: McFarland, 2011), 48, 77.

529 *"I had never met"*: Burke, *Feather,* 120.

529 *were married:* Ibid., 131.

529 *"There were no tedious reformers"*: Ibid., 213.

529 *turned Burkeley Crest into a menagerie:* Ibid., 178–80; Ziegfeld, *Ziegfelds' Girl,* 67–71.

530 *"produced those Sunday dinners"*: Ziegfeld, *Ziegfelds' Girl,* 58.

530 *"Daddy's version"*: Ibid., 101–2.

530 *"ambitionless"*: Burke, *Feather,* 152.

530 *It cost $10,000 a year:* Ziegfeld and Ziegfeld, *Touch,* 107–8.

530 *"Neither of them"*: Ziegfeld, *Ziegfelds' Girl,* 19.

530 *"Whether it was"*: Cantor and Freedman, *Glorifier,* 43.

530 *"The world"*: Quoted in Carter, *World,* 148.

531 *"I did not drink"*: Mordden, *Ziegfeld,* 207.

531 *"Flo gambled at night"*: Burke, *Feather,* 214.

531 *"Usually he did not come"*: Ibid., 215.

531 *"Everyone except Mother"*: Ziegfeld, *Ziegfelds' Girl*, 117.

531 *"I wanted to be an artist"*: Burke, *Feather*, 207.

531 *"whether the next man"*: Ziegfeld, *Ziegfelds' Girl*, 116.

531 *"One of the things"*: Burke, *Feather*, 210.

532 *He, in turn, needed Billie and Patty*: Ziegfeld and Ziegfeld, *Touch*, 61.

532 *"something of a windup toy"*: Mordden, *Ziegfeld*, 211.

532 *strapped for cash*: Carter, *World*, 127–28.

532 *"the master of allure"*: Farnsworth, *Follies*, 81.

532 *thousands of "beauties"*: Cantor and Freedman, *Glorifier*, 11.

532 *"flocks of girls"*: McEvoy, "He Knew," 11.

532 *"Most of them entered"*: Sobel, *Heartbeat*, 109.

532 *"the firecrackers"*: McEvoy, "He Knew," 11.

533 *"This is done"*: Florenz Ziegfeld, Jr., "Picking Out Pretty Girls for the Stage," *The American Magazine* 88 (December 1919): 34, 119, 128–29.

533 *"His eye for beauty"*: Burke, *Feather*, 159.

533 *"picking" process*: Quoted in Sobel, *Heartbeat*, 107.

533 *"carry herself gracefully"*: Ziegfeld, "Picking Out Pretty Girls," 34.

533 *The "secret" of selecting*: Florenz Ziegfeld, Jr., "Beauty, the Fashions and the Follies," *The Ladies' Home Journal* 40 (March 1923): 16–17, 125.

533 *twenty-dollar gold piece*: Ziegfeld, *Ziegfelds' Girl*, 191. Most Ziegfeld girls were paid from $75 to $175 per week.

534 *"forbidden"*: Michael Lasser, "The Glorifier: Florenz Ziegfeld and the Creation of the American Showgirl," *American Scholar* 63 (Summer 1994): 445.

534 *"He was the perpetual"*: Sobel, *Heartbeat*, 199.

534 *"What the girls do"*: Ziegfeld, "Beauty," 129.

534 *"No seminary students"*: Cantor and Freedman, *Glorifier*, 64.

534 *"A Ziegfeld Girl"*: Quoted in Mizejewski, *Ziegfeld Girl*, 99.

534 *"tilted upward"*: Burke, *Feather*, 158.

534 *"the first thing he did"*: Cantor and Freedman, *Glorifier*, 63.

534 *"That's enough"*: McEvoy, "He Knew," 10–11.

534 *"He has no idea"*: Seldes, "Glorifier," 60.

534 *"glorified"; "in the chorus"; "self-consciousness"*: Ibid.

535 *"American Beauties"; "a deliberate and rigid goose-step"*: Wilson, "Finale at the Follies" in *American Earthquake*, 44–52.

535 *"appear slightly inaccessible"*: Gilbert Seldes, *The Seven Lively Arts* (NY: Harper & Brothers, 1924), 136–37.

535 *"He has been at it"*: Woollcott, "Invisible," in *Portable*, 445–46.

535 *"The curtain opened"*: "Follies of 1927," http://ruthetting.com/ziegfeld-follies-1927.

535 *"stirring and glamorous"*: Alison Smith, "The Glorifying Machine," DN, August 17, 1927.

536 *"mounted a completely"*: J. Brooks Atkinson, "Affairs of the Early Season," NYT, August 28, 1927.

536 *"splendor about the Follies"*: Wilson, "Finale at the Follies," in *American Earthquake*, 51–52.

536 *"aesthetic"; "The Great Glorifier"*: Nathan, *Mirror*, 89–90.

536 *"rambling, sparkling"*: NYW, September 29, 1927.

536 *"Perhaps it will"*: "His Honor," *The Literary Digest* (October 8, 1927): 40.

536 *"a good spanking"*: Cantor and Freedman, *Glorifier,* 99–100.

536 *"Caught a little bear"*: Ziegfeld and Ziegfeld, *Touch,* 142.

536 *a Rolls-Royce convertible*: Ibid., 142–43.

536 *superhuman*: McEvoy, "He Knew," 52.

537 *"The history of the American Musical Theatre"*: Quoted in Stephen Banfield, *Jerome Kern* (New Haven: Yale University Press, 2006), 155.

537 *"It's got a million dollar title"*: Hugh Fordin, *Getting to Know Him: A Biography of Oscar Hammerstein II* (NY: Random House, 1977), 70.

537 *Ferber signed a contract*: Edna Ferber, *A Peculiar Treasure* (NY: Doubleday, Doran, 1939), 305. See also Gerald Bordman, *Jerome Kern: His Life and Music* (NY: Oxford University Press, 1980), 275.

537 *"as essential to the play"*: Fordin, *Getting,* 86.

537 *only producer in New York*: Mordden, *Ziegfeld,* 237.

538 *"It is the best musical comedy"*: Kreuger, *Show Boat,* 20.

538 *"one-man Greek chorus"*: Bordman, *Kern,* 276.

538 *"bank president"; "the most impressive production"*: Fordin, *Getting,* 72.

538 *"We had the turtles"*: Ibid.

538 *"We had fallen"*: Ibid., 79.

538 *"with a look"; "I give you my word"*: Ferber, *Peculiar,* 306.

539 *"That's the gloomiest story"*: Ziegfeld and Ziegfeld, *Touch,* 144.

539 *convinced him to use realistic effects*: Cantor and Freedman, *Glorifier,* 144.

539 *"an imposing figure"*: Ferber, *Peculiar,* 317.

539 *"Why did I ever undertake"; "Please accept"*: Cantor and Freedman, *Glorifier,* 109–10.

539 *"They don't like it"*: Fordin, *Getting,* 86.

539 *"On the contrary"*: Mordden, *Ziegfeld,* 250.

540 *"made it"*: Ferber, *Peculiar,* 317.

540 *"New York"*: Fordin, *Getting,* 86.

540 *"I couldn't bring myself"*: Ferber, *Peculiar,* 318.

540 *"thunderous applause"*: Fordin, *Getting,* 88.

540 *"a work of genius"*: Robert Coleman, *Daily Mirror,* December 28, 1927.

540 *"the best musical show ever written"*: J. Brooks Atkinson, "Show-Folk Variously," NYT, January 8, 1928.

540 *"the most beautiful girls"*: Coleman, *Daily Mirror,* December 28, 1927.

540 *"light, escapist fare"*: Miles Kreuger, quoted in Banfield, *Kern,* 155.

541 *"that's got Negro blood in him"*: Kreuger, *Showboat,* 35.

541 *"a composite"*: Farnsworth, *Follies,* 119.

541 *"came to regret"*: Quoted in Geoffrey Block, *Enchanted Evenings: The Broadway Musical from Show Boat to Sondheim* (NY: Oxford University Press, 1997), 21.

541 *"unique breakaway"*: Bordman, *Kern,* 292.

542 *a story about Ziegfeld*: Ziegfeld and Ziegfeld, *Touch,* 143. This same scene appeared in the 1936 Academy Award–winning Hollywood film, *The Great Ziegfeld.*

542 *"as something more than a ballyhooer"*: J. Brooks Atkinson, " 'All for One,'" NYT, March 25, 1928.

CHAPTER TWENTY-SEVEN: A BAG OF PLUMS

PAGE

543 "I pray to God": Arthur Garfield Hays, *City Lawyer: The Autobiography of a Law Practice* (NY: Simon & Schuster, 1942), 238.

543 *"He was doing books"*: Reminiscences of Bennett Cerf Columbia University Oral History Collection, Butler Library. Columbia University, hereafter cited as Cerf, Oral History.

543 *"With a silk hat on"*: Bennett Cerf, *At Random: The Reminiscences of Bennett Cerf* (NY: Random House, 1977), 38.

544 *"the outstanding figure"*: Sherwood Anderson, *Sherwood Anderson's Memoirs: A Critical Edition*, ed. Ray Lewis White (Chapel Hill: University of North Carolina Press, 1969), 490.

544 *"the persuasive powers of a Svengali"*: Lawrence Langner, *The Magic Curtain: The Story of a Life in Two Fields, Theatre and Invention by the Founder of the Theatre Guild* (NY: E. P. Dutton, 1951), 198.

544 *"A job with any publishing house"*: Lillian Hellman, *An Unfinished Woman: A Memoir* (Boston: Little, Brown, 1969), 33–34.

544 *"Most publishers"*: Cerf, Oral History.

544 *"He'd ask the girls"*: Cerf, *At Random*, 28.

545 *"an unforgettable look"*: Louis Kronenberger, "Gambler in Publishing: Horace Liveright," *The Atlantic Monthly* 97 (January 1965): 96, 103.

545 *"the Jazz Age in microcosm"*: Edith M. Stern, "A Man Who Was Unafraid," *The Saturday Review of Literature* 24 (June 28, 1941): 10.

545 *"branch offices"*: Kronenberger, "Gambler," 97–98.

545 *"full of lush girls"*: Hellman, *Unfinished Woman*, 33–34.

545 *"Manhattan's Maecenas"*: John Kobler, *Otto the Magnificent: The Life of Otto Kahn* (NY: Charles Scribner's Sons, 1989), 146.

545 *"waxed to fine points"*: Theresa M. Collins, *Otto Kahn: Art, Money and Modern Time* (Chapel Hill: University of North Carolina Press, 2002), 129.

545 *"Horace . . . had a compulsion"*: Cerf, Oral History.

546 *annus mirabilis*: Kronenberger, "Gambler," 97.

546 *"Never before"*: Hellman, *Unfinished Woman*, 33–34.

546 *"on the walls of buses"*: Anderson, *Memoirs*, 492.

546 *"The sympathy and attention"*: Hellman, *Unfinished Woman*, 33–34.

546 *"Most of the authors"*: Bennett A. Cerf, "Horace Liveright: An Obituary—Unedited," *Publishers Weekly* 124 (October 7, 1933): 1229.

546 *Liveright was born*: Tom Dardis, *Firebrand: The Life of Horace Liveright* (NY: Random House, 1995), 4–7.

547 *"by a succession of speculations"*: Anderson, *Memoirs*, 490.

548 *"didn't drink enough"*: Quoted in Dardis, *Firebrand*, 42.

548 *Hermann Elsas supported his profligate son-in-law*: Dardis, *Firebrand*, 50.

549 *"gave the impression"*: Donald Friede, *The Mechanical Angel: His Adventures and Enterprises in the Glittering 1920s* (NY: Alfred A. Knopf, 1948), 22.

549 *O'Neill was grateful*: Dardis, *Firebrand*, 59.

549 *"Most of the older"*: William H. Nolte, ed., *H. L. Mencken's Smart Set Criticism* (Ithaca, NY: Cornell University Press, 1968), 105.

550 *Alfred A. Knopf*: John Tebbel, "Publisher to an Era," *The Saturday Review* 47 (August 29, 1964): 132.

550 *"I love books physically"*: Geoffrey T. Hellman, "Publisher—I: A Very Dignified Pavane," TNY 24 (November 20, 1948): 46.

550 *"announce"; "a fierce mustache"*: Lurton Blassingame, "Profiles: The Trinity—And a Dog," TNY 2 (August 21, 1926): 15.

550 *"Getting talked about"*: Alfred A. Knopf, *Publishing Then and Now, 1912–1964* (NY: New York Public Library, 1964), 16–17.

550 *"I bought a couple of the [dogs]"*: Hellman, "Dignified," 52.

550 *"Alfred Knopf had one thing"*: Cerf, *At Random*, 41.

551 *to "puff" his catalogue*: Terry Teachout, "Huckster and Publisher: Horace Liveright Discovered That Publishing Is Not Enough, You've Got to Sell It Too," review of Tom Dardis, *Firebrand: The Life of Horace Liveright*, NYT July 16, 1995.

551 *"were run like conservative"*: Edward L. Bernays, "Add Liveright," unpublished Mss, Edward L. Bernays Papers, Manuscript Division, Library of Congress, Washington, DC, hereafter cited as Bernays Mss.

551 *Bernays found that "exhilarating"*: Bernays, *Biography*, 278.

551 *"an event"*: Ibid., 184.

552 *"filthy or disgusting"*: Quoted in Dardis, *Firebrand*, 163.

552 *"He is a crusader"*: Waldo Frank, "One Hundred Per Cent American," TNY 1 (October 10, 1925): 9–10.

552 *Other publishers*: For Liveright's view of censorship, see Horace Liveright, "The Absurdity of Censorship," *The Independent* 110 (March 17, 1923): 193.

552 *"these nuts"*: Quoted in Dardis, *Firebrand*, 167.

552 *"God rest her soul"*: Edward Weeks, *My Green Age* (Little, Brown, 1973), 190.

552 *"I can say without fear of denial"*: Liveright to Bertrand Russell, July 9, 1929, Horace Liveright Papers, Annenberg Rare Book and Manuscript Library, Van Pelt-Dietrich Library, University of Pennsylvania, Philadelphia, PA. Hereafter cited as HLP.

553 *"dignity and dust"*: Friede, *Mechanical*, 17.

553 *"It was for us"*: Ibid., 18.

553 *Friede's contribution*: Ibid., 21.

553 *"I have every reason"*: Ibid., 17.

553 *"a rambling hive"*: Ibid., 17–18.

554 *"sleek and dark"*: Weeks, *Green*, 189.

554 *"superior career infuriated me"*: Geoffrey T. Hellman, "Publisher—II: Big Day for Random," TNY 35 (May 16, 1959): 50.

554 *"charmed the hell out of me"*: Cerf, *At Random*, 27.

554 *"I'm bored to death"*: Quoted in ibid., 28.

554 *He withdrew the money*: Hellman, "Big Day," 49–50.

555 *"[Dick] was a superb salesman"*: Cerf, *At Random*, 30.

555 *"Dick, within ten years"*: Richard Simon, "Trade Winds: Try and Stop Them," *The Saturday Review of Literature* 33 (December 23, 1950).

555 *"Just two sips"*: Cerf, *At Random*, 31–32.

555 *"could involve stained"*: Kronenberger, "Gambler," 99.

555 *"at three o'clock"*: Bergreen, *Thousands Cheer*, 194.

555 *"Mr. Swope"*: E. J. Kahn, Jr., *The World of Swope* (NY: Simon & Schuster, 1965), 291.

555 *"[Liveright and his friends] insisted"*: Bertrand Russell to Dora Russell, October 11, 1927, Bertrand Russell Archives, McMaster University, Hamilton, Ontario.

556 *"the very upper crust"*: Anderson, *Memoirs,* 533.

556 *"Any writer on a New York visit"*: Hellman, *Unfinished Woman,* 36–37.

556 *"All the men"*: Ibid., 38.

556 *"She sailed in"; "Lucille, you have insulted me"; "We were absolutely"*: Cerf, Oral History.

557 *"Your sweetie's calling"*: Stern, "Unafraid," 24.

557 *"offering opinions"*: Hellman, *Unfinished Woman,* 38.

557 *"resembled a gossipy Alpine village"*: Kronenberger, "Gambler," 98.

557 *"madhouse"*: Anderson, *Memoirs,* 517.

557 *"harrowing duty"*: Friede, *Mechanical,* 23.

557 *"Actually nobody cared very much"*: Ibid., 27, 33.

558 *"But Liveright would necessarily"*: Ibid., 23.

558 *"wonderfully free from tension"; "the one real socialist"*: Kronenberger, "Gambler," 96–97.

558 *"There'd be a call"*: Cerf, Oral History.

558 *"who would inflate his ego"*: Cerf, *At Random,* 79–80.

558 *"The employees he chose"*: Stern, "Unafraid," 10.

558 *"flairs"; "Horace relished the scandal"*: Ibid., 14.

558 *"had a way of trusting"*: Anderson, *Memoirs,* 517.

559 *Liveright turned down*: Anderson to Liveright, June 1, 1925, in Charles E. Modlin, ed., *Sherwood Anderson: Selected Letters* (Knoxville: University of Tennessee Press, 1984), 68.

559 *Liveright's editors wanted to publish it*: Friede, *Mechanical,* 28.

559 *"I won't stand for it"*: Harry Hansen, "The First Reader," *New York World Telegram,* September 26, 1933.

559 *"It would be in extremely rotten tase"*: Jeffrey Meyers, *Hemingway: A Biography* (NY: Harper & Row, 1985), 169; Ernest Hemingway to Horace Liveright, January 19, 1926, in Carlos Baker, ed., *Ernest Hemingway: Selected Letters, 1917–1961* (NY: Charles Scribner's Sons, 1981), 190–91.

559 *"You should have printed"*: John Tebbel, *Between Covers: The Rise and Transformation of Book Publishing in America* (NY: Oxford University Press, 1987), 244.

559 *"flagship"*: Dardis, *Firebrand,* 194.

559 *convinced Liveright was cheating him*: Cerf, *At Random,* 36.

559 *"a crooked one at that"*: Dardis, *Firebrand,* 77.

560 *At a sensitive point in the negotiations*: Richard Lingeman, *Theodore Dreiser: An American Journey* (NY: John Wiley & Sons, 1993), 412–14.

560 *"I should not have said"*: Horace Liveright to Theodore Dreiser, April 2, 1926, HLP.

560 *"the most phenomenal list"*: Friede, *Mechanical,* 26.

560 *"at will"*: Ibid., 35.

561 *"Nonsense," said Liveright*: Ibid., 39.

561 *Liveright produced his biggest Broadway success*: NYT, March 23, 1928.

561 *a uniformed nurse*: Dardis, *Firebrand,* 287–88.

561 *"That brownstone house"*: Stern, "Unafraid," 10.

562 *"careless, engaging manner"*: Geoffrey T. Hellman, "How to Win Profits and Influence Literature—II," TNY 15 (October 7, 1939): 24.

562 *"with a terrifying will to win"*: Michael Korda, *Another Life: A Memoir of Other People* (NY: Random House, 2000), 43.

562 *"ridiculously small"*: Hellman, "How to Win Profits—II," 24–25.

562 *"sheer will power"*: Ibid., 25.

563 *"Of what?"*: "20,000 Per Cent Increase," *Fortune* 9 (January 1934): 48.

563 *"find people"*: Ibid., 48, 50.

563 *"planned publishing"; "Made" books*: Charles Allan Madison, *Book Publishing in America* (NY: McGraw-Hill, 1966), 347.

563 *"a suicidal notion"; "If you must publish"*: "20,000 Per Cent," 50.

563 *"We . . . did not want"*: Madison, *Book Publishing*, 347.

563 *"Ready at Last!"*: "20,000 Per Cent," 50.

564 *Orders poured in*: "20,000 Per Cent," 50–51; Peter Schwed, *Turning the Pages: An Insider's Story of Simon & Schuster, 1924–1984* (NY: Macmillan, 1984), 2–3.

564 *A traveler arriving from Europe*: Tebbel, *Covers*, 236.

564 *At the end of 1924*: Hellman, "How to Win Profits—II," 28; "20,000 Per Cent," 50. The book's three editors were F. Gregory Hartwick, Propser Buranelli, and Margaret Petherbridge.

564 *"great boom"*: "20,000 Per Cent," 51.

564 *the payroll was cut back; "Here today, back tomorrow"*: Schwed, *Turning*, 3, 6–7. Knopf's statement is attributed to him by a number of New York editors.

564 *"In April 1925"*: Simon, "Trade Winds," 4.

564 *Dr. Will Durant*: Hellman, "How to Win Profits—II," 28.

564 *read it with relish*: "20,000 Per Cent," 51, 100.

565 *It was an immediate best-seller*: Ibid., 100. It sold over half a million copies by 1930.

565 *"Richard Simon was one of the first"*: NYT, July 30, 1960.

565 *"you could learn anything"*: Korda, *Another Life*, 71.

565 *"Nobody was ever better"*: Ibid.

565 *"I'll give you a definite maybe"*: Geoffrey T. Hellman, "How to Win Profits and Influence Literature—III," TNY 15 (October 14, 1939): 29.

565 *"Is there a book in it?"; "Will it sell?"; "spark plug"*: Ibid., 28.

565 *Hard-drinking, chain-smoking Simon*: Ibid., 29; Korda, *Another Life*, 43.

566 *"The best way"*: Simon, "Trade Winds," 4.

566 *"the most innovative publisher"; "Make them want to come"*: Schwed, *Turning*, 18.

566 *"Give the reader a break"*: Ibid., 19.

566 *"a separate business venture"*: Hellman, "How to Win Profits—III," 26–27.

566 *"Max and Dick were mercurial geniuses"*: Schwed, *Turning*, 59–60.

567 *"senile drivel"*: Quoted in Hellman, "How to Win Profits—II," 29–30.

567 *an enthusiastic foreword by John Galsworthy*: Tebbel, *Covers*, 238.

567 *"There was electricity"*: Quoted in Schwed, *Turning*, 69.

567 *"blurb-infested"*: Schwed, *Turning*, 88.

567 *"We write"*: Tebbel, *Covers*, 239. The Inner Sanctum was the partners' name for the editorial room between their offices.

567 *"He read even"*: Korda, *Another Life*, 56–57.

567 *"congenial spirits"*: Ibid., 43.

567 *Barber Shop Ballads*: Tebbel, *Covers*, 316–17.

568 *Alfred Knopf hired*: Ibid., 317.

568 *"lump order"*: "20,000 Per Cent," 102.

568 *"unghost-written autobiography"*: Tebbel, *Covers,* 239–40.

568 *"laughing stock of the trade"*: Hellman, "How to Win Profits—III," 26.

569 *"completely taken in"*: Ibid.

569 *"The people who"*: Quoted in Madison, *Book Publishing in America,* 349.

569 *"Publisher's Row"*: "Those New York Publishers," *Fortune,* 15 (July 1939): 90.

569 *"economies of communication"*: W. Eric Gustafson, "Printing and Publishing," in Max Hall, ed., *Made in New York: Case Studies in Metropolitan Manufacturing* (Cambridge: Harvard University Press, 1959), 195.

569 *"The whole publishing business"*: Ibid., 196.

570 *"They could have economized"*: Tierney, "What's New York."

570 *drawing $60,000:* "Those New York Publishers," 202.

570 *"days of splendor"*: Anderson, *Memoirs,* 517.

570 *"pieces of merchandise"*: "20,000 Per Cent," 104.

570 *had published 251 books:* Ibid.

570 *"Out of politeness"*: Hellman, "How to Win Profits and Influence Literature—I," TNY 15 (September 30, 1939): 24.

571 *"And so"*: Bennett Cerf, Journal, May 1925, Bennett Cerf Papers, Rare Books and Manuscripts Library, Columbia University, New York, NY.

571 *"My father-in-law"; "One very easy way"*: Cerf, *At Random,* 44.

571 *"one of the great properties"*: Ibid., 45.

571 *get him out of the financial "hole"*: Ibid.

571 *his own trust fund:* Ralph Kirshner, "Bennett Alfred Cerf," *Dictionary of American Biography,* Supplement 9, 1971–75, p. 164; Simon, "Trade Winds," 4.

572 *would make Klopfer an equal partner:* Cerf, *At Random,* 46.

572 *Klopfer informed him:* Hellman, "Big Day," 52.

572 *sold 385,000 copies:* Simon, "Trade Winds," 5.

572 *"to dance"*: Cerf, Oral History.

572 *"The minute we gave"*: Cerf, *At Random,* 54.

572 *"diffident of the limelight"*: Hellman, "Big Day," 58.

572 *"Everyone has"*: Ibid., 62.

572 *"anything else"*: Ibid., 82.

572 *"When we went"*: Cerf, *At Random,* 62.

572 *"his nourishment"*: Hellman, "Big Day," 82.

572 *"very little work"*: Cerf, *At Random,* 62–63.

572 *wine-making machine:* Cerf, Oral History.

573 *"was a joy ride"*: Ibid.

573 *"at random"*: Cerf, *At Random,* 63–65.

573 *"Can one do this"*: Hellman, "Big Day," 54.

573 *"so even during"*: Cerf, Oral History.

573 *"It was"*: Simon, "Trade Winds," 6.

574 *guardian of free speech:* Paul S. Boyer, *Purity in Print: The Vice-Society Movement and Book Censorship in America* (NY: Charles Scribner's Sons, 1968), 255–56; "Obituaries: [Bennett Cerf]," *Publishers Weekly* (September 6, 1971): 30.

EPILOGUE: BLUE SKIES

PAGE

575   *"I was sort of"*: Cerf, *At Random,* 58; Cerf, Oral History.

575   *"pyramiding speculator"*: Friede, *Mechanical,* 25.

575   *"What brought Horace low"*: Kronenberger, "Gambler," 103.

576   *the market turned permanently against him*: Horace Liveright to Albert Wallerstein, June 5, 1929, HLP.

576   *"I'm a stubborn fool"*: Horace Liveright to Leon Amster, August 29, 1929, HLP.

576   *he began speculating heavily*: Ziegfeld and Ziegfeld, *Ziegfeld Touch,* 142.

576   *"strategy and tears"*: Burke, *Feather,* 219.

576   *"Flo never"*: Ibid., 220.

576   *Ziegfeld began to get nervous*: Carter, *World,* 149–50.

577   *"I'm through"*: Burke, *Feather,* 221–22.

577   *"another turn"; "This trait"*: Cantor and Freedman, *Great Glorifier,* 26.

577   *"Daddy and Mr. Goldwyn"*: Patricia Ziegfeld, *Ziegfeld's Girl,* 202.

577   *"Up to then"*: Ziegfeld and Ziegfeld, *Ziegfeld Touch,* 159.

577   *dodging process servers*: Mordden, *Ziegfeld,* 285.

578   *from mobsters*: Grant Hayter-Menzies, *Mrs. Ziegfeld: The Public and Private Lives of Billie Burke* (Jefferson, NC: McFarland, 2009), 130.

578   *propped up; "smile wan . . . his voice weak"*: Quoted in Ziegfeld and Ziegfeld, *Ziegfeld Touch,* 163.

578   *A. C. Blumenthal*: NYT, July 24, 1932.

578   *"Ziegfeld finally had a hit"*: Mordden, *Ziegfeld,* 290.

578   *"Would like to do"*: Ibid.

578   *"Doctor claims"*: Ziegfeld and Ziegfeld, *Ziegfeld Touch,* 166.

578   *ran up a telegraph bill*: Ibid.

578   *Television, he told Patty*: Ibid., 138.

578   *"The élan was gone"*: Burke, *Feather,* 223.

578   *cut off service*: Ziegfeld and Ziegfeld, *Ziegfeld Touch,* 167.

579   *a Broadway audience was rising*: NYT, July 23, 24, 1932. The cause of death: complications from an enlarged heart.

579   *reached them*: NYT, July 24, 1932; Hayter-Menzies, *Mrs. Ziegfeld,* 139.

579   *"Anything can happen now"*: Fitzgerald, *Great Gatsby,* 73.

579   *hired a private policeman*: NYT, July 24, 1932.

579   *"This seemed like"*: Quoted in Hayter-Menzies, *Mrs. Ziegfeld,* 141.

580   *cost Liveright nearly $100,000*: Liveright to Albert Wallerstein, June 5, 1929, HLP.

580   *"non-paying lodgers"*: Liveright to Charles Gordon, n.d., HLP.

580   *"to assist"*: *Chicago Tribune,* July 30, 1931.

580   *"Some of the old glamour"*: Hellman, *An Unfinished Woman,* 58.

580   *"As I held Dorothy"*: Horace Liveright, "The Turbulent Years," unpublished autobiography, Manuel Komroff Papers, Rare Book and Manuscript Library, Butler Library, Columbia University, New York, NY.

580   *"Moving to Forty-seventh Street"*: Kronenberger, "Gambler," 102.

581   *"tired and worn"; "Horace"*: Ibid., 104.

581 *"played . . . out his string"; "a heartbreaking farce"*: Cerf, "Horace Liveright: An Obituary—Unedited," 1230.

581 *They married . . . and divorced*: NYT, December 9, 1931, September 25, 1933.

581 *found him in his apartment*: Cerf, *At Random*, 78–79.

581 *suffering from emphysema*: NYT, January 30, 1933.

581 *Richard Simon bought*: Cerf, *At Random*, 80. Liveright's last days are chronicled in Manuel Komroff's unpublished essay, "The Liveright Story," in the Komroff Papers at Columbia University.

581 *"Horace was sitting"*: Anderson, *Memoirs*, 518–19.

582 *"If I get well"*: Liveright to E. J. Mayer, September 21, 1933, New York Public Library, for the Performing Arts, Billy Rose Theatre Division, New York, NY.

582 *"not worth more than"*: NYT, September 29, 1933.

582 *dead at forty nine*: Liveright claimed, on occasion, that he was born in 1886, not 1884.

582 *"the people"*: Cerf, "Horace Liveright: An Obituary—Unedited," 1229–30.

582 *"a deep love"; "madhouse"; "a publisher"*: Cerf, Oral History; Cerf, "Horace Liveright: An Obituary—Unedited," 1229–30.

582 *"It was all rather crazy"*: Anderson, *Memoirs*, 518.

582 *"a spectacular death"*: F. Scott Fitzgerald, "Echoes of the Jazz Age," in Wilson, ed., *Crack-Up*, 13.

582 *"bleary-eyed"*: Fitzgerald, "Crack-Up," in Wilson, ed., *Crack-Up*, 69–74.

582 *"self-autopsy"*: Glenway Wescott, "The Moral of Scott Fitzgerald," in Wilson, ed., *Crack-Up*, 327.

BIBLIOGRAPHY

Books

Adams, Thomas. *The Building of the City.* Vol. 2 of *Regional Plan of New York and Its Environs.* New York: Regional Plan of New York and Its Environs, 1931.

Agrest, Diana, ed. *A Romance with the City: Irwin S. Chanin.* New York: Cooper Union, 1982.

Aitken, Hugh G. H. *Sytony and Spark: The Origins of Radio.* Princeton: Princeton University Press, 1992.

Allen, Frederick Lewis. "New York City." In Vol. 5 of *Look at America.* Cambridge: Houghton, 1948.

———. *Only Yesterday: An Informal History of the 1920s.* New York: Harper & Brothers, 1931.

Allen, Oliver E. *The Tiger: The Rise and Fall of Tammany Hall.* Reading, MA: Addison-Wesley, 1993.

Altman, Billy. *Laughter's Gentle Soul: The Life of Robert Benchley.* New York: W. W. Norton, 1997.

Ammann, O. H. "An Engineer's Conception of the Proposed Hudson River Bridge." In *Othmar Hermann Ammann, 1879–1965: His Way to Great Bridges,* by Urs C. Widmer. n.p., 1978.

Amory, Cleveland, and Frederic Bradlee. *Cavalcade of the 1920s and 1930s.* London: Bodley Head, 1960.

Amory, Cleveland, and Frederic Bradlee, eds. "Three Americans." In *Vanity Fair: Selections from America's Most Memorable Magazine.* New York: Viking, 1960.

Anderson, Jervis. *This Was Harlem: A Cultural Portrait, 1900–1950.* New York: Farrar, Straus & Giroux, 1981.

Anderson, Sherwood. *Sherwood Anderson's Memoirs: A Critical Edition.* Edited by Ray Lewis White. Chapel Hill: University of North Carolina Press, 1969.

Andrews, Wayne. *The Vanderbilt Legend: The Story of the Vanderbilt Family, 1794–1940.* New York: Harcourt Brace, 1941.

Asbury, Herbert. *The Gangs of New York: An Informal History of the Underworld.* New York: Thunder's Mouth Press, 2001, originally published in 1928.

———. *The Great Illusion: An Informal History of Prohibition.* Garden City, NY: Doubleday, Doran, 1950.

Atkinson, Brooks. *Broadway.* New York: Macmillan, revised edition, 1974.

Auchincloss, Louis. *The Vanderbilt Era: Profiles of a Gilded Age.* New York: Charles Scribner's Sons, 1989.

Aycock, Colleen, and Mark Scott. *Tex Rickard: Boxing's Greatest Promoter.* Jefferson, NC: McFarland, 2012.

Baker, Carlos, ed. *Ernest Hemingway: Selected Letters, 1917–1961.* New York: Charles Scribner's Sons, 1981.

Ballon, Hilary. *New York's Pennsylvania Stations.* New York: W. W. Norton, 2002.

Ballon, Hilary, and Kenneth T. Jackson, eds. *Robert Moses and the Modern City: The Transformation of New York,* New York: W. W. Norton, 2007.

Banfield, Stephen. *Jerome Kern.* New Haven: Yale University Press, 2006.

Banning, William Peck. *Commercial Broadcasting Pioneer: The WEAF Experiment, 1922–1926.* Cambridge: Harvard University Press, 1946.

Bard, Erwin Wilkie. *The Port of New York Authority.* New York: AMS, 1968.

Barnes, Charles B. *The Longshoremen.* New York: Arno, 1977; originally published in 1915.

Barnouw, Erik. *The Golden Web: A History of Broadcasting in the United States, 1933–1953.* New York: Oxford University Press, 1968.

———. *A Tower in Babel: A History of Broadcasting in the United States to 1933.* New York: Oxford University Press, 1966.

———. *Tube of Plenty: The Evolution of American Television.* New York: Oxford University Press, 1975.

Bascomb, Neal. *Higher: A Historic Race to the Sky and the Making of a City.* New York: Broadway, 2004.

Bayor, Ronald H. *Neighbors in Conflict: The Irish, Germans, Jews, and Italians of New York City, 1929–1941.* Baltimore: Johns Hopkins University Press, 1978.

Bayor, Ronald H., and Timothy J. Meagher, eds. *The New York Irish.* Baltimore: Johns Hopkins University Press, 1996.

Beaton, Cecil. *Cecil Beaton's New York.* Philadelphia: J. B. Lippincott, 1938.

Beebe, Lucius. *20th Century: The Greatest Train in the World* Berkeley, CA: Howell-North Books, 1962.

Behr, Edward. *Prohibition: Thirteen Years That Changed America.* New York: Arcade, 1996.

Bell, Daniel. *The End of Ideology: On the Exhaustion of Political Ideas in the Fifties.* Glencoe, IL: Free Press, 1960.

Belle, John, and Maxinne R. Leighton. *Grand Central: Gateway to a Million Lives.* New York: W. W. Norton, 2000.

Bender, Thomas, and William R. Taylor. "Skyscraper and Skyline." In Thomas Bender, *The Unfinished City: New York and the Metropolitan Idea.* New York: New Press, 2002.

Bent, Silas. *Ballyhoo: The Voice of the Press.* NY: Boni & Liveright, 1927.

Berg, A. Scott. *Lindbergh.* New York: G. P. Putnam's Sons, 1998.

Berger, Meyer. *The Eight Million: Journal of a New York Correspondent.* New York: Columbia University Press, 1983.

———. *Meyer Berger's New York.* New York: Random House, 1960.

———. *The Story of the New York Times, 1851–1951.* New York: Simon & Schuster, 1951.

Bergreen, Laurence. *As Thousands Cheer: The Life of Irving Berlin.* New York: Da Capo, 1996; first published in 1990.

———. *Look Now, Pay Later: The Rise of Network Broadcasting.* Garden City, NY: Doubleday, Doran, 1980.

Berliner, Louise. *Texas Guinan: Queen of the Nightclubs.* Austin: University of Texas Press, 1993.

Berman, Marshall. *On the Town: One Hundred Years of Spectacle in Times Square.* New York: Random House, 2006.

Bernays, Edward L. *Biography of an Idea: Memoirs of Public Relations Counsel Edward L. Bernays.* New York: Simon & Schuster, 1965.

——. *Crystallizing Public Opinion*. New York: Boni & Liveright, 1923.

Bessie, Simon Michael. *Jazz Journalism: The Story of the Tabloid Newspapers*. New York: E. P. Dutton, 1938.

Bianco, Anthony. *Ghosts of 42nd Street: A History of New York's Most Infamous Block*. New York: William Morrow, 2004.

Bigard, Barney. *With Louis and the Duke: The Autobiography of a Jazz Clarinetist*, edited by Barry Martyn. New York: Oxford University Press, 1985.

Bilby, Kenneth. *The General: David Sarnoff and the Rise of the Communications Industry*. New York: Harper & Row, 1986.

Billington, David P. *The Tower and the Bridge: The New Art of Structural Engineering*. New York: Basic, 1983.

Bird, Frederick L. *A Study of the Port of New York Authority*. New York: Dun & Bradstreet, 1949.

Bishop, Jim. *The Mark Hellinger Story*. New York: Appleton-Century-Crofts, 1952.

Black, Mary C. *New York City's Gracie Mansion: A History of the Mayor's House*. New York: J. M. Kaplan Fund, 1984.

Block, Alan. *East Side–West Side: Organizing Crime in New York, 1930–1950*. New Brunswick, NJ: Transaction, 1983.

Block, Geoffrey. *Enchanted Evenings: The Broadway Musical from Show Boat to Sondheim*. New York: Oxford University Press, 1997.

Block, Henry Irving, and J. W. Golinkin. *New York Is Like This*. New York: Dodd, Mead, 1929.

Bloom, Ken. *The Routledge Guide to Broadway*. New York: Routledge, 2007.

——. *Broadway: Its History, People, and Places: An Encyclopedia*. 2nd ed. New York: Routledge, 2003.

Bonanno, Joseph, with Sergio Lalli. *A Man of Honor: The Autobiography of Joseph Bonanno*. New York: Simon & Schuster, 1983.

Bone, Kevin. *The New York Waterfront: Evolution and Building Culture of the Port and Harbor*. New York: Monacelli, 1997.

Bordman, Gerald. *Jerome Kern: His Life and Music*. New York: Oxford University Press, 1980.

Bossom, Alfred C. *Buildings to the Skies: The Romance of the Skyscraper*. London: The Studio, 1934.

Bourke-White, Margaret. *Portrait of Myself*. New York: Simon & Schuster, 1963.

Boyer, Paul S. *Purity in Print: The Vice-Society Movement and Book Censorship in America*. New York: Charles Scribner's Sons, 1968.

Brady, Frank. *The Publisher: Paul Block: A Life of Friendship, Power and Politics*. Lanham, MD: University Press of America, 2001.

Bragdon, Claude F. *The Frozen Fountain*. New York: Alfred A. Knopf, 1932.

Brands, H. W. *Masters of Enterprises: Giants of American Business from Jacob Astar and J. P. Margno to Bill Gates and Oprah Winfrey*. New York: Free Press, 1999.

Brandon, Ruth. *Ugly Beauty: Helena Rubinstein, L'Oréal, and the Blemished History of Looking Good*. New York: HarperCollins, 2011.

Brennan, Bill. *The Frank Costello Story: The True Story of the Underworld's Prime Minister*. Derby, CT: Monarch, 1962.

Breslin, Jimmy. *Damon Runyon*. New York: Ticknor & Fields, 1991.

Brinkley, Alan. *The Publisher: Henry Luce and His American Century.* New York: Vintage, 2010.

Brinkley, Douglas. *Wheels for the World: Henry Ford, His Company, and a Century of Progress, 1903–2003.* New York: Viking, 2003.

Brock, H. I., and J. W. Golinkin. *New York Is Like This.* New York: Dodd, Mead, 1929.

Brooks, John. *Once in Golconda.* New York: Harper & Row, 1969.

Brooks, Louise. *Lulu in Hollywood.* New York: Alfred A. Knopf, 1982.

Bruccoli, Matthew J. *Some Sort of Epic Grandeur: The Life of F. Scott Fitzgerald.* New York: Harcourt, 1981.

Bruccoli, Matthew J., ed. *F. Scott Fitzgerald: A Life in Letters.* New York: Charles Scribner's Sons, 1994.

Bruccoli, Matthew J., and Margaret M. Dugan. *Correspondence of F. Scott Fitzgerald.* New York: Random House, 1980.

Bunker, John G. *Harbor & Haven.* Woodland Hills, CA: Windsor, 1979.

Burke, Billie. *With a Feather on My Nose.* New York: Appleton-Century-Crofts, 1949.

Burlingame, Roger. *Machines That Built America.* New York: Harcourt, 1953.

Burner, David. *The Politics of Provincialism: The Democratic Party in Transition, 1918–1932.* New York: Alfred A. Knopf, 1968.

Busch, Niven Jr. *Twenty-one Americans: Being Profiles of Some People Famous in Our Time.* Garden City, NY: Doubleday, Doran, 1930.

Butler, Richard J., and Joseph Driscoll. *Dock Walloper: The Story of "Big Dick" Butler.* New York: G. P. Putnam's Sons, 1933.

Buttenweiser, Ann L. *Manhattan Water-Bound: Planning and Developing Manhattan's Waterfront from the Seventeenth Century to the Present.* New York: New York University Press, 1987.

Caldwell, Mark. *New York Night: The Mystique and Its History.* New York: Charles Scribner's Sons, 2005.

Calloway, Cab, and Bryant Rollins. *Of Minnie the Moocher and Me.* New York: Thomas Y. Crowell, 1976.

Campbell, Robert. *The Golden Years of Broadcasting.* New York: Charles Scribner's Sons, 1976.

Cannadine, David. *Mellon: An American Life.* New York: Alfred A. Knopf, 2006.

Cantor, Eddie, and David Freedman. *Ziegfeld: The Great Glorifier.* New York: Alfred H. King, 1934.

Caro, Robert A. *The Power Broker: Robert Moses and the Fall of New York.* New York: Vintage, 1975, originally published in 1974 by Knopf.

Carse, Robert. *Rum Row: The Liquor Fleet That Fueled the Roaring Twenties.* Mystic, CT: Flat Hammock, 2007.

Carter, Randolph. *The World of Flo Ziegfeld.* New York: Praeger, 1974.

Carter, Warrick L. "Edward Kennedy Ellington." In *Dictionary of American Biography* Supplement 9, 1971–75. Edited by Kenneth T. Jackson. New York: Charles Scribner's Sons, 1994.

Cartwright, Otho G. *West Side Studies: The Middle West Side, A Historical Sketch.* New York: Russell Sage Foundation, 1914.

Cashman, Sean Dennis. *Prohibition: The Lie of the Land.* New York: Free Press, 1981.

Cavanaugh, Jack. *Tunney: Boxing's Brainiest Champ and His Upset of the Great Jack Dempsey.* New York: Random House, 2006.

Cerf, Bennett. *At Random: The Reminiscences of Bennett Cerf.* New York: Random House, 1977.

Chandler, Charlotte. *She Always Knew How: Mae West, A Personal Biography.* New York: Simon & Schuster, 2009.

Chanin Building Brochure. New York Public Library.

Chapman, John. *Tell It to Sweeney: The Informal History of the New York Daily News.* Garden City, NY: Doubleday, Doran, 1961.

Charters, Samuel B., and Leonard Kunstadt. *Jazz: A History of the New York Scene.* New York: Da Capo, 1981; originally published in 1962.

Charyn, Jerome. *Gangsters and Gold Diggers: Old New York, the Jazz Age, and the Birth of Broadway.* New York: Thunder's Mouth Press, 2003.

Chase, W. Parker. *New York: The Wonder City.* New York: Wonder City Publishing, 1931.

Chauncey, George. *Gay New York: Gender, Urban Culture, and the Making of the Gay Male World, 1890–1940.* New York: Basic, 1994.

Cheney, Sheldon. *The New World Architecture.* New York: AMS, 1930.

Chesterton, G. K. *What I Saw in America.* New York: Dodd, Mead, 1922.

Chinitz, Benjamin. *Freight and the Metropolis: The Impact of America's Transport Revolutions on the New York Region.* Cambridge: Harvard University Press, 1960.

Chrysler Tower Corporation. *The Chrysler Building.* New York: Chrysler Tower Corp.

Chrysler, Walter P. *Life of an American Workman.* New York: Dodd, Mead, 1937.

Churchill, Allen. *The Great White Way.* New York: Dutton, 1962.

——. *The Upper Crust: An Informal History of New York's Highest Society.* Englewood Cliffs, NJ: Prentice Hall, 1970.

Ciucci, Giorgio, and Manfredo Tafuri. *The American City: From the Civil War to the New Deal.* Cambridge: MIT Press, 1979.

Clark, Norman H. *Deliver Us from Evil: An Interpretation of American Prohibition.* New York: W. W. Norton, 1976.

Clark, Tom. *The World of Damon Runyon.* New York: Harper & Row, 1978.

Clarke, Donald Henderson. *In the Reign of Rothstein.* New York: Grosset & Dunlap, 1929.

Clary, Martin. *Mid-Manhattan.* New York: Forty-second Street Property Owners and Merchants Association, 1929.

Cochran, Thomas C. "Walter Percy Chrysler." In *Dictionary of American Biography.* Vol. 22, Supplement 2. New York: Charles Scribner's Sons, 1955.

Cohen, Harvey G. *Duke Ellington's America.* Chicago: University of Chicago Press, 2010.

Cohen, Julius Henry. *They Builded Better than They Knew.* New York: J. Messner, 1946.

Cohen, Miriam. *Workshop to Office: Two Generations of Italian Women in New York City, 1900–1950.* Ithaca, NY: Cornell University Press, 1992.

Collier, James Lincoln. *Duke Ellington.* New York: Oxford University Press, 1987.

Collins, F. A. *The Romance of Park Avenue.* New York: Park Avenue Association, 1930.

Collins, Theresa M. *Otto Kahn: Art, Money and Modern Time.* Chapel Hill: University of North Carolina Press, 2002.

Committee on the Regional Plan of New York and Its Environs. *Buildings: Their Uses and the Spaces About Them.* Vol. 6 of the *Regional Survey of New York and Its Environs.* New York: Regional Plan of New York and Its Environs, 1931.

Condit, Carl W. *The Port of New York: A History of the Rail and Terminal System from the Grand Central Electrification to the Present.* Vol. 2 of *The Port of New York.* Chicago: University of Chicago Press, 1981.

Conklin, William R. "Manhattan Machine." In *We Saw It Happen: The News Behind the News That's Fit to Print; Thirteen Correspondents of the New York Times,* edited by Hanson W. Baldwin and Shepard Stone. New York: Simon & Schuster, 1938.

Connable, Alfred, and Edward Silberfarb. *Tigers of Tammany: Nine Men Who Ran New York.* New York: Holt, Rinehart & Winston, 1967.

Connor, Matthew R. "Lois Long." In Vol. 13 of *American National Biography,* edited by John A. Garraty and Mark C. Carnes. New York: Oxford University Press, 1999.

Cozens, Frederick W., and Florence Scovil Stumpf. "The Sports Page." In *Sport and Society: An Anthology,* edited by John T. Talamini and Charles O. Page. Boston: Little, Brown, 1973.

Creamer, Robert W. *Babe: The Legend Comes to Life.* New York: Simon & Schuster, 1992.

Crepeau, Richard C. *Baseball: America's Diamond Mind, 1919–1941.* Lincoln: University of Nebraska Press, 1980.

Cressey, Donald R. *Criminal Organization: Its Elementary Forms.* New York: Harper & Row, 1972.

Critchley, David. *The Origin of Organized Crime in America: The New York City Mafia, 1891–1931.* New York: Routledge, 2009.

Cudahy, Brian J. *The New York Subway.* New York: Fordham University Press, 1991.

Curcio, Vincent. *Chrysler: The Life and Times of an Automotive Genius.* New York: Oxford University Press, 2000.

Czitrom, Daniel J. *Media and the American Mind: From Morse to McLuhan.* Chapel Hill: University of North Carolina Press, 1982.

Dale, Rebecca M., ed. *E. B. White: Writings from The New Yorker, 1927–1976.* New York: HarperCollins, 1990.

Daley, Robert. *The World Beneath the City.* Philadelphia: J. B. Lippincott, 1959.

Dance, Stanley. *The World of Duke Ellington.* New York: Charles Scribner's Sons, 1970.

Danzig, Allison, and Peter Brandwein, eds. *Sport's Golden Age: A Close-up of the Fabulous Twenties.* New York: Harper & Brothers, 1948.

Dardis, Tom. *Firebrand: The Life of Horace Liveright.* New York: Random House, 1995.

Dash, Mike. *The First Family: Terror, Extortion, Murder, and the Birth of the American Mafia.* New York: Random House, 2009.

Davenport, Donald H., with Lawrence M. Orton and Ralph W. Roby. *The Retail Shopping and Financial Districts in New York and Its Environs.* New York: Regional Plan of New York and Its Environs, 1927.

Davis, Kenneth Sydney. *The Hero: Charles A. Lindbergh and the American Dream.* Garden City, NY: Doubleday, Doran, 1959.

Dawson, James P. "Boxing." In *Sport's Golden Age: A Close-up of the Fabulous Twenties,* edited by Allison Danzig and Peter Brandwein. New York: Harper & Brothers, 1948.

DeLillo, Don. *Underworld.* New York: Charles Scribner's Sons, 1997.

Dempsey, Jack. *Jack Dempsey: By the Man Himself.* New York: Simon & Schuster, 1960.

Dempsey, Jack, with Barbara Piattelli Dempsey. *Dempsey.* New York: Harper & Row, 1977.

Doig, Jameson W. *Empire on the Hudson: Entrepreneurial Vision and Political Power at the Port of New York Authority.* New York: Columbia University Press, 2001.

———. "Politics and the Engineering Mind: O. H. Ammann and the Hidden Story of the George Washington Bridge." In *Building the Public City: The Politics, Governance, and Finance of Public Infrastructure,* edited by David C. Perry. Thousand Oaks, CA: Sage, 1995.

Dos Passos, John. *The Best Times: An Informal Memoir.* New York: New American Library, 1966.

Douglas, Ann. *Terrible Honesty: Mongrel Manhattan in the 1920s.* New York: Farrar, Straus & Giroux, 1995.

Douglas, George H. *The Early Days of Radio Broadcasting.* Jefferson, NC: McFarland, 1987.

Douglas, Susan J. *Listening In: Radio and the American Imagination.* New York: Times Books, 1999.

Drachman, Virginia G. *Enterprising Women: 250 Years of American Business.* Chapel Hill: University of North Carolina Press, 2002.

Dreher, Carl. *Sarnoff: An American Success.* New York: Quadrangle, 1977.

Dreiser, Theodore. *The Color of a Great City.* New York: Boni & Liveright, 1923.

———. *My City.* New York: Boni & Liveright, 1929.

Duffus, R. L. *Mastering the Metropolis: Planning the Future of the New York Region.* New York: Harper & Brothers, 1930.

Duffy, Francis J., and William H. Miller. *The New York Harbor Book.* Falmouth, ME: TBW Books, 1986.

Dunlap, David W. *On Broadway: A Journey Uptown over Time.* New York: Rizzoli, 1990.

Durante, Jimmy, and Jack Kofoed. *Night Clubs.* New York: Alfred A. Knopf, 1931.

Durso, Joseph. *Madison Square Garden: 100 Years of History.* New York: Simon & Schuster, 1979.

———. *Yankee Stadium: Fifty Years of Drama.* Boston: Houghton, 1972.

Eberly, Philip K. *Music in the Air: America's Changing Tastes in Popular Music, 1920–1980.* New York: Hastings House, 1982.

Eig, Johnathan. *Luckiest Man: The Life and Death of Lou Gehrig.* New York: Simon & Schuster, 2006 edition, originally published in 2005.

Einstein, Izzy. *Prohibition Agent No. 1.* New York: Stokes, 1932.

Eliot, Marc. *Down 42nd Street: Sex, Money, Culture, and Politics at the Crossroads of the World.* New York: Warner, 2001.

Elledge, Scott. *E.B. White: A Biography.* New York: W. W. Norton, 1984.

Ellington, Edward Kennedy. *Music Is My Mistress.* Garden City, NY: Doubleday, 1973.

Ellington, Mercer, with Stanley Dance. *Duke Ellington in Person: An Intimate Memoir.* Boston: Houghton Mifflin, 1978.

English, T. J. *Paddy Whacked: The Untold Story of the Irish American Gangster.* New York: Regan, 2005.

Erenburg, Lewis A. *Steppin' Out: New York Nightlife and the Transformation of American Culture, 1890–1930.* Westport, CT: Greenwood, 1981.

Erie, Steven P. *Rainbow's End: Irish-Americans and the Dilemmas of Urban Machine Politics, 1840–1985.* Berkeley: University of California Press, 1988.

Ernst, Robert. *Weakness Is a Crime: The Life of Bernarr Macfadden.* Syracuse, NY: Syracuse University Press, 1991.

Evensen, Bruce J. *When Dempsey Fought Tunney: Heroes, Hokum, and Storytelling in the Jazz Age.* Knoxville: University of Tennessee Press, 1996.

Fabe, Maxene. *Beauty Millionaire: The Life of Helena Rubinstein.* New York: Thomas Y. Crowell, 1972.

Faber, Doris. *Printer's Devil to Publisher: Adolph S. Ochs of The New York Times.* New York: Messner, 1963.

Farley, James A. *Behind the Ballots: The Personal History of a Politician.* New York: Harcourt Brace, 1972.

Farnsworth, Marjorie. *The Ziegfeld Follies.* London: Peter Davies, 1956.

Fass, Paula S. *The Damned and the Beautiful: American Youth in the 1920's.* New York: Oxford University Press, 1977.

Federal Writers Project. *New York Panorama: A Companion to the WPA Guide to New York City.* New York: Pantheon, 1989; originally published in 1938.

———. *The WPA Guide to New York City: The Federal Writers' Project Guide to 1930s New York.* New York: Pantheon, 1982; originally published in 1939.

Ferber, Edna. *A Peculiar Treasure.* New York: Doubleday, Doran, 1939.

Ferber, Nat. *I Found Out: A Confidential Chronicle of the Twenties.* New York: Dial, 1939.

Ferriss, Hugh. *The Metropolis of Tomorrow.* Princeton: Princeton Architectural Press, 1986.

———. *Power in Buildings: An Artist's View of Contemporary Architecture.* New York: Columbia University Press, 1953.

Finney, Ben. *Feet First.* New York: Crown, 1971.

Fischer, Rudolph. "The Caucasian Storms Harlem." In *The Portable Harlem Renaissance Reader,* edited by David Levering Lewis. New York: Penguin edition, 1995.

Fishman, Robert. "The Metropolitan Tradition in American Planning," in Robert Fishman, ed., *The American Planning Tradition: Culture and Policy.* Washington, DC: Woodrow Wilson Center Press, 2000.

———. "The Regional Plan and the Transformation of the Industrial Metropolis." In *The Landscape of Modernity: Essays on New York City, 1900–1940,* edited by David Ward and Olivier Zunz. New York: Russell Sage Foundation, 1992.

Fishman, Robert, ed. *The American Planning Tradition: Culture and Policy.* Washington, DC: Woodrow Wilson Center Press, 2000.

Fitch, James Marston, and Diana S. Waite. *Grand Central Terminal and Rockefeller Center: A Historic-critical Estimate of Their Significance.* NY: New York State Parks and Recreation, Division for Historic Preservation, 1974.

Fitzgerald, F. Scott. "The Crack-Up." In *The Crack-Up,* edited by Edmund Wilson. New York: New Directions, 1993 edition.

———. "Early Success." In *The Crack-Up,* edited by Edmund Wilson. New York: New Directions, 1993 edition.

———. *The Great Gatsby.* New York: Charles Scribner's Sons, 1925.

Fitzgerald, Zelda. "The Changing Beauty of Park Avenue." In *Zelda Fitzgerald: The Collected Writings,* edited by Matthew J. Bruccoli. New York: Charles Scribner's Sons, 1991.

Fleischer, Nat. *Jack Dempsey: The Idol of Fistiana.* New York: C. J. O'Brien, 1929.

Flynn, Edward J. *You're the Boss.* New York: Viking, 1947.

Footner, Hulbert. *New York: City of Cities.* New York: J. B. Lippincott, 1937.

Ford, Ford Madox. *New York Is Not America.* New York: Boni & Liveright, 1927.

Fordin, Hugh. *Getting to Know Him: A Biography of Oscar Hammerstein II.* New York: Random House, 1977.

Fowler, Gene. *Beau James: The Life and Times of Jimmy Walker.* New York: Viking, 1949.

———. *The Great Mouthpiece: A Life Story of William J. Fallon.* New York: Grosset, 1931.

———. *Skyline: A Reporter's Reminiscence of the 1920s.* New York: Viking, 1961.

Fraser, Kennedy. *Ornament and Silence: Essays on Women's Lives.* New York: Alfred A. Knopf, 1996.

Frayne, Trent. *The Mad Men of Hockey.* New York: Dodd Mead, 1924.

Freilich, Morris, ed. *Marginal Natives at Work: Anthropologists in the Field.* New York: Schenkman, 1977.

French, Fred. *The Real Estate Investment of the Future.* New York: Fred F. French Investing Co., 1927.

French, John W., and Fred F. French. *A Vigorous Life: The Story of Fred F. French, Builder of Skyscrapers.* New York: Vantage, 1993.

Friede, Donald. *The Mechanical Angel: His Adventures and Enterprises in the Glittering 1920s.* New York: Alfred A. Knopf, 1948.

Fuller, Hector. *Abroad with Mayor Walker.* New York: Shields, 1928.

Gabler, Neal. *An Empire of Their Own: How the Jews Invented Hollywood.* New York: Crown, 1988.

———. *Winchell: Gossip, Power, and the Culture of Celebrity.* New York: Vintage, 1995, originally published in 1994.

Gaines, Steven. *The Sky's the Limit: Passion and Property in Manhattan.* New York: Back Bay, 2005.

Gallico, Paul. *Confessions of a Story Writer.* New York: Alfred A. Knopf, 1946.

———. *Farewell to Sport.* New York: Alfred A. Knopf, 1970.

———. *The Golden People.* Garden City, NY: Doubleday, Doran, 1965.

———. *Lou Gehrig: Pride of the Yankees.* New York: Grosset & Dunlap, 1942.

Garrett, Charles. *The La Guardia Years: Machine and Reform Politics in New York City.* New Brunswick, NJ: Rutgers University Press, 1961.

Gauvereau, Emile Henry. *My Last Million Readers.* New York: Dutton, 1941.

George, Carol V. R., ed., *"Remember the Ladies": New Perspectives on Women in American History.* Syracuse, NY: Syracuse University Press, 1975.

Gildea, William. *The Longest Fight: In the Ring with Joe Gans, Boxing's First African American Champion.* New York: Farrar, Straus & Geroux, 2012.

Gill, Brendan. *Here At the New Yorker.* New York: Random House, 1975.

Gill, Jonathan. *Harlem: The Four Hundred Year History from Dutch Village to Capital of Black America.* New York: Grove, 2011.

Gillespie, Angus Kress. *Crossing Under the Hudson: The Story of the Holland and Lincoln Tunnels.* New Brunswick, NJ: Rutgers University Press, 2011.

Gilmartin, Gregory F. *Shaping the City: New York and the Municipal Art Society.* New York: Clarkson N. Potter, 1995.

Gioia, Ted. *The History of Jazz.* New York: Oxford University Press, 1997.

Goldberg, Vicki. *Margaret Bourke-White: A Biography.* New York: Harper & Row, 1987.

Goldberger, Paul. *The Skyscraper.* New York: Alfred A. Knopf, 1982.

Golden, Eve. *Anna Held and the Birth of Ziegfeld's Broadway.* Lexington: University of Kentucky Press, 2000.

Goldmark, Pauline, ed. *West Side Studies: Boyhood and Lawlessness.* New York: Russell Sage Foundation, 1914.

Gordon, John Steele. *An Empire of Wealth: The Epic History of American Economic Power.* New York: Harper & Row, 2004.

Graff, Henry F. "Jacob Ruppert." In *Dictionary of American Biography.* Vol. 22. New York: Charles Scribner's Sons, 1955.

Graham, Frank. *Al Smith, American: An Informal Biography.* New York: G. P. Putnam's Sons, 1945.

——. *The New York Yankees: An Informal History.* New York: G. P. Putnam's Sons, 1943.

Graham, Stephen. *New York Nights.* New York: George H. Doran, 1927.

Granick, Harry. *Underneath New York.* New York: Fordham University Press, 1947.

Granlund, Nils Thor. *Blondes, Brunettes, and Bullets.* New York: David McKay, 1957.

Grauer, Neil A. *Remember Laughter: A Life of James Thurber.* Lincoln: University of Nebraska Press, 1994.

Gray, Carl C. *The Eighth Wonder.* Hyde Park, NY: B. F. Sturtevant, 1927.

Gray, Christopher. *New York Streetscapes: Tales of Manhattan's Significant Buildings and Landmarks.* New York: Harry N. Abrams, 2003.

Green, Nancy L. "From Downtown Tenements to Midtown Lofts." In *A Coat of Many Colors: Immigration, Globalization, and Reform in the New York City Garment Industry,* edited by Daniel Soyer. New York: Fordham University Press, 2005.

——. *Ready-to-Wear: A Century of Industry and Immigrants in Paris and New York.* Durham, NC: Duke University Press, 1997.

——. "Sweatshop Migrations: The Garment Industry Between Home and Shop." In *The Landscape of Modernity: Essays on New York City, 1900–1940,* edited by David Ward and Olivier Zunz. New York: Russell Sage Foundation, 1992.

Gribetz, Louis J., and Joseph Kaye. *Jimmie Walker: The Story of a Personality.* New York: Dial, 1932.

Gustafson, W. Eric. "Printing and Publishing." In *Made in New York: Case Studies in Metropolitan Manufacturing,* edited by Max Hall. Cambridge: Harvard University Press, 1959.

Gutfreund, Owen D. "Rebuilding New York in the Auto Age: Robert Moses and His Highways." In *Robert Moses and the Modern City: The Transformation of New York,* edited by Hilary Ballon and Kenneth T. Jackson. New York: W. W. Norton, 2007.

Guth, Dorothy Lobrano. *Letters of E. B. White.* New York: Harper & Row, 1951.

Haig, Robert Murray. *Major Economic Factors in Metropolitan Growth and Arrangement: A Study of Trends and Tendencies in the Economic Activities Within the Region of New York and Its Environs.* Vol. 1 of *Regional Survey of New York and Its Environs.* New York: Regional Plan of New York and Its Environs, 1927.

Halberstam, David. *The Powers That Be.* New York: Alfred A. Knopf, 1979.

Hall, Ben M. *The Best Remaining Seats: The Story of the Golden Age of the Movie Palace.* New York: Clarkson N. Potter, 1961.

Hall, Peter. *Cities of Tomorrow: An Intellectual History of Urban Planning and Design in the Twentieth Century.* New York: Basil Blackwell, 1988.

Haller, Mark H. "Bootleggers as Businessmen: From City Slums to City Builders." In *Law, Alcohol and Order: Perspectives on National Prohibition,* edited by David E. Kyvig. Westport, CT: Greenwood, 1985.

Hamlin, Talbot. *Architecture Through the Ages.* New York: G. P. Putnam's Sons, 1953.

Hampton, Benjamin B. *History of the American Film Industry: From Its Beginnings to 1931.* New York: Dover, 1970 edition; originally published in 1931 under the title *A History of the Movies.*

Hanson, Nils. *Lillian Lorraine, The Life and Times of a Ziegfeld Diva.* Jefferson, NC: McFarland, 2011.

Hanson, Ron. *A Wild Surge of Guilty Passion.* New York: Scribner, 2011.

Hapgood, Norman, and Henry Moskowitz. *Up from the City Streets: Alfred E. Smith, a Biographical Study in Contemporary Politics.* New York: Grosset & Dunlap, 1927.

Harper, William. *How You Played the Game: The Life of Grantland Rice.* Columbia: University of Missouri Press, 1999.

Harriman, Margaret Case. *The Vicious Circle: The Story of the Algonquin Round Table.* New York: Rinehart, 1951.

Harris, Leon. *Merchant Princes.* New York: Harper & Row, 1977.

Harvey, Carol P. "Elizabeth Arden." In Vol. 1 of *Great Lives from History: American Women Series,* edited by Frank N. Magill. Pasadena CA: Salem, 1995.

Haskins, Jim. *The Cotton Club.* New York: Random House, 1977.

Hasse, John Edward. *Beyond Category: The Life and Genius of Duke Ellington.* New York: Simon & Schuster, 1995.

Hawes, Elizabeth. *New York, New York: How the Apartment House Transformed the Life of the City, 1869–1930.* New York: Alfred A. Knopf, 1993.

Hays, Arthur Garfied. *City Lawyer: The Autobiography of a Law Practice.* New York: Simon & Schuster, 1942.

Hayter-Menzies, Grant. *Mrs. Ziegfeld: The Public and Private Lives of Billie Burke.* Jefferson, NC: McFarland, 2009.

Heimer, Mel. *The Long Count.* New York: Atheneum, 1969.

Helfgott, Roy B. "Women's and Children's Apparel." In *Made in New York; Case Studies in Metropolitan Manufacturing,* edited by Max Hall. Cambridge: Harvard University Press, 1959.

"Helena Rubinstein." In *European Immigrant Women in the United States: A Biographical Dictionary.* New York: Garland, 1994.

Heller, Peter. *"In This Corner . . . !": Fifty World Champions Tell Their Stories.* New York: Simon & Schuster, 1973.

Hellman, Lillian. *An Unfinished Woman: A Memoir.* Boston: Little, Brown, 1969.

Henderson, Mary C. *The City and the Theatre.* New York: Back Stage, 2004.

Herndon, Booton. *Bergdorf's on the Plaza: The Story of Bergdorf Goodman and a Half-Century of American Fashion.* New York: Alfred A. Knopf, 1956.

Herrick, Myron. Foreword to *"We,"* by Charles A. Lindbergh. New York: G. P. Putnam's Sons, 1928.

Higham, Charles. *Ziegfeld.* Chicago: Henry Regnery, 1972.

Hill, Richard. *Skywalkers: A History of Indian Ironworkers.* Brantford, Ontario: Woodland Indian Cultural Educational Centre, 1987.

Hilmes, Michele. *Hollywood and Broadcasting from Radio to Cable.* Urbana: University of Illinois Press, 1990.

———. *Radio Voices: American Broadcasting, 1922–1952.* Minneapolis: University of Minnesota Press, 1997.

Holli, Melvin G., and Peter d'A. Jones, eds. *Biographical Dictionary of American Mayors, 1820–1980: Big City Mayors.* Westport, CT: Greenwood, 1981.

Holtzman, Jerome. *Jerome Holtzman on Baseball: A History of Baseball Scribes.* Champaign, IL: Sports Publishing, 2005.

Holtzman, Jerome, ed. *No Cheering in the Press Box.* New York: Holt, Rinehart & Winston, 1974.

Homberger, Eric. *The Historical Atlas of New York City: A Visual Celebration of 400 Years of New York City's History.* New York: Henry Holt, 1994.

Hood, Clifton. *722 Miles: The Building of the Subways and How They Transformed New York.* New York: Simon & Schuster, 1993.

Hood, Raymond M. *Contemporary American Architects*. New York: Whittlesey House, 1931.

Hoopes, Roy. *Ralph Ingersoll: A Biography*. New York: Atheneum, 1985.

Hoover, Edgar Malone, and Raymond Vernon. *Anatomy of a Metropolis*. Cambridge: Harvard University Press, 1959.

Horowitz, Louis J., and Boyden Sparkes. *The Towers of New York: The Memoirs of a Master Builder*. New York: Simon & Schuster, 1937.

Hoyt, Edwin P. *Alexander Woollcott: The Man Who Came to Dinner*. London: Abelard-Schuman, 1968.

———. *The Vanderbilts and Their Fortunes*. Garden City, NY: Doubleday, Doran, 1962.

Hudson, Robert V. *The Writing Game: A Biography of Will Irwin*. Ames: Iowa State University Press, 1982.

Hungerford, Edward. *Men and Iron: The History of New York Central*. New York: Thomas Y. Crowell, 1938.

Huthmacher, Joseph J. *Senator Robert F. Wagner and the Rise of Urban Liberalism*. New York: Atheneum, 1971.

Hylan, John F. *Autobiography of John Francis Hylan: Mayor of New York*. New York: Rotary, 1922.

Ianni, Francis A. *A Family Business: Kinship and Social Control in Organized Crime*. New York: Russell Sage Foundation, 1972.

Inabinett, Mark. *Grantland Rice and His Heroes: The Sportswriter as Mythmaker in the 1920s*. Knoxville: University of Tennessee Press, 1994.

Irwin, Will. *Highlights of Manhattan*. New York: D. Appleton-Century-Crofts, 1937 Revised Edition; originally published in 1927.

Jackson, Kenneth T. *Crabgrass Frontier: The Suburbanization of the United States*. New York: Oxford University Press, 1985.

Jackson, Kenneth T. Foreword to *Empire on the Hudson: Entrepreneurial Vision and Political Power at the Port of New York Authority*, by Jameson W. Doig. New York: Columbia University Press, 2001.

Jackson, Kenneth T., ed. *The Encyclopedia of New York City*. New Haven: Yale University Press, 1995.

Jackson, Kenneth T., and David S. Dunbar, eds. *Empire City: New York Through the Centuries*. New York: Columbia University Press, 2002.

Jackson, Robert W. *Highway Under the Hudson: A History of the Holland Tunnel*. New York: New York University Press, 2011.

Jacobs, Jane. *The Death and Life of Great American Cities*. New York: Vintage, 1992; originally published by Random House, 1961.

———. *The Economy of Cities*. New York: Vintage, 1970.

Jaher, Frederic Cople. *The Urban Establishment: Upper Strata in Boston, New York, Charleston, Chicago and Los Angeles*. Urbana: Illinois University Press, 1982.

Jensen, Vernon H. *Strife on the Waterfront: The Port of New York Since 1945*. Ithaca, NY: Cornell University Press, 1974.

Johnson, David A. *The Emergence of Metropolitan Regionalism: An Analysis of the Regional Plan of New York and Its Environs*. Ithaca, NY: Cornell University Press, 1974.

———. *Planning the Great Metropolis: The 1929 Regional Plan of New York and Its Environs*. London: E & FN Spon, 1996.

Johnson, Malcolm. *Crime on the Labor Front*. New York: McGraw-Hill, 1950.

Jones, Pamela. *Under the City Streets*. New York: Henry Holt, 1978.

Jonnes, Jill. *Conquering Gotham: Building Penn Station and Its Tunnels.* New York: Penguin, 2008.

———. *Hep-Cats, Narcs, and Pipe-Dreams: A History of America's Romance with Illegal Drugs.* New York: Charles Scribner's Sons, 1996.

Joselit, Jenna Weissman. *Our Gang: Jewish Crime and the New York Jewish Community, 1900–1940.* Bloomington: Indiana University Press, 1983.

Kahn, E. J. Jr., *The World of Swope.* New York: Simon & Schuster, 1965.

Kahn, Ely Jacques. *Contemporary American Architects: Ely Jacques Kahn.* New York: Whittlesey House, 1931.

Kahn, Roger. *A Flame of Pure Fire: Jack Dempsey and the Roaring '20s.* Orlando FL: Harcourt/Harvest, 1999.

Katcher, Leo. *The Big Bankroll: The Life and Times of Arnold Rothstein.* New York: Da Capo, 1994; originally published in 1959.

Katz, Leonard. *Uncle Frank: The Biography of Frank Costello.* New York: Drake, 1973.

Kaufmann, Edgar, and Ben Raeburn, eds. *Frank Lloyd Wright: Writings and Buildings.* New York: World, 1960.

Kaytor, Marilyn. *"21": The Life and Times of New York's Favorite Club.* New York: Viking, 1975.

Keats, John. *You Might As Well Live: The Life and Times of Dorothy Parker.* New York: Simon & Schuster, 1970.

Keeler, Robert. *Newsday: A Candid History of the Respectable Tabloid.* New York: William Morrow, 1997.

Kellner, Bruce. *Carl Van Vechten and the Irreverant Decades.* Norman: University of Oklahoma Press, 1968.

Kelly, Thomas. *Empire Rising.* New York: Farrar, Straus & Giroux, 2005.

Kessler-Harris, Alice. *Out to Work: A History of Wage-Earning Women in the United States.* New York: Oxford University Press, 1982.

Kessner, Thomas. *Fiorello La Guardia and the Making of Modern New York.* New York: McGraw-Hill, 1989.

Kieran, John. *A Natural History of New York City.* Boston: Houghton, 1959.

Kilham, Walter H. Jr., *Raymond Hood, Architect: Form Through Function in the American Skyscraper.* New York: Architectural Book Publishing, 1973.

Kinney, Harrison. *James Thurber: His Life and Times.* New York: Henry Holt, 1995.

Kirshner, Ralph. "Bennett Alfred Cerf." In *Dictionary of American Biography.* Supplement 9, 1971–75, edited by Kenneth T. Jackson. New York: Charles Scribner's Sons, 1994.

Kisseloff, Jeff. *You Must Remember This: An Oral History of Manhattan from the 1890s to World War II.* New York: Harcourt Brace Jovanovich 1989.

Klein, Alexander, ed. *The Empire City: A Treasury of New York.* New York: Rinehart, 1955.

Klurfeld, Herman. *Winchell: His Life and Times.* New York: Praeger, 1976.

Knopf, Alfred A. *Publishing Then and Now, 1912–1964.* New York: New York Public Library, 1964.

Kobler, John. *Ardent Spirits: The Rise and Fall of Prohibition.* New York: G. P. Putnam's Sons, 1973.

———. *Luce: His Time, Life, and Fortune.* New York: Doubleday, Doran, 1968.

———. *Otto the Magnificent: The Life of Otto Kahn.* New York: Charles Scribner's Sons, 1989.

———. *The Trial of Ruth Snyder and Judd Gray.* Garden City, NY: Doubleday, Doran, 1938.

Koehn, Nancy F. *Brand New: How Entrepreneurs Earned Consumer's Trust from Wedgwood to Dell.* Boston: Harvard Business School Press, 2001.

Koolhaas, Rem. *Delirious New York: A Retroactive Manifesto for Manhattan.* New York: Monacelli, 1994.

Korda, Michael. *Another Life: A Memoir of Other People.* New York: Random House, 2000.

Koszarski, Richard. *The Astoria Studio and Its Fabulous Films.* New York: Dover, 1983.

Kramer, Dale. *Ross and The New Yorker.* Garden City: Doubleday, Doran, 1951.

Kramer, Frederick A. *Building the Independent Subway.* New York: Quadrant, 1990.

Kreuger, Miles. *Show Boat: The Story of a Classic American Musical.* New York: Oxford University Press, 1977.

Kriendler, H. Peter, with H. Paul Jeffers. *"21": Every Day Was New Year's Eve: Memoirs of a Saloon Keeper.* Dallas: Taylor, 1999.

Krismann, Carol H. *Encyclopedia of American Women in Business.* Vol. 1. Westport, CT: Greenwood, 2005.

Kunkel, Thomas. *Genius in Disguise: Harold Ross of The New Yorker.* New York: Carroll & Graf, 1995.

Kurlansky, Mark. *The Big Oyster: History on the Half Shell.* New York: Ballantine, 2006.

Kyvig, David E. "Sober Thoughts: Myths and Realities of National Prohibition After Fifty Years." In *Law, Alcohol and Order: Perspectives on National Prohibition,* edited by David E. Kyvig. Westport, CT: Greenwood, 1985.

Kyvig, David E., ed. *Law, Alcohol and Order: Perspectives on National Prohibition.* Westport, CT: Greenwood, 1985.

Lacey, Robert. *Ford: The Men and the Machine.* Boston: Little, Brown, 1986.

———. *Little Man: Meyer Lansky and the Gangster Life.* Boston: Little, Brown, 1992.

Lait, Jack, and Lee Mortimer. *New York: Confidential!* Chicago: Ziff-Davis, 1948.

Landmarks Preservation Commission. *Fred F. French Building.* Landmarks Preservation Commission Designation Report, New York Public Library, March 18, 1986.

———. *Tudor City Historic District: Designation Report.* New York: Landmarks Preservation Commission, 1988.

Lane, Wheaton J. *Commodore Vanderbilt: An Epic of the Steam Age.* New York: Alfred A. Knopf, 1942.

Langner, Lawrence. *The Magic Curtain: The Story of a Life in Two Fields, Theatre and Invention, by the Founder of the Theatre Guild.* New York: E. P. Dutton, 1951.

Lardner, James, and Thomas Reppetto. *NYPD: A City and Its Police.* New York: Henry Holt, 2000.

Lardner, John. "The Lindbergh Legends." In *Lardner: The World of John Lardner,* edited by Roger Kahn. New York: Simon & Schuster, 1961.

———. *White Hopes and Other Tigers.* Philadelphia: J. B. Lippincott, 1951.

Lardner, Rex. *The Legendary Champions.* New York: American Heritage, 1972.

Larrowe, Charles P. *Shape-Up and Hiring Hall: A Comparison of Hiring Methods and Labor Relations on the New York and Seattle Water Fronts.* Berkeley: University of California Press, 1955.

Lawrence, A. H. *Duke Ellington and His World: A Biography.* New York: Routledge & Kegan Paul, 2001.

Lawrenson, Helen. *Stranger at the Party.* New York: Random House, 1972.

Leach, William. *Land of Desire: Merchants, Power, and the Rise of a New American Culture.* New York: Pantheon, 1993.

Leckie, Janet T. *A Talent for Living: The Story of Henry Sell, an American Original.* New York: Hawthorn, 1970.

Le Corbusier. *When the Cathedrals Were White: A Journey to the Country of Timid People.* New York: Rayane & Hitchcock, 1947.

Leich, Jean Ferriss. *Architectural Visions: The Drawings of Hugh Ferriss.* New York: Watson-Guptill, 1980.

Leighton, Isabel, ed. *The Aspirin Age, 1919–1941.* New York: Simon & Schuster, 1976.

Leinwand, Gerald. *Mackerels in the Moonlight: Four Corrupt American Mayors.* Jefferson, NC: McFarland, 2004.

Lender, Mark Edward, and James Kirby Martin. *Drinking in America: A History.* New York: Free Press, 1982.

Lerner, Michael A. *Dry Manhattan: Prohibition in New York City.* Cambridge: Harvard University Press, 2007.

Levine, Louis. *The Women's Garment Workers: A History of the International Ladies Garment Workers Union.* New York: B. W. Huebsch, 1924.

Lewis, Alfred Allan. *Ladies and Not-So-Gentle Women.* New York: Penguin, 2001.

———. *Man of the World, Herbert Bayard Swope: A Charmed Life of Pulitzer Prizes, Poker and Politics.* New York: Bobbs-Merrill, 1978.

Lewis, Alfred Allan, and Constance Woodworth. *Miss Elizabeth Arden.* New York: Coward, McCann & Geoghegan, 1972.

Lewis, David Levering. *When Harlem Was in Vogue.* New York: Oxford University Press edition, 1989.

Lewis, Harold M. *Highway Traffic.* Vol. 3 of *Regional* Survey *of New York and Its Environs.* New York: Regional Plan of New York and Its Environs, 1927.

Lewis, Harold M., William J. Wilgus, and Daniel L. Turner. *Transit and Transportation, and a Study of Port and Industrial Areas and Their Relation to Transportation.* Vol. 4 of *Regional Survey of New York and Its Environs.* New York: Regional Plan of New York and Its Environs, 1928.

Lewis, Tom. *Empire of the Air: The Men Who Made Radio.* New York: Harper Perennial, 1993.

Lieb, Fred. *Baseball as I Have Known It.* New York: Coward, McCann & Geoghegan, 1977.

Liebling, A. J. *Back Where I Came From.* San Francisco: North Point, 1900, originally published in 1938.

———. "The Sea in the City." In *Back Where I Came From.* San Francisco: North Point, 1938.

Lindbergh, Charles A. *"We."* New York: G. P. Putnam's Sons, 1928.

Lingeman, Richard. *Theodore Dreiser: An American Journey.* New York: John Wiley & Sons, 1993.

Lopate, Phillip. *Waterfront: A Walk Around Manhattan.* New York: Anchor, 2005; originally published in 2004.

Lopate, Phillip, ed. *Writing New York: A Literary Anthology.* New York: Library of America, 1998.

Louvish, Simon. *Mae West: It Ain't No Sin.* New York: Thomas Dunne, 2005.

Lynch, Denis Tilden. *Criminals and Politicians.* New York: Macmillan, 1932.

Lyons, Eugene. *David Sarnoff.* New York: Harper & Row, 1966.

MacDonald, J. Fred. *Don't Touch That Dial!: Radio Programming in American Life, 1920–1960.* Chicago: Nelson-Hall, 1979.

Macfadden, Mary W., and Emile Gauvreau. *Dumbbells and Carrot Strips: The Story of Bernarr Macfadden.* New York: Henry Holt, 1953.

MacKaye, Milton. *The Tin Box Parade.* New York: McBride, 1934.

MacKellar, Landis. *The "Double Indemnity" Murder: Ruth Snyder, Judd Gray and New York's Crime of the Century.* Syracuse, NY: Syracuse University Press, 2006.

Mackey, Thomas C. *Pursuing Johns: Criminal Law Reform, Defending Character, and New York City's Committee of Fourteen, 1920–1930.* Columbus: Ohio State University Press, 2005.

MacManus, Theodore F., and Norman Beasley. *Men, Money and Motors.* New York: Harper & Brothers, 1929.

Madison, Charles A. *Book Publishing in America.* New York: McGraw-Hill, 1966.

Maeder, Jay, ed. *Big Town Biography: Lives and Times of the Century's Classic New Yorkers.* New York: Daily News Books, 1999.

Magee, Mabel A. *Trends in Location of the Women's Clothing Industry.* Chicago: University of Chicago Press, 1930.

Mahoney, Tom, and Leonard Sloane. *The Great Merchants: America's Foremost Retail Institutions and the People Who Made Them Great.* New York: Harper & Row, 1966.

Maltin, Leonard. *The Great American Broadcast: A Celebration of Radio's Golden Age.* New York: Dutton, 1997.

Mandel, Ernest. *Delightful Murder: A Social History of the Crime Story.* Minneapolis: University of Minnesota Press, 1984.

Mann, Arthur. *La Guardia: A Fighter Against His Times, 1882–1933.* New York: J. B. Lippincott, 1959.

Margolin, Leslie. *Murderess! The Chilling True Story of the Most Infamous Woman Ever Electrocuted.* New York: Pinnacle, 1999.

Markey, Morris. *Manhattan Reporter.* New York: Dodge, 1935.

Markey, Morris, and Johan Bull. *That's New York!* New York: Macy-Masius, 1927.

Marshall, Alex. *Beneath the Metropolis: The Secret Lives of Cities.* New York: Carroll & Graf, 2006.

Marshall, Bruce. *Building New York: The Rise and Rise of the Greatest City on Earth.* New York: Universe, 2005.

Marshall, David. *Grand Central.* New York: McGraw-Hill, 1946.

Martin, Richard. "Hattie Carnegie." In Vol. 4 of *American National Biography,* edited by Mark C. Carnes and John A. Garraty. New York: Oxford University Press, 1999.

Mast, Gerald. *Can't Help Singin': The American Musical on Stage and Screen.* Woodstock, NY: Overlook, 1987.

Matteson, George. *Tugboats of New York: An Illustrated History.* New York: New York University Press, 2005.

Maxtone-Graham, John. *The Only Way to Cross.* New York: Macmillan, 1972.

Maxwell, Gilbert. *Helen Morgan: Her Life and Legend.* New York: Hawthorn, 1974.

Mayer, Martin. *Emory Buckner: A Biography.* New York: Harper & Row, 1968.

McCallum, John D. *The World Heavyweight Boxing Championship: A History.* Radnor, PA: Chilton, 1974.

McCann, Colum. Foreword to *At the Fights: American Writers on Boxing*, edited by George Kimball and John Schulian. New York: Library of America, 2011.

McClausland, Elizabeth. *Changing New York*. New York: Dutton, 1939.

McEntee, Ann Marie. "Feathers, Finials, and Frou-Frou: Florenz Ziegfeld's Exoticized Follies Girls." In *Art, Glitter and Glitz: Mainstream Playwrights and Popular Theatre in 1920s America*, edited by Arthur Gewirtz and James J. Kolb. Westport, CT: Praeger, 2003.

McGivena, Leo, and Others. *The News: The First Fifty Years of New York's Picture Newspaper*. New York: News Syndicate Co., 1969.

McKay, Claude. *Harlem: Negro Metropolis*. New York: Dutton, 1940.

McKinney, Megan. *The Magnificent Medills: America's Royal Family of Journalism During a Century of Turbulent Splendor*. New York: HarperCollins, 2011.

McNamee, Graham, and Robert Gordon Anderson. *You're on the Air*. New York: Harper & Row, 1926.

McNickle, Chris. *To Be Mayor of New York: Ethnic Politics in the City*. New York: Columbia University Press, 1993.

McShane, Clay. *Down the Asphalt Path: The Automobile and the American City*. New York: Columbia University Press, 1994.

Meany, Tom. *Babe Ruth: The Big Moments of the Big Fellow*. New York: A. S. Barnes, 1947.

Meeks, Carroll L. V. *The Railroad Station: An Architectural History*. New Haven: Yale University Press, 1956.

Mellow, James R. *Invented Lives: F. Scott and Zelda Fitzgerald*. Boston: Houghton Mifflin, 1984.

Melnick, Ross. *American Showman: Samuel "Roxy" Rothafel and the Birth of the Entertainment Industry, 1908–1935*. New York: Columbia University Press, 2012.

Mencken, H. L. *Americana 1925*. New York: Alfred A. Knopf, 1925.

———. *The American Language*. New York: Alfred A. Knopf, 1937.

———. *A Choice of Days*. New York: Alfred A. Knopf, 1980.

———. "Dempsey vs. Carpentier." In *At the Fights: American Writers on Boxing*, edited by George Kimball and John Schulian. New York: Library of America, 2011.

———. *My Life as Author and Editor*. Edited by Jonathan Yardley. New York: Alfred A. Knopf, 1993.

———. *Prejudices: Sixth Series*. New York: Alfred A. Knopf, 1927.

———. *A Second Mencken Chrestomothy*. New York: Alfred A. Knopf, 1998.

Merz, Charles. *The Dry Decade*. NY: Doubleday, Doran, 1931.

Messler, Norbert. *The Art Deco Skyscraper in New York*. New York: Peter Lang, 1986.

Metz, Robert. *CBS: Reflections in a Bloodshot Eye*. Chicago: Playboy, 1975.

Meyers, Jeffrey. *Hemingway: A Biography*. New York: Harper & Row, 1985.

Middleton, William D. *Grand Central: The World's Greatest Railway Terminal*. San Marino, CA: Golden West Books, 1977.

———. *When the Steam Railroad Electrified*. Milwaukee: Kalmbach, 1974.

Milbank, Caroline Rennolds. *New York Fashion: The Evolution of American Style*. New York: Harry N. Abrams, 1989.

Miller, Benjamin. *Fat of the Land: Garbage of New York, the Last Two Hundred Years*. New York: Basic Books, 2000.

Miller, Donald L. *Lewis Mumford, A Life, New York:* Weidenfeld & Nicolson, 1989.

Miller, Ron, and Frederick C. Durant III, with Melvin H. Schuetz. *The Art of Chesley Bonestell*. London: Collins & Brown, 2001.

Mitgang, Herbert. *The Man Who Rode the Tiger.* New York: J. B. Lippincott, 1963.

———. *Once Upon a Time in New York.* New York: Free Press, 2000.

Mizejewski, Linda. *Ziegfeld Girl: Image and Icon in Culture and Cinema.* Durham, NC: Duke University Press, 1999.

Modlin, Charles E., ed. *Sherwood Anderson: Selected Letters.* Knoxville: University of Tennessee Press, 1984.

Montville, Leigh. *The Big Bam: The Life and Times of Babe Ruth.* New York: Doubleday, 2006.

Moore, Deborah Dash. *At Home in America: Second Generation New York Jews.* New York: Columbia University Press, 1981.

Morand, Paul. *New York.* New York: Henry Holt, 1930.

Mordden, Ethan. *That Jazz! An Idiosynciatic Social History of the American Twenties.* New York: Putnam, 1978.

———. *Ziegfeld: The Man Who Invented Show Business.* New York: St. Martin's, 2008.

Morland, Nigel. *Background to Murder.* London: Werner Laurie, 1955.

Morris, Jan. *Manhattan '45.* New York: Oxford University Press, 1986.

Morris, Lloyd. *Incredible New York: High Life and Low Life from 1850 to 1950.* New York: Random House, 1951.

Moscow, Warren. *The Last of the Big Time Bosses.* New York: Stein, 1971.

———. *What Have You Done for Me Lately? The Ins and Outs of New York City Politics.* Englewood Cliffs, NJ: Prentice Hall, 1967.

Mosedale, John. *The Greatest of All: The 1927 New York Yankees.* New York: Dial, 1975.

Moses, Robert. *A Tribute to Governor Smith.* New York: Simon & Schuster, 1962.

———. *Working for the People.* New York: Harper & Row, 1956.

Mujica, Francisco. *History of the Skyscraper.* New York: Da Capo, 1977.

Mumford, Lewis. *Architecture: Reading with a Purpose, No. 23.* Chicago: American Library Association, 1926.

———. *The Culture of Cities.* New York: Harcourt Brace, Jounavich, 1938.

———. "The Metropolitan Milieu." In *America and Alfred Stieglitz: A Collective Portrait,* edited by Waldo Frank, Lewis Mumford, Dorothy Norman, Paul Rosenfeld, and Harold Rugg. Garden City, NY: Doubleday, Doran, 1934.

———. "The Modern City." In *Forms and Functions of Twentieth-Century Architecture.* Volume 4, Building Types. Edited by Talbot Hamlin. New York: Columbia University Press, 1952.

———. *Sketches from Life: The Autobiography of Lewis Mumford.* New York: Dial, 1982.

Nadelhoffer, Hans. *Cartier: Jewelers Extraordinary.* New York: Harry N. Abrams, 1984.

Nasaw, David. *Going Out: The Rise and Fall of Public Amusements.* New York: Basic, 1993.

Nash, Eric P. *Manhattan Skyscrapers.* New York: Princeton Architectural Press, 1999.

Nathan, George J. "Ziegfeld." In *The Magic Mirror: Selected Writings on the Theatre.* New York: Alfred A. Knopf, 1960.

Naylor, David. *Great American Movie Theaters.* Washington, DC: Preservation Press, 1987.

Nelli, Humbert S. "American Syndicate Crime: A Legacy of Prohibition." In *Law, Alcohol and Order: Perspectives on National Prohibition,* edited by David E. Kyvig. Westport, CT: Greenwood, 1985.

———. *The Business of Crime.* New York: Oxford University Press, 1976.

Nevins, Allan, and John A. Krout, eds. *The Greater City: New York, 1898–1948.* New York: Columbia University Press, 1948.

Nevins, Deborah. "Grand Central: Architecture as a Celebration of Daily Life." In *Grand Central Terminal: City Within the City,* edited by Deborah Nevins. New York: Municipal Art Society of New York, 1982.

Nevins, Deborah, ed. *Grand Central Terminal: City Within the City.* New York: Municipal Art Society of New York, 1982.

Newman, Peter Charles. *King of the Castle: The Making of a Dynasty—Seagram's and the Bronfman Empire.* New York: Atheneum, 1979.

New York Committee of Fourteen. *Annual Report for 1928.* New York: Committee of Fourteen, 1929.

New York, New Jersey Port and Harbor Development Commission. *Joint Report with Comprehensive Plan and Recommendation.* Albany, NY: Lyon, 1920.

Nolte, William H., ed. *H. L. Mencken's Smart Set Criticism.* Ithaca, NY: Cornell University Press, 1968.

Norris, Margaret. *Heroes and Hazards: True Stories of the Careers of the Men Who Make Our Modern World Safe by Their Courage.* New York: Junior Literary Guild, 1932.

Northrop, William B., and John B. Northrop. *The Insolence of Office: The Story of the Seabury Investigations.* New York: G. P. Putnam's Sons, 1932.

Nown, Graham. *The English Godfather.* London: Ward Lock, 1987.

Oates, Joyce Carol. *On Boxing.* Garden City, NY: Dolphin/Doubleday, 1987.

O'Connor, Richard. *The First Hurrah: A Biography of Alfred E. Smith.* New York: G. P. Putnam's Sons, 1970.

———. *Hell's Kitchen.* New York: J. B. Lippincott, 1958.

O'Higgins, Patrick. *Madame: An Intimate Portrait of Helena Rubinstein.* New York: Dell, 1972.

Okrent, Daniel. *Great Fortune: The Epic of Rockefeller Center.* New York: Penguin, 2004.

———. *Last Call: The Rise and Fall of Prohibition.* New York: Charles Scribner's Sons, 2010.

O'Meara, Lauraleigh. *Lost City: Fitzgerald's New York.* New York: Routledge & Kegan Paul, 2002.

Paley, William S. *As It Happened: A Memoir.* Garden City, NY: Doubleday, Doran, 1979.

Paper, Lewis J. *Empire: William S. Paley and the Making of CBS.* New York: St. Martin's, 1987.

Paris, Barry, *Louise Brooks.* New York: Alfred A. Knopf, 1989.

Parish, James Robert. *The George Raft File: The Unauthorized Biography.* New York: Drake, 1973.

Patterson, Jerry E. *Fifth Avenue: The Best Address.* New York: Rizzoli, 1998.

Pecorella, Robert. *Community Power in a Postreform City: Politics in New York City.* Armonk, NY: M. E. Sharpe, 1994.

Peiss, Kathy. *Hope in a Jar: The Making of America's Beauty Culture.* New York: Metropolitan, 1998.

Perret, Geoffrey. *America in the Twenties: A History.* New York: Simon & Schuster, 1982.

———. *Days of Sadness, Years of Triumph; the American People, 1939–1945.* New York: Coward, 1973.

Peretti, Burton W. *Nightclub City: Politics and Amusement in Manhattan.* Philadelphia: University of Pennsylvania Press, 2007.

Perry, Clarence Arthur. *The Rebuilding of Blighted Areas: A Study of the Neighborhood Unit in Replanning and Plot Assemblage.* New York: Regional Plan Association, 1933.

Petroski, Henry. *Engineers of Dreams: Great Bridge Builders and the Spanning of America.* New York: Alfred A. Knopf, 1995.

Pietrusza, David. *Rothstein: The Life, Times, and Murder of the Criminal Genius Who Fixed the 1919 World Series.* New York: Carroll & Graf, 2003.

Pildas, Ave. Text by Lucinda Smith. *Movie Palaces.* New York: Clarkson N. Potter, 1980.

Pirone, Dorothy Ruth, and Chris Martens. *My Dad, the Babe: Growing Up with an American Hero.* Boston: Quilan, 1988.

Pistolese, Rosana, and Ruth Horsting. *History of Fashions.* New York: John Wiley & Sons, 1976.

Plunz, Richard. *A History of Housing in New York City.* New York: Columbia University Press, 1990.

Poggi, Jack. *Theater in America: The Impact of Economic Forces, 1870–1967.* Ithaca, NY: Cornell University Press, 1968.

Port of New York Authority. *George Washington Bridge: Over the Hudson River Between New York and New Jersey.* New York: Port of New York Authority, 1931.

Pound, Arthur. *The Golden Earth: The Story of Manhattan's Landed Wealth.* New York: Arno, 1975, originally published in 1935.

Powell, Kenneth. *Grand Central Terminal.* London: Phaidon, 1996.

Pringle, Henry Fowles. *Alfred E. Smith: A Critical Study.* New York: Macy-Masius, 1927.

———. *Big Frogs.* New York: Vanguard, 1928.

Proskauer, Joseph. *A Segment of My Times.* New York: Farrar, Straus & Grioux, 1950.

Puzo, Mario. *The Fortunate Pilgrim.* New York: Random House, 1997; originally published by Atheneum, 1965.

Pye, Michael. *Maximum City: The Biography of New York.* London: Sinclair-Stevenson, 1991.

Quinn, Peter. *Looking for Jimmy: A Search for Irish America.* New York: Overlook, 2007.

Raab, Selwyn. *Five Families: The Rise, Decline, and Resurgence of America's Most Powerful Mafia Empires.* New York: St. Martin's, 2006.

Rachlis, Eugene, and John E. Marqusee. *The Land Lords.* New York: Random House, 1963.

Rasenberger, Jim. *High Steel: The Daring Men Who Built the World's Greatest Skyline, 1881 to the Present.* New York: HarperCollins, 2004.

Rastorfer, Darl. *Six Bridges: The Legacy of Othmar H. Ammann.* New Haven: Yale University Press, 2000.

Rayden, Alexander. *The People's City: A History of the Influence and Contribution of Mass Real Estate Syndication in the Development of New York City.* Charleston, SC: BookSurge Publishing, 2007.

Reed, Henry Hope Jr. *The Golden City.* Garden City, NY: Doubleday, Doran, 1959.

Reier, Sharon. *The Bridges of New York.* New York: Quadrant, 1977.

Reisenberg, Felix, and Alexander Alland. *Portrait of New York.* New York: Macmillan, 1939.

Reisler, Jim, ed. *Guys, Dolls, and Curveballs: Damon Runyon on Baseball.* New York: Carroll & Graf, 2005.

Reppetto, Thomas A. *American Mafia A History of Its Rise to Power.* New York: Henry Holt, 2004.

Reps, John William. *The Making of Urban America: A History of City Planning in the United States.* Princeton: Princeton University Press, 1965.

Revell, Keith D. *Building Gotham: Culture and Public Policy in New York City, 1898–1938.* Baltimore: John Hopkins University Press, 2003.

Reynolds, Donald Martin. *The Architecture of New York City: Histories and Views of Important Structures, Sites, and Symbols.* New York: John Wiley & Sons, 1994.

Reynolds, Michael S. *Hemingway: The Paris Years.* New York: W. W. Norton, 1999; originally published in 1989.

Rice, Grantland. *The Tumult and the Shouting: My Life in Sport.* New York: A. S. Barnes, 1966.

Rickard, Maxine Elliott Hodges, and Arch Oboler. *Everything Happened to Him: The Story of Tex Rickard.* New York: Frederick A. Stokes, 1936.

Rider, Fremont. *Rider's New York City and Vicinity, Including Newark, Yankes and Jersey City.* New York: Macmillan, 1924.

Riordon, William L. *Plunkitt of Tammany Hall: A Series of Very Plain Talks on Very Practical Politics.* Terrence J. McDonald, ed. New York: St. Martin's, 1944.

Roberts, Randy. *Jack Dempsey: The Manassa Mauler.* Baton Rouge: Louisiana State University Press, 2003.

Roberts, Sam. *Grand Central: How a Train Transformed America.* New York: Grand Central, 2013.

Robertson, John G. *The Babe Chases 60.* Jefferson, NC: McFarland, 1998.

Robins, Anthony W. *Grand Central Terminal: 100 Years of a New York Landmark.* New York: Stewart, Tabori & Chang, 2013.

Robinson, Cervin. *Skyscraper Style: Art Deco New York.* New York: Oxford University Press, 1975.

Robinson, David. *From Peep Show to Palace: The Birth of American Film.* New York: Columbia University Press, 1996.

Rockland, Michael A. *The George Washington Bridge: Poetry in Steel.* New Brunswick, NJ: Rutgers University Press, 2008.

Rodgers, Cleveland. *New York Plans for the Future.* New York: Harper & Row, 1943.

Rodgers, Cleveland, and Rebecca Rankin. *New York: The World's Capital City.* New York: Harper & Row, 1948.

Rorabaugh, W. J. *The Alcoholic Republic.* New York: Oxford University Press, 1979.

Rorty, James. *Our Master's Voice: Advertising.* Garden City, NY: Doubleday, Doran, 1934.

Roscoe, Burton. *Before I Forget.* Garden City, NY: Doubleday, Doran, 1937.

———. *We Were Interrupted.* Garden City, NY: Doubleday, Doran, 1947.

Rosenblum, Constance. *Gold Digger: The Outrageous Life and Times of Peggy Hopkins Joyce.* New York: Henry Holt, 2000.

Rosenwaike, Ira. *Population History of New York City.* Syracuse, NY: Syracuse University Press, 1972.

Rosmond, Babette. *Robert Benchley: His Life and Good Times.* New York: Paragon House, 1989.

Ross, Walter Sanford. *The Last Hero: Charles A. Lindbergh.* New York: Harper & Row, 1968.

Roth, Leland M. *The Architecture of McKim, Mead, and White, 1870–1920: A Building List.* New York: Garland, 1978.

Rothstein, Carolyn. *Now I'll Tell.* New York: Vanguard, 1934.

Rubinstein, Helena. "Manufacturing Cosmetics." In *An Outline of Careers for Women.* Edited by Doris E. Fleischman. Garden City, NY: Doubleday, Doran, 1935.

———. *My Life for Beauty.* New York: Simon & Schuster, 1966.

Runyon, Damon. *The Damon Runyon Omnibus.* New York: Blue Ribbon, 1939.

———. *Guys and Dolls and Other Writings.* New York: Penguin, 2008.

———. *Runyon on Broadway.* London: Constable, 1965.

———. *A Treasury of Damon Runyon.* New York: Modern Library, 1958.

————. *Trials and Other Tribulations.* Philadelphia: J. B. Lippincott, 1933.

Rush, Thomas E. *The Port of New York.* Garden City, NY: Doubleday, Doran, 1920.

Russell, Maud. *Men Along the Shore.* New York: Brussel & Brussel, 1966.

Ruth, Babe. *Playing the Game: My Early Years in Baseball.* Mineola, NY: Dover, 2011.

Ruth, Babe, as told to Bob Considine. *The Babe Ruth Story.* New York: E. P. Dutton, 1948.

Ruth, George Herman. *Babe Ruth's Own Book of Baseball.* New York: G. P. Putnam's Sons, 1928.

Ruth, Mrs. Babe, with Bill Slocum. *The Babe and I.* Englewood Cliffs, NJ: Prentice Hall, 1959.

Ruttenbaum, Steven. *Mansions in the Clouds: The Skyscraper Palazzi of Emery Roth.* New York: Balsam, 1986.

Samuels, Charles. *The Magnificent Rube: The Life and Gaudy Times of Tex Rickard.* New York: McGraw-Hill, 1957.

Sammons, Jeffrey T. *Beyond the Ring: The Role of Boxing in American Society.* Urbana: Illinois University Press, 1988.

Sandburg, Carl. *Chicago Poems.* New York: Henry Holt, 1916.

Sarnoff, David. *Looking Ahead: The Papers of David Sarnoff.* New York: McGraw-Hill, 1968.

Sassen, Saskia. *The Global City: New York, London, Tokyo.* Princeton: Princeton University Press, 1991.

Sayre, Wallace S., and Herbert Kaufman. *Governing New York City.* New York: Russell Sage Foundation, 1960.

Schaffer, Daniel. "New York and the Garden City Movement Between the Wars." In *Berlin–New York: Like and Unlike: Essays on Architecture and Art from 1870 to the Present,* edited by Josef Paul Kleihues and Christina Rathgeber. New York: Rizzoli International Publications, 1993.

Schlichting, Kurt C. *Grand Central's Engineer: William J. Wilgus and the Planning of Modern Manhattan.* Baltimore: Johns Hopkins University Press, 2012.

————. *Grand Central Terminal: Railroads, Engineering and Architecture in New York City.* Baltimore: Johns Hopkins University Press, 2001.

Schuberth, Christopher. *The Geology of New York City and Environs.* New York: Natural History Press, 1968.

Schulian, John. "The Fist and the Pen." Introduction to *At the Fights: American Writers on Boxing,* edited by George Kimball and John Schulian. New York: Library of America, 2011.

Schwartz, Evan I. *The Last Lone Inventor: A Tale of Genius, Deceit, and the Birth of Television.* New York: Harper Perennial, 2002.

Schwartz, Joel. *The New York Approach.* Columbus: Ohio State University Press, 1993.

Schwed, Peter. *Turning the Pages: An Insider's Story of Simon & Schuster, 1924–1984.* New York: Macmillan, 1984.

Sciacca, Tony. *Luciano: The Man Who Modernized the American Mafia.* New York: Pinnacle, 1975.

Scully, Vincent Joseph. *American Architecture and Urbanism.* New York: Praeger, 1969.

Seldes, Gilbert. *The Movies Come from America.* New York: Charles Scribner's Sons, 1937.

————. *The Seven Lively Arts.* New York: Harper & Row, 1924.

Selekman, Ben Morris, Henriette Rose Walter, and Walter J. Couper. "The Clothing and Textile Industries." In *Food, Clothing, and Textile Industries, Wholesale Markets and Retail Shopping and Financial Districts, Present Trends and Probable Future Devel-*

opments, Vol. 1B of *The Regional Survey of New York and Its Environs.* New York: Regional Plan of New York and Its Environs, 1928.

Selvaggi, Giuseppe. *The Rise of the Mafia in New York.* New York: Bobbs-Merrill, 1978.

Seymour, Harold. *Baseball: The Golden Age.* New York: Oxford University Press, 1971.

Shachtman, Tom. *Skyscraper Dreams, The Great Real Estate Dynasties of New York.* Boston: Little, Brown, 1991.

Shanor, Rebecca Read. *The City That Never Was: Two Hundred Years of Fantastic and Fascinating Plans That Might Have Changed the Face of New York City.* New York: Viking, 1991.

Shapiro, Nat, and Nat Hentoff, eds. *Hear Me Talkin' to Ya: The Story of Jazz as Told by the Men Who Made It.* New York: Dover, 1955.

Shaw, Arnold. *52nd Street: The Street of Jazz.* New York: Da Capo, 1971.

———. *The Jazz Age: Popular Music in the 1920s.* New York: Oxford University Press, 1987.

Shaw, Charles G. *Nightlife: Vanity Fair's Intimate Guide to New York After Dark.* New York: John Day, 1931.

Shefter, Martin. "The Emergence of the Political Machine: An Alternative View." In *Theoretical Perspectives on Urban Politics,* edited by Willis D. Hawley and Michael Lipsky. Englewood Cliffs, NJ: Prentice Hall, 1976.

Shirley, Glenn. *"Hello, Sucker!" The Story of Texas Guinan.* Austin, TX: Eakin, 1989.

Shuker, Nancy. *Elizabeth Arden: Cosmetics Entrepreneur.* Englewood Cliffs, NJ: Silver Burdett, 1989.

Siegfried, Andre. *America Comes of Age, A French Analyst.* New York: Harcourt, 1927.

Sifakis, Carl. *The Mafia Encyclopedia.* New York: Checkmark, 2005.

Silver, Nathan. *Lost New York.* Boston: Houghton, 1967.

Simon & Schuster. *Simon & Schuster.* New York: Simon & Schuster, 2001.

Sklar, Robert. *Movie-Made America.* New York: Random House, 1975.

Slayton, Robert A. *Empire Statesman: The Rise and Redemption of Al Smith.* New York: Free Press, 2001.

Smelser, Marshall. *The Life That Ruth Built: A Biography.* New York: Quadrangle, 1975.

Smith, Alfred E. *Up to Now: An Autobiography.* New York: Viking, 1929.

Smith, H. Allen. *To Hell in a Handbasket.* New York: Doubleday, 1962.

Smith, Red. "As He Seemed to a Hick," in Phillip Lopate, ed., *Writing New York: A Literary Anthology.* New York: Library of America, 1998.

Smith, Richard Norton. *The Colonel: The Life and Legend of Robert R. McCormick, 1880–1955.* New York: Houghton Mifflin, 1997.

Smith, Sally Bedell. *In All His Glory: The Life of William S. Paley.* New York: Simon & Schuster, 1990.

Smulyan, Susan. *Selling Radio: The Commercialization of American Broadcasting, 1920–1934.* Washington DC: Smithsonian Institution Press, 1994.

Sobel, Bernard. *Broadway Heartbeat: Memoirs of a Press Agent.* New York: Hermitage House, 1953.

Sobel, Robert. *The Big Board: A History of the New York Stock Market.* New York: Free Press, 1965.

———. *The Fallen Collossus.* New York: Weybright & Talley, 1977.

———. *The Great Bull Market: Wall Street in the 1920s.* New York: W. W. Norton, 1968.

———. *RCA.* New York: Stein & Day, 1984.

Sobol, Ken. *Babe Ruth and the American Dream.* New York: Random House, 1974.

Sochen, June. *Mae West: She Who Laughs, Lasts.* Arlington Heights, IL: Harlan Davidson, 1992.

Solis, Julia. *New York Underground: The Anatomy of a City.* New York: Routledge & Kegan Paul, 2005.

Soyer, Daniel, ed. *A Coat of Many Colors: Immigration, Globalization, and Reform in New York City's Garment Industry.* New York: Fordham University Press, 2005.

Spengler, Edwin H. "Land Values in New York in Relation to Transit Facilities." In *Studies in History, Economics and Public Law,* ed. by Faculty of Political Science, Columbia University, No. 33, 1930.

Stanley, Ed. *Grand Central Terminal: Gateway to New York City.* New York: Mondo, 2003.

Starrett, Paul. *Changing the Skyline: An Autobiography.* New York: McGraw-Hill, 1938.

Starrett, Colonel W. A. *Skyscrapers and the Men Who Build Them.* New York: Charles Scribner's Sons, 1928.

Stashower, Daniel. *The Boy Genius and the Mogul: The Untold Story of Television.* New York: Broadway, 2002.

Stein, Charles W., ed. *American Vaudeville: As Seen by Its Contemporaries.* New York: Alfred A. Knopf, 1984.

Stein, Clarence S. *Toward New Towns for America.* Cambridge: MIT Press, 1966.

Stern, Jewel, and John A. Stuart. *Ely Jacques Kahn, Architect: Beaux-Arts to Modernism in New York.* New York: W. W. Norton, 2006.

Stern, Robert A. M., and Thomas P. Catalano. *Raymond Hood.* New York: Rizzoli, 1982.

Stern, Robert A. M., Gregory F. Gilmartin, and John Massengale. *New York 1900: Metropolitan Architecture and Urbanism 1890–1915.* New York: Rizzoli, 1995.

Stern, Robert A. M., Gregory F. Gilmartin, and Thomas Mellins. *New York 1930: Architecture and Urbanism Between the Two World Wars.* New York: Rizzoli, 2009.

Stevens, John D. *Sensationalism and the New York Press.* New York: Columbia University Press, 1991.

Stiles, T. J. *The First Tycoon: The Epic Life of Cornelius Vanderbilt.* New York: Alfred A. Knopf, 2009.

Still, Bayrd. *Mirror for Gotham.* New York: New York University Press, 1956.

Stoddard, Lothrop. *Luck, Your Silent Partner.* New York: Horace Liveright, 1929.

Stolberg, Benjamin. *Tailor's Progress.* New York: Doubleday, Doran, 1944.

Stolberg, Mary M. *Fighting Organized Crime.* Boston: Northeastern University Press, 1995.

Stone, Jill. *Times Square: A Pictorial History.* New York: Collier, 1982.

Stravitz, David. *The Chrysler Building: Creating a New York Icon, Day by Day.* New York: Princeton Architectural Press, 2002.

Sullivan, Mark. *Our Times: The United States, 1900–1925.* New York: Charles Scribner's Sons, 1935.

Susman, Warren. *Culture as History: The Transformation of American Society in the Twentieth Century.* New York: Pantheon, 1984.

Susman, Warren, ed. *Culture and Commitment, 1929–1945.* New York: G. Braziller, 1973.

Sussman, Carl, ed. *Planning the Fourth Migration: The Neglected Vision of the Regional Planning Association of America.* Cambridge: MIT Press, 1976.

Swantstrom, Edward E. *The Waterfront Labor Problem: A Study in Decasualization and Unemployment Insurance.* New York: Fordham University Press, 1938.

Sylvester, Robert. *No Cover Charge: A Backward Look at the Night Clubs*. New York: Dial, 1956.

Tafuri, Manfredo. "The Disenchanted Mountain: The Skyscraper and the City." In *The American City: From the Civil War to the New Deal*, by Giorgio Ciucci, et al. Cambridge: MIT Press, 1979.

Talese, Gay. *The Bridge: The Building of the Verrazano-Narrows Bridge*. New York: Harper & Row, 1964.

Talmey, Allene. *Doug and Mary and Others: A Book*. New York: Macy-Masius, 1927.

Taylor, William R., ed. *Inventing Times Square: Commerce and Culture at the Crossroads of the World*. New York: Russell Sage Foundation, 1991.

Tebbel, John. *An American Dynasty*. Garden City, NY: Doubleday, Doran, 1947.

———. *Between Covers: The Rise and Transformation of Book Publishing in America*. New York: Oxford University Press, 1987.

Teichmann, Howard. *George S. Kaufman: An Intimate Portrait*. New York: Atheneum, 1972.

Terkel, Studs. *Giants of Jazz*. New York: New Press, 1975.

Thirteen Correspondents of the New York Times. *We Saw It Happen*. New York: Simon & Schuster, 1938.

Thomas, Dana L. *The Media Moguls: From Joseph Pulitzer to William S. Paley: Their Lives and Boisterous Times*. New York: G. P. Putnam's Sons, 1981.

Thomas, Lowell. *Men of Danger*. New York: Frederick A. Stokes, 1936.

Thomas, Norman, and Paul Blanshard. *What's the Matter with New York: A National Problem*. New York: Macmillan, 1932.

Thompson, Craig, and Allen Raymond. *Gang Rule in New York: The Story of a Lawless Era*. New York: Dial, 1940.

Thompson, Warren S. *Population: The Growth of Metropolitan Districts in the United States: 1900–1940*. Washington, DC: Washington, DC: U.S. Government Printing Office, 1947.

Thurber, James. *My Life and Hard Times*. New York: Harper & Row, 1973.

———. *The Years with Ross*. Boston: Little, Brown, 1957.

Toll, Robert C. *On with the Show! The First Century of Show Business in America*. New York: Oxford University Press, 1976.

Trager, James. *Park Avenue: Street of Dreams*. New York: Atheneum, 1990.

———. *West of Fifth: The Rise and Fall and Rise of Manhattan's West Side*. New York: Atheneum, 1987.

Traub, James. *The Devil's Playground: A Century of Pleasure and Profit in Times Square*. New York: Random House, 2004.

Trimble, Patrick A. "Jacob Ruppert." In *The Scribner Encyclopedia of American Lives: Sports Figures*. Vol. 2. New York: Charles Scribner's Sons, 2002.

True, Ruth S. *West Side Studies: The Neglected Girl*. New York: Russell Sage Foundation, 1914.

Tucker, Mark, ed. *The Duke Ellington Reader*. New York: Oxford University Press, 1993.

———. *Ellington: The Early Years*. Urbana: University of Illinois Press, 1995.

Tye, Larry. *The Father of Spin: Edward L. Bernays and the Birth of Public Relations*. New York: Crown, 1998.

Tyler, David Budlong. *Steam Conquers the Atlantic*. New York: Appleton-Century-Crofts, 1939.

Ulanov, Barry. *Duke Ellington*. New York: Da Capo, 1975; originally published in 1947.

Ulrich, Kurt. *Monarchs of the Sea*. London: Tauris Parke, 1998.

United States President's Research Committee on Social Trends. *Recent Social Trends in the United States.* New York: McGraw-Hill, 1933.

Urban, Joseph. *Theatres.* New York: Theatre Arts, 1929.

Valentine, Lewis J. *Night Stick.* New York: Dial, 1947.

Vanderbilt, Arthur T. II. *Fortune's Children: The Fall of the House of Vanderbilt.* New York: William Morrow, 1989.

Vanderbilt, Cornelius Jr. *Farewell to Fifth Avenue.* New York: Simon & Schuster, 1935.

———. *Park Avenue.* New York: Macaulay, 1930.

Voigt, David Quentin. *American Baseball: From the Commissioners to Continental Expansion.* Norman: University of Oklahoma Press, 1970.

Wade, Richard C. "The Withering Away of the Party System," in Jewell Bellish and Dick Nilzer, eds. *Urban Politics, New York Style.* Armonk, NY: M. E. Sharpe, 1990.

Waggoner, Susan. *Nightclub Nights: Art, Legend, and Style, 1920–1960.* New York: Rizzoli, 2001.

Waldinger, Roger D. *Through the Eye of the Needle: Immigrants and Enterprise in New York's Garment Trades.* New York: New York University Press, 1986.

Waldrop, Frank. *McCormick of Chicago: An Unconventional Portrait of a Controversial Figure.* Englewood Cliffs, NJ: Prentice Hall, 1966.

Walker, Stanley. *City Editor.* New York: Frederick A. Stokes, Co., 1934.

———. "The Dream Prince." In *The Empire City: A Treasury of New York,* edited by Alexander Klein. Freeport, NY: Books for Libraries, 1955.

———. *The Night Club Era.* Baltimore: Johns Hopkins University Press, 1999 paperback edition.

Wallace, Stone. *George Raft: The Man Who Would Be Bogart.* Albany, GA: BearManor Media, 2008.

Walsh, Christy. *Adios to Ghosts!* Self-published, 1937.

Walsh, George. *Gentleman Jimmy Walker: Mayor of the Jazz Age.* New York: Praeger, 1974.

———. *Public Enemies: The Mayor, the Mob, and the Crime That Was.* New York: W. W. Norton, 1980.

Walsh, Michael. *And All the Saints.* New York: Warner, 2003.

Waltzer, Jim. *The Battle of the Century: Dempsey, Carpentier, and the Birth of Modern Promotion.* Santa Barbara, CA: Praeger, 2011.

Ward, David, and Oliver Zunz, eds. *The Landscape of Modernity: Essays on New York City, 1900–1940.* New York: Russell Sage Foundation, 1992.

Ward, Geoffrey C. *American Originals.* New York: Harper & Row, 1991.

———. *Unforgivable Blackness: The Rise and Fall of Jack Johnson.* New York: Alfred A. Knopf, 2004.

Ward, Geoffrey C., and Ken Burns. *Jazz: A History of America's Music.* New York: Alfred A. Knopf, 2000.

Ward, Nathan. *Dark Harbor: The War for the New York Waterfront.* New York: Farrar, Straus & Giroux, 2010.

Warner, Emily Smith, with Hawthorne Daniel. *The Happy Warrior: A Biography of My Father Alfred E. Smith.* Garden City, NY: Doubleday, Doran, 1956.

Waters, Harold. *Smugglers of Spirits: Prohibition and the Coast Guard Patrol.* New York: Hastings House, 1971.

Watts, Steven. *The People's Tycoon: Henry Ford and the American Century.* New York: Alfred A. Knopf, 2005.

Wecter, Dixon. *The Hero in America.* Harbor: University of Michigan Press, 1963.

Weeks, Edward. *My Green Age.* Boston: Little, Brown, 1973.

Weiss, Marc A. *The Rise of the Community Builders.* New York: Columbia University Press, 1987.

Weiss, Nancy Joan. *Charles Francis Murphy, 1858–1924: Respectability and Responsibility in Tammany Politics.* Northampton, MA: Smith College, 1968.

Wendt, Lloyd. *Chicago Tribune: The Rise of a Great American Newspaper.* Chicago: Rand McNally, 1984.

Werner, M. R. *Tammany Hall.* Garden City, NY: Doubleday, Doran, 1928.

Whalen, Grover A. *Mr. New York: The Autobiography of Grover A. Whalen.* New York: G. P. Putnam's Sons, 1955.

White, E. B., *Here Is New York.* New York: Harper & Brothers, 1949.

———. *Writings from the New Yorker: 1927–1976.* Edited by Rebecca M. Dale. New York: Harper Collins, 1990.

White, Norval. *New York: A Physical History.* New York: Atheneum, 1987.

Whyte, William H. *City: Rediscovering the Center.* New York: Doubleday, Doran, 1988.

Whyte, William H, ed. *The Exploding Metropolis.* Berkeley: University of California Press, 1993 edition, originally published in 1957.

Wilgus, William J. "Transportation in the New York Region." In *Transit and Transportation, and a Study of Port and Industrial Areas and Their Relation to Transportation.* Vol 4, *Regional Survey of New York and Its Environs,* by Harold M. Lewis, William J. Wilgus, and Daniel L. Turner. New York: Regional Plan of New York and Its Environs, 1928.

Willebrandt, Mabel Walker. *The Inside of Prohibition.* Indianapolis Bobbs-Merrill, 1929.

Willensky, Elliot. "Grand Central: Shaper of a City." In *Grand Central Terminal: City Within the City,* edited by Deborah Nevins. New York: Municipal Art Society of New York, 1982.

Willis, Carol. *Form Follows Finance: Skyscrapers and Skylines in New York and Chicago.* New York: Princeton Architectural Press, 1995.

Willis, Carol, ed. *Building the Empire State.* New York: W. W. Norton, 1998.

Willoughby, Malcolm F. *Rum War at Sea.* Washington, DC: U.S. Government Printing Office, 1964.

Wilson, Edmund. "Finale at the Follies." In *The American Earthquake: A Documentary of the Twenties and Thirties,* Edmund Wilson. NY: Octagon, 1971, originally published in 1958.

———. *The Twenties.* New York: Farrar, Straus & Giroux, 1975.

———. *The Thirties.* New York: Farrar, Straus & Giroux, 1980.

Winchell, Walter. *Winchell Exclusive: "Things That Happened to Me—And Me to Them."* New York: Prentice Hall, 1975.

Wolf, George, with Joseph DiMona. *Frank Costello: Prime Minister of the Underworld.* New York: William Morrow, 1974.

Wolfe, Thomas. *The Web and the Rock: A Selection from the Web and the Rock* (New York: Harper Perennial, 2009.

Woodhead, Lindy. *War Paint: Madame Helena Rubinstein and Miss Elizabeth Arden, Their Lives, Their Times, Their Rivalry.* New York: John Wiley & Sons, 2003.

Woodward, Helen. *The Lady Persuaders.* New York: Obolensky, 1960.

Woollcott, Alexander. "The Invisible Fish." In *The Portable Woollcott,* edited by Joseph Hennessey. New York: Viking, 1946.

——. *Long, Long Ago*. New York: Viking, 1943.

——. *While Rome Burns*. New York: Grosset, 1934.

Woon, Basil. *The Frantic Atlantic*. New York: Alfred A. Knopf, 1927.

Worden, Helen. *The Real New York*. Indianapolis: Bobbs-Merrill, 1932.

——. *Round Manhattan's Rim*. Indianapolis, Bobbs-Merrill, 1934.

Wright, Frank Lloyd. "The Tyranny of the Skyscraper." In Wright, *Modern Architecture, Being the Kahn Lectures for 1930*. Princeton: Princeton University Press, 1931.

Yablonsky, Lewis. *George Raft*. New York: McGraw-Hill, 1974.

Yagoda, Ben. *About Town: The New Yorker and the World It Made*. New York: Da Capo, 2001.

Yardley, Jonathan. *Ring: A Biography of Ring Lardner*. New York: Random House, 1977.

Zeitz, Joshua. *Flapper: A Madcap Story of Sex, Style, Celebrity and the Women Who Made America Modern*. New York: Crown, 2006.

Ziegfeld, Patricia. *The Ziegfelds' Girl: Confessions of an Abnormally Happy Childhood*. Boston: Little, Brown, 1964.

Ziegfeld, Richard, and Paulette Ziegfeld. *The Ziegfeld Touch: The Life and Times of Florenz Ziegfeld, Jr.* New York: Harry N. Abrams, 1993.

Zink, Harold. *City Bosses in the United States: A Study of Twenty Municipal Bosses*. Durham, NC: Duke University Press, 1930.

Articles

"America Comes to Seventh Avenue." *Fortune* 20 (July 1939).

"20,000 Per Cent Increase." *Fortune* 9 (January 1934).

"And All Because They're Smart." *Fortune* 11 (June 1935).

"An Appraisal." *Fortune* 6 (September 1932).

"A Baedeker of Business in New York." *Fortune* 20 (July 1939).

"Barnum Was Great, but 'Tex' Rickard Gets More Money." *Literary Digest* 69 (June 25, 1921).

"Blue Chip." *Fortune* 2 (September 1932).

"Booming Out: Mohawk Ironworkers Build New York." Touring photographic exhibition, Smithsonian National Museum of American Indians, first opened 2002.

"Brisbane Building Will Dominate Upper New York Skyline." *The Real Estate Record and Builders' Guide* 114 (September 13, 1924).

"Builder of Knickerbocker Village Dies." *The Real Estate Record and Builders' Guide* 138 (September 5, 1936).

"The Building of New York." *Architecture* 56 (December 1927).

"A Census of Skyscrapers." *The American City* 41 (September 1929).

"Chrysler." *Fortune* 12 (August 1935).

"Chrysler Motors." *Time*, January 7, 1929.

"The Cinematic City of the Future." *Fortune* 2 (October 1930).

"Cloak and Suit." *Fortune* 1 (June 1930).

"Congested Traffic." *The New Republic* 57 (November 28, 1928).

"Congestion of Traffic at the Grand Central Station and Its Remedy." *Scientific American* 183 (December 1, 1900).

"Construction: The Big Digger." *Time* 49 (April 7, 1947).

"Curiosities and Calamities of the Big Scrap." *The Literary Digest* 95 (October 8, 1927).

"Defends Skyscrapers as Greatest Asset to Municipality." *Real Estate Record and Builder's Guide* (November 27, 1926).

"Dempsey as a Movie Hero." *The Literary Digest* 81 (June 21, 1924).

"Dempsey-Tunney Fight: A World Spectacle." *The Literary Digest* 92 (September 17, 1927).

"Designer of World's Tallest Building Answers Critics." *Real Estate Record and Builders' Guide* 118 (December 25, 1926).

"Economics of the Great White Way." *The Literary Digest* 86 (September 12, 1925).

"Editors Analyze Selling Elements of Snyder-Gray Murder Story." *Editor & Publisher,* May 14, 1927.

"The Electrification of the New York Central's Terminal Lines." *Scientific American Supplement,* no. 1562 (December 9, 1905).

"The Ever Narrowing Home." *Housing* 18 (June 1929).

"The Fellow on the Bridge." *Time* December 27, 1971.

"Fifth Avenue Tailors." *Fortune* 6 (November 1932).

"Final Sketch of the Reynolds Building, New York." *American Architect* 135 (August 1928).

"The General." *Time* 58 (July 23, 1951).

"The Grand Central Terminal." *Fortune* 3 (February 1931).

"His Honor." *The Literary Digest* 923 (October 8, 1927).

"I Am a Famous Woman in This Industry." *Fortune* 18 (October 1938).

"In Defense of Vincent Astor." *Fortune* 8 (October 1933).

"In Praise of Congestion." *Time* 18 (December 14, 1931).

"Introducing Duke Ellington." *Fortune* 8 (August 1933).

"Jean and Jimmy." *The New Yorker* 10 (May 5, 1934).

"Jimmy Walker." *Time,* January 11, 1926.

"Joseph Patterson Dies." *Editor & Publisher* (June 1, 1946).

"Madison Square Garden." *Fortune* 12 (October 1935).

"Man of the Future." *Time* 88 (October 7, 1966).

"Manhattan Speakeasies." *Fortune* 7 (June 1933).

"A Matter of Opinion." *Time,* August 1, 1927.

"The Metropolitanites." *Fortune* 20 (July 1939).

"The Modern Apartment Hotel." *The American Architect* 131 (January 1927).

"Modern Tendencies in Theatre Design." *The American Architect* 131 (May 20, 1927).

"Mohawks Like High Steel." *Bethlehem Review* (July 1954).

"Mr. CBS." *Time,* January 31, 1964.

"Mr. Gershwin Replies to Mr. Kramer." *Singing* 1, no. 10 (October 1926).

"Mr. Goodman's 18,000 Exclusives." *Fortune* 3 (June 1931).

"The Music That Is in Every Man: An Interview with the World's Most Remarkable Entertainer, 'Roxy.'" *The Etude* (December 1927).

"The New Grand Central Terminal in New York City." *Engineering News* 69, no. 18 (May 1, 1913).

"New Roadways Around Grand Central Terminal Formally Opened." *The Real Estate Record and Builders' Guide* (September 15, 1928).

"The New Yorker." *Fortune* 10 (August 1934).

"Nineteen Thousand Cops." *Fortune* 20 (July 1939).

"Obituaries: [Bennett Cerf]." *Publishers Weekly* (September 6, 1971.

"On the Beach." *Fortune* 15 (February 1937).

"Opening of New Grand Central Terminal, NY." *Railway Age Gazette* (February 7, 1913).

"Our Modern Architecture." *The New York Times,* May 29, 1930.

"Passing of a Giant." *Time,* June 3, 1946.

"The Pennsylvania Station." *Fortune* 19 (July 1939).

"Practical Television." *Time,* January 23, 1928.

"Profile: Lois Long." *The New Yorker* 50 (August 12, 1974).

"Radio Congress." *Time* (October 20, 1924).

"Radio into Talkies." *Time,* July 15, 1929.

"Raymond Mathewson Hood." *Architectural Forum* 62 (1935).

"The Ring Editor, Six Years Ago." *The Ring* (February 1935).

"The Roxy." *The Decorative Furnisher* 52 (April 1927).

"Roxy and His Gang." *The American Magazine* (March 1925).

"The Roxy Theatre, New York City." *Architecture and Building* 59 (April 1927).

"Saks Fifth Avenue." *Fortune* 18 (November 1938).

"Sarnoff." *Newsweek* 78 (November 27, 1971).

"Screen—The Greatest." *The New York Times,* December 31, 1922.

"Skyscrapers." *Fortune* 2 (September 1930).

"Skyscrapers and Traffic Congestion." *The American Architect* 131 (March 1927).

"Skyscrapers: Builders and Their Tools." *Fortune* 2 (October 1930).

"Skyscrapers: Pyramids in Steel and Stock." *Fortune* 2 (August 1930).

"Smith-Hylan Battle." *The Literary Digest* 86 (September, 1925).

"Staff Tells Patterson's Concern for Masses." *Editor & Publisher,* June 1, 1946.

"The Talk of the Town: The Key to the Padlocks." *The New Yorker* 1 (March 21, 1925).

"Tammany in Modern Clothes." *The New Yorker* 1 (January 16, 1926).

"Television." *Time,* May 18, 1931.

"10,000 French Projects to be Ready March, 1927." *Real Estate Record and Guide* (July 17, 1926).

"The Theatre-Business." *Fortune* 17 (February 1938).

"A Theatre with Four Million Patrons a Year." *Photoplay Magazine* (April 1915).

"Thompson Model 1928 Submachine Gun." National Museum of American History, Smithsonian Institution, Washington, DC.

"Three Visions of New York: Raymond Hood." *Creative Art* 9 (August, 1931).

"Today." *Time* 8 (August 16, 1926).

"Tower Buildings and Wider Streets: A Suggested Relief for Traffic Congestion." *The American Architect* 132 (July 1927).

"Tunney and the Boxing Business." *Outlook* 149 (August 15, 1928).

"Two Miles of Millionaires." *Munsey's Magazine* 19 (June 1898)

"Under the Asphalt." *Fortune* 20 (July 1939).

"Unfit for Modern Motor Traffic." *Fortune* 14 (August 1936).

"The Union: Mother of Clubs." *Fortune* 6 (December 1932).

"The Vanishing of New York Social Citadels: Four Great Establishments on Fifth Avenue That Have Unwillingly Given Up the Ghost." *Vanity Fair* 25 (October 1925).

"What Is the Lure of the Tabloid Press?" *Editor & Publisher,* July 26, 1924.

"Where Is the World Metropolis?" *Review of Reviewers* 60 (September 1919).

"Who Are the Chanins?" *The New York Times,* January 24, 1926.

"Yes, 'Tex' Gave Them a Great Show to the End." *The Literary Digest* 100 (January 26, 1929).

Adams, Thomas. "New York Blazes a National Trail." *Survey* 63 (October 15, 1929).

Alexander, Jack. "District Leader, III." *The New Yorker* 12 (August 8, 1936).

——. "Profiles: Vox Populi—I." *The New Yorker* 14 (August 6, 1938).

——. "Profiles: Vox Populi—II." *The New Yorker* 14 (August 13, 1938).

Amber, John. "I Shall Keep My Oath: The Life Story of Emory R. Buckner." *Success* 9 (July 25, 1925).

Allen, Kenneth. "The Pollution of Tidal Harbors by Sewage with Especial Reference to New York Harbor." *Transactions of the American Society of Civil Engineers* 85 (1922).

Ammann, Othmar H. "Brobdingnagian Bridges." *Technological Review* 33 (July 1931).

——. "General Conception and Development of Design." *Transactions of the American Society of Civil Engineers* 97 (October 1933).

——. "The Hell Gate Arch Bridge and Approaches of the New York Connecting Railroad over the East River." *Transactions of the American Society of Civil Engineers* 82 (1918).

Anderson, Dave. "Sports of the Times: The Legendary Champion." *The New York Times,* June 2, 1983.

Atkinson, J. Brooks. "Affairs of the Early Season." *The New York Times,* August 28, 1927.

——. " 'All for One.' " *The New York Times,* March 25, 1928.

——. "Show-Folk Variously." *The New York Times,* January 8, 1928.

Bakeless, John. "The City of Dreadful Waste." *The Forum* 80 (1928).

Barr, Jason, Troy Tassier, and Rossen Trendafilov. "Depth of Bedrock and the Formation of the Manhattan Skyline, 1890–1915." *The Journal of Economic History* 71 (December 2011).

Bascomb, Neal. "For the Architect, a Height Never Again to Be Scaled." *The New York Times,* May 26, 2005.

Beard, Charles A. "New York, the Metropolis of To-Day." *The American Review of Reviews* 69 (June 1924).

Bell, Daniel. "The Three Faces of New York," *Dissent* (June 1961).

Berger, Meyer. "Exploded 'Big Shots.' " *The New York Times,* January 4, 1942.

Bernard, Walter. "The World's Greatest Railway Terminal." *Scientific American* 104 (June 17, 1911).

Berrol, Selma C. "Manhattan's Jewish West Side." *New York Affairs* 10 (Winter 1987).

Bigelow, Joe. "Roxy." *Variety,* January 15, 1936.

Blake, Hugh. "A Reporter at Large—The New Roxy." *The New Yorker* 8 (December 17, 1932).

Blanchard, David. "High Steel! The Kahnawake Mohawk and the High Construction Trade." *Journal of Ethnic Studies* 11 (Summer 1983).

Blassingame, Lurton. "Profiles: The Trinity—And a Dog." *The New Yorker* 2 (August 21, 1926).

——. "Type Model." *The New Yorker* 2 (January 8, 1927).

Bliven, Bruce. "How Radio Is Remaking Our World," *The Century Magazine* 108 (June 1924).

Bontemps, Arna. "The Two Harlems." *The American Scholar* 14 (Spring 1945).

Boyd, John Taylor Jr. "Wall Street Enters the Building Field 11." *Architectural Engineering and Business* (June 1929).

Boyer, Richard O. "The Hot Bach, I." *The New Yorker* 20 (June 24, 1944).

———. "The Hot Bach, III." *The New Yorker* 20 (July 8, 1944).

Bragdon, Claude. "The Shelton Hotel, New York." *The Architectural Record* 58 (July 1925).

Brock, H. I. "New Peaks in Tall Manhattan's Range." *The New York Times,* February 9, 1930.

Brundidge, Harry T. "Lou Gehrig Gives Baseball Full Credit for Rescuing Parents and Self from New York Tenement District." *Sporting News,* December 25, 1930.

Budd, Mike. "The Cabinet of Dr. Caligari: Conditions of Reception." *Cine-Tracts* 3 (Winter 1981).

Bullock, William. "Hylan." *The American Mercury* 1 (April 1924).

Busch, Niven Jr. "Skybinder." *The New Yorker* 4 (January 26, 1929).

Bush, Stephen W. "The Theatre of Realization." *Moving Picture World* 18 (November 15, 1913).

Cameron, Douglas. "Curfew Law Called Flop." *Daily News,* October 9, 1927.

Carson, Gerald. "Supreme City: New York in the 20s: 1. America's Junction," *American Heritage* 39 (November 1980).

Cerf, Bennett. "Horace Liveright: An Obituary—Unedited." *Publishers Weekly* 124 (October 7, 1933).

Chase, Stuart. "Park Avenue." *The New Republic* 51 (May 25, 1927).

Chrysler, Walter P. "Is Carelessness on Your Payroll?" *Building Age* 52 (March 1930).

Churchill, Allen. "Recalling the Heyday of the Great White Way." *The New York Times,* January 24, 1982.

Coates, Robert M. "Profiles: Realtor." *The New Yorker* 5 (June 1, 1929).

Cohen, Edward. "The Engineer and His Works: A Tribute to Othmar Hermann Ammann, P.E. (1879–1965)." *Annals of the New York Academy of Sciences* 136 (1967).

Conly, Robert L. "The Mohawks Scrape the Sky." *National Geographic Magazine* 102 (July 1952).

Corbett, Harvey Wiley. "New Heights in American Architecture." *Yale Review* 17 (July 1928).

———. "The Problem of Traffic Congestion and a Solution." *Architectural Forum* 46 (March 1927).

———. "Raymond Mathewson Hood, 1881–1934." *Architectural Forum* 61 (September 1934).

———. "The Separation of Vehicular and Pedestrian Traffic," *Creative Art* 9 (August 1931).

Curtis, Wayne. "Bootleg Paradise." *American Heritage* 58 (April 2007).

Cushing, Charles Phelps. "Where Our City Soars and Dives." *The New York Times,* July 13, 1930.

Daley, Arthur. "The Dempsey-Tunney Long Count . . . A Living Legend." *The American Legion Magazine* (April 1965).

———. "Sport Loses a Firm Friend." *The New York Times,* November 20, 1946.

Daley, John. "Last Out for the Babe." *The New York Times,* August 17, 1948.

Davenport, Walter. "Gene the Genteel." *The New Yorker* 3 (August 20, 1927).

———. "High and Mighty." *Colliers* 85 (March 1, 1930).

Davis, Elmer. "Clytemnestra: Long Island Style." *The New Yorker* 3 (May 7, 1927).

———. "Ex-Marine Gets Ovation as He Enters Ring." *New York Times,* September 24, 1926.

Dawson, James P. "Fight Fast and Furious." *The New York Times,* September 23, 1927.

De Casseres, Benjamin. "Joel's." *The American Mercury* 26 (July 1932).

de Rochemont, Richard G. "The Tabloids." *The American Mercury* 9 (October 1926).

Dempsey, David. "No Way to Run a Publishing House: Horace Liveright." Review of *Horace Liveright: Publisher of the Twenties,* by Walter Gilmer. *The New York Times,* May 31, 1970.

Dempsey, Jack, with Charles J. McGuirk. "The Golden Gates." *The Saturday Evening Post,* October 20, 1934.

Derrick, Peter. "Catalyst for Development: Rapid Transit in New York." *New York Affairs* 9 (Fall 1986).

———. "The N.Y.C. Mess: Legacy of the 5¢ Fare." *Mass Transit* 8 (July 1981).

D'Esposito, Joshua. "Some of the Fundamental Principles of Air Rights." *Railway Age* 83 (October 1927).

Doig, Jameson W., and David Billington. "Ammann's First Bridge: A Study in Engineering, Politics, and Entrepreneurial Behavior." *Technology and Culture* 35 (July 1994).

Donaldson, Wellington. "First Years of Operation of Wards Island Sewage Treatment Works." *Sewage Works Journal* 11 (January 1939).

Duffus, Robert L. "Al Smith: An East Side Portrait." *Harper's Magazine* 152 (February 1926).

———. "Metal Roots That Feed the Living City." *The New York Times,* April 13, 1930.

———. "A Rising of Traffic Rolls over New York." *The New York Times,* February 9, 1930.

Dunlap, David W. "In a City of Skyscrapers, Which Is the Mightiest of the High? Experts Say It's No Contest." *The New York Times,* September 1, 2005

———. "Irwin Chanin, Builder of Theaters and Art Deco Towers, Dies at 96." *The New York Times,* February 26, 1988.

Durrer, Margot Ammann. "Memories of My Father." *Swiss American Historical Society Review,* April 4, 1979.

Faulkner, William. "The Art of Fiction XII: William Faulkner." Interview by Jean Stein. *The Paris Review* 12 (Spring 1956).

Ferree, Barr. "The Modern Office Building: Part I." *Inland Architect* 27 (February 1896).

Ferriss, Hugh. "The New Architecture." *The New York Times Book Review and Magazine,* March 19, 1922.

Fistere, John Cushman. "No Timid Man Could Hold This Job." *The American Magazine* 111 (June 1931).

Fleming, Thomas J. "Was It Ever Fun to Be Mayor?" *New York* (November 10, 1969).

Forbes, B. C. "Chrysler Tells How He Did It." *Forbes* (January 1, 1929).

Frank, Waldo. "One Hundred Per Cent American." *The New Yorker* 1 (October 10, 1925).

Fuller, George W. "Sewage Disposal Trends in the New York City Region." *Sewage Works Journal* 4 (July 1932).

Gallico, Paul. "Dempsey Knocks Out Firpo." *Daily News,* September 15, 1923.

———. "The Golden Decade." *The Saturday Evening Post,* September 15, 1931.

———. "The Man Who Flew Alone." *Daily News,* May 23, 1927.

———. "New Sports Writer Tests His Punch." *Daily News,* September 10, 1923.

Garrett, O. H. P. "Profiles: Fourteenth Street and Broadway." *The New Yorker* 1 (August 29, 1925).

Gerard, Jeremy. "William S. Paley, Builder of CBS, Dies at 89." *The New York Times,* October 27, 1990.

Gladwell, Malcolm. "The Televisionary." *The New Yorker* 78 (May 27, 2002)

Goldberger, Paul. "Architecture: Chanin, a Master of the Skyline." *The New York Times,* December 7, 1982.

——. "The Chrysler Building at 50." *The New York Times,* August 18, 1980.

——. "Perfect Space: The Chrysler Building Lobby, New York." *Travel & Leisure* 19 (June 1989).

——. "A Steely Humanist." Review of Donald L. Miller, *Lewis Mumford, A Life. The Atlantic Monthly* 264 (July 1989).

Gordon, John Steele. "An Immense and Distant Roof." *American Heritage* (February–March 1997).

Gray, Christopher. "An Art Deco Precursor of the Daily News Building." *The New York Times,* November 12, 1995.

——. "Neighborhood: East Fifty-seventh Street, Part 1." *Avenue* 9 (April 1985).

——. "Neighborhood: East Fifty-seventh Street, Part 3." *Avenue* 9 (June–July 1985).

——. "A Race for the Skies, Lost by a Spire." *The New York Times,* November 15, 1992.

——. "Streetscapes: A Prestigious Enclave with a Name in Question." *The New York Times,* September 21, 2003.

——. "Streetscapes: The Bergdorf Goodman Building on Fifth Avenue." *The New York Times,* August 30, 1998.

——. "Streetscapes: The Grand Central Viaduct." *The New York Times,* October 29, 1989.

——. "Streetscapes: William Van Alen." *The New York Times,* March 22, 1998.

——. "When a Monster Plied the West Side." *The New York Times,* December 22, 2011.

——. "Where the Orchestras Played and the Mice Presided." *The New York Times,* February 18, 2010.

Green, Abel. "Night Club Reviews: The Cotton Club (New York)." *Variety,* December 7, 1927.

Green, Penelope, "The Rivals." Review of *War Paint: Madame Helena Rubinstein and Miss Elizabeth Arden, Their Lives, Their Times, Their Rivalry,* by Lindy Woodhead. *The New York Times,* February 15, 2004.

——. Guinan, Texas. "My Life—AND HOW!" *New York Evening Journal,* May 1–2, April 29–20, 1929.

——. "Texas Guinan Says." *New York Evening Graphic,* May 6, 1931.

Hagerty, James A. "Tammany Hall: Its Structure and Its Rule." *The New York Times,* October 5, 1930.

Hall, Gladys. "He Makes the World at Home." *Classic* (August 1923).

Hall, Mordaunt. "Iron Workers Aloft." *The New York Times,* April 9, 1928.

——. "New Roxy Theatre Has Gala Opening." *The New York Times,* March 12, 1927.

——. "A Technical Manual," *The New York Times,* May 7, 1927.

——. "The Screen." *The New York Times,* May 7, 1927.

——. "The Screen: Al Jolson and the Vitaphone." *The New York Times,* October 7, 1927.

Haller, Mark H. "Illegal Enterprise: A Theoretical and Historical Interpretation." *Criminology* 28, no. 2 (1990).

Hanley, Thomas B. "Mayor Walker Settles Down to His Sixteen-Hour-a-Day Job." *New York World,* January 31, 1926.

Hansen, Harry. "The First Reader." *New York World Telegram,* September 26, 1933.

Hardin, Nancy, and Lois Long. "Profiles: Luxury, Inc." *The New Yorker* 10 (March 31, 1934).

Harding, Allan. "What Radio Has Done and What It Will Do Next." *The American Magazine* (March 1926).

Harriman, Margaret Case. "Profiles: Glamour Inc.: Elizabeth Arden." *The New Yorker* 11 (April 6, 1935).

Harrison, James R. "Greatest Ring Spectacle." *The New York Times,* September 23, 1927.

Haskell, Douglas. "Architecture: Chrysler's Pretty Bauble." *The Nation* 131 (October 22, 1930).

——. "The Lost New York of the Pan American Airways Building." *Architectural Forum* 119 (November 1963).

——. "The Stripes of the News." *The Nation* 131 (December 24, 1930).

——. "Unity and Harmony at Rockefeller Center." *Architectural Forum* 124 (January–February, 1966).

Hecht, Ben. "A Reporter at Large: The Olympian Eye." *The New Yorker* 3 (April 30, 1927).

Hellinger, Mark. "All in a Day." *Daily News,* November 7, 1933.

Hellman, Geoffrey T. "Profiles: How to Win Profits and Influence Literature—I." *The New Yorker* 15 (September 30, 1939).

——. "Profiles: How to Win Profits and Influence Literature—II." *The New Yorker* 15 (October 7, 1939).

——. "How to Win Profits and Influence Literature—III." *The New Yorker* 15 (October 14, 1939).

——. "Publisher—I: A Very Dignified Pavane." *The New Yorker* 24 (November 20, 1948).

——. "Publisher—II: Big Day for Random." *The New Yorker* 35 (May 16, 1959).

Herzog, Catherine. "The Movie Palace and the Theatrical Sources of Its Architectural Style." *Cinema Journal* 20 (Spring 1981).

Holland, Clifford M. "Linking New York and New Jersey." *The American City* 14 (March 1921).

Hood, Raymond M. "The American Radiator Company Building, New York." *The American Architect* 126 (November 19, 1924).

——. "Architecture." *New York World,* May 13, 1930.

——. "Attempting to Build with Black Brick." *Contacts* 56 (July 1927).

——. "New York's Skyline W. "Climb Much Higher," *Liberty* 2 (April 1926)

——. "Three Visions of New York." *Creative Art* 9 (August 1931).

Hood, Raymond, as told to Tisdale, F. S. "A City Under a Single Roof." *Nation's Business* 17 (November 1929).

Howe, Jerome W. "Boring Out a Highway Under the Hudson." *The New York Times,* September 14, 1924.

Howell, Mark. "The Chrysler Six, America's First Modern Automobile." *Antique Automobile* 36 (January–February 1972).

Humphreys, Joe. "The Rickard I Knew." *Collier's* 84 (November 9, 1929).

Hungerford, Edward. "The Greatest Railway Terminal in the World." *The Outlook* 102 (December 28, 1912).

Husting, Lucille. " 'Hello, Everybody!' A Trip 'Back Stage' Elicits 'Roxy's' Personal Story." *Radio News* (December 1927).

Huthmacher, J. Joseph. "Charles Evans Hughes and Charles Francis Murphy: The Metamorphosis of Progressivism." *New York History* 46 (January 1965).

Hyman, Stanley Edgar. "The Urban New Yorker." *The New Republic* 107 (July 20, 1942).

Inglis, William. "New York's New Gateway." *Harper's Magazine* 57 (February 1, 1913).

Ivins, Molly. "Paul Gallico." *The New York Times,* July 17, 1976.

Jacobs, Harry Allan. "Architects Discuss Future Building." *The New York Times,* December 13, 1931.

——. "Raymond Hood Uses Tablecloths and Pillars in Planning Modern Skyscrapers." *The New York Times,* December 7, 1930.

James, Edwin L. "Crowd Roars Thunderous Welcome." *The New York Times,* May 22, 1927.

Johns, Orrick. "Bridge Homes—A New Vision of the City." *The New York Times,* February 22, 1925.

Johnston, Alva. "Beer and Baseball." *The New Yorker* 8 (September 24, 1932).

——. "The Jimmy Walker Era." *Vanity Fair* (December 1932).

——. "Knickerbocker Village—I." *The New Yorker* 8 (August 6, 1932).

——. "Knickerbocker Village—II." *The New Yorker* 8 (August 13, 1932).

——. "Profiles: News Photographer—I." *The New Yorker* 10 (December 1, 1934).

——. "A Reporter at Large: Gangs 'A La Mode.'" *The New Yorker* 4 (August 25, 1928).

Kaempffert, Waldemar. "Burrowing into the Roots of the City." *The New York Times,* July 17, 1927.

Kahn, Ely Jacques. "Our Skyscrapers Take Simple Forms." *The New York Times,* May 2, 1926.

——. "Raymond Mathewson Hood, 1881–1934." *Architecture* 69 (October 1934).

Kahn, Roger. "The Real Babe Ruth." *Esquire* (August 1959).

Katz, Leon. "A Poet in Steel." *Portfolio* 1 (Summer 1988).

Keiffer, Elaine Brown. "Madame Rubinstein." *Life,* July 21, 1941.

Kennedy, John B. "Under Cover: An Interview with A. Bruce Bielaski." *Collier's,* August 13, 1927.

Kieran, John. "Sports of the Times." *The New York Times,* August 26, 1927.

——. "Sports of the Times." *The New York Times,* September 24, 1927.

——. "Sports of the Times." *The New York Times,* September 26, 1927.

——. "Sports of the Times." *The New York Times,* October 26, 1927.

Kofoed, Jack. "The Master of Ballyhoo." *The North American Review* 227 (March 1929).

Konvitz, Josef W. "William J. Wilgus and Engineering Projects to Improve the Port of New York, 1900–1930." *Technology and Culture* 30 (1989).

Krinsky, Carol Herselle. "The Fred F. French Building: Mesopotamia in Manhattan." *Antiques* (January 1982).

Kronenberger, Louis. "Gambler in Publishing: Horace Liveright." *The Atlantic Monthly* 97 (January 1965).

Lasser, Michael. "The Glorifier: Florenz Ziegfeld and the Creation of the American Showgirl." *The American Scholar* 63 (Summer 1994).

Lee, Joe. "Gene Tunney, 1897–1978." *The Ring* (February 1979).

Lewis, Alfred Henry. "Joseph Medill Patterson: An Apostle of Hope." *The Saturday Evening Post,* September 15, 1906.

Lewis, Harold M. "Motorways Proposed for New York Region." *The New York Times,* January 5, 1930.

Lewis, Lloyd. "The De Luxe Picture Palace." *The New Republic* 58 (March 27, 1929).

Lewis, Michael. "Dancing to New Rules, a Rhapsody in Chrome." *The New York Times,* May 26, 2005.

Liebling, A. J. "The Wayward Press, Mamie and Mr. O'Connell Carry On." *The New Yorker* 22 (June 8, 1946).

Lippmann, Walter. "Tammany Hall and Al Smith." *The Outlook* 148 (February 1, 1928).

Littell, Edmund M. "Men Wanted." *The American Magazine* (April 1930).

Liveright, Horace. "The Absurdity of Censorship." *The Independent* 110 (March 17, 1923).

Lowry, Helen Bullit. "New York's After-Midnight Clubs." *The New York Times,* February 5, 1922.

Lubschez, Ben J. "The Two Great Railway Stations of New York." *Journal of the Royal Institute of British Architects* 27 (June 12, 1920).

MacDonald, Carlyle. "Could Have Gone 500 Miles Farther." *The New York Times,* May 22, 1927.

Macgowan, Kenneth. "Profiles: Deus Ex Cinema." *The New Yorker* 3 (May 28, 1927).

Mackay, Ellin. "Why We Go to Cabarets: A Post-Debutante Explains." *The New Yorker* 1 (November 28, 1925).

MacKaye, Milton. "Poet in Steel." *The New Yorker* 10 (June 2, 1934).

Markey, Morris. "The Broadcasting Industry." *The New Yorker* 4 (March 3, 1928).

———. "Mr. Bruckner Explains." *The New Yorker* 1 (November 14, 1925).

———. "Night: Downtown." *The New Yorker* 3 (November 19, 1927).

———. "A Reporter at Large: Booze." *The New Yorker* 3 (December 31, 1927).

———. "A Reporter at Large: Conversations on Bootlegging—II." *The New Yorker* 4 (May 12, 1928).

———. "A Reporter at Large: Deus ex Machine." *The New Yorker* 2 (April 17, 1926).

Mason, Roy. "City Under One Roof Extends Borders." *The New York Times,* August 29, 1926.

McBride, Henry. "The Palette Knife." *Creative Art* 8 (May 1931).

McClintick, David. "What Hath William Paley Wrought?" *Esquire* 100 (December 1983).

McEvoy, J. P. "He Knew What They Wanted." *The Saturday Evening Post,* September 10, 1932.

McGeehan, W. O. "Condition." *The Saturday Evening Post,* September 22, 1928.

———. "Rickard Rounds Up the Rubes." *The New Yorker* 1 (December 12, 1925).

———. "The Social Life of an Athlete." *Vanity Fair* 29 (August 1927).

McGoldrick, Joseph. "The New Tammany." *The American Mercury* 15 (September 1928).

———. "Our American Mayors, XII: 'Jimmy' Walker." *National Municipal Review* 17 (October 1928).

McGrath, Charles. "A Lunch Club for the Higher-Ups." *The New York Times,* May 26, 2005.

McHugh, F. D. "Manhattan's Mightiest 'Minaret.'" *Scientific American* 142 (April 1930).

McKenzie, Alex. "Sarnoff: Controversial Pioneer." *IEEE Spectrum* 9, no. 1 (January 1972)

Melnick, Ross. "Rethinking Rothafel: Roxy's Forgotten Legacy." *The Moving Image* (Fall 2003).

———. "Station R-O-X-Y." *Film History* 17 (2005).

Mermey, Maurice. "Croesus's Sixty Acres." *The North American Review* 227 (January 1929).

Meyers, Andrew A. "Invisible Cities: Lewis Mumford, Thomas Adams, and the Invention of the Regional City, 1923–1929." *Business and Economic History* 27 (Winter 1998).

Michaelis, David. "77 Stories: The Secret Life of a Skyscraper." *Manhattan Inc.* (June 1986)

Millard, Ruth. "Jazz Is Now Big Business." *The World Magazine* (May 22, 1927).

Mills, Chester P. "Dry Rot." *Collier's,* September 17, 1927.

———. "Where the Booze Begins." *Collier's,* October 15, 1927.

Mitchell, Joseph. "The Mohawks in High Steel." *The New Yorker* 25 (September 17, 1949).

Moscow, Warren. "Jimmy Walker's City Hall." *The New York Times Magazine* (August 22, 1976).

Mullett, Mary B. "The Chanin's of Broadway." *The American Magazine* 106 (August 1928).

———. "Roxy and His Gang." *The American Magazine* 99 (March 1925).

Mumford, Lewis. "The Barclay-Vesey Building." *The New Republic* 51 (July 6, 1927).

———. "Cities Fit to Live In." *The Nation* 167 (May 15, 1948).

———. "Culture of Cities." *Journal of the American Institute of Architects* 35 (June 1961).

———. "The Drama of the Machines." *Scribner's Magazine* 88 (August 1930).

———. "The Intolerable City: Must It Keep on Growing?" *Harper's Magazine* 157 (February 11, 1926).

———. "Is the Skyscraper Tolerable?" *Architecture* 55 (February 1927).

———. "Notes on Modern Architecture:" *The New Republic* 66 (March 18, 1931).

———. "The Plan of New York: I." *The New Republic* 71 (June 15, 1932).

———. "The Plan of New York: II." *The New Republic* 71 (June 22, 1932).

———. "The Sacred City." *The New Republic* 45 (January 27, 1926).

———. "The Sky Line: Bridges and Buildings." *The New Yorker* 7 (November 21, 1931).

———. "The Sky Line: The Regional Plan." *The New Yorker* 8 (May 21, 1932).

———. "The Theory and Practice of Regionalism." *Sociological Review* 29 (January 1928).

Murchison, Kenneth M. "The Chrysler Building, as I See It." *The American Architect* 138 (September 1930).

———. "Mr. Murchison of New York Says—Architect Tolerates French and His Building." *The Architect* 7 (January 1927).

———. "The Spires of Manhattan." *Architectural Forum* 53 (June 1930).

Murray, Jim. "A Son of St. Patrick." *Los Angeles Times,* March 17, 1971.

Muschamp, Herbert. "Architecture View: For All the Star Power, a Mixed Performance." *The New York Times,* July 12, 1992.

———. "Restoration Liberates Grand Vistas, and Ideas: An Appraisal." *The New York Times,* October 2, 1998.

New York Housing Association. "The Ever-Narrowing Home." *Housing (New York)* 18 (June 1929).

Noble, David Grant. "Mohawk Steelworkers of Manhattan." *Four Winds* 2 (Spring 1982).

Norris, Margaret, and Brenda Ueland. "Riding the Girders." *The Saturday Evening Post,* April 11, 1931.

Nugent, William Henry. "The Sports Section." *The American Mercury* (March 1929).

Ogren, Kathy J. "Roseland Ballroom." *ENYC.*

Owen, Russell. "A Boy's Day in a Big City." *The New York Times,* June 14, 1927.

———. "A Master Ditch Digger." *The New Yorker* 3 (June 4, 1927).

Parsons, William Barclay. "Twenty-Five Years of the New York Subway." *The New York Times,* October 27, 1929.

Patterson, Alicia, as told to Hal Burton. "This Is the Life I Love." *The Saturday Evening Post* 231 (February 21, 1959).

Patterson, Jim, with Bob Perrone. "Rene Paul Chambellan—One of Art Deco's Greatest Sculptors." www.louisvilleartdeco.com/feature/RenePaulChambellan.

Pedrick, Captain William J. "The Story of Fifth Avenue." *The Magazine of Business* 53 (February 1928).

Peiss, Kathy. "Making Faces: The Cosmetics Industry and the Cultural Construction of Gender, 1890–1930." *Genders* 7 (Spring 1990).

Pierpont, Claudia Roth. "The Silver Spire." *The New Yorker* 78 (November 18, 2002).

Poole, Ernest. "Cowboys of the Skies." *Everybody's Magazine* 19 (November 1908).

Poore, C. G. "Program for a Greater Port of New York." *The New York Times,* April 13, 1930.

———. "The Riveter's Panorama of New York." *The New York Times Magazine,* January 5, 1930.

———. "A Skyscraper Builder Began as a Newsboy." *The New York Times,* January 20, 1929.

Pope, Robert Anderson. "Grand Central Terminal Station." *The Town-Planning Review* 2 (April 1911).

Pope, Virginia. "Now the Penthouse Palace Is Evolving." *The New York Times,* March 23, 1930.

Price, Matlack. "Chanin Building." *Architectural Forum* 50 (May 1929).

Pringle, Henry F. "Jimmy Walker." *The American Mercury* 9 (November 1926).

———. "Profiles: The Janitor's Boy." *The New Yorker* 3 (March 5, 1927).

Ramey, Jessie. "The Bloody Blonde and the Marble Woman: Gender and Power in the Case of Ruth Snyder." *Journal of Social History* 37 (Spring 2004).

Ramsaye, Terry. "Intimate Visits to the Homes of Famous Film Magnates." *Photoplay* 32 (October 1927).

Reinitz, Bertram. "Night Sailings Are Now Events." *The New York Times,* April 1, 1928.

Reynolds, Walter. "Don't Give the People What They Want." *The Green Book Magazine* 12 (August 1914).

Rice, Grantland. "Boxing for a Million Dollars." *American Review of Reviews* (October 1926).

Roberts, Randy. "Jack Dempsey: An American Hero in the 1920s." *Journal of Popular Culture* 8 (1974).

de Rochemont, Richard G. "The Tabloids." *The American Mercury* 9 (October 1926).

Rogers, Cameron. "Youth at the Top." *World's Work* 58 (January 1929).

Rogers, Lindsay. "Fiscal Crisis of the World's Largest City," *New Outlook* (January 1933).

Rosenblatt, Maurice. "Joe Ryan and His Kingdom." *The Nation* 161 (November 24, 1945).

———. "The Scandal of the Waterfront." *The Nation* 161 (November 17, 1945).

Rozhon, Tracie. "A Scalloped Dream, a Hotelier's Fantasy." *The New York Times,* July 24, 1997.

Ruttenbaum, Steven. "Visible City, the Ritz Tower." *Metropolis* 4 (May 1985).

Rybak, T. James. "Guglielmo Marconi." *Popular Electronics* 9, no. 4 (April 1992).

Sarnoff, David. "Radio Progress Passes in Review." *The New York Times,* September 18, 1927.

Sarnoff, David, as told to Mary Margaret McBride. "Radio." *The Saturday Evening Post,* August 7, 1926.

———. "Radio, Part Two." *The Saturday Evening Post* (August 14, 1926).

Saylor, Henry H. "The Editor's Diary." *Architecture* 63 (June 1931).

Schneider, Walter E. "Fabulous Rise of N.Y. Daily News." *Editor & Publisher,* June 24, 1939.

Schnitman, L. Seth. "Statistical Analysis of New York City Construction—1919 to 1930." *Real Estate Record and Builders' Guide* 126 (October 11, 1930).

Schroeder, Walter. "New York City Starts $300,000,000 Sewage Treatment Program." *The American City* 45 (August 1931).

Schulberg, Budd. "Joe Docks, Forgotten Man of the Waterfront." *The New York Times,* December 28, 1952.

Schumach, Murray. "Babe Ruth." *The New York Times,* August 7, 1948.

Seibold, Louis. "The Morals of Tammany." *North American Review* 226 (November 1928).

Seldes, Gilbert. "The Great Glorifier." *The New Yorker* 69 (May 31, 1993); originally published in 1931.

Shepherd, William G. "At the Rum Row War." *Collier's,* May 30, 1925.

Simon, Richard L. "Trade Winds: Try and Stop Them." *The Saturday Review of Literature* 33 (December 23, 1950).

Smith, Alexander Rogers. "Greatest Shipping Port in the World." *Review of Reviews* 72 (October 1925).

Smith, Alison. "The Glorifying Machine." *Daily News,* August 17, 1927.

Smith, Red. "Jack Dempsey Is Dead Here at 87." *The New York Times,* June 1, 1983.

Sobel, Bernard. "This Was Ziegfeld." *The American Mercury* 60 (January 1945).

Solon, Leon V. "The Titan City Exhibition." *The Architectural Record* 59 (January 1926).

Sorel, Nancy Caldwell. "First Encounters: Fanny Brice and Florenz Ziegfeld." *The Atlantic Monthly* 257 (January 1986).

Sparling, Earl. "Is New York American?" *Scribner's Magazine* 90 (August 1931).

Starrett, Theodore. "The Grand Central Terminal Station." *Architecture and Building* 45 (April 1913).

Stern, Edith M. "A Man Who Was Unafraid." *The Saturday Review of Literature* 24 (June 28, 1941).

Stewart, Harry A. "Don't Keep Half Your Brain Busy Trying to Hide Something." *The American Magazine* 97 (April 1924).

Stumpf, Charles K. "Rootin', Tootin', Shootin' Texas Guinan." *Under Western Skies* 9 (January 1980).

Sullivan, Mark. "Why the West Dislikes New York." *World's Work* 51 (February 1926).

Swados, Felice. "Waterfront." *The New Republic* 93 (February 2, 1938).

Swales, Francis S. "Draftsmanship and Architecture, V: As Exemplified by the Work of William Van Alen." *Pencil Points* 10 (August 1929).

Swerling, Jo. "Profiles: Beauty in Jars and Vials." *The New Yorker* 4 (June 30, 1928).

Talese, Gay. "City Bridge Creator, 85, Keeps Watchful Eye on His Landmarks." *The New York Times,* March 26, 1964.

Talmey, Allene. "Profiles: Man Against the Sky." *The New Yorker* 7 (April 11, 1931).

Taylor, Deems. "The City That Died of Greatness." *Vanity Fair* 31 (November 1928).

Teachout, Terry. "Huckster and Publisher: Horace Liveright Discovered That Publishing Is Not Enough, You've Got to Sell It Too." Review of *Firebrand: The Life of Horace Liveright,* by Tom Dardis. *The New York Times,* 16 July 1995.

Tebbel, John. "Leon Shimkin: The Businessman as Publisher." *The Saturday Review* 49 (September 10, 1966).

———. "Publisher to an Era." *The Saturday Review* 47 (August 29, 1964).

Teitel, Nathan. "The Man Who Invented Women." *The Saturday Review* 55 (November 4, 1972).

Thomas, Norman, and Paul Blanshard. "Jimmy Walker." *The Nation* 135 (October 5, 1932).

Thompson, Hugh. "The Greatest Railroad Terminal in the World." *Munsey's Magazine* 11 (April 1911).

Tierney, John. "What's New York the Capital of Now?" *The New York Times Magazine,* November 20, 1994.

Tittle, Walter. "Ziegfeld of the Follies." *World's Work* 53 (March 1927).

T-Square. "The Sky Line: Against the Graybar." *The New Yorker* 3 (May 21, 1927).

———. "The Sky Line: A Midwinter Renaissance." *The New Yorker* 5 (January 18, 1930).

———. "The Sky Line: Roxy to the Fore." *The New Yorker* 3 (March 19, 1927).

——. "The Sky Line: Some New York Giants." *The New Yorker* 4 (November 3, 1928).

Tunis, John. "Changing Trends in Sport." *Harper's Magazine* 170 (December 1934).

Turner, Daniel L. "Is There a Vicious Circle of Transit Development and City Congestion?" *National Municipal Review* 15 (June 1926).

Tynan, Kenneth. "Profiles: The Girl in the Black Helmet." *The New Yorker* 55 (June 11, 1979).

Van Alen, William. "Architect Finds New Designs in Frame of Steel." *New York Herald Tribune,* September 7, 1930.

——. "The Chrysler Building, New York." *Architecture and Building* 62 (August 1930).

——. "The Structure and Metal Work of the Chrysler Building." *Architectural Forum* 53 (October 1930).

Villard, O. G. "Tabloid Offenses." *The Forum* 77 (March 1927).

Volse, Louis A. "An Artist in Steel Design." *Engineering News-Record* 160 (May 15, 1958).

Vorse, Mary Heaton. "The Pirates' Nest of New York." *Harper's Magazine* 204 (April 1952).

Walker, J. Bernard. "The Hudson River Vehicular Tunnel." *Scientific American* 137 (September 1927).

Walker, Waldo. "Great Express Highways for New York Zone." *The New York Times,* November 21, 1926.

Ward, John W. "The Meaning of Lindbergh's Flight." *American Quarterly* 10 (Spring 1958).

Weber, Adna F. "Rapid Transit and the Housing Problem." *Municipal Affairs* 6 (Fall 1902).

Weiner, M. R. "Fiorello's Finest Hour." *American Heritage* 12 (October 1961).

Weiss, Marc A. "Skyscraper Zoning: New York's Pioneering Role." *Journal of the American Planning Association* 58 (Spring 1992).

Welch, Richard. "The Glamorous Jimmy Walker." *American History Illustrated* 18 (1983).

Wells, George Y. "Patterson and the Daily News." *The American Mercury* 59 (December 9, 1944).

West, Donald. "Spotlight: The House That Paley Built—And Keeps." *The New York Times,* October 24, 1976.

Wheeler, William G. "Safeguarding Construction Crews in a Great Skyscraper." *Buildings and Building Management* 29 (December 2, 1929).

White, E. B. "You Can't Resettle Me!" *The Saturday Evening Post,* October 10, 1936.

Whiteside, Thomas. "David Sarnoff's Fifty Fabulous Years." *Collier's,* October 12, 1956.

Widmer, Urs C. "Othmar Hermann Ammann, 1879–1965: His Way to Great Bridges." *Review* 15 (June 1979).

Wilgus, William J. "The Grand Central Terminal in Perspective." *American Society of Civil Engineers, Transactions, Paper No. 2119* 106 (October 1940).

Williams, Alberta. "White-Collar Neighbors." *The New Yorker* 10 (November 24, 1934).

Willis, Carol. "The Titan City: Forgotten Episodes in American Architecture." *Skyline* (October 1982).

——. "Zoning and Zeitgeist: The Skyscraper City in the 1920s." *Journal of the Society of Architectural Historians* 95 (March 1986).

Wisehart, M. K. "The Greatest Bridge in the World and the Man Who Is Building It." *The American Magazine* 34 (June 1928).

Wolner, Edward. "The City-Within-a-City and Skyscraper Patronage in the 1920's." *Journal of Architectural Education* 42 (Winter 1989).

Woolf, S. J. "Jimmy Walker: Toastmaster to Our Town." *The New York Times,* April 8, 1945.

——. "A Motor Car Magnate's Rise to Power." *The New York Times,* August 19, 1928.

Young, James C. "Broadcasting Personality." *Radio Broadcast* (July 1924).

———. "Fifth Avenue's Changing Tides." *The New York Times,* July 17, 1927.

Ziegfeld, Florenz Jr. "Beauty, the Fashions and the Follies." *The Ladies' Home Journal* 40 (March 1923).

———. "Picking Out Pretty Girls for the Stage." *The American Magazine* 88 (December 1919).

———. "The Showman's Shifting Sands." *The Ladies' Home Journal* 11 (June 1923).

Manuscript Collections

Alfred E. Smith Private Papers, New York State Library, Albany, NY.

Sherwood Anderson Papers, Roger and Julie Baskes Department of Special Collections, Newberry Library, Chicago, IL.

Edward L. Bernays Papers, Manuscript Division, Library of Congress, Washington, DC.

Bennett Cerf Papers, Rare Books and Manuscripts Library, Columbia University, New York, NY.

Fred F. French Companies Records, 1902–1911, New York Public Library, New York, NY.

Harvey Wiley Corbett Architectural Drawings and Papers, Avery Architectural and Fine Arts Library, Columbia University, New York, NY.

Theodore Dreiser Papers, Annenberg Rare Book and Manuscript Library, Van Pelt-Dietrich Library, University of Pennsylvania, Philadelphia, PA.

James A. Farley Papers, Manuscript Division, Library of Congress, Washington, DC.

Hugh Ferriss Architectural Drawings and Papers Collection, Avery Architectural and Fine Arts Library, Columbia University, New York, NY.

F. Scott Fitzgerald Papers, Department of Rare Books and Special Collections, Firestone Library, Princeton University, Princeton, NJ.

Raymond M. Hood Architectural Drawings and Papers, Avery Architectural and Fine Arts Library, Columbia University, New York, NY.

John Hylan Papers, New York City Municipal Archives, New York, NY.

Otto H. Kahn Papers, Department of Rare Books and Special Collections, Firestone Library, Princeton University, Princeton, NJ.

Manuel Komroff Papers, Rare Book and Manuscript Library, Butler Library, Columbia University, New York, NY.

Horace Liveright Papers, Annenberg Rare Book and Manuscript Library, Van Pelt-Dietrich Library, University of Pennsylvania, Philadelphia, PA.

Joseph Medill Patterson Papers, Donnelley Library, Lake Forest College, Lake Forest, IL.

Lewis Mumford Papers, Annenberg Rare Book & Manuscript Library, Van Pelt-Dietrich Library, University of Pennsylvania, Philadelphia, PA.

William Patterson Papers. Lake Forest College, Lake Forest, IL.

Regional Plan Papers, Cornell University Library, Ithaca, New York.

Billy Rose Theatre Collection, New York Public Library, Library for the Performing Arts, Billy Rose Theatre Division, New York, NY.

Bertrand Russell Archives, McMaster University, Hamilton, Ontario.

David Sarnoff Papers, Hagley Library and Archives, Wilmington. Delaware. The papers were moved here after the David Sarnoff Library and Museum in Princeton, NJ, closed its doors.

Lincoln Schuster Papers, Rare Book and Manuscript Library, Butler Library, Columbia University, New York, NY.

George S. Silzer Files, New Jersey State Archives, Trenton N.J.

Richard L. Simon Papers, Rare Book and Manuscript Library, Butler Library, Columbia University, New York, NY.

James Walker Papers, New York City Municipal Archives, New York, NY.

William J. Wilgus Papers, Manuscripts and Archives Division, New York Public Library, New York, NY.

Mabel Walker Willebrandt Papers, Manuscript Division, Library of Congress, Washington, DC.

Other Collections

Columbia University Oral History Collection, Butler Library, Columbia University, New York, NY.

Department of Prints, Photographs, and Architectural Collections, New-York Historical Society, New York, NY.

Oral History, American Music, Yale University Library, Special Collections, New Haven, CT.

The Paley Center for Media, New York, NY.

Still Picture Research Room, National Archives and Records Administration, College Park, MD.

Government Documents

Report of the City Committee on Plan and Survey. (NY; 1928.)

[State of New York], Joint Legislative Committee to Investigate the Administration of Various Departments of Government of the City of New, Hearing[s] July 21, 1931 to December 8, 1932 (NY i 1931–32), New York City Municipal Archives, NY, NY.

Bureau of Census, Fifteenth Census of the United States Population, Vol. III, pt. 2 (Washington, DC, 1932).

"Remarks of the Mayor on Organization of the City Committee on Plan and Survey," June 21, 1926, James J. Walker Papers, Municipal Archives, New York, New York.

Report of the City Committee on Plan and Survey. (NY 1928). James J. Walker Papers, Municipal Archives, NY, NY.

INDEX

Page numbers in *italics* refer to illustrations.

Adair, Eleanor, 206
Adams, Franklin P., 563
Adams, Rayne, 437
Adams, Thomas, 449–52, 486
Aeolian Hall, 307, 317, 511
African Americans, 49, 326, 410
 as boxers, 3, 377, 399–400, 404–5, 427
 integration of, 519, 520
 in jazz, 499, 503–19
 segregation of, 16, 104, 176, 515
 Talented Tenth of, 517
 voting of, 16
 see also racism
Ahearn, James, 101
Ahlschlager, Walter W., 269
Albany, N.Y., 2, 9, 19–22, 27, 28, 31, 34,
 40–42, 57, 72, 156, 552
Albany Knickerbocker, 27
Alcock, John W., 133*n*
Alexander, Grover Cleveland, 388
Alexander, Jack, 106, 367
Alexanderson, Ernst F. W., 299, 303
Alger, Horatio, Jr., 251
Algonquin Round Table, 125, 211, 333–34
Alhambra Theatre, 278
Ali, Muhammad, 377
Alice's Adventures in Wonderland (Carroll),
 171
Allen, Frederick Lewis, 123, 305
Allen, Gracie, 331
Allen, Lee, 381
American Baseball League, 378–79,
 392–93, 425
American Basketball League, 408
American Federation of Labor, 320
American Institute of Architects, 164*n,*
 262

American Mercury, 118
American Radiator Building, 222, 437–39,
 442
American Revolution, 478
American Socialist Party, 27, 343, 547*n*
American Society of Civil Engineers, 163
American Telephone & Telegraph (AT&T),
 283, 285, 299, 306, 314–15, 318, 321
 radio broadcasting of, 283–85, 308–10,
 321, 322
American Tragedy, An (Dreiser), 543, 546,
 559–60, 580
Ammann, Klary, 481
Ammann, Lilly Wehrli, 472, 473, 476,
 481
Ammann, Othmar, xv, 60*n,* 471–84
Amos 'n' Andy, 326–27, 331
Anderson, Dave, 438
Anderson, Harold M., 142
Anderson, Sherwood, 344, 436, 543–44,
 546, 555, 556, 558–59, 581–82
Andrews, Lincoln C., 86, 91
Angell, Katharine Sergeant, 214
Angeluzzi, Larry, 460
Annenberg, Max, 350
Annenberg, Moses, 350
Ansonia Hotel, 381, 387, 529
anti-Catholicism, 16, 437
Anti-Saloon League, 9, 69, 72
anti-Semitism, 117, 176, 182, 304, 310,
 320, 559
Architectural League, 441
Arden, Elizabeth, xv, 202–4, 206–10, 213,
 471
Arlen, Michael, 264
Armour, Tommy, 414
Armstrong, Louis "Satchmo," 508

Army, U.S., 43, 71, 208, 211, 233
  1st Division (Big Red One) of, 345
  42nd Division (Rainbow), 345
Arno, Peter, 215
Art Deco, xi, 47, 201, 217, 222, 229, 245–46, 258, 260, 494
Art Moderne, 201, 245
Art Nouveau, 201
Asbury, Herbert, 95, 115
Astaire, Fred, 121, 406
Astor, Caroline Webster Schermerhorn, 181–82, 211
Astor, Helen Dinsmore Huntington, 66, 182, 189, 280
Astor, John Jacob, IV, 181
Astor, Madeleine, 181
Astor, Vincent, 181–82, 280
Astor family, 117, 177, 181–82, 185, 194, 287–88, 403, 409
Atkinson, Brooks, 272, 281–82, 528, 535–36, 540
Atlanta Penitentiary, 71, 89–90, 104, 105
Atlantic Monthly, 544
Atlantic Ocean, 144, 156, 197, 459
  great liners on, 179–80, 181, 300–301, 426, 465
  Lindbergh's solo flight across, 133, 139–43
  wireless communication across, 298, 300–301, 303, 313–14
Attell, Abe, 423
audion, 299
Augusta, 87
Australia, 204–5
Aylesworth, Merlin Hall, 311, 326

Babe Comes Home (film), 389
Baker, Frank "Home Run," 379
Baker, Johnny, 52
Balenciaga, 194
Ballon, Hilary, 165
Baltimore & Ohio Railroad, 246
Baltimore Orioles, 379, 384
Bank of Manhattan Building, 250, 257
Banton, Joab, 55
Barber Shop Ballads (Spaeth, ed.), 567–68

Barclay-Vesey Building, 222, 439
Barfield, Soldier, 3
Barnes, Charles, 463
Barnouw, Erik, 313
Barnum, P. T., 272
Barnum & Bailey Circus, 351
Barry, Dave, 421–23
Bartlett, Elise, 581
Barton, Bruce, 227
Barton, Enos, 232*n*
Baseball: The Golden Age (Seymour), 379*n*
Battle Row Ladies' Social and Athletic Club, 99–100
Bayonne Bridge, 477, 478, 481
Beaton, Cecil, 262
Beautiful and the Damned, The (Fitzgerald), 352
Bechet, Sidney, 506, 510
Beebe, Lucius, 39
Beekman, James, 189
Beeler, Paul, 421–22
beer
  illegal brewing of, 92, 94, 104–5, 108–9, 389
  near, 104, 389
  needle, 105
Beiderbecke, Bix, 511
Belasco, David, 22, 359, 362, 403, 424, 520
Bell, Alexander Graham, 314
Bell, Daniel, 68, 498
Belle of the Nineties (film), 94
Bellevue Hospital Psycopathic Ward, 44
Bell Labs, 315
Bellows, George, 375
Bell System, 310
Benchley, Robert, 125, 127, 211, 214
Benjamin Franklin Bridge, 476
Bennett, Floyd, 138
Bennett, James Gordon, 338, 339
Benny, Jack, 330, 331
Bent, Silas, 359
Berengaria, 25, 465
Berg, A. Scott, 137–38
Berg, Gertrude, 335
Bergdorf, Herman, 192–93

Bergdorf Goodman, xiii, 8, 147, 191–95, 202, 214

Berger, Meyer, 94, 242, 244

Berlin, 48, 143*n*

Berlin, Ellin Mackay, 117

Berlin, Irving, 21, 30, 117, 274, 275, 359, 388, 491, 522, 523, 528, 531, 536, 575

Bernays, Edward L., 324–25, 334, 547*n*, 551

Berns, Charles, 124–28

Bernstein, Leo, 512

Berry, Charles, 44, 57

Beyond the Horizon (O'Neill), 549

Bielaski, A. Bruce, 86–89, 91

Bigard, Barney, 510*n*

Billington, David P., 481

Biltmore Hotel, 263

Bing, Alexander, 174, 445

Bing, Leo, 174

Bing & Bing, 174

Biography of an Idea (Bernays), 547*n*

Bishop, Jim, 340

"Black and Tan Fantasy," 504, 513

Black Boy, 560–61

Blake, Eubie, 509

Bledsoe, Jules, 540

Block, Harry, 514

Block, Paul, 576

Bloom, Ken, 287

blues, 506, 508, 510, 516, 517

Blythe, Dick, 138

B'nai B'rith, 8

Board of Aldermen, N.Y., 38, 49

Board of Estimate and Apportionment, N.Y., 13, 38–39, 41, 42, 44, 48, 57, 58, 60

Body Heat (film), 367*n*

Bombay Bicycle Club, 123

Bonanno, Joseph, 65

Boni, Albert, 543, 548

Boni, Charles, 548

Boni & Liveright, 543–46, 548–49, 553–60, 563, 568, 571, 574, 580–81

Book-of-the-Month Club, 568

Bordman, Gerald, 541

Boston, Mass., 44, 107, 202, 285, 306, 394

Boston Evening Transcript, 562

Boston Red Sox, 146, 378–79

Bourke-White, Margaret, 256–57
    Chrysler Building studio of, 262–63
    pet alligators of, 263

Bow, Clara, 141

Bowes, Edward, 335

Boxer Rebellion, 276

Boyle, John F., 402

Boyle's Thirty Acres, 306, 402, 422

Bradley, Edward R., 531

Brady, James "Diamond Jim," 526

Brandon, Ruth, 205

Brands, H. W., 314*n*

Breer, Carl, 253

Brennan, Bill, 400–401, 404, 411

Brenner, Sam, 125–26

Breslin, Jimmy, 94

Brice, Fanny, 528, 532

Brisbane, Arthur, 172–73, 175, 348, 521

British Bahamas, 73, 77–78

Broadcasting: Its New Day (Rothafel), 285

Bronfman, Samuel, 78

Bronx-Whitestone Bridge, 481

Brooklyn Bridge, 20, 229, 456, 477, 479

Brooklyn Dodgers football team, 90

Brooklyn-Manhattan Transit Company (BMT), 14

Brooklyn Navy Yard, 125

Brooklyn Rapid Transit Company (BRT), 14*n*

Brooks, Louise, 328–29, 333, 528

Broun, Heywood, 122, 125, 377–78

Brower, John, 410

Brown, Arthur W., 133*n*

Brown, Frederick, 184–86, 190–92, 216

Brown, Josephine "Granny," 357

Brown, Rose Levy, 186

Brunswick Records, 512

Buckner, Emory Roy, 65–66, 82, 86–87, 89, 119–20, 128–30, 137

Buffalo, N.Y., 154, 156, 243

Buffalo Bill's Wild West Show, 525

Buick Motor Company, 252–53

Burkan, Nathan, 88–89

Burke, Anna Walker "Nan," 4, 5

Burke, Mary William "Billie," 521, 524, 529–32, 576–79

Burkeley Crest, 521, 529–30, 538, 576–78

Burnham, Daniel H., 163, 174, 449

Burns, George, 331

Burns, James "Bud," 108

Burr, Aaron, 16

Busch, Niven, Jr., 232–33

Byrd, Richard E., 135–39, 143n

Byron, George Gordon, Lord, 25

Cabinet of Dr. Caligari, The (film), 281

Café des Beaux Arts, 112

Cain, James M., 367n

California, 48, 136
  gold boom in, 399–400

Calloway, Cab, 514, 517

Calvary Cemetery, 34

Campbell, Maurice, 109

Canada, 72, 77, 206, 414–15, 457
  distilleries in, 78, 103

"Can't Help Lovin' Dat Man," 540

Cantor, Eddie, 330, 335, 522, 523, 528, 530, 534–36, 542, 577–78

capitalism, 45, 47, 84, 162, 188, 307, 342, 343, 491

Capitol Theatre, 270, 281–87, 292, 309

Capone, Al, 107, 137, 418, 423

Carnegie, Andrew, 183, 197, 336, 418

Carnegie, Hattie, xv, 196–99, 201, 210, 471

Caro, Robert, 452

Carpathia, SS, 300–301

Carpenter, J. E. R., 174, 264

Carpentier, Georges, 306, 321, 401–4, 408, 413

Cassatt, Alexander, 160–61

CBS World News, 337

Cellini, Benvenuto, 553

censorship, 543, 552–53

Century Club, 439

Century Theatre, 130

Cerf, Bennett Alfred, 543–46, 550–51, 581–82
  death of, 574
  publishing career of, 543–44, 554–58, 561, 570–75
  on *What's My Line?*, 574n

Cerf, Frederika Wise, 554

Cerf, Gustave, 554

Chambellan, Rene Paul, 245–46

Chamberlin, Clarence D., 135–36, 138–39, 143n

Chandler, Raymond, 367n

Chandler, Robert W., 435

Chanel, 124

"Changing Beauty of Park Avenue, The" (Z. Fitzgerald), 151–52

Chanin, Henry, 232, 234, 245, 247, 286

Chanin, Irwin S., xv, 8, 231–35, 240–41, 245–48, 251, 260, 269–70, 286

Chanin, Simon, 233

Chanin, Zenda, 233

Chanin Building, 217, 232–33, 244–47, 249, 260, 264
  construction of, 235–42, 244–45, 251, 266

Chanin Construction Company, 232, 234–35, 245–46, 269

Chaplin, Charlie, 261, 274, 283, 329, 402, 527

Chapman, John Arthur, 340, 348, 352–53, 368–69

Charles Scribner's Sons, 549, 559

Charleston (dance), 121, 140, 515, 517

Chase, Stuart, 169, 174–75, 178

Chase, W. Parker, 168, 216

Chase Securities, 254

Chesterton, G. K., 291

Chicago, Ill., 44, 114, 131, 136, 156, 161, 163, 173–74, 202, 264, 309, 417–24
  crime in, 107
  Irish in, 341
  jazz in, 504, 508, 509
  1909 Plan for, 449
  red light district in, 342
  skyscrapers in, 217, 236

Chicago & Great Western Railroad, 252

Chicago Art Institute, 344

Chicago Civic Opera, 318

Chicago Musical College, 525, 526

Chicago Tribune, 341–46, 367, 375, 437

Chicago White Sox, 379
  1919 "Black Sox" scandal of, 381

Chidwick, John P., 9–10
Children's Court, N.Y., 28
China, 276, 342, 402
Chrysler, Della Forker, 252, 261
Chrysler, Jack, 250
Chrysler, Walter, Jr., 250
Chrysler, Walter P., xv, 8, 147, 248–63, 268,
    271, 359, 370, 407
  automotive career of, 252–56, 261
  celebrity of, 255
  character and personality of, 250–52,
    255–57, 261
  childhood and adolescence of, 251–52
  marriage and family of, 250, 252, 261
Chrysler Building, 47, 217, 222, 255–64,
    271
  Cloud Club in, 260–62
  construction of, 251, 256–58
  gargoyles and eagles on, 260, 263
  height of, 257–59
  iconic Art Deco architecture of, 249–51,
    256–60
  illumination of, 259n
  interior of, 259–61, 262–63
  tower and steel needle atop, 257–58,
    260, 262, 370
Chrysler Motors, 249, 255, 261, 328
  Chrysler Six of, 253–54, 256
Churchill, Winston, 79, 189
Citizens Union, 51
City: Rediscovering the Center (Whyte),
    442n
City College of New York, 443, 546
City Committee on Plan and Survey,
    56–57
City Hall, 3, 13, 18, 30, 36–39, 41–42,
    58–59, 61, 108, 134, 145, 155, 382
City Housing Corporation, 445–46
Civil Liberties Union, 552
civil rights movement, 327n
Civil War, U.S., 16, 71, 156, 525
Clausen & Flanagan Brewing Company,
    104
Clean Books Bill, 22, 552
Clean Water Act, 58
Clinton, William Jefferson, 94, 102n

Cliquot Club Eskimos, 318
Cloak, Suit, and Skirt Manufacturers'
    Protective Association, 490
Clough, Matilda Golden "Goldie," 522–24,
    532–33, 540
Clougher, Harry J., 50–51
Club Argonaut, 103
Club Deluxe, 104
Club Durant, 103
Club Kentucky, 504, 508, 512–13, 516
Club Richmond, 117
Coast Guard, U.S., 65, 70, 73, 398
  corruption in, 85–86, 87, 88
  ships acquired by, 79–80
Coates, Robert M., 228, 230
Coats, George A., 321–23, 325
Cobb, Ty, 379–80, 381, 387
Cochran, Thomas C., 252
Cohan, George M., 403
Cohron, E. C., 80, 87–89
Coli, François, 135, 141
Collier's, 91
Collingwood, Charles, 337
Columbia, 135–36, 143n
Columbia Broadcasting System (CBS), 3,
    292, 322–28
  advertising on, 326, 327, 328, 329–32
  NBC competition with, 322, 325–27,
    329–32, 334–36
  news on, 337
  Paley's purchase of, 318–20, 323–24, 504
  programming on, 319, 322–23, 326, 327,
    329–32, 334, 335, 517
  radio stations accumulated by, 326
  television programming of, 327n, 336
Columbia Phonograph Broadcasting
    System, 322–23
Columbia Phonograph Company, 322
Columbia Records, 512
Columbia University, 30, 45, 86, 124n, 219,
    228, 372, 375, 392–94, 479
  Journalism School of, 554, 561, 562
Columbia Workshop, The, 331
Commodore Hotel, 29, 35, 146, 167, 254,
    263, 269
Communist Party, 557

Condit, Carl, 457, 483
"Confessions of a Drone" (Patterson), 343
Congress, U.S., 69–70, 87, 312
    see also House of Representatives, U.S.:
        Senate, U.S.
Congress Cigar Company, 320, 323
Conklin, William R., 10
Connolly, Maurice, 19
Conrad, Frank, 305
Constitution, U.S., 69–70
    Eighteenth Amendment to, 9, 69–72,
        123, 128
    Nineteenth Amendment to, 28
    Twenty-first Amendment to, 132
Coolidge, Calvin, 91, 134, 143, 312–13,
    390, 455
Cooper Union, 233–34, 249
Corbett, Harvey Wiley, 222, 434–36, 440,
    443, 450, 486
Corcoran, Paddy, 223
Correll, Charles, 326
Costello, Eddie, 66, 74–77, 87–89
Costello, Frank, xv, 105
    arrests and imprisonment of, 75, 82
    birth and early life of, 74–75
    bootlegging of, 66, 68, 72–85, 94, 104, 128
    criminal life of, 66, 68, 72–85, 90, 92, 104
    Dwyer and, 66, 68, 72–75, 78–85, 92,
        94, 104
    social insecurity of, 74–75, 79
    trial and acquittal of, 87–89, 91, 137
Costello, Lauretta Giegerman "Bobbie,"
    75, 83
Cotton Club, 94, 98, 106, 504, 514–19, 521,
    533
    segregation in, 104, 515
Court of Appeals, U.S., 89
Covici, Pascal, 553n, 568
Coward, Noel, 189
Cowley, Malcolm, 35, 47, 443
"Crack-Up, The" (Fitzgerald), 582
Cradle of the Deep, The (Lowell), 568–69
Cram, Goodhue & Ferguson, 436
Crane, Hart, 544, 546
Crawford, Joan, 198
"Creole Love Call," 504, 513

Critchley, David, 84
Croker, Richard, 17, 22, 62
Crosby, Bing, 330–31
Crossley Report, 335
Crossword Puzzle Book, The, 563–64
Crowninshield, Frank, 127
Croyden Aerodrome, 142
Cruise, Michael J., 52
Cuba, 25, 31
cummings, e. e., 544
Curran, Henry H., 433–34
Curry, John Francis, 9–10, 61, 62
Cushing, Harvey, 334n
Customs Service, U.S., 70, 85, 574

Daily Mirror (London), 345
Daily News Building, 369–70, 450
Dakin, Sinclair, 354–55
Daley, Arthur, 2, 3
Daley, John, 380
Damrosch, Walter, 312, 317
Danziger, Harry, 50–51
Daredevil Jack (film), 405
Dark Laughter (Anderson), 546
Dash, Mike, 75, 84
Davenport, Walter, 415
Davies, Marion, 175, 521, 534
Davis, Elmer, 367, 416
Dawson, James P., 377, 395, 404, 407
Death and Life of Great American Cities,
    The (Jacobs), 447
De Casseres, Benjamin, 118
Decca Records, 330
de Forest, Lee, 299–300
DeLillo, Don, 218
Delirious New York (Koolhaas), 441
Delmonico's, 23, 114, 117, 216
DeMange, George "Big Frenchy," 103–4,
    110, 120, 514
Democracy in America (Tocqueville), vii
Democratic National Convention of 1924,
    18
Democratic Party, 5, 6, 9–10, 15, 17–20,
    22–29, 49, 61, 108, 342, 410
    Tammany connections to, 16–34, 60, 69,
        91, 109

Dempsey, Deanna Piatelli, 427

Dempsey, Hyrum, 395, 398

Dempsey, Mary Celia Smoot, 395, 396, 398

Dempsey, Maxine Cates, 396–98

Dempsey, William Harrison "Jack," xv, 30, 142, 290, 372–77, 381, 394–98, 415–18

autobiography of, 395

birth and early years of, 395–96

Carpentier's bout with, 306, 321, 401–4, 413

character and personality of, 397–98, 413, 416

death of, 428

Firpo's bout with, 372–77, 405–6, 413, 422

Gallico and, 372–76, 414

Irish and Cherokee heritage of, 395

plastic surgery of, 406

popularity of, 394, 426

Tex Rickard and, 391, 394–95, 397–98, 400–407, 417, 419–21, 424, 426–28, 504

Tunney's bouts with, 373n, 390–91, 410–11, 415–24, 430

Willard's bout with, 373, 397–98, 400, 401, 405

World war II service of, 398

Depression, Great, 9, 57, 62, 187, 210n, 229–30, 262, 282, 289, 446, 573–74

Detroit, Mich., 44, 142, 249, 264–65, 334n, 483

DeWitt Clinton High School, 562

de Wolfe, Elsie, 173

Diablo, John, 241–42, 244

DiMaggio, Joe, 2

Dior, 194

Dixon, Mildred, 518

Doctors Hospital, 371

Dodge Brothers, 255

Dominion Bridge Company, 243

Dorset Hotel, 174

Dorsey, Tommy, 511

Dos Passos, John, 123

Doubleday, 553n

Double Indemnity (Cain), 367n

Douglas, Ann, 330

Downey, Morton, 331

Dracula (Stoker), 561

Dreiser, Theodore, 344, 463–64, 543–44, 546, 549, 554, 559–60, 580

Dry Manhattan: Prohibition in New York City (Lerner), 123n

Du Bois, W. E. B., 517

Duchin, Eddie, 511

Duke's Serenaders, 506

Dunn, Jack, 384

Dunn, Lady Mary, 334

Dunne, Edward F., 342–43

Durant, Ariel, 565

Durant, Will, 359, 564–65

Durant, William, 253

Durante, Jimmy, 21, 103, 114, 519

Dwyer, Agnes Frances, 67

Dwyer, William Vincent "Big Bill," xv, 108

arrest, trial and imprisonment of, 65–67, 82, 87–90, 92, 104, 105

bootlegging of, 65–68, 72–75, 78–85, 94, 104, 408

Costello and, 66, 68, 72–75, 78–85, 92, 94, 104

family life of, 66–67

physical appearance of, 66

sports and restaurant investments of, 66–67, 79, 83, 90

wealth of, 90

youth and education of, 67

Earl Carroll's Vanities, 528

East River, 35, 57, 80, 85, 97, 157, 165, 168, 182, 188–90, 216–17, 223, 262, 333, 459

East River National Bank Building, 66

"East Saint Louis Toodle-Oo," 513

Ecole des Beaux-Arts, 250, 437, 438

Ederle, Gertrude, 536

Edison, Thomas, 283, 302, 364n

Editor & Publisher, 366

Educational Alliance, 296, 297

Education and the Good Life (Russell), 555

Eiffel Tower, 258

elections, U.S., 69, 99
    of 1901, 17
    of 1912, 101
    of 1920, 402, 465
    of 1924, 72
    of 1925, 18, 24–29, 31, 32, 56, 536
    of 1928, 18, 28, 34, 61
    of 1929, 7, 60–62
    of 1932, 10, 370
electromagnetic waves, 297–300
El Fay, 110, 113, 114–20
Eliot, T. S., 544, 559n
Ellington, Daisy Kennedy, 505, 508, 512, 518
Ellington, Edna Thompson, 506, 512
Ellington, Edward Kennedy "Duke," xv, 47, 94, 333, 503–19
    autobiography of, 505, 508, 518
    compositions of, 504, 506, 513, 515, 520
    elegant reserve of, 504
    piano playing of, 505–8
    recordings of, 512–13, 520
Ellington, James Edward, 505, 508, 512, 518
Ellington, Mercer, 506–7, 510, 512, 513, 516, 518
Ellington, Ruth, 518
Elliott, Robert, 363
Elsas, Hermann, 548, 557
Elysée Hotel and Restaurant, 324
Empire on the Hudson (Doig), 452n
Empire State Building, 222, 259
Encyclopedia of New York City, 94
Engels, Friedrich, 343
Engineering News-Record, 478
England, 98
    Garden City movement in, 444, 449
    Midlands of, 96, 98
    tabloid journalism in, 338, 344–45
    see also Great Britain
Enoch Arden (Tennyson), 206
Equitable Coach Company, 58–60
Erie Canal, 166
Erlanger, Abraham Lincoln, 520, 521n, 527, 532, 577
Ernst, Morris, 574

Ethical Culture School, 562
Etting, Ruth, 528, 535, 542
Eveready Hour, The (radio), 309
Eveready Hour, The (television), 317
Expressionism, 281

Fadiman, Clifton, 566–67
Farber, Ann Goodman, 194–95
Farewell to Fifth Avenue (Vanderbilt), 178
Farley, James, 410
Farnsworth, Philo T., 316
Farrell, Frank, 31
Fashion Hall of Fame, 201
Faulkner, William, 546, 557–58, 574
Fay, Larry, 102–3, 106, 110–14, 116–17, 131
FDR Drive, 7, 450
Federal Communications Commission (FCC), 313
Federal Radio Act, 313
Federal Radio Commission (FRC), 313
Federal Trade Commission, 310
Ferber, Edna, 125, 537–40, 555
Ferdinand, Archduke, 178
Ferriss, Hugh, 222, 245, 434–36
Fessenden, Reginald, 299–300, 303
Field, Marshall, 342
Field, William H., 346, 347, 349
Fields, W. C., 527, 528, 532
Fifth Avenue, xi, 4, 46, 97, 117, 123, 147, 152, 154, 156, 167–68, 172, 177, 188, 479–80
    fashionable stores and salons on, xiii, 8, 147, 183, 186, 190–96, 199–210, 211, 213, 353, 491
    luxury mansions and apartments on, 175, 181–85, 187–92, 198, 203, 220, 224
Finney, Ben, 114, 122
Firebrand (Dardis), 559n
Fire Department, N.Y., 16, 43, 49, 140
Firpo, Luis Angel, 372–77, 405–6, 413, 422
First Tycoon, The: The Epic Life of Cornelius Vanderbilt (Stiles), 157n
Fitzgerald, F. Scott, xi, 30, 47, 93, 116, 133, 137, 143, 176, 211, 525, 559
    works of, 67, 95, 126, 151, 179, 352, 536, 555, 582

Fitzgerald, Zelda Sayre, 93, 137, 151–52, 161, 171, 175, 211

Fleischmann, Raoul, 211–12, 215

Flower Hospital, 101

Flynn, Edward J., 6, 17, 19, 24, 28, 29, 53, 54

Foley, Thomas F. "Big Tom," 20, 21, 23–24, 131

Folies Bergère, 527

Footner, Hulbert, 146–47, 185, 189–90, 264

Forbes, 255

Ford, Edsel, 430

Ford, Henry, 252, 254, 255, 275, 336, 403, 430–31, 482

Ford Motor Company, 253, 261, 303
  Model A of, 255, 431
  Model T of, 254, 302, 430–31

Fort Lee, 478

Fortunate Pilgrim, The (Puzo), 460

Fortune, 124, 151, 164, 167, 192, 200–201, 215, 251, 254, 257, 323, 332, 458, 488, 544

Four Hundred, 181–82

Fowler, Gene, 5, 24, 34, 39, 387, 396

Fox, William, 271–72, 290

Fox Film Corporation, 271, 435n

France, 4, 62, 134, 135, 403, 413
  Normandy, 139, 143n

Frank, Waldo, 552

Frankau, Ethel, 195

Frantic Atlantic, The (Woon), 180

Frazee, Harry H., 145–46, 178, 379

Fred F. French Building, 216–17, 220–23, 226, 228, 231, 242

Fred F. French Companies, 221, 225–26, 228, 230

Freeman, Julius, 276–77

Freeman, Milton H., 456, 468

French, Cordelia, 220, 228

French, Fred F., xi, xv, 8, 216–30, 235, 251, 369, 441, 446

French, Hazel, 219–20

French, John, 227

French Plan, 218, 224–26, 229–30

Freud, Sigmund, 327, 551

Friede, Donald, 553, 557–58, 560–61, 568, 575

Frohman, Charles, 520n

Fulton Fish Market, 460

Gable, Clark, 367n

Gabler, Neal, 289–90

Gabor, Zsa Zsa, 334

Gallico, Hortense Ehrlich, 375

Gallico, Paolo, 375

Gallico, Paul, 143, 351, 368, 425, 427, 429
  Dempsey and, 372–76, 414
  novels and children's books of, 375
  sports writing of, 140, 372–78, 383–84, 393–95, 403, 408, 414, 418, 422–23

Galli-Curci, Amelita, 317

Galsworthy, John, 567

Gambarelli, Maria, 283–84

gambling, 68, 75, 76, 84, 94, 105, 115, 281, 524–25

Gangs of New York, The (Asbury), 95

Gans, Joe, 399–400, 419

Gans, Leonard S., 224

Garbo, Greta, 189

Garden City Hotel, 137–38

Gate of Heaven Cemetery, 4

Geddes, Patrick, 443, 448

Gehrig, Henry Louis "Lou," 380, 387, 392–94, 420, 426
  home runs of, 392–93, 417, 424–25
  youth and education of, 392, 393

General Electric Corporation (GE), 163, 299, 303, 305, 314–15

General Introduction to Psychoanalysis (Freud), 551

General Motors (GM), 252–53, 255, 261
  Chevrolet line of, 430, 431

General Motors Building, 251

General Motors Family Party, The, 317

George Washington Bridge, xiii, 7, 453, 471–83, 495
  cable suspension of, 476, 49–80–81
  design and construction of, 471–78
  upper and lower decks of, 476, 479–80

George White's Scandals, 522, 528

Germans, 16, 48, 67, 97

Germany, Imperial, 186, 302, 344, 345

Germany, Nazi, 3

Gershwin, George, 307, 309, 509, 511, 519, 522, 528

Gibbons, Tommy, 405–6, 413

Gilbert, Cass, 479

Gill, Brendan, 213

Gimbel, Adam, xv, 199, 200–202, 210, 213, 245

Gimbel, Bernard, 200, 426

Gimbel, Sophie Haas Rossbach, 201–2

Gimbel Brothers, 200

Gimbels, 199, 308, 488, 568

Gioia, Ted, 503, 504, 516–17

Givena, Leo E., 354–55

Glad, Gladys, 351

Glazer, Nathan, 498

Goethals, George Washington, 477

Goethals Bridge, 477

Gold, Michael, 544, 545

Goldberger, Paul, 174, 175, 443, 482

Golden Gloves, 351, 375

Goldfield, Calif., 399–400

Goldfield Daily Sun, 399

Goldwyn, Samuel, 577, 580

Goldwyn Pictures, 281

Gomez, Lefty, 2

Gompers, Samuel, 320

Goodman, Andrew, 194–95

Goodman, Belle, 195

Goodman, Edwin, xv, 191–95, 196–97, 200–202, 210, 471, 490–91

Gophers gang, 95, 97–103, 108

Gordon, Waxey, 105, 353, 578

Gosden, Freeman, 326

Gould, Chester, 352

Gould family, 177, 184, 403

Gracie, Archibald, 35

Gracie Mansion, 35

Graham, Florence Nightingale, see Arden, Elizabeth

Graham, Stephen, 120–21, 290–91

Grand Central Depot, 154–59

1871 opening of, 147, 155, 157, 158

Grand Central Palace, 253

Grand Central Terminal, xiii, 8, 20, 29, 103, 146–47, 151–52, 159–68, 160, 202, 216–17, 265

architecture of, 163–65, 433

ceiling mural of, 164–65

Grand Concourse of, 159–60, 164–65, 259

1913 opening of, xi, 158, 165, 169, 177

1990s restoration of, 166

Oyster Bar in, 165

planning and construction of, 155, 158–62, 168, 432–33

sculptural group on south facade of, 164

substructure of, 159, 162–63, 263–64

Terminal City around, 147, 167–69, 217, 224, 248, 262, 264, 268

Grand Central Zone, 162, 167–69, 236, 245, 247, 263

Grange, "Red," 376

Granlund, Nils Thor "Granny," 112–14, 116–17

Grant's Tomb, 470

Grapes of Wrath, The (Steinbeck), 48

Gray, Christopher, 168, 247, 262

Gray, H. Judd, 355–58, 360–67

Graybar Building, 217, 231–32, 242

Great Britain, 45, 79, 82

see also England

Great Gatsby, The (Fitzgerald), 67, 95, 151, 179

Greeley, Horace, 338

Greenhaus, Sam, 36, 41

Greenspun, Hank, 423

Greer, Sonny, 506–8, 511–12, 516–17

Griffith, D. W., 283, 359

Griswold, Charles, 273

Gross, Samuel, 91

Groton, 342

Grove, Lefty, 375

Guest, Amy Phipps, 189

Guest, Frederick E., 189

Guinan, Mary Louise Cecilia "Texas," xv, 112–14, 117–22, 128–32, 137, 176, 274, 406

arrest of, 129–30

autobiography of, 113

brassy style and "Hello Sucker" trade-
    mark of, 112, 116, 119, 120–21
death of, 131, 132
film career of, 112, 113, 114, 130–31
marriage of, 114
newspaper column of, 113
physical appearance of, 120
Guinan, Tommy, 121–22
Gumps, The, 352
Guy, Freddie, 509

Hague, Frank, 402, 403
Hairy Ape, The (O'Neill), 544
Halberstam, David, 319–20
Hall, Adelaide, 509, 513
"Hall, The," 29
Halle, Louis, 82–83
Hamilton Tigers, 66
Hammerstein, Oscar, II, 537–39, 541
Handy, W. C., 506
Hanging Gardens of Babylon, 171–72
Hanley, Thomas, 39–40
Hanrahan, John, 212–13
Harcourt Brace, 552
Harding, Warren G., 402
Hardwick, Otto "Toby," 506–10
Harlan, John M., 86
Harlem, 91, 94, 104–5, 117, 140, 155, 156,
    167, 279, 333, 507, 511
    cultural renaissance of, 517
    East, 68, 74, 75, 77, 83
    nightclubs in, 94, 98, 104, 106, 140,
        504–18, 555–56
    numbers racket in, 106–7
    Sugar Hill in, 517–18
Harlem Hospital, 7
Harlem River, 153, 157
Harmon, Arthur Loomis, 222
Harper, Leonard, 508
Harper & Brothers, 549
Harper's Bazaar, 152, 498
Harriman, Margaret Case, 204
Harris, Louis I., 30, 50–51, 266, 291
Harrison, James, 419
Harvard University, 181, 467, 531
Harvest Moon Ball, 351

Haskell, Douglas, 166, 370
Hastings, John A., 58–59, 72
Hause, Frank J., 365–66
Havana, 3, 42, 130
Hayes, Patrick Joseph Cardinal, 9, 145
Hays, Arthur Garfield, 552
Health Department, N.Y., 30, 50–51
Hearst, John Randolph, 333
Hearst, William Randolph, 27, 28, 333,
    409, 474, 521, 534
Hearst, William Randolph, Jr., 3
Hearst, William Randolph, newspaper em-
    pire of, 17–18, 113, 172, 301, 338–40,
    342, 346, 348–49, 358–59, 361, 387, 404
Hearst-Brisbane Properties, 172
Hecht, Ben, 6, 359
Heeney, Tom, 426, 428
Held, Anna, 526–27, 529
Heldenleben, Ein (Strauss), 283
Helleu, Paul, 164, 165n
Hell Gate Bridge, 80, 241, 473, 478
Hellinger, Mark, 122, 339–40, 351, 406
Hellman, Geoffrey T., 568, 570, 574n
Hellman, Lillian, 544, 546, 556–57
Hell's Kitchen Gang, 93n
Hemingway, Ernest, 558–59
Hemingway (Reynolds), 559n
Henderson, Fletcher, 508, 512, 515, 517
Henry Hudson Parkway, 483–85
Henry L. Marshall, 73
Here Is New York (White), vii, 448
Herrick, Myron T., 141, 142
Hertz, Heinrich, 297–98
Highlights of Manhattan (Irwin), 152–53,
    199, 487–88
High Line, 485
High School of Commerce, 393
high steel construction workers, 236–45,
    238, 251, 256, 463
    Mohawk Indian, 241–45, 473
Hill, David B., 390
Hines, James "Jimmy"
    character and personality of, 105–7
    lifestyle of, 106, 107
    Madden and, 94, 101, 105–9
    physical appearance of, 106

Hines, Phil, 107

Hitler, Adolf, 337

Hoff, Boo Boo, 423, 514

Holland, Anna Coolidge Davenport, 456, 467

Holland, Clifford M., xv, 456, 467–69, 480, 482–83

Holland Tunnel, xiii, 7, 453–56, 467–71, 482–85, 495
  construction of, 456–57, 466–69, 493
  opening of, 455–57, 469–71
  ventilation of, 468–69, 480

Hollywood, Calif., 113, 124, 142, 198, 280, 289–90, 314, 333, 385, 389, 390, 405, 406

Hollywood Club, 508–12

Hood, Elsie Schmidt, 437–39

Hood, Raymond Mathewson, xv, 235, 436–42, 478, 486
  architecture of, 222, 317, 368–70, 433*n*, 436, 438–40, 442
  early life and education of, 436–38
  family life of, 436, 437
  Tower City plan of, 440–43, 446, 450

Hoover, Herbert, 370
  presidency of, 61, 337
  as Secretary of Commerce, 307–8, 315

Hope, Bob, 330

Horace Mann School, 219

Horne, Lena, 515

Horner, Freda, 102

Hornsby, Rogers, 387, 388

Horowitz, Harry, 75

Hotel Astor, 262, 287–88, 290, 529

Hotel Drake, 174

Hotel Knickerbocker, 287–88

Hotel Lincoln, 234–35

Hot Springs, Ark., 94, 102*n*

Hottelet, Richard C., 337

Houghton Mifflin, 549, 569*n*

Houseman, John, 331

House of Representatives, U.S., 389, 403
  Judiciary Committee of, 131

Howard, Ebenezer, 444–45, 447, 451

Howard, Thomas, 364

Howells, John Mead, 369, 437–38

Howells, William Dean, 438

Hubert's Museum and Flea Circus, 115

Hudson Dusters gang, 95, 103

Hudson River, 1, 7, 25, 26, 67, 83, 85, 93, 95, 97, 98, 108, 156, 157, 160–61, 179, 219–20, 450
  tunnels under, 402, 451, 453–56, 466–71

Hudson River Railroad, 156

Huggins, Miller, 372, 381, 385–88

Humphreys, Joe, 140, 408

Hunt, Marshall, 378, 384–86, 389, 392, 394, 424

Huntington, Collis P., 183, 203

Hurst, Fannie, 359

Huston, Tillinghast L'Hommedieu, 379–80

Hutchinson, B. E., 254

Hutton, E. F., 576

Hylan, John F. "Red Mike," 17, 18, 19, 30, 43, 44, 50–52
  Walker vs., 24, 25–29

iconoscope, 316

Igoe, Hype, 372, 387, 419–20

Illustrated Daily News, 339, 346

"In a City of Skyscrapers, Which is the Mightiest of the High? Experts Say It's No Contest" (Dunlap), 258*n*

Independent Subway System (IND), 27, 265, 266, 494

Ingersoll, Ralph, 211, 214–15

In Our Time (Hemingway), 559

Insull, Samuel, 343

Interborough Rapid Transit company (IRT), 14, 60

Interior Architecture, 173

Internal Revenue Service (IRS), 70

International Ladies' Garment Workers' Union, 490

"Intolerable City, The" (Mumford), 444–45

Ireland, 133*n*, 139
  County Kerry, 9
  County Kilkenny, 25
  County Mayo, 412
  Potato Famine in, 16

Irish Catholics, 32, 67, 113, 156, 176
  criminal activities of, 93–110, 223

in police and fire departments, 16,
    48–49
in Tammany Hall, 15–17, 20, 22–23,
    32–34, 71
Irwin, Will, 152–53, 175–77, 191, 199, 222,
    270, 287, 290–91, 487–89, 491–92,
    495
Isaacs, Stanley, 61
isolationism, 345, 371*n*
Is Sex Necessary? (Thurber and White),
    214
Italians, 16, 48, 49, 176, 496
    in organized crime, 66, 68, 72–85
Italy, 74, 75, 298
Ives, H. Douglas, 221, 228
Ives, Herbert E., 315, 316*n*

Jack Dempsey: The Manassa Mauler (Rob-
    erts), 373*n*
Jack Dempsey's Restaurant, 427
Jackson, Edward Norman, 348, 353
Jackson, Kenneth, 454, 457, 485
Jacobs, Jane, 167, 447
Jacobs, Mike, 2, 409
jazz, 47, 213, 291, 339, 498–99, 503–18
    Chicago, 504, 508, 509
    hot, 516
    "jungle style," 516
    New Orleans, 504, 506, 509, 510
    stride piano "cutting battles" in, 507
    symphonic, 511
    "White," 330, 509*n*, 510, 511
    see also blues; ragtime
Jazz Age, xi, 3, 4, 30, 111, 172, 213, 231,
    261, 339, 352, 497, 525, 529, 545, 582
Jazz Singer, The (film), 282, 314
Jersey City, N.J., 455, 469–71
Jesus Christ, 227
Jews, 40, 48, 75, 173, 355
    Eastern European, 16, 117, 182–87,
        231–35, 271, 290, 292, 295–96, 320,
        323, 487, 490–91
    in entertainment, 269–87
    in garment industry, 16, 186, 191–99,
        487–98
    German, 269–87, 324, 494, 543–61

in organized crime, 27, 52, 55, 76–79,
    83, 423
in publishing, 543–74
in real estate, 186–87
see also anti-Semitism
Jim Crow laws, 515
Joe DiMaggio Highway, 485*n*
John A. Roebling & Sons, 477
John Smith (Liveright), 547
Johnson, Howard "Stretch," 515
Johnson, Jack, 104, 400, 406
Johnson, Samuel, 430
Johnston, Alva, 8–9, 31, 109, 224, 226–27,
    353, 466
Jolson, Al, 314, 335, 403
Jones, Bobby, 375, 376
Jones, Soldier, 404, 413
Jones Beach State Park, 255
Joplin, Scott, 562
Joyce, James, 550, 574
Joyce, Peggy Hopkins, 261, 359, 528
Judaism, 295–97
    High Holy Days of, 297
    Orthodox, 295–96
    synagogues of, 296–97, 303
Judson, Arthur, 321–23, 325, 327
Justice Department, U.S., 65, 70, 86

Kaempffert, Waldemar, 266–67
Kahn, Ely Jacques, 222, 439, 492
Kahn, Otto, 329, 419, 545, 558, 582
Kahn, Roger, 401, 422, 427
Kahnawake Mohawk Reservation, 241–44
Kaltenborn, Hans von (H. V.), 332
Kaufman, George S., 120–21, 125
Kaytor, Marilyn, 126
KDKA Radio, 305
Kearns, Jack "Doc," 373, 397, 401, 405, 407
Keeler, Ruby, 519, 528
Kelley, Virginia Cassidy, 94, 102*n*
Kelly, John, 16
Kennedy, Joseph P., 314, 531
Kent, Rockwell, 573
Kern, Jerome, 537–40
Khayyám, Omar, 414
Kieran, John, 377–78, 418, 421

Kirkland & Ellis, 344
Klauber, Edward, 334
Klaw, Marc, 520, 521n, 527, 532
Klopfer, Donald S., 544, 555, 570–73
Knickerbocker Building, 82–83
Knickerbocker Village, 230
Knopf, Alfred A., 550–51, 564, 568
Knopf, Blanche Wolf, 550
Kober, Arthur, 556n
Kobler, John, 364
Koenig, Samuel S., 61
Kohler, Charles L., 51
Komroff, Manuel, 581
Koolhaas, Rem, 441
Korda, Michael, 562, 565, 567
Kraków, 203–5
Kraków University, 204
Kriendler, Carl "Jack," 124–28
Kriendler, H. Peter, 125
Kriendler, Sadie, 125, 127
Kroch, Carl A., 566
Kronenberger, Louis, 544–45, 555, 557–58,
    575, 580
Krupp Works, 260
Ku Klux Klan, 22, 540

Labor Department, U.S., 46, 209
Lackawanna Railroad, 306
Lady Gophers, 99–100
Lafayette, Marquis de, 142
Lafayette Theatre, 507, 514
La Guardia, Fiorello, 2, 7, 10, 55–56, 59
    congressional career of, 70, 91
    election of, 58
    mayoral campaigns of, 60–62
    reforms of, 5, 7
    Walker and, 5, 60–61
Landmarks Preservation Commission,
    221–22
Land of Promise, The (Maugham), 529
Lang, Fritz, 264
Lansky, Meyer, 76–77, 78–79, 94, 105
Lardner, John, 143, 404
Lardner, Ring, 143n, 375, 377–78, 406
Larkin, John A., 433
LaRocca, D. J., 509n

Lasky, Jesse L., 560, 580
Lawes, Lewis E., 102, 364
Lawrence, A. H., 514
Lawrence, D. H., 208
Le Bourget Airport, 140–42, 143n
Le Corbusier, 259, 264, 291, 450
    on George Washington Bridge, 472, 479
    Voisin Plan of, 434–35, 440
Lee, Ivy, 334
Lefcourt, Abraham E., xv, 489–95, 497–98
Lefcourt Clothing Center, 492
Lefcourt-Marlborough Building, 493
Lehman Brothers, 210n
Leipzig Conservatory, 525
Lend-Lease Act, 371n
Leonard, Benny, 403, 426
Lerner, Michael A., 123n
Levine, Charles A., 136, 143n
Levinsky, Battling, 413
Levy, Isaac, 321–23
Levy, Leon, 321–23
Lewis, Alfred Allan, 188
Lewis, David Levering, 515, 517–18
Lewis, Thomas Jenkins, 208, 210
Lieb, Frederick G., 377, 380, 382, 394
Liebling, A. J., 347, 370–71, 458
Life, 199
Lincoln, Abraham, 3, 16, 341, 370, 562
Lincoln Tunnel, 470, 483, 484
Lindbergh, Charles, Sr., 136
Lindbergh, Charles Augustus, Jr., xi, 3,
    133–37, 536
    barnstorming of, 136
    celebrity of, 133–35, 140–46, 169, 191,
        255, 313, 392
    character and personality of, 136–37,
        142–43
    first solo nonstop Atlantic flight made
        by, 133–35, 139–43, 419
    flight training of, 136
    memoirs of, 142
Lindbergh, Evangeline, 136, 142, 145–46
Lindenthal, Gustav, 473–75
Lindy Hop, 140
Lindy's, 290
Lippmann, Walter, 17, 548

Listerine Program, The, 330

Literary Guild, 568

Little, Brown, 549, 569*n*

Little Brother of the Rich, A (Patterson), 343

Little Leather Library, 548

Little Orphan Annie, 352

Liveright, Henrietta Fleisher, 547

Liveright, Henry, 546–47

Liveright, Herman, 580, 582

Liveright, Horace Brisbin, xv, 543–61, 565, 579–82

   Broadway productions of, 543, 553, 557–58, 560–61, 580

   censorship battle of, 543, 552–53

   character and personality of, 543–48, 550–51, 556–57, 576

   financial problems of, 547–48, 557–58, 561, 571, 575–76, 579–81

   illness and death of, 546, 573–74, 581–82

   marriage and children of, 548, 556–57

   publishing career of, 543–46, 548–54, 557–61, 568, 570–71, 573, 575, 582

   stock market investments of, 547, 553, 575–76

Liveright, Lucille Elsas, 548, 556–57, 561

Liveright, Otto, 547

Lloyds of London, 136

Loew, Marcus, 112, 280

Loew's theaters, 81, 112, 270, 280

London, 43, 45, 48, 65, 82, 93*n*, 142, 143, 175, 205, 291, 298, 303, 313–14

   Mayfair, 177

   Palace Theatre, 526

   traffic congestion in, 434

Long, Lois, xv, 213–15

Long Island, 22, 78, 86, 98, 133, 182, 254–55, 331

   Curtiss Field, 135, 136–38

   Mitchell Field, 144

   Montauk Point, 73, 80, 81, 85

   North Shore, 334

   Roosevelt Field, 135, 137–40, 143*n*, 419

Long Island City, N.Y., 55, 165, 289, 356, 483

Long Island Sound, 85, 253, 390, 439, 459

longshoremen, 458, 462–66

Longshoremen, The (Barnes), 463

Lopate, Phillip, 461

Lorillard Tobacco Company, 330

Lorraine, Lillian, 529

Los Angeles, Calif., 2, 390, 394, 406, 484

Los Angeles Times, 397, 427

Louis, Joe, 3, 377*n*, 427

Louise Brooks (Paris), 329*n*

Love of Sunya, The (film), 270, 275

Low, Seth, 17

Lowell, Joan, 568–69

Lubin, Herbert, 270–72, 286–87

Luce, Henry, 257, 336

Luciano, Charles "Lucky," 76–77, 83, 90, 105

"Lucky Lindy," 141

Ludwig, Emil, 568

Lugosi, Bela, 561

Lykusky, Jacob, 204

Lyons, Eugene, 300, 303–4

Lyric Theatre, 62, 540

Ma and Pa Kettle Go to Town (film), 165

McAdoo, William, 466

McAllister, Ward, 211

McAndrews, Thomas F., 3

McCooey, John, 9, 17–19, 26, 28

McCormack, William J. "Big Bill," 464–65

McCormick, Cyrus, 344

McCormick, Katherine Medill, 341, 343–44

McCormick, Robert Rutherford "Bertie," 341, 343–44, 345–46, 419, 437

McCormick, Robert Sanderson, 343–44

McCoy, "Big Bill," 73, 77, 80

McCue, Martin G., 9–10

MacDonald, Carlyle, 141

McEvoy, J. P., 523, 532

Macfadden, Bernarr, 340, 348–49, 359

McGeehan, W. O., 374, 377–78, 388, 406, 418, 421, 426, 428

McGovern, Arthur A., 386, 389

Macgowan, Kenneth, 271–72

McGraw, John, 379, 387, 413, 426

McGraw-Hill Building, 433*n*

McGuinness, Peter J., 53–54

McGuire, William Anthony, 539

Machinal: A Tragedy in Ten Episodes
    (Treadwell), 367

McHugh, Jimmy, 514, 515

Mack, Connie, 392

Mackay, Clarence, 117

MacKay, William B., 478

MacKaye, Benton, 444

MacKaye, Milton, 3, 33–34, 49, 361

McKee, Joseph V., 10

MacKellar, Landis, 360

McKim, Charles Follen, 164, 166

McKim, Mead & White, 161, 163, 173

McLaughlin, George V., 29–30, 51–54, 56

McNamee, Graham, 312, 420–21

Macon, 134, 144

McPherson, Aimee Semple, 359

Macy's, 199, 202, 308, 488, 572

Madden, Dorothy Rogers "Loretta," 99

Madden, Francis, 96, 97–98

Madden, Margaret, 100

Madden, Martin, 96

Madden, Mary, 96

Madden, Mary Agnes O'Neil, 93, 96, 98,
    100

Madden, Owen Vincent "Owney," xv,
    92–111, 120
  birth and early life of, 96–99
  business investments of, 94, 98, 104–5,
    108–10, 113, 117, 504, 514–16, 521
  criminal life of, 92–95, 97–110, 116
  death of, 98
  George Raft and, 92, 94–95, 100, 103, 117
  Hines and, 94, 101, 105–9
  illegal beer breweries of, 92, 94, 104–5,
    108–9
  illness and wounds of, 93, 101–2
  imprisonments of, 93, 94, 95, 102, 110
  Irish heritage of, 94–96, 98
  killer reputation of, 92, 96, 99–100,
    103–4
  marriages of, 94, 99
  murders of, 92–94, 100, 102
  personality and lifestyle of, 92, 94, 95,
    100, 105–6, 107–8

physical appearance of, 103, 106
  wealth of, 110

Madison Square Garden, xiii, 10, 18, 46,
    66, 90, 155, 351, 402, 430–31
  boxing matches at, 2, 3, 105, 215, 391,
    395, 400–401, 403, 408, 411
  Tex Rickard and, 400–401, 405, 407–9,
    426, 428–29

Mafia, 66, 76–79, 83–85, 108
  extortion by, 84
  Italians in, 74, 76–77, 90, 94
  labor racketeering of, 84
  narcotics and gambling rackets of, 84
  overlords of, 74, 76–77, 90
  Sicilian, 81, 84
  see also Prohibition, bootlegging in

Majestic, SS, 523

Majestic Records, 4–5

Maloney, Jim, 140

Manhattan, 38
  Battery, 134, 144–45, 180, 484
  Beekman Place, 189–90, 192, 218, 333
  Broadway theater district, 5, 20, 46,
    62, 94, 105, 141, 232, 234–35, 245,
    269–75, 279, 287–92, 324–25, 504,
    519–42
  Bryant Park, 222, 438
  Central Park, 8, 46, 101, 134, 145, 146,
    156, 168, 175, 182, 194, 215, 220, 396,
    439
  Chelsea Piers, 67, 85, 179, 426, 459–60,
    572
  Chinatown, 470
  Columbus Circle, 474
  as entertainment and communications
    center, xi, 1, 46–47, 146, 268, 290, 486
  Garment District and industry in, xii,
    xiii, 5, 8, 16, 191–95, 232, 234, 355,
    439, 485, 486–98, 503
  Gramercy Square, 188
  Greenwich Village, 4, 13, 19, 25–26, 117,
    121, 355, 390, 412, 437, 548
  Hell's Kitchen, xi, xiii, 46, 66, 67, 92, 93,
    95–100, 104, 108, 111, 125, 161, 167,
    211, 296, 459–60, 485
  Herald Square, 146, 199–200, 488, 491

Little Italy, 76, 77, 493

Lower East Side, 15, 19–20, 97, 117, 118, 125, 170, 186, 229, 234, 296, 355, 489, 491, 494, 503

Madison Square, 8, 114, 155, 391, 495

Midtown, xii, 1–4, 8, 39, 46, 66–67, 76, 80–83, 105, 108–10, 146, 168, 209, 211, 216–30, 447, 486

Murray Hill, 152, 188, 213, 215

Prospect Hill, 223–24

St. John's Park, 157

St. Luke's Place, 25, 35–36

skyscrapers in, xi, 3, 8, 45, 47, 138, 144–45, 147, 168, 171–72, 183, 216–32, 235–40, 244–51, 255–64, 289, 432–37, 448, 450, 489, 493

slums and street crime in, 96–97

Sutton Place, 182, 187–90, 192, 215, 218, 224, 562

Tenderloin vice district, 33, 167, 491–92

Terminal City, 147, 167–69

ticker tape parades in, 2–3, 134–35, 144–45

Times Square, xi, 8, 46, 105, 108, 114–115, 118, 157, 168, 234, 265, 268–71, 279–80, 287–92, 324–25

Tin Pan Alley, 21, 141, 498–99, 503, 513, 516

traffic congestion in, 14, 36–37, 432–33, 457, 466, 470, 475

Union Square, 21

Upper East Side, 53, 186–87, 389

Upper West Side, 192, 197

Wall Street, xi, 52, 67, 86, 147, 161, 187, 217, 225, 254, 255, 292, 312, 457, 543

Washington Heights, 393, 475–76, 482

Washington Square, 121, 146, 437

West Side, 61, 92–101, 104, 157, 161, 167, 482

Manhattan Bridge, 229, 480

Man Nobody Knows, The (Barton), 227

Man o' War, 376

"Man Who Flew Alone, The" (Gallico), 143

Mara, Tim, 2

Maranzano, Salvatore, 76

Marconi, Annie Jameson, 298

Marconi, Guglielmo, 297–300, 315

Marconi Wireless Telegraph Company of America, 297, 298–303, 304

Marguery apartments, 167, 173, 174–75

Marine Corps, U.S., 273, 276, 285, 390, 412, 413, 415

Markey, Morris, 92, 214, 265, 318, 414

Marshall, George, 328–29

Marx, Harpo, 125

Marx, Karl, 343, 547

Mason, Roy, 263

Masseria, Giuseppe "Joe the Boss," 76

Masters of Enterprise (Brands), 314n

Matthias, Brother, 383–84

Maugham, Somerset, 529

Mauretania, 426

Maxtone-Graham, John, 180

Maxwell House Hour, The, 317

Maxwell Motors, 253–55

Mayer, Joseph, 472–73

Medill, Joseph, 341

Mefford, Arthur, 366

Melan, Joseph, 480

Mellon, Andrew, 91, 346

Melville, Herman, 443

Memphis, 134, 143

Mencken, H. L., 47, 118, 127, 132, 344, 403, 549, 550

Mercury Theatre of the Air, 331

Messner, Julian, 549, 554, 571, 580

Methodist Board of Temperance, Prohibition and Public Morality, 9

Methodist Church, 86

Metropolis (film), 264

Metropolitan Club, 250

Metropolitan Museum of Art, 152

Metropolitan Opera Company, 312, 322, 439, 476

Metropolitan Opera House, 179

Meusel, Bob, 388

Meynell, Sir Francis, 573

Mid-Manhattan (Clary), 254n

Midnight Frolic, 528n

Mies van der Rohe, Ludwig, 258n

Miley, James "Bubber," 509–10, 513, 516

Millay, Edna St. Vincent, 211

Miller, Dave, 423

Miller, Julius, 48*n,* 484–85

Miller, Marilyn, 528, 533*n,* 542

Mills, Florence, 508–9

Mills, Irving, 503–4, 512–14, 518*n*

Mills Brothers, 331

Minsk, 295–96

Mitchell, Joseph, 238, 241*n,* 242, 244

Modern Library, 543–44, 557, 571–74

"Mohawks in High Steel, The" (Mitchell), 244

"Mohawks Who Built Manhattan, The" (Valois), 243*n*

Moisseiff, Leon, 480

Monongahela Club, 105–6

Moore, William, 102

Morand, Paul, 177, 179, 185, 264, 275, 291

Mordden, Ethan, 509, 521, 524, 539–40, 578

Morello, Giuseppe, 84

Morgan, Anne, 188, 218, 306, 376, 403

Morgan, Helen, 528, 541

Morgan, J. Pierpont, 161, 171, 188, 306

Mori, Placido, 437–39

Morland, Nigel, 362

Mormons, 395

Morris, Jan, 264

Morris, Lloyd, 516

Morse code, 80, 297, 298

Moscow, Warren, 41, 43, 59, 62

Moses, Robert, 19, 479

  high-rise projects of, 447

  parks and parkways of, 254–55, 450–53, 483–84

Motion Picture News, 282–83

Mount Sinai Hospital, 273

Mount Vernon, N.Y., 303, 448

movies, 124, 142*n,* 165, 289–90, 313, 344, 375, 385, 389, 435

  documentary, 281

  musical accompaniment to, 272–75, 278–79, 280, 282

  nickelodeon, 278, 280

  silent, 112, 113, 114, 141, 270, 275, 277–82

  talking, 47, 282, 314

  Western, 113, 114

Moving Image, The, 292*n*

Mullan-Gage Act, 72

Mullett, Mary, 284, 286

Mumford, Elvina, 443

Mumford, Geddes, 443

Mumford, Lewis, 247, 258, 261, 432, 469, 479, 546

  autobiography of, 443

  education of, 443

  urban planning philosophy of, 441, 443–49

Mumford, Sophia, 443

Munsey's Magazine, 162, 183

Murchison, Kenneth M., 226, 227, 250, 258

Murphy, Charles Francis, 17, 19, 22–23, 32–34, 53

Murray's Roman Gardens, 115

Murrow, Edward R., 337

Music Appreciation Hour, 317

Music Box Revue, 528

Music Is My Mistress (Ellington), 505, 508, 518

My Life (Clinton), 102*n*

"My Life—AND HOW!" (Guinan), 113

My Life for Beauty (Rubinstein), 204

"My New York," 536

Nally, Edward J., 301–2, 303, 307

Nanook of the North (film), 281

Nantucket Island, 300, 458

Napoleon I, Emperor of France, 370, 525, 568

narcotic drugs, 68, 84, 95, 511

Nathan, George Jean, 118, 127, 520, 536

National Association for the Advancement of Colored People (NAACP), 327*n*

National Broadcasting Company (NBC), xi, 3, 134, 292, 311–13

  CBS competition with, 322, 325–27, 329–32, 334–36

  creation of, 311–12, 317, 321

  news on, 337

  programming on, 325, 326–27, 330, 332

  Red and Blue radio networks of, 311–12, 327

  television network of, 317–18, 336

National Carbon Company, 309
National Hockey League, 408*n,* 409
National Police Gazette, 359
Native Americans, 16, 241–45
Navy, U.S., 71, 79, 302, 303, 398
Neiman Marcus, 208
Nelson, "Battling" (Oscar Mathaeus Niel-
    sen), 399–400, 419, 422
New Amsterdam Theatre, 520–22, 528,
    533–36, 542
New Jersey, 46, 98, 160, 165, 453, 454–55,
    461
    Bergen County, 471, 475–78, 482
    Highlands, 73
    Morris County, 475–76
    Palisades Cliffs, 473, 475, 482
Newman, William H., 158–59, 164
New Orleans, La., 504, 506, 509
Newport, R.I., 172, 176, 531
New Republic, 449, 484–85
Newsday, 343
Newsweek, 337
New York:
    Bronx County, 19*n*
    Dutchess County, 447
    Kings County, 19*n*
    Nassau County, 138
    New York County, 19*n,* 138
    Queens County, 19*n,* 356–59, 443–46,
        482
    Richmond County, 19*n,* 48*n*
    Suffolk County, 138
    Westchester County, 4, 138, 247
New York, N.Y.:
    annual budget and municipal debt of,
        43–44, 45
    Assembly districts of, 28, 49
    Bronx, 6, 15, 17, 18–19, 46, 48*n,* 49, 50,
        58, 92, 105, 217–19, 253–54, 301, 303
    Brooklyn, 15, 17, 18–19, 26–28, 38, 48*n,*
        49, 58, 98, 242, 247
    bus service in, 585–89
    Coney Island, 24, 351, 368
    construction and growth in, xi, 8, 9, 41,
        44, 45
    corruption in, 50–56, 59
    cosmopolitanism of, 48–49
    district leaders in, 32–34, 49–52, 54–56,
        79, 94, 99, 105
    elevated trains in, 157, 265, 266*n*
    Eleventh Assembly District, 101
    film industry in, 289
    Harbor and Port of, 46, 65–66, 79, 85,
        86, 87, 88, 133, 144, 160, 268, 271,
        301, 457–66
    high society in, 172, 176–77, 181–90,
        280, 439
    hospitals in, 43–44, 101, 273, 371
    immigrant groups in, 16, 48–49
    milk distribution scandal in, 50–51
    municipal employees in, 43
    Night Club Era in, 110–32
    1920s building boom in, 167–71, 192,
        265–68
    organized crime in, 27, 33, 52, 55,
        65–69, 72–86, 516
    polluted rivers of, 14, 57
    population growth in, 19
    post-World War I strikes in, 346
    Queens, 15, 18–19, 26, 28, 48*n,* 49, 58,
        66, 83
    railroad trunk lines into, 8, 41, 46
    saloons in, 71, 75, 96, 123
    seventeenth-century Dutch settlement
        in, 457–58
    sewage system in, 57–58, 109
    six million population of, 43
    speakeasies in, 46, 71, 81, 88, 92, 105,
        109–10, 112–31, 138, 143, 260, 381
    Staten Island, 18–19, 28, 49, 58, 144
    street gangs in, 16, 67, 75, 95, 97–102,
        223
    subway system of, 14–15, 26–27, 37, 38,
        46, 58, 60, 61, 106, 154, 159, 167, 264,
        265–68, 288, 432, 456, 493–94
    water system of, 43, 267–68
    wealth and poverty in, 46, 48
    as world's financial capital, 45
    see also Manhattan
New York, New Haven & Hartford Rail-
    road, 157
New York Age, 517

New York American, 17, 211, 301, 339, 346, 358, 387, 404

New York Americans Hockey Team, 66, 90

New York & Harlem Railroad, 155–57

New York Automobile Show, 253–54

New York Central & Hudson River Railroad, 156–57

New York Central Building, 247–48

New York Central Railroad, 8, 41, 67, 96, 99, 147, 156–57, 158–61, 167, 247, 441, 450, 455, 457, 460–62, 484

electrification of, 154, 158–59, 161, 163, 166

1902 and 1907 accidents on, 153–55, 160, 163

railyards of, 146, 152, 153–54, 158

real estate company of, 167, 170–71

20th Century Limited on, 180, 263–64, 330, 418

West Side Freight Line of, 460

New York County Republican Committee, 61

New York *Daily Mirror,* 138, 172, 340, 348–49, 359, 361, 540

New York *Daily News,* 7, 45, 53, 58–59, 129–30, 131, 133, 140, 142–43, 338–71

"About Broadway" column in, 340

advertising in, 339, 348, 349, 353–55, 365–66

circulation of, 338, 341, 349, 350, 353–54, 371

comic strips in, 351

compact size of, 339, 346

contests and promotional features of, 349, 351, 375

criticism of, 339, 340–41

editorial policy of, 347

entertainment news, scandal and gossip in, 340, 345–66, 371, 535

financial problems of, 348, 354

"A Friend in Need" column in, 340

launching of, 338–39, 341, 345–47

news and editorials in, 339, 340, 350

photographs in, 339, 347, 348, 352–54, 355, 359–60, 364–66, *365,* 385

Snyder-Gray murder covered in, 355, 359–67, *365*

sports coverage in, 372–78, 383–85, 389

staff and editors of, 340, 346–50, 352–355, 359–60, 365–66, 368–69, 372–76

"Straw Poll" feature in, 351, 368

Sunday edition of, 349

tabloid style of, 338–39, 343, 345–48, 350–51, 367

"Voice of the People" column in, 351

women's features in, 351–52

New Yorker, 31, 47, 92, 106, 117, 118, 176, 203, 210–15, 255, 256, 275, 334, 340, 449

advertising in, 212–13, 214

circulation of, 215

humor and cartoons in, 214–15, 287

"On and Off the Avenue" column in, 214

staff and contributors at, 213–15, 224, 227–28, 238, 241*n,* 265, 271–72, 318, 347, 353, 367, 414–15, 550

"Tables for Two" column in, 213

"Talk of the Town" column in, 215

New York Evening Graphic, 340, 348–49, 359

New York Evening Journal, 163, 172, 342, 372, 375

New York *Evening Mail,* 348

New York Evening Post, 33, 60, 70–71

New York *Evening World,* 346

New York Giants, 2, 379–80, 413

New York Herald, 3, 31*n,* 297, 339, 511

New York Herald Tribune, 17–18, 31, 95, 257–58, 338, 340, 362, 377–78

New York Journal, 17, 113, 339, 346, 386

New York *Journal American,* 484

New York Life Insurance Company, 401, 407

New York National Guard, 389–90

New York Philharmonic Orchestra, 331, 375, 476

New York Post, 17, 327*n*

New York Public Library, 307, 438, 474

New York Society for the Suppression of Vice, 552

New York State Assembly, 5, 20–22, 32, 552

New York State Boxing Commission, 465

New York State Bridge and Tunnel Commission, 456

New York State Senate, 5, 17, 23–24, 40, 72, 154, 347

New York Steam Corporation, 262

New York Stock Exchange, 225

New York *Sun,* 27, 142

New York Symphony Orchestra, 312

New York Telegram, 359

New York Theatre, 527

New York Times, 10, 32, 33, 53–54, 77, 80, 89, 169, 172, 182, 185, 187–88, 207, 263, 265, 280, 287–88

on bridges and tunnels, 454, 467–68, 469, 471, 481, 483

circulation of, 338, 341, 346

on construction workers, 236, 242, 244

on entertainment, 528

on Fred French, 227–28

on Hattie Carnegie, 196, 197

on Irwin Chanin, 234

on Jimmy Walker, 2, 4, 5, 7, 15, 27, 31, 40, 44, 54, 61–62

on Lindbergh, 134, 136, 140–42, 144, 145

on media, 299, 315, 331, 336, 338, 347, 565

on Rothafel, 271

on speakeasies, 110, 115, 118, 122, 123

on sports, 374, 377–78, 380, 395, 398, 404, 415, 418–19

on Walter Chrysler, 251

New York Times Building, 269, 287–88, 307, 404

New York *Tribune,* 31*n,* 402, 554

New York University, 125–26

Law School of, 17, 21

New York World, 13, 18, 30, 39, 71, 211, 287, 339, 346, 527, 536, 555, 563

New York World's Fair of 1939, 317

New York Yankees, 2, 146, 195, 374, 377–82, 385–94, 417, 425–26

"Nick the Greek," 52

Nobel Prize, 567

Nonesuch Press, 573

Northcliffe, Alfred Harmsworth, Lord, 338, 345, 347

Northern Pacific Railroad, 472

Notre Dame Cathedral, 437

Nungesser, Charles, 135, 141

Oates, Joyce Carol, 392, 406

Occupational Safety and Health Administration (OSHA), 239

Ocean Steamship Company, 412

Ochs, Adolph, 287–88, 353

O'Dwyer, William, 2

O'Higgins, Patrick, 204

"O Holy Night," 299

O'Keeffe, Georgia, 175, 436, 438*n*

Okinawa, 398

Oklahoma! (Rodgers and Hammerstein), 541

Okrent, Daniel, 278

Old Gold Program, 330

Oliver, Joe "King," 514

"Ol' Man River," 538–40, 578

Olmsted, Frederick Law, 156

Olvany, George Washington, 17, 18, 24, 28, 29, 32, 49, 52–53, 61, 221, 230

Olympic, RMS, 300

O'Neill, Eugene, 544–46, 549, 573–74

On the Waterfront (film), 464, 465

Original Amateur Hour, The, 335

Original Dixieland Jazz band, 509*n*

Ormandy, Eugene, 284

Orteig, Raymond, 135, 146

Orteig Prize, 135, 137, 146

Ossining, N.Y., 368–69, 371

Padlocks of 1927, The, 130

Palace Theatre, 280

Palais Royale, 511, 518*n*

Paley, Barbara Cushing Mortimer "Babe," 334*n*

Paley, Dorothy Hart Hearst, 333–34

Paley, Goldie Drell, 320

Paley, Isaac, 320

Paley, Jacob, 320

Paley, Samuel, 320, 323, 324
Paley, William S., xv, 3, 292, 318–37, 344, 517
　autobiography of, 320, 324, 326, 330
　CBS purchased by, 318–20, 323–24, 504
　character and personality of, 320–21, 324, 326, 328–29, 333–35
　competition of Sarnoff and, 318–20, 325–27, 329, 331–32, 334–36
　death of, 324n
　early years and education of, 320
　love affairs of, 328–29, 333, 334
　marriages and family of, 333–34
　physical appearance of, 319, 328
　radio advertising promoted by, 319, 327–28, 329–32
　wealth and opulent lifestyle of, 324n, 332–33
　see also Columbia Broadcasting System (CBS)
Palm Beach, Fla., 3, 42, 172
Palm Beach Nights, 532
Palmer, Bertha, 526
Palmolive Hour, The, 317
Panama Canal, 455, 477
Paradise Ballroom, 509n
Paramount Building, 324–25
Paramount Pictures, 271, 289, 560
　Astoria Studio of, 289
Paramount Theatre, 141, 236, 270–71, 292
Paris, xi, 42, 47, 48, 124, 133, 135–37, 139–41, 143, 146, 205, 208, 211, 245, 419
　fashions of, 193, 194, 498
　Faubourg St. Germain, 177
　Les Invalides cemetery, 370
Park Avenue, 67, 75, 117, 124, 146–47, 151–55, 158–61, 164, 166–80, 183, 215, 442
　center island of, 147, 153, 171
　early blighted industrial condition of, 155, 158
　as elevated viaduct around Grand Central, 147, 161, 164, 166, 168, 247
　luxury high rises on, 168, 170–78, 218, 224, 332–33

　as "Street of Dreams," 8
　Tunnel under, 152–55, 158–60, 168
Park Avenue Association, 178, 179
Parker, Dorothy, 125, 211, 214, 331, 546
Parlor Match, A, 526–27
Pasadena Rose Festival, 277
Paterno, Joseph V., 482
Pathé Studios, 580
Patterson, Alice Higinbotham, 342, 343, 345, 371
Patterson, Alicia, 343
Patterson, Eleanor Medill "Cissy," 341
Patterson, Elinor Medill "Nellie," 341, 343
Patterson, James, 344, 367
Patterson, Joseph Medill, xv, 338–54, 364–71, 373, 375–78, 384–85, 419
　birth and early life of, 341–42
　character and personality of, 367–68
　as copublisher of Chicago Tribune, 344–46, 367, 437
　illness and death of, 371
　marriages and family of, 342, 344–45, 371
　novels and plays of, 341, 343
　physical appearance of, 367
　politics of, 341, 343, 347, 371n
　reporting of, 341, 342, 345
　World War I combat service of, 345, 367
　see also New York Daily News
Patterson, Mary King, 344–45, 351, 367, 371
Patterson, Robert W., Jr., 341, 342, 343
Paul Whiteman Orchestra, 330
Payne, Philip A., 138–39, 349–50, 375
Peekskill Military Academy, 274
Pegler, Westbrook, 381, 409
Pell, Arthur, 546, 552, 557–58, 575, 579–81, 582n
Pennsylvania, 276, 546–47
Pennsylvania Railroad, 160–61, 167, 445, 455, 461, 466, 475
Pennsylvania Station, 103, 162, 167, 202, 396, 425, 428
　architecture of, 161, 164, 166
　1911 opening of, 165
Pennsylvania Steel Company, 473

Perkins, Max, 559
Peters, Curtis Arnoux, 215
Peterson, Dorothy, 561, 580–81
Philadelphia, Pa., 44, 107, 108, 161, 167,
    199–200, 218, 320–22, 324, 376,
    410–11, 476, 514
  Rittenhouse Square in, 321
  Warwick Hotel in, 321
Philadelphia Athletics, 379, 392
Philco, 316n
Phipps, Henry, Jr., 188–89
Phipps Corporation, 188
Phoenix Cereal Beverage Company, 104–5,
    108–9
Photophone, 314
Photoplay, 328
Pickford, Mary, 207
Pipp, Wally, 393
Pittsburgh, Pa., 252, 305, 306, 425, 437, 547
Pittsburgh Courier, 518
Pittsburgh Pirates, 425–26
Plant, Morton F., 183
Plaza Hotel, 191, 196
Plimpton, George, 375
Plunkiett, George Washington, 99, 101
Police Department, N.Y., 29–30, 43, 48–49,
    51–56, 102, 466
  Confidential Squad of, 52–55
  corruption in, 81, 85, 94, 105, 108–9, 126
  suppression of street gangs by, 95, 97,
    99–100
Polo Grounds, 2, 373–74, 377, 379–80,
    396, 398, 402, 518
Poole, Ernest, 241
Porter, Cole, 62, 259
Port of New York Authority, 452–53,
    476–79, 484
Portrait of the Artist as a Young Man
    (Joyce), 550
Pound, Arthur, 169–70
Pound, Ezra, 291, 546, 559n
Power Broker, The (Caro), 452
Pratt Institute, 506
"Pretty Girl Is Like a Melody, A," 523, 528
Princeton University, 199, 334
Princip, Gavrilo, 178

Pringle, Henry, 22, 30, 36, 41, 348
Printer's Ink, 309
  "Sweeney" campaign in, 354–55
"Prisoner's Song," 129
Procter & Gamble, 328
Prohibition, 65–94, 102–3, 108–32, 260,
    288, 528n, 536
  alcohol confiscated in, 67–68, 92
  anti-liquor laws prior to, 69n
  bootlegging in, 65–69, 71–86, 91–92,
    103–5, 109, 111, 115–16, 122–23, 260,
    333, 408
  diluting and adulterating liquor in,
    81–82, 122–23
  enforcement of, 69–70, 71, 72, 79–80,
    86–92, 108–9, 119–20, 128–30, 408
  hijacking of boats in, 73–74, 78, 110
  opposition to, 9, 31, 61, 70, 71–72, 79,
    91, 131, 347
  repeal of, 94, 132
  restrictions of, 70–71, 104
  rise of organized crime in, 68–69,
    72–86, 95–96
Prohibition Bureau, 65, 69–70
Proskauer, Joseph, 21, 24
Protestantism, 49, 75, 95, 182, 184, 227,
    241n, 326, 334
Psalms, Book of, 295
Publishers Weekly, 567, 582
Pulitzer, Joseph, 287, 338–39
Pulitzer Prize, 142n, 549
Puncheon, 124–28, 177, 570
Puritanism, 9, 31
Putnam, George Palmer, 142
Putnam's, 552
Puzo, Mario, 459, 460

Queen of the Night Clubs (film), 130
Queensboro Bridge, 151, 188, 459, 473,
    579
Queens County Prison, 356
Queens-Midtown Tunnel, 7, 483, 484
Quo Vadis (film), 282

Race to Paris, 135–41
racism, 399–400, 519, 555–56, 561

Racquet & Tennis Club, 177, 178
radio, 295, 297–99, 301–3, 305–15
  advertising on, 308–9, 319, 327–32
  commercial, 302, 305–10
  development of, 297–300, 301–3
  early demonstrations of, 299–300
  first commercial station on, 305
  as first modern mass medium, 311
  golden age of, 317
  impact of Sarnoff and Paley on, 297–337
  news on, 337–38
  nonprofit, 309
  phone line transmission of, 308, 321, 322
  public service programs on, 309
  receivers of, 302, 305–6, 310–11, 313, 319
  Rothafel broadcasts on, 271, 283–85, 287, 292, 309
  sporting events on, 306–7, 321, 380–81, 420
Radio Age, 308
Radio City Music Hall, 292n, 440
Radio City Symphony Orchestra, 282
Radio Corporation of America (RCA), 297, 303–18, 325
  competitors of, 305, 306, 308–10
  formation of, 303–5
  radio broadcasting of, 305–8, 310
  Sarnoff's leadership of, 303–18
  television development by, 315–18
  transatlantic facsimile transmission by, 313–14
Radio-Keith-Orpheum (RKO), 314
Radio Music Box (radiola), 302, 305–6, 313, 319
Radio News, 284
Raft, George, 94–95, 100
  dancing of, 103, 117, 121
  film career of, 92, 94, 290
ragtime, 505–6, 509, 540
Random House, 544, 555, 573–74, 582n
Rapée, Erno, 274–75, 282
Rastorfer, Darl, 479–80
Raymond, "Nigger Nate," 52
RCA Photophone, 314

RCA Victor Company, 313–14
  "His Master's Voice" trademark of, 313
Reader's Digest, 350
Reconstruction Finance Corporation, 230
Rector's, 114, 117
Reed, Charles, 163–64
Reed, John, 549
Reed and Stem, 163–64, 165
Regent Theatre, 279
Regional Planning Association of America (RPAA), 443–46, 449
Regional Plan of New York and Its Environs, The, 448–52
Republican National Convention of 1924, 309
Republican Party, 6, 10, 16, 17, 27, 28, 40, 57, 60, 109, 178, 342, 410, 446, 475
  bosses of, 91, 108
"Rethinking Rothafel" (Melnick), 292n
Revell, Keith D., 56, 58
Reynolds, William H., 249, 251
Rhapsody in Blue (Gershwin), 307, 511
Rialto Theatre, 270, 280–81
Rice, Grantland, 373, 375, 377–78, 381, 406, 413–14
Rickard, Edith Mae Haig, 399, 400–401, 408
Rickard, George "Tex," xv, 66, 306, 376, 397–411, 512
  arrest and trial of, 405
  death and funeral of, 428–29
  Dempsey and, 391, 394–95, 397–98, 400–407, 417, 419–21, 424, 426–28, 504
  early life of, 399
  gambling business of, 398–99
  Madison Square Garden and, 400–401, 405, 407–9, 426, 428–29
Ringling, John, 400–401, 403, 407, 530
Ringling Brothers Circus, 46
Rio Rita, 138, 146, 522, 538, 540, 542, 576
Rise of the Goldbergs, The, 335
Ritz-Carlton Hotel, 39, 173, 560
Ritz Tower, 172–75, 196
Rivoli Theatre, 280–81, 282, 314
Robertson, Thomas Markoe, 221, 231

Robeson, Paul, 538, 555, 560–61, 578
Robinson, Grace, 359–60, 362
Rochester, N.Y., 192, 193, 329n
Rockefeller, John D., 171, 275
Rockefeller, John D., Jr., 403
Rockefeller Center, 124n, 193, 292n,
    440–41, 570n, 580
Rockefeller family, 334, 441
Rockettes, 292n
Rodgers, Richard, 541
Roebling, John A., 477, 479
Roebling, Washington, 479
Rogers, Mary, 359
Rogers, Will, 104, 111, 309, 331, 528, 532,
    579
Rolland, Romain, 562
Roman Catholic Church, 4, 5, 9–10, 16,
    105, 122, 184, 241, 360, 363, 371,
    383–84, 437, 525
"Romance in the Roaring Forties" (Run-
    yon), 122
Rome, 42, 48, 483, 498
Roosevelt, Eleanor, 66
Roosevelt, Franklin Delano, 306, 368
    as Assistant Secretary of the Navy, 303
    governorship of, 6, 7, 9, 478
    New Deal of, 370, 451
    presidency of, 6, 347, 370, 371n
Roosevelt, Theodore, 86, 227, 342, 346, 403
Root, Elihu, 86, 376
Root, John Wellborn, 174
Rosalie, 539, 542
Roscoe, Burton, 344, 368
Rose, Billy, 116
Roseland Ballroom, 290, 508
Ross, Harold, 125, 210–15, 334
Roth, Emery, xv, 171–74, 175, 196, 494
Roth, Julian, 175
Roth, Richard, 175
Roth, Rose, 197
Rothafel, Beta, 274
Rothafel, Rosa Freeman, 274, 276–77, 286
Rothafel, Samuel "Roxy," xv, 269–87
    early years of, 275–76
    entertainment promotions of, 269–75,
        277–83, 314

Marine Corps service of, 276, 285
marriage and family of, 274, 276–77,
    286
personality and lifestyle of, 280–81,
    284–87
physical appearance of, 274, 285–86
radio broadcasts of, 271, 283–85, 287,
    292
writing of, 277–78, 285
Rothapfel, Gustave, 275–76, 277
Rothstein, Arnold, 27, 52, 55, 76, 103, 105,
    113, 151, 420, 496, 511
Roxy and His Gang, 271, 284–85, 287, 290,
    292n, 309, 327
Roxyettes, 282, 292n
Roxy Theatre, xi, xiii, 140, 269–75
    closing and demolition of, 292n
    construction of, 271
    grand opening of, 270–75, 287, 314
    interior features of, 272–73
    orchestra, chorus and pipe organ of,
        272, 273–75
Rubáiyát (Khayyám), 414
Rubinstein, Ceska, 205
Rubinstein, Helena, xvi, 202–10, 213, 471
Rubinstein, Manka, 205, 208
Rum Row, 72–73, 77, 80–81, 85, 87, 91
Runnin' Wild (Johnson), 509
Runyon, Damon, 30, 77, 94, 105, 122, 290,
    358, 360–62, 377–78, 387, 396, 406
Ruppert, Jacob, 379–80, 386, 389–90, 403
Russell, Bertrand, 544, 553, 555–56
Russell, Lillian, 344
Russell Sage Foundation, 97, 448–52
"Russian Lullaby, A," 275
Ruth, Claire Merritt Hodgson, 385–86, 388
Ruth, George, Sr., 383
Ruth, George Herman "Babe," xvi, 2, 4,
    30, 142, 146, 336, 377–91, 395, 398n,
    420, 504
    celebrity of, 382–83, 394
    death of, 383
    health problems of, 385
    home runs of, 378–79, 380, 385, 388–89,
        392–93, 417, 424–26
    income of, 377, 387–88, 390, 415

Ruth, George Herman "Babe" (*cont.*)
   lifestyle and personality of, 381–85, 394
   movie appearances of, 385, 389, 390
   New York Yankees career of, 374,
      377–80, 385–94
   pitching of, 378, 383
   youth and education of, 383–84
Ruth, Helen Woodford, 381, 385–86
Ruth, Julia Hodgson, 386, 387*n*
Ruth, Kate Schamberger, 383
Ruth, Mary Margaret "Mamie," 383
Ryan, Joseph Patrick, 464–65

Saarinen, Eliel, 438
"Sadie Salome," 528
St. Agnes Church, 9
St. John's, Newfoundland, 133*n*, 139
St. John's Park Terminal, 157, 460
St. Lawrence River, 241, 243, 473
St. Louis, Mo., 44, 135, 136, 146, 282
St. Louis Cardinals, 388
St. Mary's Industrial School for Boys,
   383–84
St. Michael's School, 97
St. Patrick's Cathedral, 1–4, 145, 156, 193
St. Patrick's Day Parade, 4
Saint-Pierre, 77–79, 82, 85
Saint-Pierre and Miquelon, 77–78
St. Regis Hotel, 196, 317
Saks, Andrew, 199
Saks, Horace, 199–201
Saks & Company, 199–200
Saks Fifth Avenue, xiii, 8, 186, 199–202,
   208, 215
Sally, 531, 537
Salt Lake City, Utah, 210, 396–97
Samuel H. Armstrong Technical High
   School, 505–6
Sandburg, Carl, 231
Sandow, Eugene, 525–26
San Francisco, Calif., 44, 316*n,* 526
Sanitation Department, N.Y., 58
Sardi's, 290
Sarnoff, Abraham, 295–96, 300
Sarnoff, David, xi, xvi, 3, 134, 292,
   295–318, 337, 404, 419–20

birth and early years of, 295–97, 491
boyhood singing of, 296–301
character and personality of, 302, 304,
   312, 335
death of, 297
early jobs of, 296–97
education and religious training of,
   295–96
family life of, 303, 304
as multimillionaire telecommunications
   tycoon, 297–318
NBC created by, 311–12, 317, 321, 326
Paley's competition with, 318–20,
   325–27, 329, 331–32, 334–36
physical appearance of, 304
and sinking of the *Titanic,* 300–301
and television development, 315–18
as wireless operator, 299–301
Sarnoff, Leah Privin, 295–96, 301, 303
Sarnoff, Lizette Hermant, 303
Sarnoff, Robert W., 303
Sartre, Jean-Paul, 47
Save New York Committee, 491
Savoy-Plaza Hotel, 186, 195–96
Schmeling, Max, 3
Schroeder, William, Jr., 44, 58
Schulberg, Budd, 464
Schultz, "Dutch," 92, 105, 107, 578
Schultz and Gross, 174
Schuster, Barnet, 562
Schuster, M. Lincoln "Max," 544, 554,
   561–70
   publishing career of, 563–70
Scientific American, 155, 469
Scudder, Townsend, 356, 362
Seabury, Samuel, 6, 9, 54, 59
Seabury Committee, 229–30
Seagram Building, 258*n*
Seldes, Gilbert, 270, 275, 283, 534–35
Selznick, Lewis J., 280
Senate, U.S., 403
Seneca, 88
Sensationalism and the New York Press
   (Stephens), 350*n*
settlement houses, 296, 297
Sevareid, Eric, 337

Seymour, Harold, 379n

Sharkey, Jack, 140, 394–95, 416–17, 426

Shaw, George Bernard, 344, 404

Shelton, Yvonne "Vonnie," 24–25, 31, 34

Shelton Hotel, 175, 222

Sherry-Netherlands Hotel, 186, 195–96

Sherwood, Robert E., 282

Shevlin, George J., 67–68

Shimkin, Leon, 564, 569n

Shirer, William L., 337

Shor, Bernard "Toots," 2, 83

Show Boat (Kern and Hammerstein),
  537–42, 578, 581

Show Girl, 519–20

Shreve, Lamb & Harmon, 259

Shubert Brothers syndicate, 519, 520n–21n

Shuffle Along (Sissle and Blake), 509

Siegel, Benjamin "Bugsy," 76, 79

Silver Slipper, 109–10, 117, 120, 406

Silzer, George, 474, 475–77

Simon, Andrea Louise Heineman, 565

Simon, Carly, 565n

Simon, Leo, 562

Simon, Richard Leo, 544, 554–55, 561–70,
  573

  publishing career of, 563–70

Simon & Schuster, 544, 554, 563–70, 572

  Common Sense Library of, 565–66

Sinclair, Upton, 549, 582

Sing Sing Prison, 51, 95, 102, 359n

  electric chair executions in, 362–66, 365

Singstad, Ole, 456, 468–69, 483

Sissle, Noble, 509

Sister Carrie (Dreiser), 549

Sketches from Life (Mumford), 443

Skyscraper (film), 236

"Skyscraper" (Sandburg), 231

Skyscraper Museum, 258n

Sloan, John, 221, 231

Slocum, Bill, 387

Small's Paradise, 515

Smart Set, 118

Smith, Al, Jr., 3

Smith, Alfred E. "Al," 62, 131, 402, 446,
  478

  Catholic faith of, 18, 20

as governor of New York, 17–25, 27–29,
  31–34, 52, 53, 72, 134, 230, 254,
  362–63, 380, 457, 464–65, 477

  Jimmy Walker and, 6, 9, 18, 19–20, 21,
  23–25, 27–28, 31–32, 34

  personality of, 20, 23

  political opposition to, 17, 19

  presidential campaign of, 18–19, 28,
  33–34, 53, 61

  reforms of, 5

Smith, Catherine Dunn "Katie," 20

Smith, Harry B., 527

Smith, Howard K., 337

Smith, Kate, 331

Smith, Red, 3, 376

Smith, Sally Bedell, 325

Smith, Sidney, 352

Smith, T. R. "Tommy," 549, 555, 581

Smith, Willie "The Lion," 507–8, 511

Snowden, Elmer, 508, 510

Snowden, George "Shorty," 140

Snyder, Albert, 355–58, 360–61, 366–67

Snyder, Lorraine, 356–58, 360

Snyder, Ruth Brown, xvi, 355–67, 365

Snyder-Gray murder case, 355–67, 365

Sobel, Bernard, 522, 524–25, 577

socialism, 16, 27, 341, 343–44, 547

Society of Beaux-Arts Architecture ball,
  262

Soldier Field, 417, 419–24

Soldier's Pay (Faulkner), 557

Sousa, John Philip, 317

Spaeth, Sigmund, 567–68

Spirit of St. Louis, 133, 135, 137–44

Spirit of St. Louis (film), 142n

Spirit of St. Louis (Lindbergh), 142n

Sporting News, 386

Squire, Ralph, 257–58

Stanton, Edward L., 3, 36–37, 39

Stanwyck, Barbara, 367n

Stark, Herman, 514

Starrett, W. A., 217, 222–23, 236–37

Stars and Stripes, 211

"Star-Spangled Banner, The," 140, 146, 275

State Department, U.S., 79

State Railroad Commission, N.Y., 163

Steffens, Lincoln, 23
Stein, Clarence, 444, 445
Steinbeck, John, 48
Stem, Allen, 163–64
Stern, Edith M., 545, 558
Stevens, John D., 350*n*
Stewart, James, 142*n*
Stieglitz, Alfred, 175, 435–36
Stiles, T. J., 157*n*
Stock Market Crash of 1929, 2, 60*n*, 63, 131, 170, 210*n*, 229, 262, 289, 312, 427, 490, 492, 546, 568, 575–76
Stoker, Bram, 561
Stoneham, Charles A., 380
Story of Civilization, The (Durant), 565
Story of Philosophy, The (Durant), 359, 564–65
Strand Theatre, 270, 279–80, 282
Strauss, Richard, 282, 283
Strong, George Templeton, 181
Stuyvesant High School, 443
Sullivan, Ed, 1, 107, 122
Sun Also Rises, The (Hemingway), 559
Sunday, Billy, 359
Sunnyside Gardens, Queens, 443–46
Supreme Court, N.Y., 184
Supreme Court, U.S., 60, 71–72, 86
Swanson, Gloria, 117, 270, 274, 350
Swerling, Jo, 203
Swiss Federal Institute of Technology, 472
Swope, Herbert Bayard, 555

Taft, William Howard, 301
Tafuri, Manfredo, 442
Tales of the Jazz Age (Fitzgerald), 126
Talmey, Allene, 284, 285–86, 437, 439
Talmud, 295–96, 317
Tammany Hall, 5, 6, 15–20, 88, 99, 106, 221, 351
  corrupt practices and "honest graft" of, 17, 22–23, 30–34, 44, 53–56, 60, 79, 81, 126, 239, 465
  Democratic political power of, 16–34, 60, 69, 91, 109
  headquarters of, 28
  Irish Catholics in, 15–17, 20, 33–34, 48

  leadership of, 9–10, 14, 16, 17, 22–23, 30, 32–34, 71
  reforms in, 492
Taylor, Estelle, 406, 407, 416, 418, 424, 427
telegraphy, 297–301
television, 47, 315–18
  advertising on, 317–18
  development of, 315–17
  programing on, 317–18
Ten Commandments, The (film), 282
Ten Days That Shook the World (Reed), 549
Tennyson, Alfred Lord, 206
Tenth Avenue Gang, 99–100
Terkel, Studs, 376
Teutonic, SS, 96
Texas Guinan Club, 120
Thirty Years War, 132
This Side of Paradise (Fitzgerald), 352
Thomas, Clara Fargo, 189
Thomas, Norman, 27, 29, 38, 46, 62
Thompson submachine guns "Tommy guns," 74, 79, 81
Thoreau, Henry David, 443
Thorpe, Jim, 242
300 Club, 120–22, 128–30, 176
Three Musketeers, The, 539, 542
Throgs Neck Bridge, 481
Thurber, James, 214–15, 331
Tierney, John, 570
Tilden, Bill, 376, 387
Time, 213, 274, 314, 350, 376, 544
  "Man of the Year" issue of, 255
Tinker, Edward R., 254
Titanic, RMS, 181, 300–301
Titus, Edward, 205, 208
Tocqueville, Alexis de, vii
Today, 125*n*
Torah, 295
Toscanini, Arturo, 247, 331
Town Crier, The, 334
Trader Horn (Horn), 566–67, 568
trade unions, 16, 55, 490
Treadwell, Sophie, 362, 367*n*
Treasury Department, U.S., 70, 119
Triborough Bridge, 7, 60, 481

Tribune Tower, 437–38

Trotsky, Leon, 547*n*

Trumbull, Edward, 259–60

Tudor City, 217–18, 221, 224, 227–30, 369, 446

Tunney, James Joseph "Gene," xvi, 373*n*, 390–91, 394, 404, 410–16, 426–28
  death of, 427
  Dempsey bouts with, 373*n*, 390–91, 410–11, 415–24, 430
  early life of, 412–23
  personality of, 412, 414–15
  World War I service of, 412, 413

Tunney, John, 412

Tunney, John V., Jr., 427

Tunney, Mary Josephine Lauder "Polly," 418, 426

Tunney, Mary Lydon, 412

Tweed, William Magear (Boss), 17, 62

"21," 124, 189, 215

"21": Every Day Was New Year's Eve: Memoir of a Saloon Keeper (Kriendler and Jeffers), 125*n*

Tynan, Kenneth, 328

typhoid fever, 50

Ukraine, 232, 324

Ulysses (Joyce), 574

Underworld (DeLillo), 218

Union Club, 177

Union Pacific Railroad, 251–52

United Fruit Company, 306

United Independent Broadcasters, Inc., 321–22, 325

United Nations, 188*n*, 223*n*

United Press, 337

United States:
  population of, 166
  standard of living in, 46, 377

Urban, Joseph, 106, 439, 514, 521, 528, 530, 539–40

U.S. Steel, 160

Valentine, Lewis, 52–56

Valentino, Rudolph, 282

Van Alen, William, 249–51, 256–62

Van Buren, Martin, 16

Vanderbilt, Alice, 184, 191

Vanderbilt, Anne Harriman, xvi, 182–83, 187–88, 218

Vanderbilt, Cornelius, 147, 164, 185, 460
  railroads of, 153–58, 165, 166, 182, 265
  steamship building of, 156

Vanderbilt, Cornelius, II, 147, 184

Vanderbilt, Cornelius, III, 184

Vanderbilt, Cornelius, IV, 117

Vanderbilt, Cornelius, Jr., 178

Vanderbilt, Grace Wilson, 184, 185

Vanderbilt, William Henry, 184

Vanderbilt, William Kissam, 154, 163–64, 182, 183

Vanderbilt family, 8, 97, 117, 147, 161, 172, 177, 182–85, 187, 192, 194, 403

Van Doren, Mark, 443

Vanity Fair, 119, 121, 127, 185, 213

Van Wyck, Robert A., 17

Variety, 280

Vassar College, 213

vaudeville, 21, 67, 269, 270, 278, 280, 326, 405, 406

Verrazano-Narrows Bridge, 481–82

Victor Records, 512

Victor Talking Machine Company, 322

Vienna, 197, 203, 204

Viking Press, 550

Vitaphone, 272, 275, 314

Vocalion Records, 512

Vogue, 498

Voice, 227

Volstead, Andrew J., 69

Volstead Act, 69, 71–72, 77, 87, 88, 114, 119, 131, 389

Wagner, Helen Joan, 568

Wagner, Robert F., Sr., 2, 14, 17, 19, 23, 53, 492

Waldorf-Astoria Hotel, 159, 180, 311–12, 358

Walker, Betty Compton, 4, 7, 10, 62, 534

Walker, James J. "Jimmy," xvi, 1–10, 271, 274, 444, 543
  birth and early life of, 1, 4, 5, 19–21

Walker, James J. "Jimmy" (*cont.*)
   Catholic faith of, 5, 9–10, 16
   character and personality of, 2, 3–4, 5,
     6–7, 8–10, 19, 20, 22–25, 30–31, 36–42
   civic accomplishments of, 7, 8, 40–41,
     44, 56–58
   corruption charges and resignation of,
     xi, 6–7, 9, 24, 50, 56, 57
   daily routine of, 36–39, 41–42
   declining health and death of, 5, 7, 9
   drinking and womanizing of, 4, 5, 9, 10,
     23–25, 31, 34, 41–42, 62
   education of, 21
   financial gifts and favors accepted by,
     35–36, 50, 59–60
   funeral and burial of, 1–4
   intellect and wit of, 21–22, 43
   lifestyle of, xi, 1–4, 5, 6–7, 10, 19, 23–25,
     27, 30–31, 34, 39–43, 59–60, 120, 382,
     515
   marriages of, 4
   mayoral campaigns of, 25–29, 31, 60–62
   mayoral career of, xi, 1, 2, 3–9, 13–15,
     17–18, 29–32, 34–62, 71–72, 134–35,
     140, 145, 178, 195, 245, 263, 266–67
   New York State legislative career of, 2, 5,
     9, 17, 20–27, 31, 347, 552
   perilous fiscal policy of, 44–46
   personal staff of, 36–37, 39, 41, 43
   physical appearance of, 5, 13–14, 22,
     26, 40
   physical breakdown of, 40–41, 42
   political appointments of, 29–30, 32, 49,
     51, 54
   political philosophy of, 46
   popularity of, xi, 1, 2, 4–7, 8–9, 13–14
   press relations of, 37–38, 41–42
   progressive agenda and "City Plan" of,
     14–15, 18, 29–30, 43, 56–59
   Prohibition opposed by, 9, 31, 71–72
   sartorial taste of, 14, 21, 39
   songwriting of, 20–21, 43, 503
   speeches and debates of, 3, 5, 14, 21–22,
     25, 39, 56, 536, 552
   sports interests of, 2, 3, 36, 41, 408
Walker, James John, Jr., 4

Walker, Janet Allen "Allie," 4, 14, 20, 198
   on Walker, 31, 34, 37
   Walker's relationship with, 21, 24, 31
Walker, Mary Ann, 4
Walker, Mickey, 374
Walker, Ralph, 222, 439
Walker, Stanley, 31, 43, 95–96, 102, 106,
    107, 110–11, 116, 290
   on media, 338, 340–41, 366, 377–78
Walker, William, 40
Walker, William Henry, 20–21, 25–26
Walker Act of 1920, 2
Walker Law, 22, 402
Waller, "Fats," 508, 511
Wall Street Journal, 341
Walsh, Christy, 386–88, 393–94, 504
Wanamaker, Rodman, 137
Wanamaker's Department Store, 42, 137,
    300–301
   Titan City Exhibition at, 435
War Department, U.S., 328, 475
Wards Island, 57–58
Warhol, Andy, 258
Warner Brothers, 142*n*, 272, 285
Warren, Joseph A., 54–56
Warren, Whitney, 164, 166, 167, 174, 182,
    247
Warwick Hotel, 172, 521, 577–78
Washington, D.C., 65, 85–86, 91, 108, 133,
    143–44, 306, 315, 364, 504–8, 518
Washington, George, 478
Washington Black Sox Orchestra, 508
Washingtonians, 504, 510–14
Washington Post, 98
Washington Redskins, 329
Washington Senators, 385, 424–25
Washington Times Herald, 341*n*
Waste Land, The (Eliot), 544
Waterman, Frank D., 28–29
Waterman Fountain Pen Company, 28
Watts (valet), 333
WBPI Radio, 285
WCAU Radio, 321
"*We*" (Lindbergh), 142
WEAF Radio, 283–85, 308–10, 311
Weather Bureau, U.S., 370

Weber and Fields, 312

Weissmuller, Johnny, 375

Welles, Orson, 331

West, Mae, 94, 106, 107, 290, 359, 528

Western Electric, 314

Western Union, 377, 524

Westinghouse, 305, 306, 314*n*

West Side Cowboys, 460

West Side Highway, 7, 483–85

West Side Studies (True), 97, 496*n*

Wetmore, Charles D., 164, 166, 167, 174, 182, 247

Wexler, Irving, *see* Gordon, Waxey

WGBS Radio, 568

Whalen, Grover:
  as official city greeter, 2–3, 42, 133–34, 137–39, 144–45
  as Police Commissioner, 55–56, 62

Wharton, Edith, 156

Wheeler, Wayne B., 69, 72

"When My Sugar Walks Down the Street," 515

White, E. B., vii, 214, 447–48

White, George, 522

White, J. Andrew, 306, 321–26

White House, 33, 505

Whiteman, Paul, 307, 330, 510–11

White Plains, N.Y., 153, 163

Whitney, Gertrude Vanderbilt, 117

Whitney Museum of American Art, 375

WHN Radio, 512, 513

Whoopee!, 542, 577

WHW Radio, 517

Wilder, Billy, 367*n*

Wilgus, William J., xvi, 147, 153–55, 158–63, 164*n*, 165–68
  planning of Grand Central Terminal by, 155, 158–62, 168, 432

Willard, Jess, 373, 397–98, 400, 401, 405, 410

Willebrandt, Mabel Walker, 119

Williams, Bert, 519–20, 528, 532

Wills, Harry, 404–5, 415

Wills, Helen, 375

"Will You Love Me in December as You Do in May?" (Walker), 21

Wilson, Edmund, 364, 535–36

Wilson, Woodrow, 69, 302, 426, 455, 475, 562–63

Winchell, Walter, 107, 117, 122, 340, 349, 406

Winnie Winkle, the Breadwinner, 352

Winslow, Francis A., 88–89

Winter, Benjamin, 182–87, 190, 225*n*

Wireless Age, 306

Wireless Telegraph and Signal Co.(British Marconi), 298, 303

Wise, Herbert, 554, 571–72

With Louis and the Duke (Bigard), 510*n*

WJY Radio, 307

WJZ Radio, 307, 311

WMAQ Radio, 326–27

Wolf, George, 89

Wolfe, Thomas, 47

Women's Committee for Modification of the Volstead Act, 131

women's suffrage, 28, 345

"Won't You Come and Play Wiz Me?," 526

Woollcott, Alexander, 125, 189, 211, 333–34, 366, 535

Woolworth Building, 172, 221, 249, 307, 349, 467, 479, 489

Woolwoth, Frank, 183, 221

Workman's Compensation Bill, 26

World's Columbian Exposition of 1893, 174, 525

World Series, 379
  of 1919, 27
  of 1921, 379
  of 1922, 379
  of 1923, 380–81
  of 1926, 388
  of 1927, 425–26

World War I, xi, 8, 17, 27, 44, 45, 74, 79, 133, 135, 136, 178, 205, 276, 376
  anti-espionage in, 86
  Armistice and, 140
  German submarines in, 302
  recession after, 46, 167, 169
  U.S. entry into, 302–3, 345, 402
  veterans of, 184, 401, 413

World War II, xi, 84, 175, 225, 371, 398, 451
WPA Guide to New York City, The, 93n
Wright, Henry, 444–45
Wright Company, 138
W. W. Norton, 582n
Wynn, Ed, 528

Xaverian Brothers, 383–84

Yagoda, Ben, 184–85
Yale Club, 167, 263
Yale University, 126, 200, 211, 215, 342, 468, 531
Yankee Stadium, 140, 351, 380, 391, 393, 394, 410, 416–17, 424–25
Yiddish language, 296, 528
Yorkshire Post (England), 98
Young, Owen, 303–6, 310, 311

Zeder, Fred M., 253
Ziegfeld, Florenz, Jr., xvi, 30, 112–13, 138, 258, 514, 519–43, 576–79, 582
  death of, 579
  early life of, 525–26
  gambling of, 524–25, 527, 530–31, 575–77
  marriage of, 529
  personality of, 522–25, 529–32, 539
  physical appearance of, 523, 539
  promotional talent of, 519–20, 525–27, 535, 542
  swings from wealth to insolvency of, 526–27, 542, 576–79
Ziegfeld, Florenz, Sr., 525–26
Ziegfeld, Louise, 578
Ziegfeld, Patricia, 521–22, 530–32, 577–79
Ziegfeld, Paulette, 528n
Ziegfeld, Richard, 528n
Ziegfeld, Rosalie de Hez, 525
Ziegfeld Follies, 24, 112, 439, 519–24, 527–30, 532–36, 539, 542, 577
  of 1910, 519
  of 1927, 522–24, 528n, 532–37, 542
  performers and composers connected with, 519–20, 522–23, 527, 528
Ziegfeld Girls, 520, 527, 532–35, 545, 578
Ziegfeld Theatre, xi, xiii, 146, 172, 521–22, 578–79
Ziegfeld Touch, The (R. and P. Ziegfeld), 528n
zoning law of 1916, 171
Zukor, Adolph, 271, 289–90
Zworykin, Vladimir T., 315–16

PHOTO CREDITS